FUNDAMENTALS OF INVESTING

SIXTH EDITION

LAWRENCE J. GITMAN
SAN DIEGO STATE UNIVERSITY

MICHAEL D. JOEHNK
ARIZONA STATE UNIVERSITY

HarperCollinsCollegePublishers

To our wives, Robin and Charlene

Acquisitions Editor: *Joan Cannon*
Director of Development: *Arlene Bessenoff*
Developmental Editor: *Ann Torbert*
Supplements Editor: *Julie Zasloff*
Project Coordination and Text Design: *Thompson Steele Production Services*
Cover Design: *Kay Petronio*
Cover Photographs: *Comstock, Image Club*
Art Studio: *Thompson Steele Production Services and Teshin Associates*
Photo Researcher: *Diane Kraut*
Electronic Production Manager: *Eric Jorgensen*
Manufacturing Manager: *Hilda Koparanian*
Electronic Page Makeup: *Thompson Steele Production Services*
Printer and Binder: *RR Donnelley & Sons Company*
Cover Printer: *New England Book Components, Inc.*

For permission to use copyrighted material, grateful acknowledgment is made to the copyright holders on pp. C-1–C-2 which are hereby made part of this copyright page.

Fundamentals of Investing, Sixth Edition

Library of Congress Cataloging-in-Publication Data

Gitman, Lawrence J.
    Fundamentals of investing / Lawrence J. Gitman, Michael D. Joehnk. — 6th ed.
      p.   cm.
    Includes bibliographical references and index.
    ISBN 0-673-99755-3
    1. Investments.   2. Investments—Problems, exercises, etc.
I.   Joehnk, Michael D.   II.   Title.
HG4521.G547   1996 <MRCRR>
332.6'78—dc20   95-32407
                                                         CIP

4 5 6 7 8 9 10-DOW-01 00 99 98 97

Brief Contents

v

DETAILED CONTENTS

PREFACE

"Market Hits New High." "Procter & Gamble Sustains Huge Derivatives Losses." "Money Market Yields Fall Below 3%." "Real Estate Values Remain Stable." Readers of the financial press have become accustomed to headlines such as these during the past few years. These headlines illustrate that investors operate in a dynamic environment in which the only certainty is change. This textbook, *Fundamentals of Investing*, sixth edition, reflects the realities of today's changing investment environment—from new investment vehicles, techniques, and strategies to regulations and taxes. The book serves investors who are, or will be, actively developing and monitoring their own investment portfolios. It meets the needs of professors and students in the first course in investments offered at colleges and universities, junior and community colleges, professional certification programs, and continuing education courses.

Focusing both on individual securities and on portfolios of securities, *Fundamentals of Investing* describes and explains the techniques, vehicles, and strategies for implementing investment goals in light of risk-return tradeoffs. The experiences of real-world investors demonstrate the strategies and outcomes—the successes and, sometimes, the failures—of individual investors from various walks of life. A conversational tone and liberal use of examples guide students through the material and demonstrate important points.

CHANGES IN THE SIXTH EDITION

Using information gathered from both academicians and practicing investment professionals, plus feedback from adopters, the sixth edition reflects the numerous changes in today's investment environment. General changes of a major nature include installation of a comprehensive and integrated learning system, clearer focus on the individual investor, and enhanced timeliness, breadth, and depth of coverage. Beyond that, we made important but less sweeping changes in every chapter.

COMPREHENSIVE AND INTEGRATED LEARNING SYSTEM

This edition uses proven Learning Goals to build a complete teaching/learning system. Each Learning Goal is tied by a special icon to the associated first-level head in the text, and these goals are then restated and reviewed, point by point, at the chapter's end. In addition, each goal is keyed to the end-of-chapter problems, cases, and selected supplements. To support these Learning Goals, Concepts in Review questions appear at the end of each section of the chapter (positioned before the next first-level head) and allow students to test their understanding of each section before moving on to the next section of the chapter. By focusing on the Learning Goals, students will know what material they need to learn, where they can find it in the chapter, and whether they've mastered it by the end of the chapter. In addition, instructors can build lectures and assignments around the Learning Goals.

CLEAR FOCUS ON THE INDIVIDUAL INVESTOR

Today, about one out of every four adult Americans owns stock either directly or indirectly (through mutual funds). While the focus of *Fundamentals of Investing* has always been on the individual investor, this edition sharpens that focus. Most notable are the beginning-of-chapter Investor Interviews, which relate the experiences of individual investors to the material covered in the chapter. The text has been reorganized to provide earlier coverage of the investment vehicles of greatest appeal to individual investors. Now the part of the text that includes chapters on mutual funds, real estate and other tangible investments, and tax-advantaged investments precedes the part that includes chapters on options and futures. This focus on the individual investor provides the student with a solid foundation on which subsequent courses can build understanding of the advanced concepts, tools, and techniques used by institutional investors and money managers.

TIMELY TOPICS

Various issues and developments constantly reshape the financial markets and investment vehicles. To retain the text's timeliness, we expanded coverage of the impact of foreign exchange rates on investor returns, electronic and on-line sources of investment information, mortgage-backed securities, index funds, derivatives, and international diversification. These discussions provide students with a realistic understanding of the investment arena, thereby allowing them to develop and implement effective investment strategies.

GLOBALIZATION

As a result of the growing globalization of securities markets, this edition stresses the global aspects of investing. We initially look at the growing importance of international markets, investing in foreign securities—indirectly or directly—international investment performance, and the risks of investing internationally. In later chapters, popular international investment opportunities and strategies are now described as part of the coverage of each specific type of investment vehicle. These changes should help students understand the importance of maintaining a global focus when planning, building, and managing an investment portfolio.

SPECIFIC CONTENT CHANGES BY CHAPTER

- *Chapter 1,* on the role and scope of investments, now discusses domestic and foreign investments, better emphasizes the role of individuals in the investment process, and includes a new table summarizing the basic characteristics of various types of investment vehicles.

- *Chapter 2,* on investment markets and transactions, contains expanded and updated coverage of international investment performance and foreign securities; we've also streamlined the discussion of short selling.

- *Chapter 3,* on investment plans and information, has been reorganized to begin with a discussion of making investment plans. The chapter now includes a new summary table of the most popular offerings of the dominant subscription services, a discussion of electronic and on-line investment information, and a streamlined discussion of short-term investments, including a new table of the distinguishing features of interest-paying deposit accounts.

- *Chapter 4,* on measuring investment return and risk, contains a reorganized discussion of risk that now relates interest rate risk to short-term securities and describes and demonstrates the use of the coefficient of variation (in addition to the standard deviation) for measuring risk.

- *Chapter 5,* on common stock investments, contains updated information on market performance through 1994. We have added a discussion of mid-cap stocks and expanded the material on foreign stocks to show the impact of currency exchange rates on returns in U.S. dollars.

- *Chapter 6,* on the fundamental analysis of common stock, now includes a discussion on breaking down two important measures of corporate profitability—return on assets and on return equity—into their component parts, enabling investors to see what's causing the measures to go up or down over time.

- *Chapter 7,* on stock valuation, has been expanded to include the price-earnings approach to stock valuation and a discussion on how to find the rate of growth in earnings and dividends.

- *Chapter 8,* on bond investments, includes updated information on market performance through 1994, as well as a streamlined discussion of trading bonds, especially with regard to bond ratings and bond quotes.

- *Chapter 9,* on bond valuation and analysis, now focuses more clearly on the term structure of interest rates and the pricing of bonds; we've also added some discussion of bond-equivalent yields.

- *Chapter 10,* on preferred stock and convertible securities, has been thoroughly updated to reflect the latest market trends; for example, material has been added on a special type of preferred stock, a PERC, which offers both conversion privileges and attractive dividend yields.

- *Chapter 11,* on mutual funds, has been substantially revised and now includes a new section on valuing and investing in closed-end mutual funds. Also new to this edition is coverage of index funds and asset allocation funds, as well as expanded coverage of fund charges and fees.

• *Chapter 12,* on real estate and other tangible investments, has a new introduction to investing in real estate and now logically includes a streamlined discussion of tangibles (covered with futures in the fifth edition).

• *Chapter 13,* on tax-advantaged investments, has been thoroughly updated to reflect the latest tax laws and related investment strategies and vehicles.

• *Chapter 14,* on options, now begins with a brief overview of options in general and then proceeds to a thorough discussion of puts and calls, the dominant type of options security and certainly the most actively traded. We've also strengthened the discussion of derivative securities and the various ways they can be used (without excessive technical detail). The chapter now ends with material on stock rights and warrants.

• *Chapter 15,* on futures, has been updated to include the new instruments that are available in the market. In addition, some of the basic introductory material has been consolidated to provide a more focused discussion.

• *Chapter 16,* on portfolio construction, includes a new section on the effectiveness, methods, and wisdom of international diversification.

• *Chapter 17,* on portfolio management and control, has been updated and clarified to integrate better with earlier chapters and focus more clearly on the evaluation and assessment of portfolio performance and the methods for timing portfolio transactions.

PEDAGOGICAL FEATURES

This edition includes numerous pedagogical features designed to help students focus their study of investments. Among them are a comprehensive yet flexible organization, Learning Goals, Investor Interviews, a marginal glossary, Investor Insights, Concepts in Review, boxed InvestorFacts, varied end-of-chapter materials, and a number of useful appendixes.

COMPREHENSIVE YET FLEXIBLE ORGANIZATION

The text provides a firm foundation for learning by first describing the overall investment environment, including the concepts of risk and return. It then examines each of the popular investment vehicles—common stocks, bonds, preferred stocks, convertible securities, mutual funds, real estate and other tangibles, tax-advantaged investments, options, and futures. The final section of the book focuses on investment administration—constructing, managing, and controlling portfolios of the popular investment vehicles discussed in earlier chapters. Although the first and last parts of the textbook are best covered at the start and end of the course, respectively, instructors can cover particular investment vehicles in just about any sequence.

We organized each chapter according to a decision-making perspective, and always point out the pros and cons of the various vehicles and strategies that we present. With this information, individual investors can select the investment actions that are most consistent with their objectives. In addition, we've illustrated investment vehicles and strategies in such a way that the student learns the decision-making implications and consequences of each contemplated investment action. The comprehensive yet flexible nature of the book enables instructors to customize it to their own course structure and teaching objectives.

LEARNING GOALS

Each chapter begins with six Learning Goals, labeled with numbered icons, that clearly state the concepts and materials to be covered. The Learning Goal icons are tied to first-level headings and reviewed point by point at the chapter's end, and keyed to end-of-chapter problems and cases.

INVESTOR INTERVIEWS

Each chapter begins with an Investor Interview that provides intriguing personal insights into the backgrounds, motivations, strategies, and outcomes of the investment programs of selected individual investors. Investors from all walks of life, ranging from recent college graduates to retirees, with differing family situations and degrees of financial success, are included. By introducing the reader to individual investors who explain their investment experiences in their own words, these chapter-launchers benefit the reader by breathing life into the material.

MARGINAL GLOSSARY

New terms are set in boldface type and defined when first introduced in the text. In addition, each term appears with its definition in the text margin, to facilitate student learning and review. All of the marginal glossary terms also appear in a separate end-of-book glossary.

INVESTOR INSIGHTS

Each chapter features two boxed essays, called Investor Insights, that describe real-life investing situations or events. Although we kept a few of the most popular from the previous edition, the majority are new. There are four categories of boxes: Conflicting Viewpoints, which describe both sides of a controversial issue or industry debate; Market Innovations, which discuss new investment vehicles and products; Global Issues, which focus on relevant international investment issues and opportunities; and Investing in Action, which describe timely issues of interest to the individual investor. These high-interest boxes, which have been written specifically for this textbook, demonstrate text concepts and enliven students' reading at a level consistent with their abilities.

CONCEPTS IN REVIEW

Concepts in Review questions appear at the end of each section of the chapter (positioned before the next first-level heading) and are marked with a special design element. As students progress through the chapter, they can test their understanding of each concept, tool, or technique before moving on to the next section within the chapter.

BOXED INVESTORFACTS

Each chapter also contains two to three InvestorFacts—brief sidebar items that give an interesting statistic, cite an unusual investment experience, or provide a humorous anecdote. These items provide stimulating and motivational facts and figures. For example, the InvestorFact on page 219 notes how much of the country's market is concentrated in its five largest stocks. The InvestorFact on page 666 discusses how well portfolios assembled by professional investors fare against those picked by a throw of darts.

END-OF-CHAPTER MATERIALS

A number of important elements at the end of each chapter reinforce the concepts, tools, and techniques described in the chapter and help students review and integrate chapter content. They are:

On-Track with STOCK-TRAK®

The STOCK-TRAK® portfolio management simulation enables students to construct portfolios and trade securities in real-time at today's prices by calling a "broker" at a toll-free number. A brief section at the end of each chapter describes how the STOCK-TRAK® simulation (described in more detail on page xxv) relates to the chapter topic. These sections were written by Thomas M. Krueger of the University of Wisconsin–La Crosse and are based on classroom experiences with *Fundamentals of Investing* and with STOCK-TRAK®.

Summary

Each summary lists the chapter's six key concepts and ideas, which correspond directly to the numbered Learning Goals presented at the beginning of the chapter and restated in the summary.

Discussion Questions

New to this edition, about five comprehensive and thought-provoking Discussion Questions are included at the end of each chapter. These questions guide the student to integrate, investigate, and analyze the key concepts presented in the chapter. Many questions require that students apply the tools and techniques presented in the chapter to investment information they have obtained, to make a recommendation with regard to a specific investment strategy or vehicle. These project-type questions are far broader than the Concepts in Review questions included within the chapter.

Problems

A separate set of 8 to 15 Problems is included at the end of each chapter except Chapter 1. The Problems, which are keyed to the Learning Goals, vary in complexity and scope, and thus assure professors a wide choice of assignable materials. A disk symbol 🖴 appears next to the Problems that can be solved using the *Investment Management Disk (IMD)*, described in detail below.

Case Problems

Each chapter ends with two Case Problems that are keyed to the Learning Goals. These brief accounts encourage students to apply techniques presented in the chapter and to recommend how an investor might solve a specific problem. Students can solve some of the questions in the cases with the *Investment Management Disk (IMD)*, as indicated by the disk symbol 🖴 printed next to the question.

USEFUL APPENDIXES

In addition to its 17 chapters, the book includes 4 appendixes. Appendix A is a full set of financial tables for use in making investment calculations. Appendix B describes the Black-Scholes option pricing model (OPM) for those instructors and students who want to explore this important model. Related problems are included. Appendix C lists by topic all equations found in the text and all routines on the *Investment Management Disk (IMD)*. Appendix D explains how to use the student version of AAII's *Stock Investor*.

SUPPLEMENTAL MATERIALS

We recognize the key role of a complete and creative package of materials to supplement a basic textbook. We believe that the following materials, offered with this sixth edition, will enrich the investments course for both students and professors.

 ### THE INVESTMENT MANAGEMENT DISK

Included with each new copy of the book is the *Investment Management Disk (IMD)*, which was revised and improved for this sixth edition by Donald G. Crawford of DGC Consulting. The purpose of the disk is to perform the calculation of virtually all of the formulas, ratios, and valuation procedures presented in the book and listed in Appendix C. The 3½-inch disk is user-friendly and fully interactive. More than a problem solver, it also enhances the student's understanding of the investment process. The disk is keyed to all applicable text discussions and end-of-chapter and ancillary materials with a computer disk symbol 🖫. Detailed instructions for using the disk are printed on the back left endpaper.

INVESTOR'S RESOURCE MANUAL (IRM)

Shrink-wrapped free with each new copy of the textbook, this supplement will further enrich the student's learning experience. The *Investor's Resource Manual (IRM)* has four parts: First is the "List of Sources of Financial Information," a list that includes various financial publications and advisories, academic and professional journals, books, commercial bank reports, institutional publications, and investor subscription services. The purpose of this material is to help investors gain useful information about economic and investment outlooks as well as information about specific securities.

The second part of the *Investor's Resource Manual (IRM)* includes a variety of company, industry, and economic reports obtained from *Moody's, Standard & Poor's*, and *Value Line*. These reports provide a real-world slant to the study of investments and give students the opportunity for some hands-on experience analyzing two companies: Tootsie Roll Industries and Liz Claiborne Corporation. Similarly, the third part of the *IRM* reprints several Morningstar mutual fund reports for student analysis and hands-on experience.

The fourth part of the *Investor's Resource Manual* reprints the latest annual report for Tootsie Roll Industries, in its entirety. The ready availability of this report enables students to review an actual annual report and offers the raw material for use in performing fundamental analysis of Tootsie Roll Industries, especially in Chapters 6 and 7, which cover common stock.

A series of classroom exercises and assignments that use the Tootsie Roll annual report are included in the *Instructor's Manual*. These focus on the different types of information contained in annual reports and the different ways such reports can be used. Bookstores can order extra copies of this reference guide to sell alone or with used copies of the book.

STUDY GUIDE

The student review manual, *Study Guide to Accompany Fundamentals of Investing, Sixth Edition*, prepared by Majed R. Muhtaseb of the California State Polytechnic University–Pomona, has been completely revised. Each chapter of the *Study Guide* contains a chapter summary, a chapter outline, and a programmed self-test that consists of true-false and multiple-choice questions. Following the self-test are problems with detailed solutions and, where appropriate, calculator key strokes showing use of the calculator to solve certain problems. All elements are similar in form and content to those found in the book.

ENRICHMENT TOOLS

Available to adopters of the sixth edition are two enrichment tools that allow students to gain practical experience building and managing an investment portfolio. They are:

STOCK-TRAK® Portfolio Management Simulation

STOCK-TRAK® is a mock brokerage service through which students can gain realistic portfolio management experience. Each student who registers with STOCK-TRAK® receives a STOCK-TRAK® brokerage account with up to $100,000 in imaginary cash and 6 to 12 weeks in which to buy, sell, buy on margin, sell short, and write options and trade any of the following investment vehicles: stocks, bonds, stock options, index options and futures, interest rate options and futures, commodity futures, foreign currency options and futures, and mutual funds. Students receive periodic statements of their account activity and performance, and instructors receive a summary of class results. Students who participate in STOCK-TRAK® simply call a toll-free number and speak with "brokers" to make trades. For its brokers, STOCK-TRAK® employs and carefully trains mostly graduate and undergraduate finance students from universities in the Atlanta area, so that all have a working knowledge of the subject matter.

Stock Investor: The Student Version

Stock Investor: The Student Version is a simplified version of the American Association of Institutional Investors' popular *Stock Investor* program. This basic screening and analysis program includes fundamental information on over 1000 publicly traded companies and 60 (broadly defined) industry groups. The software enables students to practice their investment skills by screening and analyzing for companies that meet specific criteria. Appendix D provides more information on *Stock Investor: The Student Version*.

INSTRUCTOR'S MANUAL

Written by the text authors, with the assistance of Karyn Williams of Arizona State University, the *Instructor's Manual* contains chapter outlines; a list of major topics discussed in each chapter; detailed chapter reviews; answers to all Concepts in Review questions, Discussion Questions and Problems; solutions to the Case Problems; and ideas for outside projects, including a series of assignments and exercises to accompany the Tootsie Roll Industries annual report. Instructions for outside projects are printed on separate sheets, for ease in duplicating them for classroom distribution. The manual contains nearly 100 transparency masters, consisting of outlines, exhibits, and Problem and Case solutions.

TEST BANK

Revised for the sixth edition by Susan Mason, the Test Bank now includes a substantial number of new questions. Each chapter now contains at least 15 true-false questions, at least 40 multiple-choice questions, and several problems and short-essay questions. The Test Bank is available on Testmaster, a highly acclaimed microcomputerized test-generating system with word processing capabilities. The system produces customized tests and allows instructors to scramble questions and add new ones. Testmaster is available in both IBM and Macintosh versions.

OVERHEAD TRANSPARENCIES

A set of 80 overhead transparencies is available free to adopters. The acetates include key art, tables, and equations from the text, solutions to Problems and Cases, and, for additional classroom practice, problems and solutions not found in the textbook.

ACKNOWLEDGMENTS Many people gave their generous assistance during the initial development and the revisions of *Fundamentals of Investing*. The expertise, classroom experience, and general advice of both colleagues and practitioners were invaluable. Reactions and suggestions from students throughout the country—comments we especially enjoy receiving—sustained our belief in the need for a fresh, informative, and teachable investments text.

A few individuals provided significant subject matter expertise in the initial development of the book. They are Terry S. Maness of Baylor University, Arthur L. Schwartz, Jr., of the University of South Florida at St. Petersburg, and Gary W. Eldred. Their contributions are greatly appreciated. In addition, HarperCollins obtained the experienced advice of a large group of reviewers. We appreciate their many suggestions and criticisms, which have had a strong influence on various aspects of this volume. Our special thanks go to the following people who reviewed all or part of the manuscripts for the previous five editions of the book.

M. Fall Ainina	Robert D. Hollinger	John Park
Gary Baker	Sue Beck Howard	Ronald S. Pretekin
Harisha Batra	Roland Hudson, Jr.	Stephen W. Pruitt
Richard B. Bellinfante	A. James Ifflander	William A. Richard
Cecil C. Bigelow	Donald W. Johnson	Linda R. Richardson
A. David Brummett	Ravindra R. Kamath	William A. Rini
Gary P. Cain	Bill Kane	Roy A. Roberson
Gary Carman	Daniel J. Kaufmann, Jr.	Edward Rozalewicz
Daniel J. Cartell	David S. Kidwell	William J. Ruckstuhl
P. R. Chandy	Phillip T. Kolbe	Gary G. Schlarbaum
David M. Cordell	Sheri Kole	Keith V. Smith
Timothy Cowling	Thomas M. Krueger	Harold W. Stevenson
Robert M. Crowe	George Kutner	Nancy E. Strickler
Clifford A. Diebold	Robert T. LeClair	Glenn T. Sweeny
James Dunn	Weston A. McCormac	Phillip D. Taylor
Betty Marie Dyatt	David J. McLaughlin	Robert C. Tueting
Steven J. Elbert	Keith Manko	Howard E. Van Auken
Frank J. Fabozzi	Kathy Milligan	John R. Weigel
Robert A. Ford	Warren E. Moeller	Peter M. Wichert
Harry P. Guenther	Homer Mohr	Glenn A. Wilt, Jr.
Gay Hatfield	Joseph Newhouse	John C. Woods
Elizabeth Hennigar	Joseph F. Ollivier	Richard H. Yanow

The following people provided extremely useful reviews and input to the sixth edition:

Paul Bolster, *Northeastern University*
Richard F. DeMong, *University of Virginia*
Thomas Eyssell, *University of Missouri–St. Louis*
Chaim Ginsberg, *Borough of Manhattan Community College*
Joel Gold, *University of Southern Maine*
Brian Grinder, *Eastern Washington University*
Mahboubul Hassan, *New Hampshire College*
Nancy Kegelman, *Brookdale Community College*
Larry A. Lynch, *Roanoke College*
Timothy Manuel, *University of Montana*
Majed R. Muhtaseb, *California State Polytechnic University–Pomona*

Because of the wide variety of topics covered in the book, we called upon many experts for advice. We thank them and their firms for allowing us to draw on their insights and awareness of recent developments, to ensure that the text is as current as possible. In particular, we want to mention Russell L. Block, San Diego, California; George Ebenhack, Oppenheimer & Co., Los Angeles, California; Richard Esposito, Prana Investments, Inc., New York; N. Arthur Hulick, Investment Planning and Management, Scottsdale, Arizona; Mike Iacampo, Donaldson, Lufkin, & Jenrette, Los Angeles, California; Martin P. Klitzner, Sunrise Capital Partners, Del Mar, California; Douglas R. Lempereur, Templeton Global Bond Managers, Ft. Lauderdale, Florida.; David M. Love, Kenmar Institutional Investment Management, Rancho Santa Fe, California; Robert Luck, CFA, Association for Investment Management and Research (AIMR), Charlottesville, Virginia; Donald R. Maescher, Seidler Amdec Realty Advisors, Inc., San Diego, California; David H. McLaughlin, Chase Investment Counsel Corp., Charlottesville, Virginia; Michael R. Murphy, Sceptre Investment Counsel, Toronto, Ontario, Canada; Mark S. Nussbaum, PaineWebber, La Jolla, California; John Richardson, Northern Trust Bank of Arizona, Phoenix, Arizona; Pat Rupp, IDS, Inc., Dayton, Ohio; Mike Smith, Economic Analysis Corporation, Los Angeles, California; Eric Sorenson, Salomon Bros., Inc., New York; Jeanine K. Volinski, La Jolla Insurance Services, La Jolla, California; Barbara Walchli, First Interstate Capital Management, Scottsdale, Arizona; Fred Weaver, Great Western Bank, Phoenix, Arizona; and Lynn Yturri, BancOne Arizona, Phoenix, Arizona.

We greatly appreciate the support of our colleagues at San Diego State University and Arizona State University. Special thanks to Robert J. Wright of Wright & Wright, CPAs, San Diego, and to Vaughn Armstrong of Washington State University–Vancouver for their help in revising and updating the many tax discussions, and to Professor Christopher M. Korth of Western Michigan University for his help in further "internationalizing" the text. Thanks, too, to Professor Frank Griggs of Grand Valley State University for his ideas on strengthening the material on the P/E approach to stock valuation and to Professor Albert J. Fredman of California State University, Fullerton, for his help in preparing the material on closed-end mutual funds. We also thank Majed R. Muhtaseb for his useful feedback and for authoring the *Study Guide* and Susan Mason for revising and updating the Test Bank. Special thanks are due Marlene G. Bellamy of Writeline Associates for her research and writing help as well as her assistance in preparing the Investor Interviews, Investor Insights, and some of the InvestorFacts. Thanks to Amy Balser Blumenthal for writing assistance in preparing the Investor Insights. Our thanks also go to Don Crawford for developing the latest version of the *Investment Management Disk*; to John Bajkowski and John Markese of the American Association of Individual Investors (AAII) for adapting and allowing us to use the *Stock Investor: The Student Version*; to Tom Krueger of the University of Wisconsin–La Crosse for his contributions of sections on how to use STOCK-TRAK® and AAII's *Stock Investor: The Student Version*; and to Kaye Coates of KDC Software Solutions, Tuscon, Arizona, for her help in adapting the AAII Stock Investor data set to our book. Thanks are also due to Mark T. Brookshire of Stock-Trak, Inc., for licensing our use of the STOCK-TRAK® service and to Tootsie Roll Industries, Inc., for allowing us to reprint its annual report. We are grateful too for the research assistance provided by Derek Krebs and Melissa Beede, and for the clerical assistance of Liz Rogers, Francis Grieshaber, and Pam Hively.

The staff of HarperCollins, particularly Joan Cannon, Arlene Bessenoff, and Kate Steinbacher, contributed their creativity, enthusiasm, and commitment to this textbook. Thanks to Diane Kraut, freelance permissions editor, who managed the important task of organizing and clearing permissions; to Julie Zasloff, supplements editor, who masterminded supplements development and packaging; and to electronic production manager Eric Jorgensen. Freelance development editor Ann Torbert and production editors Elinor Stapleton and Lisa Kinne, both of Thompson Steele Production Services, warrant special thanks for shepherding the project through the development and production stages. Without their care and concern, the text would not have evolved into the teachable and interesting text we believe it to be. A very special word of thanks is due Ann Torbert both for her outstanding development work and for her work in pulling together the numerous parts of this project.

Finally, our wives, Robin and Charlene, and our children, Jessica and Zachary, and Chris and Terry and his wife, Sara, played important roles by providing support and understanding during the book's development, revision, and production. We are forever grateful to them, and we hope that this edition will justify the sacrifices required during the many hours we were away from them working on this book.

Lawrence J. Gitman
Michael D. Joehnk

FUNDAMENTALS OF INVESTING

Sixth Edition

Lawrence J. Gitman
San Diego State University

Michael D. Joehnk
Arizona State University

Fundamentals of Investing, 6/e presents its subject as a dynamic activity rather than as a set of rules. The sixth edition describes and explains techniques, vehicles, and strategies for implementing investment goals in light of risk-return tradeoffs. Gitman and Joehnk include a wide variety of real-world examples to guide students through the material and illustrate important points. The text reflects the numerous changes in today's investment environment, such as the increased importance of international investing and the expanded role of mutual funds. This edition also includes an enhanced learning system tied to achievable, class-tested learning goals, a stronger focus on the individual investor that demonstrates the relevancy of the material to the student's own life, and computerized exercises that enable students to develop and implement investment strategies.

INVESTOR INTERVIEW

Ravi Rao began investing in 1981 when a freshman at the University of Alaska. Realizing that the earlier he started, the more his money would grow (due to the time value of money), with summer job earnings he purchased a six-month CD yielding 17 percent. "I liked the high yields and low risk of CDs but also wanted to buy stocks—more for the challenge than to make money," Ravi remembers. "Being naive, I invested without knowing what I was doing and picked stocks based on gut instinct. I didn't read the financial press, know how stocks were valued, or pay attention to the risk-return tradeoff: The greater the risk (the variability of expected returns), the higher the return an investment should provide. I had no specific return in mind."

In the early 1980s, Ravi picked good technology industries (computers, telecommunications) but poor companies and then wouldn't sell. "For example, I picked Kaypro rather than the analysts' choice, Compaq—a bad move!" he explains. "Kaypro stock dropped like a rock, but my broker urged me to hold on. When I sold, I lost 40 percent of my original investment." He watched his Hershey Oil stock go from $6 to $12 but again didn't sell; eventually, he sold at a loss.

After his early mistakes, Ravi educated himself about investing and also took finance and investment courses during his MBA studies. He studies stock fundamentals, rather than following someone else's "hot tips." He sticks to industries he understands, and he researches the company, its industry, key trends, and broader factors like the economy and market forces. Ravi seeks stocks he thinks will rise substantially (20 percent) over three to six months. Before investing, Ravi estimates his return on investment using time value of money concepts to make sure the projected return, at minimum, equals his goal after commissions. More importantly, given his early difficulties, he sells when the stock reaches his target price or hits a plateau. This can be hard, though: He bought Compaq at 30, sold at 36, then watched it go to 50.

Due to limited investment funds, Ravi buys stocks of a few major American companies at a time and is considering mutual funds. Recognizing that international investments can boost his returns, he also plans to invest in Singapore. He takes a subjective approach to risk, analyzing the company, its products, and its industry thoroughly and looking for a competitive advantage, moderate levels of risk, and stocks in different industries—like Ford (which he bought at 24¼ and sold at 45–his best stock to date) and PepsiCo—to reduce risk through limited diversification.

> I DIDN'T READ THE FINANCIAL PRESS, KNOW HOW STOCKS WERE VALUED, OR PAY ATTENTION TO THE RISK-RETURN TRADEOFF.

Ravi is essentially a patient investor who relies on his personal understanding of a company's product or service, basic financial and statistical concepts, and a firm philosophy of saving for the future. For him, investing is exciting: "It means sharing in the success of American business."

Ravi Rao grew up in Alaska and lives in Seattle, Washington. He has a B.S. degree in geology and an MBA from the University of Alaska. Prior to his current job as a junior accountant, he was a field geologist, ARCO intern, and Science Project Business Manager–Alaska Science and Technology Foundation Grant.

INVESTOR INTERVIEW

At the beginning of each chapter, *Investor Interviews* provide students with personal insights into the motivations, strategies, and outcomes of investment programs of today's individual investors.

INTEGRATED LEARNING SYSTEM

A comprehensive and integrated learning system, incorporating learning goals, points students to central concepts and helps them master the material before they move on. Learning goals are tied to each major section, are supported by "Concept in Review" questions, and are restated in the summary and reviewed in the problems and questions at the chapter's end.

LEARNING GOALS

After studying this chapter, you should be able to:

LG 1 Understand the meaning of the term *investment* and the factors commonly used to differentiate between various types of investments.

LG 2 Describe the structure of and participants in the investment process and the types of investors.

LG 3 Review the importance of, rewards from, and steps in investing.

LG 4 Discuss the principal types of investment vehicles, including short-term vehicles, common stock, fixed-income securities, and mutual funds.

LG 5 Describe other kinds of popular investment vehicles—real estate, tangibles, and tax-advantaged investments—and derivative securities—options, rights, warrants, and futures.

LG 6 Summarize the content and organizational model around which this text is structured.

INVESTMENT VEHICLES

LG 4 **LG 5**

A broad range of investment vehicles is available to individual investors. Some vehicles are securities, others are not. Even among securities there are many different types, each having different maturities or lives, costs, return and risk characteristics, and tax considerations. The same is true of property investments. We devote the bulk of this book—Chapters 5 through 15—to describing the characteristics, special features, returns and risks, and possible investment strategies that can be used with vehicles available to the individual investor. Here we will introduce the various investment outlets and give a brief description of each. Table 1.1 summarizes the information presented in this section.

SHORT-TERM VEHICLES

short-term vehicles
savings instruments that usually have lives of one year or less.

Short-term vehicles include savings instruments that usually have lives of one year or less. The most important of these are various types of deposit accounts, U.S. Treasury bills (T-bills), certificates of deposit (CDs), commer-

SUMMARY

LG 1 Understand the meaning of the term *investment* and the factors commonly used to differentiate between various types of investments. An investment is any vehicle into which funds can be placed with the expectation that they will generate positive income and/or their value will be preserved or increase. Some vehicles are securities; others are forms of property. Some investments are made directly, others indirectly. An investment can be a debt, an equity, or a derivative security such as an option. It can possess risk ranging from very low to extremely high. An individual can invest in either short-term or long-term vehicles. Today, individual investors have ready access to foreign as well as domestic investments.

LG 2 Describe the structure of and participants in the investment process and the types of investors. The investment process is structured around financial institutions and financial markets that bring together suppliers and demanders of funds. The participants are government, business, and individuals. Of these groups, only individuals are net funds suppliers. Investors can be either individual investors or institutional investors.

LG 3 Review the importance of, rewards from, and steps in investing. Investing is important because it makes available funds needed to permit our economy to function, grow, and prosper. The rewards for investing can be received either as current income or as increased value. The steps in investing involve the following: meeting investment prerequisites, establishing investment goals, evaluating investment vehicles, selecting suitable investments, constructing a diversified portfolio, and managing the portfolio.

LG 4 Discuss the principal types of investment vehicles, including short-term vehicles, common stock, fixed-income securities, and mutual funds. A broad range of investment vehicles is available. Short-term vehicles have low risk. They are used to earn a return on temporarily idle funds, as a primary investment outlet of conservative investors, and to provide liquidity. Common stocks offer dividends and capital gains. Fixed-income securities—bonds, preferred stock, and convertible securities—offer fixed periodic returns with some potential for gain in value. Mutual funds are popular investment vehicles that allow investors to conveniently buy or sell interests in a professionally managed diversified portfolio of securities.

LG 5 Describe other kinds of popular investment vehicles—real estate, tangibles, and tax-advantaged investments—and derivative securities—options, rights, warrants, and futures. Other popular investment vehicles include real estate; tangibles such as gold, other precious metals, gems, and collectibles; and tax-advantaged investments, which include various tax shelters. Derivative securities are high-risk, high-expected-return vehicles, the key ones being options—rights, warrants, puts and calls—and futures—commodity and financial.

INVESTOR INSIGHTS BOXES

"Investor Insights" boxes provide students with real-life investing situations to apply to the theories and concepts they are studying.

⚡ INVESTOR INSIGHTS: *Market Innovations*

Here Comes the Electronic Investor

Imagine being able to trade stocks, bonds, options, and mutual funds with your personal computer, in the comfort of your own home. Such on-line trading is now possible—all you need is a computer with a modem and a subscription to one of the on-line computer services, such as Prodigy, CompuServe, or America Online. Each is linked to discount brokerages that allow you to place orders electronically (once you have opened an account, of course). Three other services—Charles Schwab & Co.'s *StreetSmart*, Fidelity Investments's *On-line Xpress (FOX)*, and AccuTrade—let you trade on-line directly without using one of the subscription services.

Here's how the process works: Your order goes from your computer through the on-line service to the brokerage's computer, which notes the type of order you have made and runs the necessary compliance checks. Some brokerage houses require that a person approve the order, though this tends to be the exception. The order then goes to the floor of the stock exchange, is executed automatically or given to a specialist who matches it to a reciprocal order, and is sent back to the brokerage marked "executed." A confirmation then travels back along the same electronic path to your computer. These transactions can take as little as 10 seconds, and 70 percent of them occur within one minute.

Beyond actual trading programs, on-line services offer many other options, with more available each month. Some services offer quotes for stocks and mutual funds, databases of investment information, and stock market analyses used by professional investment analysts. At any time of day or night, subscribers can dial into the Dow Jones News/Retrieval Service or Standard & Poor's MarketScope service to get current and historical news on the companies that interest them.

On-line investing is certainly not for everyone. In fact, only a tiny percentage of investors have chosen this option over more traditional trading methods. To decide if you should invest on-line, weigh the pros and cons. Most important is your willingness to invest your time and to trust your decisions. You must master the nuances of computer trading programs (which can be complicated), do your own research, and have the confidence to complete trades electronically. Those unsure of this last requirement should know that some programs offer you the chance to practice making a trade until you have become comfortable with the mechanics involved. Also, it generally is difficult to make careless mistakes, because brokerages require that you verify your trading instructions.

Not ready to trade electronically? More than 500 investment programs can help you become a better investor. Unlike the earliest investment software, which did little more than help people keep track of their finances, the latest programs can create a portfolio and then test its composition to improve performance, examine all U.S. mutual funds to find your desired balance of risk and reward, or analyze the trading pattern of any stock to find the right time to buy or sell.

If you decide to become an on-line investor, good luck. A final word of advice: Never forget that you're playing with real money, not a computer game!

Sources: Ed Henry, "When Your Computer Is Your Broker," *Kiplinger's Personal Finance Magazine*, July 1994, pp. 93–95; Carla Koehl, "Electronic Investing," *Worth*, April 1994, pp. 76–77; Walter S. Mossberg, "The Digital Trading Post," *SmartMoney*, February 1994, pp. 126–30; and Leonard Wiener, "Your Own Private Investing Library," *U.S. News & World Report*, November 29, 1993, pp. 104–9.

street name

firms will hold the client's security certificates for safekeeping; the stocks kept by the firm in this manner are said to be held in **street name.** Because the securities are issued in the brokerage house's name and held in trust for the client (rather than issued in the client's name), they can be more easily transferred at the time of sale without having to obtain the client's signature. Street name is

Table 5.2   Holding Period Returns in the Stock Market, 1955–1994

Holding Periods	Average Annual Returns	Cumulative Returns	Amount to Which $10,000 Will Grow
5 yrs.: 1990–94	9.95%	60.68%	$ 16,068.28
10 yrs.: 1985–94	14.86	299.65	39,965.17
15 yrs.: 1980–94	14.25	638.07	73,806.79
25 yrs.: 1970–94	10.59	1139.37	123,936.70
40 yrs.: 1955–94	9.77	4064.97	416,496.92
The 1980s: 1980–89	16.5	359.3	45,933.23
The 1970s: 1970–79	5.3	67.9	16,792.04
The 1960s: 1960–69	5.2	66.0	16,602.04

Note: Average annual return figures are fully compounded returns and assume that all dividend income *and* capital gains (or losses) are automatically reinvested. All figures compiled from DJIA performance information, as obtained from *Barron's* and the *Wall Street Journal.*

Keep in mind that the numbers represent market averages; *individual* stocks can and often do perform quite differently. At least, though, the averages give us a benchmark against which we can assess current stock returns and our expectations. For example, if a return of 12 to 14 percent can be considered a good midpoint, then *sustained* returns of 18 to 20 percent can definitely be viewed as extraordinary. (Of course, if you want these higher returns, you're going to have to take on a lot more risk.) Likewise, long-run stock returns of only 6 to 8 percent should be viewed as substandard performance. If that's the best you think you can do, then you probably should stick with bonds or CDs, where you'll earn almost as much but with less risk. Actually, returns of 10 to 12 percent are not all that bad: Table 5.2 shows what a $10,000 investment would have grown to over various holding periods within the 1955–1994 time frame.

ADVANTAGES AND DISADVANTAGES OF STOCK OWNERSHIP

INVESTOR FACTS

"Investor Facts" boxes capture students' attention and help apply investment material through interesting statistics, unusual investment experiences, or humorous anecdotes.

One reason stocks are so appealing to investors is the substantial return opportunities they offer. As we just saw, stocks generally do provide attractive, highly competitive returns over the long haul. Indeed, common stock returns compare very well to alternative investment outlets, like long-term corporate bonds or U.S. Treasury securities. For example, over the 40-year period from 1955 through 1994, high-grade corporate bonds averaged annual returns of around 6 percent—*a little more than half that of common stocks.* Although long-term bonds sometimes do outperform stocks on a year-by-year basis (as they did in the mid-1980s, when interest rates were falling), the opposite is true far more often than not; that is, stocks outperform bonds, and usually by a wider margin. The main reason is that stockholders are entitled to participate fully in the residual profits of the firm. When the company prospers, so do investors—in the form of rising share prices (capital gains).

Stocks offer other benefits as well: Common stocks are easy to buy and sell, and the transactions costs are modest. Moreover, price and market information is widely disseminated in the news and financial media. A final advantage of stock ownership is that the unit cost of a share of common is usually within the reach of most individual investors. Unlike bonds, which carry minimum denominations of at least $1,000, and some mutual funds that have

I͟NVESTOR F͟ACTS

STOCK TRENDS—The third year of a president's term is historically a boom year for the stock market. The S&P 500 has risen in the third year of *every* presidential term since 1943, by an average of 18.6 percent. And the market has risen more during the third year of Democratic presidential terms than Republican ones—by 21 percent versus 16.4 percent.

(Source: *Bottom Line Personal*, December 1, 1994, p. 9.)

Questions of which stock or bond to select, when to buy, and when to sell have plagued investors for as long as there have been organized capital markets. Such concerns lie at the very heart of the mutual fund concept. They explain, in large part, the growth mutual funds have experienced. Many investors lack the time, know-how, or commitment to manage their own portfolios and, as a result, turn to others. That's why increasing numbers of investors let professional investment managers like Elizabeth Bramwell decide which stocks to buy and when to sell.

THE MUTUAL FUND PHENOMENON

mutual fund
an investment company that invests its shareholders' money in a diversified portfolio of securities.

Basically, a **mutual fund** is a type of financial service organization that receives money from its shareholders and then invests those funds on their behalf in a diversified portfolio of securities. There are mutual funds available to meet just about any investor need. Mutual funds, in fact, have been a part of our investment landscape for more than 70 years. The first one was started in Boston in 1924—and it's still in business today. By 1940, the number of mutual funds had grown to 68, and by 1980, to 564 funds. But that was only the beginning: The next dozen or so years saw unprecedented growth in the mutual fund industry. Assets under fund management grew from less than $100 billion in 1980 to *over $2 trillion in 1994*. Indeed, by 1994 *there were more than 6,000 publicly traded mutual funds in existence*. The fund industry has grown so much, in fact, that it is now the second largest financial intermediary, behind only commercial banks—but not by much. Finally, although we tend to think of mutual funds as an American phenomenon, the fact is that mutual funds, in one form or another, are found in all the major markets in the world. Indeed, in 1994 there was $2 trillion in assets under management in foreign funds, an amount nearly equivalent to the assets in U.S. funds.

What caused the extraordinary growth of mutual funds? Basically, three things: First, money market mutual funds experienced explosive growth. Second, the introduction of self-directed individual retirement accounts (IRAs) created a strong demand for mutual fund products. Third, the stock and bond markets experienced record-breaking performances (resulting from a number of factors, including sharply reduced inflation). Investors in unprecedented numbers flocked to those markets, and the mutual fund industry responded by developing new products and new funds. So many new products were created, in fact, that there are now more mutual funds in existence than there are stocks on the *New York and American stock exchanges, combined*!

AN OVERVIEW OF MUTUAL FUNDS

Mutual fund investors come from all walks of life and all income levels. They range from highly inexperienced to highly experienced investors who all share a common view: Each has decided, for one reason or another, to turn over at least a part of their investment management activities to professionals. Mutual funds are popular because they offer not only a variety of interesting investment opportunities but also a wide array of services that many investors find appealing. Investors in mutual funds are considered shareholders of the fund. An investment in a mutual fund therefore represents an ownership position in

---

EARLIER COVERAGE OF MUTUAL FUNDS

Earlier coverage of mutual funds, real estate, and other tangible investments, as well as tax-advantaged investments, provides a timely discussion of the investment vehicles of greatest appeal to individual investors.

INVESTOR INSIGHTS: *Conflicting Viewpoints*

Derivative Securities: There Are Two Sides to Every Story

Derivatives—they're an $18 trillion market that some investors shun at all costs and others use as a route to big returns: Individual investors buy puts and calls to limit their downside risk on stocks they own; risk takers use them to speculate on stock price movements. Even if you don't personally use them, the corporations, financial institutions, and mutual funds in which you invest use them to manage risk efficiently and to increase investment returns. How can you determine the effect that will have on the profitability of a company or a mutual fund in which you invest?

Derivatives vary tremendously in complexity and risk. Traditional, "conservative" derivatives like put and call options and futures are used all the time by companies and mutual funds as a type of insurance to limit risk. Recently, however, investment bankers have created increasingly complex and "toxic" synthetic derivatives. Examples include an *interest strip* (in which a bond's interest stream—the derivative—is separated from the bond and provides *only interest payments* on the underlying security), *collateralized mortgage obligations* (derived from mortgage-backed securities, themselves created from pools of home mortgages), *interest rate swaps* (in which two parties exchange fixed rates for variable rate interest payments), and even *swaptions* (options to enter into a swap).

In many cases, derivatives are the least expensive way to protect against sharp movements in currency values, commodity prices, or interest rates. Many sophisticated corporate treasurers and fund managers use them successfully to stabilize earnings and lower risk,

and funds that use derivatives often earn higher returns than those that don't. Hedging with currency forwards and futures reduces the risk of fluctuating currency prices for mutual funds holding foreign securities and companies wishing to protect foreign revenues, prices on imported products, and raw materials purchased abroad. On the other hand, betting on market movements is speculative and very risky. Even experienced, sophisticated investors can lose big; in 1994, Procter & Gamble lost $157 million pretax when it misjudged the direction of interest rates.

Should you panic if you find such derivatives as forwards, futures, and CMOs lurking in the financial reports of a corporation or mutual fund you own? Probably not, but you will need to ask some questions: How experienced is the person who's investing in derivatives? Are the derivatives used appropriately for the company or fund (i.e., to hedge currency exposure rather than to speculate on market movements)? Once you know the answers, you can judge if the derivatives are good or bad for the organization's—and your portfolio's—financial health.

Sources: Adapted from Lee Berton, "Understanding the Complex World of Derivatives," *Wall Street Journal*, June 14, 1994, pp. C1, C17; Rita Koselka, "Safe When Used Properly," *Forbes*, August 15, 1994, pp. 47–48; Lililana Nealon, "Derivatives and the Bogey Monster," *Worth*, October 1994, p. 107–8; and Maria Crawford Scott, "A Look at Derivatives and Their Use in Mutual Fund Portfolios," *AAII Journal*, September 1994, pp. 12–15.

INCREASED COVERAGE OF DERIVATIVE SECURITIES

Various issues and developments constantly reshape the financial markets and investment vehicles. A thorough discussion of derivatives gives students a realistic understanding of the investment arena, thereby allowing them to develop and implement effective investment strategies.

Puts and calls are traded on listed exchanges and, on a *much smaller scale*, in the over-the-counter market. They provide attractive leverage opportunities because they carry low prices relative to the market price of the underlying financial assets. To illustrate, consider a call on a common stock that gives the holder the right to buy 100 shares of a $50 stock at a (strike) price of $45 a share. The stock would be priced at $50, but the call would trade at an effective price of only $5 a share (or the difference between the market price of the common and the price it can be purchased at as specified on the call).

INTEGRATED STOCK-TRAK® PROBLEMS

The STOCK-TRAK® portfolio management simulation enables students to construct portfolios and trade securities in real-time prices by calling a "broker" at a toll-free number. A brief section preceding the end-of-chapter summary describes how the STOCK-TRAK® simulation relates to the chapter topic.

On Track with STOCK-TRAK®

How STOCK-TRAK® Calculates Holding Period Return

STOCK-TRAK® calculates the total portfolio value at valuation dates. It does not make any adjustments for the amount of risk incurred in the investment process. STOCK-TRAK® first calculates the portfolio's equity, or value, using the following equation:

$$Equity = cash - debit\ balance + credit\ balance + MV_{long\ position} - MV_{short\ position}$$

where:

debit balance = amount borrowed for margin trading

credit balance = proceeds from short sales

MV = current market value

The portfolio's holding period return, HPR, is then calculated using the following equation:

$$HPR = \frac{equity - beginning\ cash\ balance}{beginning\ cash\ balance}$$

If the beginning cash balance exceeds equity, the holding period return will be negative, representing a loss for the period.

SUMMARY

LG 1 Review the concept, components, and importance of return and the forces that affect the investor's level of return. Return is the reward for investing. The total return provided by an investment includes current income and capital gains (or losses). Return is commonly calculated on a historical basis and then used to project expected returns. The level of return depends on internal characteristics and external forces, which include the general level of price changes.

LG 2 Discuss the time value of money and the calculations involved in finding the future value of various types of cash flows. Because investors have opportunities to earn interest on their funds, the time value of money must be considered when evaluating investment returns. Interest can be applied using either the simple interest method or the compound interest method. The more frequently interest is compounded at a stated rate, the higher the true rate of interest. The future value of a present sum or an annuity can be found using compound interest concepts.

LG 3 Explain the concept of present value, the procedures for calculating present values, and the use of present value in determining a satisfactory investment. The present value of a future sum is the amount that would have to be deposited today, into an account earning interest at a given rate, in order to accumulate the specified future sum. The present value of streams of future returns can be found by adding the present values of the individual returns. When the stream is an annuity, its present value can be more simply calculated. A satisfactory investment is one for which the present value of benefits equals or exceeds the present value of costs.

LG 4 Describe real, risk-free, and required returns and the computation and application of holding period return, yield (internal rate of return), approximate yield, and growth rates. The required return on an investment is the rate of return an investor must earn

USING STOCK INVESTOR:
THE STUDENT VERSION

Stock Investor: The Student Version is a simplified version of the American Association of Individual Investors' popular *Stock Investor* program. Created by AAII specifically for users of HarperCollins finance textbooks, it is a basic screening and analysis program with fundamental information on 1000 publicly traded companies and 60 (broadly defined) industry groups. The software includes a stand-alone, menu-driven program that allows you to look up, analyze, and screen for companies meeting specific criteria. *Stock Investor: The Student Version* enables students of investing to practice their investment skills by selecting a manageable number of companies for further analysis.

The AAII-HarperCollins partnership demonstrates a shared commitment to bringing the latest investment tools to students of investing at affordable prices.

HOW TO USE THIS APPENDIX

Throughout this appendix, *Stock Investor: The Student Version* will be referred to simply as *Stock Investor*. This appendix is divided into three parts. The first part describes the features of Stock Investor and provides step-by-step instructions for using the program. The second part of the appendix lists the problems that are keyed to specific chapters of *Fundamentals of Investing*. The final part provides information about AAII.

ABOUT STOCK INVESTOR

DESCRIPTION
Stock Investor provides detailed historical, fundamental, and price data from Media General on hundreds of securities. This includes stocks, closed-end funds, and REITs listed on the New York Stock Exchange, American Stock Exchange, NASDAQ National Market, and NASDAQ Small Cap Market. The program includes over 200 data elements for each security; the data is organized into financial statements.

SYSTEM REQUIREMENTS
The database size and powerful screening capabilities require an IBM-compatible 386 microprocessor or higher with 3 megabytes of available RAM, and 30 megabytes of available hard disk space.

INFORMATION CONTAINED IN THE DATASET
The dataset includes the following categories of information: basic company information; current and historical market multiples; quarterly income statement data; annual income statement data; I/B/E/S earnings estimates; balance sheet data; ratios; price and share data; valuation models; and dividend reinvestment plan details.

INTEGRATION OF AAII STOCK INVESTOR: STUDENT VERSION

Exercises for *AAII's Stock Investor* allow students to practice investment skills by selecting companies for further analysis.

PRINCIPLES OF BOND PRICE BEHAVIOR

The price of a bond is a function of its coupon, its maturity, and the movement of market interest rates. As we've seen, when interest rates go down, bond prices go up, and vice versa. The relationship of bond prices to market rates is captured in Figure 8.3. Basically, the graph reinforces the *inverse relationship* between bond prices and market interest rates: *Lower* rates lead to *higher* bond prices. Figure 8.3 also shows the difference between premium and discount bonds. A **premium bond** is one that sells for more than its par value. A premium results whenever market interest rates drop below the coupon rate on the bond. A **discount bond**, in contrast, sells for less than par and is the result of market rates being greater than the issue's coupon rate. Thus, the 10 percent bond in our illustration traded as a premium bond when market rates were at 8 percent, but as a discount bond when rates stood at 12 percent.

When a bond is first issued, it is usually sold to the public at a price that equals or is very close to its par value. Likewise, when the bond matures—some 15, 20, or 30 years later—it will once again be priced at its par value. But what happens to the price of the bond in between is of considerable interest to most bond investors. In this regard, we know that the extent to which bond prices move depends not only on the *direction* of change in interest rates but also on the *magnitude* of such changes; the greater the moves in interest rates, the greater the swings in bond prices.

However, bond price volatility also varies according to the coupon and maturity of an issue. That is, bonds with *lower coupons* and/or *longer maturities* will respond more vigorously to changes in market rates and will therefore undergo sharper price swings. (Note in Figure 8.3 that for a given change in interest rates—e.g., from 10 to 8 percent—the largest change in price occurs when the bond has the greatest number of years to maturity.) Therefore, if a *decline* in interest rates is anticipated, an investor should seek lower coupons

premium bond
a bond with a market value in excess of par; occurs when interest rates drop below the coupon rate.

discount bond
a bond with a market value lower then par; occurs when market rates are greater than the coupon rate.

FIGURE 8.3 The Price Behavior of a Bond
A bond will sell at its par value so long as the prevailing market interest rate remains the same as the bond's coupon—in this case, 10 percent. However, when market rates drop (or rise), bond prices move up (or down). As a bond approaches its maturity, the price of the issue will move toward its par value, regardless of the level of prevailing interest rates.

FIGURES AND TABLES

Figures and tables graphically enhance the concepts under discussion throughout the text.

Table 6.7 Comparative Financial Statistics: MarCor Industries and Its Major Competitors ($ Millions)

Financial Measure	MarCor Industries	Regatta Group	Holbrook Industries	Bellwood, Inc.
Total assets	$338.6	$568.6	$231.9	$469.4
Long-term debt	$ 53.7	$124.8	$ 41.5	$128.1
Stockholders' equity	$170.0	$196.9	$103.7	$200.2
Stockholders' equity as a % of total assets	50.2%	34.6%	44.7%	42.6%
Total revenues	$614.9	$807.5	$505.9	$808.0
Net earnings	$ 18.0	$ 14.5	$ 10.6	$ 12.4
Net profit margin	2.9%	1.8%	2.1%	1.5%
5-year growth rates in:				
Total assets	8.9%	10.2%	8.6%	5.6%
Total revenues	8.8%	9.5%	9.0%	3.5%
Net earnings	32.0%	18.0%	7.5%	2.5%
Dividends	10.8%	N/A	8.0%	6.0%
Total asset turnover	1.79×	1.42×	2.18×	1.73×
Debt-equity ratio	0.49	0.74	0.60	0.84
Times interest earned	5.50×	2.65×	4.67×	2.26×
ROA	5.30%	4.10%	5.20%	4.50%
ROE	10.60%	6.70%	8.50%	9.20%
Price/earnings ratio	10.20×	10.20×	13.60×	12.90×
Payout ratio	48.00%	N/A	58.80%	67.00%
Dividend yield	4.70%	N/A	4.30%	6.25%
Price-to-book-value	1.08	1.07	0.95	1.17

important, MarCor is a lot less leveraged than the other manufacturers—which is a real plus in a highly volatile industry. Yet even with its low financial leverage, it is still able to maintain a highly attractive ROE. In all, Tables 6.6 and 6.7 suggest that MarCor Industries is a solid, up-and-coming business that's been able to make a real name for itself in a highly competitive industry; the company has certainly done well in the past and appears to be well managed today. Our major concern at this point (and the topic of the first part of Chapter 8) is whether MarCor will continue to produce above-average returns to investors.

CONCEPTS *in Review*

6.12 What is fundamental analysis? Does the performance of a company have any bearing on the value of its stock? Explain.

6.13 Why do investors bother to look at the historical performance of a company when future behavior is what really counts? Explain.

6.14 What is ratio analysis? Describe the role and contribution of ratio analysis to the study of a company's financial condition and operating results.

6.15 Contrast historical standards of performance with industry standards. Briefly note the role of each in analyzing the financial condition and operating results of a company.

Savings or Investment Vehicle	Minimum Balance	Yield	Federal Insurance	Method and Ease of Withdrawing Funds
a. Passbook savings account	None		Yes	In person or through teller machines; very easy
b. NOW account				Unlimited check-writing privileges
c. Money market deposit account (MMDA)				
d. Central asset account				
e. U.S. Treasury bill				
f. Certificate of deposit (CD)				
g. Commercial paper				
h. Banker's acceptance				
i. Money market mutual fund (MMMF)				
j. Series EE savings bond	Virtually none			

PROBLEMS

1. Sonia Gomez, a 45-year-old widow, wishes to accumulate $250,000 over the next 15 years in order to supplement her retirement programs that are being funded by her employer and the federal government. She expects to earn an average annual return of about 8 percent by investing in a low-risk portfolio containing about 20 percent short-term investments, 50 percent bonds, and 30 percent common stock.

Sonia currently has $31,500 that at an 8 percent annual rate of return will grow to about $100,000 at the end of 15 years (found using time-value techniques that will be described in Chapter 4). Her financial adviser indicated that for every $1,000 Sonia wishes to accumulate at the end of 15 years, she will have to make an annual investment of $36.83. (This amount is also calculated based upon an 8 percent annual rate of return using the time-value techniques that are described in Chapter 4.) Sonia plans to accumulate needed funds by making equal, annual, end-of-year investments over the next 15 years.

    a. How much money does Sonia need to accumulate by making equal, annual, end-of-year investments in order to reach her goal of $250,000?

    b. How much must Sonia deposit annually in order to accumulate at the end of year 15 the sum calculated in (a) above?

2. During 1994, the Allens and the Zells both filed joint tax returns. The Allens' taxable income was $130,000, and the Zells had total taxable income of $65,000 for the tax year ended December 31, 1994.

    a. Using the federal tax rates given in Table 3.1, calculate the taxes for both the Allens and the Zells.

    b. Calculate and compare the ratio of the Allens' to the Zells' taxable income and the ratio of the Allens' to the Zells' taxes. What does this demonstrate about the federal income tax structure?

3. Bill Shaffer estimates taht if he does 10 hours of research using data that will cost $75, there is a good chance taht he can improve his expected return on a $10,000 one-year investment from 8 percent to 10 percent. Bill feels that he must earn at least $10 per hour on the time that he devotes to his research.

    a. Find the cost of Bill's research.

    b. By how much (in dollars) will Bill's return increase as a result of the research?

END-OF-CHAPTER PROBLEMS

Varying in complexity and scope, *end-of-chapter problems* assure professors a wide choice of assignable materials.

 Summarize the content and organizational model around which this text is structured. The text contains 17 chapters, divided into six major parts. A simple model breaks the coverage into the investment environment (Part One), key investment vehicles (Parts Two through Five), and investment administration (Part Six) and is used to link each part to the investment process.

CASE PROBLEMS

1.1   INVESTMENTS OR RACQUETBALL?

Judd Read and Judi Todd are senior accounting majors at a large midwestern university. They have been good friends since high school and look forward to their graduation at the end of next semester. Each has already found a job, which will begin upon graduation. Judd has accepted a position as an internal auditor in a medium-size manufacturing firm. Judi will be working for one of the major public accounting firms. Each is looking forward to the challenge of a new career and to the prospect of achieving success both professionally and financially.

Judd and Judi are preparing to register for their final semester. Each has one free elective to select. Judd is considering taking a racquetball course offered by the physical education department; Judi is planning to take a basic investments course. Judi has been trying to convince Judd to take investments instead of racquetball. Judd believes he doesn't need to take investments, because he already knows what common stock is. He believes that whenever he has accumulated excess funds, he can invest in the stock of a company that is doing well. Judi argues that there is much more to it than simply choosing common stock. She feels that an exposure to the field of investments would certainly be more beneficial than learning how to play racquetball.

Questions

1. Explain to Judd the structure of the investment process and the economic importance of investing.

2. Describe to Judd the steps in investing and emphasize the importance of this process to his overall financial success.

3. List and discuss the other types of investment vehicles with which Judd is apparently unfamiliar.

4. Assuming Judd is in good physical condition, what arguments would you give to convince Judd to take investments rather than racquetball?

1.2   EVALUATING MOLLY PORTER'S INVESTMENT PLAN

Molly Porter's husband, Vance, was recently killed in an airplane crash. Fortunately, he had a sizable amount of life insurance, the proceeds of which should provide Molly with adequate income for a number of years. Molly is 33 years old and has two children, David and Phyllis, who are 6 and 7 years old, respectively. Although Molly does not rule out the possibility of marrying again, she feels it is best not to consider this when making her financial plans. In order to provide adequate funds to finance her children's college education as well as her own retirement, Molly has estimated that she needs to accumulate $400,000 within the next 15 years. If she continues to teach

---

END-OF-CHAPTER CASE PROBLEMS

End-of-chapter case problems encourage students to apply techniques presented in the chapter and to recommend how an investor might solve a specific problem.

PART ONE

THE INVESTMENT ENVIRONMENT

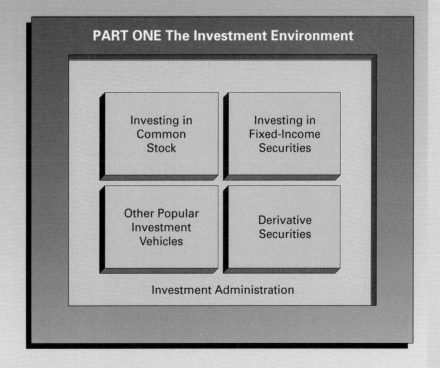

CHAPTER 1

THE ROLE AND SCOPE
OF INVESTMENTS

LEARNING GOALS

After studying this chapter, you should be able to:

LG 1 Understand the meaning of the term *investment* and the factors commonly used to differentiate between various types of investments.

LG 2 Describe the structure of and participants in the investment process and the types of investors.

LG 3 Review the importance of, rewards from, and steps in investing.

LG 4 Discuss the principal types of investment vehicles, including short-term vehicles, common stock, fixed-income securities, and mutual funds.

LG 5 Describe other kinds of popular investment vehicles—real estate, tangibles, and tax-advantaged investments—and derivative securities—options and futures.

LG 6 Summarize the content and organizational model around which this text is structured.

As *Money* magazine's 1991 mutual fund performance rankings showed, many mutual funds had five-year average annual returns exceeding 15 percent, far exceeding college student Marc Randolph's 3.5 percent savings account and EE bonds (then paying 6 percent). Realizing that investing even a small amount of his savings in such funds would lead to tremendous growth over time due to compounding, he began developing a portfolio of several types of mutual funds. As he had more money to invest and increased his knowledge of the investing process and equity markets, he sought investments with higher return potential. He identified small company, aggressive growth, and international mutual funds as good choices for a young investor who can ride out the highs and lows for the long term. The 24-year-old graduate student also began investing in individual growth stocks through NetProfits, an Internet investment club. Today, his portfolio is 68 percent stocks and equity mutual funds, 2 percent gold funds (for an inflation hedge), and 30 percent cash equivalents (for education expenses and an emergency fund).

International mutual funds now compose over half of Marc's equity investments. "I discovered that many diversified international funds earned higher historical returns than domestic growth funds with comparable risk," Marc says. "So far, I haven't been disappointed with my decision; my returns are about 20 percent, twice the return of most U.S. funds over the same two-year period." He likes the fact that international funds have a wider range of companies to choose from and that the fund manager can select what he considers the best stocks from around the world. Marc points out, "By limiting myself to only domestic stocks, I would not be able to benefit from the thousands of excellent growing companies outside of the United States." For this reason, he plans to keep a higher-than-average percentage in international investments.

Because so many additional factors are involved in analyzing international markets and individual international stocks, at the moment Marc sticks to mutual funds with at least five years of solid performance. He started with a conservative European fund but was disappointed with the results and switched to a general international growth fund to get better geographic diversification. From his research using Internet investment resources, Marc learned about the tremendous growth potential in funds focused on emerging markets like Latin America and the Far East. "They seem like the best bet for big gains over a long period of time," he explains. "But they are very volatile and can drop 20 percent or more in two weeks, so they definitely are not for the weak of heart. They show great potential for rising, however, and some emerging market funds have earned annual returns of 25 percent or more." However, Marc cautions investors to use only money they can afford to lose when buying equities, whether domestic or international. "Not even the experts can predict the market's movements correctly. No one likes losing money, but make sure that if you lose, the loss won't cause you hardship."

> BY LIMITING MYSELF TO ONLY DOMESTIC STOCKS, I WOULD NOT BE ABLE TO BENEFIT FROM THE THOUSANDS OF EXCELLENT GROWING COMPANIES OUTSIDE OF THE UNITED STATES.

Marc Randolph is a master's degree student in electrical engineering at Texas A&M University.

What is your idea of financial success? Making a million dollars? Providing for your family now and in the future? Owning an expensive house or car? Establishing a scholarship at your alma mater? Traveling around the world? The odds are probably against your achieving all the items on that list. After all, few people become millionaires. However, studying this textbook can help you make the most of your available financial resources. This book provides the information needed to establish and fulfill investment goals. You will learn how to plan your investment program and create a portfolio of investment *vehicles* (types of investments) that will produce an acceptable return for an acceptable level of risk. If you become familiar with various investment alternatives and have a set of well-developed investment plans, you should greatly increase your chance of achieving a reasonable degree of financial success.

This chapter sets the stage for an in-depth look at investing that will be presented throughout the textbook. It introduces you to essential concepts, tools, and techniques so that, like Marc Randolph, you too can embark on the rewarding journey toward financial success.

THE ROLE OF INVESTMENTS

The word *investments* can be used in a variety of ways. It can mean stocks or bonds purchased to fulfill certain financial goals; it can also mean tangible assets such as machines acquired to produce and sell a product. In the broadest sense, investments made by both individual investors and business firms provide the mechanism needed to allow our economy to grow and develop. To give you a general idea of the role of investments, we begin by defining investment and then looking at the structure of the investment process, the participants, and types of investors.

TYPES OF INVESTMENTS

investment
any vehicle into which funds can be placed with the expectation of receiving positive income and/or preserving or increasing its value.

Simply stated, an **investment** is any vehicle into which funds can be placed with the expectation that they will generate positive income and/or their value will be preserved or increase. Cash in a simple checking account is not an investment, because its value is likely to be eroded by inflation and because it fails to provide any type of income. The same cash placed in a bank savings account would be considered an investment, because the account provides income in the form of periodic interest. The various types of investments can be differentiated on the basis of a number of factors, described below.

Securities and Property

securities
investments that represent evidence of debt or ownership or the legal right to acquire or sell an ownership interest.

property
investments in real property or in tangible personal property.

Investments that represent evidence of debt or ownership (of a business or other assets) or the legal right to acquire or sell an ownership interest (in a business or other assets) are called **securities**. The most frequently used types of securities are bonds, stocks, and options. **Property,** on the other hand, is investments in real property or tangible personal property. *Real property* is land, buildings, and that which is permanently affixed to the land. *Tangible personal property* includes items such as gold, artwork, antiques, and other collectibles. Because of the existence of organized mechanisms for buying and selling securities and their widespread popularity, in this book we will focus primarily on securities.

Direct and Indirect

direct investment
investment in which an investor directly acquires a claim on a security or property.

indirect investment
investment made in a portfolio or group of securities or properties.

A **direct investment** is one in which an investor directly acquires a claim on a security or property. For example, if you buy a stock, a bond, a parcel of real estate, or a rare coin in order to earn income or preserve value, you have made a direct investment. An **indirect investment** is an investment made in a portfolio, or group of securities or properties. For example, you may purchase a share of a *mutual fund*, which is a diversified portfolio of securities issued by various firms. By doing so, you will own a claim on a fraction of the entire portfolio rather than on the security of a single firm. It is also possible to invest indirectly in property—for example, by buying an interest in a *limited partnership* that deals in real estate, oil wells, and the like. Although direct investments are preferred by many investors, indirect investments have certain attributes that make them attractive as well.

Debt, Equity, or Derivative Securities

debt
funds loaned in exchange for the receipt of interest income and the promised repayment of the loan at a given future date.

equity
an ongoing ownership interest in a specific business or property.

Usually, an investment will represent either a debt or an equity interest. **Debt** represents funds loaned in exchange for the receipt of interest income and the promised repayment of the loan at a given future date. When you buy a debt instrument like a *bond*, in effect you lend money to the issuer, who agrees to pay you a stated rate of interest over a specified period of time, at the end of which the original sum will be returned. **Equity** represents an ongoing ownership interest in a specific business or property. An equity investment may be held as a security or by title to a specific property. An investor typically obtains an equity interest in a business by purchasing securities known collectively as *common stock*.

derivative securities
securities that are structured to exhibit characteristics similar to those of an underlying security or asset and that derive their value from the underlying security or asset.

   Derivative securities are neither debt nor equity. They are structured to exhibit characteristics similar to those of an underlying security or asset. They derive their value from the securities or assets that underlie them. *Options* are an example. They provide the investor with an opportunity to sell or buy another security or asset at a specified price over a given period of time. You may, for example, pay $500 for an option to purchase 100 shares of common stock in a given firm for $50 per share for a period of six months. If the stock currently sells for $44 per share, you would not now exercise this option. Option and other derivative security investments, although not as common as debt and equity investments, have grown rapidly in popularity during recent years.

Low and High Risk

risk
the chance that an investment's value or return will be less than its expected value or return.

Investments are sometimes differentiated on the basis of risk. As used in finance, **risk** refers to the chance that the value or return on an investment will be less than its expected value or return. In other words, risk is the chance of an undesirable financial event. The broader the range of possible values or returns associated with an investment, the greater its risk, and vice versa.

Investors are confronted with a continuum ranging from low-risk U.S. government securities to high-risk futures contracts. Although each type of investment vehicle has a basic risk characteristic, the actual level of risk depends on the specific vehicle. For example, stocks are generally believed to be more risky than bonds. However, it is not difficult to find high-risk bonds that are in fact more risky than the stock of a financially sound firm such as IBM or McDonald's. *Low-risk investments* are those considered safe with regard to the receipt of a positive return. *High-risk investments* are considered speculative.

The terms *investment* and *speculation* refer to different investment approaches. As already stated, investment is the purchase of securities or property that is expected to generate positive income and/or maintain or grow in value. **Speculation** is the purchase of similar vehicles in which the levels of income and future value are highly uncertain. Both investment and speculation imply an ability to analyze and measure risk, but they differ with regard to the degree of risk. Simply stated, speculation is on the high-risk end of the investment process. Of course, due to the greater risk, the returns associated with speculation are expected to be greater. Both investment and speculation differ from gambling, which merely involves playing games of chance. In this book we will use the term *investment* for both investment and speculation. We will consider the issue of investment return and risk more closely in Chapter 4.

speculation
the purchase of investment vehicles in which the levels of expected earnings and future value are highly uncertain.

Short and Long Term

The life of an investment can be described as either short or long term. **Short-term investments** typically mature within one year. **Long-term investments** are those with longer maturities or perhaps, like common stock, with no maturity at all. A 6-month certificate of deposit (CD) would be a short-term investment, whereas a 20-year bond would be a long-term investment. Of course, by purchasing a long-term investment and selling it after a short period of time, say 6 months, an investor can use a long-term vehicle to meet a short-term goal. As will become clear later, it is not unusual to find investors matching the maturity of an investment to the period of time over which they wish to invest their funds. The classification of short term and long term may also be useful for tax purposes. Currently, the tax laws define short-term and long-term gains (and losses) in a similar fashion—short term is one year or less and long term is longer than one year. Tax considerations will be discussed briefly in Chapter 3, and tax fundamentals and various types of tax-advantaged investments will be described in Chapter 13.

short-term investments
investments that typically mature within one year.

long-term investments
investments with maturities of longer than a year or with no maturity at all.

Domestic and Foreign

As recently as 10 to 15 years ago, individuals invested almost exclusively in purely **domestic investments,** which were the debt, equity, and derivative securities and property of U.S.-based companies. Today, these same investors routinely look beyond the United States to find **foreign investments**—both direct and indirect—that offer more attractive returns or lower risk than purely domestic investments. Recent advances in communication and funds transfer technology, along with the development of new mechanisms and markets, today make it easy for individuals to invest in foreign securities. Particularly popular is indirect investment in foreign companies by purchasing shares of

domestic investments
debt, equity, and derivative securities and property of U.S.-based companies.

foreign investments
direct and indirect purchase of debt, equity, and derivative securities and property of foreign-based companies.

mutual funds that invest in foreign securities. Because of the ready availability of information on foreign companies and the ease and relatively low cost of making foreign investments, many individuals actively invest in foreign securities. All aspects of foreign investing are therefore routinely considered throughout this book.

THE STRUCTURE OF THE INVESTMENT PROCESS

The overall investment process is the mechanism for bringing together *suppliers* (those having extra funds) with *demanders* (those needing funds). Suppliers and demanders are most often brought together through a financial institution or a financial market. (Occasionally—especially in property transactions such as real estate—buyers and sellers deal directly with one another.) **Financial institutions** are organizations that channel the savings of governments, businesses, and individuals into loans or investments. Banks and insurance companies are examples of financial institutions. **Financial markets** are important forums in which suppliers and demanders of funds are brought together to make financial transactions, often through intermediaries such as organized securities exchanges.

financial institutions
organizations that channel the savings of governments, businesses, and individuals into loans or investments.

financial markets
forums in which suppliers and demanders of funds are brought together to make financial transactions.

In the United States there are a number of financial markets, such as stock markets, bond markets, and options markets. Similar markets exist in most major economies throughout the world. Their common feature is that the price of an investment vehicle at any point in time results from an equilibrium between the forces of supply and demand. As new information about returns, risk, inflation, world events, and so on, becomes available, the changes in the forces of supply and demand may result in a new equilibrium or *market price*. Financial markets streamline the process of bringing together suppliers and demanders of funds, and they allow transactions to be made quickly and at a fair price. They also publicize security prices.

Figure 1.1 diagrams the investment process. Note the suppliers of funds may transfer their resources to the demanders through financial institutions,

Figure 1.1 The Investment Process
Note that financial institutions participate in the financial markets as well as transfer funds between suppliers and demanders. Although the arrows go only from suppliers to demanders, for some transactions (e.g., the sale of a bond), the principal amount borrowed by the demander from the supplier (the lender) will eventually be returned.

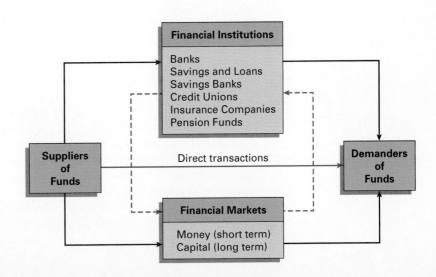

through financial markets, or directly. As the illustration shows, financial institutions can participate in financial markets as either suppliers or demanders of funds. The short-term financial market is called the *money market*; the long-term sector is the *capital market*, which is dominated by various securities exchanges. The characteristics of these markets will be discussed in greater detail in Chapter 2.

PARTICIPANTS IN THE INVESTMENT PROCESS

Government, business, and individuals are the three key participants in the investment process. Each may act as a supplier and a demander of funds.

Government

All levels of government—federal, state, and local—require vast sums of money. Some goes to finance *capital expenditures*—long-term projects related to the construction of public facilities such as schools, hospitals, public housing, and highways. Usually the financing for such projects is obtained by issuing various types of long-term debt securities. Another demand for funds comes from *operating needs*—the money needed to keep the government running. At the federal level, for example, these funds are used to pay employee and other costs associated with national defense, education, public works, welfare, Social Security, Medicare, and so on, as well as interest on the national debt. These operating needs are usually paid from tax revenue and fee collections. However, when operating expenditures exceed government revenues (a common outcome for the federal government) or when there is a timing mismatch between government receipts and payments, the government borrows funds—typically by issuing short-term debt securities.

Sometimes, governments are also suppliers of funds. If a state has temporarily idle cash, rather than just hold these resources in a checking account, it may make a short-term investment to earn a positive return. The financial activities of governments, both as demanders and suppliers of funds, significantly affect the behavior of financial institutions and financial markets. In general, government is a *net demander of funds*; that is, it demands more funds than it supplies.

Business

Most business firms, no matter what type, require large sums of money to support operations. Like government, the financial needs of business are both long and short term. On the long-term side, businesses seek funds to build plants, acquire equipment and facilities, and develop products. Short-term needs center on obtaining funds to finance inventory and accounts receivable and to meet other operating costs.

Businesses issue a wide variety of debt and equity securities to finance these needs. They also supply funds when they have excess cash. In fact, many large business firms have active and sophisticated cash-management operations and are major purchasers of short-term securities. But like government, business firms in general are *net demanders of funds*.

Individuals

You might be surprised to learn that the individual investor's role in providing the funds needed to finance economic growth is significant. Most individuals are more aware of their need to borrow than they are of the ways in which they put money into the financial system. They frequently demand funds in the form of loans to finance the acquisition of property—typically automobiles and houses. Yet the investment activities of individual investors help to satisfy the net funds demands of government and business. Individuals supply funds through the investment process in a variety of ways: They place funds in savings accounts, buy debt or equity instruments, buy insurance, make retirement plan contributions, or purchase various types of property. Although the individual demand for funds seems great, as a group individuals are *net suppliers of funds:* They put more funds into the financial system than they take out.

TYPES OF INVESTORS

Investors can be either of two types—individual or institutional. **Individual investors** manage their personal funds in order to achieve their financial goals. The individual investor usually concentrates on earning a return on idle funds, building a source of retirement income, and providing security for his or her family. As the *Investor Insights* box on page 12 discusses, the number of first-time individual investors has been increasing in recent years. The sole activity of many individual investors involves selecting the investment vehicles to be included in their employer retirement plan or individual portfolio. Individuals with large sums of money to invest or those who lack the time or expertise to make investment decisions often employ an *institutional investor*, such as a bank trust department or a professional investment adviser.

Institutional investors are investment professionals who are paid to manage other people's money. They trade large volumes of securities and include financial institutions (e.g., banks, life insurance companies, mutual funds, and pension funds), large nonfinancial corporations, and in some cases wealthy individuals and professional investors. Financial institutions invest large sums in order to earn a significant return for their customers. For example, a life insurance company must invest its premium receipts in order to earn returns that will permit the payment of benefits to policyholders or beneficiaries.

The fundamental principles used by both individual and institutional investors are similar. However, institutional investors generally invest larger sums of money on behalf of others and therefore are often more sophisticated in both investment knowledge and investment methods than individual investors. The information presented in this textbook is aimed primarily at

individual investors
investors who manage their own funds.

institutional investors
investment professionals paid to manage other people's money.

INVESTOR FACTS

HOUSEHOLD WEALTH—From 1980 to 1994, the liquid financial assets of U.S. households grew from $2.9 to $8.3 trillion. Since 1980, investors have shifted a larger percentage from cash to stocks and bonds. Today, they have 36.9 percent in cash and cash equivalents (compared with 54.8 percent in 1980), 34.0 percent in stocks (32.5 percent in 1980), 17.5 percent in bonds (11.1 percent), and 11.6 percent in mutual fund shares (1.6 percent).

(Source: *Fortune*, December 26, 1994, p. 60.)

INVESTOR INSIGHTS: *Investing in Action*

Investing: The New American Pastime

In recent years, a new player has burst upon the financial scene: the first-time individual investor. The proportion of U.S. households that own stocks either directly or through mutual funds has increased to almost 40 percent since the beginning of 1990. Savers who used to stash their money in bank savings accounts, money market funds, and certificates of deposit (CDs) now invest in stocks—especially mutual funds managed by financial services companies. This surge of small investors, and the resulting growth in the influence of mutual funds, is the most profound change the market has experienced in years. According to a Goldman Sachs review of Federal Reserve figures, mutual funds now dominate the equity market, buying 84 percent of all shares acquired in 1993.

What is behind this major market shift? In the early 1980s, CDs yielded as much as 14 percent, and the interest on long-term bonds rivaled what stocks could offer. A decade later, CD yields had collapsed to a mere 3 to 4 percent—barely above the rate of inflation. In early 1994, the Federal Reserve started raising interest rates, ending the potential for big bond returns. People accustomed to a high yield on these investments began to search for ways to replace their lost income.

An obvious solution presented itself: Domestic stocks returned nearly 16 percent annually in the early 1990s, with some global mutual funds soaring 40 percent a year, yet many small investors, especially those new to the market, were afraid to buy shares of stock directly. They chose instead to buy mutual funds, which were regularly cited in the financial press for their diverse holdings and talented managements.

Who are these new investors? They tend to fall into one of several categories:

1. Young Investors. A 1993 Merrill Lynch poll found that today's 25- to 44-year-olds started saving or planning for retirement at an average age of 26. It's no wonder: They are earning 20 percent less than those their age a generation ago, and many realize that they cannot depend on Social Security and corporate pension plans for their long-term financial security.

2. Bank Dropouts. From 1991 through 1993, the banking system lost $256 billion to mutual funds, for the reasons listed above. Many bank dropouts are older people whose Great Depression–era parents taught them that banks were the only safe place to keep their money. As a result, these reluctant investors are unaccustomed to taking financial risks, and mutual funds seem less risky than direct investments in stock.

3. Lump-Sum Investors. In the last decade, the nation's companies thinned their ranks of employees, looking for lower costs and a better "bottom line." Many of those who lost their jobs are far from retirement age and still need years of growth from their money. When they were laid off, many received large lump-sum payments from their 401(k) plans (retirement funds). By investing these funds in the market, they can build portfolios that will assure them of a comfortable future.

4. Minority Investors. Asian Americans, African Americans, and Hispanic Americans, an increasing percentage of whom are earning middle-class incomes, have just begun to invest in stocks, and financial services companies are targeting this previously untapped market. Still, in 1993 just 15 percent of Asian Americans, 13 percent of African Americans, and 3 percent of Hispanic Americans owned stocks or funds.

Sources: Adapted from Shelly Branch, "Today's New Investors," *Money,* May 1994, pp. 80–90; Susan E. Kuhn, "The New Perilous Stock Market," *Fortune,* December 27, 1993, pp. 48–62; and Michael Sivy, "Buy Stocks Now!" *Money,* June 1994, pp. 72–79.

individual investors; it represents only the first step toward developing the expertise needed to qualify as an institutional investor.

CONCEPTS *in Review*

1.1   Define the term *investment* and explain why individuals invest. What alternatives exist for investing idle funds?

1.2   Differentiate between securities and property investments. Which form of investment is more popular among individual investors?

1.3   What is the difference between direct and indirect investments? Cite an example of each. Differentiate among debt, equity, and derivative securities. Give an example of each.

1.4   Define *risk* and explain how it is used to differentiate between investments. Explain how investment, speculation, and gambling differ.

1.5   How are short-term investments differentiated from long-term investments? What are foreign investments and what role do they play today for the individual investor?

1.6   Describe the structure of the overall investment process. Define and explain the role played by *financial institutions* and *financial markets.*

1.7   Classify the role of (a) government, (b) business, and (c) individuals as net suppliers or net demanders of funds. Discuss the impact of each on the investment process.

1.8   Define and differentiate between *individual investors* and *institutional investors.* Which group often tends to be more sophisticated? Why?   ▄▄▄

INVESTING

investing
the process of placing funds in selected investment vehicles with the expectation of generating positive income and/or preserving and increasing their value.

We've seen, generally, that investments are vehicles for generating positive income and/or for preserving and increasing value. Naturally, then, the process of placing funds in selected investment vehicles is called **investing.** This activity has broad economic importance, provides rewards, should be guided by well-developed plans, and can be pursued by following a logical progression of steps.

THE ECONOMIC IMPORTANCE OF INVESTING

The functioning and growth of our economy depend on the ready availability of funds. As we've seen, governments and businesses, as well as individuals, need funds to finance their activities. For example, without mortgage loans, very few homes would be purchased. A lack of mortgage money would result in fewer people being employed to build homes as well as to manufacture the needed components (lumber, nails, glass, etc.). Likewise, manufacturers of goods such as furniture, carpeting, and major appliances would suffer decreased sales. The net effect of decreased mortgage financing would thus contribute to a general slowdown in economic activity. The availability of funds to qualified individuals (as well as to government and business) is needed to allow the economy to grow and prosper. Because individuals as a group are net suppliers of such funds while government and business are net demanders, the process of investing has a profound impact: If individuals began suddenly hiding their excess funds under floorboards rather than putting them in financial institutions or investing them in various vehicles in the financial markets, government, business, and other individuals demanding funds would have difficulty obtaining them. As a result, the levels of government spending, business expansion, and consumer purchases would decline and economic activity would be greatly retarded.

THE REWARDS FROM INVESTING

The rewards, or returns, from investing are received in either of two basic forms—current income or increased value. For example, money placed in a bank savings account would provide current income in the form of periodic interest payments. On the other hand, investment in a piece of raw land would be expected to offer an increase in value between the time of purchase and the time the land is sold. Those needing funds must provide a reward or return adequate to compensate the owners of those funds for the risk involved in supplying them. Simply stated, in order for the investment process to function smoothly, funds suppliers must be rewarded and funds demanders must provide these rewards. The magnitude and form of such rewards depend on factors such as the type of security or property transaction, the length of time involved, and the risks embedded in the transaction.

STEPS IN INVESTING

Investing can be conducted in various ways. One approach is to rely on plans carefully developed to achieve specific goals. Another approach—exactly opposite to the first—is a haphazard, "seat of the pants" method in which actions are taken on a strictly intuitive basis. Evidence suggests that the more logical approach usually results in better returns. The serious investor should therefore first establish a set of overall financial goals and then develop and execute an investment program consistent with those goals.

The following brief overview of the steps in investing will help to set the stage for the more detailed discussion of goals and plans in Chapter 3 and the discussions of investment concepts, tools, and techniques presented throughout the book.

Step 1: Meeting Investment Prerequisites

Before investing, an individual must make certain that the *necessities of life* are adequately provided for. This category would include funds for housing, food, transportation, taxes, and clothing. In addition, a pool of easily accessible funds should be established for meeting emergency cash needs. Funds for this

INVESTOR FACTS

YOUNGER INVESTORS— People are starting to invest at a younger age. Surveys done by the New York Stock Exchange revealed that the median age of shareholders declined from 53 in 1975 to 43 in 1990. And a 1993 Merrill Lynch poll found that 26 is the average age at which those in the 25- to 44-year-old age-group start investing for retirement.

(Source: *Money*, June 1994, p. 76.)

purpose are typically held in some form of liquid, short-term investment vehicle.

Another prerequisite would be adequate protection against the losses that could result from death, illness or disability, damage to property, or a negligent act. Protection against such risks can be acquired through life, health, property, and liability insurance. Although some types of insurance possess certain investment attributes, provision for adequate insurance protection is a necessary prerequisite to investing.

Planning for adequate retirement income may also be viewed as an investment prerequisite. Achieving this goal may partially depend on the success of one's investment program. At a minimum, the individual needs to establish certain retirement goals prior to setting specific investment goals.

Step 2: Establishing Investment Goals

investment goals
statements of the timing, magnitude, form, and risk associated with a desired return.

Once the investor has satisfied the prerequisites and has clearly defined financial goals, he or she must establish **investment goals**—specific statements of the timing, magnitude, form, and risk associated with a desired return. For example, an investment goal might be to accumulate $15,000 for the down payment on a summer home to be purchased in the year 2000, or to accumulate $250,000 for use at retirement in 2012. These goals should be not only consistent with overall financial goals but also realistic. The investor must have adequate funds available for investment and must assume an attainable rate of return to achieve them. For example, it would be unrealistic (and unwise) to base one's retirement expectations on receiving a return of 15 percent (without assuming enormous risk) when 10 percent is the prevailing return.

Step 3: Evaluating Investment Vehicles

valuation
procedure for estimating the perceived worth of an investment vehicle, using measures of return and risk.

Before selecting investment vehicles, the investor must evaluate them in terms of his or her investment goals. Evaluation involves assessing the potential return and risk offered by each vehicle. This process typically involves **valuation,** a procedure for estimating the perceived worth of an investment vehicle. The valuation process uses measures of return and risk to estimate the value of an investment vehicle. A general discussion of the procedures for measuring these key dimensions of potential investments is included in Chapter 4. Subsequent chapters focus on the valuation of specific vehicles.

Step 4: Selecting Suitable Investments

The specific investment vehicles selected determine one's course of action and can significantly affect the investor's success in achieving planned goals. As we'll see as we progress through this book, the best investments may not be those that simply maximize return; other factors, such as risk and tax considerations, may also be relevant. For example, an investor wishing to receive maximum annual dividends might purchase the common stock of a firm expected to pay high dividends. However, if the firm whose stock was purchased goes bankrupt, the investor could lose the money. The stock of a firm that pays lower dividends but with less risk of becoming bankrupt might have been a better choice. Careful selection of investment vehicles consistent with established goals and with acceptable levels of return, risk, and value is key to successful investing.

Step 5: Constructing a Diversified Portfolio

portfolio
a collection of investment vehicles assembled to meet one or more investment goals.

An investment **portfolio** is a collection of investment vehicles assembled to meet one or more investment goals. For example, an investment portfolio might contain common stock, government bonds, and short-term investments. Using a variety of available tools and techniques, the investor can combine vehicles in such a way that investment goals can be achieved and return, risk, and investment values are optimized.

diversification
the inclusion of a number of different investment vehicles in a portfolio, to increase returns or incur less risk.

Diversification, the inclusion of a number of different investment vehicles, is fundamental to constructing an effective portfolio. By diversifying, investors are able to earn higher returns or be exposed to less risk than if they limit their investments to just one or two vehicles. Diversification is the financial term for the age-old advice "Don't put all your eggs in one basket."

A diversified portfolio surprisingly exhibits a different risk-return behavior from those of the individual investment vehicles that compose it. For example, the common stocks of young, high-tech companies are by themselves extremely risky investments—their prices fluctuate constantly and often dramatically. Yet when they are held with common stocks of large, established companies in a diversified portfolio, over time the portfolio exhibits lower risk or a higher return than if common stock of only one type (high-tech or established company) were held. Chapter 16 is devoted to the topic of portfolio construction.

Step 6: Managing the Portfolio

Once a portfolio has been constructed, the investor must measure and evaluate its actual behavior in relation to expected performance. If, for example, the investment return, risk, or value is not consistent with his or her objectives, the investor may need to take corrective action. Such action usually involves selling certain investments and using the proceeds to acquire other vehicles for the portfolio. Portfolio management therefore involves not only selecting a compatible group of investments that meet the investor's goals but also monitoring and restructuring the portfolio as dictated by the actual behavior of the investments. Chapter 17 is devoted to portfolio management and control. The *Investor Insights* box on page 17 outlines some practical tips that investors have found useful in planning and managing their investment portfolios.

Now that we have considered the role of investments and the process of investing, we will turn our attention to an overview of investment vehicles.

CONCEPTS *in Review*

1.9   Briefly discuss the economic importance of investing, and describe the rewards available to those placing funds in the investment process.

1.10   What should an investor first establish before developing and executing an investment program? List and briefly describe each of the six steps involved in investing.

INVESTOR INSIGHTS: *Investing in Action*

Strategies for Investment Success

Becoming a successful investor takes time and effort. There are no surefire schemes for beating the market. Here are some tips to help you get started on the road to investment success and financial security.

Start saving and investing now. Yes, you can wait—but it will cost you money. Due to the power of compound interest, time is your biggest ally. If you invest $2,000 at the end of each year for 10 years ($20,000 total), at 8 percent per year, you'll have $198,422 in 35 years. But wait 10 years, invest $2,000 at the end of each year for *25* years at 8 percent per year, and your $50,000 investment will be only $146,212. You don't need a large sum, either. Just $200 a year invested at 10 percent—the long-term annualized return on stocks—will grow to over $6,000 in 15 years; in 25 years, you'll have almost $20,000! So make investing a habit now.

There's no "best" time to invest. You can always find a reason to put off taking the plunge: It's an election year, the market is too high, there's a crisis somewhere in the world. But studies show that it's more important to invest than to pick the right time. Even the experts don't predict the market's ups and downs accurately all the time.

Don't let excuses get in your way. It's easy to think that you're too busy, that investing is too hard, or that you can't possibly save enough for a down payment or retirement. Investing is one of the best uses of your time. Rethink your priorities: Is it more important to go to the movies or to plan for your financial future? And don't be intimidated by the investment process. Set realistic goals, learn the basics, and start with simple investments that you understand. Once you gain control of your finances, your confidence will increase.

Say no to "once in a lifetime" stock tips. Your broker calls to say that you *must* buy this hot initial public offering (IPO) or stock that

analysts say will grow 30 percent a year. No matter how good it sounds, don't jump in without doing your homework. By the time a mutual fund or company gets noticed, the biggest gains may already be realized. About half of all IPOs fall below the offering price in six months, and companies that analysts tout often fail to meet those very high expectations.

Include target prices in your investment strategy. When you buy a stock, set a reasonable target price to sell. When it reaches that price, reevaluate it as you would a new investment. If the company is improving, keep it; otherwise, sell it. If you bought at $45 and the stock is now $38, you may be tempted to wait for it to rebound. However, you may be better off cutting your losses and looking for a more attractive opportunity.

Diversify your portfolio. Don't put all your eggs in one investment basket. Diversification reduces your risk, so invest in several types of securities: short-term vehicles like money market funds, intermediate-term bonds or bond funds, and, for the long term, growth stocks or growth mutual funds. You should also have some international stocks or mutual funds. Also, don't concentrate too heavily in one industry or buy just one or two stocks.

Monitor your investments. Don't just buy securities and hold them forever. Review your portfolio monthly to check its progress against your goals. Weed out the poor performers, and evaluate current holdings relative to other investment opportunities.

Sources: Lynn Asinof, "Money Blunders of the Otherwise Intelligent," *Wall Street Journal,* September 23, 1994, pp. C1–C2; Ken and Daria Dolan, "Six Investing Resolutions to Make (and Keep) in 1994," *Money,* January 1994, p. 29; Elizabeth Fenner, "Avoiding the Seven Biggest Investor Mistakes," *Money,* May 1994, pp. 74–79; Ann Perry, "Road to Frustration Paved with Good Excuses," *San Diego Union-Tribune,* January 3, 1994, pp. C1–C2.

INVESTMENT VEHICLES

A broad range of investment vehicles is available to individual investors. Some vehicles are securities, others are not. Even among securities there are many different types, each having different maturities or lives, costs, return and risk characteristics, and tax considerations. The same is true of property investments. We devote the bulk of this book—Chapters 5 through 15—to describing the characteristics, special features, returns and risks, and possible investment strategies that can be used with vehicles available to the individual investor. Here we will introduce the various investment outlets and give a brief description of each. Table 1.1 summarizes the information presented in this section.

SHORT-TERM VEHICLES

short-term vehicles
savings instruments that usually have lives of one year or less.

Short-term vehicles include savings instruments that usually have lives of one year or less. The most important of these are various types of deposit accounts, U.S. Treasury bills (T-bills), certificates of deposit (CDs), commer-

Table 1.1　Overview of Investment Vehicles

Type	Description	Examples	Where Covered in This Book
Short-term vehicles	Savings instruments with lives of one year or less. Used to warehouse idle funds and to provide liquidity.	Deposit accounts U.S. Treasury bills (T-bills) Certificates of deposit (CDs) Commercial paper Banker's acceptances Money market mutual funds Series EE savings bonds	Ch. 3 Ch. 3 Ch. 3 Ch. 3 Ch. 3 Ch. 3 Ch. 3
Common stock	Equity investment vehicles that represent ownership in a corporation.		Chs. 5, 6, 7
Fixed-income securities	Investment vehicles that offer a fixed periodic return.	Bonds Preferred stock Convertible securities	Chs. 8, 9 Ch. 10 Ch. 10
Mutual funds	Companies that raise money from sale of shares and invest in and professionally manage a diversified portfolio of securities.		Ch. 11
Other popular investment vehicles	Various other investment vehicles that are widely used by investors.	Real estate Tangibles Tax-advantaged investments	Ch. 12 Ch. 12 Ch. 13
Derivative securities	Securities that are neither debt nor equity but are structured to exhibit the characteristics of the underlying securities or assets from which they derive their value.	Options Futures	Ch. 14 Ch. 15

cial paper, banker's acceptances, money market mutual funds, and Series EE savings bonds. Often such instruments are used to "warehouse" idle funds and earn a return while suitable long-term vehicles are being evaluated. Because these vehicles generally carry little or no risk, they tend to be popular among those wishing to earn something on temporarily idle funds. They are also popular among conservative investors, who may use short-term vehicles as a primary investment outlet.

liquidity
the ability to convert an investment into cash quickly and with little or no loss in value.

In addition to their "warehousing" function and use by conservative investors, short-term vehicles provide **liquidity**—an ability to convert them into cash quickly and with little or no loss in value. Provision for liquidity is an important part of any financial plan because it allows one to obtain funds quickly either to meet unexpected obligations or to take advantage of attractive opportunities. As a rule of thumb, financial planners often suggest that anywhere from three to six months' worth of after-tax income should be held in short-term vehicles to meet unexpected needs. A serious illness or loss of a job could create a need for immediate cash. Being forced to sell one's long-term securities at a time when security prices are low can result in substantial losses. A closer look at meeting liquidity needs is provided in Chapter 3.

COMMON STOCK

common stock
equity investment representing ownership in a corporation; each share represents a fractional ownership interest in the firm.

Common stock is an equity investment that represents ownership in a corporation. Each share of common stock represents a fractional ownership interest in the firm. For example, one share of common stock in a corporation that has 10,000 shares outstanding would represent 1/10,000 ownership interest.

dividends
periodic payments made by firms to their stockholders.

capital gains
the amount by which the sale price of an asset exceeds its purchase price.

The return on common stock investment comes from either of two sources. One source of return is the receipt of **dividends**, which are periodic payments made by the firm to its shareholders from its current and past earnings. The second source of return is **capital gains**, which result from selling the stock at a price above that originally paid. For example, imagine you purchased a single share of M and N Industries common stock for $40 per share. During the first year you owned it, you received $2.50 per share in cash dividends; at the end of the year, you sold the stock for $44 per share. If we ignore the costs associated with buying and selling the stock, you would have earned $2.50 in dividends and $4 in capital gains ($44 sale price – $40 purchase price).

Next to short-term vehicles and home ownership, common stock is the most popular form of investment vehicle. One reason for its popularity is that it offers a broad range of return-risk combinations. Because of the widespread popularity of common stock, three chapters—Chapters 5, 6, and 7—are devoted to the study of this investment vehicle.

FIXED-INCOME SECURITIES

fixed-income securities
investment vehicles that offer a fixed periodic return.

Fixed-income securities are a group of investment vehicles that offer a fixed periodic return. Some forms offer contractually guaranteed returns; others have specified, but not guaranteed, returns. Due to their fixed returns, fixed-income securities tend to be popular investments during periods of high interest rates, such as those during the late 1970s and early 1980s, as investors seek to "lock in" high returns. The key forms of fixed-income securities are bonds, preferred stock, and convertible securities.

Bonds

bonds
long-term debt instruments (IOUs), issued by corporations and governments, that offer a known interest return plus return of the bond's face value at maturity.

Bonds are the long-term debt instruments—IOUs—of corporations and governments. A bondholder has a contractual right to receive a known interest return, typically paid semiannually, plus return of the bond's *face value*—the stated value given on the certificate—at maturity (typically 20 to 40 years). If you purchased a $1,000 bond paying 9 percent interest in semiannual installments, you would expect to be paid $45 (i.e., $9\% \times \frac{1}{2}$ year $\times$ $1,000) every six months; at maturity you would receive the $1,000 face value of the bond. An investor may be able to buy or sell a bond prior to maturity at a price different from its face value. As with common stock, a wide range of return-risk combinations is available to the bond investor. We will examine bond investments in detail in Chapters 8 and 9.

Preferred Stock

preferred stock
ownership interest in a corporation; has a stated dividend rate, payment of which is given preference over common stock dividends of the same firm.

Like common stock, **preferred stock** represents an ownership interest in a corporation. Unlike common stock, preferred stock has a stated dividend rate; payment of this dividend is given preference over common stock dividends of the same firm. Preferred stock has no maturity date. Investors typically purchase it for the dividends it pays, but it may also provide capital gains. The key aspects of preferred stock are described in Chapter 10.

Convertible Securities

convertible security
a fixed-income obligation (bond or preferred stock) with a feature permitting conversion into a specified number of shares of common stock.

A **convertible security** is a special type of fixed-income obligation (bond or preferred stock) with a feature permitting the investor to convert it into a specified number of shares of common stock. Convertible bonds and convertible preferreds provide the fixed-income benefit of a bond (interest) or preferred stock (dividends) while offering the price-appreciation (capital gain) potential of common stock. A detailed discussion of convertibles appears in Chapter 10.

MUTUAL FUNDS

mutual fund
a company that raises money from sale of its shares and invests in and professionally manages a diversified portfolio of securities.

A company that raises money from sale of its shares and invests in and professionally manages a diversified portfolio of securities is called a **mutual fund.** Investors in the fund have an interest in the portfolio of securities that the fund owns and manages. All mutual funds issue and repurchase shares as demanded at a price reflecting the value of the portfolio at the time the transaction is

money market mutual funds
mutual funds that invest solely in short-term investment vehicles.

made. **Money market mutual funds,** mentioned earlier as short-term investment vehicles, are mutual funds that invest solely in other short-term vehicles. Chapter 11 is devoted to study of mutual funds.

OTHER POPULAR INVESTMENT VEHICLES

Various other investment vehicles are also widely used by investors. The most common are real estate, tangibles, and tax-advantaged investments.

Real Estate

real estate
entities such as residential homes, raw land, and income property.

The term **real estate** refers to entities such as residential homes, raw land, and a variety of forms of income property, including warehouses, office and apartment buildings, cooperatives (co-ops), and condominiums. As a result of generally increasing values and favorable tax treatments since World War II, real estate was a popular investment vehicle through the 1970s and much of the 1980s. Although its popularity has waned a bit in recent years, it is likely that as economic conditions improve, real estate will experience a resurgence in popularity. Historically, the appeal of real estate investment stemmed from the fact that it offered returns in the form of rental income, tax write-offs, and capital gains that were not available from alternative investment vehicles. A detailed look at the role real estate can play in the investment portfolio is presented in Chapter 12.

Tangibles

tangibles
investment assets, other than real estate, that can be seen or touched.

Tangibles, in contrast, are investment assets, other than real estate, that can be seen or touched. They include gold and other precious metals, gemstones, and collectibles such as coins, stamps, artwork, and antiques. These vehicles are purchased as investments in anticipation of price increases. During the ownership period, some may also provide the investor with psychological or aesthetic enjoyment. Tangibles are discussed in more detail in Chapter 12.

Tax-Advantaged Investments

tax-advantaged investments
investment vehicles and strategies for legally reducing one's tax liability.

Due to provisions in the federal tax law, some investment vehicles offer certain tax advantages over others. For example, interest received on most municipal bonds is not taxed at all, and income from individual retirement arrangements (IRAs) is deferred from taxes until the money is actually taken out of the account. Because the federal income tax rate for an individual can be as high as 39.6 percent, many investors look for **tax-advantaged investments**—investment vehicles and strategies for legally reducing one's tax liability. With these, they find that their after-tax rates of return can be far higher than with conventional investments. A comprehensive review of some common tax-advantaged investments is presented in Chapter 13.

DERIVATIVE SECURITIES

Derivative securities typically possess high levels of risk. They usually have nonexistent or imperfect records of success, uncertain returns, or unstable market values. Because of their typically above-average risk, these vehicles also have high levels of expected return. The key derivative securities are options and futures.

Options

options
securities that provide the investor with an opportunity to sell or buy another security or property at a specified price over a given period of time.

As noted earlier, **options** are securities that provide the investor with an opportunity to sell or buy another security or property at a specified price over a given period of time. They are acquired and used by investors in a variety of ways and for a variety of reasons. Most often, options are purchased in order to take advantage of an anticipated decrease or increase in the price of common stock. However, the purchaser of an option is not guaranteed any return and could lose the entire amount invested, either because the option never becomes attractive enough to use or because the option expires. Aside from their speculative use, options are sometimes used to protect existing investment positions against losses. Three common types of options are *puts* and *calls*, *rights*, and *warrants*, which we will discuss in detail in Chapter 14.

Futures

futures
legally binding obligations that the sellers of such contracts will make delivery and the buyers of the contracts will take delivery of a specified commodity or financial instrument at some specific date in the future at a price agreed upon at the time the contract is sold.

Futures are legally binding obligations that the sellers of such contracts will make delivery and the buyers of the contracts will take delivery of a specified commodity or financial instrument at some specific date in the future at a price agreed upon at the time the contract is sold. Examples of commodities sold by contract include soybeans, pork bellies, platinum, and cocoa. Examples of financial futures are contracts for Japanese yen, U.S. Treasury securities, interest rates, and stock indexes. Trading in commodity and financial futures is generally a highly specialized, high-risk proposition. An expanded discussion of commodity and financial futures is presented in Chapter 15.

CONCEPTS *in Review*

1.11 Discuss the role of short-term vehicles in an individual's investment plans and portfolio. Why is a provision for liquidity important in a financial plan?

1.12 What is *common stock?* Briefly describe the two sources of potential return from a common stock investment.

1.13 Briefly define and differentiate the following fixed-income securities:
     a. Bonds
     b. Preferred stock
     c. Convertible securities

1.14 What is a *mutual fund?* Why is this form of investment popular among individual investors? What is a *money market mutual fund?*

1.15 Briefly describe each of the following popular investment vehicles:
   a. Real estate
   b. Tangibles
   c. Tax-advantaged investments

1.16 Briefly describe each of the following types of derivative securities, and indicate some factors that are likely to affect the returns on each:
   a. Options
   b. Futures

AN OVERVIEW OF THE TEXT

The textbook contains 17 chapters, divided into six major parts:

One: The Investment Environment

Two: Investing in Common Stock

Three: Investing in Fixed-Income Securities

Four: Other Popular Investment Vehicles

Five: Derivative Securities

Six: Investment Administration

We begin with an overview of the investment environment (Part One), then describe the key aspects of the most popular investment vehicles (Parts Two through Five), and conclude with a discussion of investment administration (Part Six). Each part, which is introduced with a listing of its chapters as well as its relationship to the overall investment process, explains an important aspect of investing. Figure 1.2 (page 24) depicts the relationships among the six parts of the text. This plan of organization links the investor's activities in developing, implementing, and monitoring investment plans. It is intended to provide the understanding needed to establish an investment portfolio that earns an acceptable return for an acceptable level of risk.

Each chapter is a separate learning unit that begins with a list of Learning Goals. The Learning Goals are part of an integrated teaching/learning system and are keyed to text discussions and end-of-chapter materials by a special icon, **LG 1**. Each section of the chapter is immediately followed with review questions, called Concepts in Review, that encourage you to test your understanding of the material before moving on. The Summary at the end of the chapter is also tied to the Learning Goals, for a complete chapter review.

Other features of the book are intended to improve the learning process. Chapters open with an interview with an actual investor, who discusses his or her experiences as they relate to the chapter topic. Two Investor Insight boxes per chapter describe real-life situations or events in various categories: Conflicting Viewpoints on an investment issue, Global Issues, Market Innovations, and a catchall category of interesting topics called Investing in Action. Several *Investor Facts* in each chapter provide interesting, sometimes humorous bits of information. All figures have explanatory captions that simplify their interpretation and review. Following the end-of-chapter Summary, Discussion Questions, Problems, and two Case Problems (with questions)—all tied by icon to the Learning Goals—are included for review of concepts and practice of techniques presented in the chapter.

Figure 1.2 An Overview of the Major Parts of the Text
The text approaches the individual investment process in a logical fashion, beginning with an overview of the investment environment (Part One). Next comes a description of the key aspects of the most popular investment vehicles (Parts Two through Five). The text concludes with a discussion of investment administration (Part Six).

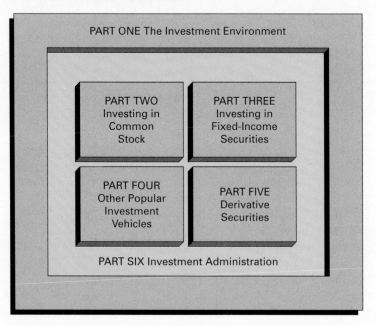

To enhance the topical coverage and practical utility of the text, the computer has been introduced where appropriate as an investment decision-making aid. The Investment Management Disk (IMD), a menu-driven computer disk, can be used to help perform many of the routine investment calculations and procedures presented in the book. For convenience, it is keyed to text discussions and to end-of-chapter Discussion Questions, Problems, and Case Problems that can be solved with it. These items are clearly denoted by a disk symbol: ▄. Appendix C describes this tool in more detail.

Two additional features are designed to help you enhance your skills in managing investment data. The STOCK-TRAK® portfolio management simulation enables you to construct portfolios and trade securities in real-time at today's prices by calling a "broker" at a toll-free number. A brief section at the end of each chapter describes how the STOCK-TRAK® simulation relates to the chapter topic. *Stock Investor: The Student Version* is a simplified version of the American Association of Institutional Investors' popular Stock Investor program. This basic screening and analysis program includes fundamental information on over 1000 publicly traded companies and 60 (broadly defined) industry groups. The software enables you to practice your investment skills by screening and analyzing for companies that meet specific criteria. Appendix D provides more information on using *Stock Investor: The Student Version*.

On Track with *STOCK-TRAK*®

Trading with *STOCK-TRAK*®

STOCK-TRAK® is the most comprehensive portfolio simulation available. With STOCK-TRAK®, you can manage an imaginary portfolio with an initial value that can be in the hundreds of thousands of dollars. You can select from a wide variety of securities, including shares of stock priced at or above $5,000. A broad range of government and corporate bonds are available for investment. In addition, you can put your funds into options and futures. If you seek less risk in the commodities arena, several assets can be bought on the spot market.

After you have read Chapter 1, if you are planning to participate in STOCK-TRAK® you should review the registration materials, looking especially at the types and specific investment alternatives available. The better you understand STOCK-TRAK®'s operations and procedures, the more you'll be able to use its various features.

SUMMARY

LG 1 Understand the meaning of the term *investment* and the factors commonly used to differentiate between various types of investments. An investment is any vehicle into which funds can be placed with the expectation that they will generate positive income and/or their value will be preserved or increase. Some vehicles are securities; others are forms of property. Some investments are made directly, others indirectly. An investment can be a debt, an equity, or a derivative security such as an option. It can possess risk ranging from very low to extremely high. An individual can invest in either short-term or long-term vehicles. Today, individual investors have ready access to foreign as well as domestic investments.

LG 2 Describe the structure of and participants in the investment process and the types of investors. The investment process is structured around financial institutions and financial markets that bring together suppliers and demanders of funds. The participants are government, business, and individuals. Of these groups, only individuals are net funds suppliers. Investors can be either individual investors or institutional investors.

LG 3 Review the importance of, rewards from, and steps in investing. Investing is important because it makes available funds needed to permit our economy to function, grow, and prosper. The rewards from investing can be received either as current income or as increased value. The steps in investing involve the following: meeting investment prerequisites, establishing investment goals, evaluating investment vehicles, selecting suitable investments, constructing a diversified portfolio, and managing the portfolio.

LG 4 Discuss the principal types of investment vehicles, including short-term vehicles, common stock, fixed-income securities, and mutual funds. A broad range of investment vehicles is available. Short-term vehicles have low risk. They are used to earn a return on temporarily idle funds, as a primary investment outlet of conservative investors, and to provide liquidity. Common stocks offer dividends and capital gains. Fixed-income securities—bonds, preferred stock, and convertible securities—offer fixed periodic returns with some potential for gain in value. Mutual funds are popular investment vehicles that allow investors to conveniently buy or sell interests in a professionally managed diversified portfolio of securities.

Describe other kinds of popular investment vehicles—real estate, tangibles, and tax-advantaged investments—and derivative securities—options and futures. Other popular investment vehicles include real estate; tangibles such as gold and other precious metals, gemstones, and collectibles; and tax-advantaged investments, which reduce one's tax liability and thereby increase the after-tax rate of return. Derivative securities are high-risk, high-expected-return vehicles, the key ones being options—puts and calls, rights, and warrants—and futures—commodity and financial.

LG 6 Summarize the content and organizational model around which this text is structured. The text contains 17 chapters, divided into six major parts. A simple model breaks the coverage into the investment environment (Part One), popular investment vehicles (Parts Two through Five), and investment administration (Part Six) and is used to link each part to the overall investment process.

CASE PROBLEMS

1.1   INVESTMENTS OR RACQUETBALL?

Judd Read and Judi Todd are senior accounting majors at a large midwestern university. They have been good friends since high school and look forward to their graduation at the end of next semester. Each has already found a job, which will begin upon graduation. Judd has accepted a position as an internal auditor in a medium-size manufacturing firm. Judi will be working for one of the major public accounting firms. Each is looking forward to the challenge of a new career and to the prospect of achieving success both professionally and financially.

Judd and Judi are preparing to register for their final semester. Each has one free elective to select. Judd is considering taking a racquetball course offered by the physical education department; Judi is planning to take a basic investments course. Judi has been trying to convince Judd to take investments instead of racquetball. Judd believes he doesn't need to take investments, because he already knows what common stock is. He believes that whenever he has accumulated excess funds, he can invest in the stock of a company that is doing well. Judi argues that there is much more to it than simply choosing common stock. She feels that an exposure to the field of investments would certainly be more beneficial than learning how to play racquetball.

Questions

1. Explain to Judd the structure of the investment process and the economic importance of investing.

2. Describe to Judd the steps in investing and emphasize the importance of this process to his overall financial success.

3. List and discuss the other types of investment vehicles with which Judd is apparently unfamiliar.

4. Assuming Judd is in good physical condition, what arguments would you give to convince Judd to take investments rather than racquetball?

 ### 1.2 EVALUATING MOLLY PORTER'S INVESTMENT PLAN

Molly Porter's husband, Vance, was recently killed in an airplane crash. Fortunately, he had a sizable amount of life insurance, the proceeds of which should provide Molly with adequate income for a number of years. Molly is 33 years old and has two children, David and Phyllis, who are 6 and 7 years old, respectively. Although Molly does not rule out the possibility of marrying again, she feels it is best not to consider this when making her financial plans. In order to provide adequate funds to finance her children's college education as well as her own retirement, Molly has estimated that she needs to accumulate $400,000 within the next 15 years. If she continues to teach school, she believes sufficient excess funds will be available each year (salary plus insurance proceeds minus expenses) to permit her to achieve this goal. She plans to make annual deposits of these excess funds into a money market mutual fund, which is currently earning 6 percent interest.

Questions

1.   In view of Molly's long-term investment goals, assess her choice of a money market mutual fund as the appropriate investment vehicle.

2.   What alternative investment vehicles might Molly consider prior to committing her money to the money market mutual fund?

3.   If you were Molly, given your limited knowledge of investments, in what vehicles would you invest the excess funds? Explain.

CHAPTER 2

INVESTMENT MARKETS AND TRANSACTIONS

LEARNING GOALS

After studying this chapter, you should be able to:

LG 1 Review the basic types of securities markets and the characteristics of both organized exchanges and the over-the-counter market.

LG 2 Discuss globalization, trading hours, regulation, ethical issues, and the general conditions of securities markets.

LG 3 Explain the role of stockbrokers in security transactions—services provided, selection, opening an account, account types, and transaction sizes.

LG 4 Describe the basic types of orders—market, limit, and stop-loss—transaction costs, and the legal aspects of investor protection.

LG 5 Understand long purchases and the motives, regulations, procedures, and calculations involved in making margin transactions.

LG 6 Summarize the essentials of short selling—motives, procedures, and advantages and disadvantages—and discuss its uses—speculation and hedging.

Computer systems developer Mark Marcellus, like many novice investors, kept his savings in low-risk certificates of deposit (CDs) because he found investing with a stockbroker intimidating. After his first child was born about ten years ago, he realized that CDs alone wouldn't provide a solid financial foundation for his family and for retirement. So he took an investments course and began investing toward the two goals he and his wife, Marsha, set: a larger house (a short-term goal) and a college education for their children (a long-term goal). Five years later, they bought the new house. They are still working toward the education fund, and financial security in retirement has been added as a key long-term goal.

Mark's first bonds and common stocks were recommended by a stockbroker. Mark also educated himself by reading the *Wall Street Journal*, *Barron's*, and every investing book in the library. Two 1989 events changed his investment approach: reading Peter Lynch's book *One Up on Wall Street* and joining an investment club where he learned about basic investment analysis. Following Lynch's advice—"invest where you spend your money"—his first analysis for the club was Microsoft. Mark remembers: "The numbers jumped off the page; I immediately bought the stock. If I'd known how rare these situations are, I'd have invested much, much more!" He credits the investment club and membership in the American Association of Individual Investors (AAII) with giving him many of the tools to take charge of his own investment decisions.

> **THE NUMBERS JUMPED OFF THE PAGE; I IMMEDIATELY BOUGHT THE STOCK.**

Today, about 15 percent of Mark's portfolio is in short-term investments (money market funds, CDs)—liquid assets for short-term needs and emergencies. Individual stocks and stock mutual funds account for another 60 percent, with 10 percent of that amount in international stock funds for more diversification. He focuses on companies he understands, especially computer-related stocks. He plans to gradually replace some of the 15 percent he currently has in long-term bonds with stocks. The remaining 10 percent is specialty mutual funds (gold and real estate), long-term investments that further diversify his portfolio.

For short-term goals, Mark invests conservatively, looking for fixed returns and maturities. He prefers an extended investment horizon of at least five years. "It suits my temperament better than trading in and out of stocks," he explains. Originally, he balanced conservative investments such as corporate bonds and Treasury bills with more aggressive stock investments. His philosophy has since changed, and his goal for long-term investment portfolios is to remain 80 to 90 percent invested in stocks, using the balance to buy more stocks during market dips.

Investing has paid off in many ways for Mark. Overall, his annualized returns have been about 10 percent on fixed-income investments and 15 percent on equity investments. "What I thought would be a boring but necessary duty has turned into a fascinating experience," he says. "And the most surprising reward has been the intellectual and personal growth I've gained."

Mark Marcellus, a computer systems developer, is married with two children and lives near New York City on Long Island.

In general, it would be difficult to drive cross country from one city to another without knowing how to read a map. In addition, an understanding of traffic regulations would be needed to make such a trip safely. Despite the fact that you were able to drive a car, without these other skills you would probably be unable to complete the cross-country drive. The same logic applies to investing. Although investing is far more challenging than driving, it too involves a number of important procedures and rules that you need to know. Regardless of how well prepared you might be to select the best vehicle for achieving your particular investment goals, you must know other things as well, as Mark Marcellus's story demonstrates: You need to understand the workings of the market in which that vehicle is bought and sold. You must know how to find and enter the market. You should understand the basic types of transactions required.

In this chapter we will look at the key aspects of the investment environment so that you will know which market to enter for your purposes, how to enter your chosen market, and which basic types of transactions you can make.

SECURITIES MARKETS

securities markets
a mechanism that allows suppliers and demanders of funds to make transactions; include both the *money market* and the *capital market.*

Securities markets are a mechanism that allows suppliers and demanders of funds to make transactions. They permit such transactions to be made quickly and at a fair price. Before describing the methods used to enter these markets, we will look at the various types of markets, their organization, their globalization, their regulation, and their general behavior.

TYPES OF SECURITIES MARKETS

money market
market in which short-term securities are bought and sold.

capital market
market in which long-term securities such as stocks and bonds are bought and sold.

Securities markets may be classified as either money markets or capital markets. In the **money market,** short-term securities are bought and sold. In the **capital market,** transactions are made in longer-term securities such as stocks and bonds. In this book we will devote most of our attention to the capital market, through which stock, bond, options, and futures investments can be made. Capital markets can be classified as either primary or secondary, depending on whether securities are initially being sold by their issuing company or by intervening owners.

The Primary Market

primary market
market in which new issues of securities are sold to the public.

initial public offering (IPO)
the public sale of stock by a privately owned company.

Securities and Exchange Commission (SEC)
federal agency that regulates securities offerings and markets.

public offering
the sale of a firm's securities to the general public.

The market in which new issues of securities are sold to the public is the **primary market.** It is the market in which the proceeds of sales go to the issuer of the securities. Every year, about 900 stocks are offered for sale in the primary market. The main vehicle in the primary market is the **initial public offering (IPO)**—the public sale of stock by a privately owned company. Before securities can be offered for public sale, the issuer must register them with and obtain approval from the **Securities and Exchange Commission (SEC).** The SEC is a federal regulatory agency that must confirm both the adequacy and the accuracy of information provided to potential investors before a security is publicly offered for sale. In addition, it regulates the securities markets.

To market its securities, a firm has three choices: It can make a **public offering,** in which it offers its securities for sale to the general public; it can

rights offering
an offer of shares of stock to existing stockholders on a pro rata basis.

private placement
the sale of new securities directly to selected groups of investors, without SEC registration.

investment banker
financial intermediary that purchases new securities from the issuing firm at an agreed-upon price and resells them to the public.

underwriting
the role of the investment banker in bearing the risk of reselling at a profit the securities purchased from an issuing corporation at an agreed-upon price.

underwriting syndicate
a group formed by an *investment banker* to spread the financial risk associated with the selling of new securities.

selling group
a large number of brokerage firms that join and accept responsibility for selling a certain portion of a new security issue.

make a **rights offering,** in which it offers shares to existing stockholders on a pro rata basis; or it can make a **private placement,** in which new securities are sold directly, without SEC registration, to selected groups of investors, such as insurance companies and pension funds.

Most public offerings are made with the assistance of an **investment banker**—a financial intermediary (e.g., Salomon Brothers or Goldman Sachs) that specializes in selling new security issues. The main activity of the investment banker is **underwriting.** This process involves purchasing the security issue from the issuing firm at an agreed-upon price and bearing the risk of reselling it to other investors at a profit. The investment banker also provides the issuer with advice about pricing and other important aspects of the issue.

In the case of very large security issues, the investment banker will bring in other bankers as partners to form an **underwriting syndicate,** to spread the financial risk associated with buying the entire issue from the issuer and reselling the new securities at a profit to other investors. The originating investment banker and the syndicate members put together a **selling group,** normally made up of themselves and a large number of brokerage firms. Each member of the selling group accepts the responsibility for selling a certain portion of the issue and is paid a commission on the securities it sells. The selling process for a large security issue is depicted in Figure 2.1.

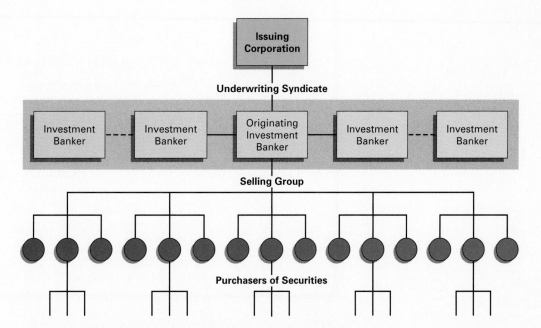

Figure 2.1 The Selling Process for a Large Security Issue
The investment banker hired by the issuing corporation may form an underwriting syndicate. The underwriting syndicate buys the entire security issue from the issuing corporation at an agreed-upon price and bears the risk of reselling it to other investors at a profit. Both the originating investment banker and the other syndicate members put together a selling group to sell the issue on a commission basis to investors.

The relationships among the participants in this process can also be seen in the so-called tombstone announcements of new security issues. An announcement for American Sensors' 1995 common stock offering is shown in Figure 2.2. The layout of the announcement indicates the roles of the various participating firms. Isolated firm names or a larger typeface differentiate the underwriter and the underwriting syndicate from the selling group. (In the figure, the key participants in the offering are labeled in the margin at the right.)

This announcement is not an offer to sell or a solicitation of an offer to buy any of these securities. The offering is made only by the Prospectus, copies of which may be obtained in any State in which this announcement is circulated only from such of the several underwriters as may lawfully offer these securities in such State.

February 2, 1995

2,000,000 Shares

Common Shares

Price $15.00 Per Share

1,600,000 Shares

		Underwriting Syndicate

PaineWebber Incorporated   **Wertheim Schroder & Co.**
                                          Incorporated

Alex. Brown & Sons   Dillon, Read & Co. Inc.   A.G. Edwards & Sons, Inc.
   Incorporated
C.J. Lawrence/Deutsche Bank   Lehman Brothers
      Securities Corporation
Oppenheimer & Co., Inc.   Prudential Securities Incorporated

The Chicago Corporation   Josephthal Lyon & Ross
                                                        Incorporated
Ladenburg, Thalmann & Co. Inc.   Sutro & Co. Incorporated

Commonwealth Associates   Dickinson & Co.

First Colonial Securities Group, Inc.   Mabon Securities Corp.

Pennsylvania Merchant Group Ltd   Southwest Securities, Inc.

Selling Group

This tranche is being offered in the United States.

400,000 Shares

PaineWebber International   J. Henry Schroder Wagg & Co. Limited

This tranche is being offered outside the United States and Canada.

Figure 2.2 An Offering Announcement
This form of offering announcement is commonly referred to as a "tombstone." The participants in both the underwriting syndicate and the selling group established to sell the common stock of American Sensors are clearly noted on the tombstone. (Source: *Wall Street Journal*, February 2, 1995, p. C19.)

Compensation for underwriting and selling services typically comes in the form of a discount from the sale price of the securities. For example, an invest-ment banker may pay the issuing firm $24 per share for stock that will be sold for $26 per share. The investment banker may then sell the shares to members of the selling group for $25.25 per share. In this case, the original investment banker earns $1.25 per share ($25.25 sale price − $24 purchase price), and the members of the selling group earn 75 cents for each share they sell ($26 sale price − $25.25 purchase price). Although some primary security offerings are directly placed by the issuer, the majority of new issues are sold through public offering using the mechanism just described.

Secondary Markets

secondary market
the market in which securities are traded after they have been issued.

The market in which securities are traded after they have been issued is the **secondary market,** or the *aftermarket.* The secondary market exists because some purchasers of already issued securities may wish to sell them and others may wish to buy them. In the secondary market, unlike the primary market, the corporation whose securities are traded is not involved in the transaction. Instead, money and securities are exchanged between investors—the seller exchanges securities for cash paid by the buyer. The secondary market gives security purchasers *liquidity.* It also provides a mechanism for continuous pricing of securities to reflect their value at each point in time based upon the best information then available.

organized securities exchanges
centralized institutions in which transactions are made in already outstanding securities.

over-the-counter (OTC) market
widely scattered telecommunica-tions network through which sellers and buyers of certain securities can be brought together.

Included among secondary markets are the various organized securities exchanges and the over-the-counter market. **Organized securities exchanges** are centralized institutions in which the forces of supply and demand for already outstanding securities are brought together. The **over-the-counter (OTC) market,** on the other hand, is a widely scattered telecommunications network through which sellers and buyers of certain securities can be brought together. Organized securities exchanges are auction markets in which order systems are used. Price is determined by the flow of buy and sell orders. The over-the-counter markets use a quote system in which negotiation and dealer quotes determine the price. Because popular investment vehicles are traded on both the organized exchanges and the over-the-counter market, the individual investor will probably make transactions in both of these markets.

ORGANIZED SECURITIES EXCHANGES

Securities traded on organized securities exchanges account for about 62 per-cent of the total *dollar volume* of domestic shares traded. All trading at a given exchange is carried out in one place (e.g., the New York Stock Exchange on Wall Street) and under a broad set of rules by persons who are members of that exchange. The best-known exchanges on which stock and bond transac-tions are made are the New York Stock Exchange (NYSE) and the American Stock Exchange (AMEX), both located in New York City. They account for approximately 89 and 2 percent, respectively, of the total annual dollar volume of shares traded on organized U.S. exchanges. Other domestic exchanges include *regional exchanges,* such as the Chicago Stock Exchange and the Pacific Stock Exchange. These exchanges deal primarily in securities with regional or local appeal. Together, the regional exchanges account for about 9 percent of the annual dollar share volume on organized U.S. exchanges. In addition, *foreign stock exchanges* list and trade shares of firms in their own foreign markets. Separate domestic exchanges exist for options trading and trading in futures. Here we will consider the basic structure, rules, and operations of each of these organized domestic securities exchanges. (Foreign exchanges are discussed later.)

The New York Stock Exchange

Most organized securities exchanges are modeled after the New York Stock Exchange (NYSE)—the dominant organized exchange. In order to be a member, an individual or firm must own or lease a "seat" on the exchange. The word *seat* is used only figuratively, because members trade securities standing up. There are a total of 1,366 seats on the NYSE. During this century, seats on the exchange have sold for as much as $1.15 million (in 1987) and as little as $17,000 (in 1947). Recently, seats have sold for around $750,000. The majority of seat holders are brokerage firms, each typically owning more than one seat. The largest brokerage firm, Merrill Lynch Pierce Fenner & Smith, Inc., owns over 20 seats.

Firms such as Merrill Lynch designate officers to occupy seats. Only such designated individuals are permitted to make transactions on the floor of the exchange. Membership is often divided into broad classes based on the members' activities. Although the majority of members make purchase and sale transactions on behalf of their customers, some members specialize in making transactions for other members or for their own account. Table 2.1 classifies and briefly describes member activities. You can see that commission brokers and specialists perform the majority of the activities on the exchange.

Listing Policies   To become listed on an organized stock exchange, a firm must file an application. Some firms are listed on more than one exchange; they are said to have **dual listing.** Currently, over 2,300 firms, accounting for about 2,900 stocks (common and preferred) and 2,100 bonds, are listed on the NYSE.

dual listing
listing of a firm's shares on more than one exchange.

The New York Stock Exchange has the most stringent listing requirements. In order to be eligible for listing on the NYSE, a firm must have at least 2,000 stockholders owning 100 or more shares. It must have a minimum of 1.1 million shares of publicly held stock, a demonstrated earning power of $2.5 million before taxes at the time of the listing and $2 million before taxes for each of the preceding two years, net tangible assets of $18 million, and a total of $18 million in market value of publicly traded shares. It also must pay a listing fee. Once a firm's securities have been accepted for listing, it must meet the requirements of the federal Securities and Exchange Commission (SEC), which regulates certain aspects of listed securities. If listed firms do not continue to meet specified requirements, they may be **de-listed** from the exchange.

de-listed
removed from listing on an organized stock exchange.

Trading Activity   Trading is carried out on the floor of the organized exchanges. The largest—the floor of the NYSE—is an area about the size of a

Table 2.1 NYSE Member Activities

Type of Member	Approximate Percentage of Total Membership*	Primary Activities
A. Make transactions for customers		
Commission brokers	52	Make purchase and sale transactions of stocks and bonds as requested by customers.
Bond brokers	2	Commission brokers who make only bond transactions for customers.
B. Make transactions for other members		
Floor brokers ("two-dollar brokers")	10	Execute orders for other brokers who are unable to do so due to excessive market activity.
Specialists	29	Make a continuous, fair, and orderly market in the one or more issues assigned to them. Also make purchase and sale transactions of less than 100 shares (odd lots) for members of the exchange.
C. Make transactions for their own account		
Registered traders	4	Purchase and sell securities for their own accounts. Must abide by certain regulations established to protect the public.

*Because approximately 3 percent of the members are inactive, the percentages given total to only 97 percent.

football field. Its operation is typical of the various exchanges (though details vary): On the NYSE floor are 18 trading posts. Certain stocks are traded at each of the posts. Bonds and less active stocks are traded in an annex. All trades are made on the floor of the exchange by members of the exchange. Around the perimeter are telephones and electronic equipment used to transmit buy and sell orders from brokers' offices to the exchange floor and back again once an order has been executed.

All transactions on the floor of the exchange are made through an auction process. The goal is to fill all buy orders at the lowest price and to fill all sell orders at the highest price. The price is in effect determined by the flow of buy and sell orders. The actual auction takes place at the post where the particular security is traded. Members interested in purchasing a given security publicly negotiate a transaction with members interested in selling that security. The job of the **specialist**—an exchange member who specializes in making transactions in one or more stocks—is to provide for a continuous and orderly market in that security. The specialist offers to buy or sell (at specified prices) whenever there is a lack of continuity or order in the market for the security.

specialist
stock exchange member who specializes in making transactions in one or more stocks.

The American Stock Exchange

The American Stock Exchange (AMEX) is the second largest organized U.S. security exchange in terms of the number of listed companies. In terms of dollar volume of trading, the AMEX is actually smaller than the two largest regional exchanges—the Chicago and the Pacific. Its organization and its procedures are similar to those of the NYSE, except that its listing requirements are not as stringent. There are approximately 660 seats on the AMEX, with over 1,000 listed stocks and 125 (corporate) listed bonds.

Regional Stock Exchanges

The number of companies having securities listed on each of the regional exchanges is typically in the range of 100 to 500. As a group, these exchanges handle about 9 percent of the dollar volume of all shares traded on organized U.S. exchanges. The best-known regional exchanges are the Chicago, Pacific (co-located in Los Angeles and San Francisco), Philadelphia, Boston, and Cincinnati exchanges. Most are modeled after the NYSE, but their membership and listing requirements are considerably more lenient.

It is not uncommon for the regional exchanges to list securities that are also listed on the NYSE or AMEX. This dual listing is often done to enhance a security's trading activity. In addition, a number of the regional exchanges, along with the NYSE, AMEX, and the over-the-counter market, are linked together through an electronic communications network—the *Intermarket Trading System (ITS)*—that allows brokers and other traders to make transactions at the best prices.

Options Exchanges

Options allow the holder to sell or to buy another security or property at a specified price over a given period of time. Securities options are listed and traded on the Chicago Board Options Exchange (CBOE), as well as on the American Stock Exchange, the New York Stock Exchange, the Pacific Stock Exchange, and the Philadelphia Stock Exchange. The dominant options exchange is the CBOE. Usually, an option to sell or buy a given security is listed on only one of the options exchanges, although dual listing does sometimes occur. Options exchanges deal only in security options; options to sell or buy property are not traded in this marketplace.

Futures Exchanges

Futures contracts guarantee the delivery of a specified commodity or financial instrument at some specific future date at an agreed-upon price. The dominant exchange on which commodity and financial futures are traded is the Chicago Board of Trade (CBT). There are a number of other futures exchanges, some of which specialize in certain commodities and financial instruments rather than the broad spectrum listed on the CBT. The largest of these exchanges include the New York Mercantile Exchange, the Chicago Mercantile Exchange, the Commodity Exchange of New York, the London International Financial Futures Exchange, the New York Coffee, Sugar & Cocoa Exchange, the New York Cotton Exchange, the Kansas City Board of Trade, and the Minneapolis Grain Exchange.

THE OVER-THE-COUNTER MARKET

The *over-the-counter (OTC) market* is not a specific institution; rather, it is another way of trading securities. The OTC market is the result of an intangible relationship among sellers and purchasers of securities, who are linked by a telecommunications network. It accounts for about 38 percent of the total dollar volume of domestic shares traded. Securities traded in this market are sometimes called *unlisted securities*. The prices at which securities are traded in the OTC market are determined using a quote system that involves negotiation and dealer quotes. The actual process—described later—depends on the general activity of the security.

A numerical majority of stocks are traded over the counter, as are most government and corporate bonds. Of the over 35,000 issues traded over the counter, about 5,400 have an active market in which frequent transactions take place. A numerical majority of all corporate bonds, some of which are also listed on the NYSE, are traded in the OTC market.

New Issues and Secondary Distributions

To create a continuous market for unlisted securities, the OTC market also provides a forum in which initial public offerings (IPOs), both listed and unlisted, are sold. If they are listed, subsequent transactions will be made on the appropriate organized securities exchange; unlisted securities will continue to trade in the OTC market. **Secondary distributions**—the public sales of large blocks of previously issued securities held by large investors—are also made in the OTC market to minimize the potentially negative effects of such transactions on the price of listed securities. These transactions are forms of third- or fourth-market trades, which are described below.

The Role of Dealers

The market price of OTC securities results from a matching of supply and demand for securities by traders known as **dealers.** Each "makes markets" in certain securities by offering to buy or sell them at stated prices. Thus, unlike the organized exchanges (where the buyer and seller of a security are brought together by a broker), the OTC market links a buyer or seller with a dealer. That is, the second party to an OTC transaction is always a dealer. For example, a dealer making a market in Raco Enterprises might offer to buy shares from investors at $29.50 and sell shares to other investors at $31. The **bid price** is the highest price offered by the dealer to purchase a given security; the **ask price** is the lowest price at which the dealer is willing to sell the security. Because more than one dealer frequently makes a market in a given security, dealers compete. Buyers and sellers attempt to find and negotiate the best price—lowest buy price or highest sell price—when making OTC market transactions. The dealer makes a profit from the spread between the bid and the ask prices.

Nasdaq

OTC dealers are linked with the sellers and purchasers of securities through the **Nasdaq (National Association of Securities Dealers Automated Quotation) system.** Nasdaq is an automated system that provides up-to-date bid and ask

---

secondary distributions
the public sales of large blocks of previously issued securities held by large investors.

dealers
traders who "make markets" by offering to buy or sell certain over-the-counter securities at stated prices.

bid price
the highest price offered by a dealer to purchase a given security.

ask price
the lowest price at which a dealer is willing to sell a given security.

Nasdaq (National Association of Securities Dealers Automated Quotation) system
an automated system that provides up-to-date bid and ask prices on certain selected, highly active OTC securities.

prices on about 5,400 selected, highly active OTC securities. It enables buyers and sellers to locate one another easily. Not all OTC securities are listed on Nasdaq, however. To trade in securities not quoted on Nasdaq, buyers and sellers must find each other through references or through known dealers in the securities involved.

About 3,400 of the Nasdaq stocks are included in the **Nasdaq/National Market System (Nasdaq/NMS)**. These are stocks that meet certain qualification standards relative to financial size, performance, and trading activity. Transactions in stocks on this list are reported more quickly (immediately) and in more detail (similar to NYSE and AMEX trades) than non-Nasdaq/NMS issues are. Their more detailed quotations are isolated from other OTC stocks when published in the financial press.

Nasdaq/National Market System (Nasdaq/NMS)
a list of Nasdaq stocks meeting certain qualification standards relative to financial size, performance, and trading activity.

THIRD AND FOURTH MARKETS

The **third market** is the name given to over-the-counter transactions made in securities listed on the New York Stock Exchange, the American Stock Exchange, or one of the other organized exchanges. It exists to serve the needs of large institutional investors, such as mutual funds, pension funds, and life insurance companies, by allowing them to make large transactions at a reduced cost. These transactions are typically handled by firms or dealers that are not members of an organized securities exchange. For bringing together large buyers and sellers, dealers charge commissions below those charged for making similar transactions on the associated securities exchange. Institutional investors are thus often able to realize sizable savings in brokerage commissions as well as to have minimal impact on the price of the transaction.

third market
over-the-counter transactions made in securities listed on the NYSE, AMEX, or other organized exchanges.

The **fourth market** is the name given to transactions made directly between large institutional buyers and sellers of securities. Unlike third-market transactions, fourth-market transactions bypass the dealer. But in order to find a suitable seller or buyer, an institution may hire a firm to facilitate the transaction.

fourth market
transactions made directly between large institutional buyers and sellers.

GLOBALIZATION OF SECURITIES MARKETS

Today, investors, issuers of securities, and securities firms look beyond the markets of their home countries to find the best returns, lowest costs, and best international business opportunities. The basic goal of most investors is to earn the highest return with the lowest risk. This outcome is achieved through diversification. The inclusion of foreign investments in a portfolio can greatly increase the potential for diversification by holding (1) a wider range of industries and securities, (2) securities traded in a larger number of markets, and (3) securities denominated in different currencies. The smaller and less diversified an investor's home market is, the greater the potential benefit from prudent international diversification. However, even investors from the United States and other highly developed markets can benefit from global diversification.

Advances in technology and communications, together with the elimination of many political and regulatory barriers, allow investors to make cross-border securities transactions with relative ease. More and more financial markets are opening and integrating with the rest of the world's markets. Both investors and seekers of funds can view the world's markets as integrated and available to them. In short, we are experiencing a globalization of the securities markets, enabling investors to seek out opportunities to profit from rapidly expanding economies throughout the world. To enter the international investment arena, today's investors need to understand how international securities markets operate, ways to invest in foreign securities, and the rewards and risks of international investing.

Growing Importance of International Markets

Organized securities exchanges now operate in more than 30 countries worldwide. They are located not only in the major industrialized nations such as Japan, Great Britain, Canada, and Germany but also in emerging economies such as Brazil, Chile, India, Korea, Kuwait, Malaysia, Mexico, Taiwan, Thailand, and Turkey. The top three securities markets worldwide are the New York, Tokyo, and London stock exchanges. Other important foreign exchanges include Frankfurt, Paris, Toronto, Montreal, Sydney, Hong Kong, Zurich, and Buenos Aires. The European stock markets are expected to take on additional importance with economic integration of the European Community (EC) during the 1990s. Among the EC's major goals are the development of a central capital market, a central bank, and a single currency unit for the 12 member countries. The current market capitalization of the combined EC markets represents a market competitive with New York and Tokyo.

Bond markets too are going global as investors are purchasing government and corporate fixed-income securities in foreign markets. The United States dominates the international government bond market, followed by Japan, Germany, and Great Britain.

International Investment Performance

A primary motive for investing overseas is the lure of high returns. In fact, only once since 1980 did the United States finish number one among the major stock markets of the world. For example, in 1993, investors would have earned higher returns in such markets as Germany, Hong Kong, and Mexico than in the United States. During that year the stock price index for Germany increased by 33.6 percent, that for Hong Kong by 109 percent, and that for Mexico by 46.9 percent, compared to a 7 percent increase in the U.S. stock price index. Of course, foreign securities markets tend to be more risky than U.S. markets. A market with high returns in one year may not do so well in the next year.

Investors can compare activity on U.S. and foreign exchanges by following market indexes that track the performance of those exchanges. (We'll discuss indexes in more detail in Chapter 3.) Most of the major indexes, trading activity in selected stocks on major foreign exchanges, and foreign exchange rates are reported daily in the *Wall Street Journal* and regularly in other financial publications such as *Barron's* and *Business Week*. Also, the *Wall Street Journal*'s "Investment Insight" section frequently compares performance of the U.S. and selected foreign markets.

INVESTOR FACTS

THE RUSSIANS ARE COMING, THE RUSSIANS ARE COMING—To Wall Street, that is. On November 30, 1994, the first newly privatized Russian company filed an application to issue American Depositary Receipts (ADRs). AvtoVAZbank, a regional bank owned primarily by Russia's biggest car manufacturer, plans to sell its ADRs in the over-the-counter market. Other Russian companies are expected to follow in quest of Western capital. Eager investors see this as a major step toward opening up the Russian market, which despite high risks has tremendous profit potential.

(Source: *Wall Street Journal*, December 1, 1994, p. C1.)

Yankee bonds
dollar-denominated debt securities issued by foreign governments or corporations and traded in U.S. securities markets.

American Depositary Receipts (ADRs)
dollar-denominated negotiable receipts for the stocks of foreign companies that are held in the vaults of banks in the companies' home countries.

Investing in Foreign Securities

Foreign security investments can be made either indirectly or directly. Indirect investment results from the purchase of either the shares of a U.S.-based multinational with substantial foreign operations or the shares of an international mutual fund. Many U.S.-based multinational firms such as Exxon, IBM, Citicorp, Dow Chemical, Coca-Cola, Colgate-Palmolive, and Hewlett-Packard, receive more than 50 percent of their revenues from overseas operations. By investing in the securities of such firms, an investor can achieve a degree of international diversification. Such diversification can also be achieved by purchasing shares in a mutual fund that invests primarily in foreign securities. These indirect foreign security investment transactions are made in a conventional fashion through a stockbroker, as explained later in this chapter and in Chapter 11, which is devoted to mutual funds.

Direct investment in foreign companies can be achieved in three ways— by purchasing securities on foreign exchanges, by buying securities of foreign companies that are traded on U.S. exchanges, or by buying *American Depositary Receipts (ADRs)*. Purchasing securities on foreign exchanges involves additional risks because they are not traded in U.S. dollars. This approach is not for the timid or inexperienced investor. Because each country's exchange has its own regulations and procedures, investors must be prepared to cope not only with varying degrees of market regulation and efficiency but also with different securities exchange rules, transaction procedures, accounting standards, tax laws, and language barriers. These transactions are best handled either through brokers at major U.S. Wall Street firms with large international operations or through major banks, such as Bankers Trust and Citicorp, that have special units to handle foreign securities transactions. Brokers at these firms provide information and advice and make foreign security transactions for their clients. Investors could alternatively deal with foreign broker-dealers, but such an approach is more complicated and risky.

Investors can buy the securities of foreign companies that are traded on both organized and over-the-counter exchanges. These securities are issued by large, well-known foreign (particularly Canadian) companies. Stocks of companies such as Alcan, KLM, Sony, and Volvo trade directly on U.S. exchanges. In addition, **Yankee bonds**—dollar-denominated debt securities issued by foreign governments or corporations and traded in U.S. securities markets—are traded on organized exchanges and in the over-the-counter market in the United States. Transactions in foreign securities that are traded on U.S. exchanges are handled in the same way as exchange-traded domestic securities.

Foreign stocks are also traded on U.S. exchanges in the form of **American Depositary Receipts (ADRs)**, which are dollar-denominated negotiable receipts for the stocks of foreign companies that are held in the vaults of banks in the companies' home country. Today, nearly 1,200 ADRs representing about 40 different home countries are traded on U.S. exchanges. About one-fourth of them are actively traded. Included are ADRs of well-known companies such as Daimler-Benz, Fuji Photo, Sanyo, and Toyota. ADRs trade and are transacted in the same fashion as standard domestic securities. ADRs are further discussed in Chapter 5.

Risks of Investing Internationally

Investing abroad is not without its pitfalls. In addition to the usual risks involved in making any security transaction, the international investor must consider the risks associated with doing business in a particular foreign country. Changes in government regulations such as trade policies, labor laws, and taxation may affect operating conditions for the country's firms. The government itself may not be stable. Therefore, when making investments in foreign markets, investors must watch similar environmental factors in each foreign country. That is, of course, more difficult than at home because of the lack of familiarity with the foreign economic and political environments, as well as the number of countries involved.

U.S. securities markets are generally viewed as highly regulated, efficient, and reliable. This is not always the case in foreign markets, many of which lag substantially behind the United States in both operations and regulation. Some countries place various restrictions on foreign investment. In Korea, Brazil, and Thailand, for example, mutual funds are the only way for foreigners to invest; Mexico has a two-tier market, with some securities restricted to foreigners. Some countries make it difficult for foreigners to get their funds out, and many impose taxes on dividends. For example, Swiss taxes are about 20 percent on dividends paid to foreigners. Accounting standards vary from country to country. These differences in accounting practices can affect the apparent profitability, conceal other attractive assets (e.g., hidden reserves and undervalued assets that are permitted in many countries), and fail to disclose other risks. As a result, it is difficult to compare fairly the financial performances and positions of firms operating in different foreign countries. Other difficulties include illiquid markets and an inability to obtain reliable investment information due to a lack of reporting requirements.

Furthermore, because international investing involves securities denominated in foreign currencies, trading profits and losses are affected not only by a security's price changes but also by changes in foreign exchange rates. The values of the world's major currencies fluctuate with respect to each other on a daily basis, and the relationship between two currencies at a specified date is called the **foreign exchange rate.** On September 15, 1994, the foreign exchange rate for the French franc (Ff) and the U.S. dollar (US$) was expressed as follows:

foreign exchange rate
the relationship between two currencies at a specific date.

US$1.00 = Ff 4.95
Ff 1.00 = US$.202

On that day, you would have received 4.95 French francs for every $1. Conversely, each French franc was worth $.202.

Changes in the value of a particular foreign currency with respect to the US$—or any other currency—are called *appreciation* and *depreciation*. For example, on March 15, 1995, the Ff/US$ exchange rate was 5.29, indicating that in six months the French franc *depreciated* relative to the dollar (and the dollar *appreciated* relative to the franc). On March 15, it took more francs to buy $1 (5.29 versus 4.95), so each franc was worth less in dollar terms ($.189 versus $.202). Had the French franc instead *appreciated* (and the dollar *depreciated* relative to the franc), each franc would have been worth more in dollar terms.

foreign exchange risk
the risk caused by varying exchange rates between the currencies of two countries.

Foreign exchange risk is the risk caused by the varying exchange rates between the currencies of two countries. For example, assume that on September 15, 1994, you bought 100 shares of a French stock at 100 Ff per share, held it for six months, and then sold it for 105 French francs. The following table summarizes the transactions:

Date	Transaction	Number of Shares	Price in Ff	Value of Transaction Ff	Exchange Rate Ff/US$	Value in US$
9/15/94	Purchase	100	100	10,000	4.95	$2,020.20
3/15/95	Sell	100	105	10,500	5.29	$1,984.88

Although you realized a gain of 500 French francs, in dollar terms the transaction resulted in a loss of $35.32 ($2,020.20 – $1,984.88). The value of the stock in dollars decreased because the French franc was worth less (had depreciated) relative to the dollar. Therefore, investors in foreign securities must be aware that the value of the foreign currency in relationship to the dollar can have a profound effect on returns from foreign security transactions.

TRADING HOURS OF SECURITIES MARKETS

To compete more effectively with foreign securities markets, in which investors can execute trades when U.S. markets are closed, both the organized U.S. exchanges and Nasdaq recently expanded trading hours beyond the traditional session (9:30 A.M. to 4:00 P.M., Eastern time). In mid-1991, the NYSE added two short electronic trading sessions that begin after the 4:00 P.M. closing bell. The first, from 4:15 to 5:00 P.M., trades stocks at that day's closing prices via a computer-matching system. Transactions occur only if a match can be made, and they are handled on a first-come, first-served basis. The second session lasts from 4:00 to 5:15 P.M. and allows institutional investors to trade large blocks of stock valued at $1 million or more. Since their inception, the NYSE has experienced growing interest in both sessions.

Nasdaq began its own expanded-hours electronic trading session in January 1992. Called *Nasdaq International,* it runs from 3:30 A.M. (when the London Exchange opens) to 9:00 A.M. Eastern time, one-half hour before the start of regular trading sessions in U.S. markets. Because it lists NYSE stocks as well as other U.S. equities and has less stringent disclosure requirements than other markets, Nasdaq International is designed to attract traders from both the New York and London exchanges. The Pacific Stock Exchange also conducts an after-hours trading session, from 4:00 to 4:50 P.M., Eastern time. Unlike the NYSE and Nasdaq, the Pacific Stock Exchange's after-hours session is run on an auction basis. It continues to make markets, rather than trading electronically at fixed prices. Other U.S. markets are expected eventually to expand hours as well.

These actions represent the first steps toward the development of 24-hour global trading of securities, both electronically and at auction through organized exchanges. Actually, large institutional investors are already able to trade securities after hours (from 4:00 P.M. to 9:30 A.M., Eastern time) through *Instinet,* a private electronic trading system owned by Reuters, the British communications conglomerate. This system facilitates *fourth-market* transactions in about 10,000 U.S. and European stocks. In addition, in 1992 the Chicago Board of Trade and the Chicago Mercantile Exchange for competitive reasons established *Globex*. It is a computerized electronic trading system that creates a 24-hour global marketplace in which options and futures listed on those exchanges can be traded at times when they are closed. Some people believe that if it's successful, Globex could become the model for the 24-hour global stock exchange of the future. Many experts expect longer trading sessions to be used primarily by institutional investors, but they question their value for the average individual investor.

REGULATION OF SECURITIES MARKETS

Securities laws are passed to protect investors and meet the needs of the financial marketplace as it grows in both size and complexity. A number of state and federal laws provide that adequate and accurate disclosure of information be made to potential and existing investors. Such laws also regulate the activities of various participants in the securities markets. State laws, which regulate the sale of securities within state borders, are commonly called "blue sky laws" because they are intended to prevent investors from being sold nothing but "blue sky." These laws typically establish procedures for regulating both security issues and sellers of securities doing business within the state. As part of this process, most states have a regulatory body, such as a state securities commission, that is charged with the enforcement of the related state statutes. However, the most important securities laws, briefly summarized below, are those enacted by the federal government.

Securities Act of 1933

The *Securities Act of 1933* was passed by Congress to ensure full disclosure of information about new security issues and prevent a stock market collapse similar to that of 1929–1932. The act requires the issuer of a new security to file with the Securities and Exchange Commission (SEC) a registration statement containing information about the new issue. The firm cannot sell the security until the SEC approves the registration statement, a process that usually takes about 20 days.

prospectus
a portion of a security registration statement that details the key aspects of the issue, the issuer, and its management and financial position.

red herring
a preliminary prospectus made available to prospective investors after a registration statement's filing but before its approval.

One portion of the registration statement, called the **prospectus,** details the key aspects of the issue, the issuer, and its management and financial position. During the waiting period between the statement's filing and its approval, a preliminary prospectus is made available to prospective investors. It is often called a **red herring** because a notice printed in red on the front cover indicates the tentative nature of the offer. If the statement has been approved, the new security issue can be offered for sale. If the registration statement is found to be fraudulent, the SEC will reject the issue and may also sue the directors and others responsible for the misrepresentation. The cover of the preliminary prospectus describing the 1995 stock issue of American Sensors is shown in Figure 2.3. Note the red herring printed vertically on its left edge.

As an investor, you should realize that approval of the registration statement by the SEC does not mean the security is a good investment; it merely

Figure 2.3 Cover of a Preliminary Prospectus for a Stock Issue
Some of the key factors relating to the 1995 stock issue by
American Sensors are summarized on the cover of its 36-page
preliminary prospectus. Note the type printed vertically on the left
edge is normally red, a *red herring*. (Source: *American Sensors,*
December 29, 1994, p. 1.)

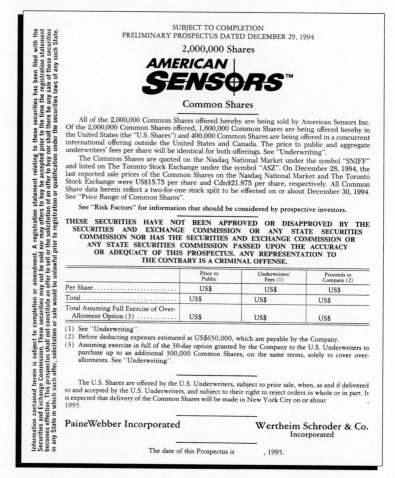

indicates that the facts presented in the statement appear to reflect the firm's
true position.

Securities Exchange Act of 1934

The *Securities Exchange Act of 1934* formally established the SEC as the
agency in charge of the administration of federal securities laws. The act gave
the SEC the power to regulate the organized securities exchanges and the over-
the-counter market by extending disclosure requirements to outstanding securities. It required the stock exchanges as well as the stocks traded on them to
be registered with the SEC.

As a result of this act, the SEC covers the organized exchanges and the
OTC market, their members, brokers and dealers, and the securities traded in
these markets. Each of these participants must file reports with the SEC and
must periodically update them. The act has been instrumental in providing

adequate disclosure on issues that are traded in the secondary markets. The 1934 act, which has been amended several times over the years, and the Securities Act of 1933, remain the key pieces of legislation that protect participants in the securities markets.

Maloney Act of 1938

The *Maloney Act of 1938*, an amendment to the Securities Exchange Act of 1934, provided for the establishment of trade associations to self-regulate the securities industry. Since its passage, only one such trade association, the National Association of Securities Dealers (NASD), has been formed. NASD members include nearly all of the nation's securities firms that do business with the public. The NASD, operating under SEC supervision, establishes standardized rules and procedures for security trading and ethical behavior, monitors and enforces compliance with these rules and procedures, and serves as the industry spokesperson. Membership in the NASD allows member firms to make transactions with other member firms at rates below those charged to nonmembers. Today, any securities firms that are not members of the NASD must agree to be supervised directly by the SEC. Because the SEC has the power to revoke the NASD's registration, its power over this organization is the same as over the exchanges. In addition to its self-regulatory role, the NASD has greatly streamlined the functioning of the over-the-counter market by creating Nasdaq.

Investment Company Act of 1940

The *Investment Company Act of 1940* was passed to protect those purchasing investment company shares. An *investment company* is one that obtains funds by selling its shares to numerous investors and uses the proceeds to purchase securities. The dominant type of investment company is the *mutual fund* (which is discussed in detail in Chapter 11). The Investment Company Act of 1940 established rules and regulations for investment companies and formally authorized the SEC to regulate their practices and procedures. It required the investment companies to register with the SEC and to fulfill certain disclosure requirements. The act was amended in 1970 to prohibit investment companies from paying excessive fees to their advisers and from charging excessive commissions to purchasers of company shares.

Investment Advisers Act of 1940

The *Investment Advisers Act of 1940* was passed to protect investors against potential abuses by *investment advisers*—persons hired by investors to advise them about security investments. It requires that advisers disclose all relevant information about their backgrounds, conflicts of interest, and so on, as well as about any investments they recommend. The act requires advisers to register and file periodic reports with the SEC. A 1960 amendment extended the SEC's powers to permit inspection of the records of investment advisers and revocation of the registration of advisers who violate the act's provisions. *This act does not provide any guarantee of competence on the part of advisers*; it merely helps to protect the investor against *fraudulent and unethical practices* by the adviser.

Securities Acts Amendments of 1975

In 1975, Congress amended the securities acts to require the SEC and the securities industry to develop a competitive national system for trading securities. As a first step, the SEC abolished fixed-commission schedules, thereby providing for negotiated commissions. (Commissions are discussed in more detail later in this chapter.) A second action was the establishment of the *Intermarket Trading System (ITS)*. Today, this electronic communications network links nine markets, including the NYSE, AMEX, major regional exchanges, and the Nasdaq market, and trades over 2,900 eligible issues. Unquestionably, the *Securities Acts Amendments* have been highly effective in initiating a national market system. However, many institutional and organizational barriers remain to be overcome before a truly competitive national market system can be established.

ETHICAL ISSUES

The 1980s were a decade of general economic prosperity and rapidly rising stock prices. As typically happens during periods of excess in the financial markets, the decade also witnessed a takeover and buyout mania that spawned a host of speculators intent on profit. Many times these speculators operated without regard for the legality of their actions. Although the tactics varied, many of the illegal gains were achieved through insider-trading practices. **Insider trading** involves using private information to make profitable securities transactions. It is both illegal and unethical. The *Insider Trading and Fraud Act of 1988* defined an *insider* as one who possesses material nonpublic information, and it established penalties for insider trading. Insiders are typically a company's directors, officers, major shareholders, bankers, investment bankers, accountants, or attorneys.

The prosecution and conviction of a number of high-profile insiders during the 1980s and early 1990s has created a body of case law that more clearly defines illegal and unethical acts. The definition of insider, which originally referred only to a company's employees, directors, and their relatives, was expanded to include anyone who obtains private information about a company. Recent legislation substantially increased the penalties for insider trading and gave the SEC greater power to investigate and prosecute claims of illegal insider-trading activity.

Clearly, the many insider-trading cases of the 1980s and early 1990s heightened the public's awareness of **ethics**—standards of conduct or moral judgment—in business. The financial community is continuing to develop and enforce ethical standards that will motivate market participants to adhere to laws and regulations. Although it is indeed difficult to enforce ethical standards, it appears that opportunities for abuses in the financial markets will be reduced, thereby providing a more level playing field for all investors.

GENERAL MARKET CONDITIONS: BULL OR BEAR

Conditions in the securities markets are commonly classified as "bull" or "bear," depending on whether securities prices are rising or falling over time. Changing market conditions generally stem from changes in investor attitudes,

insider trading
the illegal use of material non-public information about a company to make profitable securities transactions.

ethics
standards of conduct or moral judgment.

bull markets
favorable markets normally associated with rising prices, investor optimism, economic recovery, and governmental stimulus.

bear markets
unfavorable markets normally associated with falling prices, investor pessimism, economic slowdowns, and government restraint.

changes in economic activity, and government actions aimed at stimulating or slowing down economic activity. **Bull markets** are favorable markets normally associated with rising prices, investor optimism, economic recovery, and governmental stimulus. **Bear markets** are unfavorable markets normally associated with falling prices, investor pessimism, economic slowdowns, and government restraint.

Over the past 50 or so years, the behavior of the stock market has been generally bullish, reflecting the growth and prosperity of the economy. Figure 2.4 shows the stock price movements from 1950 to mid-1995. Both bull (upward lines) and bear (downward lines) markets can be seen. The most famous bull market was surely the one that started in August 1982 and peaked in August 1987. It ended in a dramatic way with the big market crash of October 19, 1987. Actually, the market had started dropping in late August 1987 and by mid-October had already fallen about 15 percent. Then came "black Monday," when the market experienced its biggest and hardest crash in history: In one day, the market fell nearly 23 percent and lost roughly half a trillion dollars in value. The bear market initiated with this decline was the result of major federal budget deficits, unfavorable trade balances, and congressional discussions directed at regulating acquisitions and the issuance of junk bonds. Figure 2.4 shows that since early 1991, the stock market has been bullish primarily as a result of low inflation, improving trade balances, shrinking budget deficits, and economic recovery.

Figure 2.4 Bull and Bear Markets, 1950–mid-1995 Rising stock prices, shown here by increases in the Standard & Poor's 500 Composite Index (upward lines), are called *bull markets. Bear markets* are periods of falling prices (downward lines). Most recently, a bull market began in early 1991 and continued through the middle of 1995. (Source: *Federal Reserve Bulletin*, various issues.)

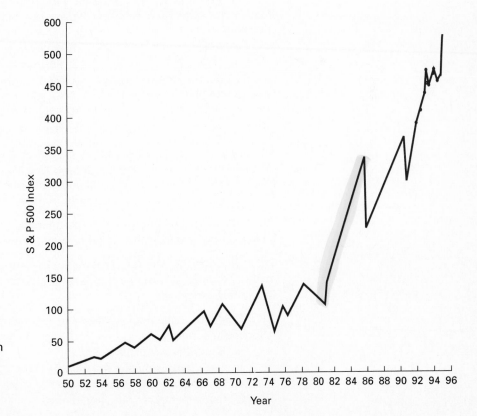

In general, investors experience higher (or positive) returns on common stock investments during a bull market. However, some securities are bullish in a bear market or bearish in a bull market. Of course, during bear markets many investors will invest in vehicles other than securities to obtain higher and less risky returns. Market conditions are difficult to predict and usually can be identified only after they exist. The actual assessment of market conditions and the use of this information by investors are described in Chapter 3.

CONCEPTS *in Review*

2.1   Define and differentiate between each of the following pairs of words:
   a. *Money market* and *capital market*
   b. *Primary market* and *secondary market*
   c. *Organized securities exchanges* and *over-the-counter (OTC) market*

2.2   Define and differentiate between a *public offering,* a *rights offering,* and a *private placement.* Briefly describe the role of the investment banker in underwriting a public offering.

2.3   Briefly describe the following aspects of the New York Stock Exchange (NYSE):
   a. Membership
   b. Listing policies
   c. Trading activity

2.4   For each of the items in the left-hand column, match the most appropriate item in the right-hand column. Explain the relationship between the items matched.

a. AMEX	1. Unlisted securities are traded
b. CBT	2. Futures exchange
c. Boston Stock Exchange	3. Options exchange
d. CBOE	4. Receipt for stock of foreign company
e. OTC	5. Second largest security exchange
f. ADR	6. Regional stock exchange

2.5   Describe the over-the-counter market, and explain how it works. Be sure to mention dealers, bid and ask prices, Nasdaq, and the Nasdaq/NMS. What role does this market play in initial public offerings (IPOs) and secondary distributions? What are the third and fourth markets?

2.6   Why is globalization of securities markets an important issue today? How have international investments performed in recent years?

2.7   Describe the way foreign security investments can be made, both indirectly and directly. Describe the risks of investing internationally, particularly foreign exchange risk.

2.8   Briefly describe the key rules and regulations resulting from each of the following securities acts:
   a. Securities Act of 1933
   b. Securities Exchange Act of 1934
   c. Maloney Act of 1938
   d. Investment Company Act of 1940

e. Investment Advisers Act of 1940

f. Securities Acts Amendments of 1975

2.9   What is the general trend with regard to trading hours in U.S. markets? Why? Describe the legal and ethical issues surrounding insider trading. Differentiate between a bull market and a bear market.   ━━━

MAKING SECURITIES TRANSACTIONS

Understanding how the securities markets are structured and how they function is only the first step in developing a sound investment program. The individual investor must also understand the procedures required to make transactions. In this section of the chapter, we will look at the role of stockbrokers, the basic types of orders that can be placed, the costs of making investment transactions, and investor protection.

THE ROLE OF STOCKBROKERS

stockbrokers
individuals licensed by stock exchanges to facilitate transactions between buyers and sellers of securities; also called *account executives, investment executives, or financial consultants.*

Stockbrokers—also called *account executives, investment executives,* or *financial consultants*—act as intermediaries between buyers and sellers of securities. They typically charge a commission for facilitating these securities transactions. Stockbrokers must be licensed by the exchanges on which they place orders and must abide by the ethical guidelines of the exchanges and the SEC. Stockbrokers work for the brokerage firms that own seats on the organized securities exchanges. Members of the securities exchange actually execute orders transmitted to them by the brokers in the various sales offices. For example, the largest U.S. brokerage firm, Merrill Lynch Pierce Fenner & Smith, has offices in most major cities throughout the country. Orders from these offices are transmitted to the main office of Merrill Lynch and then to the floor of the stock exchanges (NYSE and AMEX) or to the OTC market, where they are executed. Confirmation of the order is sent back to the broker placing the order, who then relays it to the customer. This process can be carried out in a matter of minutes with the use of sophisticated telecommunications networks. Personal computers have opened up new ways of making security transactions, as the *Investor Insights* box on page 50 describes.

Orders for over-the-counter securities must be executed through *market makers,* who are dealers specializing in that security. The Nasdaq system, along with the available information on who makes markets in certain securities, enables brokers to execute orders in OTC securities. Normally, OTC transactions can be executed rapidly, because market makers maintain inventories of the securities in which they deal. Although the procedure for executing orders on organized exchanges may differ from that in the OTC market, an investor always places orders with his or her broker in the same manner, regardless of the market in which the security is traded.

Brokerage Services

The primary activity of stockbrokers involves making the purchase and sale transactions requested by clients. Brokers do not actually buy or sell securities; they simply execute clients' transactions at the best possible price. Brokerage

Investor Insights: *Market Innovations*

Here Comes the Electronic Investor

Imagine being able to trade stocks, bonds, mutual funds, and options with your personal computer, in the comfort of your own home. Such on-line trading is now possible—all you need is a computer with a modem and a subscription to one of the on-line computer services, such as Prodigy, CompuServe, or America Online. Each service is linked to discount brokerages that allow you to place orders electronically (once you have opened an account, of course). Three other on-line computer services—Charles Schwab & Co.'s *StreetSmart,* Fidelity Investments' *On-line Xpress (FOX)*, and *AccuTrade*—let you trade on-line directly without using one of the subscription services.

Here's how the process works: Your order goes from your computer through the on-line service to the brokerage's computer, which notes the type of order you have made and runs the necessary compliance checks. Some brokerage houses require that a person approve the order, though this tends to be the exception. The order then goes to the floor of the stock exchange, is executed automatically or given to a specialist who matches it to a reciprocal order, and is sent back to the brokerage marked "executed." A confirmation then travels back along the same electronic path to your computer. These transactions can take as little as 10 seconds, and 70 percent of them occur within one minute.

Beyond actual trading programs, on-line services offer many other options, with more available each month. Some services offer quotes for stocks and mutual funds, databases of investment information, and stock market analyses used by professional investment analysts. At any time of day or night, subscribers can dial into the Dow Jones *News/Retrieval Service* or Standard & Poor's *MarketScope*

service to get current and historical news on the companies that interest them.

On-line investing is certainly not for everyone. In fact, only a tiny percentage of investors have chosen this option over more traditional trading methods. To decide if you should invest on-line, weigh the pros and cons. Most important is your willingness to invest your time and to trust your decisions. You must master the nuances of computer trading programs (which can be complicated), do your own research, and have the confidence to complete trades electronically. Those unsure of this last requirement should know that some programs offer you the chance to practice making a trade until you have become comfortable with the mechanics involved. Also, it generally is difficult to make careless mistakes, because brokerages require that you verify your trading instructions.

Not ready to trade electronically? More than 500 investment programs can help you become a better investor. Unlike the earliest investment software, which did little more than help people keep track of their investments, the latest programs can create a portfolio and then test its composition to improve performance, examine all U.S. mutual funds to find your desired balance of risk and reward, or analyze the trading pattern of any stock to find the right time to buy or sell.

If you decide to become an on-line investor, good luck. A final word of advice: Never forget that you're playing with real money, not a computer game!

Sources: Ed Henry, "When Your Computer Is Your Broker," *Kiplinger's Personal Finance Magazine*, July 1994, pp. 93–95; Carla Koehl, "Electronic Investing," *Worth*, April 1994, pp. 76–77; Walter S. Mossberg, "The Digital Trading Post," *SmartMoney*, February 1994, pp. 126–30; and Leonard Wiener, "Your Own Private Investing Library," *U.S. News & World Report*, November 29, 1993, pp. 104–9.

---

street name
stock certificates issued in the brokerage house's name but held in trust for its client, who actually owns them.

firms will hold the client's security certificates for safekeeping; the stocks kept by the firm in this manner are said to be held in **street name.** Because the securities are issued in the brokerage house's name and held in trust for the client (rather than issued in the client's name), they can be more easily transferred at the time of sale without having to obtain the client's signature. Street name is actually a common way of buying securities, because many investors do not want to be bothered with handling and safeguarding stock certificates. In such cases, the brokerage firm records the details of the client's transaction and keeps track of his or her investments through a series of bookkeeping entries. When dividends, notices, and so on, are received by the broker, they are forwarded to the client who owns the securities.

In addition, stockbrokers offer clients a variety of other services. For example, the brokerage firm normally provides free information about investments. Quite often, the firm will have a research staff that periodically issues analyses of economic, market, industry, or company behavior and makes recommendations to buy or sell certain securities. As a client of a large brokerage firm, you can expect to receive regular bulletins discussing market activity and possibly a recommended investment list. You will also receive a statement describing your transactions for the month and showing commission and interest charges, dividends and interest received, and your account balance.

Today, most brokerage firms will invest surplus cash left in a customer's account in a money market mutual fund, allowing the customer to earn a reasonable rate of interest on these balances. Such arrangements help the investor earn as much as possible on temporarily idle funds. Most brokerage offices also have electronic equipment that provides up-to-the-minute stock price quotations and world news. Price information can be obtained from the *ticker* (a lighted screen that displays all NYSE, AMEX, and regional exchange security transactions as they occur) or by keying into a computer system that provides a capsulized description of almost all securities and their prices. World news, which can significantly affect the stock market, is obtained from a wire service subscribed to by the brokerage office. Finally, most offices have a reference library available for use by clients.

Selecting a Stockbroker

It is of primary importance to select a stockbroker who understands your investment goals and who can effectively assist you in pursuing these goals. If you choose a broker whose own disposition toward investing is similar to yours, you should be able to establish a solid working relationship. In addition, when selecting a broker you should consider the cost and types of services available from the firm with which he or she is affiliated. Often, significant differences can be found among firms. The broker you select should be the person you believe best understands your investment goals and will provide the best service at the lowest possible cost to you.

It is probably wise to ask friends or business associates to recommend a broker. However, it is not important—and often not even advisable—to know your stockbroker personally. A strictly business relationship eliminates the possibility that social concerns will interfere with the achievement of your investment goals. This does not mean that your broker's sole interest should be commissions. Responsible brokers do not engage in **churning**—that is, causing excessive trading of their clients' accounts in order to increase commissions. Churning is both illegal and unethical under SEC and exchange rules. However, it is often difficult to prove.

Investors who wish merely to make transactions and are not interested in obtaining the full array of brokerage services should consider a **discount**

churning
an illegal and unethical act by a broker to increase commissions by causing excessive trading of clients' accounts.

discount broker
broker who charges low commissions to make transactions for customers but provides little or no research information or investment advice.

broker. These brokers merely make transactions for customers—they provide little or no research information or investment advice. The investor calls a toll-free number to initiate a transaction, and the discount broker confirms the transaction by phone or return mail. Discount brokers that charge the lowest commissions and provide virtually no services are commonly referred to as *deep discounters.* The rapidly growing volume of business done by discount brokers attests to their success. Today, many banks and savings institutions are making discount brokerage services available to their depositors who wish to buy stocks, bonds, mutual funds, and other investment vehicles.

Opening an Account

To open an account, the customer must fill out various documents that establish a legal relationship between the customer and the brokerage firm. A signature card and a personal data card provide the information needed to identify the client's account. The stockbroker must also have a reasonable understanding of a client's personal financial situation to assess his or her investment goals—and also to be sure that the client can pay for the securities purchased. Instructions regarding the transfer and custody of securities must also be given to the broker. If the customer wishes to borrow money to make transactions, a *margin account* (described below) must be established. If the customer is acting as a trustee or an executor or is a corporation, additional documents will be required. No laws or rules prohibit an investor from having accounts with more than one stockbroker. Many investors establish accounts at different firms to obtain the benefit and opinions of a diverse group of brokers.

Types of Accounts

A number of different types of accounts can be established with a stockbroker. We will briefly consider several of the more popular types.

Single or Joint   A brokerage account may be either single or joint. *Joint accounts* are most common between husband and wife or parent and child. The account of a minor (a person less than 18 years of age) is a **custodial account,** in which a parent or guardian must be part of all transactions. Regardless of which form of account is maintained, the name(s) of the account holder(s) and an account number are used to identify the account.

custodial account
the brokerage account of a minor; requires a parent or guardian to be part of all transactions.

Cash or Margin   A **cash account,** the more common type, is one in which the customer can make only cash transactions. Customers can initiate cash transactions via phone and are given three business days in which to get the cash to the brokerage firm. The firm is likewise given three business days in which to deposit the proceeds from the sale of securities in the customer's cash account.

cash account
a brokerage account in which a customer can make only cash transactions.

    A **margin account** is an account in which a creditworthy customer has been extended borrowing privileges by the brokerage firm. By leaving securities with the firm to be held as collateral, the customer is permitted to borrow a prespecified proportion of the purchase price. The brokerage firm will, of course, charge the customer a specified rate of interest on borrowings. (More discussion of margin trading is included later in this chapter.)

margin account
a brokerage account in which the customer has been extended borrowing privileges by the brokerage firm.

wrap account
a brokerage account in which customers with large portfolios pay a flat annual fee that covers the cost of a money manager's services and the commissions on *all* trades.

Wrap The **wrap account** allows brokerage customers with large portfolios (generally $100,000 or more) to conveniently shift stock-selection decisions to a professional money manager—either in-house or independent. In return for a flat annual fee equal to between 2 and 3 percent of the portfolio's total asset value, the brokerage firm helps the investor select a money manager, pays the manager's fee, and executes the money manager's trades. Of course, the investor's overall goals are initially communicated to the manager. Wrap accounts are appealing for a number of reasons other than convenience. Because the annual fee in most cases covers commissions on *all* trades, the chance of the broker churning the account is virtually eliminated. In addition, the broker monitors the manager's performance and provides the investor with detailed reports, typically quarterly.

Odd-Lot or Round-Lot Transactions

odd lot
less than 100 shares of stock.

round lot
100 share units of stock or multiples thereof.

Stock transactions can be made in either odd or round lots. An **odd lot** consists of less than 100 shares of a stock; a **round lot** is a 100-share unit or multiple thereof. You would be dealing in an odd lot if you bought, say, 25 shares of stock, but in a round lot if you bought 200 shares. A trade of 225 shares would be a combination of an odd and two round lots. Because transactions in odd lots require either additional processing by the brokerage firm or the assistance of a specialist, an added fee—known as an *odd-lot differential*—is tacked on to the normal commission charge, driving up the costs of these small trades. Small investors in the early stages of their investment programs are primarily responsible for odd-lot transactions.

BASIC TYPES OF ORDERS

Different types of orders are used in making security transactions. The type placed normally depends on the investor's goals and expectations. The three basic types of orders are the market order, the limit order, and the stop-loss order.

Market Order

market order
an order to buy or sell stock at the best price available when the order is placed.

An order to buy or sell stock at the best price available when the order is placed is a **market order.** It is usually the quickest way to have orders filled, because market orders are usually executed as soon as they reach the exchange floor or are received by the dealer. Because of the speed with which market orders are executed, the buyer or seller of a security can be sure that the price at which the order is transacted will be very close to the market price prevailing at the time the order was placed.

Limit Order

limit order
an order to buy at or below a specified price or to sell at or above a specified price.

An order to buy at or below a specified price or to sell at or above a specified price is known as a **limit order.** When a limit order is placed, the broker transmits it to a specialist dealing in the security. The specialist makes a notation in his or her book, indicating the number of shares and price of the limit order.

The order is executed as soon as the specified market price (or better) exists and all other orders with precedence—similar orders received earlier, buy orders at a higher specified price, or sell orders at a lower specified price—have been satisfied. The limit order can be placed as one of the following:

1. A *fill-or-kill order*, which if not immediately executed is canceled.

2. A *day order*, which if not executed is automatically canceled at the end of the day.

3. A *good-'till-canceled (GTC) order*, which generally remains in effect for six months unless executed, canceled, or renewed.

Assume, by way of example, that you place a limit order to buy 100 shares of a stock currently selling at 30½ (security market terminology for $30.50) at a limit price of $30. Once the specialist has cleared all similar orders received before yours, and once the market price of the stock has fallen to $30 or less, the order is executed. It is possible, of course, that your order might expire (if it is not a GTC order) before the stock price drops to $30.

Although a limit order can be quite effective, it can also keep you from making a transaction. If, for instance, you wish to buy at $30 or less and the stock price moves from its current $30.50 price to $42 while you are waiting, you have missed the opportunity to make a profit of $11.50 per share ($42 − $30.50). Had you placed a market order to buy at the best available price ($30.50), the profit of $11.50 would have been yours. Limit orders for the sale of a stock are also disadvantageous when the stock price closely approaches but does not attain the minimum sale price limit before dropping substantially. Generally speaking, limit orders are most effective when the price of a stock is known to fluctuate greatly, because there is then a better chance that the order will be executed.

Stop-Loss Order

stop-loss (stop) order
an order to sell a stock when its market price reaches or drops below a specified level; can also be used to buy stock when its market price reaches or rises above a specified level.

An order to sell a stock when its market price reaches or drops below a specified level is called a **stop-loss** or **stop order**. Stop-loss orders are *suspended orders* that are placed on stocks when and if a certain price is reached. The stop-loss order is placed on the specialist's book and becomes active once the stop price has been reached. Like limit orders, stop-loss orders are typically day or GTC orders. When activated, the stop order becomes a *market order* to sell the security at the best price available. Because of this, it is possible that the actual price at which the sale is made could be well below the price at which the stop was initiated. These orders are used to protect investors against the adverse effects of a rapid decline in share price.

For example, assume you own 100 shares of Ballard Industries, which is currently selling for $35 per share. Because you believe the stock price could decline rapidly at any time, you place a stop order to sell at $30. If the stock price does in fact drop to $30, the specialist will sell the 100 shares at the best price available at that time. If the market price declines to $28 by the time your stop-loss order comes up, you will receive less than $30 per share. Of course, if the market price stays above $30 per share, you will have lost nothing as a result of placing the order, because the stop order will never be initiated. Often investors will raise the level of the stop as the price of the stock rises; such action helps to lock in a higher profit when the price is increasing.

Stop orders can also be placed to *buy* a stock, although they are far less common than sell orders. For example, an investor may place a stop order to buy 100 shares of MJ Enterprises, currently selling for $70 per share, once its price rises to, say, $75—the stop price. These orders are commonly used either to limit losses on short sales (discussed later) or to buy a stock just as its price begins to rise.

To avoid the risk of the market moving against you when your stop order becomes a market order, you can place a *stop-limit order*, rather than a plain stop order. It is an order to buy or sell stock at a given price or better once a stipulated stop price has been met. For example, in the Ballard Industries illustration above, had a stop-limit order been in effect, when the market price of Ballard dropped to $30 the broker would have entered a limit order to sell your 100 shares at $30 a share, *or better*. Thus, there would be no risk of getting less than $30 a share for your stock—*unless the price of the stock kept right on falling*. In that case, as is true for any limit order, you might miss the market altogether and end up with stock worth much less than $30. Even though the stop order to sell was triggered (at $30), the stock will *not* be sold, with a limit order, if it keeps falling in price.

TRANSACTION COSTS

Making transactions through brokers or dealers is considerably easier for investors than it would be to negotiate directly, trying to find someone who wants to buy that which they want to sell (or vice versa). To compensate the broker for executing the transaction, investors pay transaction costs, which are usually levied on both the purchase and the sale of securities. When making investment decisions, investors must consider the structure and magnitude of transaction costs, because they affect returns.

Since the passage of the Securities Acts Amendments of 1975, brokers have been permitted to charge whatever commission they deem appropriate. Most firms have established **fixed-commission schedules** that apply to small transactions, the ones most often made by individual investors. An example of such a schedule is given in Table 5.3 on page 200. On large institutional transactions, **negotiated commissions**—commissions mutually agreed upon by the client and broker—are usually used. Negotiated commissions are also available to individual investors who maintain sizable accounts—typically in the range of $25,000 or more.

The commission structure varies depending upon type of security and type of broker. The basic commission structures for various types of securities are described in subsequent chapters as part of the detailed discussion of those securities. The commissions charged on differing size transactions, shown in Table 5.4 on page 201, clearly demonstrate varying transactions costs among full-service and discount brokers. Obviously, discount brokers charge substantially less than full-service brokers for the same transaction. However, most discounters charge a minimum fee to discourage small orders. For example, Charles Schwab, the nation's largest discounter, charges a minimum fee of about $40 for any stock transaction. The savings from the discounter are substantial: Depending on the size and type of transaction, the discount broker can typically save investors between 30 and 80 percent of the commission charged by the full-service broker. Investors must weigh the added

fixed-commission schedules
fixed brokerage commissions that typically apply to small transactions.

negotiated commissions
brokerage commissions agreed upon by the client and the broker as a result of their negotiations.

commissions they pay a full-service broker against the value of the advice they receive, because the advice is the only major difference between the discount and the full-service broker.

INVESTOR PROTECTION: SIPC AND ARBITRATION

Although most investment transactions take place safely, it is important for investors to know what protection they have if things don't go smoothly. As a client, you are protected against the loss of the securities or cash held by your broker. The **Securities Investor Protection Corporation (SIPC)**, a nonprofit membership corporation, was authorized by the *Securities Investor Protection Act of 1970* to protect customer accounts against the consequences of financial failure of the brokerage firm. The SIPC currently insures each customer's account for up to $500,000, except that claims for cash are limited to $100,000 per customer. Note that SIPC insurance does not guarantee that the dollar value of the securities will be recovered; it guarantees only that the securities themselves will be returned. Some brokerage firms also insure certain customer accounts for amounts in excess of the required $500,000 of SIPC insurance. Certainly, in light of the diversity and quality of services available among brokerage firms, careful consideration should be given not only to the selection of an individual broker but also to the choice of a firm.

SIPC provides protection in case your brokerage firm fails. But what happens if your broker gave you bad advice and, as a result, you lost a lot of money on an investment? SIPC won't help. It's not intended to insure you against bad investment advice. Instead, if you have a dispute with your broker, the first thing you should do is discuss the situation with the managing officer at the branch where you do business. If that doesn't do any good, then contact the firm's compliance officer and the securities commission in your home state.

If you still don't get any satisfaction, you may have no choice but to take the case to **arbitration,** a process whereby you and your broker present the two sides of the argument before an arbitration panel. The panel then decides the case. Many brokerage firms require you to resolve disputes by *binding arbitration*; in this case, you don't have the option to sue. You must accept the arbitrator's decision, and you cannot go to court to appeal your case. Thus, before you open an account, check whether the brokerage agreement contains a binding arbitration clause.

Settling securities disputes through arbitration rather than litigation has advantages and disadvantages. Arbitration proceedings typically cost less and are resolved more quickly than litigation. However, until recently, the brokerage agreements that required investors to submit to binding arbitration also specified the use of securities-industry arbitration panels. Many questioned whether these panels, which before 1989 were often composed entirely of persons with relationships to the securities industry, were fair to investors. As a result of pressure from the SEC and a 1990 court decision in New York State, many investors now have the option of using either securities-industry panels or independent arbitration panels such as those sponsored by the American Arbitration Association (AAA), which are considered more sympathetic toward investors. In addition, only one of the three arbitrators on a panel can be connected with the securities industry.

Securities Investor Protection Corporation (SIPC)
a nonprofit membership corporation, authorized by the federal government, that insures each brokerage customer's account for up to $500,000, with claims for cash limited to $100,000.

arbitration
a dispute resolution process in which a customer and a broker present their argument before a panel, which then decides the case.

Recently, the NASD and other securities-related organizations began encouraging investors to *mediate* disputes and voluntarily negotiate a settlement rather than immediately start arbitration proceedings. Although mediation is not binding, it can further reduce costs and time for both investors and brokers. Even so, probably the best thing you can do to avoid such a situation is to use care when selecting a broker, understand the financial risks involved in the broker's recommendations, and carefully evaluate the advice he or she offers.

CONCEPTS *in Review*

2.10 What role does the stockbroker play in the overall investment process? Describe the types of services offered by brokerage firms, and discuss the criteria for selecting a suitable stockbroker.

2.11 What must one do in order to open a brokerage account? Briefly differentiate among the following types of brokerage accounts:
  a. Single or joint   d. Margin
  b. Custodial   e. Wrap
  c. Cash

2.12 Differentiate between a market order, a limit order, and a stop-loss order. What is the rationale for using a stop-loss order rather than a limit order?

2.13 In what two ways are commissions typically charged by brokers for executing their clients' transactions? Differentiate between the services and costs associated with full-service and discount brokers.

2.14 What protection does the Securities Investor Protection Corporation (SIPC) provide securities investors? How are arbitration procedures used to settle disputes between investors and their brokers?   ■■

BASIC TYPES OF TRANSACTIONS

An investor can make a number of basic types of security transactions. Each type is available to those who meet certain requirements established by various government agencies as well as by brokerage firms. Although the various types of transactions can be used in a number of ways to meet investment objectives, we describe only the most popular use of each transaction here. The three most common types of transaction are the long purchase, margin trading, and short selling.

LONG PURCHASE

long purchase
a transaction in which investors buy securities in the hope that they will increase in value and can be sold at a later date for profit.

The **long purchase** is a transaction in which investors buy securities in the hope that they will increase in value and can be sold at a later date for profit. The object, then, is to buy low and sell high. A long purchase is the most common type of transaction. Each of the basic types of orders described above can be used with long transactions. Because investors generally expect the price of a security to rise over the period of time they plan to hold it, their return comes from any dividends or interest received during the ownership period, *plus* the difference between the price at which they sell the security and the price paid to purchase it (capital gain). This return, of course, is reduced by the transaction costs.

Ignoring any dividends (or interest) and transaction costs, the long purchase can be illustrated by a simple example. After studying various aspects of Varner Industries, Fae Johnson is convinced that its common stock, which currently sells for $20 per share, will increase in value over the next few years. Based on her analysis, Fae expects the stock price to rise to $30 per share within two years. She places a limit order and buys a round lot (100 shares) of Varner for $20. If the stock price rises to, say, $40 per share, Fae will profit from her long purchase; if it drops below $20 per share, she will experience a loss on the transaction. Obviously, one of the major motivating factors in making a long transaction is an expected rise in the price of the security.

MARGIN TRADING

margin trading
the use of borrowed funds to purchase securities; magnifies returns by reducing the amount of capital that must be put up by the investor.

Security purchases do not have to be made on a cash basis; borrowed funds can be used instead. This activity is referred to as **margin trading,** and it is used for one basic reason: to magnify returns. As peculiar as it may sound, the term *margin* refers to the amount of equity (stated as a percentage) in an investment, or the amount that is *not* borrowed. If an investor uses 75 percent margin, for example, it means that 75 percent of the investment position is being financed with the person's own capital and the balance (25 percent) with borrowed money. The Federal Reserve Board ("the Fed"), which governs our banking system, sets the **margin requirement,** specifying the minimum amount of equity (stated as a percentage) that must be the margin investor's own funds. By raising or lowering the margin requirement, the Fed can depress or stimulate activity in the securities markets.

margin requirement
the minimum amount of equity (stated as a percentage) that must be a margin investor's own funds; set by the Federal Reserve Board.

Margin purchases must be approved by a broker. The brokerage firm then lends the purchaser the needed funds and retains the purchased securities as collateral. Margin requirements for stocks have been at 50 percent for some time. It is important to recognize that margin purchasers must pay a specified rate of interest on what they borrow.

A simple example will help to clarify the basic margin transaction. Jeffrey Lawrence wishes to purchase 70 shares of common stock, which is currently selling for $63.50 per share. With the prevailing margin requirement of 50 percent, Jeffrey must put up only $2,222.50 in cash ($63.50 per share × 70 shares × .50). The remaining $2,222.50 will be lent to Jeffrey by his brokerage firm. Jeffrey will, of course, have to pay interest on the amount he borrows, plus the applicable brokerage fees. It should be clear that with the use of margin, an investor can purchase more securities than he or she could afford on a strictly cash basis. In this way, investors can magnify their returns.

Although margin trading can lead to increased returns, it also presents substantial risks. One of the biggest is that the issue may not perform as expected. If this occurs, no amount of margin trading can correct matters. Margin trading can only *magnify* returns, not *produce* them. Because the security being margined is always the ultimate source of return, *the security selection process (discussed in Chapters 6 and 7) is critical to this trading strategy.*

Essentials of Margin Trading

Margin trading can be used with most kinds of securities. It is regularly used, for example, with both common and preferred stocks, most types of bonds, mutual funds, warrants, and futures. It is not normally used with tax-exempt municipal bonds, because the interest paid on such margin loans is not deductible for income tax purposes. For simplicity, we will use common stock as the vehicle in our discussion of margin trading.

Magnified Profits and Losses   Using an investor's equity as a base, the idea of margin trading is to employ **financial leverage**—the use of debt financing to magnify investment returns. Here is how it works: Suppose you have $5,000 to invest and are considering the purchase of 100 shares of stock at $50 per share because you feel the stock in question will go up in price. If you do not margin, you can buy outright 100 shares of the stock (ignoring brokerage commissions). However, if you margin the transaction—for example, at 50 percent—you could acquire the same $5,000 position with only $2,500 of your own money. This would leave you with $2,500 to use for other investments or to buy on margin another 100 shares of the same stock. Either way, by margining you will reap greater benefits from the stock's price appreciation.

The concept of margin trading is more fully illustrated in Table 2.2. An unmargined (100 percent equity) transaction is depicted along with the same

financial leverage
the use of debt financing to magnify investment returns.

Table 2.2   The Effect of Margin Trading on Security Returns

	Without Margin (100% Equity)	With Margins of 80%	With Margins of 65%	With Margins of 50%
Number of $50 shares purchased	100	100	100	100
Cost of investment	$5,000	$5,000	$5,000	$5,000
Less: borrowed money	0	1,000	1,750	2,500
Equity in investment	$5,000	$4,000	$3,250	$2,500
A. Investor's position if price rises by $30 to $80/share				
Value of stock	$8,000	$8,000	$8,000	$8,000
Less: cost of investment	5,000	5,000	5,000	5,000
Capital gain	$3,000	$3,000	$3,000	$3,000
Return on investor's equity (capital gain/ equity in investment)	60%	75%	92.3%	120%
B. Investor's position if price falls by $30 to $20/share				
Value of stock	$2,000	$2,000	$2,000	$2,000
Less: cost of investment	5,000	5,000	5,000	5,000
Capital loss	$3,000	$3,000	$3,000	$3,000
Return on investor's equity (capital loss/ equity in investment)*	(60%)	(75%)	(92.3%)	(120%)

*With a capital loss, return on investor's equity is *negative*.

transaction using various margins. Remember that the margin rates (e.g., 65 percent) indicate the investor's equity in the investment. When the investment is unmargined and the price of the stock goes up by $30 per share (see Table 2.2, part A), the investor enjoys a very respectable 60 percent rate of return. However, observe what happens when margin is used: The rate of return shoots up to as high as 120 percent, depending on the amount of equity in the investment. This is so because the gain is the same ($3,000) *regardless of how the transaction is financed*. Clearly, as the investor's equity in the investment *declines* (with lower margins), the rate of return *increases* accordingly.

Three facets of margin trading become obvious from the table: (1) The price of the stock will move in whatever way it is going to regardless of how the position is financed; (2) the lower the amount of the investor's equity in the position, *the greater the rate of return* the investor will enjoy when the price of the security rises; and (3) *the risk of loss is also magnified* (by the same rate) when the price of the security falls (see Table 2.2, part B).

Advantages and Disadvantages   A magnified return is the major advantage of margin trading. The size of the magnified return will depend on both the price behavior of the security being margined and the amount of margin being used. Another, more modest benefit of margin trading is that it allows for greater diversification of security holdings, because investors can spread their capital over a greater number of investments.

The major disadvantage of margin trading, of course, is the potential for magnified losses if the price of the security falls. Another disadvantage is the cost of the margin loans themselves. A **margin loan** is the official vehicle through which the borrowed funds are made available in a margin transaction. All margin loans are made at a stated interest rate, which depends on prevailing market rates and the amount of money being borrowed. This rate is usually 1 to 3 percent above the **prime rate**—the lowest interest rate charged the best business borrowers; for large accounts, it may be at the prime rate. The loan cost, which must be paid by the investor, will increase daily, thereby reducing the level of profits (or magnifying losses) accordingly.

Making Margin Transactions

To execute a margin transaction, it is necessary to establish a **margin account**. It is opened with a minimum of $2,000 in equity, in the form of either cash or securities. Margin credit can be obtained from a broker or a banker, although nearly all margin trading is done through brokers. The broker will retain any securities purchased on margin as collateral for the loan.

The margin requirement established by the Federal Reserve Board sets the minimum amount of equity for margin transactions. This does not mean, of course, that investors must execute all margin transactions by using exactly the minimum amount of margin; they can use more than the minimum if they wish. Moreover, it is not unusual for brokerage firms and the major exchanges to establish their own margin requirements, which are more restrictive than those of the Federal Reserve. There are basically two types of margin requirements: initial margin and maintenance margin.

Initial Margin   The minimum amount of equity that must be provided by the investor *at the time of purchase* is the **initial margin**. It is used to prevent

---

margin loan
vehicle through which borrowed funds are made available, at a stated interest rate, in a margin transaction.

prime rate
the lowest interest rate charged the best business borrowers.

margin account
a brokerage account authorized for margin trading.

initial margin
the minimum amount of equity that must be provided by a margin investor *at the time of purchase.*

Table 2.3   Initial Margin Requirements for Various Types of Securities (December 1994)

Security	Minimum Initial Margin (Equity) Required
Listed common and preferred stock	50%
OTC stocks traded on Nasdaq/NMS	50%
Convertible bonds	50%
Corporate bonds	30%
U.S. Treasury bills, notes, and bonds	8% of principal
Other federal government issues	10% of principal
Federal government guaranteed issues	15% of principal

overtrading and excessive speculation. Generally, it is this margin requirement that investors refer to when discussing margin trading. All securities that can be margined have specific initial requirements, which can be changed at the discretion of the governing authorities. Table 2.3 shows initial margin requirements for various types of securities. The more stable investment vehicles, such as Treasury issues, generally enjoy substantially lower margin requirements and therefore offer greater magnification opportunities. Note that OTC stocks traded on the Nasdaq/NMS can be margined like listed securities. All other OTC stocks are considered to have no collateral value and therefore *cannot be margined*.

As long as the margin in an account remains at a level equal to or greater than prevailing initial requirements, the investor may use the account in any way he or she wants. However, if the value of the investor's holdings declines, the margin in his or her account will also drop. In this case, the investor will have what is known as a **restricted account,** one whose equity is less than the initial margin requirement. It does not mean that the investor must put up additional cash or equity, but the investor may not make further margin purchases and must bring the margin back to the initial level when securities are sold, as long as the account is restricted.

Maintenance Margin   The absolute minimum amount of margin (equity) that an investor must maintain in the margin account at all times is the **maintenance margin.** When an insufficient amount of maintenance margin exists, an investor will receive a **margin call** to remedy the situation. This call gives the investor a short period of time (perhaps 72 hours) to bring the equity up to the initial margin. If this is not done, the broker is authorized to sell enough of the investor's margined holdings to bring the equity in the account up to this standard.

The maintenance margin protects both the brokerage house and investors: Brokers avoid having to absorb excessive investor losses, and investors avoid being wiped out. The maintenance margin on equity securities is currently 25 percent. It rarely changes, although it is often set slightly higher by brokerage firms for the added protection of both brokers and their customers. For straight debt securities like Treasury bonds, there is no official maintenance margin except that set by the brokerage firms themselves.

restricted account
a margin account whose equity is less than the initial margin requirement; the investor may not make further margin purchases and must bring the margin back to the initial level when securities are sold, as long as the account is restricted.

maintenance margin
the minimum amount of margin (equity) that an investor must maintain in the margin account at all times.

margin call
notification of the need to bring the equity of an account whose margin is below the maintenance level up to the initial margin level or have margined holdings sold to reach this point.

The Basic Margin Formula

The amount of margin is always measured in terms of its relative amount of equity, which is considered the investor's collateral. A simple formula can be used with all types of *long purchases* to determine the amount of margin in the transaction (or account) at any given point. Basically, only two pieces of information are required: (1) the prevailing market value of the securities being margined, and (2) the amount of money being borrowed, or the size of the margin loan, which is known as the **debit balance.** Given this information, we can compute margin according to Equation 2.1:

debit balance
the amount of money being borrowed; the size of a margin loan.

Equation 2.1

$$\text{Margin} = \frac{\text{value of securities} - \text{debit balance}}{\text{value of securities}}$$

Equation 2.1a

$$= \frac{V - D}{V}$$

To illustrate the use of this formula, consider the following example. Assume you want to purchase 100 shares of stock at $40 per share, at a time when the initial margin requirement is 70 percent. First we must determine how this $4,000 transaction will be financed. Because we know that 70 percent of it (the stated prevailing initial margin requirement) must be financed with equity, the balance (30 percent) can be financed with a margin loan. Therefore, you will borrow $1,200 (.30 × $4,000 = $1,200); this, of course, is the debit balance. The remainder ($2,800) represents your equity in the transaction. This amount is measured as the difference between the value of the securities being margined ($4,000) and the amount being borrowed ($1,200). In other words, equity is represented by the numerator $(V - D)$ in the margin formula.

Let's consider what happens to the margin as the value of the security changes. If over time the price of the stock moves to $65, the margin would then be:

$$\text{Margin} = \frac{V - D}{V} = \frac{\$6,500 - \$1,200}{\$6,500} = .815 = \underline{81.5\%}$$

Note that the margin (equity) in this investment position has now risen to 81.5 percent. *When the price of the stock goes up, the investor's margin also increases.* On the other hand, *when the price of the security goes down, so does the amount of margin.* For instance, if the price of the stock in our illustration drops to $30 per share, the new margin would equal only 60 percent [($3,000 − $1,200) ÷ $3,000]. In that case, we would be dealing with a *restricted account,* because the margin level has dropped below the prevailing initial margin.

Finally, note that although our discussion has been couched mostly in terms of *individual transactions,* the same margin formula is used with *margin accounts.* The only difference is that we would be dealing with input that applies to the account as a whole—the value of *all securities* held in the account and the *total amount* of margin loans.

Return on Invested Capital

When assessing the return on margin transactions, we must take into account the fact that the individual puts up only part of the funds. Therefore, we are concerned with the rate of profit earned on only that portion of the funds provided by the investor. Using both current income received from dividends or interest and total interest paid on the margin loan, we can apply Equation 2.2 to determine the return on invested capital from a margin transaction:

Equation 2.2

$$\text{Return on invested capital from a margin transaction} = \frac{\substack{\text{total} \\ \text{current} \\ \text{income} \\ \text{received}} - \substack{\text{total} \\ \text{interest} \\ \text{paid on} \\ \text{margin loan}} + \substack{\text{market} \\ \text{value of} \\ \text{securities} \\ \text{at sale}} - \substack{\text{market} \\ \text{value of} \\ \text{securities} \\ \text{at purchase}}}{\text{amount of equity invested}}$$

This equation can be used to compute either the expected or actual return from a margin transaction. To illustrate: Consider an investor who wants to buy 100 shares of stock at $50 per share because she feels it will rise to $75 within 6 months. The stock pays $2 per share in annual dividends (though with the 6-month holding period, the investor will receive only half of that amount, or $1 per share). The investor is going to buy the stock with 50 percent margin and will pay 10 percent interest on the margin loan. Thus, she is going to put up $2,500 equity to buy $5,000 worth of stock that she hopes will increase to $7,500 in 6 months. Because the investor will have a $2,500 margin loan outstanding at 10 percent for 6 months, she will pay $125 in total interest costs ($2,500 × .10 × 6/12 = $125). We can substitute this information into Equation 2.2 to find the expected return on invested capital from this margin transaction:

$$\text{Return on invested capital from a margin transaction} = \frac{\$100 - \$125 + \$7,500 - \$5,000}{\$2,500} = \frac{\$2,475}{\$2,500} = .99 = \underline{\underline{99\%}}$$

Keep in mind that the 99 percent figure represents the rate of return earned over a 6-month holding period. If we wanted to compare this rate of return to other investment opportunities, we could determine the transaction's annualized rate of return by multiplying by 2 (the number of 6-month periods in a year). This would amount to 198 percent (99% × 2 = 198%).

Uses of Margin Trading

Margin trading is most often used in one of two ways. As we have seen, one of its uses is to magnify transaction returns. Another major margin tactic is called pyramiding, which takes the concept of magnified returns to its limits. Pyramiding uses the paper profits in margin accounts to partly or fully finance the acquisition of additional securities. This allows such transactions to be made at margins below prevailing initial margin levels, and sometimes substantially so. In fact, with this technique it is even possible to buy securities

pyramiding
the technique of using paper profits in margin accounts to partly or fully finance the acquisition of additional securities.

excess margin
more equity than is required in a margin account.

with no new cash at all; rather, they can all be financed entirely with margin loans. The reason is that the paper profits in the account lead to **excess margin,** more equity in the account than necessary. For instance, if a margin account holds $60,000 worth of securities and has a debit balance of $20,000, it is at a margin level of 66⅔ percent [($60,000 − $20,000) ÷ $60,000]. This account would hold a substantial amount of excess margin if the prevailing initial margin requirement were only 50 percent.

The principle of pyramiding is to use the excess margin in the account to purchase additional securities. The only constraint, and the key to pyramiding, is that when the additional securities are purchased, the investor's margin account must be at or above the prevailing required initial margin level. Remember that it is the account, and not the individual transactions, that must meet the minimum standards. If the account has excess margin, the investor can use it to build up security holdings. Pyramiding can continue as long as there are additional paper profits in the margin account and as long as the margin level exceeds the prevailing initial requirement when purchases are made. The tactic is somewhat complex but also profitable, especially because it minimizes the amount of new capital required in the investor's account.

In general, margin trading is simple, but it is also risky. Risk is primarily associated with potential price declines in the margined securities. A decline in prices can result in a *restricted account.* If prices fall enough to cause the actual margin to drop below the maintenance margin, the resulting *margin call* will force the investor to almost immediately deposit additional equity into the account. In addition, losses (resulting from the price decline) are magnified in a fashion similar to that demonstrated in Table 2.2, part B. Clearly, the chance of a margin call and the magnification of losses make margin trading more risky than nonmargined transactions. Margin therefore should be used only by investors who fully understand its operation and appreciate its pitfalls.

SHORT SELLING

Short selling is used when a decline in security prices is anticipated. This technique enables investors to profit from falling security prices. However, as we shall see, it can also be used to *protect* investors from falling security prices. Almost any type of security can be "shorted": Common and preferred stocks, all types of bonds, convertible securities, listed mutual funds (called "closed-end investment companies"), options, and warrants can all be sold short. In practice, though, the short-selling activities of most investors are limited almost exclusively to common stock and to options.

Essentials of Short Selling

short selling
the sale of borrowed securities, their eventual repurchase by the short seller, and their return to the lender.

Short selling is generally defined as the practice of selling borrowed securities. Short sales start when securities that have been borrowed from a broker are sold in the marketplace. Later, when the price of the issue has declined, the short seller buys back the securities, which are then returned to the lender. A short seller must make an initial equity deposit with the broker in a fashion and subject to rules similar to those for margin trading. The deposit coupled with the proceeds from sale of the borrowed shares assures the broker that sufficient funds are available to buy back the shorted securities at a later date, even if their price increases. Because short sales, like long and margin transactions,

Table 2.4   The Mechanics of a Short Sale

Step 1—Short sale initiated:	
100 shares of borrowed stock are *sold* at $50/share:	
Proceeds from sale to investor	$5,000
Step 2—Short sale covered:	
Later, 100 shares of the stock are *purchased*	
at $25/share and returned to broker from	
whom stock was borrowed:	
Cost to investor	2,500
Net profit	$2,500

require investors to work through a broker, it is important find a stockbroker you trust. The *Investor Insights* box on page 66 offers some tips for finding a stockbroker.

Making Money When Prices Fall   Making money when security prices fall is what short selling is all about. Like their colleagues in the rest of the investment world, short sellers are also trying to make money by buying low and selling high. The only difference is that they reverse the investment process: They start the transaction with a sale and end it with a purchase.

Table 2.4 shows how a short sale works and how investors can profit from such transactions. (For simplicity, we ignore transaction costs.) The transaction shown results in a net profit of $2,500 as a result of an initial sale of 100 shares of stock at $50 per share (step 1) and subsequent covering (i.e., purchase) of the 100 shares for $25 per share (step 2). The amount of profit or loss generated in a short sale depends on the price at which the short seller can buy back the stock. Short sellers earn profit only when the proceeds from the sale of the stock are greater than the cost of buying it back.

Who Lends the Securities?   Acting through their brokers, short sellers obtain securities from the brokerage firm or from other investors. Of the two, brokers are the principal source of borrowed securities. As a service to their customers, they lend securities held in the brokers' portfolios or in *street name* accounts. It is important to recognize that when the broker lends street name securities, it is lending the short seller the securities of other investors. Individual investors typically do not pay fees to the broker for the privilege of borrowing the shares and, as a result, do not earn interest on the funds they leave on deposit with the broker.

Advantages and Disadvantages   The major advantage of selling short is, of course, the chance to profit from a price decline. In addition, the technique can be used by investors to protect profits that have already been earned and to defer the taxes on such profits. As we will see, when used in this manner, short selling becomes a highly conservative investment strategy.

The key disadvantage of many short-sale transactions is that the investor faces limited return opportunities, along with high risk exposure. The price of a security can fall only so far (to a value of or near zero), yet there is really no limit to how far such securities can rise in price. (Remember, a short seller is

INVESTOR INSIGHTS: *Investing in Action*

Finding the Right Broker for You

Smart investors do not entrust their hard-earned savings to just anyone, but take the time to find a trustworthy, dependable stockbroker. How should you go about doing this?

Begin by seeking referrals from friends, relatives, or business associates with incomes and financial goals similar to yours. Check the records of your candidates: Call the National Association of Securities Dealers, which catalogs disciplinary and legal actions taken against brokers, including pending actions and settlements through arbitration decisions (the way that complaints against brokers are most frequently resolved). You can also contact your state regulator. It's not enough to investigate just the brokers themselves—make sure they are backed by financially sound firms.

Next, make an appointment to see each broker. In the course of the interview, ask him or her the following five important questions:

1. *"How long have you been in business?"* Avoid a broker who has been practicing for fewer than three years; you don't want a novice learning the trade with your money. Also check out the broker's education, professional training, and work history. Avoid those who change jobs frequently.

2. *"Describe your typical client."* You'll be best served by someone whose clients' investment objectives match yours. If you favor mutual funds, don't choose a broker who specializes in hot growth stocks.

3. *"What kind of contact will we have?"* Make sure the broker wants to get together at least quarterly to review your portfolio, more often if your account will be active. The broker should also be willing to give you research reports on investments you're considering.

4. *"How well have your clients' portfolios performed?"* Ask the broker to show you the investment histories of three clients with objectives like yours. Then check to make sure the returns have exceeded appropriate yard-sticks (e.g., the Standard & Poor's 500 index for stocks).

5. *"How much will you make from my investments?"* A reputable broker should disclose all fees and commissions to you. In general, brokers collect the highest commissions on complicated and risky investments and frequent account activity, so you must find one who will place your best interests over his or her own potential for gain. Avoid a broker who over-emphasizes trading, because the commissions on frequent trades will eat up your profits.

Choosing a good broker isn't everything, though; it is up to you to monitor your account. Review your statement every month and look for any problems. Some further guidelines:

• Don't routinely sign documents your broker gives you without understanding what they say and their financial implications.

• Know your rights if your broker has made an unsuitable recommendation. Securities brokers are bound by regulations to make recommendations that are appropriate for each customer. They can be held liable for losses resulting from an unsuitable suggestion.

• Watch for unauthorized transactions, one of the worst offenses in the industry. If you spot one, complain immediately. Otherwise, your broker could claim that you approved of the trade because you waited to see how it turned out before taking action.

• Most importantly, *always document everything*! By keeping detailed records, you will be prepared to defend yourself if any dispute arises.

Sources: Lloyd S. Clareman, "Keep Your Broker Honest," *Fortune*, 1994 Investor's Guide, pp. 167–68; Daria and Ken Dolan, "How to Find A Stockbroker You Can Really Trust," *Money*, August 1994, p. 23; Dean Foust, "Avoiding the Broker from Hell," *Business Week*, 12 July 1993, p. 154; Ruth Simon, "7 Savvy Questions to Ask Your Broker," *Money*, November 1994, pp. 198–207.

hoping for a price *decline*; when a security goes *up* in price, a short seller loses.) For example, notice in Table 2.4 that the stock in question cannot possibly fall by more than $50, yet who is to say how high its price can go?

A less serious disadvantage is that short sellers never earn dividend (or interest) income. In fact, short sellers owe the lender any dividends (or interest) that are paid while the transaction is outstanding. That is, if a dividend is paid during the course of a short-sale transaction, the short seller must pay an equal amount to the lender of the stock. (The mechanics of these payments are taken care of automatically by the short seller's broker.)

Uses of Short Selling

Investors short sell for one of two reasons: to seek speculative profits when the price of a security is expected to drop or to protect a profit and defer taxes by "hedging" their position. The first use is the standard short-sale transaction. The hedge tactic, in contrast, is a conservative use of short selling, employed to lock in a given profit level.

Speculating with Short Sales   The first use of selling short—speculation—is perhaps the most common use of this trading technique. Because the short seller is betting against the market, this approach is subject to a considerable amount of risk exposure. It works like this: Assume an investor has uncovered a stock that she feels is about to tumble over the next eight months from its present level of $50 per share to somewhere around $30. She therefore decides to short sell 300 shares of the stock at $50. Table 2.5 shows the basics of this hypothetical transaction. Note that the transaction generates a profit of $6,000 to the investor (ignoring dividends and brokerage commissions). However, if the market moves against the short seller, all or most of her $15,000 investment could be lost.

shorting-against-the-box
a conservative hedging technique used to protect existing security profits by following a profitable long purchase with a short sale of an equivalent number of the same shares.

Hedging with Short Sales   The second use of selling short—hedging—is a conservative technique used to protect existing security profits. Like insurance, the purpose of this hedge is to minimize or eliminate exposure to loss. Called **shorting-against-the-box,** it is initiated after an investor has generated a profit in an earlier long purchase by selling short an equivalent number of the same

Table 2.5   Speculating with a Short Sale*

Step 1—Short sale initiated:	
300 shares of borrowed stock are *sold* at $50/share:	
Proceeds from sale to investor	$15,000
Step 2—Short sale covered:	
Later, 300 shares of the stock are *purchased* at $30/share and returned to broker from whom stock was borrowed:	
Cost to investor	9,000
Net profit	$ 6,000

*Assume the stock pays no dividends and therefore the short seller has no dividend liability.

shares. An investor who already owns, say, 100 shares of stock (the long transaction) would short an equal number of shares of stock in the same company. The investor would then have two positions—one long and one short—both involving an equal number of shares. By doing this, he or she is able to protect the profit already made in the long position, and, as a by-product, can defer the taxes on this profit until the next taxable year. (The tax benefits of this strategy are discussed in more detail in Chapter 13.) The cost of shorting-against-the-box is reasonably low and involves only the brokerage commissions associated with initiating and covering the short sale.

Shorting-against-the-box works like this: Suppose that early last year, you bought 100 shares of NuLox at $20 per share and have since watched the price of NuLox rise to $50. You currently have a $3,000 net profit. Although you do not want to sell the stock right now, neither do you want to lose any of your profit. In essence, you would like to ride things out for a while and still protect the profit you have earned up to now. A simple "short sale against the box" will allow you to do this. By shorting 100 shares of NuLox at $50 per share, you have locked in your profit of $3,000. No matter what happens to the price of the stock. you are guaranteed a profit of $3,000.

CONCEPTS *in Review*

2.15 What is a *long purchase?* What expectation underlies such a purchase? What is *margin trading,* and what is the key reason it's sometimes used as part of a long purchase?

2.16 How does margin trading magnify profits and losses? What are the key advantages and disadvantages of margin trading?

2.17 Describe the procedures and regulations associated with margin trading. Be sure to mention a restricted account, maintenance margin, and the margin call. Define the *debit balance,* and describe the common uses of margin trading.

2.18 What is the primary motive for short selling? Describe the basic short-sale procedure. Why must the short seller make an initial equity deposit?

2.19 Describe the key advantages and disadvantages of short selling. How are short sales used to earn speculative profits? How is shorting-against-the-box used as a conservative hedging technique to protect existing security profits?

On Track with STOCK-TRAK®

STOCK-TRAK®'s Trading Procedures

STOCK-TRAK®'s offers three methods for placing trades: by telephone, by electronic mail (E-mail), and by fax. Telephone orders are split into two time-sensitive classifications. Calls made between 2:00 and 6:00 P.M. Eastern time are too early for the caller to receive closing prices. Confirmation of prices on such trades will be made in your biweekly report. During the primary trading period, which lasts for approximately four hours after 6:00 P.M. Eastern time, brokers are able to provide immediate quotes as they make trades. Orders may be placed by E-mail or by fax 24 hours a day. Transactions E-mailed or faxed after 9:00 P.M. Eastern time will be recorded on the following day. Limit orders are not accepted.

SUMMARY   Review the basic types of securities markets and the characteristics of both organized exchanges and the over-the-counter market. Short-term investment vehicles are traded in the money market, whereas longer-term securities, such as stocks and bonds, are traded in the capital market. The organized securities exchanges are auction markets. They include the New York Stock Exchange (NYSE), the American Stock Exchange (AMEX), regional stock exchanges, foreign stock exchanges, and other specialized exchanges. The organized exchanges act as secondary markets in which existing securities are traded. The over-the-counter (OTC) market acts as a primary market in which initial public offerings (IPOs) are made, and it also handles secondary trading in unlisted securities. It is a dealer market in which negotiation and dealer quotes, often obtained through its automated system, Nasdaq, determine price.

LG 2   Discuss globalization, trading hours, regulation, ethical issues, and the general conditions of securities markets. Today, securities market must be viewed globally due to the growing importance of international markets and foreign security transactions. Foreign security investments can be made either indirectly or directly in a variety of ways, including American Depositary Receipts (ADRs). International investments can enhance returns but bring with them added risk, particularly foreign exchange risk. Recently, some U.S. exchanges have expanded their trading hours in order to compete more effectively with foreign markets. The securities markets are regulated by the federal Securities and Exchange Commission (SEC) and by state commissions. The key federal laws regulating the securities industry are the Securities Act of 1933, the Securities Exchange Act of 1934, the Maloney Act of 1938, the Investment Company Act of 1940, the Investment Advisers Act of 1940, and the Securities Acts Amendments of 1975. During the 1980s, the blatant violation of these laws, particularly with regard to insider trading, raised important ethical issues. Market conditions are commonly classified as "bull" or "bear," depending upon whether security prices are generally rising or falling over a given time period.

LG 3   Explain the role of stockbrokers in security transactions—services provided, selection, opening an account, account types, and transaction sizes. Stockbrokers act as intermediaries between buyers and sellers of securities, and they provide a variety of other services to their clients. An investor should select a stockbroker who has a compatible disposition toward investing and whose firm offers the desired services at competitive costs. A variety of types of brokerage accounts, such as single, joint, custodial, cash, margin, and wrap, may be established. An investor can make odd-lot transactions (less than 100 shares) and round-lot transactions (100 shares or multiples thereof). Because odd-lot transactions require either additional processing by the brokerage firm or the assistance of a specialist, an added fee is typically charged on these transactions.

LG 4   Describe the basic types of orders—market, limit, and stop-loss—transaction costs, and the legal aspects of investor protection. A variety of types of orders can be used in making security transactions. A market order is an order to buy or sell stock at the best price available. A limit order is an order to buy at a specified price or below or sell at a specified price or above. Stop-loss orders become market orders as soon as the minimum sell price or the maximum buy price is hit. Limit and stop-loss orders can be placed as fill-or-kill orders, day orders, or good-'till-canceled (GTC) orders. On small transactions, most brokers have fixed-commission schedules; on larger transactions, they will negotiate commissions. Commissions also vary by type of security and type of broker—full-service or discount broker. The Securities Investor Protection Corporation (SIPC) insures customers' accounts against the brokerage firm's failure. Arbitration procedures are frequently employed to resolve disputes between an investor and broker.

LG 5   Understand long purchases and the motives, regulations, procedures, and calculations involved in making margin transactions. Most investors make long purchases—buy low, sell high—in expectation of price increases. Many investors establish margin accounts to use borrowed funds to enhance their buying power. The Federal Reserve Board establishes the margin requirement—the minimum investor equity in a margin transaction, both initially and during the margin transaction. A restricted account has actual margin below the initial margin requirement. When the actual margin falls below the maintenance margin, an investor will receive a margin call. The return on invested capital in a margin transaction is magnified; that is, positive returns are larger and negative returns are larger than in a comparable unmargined transaction. Paper profits can be used to pyramid a margin account by investing its excess margin. The risks of margin trading are the chance of a restricted account or margin call and the consequences of magnification of losses due to price declines.

LG 6   Summarize the essentials of short selling—motives, procedures, and advantages and disadvantages—and discuss its uses—speculation and hedging. Short selling is used when a decline in security prices is anticipated or to protect against falling security prices. It involves selling borrowed securities with the expectation of earning a profit by repurchasing them at a lower price in the future. To execute a short sale, the investor must make an initial equity deposit with the broker, similar to what is done in margin trading. The investor borrows the shares from the broker, who provides them from its own portfolio or from street name accounts of its clients. The major advantages of selling short are the chance to profit from a price decline, the protection of profits that have already been earned, and deferral of taxes. The disadvantages of short selling are the limited return opportunities with the high risk of unlimited loss potential and the fact that short sellers never earn dividend (or interest) income. Short selling may be used either to seek speculative profits from an anticipated share price decline or as a conservative hedging technique to protect earned profits by shorting-against-the-box.

DISCUSSION QUESTIONS

1. Why do you think some large, growing companies such as Apple Computer, Intel, and Microsoft are traded on the Nasdaq/NMS rather than listed and traded on a major organized exchange such as the NYSE (for which they easily meet the listing requirements)? Discuss the pros and cons of listing on a major organized exchange.

2. Based on the current structure of the world's financial markets and your knowledge of the NYSE and OTC, describe the key features, functions, and problems faced by a single global market (exchange) on which transactions can be made in all securities of all of the world's major companies. Discuss the likelihood of such a market developing.

3. Prepare a checklist of questions and issues you would use when shopping for a stockbroker. Describe both the ideal broker and the ideal brokerage firm given your investment goals and disposition. Discuss the pros and cons of using a full-service rather than a discount broker.

4. Describe how a conservative and an aggressive investor might use, if at all, each of the following types of orders and types of transactions as part of their investment programs. Contrast these two types of investors in view of these preferences.
   a. Types of orders
      (1) Market
      (2) Limit
      (3) Stop-loss

b. Types of transactions
(1) Long purchase
(2) Margin
(3) Short sale

PROBLEMS `LG 1` `LG 2`   1. In each of the following cases, calculate the price of one share of the foreign stock measured in US$.
a. A Belgian stock priced at 9,000 Belgian francs (Bf) when the exchange rate is 35.3 Bf/US$
b. A French stock priced at 700 French francs (Ff) when the exchange rate is 5.60 Ff/US$
c. A Japanese stock priced at 1,350 yen (¥) when the exchange rate is 125 ¥/US$

`LG 1` `LG 2`   2. Lola Paretti purchased 50 shares of BMW, a German stock traded on the Frankfurt Exchange, for 500 marks (DM) per share exactly one year ago, when the exchange rate was 1.60 DM/US$. Today, the stock is trading at 530 DM per share and the exchange rate is 1.30 DM/US$.
a. Did the DM depreciate or appreciate relative to the US$ during the past year? Explain.
b. How much in US$ did Lola pay for her 50 shares of BMW when she purchased them a year ago?
c. How much in US$ can Lola sell her BMW shares for today?
d. Ignoring brokerage fees and taxes, how much profit (or loss) in US$ would Lola realize on her BMW stock if she sells it today?

`LG 3` `LG 4`   3. Al Cromwell places a market order to buy a round lot of Thomas, Inc., common stock, which is traded on the NYSE and is currently quoted at $50 per share. Ignoring brokerage commissions, how much money would Cromwell most likely have to pay? If he had placed a market order to sell, how much money would he receive? Explain.

`LG 3` `LG 4`   4. Imagine that you have placed a limit order to buy 100 shares of Sallisaw Tool at a price of $38, though the stock is currently selling for $41. Discuss the consequences, if any, of each of the following:
a. The stock price drops to $39 per share two months prior to cancellation of the limit order.
b. The stock price drops to $38 per share.
c. The minimum stock price achieved prior to cancellation of the limit order was $38.50, and when canceled the stock was selling for $47.50 per share.

`LG 3` `LG 4`   5. If you place a stop-loss order to sell at $23 on a stock currently selling for $26.50 per share, what is likely to be the minimum loss you will experience on 50 shares if the stock price rapidly declines to $20.50 per share? Explain. What if you had placed a stop-limit order to sell at $23, and the stock price tumbles to $20.50?

`LG 3` `LG 4`   6. Elmo Inc.'s stock is currently selling at $60 per share. For each of the following situations (ignoring brokerage commissions), calculate the gain or loss realized by Maureen Katz if she makes a round-lot transaction.
a. She sells short and repurchases the borrowed shares at $70 per share.
b. She takes a long position and sells the stock at $75 per share.
c. She sells short and repurchases the borrowed shares at $45 per share.
d. She takes a long position and sells the stock at $60 per share.

7. Assume an investor buys 100 shares of stock at $50 per share, putting up a 70 percent margin.
    a. What would be the debit balance in this transaction?
    b. How much equity capital would the investor have to provide to make this margin transaction?
    c. If the stock rises to $80 per share, what would be the investor's new margin position?

8. Jerri Kingston bought 100 shares of stock at $80 per share using an initial margin of 60 percent. Given a maintenance margin of 25 percent, how far does the stock have to drop before Ms. Kingston faces a margin call? (Assume there are no other securities in the margin account.)

9. An investor buys 200 shares of stock selling for $80 per share, using a margin of 60 percent. If the stock pays annual dividends of $1 per share and a margin loan can be obtained at an annual interest cost of 8 percent, determine the return on invested capital the investor would realize if the price of the stock increases to $104 within 6 months. What is the annualized rate of return on this transaction?

10. Marlene Bellamy purchased 300 shares of Writeline Communications stock at $55 per share using the prevailing minimum initial margin requirement of 50 percent. She held the stock for exactly 4 months and sold it without any brokerage costs at the end of that period. During the 4-month holding period, the stock paid $1.50 per share in cash dividends. Marlene was charged 9 percent annual interest on the margin loan. The minimum maintenance margin was 25 percent.
    a. Calculate the initial value of the transaction, the debit balance, and the equity position on Marlene's transaction.
    b. For each of the following share prices, calculate the actual margin percentage and indicate whether Marlene's margin account would have excess equity, be restricted, or be subject to a margin call:
    (1) $45
    (2) $70
    (3) $35
    c. Calculate the dollar amount of (1) dividends received and (2) interest paid on the margin loan during the 4-month holding period.
    d. Use each of the following sale prices at the end of the 4-month holding period to calculate Marlene's annualized rate of return on the Writeline Communications stock transaction:
    (1) $50
    (2) $60
    (3) $70

11. Not long ago, Dave Edwards bought 200 shares of Almost Anything, Inc., at $45 per share; he bought the stock on margin of 60 percent. The stock is now trading at $60 per share, and the Federal Reserve has recently lowered initial margin requirements to 50 percent. Dave now wants to do a little pyramiding and buy another 300 shares of the stock. What's the minimum amount of equity he'll have to put up in this transaction?

12. Assume an investor short sells 100 shares of stock at $50 per share, putting up an initial equity deposit equal to 70 percent of the short-sale proceeds.
    a. How much cash will the investor have to deposit in order to execute this short-sale transaction?
    b. What is the new margin for this transaction if the price of the stock falls to $20 per share?

13. Bob Barloe recently short sold 200 shares of stock at $72 per share, putting up an initial equity deposit equal to 50 percent of the short-sale proceeds.
   a. Determine the size of the initial equity deposit required to make this transaction.
   b. What would the new margin (in percent) be if the stock price drops to $50 a share?
   c. What kind of net profit (in dollars) would Bob realize if he covered this short sale at $50 a share?
   d. What would the new margin position (in percent) be if, instead of dropping, the price of the stock rose to $86.50 a share? Given a 30 percent maintenance margin, would this account be subject to a margin call?

  14. Susan Davidson strongly believed that the price of BBP Inc. stock was about to experience a significant decline. As a result, she decided to short sell 400 shares at the current price of $35 per share. An initial equity deposit equal to 60 percent of the short sale proceeds is required, and the maintenance margin requirement is 30 percent.
   a. How large an initial equity deposit must Susan make to short sell the BBP Inc. shares?
   b. For each of the following share prices, calculate the actual margin percentage and indicate whether Susan's margin deposit will be in excess, be restricted, or be subject to a margin call:
      (1) $80
      (2) $50
      (3) $30
   c. Calculate Susan's net profit if she buys back the shares of BBP Inc. at the following share prices:
      (1) $20
      (2) $40
      (3) $60

 15. A well-heeled investor, Oliver Stanley, recently purchased 1,000 shares of stock at $48 per share. They have since risen to $55 per share. Although Mr. Stanley wants to sell out, he hesitates to do so because it is near the end of year and he wants to defer the tax liability until next year. As a result, he decides to short-against-the-box, by shorting 1,000 shares of the stock at its current price of $55.
   a. What total profit will Mr. Stanley make if the price of the stock continues to rise to $60 per share?
   b. How much of this will come from the long transaction and how much from the short sale?

CASE PROBLEMS   **2.1 DARA'S DILEMMA: HOLD, SELL, OR . . . ?**

As a result of her recent divorce, Dara Simmons—a 40-year-old mother of two teenage children—received 400 shares of Casinos International common stock. The stock is currently selling for $54 per share. After a long discussion with a friend who is an economist with a major commercial bank, Dara believes that the economy is turning down and a bear market is likely. With the aid of her stockbroker, Dara has researched Casinos International's current financial situation and finds that the future success of the company may hinge on the outcome of pending court proceedings on the firm's application to open a new floating casino on a nearby river. If the permit is granted, it seems likely that the firm's stock will experience a rapid increase in value, regardless of economic conditions. On the other hand, if the permit is not granted, the stock value is likely to be adversely affected.

Dara felt that, based upon the available information, the price of Casinos was likely to fluctuate a great deal over the near future. Her first reaction was to sell the stock and invest the money in a safer security, such as a high-rated corporate bond. At the same time, she felt that she might be overly pessimistic due to her recent divorce. She realized that if Casinos had its floating casino application granted, she would make a killing on the stock. As a final check before making any decision, Dara talked with her accountant, who suggested that for tax purposes it would be best to delay the sale of the stock for an additional 4 months. After making a variety of calculations, the accountant indicated that the consequences of selling the stock now at $54 per share would be approximately equivalent to receiving $48 per share any time after the 4-month period had elapsed.

Dara felt that following four alternatives were open to her:

Alternative 1: Sell now at $54 per share and use the proceeds to buy high-rated corporate bonds.

Alternative 2: Keep the stock and place a limit order to sell the stock at $60 per share.

Alternative 3: Keep the stock and place a stop-loss order to sell at $45 per share.

Alternative 4: Hold the stock for an additional 4 months prior to making any decision.

Questions

1. Evaluate each of these alternatives. Based on the limited information presented, recommend the one you feel is best.

2. If the stock price rises to $60, what will happen under alternatives 2 and 3? Evaluate the pros and cons of these outcomes.

3. If the stock price drops to $45, what will happen under alternatives 2 and 3? Evaluate the pros and cons of these outcomes.

4. In light of the rapid fluctuations anticipated in the price of Casinos' stock, how might a stop-limit order to sell be used by Dara to reduce the risk associated with the stock? What is the cost of such a strategy? Explain.

| LG 5 | LG 6 | ## 2.2 RAVI DUMAR'S HIGH-FLYING MARGIN ACCOUNT

Ravi Dumar is a stockbroker who lives with his wife, Sasha, and their five children in Milwaukee, Wisconsin. Ravi firmly believes that the only way to make money in the market is to follow an aggressive investment posture—for example, to use margin trading. In fact, Ravi himself has built a substantial margin account over the years. He currently holds $75,000 worth of stock in his margin account, though the debit balance in the account amounts to only $30,000. Recently, Ravi uncovered a stock that, based on extensive analysis, he feels is about to take off. The stock, Running Shoes (RS), currently trades at $20 per share. Ravi feels it should soar to at least $50 within a year. RS pays no dividends, the prevailing initial margin requirement is 50 percent, and margin loans are now carrying an annual interest charge of 10 percent. Because Ravi feels so strongly about RS, he wants to do some pyramiding by using his margin account to purchase 1,000 shares of the stock.

Questions

1. Discuss the concept of pyramiding as it applies to this investment situation.

2. What is the present margin position (in percent) of Ravi's account?

3. Ravi buys the 1,000 shares of RS through his margin account (bear in mind that this is a $20,000 transaction). Now:
   a. What will the margin position of the account be after the RS transaction if Ravi follows the prevailing initial margin (50 percent) and uses $10,000 of his money to buy the stock?
   b. What if he uses only $2,500 equity and obtains a margin loan for the balance ($17,500)?
   c. How do you explain the fact that the stock can be purchased with only 12.5 percent margin when the prevailing initial margin requirement equals 50 percent?

4. Assume that Ravi buys 1,000 shares of RS stock at $20 per share with a minimum cash investment of $2,500 and that the stock does take off and its price rises to $40 per share in a year.
   a. What is the return on invested capital for this transaction?
   b. What return would Ravi have earned had he bought the stock without margin—if he had used all of his own money?

5. What do you think of Ravi's idea to pyramid? What are the risks and rewards of this strategy?

CHAPTER 3

INVESTMENT PLANS AND INFORMATION

LEARNING GOALS

After studying this chapter, you should be able to:

LG 1 Describe common investment goals, the importance of meeting life insurance needs, and fundamental personal tax considerations.

LG 2 Discuss the development of an investment program, investing over the life cycle, and investing in different economic environments.

LG 3 Identify the types and sources of investment information.

LG 4 Evaluate electronic and on-line investment information, the use of investment advisers, and the role of investment clubs.

LG 5 Explain the characteristics, interpretation, and uses of the commonly cited market averages and indexes.

LG 6 Understand the role, types, and key features of the popular short-term investment vehicles available for meeting liquidity needs.

In his first ten years as an investor, Jeff Robinson was a casual investor who termed his results "unremarkable." This changed in November 1993, when he faced the impending loss of his environmental consulting firm's biggest client and wanted another source of income. He began actively trading different stocks to increase returns, opened a margin account, discovered the library of investment information available through on-line services, and began executing trades electronically. "My goal is to make enough profit from my portfolio to retire from consulting and invest full-time—and have fun doing it," Jeff says. He's off to a good start: In 1994, his realized return was about 35 percent.

Jeff takes both long and short positions in individual stocks; mutual funds don't move quickly enough for his purposes. Ideally, he sells when his long positions double and his short positions provide a 20 percent return. For maximum appreciation on limited investment dollars, he focuses on companies that suffer from bad news but should rebound and those with near-term growth potential.

The success of Jeff's aggressive investment strategy depends on accurate, timely investment information. To find investment prospects, he reads such publications as the *Wall Street Journal*, *Investor's Business Daily*, *Individual Investor*, *Forbes*, and *Business Week*, and he browses the investment message boards on America Online (AOL). After identifying an interesting stock, he requests the company's investor's package (annual reports, press releases, analysts' reports) and gathers as much information as possible. One source he consults is AOL, where he can access investment publication databases for articles on the company and read message boards to discover what other investors think about the stock. Jeff prefers on-line information to monthly investment newsletters—he likes the interactive nature and timeliness of on-line information, with quick feedback on a particular stock and answers to investing questions. With data in hand, he does a thorough analysis, often using a healthy dose of common sense to evaluate the numbers. Then he decides whether to buy, if he thinks the stock will appreciate, or whether to short, if he thinks the price will fall.

Jeff cautions that it's easy to be swayed by what one reads, whether in the financial press or on-line. Novice investors can easily suffer from "informa-

THERE'S NO SUBSTITUTE FOR DOING YOUR OWN HOMEWORK AND VERIFYING THE NUMBERS.

tion overload" and can be swamped by the enormous amount of information available from message boards and databases of investment publications. "That's why it is critical to find out for yourself what the facts are and to make up your own mind," Jeff says.

After receiving his Ph.D. in chemistry from the University of Maryland in 1982, Jeff Robinson taught at the U.S. Naval Academy and then did environmental consulting for the government and his own firm. In addition to his personal investing activities and being on the staff of the Motley Fool, *he writes satire, humor, and science fiction.*

Generally speaking, it takes more than money to be a successful investor. You also need to have a carefully developed investment plan and know where to find useful investment information. Although there are people who have made a lot of money with neither investment plans nor information, an investor with good plans and information will normally be more effective than one who operates solely on the basis of intuition. Just as a space vehicle needs navigational aids and expertise to reach its desired destination, so investors need carefully developed investment plans to achieve their financial goals in life. In addition, individuals who buy a particular stock because they like the firm's product often fail to address numerous relevant questions, such as, How will the economy change? What behavior is the stock market expected to exhibit over the near term? Is the company profitable, and will it continue to be so? Answers to these and other relevant questions can be obtained by acquiring and analyzing investment information, which is available from a variety of sources.

Chapter 3 will help you to develop your investment goals and plans and, like Jeff Robinson, to discover where to find the investment information you need. In the first part of the chapter, we look at investment plans; in the second part, we examine the important aspects of investment information.

MAKING INVESTMENT PLANS

The first step in investment planning is to establish investment goals consistent with overall financial objectives. From the general list of goals, an investment plan can then be developed. Investment plans should make adequate provision for life insurance coverage and consider taxes. They serve as the backbone of an investment program, which must be responsive to the investor's stage of the life cycle and the changing economic environment.

INVESTMENT GOALS

investment goals
the financial objectives that one wishes to achieve by investing in any of a wide range of potential investment vehicles.

Investment goals are the financial objectives that one wishes to achieve by investing in any of a wide range of potential investment vehicles. Clearly, your investment goals will determine the types of investments you will make. Common investment goals include:

1. *Accumulating Retirement Funds.* Accumulating funds for retirement is the *single most important reason for investing.* Too often, however, people tend to rely heavily on Social Security and employers for retirement funds. It is of the utmost importance to review the amounts that can realistically be expected from these sources and to decide, based on your retirement goals, *whether they will be adequate to meet your needs.* If they are not, they must be supplemented through your own investment program. The earlier in life you assess your retirement needs, the greater your chance of accumulating sufficient funds to meet them. (Some tax-advantaged individual retirement plans are discussed in more detail in Chapter 13.)

2. *Enhancing Current Income.* Investments enhance current income by earning dividends or interest. Retirees frequently choose investments offering

investment plan
a written document describing how funds will be invested, the target date for achievement of each investment goal, and the associated amount of tolerable risk.

insurance policy
a contract between the insured and the insurer that requires the insured to make periodic premium payments in exchange for the insurer's promise to pay for losses according to specified terms.

high current income at low risk. The idea of a retired person "clipping coupons"—collecting interest—from high-yield bonds is a fair description of what most senior citizens *should* be doing at that point in their lives.

3. *Saving for Major Expenditures.* Families often put aside money over the years to accumulate the funds needed to make major expenditures. The most common of these are the down payment on a home, education, a "once in a lifetime" vacation, capital to start a business, and the purchase of a special item (perhaps jewelry or an antique). The appropriate types of investment vehicles to be selected depend on the purpose and the amount of money needed. For purposes such as the down payment on a home or a child's education, for example, much less risk should be tolerated than for other goals. The attainment of such basic goals should not, if possible, be placed in jeopardy.

4. *Sheltering Income from Taxes.* As will be explained in Chapter 13, federal income tax law allows certain noncash charges to be deducted from specified sources of income, thereby reducing the amount of final taxable income. Obviously, if a person can avoid (or defer) paying taxes on the income from an investment, he or she will have more funds left for reinvestment.

Once the general goals have been established, an **investment plan**—a written document describing how funds will be invested—should be adopted. A series of supporting investment goals can be developed for each long-run goal. For each goal, the target date of achievement and the amount of tolerable risk must be specified. Generally, the more important the financial objective, the lower the risk that should be assumed. Suppose, for example, one long-run goal is to accumulate $80,000 in cash at the end of ten years. Our example could be more precisely stated as an investment goal to accumulate $80,000 in cash by investing in a portfolio evenly divided between low-risk and speculative stocks providing a total return of 10 percent per year. The more specific you can be in the statement of investment goals, the easier it will be to establish an investment plan consistent with your goals. The *Investor Insights* box on page 80 describes the benefits of using a professional financial planner to help formulate investment goals and plans.

MEETING LIFE INSURANCE NEEDS

With investment goals and plans laid out, the would-be investor needs to make sure that his or her insurance needs are met. Insurance is an important prerequisite for two reasons: (1) It provides protection against consequences that can adversely affect finances, and (2) it can provide certain long-term cash benefits. An **insurance policy** is a contract between the insured (you) and the insurer (an insurance company) that requires the insured to make periodic premium payments in exchange for the insurer's promise to pay for losses according to specified terms. Decisions regarding insurance purchases may affect the amount of funds available for investment.

The many different types of insurance available can be broken down into three basic forms: life insurance, health insurance, and property and liability insurance. Although many types of health, property, and liability insurance are essential, here we focus on life insurance because of its investment attributes.

INVESTOR INSIGHTS: *Investing in Action*

Benefiting from a Financial Planner

Today, professional financial planners are helping more people than ever to manage their personal finances. According to Barbara Roper of the Consumer Federation of America, about 250,000 people in the United States now represent themselves as financial planners. They provide a wide range of services, including managing clients' assets, making investments, preparing comprehensive personal financial plans, or focusing on a particular concern such as retirement planning. The industry, however, is very loosely regulated, so that just about anyone can offer financial planning services. In fact, up to half of the nation's financial planners have no formal training. Often, insurance salespeople or securities brokers without special training call themselves financial planners. Obviously, you must take time to find a trustworthy, competent adviser.

Financial planners are compensated in two basic ways: fees and commissions. *Fee-only planners* charge either a flat or an hourly rate to create a personalized plan for you. If they implement the plan by managing your investment portfolio, they also collect a fee of between 1 and 3 percent of the dollar amount of assets you've entrusted to them. *Fee-based planners* charge lower fees than the fee-only planners and supplement them with commissions. *Commission-only planners* charge you nothing for advice and receive commissions on the products—insurance policies, stocks, bonds, mutual funds, annuities, and tax shelters—they sell you.

Many consumer groups say that fee-only planners are always preferable, because they do not have the conflict of interest that faces commission-charging advisers: choosing the plan that is right for the client or the one that maximizes their own profit. Still, fee-only planners with a high hourly rate can run up huge fees that might exceed those charged by a commission-only planner.

Before you start your search, you should define your personal financial goals and decide what you want to accomplish with the planner. Do you want help with specific topics like budgeting, managing investments, retirement plans, or do you want a comprehensive personal financial plan? Clearly, you'll need to select a planner who can meet your particular needs and has other clients whose financial circumstances and investment goals are similar to yours. Ask friends for recommendations, then interview two or three planners before making up your mind. Ask about their educational and training background, and talk to their current and former clients. Also, check their criminal and disciplinary records by calling the SEC and your state securities agency. (If you feel hesitant to do this, remember: This person will be entrusted with your money and your life plans.) To find a planner with a formal background in finance, consult a directory issued by a trade association such as the Institute of Certified Financial Planners (ICFP), the International Association for Financial Planning (IAFP), the American Society of CLU & ChFC, or the National Association of Personal Financial Advisors (NAPFA). All that this indicates, though, is that a planner has made the effort to get some training; certification is no guarantee of competence, integrity, or honesty. Finally, you should be able to develop a good rapport with the planner and feel comfortable with his/her personal style.

The cost of financial planning services depends on the type of planner you choose, the complexity of your financial situation, and the services you require. Fees for a comprehensive personal financial plan can top $5,000, whereas an abbreviated plan usually costs several hundred dollars. Any planner should be willing to give you an estimate of fees up front. If you're looking for a commission-only planner, hire only someone who will disclose all the money he or she will make from an investment recommendation.

Sources: Adapted from Francis Flaherty, "Searching for a Trustworthy Planner," *San Diego Union-Tribune*, November 22, 1993, pp. C1– C2; William Giese, "What to Expect from a Financial Planner," *Kiplinger's Personal Finance Magazine*, August 1994, pp. 73–76; and Terence P. Paré, "How to Find a Financial Planner," *Fortune*, May 16, 1994, pp. 103–6.

Types of Life Insurance

life insurance
a contract that provides financial protection for a family if the primary breadwinner or any other family member dies prematurely.

Life insurance is a contract that provides financial protection for a family if the primary breadwinner or any other family member dies prematurely. Some types of life insurance provide only death benefits; others also allow for the accumulation of savings. The four basic types of life insurance are term, whole life, universal life, and variable life.

term life insurance
a policy in which the insurer is obligated to pay a specified amount if the insured dies within the policy period; does not contain a savings feature.

Term A **term life insurance** policy covers the insured for a specific period (typically 5 to 20 years). The insurer is obligated to pay a specified amount if the insured dies within the policy period. *Term is the least expensive form of life insurance*, although its cost rises as the insured ages. It provides protection but does not contain a savings feature.

Many employers offer free or low-cost *group term insurance* protection for their employees. Frequently, this benefit is the least expensive way to obtain life insurance. If you need to increase your term life insurance, you may be able to purchase additional amounts at low cost through group insurance. Keep in mind that many of these plans are not transportable, however. That means that you can't take your term protection with you if you leave your job.

whole life insurance
a policy that provides coverage over the entire life of the insured; offers a savings benefit.

cash value
the amount of money set aside by an insurer to provide for the payment of the death benefit.

Whole Life As the name implies, **whole life insurance** provides coverage over the entire life of the insured. The insured pays a fixed (or level) premium each year until death or termination of the policy. Whole life also offers a savings benefit commonly called the **cash value**. The cash value is the amount of money set aside by the insurer to provide for the payment of the death benefit. It increases over time. From the insurer's view, increased cash values are necessary as the insured's probability of death increases with age. Either the beneficiaries of the insured will receive the amount of the death benefit upon his or her death, or the policyholder at some predetermined time can terminate the policy and receive its cash value.

The advantage of whole life insurance is that the premium payments contribute toward the tax-sheltered accumulation of value. It also provides insurance protection for a fixed annual premium over the whole life of the insured. However, the actual cash value accumulation of a whole life policy reflects an annual rate of return generally *below* what could be earned on alternative investments. For this reason, some financial advisers recommend purchasing the cheaper term insurance and investing the premium savings.

universal life insurance
a policy that combines term insurance with a tax-sheltered savings/investment account that pays interest at competitive rates.

Universal Life **Universal life insurance** retains the savings feature of whole life but provides a higher rate of return on the cash value portion of the policy than most whole life policies. Basically, universal life combines *term insurance*, which provides the death benefits, with a tax-sheltered savings/investment account that pays interest at *competitive money market rates*.

A key advantage of universal life over whole life is that the purchaser is more aware of what he or she is buying than the whole life policyholder is. In contrast to whole life, universal life insurance carries a detailed breakdown of policy costs as well as benefits. All charges for costs, such as sales commissions, insurance company service fees, and actual insurance protection, are explicitly listed. (Usually, whole life sellers quote the premium amount and little else.) Another advantage of universal life is that many policies allow a buyer, under certain conditions, to skip or reduce a premium payment.

variable life insurance
a policy that combines insurance coverage with a savings account that allows the insured to decide how it is invested; the amount of insurance coverage varies with the profit generated in the investment (savings) account.

Variable Life   **Variable life insurance** is like whole life and universal life in that it combines insurance coverage with a savings account. It differs from them in two respects: (1) It allows the insured to decide how the money in the savings account (cash value account) is invested, and (2) it does *not* specify a guaranteed minimum return. Variable life offers the highest level of investment returns. As its name implies, the amount of insurance coverage provided will vary with the profit (and losses) generated in the investment (savings) account. Thus, the amount of death benefit payable is, for the most part, related to the policy's investment returns, though it can never fall below the policy's stated *minimum death benefit*. As with all other forms of life insurance, the investment earnings can grow within the policy free of any current taxation, and the policy's death benefit passes tax-free to beneficiaries. Because variable life is really an investment vehicle wrapped in an insurance policy, it is *probably better used as a tax-sheltered investment vehicle* than as a source of primary life insurance coverage.

Estimating Life Insurance Needs

multiple earnings approach
technique for estimating life insurance needs by applying a specified multiple to current gross annual earnings.

Two techniques are commonly used for estimating a person's life insurance needs. One is a simple technique—the **multiple earnings approach**—that determines the amount of life insurance as a multiple of current gross annual earnings. Tables of multiples can be obtained from life insurance agents and companies. They typically provide values based on age, family structure, and gross annual pay. For example, to replace 75 percent of the $60,000 gross annual earnings of a 40-year-old breadwinner in a family of four, a multiple of 8.5 might be specified. Multiplying $60,000 by 8.5 results in $510,000 of needed life insurance coverage.

needs approach
technique for estimating life insurance needs by considering a person's financial obligations and the financial resources currently available for meeting them.

The second and much more widely accepted approach—the **needs approach**—specifically considers a person's financial obligations and the financial resources currently available for meeting them. The approach involves (1) estimating total financial resources needed; (2) determining all financial resources currently available, including life insurance and pension plan death benefits already in force; and (3) subtracting the amount of financial resources available from the amount needed, to determine the amount of additional life insurance required. This approach involves fairly detailed forecasts of resources needed and available, and it uses time value of money techniques (discussed in Chapter 4). Therefore, it is far more difficult to apply than the multiple earnings approach. Many insurance companies have forms available that can be used to simplify application of the needs approach. Regardless of which method is used, investors must make sure that they have enough life insurance to provide adequate financial protection.

CONSIDERING PERSONAL TAXES

Besides having one's investment goals and plans outlined and one's insurance needs met, it's also important to consider the tax consequences associated with various investment vehicles and strategies. A knowledge of the tax laws can help you reduce taxes and thereby increase the amount of after-tax dollars available for achieving your investment goals. Because tax laws are complicated and subject to frequent revision, here we will present only the key concepts and their applications to popular investment transactions.

Basic Sources of Taxation

The two major types of taxes are those levied by the federal government and those levied by state and local governments. The major federal tax is the *income tax*, which is also the major form of personal taxation. Federal rates currently range from 15 to 39.6 percent of taxable income.

State and local taxes vary from area to area. Some states have income taxes that may range as high as 15 percent or more of income. Some cities, especially large East Coast cities, also have local income taxes that typically range between 1 and 5 percent of income. In addition to income taxes, state and local governments rely heavily on sales and property taxes as a source of revenue. Although sales taxes vary from state to state, most are between 3 and 7 percent. Property taxes are levied on real estate and personal property, such as automobiles, boats, and furniture. These taxes vary from community to community.

Income taxes at the federal, state, and local levels have the greatest impact on security investments, whose returns are in the form of dividends, interest, and increases in value. Property taxes can have a sizable impact on real estate and other forms of property investment.

Types of Income

The income of individuals used to be classified simply as either ordinary or capital gain (or loss). That classification changed with the *Tax Reform Act of 1986*. One of the major revisions of the sweeping 1986 tax law was the creation of *three basic categories of income*. Devised as a way to reduce or eliminate the tax-advantaged treatment of certain types of investments, they are:

1. *Active income,* consisting of everything from wages and salaries to bonuses, tips, pension income, and alimony. Active income is made up of income earned on the job as well as most other forms of *noninvestment* income.

2. *Portfolio income*, comprising earnings generated from various types of investment holdings. This category of income covers most (but not all) types of investments, from savings accounts, stocks, bonds, and mutual funds to options and futures. For the most part, portfolio income consists of interest, dividends, and capital gains (i.e., the profit on the sale of an investment).

3. *Passive income*, a special category of income composed chiefly of income derived from real estate, limited partnerships, and other forms of tax-advantaged investments. (Chapter 13 presents detailed discussions and illustrations of the basic mechanics of tax-advantaged investments.)

The key feature of these categories is that they limit the amount of deductions (write-offs) that can be taken, particularly with regard to portfolio and passive income. Specifically, the amount of allowable deductions associated with portfolio and passive income is *limited to the amount of income derived from these two sources.* For example, if you had a total of $380 in portfolio income for the year, you could deduct no more than $380 in investment-related interest expense. For deduction purposes, the portfolio and passive income categories cannot be mixed or combined with each other or with active income. *Investment-related expenses can be used only to offset portfolio income*, and with a few exceptions, *passive investment expenses can be used only to offset the income from passive investments.*

Ordinary Income   Regardless of whether it's classified as active, portfolio, or passive, ordinary income—after certain computations—is taxed at one of five rates: 15, 28, 31, 36, or 39.6 percent. There is one structure of tax rates for taxpayers who file *individual* returns and another for those who file *joint* returns with a spouse. Table 3.1 shows the tax rates and income brackets for these two filing categories. Notice that the rates are *progressive*—taxpayers with taxable income above a specified amount are taxed at a higher rate.

An example will demonstrate how ordinary income is taxed. Consider the Ellis sisters, Joni and Cara. Both are single. Joni's taxable income is $18,000; Cara's is $36,000. Using Table 3.1, we can calculate their taxes as follows:

Joni:
$(.15 \times \$18,000) = \underline{\$2,700}$

Cara:
$(.15 \times \$22,750) + [.28 \times (\$36,000 - \$22,750)] = \$3,413 + \$3,710 = \underline{\$7,123}$

The progressive nature of the federal income tax structure can be seen by the fact that although Cara's taxable income is twice that of Joni, her income tax is nearly 2.7 times Joni's.

Capital Gains and Losses   A *capital asset* is property owned and used by the taxpayer for personal reasons, pleasure, or investment. The most common types are securities and real estate, including one's home. A **capital gain** represents the amount by which the proceeds from the sale of a capital asset exceed its original purchase price. The amount of any capital gain realized is added to other sources of income and the total is taxed at the rates given in Table 3.1, but the *maximum tax rate on the capital gain is 28 percent.* For example, imagine that James McFail, a single person who has other taxable income totaling $40,000, sold at $12 per share 500 shares of stock originally

capital gain
the amount by which the proceeds from the sale of a capital asset exceed its original purchase price.

Table 3.1   Tax Rates and Income Brackets for Individual and Joint Returns (1994)

Tax Rates	Taxable Income	
	Individual Returns	Joint Returns
15%	$0 to $22,750	$0 to $38,000
28%	$22,751 to $55,100	$38,001 to $91,850
31%	$55,101 to $115,000	$91,851 to $140,000
36%	$115,001 to $250,000	$140,001 to $250,000
39.6%	Over $250,000	Over $250,000

purchased for $10 per share. The total capital gain on this transaction was $1,000 [500 shares $\times$ ($12/share $-$ $10/share)]. Thus, McFail's taxable income would total $41,000. His total tax would be $8,523 [(.15 $\times$ $22,750) + (.28 $\times$ ($41,000 $-$ $22,750))]. Had McFail's other taxable income been, say, $60,000, all of his income over $55,100 would have been taxable at 31 percent (see Table 3.1). In spite of this, the $l,000 capital gain would be taxed at the maximum 28 percent rate for capital gains rather than at the 31 percent rate.

Capital gains are appealing to investors because they are not taxed until actually realized. For example, if you own a stock originally purchased for $50 per share that at the end of the tax year has a market price of $60 per share, you have a "paper gain" of $10 per share. This *paper*, or *unrealized, gain* is not taxable, because you still own the stock. *Only realized gains are taxed.* If you sold the stock for $60 per share during the tax year, you would have a realized—and therefore taxable—gain of $10 per share.

A **capital loss** results when a capital asset is sold for *less than* its original purchase price. Before taxes are calculated, all gains and losses must be netted out. Up to $3,000 of **net losses** can be applied against ordinary income in any year. Losses that cannot be applied in the current year may be carried forward and used to offset future income, subject to certain conditions.

Investments and Taxes

From an investor's point of view, the key dimensions of taxes revolve around current (ordinary) income, capital gains, tax shelters, and tax planning. Investors in vehicles providing current income tend to be those in the lower two tax brackets (15 and 28 percent)—especially retirees. The predominant form of current investment income is interest and dividends. To a lesser degree, another source of current income is rental income from various types of real estate investment. From a tax point of view, capital gains are appealing to many investors. The fact that these gains are not taxed until actually realized allows the investor to defer as well as control the timing of the tax payments on them. In addition, because capital gains are taxed as ordinary income up to a maximum tax rate of 28 percent, they provide a small *tax rate advantage* to taxpayers in the top (31, 36, and 39.6 percent) tax brackets.

However, investments that are likely to lead to capital gains income generally have higher risk than those that provide only current investment income. Therefore, the choice of investment vehicles cannot be made solely on the basis of the timing and possible reduction of tax payments. The levels of return and risk need to be viewed in light of their tax effects. *It is the after-tax return and associated risk that should be considered.*

The opportunities created by the tax laws make tax planning important in the investment process. **Tax planning** involves looking at an individual's earnings, both current and projected, and developing strategies that will defer and minimize the level of taxes. The tax plan should guide an investor's activities in such a way that over the long run he or she will achieve maximum after-tax returns for an acceptable level of risk.

Tax plans should also reflect the desired form in which returns are to be received—current income, capital gains, or tax-advantaged income. One common strategy is to claim losses as soon as they occur and to delay profit

capital loss
the amount by which the proceeds from the sale of a capital asset are *less than* its original purchase price.

net losses
the amount by which capital losses exceed capital gains; up to $3,000 of net losses can be applied against ordinary income in any year.

tax planning
the development of strategies that will defer and minimize an individual's level of taxes over the long run.

taking. Such an approach allows you to benefit from the tax deductibility of a loss and to delay having to claim income from gains. Tax planning, which is usually done in coordination with an accountant, tax expert, or tax attorney, is most common among individuals with high levels of income ($75,000 or more annually). Yet sizable savings can result for investors with lower incomes as well.

THE INVESTMENT PROGRAM

When investment goals have been specified, an investment program can be developed. The backbone of the program is the investment plan, which indicates the general strategy that will be used to achieve each goal. Investors should remember that some portion of the goals may be achieved through government or employer pension programs outside the individual's control. Any contribution of such plans toward goal achievement must be recognized.

diversification
holding a variety of investment vehicles in a portfolio to minimize risk.

The overriding consideration in the investment plan is **diversification**. This concept, which is fully developed in Chapter 16, emphasizes the need to hold a variety of investment vehicles to minimize risk. A well-balanced portfolio makes it less likely that one bad investment will hinder the goal of accumulating a specified amount.

As the investment program progresses, checkpoints should be established to assess progress at various time intervals. Adjustments in either goals or plans may be required as new information is received; goals may be too lax or too restrictive, or plans unrealistic. By monitoring actual outcomes and making needed adjustments, you should be better able to establish and achieve realistic financial goals over the long run.

INVESTING OVER THE LIFE CYCLE

Investors tend to follow different investment philosophies as they move through different stages of the life cycle. Generally speaking, most investors tend to be more aggressive when they're young and more conservative as they grow older. Typically, investors tend to move through the following investment stages:

Most young investors, in their twenties and thirties, tend to prefer growth-oriented investments that stress *capital gains* rather than current income. Often young investors don't have much in the way of investable funds, so capital gains are viewed as the quickest (if not necessarily the surest) way to build up investment capital. Such investors tend to favor growth-oriented and speculative vehicles, particularly high-risk common stocks, options, and futures.

As investors approach the middle-age consolidation stage of life (the mid-forties), family demands and responsibilities such as educational expenses and retirement contributions become more important, and the approach to investing changes. Thus, the whole portfolio goes through a transition to *higher-*

quality securities. Low-risk growth and income stocks, preferred stocks, convertibles, high-grade bonds, and mutual funds are all widely used at this stage in life.

Finally, investors move into their retirement years. Preservation of capital and current income become the principal concerns. A secure, high level of income is paramount, and capital gains are viewed as merely a pleasant, occasional by-product of investing. The investment portfolio now becomes *highly conservative*, consisting of low-risk income stocks, high-yielding government bonds, quality corporate bonds, bank certificates of deposit (CDs), and other money market investments. It's at this stage that you should be able to reap the rewards of a lifetime of saving and investing.

INVESTING IN DIFFERENT ECONOMIC ENVIRONMENTS

Despite the government's arsenal of weapons for moderating economic swings, numerous changes are sure to occur in the economy during your lifetime of investing. At all stages of the life cycle, your investment program must be flexible enough to allow you to recognize and react to changing economic conditions. While the first rule of investing is to know *where* to put your money, the second is to know *when* to make your moves. The first question is easier to deal with because it basically involves matching the risk and return objectives of your investment plan with the available investment alternatives. For example, if you're a seasoned investor who can tolerate the risk, then speculative stocks may be right for you; on the other hand, if you're a novice who wants a fair return on your capital, perhaps you should consider a good growth-oriented mutual fund. Unfortunately, although stocks or growth funds may do well when the economy is expanding, they can turn out to be disasters at other times. This leads to our second, and more difficult, question: What effect do economic/market conditions have on investment returns?

The question of when to invest is difficult because it deals with *market timing*. The fact is that most investors, even professional money managers, cannot predict the peaks and troughs in the market with much consistency. It's a lot easier to get a handle on the *current state* of the economy/market. That is, knowing whether the economy/market is in a state of expansion or decline is considerably different from being able to pinpoint when it's about to change course. Thus, for our purposes we can define market timing as the *process through which we identify the current state of the economy/market and assess the likelihood of its continuing on its present course.*

As an investor, it's probably best to confine your assessment of the market to three distinct conditions: (1) a state of recovery or expansion, (2) a state of decline or recession, or (3) uncertainty as to the direction of its movement. These different stages are illustrated in Figure 3.1 on page 88. It's easy to see when things are moving up (recovery/expansion) or when they're moving down (decline/recession). The difficulty comes with the peaks and troughs. At those points, you don't know whether the market will continue its current direction, up or down, or whether it will change direction. That is why these areas in the figure are shaded, depicting *uncertainty*. How you will respond to these conditions depends on whether your investments are in stocks, bonds, or real estate and other tangible investments.

Figure 3.1   Different Stages of an Economic/Market Cycle
The economic/market cycle shows three different conditions:
(1) a state of recovery/expansion, (2) a state of decline/reces-
sion, and (3) uncertainty as to the direction in which the
economy/market is going to move (shown by the shaded
areas at peak and troughs).

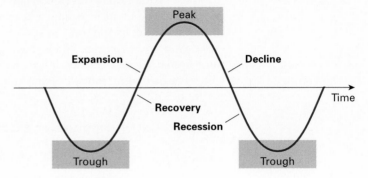

Stocks and the Business Cycle

Common stocks and other equity-related securities (e.g., stock mutual funds,
convertible securities, stock options, and stock index futures) are highly
responsive to conditions in the economy. Economic conditions are described
generically as the *business cycle*. The business cycle reflects the current status
of a variety of economic variables, including GDP (gross domestic product),
industrial production, personal disposable income, the unemployment rate,
and more. A strong economy is reflected in an expanding business cycle. When
business is good and profits are up, stocks react accordingly, by increasing in
value and return. Growth-oriented and speculative stocks tend to do especially
well in strong markets, as, to a lesser extent, do low-risk and income-oriented
stocks. In contrast, when economic activity is declining, the values and returns
on common stocks tend to be off as well.

Bonds and Interest Rates

Bonds and other forms of fixed-income securities (e.g., preferred stocks and
bond funds) are highly sensitive to movements in interest rates. In fact, interest
rates are the single most important variable in determining bond price
behavior and returns to investors. Because interest rates and bond prices move
in opposite directions (as will be explained in Chapters 8 and 9), it follows that
rising interest rates are unfavorable for outstanding bonds already held in an
investor's portfolio. Of course, high interest rates enhance the attractiveness of
new bonds because they offer high returns.

Real Estate, Other Tangible Investments, and Inflation

Real estate and other tangible investments, including gold and other precious
metals, gemstones, and collectibles such as artwork and antiques, are generally responsive more to the *rate of inflation* than to anything else. Housing
prices and the prices of commodities like coffee, oil, meat, corn, and sugar are

components of the consumer price index (CPI). *When consumer prices start to rise, the returns on real estate and other tangible investments start to go up as well.* For example, consider what happened over the 18-year period from 1977 to 1995. In the first 5 years of that period, inflation was running high, hitting 13.5 percent. At the same time, investments in real estate, and other tangible assets were generating correspondingly high rates of return, and indeed out-performing all other forms of investments. But when inflation was brought back down to more normal levels (3 to 5 percent) beginning around 1982, returns on real estate and other tangible investments plummeted. (*Note*: As will be discussed in Chapter 12, changes in the tax laws and rising interest rates also contributed to the declining real estate returns during this period.) Certainly, the rate of inflation significantly affects the returns on real estate and other tangible investments.

CONCEPTS *in Review*

3.1   What are investment goals? Briefly describe each of the following commonly cited investment goals:

    a. Accumulating retirement funds

    b. Enhancing current income

    c. Saving for major expenditures

    d. Sheltering income from taxes

3.2   Why is insurance an important prerequisite to investment planning? Briefly define and differentiate among the following types of life insurance. Describe the basic motives that should underlie the use of each of these types.

    a. Term life insurance

    b. Whole life insurance

    c. Universal life insurance

    d. Variable life insurance

3.3   Define, differentiate, and compare the two common approaches for estimating life insurance needs.

    a. Multiple earnings approach

    b. Needs approach

3.4   Define, differentiate, and explain how the following items relate to federal income taxes:

    a. Active income

    b. Portfolio and passive income

    c. Capital gain

    d. Capital loss

    e. Tax planning

3.5   Explain how existing government or employer pension programs must be considered when estimating the amount of annual income that must be contributed to achieve a given goal. Comment on the role that monitoring an investment plan plays in the total investment program.

3.6   Describe the differing investment philosophies typically observed during each of the following stages of an investor's life cycle:

    a. Youth (ages 20 to 45)

    b. Middle-age (ages 45 to 60)

    c. Retirement years (ages 60 on)

3.7 Describe the four stages of the economic/market cycle, and discuss the impact of this cycle on each of the following forms of investment:
   a. Stocks
   b. Bonds
   c. Real estate and other tangible investments

TYPES AND SOURCES OF INVESTMENT INFORMATION

descriptive information
factual data on the past behavior of the economy, the market, the industry, the company, or a given investment vehicle.

analytical information
available current data in conjunction with projections and recommendations about potential investments.

Once investors have developed their investment plans, they can begin searching for the right investments. The search should start with the examination of investment information of various kinds. Investment information allows the investor to formulate expectations of the risk-return behaviors of potential investments. It can be considered either descriptive or analytical. **Descriptive information** presents factual data on the past behavior of the economy, the market, the industry, the company, or a given investment vehicle. **Analytical information** presents available current data in conjunction with projections and recommendations about potential investments. The sample page from *Value Line* included in Figure 3.2 provides both descriptive and analytical information on Hewlett-Packard. Items that are primarily descriptive are keyed with a *D*; analytical items are noted with an *A*. Examples of descriptive information are the company's capital structure and monthly stock price ranges for the past 13 years. Examples of analytical information are rank for timeliness and estimated average price range for the next 3 to 5 years.

Some forms of investment information are free; others must be purchased individually or by annual subscription. Free information can be obtained from newspapers, magazines, and brokerage firms, and more can be found in public, university, and brokerage firm libraries. Alternatively, an investor can subscribe to services that provide periodic reports summarizing the investment outlook and recommending certain actions. Such services cost the investor money, but obtaining, reading, and analyzing free information all cost time. So it is necessary to evaluate the worth of potential information. For example, paying $40 for information that increases one's return by $27 would not be economically sound. The larger an individual's investment portfolio, the easier it is to justify information purchases, because their benefit can usually be applied to a number of investments.

TYPES OF INFORMATION

Investment information can be classed into five types, each concerned with an important aspect of the investment process.

1. *Economic and current event information* provides background as well as forecast data related to economic, political, and social trends, on a domestic as well as a global basis. Such information provides a basis for assessing the environment in which decisions are made.

2. *Industry and company information* provides background as well as forecast data on specific industries and companies. Investors use such information to assess the outlook in a given industry or specific company. Due to its company orientation, it is most relevant to stock, bond, or options investments.

Figure 3.2   A Report Containing Descriptive and Analytical Information
This report—*Value Line's* full-page report on Hewlett-Packard from January 27, 1995—contains both descriptive (marked *D*) and analytical (marked *A*) information. (Source: Adapted from *The Value Line Investment Survey, Ratings and Reports*, Edition 1, January 27, 1995, p. 1092. © Value Line Publishing, Inc.)

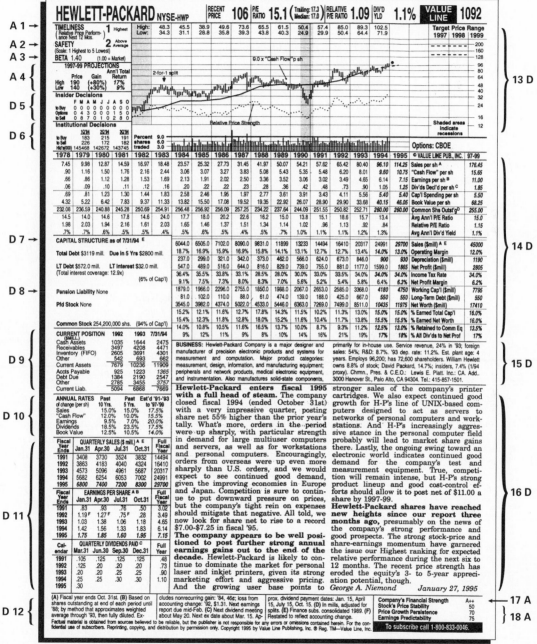

1. Rank for timeliness (price performance in next twelve months)—from 1 (highest) to 5 (lowest)

2. Rank for long-term safety—1 (highest) down to 5 (lowest)

3. Beta (the stock's sensitivity to market fluctuation—NYSE average = 1.00)

4. Estimated average price range—3–5 years ahead

5. Insider decisions

6. Institutional decisions

7. Company's capital structure

8. Pension liability

9. Working capital

10. Growth rates

11. Quarterly sales, earnings, dividends—actual past, estimated future

12. Footnotes—including estimated constant dollar earnings, dividend payment dates.

13. Monthly price ranges—past 13 years and value line (cash flow line)

14. Statistical milestones—on a per share basis and a company basis—historical past and estimated future

15. Brief summary of company's business

16. Critique—of recent developments and prospects

17. Company's financial strength

18. Important indices of quality

3. *Information on alternative investment vehicles* provides background and predictive data for various forms of real estate and other tangible investments as well as for securities other than stocks, bonds, and options—such as futures.

4. *Price information* contains current price quotations on certain investment vehicles, particularly securities. These quotations are commonly accompanied by statistics on the recent price behavior of the vehicle.

5. *Information on personal investment strategies* provides recommendations on investment strategies or specific purchase or sale actions. In general, this information tends to be educational or analytical rather than descriptive.

SOURCES OF INFORMATION

A complete listing of the sources of each type of investment information is beyond the scope of this book; we can consider only the basic forms of investment information here. For those desiring expanded source information, the *Investor's Resource Manual* that accompanies this textbook provides an annotated listing. The discussion here is concerned with the most common sources of information on economic and current events, industries and companies, and prices.

Economic and Current Event Information

It is clearly important for investors to stay abreast of major economic and current events. An awareness of events should translate into better investment decisions. Popular sources of economic and current event information include financial journals, general newspapers, institutional news, business periodicals, government publications, and special subscription services.

Wall Street Journal
a daily business newspaper, published regionally; the most popular source of financial news.

Financial Journals   The *Wall Street Journal* is the most popular source of financial news. It is published daily, in a number of locations around the country; European and Asian editions are also published. In addition to giving daily price quotations on thousands of investment vehicles, it reports world, national, regional, and corporate news. The first page of the third section of the *Journal* usually contains a column, "Your Money Matters," that addresses personal finance issues and topics.

Barron's
a weekly business newspaper; a popular source of financial news.

A second popular source of financial news is *Barron's,* which is published weekly. *Barron's* generally offers lengthier articles on a variety of topics of interest to individual investors than the *Journal* does. Probably the most popular column in *Barron's* is Alan Abelson's "Up & Down Wall Street," which provides a critical and often humorous assessment of major developments affecting the stock market and business. Current price quotations and a summary of statistics on a range of investment vehicles also are included.

Investor's Business Daily, a third national business newspaper, is published daily Monday through Friday. It is similar to the *Wall Street Journal* but contains more detailed price and market data. Other sources of financial news are the *Commercial and Financial Chronicle*, the *Financial Times*, and the *Journal of Commerce*.

General Newspapers   Another popular source of financial news is *USA Today*—the national newspaper published Monday through Friday. Each issue contains a "Money" section (Section B) devoted to business and personal financial news and to current security price quotations and summary statistics.

Local newspapers provide still another convenient source of financial news. In most large cities, the daily newspaper devotes at least a few pages to financial and business news. Major metropolitan newspapers such as the *New York Times* and the *Los Angeles Times* provide investors with a wealth of financial information. Most major newspapers contain stock price quotations for major exchanges, price quotations on stocks of local interest, and a summary of the major stock market averages and indexes.

Institutional News   The monthly economic letters of the nation's leading banks, such as Bank of America (based in San Francisco), Citibank (New York), and Harris Trust (Chicago), provide useful economic information. To keep customers abreast of important news developments, most brokerage firms subscribe to a number of wire services such as the Dow Jones, Bloomberg Financial Services, AP (Associated Press), and UPI (United Press International) services. Access to these services is best obtained through a stockbroker.

Business Periodicals   Business periodicals range in scope. Some present general business and economic articles, others cover securities markets and related topics, and still others focus solely on specific industries or property investments. Regardless of the subject matter, most business periodicals present descriptive information, and some also include analytical information. However, they rarely offer recommendations.

General business and economic articles are presented in the business sections of general-interest periodicals such as *Newsweek, Time*, and *U.S. News & World Report*. A number of strictly business- and finance-oriented periodicals are also available. These include *Business Week, Fortune, Business Month*, and *Nation's Business*.

Securities and marketplace articles can be found in a number of financial periodicals. The most basic, commonsense articles appear in *Forbes, Kiplinger's Personal Finance Magazine, Money, Smart Money*, and *Worth*. *Forbes*, published every two weeks, is the most investment oriented. Each January, it publishes an "Annual Report on American Industry," which compares the growth and performance of key industries over the past five years. In August of each year, *Forbes* also publishes a comparative evaluation of mutual funds. *Kiplinger's Personal Finance Magazine, Money, Smart Money*, and *Worth* are published monthly and contain articles on managing personal finances and on investments.

Other periodicals aimed at the sophisticated investor are listed and described in the *Investor's Resource Manual* that accompanies this book.

Government Publications   A number of government agencies publish economic data and reports useful to investors. A broad view of the current and expected state of the economy can be found in the annual *Economic Report* *of the President.* This document reviews and summarizes economic policy and conditions and includes data on important aspects of the economy. The *Federal Reserve Bulletin,* published monthly by the Board of Governors of the Federal Reserve System, and periodic reports published by each of the 12 Federal Reserve District Banks provide articles and data on various aspects of economic and business activity. A useful Department of Commerce publication is the *Survey of Current Business.* It is published monthly and includes indicators and data relating to economic and business conditions. A good source of financial statement information on all manufacturers, broken down by industry and asset size, is the *Quarterly Financial Report for Manufacturing Corporations*, published jointly by the Federal Trade Commission and the Securities and Exchange Commission.

Special Subscription Services   For those who want additional insights into business and economic conditions, special subscription services are available. These reports include business and economic forecasts and give notice of new government policies, union plans and tactics, taxes, prices, wages, and so on. One popular service is the *Kiplinger Washington Letter*, a weekly publication that provides a wealth of economic information and analyses.

Industry and Company Information

Of special interest to investors is information on particular industries and companies. Often, after choosing an industry in which to invest, the investor will want to analyze specific companies. General articles related to the activities of specific industries can be found in trade publications such as *Chemical Week, American Banker, Computer, Oil and Gas Journal,* and *Public Utilities Fortnightly.* More specific popular sources are discussed below.

Stockholders' Reports   An excellent source of data on an individual firm is its **stockholders'**, or **annual, report,** published yearly by publicly held corporations. These reports contain a wide range of information, including financial statements for the most recent period of operation, along with summarized statements for several prior years. These reports are free and may be obtained from the companies themselves or from brokers. A sample page from Hewlett-Packard's 1994 stockholders' report is shown in Figure 3.3. In addition to the stockholders' report, many serious investors will review a company's **Form 10-K**, a statement that firms having securities listed on an organized exchange or traded in the national OTC market must file with the SEC.

stockholders' (annual) report
a report published yearly by a publicly held firm; contains a wide range of information, including financial statements for the most recent fiscal year.

Form 10-K
a statement that must be filed with the SEC by all firms having securities listed on an organized exchange or traded in the national OTC market.

Comparative Data Sources   A number of useful sources of comparative data, typically broken down by industry and firm size, are available for use in analyzing the financial conditions of companies. Among these sources are Dun & Bradstreet's *Key Business Ratios*, Robert Morris and Associates' *Annual Statement Studies*, the *Quarterly Financial Report for Manufacturing Corporations* (cited above), and the *Almanac of Business and Industrial Financial Ratios*. The data provided by these sources, which are typically available in public and university libraries, are used as a benchmark for evaluating the financial outcomes and conditions of a company.

Figure 3.3   A Page from a Stockholders' Report
The first page of Hewlett-Packard's report quickly acquaints the investor with the key information on the firm's operations over the past year, in textual, tabular, and graphic form. (Source: *Hewlett-Packard 1994 Stockholders' Report.* Palo Alto, California: Hewlett-Packard, 1995.)

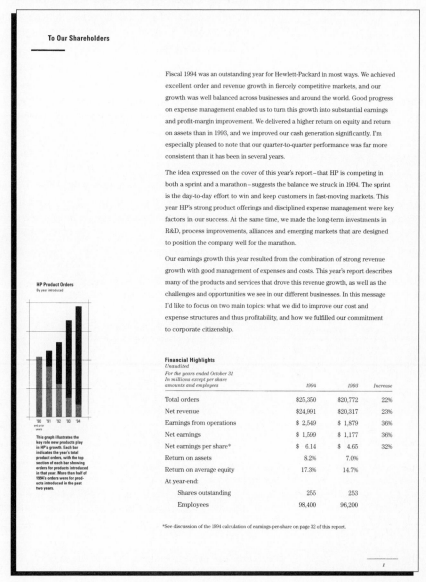

Subscription Services   A variety of subscription services provide information on specific industries and companies. Today, many of these services are available on computer diskette or CD-ROM with accompanying software, and much of the data are available using a computer modem. Generally, a subscriber pays a basic fee that entitles him or her to information periodically published by the service. In addition to the basic service, a subscriber can purchase other services that provide information of greater depth or range. The major subscription services provide both descriptive and analytical information, but

Standard & Poor's Corporation (S&P)
publisher of a variety of financial reports and services, including *Corporation Records* and *Stock Reports*.

Moody's Investor Services
publisher of a variety of financial reference manuals, including *Moody's Manuals*.

they generally do not make recommendations. Most investors, rather than subscribing to these services, gain access to them through their stockbrokers or a large public or university library.

The dominant subscription services are those offered by Standard & Poor's Corporation, Moody's Investor Services, and Value Line. **Standard & Poor's Corporation (S&P)** offers approximately 25 different financial reports and services. Five of the most popular services are briefly summarized in Table 3.2. **Moody's Investor Services** publishes a variety of materials. Five of its most

Table 3.2 Most Popular Offerings of the Most Dominant Subscription Services

Subscription Service Offerings	Coverage	Frequency of Publication
Standard & Poor's Corporation		
Corporation Records	Detailed descriptions of publicly traded securities of over 10,000 public corporations.	Annual with updates throughout the year
Stock Reports (sample shown in Figure 6.3, page 264)	Summary of financial history, current finances, and future prospects for thousands of companies.	Annual with updates throughout the year
Stock Guide	Statistical data and analytical rankings of investment desirability for major stocks.	Monthly
Bond Guide	Statistical data and analytical rankings of investment desirability for major bonds.	Monthly
The Outlook	Analytical articles with investment advice on the market, industries, and securities.	Weekly magazine
Moody's Investor Services		
Moody's Manuals	Eight reference manuals—*Bank and Finance, Industrial, International, Municipal and Government, OTC Industrial, OTC Unlisted, Public Utility,* and *Transportation.* Contain a wealth of historical and current financial, organizational, and operational data on major firms.	Annual, with biweekly updates
Handbook of Common Stocks	Provides financial information on over 1,000 common stocks.	Quarterly
Dividend Record	Recent dividend announcements and payments by thousands of companies.	Twice weekly, with annual summary
Bond Survey	Assesses bond market condition and new offerings.	Weekly
Bond Record	Price and interest rate behavior of thousands of bonds.	Monthly
Value Line Investment Survey		
Includes three reports:	Covers 1,700 of the most widely held stocks.	Weekly
1. *Summary and Index*	Current ratings for each stock.	
2. *Ratings and Reports* (sample shown in Figure 3.2, page 91)	Full-page report including financial data, descriptions, analysis, and.ratings for each of about 130 stocks	
3. *Selection and Opinion*	Selected investment, business, and stock market prospects, and investment strategy advice.	

Value Line Investment Survey
one of the most popular sub-scription services used by individual investors; subscribers receive three basic reports.

popular services are also briefly described in Table 3.2 The *Value Line Investment Survey* is one of the most popular subscription services used by individual investors. Its subscribers receive the three basic reports briefly described in Table 3.2.

Brokerage Reports   Brokerage firms often make available to their clients reports from the various subscription services. They also provide clients with prospectuses for new security issues and *back-office research reports*. As noted in Chapter 2, a *prospectus* is a document that describes in detail the key aspects of the issue, the issuer, and its management and financial position. The cover of the prospectus describing the 1995 stock issue of American Sensors was shown in Chapter 2, in Figure 2.3 on page 44. **Back-office research reports** include the brokerage firm's analyses of and recommendations on prospects for the securities markets, specific industries, or specific securities. Usually a brokerage firm will publish lists of securities classified by its research staff as either "buy" or "sell." Brokerage research reports are available upon request at no cost to existing and to potential clients.

back-office research reports
brokerage firm's analyses of and recommendations on investment prospects; made available on request at no cost to existing and potential clients.

investment letters
provide, on a subscription basis, the analyses, conclusions, and recommendations of experts in securities investment.

Investment Letters   **Investment letters** provide, on a subscription basis, the analyses, conclusions, and recommendations of experts in securities invest-ment. Some letters concentrate on specific types of securities, whereas others are concerned solely with assessing the economy or security markets. Among the more popular investment letters are the *Addison Report, Bob Nurock's Advisory*, the *Dick Davis Digest*, the *Growth Stock Outlook*, the *Holt Investment Advisory, Investment Quality Trends*, the *Prudent Speculator*, the *Professional Tape Reader*, and the *Zweig Forecast*. The more popular ones are generally issued monthly or weekly and usually cost from $75 to $400 a year. Advertisements for many of these investment letters can be found in *Barron's* and in various business periodicals. The *Hulbert Financial Digest*, which mon-itors the performance of investment letters, is an excellent source of objective information on investment letters.

Price Information

quotations
price information about various types of securities, including cur-rent price data and statistics on recent price behavior.

Price information about various types of securities is contained in their **quota-tions**, which include current price data and statistics on recent price behavior. Price quotations are readily available for actively traded securities. The most up-to-date quotations can be obtained from a stockbroker. Some brokerage offices have equipment that allows customers to key into a computer terminal to obtain quotations. Another automated quotation device found in most bro-kerage offices is the *ticker*, a lighted screen on which stock transactions made on the NYSE, AMEX, and regional exchanges are consolidated and reported as they occur. The ticker symbols for some well-known companies are listed in Table 3.3. Access to price information via personal computers is also now available on a fee basis through a variety of on-line services.

Investors can easily find the prior day's security price quotations in the published news media, both nonfinancial and financial. The major source of security price quotations is the *Wall Street Journal*, which presents quotations for each previous business day's activities in all major markets. Actual price quotations will be demonstrated and discussed as part of the coverage of spe-cific investment vehicles in later chapters.

Table 3.3 Ticker Symbols for Some Well-Known Companies

Company	Symbol	Company	Symbol
Aluminum Co. of America	AA	Mobil Corporation	MOB
AT&T	T	Occidental Petroleum	OXY
Coca-Cola	KO	Pepsico, Inc.	PEP
Disney (Walt)	DIS	Polaroid Corporation	PRD
Eastman Kodak	EK	Procter & Gamble	PG
Ford Motor	F	Quaker Oats	OAT
General Electric	GE	Safeway	SWY
General Motors	GM	Sears, Roebuck	S
Hewlett-Packard	HWP	Texas Instruments	TXN
International Business Machines	IBM	Upjohn	UPJ
McDonalds Corporation	MCD	Wendy's International	WEN
Microsoft	MSFT	Westinghouse	WX
Merrill Lynch	MER	Xerox Corporation	XRX

ELECTRONIC AND ON-LINE INVESTMENT INFORMATION

Today, many investors use their personal computers to obtain current, often up-to-the-minute, investment information provided on diskette, on CD-ROM, or on-line. Accompanying these data sets is software that can be used to access and, in many cases, analyze the data in a variety of ways. For example, the *Media General Standard Data Diskette* contains financial data on 7,000 companies and is revised monthly. The AAII's *Stock Investor: The Student Version* that accompanies this textbook is another example of a historical database of company information.

A more popular approach to obtaining investment information is on-line either directly from the data service, such as *Dow Jones News/Retrieval*, or through one of the established on-line services, such as America Online, CompuServe, Prodigy, or the Internet. All of these on-line services are accessed by personal computer using a modem. Often the on-line service subscriber must pay extra for an "extended" or "premium" service that includes particular investment/financial data. For example, CompuServe subscribers can access stock quotes, a variety of stock databases, selected SEC filings, corporate insider-trading information, and articles from more than 800 periodicals. (Except for delayed stock quotes, all of these CompuServe offerings entail an hourly surcharge.) Dow Jones's News/Retrieval is a popular on-line service that provides stock quotes, extensive financial data, and same-day access to the *Wall Street Journal* and *Barron's* articles. In addition to databases and analysis software, some of the major on-line services—America Online, CompuServe, and Prodigy—have on-line trading facilities that allow subscribers to execute orders through a discount broker.

An obvious advantage of electronic and on-line services is convenience—having data at one's fingertips. Another advantage is currency: Investment analysis requires considerable amounts of economic and financial information, and the more current it is, the better. However, as is true of investment information from any source, one needs to be aware of the potential for high-tech fraud, as the *Investor Insights* box on page 99 explains.

Most electronic and on-line investment information services have a basic monthly charge that may cover a specified number of hours' usage beyond which additional hourly charges are levied. Charges also sometimes vary

INVESTOR INSIGHTS: *Market Innovations*

On-Line Investing Advice: Good Tips or Cyberscam?

Thanks to new technology, millions of small investors can now offer tips on their favorite stocks or look for investment ideas by logging on to their computers. The three leading commercial on-line services (America Online, CompuServe, and Prodigy) as well as the Internet feature "investor bulletin boards," providing popular open forums organized by such topics as equities, bonds, annuities, and mutual funds. Investors can ask questions, offer advice, or simply read what others have written.

Unfortunately, these bulletin boards have also empowered a growing number of hustlers and con artists, according to securities regulators in the United States and Canada. A popular scam is the price manipulation of small, thinly traded stocks called "penny stocks" that usually aren't listed on major exchanges. The perpetrator claims to have "inside information" on a hot prospect or signs on with different names to create the appearance of a run on the stock. If even a tiny fraction of a bulletin board's users responds to the tip, the price of the stock zooms skyward and the schemer makes a quick buck by selling out. Other examples of misconduct include illegal promotions by phony or unlicensed brokers, pyramid schemes—electronic chain letters offering the chance to "get rich quick" in exchange for a small amount of money—and the promotion of dubious investments in diamond and gold mines and wireless cable.

In the past, these con artists had to peddle their scams by word of mouth or by "cold calling" strangers from telephone "boiler rooms," makeshift operations set up to be moved quickly if regulators became suspicious. Now, with the push of a few computer keys, they can tout their schemes anonymously and reach millions of people at once. They also know that, in all probability, they won't be caught. With the sheer volume of messages posted on computer bulletin boards each day, regulators can do little more than scan for obscenity and profanity.

In addition, the prosecution of on-line fraud is a tricky issue. Because the crimes occur in cyberspace, there are questions of jurisdiction, privacy, and First Amendment rights, and there is no legal precedent establishing liability. Nevertheless, the first legal actions against cyberscams were taken in July 1994, when New Jersey securities authorities filed cease-and-desist orders against the purveyors of two electronic pyramid schemes, and Missouri regulators stopped an unlicensed broker from hawking unregistered penny stocks.

Despite all these dangers, potential investors should not give up on computer bulletin boards. Instead, they can avoid falling into any traps by taking a few precautions: Don't buy stocks you haven't researched, be especially careful when perusing messages in the low-priced stock sections, and don't assume that other people using the investor bulletin board have your best interests at heart. Most importantly, take all the information you receive with a grain of salt. Remember, you're taking advice from people you don't know. After all, says Jack Rickard, editor of *Boardwatch Magazine,* a monthly devoted to on-line services, "If you see a tip, it may be from one of the top brokers in the country, or it could be from an 11-year-old kid."

Sources: Susan Brink, Anne Kates Smith, and Rita Rubin, "Information-Highway Robbery," *U.S. News & World Report,* July 11, 1994, p. 67; Earl C. Gottschalk, Jr., "Stock Hustlers Exploit On-Line Services," *Wall Street Journal,* June 21, 1994, pp. C1, C24; Justin Martin, "Investors Go Online for Talk and Tips," *Fortune,* December 12, 1994, p. 48; and Linda Stern, "On-line Fiscal Tips Can Be Out of Line," *San Diego Union-Tribune,* July 11, 1994, p. C2.

depending upon the time of day the service is accessed. Additional charges are frequently imposed for access to certain premium services that may include specified or expanded databases, analytical software, advisory services, or order execution facilities. In addition, some of the more specialized on-line services, like Dow Jones News/Retrieval, charge a one-time start-up fee. Of course, upon initiation of these services, subscribers are given a user's guide that describes the procedures for access, how to obtain help, the services available, and the associated fees. The growing use of on-line services as a source of both investment information and software is expected to accelerate as investors become more familiar and comfortable with them, as their accessibility and offerings expand, and as their costs moderate. Clearly, investment information is an important vehicle on the emerging information highway.

USING INVESTMENT ADVISERS

investment advisers
individuals or firms that provide investment advice—typically for a fee.

Although numerous sources of financial information are available, many investors have neither the time nor the expertise to analyze it and make decisions on their own. Instead, they turn to an investment adviser. **Investment advisers** are individuals or firms that provide investment advice—typically for a fee.

The Adviser's Product

The "product" provided by investment advisers ranges from broad general advice to detailed specific analyses and recommendations. The most general form of advice is a newsletter published by the adviser. These letters offer general advice on the economy, current events, market behavior, and specific securities. Investment advisers also provide complete investment evaluation, recommendation, and management services.

Regulation of Advisers

As pointed out in Chapter 2, the Investment Advisers Act of 1940 ensures that investment advisers make full disclosure of information about their backgrounds, about conflicts of interest, and so on. The act requires professional advisers to register and file periodic reports with the SEC. A 1960 amendment permits the SEC to inspect the records of investment advisers and to revoke the registration of those who violate the act's provisions. However, financial planners, stockbrokers, bankers, lawyers, and accountants who provide investment advice *in addition to their main professional activity* are not regulated by the act. Many states have also passed similar legislation, requiring investment advisers to register and to abide by the guidelines established by the state law.

Be aware that the federal and state laws regulating the activities of professional investment advisers *do not guarantee competence*. Rather, they are intended to protect the investor against fraudulent and unethical practices. It is important to recognize that, at present, *no law or regulatory body controls entrance into the field*. Therefore, investment advisers can range from highly informed professionals to totally incompetent amateurs. Advisers possessing a professional designation are usually preferred because they have completed academic courses in areas directly or peripherally related to the investment process. Such designations include CFA (Chartered Financial Analyst), CIC (Chartered Investment Counselor), CFP (Certified Financial Planner), ChFC (Chartered Financial Consultant), CLU (Chartered Life Underwriter), and CPA

(Certified Public Accountant). The *Investor's Resource Manual* that accompanies this text provides a guide to these professional certification programs.

The Cost and Use of Investment Advice

Professional investment advice typically costs between ¼ of 1 percent and 3 percent annually of the amount of money being managed. For large portfolios, the fee is typically in the range of ¼ to ¾ percent. For small portfolios (less than $100,000), an annual fee ranging from 2 to 3 percent of the amount of funds managed would not be unusual. These fees generally cover complete management of a client's money, excluding any purchase or sale commissions. The cost of periodic investment advice not provided as part of a subscription service could be based on a fixed-fee schedule or quoted as an hourly charge for consultation.

Like most services, some investment advisory services are better than others. More expensive services do not necessarily provide better advice. It is best to study carefully the track record and overall reputation of an investment adviser prior to purchasing his or her services. Not only should the adviser have a good performance record, but also he or she should be responsive to the investor's personal goals.

INVESTMENT CLUBS

investment club
a legal partnership through
which a group of investors are
bound to an organizational
structure, operating procedures,
and purpose, which is typically
to earn favorable long-term
returns from moderate-risk
investments.

Another way to obtain investment advice—and experience—is to join an investment club. This route can be especially useful for those of moderate means who do not want to incur the cost of an investment adviser. An **investment club** is a legal partnership binding a group of investors (partners) to a specified organizational structure, operating procedures, and purpose. The goal of most clubs is to earn favorable long-run returns by making investments in vehicles of moderate risk.

Investment clubs are usually formed by a group of individuals with similar goals who wish to pool their knowledge and money to create a jointly owned and managed portfolio. Certain members are responsible for obtaining and analyzing data on a specific investment vehicle or strategy. At periodic meetings, the members present their findings and recommendations, which are discussed and further analyzed by the membership. The group decides whether the proposed vehicle or strategy should be pursued. Most clubs require members to make scheduled contributions to the club's treasury, thereby providing for periodic increases in the pool of investable funds. Although most clubs concentrate on investments in stocks and bonds, they are occasionally formed to invest in real estate, options, or futures.

Membership in an investment club provides an excellent way for the novice investor to learn the key aspects of portfolio construction and investment management, while (one hopes) earning a favorable return on funds. The National Association of Investors Corporation (NAIC) publishes a variety of useful materials and also sponsors regional and national meetings. (A free information package on how to start an investment club can be obtained by writing NAIC, P.O. Box 220, Royal Oak, MI 48068, or by calling 810–583–6242.)

CONCEPTS *in Review*

3.8   Define and differentiate between *descriptive information* and *analytical information*. How might one logically assess whether the acquisition of investment information or advice is economically justified?

3.9   What popular financial business periodicals would you use to follow the financial news? General news? Business news?

3.10   Briefly describe the following sources of company information and indicate the types of information they provide:
   a. Stockholders' report
   b. Comparative data sources
   c. *Standard & Poor's Stock Reports*
   d. *Moody's Handbook of Common Stocks*

3.11   List and briefly describe the subscription services and types of information available from:
   a. Standard & Poor's Corporation
   b. Moody's Investor Services
   c. *Value Line Investment Survey*

3.12   Briefly describe the content and source of each of the following types of information:
   a. Prospectuses
   b. Back-office research reports
   c. Investment letters
   d. Price quotations

3.13   What role does electronic and on-line investment information play in the use of personal computers by many professional and individual investors? Briefly describe the types of such information currently available.

3.14   What are professional *investment advisers*? Describe the services they perform, how they are regulated, and the cost of investment advice.

3.15   What is an *investment club*? What benefits does it offer the small investor?

MARKET AVERAGES AND INDEXES

The investment information just discussed helps investors understand when the economy is moving up or down and how individual investments have performed. Additionally, this and other information can be used to formulate expectations about future investment performance. It is also important to know whether market behavior is favorable or unfavorable. The ability to interpret various market measures should help an investor to select and time investment actions.

A widely used way of assessing the behavior of securities markets is to study the performance of market averages and indexes. These measures allow investors conveniently to (1) gauge general market conditions, (2) compare their portfolio's performance to that of a large diversified (market) portfolio, and (3) study market cycles, trends, and behaviors in order to forecast future market behavior. Here we discuss key measures of stock and bond market activity and the small investor's portfolio; in later chapters we discuss averages and indexes associated with other forms of investments.

STOCK MARKET AVERAGES AND INDEXES

averages
numbers used to measure the general behavior of stock prices by reflecting the arithmetic average price behavior of a representative group of stocks at a given point in time.

indexes
numbers used to measure the general behavior of stock prices by measuring the current price behavior of a representative group of stocks in relation to a base value set at an earlier point in time.

Stock market averages and indexes are used to measure the general behavior of stock prices over time. Although the terms "average" and "index" tend to be used interchangeably when discussing market behavior, technically they are different types of measures. **Averages** reflect the arithmetic average price behavior of a representative group of stocks at a given point in time. **Indexes** measure the current price behavior of a representative group of stocks in relation to a base value set at an earlier point in time.

Averages and indexes provide a convenient method of capturing the general mood of the market. They also can be compared at different points in time to assess the relative strength or weakness of the market. Current and recent values of the key averages and indexes are quoted daily in the financial news; most local newspapers and many radio and television news programs also quote their prevailing values. Figure 3.4, published daily in the *Wall Street*

STOCK MARKET DATA BANK   12/7/94

MAJOR INDEXES

HIGH	LOW (†365 DAY)		CLOSE	NET CHG	% CHG	†365 DAY CHG	% CHG	FROM 12/31	% CHG
DOW JONES AVERAGES									
3978.36	3593.35	30 Industrials	3735.52 −	10.43 −	0.28	+ 0.99 +	0.03	− 18.57 −	0.49
1862.29	1415.67	20 Transportation	1415.67 −	14.91 −	1.04	− 351.79 −	19.90	− 346.65 −	19.67
231.48	173.94	15 Utilities	180.46 −	0.27 −	0.15	− 45.68 −	20.20	− 48.84 −	21.30
1447.06	1232.11	65 Composite	1244.48 −	6.19 −	0.49	− 131.38 −	9.55	− 136.55 −	9.89
456.27	416.31	Equity Mkt. Index	425.56 −	1.84 −	0.43	− 15.82 −	3.58	− 16.63 −	3.76
NEW YORK STOCK EXCHANGE									
267.71	243.14	Composite	246.85 −	1.00 −	0.40	− 11.12 −	4.31	− 12.23 −	4.72
327.93	298.30	Industrials	311.12 −	1.19 −	0.38	− 2.21 −	0.71	− 4.14 −	1.31
233.17	197.30	Utilities	199.46 −	0.34 −	0.17	− 29.96 −	13.06	− 30.46 −	13.25
285.03	219.95	Transportation	219.95 −	2.05 −	0.92	− 47.17 −	17.66	− 50.53 −	18.68
224.90	190.17	Finance	194.37 −	1.25 −	0.64	− 23.14 −	10.64	− 22.45 −	10.35
STANDARD & POOR'S INDEXES									
482.00	438.92	500 Index	451.23 −	1.88 −	0.41	− 15.06 −	3.23	− 15.22 −	3.26
562.99	510.05	Industrials	535.72 −	2.16 −	0.40	− 3.10 −	0.58	− 4.47 −	0.83
453.63	343.66	Transportation	344.65 −	3.46 −	0.99	− 79.00 −	18.65	− 80.95 −	19.02
176.81	147.85	Utilities	150.03 −	0.19 −	0.13	− 23.54 −	13.56	− 22.55 −	13.07
46.94	39.87	Financials	41.23 −	0.28 −	0.67	− 3.43 −	7.68	− 3.04 −	6.87
184.79	162.44	400 MidCap	165.51 −	0.95 −	0.57	− 9.74 −	5.56	− 13.87 −	7.73
NASDAQ									
803.93	693.79	Composite	734.27 −	6.96 −	0.94	− 33.62 −	4.38	− 42.53 −	5.48
851.80	703.27	Industrials	736.26 −	8.06 −	1.08	− 61.15 −	7.67	− 69.58 −	8.63
949.10	858.96	Insurance	886.69 −	8.74 −	0.98	− 19.25 −	2.12	− 33.90 −	3.68
787.92	662.57	Banks	685.99 −	4.75 −	0.69	+ 1.58 +	0.23	− 3.44 −	0.50
356.61	307.55	Nat. Mkt. Comp.	326.86 −	3.14 −	0.95	− 12.54 −	3.69	− 16.75 −	4.87
342.72	282.87	Nat. Mkt. Indus.	298.07 −	3.32 −	1.10	− 21.06 −	6.60	− 24.69 −	7.65
OTHERS									
487.89	422.67	Amex	429.19 −	1.82 −	0.42	− 39.68 −	8.46	− 47.96 −	10.05
305.87	270.81	Value-Line(geom.)	270.81 −	1.32 −	0.49	− 20.18 −	6.93	− 24.47 −	8.29
271.08	238.96	Russell 2000	240.17 −	1.83 −	0.76	− 14.20 −	5.58	− 18.42 −	7.12
4804.31	4373.58	Wilshire 5000	4449.97 −	20.94 −	0.47	− 188.75 −	4.07	− 207.86 −	4.46

†-Based on comparable trading day in preceding year.

Figure 3.4 Major Stock Market Averages and Indexes
The "Stock Market Data Bank" summarizes the key indexes and includes statistics showing the change from the previous day, the annual change, and the year-to-date change. (Source: *Wall Street Journal*, December 8, 1994, p. C2.)

Journal, provides a summary and statistics on the major stock market averages and indexes. Let's look at the key averages and indexes.

The Dow Jones Averages

Dow Jones & Company, publisher of the *Wall Street Journal*, prepares four stock averages. The most popular is the **Dow Jones Industrial Average (DJIA)**, which is made up of 30 stocks selected for total market value and for broad public ownership. The group consists of high-quality industrial stocks whose behaviors are believed to reflect overall market activity. The box within Figure 3.5 lists the stocks currently included in the DJIA. Occasionally, a merger, bankruptcy, or extreme lack of activity causes a particular stock to be dropped from the average. In that case, a new stock is added, and the average is

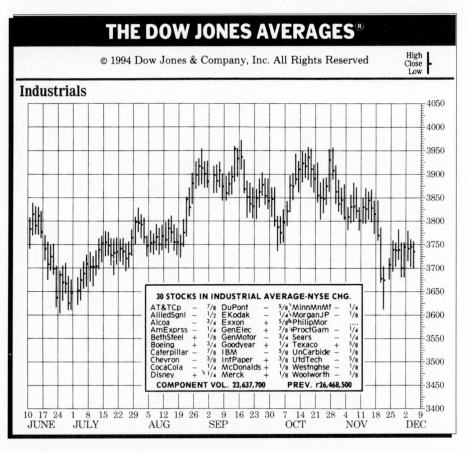

Figure 3.5　The DJIA from June 10, 1994 to December 7, 1994
From early July through early October 1994 the stock market was bullish. As measured by the DJIA, it moved from 3650 to 3950, a gain of over 8 percent, within 90 days. During the following 60 days, the market turned bearish, with the DJIA falling to about 3700, a drop of about 6 percent. (Source: *Wall Street Journal*, December 8, 1994, p. C3. Reprinted by permission of the *Wall Street Journal*. © Dow Jones & Company, Inc., 1994. All rights reserved.)

readjusted so that it continues to behave in a manner consistent with the immediate past.

The value of the DJIA is calculated each business day by substituting the *closing share prices* of each of the 30 stocks in the average into the following equation:

$$\text{Equation 3.1} \qquad \text{DJIA} = \frac{\substack{\text{closing share price} \\ \text{of stock 1}} + \substack{\text{closing share price} \\ \text{of stock 2}} + \cdots + \substack{\text{closing share price} \\ \text{of stock 30}}}{\text{DJIA divisor}}$$

The value of the DJIA is merely the sum of the closing share prices of the 30 stocks included in it, divided by a "divisor." For example, on December 7, 1994, the sum of the closing prices of the 30 industrials was 1389.61, which when divided by the divisor of 0.372 resulted in a DJIA value of 3735.52 (i.e., 1389.61 ÷ 0.372). The purpose of the divisor is to adjust for any stock splits, company changes, or other events that have occurred over time, thereby allowing the DJIA to be used to make time-series comparisons.

Because the DJIA results from summing the prices of the 30 stocks, higher-priced stocks tend to affect the index more greatly than lower-priced stocks do. For example, a 5 percent change in the price of a $50 stock (i.e., $2.50) will have less impact on the index than a 5 percent change in a $100 stock (i.e., $5.00). In spite of this and other criticisms leveled against the DJIA, it remains the most widely cited stock market indicator.

The actual value of the DJIA is meaningful only when compared to earlier values. For example, the DJIA on December 7, 1994, closed at 3735.52. This value is meaningful only when compared to the previous day's closing value of 3745.95. Many people mistakenly believe that one DJIA "point" equals $1 in the value of an average share; actually, one point currently translates into about 1.24 cents in average share value. Figure 3.5 shows the DJIA over the six-month period June 10, 1994, to December 7, 1994. Beginning in early July 1994, the DJIA increased through early October 1994 and then declined through December 7, 1994.

The three other Dow Jones averages are the transportation, the utilities, and the composite. The *Dow Jones Transportation Average* is based on 20 stocks, including railroads, airlines, freight forwarders, and mixed transportation companies. The *Dow Jones Utilities Average* is computed using 15 public utility stocks. The *Dow Jones 65 Stocks Composite Average* is made up of the 30 industrials, the 20 transportations, and the 15 utilities. Like the DJIA, each of the other Dow Jones averages is calculated to allow for continuity of the average over time. The transportation, utilities, and 65 stocks composite averages are often cited in the financial news along with the DJIA, as shown in Figure 3.4.

Standard & Poor's Indexes

Standard & Poor's indexes
true indexes that measure the current price of a group of stocks relative to a base having an index value of 10.

Standard & Poor's Corporation, another leading financial publisher, publishes six major common stock indexes. One often cited S&P index is the 500 stock composite index. Unlike the Dow Jones averages, **Standard & Poor's indexes** are true indexes. They are calculated each business day by substituting the *closing market value of each stock* (i.e., closing price × number of shares outstanding) into the following equation:

Equation 3.2

$$\text{S\&P Index} = \frac{\begin{array}{c}\text{current closing} \\ \text{market value} \\ \text{of stock 1}\end{array} + \begin{array}{c}\text{current closing} \\ \text{market value} \\ \text{of stock 2}\end{array} + \cdots + \begin{array}{c}\text{current closing} \\ \text{market value} \\ \text{of last stock}\end{array}}{\begin{array}{c}\text{base period} \\ \text{closing market} \\ \text{value of stock 1}\end{array} + \begin{array}{c}\text{base period} \\ \text{closing market} \\ \text{value of stock 2}\end{array} + \cdots + \begin{array}{c}\text{base period} \\ \text{closing market} \\ \text{value of last stock}\end{array}} \times 10$$

The value of the S&P index is found by dividing the sum of the market values of all stocks included in the index by the market value of the stocks in the base period and then multiplying the resulting quotient by 10—the base value of the S&P indexes. Most indexes are calculated in a similar fashion; the main differences lie in the stocks included in the index, the base period, and the base value of the index. For example, on December 7, 1994, the ratio of the closing market values of the S&P 500 composite stocks to the 1941–1943 base-period closing market values was 45.123, which when multiplied by the base value of the S&P index of 10 results in an index value of 451.23 (as shown in Figure 3.4).

Certain of the S&P indexes contain many more shares than the Dow averages do, and all of them are based upon *market values* rather than *share prices*. Therefore, many investors feel that the S&P indexes provide a more broad-based and representative measure of general market conditions than the Dow averages do. Although some technical computational problems exist with these indexes, they are widely used—frequently as a basis for estimating the "market return," an important concept that will be introduced in Chapter 4.

Like the Dow averages, the S&P indexes are meaningful only when compared to values in other time periods or the 1941–1943 base period value of 10. For example, the December 7, 1994, value of the S&P 500 stock composite index of 451.23 means that the market values of the stocks in the index increased by a factor of 45.12 (451.23 ÷ 10) since the 1941–1943 period. The December 7, 1994, market value of the stocks in the index was 1.03 times the lowest index value of 438.92 in the preceding 365-day period (451.23 ÷ 438.92), or an increase of 3 percent.

The six major common stock indexes published by Standard & Poor's are as follows: the *industrials index*, made up of the common stock of 400 industrial firms; the *transportation index*, which includes the stock of 20 transportation companies; the *utilities index*, made up of 40 public utility stocks; the *financials index*, which contains 40 financial stocks; the *composite index* (used above), which consists of the total of 500 stocks that make up the industrials, transportation, utilities, and financials indexes; and the *midcap index*, made up of the stocks of 400 medium-size companies—stock market values between about $225 million and $6 billion, with a median value of about $775 million. The S&P midcap index, launched in June 1991, is the newest. Its popularity results from strong investor interest in the stocks of medium-size companies. Like the Dow, the S&P indexes are frequently quoted in the financial news, as shown in Figure 3.4.

Although the Dow Jones averages and S&P indexes tend to behave in a similar fashion over time, their day-to-day magnitude and even direction (up or down) can differ from one another significantly, because the Dows are averages and the S&Ps are indexes.

NYSE, AMEX, and Nasdaq Indexes

Three indexes are based on the daily results of the New York Stock Exchange (NYSE), the American Stock Exchange (AMEX), and the National Association of Securities Dealers Automated Quotation (Nasdaq) system. Each reflects the movement of stocks listed on its exchange. The **NYSE composite index** includes all of the 2,900 or so stocks listed on the "Big Board." The base of 50 reflects the December 31, 1965, value of stocks listed on the NYSE. In addition to the composite index, the NYSE also publishes indexes for industrials, utilities, transportation, and finance subgroups. The behavior of the NYSE industrial index is normally similar to that of the DJIA and the S&P 500 indexes.

The **AMEX index** reflects the price of all shares traded on the American Stock Exchange, relative to a base of 100, set August 31, 1973. Although it does not always closely follow the S&P and NYSE indexes, the AMEX index tends to move in the general direction they do.

The **Nasdaq indexes** reflect over-the-counter market activity. They are based on a value of 100, set February 5, 1971. The most comprehensive of the Nasdaq indexes is the *OTC composite index*, which is calculated using the 5,400 or so domestic common stocks traded on the Nasdaq system. The other five commonly quoted Nasdaq indexes are the *industrials*, the *insurance*, the *banks*, the *national market composite*, and the *national market industrials*. Although their degrees of responsiveness may vary, the Nasdaq indexes tend to move in the same direction at the same time as the other major indexes.

Value Line Indexes

Value Line publishes a number of stock indexes constructed by equally weighting the price of each stock included. This is accomplished by considering only the percentage changes in stock prices. This approach eliminates the effects of differing market price and total market value on the relative importance of each stock in the index. The **Value Line composite index** includes the approximately 1,700 stocks in the *Value Line Investment Survey* that are traded on the NYSE, AMEX, and OTC market. The base of 100 reflects the June 30, 1961, stock prices. In addition to its composite index, Value Line publishes indexes for *industrials, rails,* and *utilities*.

Other Averages and Indexes

In addition to the major indexes just described, a number of others are available. The **Wilshire 5000 Index**, published by Wilshire Associates, Inc., is reported daily in the *Wall Street Journal*. It represents the total dollar value (in billions of dollars) of 5,000 actively traded stocks, including all those on the NYSE and the AMEX in addition to active OTC stocks. *Barron's* publishes a *50-Stock Average*. The *New York Times* publishes its own average, which is similar to the Dow Jones averages. Moody's Investor Services prepares market indicators for a variety of groupings of common stock. In addition, a list of stock market indexes for 20 foreign stock markets, including the widely followed Tokyo *Nikkei Average* and Morgan Stanley Capital International's *Europe/Australia/Far East (EAFE) index*, are published daily in the *Wall Street Journal's* "World Markets" column.

NYSE composite index
measure of the current price behavior of the stocks listed on the NYSE.

AMEX index
measure of the current price behavior of the stocks listed on the AMEX.

Nasdaq indexes
measures of current price behavior of securities sold OTC.

Value Line composite index
a stock index, published by Value Line, that reflects the percentage changes in share price of about 1,700 stocks traded on the NYSE, AMEX, and OTC market relative to a base of 100.

Wilshire 5000 Index
measure of the total dollar value of 5,000 actively traded stocks, including all those on the NYSE and the AMEX in addition to active OTC stocks.

BOND MARKET INDICATORS

A number of indicators are available for assessing the general behavior of the bond markets. However, there are not nearly as many indicators of overall bond market behavior as there are of stock market behavior. The key measures are bond yields, the Dow Jones bond averages, and the New York Stock Exchange bond statistics.

Bond Yields

bond yield
summary measure of the return an investor would receive on a bond if it were purchased at its current price and held to maturity; reported as an annual rate of return.

A **bond yield** is a summary measure of the return an investor would receive on a bond if it were purchased at its current price and held to maturity. They are reported as an annual rate of return. For example, a bond with a yield of 8.50 percent will provide its owner with a return in the form of periodic interest and capital gain or loss that would be equivalent to an 8.50 percent annual rate of earnings on the amount invested, if the bond were purchased at its current price and held to maturity.

Typically, bond yields are quoted for a group of bonds that are similar with respect to type and quality. For example, *Barron's* quotes the yields on the Dow Jones bond averages of 10 utilities, 10 industrials, and 20 bond composites, as well as for specified grades of corporate bonds. In addition, it quotes numerous other bond indexes and yields, including those for Treasury and municipal bonds. Similar bond yield data are also available from S&P, Moody's, and the Federal Reserve. Like stock market averages and indexes, bond yield data are especially useful when viewed over time.

Dow Jones Bond Averages

Dow Jones bond averages
mathematical averages of the closing prices for groups of utility, industrial, and composite bonds.

The **Dow Jones bond averages** include a utility, an industrial, and a composite bond average. Each average reflects the simple mathematical average of the *closing prices*, rather than yields, for each group of bonds included. The utility bond average is based on the closing prices of 10 utility bonds, the industrial bond average is based on the closing prices of 10 industrial bonds, and the composite bond average is based on the closing prices of 10 utility and 10 industrial bonds.

Like bond price quotations, the bond averages are presented in terms of the percentage of face value at which the bond sells. For example, the December 7, 1994, Dow Jones 20 bond composite average of 93.61 indicates that, on average, bonds were on the day reported selling for 93.61 percent of their face or maturity value. For a $1,000 bond, the average price of an issue would equal about $936.10. The Dow Jones bond averages are published daily in the *Wall Street Journal* and summarized weekly in *Barron's*.

NYSE Bond Statistics

The New York Stock Exchange is the dominant organized exchange on which bonds are traded. Thus, certain summary statistics on daily bond-trading activity on the NYSE provide useful insight into the behavior of the bond markets in general. These statistics include the number of issues traded; the number that advanced, declined, or remained unchanged; the number of new highs and new lows; and total sales volume in dollars. For example, on December 7, 1994, 380 domestic issues were traded; 130 advanced, 166 declined, and 84 remained unchanged. Of the issues traded, 1 achieved a new price high for the year, and 34 fell to new price lows. Total sales volume was $26,335,000. NYSE bond statistics are published daily in the *Wall Street Journal* and summarized weekly in *Barron's*.

SMALL INVESTOR'S PORTFOLIO INDEX

Small Investor Index
an index that measures gains and losses of the average investor relative to a base of 100; based on a portfolio that includes five types of investments held in proportions consistent with what the average small investor owns.

Money magazine's **Small Investor Index** measures the average investor's gains and losses in the market. The Small Investor Index is based on a portfolio that includes five types of investments held in proportions consistent with Federal Reserve data on what the average household owns. The investments and their approximate proportions on November 1, 1994, were as follows: stocks, 41 percent; bonds, 22 percent; cash, 35 percent; real estate, 1 percent; and gold, 1 percent. The index is based on a value of 100 set at the end of the immediately preceding year. It is reported monthly in *Money*'s "Wall Street Newsletter" section. On November 1, 1994, the index value of 100.55 indicated that the average investor would have gained a mere .55 percent in the first 10 months of 1994 (January 1 through October 31, 1994). Although this index is not widely used on Wall Street, it does provide the individual investor with a standard against which he or she can assess both the composition and the performance of his or her portfolio.

CONCEPTS *in Review*

3.16 Describe the basic philosophy and use of stock market averages and indexes. Explain how the behavior of an average or index can be used to classify general market conditions as bull or bear.

3.17 List each of the major averages or indexes prepared by (a) Dow Jones & Company and (b) Standard & Poor's Corporation. Indicate the number and source of the securities used in calculating each average or index.

3.18 Briefly describe the composition and general thrust of each of the following indexes:
  a. NYSE composite index
  b. AMEX index
  c. Nasdaq indexes
  d. Value Line composite index
  e. *Money's* Small Investor Index

3.19 Discuss each of the following as they relate to assessing bond market conditions:
  a. Bond yields
  b. Dow Jones bond averages
  c. NYSE bond statistics

MEETING LIQUIDITY NEEDS: INVESTING IN SHORT-TERM SECURITIES

liquidity
the ability to convert an investment into cash quickly and with little or no loss in value.

Once an investor has developed investment plans and gained a basic understanding of the types and sources of investment information, action can be taken to ensure adequate liquidity. Such a provision is an important part of an investment plan and a prerequisite to implementing its long-term provisions. **Liquidity** as used here refers to the ability to convert an investment into cash quickly and with little or no loss in value. A checking account is highly liquid. Stocks and bonds are not liquid, because there is no definite assurance of being able to sell the securities at a price equal to or greater than their purchase price.

THE ROLE OF SHORT-TERM SECURITIES

Short-term securities are an important part of most savings and investment programs. They generate income—which can be quite high during periods of high interest rates. However, their primary function is to provide a pool of reserves that can be used for emergencies or simply to accumulate funds for some specific purpose. When viewed as part of an investment portfolio, short-term securities are usually held as a *temporary*, highly liquid investment until something better comes along. Some individuals choose to hold short-term securities because they simply are more comfortable with these vehicles. In fact, this approach has had considerable merit during periods of economic (and investment) instability, such as those experienced during the 1970s and early 1980s. Regardless of the motives for holding short-term securities, investors should evaluate them in terms of their risk and return.

Determining Interest on Short-Term Securities

discount basis
a method of earning interest on a security by purchasing it at a price below its redemption value; the difference is the interest earned.

bond equivalent yield (BEY)
the annual percentage rate that would be earned by an investor in a short-term security sold at a discount were it purchased today at its current price and held to its maturity.

Short-term investments earn interest in one of two ways. First, some investments, such as savings accounts, pay a *stated rate of interest*. In this case, the interest rate is easily obtained by the investor—it's the stated rate on the account. Second, interest is earned on short-term investments on a **discount basis**. This means that the security is purchased at a price below its redemption value, and the difference is the interest earned. U.S. Treasury bills (T-bills), for example, are issued on a discount basis.

It is desirable, of course, to be able to compare a vehicle with a stated rate of interest to one sold on a discount basis. To do that, the return on a discount basis can be expressed as a **bond equivalent yield (BEY)**. The BEY is the annual percentage rate that would be earned by an investor in a short-term security sold at a discount were it purchased today at its current price and held to its maturity. The following equation gives the BEY:

Equation 3.3

$$\begin{array}{l}\text{Bond equivalent yield} \\ \text{on a discount security}\end{array} = \left(\dfrac{365}{\begin{array}{c}\text{number of days} \\ \text{to maturity}\end{array}}\right) \times \left(\dfrac{\begin{array}{c}\text{redemption} \\ \text{value}\end{array} - \begin{array}{c}\text{current} \\ \text{price}\end{array}}{\text{current price}}\right)$$

Equation 3.3a

$$BEY = \left(\frac{365}{n}\right) \times \left(\frac{R - P}{P}\right)$$

To illustrate, suppose you buy a T-bill for $9,905 that can be redeemed for $10,000 at the end of 91 days. The total interest on this security is $95 (redemption value − current price), and its bond equivalent yield (BEY) is:

$$BEY = \left(\frac{365}{91}\right) \times \left(\frac{\$10,000 - \$9,905}{\$9,905}\right)$$

$$= (4.011) \times (.0096)$$

$$= \underline{.0385, \text{ or } 3.85\%}$$

Risk Characteristics

Short-term investments are generally considered low in risk. The primary risk results from the *loss of potential purchasing power* that occurs when the rate of return on these investments falls short of the inflation rate. Unfortunately, this has often been the case with such vehicles as **passbook savings accounts.** Most other short-term investments have averaged, over long periods of time, rates of return that are about equal to, or maybe even slightly higher than, the average inflation rate.

passbook savings account
a savings account, offered by banks, that generally pays a low rate of interest and has no minimum balance.

The *risk of default*—nonpayment—is virtually nonexistent with short-term investment vehicles. The principal reason is that the primary issuers of most money market securities are highly reputable institutions, such as the U.S. Treasury, large banks, and major corporations. Furthermore, deposits in commercial banks, savings and loans, savings banks, and credit unions are insured for up to $100,000 per account by government agencies. Finally, because the value of short-term investments does not change much in response to changing interest rates, exposure to capital loss is correspondingly low. These securities have short maturities (often measured in days and never exceeding a year), and the shorter the maturity of an issue, the less volatile is its market price.

Advantages and Disadvantages of Short-Term Investments

As noted, the major advantages of short-term investments are their high liquidity and low risk. Most are available from local financial institutions and can be readily converted to cash with minimal inconvenience. Finally, because the returns on most short-term investments vary with inflation and market interest rates, investors can readily capture higher returns as rates move up. Of course, on the negative side, when interest rates go down, returns drop as well.

Although a decline in market rates has undesirable effects on most short-term vehicles, perhaps their biggest disadvantage is their relatively low return. Because these securities are generally so low in risk, you can expect the returns on short-term investments generally to average less than the returns on long-term investments.

POPULAR SHORT-TERM INVESTMENT VEHICLES

Over the past 20 years or so, there has been a proliferation of savings and short-term investment vehicles, particularly for the individual investor of modest means. Saving and investing in short-term securities is no longer the easy task it once was, when the decision for most people amounted to whether funds should be placed in a passbook savings account or in Series E savings bonds. Today, even some checking accounts pay interest on idle balances. Along with the dramatic increase in investment alternatives has come greater sophistication in short-term investment management. Short-term vehicles can be used as secure investment outlets for the long haul or as a place to hold cash until the market becomes stronger and a more permanent outlet for the funds can be found.

In the material that follows, we will first examine each of the major short-term investment deposits and vehicles; we will then briefly look at several ways in which these deposits/securities can be used in an investment portfolio. (Note that all the *deposit accounts* discussed below are issued by commercial banks, savings and loans [S&Ls], savings banks, and credit unions; often we will simply use the term *bank* to refer to any one or all of these financial institutions and not necessarily to commercial banks alone.)

Deposit Accounts

NOW (negotiated order of with-drawal) account
a bank checking account that pays interest; has no legal minimum balance, but many banks impose their own.

money market deposit accounts (MMDAs)
a bank deposit account with limited check-writing privileges; has no legal minimum balance, but many banks impose their own.

central asset account
a comprehensive deposit account that combines checking, investing, and borrowing activities; it automatically "sweeps" excess balances into short-term investments and borrows to meet shortages.

Banks offer investors several forms of deposit accounts that pay interest on account balances. Four such accounts are passbook savings accounts, **NOW (negotiated order of withdrawal) accounts, money market deposit accounts (MMDAs),** and **central asset accounts.** Some of the distinguishing features of these accounts are summarized in Table 3.4. The first two—passbook savings accounts and NOW accounts—are primarily used as savings vehicles; they provide the individual investor with a highly liquid pool of funds that can be easily accessed to meet scheduled as well as unexpected expenditures. The second two—MMDAs and central asset accounts—are more likely to be used for investment purposes, to earn a reasonably competitive short-term return while maintaining sufficient liquidity to quickly meet unexpected needs and seize attractive investment opportunities.

U.S. Treasury Bills

U.S. Treasury bills (T-bills)
obligations of the U.S. Treasury, sold on a discount basis, and having varying short-term maturities; regarded as the safest of all investments.

For many years, before recent market innovations, **U.S. Treasury bills** (T-bills) were the key short-term investment for those with sufficient funds to meet the rather high minimum investment requirement. T-bills are obligations of the U.S. Treasury issued as part of its ongoing process of funding the national debt. T-bills are sold on a discount basis in minimum denominations of $10,000, with $1,000 increments thereafter. They are issued with three-month (13-week or 91-day), six-month (26-week or 182-day), and one-year maturities. The three- and six-month bills are auctioned off every Monday (for delivery on the following Thursday), and there is an auction for one-year bills approximately every four weeks.

Purchasing T-Bills An individual investor can purchase T-bills *directly* (through participation in the weekly Treasury auctions) or *indirectly* (through local commercial banks, security dealers, or brokers who buy bills for investors on a commission basis). Outstanding Treasury bills can also be purchased in the secondary market through banks or brokers. The biggest advantage of the secondary market is that the investor has a much wider selection of maturities to choose from, ranging from less than a week to as long as a year.

Table 3.4   Distinguishing Features of Interest-Paying Deposit Accounts

Type of Account	Brief Description*	Minimum Balance	Interest Rate	Federal Insurance
Passbook savings account	Savings accounts offered by banks. Used primarily for convenience or if investors lack sufficient funds for other short-term vehicles.	Typically none	2–6% depending on economy	Yes, up to $100,000 per deposit.
NOW account (negotiated order of withdrawal)	Bank checking account that pays interest on balances.	No legal minimum, but often set at $500 to $1,000	At or near passbook rates	Yes, up to $100,000 per deposit.
Money market deposit account (MMDA)	Bank deposit account with limited check-writing privileges.	No legal minimum, but often set at about $2,500	Typically about 1% above passbook rate	Yes, up to $100,000 per deposit.
Central asset account	Deposit account at bank, brokerage house, mutual fund, or insurance company that combines checking, investing, and borrowing. Automatically "sweeps" excess balances into short-term investments and borrows to meet shortages.	Typically $5,000 to $20,000	Similar to MMDAs	Yes, up to $100,000 per deposit in banks. Varies in other institutions.

*The term *bank* refers to commercial banks, savings and loans (S&Ls), savings banks, and credit unions.

It is relatively simple to buy T-bills directly. All one need do is submit a tender offer to the nearest Federal Reserve Bank or branch, specifying both the amount and the maturity of T-bills desired. (Tender forms can be obtained by writing the Bureau of the Public Debt, Department N, Washington, DC 20239–1500, or by calling 202-874-4000.) The Treasury tries to accommodate individual investors through its noncompetitive bidding system, which most individual investors use because of its simplicity. In essence, all noncompetitive tender offers are awarded T-bills at a price equal to the average of all the accepted competitive bids. Thus, the investor is assured of buying bills in the quantity desired, while obtaining the benefits of an open auction system—all without going through the hassle of a competitive bid. Note, though, that T-bills bought directly through noncompetitive bidding are meant to be held to maturity; they should not be purchased by investors who may want to trade them. It's a difficult and time-consuming process to sell them in the aftermarket.

bank discount yield (BDY) the rate at which T-bills are quoted in the *Wall Street Journal* and other financial media; represents the annualized percentage discount (redemption value − current price) at which the T-bill can be currently purchased.

Calculating T-Bill Yields   Treasury bill rates are quoted in the *Wall Street Journal* and other major financial media at the **bank discount yield** (BDY). This is the annualized percentage discount (redemption value − current price) at which the T-bill can be currently purchased. The formula for BDY is given by Equation 3.4:

Equation 3.4

$$\text{Bank discount yield} = \left(\frac{360}{\text{number of days to maturity}} \right) \times \left(\frac{\text{redemption value} - \text{current price}}{\text{redemption value}} \right)$$

Equation 3.4a

$$BDY = \left(\frac{360}{n}\right) \times \left(\frac{R - P}{R}\right)$$

Substituting the data for the T-bill discussed earlier into Equation 3.4, we get a bank discount yield of:

$$BDY = \left(\frac{360}{91}\right) \times \left(\frac{\$10{,}000 - \$9{,}905}{\$10{,}000}\right)$$

$$= (3.956) \times (.0095)$$

$$= .0376, \text{ or } 3.76\%$$

Equation 3.5 can be used to convert a bank discount yield (BDY) to the *bond equivalent yield (BEY)*, which (as noted earlier) is the annual percentage rate earned by purchasing the T-bill today at its current price and holding it to maturity:

Equation 3.5

$$\text{Bond equivalent yield} = \frac{365 \times \text{bank discount yield}}{360 - \left(\text{bank discount yield} \times \text{number of days to maturity}\right)}$$

Equation 3.5a

$$BEY = \frac{365 \times BDY}{360 - (BDY \times n)}$$

Substituting the T-bill data into Equation 3.5, we get a bond equivalent yield of:

$$BEY = \frac{365 \times .0376}{360 - (.0376 \times 91)}$$

$$= \frac{13.72}{356.58}$$

$$= .0385, \text{ or } 3.85\%$$

Note that the 3.85 percent BEY is the same value calculated for the T-bill in Equation 3.3, which calculated BEY using the bond's price data rather than its bank discount yield (BDY). In this case, the T-bill, which is quoted at an annualized bank discount yield (BDY) of 3.76 percent, will provide the investor with a bond equivalent yield (BEY), or annual percentage rate of 3.85 percent.

Evaluating T-bills   A particularly attractive feature of T-bills is that they are *exempt from state and local income taxes*, which in some areas can be as high as 20 percent. Federal taxes are not due until the interest is actually received at maturity (the same is true for CDs and commercial paper). Because they are issued by the U.S. Treasury, T-bills are regarded as the safest, but generally lowest yielding, of all investments. Furthermore, there is a highly active secondary market for Treasury bills (other than those bought through noncompetitive bidding), so they can easily be sold if the investor needs the cash.

certificates of deposit (CDs)
savings instruments in which funds must remain on deposit for a specified period; withdrawals prior to maturity incur interest penalties.

Certificates of Deposit

Certificates of deposit (CDs) differ from the deposit accounts discussed earlier in that funds must remain on deposit for a specified period, which can range from 7 days to a year or more. Although it is possible to withdraw funds prior to maturity, an interest penalty (equal to 31 to 90 days of interest, depending on the original maturity of the CD) usually makes withdrawal costly. Banks today are free to offer any rate and maturity on these securities. The interest rate on them is fixed over their stated maturity. A wide variety of CDs are offered by most banks and thrift institutions, and these go by an equally wide variety of names.

CDs are convenient to buy and hold, and all offer attractive and highly competitive returns plus federal insurance protection. The decision whether to invest in a CD or in a more liquid short-term investment vehicle, such as a MMDA or a T-bill, generally depends on the length of the holding period and interest rate expectations. Uncertain holding periods and expected interest rate increases would favor MMDAs and T-bills; certain holding periods and expected interest rate declines would favor CDs.

brokered CDs
certificates of deposit sold by stockbrokers; offer slightly higher yields than other CDs and typically can be sold prior to maturity without incurring a penalty.

CDs can also be purchased from stockbrokers, in the form of **brokered CDs**. The brokerage house looks around the country for the highest yield it can get, buys these CDs, and then resells them to its clients. In essence, a bank issues the CDs, and the brokerage house places them with the investing public. There's usually no commission to pay, because the broker earns its commission from the issuing bank. The minimum denomination is usually $1,000.

Brokered CDs are attractive for two reasons: First, they can be sold prior to maturity without incurring a penalty, because the brokerage firms maintain active secondary markets. Of course, there are no guarantees—the market prevails. If rates go up, the relative value of a CD falls, and its return will decline if it is sold prior to maturity. Second, brokered CDs may provide higher yields—frequently ¼ to ¾ of a percent higher—than those available from a local bank. But because a broker can always get higher yields by selling CDs issued by troubled financial institutions, it is best to buy *only those brokered CDs that are issued by a federally insured institution.*

Commercial Paper

commercial paper
short-term, unsecured promissory notes (IOUs) issued by corporations with very high credit standings.

Commercial paper is short-term, unsecured promissory notes (IOUs) issued by corporations with very high credit standings. These notes are typically sold by firms in need of short-term loans. Although sometimes issued in denominations as small as $25,000 or $50,000, most commercial paper is initially sold in multiples of $100,000. Typical maturities range from a few days up to 270 days, the maximum maturity that does not require registration with the Securities and Exchange Commission (SEC). Because the secondary market for commercial paper is limited, most investors hold commercial paper to maturity. Commercial paper is rated as to its quality by independent agencies. Its yield is comparable to the rate of return earned on large-denomination CDs. A popular strategy is to buy high-rated paper with a maturity closely matched to the desired investment horizon.

Typically, only larger institutions deal directly in commercial paper, due to its large denominations. Individual investors who obtain commercial paper mostly do so from a bank or broker, who will "break down" the paper and sell the investor a small portion. However, individual investors can generally earn returns competitive with commercial paper by purchasing CDs, which, like commercial paper, have a fixed maturity but in addition have federal insurance protection.

Banker's Acceptances

Banker's acceptances arise from short-term credit arrangements used by business firms to finance transactions, most often involving firms in foreign countries or firms with unknown credit capacities. Typically, an importer's bank agrees to pay its foreign supplier on behalf of the importer, who is contractually obligated to repay the bank within the three to six months it takes to receive and sell the merchandise involved in the transaction. The importer's bank may either hold the acceptance to maturity or sell it at a discount to obtain immediate cash. An investor who buys a banker's acceptance is therefore promised payment of its face value by the importer at the specified future date. As a result of its sale, the banker's acceptance becomes a marketable security. The initial maturities of banker's acceptances are typically between 30 and 180 days, 90 days being most common. If the importer fails to pay the amount due at maturity, the bank is liable for the payment. Because of this, banker's acceptances, which typically have a minimum denomination of $100,000, are low-risk securities with good secondary markets. The yields on banker's acceptances are generally slightly below those of CDs and commercial paper; they can usually be purchased through a bank or stockbroker.

Money Market Mutual Funds

A **money market mutual fund (MMMF)** is simply a mutual fund that pools the capital of a large number of investors and uses it to invest exclusively in high-yielding, short-term securities, such as Treasury bills, large certificates of deposit, and commercial paper. Because such securities are sold in denominations of $10,000 to $1 million (or more), most small investors cannot purchase them individually. The MMMF makes these vehicles, which very often offer the highest short-term returns, available to even small investors. Shares of MMMFs can be purchased (through brokers and investment dealers or directly from the fund) in initial amounts as small as $500 to $1,000 (although $1,000 to $5,000 is a more typical amount). MMMFs provide convenient and easy access to funds through check-writing privileges; the nice feature of this privilege is that you continue to earn interest while the check is being cleared through the banking system. Almost every major brokerage firm has a money fund of its own; another 600 or so are unaffiliated with a specific brokerage firm.

The returns on money funds amount to what fund managers are able to earn from their investment activity in various short-term securities. Thus, the returns rise and fall with money market interest rates. As Figure 3.6 shows, these are *highly volatile* rates that cause investor yields to vary accordingly. The returns on MMMFs are closely followed in the financial media. In fact, the current yields on about 650 of the largest funds are reported every Thursday in the *Wall Street Journal*, and the yields on other large funds are reported regularly in most major newspapers (see Figure 3.7 on page 118). Note in this case that not only are yields reported, but so are average maturities and total assets.

We will describe mutual funds more fully in Chapter 11; however, several characteristics of money funds should be noted here. One concern of many investors is safety. Though they are not federally insured, MMMFs have been virtually free of even the threat of failure for as long as they have existed.

Figure 3.6 The Behavior of Short-Term Market Rates over Time
The yields on marketable short-term securities (such as Treasury bills) are highly unstable. They therefore have a dramatic effect on returns to investors in money funds and other short-term vehicles (like MMDAs).

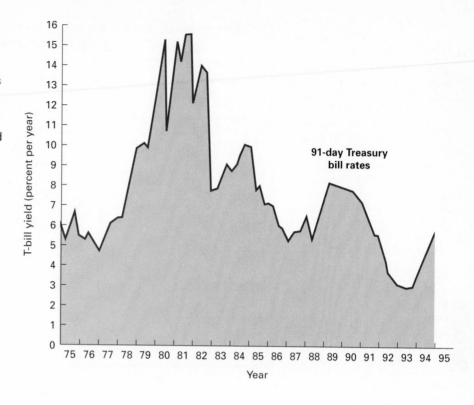

Default risk is almost zero, because the securities the funds purchase are very low in risk to begin with and diversification by the funds lowers risk even more. Despite this remarkable safety record, it is impossible to say with certainty that MMMFs are as risk-free as federally insured deposits. In the event of a massive financial crisis, they probably are not. On the other hand, the amount of extra risk might be viewed as so minimal as to be easily offset by a slightly higher yield. This is a choice the individual investor must make within his or her own risk-return framework.

government securities money funds
money market mutual funds that confine their investments to Treasury bills and other short-term securities of the U.S. government and its agencies.

Government securities money funds were established as a way to meet investor concerns for safety. These funds effectively eliminate any risk of default by confining their investments to Treasury bills and other short-term securities of the U.S. government and its agencies. They are like standard MMMFs in all other respects except for slightly lower yields (which is the price you pay for the higher quality).

In addition to standard money market mutual funds and government securities money funds, there are over 350 tax-exempt money funds. The **tax-exempt money fund** limits its investments to tax-exempt municipal securities with very short (30 to 90 days) maturities. Except for this feature, they are like the standard money market funds. Because their income is free from federal (and some state) income tax, they yield less than standard, fully taxable money funds do. They appeal predominantly to investors in the higher tax brackets for whom the lower tax-free yield is better than the after-tax return they could earn on standard money funds. The current yields on most major tax-exempt money funds are separately reported every Thursday in the *Wall Street Journal* and in other major newspapers.

tax-exempt money fund
a money market mutual fund that limits its investments to tax-exempt municipal securities with very short (30 to 90 days) maturities.

Figure 3.7 Published Yield Information on Major Money Market Mutual Funds

Data on money funds are widely quoted in the financial press. Here we see that the information includes the portfolios' average maturity (in days), the seven-day average of the annualized yield currently available, and the total assets in the portfolio measured in million of dollars. (Source: *Wall Street Journal*, December 8, 1994, p. C11. Reprinted by permission of the *Wall Street Journal*. © Dow Jones & Company, Inc., 1994. All rights reserved.)

MONEY MARKET MUTUAL FUNDS

The following quotations, collected by the National Association of Securities Dealers Inc., represent the average of annualized yields and dollar-weighted portfolio maturities ending Wednesday, December 7, 1994. Yields don't include capital gains or losses.

Fund	Avg. Mat.	7Day Yld.	Assets	Fund	Avg. Mat.	7Day Yld.	Assets
QityCsh	50	4.57	102	FidInTxEx	45	3.49	2235
QuestCshGov	39	4.53	112	FidCA	34	3.02	690
QuestCshPr	44	4.67	1468	FidCT	66	3.01	303
RNC Liq	56	4.76	34	FidDlyTE	50	3.10	471
RegisDSI	17	4.76	114	FidMA	36	2.85	709
RemTaxTr	38	5.15	465	FidMI	47	3.05	212
RemTreasTr	38	4.67	112	FidNJ	63	3.05	402
RemGovtTr	36	5.02	169	FidNY	51	2.99	703
RenaisGvt	44	4.69	50	FidOH	51	3.07	296
RenaisMM	31	4.85	356	FidSpCA	34	3.35	1248
ResrveFd Gvt	26	4.63	745	FidSpCT	66	3.09	168
ReserveFd	36	4.64	1436	FidSpNJ	64	3.33	408
RetirGv	20	4.68	245	FidSpNY	50	3.13	549
RimcoTrs	65	4.56	86	FidSpPA	56	3.27	231
RIMCOPrm	60	5.04	346	FidTxEx	45	3.19	3651
RiverUSGv	43	4.78	136	FidSpFL	25	3.14	347
RiversdeCap	54	4.38	166	FidSpMA	36	3.02	381
RdSaMM	29	5.07	707	FidSpMu	45	3.36	2322
RdSqUS	30	5.11	379	FtInvTax	53	2.89	27
RydexUSGv	3	4.41	175	FtPraMu	39	2.91	198
SBSF MM	81	4.66	27	FLMuniCash	34	3.42	134
SEICshTrea	12	5.12	37	FrkCal	32	2.76	708
SEI CsPrB	31	5.24	23	FrkNYTE	21	2.60	65
SEI CshGvII	23	5.34	743	FrkTx c	30	2.66	201
SEI CsMM	34	5.44	223	Free CA	50	2.94	76
SEI CsPr	31	5.54	2045	FreeTE	47	2.86	274
SEI DlvInGvC	48	5.07	260	FtBostInTE	29	3.44	82
SEI LaGv	19	5.23	268	FirstUnTFI	49	3.29	462
SEI LaPr	36	5.36	943	FirstUnTFT	49	3.59	57
SEI LaTr	25	4.90	1259	FundmentTF	53	.91	9
SEI CsTrIIA	56	5.10	348	GalaxyTE Tr	52	2.82	178
SEI CsTrIIB	56	4.80	16	GalaxyTE R	52	2.72	108
SITMMkt	32	5.08	24	GnTxEx	69	2.98	296
STIPrQuTr	44	4.77	635	GnCalMu	58	2.88	593
STIUSGvtr	43	4.66	285	GnNYMu	68	2.77	689
STIUSGvIv	43	4.46	36	GinmdTECsh	39	3.16	227
Safeco f	30	4.53	181	GSITNY	26	3.00	113
SalomonUST	51	4.68	24	GSITCA c	33	3.09	293
SchbValAdv	50	5.24	3633	GSITDv c	41	3.39	1657

Fund	Avg. Mat.	7Day Yld.	Assets	Fund	Avg. Mat.	7Day Yld.	Assets
AALMny	40	4.23	67	HTInsgtGv	28	5.05	250
AARP HQ	25	4.78	367	HanvCsh	55	4.99	1182
AIM MM C	14	4.69	388	HanvGov	36	5.10	1183
AIM MMA	14	4.71	160	HanvUSTr	22	4.74	1324
AVESTA Tr	52	5.05	53	HanvTreas	22	4.66	1074
AccUSGov	72	4.52	12	Harbor	24	4.99	68
ActAsGv	46	4.64	516	HrtgCsh	27	4.89	1034
ActAsMny	62	5.04	4919	HiMrkUSFid	42	4.65	158
AetnaAdvs	36	5.38	54	HiMrkTrsFid	55	4.46	241
Aetna Sel	36	5.38	168	HiMrkDvFid	48	4.78	381
AlexBwn	50	4.92	1380	HilrdGovt	40	4.51	232
AlxBTr	45	4.48	537	HmestdDlv	38	4.68	35
AlgerMM	61	5.46	172	HorznPr	13	5.32	2621
AlliaCpRs	43	4.44	2398	HorznTr	37	5.05	1975
AliaGvR	37	4.48	2097	Hummer	38	4.70	150
AlliMny	36	4.40	1854	IAATrMM	30	4.89	37
AmAAdTrl	1	5.25	96	IAIMnyMktFd	17	5.10	31
AmAAdMMI	39	5.37	1339	IDS CshM	34	4.82	1323
AmCRes	38	4.89	510	IMGLiq	44	4.71	157
AmPerCsh	47	5.00	217	IndCaGv	47	4.69	254
AmPerTrs	11	4.63	161	IndCaMM	35	4.69	334
AmSouth Pr	43	4.88	496	IndOnPr	23	4.81	281
AmSouth US	44	4.81	304	IndOnUS	26	4.77	279
AmbMMF	33	4.99	337	InfnAIGv	28	4.59	50
AmbTreas F	48	4.67	230	InfnCCR Inst	33	5.11	37
AmbTreasl	48	4.52	88	InfCCR	33	4.56	480
AmbMMI	33	4.84	503	InsfCsh	19	5.12	268
Amcore Gv	11	4.82	104	InstFd	4	3.73	12
AmAAdMMM	39	5.02	62	InstGov	25	5.36	103
ArchUSTr	24	4.29	2	InstDailyInc	34	5.46	59
ArchFd	30	4.68	49	InvCshTrGv	30	5.44	138

Series EE Savings Bonds

Series EE savings bonds
savings bonds issued by the U.S. Treasury and sold at banks and through payroll deduction plans, in varying denominations, at 50% of face value; pay a variable rate of interest tied to U.S. Treasury securities and calculated every six months in May and November.

accrual-type securities
securities for which interest is paid when the bond is cashed, on or before maturity, rather than periodically over the life of the bond.

Series EE savings bonds are the well-known savings bonds that have been available for decades. (First issued in 1941, they used to be called Series E bonds.) EE bonds are often purchased through payroll deduction plans. Although issued by the U.S. Treasury, they are quite different from T-bills. In fact, perhaps their only similarity to the latter is that they are sold on a discount basis and are also exempt from state and local income taxes.

Series EE bonds are **accrual-type securities**, which means that interest is paid when the bond is cashed, on or before maturity, rather than periodically over the life of the bond. (The government does issue bonds that pay interest semiannually: One such form is Series HH bonds, which are issued at their full face value and pay semiannual interest at the current fixed rate of 4 percent. Series HH bonds can be obtained only through the exchange of Series E or Series EE bonds, have an initial 10-year maturity and can be extended for an additional 10 years, and are available in denominations of $500 to $10,000.) The purchase price of all denominations is 50 percent of the face amount. Thus, a $100 bond will cost $50 and be worth $100 at maturity. Series EE bonds are backed by the full faith and credit of the U.S. government and can be replaced without charge in case of loss, theft, or destruction. They can be purchased at banks or other thrift institutions, or through payroll deduction plans. They are issued in denominations of $50 through $10,000. A person is limited to maximum annual Series EE bond purchases of $15,000 (i.e., $30,000 face value).

The actual maturity date on EE bonds is unspecified because they pay a variable rate of interest. The higher the rate of interest being paid, the shorter the period of time it takes for the bond to accrue from its discounted purchase price to its maturity value. As of May 1, 1995, there are new rules for savings bonds. All EE bonds held six months to five years—bonds can be redeemed any time after the first six months—earn interest at 85 percent of the average yield on six-month Treasury bills. After five years, the rate of interest is 85 percent of the average yield on five-year Treasury notes. Interest rates are calculated every six months in May and November and change in accordance with prevailing Treasury security yields. Current rates on Series EE bonds can be obtained from your bank or simply by calling 800-487-2663. (Note: For bonds purchased after May 1, 1995, the rates for the six-month period ending October 31, 1995 were as follows: bonds held less than five years, 5.25 percent; bonds held five through 17 years, 6.31 percent. The long-term rate is quoted for reference only, because no bonds currently fall into this category.) Interest is credited every six months.

In addition to being exempt from state and local taxes, Series EE bonds provide an appealing tax twist: *Investors need not report the interest earned on their federal tax returns until the bonds are redeemed.* Although interest can be reported annually (this might be done, e.g., if the bonds are held in the name of a child who has limited interest income), most investors choose to defer it. In effect, this means the funds are being reinvested at an after-tax rate equal to the bond's current rate. Another attractive tax feature allows partial or complete tax avoidance of EE bond earnings when proceeds are used to pay education expenses, such as college tuition, for the bond purchaser, a spouse, or other IRS-defined dependent. To qualify the purchaser must be age 24 or older and as of 1994, have adjusted gross income below $56,200 for single filers and $91,850 for married couples. (The maximum income levels are adjusted annually.)

What's more, it is even possible to defer the tax shelter *beyond* the redemption date of your Series EE bond. You can extend your tax shelter if, instead of cashing in the bonds, you exchange them for Series HH bonds. The accumulated interest on the Series EE bonds remains free of federal income tax for a while longer, because you will not have to pay the tax on those interest earnings until the HH bonds reach maturity (up to 20 years) or until you cash *them* in. Thus, in contrast to their predecessors, today's Series EE bonds not only represent a safe and secure form of investment but also provide highly competitive yields and offer attractive tax incentives.

INVESTMENT SUITABILITY

The deposit accounts and short-term securities discussed above are widely used by individuals as both savings and investment vehicles. They are used to build up or maintain a desired level of savings to meet scheduled as well as unexpected expenditures. Whatever the reason, savings are viewed chiefly as a means of accumulating funds that will be readily available when and if the need arises—in essence, to provide safety and security. In this case, high yield is less important than safety, liquidity, and convenience. Passbook savings accounts, NOW accounts, and Series EE savings bonds are popular savings vehicles. To a lesser extent, so are money market deposit accounts, central asset accounts, T-bills, CDs, commercial paper, banker's acceptances, and money market mutual funds.

Yield is often just as important as liquidity when these vehicles are used for *investment purposes*. However, because the objective is different, the securities tend to be used much more aggressively as investments than in savings programs. Most investors will hold at least a part of their portfolio in short-term, highly liquid securities, if for no other reason than to be able to act on unanticipated investment opportunities. Some investors, in fact, may as a matter of practice devote all or most of their portfolios to such securities. They do so in the belief that these investments provide attractive rates of return for the risk, because they are unfamiliar with other investment vehicles, or simply because they do not wish to devote the time necessary to managing their portfolios.

One of the most common uses of short-term securities as investment vehicles is as temporary outlets. This is done for two reasons: either to warehouse funds until an attractive permanent investment can be found or to sit on the sidelines in times of unsettled or undesirable market conditions. For example, an investor who has just sold some stock but does not have a suitable long-term investment alternative might place the proceeds in a money fund until he finds a more permanent use for them. Or an investor who feels that interest rates are about to rise sharply might sell her long-term bonds and use the proceeds to buy T-bills. The high-yielding securities—like MMDAs, CDs, commercial paper, banker's acceptances, and money funds—are generally preferred for use as part of an investment program, as are central asset accounts at major brokerage firms.

Deciding which securities are most appropriate for a particular situation requires consideration of such issue characteristics as availability, safety, liquidity, and yield. Although all the investments we have discussed satisfy the basic liquidity demand, they do so to varying degrees. A NOW account is unquestionably the most liquid of all, because you can write as many checks as you wish and for any amount. A certificate of deposit, on the other hand, is not as liquid, because early redemption involves an interest penalty. Table 3.5 summarizes the key characteristics for most of the short-term investments

Table 3.5   A Scorecard for Short-Term Accounts and Securities

Savings or Investment Vehicle	Availability	Safety	Liquidity	Yield (Average Rate)*
Passbook savings account	A+	A+	A	C− (2.0%)
NOW account	A−	A+	A+	F (1.0%)
Money market deposit account (MMDA)	B	A+	A	B− (2.3%)
Central asset account	B−	A	A+	C− (2.3%)
U.S. Treasury bill (91-day)	B−	A++	A−	A− (5.7%)
Certificate of deposit (3-month, large denomination)	B	A+	C	A (5.4%)
Commercial paper (90-day)	B−	A−	C	A (6.2%)
Banker's acceptance (90-day)	B−	A	B	A− (6.1%)
Money market mutual fund (MMMF); standard and government security funds	B	A/A+	B+	B (4.6%)
Series EE savings bond	A+	A++	C−	B+ (5.9%)

*The average rates reflect representative or typical rates that existed in late 1994.

discussed here. The letter grade assigned the investments for each characteristic reflects an estimate of the investment's quality in that area. For example, MMMFs received only a B+ on liquidity, because withdrawals usually require a minimum of $500. NOW accounts, on the other hand, are judged somewhat better in this respect, because a withdrawal can be for any amount. Yields are self-explanatory, although you should note that if an investment scores lower on availability, safety, or liquidity, it will generally offer a higher yield.

CONCEPTS in Review

3.20   What makes an asset liquid? Why hold liquid assets? Would 100 shares of IBM stock be considered a liquid investment? Explain.

3.21   Explain the characteristics of short-term investments with respect to both purchasing power and default risk.

3.22   Briefly describe the key features and differences among the following deposit accounts:
   a. Passbook savings account
   b. NOW account
   c. Money market deposit account
   d. Central asset account

3.23   Define, compare, and contrast the following short-term investments:
   a. U.S. Treasury bills
   b. Certificates of deposit
   c. Commercial paper
   d. Banker's acceptances
   e. Money market mutual funds
   f. Series EE savings bonds

On Track with STOCK-TRAK®

STOCK-TRAK® Information Requirements

STOCK-TRAK® is a portfolio valuation service and therefore does not assist "investors" in developing investment programs. Two comparison benchmarks are provided, however: (1) Weekly class rankings include an "Interest Only" account that shows the rate of return available from money market accounts, and (2) biweekly portfolio statements report the return on the Standard & Poor's 500 Stock Composite Index over the relevant simulation period.

   When making transactions, users must locate and communicate the proper ticker symbol for the security they want to buy or sell. Stock ticker symbols can be found in the *Wall Street Journal*. Complete mutual fund names are required when making mutual fund investments; they can be found in electronic databases, such as the Dow Jones News/Retrieval. Information about the bonds that can be purchased, as listed in the STOCK-TRAK® registration materials, can be found in Standard & Poor's *Bond Guides*.

SUMMARY

LG 1 Describe common investment goals, the importance of meeting life insurance needs, and fundamental personal tax considerations. Investment goals determine the types of investments made. Common investment goals include (1) accumulating retirement funds, (2) enhancing current income, (3) saving for major expenditures, and (4) sheltering income from taxes.

Provision for adequate life insurance is an important prerequisite to investment planning. Life insurance may be bought in any of four basic forms: term, whole life, universal life, and variable life insurance. Life insurance needs can be estimated using the multiple earnings approach and the needs approach.

The tax consequences associated with various investment vehicles and strategies must also be considered. The key dimensions are ordinary income, capital gains and losses, and tax shelters and tax planning.

LG 2 Discuss the development of an investment program, investing over the life cycle, and investing in different economic environments. Investment plans should consider any known employer pension benefits as well as available funds, to determine the level of annual investment required to meet each goal. Diversification is the overriding consideration. Investors tend to begin aggressively and become more conservative as they approach retirement. The actual investment vehicles selected will be affected by both the investor's stage in the life cycle and economic/market cycles.

LG 3 Identify the types and sources of investment information. Investment information, descriptive or analytical, can be classified as economic and current event, industry and company, alternative investment vehicles, price information, and personal investment strategies. It can be obtained from financial journals, newspapers, institutional news, business periodicals, government publications, special subscription services, stockholders' reports, comparative data sources, brokerage reports, investment letters, price quotations, and electronic and on-line sources.

LG 4 Evaluate electronic and on-line investment information, the use of investment advisers, and the role of investment clubs. On-line data services and databases provide PC-based access to both current and historical investment information. There are a variety of different types of investment advisers, who charge an annual fee ranging from .25 percent to 3 percent of the amount being managed and are often regulated by federal and state law. Investment clubs are used by individual investors to obtain investment advice and experience.

LG 5 Explain the characteristics, interpretation, and uses of the commonly cited market averages and indexes. Investors commonly rely on stock market averages and indexes to stay abreast of market behavior. The most cited averages are the Dow Jones, which includes the Dow Jones Industrial Average (DJIA). Other popular averages and indexes are Standard & Poor's, the NYSE composite index, the AMEX index, the Nasdaq indexes, and the Value Line indexes.

Bond market indicators are most often reported in terms of average bond yields and average prices. The Dow Jones bond averages are among the most popular. Both stock and bond market statistics are published daily in the *Wall Street Journal* and summarized weekly in *Barron's*. *Money* magazine's Small Investor Index provides the individual investor with a standard that can be used to assess his or her portfolio.

LG 6 Understand the role, types, and key features of the popular short-term investment vehicles available for meeting liquidity needs. Investment goals and plans should provide adequate liquidity, which can be met by holding a variety of short-term securities.

These securities can earn interest at a stated rate or on a discount basis. They carry a low risk; the primary risk results from a potential loss in purchasing power. Numerous short-term investment vehicles are available from banks, brokerage firms, and the government. Their suitability depends on the investor's attitude toward availability, safety, liquidity, and yield.

DISCUSSION QUESTIONS

1. Assume that you are 35 years old, are married with two young children, are renting a condo, and have an annual income of $50,000. Use the following questions to guide your preparation of a rough investment plan consistent with these facts.
    a. What are your key investment goals?
    b. How much life insurance do you need to protect your family? What type of insurance would you buy?
    c. How might personal taxes affect your investment plans? Use current tax rates to assess their impact.
    d. How might your stage in the life cycle affect the types of risk you might take?
    e. What impact might the current economic environment have on the investment vehicles you might choose?
    f. Can you realistically expect to achieve the goals you specified in (a)?

2. During 1994, the common stock of a successful snowboard manufacturer—Ride Inc.—was initially sold. Gather appropriate information from relevant sources to assess the following with an eye toward investing in Ride.
    a. Economic conditions and the key current events during the immediate past 12 months
    b. Information on the status and growth—past and future—of the snowboarding industry and specific information on Ride and its major competitors
    c. Brokerage reports and analysts' recommendations with respect to Ride
    d. A history of past and recent dividends and price behavior of Ride, which is traded on the Nasdaq National Market
    e. A recommendation with regard to the advisability of investing in Ride

3. Survey the market and isolate the most popular on-line services that offer investment information. For each of these services compile a list of the types of investment information, decision models, advisory services, and order execution services it provides. Also catalog the costs, if any, of obtaining these services. Then compare the services on a benefit-cost basis, and choose and justify the on-line service you would subscribe to given your investment plans.

4. Gather and evaluate relevant market averages and indexes over the past 6 months to assess recent stock and bond market conditions. Describe the conditions in each of these markets. Using recent history, coupled with relevant economic and current event data, forecast near-term market conditions. Based on your assessment of market conditions, would you recommend investing in stocks, in bonds, or in neither at this point in time? Explain the reasoning underlying your recommendation.

5. What role, if any, will short-term investments play in your portfolio? Why? Complete the following table for the short-term investments listed. Find their yields in

a current issues of the *Wall Street Journal*, and explain which, if any, you would include in your investment portfolio.

Savings or Investment Vehicle	Minimum Balance	Yield	Federal Insurance	Method and Ease of Withdrawing Funds
a. Passbook savings account	None		Yes	In person or through teller machines; very easy
b. NOW account				Unlimited check-writing privileges
c. Money market deposit account (MMDA)				
d. Central asset account				
e. U.S. Treasury bill				
f. Certificate of deposit (CD)				
g. Commercial paper				
h. Banker's acceptance				
i. Money market mutual fund (MMMF)				
j. Series EE savings bond	Virtually none			

PROBLEMS   1. Sonia Gomez, a 45-year-old widow, wishes to accumulate $250,000 over the next 15 years to supplement her retirement programs that are being funded by her employer and the federal government. She expects to earn an average annual return of about 8 percent by investing in a low-risk portfolio containing about 20 percent short-term investments, 30 percent common stock, and 50 percent bonds.

Sonia currently has $31,500 that at an 8 percent annual rate of return will grow to about $100,000 at the end of 15 years (found using time-value techniques that will be described in Chapter 4). Her financial adviser indicated that for every $1,000 Sonia wishes to accumulate at the end of 15 years, she will have to make an annual investment of $36.83. (This amount is also calculated based upon an 8 percent annual rate of return using the time-value techniques that are described in Chapter 4.) Sonia plans to accumulate needed funds by making equal, annual, end-of-year investments over the next 15 years.

    a. How much money does Sonia need to accumulate by making equal, annual, end-of-year investments to reach her goal of $250,000?

    b. How much must Sonia deposit annually to accumulate at the end of year 15 the sum calculated in (a) above?

LG 1 LG 2   2. During 1994, the Allens and the Zells both filed joint tax returns. The Allens' taxable income was $130,000, and the Zells had total taxable income of $65,000 for the tax year ended December 31, 1994.

    a. Using the federal tax rates given in Table 3.1, calculate the taxes for both the Allens and the Zells.

    b. Calculate and compare the ratio of the Allens' to the Zells' taxable income and the ratio of the Allens' to the Zells' taxes. What does this demonstrate about the federal income tax structure?

LG 3 LG 4   3. Bill Shaffer estimates that if he does 10 hours of research using data that will cost $75, there is a good chance that he can improve his expected return on a $10,000 one-year investment from 8 percent to 10 percent. Bill feels that he must earn at least $10 per hour on the time he devotes to his research.

    a. Find the cost of Bill's research.

    b. By how much (in dollars) will Bill's return increase as a result of the research?

    c. On a strict economic basis, should Bill perform the proposed research?

4. Imagine the Mini-Dow Average (MDA) is based on the closing prices of five stocks. The divisor used in the calculation of the MDA is currently .765. The closing prices for each of the five stocks in the MDA today and exactly one year ago when the divisor was .790 are as follows:

	Closing Stock Price	
Stock	Today	One Year Ago
Ace Computers	$ 65	$74
Coburn Motor Company	37	34
National Soap & Cosmetics	110	96
Ronto Foods	73	72
Wings Aircraft	96	87

    a. Calculate the MDA both today and one year ago.

    b. Compare the values of the MDA calculated in (a) and describe the apparent market behavior over the last year. Was it a *bull* or a *bear* market?

5. The SP-6 index (a fictitious index) is used by many investors to monitor the general behavior of the stock market. It has a base value set equal to 100 on January 1, 1970. The closing market values for each of the six stocks included in the index are given below for three dates.

	Closing Market Value of Stock		
Stock	June 30, 1996 (Thousands)	January 1, 1996 (Thousands)	January 1, 1970 (Thousands)
1	$ 430	$ 460	$240
2	1,150	1,120	630
3	980	990	450
4	360	420	150
5	650	700	320
6	290	320	80

    a. Calculate the value of the SP-6 index both on January 1, 1996, and June 30, 1996, using the data presented above.

    b. Compare the values of the SP-6 index calculated in (a) and relate them to the base index value. Would you describe the general market condition during the 6-month period January 1 to June 30, 1996, as a *bull* or a *bear* market?

6. Carla Sanchez wishes to develop an average or index that can be used to measure the general behavior of stock prices over time. In this regard, she has decided to include six closely followed, high-quality stocks in the average or index. She plans to use August 15, 1975, as the base and is interested in measuring the value of the average or index on August 15, 1993, and August 15, 1996. She has found the closing prices for each of the six stocks, A through F, at each of the three dates and has calculated a divisor that can be used to adjust for any stock splits, company changes, and so on, that

| | Closing Stock Price | | |
Stock	August 15, 1996	August 15, 1993	August 15, 1975
A	$46	$40	$50
B	37	36	10
C	20	23	7
D	59	61	26
E	82	70	45
F	32	30	32
Divisor	.70	.72	1.00

Note: The number of shares of each stock outstanding has remained unchanged at each of the three dates. Therefore, the closing stock prices will behave identically to the closing market values.

have occurred since the base year, which has a divisor equal to 1.00.

    a. Using the data given above, calculate the market average, using the same methodology used to calculate the Dow averages, at each of the three dates—the fifteenth of August 1975, 1993, and 1996.

    b. Using the data given above and assuming a base index value of 10 on August 15, 1975, calculate the market index, using the same methodology used to calculate the S&P indexes, at each of the three dates.

    c. Use your findings in (a) and (b) to describe the general market condition—*bull* or *bear*—that existed between August 15, 1993, and August 15, 1996.

    d. Calculate the percentage changes in the average and index values between August 15, 1993, and August 15, 1996. Why do they differ?

LG 6   7. A short-term investment vehicle with a $10,000 redemption value and 182 days to maturity can be purchased at its current price of $9,700.

    a. Use Equation 3.3 to find the security's bond equivalent yield (BEY).

    b. What effect would a drop in the current price to $9,600 have on the BEY calculated in (a)? Why?

LG 6   8. A Treasury bill (T-bill) with a $10,000 redemption value and 91 days to maturity can currently be purchased for $9,800.

    a. Use Equation 3.4 to find the T-bill's bank discount yield (BDY).

    b. What effect would the fact that the T-bill has 182 days to maturity have on the BDY calculated in (a)? Why?

LG 6   9. Chaim Begin is considering the purchase of a Treasury bill that has a bank discount yield (BDY) of 5.74 percent and has 182 days until it matures to its $10,000 redemption value.

    a. Use Equation 3.5 to find the bond equivalent yield (BEY) of this T-bill.

    b. What effect would a drop in the BDY to 5.10 percent have on the BEY calculated in (a)? Why?

LG 6   10. The O'Sheas are considering a short-term investment that has a redemption value of $50,000 at the end of 120 days. The investment can be purchased at a current price of $48,700.

    a. Use Equation 3.3 to find the bond equivalent yield (BEY) on the O'Sheas' proposed investment.

    b. Use Equation 3.4 to find the bank discount yield (BDY) on the proposed investment.

    c. Use Equation 3.5 to convert the bank discount yield (BDY) found in (b) to a bond equivalent yield (BEY).

    d. Compare the comment on the values for BEY found in (a) and (c).

**CASE
PROBLEMS**

3.1 PREPARING CAROLYN BOWEN'S INVESTMENT PLAN

Carolyn Bowen, who just turned 55, is a widow currently employed as a receptionist for the Xcon Corporation, where she has worked for the past 20 years. She is in good health, lives alone, and has two grown children. A few months ago, her husband, who was an alcoholic, died of liver disease. Although at one time a highly successful automobile dealer, Carolyn's husband left her with only their home and the proceeds from a $50,000 life insurance policy. After paying medical and funeral expenses, $30,000 of the life insurance proceeds remain. In addition to the life insurance proceeds, Carolyn has $25,000 in a savings account, which she had secretly built over the past 10 years. Recognizing that she is within 10 years of retirement, Carolyn wishes to use her limited resources to develop an investment program that will allow her to live comfortably once she retires.

Carolyn is quite superstitious. After consulting with a number of psychics and studying her family tree, she feels certain she will not live past 80. She plans to retire at either 62 or 65, whichever will better allow her to meet her long-run financial goals. After talking with a number of knowledgeable individuals—including, of course, the psychics—Carolyn estimates that to live comfortably, she will need $30,000 per year before taxes once she retires. This amount will be required annually for each of 18 years if she retires at 62 or for each of 15 years if she retires at 65. As part of her financial plans, Carolyn intends to sell her home at retirement and rent an apartment. She has estimated that she will net $75,000 if she sells the house at 62 and $85,000 if she sells it at 65. Carolyn has no financial dependents and is not concerned about leaving a sizable estate to her heirs.

If Carolyn retires at age 62, she will receive from Social Security and an employer-sponsored pension plan a total of $906 per month ($10,872 annually); if she waits until age 65 to retire, her total retirement income would be $1,125 per month ($13,500 annually). For convenience, Carolyn has already decided that to convert all her assets at the time of retirement into a stream of annual income, she will at that time purchase an annuity by paying a single premium. The annuity will have a life just equal to the number of years remaining until her 80th birthday. Because Carolyn is uncertain as to the actual age at which she will retire, she obtained the following interest factors from her insurance agent in order to estimate the annual annuity benefit provided for a given purchase price.

Life of Annuity	Interest Factor
15 years	11.118
18 years	12.659

By dividing the factors into the purchase price, the yearly annuity benefit can be calculated. Carolyn plans to place any funds currently available into a savings account paying 6 percent compounded annually until retirement. She does not expect to be able to save or invest any additional funds between now and retirement. To calculate the future value of her savings, she will need to multiply the amount of money currently available to her by one of the following factors, depending upon the retirement age being considered.

Retirement Age	Time to Retirement	Future-Value Interest Factor
62	7 years	1.504
65	10 years	1.791

Questions

1. Assume that Carolyn places currently available funds in the savings account. Determine the amount of money Carolyn will have available at retirement once she sells her house if she retires at (a) age 62 and (b) age 65.

2. Using the results from question 1 and the interest factors given above, determine the level of annual income that will be provided to Carolyn through purchase of an annuity at (a) age 62 and (b) age 65.

3. With the results found in the preceding questions, determine the total annual retirement income Carolyn will have if she retires at (a) age 62 and (b) age 65.

4. From your findings, do you think Carolyn will be able to achieve her long-run financial goal by retiring at (a) age 62 or (b) age 65? Explain.

5. Evaluate Carolyn's investment plan in terms of her use of a savings account and an annuity rather than some other investment vehicles. Comment on the risk and return characteristics of her plan. What recommendations might you offer Carolyn? Be specific.

3.2 A RICH UNCLE—THE PEREZES' GOOD FORTUNE

Angel and Marie Perez own a small pool hall located in southern New Jersey. They enjoy running the business, which they have owned for nearly 3 years. Angel, a retired professional pool shooter, saved for nearly 10 years to buy this business, which he and his wife own free and clear. The income from the pool hall is adequate to allow Angel, Marie, and their two children, Mary (age 10) and José (age 4), to live comfortably. Although lacking any formal education beyond the tenth grade, Angel has become an avid reader. He enjoys reading about current events and consumer affairs. He especially likes *Consumer Reports*, from which he has gained numerous insights for making various purchase transactions. Because of the long hours required to run the business, Angel can devote 3 to 4 hours a day (on the job) to reading.

Recently, Angel and Marie were notified that Marie's uncle had died and left them a portfolio of stocks and bonds having a current market value of $300,000. They were elated to learn of their good fortune but decided it would be best not to change their lifestyle as a result of this inheritance. Instead, they want their newfound wealth to provide for their children's college education as well as their own retirement. They decided that, like their uncle, they would keep these funds invested in stocks and bonds. Angel felt that in view of this, he needed to acquaint himself with the securities currently in the portfolio. He knew that if he were to manage the portfolio himself, he would have to stay abreast of the securities markets as well as the economy in general. He also realized he would need to follow each security in the portfolio and continuously evaluate possible alternative securities that could be substituted as conditions warrant. Because Angel had plenty of time in which to follow the market, he strongly believed that, with proper information, he could manage the portfolio. Given the amount of money involved, Angel was not too concerned with the information costs; rather, he wanted the best information he could get at a reasonable price.

Questions

1. Explain what role the *Wall Street Journal* and/or *Barron's* might play in fulfilling Angel's needs. What other general sources of economic and current event information might you recommend to Angel? Explain.

2. How might Angel be able to use the services of Standard & Poor's Corporation, Moody's Investor Services, and the *Value Line Investment Survey* to acquaint himself with securities in the portfolio? Indicate which, if any, of these services you would recommend, and why.

3. Explain to Angel the need to find a good stockbroker and the role the stockbroker could play in providing information and advice.

4. Describe the services and sources of investment advice available to Angel. Would you recommend that he hire an adviser to manage the portfolio? Explain the potential costs and benefits of such an alternative.

5. Give Angel a summary prescription for obtaining information and advice that will help to ensure the preservation and growth of the family's newfound wealth.

CHAPTER 4

MEASURING INVESTMENT RETURN AND RISK

LEARNING GOALS

After studying this chapter, you should be able to:

LG 1 Review the concept, components, and importance of return and the forces that affect the investor's level of return.

LG 2 Discuss the time value of money and the calculations involved in finding the future value of various types of cash flows.

LG 3 Explain the concept of present value, the procedures for calculating present values, and the use of present value in determining a satisfactory investment.

LG 4 Describe real, risk-free, and required returns and the computation and application of holding period return, yield (internal rate of return), approximate yield, and growth rates.

LG 5 Discuss the major sources of risk, the components of risk, and the risk of a single asset in both absolute and relative terms.

LG 6 Understand beta and the capital asset pricing model (CAPM) and how they can be used in the selection process to evaluate the risk-return characteristics of alternative investment vehicles.

Ravi Rao began investing in 1981 during his freshman year at the University of Alaska. Realizing that the earlier he started, the more his money would grow (due to the time value of money), with summer job earnings he purchased a six-month CD yielding 17 percent. "I liked the high yields and low risk of CDs but also wanted to buy stocks—more for the challenge than to make money," Ravi remembers. "Being naive, I invested without knowing what I was doing and picked stocks based on gut instinct. I didn't read the financial press, know how stocks were valued, or pay attention to the risk-return tradeoff: The greater the risk (the variability of expected returns), the higher the return an investment should provide. I had no specific return in mind."

In the early 1980s, Ravi picked good technology industries (computers, telecommunications) but poor companies and then wouldn't sell. "For example, I picked Kaypro rather than the analysts' choice, Compaq—a bad move!" he explains. "Kaypro stock dropped like a rock, but my broker urged me to hold on. When I sold, I lost 40 percent of my original investment." He watched his Hershey Oil stock go from $6 to $12 but again didn't sell; eventually, he sold at a loss.

After his early mistakes, Ravi educated himself about investing and also took finance and investment courses during his MBA studies. He studies stock fundamentals, rather than following someone else's "hot tips." He sticks to industries he understands, and he researches the company, its industry, key trends, and broader factors like the economy and market forces. Ravi seeks stocks he thinks will rise substantially (20 percent) over three to six months. Before investing, Ravi estimates his return on investment using time value of money techniques to make sure the projected return, at minimum, equals his goal after commissions. More importantly, given his early difficulties, he sells when the stock reaches his target price or hits a plateau. This can be hard, though: He bought Compaq at 30, sold at 36, then watched it go to 50.

Due to limited investment funds, Ravi buys stocks of a few major American companies at a time and is considering mutual funds. Recognizing that international investments can boost his returns, he also plans to invest in Singapore. He takes a subjective approach to risk, analyzing the company, its products, and its industry thoroughly and looking for a competitive advantage, moderate levels of risk, and stocks in different industries—like Ford (which he bought at 24⅛ and sold at 45—his best stock to date) and PepsiCo—to reduce risk through limited diversification.

> **I DIDN'T READ THE FINANCIAL PRESS, KNOW HOW STOCKS WERE VALUED, OR PAY ATTENTION TO THE RISK-RETURN TRADEOFF.**

Ravi is essentially a patient investor who relies on his personal understanding of a company's product or service, basic financial and statistical concepts, and a firm philosophy of saving for the future. For him, investing is exciting: "It means sharing in the success of American business."

Ravi Rao grew up in Alaska and lives in Seattle, Washington. He has a B.S. degree in geology and an MBA from the University of Alaska. Currently pursuing an investment and financial planning career, he has been a field geologist, ARCO intern, and science project business manager–Alaska Science and Technology Foundation Grant.

When buying goods and services, most people have preconceived notions of value. For relatively inexpensive goods and services, they will pay the marked or quoted price if it falls within the range of their preconceived notion. For instance, most people are willing to pay 50 cents to $1.00, and possibly $1.25, for a cup of coffee. But at prices in excess of $1.00, they are likely to decide to make their own coffee, forgo it altogether, or switch to another beverage. In the purchase of more expensive items, considerations of price and value become more important. For example, when shopping for a used car, most people will be unwilling to pay more than its "book value" as reflected in a widely circulated used-car price guide. It is unlikely you would be willing to pay, say, $9,500 for a used car that for its age, mileage, and condition has a book value of $8,750. The value of a good or service to individuals largely depends on the satisfaction they expect to receive from it. Because price and value are not necessarily the same, an economically rational individual would try to pay a price at or below perceived value. When making investment decisions, the same logic should apply.

An investment can be viewed as a financial commodity. Just as a physical commodity, such as an automobile, has certain characteristics (age, mileage, condition) that determine its value, so does an investment vehicle. Those key characteristics of an investment are *return* and *risk*; together, they determine its value. An understanding of these dimensions, their measurement, and their linkage to value is an important prerequisite to making wise investment decisions. Like Ravi Rao, you need to consider risk and return when making investment decisions. Chapter 4 introduces you to these important concepts. In subsequent chapters we consider the use of these factors to value specific investment vehicles. Here we look first at the concept of return.

THE CONCEPT OF RETURN

return
the level of profit from an investment, i.e., the reward for investing.

Investors are motivated to invest in a given vehicle by its expected return. The **return** is the level of profit from an investment, i.e., the reward for investing. Suppose, for example, you have $1,000 in an insured savings account paying 5 percent annual interest and a business associate asks you to lend her that much money. If you lend her the money for one year, at the end of which she pays you back, your return will depend on the amount of interest you charge. If you make an interest-free loan, your return will be zero. If you charge 5 percent interest, your return will be $50 (.05 × $1,000). Because you are already earning a safe 5 percent on the $1,000, it seems clear that you should charge your associate a minimum of 5 percent interest.

Some investment vehicles guarantee a return; others do not. For example, the $1,000 deposited in an insured savings account at a large bank can be viewed as a certain return. The $1,000 loan to your business associate might be less certain: What is your return if she runs into financial difficulty? Assume that she can repay you only $850. In this case, your return will be minus $150 ($850 − $1,000) or minus 15 percent ($150 ÷ $1,000). Thus, the size of the expected return is one important factor in choosing a suitable investment.

COMPONENTS OF RETURN

The return on an investment may come from more than one source. The most common source is periodic payments such as dividends or interest. The other source of return is appreciation in value—the gain from selling an investment vehicle for more than its original purchase price. We will call these two sources of return *current income* and *capital gains* (or *capital losses*).

Current Income

Current income may take the form of dividends from stocks, interest received on bonds, rent received from real estate, and so on. To be considered income, it must be received in the form of cash or be readily convertible into cash. For our purposes, **current income** is usually cash or near-cash that is periodically received as a result of owning an investment.

Using the data in Table 4.1, we can calculate the current income from investments A and B—both purchased for $1,000—over a one-year period of ownership. Investment A would provide current income of $80; investment B would provide current income of $120. On the basis of the current income received over the one-year period, investment B seems preferable. Of course, the market value of the invested funds may have changed, so it would be premature to declare now which investment is better.

Capital Gains (or Losses)

The second dimension of return is concerned with the change, if any, in the market value of an investment. Investors pay a certain amount for an investment, from which they expect to receive not only current income but also the return of the invested funds sometime in the future. As noted in Chapter 3, the amount by which the proceeds from the sale of an investment exceed its original purchase price is called a *capital gain*. If an investment is sold for less than its original purchase price, a *capital loss* results.

Let's calculate the capital gain or loss of investments A and B in Table 4.1. For investment A, a capital gain of $100 ($1,100 sale price − $1,000 purchase price) is realized over the one-year period. In the case of investment B, a $40 capital loss ($960 sale price − $1,000 purchase price) results. Combining the

current income
usually cash or near-cash that is periodically received as a result of owning an investment.

Table 4.1   Profiles of Two Investments

	Investment	
	A	B
Purchase price (beginning of year)	$1,000	$1,000
Cash received		
1st quarter	$ 10	$ 0
2nd quarter	20	0
3rd quarter	20	0
4th quarter	30	120
Total current income (for year)	$ 80	$ 120
Sale price (end of year)	$1,100	$ 960

total return
the sum of the current income and the capital gain (or loss) earned on an investment over a specified period of time.

capital gain (or loss) with the current income (calculated in the preceding section) gives the **total return** on each investment:

| | Investment | |
Return	A	B
Current income	$ 80	$120
Capital gain (loss)	100	(40)
Total return	$180	$ 80

In terms of the total return earned on the $1,000 investment over the one-year period, investment A is superior to investment B.

The use of percentage returns is generally preferred over the use of dollar returns because percentages allow direct comparison of different sizes and types of investments. Stated as a percentage of the initial investment, an 18 percent return ($180 ÷ $1,000) was earned on investment A, whereas B yielded only an 8 percent return ($80 ÷ $1,000). Although at this point investment A appears preferable, differences in risk as well as certain tax factors might cause some investors to prefer B. (We will see why later in this chapter.)

WHY RETURN IS IMPORTANT

Return is a key variable in the investment decision: It allows us to compare the actual or expected gains provided by various investments with the levels of return required to justify them. For example, an investor would be satisfied with an investment that earns 12 percent if he or she requires it to earn only 10 percent. Return can be measured in a historical sense, or it can be used to formulate future expectations.

Historical Performance

Although most people recognize that future performance is not guaranteed by past performance, they would agree that past data often provide a meaningful basis for formulating future expectations. A common practice in the investment world is to look closely at the historical performance of a given vehicle when formulating expectations about its future. Because interest rates and other financial return measures are most often cited on an annual basis, evaluation of past investment returns is typically done on the same basis. Consider the data for a hypothetical investment presented in Table 4.2. Two aspects of these data are important: First, we can determine the average level of return generated by this investment over the past 10 years. Second, we can analyze the trend in this return. As a percentage, the average total return (column 6) over the past 10 years was 8.10 percent. Looking at the yearly returns, we can see that after the negative return in 1987, 4 years of positive and generally increasing returns occurred before the negative return was repeated in 1992. From 1993 through 1996, positive and increasing returns were again realized.

Expected Return

expected return
the return an investor thinks an investment will earn in the future.

In the final analysis, when making investment decisions it's the future that matters; **expected return** is a vital measure of performance. It's what you think the investment will earn in the future (in terms of current income and capital

Table 4.2   Historical Investment Data for a Hypothetical Investment

Year	(1) Income	Market Value (Price)			Total Return	
		(2) Beginning of Year	(3) End of Year	(4) (3) − (2) Capital Gain	(5) (1) + (4) ($)	(6) (5) ÷ (2) (%)*
1987	$4.00	$100	$ 95	−$ 5.00	−$ 1.00	−1.00%
1988	3.00	95	99	4.00	7.00	7.37
1989	4.00	99	105	6.00	10.00	10.10
1990	5.00	105	115	10.00	15.00	14.29
1991	5.00	115	125	10.00	15.00	12.00
1992	3.00	125	120	− 5.00	−2.00	−1.60
1993	3.00	120	122	2.00	5.00	4.17
1994	4.00	122	130	8.00	12.00	9.84
1995	5.00	130	140	10.00	15.00	11.54
1996	5.00	140	155	15.00	20.00	14.29
Average	$4.10			$ 5.50	$ 9.60	8.10%

*Percent return on beginning-of-year market value of investment.

gains) that determines what you should be willing to pay for it. To see how, let's return to the data in Table 4.2. Looking at the historical return figures in the table, an investor would note the increasing trend in returns from 1993 through 1996. But to project future returns, we need insights into the investment's prospects. If the trend in returns seems likely to continue, an expected return in the range of 12 to 15 percent for 1997 or 1998 would seem reasonable. On the other hand, if future prospects seem poor, or if the investment is subject to cycles, an expected return of 8 to 9 percent may be a more reasonable estimate. Over the past ten years, the investment's returns have cycled from one poor year (1987 and 1992) to four years of increasing return (1988–1991 and 1993–1996). We might therefore expect low returns in 1997 to be followed by increasing returns in the 1998–2001 period.

LEVEL OF RETURN

The level of return achieved or expected from an investment will depend on a variety of factors. The key factors are internal characteristics and external forces.

Internal Characteristics

Certain characteristics of an investment affect its level of return. Examples include the type of investment vehicle, the quality of management, the way the investment is financed, and the customer base of the issuer. For example, the common stock of a large, well-managed, completely equity-financed plastics manufacturer whose major customer is Apple Computer would be expected to provide a level of return different from that of a small, poorly managed, largely debt-financed clothing manufacturer whose customers are small specialty stores. As we will see in later chapters, an assessment of internal factors and their impact on return is one important step in the process of analyzing potential investments.

External Forces

External forces such as war, shortages, price controls, Federal Reserve actions, and political events may also affect the level of return. None of these are under the control of the issuer of the investment vehicle. Because investment vehicles are affected differently by these forces, it is not unusual to find two vehicles with similar internal characteristics offering significantly different returns. As a result of the same external force, the expected return from one vehicle may increase, while that of another decreases. Likewise, the economies of various countries respond to external forces in different ways. As the *Investor Insights* box on page 137 demonstrates, investors can increase their portfolio returns by spreading investments among several global economies that are expected to move in different directions.

Another external force is the *general level of price changes*, either up—**inflation**—or down—**deflation**. Inflation tends to have a favorable impact on certain types of investment vehicles, such as real estate, and a negative one on others, such as stocks and fixed-income securities. Rising interest rates, which normally accompany increasing rates of inflation, can significantly affect returns. Depending upon which actions, if any, are taken by the federal government to control inflation, its presence can increase, decrease, or have no effect on investment returns. Furthermore, the return on each *type* of investment vehicle exhibits its own unique response to inflation.

inflation
a period of generally rising prices.

deflation
a period of generally declining prices.

CONCEPTS *in Review*

4.1   Define what is meant by the *return* on an investment. Define and differentiate between the two components of return—current income and capital gains (or losses).

4.2   What role does historical performance data play in estimating the expected return from a given investment? Describe and differentiate between the key factors affecting investment returns—internal characteristics and external forces.

THE TIME VALUE OF MONEY*

time value of money
the fact that as long as an opportunity exists to earn interest, the value of money is affected by the point in time when the money is expected to be received.

Imagine that at age 25, you begin making annual cash deposits of $1,000 into a savings account that pays 5 percent annual interest. After 40 years, at age 65, you will have made deposits totaling $40,000 (40 years × $1,000 per year). Assuming you make no withdrawals, what do you think your account balance will be—$50,000? $75,000? $100,000? The answer is none of the above; your $40,000 will have grown to nearly $121,000! Why? Because the time value of money allows the deposits to earn interest that is compounded over the 40 years. **Time value of money** refers to the fact that as long as an opportunity exists to earn interest, the value of money is affected by the point in time when the money is expected to be received.

Because opportunities to earn interest on funds are readily available, *the sooner one receives a return on a given investment, the better*. For example, two investments each requiring a $1,000 outlay and each expected to return $100 over a two-year holding period are *not necessarily* equally desirable.

---

*This section presents the fundamental concepts and techniques of time value of money. Those who have already mastered these important materials may wish to skip this discussion and continue at the heading "Determining a Satisfactory Investment" on page 145.

Global Securities: A Smart Investment

During the past few years, U.S. investors have been buying record amounts of foreign stocks. They poured an estimated $230 billion into foreign equities from January 1991 through December 1994, seven and a half times the amount invested abroad between 1986 and 1991. Almost 10 percent of American institutional portfolios are now invested internationally, and mutual funds that specialize in foreign markets have been the fastest growing segment of the fund industry.

It's no wonder: In the first third of 1993, the Dow Jones World Stock Index, minus the U.S. portion, was up 21.27 percent, compared with just 3.88 percent for the Dow Jones Industrial Average. According to Nick Carn, chief investment officer at Draycott Partners Ltd. in London, "You are probably at the beginning of quite a long period during which non-U.S. markets will meaningfully outperform U.S. markets." Indeed, rising interest rates in the United States and the likelihood that American economic growth will slow make foreign stocks look more attractive.

Stock markets are flourishing in emerging economies such as China, India, Africa, Latin America, Russia, and Vietnam. These markets can soar upward by over 100 percent in a year, but the drops are just as dramatic. The Philippines market, for instance, was up 155 percent in 1993 but had gone down 34 percent just three years earlier.

Many investors, lured by sky-high returns, attempt to guess which foreign markets will soar and which will plummet. Such speculation on short-term price movements is a dangerous game to play; some of the best-performing markets, such as Asia and Latin America, are incredibly volatile, and the politics of these regions are unstable. Also, many markets have shot upward because of an incoming flood of American investor dollars, not because of underlying economic factors. Investors must also keep in mind that currency swings can more than erase the gains on foreign investments when those gains are converted into U.S. dollars; if you buy a Japanese stock and the yen goes up relative to the dollar, the dollar value of the stock decreases.

Despite these dangers, adding foreign stocks to a portfolio of U.S. securities can be a conservative, prudent act. National markets tend to move in different directions, so that some markets will be doing better than others at any given time. A diversified portfolio with investments in several countries therefore spreads (i.e., reduces) risk and can earn a superior long-term return. Accordingly, an American with well-chosen investments abroad is likely to achieve higher returns with less risk than the stay-at-home investor.

The secret to successful global investing is achieving the proper mixture of risk and return. Professor Albert Fredman of California State University at Fullerton recommends allocating 10 to 40 percent of a portfolio to foreign holdings. Although shares of individual stocks might bring larger rewards than an international mutual fund, most pros discourage that approach for anyone with less than $200,000 to put into foreign investment; it takes at least that much to achieve a prudent degree of diversification. Perhaps most importantly, consider global investments part of a broad, long-term strategy, and always move with caution.

Sources: Gregory J. Millman, "The Global Advantage," *Worth*, March 1994, pp. 52–63; Carla Rapoport, "How to Win the Global Game," *Fortune*, December 26, 1994, pp. 82–86; and Michael R. Sesit, "Why It's Time for Investors to Think Globally," *Wall Street Journal*, April 23, 1993, pp. C1, C14.

Assuming the base value of each investment remains at $1,000, if the first investment returns $100 at the end of the first year and the second investment returns the $100 at the end of the second year, the first investment is preferable. This is so because the $100 interest earned by investment 1 could be *reinvested to earn more interest* while the initial $100 from investment 2 is still accruing. Thus, time-value concepts should be considered when making investment decisions.

INTEREST: THE BASIC RETURN TO SAVERS

interest
the "rent" paid by a borrower to a lender for use of the lender's money.

A savings account at a bank is one of the most basic forms of investment. The saver receives interest in exchange for placing idle funds in an account. **Interest** can be viewed as the "rent" paid by a borrower to a lender for the use of the lender's money. The saver will experience neither a capital gain nor a capital loss, because the value of the investment (the initial deposit) will change only by the amount of interest earned. For the saver, the interest earned over a given time frame is that period's current income.

Simple Interest

simple interest
interest paid only on the initial deposit for the amount of time it is held.

The income paid on such vehicles as certificates of deposit (CDs), bonds, and other forms of investment that pay interest is most often calculated using the **simple interest** method. Interest is paid only on the initial deposit for the amount of time it is held. If you held a $100 initial deposit in an account paying 6 percent interest for 1½ years, you would earn $9 in interest (1½ × .06 × $100) over this period. Had you withdrawn $50 at the end of half a year, the total interest earned over the 1½ years would be $6, because you would earn $3 interest on $100 for the first half-year (½ × .06 × $100) and $3 interest on $50 for the next full year (1 × .06 × $50).

Using the simple interest method, the stated rate of interest is the *true rate of interest (or return)*. In the example above, the true rate of interest would be 6 percent. Because the interest rate reflects the rate at which current income is earned regardless of the size of the deposit, it is a useful measure of current income.

Compound Interest

compound interest
interest paid not only on the initial deposit but also on any interest accumulated from one period to the next.

Compound interest is paid not only on the initial deposit but also on any interest accumulated from one period to the next. This is the method usually used by savings institutions. When interest is compounded annually over a single year, compound and simple interest calculations provide similar results; in this case, the stated interest rate and the true interest rate would be equal. The data in Table 4.3 illustrate compound interest. In this case, the interest earned each year is left on deposit rather than withdrawn. The $50 of interest earned on the $1,000 initial deposit during 1995 becomes part of the beginning (i.e., initial) balance on which interest is paid in 1996, and so on. *Note that the simple interest method is used in the compounding process*; that is, interest is paid only on the initial balance held during the given time period.

When compound interest is used, the stated and true interest rates are equal *only* when interest is compounded annually. In general, *the more frequently interest is compounded at a stated rate, the higher will be the true rate*

Table 4.3 Savings Account Balance Data
(5% interest compounded annually)

Date	(1) Deposit (Withdrawal)	(2) Beginning Account Balance	(3) .05 × (2) Interest for Year	(4) (2) + (3) Ending Account Balance
1/1/95	$1,000	$1,000.00	$50.00	$1,050.00
1/1/96	(300)	750.00	37.50	787.50
1/1/97	1,000	1,787.50	89.38	1,876.88

Table 4.4 Savings Account Balance Data
(5% interest compounded semiannually)

Date	(1) Deposit (Withdrawal)	(2) Beginning Account Balance	(3) .05 × 1/2 × (2) Interest for 6 Months	(4) (2) + (3) Ending Account Balance
1/1/95	$1,000	$1,000.00	$25.00	$1,025.00
7/1/95		1,025.00	25.63	1,050.63
1/1/96	(300)	750.63	18.77	769.40
7/1/96		769.40	19.24	788.64
1/1/97	1,000	1,788.64	44.72	1,833.36
7/1/97		1,833.36	45.83	1,879.19

of interest. The interest calculations for the deposit data in Table 4.3, assuming that interest is compounded semiannually (twice a year), are shown in Table 4.4. The interest for each 6-month period is found by multiplying the beginning (i.e., initial) balance for the 6 months by half of the stated 5 percent interest rate (see column 3 of Table 4.4). We can see that larger returns are associated with more frequent compounding: Compare the end of 1997 account balance of $1,876.88 (calculated in Table 4.3) at 5 percent compounded annually with the end of 1997 account balance of $1,879.19 (calculated in Table 4.4) at 5 percent compounded semiannually. Clearly, with semiannual compounding, the true rate of interest is greater than the 5 percent rate associated with annual compounding. A summary of the true rates of interest associated with a 5 percent stated rate and various compounding periods is given in Table 4.5.

continuous compounding
interest calculation in which interest is compounded over the smallest possible interval of time.

Continuous compounding, which is compounding over the smallest possible interval of time, results in the maximum true rate of interest that can be achieved with a given stated rate of interest. The data in Table 4.5 show that the more frequently interest is compounded, the higher the true rate of interest. Due to the impact that differences in compounding periods have on return, an investor should evaluate the true rate of interest associated with various alternatives before making a deposit.

FUTURE VALUE: AN EXTENSION OF COMPOUNDING

future value
the amount to which a current deposit will grow over a period of time when it is placed in an account paying compound interest.

Future value is the amount to which a current deposit will grow over a period of time when it is placed in an account paying compound interest. Consider a deposit of $1,000 that is earning 8 percent (.08 in decimal form) compounded

Table 4.5 True Rate of Interest for Various Compounding Periods
(5% stated rate of interest)

Compounding Period	True Rate of Interest
Annually	5.000%
Semiannually	5.063
Quarterly	5.094
Monthly	5.120
Weekly	5.125
Continuously	5.127

annually. To find the future value of this deposit at the end of one year, the following calculation would be made:

Equation 4.1

$$\text{Future value at end of year 1} = \$1,000 \times (1 + .08) = \underline{\underline{\$1,080}}$$

If the money were left on deposit for another year, 8 percent interest would be paid on the account balance of $1,080. Thus, at the end of the second year, there would be $1,166.40 in the account. This $1,166.40 would represent the beginning-of-year balance of $1,080 plus 8 percent of the $1,080 ($86.40) in interest. The future value at the end of the second year would be calculated as follows:

Equation 4.2

$$\text{Future value at end of year 2} = \$1,080 \times (1 + .08) = \underline{\underline{\$1,166.40}}$$

To find the future value of the $1,000 at the end of year *n*, the procedure illustrated above would have to be repeated *n* times. Future values, like present values (discussed later), can be determined either mathematically or by using a financial calculator, a computer, or appropriate financial tables. Here we use tables of future-value interest factors. A complete set of these tables is included in Appendix A, Table A.1; a portion of Table A.1 is shown in Table 4.6. The factors in the table represent the amount to which an initial $1 deposit would grow for various combinations of periods (typically years) and interest rates. For example, a dollar deposited in an account paying 8 percent interest and left there for 2 years would accumulate to $1.166. Using the future-value interest factor for 8 percent and 2 years (1.166), the future value of an investment (deposit) that can earn 8 percent over 2 years is found by *multiplying* the amount invested (or deposited) by the appropriate interest factor. In the case of $1,000 left on deposit for two years at 8 percent, the resulting future value is $1,166 (1.166 × $1,000), which agrees (except for a slight rounding difference) with the value calculated in Equation 4.2.

Table 4.6   Future-Value Interest Factors for One Dollar

| Period | Interest Rate | | | | | |
	5%	6%	7%	8%↓	9%	10%
1	1.050	1.060	1.070	1.080	1.090	1.100
→ 2	1.102	1.124	1.145	1.166	1.188	1.210
3	1.158	1.191	1.225	1.260	1.295	1.331
4	1.216	1.262	1.311	1.360	1.412	1.464
5	1.276	1.338	1.403	1.469	1.539	1.611
6	1.340	1.419	1.501	1.587	1.677	1.772
7	1.407	1.504	1.606	1.714	1.828	1.949
8	1.477	1.594	1.718	1.851	1.993	2.144
9	1.551	1.689	1.838	1.999	2.172	2.358
10	1.629	1.791	1.967	2.159	2.367	2.594

Note: All table values have been rounded to the nearest one-thousandth; thus, calculated values may differ slightly from the table values.

A few points with respect to the table of future-value interest factors should be highlighted. First, values in the table represent factors for determining the future value of one dollar at the *end* of the given year. Second, as the interest rate increases for any given year, the future-value interest factor also increases. Thus, the higher the interest rate, the greater the future value. Third, note that for a given interest rate, the future value of a dollar increases with the passage of time. Finally, it is also important to recognize that the future-value interest factor is always greater than 1. Only if the interest rate were zero would this factor equal 1, and the future value would therefore equal the initial deposit.

FUTURE VALUE OF AN ANNUITY

annuity
a stream of equal cash flows that occur in equal intervals over time.

ordinary annuity
an annuity for which the cash flows occur at the *end* of each period.

An **annuity** is a stream of equal cash flows that occur in equal intervals over time. Receiving $1,000 per year at the end of each of the next 8 years is an example of an annuity. The cash flows can be *inflows* of returns earned from an investment or *outflows* of funds invested (deposited) to earn future returns. Investors are sometimes interested in finding the future value of an annuity. Their concern is typically with what's called an **ordinary annuity**—one for which the cash flows occur at the *end* of each period. (We will concern ourselves only with this type of annuity.) Here we simplify our calculations by using tables of these factors for an annuity. A complete set of these tables is included in Appendix A, Table A.2. A portion is shown in Table 4.7.

The factors in Table 4.7 represent the amount to which annual end-of-year deposits of $1 would grow for various combinations of periods (years) and interest rates. For example, a dollar deposited at the end of each year for 8 years into an account paying 6 percent interest would accumulate to $9.897. Using the future-value interest factor for an 8-year annuity earning 6 percent (9.897), we can find the future value of this cash flow by *multiplying* the annual investment (deposit) by the appropriate interest factor. In the case of $1,000 deposited at the end of each year for 8 years at 6 percent, the resulting future value is $9,897 (9.897 × $1,000).

Table 4.7   Future-Value Interest Factors for a One-Dollar Annuity

Period	Interest Rate					
	5%	6%↓	7%	8%	9%	10%
1	1.000	1.000	1.000	1.000	1.000	1.000
2	2.050	2.060	2.070	2.080	2.090	2.100
3	3.152	3.184	3.215	3.246	3.278	3.310
4	4.310	4.375	4.440	4.506	4.573	4.641
5	5.526	5.637	5.751	5.867	5.985	6.105
6	6.802	6.975	7.153	7.336	7.523	7.716
7	8.142	8.394	8.654	8.923	9.200	9.487
→8	9.549	9.897	10.260	10.637	11.028	11.436
9	11.027	11.491	11.978	12.488	13.021	13.579
10	12.578	13.181	13.816	14.487	15.193	15.937

Note: All table values have been rounded to the nearest one-thousandth; thus, calculated values may differ slightly from the table values.

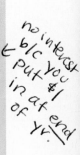
(handwritten note:) no interest b/c you put $1 in at end of yr.

PRESENT VALUE: AN EXTENSION OF FUTURE VALUE

present value
the *value today* of a sum to be received at some future date; the inverse of future value.

Present value is the inverse of future value. That is, rather than measuring the value of a present amount at some future date, **present value** finds the *current value of a future sum*. By applying present-value techniques, we can calculate the *value today* of a sum to be received at some future date.

When determining the present value of a future sum, the basic question being answered is, How much would have to be deposited today into an account paying y percent interest in order to equal a specified sum to be received so many years in the future? The applicable interest rate when finding present value is commonly called the **discount rate** (or *opportunity cost*). It represents the annual rate of return that could be earned currently on a similar investment.

discount rate
the annual rate of return that could be earned currently on a similar investment; used when finding present value; also called *opportunity cost*.

The basic present-value calculation is best illustrated using a simple example. Imagine that you are offered an opportunity that will provide you with exactly $1,000 one year from today. If you could earn 8 percent on similar types of investments, how much is the most you would pay for this opportunity? In other words, what is the present value of $1,000 to be received one year from now discounted at 8 percent? Letting x equal the present value, we can use Equation 4.3 to describe this situation:

Equation 4.3 $x \times (1 + .08) = \$1,000$

Solving Equation 4.3 for x, we get:

Equation 4.4 $x = \dfrac{\$1,000}{(1 + .08)} = \underline{\underline{\$925.93}}$

Thus, the present value of $1,000 to be received one year from now, discounted at 8 percent, is $925.93. In other words, $925.93 deposited today into an account paying 8 percent interest will accumulate to $1,000 in one year. To check this conclusion, *multiply* the future-value interest factor for 8 percent and one year, or 1.080 (from Table 4.6), by $925.93. The result is a future value of $1,000 (1.080 $\times$ $925.93).

The calculations involved in finding the present value of sums to be received in the distant future are more complex than for a one-year investment. Here we use tables of present-value interest factors to simplify these calculations. A complete set of these tables is included in Appendix A, Table A.3; a portion of Table A.3 is shown in Table 4.8. The factors in the table represent the present value of $1 associated with various combinations of periods (years) and discount (interest) rates. For example, the present value of $1 to be received one year from now discounted at 8 percent is $.926. Using this factor (.926), the present value of $1,000 to be received one year from now at an 8 percent discount rate can be found by *multiplying* it by $1,000. The resulting present value of $926 (.926 $\times$ $1,000) agrees (except for a slight rounding difference) with the value calculated in Equation 4.4.

Another example may help clarify the use of present-value tables. The present value of $500 to be received 7 years from now, discounted at 6 percent, would be calculated as follows:

Present value = .665 $\times$ $500 = $\underline{\underline{\$332.50}}$

Table 4.8   Present-Value Interest Factors for One Dollar

Period	| Discount (Interest) Rate					
	5%	6%↓	7%	8%↓	9%	10%
→ 1	.952	.943	.935	.926	.917	.909
2	.907	.890	.873	.857	.842	.826
3	.864	.840	.816	.794	.772	.751
4	.823	.792	.763	.735	.708	.683
5	.784	.747	.713	.681	.650	.621
6	.746	.705	.666	.630	.596	.564
→ 7	.711	.665	.623	.583	.547	.513
8	.677	.627	.582	.540	.502	.467
9	.645	.592	.544	.500	.460	.424
10	.614	.558	.508	.463	.422	.386

Note: All table values have been rounded to the nearest one-thousandth; thus, calculated values may differ slightly from the table values.

The .665 represents the present-value interest factor for 7 years discounted at 6 percent.

A few points with respect to the table of present-value interest factors should be highlighted. First, the present-value interest factor for a single sum is always less than 1; only if the discount rate were zero would this factor equal 1. Second, the higher the discount rate for a given year, the smaller the present-value interest factor. In other words, the greater your opportunity cost, the less you have to invest today in order to have a given amount in the future. Third, the further in the future a sum is to be received, the less it is worth at present. Finally, remember that given a discount rate of 0 percent, the present-value interest factor always equals 1; therefore, in such a case the future value of a sum equals its present value.

THE PRESENT VALUE OF A STREAM OF INCOME

mixed stream
a stream of returns that, unlike an annuity, exhibits no special pattern.

In the material above we illustrated the technique for finding the present value of a single sum to be received at some future date. Because the returns from a given investment are likely to be received at various future dates rather than as a single lump sum, we need to be able to find the present value of a *stream of returns*. A stream of returns can be viewed as a package of single-sum returns; it may be classified as a mixed stream or an annuity. A **mixed stream** of returns is one that exhibits no special pattern. As noted earlier, an *annuity* is a stream of equal periodic returns. Table 4.9 shows the end-of-year returns illustrating each of these types of patterns. To find the present value of each of these streams (measured at the *beginning* of 1996), we must calculate the total of the present values of the individual annual returns. Because shortcuts can be used for an annuity, the calculation of the present value of each type of return stream will be illustrated separately.

Table 4.9 Mixed and Annuity
Return Streams

	Returns	
Year	Mixed Stream	Annuity
1996	$30	$50
1997	40	50
1998	50	50
1999	60	50
2000	70	50

Mixed Stream

To find the present value of the mixed stream of returns given in Table 4.9, we must find and then total the present value of the individual returns. Assuming a 9 percent discount rate, the calculation of the present value of the mixed stream is shown (using present-value interest factors) in Table 4.10. The resulting present value of $187.77 represents the amount today (*beginning* of 1996) invested at 9 percent that would provide the same cash flows as the stream of returns in column 1 of Table 4.10. Once the present value of each return is found, the values can be added, because each is measured at the same point in time—the beginning of 1996.

Annuity

The present value of an annuity can be found in the same way as the present value of a mixed stream. Fortunately, however, there are simpler approaches. Here we use tables of present-value interest factors for annuities to simplify these calculations. A complete set of these tables is included in Appendix A, Table A.4; a portion of Table A.4 is shown in Table 4.11. The factors in the table represent the present value of a one-dollar annuity associated with various combinations of periods (years) and discount (interest) rates. For example, the present value of $1 to be received at the end of each year for the next 5 years discounted at 9 percent is $3.890. Using this factor, we can find the present value of the $50, 5-year annuity (given in Table 4.9) at a 9 percent discount rate by *multiplying* the annual return by the appropriate interest factor. The resulting present value is $194.50 (3.890 × $50).

Table 4.10 Mixed-Stream Present-Value
Calculation

Year	(1) Return	(2) 9% Present-Value Interest Factor	(3) (1) × (2) Present Value
1996	$30	.917	$ 27.51
1997	40	.842	33.68
1998	50	.772	38.60
1999	60	.708	42.48
2000	70	.650	45.50
		Present value of stream	$187.77

Note: Column (1) values are from Table 4.9. Column (2) values are from Table 4.8 for a 9 percent discount rate and 1 through 5 years.

Table 4.11   Present-Value Interest Factors for a One-Dollar Annuity

	Discount (Interest) Rate					
Period	5%	6%	7%	8%	9%↓	10%
1	.952	.943	.935	.926	.917	.909
2	1.859	1.833	1.808	1.783	1.759	1.736
3	2.723	2.673	2.624	2.577	2.531	2.487
4	3.546	3.465	3.387	3.312	3.240	3.170
→ 5	4.329	4.212	4.100	3.993	3.890	3.791
6	5.076	4.917	4.767	4.623	4.486	4.355
7	5.786	5.582	5.389	5.206	5.033	4.868
8	6.463	`6.210	5.971	5.747	5.535	5.335
9	7.108	6.802	6.515	6.247	5.995	5.759
10	7.722	7.360	7.024	6.710	6.418	6.145

Note: All table values have been rounded to the nearest one-thousandth; thus, calculated values may differ slightly from the table values.

DETERMINING A SATISFACTORY INVESTMENT

satisfactory investment
an investment whose present value of benefits (discounted at the appropriate rate) *equals or exceeds* the present value of its costs.

Time value of money techniques can be used to determine an acceptable investment. Ignoring risk at this point, a **satisfactory investment** would be one for which the present value of benefits (discounted at the appropriate rate) *equals or exceeds* the present value of its costs. Because the cost (or purchase price) of the investment would be incurred initially (at time zero), the cost and its present value are viewed as one and the same. If the present value of the benefits *just equals the cost*, an investor would earn a rate of return equal to the discount rate. If the present value of benefits *exceeds the cost*, the investor would earn a rate of return greater than the discount rate. If the present value of benefits is *less than the cost*, the investor would earn a rate of return less than the discount rate. It should be clear that *an investor would prefer only those investments for which the present value of benefits equals or exceeds its cost*. In these cases, the rate of return would be equal to or greater than the discount rate.

The information in Table 4.12 demonstrates the application of present value to investment decision making. Assuming an 8 percent discount rate, we can see that the present value (at the beginning of 1996) of the income (returns) to be received over the assumed 7-year period (year-end 1996

Table 4.12   Present Value Applied to an Investment

Year	(1) Income	(2) 8% Present-Value Interest Factor	(3) (1) × (2) Present Value
1996	$ 90	.926	$ 83.34
1997	100	.857	85.70
1998	110	.794	87.34
1999	120	.735	88.20
2000	100	.681	68.10
2001	100	.630	63.00
2002	1,200	.583	699.60
		Present value of income	$1,175.28

through year-end 2002) is $1,175.28. If the cost of the investment (beginning of 1996) were any amount less than or equal to $1,175.28, it would be acceptable. At a cost above $1,175.28, the investment would not be acceptable. At a cost less than or equal to the $1,175.28 present value of income, a rate of return equal to at least 8 percent would be earned; at a cost greater than $1,175.28, the rate of return would be less than 8 percent.

CONCEPTS *in Review*

4.3   What is the *time value of money*? Explain why a person wishing to invest should be able to earn a positive return.

4.4   Define, discuss, and contrast the following terms:
   a. Interest
   b. Simple interest
   c. Compound interest

4.5   When interest is compounded more frequently than annually at a stated rate, what happens to the true rate of interest? Under what condition would the stated and true rates of interest be equal? What is *continuous compounding*?

4.6   Describe, compare, and contrast the concepts of future value and present value. Explain the role of the discount rate (or opportunity cost) in the present-value calculation.

4.7   What is an *annuity*? How can calculation of the future value of an annuity be simplified? What about the present value of an annuity?

4.8   What's a *mixed stream* of returns? Describe the procedure used to find the present value of such a stream.

4.9   What is a *satisfactory investment*? When the present value of benefits exceeds the cost of an investment, what's true about the rate of return earned by the investor relative to the discount rate?

MEASURING RETURN

LG 4

Thus far, we have discussed the concept of return in terms of its two components (current income and capital gains), its importance, and the key factors affecting the level of return (internal characteristics and external forces). These discussions intentionally oversimplified the computations usually involved in determining the historical or expected return. To compare returns from different investment vehicles, we need to apply a consistent measure. Such a measure must somehow incorporate time value of money concepts that explicitly consider differences in the timing of investment income and capital gains (or losses). It must also allow us to place a current value on future benefits. Here we will look at several measures that allow us to assess and compare alternative investment vehicles effectively. First, we will define and consider the relationships among various rates of return.

 ### REAL, RISK-FREE, AND REQUIRED RETURNS

The rational investor will choose investments that fully compensate him or her for the risk involved. The greater the risk, the greater the return required by the investor. The return that fully compensates for an investment's risk is

required return
the rate of return an investor must earn on an investment to be fully compensated for its risk.

called the **required return**. To better understand the required returns upon which investors focus, it is helpful to consider their makeup. The required return on any investment i consists of three basic components—the real rate of return, an expected inflation premium, and a risk premium, as noted in Equation 4.5:

Equation 4.5

$$\text{Required return on investment } i = \text{real rate of return} + \text{expected inflation premium} + \text{risk premium for investment } i$$

Equation 4.5a

$$r_i = r^* + IP + RP_i$$

real rate of return
the rate of return that could be earned in a perfect world where all outcomes are known and certain.

The **real rate of return** is the rate of return that could be earned in a perfect world where all outcomes are known and certain—where there is no risk. In such a world, the real rate of return would create an equilibrium between the supply of savings and the demand for funds. The real rate of return changes with changing economic conditions, tastes, and preferences. Historically, it has been relatively stable and in the range of 1 to 2 percent. For convenience, we'll assume a real rate of return of 2 percent.

expected inflation premium
the average rate of inflation expected in the future.

The **expected inflation premium** represents the average rate of inflation expected in the future. By adding the expected inflation premium to the real rate of return, we get the **risk-free rate**—the rate of return that can be earned on a risk-free investment, most commonly a U.S. Treasury bill. This rate is shown in Equation 4.6:

risk-free rate
the rate of return that can be earned on a risk-free investment; the sum of the real rate of return and the expected inflation premium.

Equation 4.6

$$\text{Risk-free rate} = \text{real rate of return} + \text{expected inflation premium}$$

Equation 4.6a

$$R_F = r^* + IP$$

To demonstrate, a real rate of return of 2 percent and an expected inflation premium of 4 percent would result in a risk-free rate of return of 6 percent (2% + 4%).

The required return can be found by adding to the risk-free rate a **risk premium**, which reflects the issue and issuer characteristics. The risk premium varies depending upon the specific issue and issuer characteristics. *Issue characteristics* refer to the type of vehicle (stock, bond, etc.), its maturity (two years, five years, infinity, etc.), and its features (voting/nonvoting, callable/noncallable, etc.). *Issuer characteristics* refer to industry and company factors such as the line of business and financial condition of the issuer. Together, these factors cause investors to require a risk premium above the risk-free rate.

risk premium
a return premium that reflects the issue and issuer characteristics associated with a given investment vehicle.

Substituting the risk-free rate, R_F, from Equation 4.6a, into Equation 4.5a for the first two terms to the right of the equal sign ($r^* + IP$), we get Equation 4.7:

Equation 4.7

$$\text{Required return on investment } i = \text{risk-free rate} + \text{risk premium for investment } i$$

Equation 4.7a

$$r_i = R_F + RP_i$$

For example, if the required return on IBM common stock is 11 percent when the risk-free rate is 6 percent, investors require a 5 percent risk premium (11% − 6%) as compensation for the risk associated with common stock (the issue) and IBM (the issuer). Later in this chapter, the relationship between the risk premium and required returns is further developed. Next, we consider the specifics of return measurement.

HOLDING PERIOD RETURN

The return to a saver is the amount of current income (interest) earned on a given deposit. However, the amount "invested" in a savings account is not subject to change in value, as it is for investments such as stocks, bonds, mutual funds, and real estate. Because we are concerned with a broad range of investment vehicles, most of which have some degree of marketability, we need a measure of return that captures both periodic benefits and changes in value. One such measure is *holding period return*.

holding period
the period of time over which one wishes to measure the return on an investment vehicle.

The **holding period** is the period of time over which one wishes to measure the return on an investment vehicle. When making return comparisons, investors should use holding periods of the same length of time. For example, comparing the return on a stock over a six-month period ended December 31, 1995, with the return on a bond over a one-year holding period ended June 30, 1995, could result in a poor investment decision. To avoid this problem, the holding period should be defined and consistently applied or annualized to create a standard, and similar periods in time should be used when comparing the returns from alternative investment vehicles.

Understanding Return Components

realized return
current income actually received by an investor during a given period.

paper return
a return that has been achieved but not yet realized by an investor during a given period.

Earlier in this chapter we identified the two components of investment return: current income and capital gains (or losses). The portion of current income received by the investor during the period is a **realized return**. Most but not all current income is realized (e.g., accrued interest on taxable zero-coupon bonds is treated as current income for tax purposes but is *not* a realized return until the bond is sold or matures). On the other hand, capital gains returns are realized *only* when the investment vehicle is actually sold at the end of the holding period. Until the vehicle is sold, the capital gain is merely a **paper return**. For example, the capital gain return on an investment that increases in market value from $50 to $70 during a year is $20. For that capital gain to be realized, the investor would have to have sold the investment for $70 at the end of that year. The investor who purchased the same investment but plans to hold it for another three years would also have experienced the $20 capital gain return during the year specified, although he or she *would not have realized the gain in terms of cash flow*. However, *despite the fact that the capital gains return may not be realized during the period over which the total return is measured, it must be included in the return calculation*.

A second point to recognize about returns is that *both* the current income and the capital gains component can have a negative value. Occasionally, an investment may have negative current income, which means that the investor may be required to pay out cash to meet certain obligations. This situation is most likely to occur in various types of property investments. For example, an investor may purchase an apartment complex whose rental income, due to poor occupancy, may be inadequate to meet the payments associated with its operation. In such a case, the investor would have to pay the deficit in operating costs, and such a payment would represent negative current income. A capital loss can occur on *any* investment vehicle: Stocks, bonds, mutual funds, real estate, gold, options, and futures can all decline in market value over a given holding period.

Computing the Holding Period Return (HPR)

holding period return (HPR)
the total return earned from
holding an investment for a
specified holding period (usually
one year or less).

The **holding period return** (**HPR**) is the total return earned from holding an investment for a specified period of time (the holding period). *It is customarily used with holding periods of one year or less* (we'll explain why later). It represents the sum of current income and capital gains (or losses) achieved over the holding period, divided by the beginning investment value. The equation for HPR is as follows:

Equation 4.8

$$\text{Holding period return} = \frac{\substack{\text{current income} \\ \text{during period} } + \substack{\text{capital gain (or loss)} \\ \text{during period}}}{\text{beginning investment value}}$$

Equation 4.8a

$$\text{HPR} = \frac{C + CG}{V_0}$$

where

Equation 4.9

$$\substack{\text{Capital gain (or loss)} \\ \text{during period}} = \substack{\text{ending investment} \\ \text{value}} - \substack{\text{beginning investment} \\ \text{value}}$$

Equation 4.9a

$$CG = V_n - V_0$$

The HPR equation provides a convenient method for either measuring the total return realized or estimating the total return expected on a given investment. For example, Table 4.13 summarizes the key financial variables for four investment vehicles over the past year. The total current income and capital gain or loss for each during the holding period are given in the lines labeled (1) and (3), respectively. The total return over the year is calculated, as shown in line (4), by adding these two sources of return. Dividing the total return value [line (4)] by the beginning-of-year investment value [line (2)], we find the holding period return, given in line (5). Over the one-year holding period, the common stock had the highest HPR, 12.25 percent, and the savings account

Table 4.13   Key Financial Variables for Four Investment Vehicles

	Investment Vehicle			
	Savings Account	Common Stock	Bond	Real Estate
Cash received				
1st quarter	$15	$10	$ 0	$0
2nd quarter	15	10	70	0
3rd quarter	15	10	0	0
4th quarter	15	15	70	0
(1) Total current income	$60	$45	$140	$0
Investment value				
End-of-year	$1,000	$2,200	$ 970	$3,300
(2) Beginning-of-year	1,000	2,000	1,000	3,000
(3) Capital gain (loss)	$ 0	$ 200	($ 30)	$ 300
(4) Total return [(1) + (3)]	$ 60	$ 245	$ 110	$ 300
(5) Holding period return [(4) ÷ (2)]	6.00%	12.25%	11.00%	10.00%

had the lowest, 6 percent. As these calculations show, all that is needed to find the HPR are beginning- and end-of-period investment values, along with the value of current income received by the investor during the period. Note that had the current income and capital gain (or loss) values in lines (1) and (3) of Table 4.13 been drawn from a six-month rather than a one-year period, the HPR values calculated in line (5) would be *the same*.

Holding period return can be negative or positive. HPRs can be calculated using either historical data (as in the preceding example) or forecast data. Regardless of whether historical or forecast data are used, the HPR formula in Equation 4.8 still applies.

Using the HPR in Investment Decisions

The holding period return is easy to use in making investment decisions. Because it considers both current income and capital gains relative to the beginning investment value, it tends to overcome any problems that might be associated with comparing investments of different size. If we look only at the *total returns* calculated for each of the four investments in Table 4.13 [line (4)], the real estate investment appears best, because it has the highest total return. However, the real estate investment would require the largest dollar outlay ($3,000). The holding period return offers a *relative comparison*, by dividing the total return by the amount of the investment. Comparing HPRs, we find the investment alternative with the *highest return per invested dollar*: the common stock's HPR of 12.25 percent. Because the return per invested dollar reflects the efficiency of the investment, the HPR provides a logical method for evaluating and comparing the investment returns.

YIELD: THE INTERNAL RATE OF RETURN

yield (internal rate of return)
the compounded annual rate of return earned by a long-term investment; the discount rate that produces a present value of the investment's benefits that just equals its cost.

An alternative way to define a satisfactory investment is in terms of the compounded annual rate of return it earns. Why is an alternative measure to the HPR needed? Because *HPR fails to consider the time value of money*. While the holding period return is useful with investments held for one year or less, it is generally inappropriate for longer holding periods. Sophisticated investors typically do not use HPR when the time period is greater than one year. Instead, they use a present-value-based measure, called **yield** or **internal rate of return**, to determine the compounded annual rate of return on investments held for more than a year. The yield on an investment can also be defined as the discount rate that produces a present value of benefits just equal to its cost.

Once the yield has been determined, acceptability can be decided. If the yield on an investment is *equal to or greater than the required return*, the investment would be acceptable. An investment with a yield *below the required return* would be unacceptable: It fails to adequately compensate the investor for the risk involved.

The yield on an investment providing a single future cash flow is relatively easy to calculate. The yield on an investment providing a stream of future cash flows generally involves more time-consuming calculations. Note that many hand-held calculators as well as computer software programs are available for simplifying these calculations.

For a Single Cash Flow

Some investments, such as U.S. savings bonds, stocks paying no dividends, zero-coupon bonds, and gold, are made by paying a fixed amount up front to purchase them. The investor expects them to provide *no periodic income*, but rather a single—hopefully, large—future cash flow at maturity or when the investment is sold. The yield on investments expected to provide a single future cash flow can be estimated using either future-value or present-value interest factors. Here we will use the present-value interest factors given in Appendix A, Table A.3.

To illustrate the yield calculation, assume an investor wishes to find the yield on an investment costing $1,000 today and expected to be worth $1,400 at the end of a 5-year holding period. We can find the yield on this investment by solving for the discount rate that causes the $1,400 to be received 5 years from now to equal the initial investment of $1,000. The first step involves dividing the present value ($1,000) by the future value ($1,400), which results in a value of .714. The second step is to find in the table of present-value interest factors the 5-year factor that is closest to .714. Referring to the abbreviated present-value table (see Table 4.8), we find that for 5 years the factor closest to .714 is .713, which occurs at a 7 percent discount rate. Therefore, the yield on this investment is about 7 percent. (The precise value found using a financial calculator is 6.96 percent.) If the investor requires a 6 percent return, this investment would be acceptable (7 percent expected return ≥ 6 percent required return).

For a Stream of Income

Investment vehicles such as income-oriented stock, bonds, and income properties typically provide the investor with a *stream of income*. The yield for a stream of income (returns) is generally more difficult to estimate. The most accurate approach is based on searching for the discount rate that produces a present value of income just equal to the cost of the investment.

If we use the investment in Table 4.12 on page 145 and assume that its cost is $1,100, we find that the yield must be greater than 8 percent, because at an 8 percent discount rate, the present value of income is greater than the cost ($1,175.28 vs. $1,100). The present values at both 9 percent and 10 percent discount rates are calculated in Table 4.14. If we look at the present value of income calculated at the 9 and 10 percent rates ($1,117.61 and $1,063.08,

Table 4.14   Yield Calculation for a $1,100 Investment

Year	(1) Income	(2) 9% Present-Value Interest Factor	(3) (1) × (2) Present Value at 9%	(4) 10% Present-Value Interest Factor	(5) (1) × (4) Present Value at 10%
1996	$ 90	.917	$ 82.53	.909	$ 81.81
1997	100	.842	84.20	.826	82.60
1998	110	.772	84.92	.751	82.61
1999	120	.708	84.96	.683	81.96
2000	100	.650	65.00	.621	62.10
2001	100	.596	59.60	.564	56.40
2002	1,200	.547	656.40	.513	615.60
	Present value of income		$1,117.61		$1,063.08

respectively), we see that the yield on the investment must be somewhere between 9 and 10 percent. At 9 percent, the present value is too high, and at 10 percent, it's too low. Somewhere in between we'll end up with a present value of $1,100. The discount rate that causes the present value of income to be closer to the $1,100 cost is 9 percent, because it is only $17.61 away from $1,100. At the 10 percent rate, the present value of income is $36.92 away from the $1,100. (The precise yield value found using a financial calculator is 9.32 percent.) Thus, if the investor requires an 8 percent return on the investment, it is clearly acceptable.

Interest-on-Interest: The Critical Assumption

The critical assumption underlying the use of yield as a return measure is an ability to earn a return equal to the yield on *all income* received from the investment during the holding period. This concept can be best illustrated using a simple example. Suppose you buy a $1,000 U.S. Treasury bond that pays 8 percent annual interest ($80) over its 20-year maturity. Each year you receive $80, and at maturity the $1,000 in principal is repaid. There is no loss in capital, no default; all payments are made right on time. But if you are unable to *reinvest* the $80 annual interest receipts, you end up earning only 5 percent—rather than 8 percent—on this investment.

Figure 4.1, which shows the elements of return on this investment, can be used to demonstrate. If you *don't reinvest* the interest income of $80 per year, you'll end up on the 5 percent line; you'll have $2,600—the $1,000 principal plus $1,600 interest income (i.e., $80/year × 20 years)—at the end of 20 years. (The yield on a single cash flow of $1,000 today that will be worth $2,600 in 20 years is about 5 percent.) To move to the 8 percent line, you have to earn 8 percent on the annual interest receipts. If you do, you'll have $4,661—the $1,000 principal plus the $3,661 future value of the 20-year $80 annuity of interest receipts invested at 8 percent (i.e., $80/year × 45.762 [the 8%, 20-year factor from Table A.2])—at the end of 20 years. (The yield on a single cash flow of $1,000 today that will be worth $4,661 in 20 years is 8 percent.) The

Figure 4.1 Earning Interest-on-Interest
An investor in a $1,000, 20-year bond with an 8 percent coupon would have only $2,600 at the end of 20 years if he or she *did not reinvest* the $80 annual interest receipts—only about a 5 percent rate of return. If the interest were reinvested at the 8 percent interest rate, the investor would have $4,661 at the end of 20 years—an 8 percent rate of return. To achieve the calculated yield of 8 percent, the investor must therefore be able to earn interest-on-interest at that rate.

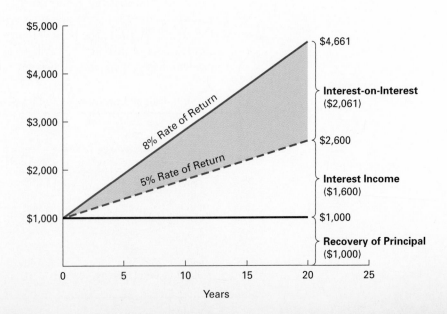

future value of the investment would be $2,061 greater (i.e., $4,661 − $2,600) by earning interest-on-interest than it would be without reinvestment of the interest receipts.

From this illustration, it should be clear that because you started out with an 8 percent investment, *you have to earn that same rate of return when reinvesting your income.* The rate of return you start with, in effect, is the required, or minimum, **reinvestment rate**—the rate of return earned on interest or other income received over the relevant investment horizon. By putting your current income to work at this rate you'll earn the rate of return you set out to. If you fail to do so, your return will decline accordingly. Even though a bond was used in this illustration, the same principle applies to any other type of investment vehicle. It's just as relevant to T-bills, common stocks, or mutual funds as it is to long-term bonds. The notion of earning interest-on-interest is what the market refers to as a **fully compounded rate of return**. It's an important concept: You can't start reaping the full potential from your investments until you start earning a fully compounded rate of return on them.

As long as periodic investment income is involved, the reinvestment of that income and interest-on-interest are matters that have to be dealt with. In fact, *interest-on-interest is a particularly important element of return for investment programs that involve a lot of current income.* In contrast to capital gains, current income has to be reinvested by the individual investor. (With capital gains, the investment vehicle itself is automatically doing the reinvesting.) It follows, therefore, that for investment programs that lean toward income-oriented securities, interest-on-interest—and the continued reinvestment of income—plays an important role in defining the amount of investment success achieved.

reinvestment rate
the rate of return earned on interest or other income received from an investment over its investment horizon.

fully compounded rate of return
the rate of return that includes interest earned on interest.

APPROXIMATE YIELD

For a given investment, the *present value (of benefits versus cost) and the yield will provide the same conclusion with respect to acceptability.* It is clearly simpler to calculate present value than to calculate the yield, although many calculators provide the capability to find yields quickly. Even without a calculator, it is possible to estimate accurately the yield on an investment if the annual benefits do not differ radically from year to year. This estimate is made using the following *approximate yield formula*:

Equation 4.10

$$\text{Approximate yield} = \frac{\text{average annual income over investment horizon} + \dfrac{\text{ending investment value} - \text{beginning investment value}}{\text{number of years in investment horizon}}}{\dfrac{\text{ending investment value} + \text{beginning investment value}}{2}}$$

Equation 4.10a

$$AY = \frac{\overline{C} + \dfrac{V_n - V_0}{n}}{\dfrac{V_n + V_0}{2}}$$

This formula can be applied to estimate the yield for both single cash flows and streams of income.

For a Single Cash Flow

Using our earlier example of the $1,000 investment that will be worth $1,400 in 5 years (see page 151), we can demonstrate the approximate yield formula for a single cash flow. Because the investment involves a single future cash flow, the average annual income ($\overline{C}$) is zero. Substituting this value along with a future value (V_n) of $1,400, current cost ($V_0$) of $1,000, and an investment horizon (n) of 5 years into Equation 4.10a's approximate yield formula, we get:

$$AY = \frac{\$0 + \dfrac{\$1,400 - \$1,000}{5}}{\dfrac{\$1,400 + \$1,000}{2}} = \frac{\$0 + \$80}{\$1,200} = \frac{\$80}{\$1,200} = \underline{\underline{0.0667, \text{ or } 6.67\%}}$$

The approximate yield of 6.67 percent is reasonably close to the precise yield of about 7 percent calculated earlier.

For a Stream of Income

To calculate the approximate yield for a stream of income, we would substitute the data in Table 4.12 on page 145 into Equation 4.10a. Suppose that in the year 2002, the $1,000 investment is sold for the future price of $1,200 ($V_n$), shown in the table, and that it is the only income in that year. Assume further that the current price of the investment is $1,175.28 ($V_0$). (*Note:* Setting up the investment this way should lead to an exact 8 percent yield, because that is the rate used to discount the income in Table 4.12 to obtain the $1,175.28 value.) The average annual income is calculated by dividing the $620 of total annual benefits from 1996 through 2001 ($90 + $100 + $110 + $120 + $100 + $100) by 7—the number of years in the investment horizon (n). Average annual income ($\overline{C}$) of $88.57 ($620 ÷ 7) results. (*Note:* To apply the approximate yield formula, Equation 4.10a, the income in the final year n is treated as the "ending investment value" (V_n) and the income in the $n - 1$ prior years is averaged over the n-year period to find the "average annual income over investment horizon" ($\overline{C}$).) Substituting the data into Equation 4.10a results in the following calculations:

$$AY = \frac{\$88.57 + \dfrac{\$1,200 - \$1,175.28}{7}}{\dfrac{\$1,200 + \$1,175.28}{2}}$$

$$= \frac{\$88.57 + \$3.53}{\$1,187.64} = \frac{\$92.10}{\$1.187.64}$$

$$= \underline{\underline{0.0776, \text{ or } 7.76\%}}$$

The approximate yield of 7.76 percent is reasonably close to the precise yield of 8 percent. The approximate yield formula will be used at numerous points throughout the text to simplify what may otherwise be tedious yield calculations.

Table 4.15 Dividends Per Share

Year	Year Number	Dividends per Share	Year	Year Number	Dividends per Share
1987	0	$2.45	1992	5	$3.15
1988	1	2.60	1993	6	3.20
1989	2	2.80	1994	7	3.20
1990	3	3.00	1995	8	3.40
1991	4	3.20	1996	9	3.50

FINDING GROWTH RATES

rate of growth
the compounded annual rate of change in the value of a stream of income.

In addition to finding compounded annual rates of return, we frequently need to find the **rate of growth**—the compounded annual rate of change in the value of a stream of income, particularly dividends or earnings. Here we describe a simple technique for estimating growth rates that relies on the use of the present-value interest factors presented in Table A.3. The technique can best be demonstrated using an example.

Imagine that you wish to find the rate of growth for the dividends given in Table 4.15. The year numbers in the table show that 1987 is viewed as the base year (year 0) and the subsequent years, 1988–1996, are considered years 1 through 9, respectively. Although 10 years of data are presented in Table 4.15, they represent only 9 years of growth because the value for the earliest year must be viewed as the initial value at time zero. To find the growth rate, we first divide the dividend for the earliest year (1987) by the dividend for the latest year (1996). The resulting quotient is .700 ($2.45 ÷ $3.50); it represents the value of the present-value interest factor for 9 years. To find the compound annual dividend growth rate, we find the discount rate in Table A.3 associated with the factor closest to .700 for 9 years. Looking across year 9 in Table A.3 shows that the factor for 4 percent is .703—very close to the .700 value. Therefore, the growth rate of the dividends in Table 4.15 is approximately 4 percent. (The precise value found using a financial calculator is 4.04 percent.) The use of growth rates, which are often an important input to the common stock valuation process, is explored in much more detail in Chapter 7.

CONCEPTS *in Review*

4.10 Define each of the following terms and describe how they are used to find the risk-free rate of return and the required rate of return for a given investment:
   a. *Real rate of return*
   b. *Expected inflation premium*
   c. *Risk premium* for a given investment

4.11 Define what is meant by the *holding period,* and explain why it is advisable to use equal-length holding periods (covering the same period in time) when comparing alternative investment vehicles. Define the *holding period return (HPR)* and explain for what length holding periods it is typically used.

4.12 Define *yield* or *internal rate of return* and explain when it is appropriate to use yield rather than the holding period return (HPR) to measure the return on an investment. How can the yield be conveniently approximated?

4.13 Explain why you must earn 10 percent on all income received from an investment during its holding period in order for its yield actually to equal the 10 percent value you've calculated.

4.14 Explain how either the present value (of benefits versus cost) or the yield measure can be used to find a satisfactory investment. Given the following data, indicate which, if any, of the following investments is acceptable. Explain your findings.

| | Investment | | |
	A	B	C
Cost	$200	$160	$500
Appropriate discount rate	7%	10%	9%
Present value of benefits	—	$150	—
Yield	8%	—	8%

RISK: THE OTHER SIDE OF THE COIN

risk
the chance that the actual return from an investment may differ from what is expected.

risk-return tradeoff
the relationship between risk and return, in which investments with more risk should provide higher returns, and vice versa.

Thus far, the primary concern of this chapter has been return. However, we cannot consider return without also looking at **risk**, the chance that the actual return from an investment may differ from what is expected. The risk associated with a given investment is directly related to its expected return. In general, the broader the range of possible returns associated with a given investment, the greater its risk, and vice versa. Put another way, riskier investments should provide higher levels of return. Otherwise, what incentive is there for an investor to risk his or her capital? In general, an investor will attempt to minimize risk for a given level of return or maximize return for a given level of risk. This relationship between risk and return, called the **risk-return tradeoff**, will be discussed later in this chapter.

In this part of the chapter, we will first examine various aspects of risk: sources of risk; the components of risk; the risk of a single asset; beta, a popular measure of risk; and the capital asset pricing model (CAPM), which uses beta to estimate return. We will then discuss how to evaluate the risk associated with a potential investment and the steps in the decision process.

SOURCES OF RISK

The risk associated with a given investment vehicle may result from a combination of any of a variety of possible sources. A prudent investor will consider how the major sources of risk, discussed below, might affect potential investment vehicles. Of course, as discussed in Chapter 2, *foreign exchange risk* should also be considered when investing internationally.

Business Risk

business risk
the degree of uncertainty associated with an investment's earnings and the investment's ability to pay investors the returns owed them.

In general, **business risk** is concerned with the degree of uncertainty associated with an investment's earnings and the investment's ability to pay investors dividends, interest, principal, and any other returns owed them. For example, a business firm may experience poor earnings and fail to fully pay investors as a result. In this case, business owners might receive no return if earnings are not adequate to meet obligations. Debtholders, on the other hand, are likely to receive some—but not necessarily all—of the amount owed them, due to the preferential treatment legally given debt.

Much of the business risk associated with a given investment vehicle is related to its kind of business. For example, the business risk of a common stock of a public utility differs from that of a high-fashion clothing manufacturer or a parcel of commercial real estate. Generally, investments in similar types of firms or properties have similar business risk, although differences in management, costs, and location can cause varying levels of risk.

Financial Risk

financial risk
the degree of uncertainty associated with the mix of debt and equity used to finance a firm or property; the larger the proportion of debt financing, the greater this risk.

The risk associated with the mix of debt and equity used to finance a firm or property is **financial risk**. The larger the proportion of debt used to finance a firm or property, the greater its financial risk. Debt financing obligates the firm to make interest payments as well as to repay the debts, thus increasing the firm's risk. These fixed-payment obligations must be met prior to distributing any earnings to the owners of such firms or properties. Inability to meet obligations associated with the use of debt could result in business failure, and in losses for bondholders as well as stockholders and owners.

Purchasing Power Risk

purchasing power risk
the chance that changing price levels in the economy (inflation or deflation) will adversely affect the returns on a given investment.

The possibility of changes in price levels within the economy (inflation or deflation) results in **purchasing power risk**. Specifically, this risk is the chance that generally rising prices (inflation) will reduce *purchasing power*—the amount of a given commodity that can be purchased with a dollar. For example, if last year a dollar would buy three candy bars, an increase in the price of a candy bar to 50 cents would mean that only two candy bars could be bought with the same dollar today. In periods of declining price levels (deflation), the purchasing power of the dollar will increase. In general, investments whose values move with general price levels have low purchasing power risk and are most profitable during periods of rising prices; those that provide fixed returns have high purchasing power risk and are most profitable during periods of declining price levels or low inflation. The returns on real and tangible personal property investments, for example, tend to move with the general price level, whereas returns from savings accounts and bonds do not.

Interest Rate Risk

interest rate risk
the chance that changes in interest rates will adversely affect a security's value.

Securities are especially affected by interest rate risk; this is especially true for those securities that offer purchasers a fixed periodic return. **Interest rate risk** is the chance that changes in interest rates will adversely affect a security's value. The interest rate changes themselves result from changes in the general relationship between the supply of and demand for money. As interest rates change, the prices of some securities fluctuate: They typically decrease with increasing interest rates and increase with decreasing interest rates. As we will see in greater detail in Chapters 8, 9, and 10, the prices of fixed-income securities (bonds and preferred stock) drop when interest rates rise. They thus provide purchasers with the same rate of return that would be available at prevailing rates. The opposite occurs when interest rates fall: The return on a fixed-income security is adjusted downward to a competitive level by an upward adjustment in its market price.

A second, more subtle aspect of interest rate risk is associated with reinvestment of income received from an investment. As noted in the earlier discussion of interest-on-interest, only if the investor can earn the initial rate of return on income received from an investment can he or she achieve a *fully compounded rate of return* equal to the initial rate of return. In other words, if a bond pays 8 percent annual interest, the investor must be able to earn 8 percent on the income received during the bond's holding period in order to earn a fully compounded 8 percent rate of return over that period. This same aspect of interest rate risk applies to reinvestment of the proceeds received from a bond or other investment at its maturity or sale.

A final aspect of interest rate risk relates to investing in short-term securities such as T-bills, certificates of deposit, commercial paper, and banker's acceptances (discussed in Chapter 3). Some investors include these securities in their portfolios rather than investing in long-term securities. With short-term securities, investors face the risk that when they mature, their proceeds may have to be invested in lower-yielding, new short-term securities. By initially making a long-term investment, an investor can lock in a return for a period of years, rather than face the risk of short-term interest rate declines. Clearly, when interest rates are declining, the returns from a short-term security investment strategy are adversely affected. On the other hand, interest rate increases have a positive impact on such a strategy. The chance that interest rates will decline is therefore the interest rate risk of a short-term security investment strategy.

All investment vehicles are actually subject to interest rate risk. Although fixed-income securities are most directly affected by interest rate movements, other long-term vehicles such as common stock and property are also influenced by them. *Generally, the higher the interest rate, the lower the value, and vice versa.*

Liquidity Risk

liquidity risk
the risk of not being able to liquidate an investment conveniently and at a reasonable price.

The risk of not being able to liquidate an investment conveniently and at a reasonable price is called **liquidity risk**. The liquidity of a given investment vehicle is an important consideration for an investor. In general, investment vehicles traded in *thin markets*, where demand and supply are small, tend to be less liquid than those traded in *broad markets*.

One can generally sell an investment vehicle merely by significantly cutting its price. However, to be liquid, an investment must be easily sold *at a reasonable price*. For example, a security recently purchased for $1,000 would not be viewed as highly liquid if it could be quickly sold only at a greatly reduced price, such as $500. Vehicles such as stocks and bonds of major companies listed on the New York Stock Exchange are generally highly liquid; others, such as an isolated parcel of raw land, are not.

Tax Risk

tax risk
the chance that Congress will make unfavorable changes in the tax laws that drive down the after-tax returns and market values of certain investments.

The chance that Congress will make unfavorable changes in tax laws is known as **tax risk**. The greater the chance that tax-law changes will drive down the after-tax returns and market values of certain investments, the greater the tax risk. Undesirable tax-law changes include elimination of tax exemptions, limitation of deductions, and increases in tax rates. During recent years, Congress has passed numerous tax-law changes. One of the most significant was the Tax

Reform Act of 1986, which contained provisions that reduced the attractiveness of many investment vehicles, particularly real estate and other tax shelters. While virtually all investments are vulnerable to tax rate increases, certain tax-advantaged investments, such as municipal and other bonds, real estate, and natural resources, generally have greater risk.

Market Risk

market risk
risk of decline in investment returns due to market factors independent of the given security or property investment.

Market risk is the risk that investment returns will decline due to market factors independent of the given security or property investment. Examples include political, economic, and social events, or changes in investor tastes and preferences. Market risk actually embodies a number of different risks: purchasing power, interest rate, and tax risks, described above.

The impact of market factors on investment returns is not uniform; the degree as well as the direction of change in return differs among investment vehicles. For example, legislation placing restrictive import quotas on Japanese goods may result in a significant increase in the value (and therefore the return) of domestic automobile and electronics stocks. Essentially, market risk is reflected in the *price volatility* of a security—the more volatile the price of a security, the greater its perceived market risk.

Event Risk

event risk
risk that comes from a largely (or totally) unexpected event that has a significant and usually immediate effect on the underlying value of an investment.

Event risk occurs when something happens to a company or property that has a sudden and substantial impact on its financial condition. Event risk goes beyond business and financial risk. It does not necessarily mean the company or market is doing poorly. Instead, it involves an event that is largely (or totally) unexpected and that has a significant and usually immediate effect on the underlying value of an investment. An example of event risk is the 1992 action by the Food and Drug Administration (FDA) to halt the use of silicone breast implants. The stock price of Dow Chemical—the dominant producer of this product—was quickly and negatively affected. Event risk can take many forms and affect all types of investment vehicles. Fortunately, its impact tends to be isolated in most cases, affecting only certain companies or properties. For instance, as a result of the FDA's silicone breast implant actions, the stocks of only a small number of companies were affected.

diversifiable (unsystematic) risk
the portion of an investment's risk resulting from uncontrollable or random events that can be eliminated through diversification; also called *unsystematic risk*.

nondiversifiable (systematic) risk
the inescapable portion of an investment's risk attributable to forces that affect all investments and therefore are not unique to any given vehicle; also called *systematic risk*.

total risk
the sum of an investment's nondiversifiable risk and diversifiable risk.

COMPONENTS OF RISK

The risk of an investment consists of two components: diversifiable and nondiversifiable risk. **Diversifiable risk**, sometimes called **unsystematic risk**, results from uncontrollable or random events, such as labor strikes, lawsuits, and regulatory actions. Such risk affects various investment vehicles differently. It represents the portion of an investment's risk that can be eliminated through diversification. **Nondiversifiable risk**, also called **systematic risk**, is attributed to forces like war, inflation, and political events that affect all investments and therefore are not unique to a given vehicle. The sum of nondiversifiable risk and diversifiable risk is called **total risk**, as given by Equation 4.11:

Equation 4.11   Total risk = nondiversifiable risk + diversifiable risk

Any intelligent investor can virtually eliminate or reduce diversifiable risk by holding a diversified portfolio of securities. Studies have shown that on average by carefully selecting 8 to 15 securities for a portfolio, investors can eliminate most diversifiable risk. Therefore, *the only relevant risk is nondiversifiable risk*. Nondiversifiable risk is inescapable. Each security possesses its own unique level of nondiversifiable risk, which we can measure, as we'll show later. (The concept of diversification and its implications are fully developed in Chapter 16 on portfolio construction.)

RISK OF A SINGLE ASSET

Most people have in their lives asked themselves how risky some anticipated course of action is. In such cases, the answer is usually a subjective judgment, such as "not very" or "quite risky," which may or may not help one's decision making. In finance, we are able to put numbers to the measurement of risk, which improves comparison between investments and helps decision making. The risk or variability of both single assets and portfolios of assets can be measured statistically. Here we focus solely on the risk of single assets. We first consider standard deviation, an absolute measure of risk, and then consider the coefficient of variation, a relative measure of risk.

standard deviation, *s*
a statistic used to measure the dispersion (variation) of returns around an asset's average or expected return, and the most common single indicator of an asset's risk.

Standard Deviation: An Absolute Measure of Risk

The most common single indicator of an asset's risk is the **standard deviation,** *s*, which measures the dispersion (variation) of returns around an asset's average or expected return. The formula is given in Equation 4.12:

Equation 4.12

$$\text{Standard deviation} = \sqrt{\frac{\sum\limits_{i=1}^{n}\left(\begin{array}{c}\text{return for} \\ \text{outcome } i\end{array} - \begin{array}{c}\text{average or} \\ \text{expected return}\end{array}\right)^2}{\begin{array}{c}\text{total number} \\ \text{of outcomes}\end{array} - 1}}$$

Equation 4.12a

$$s = \sqrt{\frac{\sum\limits_{i=1}^{n}(r_i - \bar{r})^2}{n-1}}$$

Consider two competing investments—A and B—described in Table 4.16. Notice that both investments earned an average return of 15 percent over the six-year period 1991–1996. Reviewing the returns shown for each investment

Table 4.16 Returns on Investments A and B

Year	Rate of Return	
	Investment A	Investment B
1991	15.6%	8.4%
1992	12.7	12.9
1993	15.3	19.6
1994	16.2	17.5
1995	16.5	10.3
1996	13.7	21.3
Average	15.0%	15.0%

Table 4.17 Calculation of Standard Deviations of Returns for Investments A and B

	Investment A			
Year (i)	**(1)** Return, r_i	**(2)** Average Return, $\bar{r}$	**(3)** (1) − (2) $r_i - \bar{r}$	**(4)** (3)² $(r_i - \bar{r})^2$
1991	15.6%	15.0%	.6%	0.36%
1992	12.7	15.0	−2.3	5.29
1993	15.3	15.0	.3	0.09
1994	16.2	15.0	1.2	1.44
1995	16.5	15.0	1.5	2.25
1996	13.7	15.0	−1.3	1.69

$$\sum_{i=1}^{6} (r - \bar{r})^2 = 11.12$$

$$s_A = \sqrt{\frac{\sum_{i=1}^{6} (r - \bar{r})^2}{n - 1}} = \sqrt{\frac{11.12}{6 - 1}} = \sqrt{2.224} = \underline{1.49\%}$$

	Investment B			
Year (i)	**(1)** Return, r_i	**(2)** Average Return, $\bar{r}$	**(3)** (1) − (2) $r_i - \bar{r}$	**(4)** (3)² $(r_i - \bar{r})^2$
1991	8.4%	15.0%	−6.6%	43.56%
1992	12.9	15.0	−2.1	4.41
1993	19.6	15.0	4.6	21.16
1994	17.5	15.0	2.5	6.25
1995	10.3	15.0	−4.7	22.09
1996	21.3	15.0	6.3	39.69

$$\sum_{i=1}^{6} (r - \bar{r})^2 = 137.16$$

$$s_B = \sqrt{\frac{\sum_{i=1}^{6} (r - \bar{r})^2}{n - 1}} = \sqrt{\frac{137.16}{6 - 1}} = \sqrt{27.432} = \underline{5.24\%}$$

in light of their 15 percent averages, we can see that the returns for investment B vary more from this average than the returns for investment A do.

The standard deviation provides a quantitative tool for use in assessing and comparing investment risk. Table 4.17 demonstrates the calculation of the standard deviations, s_A and s_B, for investments A and B, respectively. Evaluating the calculations, we can see that the standard deviation of 1.49 percent for the returns on investment A is, as expected, considerably below the standard deviation of 5.24 percent for investment B. The greater absolute dispersion of investment B's return, reflected in its larger standard deviation, indicates that it is the more risky investment. Of course, these values are absolute measures based upon historical data. There is no assurance that the risks of these two investments will be the same in the future.

coefficient of variation, *CV*
a statistic used to measure the *relative* dispersion of an asset's returns; it is useful in comparing the risk of assets with differing average or expected returns.

Coefficient of Variation: A Relative Measure of Risk

The **coefficient of variation, *CV***, is a measure of the *relative* dispersion of an asset's returns. It is useful in comparing the risk of assets with differing average or expected returns. Equation 4.13 gives the formula for the coefficient of variation:

Equation 4.13

$$\text{Coefficient of variation} = \frac{\text{standard deviation}}{\text{average or expected return}}$$

Equation 4.13a

$$CV = \frac{s}{r}$$

Like standard deviation, the higher the coefficient of variation, the greater is the risk.

Substituting the standard deviation values (from Table 4.17 on page 161) and the average returns (from Table 4.16 on page 160) for investments A and B into Equation 4.13a results in coefficients of variation for A and B of .099 (1.49% ÷ 15%) and .349 (5.24% ÷ 15%), respectively. Investment B has the higher coefficient of variation and, as expected, has more relative risk than investment A. Because both investments have the same average return, the coefficient of variation in this case has not provided any more information than the standard deviation.

The real utility of the coefficient of variation is in comparing investments that have *different* expected returns. For example, assume you want to select the less risky of two alternative investments—X and Y. The average return, the standard deviation, and the coefficient of variation for each of these investments are:

Statistics	Investment X	Investment Y
(1) Average return	12%	20%
(2) Standard deviation	9%*	10%
(3) Coefficient of variation [(2) ÷ (1)]	.75	.50*

* Preferred investment using the given risk measure.

If you compare the investments solely on the basis of their standard deviations, you would prefer investment X, because it has a lower standard deviation than investment Y (9% vs. 10%). However, by comparing the coefficients of variation of the investments, you can see that you would be making a serious error in choosing investment X over investment Y, because the *relative* dispersion, or risk, of the investments, as reflected in the coefficient of variation, is lower for Y than for X (.50 vs. .75). Clearly, the use of the coefficient of variation to compare investment risk is effective because it also considers the relative size, or average return, of each investment.

BETA: A POPULAR MEASURE OF RISK

During the past 30 years, much theoretical work has been done on the measurement of risk and its use in assessing returns. The two key components of this theory are *beta*, which is a measure of risk, and the *capital asset pricing model (CAPM)*, which relates the risk measured by beta to the level of required or expected return. First we will look at **beta**, a number that measures *nondiversifiable, or market, risk*. That is, beta indicates how the price of a security responds to market forces. The more responsive the price of a security is to changes in the market, the higher will be that security's beta. Beta is found by relating the historical returns on a security with the historical returns for the market.

beta
a measure of *nondiversifiable risk* that indicates how the price of a security responds to market forces; found by relating the historical returns on a security with the historical returns for the market.

market return
the average return on all (or a large sample of) stocks, such as those in Standard & Poor's 500 stock composite index.

Market return is typically measured by the average return for all (or a large sample of) stocks. The average return on all stocks in the Standard & Poor's 500 stock composite index or some other broad stock index is commonly used to measure market return. Although betas for actively traded securities can be obtained from a variety of sources, it is important to understand their derivation, interpretation, and use.

 ### Deriving Beta

The relationship between a security's return and the market return, and its use in deriving beta, can be demonstrated graphically. Figure 4.2 plots the relationship between the returns of two securities—C and D—and the market return. Note that the horizontal (x) axis measures the market returns and the vertical (y) axis measures the individual security's returns. The first step in deriving beta involves plotting the coordinates for the market return and security return at various points in time. Such annual market-return and security-return coordinates are shown in Figure 4.2 for security D for the years 1989 through 1996 (with the years noted in parentheses). For example, in 1996

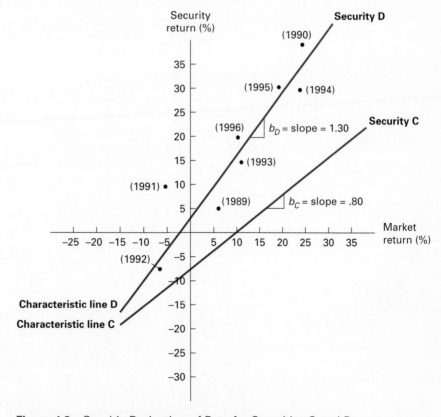

Figure 4.2 Graphic Derivation of Beta for Securities C and D
Betas can be derived graphically by plotting the coordinates for the market return and security return at various points in time and using statistical techniques to fit the "characteristic line" to the data points. The slope of the characteristic line is beta. For securities C and D, beta is found to be .80 and 1.30, respectively.

Table 4.18   Selected Betas and Associated Interpretations

Beta	Comment	Interpretation*
2.00 1.00 .50	Move in same direction as market	Twice as responsive as the market Same response or risk as the market Only half as responsive as the market
0		Unaffected by market movement
− .50 −1.00 −2.00	Move in opposite direction to market	Only half as responsive as the market Same response or risk as the market Twice as responsive as the market

*A stock that is twice as responsive as the market will experience a 2 percent change in its return for each 1 percent change in the return of the market portfolio. The return of a stock that is half as responsive as the market will change by ½ of 1 percent for each 1 percent change in the return of the market portfolio.

security D's return was 20 percent when the market return was 10 percent. By use of statistical techniques, the "characteristic line" that best explains the relationship between security-return and market-return coordinates is fit to the data points. *The slope of this line is beta.* The beta for security C is about .80, and for security D it is about 1.30. Security D's *steeper characteristic line slope indicates that its return is more responsive to changing market returns: it has a higher beta and therefore is more risky.*

Interpreting Beta

The beta for the overall market is considered to be equal to 1.00. All other betas are viewed in relation to this value. Table 4.18 shows some selected beta values and their associated interpretations. As can be seen, betas can be positive or negative, though nearly all betas are positive. The positive or negative sign preceding the beta number merely indicates whether the stock's return changes in the *same direction as the general market* (positive beta) or in the *opposite direction* (negative beta). Most stocks have betas that fall between 0.50 and 1.75. Listed below, for illustration purposes, are the actual betas for some popular stocks, as reported by *Value Line* on August 4, 1995:

Stock	Beta	Stock	Beta
American Greetings	1.15	B. F. Goodrich	1.05
Atlantic Energy	.70	Hawaiian Electric	.75
Bank of Boston	1.75	Hewlett-Packard	1.40
Briggs & Stratton	1.05	Lilly (Eli)	1.00
Cincinnati Bell	.85	Maytag	1.15
Compaq Computer	1.50	Microsoft	1.40
Disney	1.15	Quaker Oats	.90
Dow Chemical	1.30	Southwestern Energy	.65
Ford Motor	1.20	Timberland	1.35
General Electric	1.10	Winnebago	1.30

Many large brokerage firms as well as subscription services like *Value Line* publish betas for a broad range of securities. The ready availability of security betas has enhanced their use in assessing investment risks. *In general,*

<u>the higher the beta, the riskier the security</u>. The importance of beta in planning and building portfolios of securities will be discussed in greater detail in Chapter 16.

Using Beta

Individual investors will find beta useful in assessing market risk and understanding the impact the market can have on the return expected from a share of stock. Beta reveals how a security responds to market forces. For example, if the market is expected to experience a 10 percent *increase* in its rate of return over the next period, a stock having a beta of 1.50 would be expected to experience an *increase* in return of approximately 15 percent (1.50 × 10%) over the same period. Because the beta of this particular stock is greater than 1.00, it is more volatile than the market as a whole.

For stocks having positive betas, increases in market returns result in increases in security returns. Unfortunately, decreases in market returns are likewise translated into decreasing security returns—and this is where the risk lies. In the preceding example, if the market is expected to experience a 10 percent *decrease*, then the stock with a beta of 1.50 should experience a 15 percent *decrease* in its return. Because the stock has a beta of greater than 1.00, it is more responsive than the market, either way.

Stocks having betas of less than 1.00 will, of course, be less responsive to changing returns in the market. They are therefore considered less risky. For example, a stock having a beta of 0.50 will experience an increase or decrease in its return of about half that in the market as a whole. Thus, as the market goes down by 8 percent, such a stock will probably experience only about a 4 percent (0.50 × 8%) decline.

Here are some important points to remember about beta:

1. Beta measures the nondiversifiable, or market, risk of a security.

2. The beta for the market is 1.00.

3. Stocks may have positive or negative betas; nearly all are positive.

4. Stocks with betas of greater than 1.00 are more responsive to changes in market return—and therefore more risky—than the market. Stocks with betas of less than 1.00 are less risky than the market.

5. Due to its greater risk, the higher a stock's beta, the greater should be its level of expected return, and vice versa.

THE CAPM: USING BETA TO ESTIMATE RETURN

capital asset pricing model (CAPM)
model that uses beta, the risk-free rate, and the market return to help investors define the required return on an investment; it formally links together the notions of risk and return.

About 30 years ago, William F. Sharpe and John Lintner developed a model that uses beta to link together formally the notions of risk and return. Called the **capital asset pricing model (CAPM)**, it was developed to explain the behavior of security prices and to provide a mechanism whereby investors can assess the impact of a proposed security investment on their portfolio's risk and return. We can use the CAPM to understand the basic risk-return trade-offs involved in various types of investment decisions. The CAPM can be viewed both as an equation and as a graph.

The Equation

With beta, b, as the measure of nondiversifiable risk, the capital asset pricing model defines the required rate of return on an investment according to the following equation:

Equation 4.14

$$\text{Required return on investment } i = \text{risk-free rate} + \left[\begin{pmatrix} \text{beta for} \\ \text{investment } i \end{pmatrix} \times \begin{pmatrix} \text{market} \\ \text{return} \end{pmatrix} - \begin{pmatrix} \text{risk-free} \\ \text{rate} \end{pmatrix} \right]$$

Equation 4.14a

$$r_i = R_F + [b_i \times (r_m - R_F)]$$

where

r_i = the required return on investment i given its risk as measured by beta

R_F = the risk-free rate of return; the return that can be earned on a risk-free investment

b_i = beta coefficient or index of nondiversifiable risk for investment i

r_m = the market return; the average return on all securities (typically measured by the average return on all securities in the Standard & Poor's 500 stock composite index or some other broad stock market index)

The equation shows that *as beta increases, the required return for a given investment increases.*

Application of the CAPM can be demonstrated with the following example. Assume security Z with a beta (b_Z) of 1.25 is being considered at a time when the risk-free rate (R_F) is 6 percent and the market return (r_m) is 10 percent. Substituting these data into the CAPM equation, Equation 4.14a, we get:

$$r_z = 6\% + [1.25 \times (10\% - 6\%)] = 6\% + [1.25 \times 4\%]$$

$$= 6\% + 5\% = \underline{\underline{11\%}}$$

The investor should therefore expect—indeed, require—an 11 percent return on this investment as compensation for the risk he or she has to assume, given the security's beta of 1.25. If the beta were lower, say 1.00, the required return would be lower:

$$r_z = 6\% + [1.00 \times (10\% - 6\%)] = 6\% + 4\% = \underline{\underline{10\%}}$$

If the beta were higher, say 1.50, the required return would be higher:

$$r_z = 6\% + [1.50 \times (10\% - 6\%)] = 6\% + 6\% = \underline{\underline{12\%}}$$

Clearly, the CAPM reflects the positive mathematical relationship between risk and return, because the higher the risk (beta), the higher the required return.

The Graph: The Security Market Line (SML)

When the capital asset pricing model is depicted graphically, it is called the **security market line (SML)**. Plotting the CAPM, we would find that the SML will, in fact, be a straight line. For each level of nondiversifiable risk (beta), the SML, like the CAPM, reflects the required return the investor should earn in the marketplace. The CAPM at a given point in time can be plotted by simply calculating the required return for a variety of betas; of course, at the given point in time the risk-free rate and market return would be constant. For example, as we saw above, using a 6 percent risk-free rate and a 10 percent market return, the required return is 11 percent when beta is 1.25. Increase the beta to 2.00, and the required return equals 14 percent (6% + [2.00 × (10% − 6%)]). Similarly, we can find the required return for a number of betas and end up with the following combinations of risk (beta) and required return:

Risk (Beta)	Required Return (Percent)
0.0	6
0.5	8
1.0	10
1.5	12
2.0	14
2.5	16

Plotting these values on a graph (with beta on the horizontal axis and required returns on the vertical axis), we would have a straight line like the one in Figure 4.3. It is clear from the SML that as risk (beta) increases, so does the required return, and vice versa.

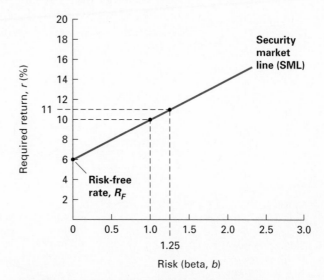

Figure 4.3 The Security Market Line (SML)
The security market line (SML) clearly depicts the tradeoff between risk and return. At a beta of 0, the required return is the risk-free rate of 6 percent; at a beta of 1.0, the required return is the market return of 10 percent. Given these data, the required return on an investment with a beta of 1.25 is 11 percent.

EVALUATING RISK

Techniques for quantifying the risk of a given investment vehicle will, however, be of little use to the investor who is unaware of his or her feelings
toward risk. Investors must somehow relate the risk perceived in a given
vehicle not only to the expected return but also to their own dispositions
toward risk. The individual investor typically tends to seek answers to these
questions: "Is the amount of perceived risk worth taking to get the expected
return?" "Can I get a higher return for the same level of risk or a lower risk
for the same level of return?" A look at the general risk-return characteristics
of alternative investment vehicles and the question of an acceptable level of
risk will help shed light on the nature of risk evaluations.

Risk-Return Characteristics of Alternative Investment Vehicles

A wide variety of risk-return behaviors is associated with each type of investment vehicle. Some common stocks offer low returns and low risk; others offer
high returns and high risk. In general the risk-return characteristics of each of
the major investment vehicles can be depicted on a set of risk-return axes, as
shown in Figure 4.4. Of course, for each type of investment vehicle, a broad
range of risk-return behaviors exists for specific investments. In other words,
once the appropriate type of vehicle has been selected, the decision as to which
specific security or property to acquire must still be made.

An Acceptable Level of Risk

Because of differing investor preferences, it is impossible to specify a general
acceptable level of risk. The three basic risk-preference behaviors—risk-indifferent, risk-averse, and risk-seeking—are depicted graphically in Figure 4.5. As
risk goes from x_1 to x_2 on the graph, the required return does not change for

Figure 4.4 Risk-Return
Tradeoffs for Various
Investment Vehicles
A risk-return tradeoff exists
such that for a higher risk
one expects a higher return,
and vice versa. Low-risk–low-
return investment vehicles
are U.S. government securities, savings accounts, and
so on. High-risk–high-return
vehicles include real estate
and other tangible investments, options, and futures.

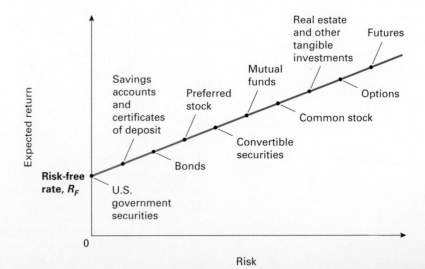

Figure 4.5 Risk Preferences
The risk-indifferent investor requires no change in return for a given increase in risk; the risk-averse investor requires an increase in return for a given risk increase; and the risk-seeking investor gives up some return for more risk. The majority of investors are risk-averse.

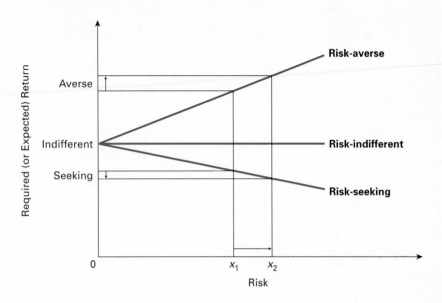

risk-indifferent
describes an investor who does not require a change in return as compensation for greater risk.

risk-averse
describes an investor who requires greater return in exchange for greater risk.

risk-seeking
describes an investor who will accept a lower return in exchange for greater risk.

the **risk-indifferent** investor: in essence, no change in return would be required as compensation for the increase in risk. For the **risk-averse** investor, the required return increases for an increase in risk. Because they shy away from risk, these investors require higher expected returns to compensate them for taking greater risk. For the **risk-seeking** investor, the required return decreases for an increase in risk. Theoretically, because they enjoy risk, these investors are willing to give up some return to take more risk.

Most investors are risk-averse: for a given increase in risk, they require an increase in return. Note that the security market line (SML) in Figure 4.3 on page 167 clearly depicts the risk-averse behavior of investors who require increasing returns, r, for increased levels of nondiversifiable risk as measured by beta, b. The risk-averse behavior is also depicted in Figure 4.4. Of course, the amount of return required by each investor for a given increase in risk differs depending upon the investor's degree of risk aversion (reflected in the slope of the line). Investors generally tend to be conservative rather than aggressive when accepting risk. To get a feel for your own risk-taking orientation, read the *Investor Insights* box on page 170.

STEPS IN THE DECISION PROCESS: COMBINING RETURN AND RISK

In the decision process, investors should take the following steps, which combine return and risk, when selecting from among alternative investments:

1. Using historical or projected return data, estimate the expected return over a given holding period. Use yield (or present-value) techniques to make sure that the time value of money is given adequate consideration.

2. Using historical or projected return data, assess the risk associated with the investment. Use of subjective risk assessment, use of the standard deviation or coefficient of variation of returns, and use of beta (for securities) are the primary approaches available to the individual investor.

INVESTOR INSIGHTS: *Conflicting Viewpoints*

How Much Investment Risk Can You Handle?

An effective investment plan is based on a balance between the risks you are willing to take and the returns you need to achieve your goals. The conservative investor saving for retirement or college funding might want to buy only "safe" investments such as bank CDs or U.S. Treasury bills. Historically, though, these fixed-rate investments have barely kept pace with inflation, and taxes lessen returns even further. On the other hand, the stock market— a riskier choice—has far outperformed other investments over the long run. Many financial experts advise having at least 30 to 40 percent of your portfolio in equities (some suggest even 50 to 75 percent) if you want to accumulate assets over the long term (more than five to ten years).

The key to risk taking is to determine your personal level of risk tolerance—how comfortable you feel with the volatility of your investments. Understanding your risk tolerance will prevent you from taking more risk than you can handle and will reduce the likelihood that you will panic and abandon your plan midstream.

One way to assess your risk tolerance is to ask yourself how much you could lose on your investments over a one-year period and still stick to your plan. In general, investors with low risk tolerance can withstand annual losses of no more than 5 percent, those with moderate tolerance can withstand losses of 6 to 15 percent, and those with high tolerance will accept losses of 16 to 25 percent.

The following quiz can help you evaluate your personal capacity for risk.

What Is Your Investment Risk Tolerance?

1. Which best describes your feelings about investing?
   a. "Better safe than sorry."
   b. "Moderation in all things."
   c. "Nothing ventured, nothing gained."

2. Which is the most important to you as an investor?
   a. Steady income
   b. Steady income and growth
   c. Rapid price appreciation

3. You won! Which prize would you select?
   a. $4,000 in cash
   b. A 50 percent chance to win $10,000
   c. A 20 percent chance to win $100,000

4. The stocks in your retirement account have dropped 20 percent since last quarter. The market experts are optimistic. What would you do?
   a. Transfer out of stock to avoid losing more.
   b. Stay in stock and wait for them to come back.
   c. Shift more money into stocks. If they made sense before, they're a bargain now.

5. The stocks in your retirement account have suddenly gone up 20 percent. You have no more information. What would you do?
   a. Transfer out of stocks and lock in my gains.
   b. Stay in stocks, hoping for more gains.
   c. Transfer more money into stocks. They might go higher.

6. Would you borrow money to take a good investment opportunity?
   a. Never
   b. Maybe
   c. Yes

7. How would you characterize yourself as an investor?
   a. Conservative
   b. Moderate risk taker
   c. Aggressive

How to determine your score:

Each (a) answer is worth 1 point. Each (b) is worth 2 points. Each (c) is worth 3 points. Add them up to find your total score.

  7–11 points: a conservative investor
12–16 points: a moderate risk taker
17–21 points: an aggressive investor

Sources: Maria Crawford Scott, "Life-Cycle Investing: Investment Decisions and Your Personal Investment Profile," *AAII Journal*, March 1993, pp. 16–19 (downloaded from America Online); and Ann Perry, "Putting Stock in the Market," *San Diego Union-Tribune*, July 18, 1993, pp. I1–I2.

3. Evaluate the risk-return behavior of each alternative investment to make sure that the return expected is reasonable given its level of risk. If other vehicles with equal or lower levels of risk provide equal or greater returns, the investment would not be acceptable.

4. Select the investment vehicles that offer the highest returns associated with the level of risk the investor is willing to take. Because most investors are risk-averse, they will acquire lower-risk vehicles, thereby receiving lower investment returns. As long as they get the highest return for the acceptable level of risk, they have made a "good investment."

Probably the most difficult step in this process is assessing risk. Aside from return and risk considerations, other factors, such as taxes, liquidity, and portfolio considerations, will affect the investment decision. We will look at these in later chapters.

CONCEPTS *in Review*

4.15 Define *risk*. Explain what is meant by the *risk-return tradeoff*. What happens to the required return as risk increases? Explain.

4.16 Define and briefly discuss each of the following sources of risk:
a. Business risk
b. Financial risk
c. Purchasing power risk
d. Interest rate risk
e. Liquidity risk
f. Tax risk
g. Market risk
h. Event risk

4.17 Briefly define and give examples of each of the following components of total risk. Be sure to indicate which is the relevant risk and explain why.
a. Diversifiable risk
b. Nondiversifiable risk

4.18 Briefly describe each of the following measures of risk or variability, and explain their similarity and under what circumstances each is preferred when comparing the risk of competing investments.
a. Standard deviation
b. Coefficient of variation

4.19 Explain what is meant by *beta*. What is the relevant risk measured by beta? What is the *market return*? How does the interpretation of beta relate to the market return?

4.20 What range of values does beta typically exhibit? Are positive or negative betas more common? Explain.

4.21 What is the *capital asset pricing model (CAPM)*? What role does beta play in it? How does the *security market line (SML)* relate to the CAPM?

4.22 Differentiate among the three basic risk preferences—risk-indifferent, risk-averse, and risk-seeking. Which of these behaviors best describes most investors? Explain. How does an investor's risk preference typically enter the investment decision process?

4.23 Describe the steps involved in the investment decision process. Be sure to mention how returns and risks can be measured and combined to determine the group of reasonable or acceptable investments from which the final selection can be made.

On Track with STOCK-TRAK®

How STOCK-TRAK® Calculates Holding Period Return

STOCK-TRAK® calculates the total portfolio value at valuation dates. It does not make any adjustments for the amount of risk incurred in the investment process. STOCK-TRAK® first calculates the portfolio's equity, or value, using the following equation:

Equity = cash − debit balance + credit balance
$$+ \ MV_{\text{long position}} - MV_{\text{short position}}$$

where:

debit balance = amount borrowed for margin trading

credit balance = proceeds from short sales

MV = current market value

The portfolio's holding period return, HPR, is then calculated using the following equation:

$$HPR = \frac{\text{equity} - \text{beginning cash balance}}{\text{beginning cash balance}}$$

If the beginning cash balance exceeds equity, the holding period return will be negative, representing a loss for the period.

SUMMARY

LG 1   **Review the concept, components, and importance of return and the forces that affect the investor's level of return.** Return is the reward for investing. The total return provided by an investment includes current income and capital gains (or losses). Return is commonly calculated on a historical basis and then used to project expected returns. The level of return depends on internal characteristics and external forces, which include the general level of price changes.

LG 2   **Discuss the time value of money and the calculations involved in finding the future value of various types of cash flows.** Because investors have opportunities to earn interest on their funds, the time value of money must be considered when evaluating investment returns. Interest can be applied using either the simple interest method or the compound interest method. The more frequently interest is compounded at a stated rate, the higher the true rate of interest. The future value of a present sum or an annuity can be found using compound interest concepts.

LG 3   **Explain the concept of present value, the procedures for calculating present values, and the use of present value in determining a satisfactory investment.** The present value of a future sum is the amount that would have to be deposited today, into an account earning interest at a given rate, to accumulate the specified future sum. The present value of streams of future returns can be found by adding the present values of the individual returns. When the stream is an annuity, its present value can be more simply calculated. A satisfactory investment is one for which the present value of benefits equals or exceeds the present value of its costs.

LG 4   **Describe real, risk-free, and required returns and the computation and application of holding period return, yield (internal rate of return), approximate yield, and growth rates.** The required return on an investment is the rate of return an investor must earn to be fully compensated for its risk. It represents the sum of the real rate of return and the inflation premium, which together represent the risk-free rate, and the risk premium for the investment. The risk premium varies depending upon issue and issuer characteristics. The holding period return (HPR) is the return earned over a specified period of time. It is frequently used to compare returns earned in periods of one year or less.

Yield or internal rate of return is the compounded annual rate of return earned on investments held for more than one year. If the yield is greater than or equal to the required return, the investment would be acceptable. Implicit in the use of yield is an ability to earn a return equal to the calculated yield on all income received from the investment during the holding period. The yield on an investment can be estimated using the approximate yield formula. Present-value techniques can be used to find a rate of growth—the compounded annual rate of change in the value of a stream of income, particularly dividends or earnings.

LG 5 **Discuss the major sources of risk, the components of risk, and the risk of a single asset in both absolute and relative terms.** Risk is the chance that the actual return from an investment will differ from what is expected. The total risk associated with a given investment vehicle may result from a combination of a variety of sources, such as business risk, financial risk, purchasing power risk, interest rate risk, liquidity risk, tax risk, market risk, and event risk. The two basic components of total risk are diversifiable (unsystematic) and nondiversifiable (systematic); nondiversifiable risk is the relevant risk. The risk of both single assets and portfolios of assets can be measured statistically on an absolute basis by the standard deviation and on a relative basis by the coefficient of variation.

LG 6 **Understand beta and the capital asset pricing model (CAPM) and how they can be used in the selection process to evaluate the risk-return characteristics of alternative investment vehicles.** Beta can be used to measure the nondiversifiable, or market, risk associated with a security investment. It is derived from the historical relationship between a security's return and the market return. The capital asset pricing model (CAPM), which can be depicted graphically as the security market line (SML), relates risk (as measured by beta) to return. The CAPM reflects increasing required returns for increasing risk.

There is a tradeoff between risk and return. Generally, each type of investment vehicle displays certain risk-return characteristics. Most investors are risk-averse: In exchange for a given increase in risk, they require an increase in return. The investment decision involves estimating the return and risk of each alternative investment and then selecting those that offer the highest returns associated with the level of risk the investor is willing to take.

DISCUSSION QUESTIONS

1. Choose a publicly traded company that has been listed on a major exchange or in the over-the-counter market for at least 5 years. Use any data source of your choice to find the annual cash dividend, if any, paid by the company in each of the immediate past 5 calendar years. Also find the closing price of the stock at the end of each of the immediately preceding 6 years.
   a. Calculate the return for each of the 5 one-year periods.
   b. Graph the returns on a set of year (x-axis)–return (y-axis) axes.
   c. Based on the graph in (b), estimate the return for the coming year, and explain your answer.

2. Estimate the amount of cash you will need each year over the next 20 years to live at the standard you desire. Also estimate the rate of return you can reasonably expect to earn annually, on average, during that 20-year period.

    a. How large a single lump sum would you need today to provide the annual cash required to allow you to live at the desired standard over the next 20 years? (*Hint:* Be sure to use the appropriate discount rate.)

    b. Would the lump sum amount calculated in (a) be larger or smaller if you could earn a higher return during the 20-year period? Explain.

    c. If you had the lump sum amount calculated in (a) but decided to delay your planned retirement in 20 years for another 3 years, how much extra cash would you have accumulated over the 3-year period if you could invest it to earn a 7 percent annual rate of return?

3. Choose three NYSE-listed stocks and maintain a record of their dividend payments, if any, and closing prices each week over the next 6 weeks.

    a. At the end of the 6-week period, calculate the 1-week holding period returns (HPRs) for each stock for each of the 6 weeks.

    b. For each stock, average the six weekly HPRs calculated in (a) and compare them.

    c. Use *Value Line* to find the beta for each of the three stocks, and compare and discuss their relative risk-return behaviors over the 6-week period.

    d. Based on your findings in (c), did the stock perform as expected (higher risk–higher return) over the 6-week period? What explanations can you suggest for any observed discrepancies?

4. Access appropriate government and economic data at your college or public library to obtain current estimates of the real rate of return and the expected inflation premium. Also find the current market return. Find both the most recent holding period return and beta (from *Value Line*) for each of the following stocks:

    Chrysler (autos)

    Compaq (computers)

    Kroger (groceries)

    Paine Webber (financial services)

    San Diego Gas & Electric (utilities)

    a. Use the appropriate data you have gathered to estimate the current risk-free rate.

    b. Find the required return for each of the five stocks using the capital asset pricing model (CAPM) and the relevant values gathered earlier and calculated in (a).

    c. Discuss, compare, and contrast the relative risks and returns for each of the five stocks.

5. Find the current risk-free rate and market return. Use *Value Line* to find current betas for each of the companies listed on page 164.

    a. Compare, contrast, and comment on the current betas in light of the August 4, 1995, betas given in the chapter for each of the companies.

    b. Do you think the betas should remain the same over time? What might cause them to change, even in a stable economic environment?

    c. Use the current betas and the capital asset pricing model (CAPM) to estimate each stock's required return.

    d. Compare and discuss your findings in (c) with regard to the specific business that each company is involved in.

PROBLEMS   LG 1   1. How much would an investor earn on a stock purchased one year ago for $63 if it paid an annual cash dividend of $3.75 and had just been sold for $67.50? Would the investor have experienced a capital gain? Explain.

LG 1   2. Assuming you purchased a share of stock for $50 one year ago, sold it today for $60, and during the year received three dividend payments totaling $2.70, calculate:
   a. Current income
   b. Capital gain (or loss)
   c. Total return
      (1) In dollars
      (2) As a percentage of the initial investment

LG 1   3. Given the historical data below:
   a. Calculate the total return (in dollars) for each year.
   b. Indicate the level of return you would expect in 1997 and 1998.
   c. Comment on your forecast.

| | | Market Value (Price) | |
Year	Income	Beginning	Ending
1992	$1.00	$30.00	$32.50
1993	1.20	32.50	35.00
1994	1.30	35.00	33.00
1995	1.60	33.00	40.00
1996	1.75	40.00	45.00

LG 2 LG 3   4. For the following savings account transactions, calculate:
   a. End-of-year account balance (assume that the account balance at December 31, 1995, is zero).
   b. Annual interest, using 6 percent simple interest and assuming all interest is withdrawn from the account as it is earned.
   c. True rate of interest, and compare it to the stated rate of interest. Discuss your finding.

Date	Deposit (Withdrawal)
1/1/96	$5,000
1/1/97	(4,000)
1/1/98	2,000
1/1/99	3,000

 LG 2 LG 3   5. Using the appropriate table of interest factors found in Appendix A, calculate:
   a. The future value of a $300 deposit left in an account paying 7 percent annual interest for 12 years.
   b. The future value at the end of 6 years of an $800 annual end-of-year deposit into an account paying 7 percent annual interest.

 LG 2 LG 3   6. For each of the following initial investment amounts, calculate the future value at the end of the given investment period if interest is compounded annually at the specified rate of return over the given investment period.

Investment	Investment Amount	Rate of Return	Investment Period
A	$ 200	5%	20 years
B	4,500	8	7
C	10,000	9	10
D	25,000	10	12
E	37,000	11	5

7. For each of the following annual deposits into an account paying the stated annual interest rate over the specified deposit period, calculate the future value of the annuity at the end of the given deposit period.

Deposit	Amount of Annual Deposit	Interest Rate	Deposit Period
A	$ 2,500	8%	10 years
B	500	12	6
C	1,000	20	5
D	12,000	6	8
E	4,000	14	30

8. If you could earn 9 percent on similar-risk investments, what is the least you would accept at the end of a 6-year period given the following amounts and timing of your investment?
   a. Invest $5,000 as a lump sum today.
   b. Invest $2,000 at the end of each of the next 5 years.
   c. Invest a lump sum of $3,000 today and $1,000 at the end of each of the next 5 years.
   d. Invest $900 at the end of years 1, 3, and 5.

9. For each of the following investments, calculate the present value of the future sum using the specified discount rate and assuming the sum will be received at the end of the given year.

Investment	Future Sum	Discount Rate	End of Year
A	$ 7,000	12%	4
B	28,000	8	20
C	10,000	14	12
D	150,000	11	6
E	45,000	20	8

10. A Florida State savings bond can be converted to $1,000 at maturity 8 years from purchase. If the state bonds are to be competitive with U.S. savings bonds, which pay 6 percent interest compounded annually, at what price will the state's bonds sell, assuming they make no cash payments prior to maturity?

11. Find the present value of each of the following streams of income assuming a 12 percent discount rate.

A		B		C	
End of Year	Income	End of Year	Income	End of Year	Income
1	$2,200	1	$10,000	1–5	$10,000/yr.
2	3,000	2–5	5,000/yr.	6–10	8,000/yr.
3	4,000	6	7,000		
4	6,000				
5	8,000				

12. Given the following streams of income:

	Income Stream	
End of Year	A	B
1	$ 4,000	$ 1,000
2	3,000	2,000
3	2,000	3,000
4	1,000	4,000
Totals	$10,000	$10,000

a. Find the present value of each income stream using a 15 percent discount rate.

b. Compare the calculated present values and discuss them in light of the fact that the undiscounted total income amounts to $10,000 in each case.

LG 2 **LG 3** 13. For each of the following investments, calculate the present value of the annual end-of-year returns at the specified discount rate over the given period.

Investment	Annual Returns	Discount Rate	Period
A	$ 1,200	7%	3 years
B	5,500	12	15
C	700	20	9
D	14,000	5	7
E	2,200	10	5

LG 2 **LG 3** 14. Using the appropriate table of interest factors found in Appendix A, calculate:

a. The present value of $500 to be received 4 years from now, using an 11 percent discount rate.

b. The present value of the following end-of-year income streams, using a 9 percent discount rate and assuming it is now the beginning of 1997.

End of Year	Income Stream A	Income Stream B
1997	$80	$140
1998	80	120
1999	80	100
2000	80	80
2001	80	60
2002	80	40
2003	80	20

LG 2 **LG 3** 15. Terri Allessandro has an opportunity to make any of the following investments. The purchase price, the amount of its lump-sum future value, and its year of receipt are given below for each investment. Terri can earn a 10 percent rate of return on investments similar to those currently under consideration. Evaluate each investment to determine if it is satisfactory and make an investment recommendation to Terri.

Investment	Purchase Price	Future Value	Year of Receipt
A	$18,000	$30,000	5
B	600	3,000	20
C	3,500	10,000	10
D	1,000	15,000	40

LG 2 **LG 3** 16. Kent Weitz wishes to assess whether or not the following two investments are satisfactory. Use his required return (discount rate) of 17 percent to evaluate each investment. Make an investment recommendation to Kent.

	Investment	
	A	B
Purchase price	$13,000	$8,500
End of Year	Income Stream	
1	$ 2,500 ✓	$4,000
2	3,500	3,500
3	4,500	3,000
4	5,000	1,000
5	5,500	500

LG 4   17. Given a real rate of interest of 3 percent, an expected inflation premium of 5 percent, and risk premiums for investments A and B of 3 percent and 5 percent, respectively, find:
a. The risk-free rate of return, R_F.
b. The required returns for investments A and B.

LG 4   18. Calculate the holding period return (HPR) for the following two investment alternatives. Which, if any, of the return components is likely not to be realized if you continue to hold each of the investments beyond one year? Which vehicle would you prefer, assuming they are of equal risk? Explain.

	Investment Vehicle	
	X	Y
Cash received		
1st quarter	$ 1.00	$ 0
2nd quarter	1.20	0
3rd quarter	0	0
4th quarter	2.30	2.00
Investment value		
End-of-year	$29.00	$56.00
Beginning-of-year	30.00	50.00

LG 4   19. Assume that you invest $5,000 today in an investment vehicle that promises to return to you $9,000 in exactly 10 years.
a. Use the present-value technique to estimate the yield on this investment.
b. Apply the approximate yield formula to estimate the yield on this investment.
c. If a minimum return of 9 percent is required, would you recommend this investment?

LG 4   20. Use the appropriate present-value interest factor table to estimate the yield to the nearest 1 percent for each of the following investments:

Investment	Initial Investment	Future Value	End of Year
A	$ 1,000	$ 1,200	5
B	10,000	20,000	7
C	400	2,000	20
D	3,000	4,000	6
E	5,500	25,000	30

LG 4   21. Rosemary Santos must earn a return of 10 percent on an investment that requires an initial outlay of $2,500 and promises to return $6,000 in 8 years.
a. Use present-value techniques to estimate the yield on this investment to the nearest 1 percent.
b. Use the approximate yield formula to estimate the yield on this investment.
c. Based on your findings in (a) and (b), should Rosemary make the proposed investment? Explain.

LG 4   22. Use the appropriate present-value interest factors to estimate the yield to the nearest 1 percent for the two investments on the next page.

	Investment	
	A	B
Initial investment	$8,500	$9,500
End of Year	Income	
1	$2,500	$2,000
2	2,500	2,500
3	2,500	3,000
4	2,500	3,500
5	2,500	4,000

23. Elliott Dumack must earn a minimum rate of return of 11 percent to be adequately compensated for the risk of the following investment:

Initial investment	$14,000
End of Year	Income
1	$ 6,000
2	3,000
3	5,000
4	2,000
5	1,000

a. Use present-value techniques to estimate the yield on this investment to the nearest 1 percent.
b. Use the approximate yield formula to estimate the yield on this investment.
c. Based on your findings in (a) and (b), should Elliott make the proposed investment? Explain.

24. Assume the investment generating income stream B in question 14 can be purchased at the beginning of 1997 for $1,000 and sold at the end of 2003 for $1,200. Calculate the approximate yield for this investment. If a minimum return of 9 percent is required, would you recommend this investment? Explain.

25. For each of the following streams of dividends, estimate (to the nearest 1 percent) the compound annual rate of growth between the earliest year for which a value is given and 1996.

	Dividend Stream		
Year	A	B	C
1987		$1.50	
1988		1.55	
1989		1.61	
1990		1.68	$2.50
1991		1.76	2.60
1992	$5.00	1.85	2.65
1993	5.60	1.95	2.65
1994	6.40	2.06	2.80
1995	7.20	2.17	2.85
1996	8.00	2.28	2.90

26. The historic returns for two investments—A and B—are summarized below for the period 1992 to 1996. Use the data to answer the questions that follow them.

	Investment	
	A	B
Year	Rate of Return	
1992	19%	8%
1993	1	10
1994	10	12
1995	26	14
1996	4	16
Average	12%	12%

a. Based upon a review of the return data, which investment appears to be more risky? Why?

b. Calculate the standard deviation and coefficient of variation for each investment.

c. Based upon your calculations in (b), which investment is most risky? Compare the conclusion to your observation in (a).

d. Does the coefficient of variation provide improved risk comparison over the standard deviation in this case? Why or why not?

27. Imagine you wish to estimate the betas for two investments, A and B. In this regard, you have gathered the following return data for the market and each of the investments over the past 10 years, 1987–1996.

	Historic Returns		
		Investment	
Year	Market	A	B
1987	6%	11%	16%
1988	2	8	11
1989	−13	−4	−10
1990	−4	3	3
1991	−8	0	−3
1992	16	19	30
1993	10	14	22
1994	15	18	29
1995	8	12	19
1996	13	17	26

a. On a set of market return (x-axis)–investment return (y-axis) axes, use the data to draw the characteristic lines for investments A and B on the same set of axes.

b. Use the characteristic lines from (a) to estimate the betas from investments A and B.

c. Use the betas found in (b) to comment on the relative risks of investments A and B.

28. A security has a beta of 1.20. Is this security more or less risky than the market? Explain. Assess the impact on the required return of this security in each of the following cases:

a. The market return increases by 15 percent.

b. The market return decreases by 8 percent.

c. The market return remains unchanged.

29. Assume the betas for securities A, B, and C are as given below:

Security	Beta
A	1.40
B	.80
C	−.90

a. Calculate the change in return for each security if the market experiences an increase in its rate of return of 13.2 percent over the next period.
b. Calculate the change in return for each security if the market experiences a decrease in its rate of return of 10.8 percent over the next period.
c. Rank and discuss the relative risk of each security based on your findings. Which security might perform best during an economic downturn? Explain.

30. Use the capital asset pricing model (CAPM) to find the required return for each of the following securities in light of the data given below:

Security	Risk-Free Rate	Market Return	Beta
A	5%	8%	1.30
B	8	13	.90
C	9	12	−20
D	10	15	1.00
E	6	10	.60

31. The risk-free rate is currently 7 percent and the market return is 12 percent. Assume you are considering the following investment vehicles with the betas noted below:

Investment Vehicle	Beta
A	1.50
B	1.00
C	.75
D	0
E	2.00

a. Which vehicle is most risky? Least risky?
b. Use the capital asset pricing model (CAPM) to find the required return on each of the investment vehicles.
c. Draw the security market line (SML) using your findings in (b).
d. Based on your findings in (c), what relationship exists between risk and return? Explain.

CASE PROBLEMS   **4.1 SOLOMON'S DECISION**

Dave Solomon, a 23-year-old mathematics teacher at Xavier High School, recently received a tax refund of $1,100. Because Dave doesn't currently have any need for this money, he decided to make a long-term investment. After surveying a large number of alternative investments costing no more than $1,100, Dave isolated two that seemed most suitable to his needs. Each of the investments cost $1,050 and was expected to provide income over a 10-year period. Investment A provided a relatively certain stream of income, while Dave was a little less certain of the income provided by investment B. From his search for suitable alternatives, Dave found that the appropriate discount rate for a relatively certain investment was 12 percent. Because he felt a bit uncomfortable with an investment like B, he estimated that such an investment would have to provide a return at least 4 percent *higher* than investment A. Although Dave planned to reinvest funds returned from the investments in other vehicles providing similar returns, he wished to keep the extra $50 ($1,100 − $1,050) invested for the full 10 years in a savings account paying 5 percent interest compounded annually. To make his investment decision, Dave has asked for your help in answering the questions that follow the expected return data for each investment.

	Expected Returns	
Year	A	B
1997	$ 150	$100
1998	150	150
1999	150	200
2000	150	250
2001	150	300
2002	150	350
2003	150	300
2004	150	250
2005	150	200
2006	1,150	150

Questions

1. Assuming investments A and B are equally risky, using the 12 percent discount rate apply the present-value technique to assess the acceptability of each investment as well as the preferred investment. Explain your findings.

2. Recognizing the fact that investment B is more risky than investment A, reassess the two alternatives applying a 16 percent discount rate to investment B. Compare your findings relative to acceptability and preference to those found for question 1.

3. From your findings in questions 1 and 2, indicate whether the yield for investment A is above or below 12 percent and for investment B is above or below 16 percent. Explain.

4. Use both the present-value technique and the approximate yield formula to find the yield on each investment. Compare your findings and contrast them with your response to question 3.

5. From the information given, which, if either, of the two investments would you recommend Dave make? Explain your answer.

6. Indicate to Dave how much money the extra $50 will have grown to by the end of 2006, given that he makes no withdrawals from the savings account.

LG 4 LG 5 LG 6   **4.2 THE RISK-RETURN TRADEOFF: MOLLY O'ROURKE'S STOCK PURCHASE DECISION**

Over the past 10 years, Molly O'Rourke has slowly built a diversified portfolio of common stock. Currently, her portfolio includes 20 different common stock issues and has a total market value of $82,500. Molly is at present considering the addition of 50 shares of one of two common stock issues—X or Y. To assess the return and risk of each of these issues, she has gathered dividend income and share price data for both over each of the last 10 years (1987 through 1996). Molly's investigation of the outlook for these issues suggests that each will, on average, tend to behave in the future just as it has in the past. She therefore believes that the expected return can be estimated by finding the average holding period return (HPR) over the past 10 years for each of the stocks.

Molly plans to use betas to assess the risk and required return of each stock. Her broker, Jim McDaniel, indicated that the betas for stocks X and Y are 1.60 and 1.10, respectively. In addition, currently the risk-free rate is 7 percent and the market return is 10 percent. The historical dividend income and stock price data collected by Molly are given below.

	Stock X			Stock Y		
		Share Price			Share Price	
Year	Dividend Income	Beginning	Ending	Dividend Income	Beginning	Ending
1987	$1.00	$20.00	$22.00	$1.50	$20.00	$20.00
1988	1.50	22.00	21.00	1.60	20.00	20.00
1989	1.40	21.00	24.00	1.70	20.00	21.00
1990	1.70	24.00	22.00	1.80	21.00	21.00
1991	1.90	22.00	23.00	1.90	21.00	22.00
1992	1.60	23.00	26.00	2.00	22.00	23.00
1993	1.70	26.00	25.00	2.10	23.00	23.00
1994	2.00	25.00	24.00	2.20	23.00	24.00
1995	2.10	24.00	27.00	2.30	24.00	25.00
1996	2.20	27.00	30.00	2.40	25.00	25.00

Questions

1. Determine the holding period return (HPR) for each stock in each of the preceding 10 years. Find the expected return for each stock using the approach specified by Molly.

2. Use the HPRs and expected return calculated in question 1 to find both the standard deviation and the coefficient of variation of the HPRs for each stock over the 10-year period 1987 to 1996.

3. Use your findings above to evaluate and discuss the return and risk associated with stocks X and Y. Which stock seems preferable? Explain.

4. Use the capital asset pricing model (CAPM) to find the required return for each stock. Compare this value with the average HPRs calculated in question 1.

5. Compare and contrast your findings in questions 3 and 4. What recommendations would you give Molly in light of the investment decision currently under consideration? Explain why Molly is better off using beta rather than either a subjective approach or the standard deviation or coefficient of variation to assess investment risk.

PART TWO

INVESTING IN
COMMON STOCK

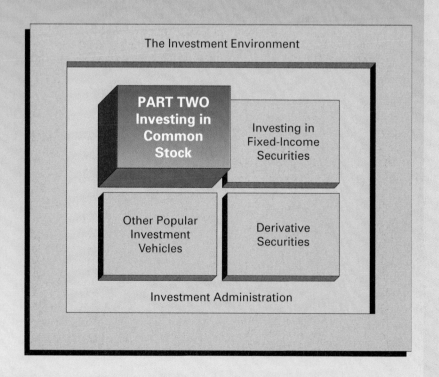

CHAPTER 5

COMMON STOCK

INVESTMENTS

LEARNING GOALS

After studying this chapter, you should be able to:

LG 1 Explain the investment appeal of common stocks and why individuals like to invest in them.

LG 2 Describe stock returns from a historical perspective and gain an appreciation of how current returns measure up to historical standards of performance.

LG 3 Discuss the basic features of common stocks, including issue characteristics, stock quotations, and transaction costs.

LG 4 Gain an understanding of the different kinds of common stock values and the ability of common stocks to serve as an inflation hedge.

LG 5 Discuss common stock dividends, including how dividend decisions are made, types of dividends, and dividend reinvestment plans.

LG 6 Describe various types of common stocks, including foreign stocks, and note the different ways stocks can be used as investment vehicles.

INVESTOR INTERVIEW

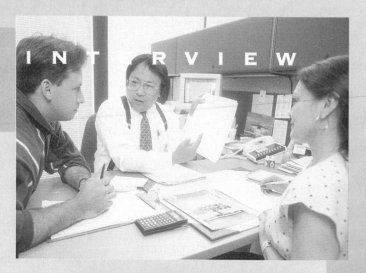

Charles and Jenny Richards started investing in common stocks about five years ago. A dual-career couple—he's a business professor and she's a nurse—they had surplus funds each month after paying off all debts (except the mortgage). After first establishing an emergency fund, they were ready to put their money to work. Charles had taken an investments course in his junior year in college. He recalls, "I remember the professor stressing the risk-return tradeoff: Although common stocks are riskier, they have the potential to earn higher returns. Over the long term, he told us, stocks have earned about 6 percent more per year than risk-free investments. Given the power of compounding, that extra annual return makes an incredible difference over time."

The Richardses' primary investment goal is growth. They select good, solid companies that they believe have excellent growth potential. Because they understand the importance of diversification, their current 15-stock portfolio is diversified across industries and includes stocks in a bank, a petroleum company, a retailer, a soft drink company, a fast-food restaurant, a chemical company, and companies in several other industries. When one of their stocks took a nosedive last year, the other 14 stocks still performed well.

They describe their method of investing as "a little out of the ordinary." Jenny explains, "We take small positions in companies by using a discount broker. Because discount brokers do not give advice—they only perform transactions for you—we pay lower commissions." The Richardses purchase shares in companies that offer dividend reinvestment plans (nicknamed "DRIPs") and then enroll their shares in the company's DRIP. In addition to reinvesting dividends, the plans also accept voluntary cash contributions, so Charles can simply send a check to buy more shares. "The beauty is that these plans charge only a small fee or no fee whatsoever," Charles says. By using the DRIPs and sending in small payments at many different dates, they are also diversifying their purchases across time. "We don't make the mistake of making a large investment in a company right before the price goes down," he adds.

> ALTHOUGH COMMON STOCKS ARE RISKIER, THEY HAVE THE POTENTIAL TO EARN HIGHER RETURNS.

This method of investing is not for everyone. Sometimes, the record keeping is tedious, but the Richards treat it as a hobby. Thus far, they are doing quite well: Their portfolio has grown from zero to over $30,000 in five years and has consistently performed about as well as the market. They invest a certain amount of money each month through the DRIPs and buy for the long term. Of course, the Richardses have made some mistakes along the way, but their rule is "keep the winners, sell the dogs." When a financially conservative friend recently told Charles, "You can't afford to be in something that risky," he responded, "I can't afford *not* to be in common stocks."

Charles and Jenny Richards (not their real names) are in their midthirties. He teaches business courses at an urban university in the Southeastern United States, and she is a registered nurse at a community hospital.

Common stocks appeal to investors for a variety of reasons. For some, investing in stocks is a way to "hit it big"; for others, it's their steady stream of dividends. And as we saw, for Charles and Jenny, stocks are a way to build up capital. However, investing in stocks is by no means a one-way street: Losses can and often do occur. There are no guarantees of success in this market. Therefore, it's in your best interests to learn as much as possible about stocks before you invest in them. This chapter, one of three on equity investing, explains the basic principles of investing in common stock. In the following two chapters, we'll look at how stocks can be valued and how to judge whether an issue will make an acceptable investment candidate.

THE INVESTMENT APPEAL OF COMMON STOCKS

residual owners
owners/stockholders of a firm, who are entitled to dividend income and a prorated share of the firm's earnings only after all the firm's other obligations have been met.

The basic investment attribute of common stocks is that they enable investors to participate in the profits of the firm. Every shareholder, in effect, is a part owner of the firm and is entitled to a piece of the firm's profit. This claim on income has limitations, though, for common stockholders are the **residual owners** of the company. That is, they are entitled to dividend income and a share of the company's earnings only after all other corporate obligations have been met. Equally important, as residual owners, holders of common stock have no guarantee that they will ever receive any return on their investment. The challenge, of course, is to find stocks that will provide the kind of return you're looking for. As anyone who has ever purchased stock can attest, that's no easy task, for there are literally thousands of actively traded stocks to choose from.

WHAT STOCKS HAVE TO OFFER

Common stocks are used by literally millions of individual investors. Their popularity stems in large part from the fact that they enable investors to tailor their investment programs to meet individual needs and preferences. In fact, given the size and diversity of the stock market, no matter what the investment objective, there are common stocks to fit the bill. For retired people, stocks provide an excellent way of earning a steady stream of current income (from dividends). For investors less concerned about current income, common stocks offer not only dividends but also a healthy dose of capital gains. These investors recognize that stocks have a tendency to go up in price over time. Indeed, the potential for capital gains is the real draw for most investors. Few securities can match common stocks when it comes to capital gains.

PUTTING STOCK PRICE BEHAVIOR INTO PERSPECTIVE

Given the nature of common stocks, when the market is strong, investors can generally expect to benefit in the form of steady price appreciation. When the market falters, so do investor returns. A good example of the former is 1993, when the market, as measured by the Dow Jones Industrial Average, went up almost 14 percent. Unfortunately, as Figure 5.1 shows, the market did not perform so well in 1994: All it could manage was a meager 2 percent gain. By comparison, though, that performance wasn't so bad. Indeed, it was nothing compared to the hair-raising market of 1987. In that year, stock prices had shot up almost 30 percent in the first six months, only to experience a terrible

Dow Jones Industrial Average

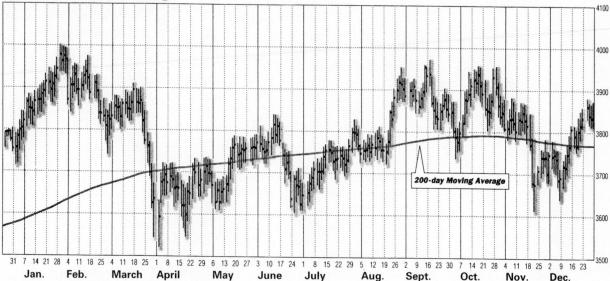

Figure 5.1   The Stock Market in 1994
As far as the stock market was concerned, 1994 was not exactly a stellar year! This was really a market
that was driven by the Federal Reserve Board, as that organization raised interest rates no less than six
times during the year, with just about every rate hike resulting in a sharp drop in the Dow Jones Industrial
Average. In spite of all the ups and downs, the market ended the year with the Dow at 3834.44, just 80.35
points (or 2.1%) above where it opened in January (3754.90).

crash on October 19. That day was not just another bad day in the market—
it was history, as stock prices (measured by the Dow Jones Industrial Average)
fell 508 points on volume of over 600 million shares. That drop easily set a
record, as did the one-day volume of shares traded. The percentage decline—
23 percent—was almost twice the previous single-day record.

The reasons for the October 19, 1987, crash are still being discussed.
Some argue that the cause was the government's inability to control the enormous budget and trade deficits facing the country. Others say the crash was
caused by inflation fears and sharply rising interest rates. Still others feel that,
although both of those factors probably played a role, the extent of the market
drop was grossly magnified by a handful of institutional traders using fancy,
computer-driven techniques (like "program trading") that ultimately drove
prices down *much farther* than they would otherwise have gone.

Fortunately, the October nineteenths of this world are the exceptions,
rather than the rule. The stock market is not all risk and wild price volatility.
As the interview of Charles and Jenny Richards indicates, it also offers some
attractive rewards. Indeed, even though the last quarter of 1987 was a wild
one, the market ended the year on the *plus* side—but not by much, as it was
up just 2 percent. And in subsequent years, the market continued to climb:
another 12 percent in 1988, followed by an even better 27 percent jump
during 1989. Indeed, in the eight years from August 1982 (generally regarded
as the beginning of the great bull market of the 1980s) through July 1990
(about the time Iraq invaded Kuwait), the market went up an impressive 280
percent. Clearly, it's this kind of resiliency and overall market performance
that explains the appeal of common stocks.

A Look at the Record: 1955–1994

What would you consider an acceptable rate of return on common stocks? It's difficult to know what's good or bad, high or low, unless you understand the kinds of returns common stocks are capable of producing. Probably the best way to develop a feel for the market is to look at its past. Table 5.1 uses the DJIA to show average market returns over the 40-year period from 1955 through 1994. In addition to total annual returns, note that market performance is also broken out between the two basic sources of return: dividends and capital gains. These figures, of course, reflect the *general behavior of the market as a whole*, and not necessarily that of *individual* stocks. Think of them as the return behavior on a well-balanced portfolio of common stocks.

The numbers show a market that over the 40-year period has provided annual returns ranging from a low of −21.45 percent to a high of +42.71 percent. Breaking out the returns between dividends and capital gains, it's clear that the big returns (or losses) come from capital gains. And in that regard, note that prices went up far more often than they went down. (As a point of reference, the DJIA moved from just over 400 in January 1955 to nearly 3900 by the end of 1994.) Overall, as seen in Table 5.2, *stocks provided average annual returns of around 10 percent over the full 40-year period*. And if you look at just the last 5 to 10 years, you'll find average returns have been more like 10 to 15 percent.

Now keep in mind that the numbers represent market averages; *individual* stocks can and often do perform quite differently. At least, though, the averages give us a benchmark against which we can assess current stock returns

Table 5.1 Annual Returns in the Stock Market, 1955–1994 (Returns based on performance of the DJIA)

Year	Rate of Return from Dividends	Rate of Return from Capital Gains	Total Rate of Return	Year	Rate of Return from Dividends	Rate of Return from Capital Gains	Total Rate of Return
1994	2.75%	2.14%	4.89%	1974	6.12%	−27.57%	−21.45%
1993	2.65	13.72	16.37	1973	4.15	−16.58	−12.43
1992	3.05	4.17	7.22	1972	3.16	14.58	17.74
1991	3.00	20.32	23.32	1971	3.47	6.11	9.58
1990	3.90	−4.34	−0.44	1970	3.76	4.82	8.58
1989	3.74	26.96	30.70	1969	4.24	−15.19	−10.95
1988	3.67	11.85	15.52	1968	3.32	4.27	7.59
1987	3.67	2.26	5.93	1967	3.33	15.20	18.53
1986	3.54	22.58	26.12	1966	4.06	−18.94	−14.88
1985	4.01	27.66	31.67	1965	2.95	10.88	13.83
1984	5.00	−3.74	1.26	1964	3.57	14.57	18.14
1983	4.47	20.27	24.74	1963	3.07	17.00	20.07
1982	5.17	19.60	24.77	1962	3.57	−10.81	−7.24
1981	6.42	−9.23	−2.81	1961	3.11	18.71	21.82
1980	5.64	14.93	20.57	1960	3.47	−9.34	−5.87
1979	6.08	4.19	10.27	1959	3.05	16.40	19.45
1978	6.03	−3.15	2.88	1958	3.43	33.96	37.39
1977	5.51	−17.27	−11.76	1957	4.96	−12.77	−7.81
1976	4.12	17.86	21.98	1956	4.60	2.27	6.87
1975	4.39	38.32	42.71	1955	4.42	20.77	25.19

Note: Total return figures are based on both dividend income *and* capital gains (or losses); all figures are compiled from DJIA performance information, as obtained from *Barron's* and the *Wall Street Journal*.

Table 5.2   Holding Period Returns in the Stock Market, 1955–1994

Holding Periods	Average Annual Returns	Cumulative Returns	Amount to Which $10,000 Will Grow
5 yrs.: 1990–94	9.95%	60.68%	$ 16,068.28
10 yrs.: 1985–94	15.62	326.77	42,676.80
15 yrs.: 1980–94	14.76	688.15	78,814.58
25 yrs.: 1970–94	10.88	1223.46	132,345.78
40 yrs.: 1955–94	9.95	4347.56	444,756.18
The 1980s: 1980–89	17.2	390.5	49,049.80
The 1970s: 1970–79	5.3	67.9	16,792.04
The 1960s: 1960–69	5.2	66.0	16,602.04

Note: Average annual return figures are fully compounded returns and assume that all dividend income *and* capital gains (or losses) are automatically reinvested. All figures compiled from DJIA performance information, as obtained from *Barron's* and the *Wall Street Journal.*

and our expectations. For example, if a return of 12 to 14 percent can be considered a good midpoint, then *sustained* returns of 18 to 20 percent can definitely be viewed as extraordinary. (Of course, if you want those higher returns, you're going to have to take on a lot more risk.) Likewise, long-run stock returns of only 6 to 8 percent should be viewed as substandard performance. If that's the best you think you can do, then you probably should stick with bonds or CDs, where you'll earn almost as much but with less risk. Actually, returns of 10 to 12 percent are not all that bad: Table 5.2 shows what a $10,000 investment would have grown to over various holding periods within the 1955–1994 time frame.

ADVANTAGES AND DISADVANTAGES OF STOCK OWNERSHIP

One reason stocks are so appealing to investors is the substantial return opportunities they offer. As we just saw, stocks generally do provide attractive, highly competitive returns over the long haul. Indeed, common stock returns compare very favorably to alternative investment outlets, like long-term corporate bonds or U.S. Treasury securities. For example, over the 40-year period from 1955 through 1994, high-grade corporate bonds averaged annual returns of around 6 percent—*less than two-thirds that of common stocks.* Although long-term bonds sometimes do outperform stocks on a year-by-year basis (as they did in the mid-1980s, when interest rates were falling), the opposite is true far more often than not; that is, stocks outperform bonds, and usually by a wide margin. The main reason for this is because, with equity securities, stockholders are entitled to participate fully in the residual profits of the firm. When the company prospers, so do investors—in the form of rising share prices (capital gains).

Stocks offer other benefits as well: Common stocks are easy to buy and sell, and the transactions costs are modest. Moreover, price and market information is widely disseminated in the news and financial media. A final advantage of stock ownership is that the unit cost of a share of common is usually within the reach of most individual investors. Unlike bonds, which carry minimum denominations of at least $1,000, and some mutual funds that have fairly hefty minimum requirements, common stocks present no such invest-

INVESTOR
FACTS

STOCK TRENDS—The third year of a president's term is historically a boom year for the stock market. The S&P 500 has risen in the third year of *every* presidential term since 1943, by an average of 18.6 percent. And the market has risen more during the third year of Democratic presidential terms than Republican ones—by 21 percent versus 16.4 percent.

(Source: *Bottom Line Personal,* December 1, 1994, p. 9.)

ment hurdles. Instead, most stocks today are priced at less than $75 a share—and any number of shares, no matter how few, can be bought or sold.

There are also some disadvantages to common stock. Risk is perhaps the most significant disadvantage. Stocks are subject to a number of different types of risk, including business and financial risk, purchasing power risk, market risk, and possibly even event risk. All of these can adversely affect a stock's earnings and dividends, its price appreciation, and, of course, the rate of return earned by an investor. Even the best of stocks possess elements of risk that are difficult to overcome, because company earnings are subject to many factors, including government control and regulation, foreign competition, and the state of the economy. Because such factors affect sales and profits, they also affect the price behavior of the stock and possibly even dividends, all of which leads to another disadvantage: Since the earnings and general performance of stocks are subject to wide swings, it is difficult to value common stocks and consistently select top performers. The selection process is complex because so many elements go into formulating expectations of how the price of the stock will perform in the future. In other words, not only is the future outcome of the company and its stock uncertain, but the evaluation and selection process itself is far from perfect.

A final disadvantage to stocks is the sacrifice of current income. Several types of investments—bonds, for instance—not only pay higher levels of income but do so with much greater certainty. Figure 5.2 compares the dividend yield of common stocks with the coupon yield of bonds. It shows how the spread in current income has behaved over time and reveals the degree of sacrifice common stock investors make. Although the spread has improved lately, common stocks still have a long way to go before they catch up with the *current income levels* available from other investment vehicles.

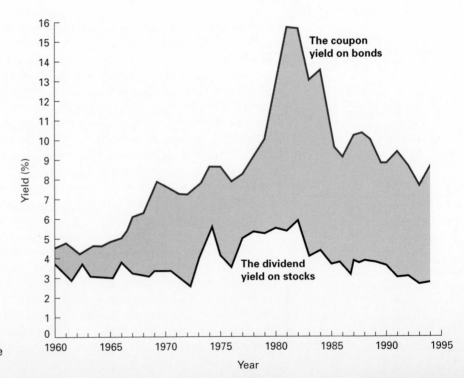

Figure 5.2 The Current Income of Stocks Versus Bonds
Clearly, the level of current income (dividends) paid to stockholders falls far short of the amount of interest income paid to bondholders.

CONCEPTS *in Review*

5.1   What is a *common stock?* What is meant by the statement that holders of common stock are the *residual owners* of the firm?

5.2   What are two or three of the major investment attributes of common stocks?

5.3   What are some of the advantages *and* disadvantages of owning common stock? What are the major types of risk to which stockholders are exposed?

5.4   How important are dividends as a source of return? What about capital gains? Which is more important to total return? Which causes wider swings in total return?

BASIC CHARACTERISTICS OF COMMON STOCK

equity capital
evidence of ownership position in a firm, in the form of shares of common stock.

Each share of common stock represents ownership (equity) in a company. Indeed, it's this equity position that explains why common stocks are often referred to as *equity securities or* **equity capital**. Every share entitles the holder to an equal ownership position and participation in the corporation's earnings and dividends, an equal vote, and an equal voice in management. Together, the common stockholders own the company, and the more shares an investor owns, the bigger his or her ownership position. Common stock has no maturity date—it remains outstanding indefinitely.

COMMON STOCK AS A CORPORATE SECURITY

publicly traded issues
shares of stock readily available to the general public and bought and sold in the open market.

While all corporations (technically, at least) must "issue" some type of common stock, the shares of many, if not most, corporations are never traded, because the firms are either too small or are family-controlled. The stocks of interest to us in this book are **publicly traded issues**—the shares that are readily available to the general public and that are bought and sold in the open market. The issuing firms of such shares range from giants like AT&T and IBM to much smaller regional or local firms, whose securities are traded either over-the-counter or on one of the regional exchanges. The market for publicly traded stocks is enormous: The value of all actively traded listed and OTC stocks in 1994 was nearly *$5 trillion.*

public offering
an offering to sell to the investing public a set number of shares of a firm's stock at a specified price.

Shares of common stock can be issued in several different ways. The most widely used procedure today is the **public offering**, whereby the corporation, working with an underwriter, offers the investing public a certain number of shares of its stock at a certain price. Figure 5.3 shows an announcement for such an offering: in this case, Cardinal Health, a major health care provider, sold more than 8 million shares of stock (both in the United States and abroad) at a price of $39 a share.

rights offering
an offering of a new issue of stock to existing stockholders, who may purchase new shares in proportion to their current ownership position.

New shares of stock can also be issued using what is known as a **rights offering**. In a rights offering, existing stockholders are given the first opportunity to buy the new issue and can purchase new shares in proportion to their current ownership position. For instance, if a stockholder currently owns 1 percent of a firm's stock and the firm issues 10,000 additional shares, the rights offering will give that stockholder the opportunity to purchase 1 percent (or 100 shares) of the new issue. The net result of a rights offering is the same as a public offering: The firm ends up with more equity in its capital structure, and the number of shares outstanding increases.

Figure 5.3 An Announcement of a New Stock Issue
Here Cardinal Health, Inc., is issuing more than 8 million shares of stock at a price of $39 a share, which will mean over $300 million in new capital to the firm. Note that in addition to the 6.65 million shares offered in the United States and Canada, 1.4 million shares are being offered outside the United States and Canada to foreign investors. Such international offerings are becoming fairly common, as companies go global in their search for capital. (Source: *Wall Street Journal,* September 26, 1994.)

Number of shares being offered in U.S. & Canada

Number of shares being offered in foreign markets

Stock Splits

stock split
a maneuver in which a company increases the number of shares outstanding by exchanging a specified number of new shares of stock for each outstanding share.

Companies can also increase the number of shares outstanding by executing a **stock split**. In declaring a split, a firm merely announces that it will increase the number of shares outstanding by exchanging a specified number of new shares for each outstanding share of stock. For example, in a 2-for-1 stock split, two new shares of stock are exchanged for each old share; in a 3-for-2 split, three new shares are exchanged for every two shares outstanding. A stockholder who owned 200 shares of stock before a 2-for-1 split automatically becomes the owner of 400 shares; the same investor would hold 300 shares had there been a 3-for-2 split.

Stock splits are used when a firm wants to enhance its stock's trading appeal by lowering its market price. Normally, the firm gets the desired result, as the price of the stock tends to fall in close relation to the terms of the split (unless the stock split is accompanied by a big increase in the level of dividends). Thus, using the ratio of the number of old shares to new, we can expect a $100 stock, for example, to trade at or close to $50 after a 2-for-1 split. Specifically, dividing the original price of $100 a share by the ratio of new shares to old (2/1), we have: $100 ÷ 2/1 = $100 ÷ 2 = $50. That same $100 stock would trade at about $67 after a 3-for-2 split—that is, $100 ÷ 3/2 = $100 ÷ 1.5 = $67. (A variation of the stock split, known as a stock dividend, will be discussed later in this chapter.)

Treasury Stock

treasury stock
shares of stock that have been sold and subsequently repurchased (and held) by the issuing firm.

On the other hand, corporations sometimes find it desirable to *reduce* the number of shares in the hands of the investing public by buying back their own stock. Generally speaking, firms repurchase their own stocks when they view them as undervalued (i.e., underpriced) in the marketplace. When that happens, the company's own stock becomes an attractive investment candidate. Those firms that can afford to do so begin acquiring their stock in the open market by becoming an investor, like any other individual or institution. When these shares are acquired, they become known as **treasury stock**. Technically, treasury stocks are simply shares of stock that have been issued and subsequently repurchased by the issuing firm. Treasury stocks are kept by the corporation and can be used for mergers and acquisitions, to meet employee stock option plans, or as a means of paying stock dividends—or the shares can simply be held in treasury for an indefinite period of time.

The impact of these share repurchases—or *buybacks*—is really not all that clear. Generally speaking, the feeling seems to be that if the buyback plan is substantial (involving a significant number of shares), the stockholder's equity position and claim on income will increase. This result, in turn, is likely to benefit stockholders to the extent that such action has a positive effect on the market price of the stock. However, it has also been suggested that too often buybacks seem to be used more as a way to prop up the price of an overvalued stock than to produce true, long-lasting benefits for stockholders.

Classified Common Stock

For the most part, all the stockholders in a corporation enjoy the same benefits of ownership. Occasionally, though, a company will issue different classes

classified common stock
common stock issued in different classes, each of which offers different privileges and benefits to its holders.

of common stock, each of which entitles the holder to different privileges and benefits. These issues are known as **classified common stock**. Literally hundreds of publicly traded firms have created such stock classes. Even though offered by the same company, each class of common stock is different and has its own value.

Classified common stock is customarily used to denote either different voting rights or different dividend obligations. For instance, class A could be used to designate nonvoting shares, and class B would carry normal voting rights. Or the class A stock would receive no dividends, whereas class B would receive regular cash dividends. Notable for its use of classified stock is the Ford Motor Company, which has two classes of stock outstanding: Class A stock is owned by the investing public, and class B stock is owned by the Ford family and their trusts or corporations. The two classes of stock share equally in the dividends, but class A stock has one vote per share and the voting rights of the class B stock are structured to give the Ford family a 40 percent absolute control of the company. Similar stock classes are used at the Washington Post, Dillards Department Stores, General Media, Dow Jones & Co., and the Adolph Coors Company. Regardless of the specifics, whenever there is more than one class of common stock outstanding, investors should take the time to determine the privileges, benefits, and limitations of each class.

BUYING AND SELLING STOCKS

Whether buying or selling stocks, investors should be familiar with the way stocks are quoted and with the costs of executing common stock transactions. Certainly, keeping track of current prices is essential: *Current price* is the link in the decision process that lets the investor know when the time is right to buy or sell a stock; it also helps investors monitor the market performance of their security holdings. Similarly, *transaction costs* are important because of the impact they can have on investment returns. Indeed, sometimes just the costs of executing stock transactions can consume most (or all) of the profits from an investment. Thus, these costs should not be taken lightly.

Stock Quotes

Investors in the stock market have come to rely on a highly efficient information system that quickly disseminates market prices to the public. The stock quotes that appear daily in the financial press are a vital part of that information system. To see how price quotations work and what they mean, consider the quotes that appear daily (Monday through Friday) in the *Wall Street Journal*. As we'll see, these quotes give not only the most recent prices of each stock but also a great deal of additional information.

Some NYSE stock quotes are presented in Figure 5.4—let's use the *Disney* quotations for purposes of illustration. These quotes were published in the *Wall Street Journal* on Monday, August 29, 1994. They describe the trading activity that occurred the day before, which in this case, was Friday, August 26. A glance at the quotations shows that stock prices are expressed in eighths of a dollar, where each eighth of a point is worth 12½ cents. Other information conveyed in the stock quote is:

| | 52 Weeks | | | | | Yld | | Vol | | | | Net |
	Hi	Lo	Stock	Sym	Div	%	PE	100s	Hi	Lo	Close	Chg
	33⁵/₈	25⁵/₈	DeluxeCp	DLX	1.48	4.6	19	1171	32³/₄	32¹/₄	32¹/₄	−¹/₂
	42	29	Dept56	DFS		...	22	954	39⁵/₈	38³/₈	39¹/₂	−³/₈
n	34¹/₄	5³/₄	DescSA	DES		...	...	309	13	12⁵/₈	13	+¹/₈
	6⁷/₈	3	DeSoto	DSO		...	dd	84	4⁷/₈	4³/₄	4³/₄	−¹/₈
	14³/₈	9	DestecEngy	ENG		...	8	598	13¹/₈	13	13	...
	27⁷/₈	18¹/₈	DetroitDisl	DDC		...	12	389	20³/₈	20	20¹/₈	−¹/₈
▲	29⁷/₈	24¹/₄	DetEd	DTE	2.06	6.9	11	1624	29⁷/₈	29¹/₂	29⁷/₈	−¹/₈
	96	80	DetEd pfE		7.36	7.9	...	z10	93¹/₂	93¹/₂	93¹/₂	...
	25¹/₂	21	DetEd pfl			...	...	5	24⁷/₈	24¹/₂	24⁷/₈	+¹/₄
	25⁵/₈	20¹/₂	DetEd dep pfF			...	...	5	24¹/₂	24³/₈	24¹/₂	+¹/₈
	32¹/₄	26¹/₈	DevDivrsRlty	DDR	2.16	7.4	21	256	29¹/₈	29	29¹/₈	...
	26	19⁷/₈	Dexter	DEX	.88	3.7	15	1604	24¹/₈	23⁷/₈	24	−¹/₄
	25³/₄	12⁵/₈	Diagnstek	DXK		...	40	278	17³/₄	17⁵/₈	17⁵/₈	−¹/₄
	40³/₈	20³/₈	DiagnstPdt	DP	.481	1.3	26	101	37³/₈	36³/₈	37	−¹/₈
x	26³/₈	19¹/₄	DialCp	DL	.60	2.4	15	4149	25¹/₈	24³/₈	24³/₄	−⁵/₈
	29¹/₈	23¹/₈	DiaSham	DRM	.56	2.1	12	385	26¹/₂	26¹/₄	26³/₈	...
	9³/₄	4	DianaCp	DNA	stk	...	13	88	5⁷/₈	5⁵/₈	5⁷/₈	+¹/₈
s	46³/₄	33	Diebold	DBD	.96	2.2	20	613	44	43⁵/₈	44	+³/₄
	49¹/₈	18	DigitalEqp	DEC		...	dd	42788	42¹/₄	40³/₈	41³/₈	−⁷/₈
n	25¹/₄	18⁷/₈	DigitalEqp pfA		2.22e	8.8	...	373	25¹/₈	25	25¹/₈	+¹/₈
	34¹/₄	24	DillardStrs	DDS	.12	.4	13	4903	29³/₈	28³/₄	29¹/₄	+⁵/₈
	10³/₄	7³/₈	DimeBcp	DME		...	8	2645	10³/₈	10¹/₄	10¹/₄	−¹/₈
n	18⁵/₈	14	DiMon	DMN	.14p	...		1805	17³/₈	16⁷/₈	17	−³/₈
	15	2¹/₄	CG Dina	DIN	.28e	9.3		816	3¹/₄	3	3	−¹/₈
n	13¹/₈	1³/₈	CG Dina L	DINL	.28e	14.9	...	202	2	1⁷/₈	1⁷/₈	−¹/₈
	28¹/₂	13⁷/₈	DiscountAuto	DAP		...	20	238	27³/₄	27³/₈	27¹/₂	−¹/₂
	48⁵/₈	37¹/₈	Disney	DIS	.30	.7	29	14513	43¹/₈	42¹/₂	42⁵/₈	−¹/₈
	31	22¹/₂	DoleFood	DOL	.40	1.4	28	1708	29¹/₄	29	29	−¹/₄
s	33	16³/₁₆	DirGen	DG	.20	.6	30	3453	32⁵/₈	32	32³/₈	−¹/₄
	20¹/₈	16⁷/₈	DominRes ubi	DOM	2.24e	12.5	...	413	18	17⁵/₈	17⁷/₈	...
	39¹/₄	34⁷/₈	DominRes	D	2.58	6.9	14	1920	37⁷/₈	37³/₈	37⁵/₈	−³/₈
	9⁵/₈	4⁷/₈	Domtar g	DTC		...	...	249	9³/₈	9	9¹/₄	+¹/₄
	31³/₄	26⁷/₈	Donelley	DNY	.64f	2.1	19	1719	30¹/₈	29¹/₈	30¹/₈	+³/₄
	66⁷/₈	50⁷/₈	Dover	DOV	1.04f	1.8	19	1257	58¹/₄	57³/₄	58¹/₄	+⁷/₈
	72⁵/₈	53¹/₂	DowChem	DOW	2.60	3.6	39	7615	72¹/₈	70⁵/₈	71⁵/₈	+¹/₂
	41⁷/₈	28³/₈	DowJones	DJ	.84	2.6	19	1687	32	31⁵/₈	31⁷/₈	−¹/₄
	28⁵/₈	18⁵/₈	DrPepper	DPS		...	18	1071	24	23³/₈	23⁵/₈	−¹/₈
	13³/₈	9³/₈	Dravo	DRV		...	dd	144	10¹/₂	10¹/₄	10¹/₂	+¹/₈

Annotation callouts (right side):
- High and low prices for previous 52 weeks
- Company name
- Stock symbol used to identify company
- Annual dividends per share for past 12 months
- Dividend yield (dividends as percent of share price)
- Price/earnings ratio: $\left(\dfrac{\text{market price}}{\text{earnings per share}}\right)$
- Share volume, in hundreds
- High and low prices for the day
- Closing (final) price for the day—this is also the price used to compute dividend yield and the P/E ratio
- Net change in price from previous day

Figure 5.4 Stock Quotations
Shown in this figure are the quotations for a small sample of stocks traded on the NYSE; these quotes provide a summary of the transactions that occurred on one day. (Source: *Wall Street Journal*, August 29, 1994.)

• The first two columns, labeled "Hi" and "Lo," show the highest and lowest prices at which the stock sold during the past 52 weeks; note that Disney traded between 48⁵/₈ and 37¹/₈ during the preceding 52-week period.

• Listed to the right of the company's name is its *stock symbol*; Disney goes by the three-letter abbreviation DIS. These stock symbols are the abbreviations used on the *market tapes* seen in brokerage offices and on CNBC television to identify specific companies. Every common stock (or mutual fund) has a unique three- to five-letter symbol that distinguishes it from any other security and that is used to execute market trades.

- The figure listed after the stock symbol is the annual cash dividend paid on each share of stock, which in the case of Disney amounts to 30 cents a share. This is followed by the stock's dividend yield (0.7 percent for Disney) and its price/earnings (P/E) ratio—note that Disney was trading at 29 times earnings.

- The daily volume follows the P/E ratio: The sales numbers are listed in lots of 100 shares, so the figure 14513 means there were actually 1,451,300 shares of Disney stock traded on August 26.

- The next three entries, in the "Hi," "Lo," and "Close" columns, contain the highest, lowest, and last (closing) prices at which the stock sold on the day in question.

- Finally, as the last ("Net Change") column shows, Disney closed down ⅛ of a point (12½ cents a share) on August 26, which means the stock closed an eighth of a point higher, at 42¾, the day before (August 25).

The same basic quotation system is used for AMEX stocks and for *some* OTC stocks. Actually, for quotation purposes, OTC stocks can be divided into two groups: Nasdaq National Market issues and other OTC stocks. The National Market stocks are those of major, actively traded companies; *they are quoted just like NYSE issues*. Other OTC stocks either are quoted in highly abbreviated form (as in the case of Nasdaq Small Cap issues) or are listed on the basis of their *bid* and *ask* prices.

A key part of the stock quotations are the footnotes that accompany the quotes. You'll notice in the NYSE quotes shown in Figure 5.4 that various symbols and initials appear with some of the quotations. For example, looking down the first column, next to the stock's 52-week high, you'll see the following initials or symbols: s, n, x, and ▲. To translate:

- The *s* means that the stock (e.g., *Diebold*) has recently gone through a *stock split* or paid a major *stock dividend*.

- The *n* means that *DigitalEqp pfA* is a *new* stock that's been issued sometime in the past 12 months.

- The *x* means the stock is trading *ex-dividend* (the buyer will *not* receive the recently declared cash dividend).

- The ▲ means the stock has just hit a *new 52-week high* (as you might expect, if the arrowhead points down, it means a new 52-week *low*).

- The letters *pf* listed after the name of the company (e.g., in the *Digital Eqp* entry) indicates the stock is a *preferred stock*.

- The *f* behind the dividends (e.g., both *Donnelley* and *Dover*) means the companies have *recently raised their dividend payouts*, whereas a *dd* in the P/E column means the company (e.g., *Dravo*) doesn't have any earnings to report since *it's lost money* in the last four quarters.

These and the various other symbols and footnotes that are sprinkled throughout the quotes are meant to provide investors with additional, valuable information about a particular security. In essence, these footnotes help to put the quotes in proper perspective.

INVESTOR INSIGHTS: *Investing in Action*

Pink Sheets: The Hidden Stock Market

Looking for a stock that's not on the New York Stock Exchange or even the Nasdaq bid/ask quotes? Chances are you'll find it in the pink sheets, a daily list of over-the-counter stocks that, for the most part, are not actively traded. Pink-sheet companies run the gamut from names that you'll recognize—for example, Churchill Downs, Manischewitz, Rand McNally—to high-growth firms, bankrupt companies, and "penny stocks" being pushed by brokers promising to make you rich. You'll also find the ADRs of major international corporations like Nestlé and A .G. Siemans and the stock of closely held companies such as Kohler, Inc., whose preshare price was $90,000 in October 1994. There are some 13,000 pink-sheet companies. About 7,500 companies list only in the pink sheets because they don't meet exchange or Nasdaq listing requirements, don't want to pay listing fees, or don't want to disclose operating and financial information. Another 5,500 listings are Nasdaq stocks advertised by market makers.

The pink-sheet market began in 1913, when Wall Street pioneers Roger Babson and Arthur Elliott formed the National Quotation Bureau (NQB) to distribute stock prices gathered from brokerage firm traders. In 1930, the NQB began printing the daily price updates on pink paper and delivering them by messenger to brokerages in major financial districts—practices still used today. (Other cities receive their pink sheets by overnight delivery.) In 1986, the NQB joined the information age by offering pink-sheet stock quotes over the Quotron computer network.

Today, many other on-line financial service companies also carry pink-sheet quotes. However, these quotes don't represent the ac-tual prices at which you can buy or sell the stock. Market makers who wish to buy or sell a stock submit bid/ask prices to the quotation service to let other dealers know what is available. The quotes for these thinly traded securities reflect the value set by the market maker, not by market forces. In addition, dealers mark up prices, often by large amounts. Your final price may be much higher than the actual selling price, making it harder to earn a profit when you sell the stock. If you decide to buy a pink-sheet stock, make sure your broker is prepared to negotiate long and hard on your behalf when he or she calls the market maker.

Until recently, the pink-sheet market offered investors little protection against unscrupulous brokers and market makers. Limited price information, often based on one or two market makers, made it hard to discover the dealer's markup—which could go as high as 200 percent. Starting in 1989, securities regulators took steps to reduce investor abuses. The SEC now requires market makers to report major trading activity. Customers must provide brokers with a signed statement verifying personal financial information and acknowledging the high-risk nature of the investment. Before closing a trade, brokers must disclose their markup and commission to customers, who can cancel the transaction if they are not satisfied. Even with these new rules, however, caution is the watchword for investors before buying risky pink-sheet stocks.

Sources: Based on information from phone interviews with John Condon and Evelyn Walsh, National Quotation Bureau; "Penny Stock Swindles Die Hard," Worth Online, downloaded from American Online, transmitted January 2, 1993; and Dan Ruck, "The Hidden Stock Market," *Money Maker*, December/January 1989, pp. 46–48.

Although the quotation systems described above apply to major listed and OTC stocks, a big piece of the market is not included in these quotes. Indeed, literally thousands of small, thinly traded stocks never show up in the published quotes; instead, the only place you will find them is in the so-called *pink sheets*. These sheets, so named because of the color of the paper the bid/ask quotes are printed on, are published daily and are available from brokers. The above *Investor Insights* box sheds more light on this little-known and often overlooked segment of the market.

Transaction Costs

Common stock can be bought and sold in round or odd lots. A *round lot* is 100 shares of stock or multiples thereof. An *odd lot* is a transaction involving less than 100 shares. The sale of 400 shares of stock would be considered a round-lot transaction; the sale of 75 shares would be an odd-lot transaction. Trading 250 shares of stock would involve a combination of two round lots and an odd lot.

negotiated commissions
transactions costs for the sale and purchase of securities that are negotiated between brokers and institutional investors or individuals with large accounts.

The cost of executing common stock transactions has risen dramatically since the introduction—on May 1, 1975—of **negotiated commissions**. As explained in Chapter 2, negotiated commissions mean, in effect, that brokerage fees are not fixed. In practice, however, most brokerage firms have fixed-fee schedules that apply to small transactions. The fact is that negotiated commissions have reduced the costs of trading for large institutional investors and individuals with substantial capital, but they have not proved so beneficial for investors of more modest means.

An investor incurs certain transaction costs when buying or selling stock. In addition to some modest transfer fees and taxes paid by the *seller*, the major cost is the brokerage fee paid—by both the *buyer and the seller*—at the time of the transaction. As a rule, brokerage fees equal between 1 and 5 percent of most transactions—though they can go much higher, particularly for very small trades. Table 5.3 shows a commission schedule used by one major brokerage house. Not surprisingly, the amount of the commission increases as the number and price of the shares traded increases. Thus, the cost of selling 50 shares of stock trading at $10 per share amounts to $35, whereas the cost of trading 200 shares of a $10 stock is $66.77. However, on a relative basis the dollar cost actually declines: In our example, the brokerage fee for the 50-share transaction amounts to 7 percent of the transaction, whereas that for the 200-share trade represents a cost of only 3.3 percent. Clearly, dealing in odd lots quickly adds to the cost of a transaction. This is so because the purchase

Table 5.3   A Schedule of Brokerage Commissions Paid in Common Stock Transactions

Share Price	Number of Shares						
	5	10	25	50	100	200	500
$ 1	$35.00	$35.00	$35.00	$35.00	$35.00	$ 35.00	$ 59.81
5	35.00	35.00	35.00	35.00	35.00	44.90	101.13
10	35.00	35.00	35.00	35.00	35.92	66.77	129.73
25	35.00	35.00	35.00	37.52	58.71	103.63	225.03
35	35.00	35.00	35.00	45.79	70.15	132.11	284.83
50	35.00	35.00	37.26	58.18	84.77	168.00	354.60
75	35.00	35.00	47.58	72.48	88.52	175.97	434.33
100	35.00	35.00	57.91	84.23	88.52	175.97	438.33
125	35.00	37.10	65.06	87.99	88.52	175.97	438.33
150	35.00	41.22	72.21	87.99	88.52	175.97	438.33

Source: A major full-service brokerage house. (These commissions are, of course, subject to change; also, some brokers/dealers may charge more than the indicated commission, others less.)

or sale of odd lots requires the assistance of a specialist, known as an *odd-lot dealer*. This usually results in an *odd-lot differential* of 12.5 to 25 cents per share, which is tacked on to the normal commission charge, driving up the costs of these small trades. Indeed, the relatively high cost of an odd-lot trade makes it better to deal in round lots whenever possible.

The commission schedule in Table 5.3 is that used by a full-service brokerage firm. Security transactions can also be made through *discount brokers*. Discounters are in business to execute orders for their customers at *substantially reduced commissions*. Some of the major discount and full-service brokerage houses are:

Discount Brokers	Full-Service Brokers
Brown & Company*	A. G. Edwards & Sons
Charles Schwab	Dean Witter Reynolds
Fidelity Brokerage Services	Kemper Securities
Muriel Siebert & Company*	Merill Lynch
National Discount Brokers*	Paine Webber
Quick & Reilly	Prudential Securities
York Securities*	Smith Barney Shearson

(Those companies marked with an asterisk indicate bare-bones, deep-discount brokers.)

As a rule, discount brokers are best suited to active traders who deal in round lots and who are not all that interested in obtaining other broker services. To keep overhead low, discount brokers may offer little or nothing in the way of customer services. The investor initiates a transaction by calling a toll-free number and placing the desired buy or sell order. The order is then executed by the broker at the best possible price, with details of the transaction confirmed shortly thereafter by mail. In order to discourage small orders, most discounters charge a minimum transaction fee of $25 to $40. Depending on the size of the transaction, discount brokers can normally save investors from 30 to 80 percent of the commissions charged by full-service brokers. A brief comparison of full-service versus discount brokerage commissions is provided in Table 5.4.

Table 5.4 Comparative Commissions: Full-Service Brokers Versus Discounters

	Size of Stock Transaction				
Type of Broker	$3,000 (100 shares at $30)	$5,000 (500 shares at $10)	$10,000 (1,000 shares at $10)	$15,000 (300 shares at $50)	$25,000 (500 shares at $50)
Typical full-service broker	$65	$130	$240	$235	$355
Typical discount broker	$40	$ 60	$ 80	$ 60	$ 80
Discount broker commissions as percentage of full-service broker commissions	61%	46%	33%	25%	22%

COMMON STOCK VALUES

The worth of a share of common stock can be described in a number of ways. Terms such as *par value, book value, market value,* and *investment value* are all found in the financial media. Each designates some accounting, investment, or monetary attribute of the stock in question.

Par Value

par value
the stated, or face, value of a stock.

The term **par value** refers to the stated, or face, value of a stock. It is not really a measure of anything, and except for accounting purposes, it is relatively useless. In many ways, par value is a throwback to the early days of corporate law, when it was used as a basis for assessing the extent of a stockholder's legal liability. Since the term holds little or no significance for investors, many stocks today are issued as no-par or low-par stocks—that is, they may have par values of only a penny or two.

Book Value

book value
the amount of stockholders' equity in a firm; equals the amount of the firm's assets minus the firm's liabilities and preferred stock.

market value
the prevailing market price of a security.

investment value
the amount that investors believe a security should be trading for, or what they think it's worth.

Book value, another accounting measure, represents the amount of stockholders' equity in the firm. As we will see in the next chapter, it is commonly used in security analysis and stock valuation. Book value indicates the amount of stockholder funds used to finance the firm; it is calculated by subtracting the firm's liabilities and preferred stock from its assets. Let's assume that a corporation has $10 million in assets, owes $5 million in various forms of short- and long-term debt, and has $1 million worth of preferred stock outstanding. The book value of this firm would be $4 million. This amount can be converted to a per share basis—*book value per share*—by dividing the book value by the number of common shares outstanding. For example, if this firm has 100,000 shares of common stock outstanding, then its book value per share would be $40. As a rule, you'd expect most stocks to have market prices that are above their book values.

Market Value

Market value is one of the easiest common stock values to determine, since it is simply the prevailing market price of an issue. In essence, market value indicates how the market participants as a whole have assessed the worth of a share of stock. By multiplying the market price of the stock by the number of shares outstanding, we can also find the market value of the firm itself—or what is known as the firm's *market capitalization*. For example, if a firm has 1 million shares outstanding and its stock is trading at $50 per share, the company has a market value (or "market cap") of $50 million. Because investors are always interested in an issue's market price, the market value of a share of stock is generally of considerable importance to most stockholders as they formulate their investment policies and programs.

Investment Value

Investment value is probably the most important measure for a stockholder. It indicates the worth investors place on the stock—in effect, what they think the stock *should* be trading for. Determining a security's investment worth is a fairly complex process, but in essence it is based on expectations of the return and risk behavior of a stock. Any stock has two potential sources of return:

annual dividend payments and the capital gains that arise from appreciation in market price. In establishing investment value, investors try to determine how much money they will make from these two sources, and they then use that estimate as the basis for formulating the return potential of the stock. At the same time, they try to assess the amount of risk to which they will be exposed by holding the stock. Together, such return and risk information helps them place an investment value on the stock. This value represents a maximum price they would be willing to pay for the issue—and is the major topic of discussion in Chapter 7.

STOCKS AS AN INFLATION HEDGE

For many years, conventional wisdom held that common stocks were the ideal inflation hedge. This line of reasoning followed from the belief that common stocks, on average, could provide rates of return that were large enough to cover the annual rate of inflation and still leave additional profits for the stockholder. Stated another way, stocks could be counted on to provide rates of return that consistently exceeded the annual inflation rate.

Through the mid-1960s, stocks did indeed perform as inflation hedges. But then U.S. inflation rates rose alarmingly, and most stocks simply could not keep up. Instead, many other investment vehicles, such as fixed-income securities and even short-term Treasury bills, began to outperform common stocks. With the quality of earnings declining in an inflationary economy, stock prices reacted predictably: They began to stagnate. The net result, as seen in Figure 5.5, was a market that went nowhere from 1965 to 1982. Even more alarming

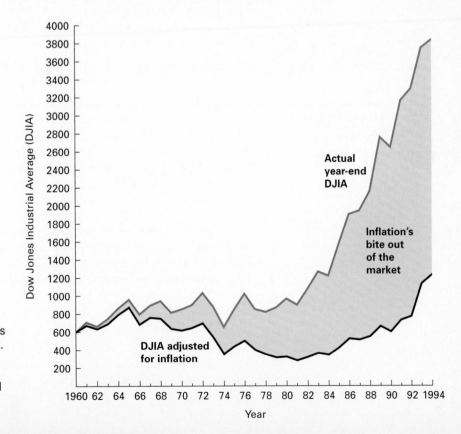

Figure 5.5 Stocks in Real Terms
From 1965 through 1981, stocks were losing ground to inflation. Finally, in 1982, the returns from stocks again began to exceed the rate of inflation and the inflation-adjusted DJIA began to rise sharply.

was the effect inflation had on the "real" value of stocks. Note that two lines appear in Figure 5.5: The upper line indicates the actual reported behavior of the Dow; the other, lower line shows the DJIA adjusted for inflation. In real terms (i.e., adjusted for inflation), *the Dow fell almost without interruption for 17 years*. Clearly, during this period, stocks were anything but an inflation hedge. However, in 1982 a major bull market began. As inflation subsided, stocks were once again able to produce attractive inflation-adjusted returns. Indeed, stocks have done quite well against inflation during the past decade or so. And it's very likely, so long as the annual rate of inflation remains at reasonably low levels of 3 to 4 percent (or less), that stocks will continue to act as an inflation hedge.

CONCEPTS *in Review*

5.5   What is a *stock split?* How does a stock split affect the market value of a share of stock? Do you think it would make any difference (in price behavior) if the company also changed the dividend rate on the stock? Explain.

5.6   Define and differentiate among each of the following pairs of terms:
   a. *Treasury stock* versus *classified stock*
   b. *Round lot* versus *odd lot*
   c. *Par value* versus *market value*
   d. *Book value* versus *investment value*

5.7   What's an *odd-lot differential* and does it really add to the cost of buying and selling stocks? How can you avoid odd-lot differentials? Which of the following transactions would involve an odd-lot differential?
   a. Buy 90 shares of stock
   b. Sell 200 shares of stock
   c. Sell 125 shares of stock

5.8   Are stocks a good inflation hedge? Explain.

COMMON STOCK DIVIDENDS

In 1994, American corporations paid out over $200 billion in dividends—more than three times the amount paid in 1981. Yet, in spite of these numbers, dividends still don't seem to get any respect. That's unfortunate, since dividend income is one of the two basic sources of return to investors. In fact, dividends on some stocks represent a substantial source of income and can add a real lift to investor returns. And although dividends are subject to higher taxes than capital gains (if you're in one of the higher tax brackets), they're also far *less risky*. That is, the stream of annual dividends is far more predictable than the capital gains that may or may not occur sometime in the future. Let's now take a closer look at this important source of income and examine several procedural aspects of the corporate dividend decision.

THE DIVIDEND DECISION

By paying out dividends, typically on a quarterly basis, companies share with their stockholders the profits they earn. Actually, the question of how much to pay in dividends is decided by a firm's board of directors. The directors eval-

spot in all this: Unlike cash dividends, these dividends are not taxed *until the stocks are actually sold.*

Dividend Reinvestment Plans

dividend reinvestment plans (DRIPs)
plans in which shareholders have cash dividends automatically reinvested in additional shares of the firm's common stock.

In recent years, a growing number of firms have established **dividend reinvestment plans (DRIPs)**, whereby shareholders can have their cash dividends automatically reinvested into additional shares of the company's common stock. (These were the vehicle used by Charles and Jenny Richards, in the interview at the start of this chapter, to build their portfolio.) The basic investment philosophy at work here is that *if the company is good enough to invest in, it's good enough to reinvest in.* As Table 5.5 demonstrates, such an approach can have a tremendous impact on your investment position over time. Today, over 1,000 companies (including most major corporations) offer dividend reinvestment plans, and each one provides investors with a convenient and inexpensive way to accumulate capital. Stocks in most DRIPs are acquired free of any brokerage commissions. Some plans even sell stocks to their DRIP investors at below-market prices—often at discounts of 3 to 5 percent. In addition, most plans will credit fractional shares to the investor's account, and many will even allow investors to buy additional shares of the company's stock. For example, once enrolled in Motorola's plan, investors can purchase up to $5,000 worth of the company's stock each quarter.

Shareholders can join dividend reinvestment plans simply by sending a completed authorization form to the company. (Generally, it takes about 30 to 45 days for all the paperwork to be processed.) Once you're in the plan, the number of shares you hold will begin to accumulate with each dividend date. There is a catch, however: Even though these dividends take the form of additional shares of stock, taxes must be paid on them *as though they were cash dividends.* Don't confuse these dividends with stock dividends—*reinvested dividends are taxable as ordinary income in the year they're received*, just as if they had been received in cash.

Table 5.5 Cash or Reinvested Dividends?

Situation: Buy 100 shares of stock at $25 a share (total investment $2,500); stock currently pays $1 a share in annual dividends. Price of the stock increases at 8% per year; dividends grow at 5% per year.

Investment Period	Number of Shares Held	Market Value of Stock Holdings	Total Cash Dividends Received
		Take Dividends in Cash	
5 years	100	$ 3,672	$ 552
10 years	100	5,397	1,258
15 years	100	7,930	2,158
20 years	100	11,652	3,307
		Participate in Dividend Reinvestment Plan	
5 years	115.59	$ 4,245	$ 0
10 years	135.66	7,322	0
15 years	155.92	12,364	0
20 years	176.00	20,508	0

CONCEPTS *in Review*

5.9 Why is the ex-dividend date important to stockholders? If a stock is sold *on* the ex-dividend date, who receives the dividend—the buyer or the seller? Explain.

5.10 What's the difference between a cash dividend and a stock dividend? Which would be more valuable to you? How does a stock dividend compare to a stock split? Is a 200 percent stock dividend the same as a 2-for–1 stock split? Explain.

5.11 What are *dividend reinvestment plans* and what benefits do they offer to investors? Are there any disadvantages?

TYPES AND USES OF COMMON STOCK

LG 6

Common stocks appeal to investors because they offer the potential for everything from current income and stability of capital to attractive capital gains. The market contains a wide range of stock, from the most conservative to the highly speculative. Generally, the kinds of stock sought by investors will depend on their investment objectives and investment programs. We will examine several of the more popular kinds of common stock here, as well as the various ways such securities can be used in different types of investment programs.

KINDS OF STOCK

As an investor, you will find it helpful to understand the market system used to classify common stock. This is so because a stock's general classification denotes not only its fundamental source of return but also the quality of the company's earnings, the issue's susceptibility to market risks, the nature and stability of its earnings and dividends, and even the susceptibility of the stock to adverse economic conditions. Such insight is useful in selecting stocks that best fit one's overall investment objectives. Among the many different types of stock, blue chips, income stocks, growth stocks, speculative stocks, cyclical stocks, defensive stocks, mid-cap stocks, and small-cap stocks are the most common. We will look at each of these to see what they are and how they might be used.

Blue-Chip Stocks

Blue chips are the cream of the common stock crop: They are stocks that are unsurpassed in quality and have a long and stable record of earnings and dividends. They are issued by large, well-established firms that have impeccable financial credentials. These companies hold important, often leading positions in their industries and frequently determine the standards by which other firms are measured. Not all blue chips are alike, however. Some provide consistently high dividend yields; others are more growth oriented. Good examples of blue-chip growth firms are Merck, Procter & Gamble, Abbott Labs, Johnson & Johnson, McDonald's, and Coca-Cola (shown here); examples of high-yielding blue chips include companies like American Home Products, Eli Lilly, Philip Morris, Dun & Bradstreet, and ServiceMaster.

Coca-Cola

NYSE Symbol KO Options on CBOE (Feb-May-Aug-Nov) In S&P 500

Price	Range	P–E Ratio	Dividend	Yield	S&P Ranking	Beta
Apr. 21'94	1994					
40½	44¾–38⅞	24	0.78	1.9%	A+	1.14

Summary

Coca-Cola is the world's largest soft-drink company and has a sizable fruit juice business. Its bottling interests include 44% ownership of NYSE-listed Coca-Cola Enterprises. About 79% of 1993 operating profits came from international operations. Earnings are expected to continue in a strong uptrend in 1994, led by further aggressive worldwide expantion.

Source: Standard & Poor's *NYSE Stock Reports*, April 29, 1994.

Blue chips are particularly attractive to investors who seek quality investment outlets that offer decent dividend yields and respectable growth potential. Many use them for long-term investment purposes and, because of their relatively low-risk exposure, as a way of obtaining modest but dependable rates of return on their investment dollars. Blue chips are popular with a large segment of the investing public and, as a result, are often relatively high priced, especially when the market is unsettled and investors become more quality-conscious.

Income Stocks

Some stocks are appealing simply because of the dividends they pay. This is the case with *income stocks*—issues that have a long and sustained record of regularly paying higher than average dividends. Income stocks are ideally suited for those who seek a relatively safe and high level of current income from their investment capital. There's more: Holders of income stocks (unlike bonds and preferred stocks) can expect the dividends they receive to increase regularly over time. Take Atlanta Gas Light, for example. It paid dividends of $1.08 a share in 1984; ten years later, in 1994, it was paying almost twice as much: $2.08 a share. Percentage-wise, that's a big jump in dividends, and it's something that can have quite an impact on total return.

The major disadvantage of income stocks is that some of them may be paying high dividends because of limited growth potential. Indeed, it's not

Duke Power

NYSE Symbol DUK Options on Phila In S&P 500

Price	Range	P–E Ratio	Dividend	Yield	S&P Ranking	Beta
Jul. 26'94	1994					
37¼	43–32⅞	12	1.96	5.3%	A–	0.46

Summary

This major electric utility serves the Piedmont region of North and South Carolina. Share earnings are expected to increase in 1994, as flat kwh sales are outweighed by several positive factors. Long-term prospects are enhanced by the company's nonutility businesses and a regional economy that should result in energy sales increases of more than 2% annually over the next 10 years.

Source: Standard & Poor's *NYSE Stock Reports*, August 2, 1994.

unusual for income securities to exhibit only low or modest rates of growth in earnings. This does not mean that such firms are unprofitable or lack future prospects. Quite the contrary: Most firms whose shares qualify as income stocks are highly profitable organizations with excellent future prospects. A number of income stocks are among the giants of American industry, and many are also classified as quality blue chips. Many public utilities, like Baltimore Gas & Electric, PacifiCorp, Carolina Power & Light, and Duke Power (shown on page 211), are found in this group, as are phone company stocks (e.g., Ameritech and U.S. West) and selected industrial and financial issues, like Bristol-Myers Squibb, Texaco, Upjohn Co., PNC Bank Corp., and CoreStates Financial. By their nature, income stocks are not exposed to a great deal of business and market risk. They are, though, subject to a fair amount of interest rate risk.

Growth Stocks

Shares that have experienced, and are expected to continue experiencing, consistently high rates of growth in operations and earnings are known as *growth stocks*. A good growth stock might exhibit a *sustained* rate of growth in earnings of 15 to 18 percent a year over a period when common stocks, on average, are experiencing growth rates of only 5 to 6 percent. Generally speaking, established growth companies combine steady earnings growth with high returns on equity. In addition, they have high operating margins and plenty of cash flow to service their debt. Microsoft (shown here), U.S. Healthcare, Blockbuster Entertainment, Gap, Mylan Labs, Equifax, American Management Systems, and Schering-Plough are all prime examples of growth stocks. As this list suggests, some growth stocks also rate as blue chips and provide quality growth, whereas others possess higher levels of speculation.

Growth stocks normally pay little or no dividends, and their payout ratios seldom exceed 15 to 20 percent of earnings. Rather, all or most of the profits are reinvested in the company and used to at least partially finance rapid growth. Thus, the major source of return to investors is price appreciation. Growth shares generally appeal to investors who are looking for attractive capital gains rather than dividends and who are therefore willing to assume a higher element of risk. Most growth stock investors, however, view this added risk as acceptable in light of the relatively high potential return these securities offer.

Microsoft Corp.
NASDAQ Symbol MSFT (Incl. in Nat'l Market) Options on ASE, Pacific

Price	Range	P–E Ratio	Dividend	Yield	S&P Ranking	Beta
May 4'94	1994					
95⅛	95⅝–78	28	None	None	B+	1.01

Summary
Microsoft develops and markets a diverse line of systems and applications microcomputer software, including the MS-DOS operating system—the most widely used operating system for IBM PC and IBM-compatible microcomputers. Results through fiscal 1995 should benefit from strong underlying demand for Windows (an enhanced graphical operating environment that runs with MS-DOS) and associated applications software programs, and from the introduction of new products.

Source: Standard & Poor's *Nasdaq Stock Reports*, May 11, 1994.

Marvel Entertainment Group

NYSE Symbol MRV Options on NYSE (Jan-Apr-Jul-Oct)

Price	Range	P–E Ratio	Dividend	Yield	S&P Ranking	Beta
May 27'94	1994					
$16\frac{1}{8}$	$30\frac{3}{8}$–$13\frac{7}{8}$	28	None	None	NR	NA

Summary

Marvel creates, distributes and licenses youth and entertainment products based on Marvel Super Heroes action adventure characters; professional sports teams, stars and leagues; and other properties. Products and operations include Marvel Comics, Fleer sports and action figure trading cards, Toy Biz toys, and Dubble Bubble and Razzles candy and gum products. Strong revenue and earnings growth should continue in 1994 and beyond. MacAndrews & Forbes Holdings, controlled by R.O. Perelman, owns 81% of the common shares.

Source: Standard & Poor's *NYSE Stock Reports*, June 6, 1994.

Speculative Stocks

Shares that lack sustained records of success but still offer the potential for substantial price appreciation are known as *speculative stocks*. Perhaps investors' hopes are spurred by a new management team that has taken over a troubled company or the introduction of a promising new product. Other times, it's the hint that some new information, discovery, or production technique will favorably affect the growth prospects of the firm and inflate the price of the stock. Speculative stocks are a special breed of securities, and they enjoy a wide following, particularly when the market is bullish.

Generally speaking, the earnings of speculative stocks are uncertain and highly unstable. They are subject to wide swings in price, and they usually pay little or nothing in dividends. On the plus side, speculative stocks like Cisco Systems, Tyco Toys, Fair•Isaac & Co., Wall Street Deli, Community Psychiatric, and Marvel Entertainment (shown above) offer attractive growth prospects and the chance to "hit it big" in the market. However, to be successful, an investor has to identify the big-money winners before the rest of the market does, and before the price of the stock is driven up. Speculative stocks are highly risky; they require not only a strong stomach but also a considerable amount of investor know-how. They are used to seek capital gains, and investors will often aggressively trade in and out of these securities as the situation demands.

Cyclical Stocks

Cyclical stocks are issued by companies whose earnings are closely linked to the general level of business activity. They tend to reflect the general state of the economy and move up and down as the business cycle moves through its peaks and troughs. Companies that serve markets tied to capital-equipment spending on the part of business, or consumer spending for big-ticket, durable items like houses and cars, typically head the list of cyclical stocks. These include companies like Caterpillar, Premark International, Georgia-Pacific, Deere, Allied Signal, and Eaton Corp. (shown on page 214).

For obvious reasons, cyclical stocks have the most appeal when the economic outlook is strong (i.e., when the country is in the early stages of a recovery). They are perhaps best avoided when the economy begins to weaken.

Eaton Corp.

NYSE Symbol ETN Options on CBOE (Jan-Apr-Jul-Oct) In S&P 500

Price	Range	P–E Ratio	Dividend	Yield	S&P Ranking	Beta
Mar. 28'94	1994					
60⅜	62⅛–50⅜	23	1.20	2.0%	B	1.21

Summary
Eaton Corp. manufactures a wide range of products serving the automotive, industrial, commercial and defense markets. Principal products include truck transmissions and axles, engine components, and electrical equipment and controls. Earnings should rise further in 1994 as ETN benefits from greater North American car and light truck production and faster economic growth. ETN recently acquired Westinghouse Electric's distribution and controls business for $1.1 billion, plus assumption of certain liabilities.

Source: Standard & Poor's *NYSE Stock Reports,* April 5, 1994.

Because their prices have a tendency to move with the level of economic activity, they are probably most suitable for investors who are willing to trade in and out of these issues as the economic outlook dictates and who can tolerate the accompanying exposure to risk.

Defensive Stocks

Sometimes, it is possible to find stocks whose prices will remain stable or even prosper when general economic activity is tapering off. These securities are known as *defensive stocks*. They tend to be less affected by downswings in the business cycle than the average issue. Examples of defensive stocks include the shares of many public utilities, as well as industrial and consumer goods companies that produce or market such staples as beverages, foods, and drugs. An excellent example of a defensive stock is Bandag; this recession-resistant company is the world's leading manufacturer of rubber used to retread tires. Other examples include Loctite, the producers of Super Glue; Checkpoint Systems, a manufacturer of antitheft clothing security clips; and Union Corp., a debt collection company (shown below). Perhaps the best known of all defensive stocks, particularly in inflationary periods, are gold mining shares; these stocks literally flourish when inflation becomes a serious problem.

Union Corp.

NYSE Symbol UCO

Price	Range	P–E Ratio	Dividend	Yield	S&P Ranking	Beta
May 25'94	1994					
10⅜	13¼–10¼	16	None	None	B–	0.79

Summary
This company provides accounts receivable management and debt collection services on a fixed-rate and contingency-fee basis to a wide range of institutional, commercial and government customers through its Transworld Systems, Capital Credit and Allied Bond & Collection subsidiaries. Earnings have been depressed since early 1992.

Source: Standard & Poor's *NYSE Stock Reports,* June 2, 1994.

Defensive shares are commonly used by more aggressive investors. For the most part, such investors tend to "park" their funds temporarily in defensive stocks while the market and/or the economy is off, and until the investment atmosphere improves.

Mid-Cap Stocks

A stock's size is based on its market value—or, more commonly, on what is known as its *market capitalization* (the market price of the stock times the number of shares outstanding). Generally speaking, the U.S. stock market can be broken into three segments, as measured by a stock's market "cap":

small	less than $500 million
medium	$500 million to $2–$3 billion
large	more than $2–$3 billion

The large-cap stocks are the real biggies—the AT&Ts, GMs, and Exxons of the investment world. Although there are far fewer large-cap stocks than any other, these companies account for about 60 percent of the total value of U.S. equity markets. But as the saying goes, bigger isn't necessarily better. And nowhere is that statement more accurate than in the stock market. Indeed, *both* the small and the medium segments of the market tend to outperform the large stocks over time.

Mid-caps are a special breed of stock, and they offer investors some attractive return opportunities. They provide much of the sizzle of small-stock returns, but without all the price volatility. (We'll look at small-cap stocks below.) At the same time, because mid-caps are fairly good-size companies and many of them have been around for a long time, they offer some of the safety of the big, established stocks. Among the ranks of the mid-caps are such well-known companies as Justin Industries, Starbucks, Tyson Foods, International Dairy Queen, Cooper Tire and Rubber, Wendy's International, and Briggs & Stratton, in addition to some not-so-well-known names. For the most part, while these securities offer a nice alternative to large stocks without the drawbacks and uncertainties of small-caps, they probably are most appropriate for investors who are willing to tolerate a bit more risk and price volatility.

One type of mid-cap stock that is particularly interesting is the so-called *baby blue chip*. Also known as "baby blues," these companies have all the

Tootsie Roll Industries

NYSE Symbol TR

Price	Range	P–E Ratio	Dividend	Yield	S&P Ranking	Beta
Mar. 28'94	1994					
69½	75–68⁷/₃₂	21	[1]0.38	[1]0.5%	A	1.15

Summary
This company is a major manufacturer and distributor of candy, sold primarily under the Tootsie Roll brand name, and is the largest U.S. confectioner of lollipops, sold mainly under the Charms and Blow-Pop names. Sales and earnings have risen steadily over the past decade, aided by successful promotional programs and product line extensions. Return on equity has remained close to 20%. The company has supplemented its cash dividend with an annual 3% stock extra for many years.

Source: Standard & Poor's *NYSE Stock Reports*, April 6, 1994.

characteristics of a regular blue chip, *except size*. Like their larger counterparts, baby blues have rock-solid balance sheets, with only modest levels of debt, and long histories of steady profit growth. For the most part, they've been able to secure niches in fast growing specialty markets. Some of these companies, in fact, have been posting annual earnings gains for 30 to 40 years in a row. Baby blues normally pay a modest level of dividends, but like most mid-caps, they tend to emphasize growth. Thus, they're considered ideal for investors seeking quality long-term growth. Some well-known baby blues include Tootsie Roll (shown on page 215), Pall Corp., Reynolds & Reynolds, Hormel, and RPM.

Small-Cap Stocks

Some investors consider small companies to be in a class by themselves in terms of attractive return opportunities. In many cases, this has turned out to be true. Known as *small-cap stocks,* these companies generally have annual revenues of less than $250 million. Because of their size, spurts of growth can have dramatic effects on their earnings and stock prices. ShowBiz Pizza Time, Mail Boxes Etc., President Riverboat Casinos, Checkers Drive-In Restaurants, Boston Celtics (the NBA basketball team), Heartland Express, and Ben & Jerry's (shown below) are just a few examples of some of the better-known small-cap stocks. Although some small-caps (like Ben & Jerry's) are solid companies with equally solid financials, that's not the case with most of them. Indeed, because many of these companies are so small, they don't have a lot of stock outstanding, and their shares are not widely traded. In addition, small-company stocks have a tendency to be "here today and gone tomorrow." Although some of these stocks may hold the potential for high returns, investors should also be aware of the very high risk exposure that comes with many of them.

initial public offering (IPO)
a special category of common stocks issued by (relatively) new firms going public for the first time.

A special category of small-company stock is the so-called **initial public offering (IPO)**. Most of these IPOs are small, relatively new companies that are going public for the first time. (Prior to their public offering, these stocks were privately held and *not* publicly traded.) Like other small-cap stocks, IPOs are attractive because of the substantial—sometimes phenomenal—capital gains that can be earned by investors. Of course, there is a catch: In order to even stand a chance of buying some of the better, more attractive IPOs, you need to

Ben & Jerry's Homemade

NASDAQ	Price Mar. 10'94	P–E Ratio	Dividend	Yield	Range 1994	1993	S&P Ranking
BJICA	17½	17	None	None	21–14½	32–15¾	B+

Business: Ben & Jerry's Homemade makes and markets Ben & Jerry's super premium ice cream in unique as well as regular flavors to supermarkets, grocery and convenience stores, and restaurants in major markets throughout the country. The company also sells its ice cream through 86 franchised Ben & Jerry's ice cream parlors. In September 1992, the company offered 1.1 million common shares at $30.50 each. Officers and directors own approximately 25% of the Class A common shares.

Source: Standard & Poor's *Corporate Rankings,* April 1994.

be either a big-time trader or a (highly) preferred client of the broker. Otherwise, the only IPOs you're going to be offered are the ones the big guys don't want—which should tell you something about that particular IPO. More often than not, the small individual investor gets a chance to buy a new issue only after it's been driven way up in price and the initial investors start bailing out, taking their profits with them. Surprisingly, this activity may take only a few hours or a few days to happen. If you're not in on the first day, the odds are that your returns will be mediocre, at best. It's an open secret on Wall Street that when it comes to hot IPOs, most individual investors stand little chance of playing the game, much less winning.

Without a doubt, IPOs are extremely high-risk investments, with the odds stacked against the investor. Since there's no market record to rely on, these stocks should be used only by investors who know what to look for in the company and who can tolerate the substantial exposure to risk. IPOs tend to flourish when the market heats up, and they very definitely are faddish, often dominated by trendy retail outlets, food chains, and high-tech firms.

INVESTING IN FOREIGN STOCKS

One of the most dramatic changes in our financial markets in the 1980s was the trend toward globalization. Indeed, globalization has become the buzz-word of the 1990s, and nowhere is that more evident than in the world equity markets. Consider, for example, that in 1970, the U.S. stock market accounted for fully *two-thirds of the world market*. In essence, our stock market was twice as big as all the rest of the world's stock markets *combined*. That's no longer true: In 1994, the U.S. share of the world equity market had dropped to less than 30 percent.

Today, the world equity markets are dominated by six countries, which, together, account for about 80 percent of the total market:

	Approximate Market Value (1994)
United States	$ 4.9 trillion
Japan	3.7 trillion
United Kingdom/ Britain	1.1 trillion
France	450 billion
Germany	425 billion
Canada	300 billion

The United States is still the biggest player. And along with Japan and England, it is one of only three countries with trillion-dollar stock markets. In addition to these six, another half-dozen or so markets are also regarded as major world players. Included in this second tier are Switzerland, Australia, Italy, the Netherlands, Hong Kong, Spain, and Singapore. Finally, a number of relatively small, emerging markets—South Korea, Sweden, Austria, Denmark, Norway, and Mexico—are beginning to make their presence felt. Clearly, the landscape has changed a lot in the last 20 years, and there's every reason to believe—with the historic changes taking place in Eastern Europe and the former Communist bloc—that even greater changes lie ahead.

But a question remains: How has the U.S. equity market performed in comparison to the rest of the world's major stock markets? Unfortunately, not too well. Table 5.6 provides a summary of total annual returns (in U.S. dollars) for the 15-year period from 1980 through 1994, for ten of the world's major equity markets. Note that the United States finished first only once (in 1982), and in 6 out of the 15 years, the U.S. equity markets finished in the bottom five! The message is clear: Investors who concentrate solely on U.S. stocks are overlooking more than two-thirds of the world's publicly traded equity markets. Equally important, they're missing out on investment returns that often exceed those obtained on U.S securities.

Going Global: Direct Investments Versus ADRs

Basically, there are two ways to invest in foreign stocks: through direct investment and through ADRs. (There *is* a third way—international mutual funds— which we'll discuss in Chapter 11.) Without a doubt, the most adventuresome way is to *buy shares directly in foreign markets*. Investing directly is *not* for the uninitiated, however. You have to know what you're doing and be pre-

Table 5.6   Comparative Annual Returns in the World's Major Equity Markets, 1980–1994

	Australia	Canada	France	Germany	Hong Kong	Japan	Singapore	Switzer-land	United Kingdom	United States	Rank*
					Annual Total Returns (in U.S. Dollars)						
1994	1.4%	−5.1%	−7.3%	3.1%	−32.0%	21.4%	−0.7%	30.0%	−4.4%	4.9%	3rd
1993	33.4	17.4	19.6	34.8	120.9	23.9	72.3	41.7	19.0	16.4	10th
1992	−6.1	−4.6	5.2	−2.1	28.0	−26.0	N/A	26.0	14.0	7.2	4th
1991	35.8	12.1	18.6	8.7	49.6	9.0	24.6	16.8	16.0	23.3	4th
1990	−16.2	−12.2	−13.3	−8.8	9.2	−35.9	−11.5	−5.1	10.4	−0.4	3rd
1989	10.8	25.2	37.6	48.2	8.4	2.3	42.4	28.0	23.1	30.7	4th
1988	38.2	17.9	37.1	19.8	28.0	35.4	33.1	5.8	4.1	15.5	8th
1987	9.5	14.8	−13.9	−24.6	−4.0	41.0	2.3	−9.2	35.2	5.9	5th
1986	45.0	10.8	79.9	36.4	56.2	101.2	45.1	34.7	27.7	26.1	10th
1985	21.1	16.2	84.2	138.1	51.7	44.0	−22.2	109.2	53.4	31.7	7th
1984	−12.4	−7.1	4.8	−5.2	46.9	17.2	−26.8	−11.1	5.3	1.2	5th
1983	55.2	32.4	33.2	23.9	−3.1	24.8	31.3	19.9	17.3	24.7	6th
1982	−22.2	2.6	−4.2	10.5	−44.2	−0.6	16.2	2.9	9.0	24.8	1st
1981	−23.8	−10.1	−28.5	−10.3	−16.2	15.7	18.0	−9.5	−10.2	−2.8	3rd
1980	54.7	21.6	−2.0	−10.7	73.8	30.4	62.4	−7.8	42.0	20.6	7th
					Average Annual Returns Over Extended Holding Periods						
5 years:											
1980–1984	4.5%	6.6%	−1.3%	0.8%	3.0%	17.0%	16.4%	−1.8%	11.4%	13.0%	
1985–1989	24.1	16.9	40.0	34.2	25.8	41.4	17.0	28.2	27.7	21.6	
1990–1994	7.6	0.9	3.7	6.2	25.7	−4.9	17.2	20.8	10.7	10.0	
10 years:											
1985–1994	15.6	8.6	20.5	19.3	25.8	16.0	17.1	24.5	18.9	15.6	
15 years:											
1980–1994	11.8	7.9	12.7	12.8	17.7	16.3	16.8	15.0	16.3	14.8	

Note: Total return = coupon income + capital gain (or loss) + profit (or loss) from changes in currency exchange rates.

*"Rank " shows how U.S. returns ranked among the listed major markets, (e.g., in 1994, the United States ranked 3rd out of the 10 markets listed in the table).

Source: International returns obtained from Morgan Stanley Capital International and Templeton International; U.S. returns based on DJIA.

INVESTOR FACTS

MARKET CONCENTRA-TION—One of the problems with foreign markets is that value tends to be concentrated in just a handful of companies. That's not a problem in the United States, where the five largest stocks (as measured by market value) account for just 7 percent of the total market. The only other developed market that even comes close to that is Japan, whose five biggest stocks account for 11 percent of its market. Market concentration percentages in some other countries: the United Kingdom, 14 percent; Germany, 26 percent; Australia, 34 percent; Switzerland, an eye-popping 43 percent; and the Netherlands, a whopping 60 percent.

pared to tolerate a good deal of market risk, for, with the possible exception of Canada, buying stocks in a foreign market can be challenging, to say the least. Although most major U.S. brokerage houses are set up to accommodate investors interested in buying foreign securities, there are still many *logistical* problems to be faced. To begin with, you have to cope with currency fluctuations and changing foreign exchange rates. As we'll see below, these can have a dramatic impact on investor returns. But that's just the start: You also have to deal with a different set of regulatory and accounting standards. The fact is that most foreign markets, even the bigger ones, are not as closely regulated as U.S. exchanges. Investors in foreign markets thus have to put up with insider trading and other practices that can cause wild swings in market prices. Further, accounting standards are often much looser, making detailed information about a company's financial condition and operating results a lot harder to come by. Finally, there are the obvious language barriers, tax problems, and general "red tape" that all too often seem to be a part of international transactions. There's no doubt that the returns from direct foreign investments can at times be substantial, but so can many of the hurdles that are placed in your way.

Fortunately, there is an easier way to invest in foreign stocks and that is to buy *American Depositary Receipts (ADRs)*—or American Depositary *Shares*, as they're sometimes called. As we saw in Chapter 2, ADRs are negotiable instruments, with each ADR representing a specific number of shares in a specific foreign company. (Actually, the number of shares held can range from just a fraction of a share to 20 shares or more.) ADRs are great for individual investors who want foreign stocks but don't want the hassles that usually come with them. That's because ADRs are bought and sold on American markets just like stocks in U.S. companies—and their prices are quoted in U.S. dollars, not British pounds, Japanese yen, or German marks. Furthermore, dividends too are paid in dollars. While there are about 350 foreign companies *whose shares are directly listed on U.S. exchanges* (over 200 of which are Canadian), most foreign companies are traded in this country as ADRs. Indeed, shares of about 1,000 companies, from some 40 countries, are traded as ADRs on the NYSE, AMEX, and Nasdaq/OTC markets.

To see how ADRs are structured, take a look at Cadbury Schweppes, the British food and household products firm. Each Cadbury ADR represents

Hitachi, Ltd.
NYSE Symbol HIT Options on CBOE (Jan-Apr-Jul-Oct)

Price	Range	P–E Ratio	Dividend	Yield	S&P Ranking	Beta
Apr. 22'94	1994					
92⅝	95⅝–72	47	[1]0.87	[1]0.9%	NR	0.53

Summary
This large Japanese company manufactures a wide range of products, including electrical and electronic equipment, industrial machinery and consumer appliances. Sales outside Japan accounted for 24% of sales in fiscal 1992–93. In recent years, in response to earlier pressures resulting from a strong yen, HIT directed efforts toward reducing costs, raising productivity and increasing overseas production of products that have a high dependency on exports. Earnings declined in fiscal 1993–4's first half.

Source: Standard & Poor's *NYSE Reports*, April 29, 1994.

INVESTOR INSIGHTS: *Global Issues*

The Ins and Outs of Investing in ADRs

American investors seeking attractive returns in overseas capital markets are buying American Depositary Receipts (ADRs) in record numbers. These negotiable certificates issued by major U.S. banks represent shares of a foreign company. ADRs are quoted in dollars and trade like domestic stocks. The issuing bank handles all the details (for a fee): settlement procedures, custody, dividend payments, and taxes. Thus, ADRs provide an easy, cost-efficient way for individual investors to buy foreign equities.

With over 1,000 ADRs to choose from, representing large and small companies in both industrialized countries and emerging markets, investors can allocate investments to specific markets. Such global diversification is a sound strategy, leading over time to higher returns, less risk, and lower volatility. Many foreign economies are growing much faster than the U.S. economy. And the world's economies—and their stock markets—move at different rates; one grows while another is in recession. This countercyclicality spreads risk among several markets. When the U.S. market is down, in all likelihood a foreign market will be rising.

Despite these advantages, ADRs—like any foreign investment—carry certain risks. Trading environments, accounting practices, and reporting requirements vary from country to country. What's more, ADRs may be less liquid than their underlying stocks. They also involve currency risk: A sudden change in the value of the dollar can wipe out your profits—or increase them.

Successful ADR investors depend on good information—information that is not always easy to find. Market knowledge is essential. Before investing in an ADR, investigate the country's current and projected economic and political environment (e.g., fiscal policies, currency valuation, and attitudes toward business), its stock market (regulations, liquidity, capitalization, index components), and the industrial sector. Good resources available in most university and public libraries include *Barron's*, the *Economist*, the *Financial Times*, the *Asian Wall Street Journal*, the *International Herald Tribune*, the *South China Morning Post*, and *Latin Finance*.

Sponsored, large-capitalization ADRs are a good way to invest in a particular country. They generally provide the lowest risk and good liquidity, and their prices reflect home market trends. For example, Australia's Broken Hill Propriety represents 6 percent of the Australian stock market and moves with the market 96 percent of the time.

Once you've chosen your ADRs, plan to hold them for a while. Don't try to second-guess currency movements or similar short-term developments; even experienced currency traders make mistakes. Trading raises transaction costs and reduces your profits. Do your homework and your ADR portfolio will balance out the ups and downs of the U.S. stock market.

ownership of four shares of Cadbury stock. These shares are held in a custodial account by a U.S. bank (or its foreign correspondent), which receives dividends, pays any foreign withholding taxes, and then converts the net proceeds to U.S. dollars, which it passes on to investors. In addition to Cadbury Schweppes, other foreign stocks that can be purchased as ADRs include Sony, L'Oréal, Daimler-Benz, Hanson plc, Elf Aquitaine, SmithKline Beecham, and Hitachi (shown on page 219). American Depositary Receipts are an interesting investment vehicle and hold a lot of appeal for U.S. investors. However, as the above *Investor Insights* box suggests, individual investors should be aware of certain ins and outs to investing in ADRs.

Stock Returns in a Global Perspective

Whether an investor is buying foreign stocks directly or ADRs, the whole process of global investing is a bit more complex and more risky than domestic investing, for, when investing globally, *the investor has to pick not only the right stock but also the right market.* Basically, foreign stocks are valued much the same way as American stocks. Indeed, the same variables that drive U.S. share prices (earnings, dividends, etc.) also drive stock values in foreign markets. On top of this, each market reacts to its own set of economic forces (inflation, interest rates, the level of economic activity, etc.), which sets the tone of the market. At any given point in time, therefore, some markets are performing better than others. The challenge facing global investors is to be in the right market at the right time. As with American stocks, foreign shares produce the same two basic sources of stock returns: dividends and capital gains (or losses).

But with global investing, there's a third variable—*currency exchange rates*—that plays an important role in defining returns to U.S. investors. For, as the U.S. dollar becomes weaker or stronger relative to a foreign currency, the returns to U.S. investors from foreign stocks will increase or decrease accordingly. Essentially, in a global context, total return to U.S. investors in foreign securities is defined as follows:

Equation 5.4

$$\begin{matrix} \text{Total Return} \\ \text{(in U.S. dollars)} \end{matrix} = \begin{matrix} \text{current income} \\ \text{(dividends)} \end{matrix} + \begin{matrix} \text{capital gains} \\ \text{(or loss)} \end{matrix} \pm \begin{matrix} \text{changes in currency} \\ \text{exchange rates} \end{matrix}$$

Since current income and capital gains are in "local currencies" (i.e., the currency in which the foreign stock is denominated, such as the German mark or the Japanese yen), we can shorten the total return formula to:
Thus, the two basic components of total return are *those generated by the stocks themselves* (dividends plus change in share prices) and *those derived from movements in currency exchange rates.*

Equation 5.5

$$\begin{matrix} \text{Total return} \\ \text{(in U.S. dollars)} \end{matrix} = \begin{matrix} \text{returns from current} \\ \text{income \& capital gains} \\ \text{(in local currency)} \end{matrix} \pm \begin{matrix} \text{returns from} \\ \text{changes in currency} \\ \text{exchange rates} \end{matrix}$$

Employing the same two basic components noted above in Equation 5.5, we can compute total return in U.S. dollars by using the following holding period return (HPR) formula, as modified for changes in currency exchange rates:

Equation 5.6

$$\begin{matrix} \text{Total return} \\ \text{(in U.S. dollars)} \end{matrix} = \left[\frac{\begin{matrix} \text{ending value of} \\ \text{stock in foreign} \\ \text{currency} \end{matrix} + \begin{matrix} \text{amount of dividends} \\ \text{received in} \\ \text{foreign currency} \end{matrix}}{\begin{matrix} \text{beginning value of stock} \\ \text{in foreign currency} \end{matrix}} \times \frac{\begin{matrix} \text{exchange rate} \\ \text{at } end \text{ of} \\ \text{holding period} \end{matrix}}{\begin{matrix} \text{exchange rate} \\ \text{at } beginning \text{ of} \\ \text{holding period} \end{matrix}} \right] - 1.00$$

where the "exchange rate" represents *the value of the foreign currency in U.S. dollars*—that is, how much one unit of the foreign currency is worth in U.S. money.

Note that because this is a (modified) HPR formula, it's best used over investment periods of one year or less. Also, since it's assumed that dividends are received at the same exchange rate as the ending price of the stock, this equation provides only an *approximate* measure of return—albeit a fairly close one. Essentially, the first component of Equation 5.6 provides returns on the stock, in local currency, and the second element accounts for the impact of changes in currency exchange rates.

To see how this formula works, consider an American investor who buys several hundred shares of Petrofina, a large Belgium petroleum and chemical company that trades on the Brussels stock exchange. The investor paid a price *per share* of 9,140 Belgium francs (Bf) for the stock, at a time when the exchange rate between the U.S. dollar and the Belgium franc (U.S.$/Bf) was $0.0307, meaning the Bf was worth a little more than 3 cents. Put another way, this exchange rate amounts to 32.55 Bf per U.S. dollar, so 1 U.S.$/32.55 Bf = $0.0307. The stock paid *annual* dividends of 275 Bf per share, and at the end of the year it was trading at 9,500 Bf per share, when the U.S.$/Bf exchange rate was $0.0336 (which is equivalent to 29.75 Bf per U.S. dollar). The stock clearly went up in price, so the investor must have done all right. To find out just what kind of return this investment generated (in U.S. dollars), we'll have to use Equation 5.6:

$$\begin{aligned}\text{Total return} \atop \text{(in U.S. dollars)} &= \left[\frac{9{,}500 + 275}{9{,}140} \times \frac{\$0.0336}{\$0.0307} \right] - 1.00 \\ &= [1.0695 \times 1.0945] - 1.00 \\ &= [1.1705] - 1.00 \\ &= \underline{\underline{17.05\%}} \end{aligned}$$

Actually, at a return of 17.05 percent, the investor seems to have done quite well. However, as it turns out, *most of this return was due to currency movements and not to the behavior of the stock*. Look at just the first part of the equation: it shows the return (in local currency) *earned on the stock* from dividends and capital gains—that is, 1.0695 − 1.00 = 6.95%. Thus, the stock itself produced a return of less than 7 percent, and all the rest—more than 10 percent (i.e., 17.05 − 6.95)—came from the change in currency values. In this case, the value of the U.S. dollar went down relative to the Belgian franc and thus added to the return.

As we've just seen, exchange rates can have a dramatic impact on investor returns. Quite often, they can convert mediocre returns or even losses into very attractive returns—and vice versa. There's really only one thing that determines whether the so-called *currency effect* is going to be positive or negative, and that's the behavior of the U.S. dollar relative to the currency in which the foreign security is denominated. In essence, *a stronger dollar has a negative impact on total returns to U.S. investors, and a weaker dollar has a positive impact*. Thus, other things being equal, the best time to be in foreign securities is when the dollar is *falling*, because that *adds* to returns to U.S. investors. Of course, the greater the amount of fluctuation in the currency exchange rate, the greater the impact on total returns. The challenge facing global investors, therefore, is to find not only the best performing foreign stock(s) but also the best performing foreign currencies. That means you want *the value of both the foreign stock and the foreign currency to go up over your investment horizon*. And this rule applies both to the direct investment in foreign stocks and to the purchase of ADRs (because even though ADRs are denominated in dollars, their quoted prices vary with ongoing changes in currency exchange rates).

ALTERNATIVE INVESTMENT STRATEGIES

Basically, common stocks can be used (1) as a "storehouse" of value, (2) to accumulate capital, and (3) as a source of income. Storage of value is important to all investors, since nobody likes to lose money. However, some investors are more concerned about it than others and therefore rank safety of principal first in their stock selection criteria. These investors are more quality-conscious and tend to gravitate toward blue chips and other nonspeculative shares. Accumulation of capital, in contrast, is generally an important goal to those with long-term investment horizons. These investors use the capital gains and/or dividends that stocks provide to build up their wealth. Some use growth stocks for such purposes, others do it with income shares, and still others use a little of both. Finally, some investors use stocks as a source of income. To them, a dependable flow of dividends is essential. High-yielding, good-quality income shares are usually the preferred investment vehicle for these people.

Individual investors can use a number of different *investment strategies* to reach one or more of their investment goals. These include buy-and-hold, high income, quality long-term growth, aggressive stock management, and speculation and short-term trading. The first three strategies would probably appeal to investors who consider storage of value important. Depending on the temperament of the investor and the time he or she has to devote to an investment program, any of the strategies might be used to accumulate capital. In contrast, the high-income strategy is the most logical choice for those using stocks as a source of income.

Buy-and-Hold

Buy-and-hold is the most basic and certainly one of the most conservative of all investment strategies. The objective is to place money in a secure investment outlet (safety of principal is vital) and watch it grow over time. High-quality stocks that offer attractive current income and/or capital gains are selected and held for extended periods—perhaps as long as 10 to 15 years. This strategy is often used to finance future retirement plans, to meet the educational needs of children, or simply as a convenient way to accumulate capital over the long haul. Generally, investors will pick out a few good stocks and then invest in them on a regular basis for long periods of time, until either the investment climate or corporate conditions change dramatically.

Not only do buy-and-hold investors regularly add fresh capital to their portfolios (many treat them like savings plans), but most also plow the income from annual dividends back into the portfolio and reinvest in additional shares (often through dividend reinvestment plans). Long popular with so-called *value-oriented investors*, this approach is used by quality-conscious individuals who are looking for highly competitive returns over the long haul.

High Income

Individual investors often use common stocks to seek high levels of current income. Common stocks are viewed as desirable outlets for such purposes not only because of their current yields but also because their *dividend levels tend to increase over time*. Safety of principal and stability of income are vital, and capital gains are of secondary importance. Quality income shares are the popular investment medium for this kind of strategy. Because of the high yields available from many income shares, some investors adopt this strategy simply as a way of earning high (and relatively safe) returns on their investment capital. More often than not, however, high-income strategies are used by those trying to supplement their income and who plan to use the added income for consumption purposes, such as a retired couple supplementing their retirement benefits with income from stocks.

Quality Long-Term Growth

This strategy is *less* conservative than either of the first two in that it seeks capital gains as the primary source of return. A fair amount of trading takes place with this approach, most of it confined to quality growth stocks (including baby blues and other mid-caps) that offer attractive growth prospects and the chance for considerable price appreciation. Dividends are not ignored, however, since a number of growth stocks also pay dividends, which many growth-oriented investors consider *an added source of return*. But, even with dividend-paying growth stocks, this strategy still emphasizes capital gains as the principal way to earn the big returns. The approach involves a greater element of risk, due to its heavy reliance on capital gains. Therefore, a good deal of diversification is often used. Long-term accumulation of capital is the most common reason for using this approach, but compared to the buy-and-hold tactic, the investor aggressively seeks a bigger payoff by doing considerably more trading and assuming more market risk.

A variation of this investment theme—one that involves a combination of both the quality long-term growth and the high-income strategies—is the so-called *total return approach* to investing. With the total return approach, investors seek attractive long-term returns from *both* dividend income *and* capital gains. These investors will hold both income stocks and growth stocks in their portfolios, or they may hold stocks that provide both dividends and capital gains (in which case, the investor doesn't necessarily look for high-yielding stocks, but rather for stocks that offer the potential for *high rates of growth in their dividend streams*). Like their counterparts who employ high-income or quality long-term growth strategies, these investors are very concerned about quality. Indeed, about the only thing that separates these investors from high-income or quality long-term growth investors is that to them, what matters is not so much the *source of return* as the *amount of return*. For this reason, total return investors seek the most attractive returns wherever they can find it—be it from a growing stream of dividends or appreciation in the price of a stock.

Aggressive Stock Management

Aggressive stock management also uses quality issues but, this time, to seek attractive rates of return through a fully managed portfolio—that is, one in which the investor aggressively trades in and out of various stocks in order to achieve eye-catching returns, primarily from capital gains. Blue chips, growth stocks, mid-caps, and cyclical issues are the primary investment vehicles; more aggressive investors might even consider small-cap stocks, foreign shares, or ADRs.

This approach is somewhat similar to the quality long-term growth strategy, but it involves considerably more trading, and the investment horizon is generally much shorter. For example, rather than waiting two or three years for a stock to move, an aggressive stock trader would go after the same investment payoff in six months to a year. Timing security transactions and turning investment capital over fairly rapidly are both key elements of this strategy: These investors try to stay fully invested in stocks when the market is bullish, and when it weakens, they will often shift to a more defensive posture by putting a big chunk of their money into defensive stocks, or even cash and other short-term debt instruments. This strategy has obvious and substantial risks, and it also places real demands on the individual's time and investment skills, but the rewards can be equally substantial.

Speculation and Short-Term Trading

Speculation and short-term trading is the least conservative of all investment strategies, especially when carried to its extreme. The sole investment objective is capital gains; and if the objective can be achieved in two weeks, all the better. Although such investors confine most of their attention to speculative or small-cap stocks, they are not averse to using foreign shares (especially the ones found in so-called *emerging markets*) or other forms of common stock if they offer attractive short-term capital gains opportunities. Many speculators find that information about the industry or company is much less important in this kind of strategy than market psychology or the general tone of the market itself. It is a process of constantly switching from one position to another as new investment opportunities unfold. Because the strategy involves so much risk, many transactions end up with little or no profit, or even substantial losses. The hope is, of course, that when one does hit, it will be in a big way and returns will be more than sufficient to offset losses. This strategy obviously requires considerable knowledge, time, and—perhaps most important—the psychological and financial fortitude to withstand the shock of financial losses.

CONCEPTS *in Review*

5.12 Define and briefly discuss the investment merits of each of the following:
   a. *Blue chips*
   b. *Income stocks*
   c. *Mid-cap stocks*
   d. *American Depositary Receipts*
   e. *IPOs*

5.13 Why do most income stocks offer only limited capital gains potential? Does this mean the outlook for continued profitability is also limited? Explain.

5.14 With all the securities available in this country, why would a U.S. investor want to buy foreign stocks? Briefly describe the two ways that a U.S. investor can buy stocks in a foreign company. As an American investor, which approach would you prefer? Explain.

5.15 Which investment approach (or approaches) do you feel would be most appropriate for a quality-conscious investor? Explain. How about someone who's willing to tolerate a good deal of risk?

On Track with *STOCK-TRAK*®

STOCK-TRAK® Common Stock Trades and Dividends

STOCK-TRAK® requires that all stock trades be in round lots of 100 shares. Common shares must be traded on the New York Stock Exchange, the American Stock Exchange, or the National Association of Securities Dealers Automated Quotation (Nasdaq) system. Nasdaq shares must be listed in major financial publications, such as the *Wall Street Journal*. Common shares sold solely on foreign exchanges, such as Toyota, cannot be traded. Dual-listed foreign stock, where one of the listings is the NYSE, AMEX, or Nasdaq markets, can, however, be purchased. An example is ELF Aquitaine, the French oil conglomerate listed on both the Paris and New York exchanges.

Dividends of sufficient size are included in the investor's cash balance. Cash dividends must equal at least half a penny per share (e.g., 50 cents on 100 shares). Stock dividends of 2 percent or more are handled by increasing the number of shares held.

SUMMARY

LG 1 Explain the investment appeal of common stocks and why individuals like to invest in them. Common stocks have long been a popular investment vehicle, due in large part to the attractive return opportunities they provide. From current income to capital gains, there are common stocks available to fit just about any investment need.

LG 2 Describe stock returns from a historical perspective and gain an appreciation of how current returns measure up to historical standards of performance. Historically (over the past 40 or so years), stocks have provided investors with annual returns of around 10 to 15 percent. These returns consist of both dividends and capital gains and are fairly reflective of what you can expect from stocks over the long haul. Of course, higher returns may be possible over shorter periods of time, or for those willing to assume a greater amount of risk.

LG 3 Discuss the basic features of common stocks, including issue characteristics, stock quotations, and transaction costs. Common stocks are a form of equity capital, each share being evidence of partial ownership of a company. Publicly traded stock can be issued via public offering or through a rights offering to existing stockholders. Companies can also increase the number of shares outstanding through a stock split. To reduce the number of shares of stock in circulation, companies can buy back shares, which are then held as treasury stock. Occasionally, a company will issue different classes of common stock, known as classified common stock.

LG 4   **Gain an understanding of the different kinds of common stock values and the ability of common stocks to serve as an inflation hedge.** There are several ways to calculate the value of a share of stock, from book value, which represents accounting value, to market and investment values, which are most important to investors. These latter two represent what the stock is or should be worth. Although common stocks are often considered the ideal inflation hedge, the fact is that when inflation really starts heating up, stocks generally do a rather unsatisfactory job of protecting the investor from inflation.

LG 5   **Discuss common stock dividends, including how dividend decisions are made, types of dividends, and dividend reinvestment plans.** Companies often share their profits by paying out cash dividends to stockholders. Such actions are normally taken only after carefully considering a variety of corporate and market factors. Sometimes companies declare stock dividends rather than or in addition to cash dividends. Many firms that pay cash dividends have automatic dividend reinvestment plans, whereby shareholders can have cash dividends automatically reinvested in the company's stock.

LG 6   **Describe various types of common stocks, including foreign stocks, and note the different ways stocks can be used as investment vehicles.** The type of stock selected depends on an investor's needs and preferences. In today's market, the investor has a full range of stocks to choose from, including blue chips, income stocks, growth stocks, speculative issues, cyclicals, defensive shares, mid-cap stocks, small-cap stocks, and initial public offerings. In addition to stocks in U.S. companies, there's a growing interest in foreign securities. American investors can buy the common stocks of foreign companies either directly on foreign exchanges or on U.S. exchanges and OTC markets as American Depositary Receipts (ADRs). Generally speaking, common stocks can be used as a storehouse of value, to accumulate capital, and as a source of income. Different investment strategies—buy-and-hold, high income, quality long-term growth, aggressive stock management, and speculation and short-term trading—can be followed to achieve these objectives.

DISCUSSION QUESTIONS

1. Look at the record of stock returns in Tables 5.1 and 5.2, particularly the return performance during the 1970s and 1980s.
    a. How would you characterize the returns during the 1970s versus those produced in the 1980s?
    b. Considering the average annual returns that have been generated over *holding periods* of 5 years or more, what rate of return do you feel is typical for the stock market in general? Is it unreasonable to expect this kind of return, on average, in the future? Does this mean that higher rates of return aren't possible? Explain.

2. Assume that the following quote for the Alpha Beta Corp. (a NYSE stock) was obtained from the Thursday, April 10, issue of the *Wall Street Journal*:

254   150½   AlphaBet   ALF   6.00   3.1   15   755   194¼   189   189⅛   − 3⅞

Given this information, answer the following questions:
    a. On what day did the trading activity occur?
    b. At what price did the stock sell at the end of the day on Wednesday, April 9?
    c. What are the highest and lowest prices at which the stock sold on the date quoted?
    d. What is the firm's price/earnings ratio? What does that indicate?
    e. What is the last price at which the stock traded on the date quoted?
    f. How large a dividend is expected in the current year?

g. What are the highest and the lowest prices at which the stock traded during the latest 52-week period?

h. How many shares of stock were traded on the day quoted?

i. How much, if any, of a change in stock price took place between the day quoted and the immediately preceding period? What did the stock close at on the immediately preceding day?

3. Listed below are three pairs of stocks. Look at each pair and select the security you would like to own, given that you want to *select the one that's worth the most money.* Then, *after* you make all three of your selections, use the *Wall Street Journal* or some other source to find the latest market value of the two securities in each pair.

   a. 50 shares of Berkshire Hathaway (stock symbol: BRK) or 150 shares of Coca-Cola (stock symbol: KO). (Both are listed on the NYSE.)

   b. 100 shares of WD-40 (symbol: WDFC—a Nasdaq National Market issue) or 100 shares of Marvel Entertainment (symbol: MRV—an NYSE stock).

   c. 150 shares of Wal-Mart (symbol: WMT) or 50 shares of Sears (symbol: S). (Both are listed on the NYSE.)

How many times did you pick the one that was worth the most money? Did the price of any of these stocks surprise you? If so, which one(s)? Does the price of a stock represent its value? Explain.

4. Assume that a wealthy individual comes to you looking for investment advice. He is in his early forties and has $250,000 to put into stocks. He wants to build up as much capital as he can over a 15-year period and is willing to tolerate a "fair amount" of risk.

   a. What types of stocks do you think would be most suitable for this investor? Come up with at least three different types of stocks and briefly explain the rationale for each.

   b. Would your recommendations change if you were dealing with a smaller amount of money—say, $50,000? What if the investor were more risk-averse? Explain.

5. Identify and briefly describe the three sources of return to U.S. investors in foreign stocks. How important are currency exchange rates, and, with regard to currency exchange rates, when's the best time to be in foreign securities?

   a. Listed below are exchange rates (for the beginning and end of a one-year investment horizon) for three currencies: the British pound (B£), Australian dollar (A$), and Mexican peso (Mp).

	Currency Exchange Rates at	
Currency	Beginning of Investment Horizon	End of One-Year Investment Horizon
British pound (B£)	1.55 U.S. dollars per B£	1.75 U.S. dollars per B£
Australian dollar (A$)	1.35 A$ per U.S. dollar	1.25 A$ per U.S. dollar
Mexican peso (Mp)	$0.30 U.S. dollars per Mp	$0.40 U.S. dollars per Mp

   From the perspective of an American investor holding a foreign (British, Australian, or Mexican) stock, which of the above changes in currency exchange rates would have a positive effect on returns (in U.S. dollars) and which would have a negative effect?

   b. Since ADRs are denominated in U.S. dollars, are their returns affected by currency exchange rates? Explain.

6. Briefly define each of the following types of investment programs, and note the kinds of stock (blue chip, speculative stocks, etc.) that would best fit with each:

a. A buy-and-hold strategy
b. A high-income portfolio
c. Long-term total return
d. Aggressive stock management

PROBLEMS   1. An investor owns some stock in General Refrigeration & Cooling. The stock recently underwent a 5-for–2 stock split. If the stock was trading at $50 per share just before the split, how much would each share most likely be selling for right after the split? If the investor owned 200 shares of the stock before the split, how many shares would she own afterward?

  2. The Kracked Pottery Company has total assets of $2.5 million, total short- and long-term debt of $1.8 million, and $200,000 worth of 8 percent preferred stock outstanding. What is the firm's total book value? What would its book value per share amount to if it had 50,000 shares of common stock outstanding?

3. The W. C. Fields Beverage Company recently reported net profits after taxes of $15.8 million. It has 2.5 million shares of common stock outstanding and pays preferred dividends of $1 million per year.
   a. Compute the firm's earnings per share (EPS).
   b. Assuming the stock currently trades at $60 per share, what would the firm's dividend yield be if it paid $2 per share to common stockholders?
   c. What would the firm's dividend payout ratio be if it paid $2 a share in dividends?

   4. You're given the following information about Associated Industries, Inc.:

Total assets	$240 million
Total debt	$115 million
Preferred stock	$25 million
Common stockholders equity	$100 million
Net profits after taxes	$22.5 million
Number of preferred stock outstanding	1 million shares
Number of common stock outstanding	10 million shares
Preferred dividends paid	$2/share
Common dividends paid	$0.75/share
Market price of the preferred stock	$30.75/share
Market price of the common stock	$25.00/share

Use this information to find the following:
a. The company's book value
b. Its book value per share
c. The stock's earnings per share (EPS)
d. The dividend payout ratio
e. The dividend yield on the common stock
f. The dividend yield on the preferred stock

5. Angus Hoffmeister owns 200 shares of Consolidated Glue. The company's board of directors recently declared a cash dividend of 50 cents a share payable April 18 (a Wednesday) to shareholders of record on March 22 (a Thursday).
   a. How much in dividends, if any, will Angus receive if he *sells* his stock on March 20?

b. Assume Angus decides to hold on to the stock rather than sell it. If he belongs to the company's dividend reinvestment plan, how many new shares of stock will he receive if the stock is at present trading at 40 and the plan offers a 5 percent discount on the share price of the stock? (Assume all of Angus's dividends are diverted to the plan.) Will Angus have to pay any taxes on these dividends, since he's taking them in stock rather than cash?

LG 5   6. Southwest Investments Corp. has the following 5-year record of earnings per share:

Year	EPS
1991	$1.40
1992	2.10
1993	1.00
1994	3.25
1995	0.80

Which of the following procedures would produce the greatest amount of dividends to stockholders over this 5-year period?
a. Paying out dividends at a fixed payout ratio of 40 percent of EPS
b. Paying out dividends at the fixed rate of $1 per share

LG 4 LG 5   7. Using the resources available at your campus or public library, select any three common stocks you like and determine the latest book value per share, earnings per share, dividend payout ratio, and dividend yield for each. (Show all your calculations.)

LG 4 LG 5   8. In January 1990, an investor purchased 800 shares of Engulf & Devour, a rapidly growing high-tech conglomerate. Over the 5-year period from 1990 through 1994, the stock turned in the following dividend and share price performance:

Year	Share Price at Beginning of Year	Dividends Paid During Year	Share Price at End of Year
1990	$42.50 *	$0.82	$ 54.00
1991	54.00	1.28	74.25
1992	74.25	1.64	81.00
1993	81.00	1.91	91.25
1994	91.25	2.30	128.75

*Investor purchased stock in 1990 at this price.

a. Based on this information, find the *annual* holding period returns for 1990 through 1994. (*Hint:* See Chapter 4 for the HPR formula.)
b. Use the return information in Table 5.1 to evaluate the investment performance of this stock. How do you think Engulf & Devour stacks up against the market? Would you consider this a good investment? Explain.

LG 6   9. George Robbins considers himself to be a pretty aggressive investor. At the present time, he's thinking about investing in some foreign securities; in particular, he's looking at two stocks: (1) Löwenbräu, the famous German beer maker, and (2) Ciba-Geigy, the big Swiss pharmaceutical firm.

Löwenbräu, which trades on the Frankfurt Exchange, is currently priced at 2,400 German marks (Dm) per share and pays annual dividends of 25 Dm per share. Robbins expects the stock to climb to 2,700 Dm within a period of 12 months. The current exchange rate is 1.58 Dm/U.S.$ but that's expected to rise to 1.75 Dm/U.S.$. The other company, Ciba-Geigy, trades on the Zurich Exchange and is currently priced at 715 Swiss francs (Sf) per share. The stock pays annual dividends of 15 Sf per share, and its share price is expected to go up to 760 Sf within a year. At current exchange rates, one Sf is worth $0.75 U.S., but that's expected to go to $0.85 by the end of the one-year holding period.

    a. *Ignoring the currency effect*, which of the two stocks promises the higher total return (in its local currency)? Based on this information, which of the two stocks looks like the better investment?

    b. Now, which of the two stocks has the better *total return, in U.S. dollars*? Did currency exchange rates affect their returns in any way? Do you still want to stick with the same stock you selected in (a)? Explain.

CASE PROBLEMS   **5.1 SARA CONTEMPLATES THE STOCK MARKET**

Sara Thomas is a child psychologist who has built up a thriving practice in her home-town of Phoenix, Arizona. Her practice has been so lucrative, in fact, that over the past several years she has been able to accumulate a substantial sum of money. She has worked long and hard to be successful, but she never imagined anything like this. Fortunately, success has not spoiled Sara. Still single, she keeps to her old circle of friends. One of her closest friends is Terry Jenkins, who happens to be a stockbroker. Sara sees a lot of Terry, who has acted as her financial adviser.

    Not long ago, Sara attended a public seminar on investing in the stock market. Like a lot of other people, Sara was beginning to feel that holding all her money in low-yielding savings accounts was a serious mistake. One evening, Sara confided to Terry that she had been doing some reading lately about the stock market and had found several stocks she thought looked "sort of interesting." She described them as follows:

- *North Atlantic Swimsuit Company.* It's a highly speculative stock and pays no dividends. Although the earnings of NASS have been a bit erratic, Sara feels that its growth prospects have never been brighter—"what with more people than ever going to the beaches the way they are these days," she says.

- *Town and Country Computer.* This is a long-established computer firm that pays a modest dividend yield (of about 2½ percent). It's considered a quality growth stock. From one of the stock reports she'd read, Sara understands that it offers excellent long-term growth and capital gains potential.

- *Southeastern Public Utility Company.* An income stock, it pays a nice dividend yield of around 5 percent. Although it's a solid company, it has limited growth prospects because of its location.

- *International Gold Mines, Inc.* This stock performed quite well several years ago. Sara feels that if it can do so well in inflationary times, it will do even better in a strong economy. Unfortunately, the stock has experienced wide price swings in the past and pays almost no dividends.

Questions

1. What do you think of the idea of Sara keeping "substantial sums" of money in savings accounts? Would common stocks make better investments than savings accounts?

2.   What is your opinion of the four stocks Sara has described? Do you think they are suitable for her investment needs?

3.   What kind of common stock investment program would you recommend for Sara? What investment objectives do you think she should set for herself, and how can common stocks help her achieve her goals?

LG 5 **LG 6**   ### 5.2 DAVE GOES AFTER DIVIDEND YIELD

Dave Peterson is a commercial artist who make a good living by doing freelance work—mostly layout and illustration work for local ad agencies and major institutional clients (e.g., large department stores). Dave has been investing in the stock market for some time, buying mostly high-quality growth stocks. He has been seeking long-term growth and capital appreciation and feels that with the limited time he has to devote to his security holdings, high-quality issues are his best bet. He has become a bit perplexed lately with the market, disturbed that some of his growth stocks aren't doing even as well as many good-grade income shares. He therefore decides to have a chat with his broker, Al Fried.

During the course of their conversation, it becomes clear that both Al and Dave are thinking along the same lines. Al points out that dividend yields on income shares are, indeed, way up and, because of the state of the economy, the outlook for growth stocks is not particularly bright. He suggests that Dave seriously consider putting some of his money into income shares to capture some of the high dividend yields that are available. After all, as Al points out, "the bottom line is not so much where the payoff comes from as how much it amounts to!" They then talk about a high-yield public utility stock, Hydro-Electric Light and Power. Al digs up some forecast information about Hydro-Electric and presents it to Dave for his consideration:

Year	Expected EPS	Expected Dividend Payout Ratio
1995	$3.25	40%
1996	3.40	40
1997	3.90	45
1998	4.40	45
1999	5.00	45

The stock at present trades at $60 per share, and Al thinks that within 5 years it should be trading at a level of $75 to $80. Dave realizes that in order to buy the Hydro-Electric stock, he will have to sell his holdings of CapCo Industries—a highly regarded growth stock that Dave has become disenchanted with because of recent substandard performance.

Questions

1.   How would you describe Dave's present investment program? How do you think it fits him and his investment objectives?

2.   Looking at the Hydro-Electric stock:
   a. Determine the amount of annual dividends Hydro-Electric is expected to pay over the years 1995 to 1999.
   b. Compute the total dollar return Dave would make from Hydro-Electric if he invests $6,000 in the stock and all the dividend and price expectations are realized.

c. If Dave participates in the company's dividend reinvestment plan, how many
    shares of stock would he have by the end of 1999, and what would they be
    worth, given that the stock trades at $80 on December 31, 1999? Assume the
    stock could have been purchased through the dividend reinvestment plan at a
    net price of $50 a share in 1995, $55 in 1996, $60 in 1997, $65 in 1998, and
    $70 in 1999. Use fractional shares, to two decimals, in your computations.
    Also, assume as in (b) above that Dave starts with 100 shares of stock and all
    dividend expectations are realized.

3. Would Dave be going to a different investment strategy if he decided to buy shares
in Hydro-Electric? If the switch is made, how would you describe his new investment
program? What do you think of this new approach, and is it likely to lead to more
trading on Dave's behalf? If so, how do you think that stacks up with the limited
amount of time he has to devote to his portfolio?

CHAPTER 6

FUNDAMENTAL ANALYSIS
OF COMMON STOCK

LEARNING GOALS

After studying this chapter, you should be able to:

LG 1 Discuss the security analysis process, including its goals and the functions it performs.

LG 2 Gain an appreciation of the purpose and contribution of economic analysis to the stock valuation process.

LG 3 Describe industry analysis and note the role it plays in stock valuation.

LG 4 Gain a basic understanding of how fundamental analysis fits into the stock valuation process and why company analysis is used to assess the financial condition and operating results of the firm.

LG 5 Calculate a variety of financial ratios and describe how financial statement analysis can be used to determine the financial vitality of a company.

LG 6 Use various financial measures to compare a company's recent performance with its own past and with other companies in the same industry, and explain how the insights derived from such analysis form the basic input for the valuation process.

For Paul and Ann Albach, investing is a team effort that began when they married 18 years ago. Their primary goal is saving for a comfortable and prosperous retirement. Through a disciplined program of saving and investing, they expect to meet their goal ahead of schedule. Over time, they moved gradually from CDs to mutual funds to individual common stocks. Because the Albachs believe that stocks can provide a better return on investment than fixed-income securities, their target portfolio is about 90 percent equities (split 70:30 between stocks and mutual funds), with 10 percent in fixed-income investments and cash. They take a long-term view of investing and don't panic over market setbacks. By investing regularly, they have achieved substantial portfolio and net worth growth.

After discovering that investing is an activity they could share, the Albachs began investing directly in common stocks, and their common stock returns so far have been higher than those of their stock mutual funds. Taking advantage of Ann's computer industry expertise, they look for high-tech growth stocks and perform a rigorous analysis before investing, blending their somewhat different approaches to stocks. Ann reads trade magazines, focuses on the quality of a company's products, and prefers companies with rapid growth. Paul's approach is more fundamental and value-based. He likes companies with a low ratio of price to earnings (a low P/E ratio), sound balance sheets, little debt, and steady earnings growth. Paul sets a target price for a stock and generally sells when it gets near that target.

Once they identify a company that interests them, Paul researches the company using *Value Line*, *Investext* (for brokerage evaluations of the company), annual and quarterly reports, and articles about the company in the financial press. "We also look for a company's products in stores and talk to people familiar with the industry or company," Ann says. Paul analyzes the company's financial statements to understand how the firm makes money, and he develops several scenarios about future earnings per share and price/earnings ratios, based on different assumptions about product success and earnings growth rates. He uses the scenarios to estimate the future stock price. After discussing scenarios for various companies, Paul and Ann each invest their own funds and compete on the outcome.

The Albachs believe they do better as a team than either would do individually. Ann says, "It is crucial to know the companies and their products, but Paul's research helps with timing." Paul thinks it's important to be objective about investing: "When an investment is successful, I ask, 'Were we rewarded for making a sound judgment, or did we just get lucky?' When we lose money, I look for flaws in my analysis. If I'd make the same investment again in the same circumstances, I don't worry about losing money."

> **WHEN AN INVESTMENT IS SUCCESSFUL, I ASK, "WERE WE REWARDED FOR MAKING A SOUND JUDGMENT, OR DID WE JUST GET LUCKY?"**

The Albachs live in central Texas. Paul, a former professor of technical and professional writing, is on the staff of a Texas higher education agency. Ann is a former editor for a magazine about computer-aided design (CAD) and is taking time off to start a family.

To many individuals, common stocks are synonymous with investments. Stories recounting shrewd market plays seem to fascinate people from all walks of life, as the prospect of seeing a small sum grow into a vast fortune has the same attraction for the homemaker, the service station attendant, or the college professor as it does for the Wall Street tycoon. However, as you know by now, successful investments are more often than not a matter of planning than of luck. Paul and Ann Albach, for example, credit much of their success to thorough security analysis. In this, the first of two chapters dealing with security analysis, we will introduce some of the principles and techniques used to evaluate the investment suitability of common stocks. These basic analytical techniques should help you, too, develop your own framework for stock selection.

SECURITY ANALYSIS

Consider the case of Circuit City Stores. If an investor had put $2,600 into Circuit City stock on January 1, 1980, that investment would have soared to over a half-million dollars by September 1994. Not bad for a 15-year period of time—indeed, not bad for a lifetime! Unfortunately, for every story of great success in the market, there are dozens more that don't end so well. Most of the disasters can be traced to bad timing, greed, poor planning, or failure to use common sense in making investment decisions. Although these chapters on stock investments cannot offer the keys to sudden wealth, they do provide sound principles for formulating a successful long-range investment program. The techniques described are quite traditional; they are the same (proven) methods that have been used by literally millions of investors to achieve attractive rates of return on their capital.

PRINCIPLES OF SECURITY ANALYSIS

security analysis
the process of gathering and organizing information and then using it to determine the value of a share of common stock.

intrinsic value
the underlying or inherent value of a stock, as determined through fundamental analysis.

Security analysis consists of gathering information, organizing it into a logical framework, and then using the information to determine the inherent or intrinsic value of a common stock. That is, given a rate of return that's compatible to the amount of risk involved in a proposed transaction, **intrinsic value** provides a measure of the underlying worth of a share of stock. It provides a standard for helping you judge whether a particular stock is undervalued, fairly priced, or overvalued. The entire concept of stock valuation is based on the belief that all securities possess an intrinsic value that their current market or trading values must approach over time.

In investments, the question of value centers on return. In particular, a satisfactory investment candidate is one *that offers a level of expected return that's commensurate with the amount of risk involved*. That is, there's a *desired or minimum rate of return* that you should be able to earn on an investment, and that rate varies with the amount of risk you have to assume. As a result, not only must an investment candidate be profitable; it must be *sufficiently* profitable—in the sense that you'd expect it to generate a return that's high enough to offset the perceived exposure to risk.

If you could have your way, you'd probably like to invest in something that offers complete preservation of capital, along with sizable helpings of current income and capital gains. The problem, of course, is finding such a security. One approach is to buy whatever strikes your fancy. A more rational approach—and one used by the Albachs—is to use security analysis to seek out promising investment candidates. Security analysis addresses the question of *what to buy* by determining what a stock *ought to be worth*. Presumably, an investor would buy a stock *only if its prevailing market price does not exceed its worth*—its intrinsic value. Ultimately, intrinsic value will depend on several factors:

1. Estimates of the stock's future cash flows (the amount of dividends the investor can expect to receive over the holding period and the estimated price of the stock at time of sale)
2. The discount rate used to translate these future cash flows into a present value
3. The amount of risk embedded in achieving the forecasted level of performance

Traditional security analysis usually takes a "top-down" approach: It begins with economic analysis, then moves to industry analysis and finally to fundamental analysis. *Economic analysis* is concerned with assessing the general state of the economy and its potential effects on security returns. *Industry analysis* deals with the industry within which a particular company operates, how the company stacks up against the major competitors in the industry, and the general outlook for that industry. *Fundamental analysis* looks in depth at the financial condition and operating results of a specific company and the underlying behavior of its common stock. In essence, it looks at the "fundamentals of the company"—at the company's investment decisions, the liquidity of its assets, its use of debt, its profit margins and earnings growth, and ultimately at the future prospects of the company and its stock. Fundamental analysis is closely linked to the notion of intrinsic value, since it *provides the basis for projecting a stock's future cash flows*. A key part of this analytical process is *company analysis*, which takes a close look at the actual financial performance of the company. Such analysis is not meant simply to provide interesting tidbits of information about how the company has performed in the past; rather, it's done to *help investors formulate expectations about the future performance of the company and its stock*. Make no mistake about it: In the field of investments, it's the future that matters. But in order to understand the future prospects of the firm, an investor should have a good handle on the company's current condition and its ability to produce earnings. And that's just what company analysis does: It helps investors predict the future by looking at the past and determining how well the company is situated to meet the challenges that lie ahead.

THE ROLE OF SECURITY ANALYSIS IN AN EFFICIENT MARKET ENVIRONMENT

The concept of security analysis in general and fundamental analysis in particular is based on the assumption that investors are capable of formulating reliable estimates of a stock's future behavior. Fundamental analysis operates on the broad premise that some securities may be mispriced in the marketplace at any given time. Further, fundamental analysis assumes that it is possible to distinguish those securities that are correctly priced from those that are not, by undertaking a careful analysis of the inherent characteristics of each of the firms in question.

To many, those two assumptions of fundamental analysis seem reasonable. However, there are others who, for one reason or another, just don't accept the assumptions of fundamental analysis. These are the so-called *efficient market* advocates. They believe that the market is so efficient in processing new information that securities trade very close to or at their correct values (proper prices) at all times. Thus, they argue, it is virtually impossible to outperform the market on a consistent basis. In its strongest form, the *efficient market hypothesis* asserts (1) that securities are rarely, if ever, substantially mispriced in the marketplace and (2) that any security analysis, however detailed, is not capable of identifying mispriced securities with a frequency greater than that which might be expected by random chance alone. Is the efficient market hypothesis correct? Is there a place for fundamental analysis in modern investment theory? Interestingly, most financial theorists and practitioners would answer yes to both of these questions.

The solution to this apparent paradox is really quite simple. Basically, fundamental analysis is of value in the selection of alternative investment vehicles for two important reasons: First, financial markets are as efficient as they are merely because a large number of people and powerful financial institutions invest a great deal of time and money in analyzing the fundamentals of most widely held investments. In other words, markets tend to be efficient—and securities tend to trade at or near their intrinsic values—simply because a great many people have done the research necessary to determine just what their intrinsic values should be. A second reason fundamental analysis is of value in investment research is that although the financial markets are generally quite efficient, they are by no means perfect. Pricing errors are inevitable, and those individuals who have conducted the most thorough studies of the underlying fundamentals of a given security are the ones most likely to be able to profit when errors do occur. We will study the ideas and implications of efficient markets in some detail in Chapter 7. For now, however, we will assume that traditional security analysis is useful in identifying attractive equity investments.

CONCEPTS *in Review*

6.1   Identify the three major parts of security analysis and explain why security analysis is important to the stock selection process.

6.2   What is *intrinsic value,* and how does it fit into the security analysis process?

6.3   What is a satisfactory investment vehicle? How does security analysis help in identifying such investment candidates?

6.4   Would there be any need for security analysis if we operated in an efficient market environment? Explain.

ECONOMIC ANALYSIS

If we lived in a world where economic activity had absolutely no effect on the stock market or security prices, we could avoid studying the economy altogether. The fact is, of course, that we do not live in such a world. Rather, stock prices are heavily influenced by the state of the economy and by economic events. As a rule, stock prices tend to move up when the economy is strong, and they retreat when the economy starts to soften. Of course, it's not a perfect relationship, but it is a powerful one.

The reason the economy is so important to the market is simple: The overall performance of the economy has a significant bearing on the performance and profitability of the companies that issue common stock. As the fortunes of the issuing firms change with economic conditions, so will the prices of their stocks. Of course, not all stocks are affected in the same way or to the same extent. Some sectors of the economy, like food retailing, may be only mildly affected by the economy; others, like the construction and auto industries, are often hard hit when times get rough.

economic analysis
a study of general economic conditions that is used in the valuation of common stock.

Economic analysis—which involves a general study of the economy—should not only give an investor a grasp of the *underlying nature of the economic environment* but also enable him or her to assess the *current state of the economy* and formulate expectations about its *future course*. It can go so far as to include a detailed examination of each sector of the economy, or it may be done on a very informal basis. Regardless of how it is performed, however, the purpose—from a security analysis perspective—is always the same: to establish a sound foundation for the valuation of common stock.

ECONOMIC ANALYSIS AND THE BUSINESS CYCLE

Economic analysis sets the tone for security analysis. If the economic future looks bleak, you can probably expect most stock returns to be equally dismal. If the economy looks strong, stocks should do well. As we saw in Chapter 3, the behavior of the economy is captured in the **business cycle**, which reflects changes in total economic activity over time. Two widely followed measures of the business cycle are gross domestic product and industrial production. *Gross domestic product* (GDP) represents the market value of all goods and services produced in a country over the period of a year. *Industrial production*, in contrast, is a measure (actually, it's an index) of the activity/output in the industrial or productive segment of the economy. Normally, GDP and the index of industrial production move up and down with the business cycle.

business cycle
an indication of the current state of the economy, reflecting changes in total economic activity over time.

Actually, the business cycle is more than just an indicator of the current state of economic activity. It's also a force that heavily influences the behavior of the stock market—so much so, in fact, that a special approach to investing has evolved around it. Known as *sector rotation*, the approach is based on the fact that some types of stocks (or market "sectors") do better at different stages of the business cycle than others. However, as the *Investor Insights* box on page 240 suggests, playing the business cycle is sometimes easier said than done.

KEY ECONOMIC FACTORS

Several parts of the economy are especially important because of the impact they have on total economic activity. These include:

> *Government fiscal policy:*
> Taxes
> Government spending
> Debt management

INVESTOR INSIGHTS: *Market Innovations*

Playing the Business Cycle

Sector rotation is an investment strategy based on the theory that certain sectors of the market tend to be strong at different points in the business cycle. It involves anticipating changes in the economic cycle—from recession to recovery to expansion—and buying stocks that are expected to do well at each stage. As shown in the accompanying exhibit, during a recession *defensive* companies that produce basic consumer products—food, drugs, tobacco, utilities—prosper, or at least tend to do better than the rest of the market, because the need for their products is reasonably constant. On the other hand, earnings of *cyclical* companies—producers of discretionary consumer goods and services such as cars, apparel, entertainment; providers of consumer credit services; housing and transportation companies—track the economic cycle and therefore fall when the economy does. Once the economy begins to recover, cyclical companies gain favor; their earnings often rise at a faster rate than defensive stocks. Stock prices for basic materials and capital goods producers rise as economic expansion increases business activity throughout the economy. For example, steel manufacturers' output rises to meet increased demand from auto companies.

Does playing the business cycle work? As with any market timing strategy, the answer is "sometimes." Despite the strong correlation between specific sector stocks and the different stages of the business cycle, it is no easy task to accurately predict changing economic trends. Doing well with a sector rotation strategy depends not only on forecasting but also on getting in and out of the sectors ahead of the market in general. Also, there are no guarantees that a particular stock—or even the whole sector—will follow the pattern described above.

Sector rotation is a longer-term form of *market timing*. Market timers move in and out

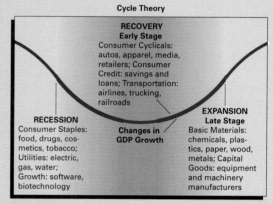

Source: "How to Play the Recovery," *Worth*, August/September 1992, p.32.

of the market frequently (an average of four buy/sell cycles per year). They make their moves when certain market signals, historical patterns, or even seasonal changes predict changes in market trends. If their signals point to a rising market, they buy. If they point to a falling market, they sell their stocks and hold cash equivalents. Sector rotation investors definitely take a longer view than most market timers because business cycles change less often than price swings in the market. Moreover, sector rotation investors aren't getting in and out of the market like market timers. Instead, they're merely changing the types of stocks they hold. Whether this strategy holds promise for you depends on how good you are at tracking the business cycle and picking the group(s) of stocks that's likely to do well in a given economic environment. It's no easy task, to say the least, but many feel it's worth a shot.

Source: Based on information from Pam Black, "The Right Time for Market Timers?" *Business Week*, July 12, 1993, pp. 152–53; "How to Play the Recovery," *Worth*, August/September 1992, p. 32; and Jeffrey M. Laderman, "Time for Market Timers to Get Some Respect?" *Business Week*, August 22, 1994, pp. 63–64.

Monetary policy:
Money supply
Interest rates

Other factors:
Inflation
Consumer spending
Business investments
Foreign trade and foreign
    exchange rates

Government fiscal policy tends to be expansive when it encourages spending—when the government reduces taxes and/or increases the size of the budget. Similarly, monetary policy is said to be expansive when money is readily available and interest rates are relatively low. An expansive economy also depends on a generous level of spending by consumers and business concerns. These same variables moving in a reverse direction can have a contractionary (recessionary) impact on the economy—for example, when taxes and interest rates increase, or when spending by consumers and businesses falls off.

The impact of these major forces filters through the system and affects several key dimensions of the economy. The most important of these are industrial production, corporate profits, retail sales, personal income, the unemployment rate, and inflation. For example, a strong economy exists when industrial production, corporate profits, retail sales, and personal income are moving up and unemployment is down. Thus, when conducting an economic analysis, an investor will want to keep an eye on fiscal and monetary policies, consumer and business spending, and foreign trade *for the potential impact they have on the economy*. At the same time, he or she must stay abreast of the level of industrial production, corporate profits, retail sales, personal income, unemployment, and inflation *in order to assess the state of the business cycle*.

To help you keep track of the economy, Table 6.1 provides a brief description of some key economic measures. These economic statistics are compiled by government agencies and are widely reported in the financial media. (Most of the reports are released monthly.) Take the time to read carefully about the various economic measures and reports cited in Table 6.1. When you understand the behavior of these statistics, you can make your own educated guess as to the current state of the economy and where it's headed.

One final point: As noted in Chapter 5, inflation can have devastating effects on common stocks (and on many other investment vehicles as well). In an inflationary environment, many companies may report higher profits, but the *quality* of those earnings actually declines as profit margins are "squeezed" and the purchasing power of the dollar deteriorates. Furthermore, the high interest rates that accompany inflation not only contribute to rising costs but also reduce the competitive edge of common stocks. That is, as interest rates rise, the returns to bonds and preferred stock improve and make the investment merits of common stock look relatively less attractive. Because of the serious consequences inflation holds for stock prices, investors should devote special attention to this factor as they analyze the economy and its prospects. By the same token, as we saw in the early to middle 1980s, when inflation

Table 6.1 Keeping Track of the Economy

To sort out the confusing array of figures that flow almost daily from Washington, D.C., and to help you keep track of what's happening in the economy, here are some of the most important economic measures and reports to watch.

- **Gross domestic product.** This is the broadest measure of the economy's performance (and replaces the old "GNP" measure). Issued every three months by the Commerce Department, it is an estimate of the total dollar value of all the goods and services produced in this country. Movements in many areas of the economy are closely related to changes in GDP, making it a good analytic tool. In particular, watch the annual rate of growth or decline in "real" or "constant" dollars. This number eliminates the effects of inflation, so that the actual volume of production is measured. Remember, though, that frequent revisions of GDP figures sometimes change the picture of the economy.

- **Industrial production.** Issued monthly by the Federal Reserve Board, this index shows changes in the physical output of America's factories, mines, and electric and gas utilities. The index tends to move in the same direction as the economy, making it a good guide to business conditions between reports on GDP. Detailed breakdowns of the index give a reading on how individual industries are faring.

- **Leading indicators.** This boils down to one number, which summarizes the movement of a dozen statistics that tend to predict—or "lead"—changes in the GDP. The monthly index, issued by the Commerce Department, includes such things as layoffs of workers, new orders placed by manufacturers, changes in the money supply, and the prices of raw materials. If the index moves in the same direction for several months, it's a fairly good sign that total output will move the same way in the near future.

- **Personal income.** A monthly report from the Commerce Department, this shows the before-tax income received by people in the form of wages and salaries, interest and dividends, rents, and other payments such as Social Security, unemployment compensation, and pensions. As a measure of individuals' spending power, the report helps explain trends in consumer buying habits, a major part of total GDP. When personal income rises, it often means that people will increase their buying. But note a big loophole: Excluded are the billions of dollars that change hands in the so-called underground economy—cash transactions that are never reported to tax or other officials.

- **Retail sales.** The Commerce Department's monthly estimate of total sales at the retail level includes everything from cars to bags of groceries. Based on a sample of retail establishments, the figure gives a rough clue to consumer attitudes. It can also indicate future conditions: A long slowdown in sales can lead to cuts in production.

- **Money supply.** A measure of the amount of money in circulation as reported weekly by the Federal Reserve. Actually, there are three measures of the money supply: *M1*, which is basically currency, demand deposits, and NOW accounts; *M2*, the most widely followed measure, which equals M1 plus savings deposits, money market deposit accounts, and money market mutual funds; and *M3*, which is M2 plus large CDs and a few other less significant types of deposits/transactions. It's felt that reasonable growth in the money supply, as measured by M2, is necessary to accommodate an expanding economy. Such growth should have a positive impact on the economy—*unless* the money supply is growing too rapidly. A rapid rate of growth in money is considered to be inflationary; in contrast, a sharp slowdown in the growth rate is viewed as recessionary.

- **Consumer prices.** Issued monthly by the Labor Department, this index shows changes in prices for a fixed market basket of goods and services. The most widely publicized figure is for all urban consumers. A second, used in labor contracts and some government programs, covers urban wage earners and clerical workers. Both are watched as a measure of inflation, but many economists believe that flaws cause them to be wide of the mark.

- **Producer prices.** This is a monthly indicator from the Labor Department showing price changes of goods at various stages of production, from crude materials such as raw cotton to finished goods like clothing and furniture. An upward surge may mean higher consumer prices later. The index, however, can miss discounts and may exaggerate rising price trends. Watch particularly changes in the prices of finished goods. These do not fluctuate as widely as crude materials and thus are a better measure of inflationary pressures.

- **Employment.** The percentage of the workforce that is involuntarily out of work is a broad indicator of economic health. But another monthly figure issued by the Labor Department—the number of payroll jobs—may be better for spotting changes in business. A decreasing number of jobs is a sign that firms are cutting production.

- **Housing starts.** A pickup in the pace of housing starts usually follows an easing of credit conditions—the availability and cost of money—and is an indicator of improvement in economic health. This monthly report from the Commerce Department also includes the number of new building permits issued across the country, an even earlier indicator of the pace of future construction.

slows down, the stock market is often one of the major beneficiaries. Certainly, the great bull market that began in 1982 was fueled by a dramatic drop in the rate of inflation, with the economy, corporate profits, and interest rates all benefiting.

DEVELOPING AN ECONOMIC OUTLOOK

Conducting an economic analysis involves studying fiscal and monetary policies, inflationary expectations, consumer and business spending, and the state of the business cycle. Often investors do this on a fairly informal basis. Many rely on one or more of the popular published sources (e.g., the *Wall Street Journal, Barron's, Fortune,* and *Business Week*) as well as on periodic reports from major brokerage houses to form their economic judgments. These sources provide a convenient summary of economic activity and enable investors to develop a general feel for the condition of the economy.

Once you have developed a general economic outlook, you can use the information in one of two ways. One approach is to construct an economic outlook and then consider where it leads in terms of possible areas for further analysis. For example, suppose you uncover information that strongly suggests the outlook for business spending is very positive. Based on such an analysis, you might want to look more closely at capital goods producers, such as machine tool manufacturers, as investment candidates. Similarly, if you feel that because of the sweeping changes taking place in Eastern Europe and what used to be the USSR, U.S. government defense spending is likely to drop off substantially, you might want to avoid the stocks of major defense contractors.

A second way to use information about the economy is to consider specific industries or companies and ask, "How will they be affected by expected developments in the economy?" Consider, for example, an investor with an interest in *apparel stocks.* Due to the nature of the business (durable fashion goods), these stocks are susceptible to changing economic conditions. Especially important here is the level of discretionary consumer spending: Normally such spending tends to accelerate when the economy picks up steam and slackens when the economy slows down. In this instance, our imaginary investor would first want to assess the current state of the business cycle. Using that insight, he or she would then formulate some expectations about the future of the economy and the potential impact it holds for the stock market in general and apparel stocks in particular.

Table 6.2 (on page 244) shows how some important economic variables can affect the behavior of the stock market. It should be clear that the market is not immune to the economy but, rather, reacts to different economic forces in different ways. At the same time, the investor has to determine how the economy may affect particular segments of the market—in this case, apparel stocks. To see how this might be done, let's assume that the economy has just recently entered the recovery stages of the business cycle. Employment is starting to pick up, inflation and interest rates have dropped to their lowest levels in years, both GDP and industrial production have experienced sharp increases in the past two quarters, and Congress is putting the finishing touches on a major piece of legislation that would lead to reduced taxes. More importantly, because the economy now seems to be in the early stages of a recovery, it should strengthen in the future and both personal income and

Table 6.2 Economic Variables and the Stock Market

Economic Variable	Potential Effect on the Stock Market
Real growth in GDP	Positive impact—it's good for the market.
Industrial production	Continued increases are a sign of strength, which is good for the market.
Inflation	Detrimental to stock prices. Higher inflation leads to lower price/earnings multiples and makes equity securities less competitive.
Corporate profits	Strong corporate earnings are good for the market.
Unemployment	A downer—an increase in unemployment means business is starting to slow down.
Federal deficit	May be positive for a depressed economy but can lead to inflation in a stronger economic environment and therefore have a negative impact.
Weak dollar	Often the result of big trade imbalances, a weak dollar has a negative effect on the market because it makes our markets less attractive to foreign investors. On the other hand, it also makes our products more affordable in overseas markets and therefore can have a positive impact on our economy.
Interest rates	Another downer—rising rates tend to have a negative effect on the market for stocks.
Money supply	Moderate growth can have a positive impact on the economy and the market. Rapid growth, however, is inflationary and therefore detrimental to the stock market.

consumer spending should increase. All of these predictions should be good news for the producers of men's and women's apparel, since a good deal of their sales and an even larger portion of their profits depend on the level of consumer income and spending. In short, our investor sees an economy that appears to be in good shape and set to become even stronger, the consequences of which are favorable not only for the market but for apparel stocks as well.

Note that these conclusions were reached by relying on sources no more sophisticated than *Barron's* or *Business Week*. In fact, about the only "special thing" this investor did was to pay careful attention to those economic forces that are important to the apparel industry (e.g., personal income). The economic portion of the analysis, in effect, has set the stage for further evaluation by indicating the type of economic environment to expect in the near future. The next step is to narrow the focus a bit and conduct the industry phase of the analysis.

However, before we continue with our analysis, it is vital to clarify further the relationship between the stock market and the economy. The economic outlook is used to get a handle on the market and to direct investors to developing industry sectors. Yet it is important to note that changes in stock prices normally occur *before* the actual forecasted changes become apparent in the economy. To go a bit further, we can say the current trend of stock prices is frequently used to help *predict* the course of the economy itself. The apparent conflict here can be resolved somewhat by noting that because of this relationship, it is even more important to derive a reliable economic outlook and to be sensitive to underlying economic changes that may mean the current outlook is becoming dated. Investors in the stock market tend to look into the future in order to justify the purchase or sale of stock. If their perception of the future is changing, stock prices will most likely also be changing. Therefore, watching the course of stock prices as well as the course of the general economy can make for more accurate investment forecasting.

CONCEPTS *in Review*

6.5   Describe the general concept of *economic analysis.* Is this type of analysis necessary, and can it help the individual investor make a decision about a stock? Explain.

6.6   Why is the business cycle important to economic analysis? Does the business cycle have any bearing on the stock market?

6.7   Briefly describe each of the following:
   a. *Gross domestic product*
   b. *Leading indicators*
   c. *Money supply*
   d. *Producer prices*

6.8   What effect, if any, does inflation have on common stocks?

INDUSTRY ANALYSIS

Have you ever thought about buying oil stocks, or autos, or chemicals? How about conglomerates or electric utility stocks? Looking at securities in terms of industry groupings is a popular way of viewing stocks and is widely used by both individual and institutional investors. This is a sensible approach too because stock prices are influenced, at least in part, by industry conditions. The level of demand in an industry and other industry forces set the tone for individual companies. Clearly, if the outlook is good for an industry, then the prospects are likely to be strong for the companies that make up that industry.

KEY ISSUES

industry analysis
study of industry groupings that looks at the competitive position of a particular industry in relation to others and identifies companies holding particular promise within an industry.

The first step in **industry analysis** is to establish the competitive position of a particular industry *in relation to others*, for, as Figure 6.1 (on the next page) indicates, not all industries perform alike. The next step is to identify companies *within the industry* that hold particular promise. This sets the stage for a more thorough analysis of individual companies and securities. Analyzing an industry means looking at such things as its makeup and basic characteristics, the key economic and operating variables that are important in defining industry performance, and the outlook for the industry. The investor will also want to keep an eye out for specific companies that appear well situated to take advantage of industry conditions. Companies with strong market positions should be favored over those with less secure positions. Such dominance provides the ability to maintain pricing leadership and suggests that the firm will be in a position to enjoy economies of scale and low-cost production. Market dominance also enables a company to support a strong research and development effort, thereby helping it secure its leadership position for the future.

Figure 6.1 A Look at the Stock Performance of Key Industry Groups

In the search for value in the stock market, an early step is to look at the big picture: *industry-group trends*. The data shown here present a broad overview of 35 key industries from Standard & Poor's list of 87 industry groups. Each of these industry groups has its own market index that measures the performance of stocks within that group. As is apparent, some industries simply do much better than others, at least over certain time periods. (Source: 1994 *Analyst's Handbook*, Standard & Poor's Corporation.)

	Stock Price Index		Change in Index			1993
	12/31/83	12/31/93	10 Years	5 Years	1 Year	P/E Ratio
S & P 400 Industrials	174.90	520.21	71.9%	197.4%	5.4%	24.15
Aerospace	218.47	479.29	61.8%	119.4%	18.2%	11.29
Airlines	155.11	270.23	28.1%	74.2%	−4.2%	def
Automobiles	89.62	208.68	27.2%	132.9%	41.1%	11.21
Beverages (Alcoholic)	86.71	350.43	68.1%	304.2%	−7.0%	28.33
Beverages	145.59	1375.33	269.1%	844.7%	4.5%	22.53
Broadcast Media	995.01	6739.44	107.0%	577.3%	35.7%	42.19
Building Materials	90.26	312.42	52.6%	246.1%	21.0%	19.95
Chemicals	69.85	199.94	42.9%	186.2%	0.6%	30.11
Communication Equip. Mfgrs.	39.75	70.17	120.6%	76.6%	3.4%	def
Computers	30.63	128.00	90.6%	318.2%	34.0%	32.79
Conglomerates	28.73	70.77	46.9%	146.3%	23.4%	13.93
Cosmetics	54.48	288.76	170.9%	430.0%	6.5%	23.40
Electric Utilities	38.89	82.29	59.6%	111.6%	−44.7%	15.89
Electrical Equipment	500.52	1242.61	79.6%	148.3%	13.5%	19.96
Electronics (Semiconductors)	48.34	164.26	200.2%	239.8%	67.7%	14.14
Entertainment	291.01	1924.81	163.2%	561.4%	19.0%	32.76
Foods	120.38	780.86	104.0%	548.7%	−2.0%	27.93
Homebuilding	54.56	96.94	146.8%	77.7%	27.5%	22.54
Hospital Management	67.97	64.11	27.0%	−5.7%	−3.1%	25.54
Hotel-Motel	103.70	265.37	35.1%	155.9%	64.6%	24.87
Household Furnishings	304.65	569.58	32.8%	87.0%	22.8%	31.59
Leisure	97.43	159.55	−17.0%	63.8%	7.4%	def
Natural Gas	204.37	419.60	29.2%	105.3%	24.9%	18.96
Oil: Domestic	323.10	613.72	18.6%	89.9%	6.0%	49.14
Oil: International	111.33	380.61	57.3%	241.9%	9.2%	15.63
Pollution Control	66.79	281.36	41.8%	321.3%	−14.9%	32.53
Publishing	794.30	2053.74	31.5%	158.6%	25.7%	26.65
Publishing Newspapers	62.11	124.19	21.7%	100.0%	7.5%	23.79
Restaurant	67.98	301.41	130.5%	343.4%	14.5%	17.77
Retail: Drug Chains	56.70	162.19	74.3%	186.0%	1.6%	22.88
Retail: Food Chains	93.01	542.90	121.4%	483.7%	9.0%	17.06
Telephone	106.68	291.81	50.1%	173.5%	8.7%	28.20
Textile, Apparel Mfgrs.	76.38	235.12	53.1%	207.8%	−10.5%	17.03
Tobacco	144.77	1108.32	164.0%	665.6%	−20.3%	14.50
Toys	21.05	67.70	287.4%	221.7%	8.9%	19.40

Normally, an investor can gain valuable insight about an industry by seeking answers to these questions:

1. *What is the nature of the industry?* Is it monopolistic, or are there many competitors? Do a few set the trend for the rest?

2. *To what extent is the industry regulated?* Is it regulated (e.g., public utilities)? If so, how "friendly" are the regulatory bodies?

3. *What role, if any, does labor play in the industry?* How important are labor unions? Are there good labor relations within the industry? When is the next round of contract talks?

4. *How important are technological developments?* Are any new developments taking place, and what is the likely impact of potential breakthroughs?

5. *Which economic forces are especially important to the industry?* Is demand for the industry's goods and services related to key economic variables? If so, what is the outlook for those variables? How important is foreign competition to the health of the industry?

6. *What are the important financial and operating considerations?* Is there an adequate supply of labor, material, and capital? What are the capital spending plans and needs of the industry?

growth cycle
a reflection of the amount of business vitality that occurs within an industry (or company) over time.

The preceding questions can sometimes be answered in terms of an industry's **growth cycle**, which reflects the vitality of the industry over time. In the first phase—*initial development*—investment opportunities are not usually available to most investors. The industry is new and untried, and the risks are very high. The second stage is *rapid expansion*, during which product acceptance is spreading and investors can foresee the industry's future more clearly. At this stage, economic variables have little to do with the industry's overall performance. Investors will be interested in investing almost regardless of the economic climate. This is the phase that is of considerable interest to investors, and a good deal of work is done to find such opportunities. Unfortunately, not all industries experience rapid growth for a long period of time. Most eventually slip into the category of *mature growth*, which is the third stage and the one most influenced by economic developments. In this stage, expansion comes from growth of the economy. It is a slower source of overall growth than the growth in phase 2. In stage 3, the long-term nature of the industry becomes apparent. Industries in this category include defensive ones, like food and apparel, and cyclical industries, like autos and heavy equipment. The last phase is either *stability* or *decline*. In the decline phase, demand for the industry's products is diminishing, and companies are leaving the industry. Investment opportunities at this stage are almost nonexistent, unless the investor is seeking only dividend income. Investors obviously wish to avoid this stage. However, few really good companies ever reach this final stage because they continually bring new products to the market and in so doing remain, at least, in the mature growth phase.

DEVELOPING AN INDUSTRY OUTLOOK

Industry analysis can be conducted by individual investors themselves or, as is more often the case, with the help of published industry reports such as the popular S&P *Industry Surveys*. These surveys cover all the important economic, market, and financial aspects of an industry, providing commentary as well as vital statistics. Other widely used sources of industry information include brokerage house reports and various write-ups in the popular financial media. An example of a widely used industry report (in this case, an S&P *Industry Survey*) is provided in Figure 6.2 (page 248).

Let's resume our example of the investor who's thinking about buying apparel stocks. Recall from our prior discussion that the economic phase of the analysis suggested a strong economy for the foreseeable future—one in which the level of personal disposable income would be expanding. Now the investor is ready to shift attention to the apparel industry. A logical starting point is to assess the expected industry response to forecasted economic developments. Demand for the product and industry sales would be especially important. The industry is made up of many large and small competitors; and, although it is unregulated, the industry is labor-intensive, and labor unions are an important force. Thus, our investor may want to look closely at these factors and especially at their potential effect on the industry's cost structure. Also important would be the outlook for imported fashion goods and foreign competition.

Industry analysis provides an understanding of the nature and operating characteristics of an industry, which can then be used to form judgments about

Figure 6.2 A Popular Source of Industry Information
Reports like the one shown here provide easy-to-digest industry overviews, including the dynamics of an industry and what makes it tick, the outlook for the industry, and a wide array of vital industry statistics. (Source: *S&P Industry Surveys*, August 1994.)

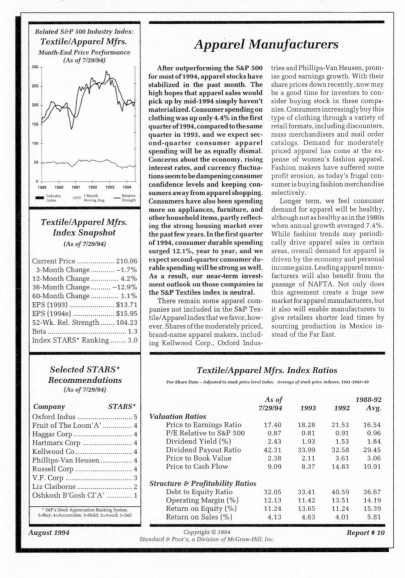

Apparel Manufacturers

After outperforming the S&P 500 for most of 1994, apparel stocks have stabilized in the past month. The high hopes that apparel sales would pick up by mid-1994 simply haven't materialized. Consumer spending on clothing was up only 4.4% in the first quarter of 1994, compared to the same quarter in 1993, and we expect second-quarter consumer apparel spending will be as equally dismal. Concerns about the economy, rising interest rates, and currency fluctuations seem to be dampening consumer confidence levels and keeping consumers away from apparel shopping. Consumers have also been spending more on appliances, furniture, and other household items, partly reflecting the strong housing market over the past few years. In the first quarter of 1994, consumer durable spending surged 12.1%, year to year, and we expect second-quarter consumer durable spending will be strong as well. As a result, our near-term investment outlook on those companies in the S&P Textiles index is neutral.

There remain some apparel companies not included in the S&P Textile/Apparel index that we favor, however. Shares of the moderately priced, brand-name apparel makers, including Kellwood Corp., Oxford Indus-

tries and Phillips-Van Heusen, promise good earnings growth. With their share prices down recently, now may be a good time for investors to consider buying stock in these companies. Consumers increasingly buy this type of clothing through a variety of retail formats, including discounters, mass merchandisers and mail order catalogs. Demand for moderately priced apparel has come at the expense of women's fashion apparel. Fashion makers have suffered some profit erosion, as today's frugal consumer is buying fashion merchandise selectively.

Longer term, we feel consumer demand for apparel will be healthy, although not as healthy as in the 1980s when annual growth averaged 7.4%. While fashion trends may periodically drive apparel sales in certain areas, overall demand for apparel is driven by the economy and personal income gains. Leading apparel manufacturers will also benefit from the passage of NAFTA. Not only does this agreement create a huge new market for apparel manufacturers, but it also will enable manufacturers to give retailers shorter lead times by sourcing production in Mexico instead of the Far East.

Related S&P 500 Industry Index:
Textile/Apparel Mfrs.
Month-End Price Performance
(As of 7/29/94)

Legend: Industry Index | 7-Month Moving Avg. | Relative Strength

Textile/Apparel Mfrs.
Index Snapshot
(As of 7/29/94)

Current Price	210.06
3-Month Change	−1.7%
12-Month Change	4.2%
36-Month Change	−12.9%
60-Month Change	1.1%
EPS (1993)	$13.71
EPS (1994e)	$15.95
52-Wk. Rel. Strength	104.23
Beta	1.3
Index STARS* Ranking	3.0

Selected STARS*
Recommendations
(As of 7/29/94)

Company	STARS*
Oxford Indus	5
Fruit of The Loom 'A'	4
Haggar Corp	4
Hartmarx Corp	4
Kellwood Co	4
Phillips-Van Heusen	4
Russell Corp	4
V.F. Corp	3
Liz Claiborne	2
Oshkosh B'Gosh Cl'A'	1

* S&P's Stock Appreciation Ranking System.
5=Buy; 4=Accumulate; 3=Hold; 2=Avoid; 1=Sell

Textile/Apparel Mfrs. Index Ratios
Per-Share Data – Adjusted to stock price level index. Average of stock price indexes, 1941-1943=10

	As of 7/29/94	1993	1992	1988-92 Avg.
Valuation Ratios				
Price to Earnings Ratio	17.40	18.28	21.53	16.54
P/E Relative to S&P 500	0.87	0.81	0.91	0.96
Dividend Yield (%)	2.43	1.93	1.53	1.84
Dividend Payout Ratio	42.31	33.99	32.58	29.45
Price to Book Value	2.38	2.11	3.61	3.06
Price to Cash Flow	9.09	8.37	14.83	10.91
Structure & Profitability Ratios				
Debt to Equity Ratio	32.05	33.41	40.59	36.67
Operating Margin (%)	12.13	11.42	13.51	14.19
Return on Equity (%)	11.24	13.65	11.24	15.39
Return on Sales (%)	4.13	4.63	4.01	5.81

August 1994

Report # 10

the prospects for industry growth. Let's assume that our investor, by using various types of published reports, has examined the key elements of the apparel industry and has concluded that it is indeed well positioned to take advantage of the improving economy. Apparel demand should increase, and although profit margins may tighten a bit, the level of profits should move up smartly, providing a healthy growth outlook. Several companies within this industry stand out, but one looks particularly attractive: MarCor Industries, a moderately sized, but rapidly growing producer of medium- to high-priced apparel for men and women. Everything about the economy and the industry looks favorable, so our investor decides to study MarCor more closely.

CONCEPTS *in Review*

6.9   What is industry analysis, and why is it important?

6.10   Identify and briefly discuss several aspects of an industry that are important to its behavior and operating characteristics; note especially how economic issues fit into industry analysis.

6.11   What are the four stages of an industry's growth cycle? Which of these stages offers the biggest payoff to investors? Which stage is most influenced by forces in the economy?

FUNDAMENTAL ANALYSIS

fundamental analysis
the in-depth study of the financial condition and operating results of a firm.

Fundamental analysis is the study of the financial affairs of a business for the purpose of better understanding the nature and operating characteristics of the company that issued the common stock. In this part of the chapter, we will deal with several aspects of fundamental analysis: We will examine the general concept of fundamental analysis, introduce the several types of financial statements that provide the raw material for this phase of the analytical process, describe the key financial ratios widely used in company analysis, and conclude with an interpretation of those financial ratios.

THE CONCEPT

Fundamental analysis rests on the belief that *the value of a stock is influenced by the performance of the company that issued the stock.* If a company's prospects look strong, the market price of its stock is likely to reflect that and be bid up. However, the value of a security depends not only on the return it promises but also on the amount of its risk exposure. Fundamental analysis captures these dimensions and conveniently incorporates them into the valuation process. It begins with a historical analysis of the financial strength of a firm—the so-called *company analysis* phase. Using the insights obtained, along with economic and industry figures, the investor can then formulate expectations about the future growth and profitability of a company.

In the historical (or company analysis) phase, the investor would study the financial statements of the firm. The purpose of such study would be to learn the strengths and weaknesses of the company, identify any underlying trends and developments, evaluate operating efficiencies, and gain a general understanding of the nature and operating characteristics of the firm. The following points are of particular interest:

1.   The competitive position of the company
2.   Its composition and growth in sales
3.   Profit margins and the dynamics of company earnings
4.   The composition and liquidity of corporate resources (the company's asset mix)
5.   The company's capital structure (its financing mix)

The historical phase is, in many respects, the most demanding and the most time-consuming. Most investors, however, have neither the time nor the inclination to conduct such an extensive study, and thus many rely on published reports for the needed background material. Individual investors have a variety of sources to choose from, including the reports and recommendations of major brokerage houses, the popular financial media, and/or financial subscription services like S&P and *Value Line*–not to mention a whole array of computer-based software and on-line financial services. These are all valuable sources of information, and the paragraphs that follow are not intended to replace them. Yet to be an intelligent investor, it is important to fully understand the content and implications of such financial reports and, in the final analysis, be able to use the information to develop your own judgment about the company and its stock.

FINANCIAL STATEMENTS

Financial statements are a vital part of company analysis, since they enable investors to develop an opinion about the operating results and financial condition of a firm. Three types of financial statements are used in company analysis: the balance sheet, the income statement, and the statement of cash flows. The first two statements are essential to carrying out basic financial analysis (in particular, to compute many of the financial ratios). The third statement—the cash flow statement—is critical because it's used to assess the cash/liquidity position of the firm. Company statements are prepared on a quarterly basis (these are *abbreviated* statements, compiled for each 3-month period of operation) and again at the end of each calendar year or *fiscal year* (a 12-month period the company has defined as its operating year, which may or may not end on December 31). Annual financial statements must be fully verified by independent certified public accountants (CPAs), filed with the U.S. Securities and Exchange Commission, and distributed on a timely basis to all stockholders in the form of annual reports. By themselves, corporate financial statements are a most important source of information to the investor; when used with financial ratios and in conjunction with fundamental analysis, they become even more powerful.

The Balance Sheet

balance sheet
a financial summary of a firm's assets, liabilities, and shareholders' equity at a single point in time.

The **balance sheet** is a statement of the company's assets, liabilities, and shareholders' equity. The *assets* represent the resources of the company (the things the company owns), the *liabilities* are its debts, and *equity* is the amount of stockholders' capital in the firm. A balance sheet may be thought of as a summary of the firm's assets balanced against its debt and ownership positions *at a single point in time* (on the last day of the calendar or fiscal year, or at the end of the quarter). In order to balance, the total assets must equal the total amount of liabilities and equity. A typical balance sheet is illustrated in Table 6.3. It shows the comparative 1994–1995 figures for MarCor Industries, the apparel firm our investor is interested in analyzing. Note that although the MarCor name is fictitious, the financial statements are not—*they are the actual financial statements of a real company*. While some of the entries have been slightly modified for pedagogical purposes, they are an accurate depiction of what real financial statements look like and how they're used in financial statement analysis.

Table 6.3 Corporate Balance Sheet, MarCor Industries
($ Thousands, Fiscal Year Ended December 31)

	1995	1994	
Current assets	$ 7,846	$ 16,279	Cash and short-term investments
	105,400	102,889	Accounts receivable
	164,356	159,238	Inventories
	1,778	16,279	Prepaid expenses
	$279,380	$278,697	Total current assets
Long-term assets	$ 1,366	$ 1,317	Land
	13,873	13,889	Buildings
	75,717	73,199	Furniture, fixtures, and equipment
	49,412	50,209	Leasehold improvements
	$140,368	$138,614	Gross long-term assets
	(85,203)	(80,865)	Accumulated depreciation
	$ 55,165	$ 57,749	Net long-term assets
	$ 4,075	$ 4,108	Other assets
Total assets	$338,620	$340,554	
Current liabilities	$ 2,000	$ 11,500	Notes payable
	4,831	1,090	Current maturities
	68,849	69,696	Accounts payable and accrued expenses
	3,806	3,119	Taxes on earnings
	5,460	4,550	Other accrued taxes
	$ 84,946	$ 89,955	Total current liabilities
Long-term debt	$ 83,723	$ 91,807	Long-term debt, less current maturities
Stockholders' equity	$ 21,787	$ 21,777	Common shares, $2.50 par value
	10,068	10,028	Capital surplus
	138,096	126,987	Retained earnings
	$169,951	$158,792	Stockholders' equity
Total liabilities and stockholders' equity	$338,620	$340,554	

The Income Statement

income statement
a financial summary of the operating results of a firm covering a specified period of time, usually one year.

The **income statement** provides a financial summary of the operating results of the firm. It is a summary of the amount of revenues (sales and income) generated over the period, the cost and expenses incurred over the same period, and the company's profits (obtained by subtracting all costs and expenses, including taxes, from revenues). Unlike the balance sheet, the income statement covers activities that have occurred over the course of time, or for a given operating period. Typically, this period extends no longer than a fiscal or calendar year. Table 6.4 (on page 252) shows MarCor Industries' income statements for 1994 and 1995. Note that these annual statements cover operations for a 12-month period ending on December 31, which corresponds to the date of the balance sheet. The income statement indicates how successful the firm has been in using the assets listed on the balance sheet. That is, management's success in operating the firm is reflected in the profit or loss the company generates during the year.

Table 6.4 Corporate Income Statement, MarCor Industries
($ Thousands, Fiscal Year Ended December 31)

1995	1994	
$606,610	$567,986	Net sales
6,792	6,220	Other income
1,504	895	Interest income
$614,906	$575,101	Total revenues
$377,322	$354,424	Cost of goods sold
205,864	194,419	Selling, administrative, and other operating expenses
5,765	5,523	Interest expense
$588,951	$554,366	Total costs and expenses
$ 25,955	$ 20,735	Earnings before taxes
$ 7,950	$ 5,230	Taxes on earnings
$ 18,005	$ 15,505	Net earnings (net profit after taxes)
$ 4.74	$ 4.08	Earnings per share
3,800	3,800	Number of common shares outstanding (in thousands)

The Statement of Cash Flows

statement of cash flows
a financial summary of a firm's cash flow and other events that caused changes in the company's cash position.

The **statement of cash flows** provides a summary of the firm's cash flow and other events that caused changes in the cash position. A relatively new report, first required in 1988, it is also one of the most useful, because it shows how the company is doing in generating cash. The fact is, a company's reported earnings may have little resemblance to the firm's cash flow. Whereas profits are simply the difference between revenues and the accounting costs that have been charged against them, *cash flow is the amount of money a company takes in as a result of doing business.*

Table 6.5 presents the 1994–1995 statement of cash flows for MarCor Industries. Notice that this report brings together items from *both* the balance sheet and the income statement to show how the company obtained its cash and how it used this valuable liquid resource. The statement is broken into three parts, the most important of which is the first one, labeled "Cash from Operations." It's important because it captures the *net cash flow from operations*—the line highlighted on the statement. This is what is generally ment by the term *cash flow,* since it represents the amount of cash generated by the company and available for investment and financing activities.

Note that MarCor's 1995 cash flow from operations was nearly $19 million—way up from the year before. However, because the company spent more on its investments and financing activities than it took in, its actual cash position declined by some $8.4 million. That change is shown near the bottom of the statement, in the line labeled "Net Increase (Decrease) in Cash." Ideally, you'd like to see a high (and preferably increasing) cash flow, since that would mean the company has plenty of money to pay dividends, service debt, and finance growth. In addition, you'd like to see the firm's cash position increase over time because of the positive impact that has on the company's liquidity and its ability to meet operating needs in a prompt and timely fashion.

INVESTOR FACTS

NO THANKS, WE'LL PASS—Most companies today use long-term debt as a major source of financing. That's not true in all cases, however. Some big, well-known companies get along quite well without it, or use very little of it. Among them are Nike, whose capital structure is made up of less than 1 percent long-term debt, and Rubbermaid, with less than 2 percent long-term debt. Some firms that have *no long-term debt* are H&R Block, Gap, Luby's Cafeterias, and St. Jude Medical.

Table 6.5 Statement of Cash Flows, MarCor Industries
($ Thousands, Fiscal Year Ended December 31)

1992	1991	
		Cash from Operations
$18,005	$15,505	Net earnings
8,792	8,202	Depreciation and amortization
560	54	Other noncash charges
(7,296)	(21,696)	Increase in current assets
(1,268)	3,041	Increase (decrease) in current liabilities
$18,793	$ 5,106	Net cash flow from operations
		Cash from Investment Activities
($ 6,685)	($ 4,686)	Acquisitions of property, plant, and equipment—net
($ 6,685)	($ 4,686)	Net cash flow from investing
		Cash from Financing Activities
—	$ 7,950	Proceeds from long-term borrowing
($11,825)	(1,240)	Reduction in long-term debt, including current maturities and early retirements
(8,626)	(7,287)	Payment of dividends to common stock
($20,451)	($ 557)	Net cash flow from financing
($ 8,433)	($ 157)	**Net Increase (Decrease) in Cash**
$16,279	$16,436	Cash and short-term investments at beginning of period
$ 7,846	$16,279	Cash and short-term investments at end of period

KEY FINANCIAL RATIOS

To see what accounting statements really have to say about the financial condition and operating results of the firm, it is necessary to turn to *financial ratios*. Such ratios are useful because they provide a different perspective on the financial affairs of the firm—particularly with regard to the balance sheet and income statement—and thus expand the information content of the company's financial statements. Ratios lie at the very heart of company analysis. Indeed, company analysis as a system of information would be incomplete without this key ingredient.

ratio analysis
the study of the relationships among and between various financial statement accounts.

Ratio analysis is the study of the relationships among and between various financial statement accounts. The mechanics of ratio analysis are actually quite simple: Selected information is obtained from annual financial statements and used to compute a set of ratios. Each measure relates one item on the balance sheet or the income statement to another, or, as is more often the case, it relates a balance sheet account to an operating (income statement) element. In this way, the investor looks not so much at the absolute size of the financial statement accounts but, more importantly, at the liquidity, activity, and profitability of the firm. However, as the Investor Insights box on page 254 suggests, to get the most from ratio analysis, you must have a good understanding of the uses and limitations of the financial statements themselves.

The most significant contribution of financial ratios is that they enable an investor to assess the firm's past and present financial condition and operating

INVESTOR **I**NSIGHTS: *Investing in Action*

The Ten Commandments of Financial Statement Analysis

Individuals must pass a test before obtaining a driver's license, but investors don't need to pass any type of test before trying to use financial statements as part of their investment analyses. Yet analyzing financial statements requires at least as much knowledge and skill as driving an automobile. Perhaps each financial statement should contain a warning to potential users, similar to those found on many products. As a starter, the warning might include these ten commandments:

1. Thou shalt not use financial statements in isolation. Instead, use them with other available information, such as data on economy-wide conditions and industrywide conditions.

2. Thou shalt not use financial statements as the only source of firm-specific information. There are many other sources of information about the company. Consider, for example, financial periodicals and analysts' reports.

3. Thou shalt not avoid reading footnotes, which are an integral part of financial statements. Financial statements cannot be reasonably analyzed without reading and understanding the footnotes.

4. Thou shalt not focus on a single number. Financial statements are not designed to be reduced to a single number. Net income is not intended to be the number that summarizes all the information relevant to making an investment decision. A user must analyze growth and leverage, among other factors, as well as profitability.

5. Thou shalt not overlook the implications of what is read. It is not sufficient simply to know that a company is a high-growth or highly leveraged firm; one must also know

that such characteristics typically imply higher risk as well.

6. Thou shalt not ignore events subsequent to the financial statements. Financial statements are not forecasts of the future; rather, they report the financial condition of the company as of year-end. They do not capture the effects of events that occur after year-end. They thus become increasingly out of date as the year progresses.

7. Thou shalt not overlook the limitations of financial statements. Financial statements report on only a specified set of events, not all events or all possible financial effects of a single event. Financial statements do not generally represent estimates of the market values of the reported assets and liabilities; nor do they reflect changes in the market values of those assets and liabilities.

8. Thou shalt not use financial statements without adequate knowledge. Investors should be sufficiently competent to read, understand, and analyze financial statements.

9. Thou shalt not shun professional help. If unwilling or unable to attain adequate knowledge, the investor should defer to someone who does have such ability, such as a financial analyst or a professional money manager.

10. Thou shalt not take unnecessary risks. If unwilling or unable to obtain professional help, the investor should undertake investments where investment risk is minimal or where analysis of financial statements is not an issue.

Source: Based on William H. Beaver, "Ten Commandments of Financial Statement Analysis," *Financial Analysts Journal*, January/February 1991, pp. 9, 18.

results. The mechanics of ratio analysis are actually quite simple: Selected information is obtained from annual financial statements and used to compute a set of ratios, which are then compared to historical and/or industry standards to evaluate the financial condition and operating results of the company. When historical standards are used, the company's ratios are compared and studied from one year to the next. Industry standards, in contrast, involve a comparison of a particular company's ratios to the performance of other companies in the same line of business. And, remember, the reason we're doing all this is to *develop information about the past that can be used to get a handle on the future*. It's only from a thorough understanding of a company's past performance that an investor can forecast its future with some degree of accuracy. For example, even if sales have been expanding rapidly over the past few years, an investor must carefully assess the reasons for the growth before naively assuming that past growth-rate trends will continue into the future. Such insights are obtained from financial ratios and financial statement analysis.

Financial ratios can be divided into five groups: (1) liquidity, (2) activity, (3) leverage, (4) profitability, and (5) common stock, or market, measures. Using the 1995 figures from the MarCor financial statements (Tables 6.3 and 6.4), we will now identify and briefly discuss some of the widely used measures in each of these five categories.

Measures of Liquidity

liquidity measures
financial ratios concerned with a firm's ability to meet its day-to-day operating expenses and satisfy its short-term obligations as they come due.

Liquidity is concerned with the firm's ability to meet its day-to-day operating expenses and satisfy its short-term obligations as they come due. Of major concern is whether a company has adequate cash and other liquid assets on hand to service its debt and operating needs in a prompt and timely fashion. A general overview of a company's liquidity position can often be obtained from two simple measures: current ratio and net working capital.

Current Ratio   One of the most commonly cited of all financial ratios, the *current ratio* is computed as follows:

Equation 6.1
$$\text{Current ratio} = \frac{\text{current assets}}{\text{current liabilities}}$$

In 1995, MarCor Industries had a current ratio of:

$$\text{Current ratio for MarCor} = \frac{\$279,380}{\$84,946} = \underline{\underline{3.29}}$$

This figure indicates that MarCor had $3.29 in short-term resources to service every dollar of current debt. This is a fairly high number and, by most standards, would be considered very strong.

Net Working Capital   Though technically not a ratio in the formal sense of the word, net working capital is nonetheless often viewed as such. Actually, *net working capital* is an *absolute measure* of liquidity that indicates the dollar amount of equity in the working capital position of the firm. It is the difference between current assets and current liabilities. For 1995, the net working capital figure for MarCor Industries equaled:

Equation 6.2
$$\text{Net working capital} = \text{current assets} - \text{current liabilities}$$

$$\text{For MarCor} = \$279,380 - \$84,946 = \underline{\underline{\$194,434}}$$

A net working capital figure that approaches the $200 million mark is substantial (for a company this size) and suggests that the liquidity position of this firm is good—so long as it is not made up of slow-moving and obsolete inventories and/or past due accounts receivable.

Activity Ratios

activity ratios
financial ratios that are used to measure how well a firm is managing its assets.

Measuring general liquidity is only the beginning of the analysis; we must also assess the composition and underlying liquidity of key current assets and evaluate how effectively the company is managing these assets. **Activity ratios** compare company sales to various asset categories in order to measure how well the company is utilizing its assets. Three of the most widely used activity ratios deal with accounts receivable, inventory, and total assets.

Accounts Receivable Turnover   A glance at most financial statements will reveal that the asset side of the balance sheet is dominated by just a few accounts that make up 80 to 90 percent, or even more, of total resources. Certainly, this is the case with MarCor, where, as can be seen in Table 6.3, three entries (accounts receivable, inventory, and net long-term assets) accounted for about 95 percent of total assets in 1995. Most firms invest a significant amount of capital in accounts receivable, and for this reason they are viewed as a crucial corporate resource. *Accounts receivable turnover* is a measure of how these resources are being managed. It is computed as follows:

Equation 6.3
$$\text{Accounts receivable turnover} = \frac{\text{annual sales}}{\text{accounts receivable}}$$

$$\text{For MarCor} = \frac{\$606,610}{\$105,400} = \underline{\underline{5.76}}$$

In essence, this turnover figure indicates the kind of return the company is getting from its investment in accounts receivable. Other things being equal, the higher the turnover figure, the more favorable it is. In 1995, MarCor turned its receivables over about 5.8 times; put another way, each dollar invested in receivables supported $5.76 in sales.

Inventory Turnover   Another important corporate resource—and one that requires a considerable amount of management attention—is inventory. Control of inventory is important to the well-being of a company and is commonly assessed with the *inventory turnover* measure:

Equation 6.4
$$\text{Inventory turnover} = \frac{\text{annual sales}}{\text{inventory}}$$

$$\text{For MarCor} = \frac{\$606,610}{\$164,356} = \underline{\underline{3.69}}$$

Again, the more mileage (sales) the company can get out of its inventory, the better the return on this vital resource. A figure of 3.69 for MarCor reveals its goods were bought and sold out of inventory about 3.7 times a year. Generally, the higher the turnover figure, the less time an item spends in inventory and, thus, the better the return the company is able to earn from funds tied up in inventory.

Total Asset Turnover   *Total asset turnover* indicates how efficiently assets are being used to support sales. It is calculated as follows:

Equation 6.5
$$\text{Total asset turnover} = \frac{\text{annual sales}}{\text{total assets}}$$

$$\text{For MarCor} = \frac{\$606,610}{\$338,620} = \underline{\underline{1.79}}$$

Note in this case that MarCor is generating about $1.80 in revenues from every dollar invested in assets. This is a fairly high number and is important because it has a direct bearing on corporate profitability. The principle at work here is much like the return to an individual investor: Earning $100 from a $1,000 investment is far more desirable than earning the same $100 from a $2,000 investment. A high total asset turnover figure suggests that corporate resources are being well managed and that the firm is able to realize a high level of sales (and, ultimately, profits) from its asset investments.

Leverage Measures

leverage measures
financial ratios that measure the amount of debt being used to support operations and the ability of the firm to service its debt.

Leverage deals with the firm's different types of financing and indicates the amount of debt being used to support the resources and operations of the company. The amount of indebtedness within the financial structure and the ability of the firm to service its debt are major concerns in leverage analysis. There are two widely used leverage ratios: The first, the debt-equity ratio, measures the *amount of debt* being used by the company, and the second, times interest earned, assesses how well the company can *service its debt*.

Debt-Equity Ratio   A measure of leverage, or the relative amount of funds provided by lenders and owners, the *debt-equity ratio* is computed as follows:

Equation 6.6
$$\text{Debt-equity ratio} = \frac{\text{long-term debt}}{\text{stockholders' equity}}$$

$$\text{For MarCor} = \frac{\$83,723}{\$169,951} = \underline{\underline{.49}}$$

Since highly leveraged firms (those using large amounts of debt) run an increased risk of defaulting on their loans, this ratio is particularly helpful in assessing a stock's risk exposure. The 1995 debt-equity ratio for MarCor is reasonably low (at 49 percent) and shows that most of the company's capital comes from its owners. Stated another way, this figure means there was only 49 cents of debt in the capital structure for every dollar of equity.

Times Interest Earned   *Times interest earned* is a so-called coverage ratio and measures the ability of the firm to meet its fixed interest payments. It is calculated as follows:

Equation 6.7
$$\text{Times interest earned} = \frac{\text{earnings before interest and taxes}}{\text{interest expense}}$$

$$\text{For MarCor} = \frac{\$25,955 + \$5,765}{\$5,765} = \underline{\underline{5.50}}$$

The ability of the company to meet its interest payments (which, with bonds, are fixed contractual obligations) in a timely and orderly fashion is an important consideration in evaluating risk exposure. MarCor's times interest earned ratio indicates that the firm has about $5.50 available to cover every dollar of interest expense. As a rule, a coverage ratio of 6 to 7 times earnings is considered pretty strong. There's usually little concern until the measure drops to something less than 2 or 3 times earnings.

Measures of Profitability

profitability measures
financial ratios that measure returns by relating the relative success of a firm through comparison of profits to sales, assets, or equity.

Profitability is a relative measure of success. Each of the various profitability measures relates the returns (profits) of a company to its sales, assets, or equity. There are three widely used profitability measures: net profit margin, return on assets, and return on equity.

Net Profit Margin   This is the "bottom line" of operations. *Net profit margin* indicates the rate of profit from sales and other revenues. It is computed as follows:

Equation 6.8

$$\text{Net profit margin} = \frac{\text{net profit after taxes}}{\text{total revenues}}$$

$$\text{For MarCor} = \frac{\$18,005}{\$614,906} = \underline{\underline{2.9\%}}$$

The net profit margin looks at profits as a percentage of sales (and other revenues). Because it moves with costs, it also reveals the type of control management has over the cost structure of the firm. Note that MarCor has a net profit margin of 2.9 percent in 1995—that is, the company's return on sales was roughly 3 cents on the dollar. Although this is a bit below average for U.S. corporations in general, a net profit margin of nearly 3 percent is good (i.e., above average) for a fashion apparel firm.

Return on Assets   As a profitability measure, *return on assets (ROA)* looks at the amount of resources needed to support operations. Return on assets reveals management's effectiveness in generating profits from the assets it has available—and *is perhaps the single most important measure of return*. It is computed as follows:

Equation 6.9

$$\text{ROA} = \frac{\text{net profit after taxes}}{\text{total assets}}$$

$$\text{For MarCor} = \frac{\$18,005}{\$338,620} = \underline{\underline{5.3\%}}$$

In the case of MarCor Industries, the company earned 5.3 percent on its asset investments in 1995. A return of 5.3 percent is certainly not spectacular, but for an apparel stock, it's not too bad—indeed, as we'll see below, it's actually above average. As a rule, you'd like to see a company maintain as high an ROA as possible, since the higher the ROA, the more profitable the company.

Return on Equity   A measure of the overall profitability of the firm, *return on equity (ROE)* is closely followed by investors because of its direct link to the profits, growth, and dividends of the company. Return on equity—or return on investment (ROI), as it's sometimes called—measures the return to the firm's stockholders, by relating profits to shareholder equity:

Equation 6.10

$$\text{ROE} = \frac{\text{net profit after taxes}}{\text{stockholders' equity}}$$

$$\text{For MarCor} = \frac{\$18,005}{\$169,951} = \underline{\underline{10.6\%}}$$

ROE shows the annual payoff to investors, which in the case of MarCor amounts to nearly 11 cents for every dollar of equity. Generally speaking, look for a high or increasing ROE; in contrast, watch out for a falling ROE, as that could spell trouble later on.

Breaking Down ROA and ROE

Both ROA and ROE are important measures of corporate profitability. But to get the most from these two measures, we have to break them down into their component parts. ROA, for example, is made up of two key components: the firm's net profit margin and its total asset turnover. Thus, rather than use Equation 6.9 to find ROA, we can use the following expanded format:

Equation 6.11 $\text{ROA} = \text{net profit margin} \times \text{total asset turnover}$

Using the net profit margin and total asset turnover figures we computed above (Equations 6.8 and 6.5, respectively), we can find MarCor's 1995 ROA as follows:

$$\text{ROA} = 2.9\% \times 1.79 = \underline{\underline{5.2\%}}$$

Small rounding errors account for the difference between the number computed here and the one computed earlier (5.2% here vs. 5.3% in Equation 6.9).

Why use the expanded version of ROA? *The major reason is that it shows you what's driving company profits.* That is, as an investor, you want to know if ROA is moving up (or down) because of improvements (or deteriorations) in the company's profit margin and/or its total asset turnover. Ideally, you'd like to see ROA moving up (or staying high) because the company does a good job of managing *both* its profits and its assets.

Just as ROA can be broken into its component parts, so too can the return on equity (ROE) measure. Actually, ROE is nothing more than an extension of ROA, as it introduces the company's financing decisions to nothing more than the profitability assessment. That is, the expanded ROE measure indicates the extent to which financial leverage (or "trading on the equity") can increase return to stockholders. The use of debt in the capital structure, in effect, means that *ROE will always be greater than ROA.* The question is, How much greater? Rather than use the abbreviated version of ROE (in Equation 6.10), we can compute ROE as follows:

Equation 6.12 $\text{ROE} = \text{ROA} \times \text{equity multiplier}$

where:

$$\text{Equity multiplier} = \frac{\text{total assets}}{\text{total stockholders' equity}}$$

To find ROE according to Equation 6.12, we first have to find the equity multiplier:

$$\text{Equity multiplier for MarCor} = \frac{\$338,620}{\$169,951} = 1.99$$

Now, we can find the 1995 ROE for MarCor, as follows:

$$\text{ROE} = 5.3\% \times 1.99 = \underline{\underline{10.6\%}}$$

Here we can see that the use of debt (the equity multiplier) has magnified—in this case, doubled—returns to stockholders.

Alternatively, we can expand Equation 6.12 still further by breaking ROA in the equation *into its component parts*. In that case, we could compute ROE as:

Equation 6.13

$$\text{ROE} = \text{ROA} \times \text{equity multiplier}$$
$$= (\text{net profit margin} \times \text{total asset turnover}) \times \text{equity multiplier}$$

$$\text{For MarCor} = 2.9\% \times 1.79 \times 1.99 = \underline{\underline{10.6\%}}$$

This expanded version of ROE is especially helpful, since it enables investors to assess the company's profitability in terms of three key components: net profit margin, total asset turnover, and financial leverage. In this way, an investor can determine if ROE is moving up simply because the firm is employing more debt (which isn't necessarily beneficial) or because of the way it's managing its assets and operations—which certainly does have positive long-term implications. To stockholders, ROE is a critical measure of performance (and thus demands careful attention) because of the impact it has on growth and earnings—both of which, as we'll see in Chapter 7, play vital roles in the stock valuation process.

Common Stock Ratios

common stock (market) ratios
financial ratios that convert key information about a firm to a per share basis.

There are a number of **common stock,** or so-called **market, ratios** that convert key bits of information about the company to a per share basis. They are used to assess the performance of a company for stock valuation purposes. These ratios tell the investor exactly what portion of total profits, dividends, and equity is allocated to each share of stock. Popular common stock ratios include earnings per share, price/earnings ratio, dividends per share, dividend yield, payout ratio, and book value per share. We have already examined two of these measures in Chapter 5 (earnings per share and dividend yield); let's look now at the other four.

Price/Earnings Ratio   This measure is an extension of the earnings-per-share ratio and is used to determine how the market is pricing the company's common stock. The *price/earnings (P/E) ratio* relates the company's earnings per share (EPS) to the market price of its stock:

Equation 6.14

$$\text{P/E} = \frac{\text{market price of common stock}}{\text{EPS}}$$

To compute the P/E ratio, it is necessary to first calculate the stock's EPS. Using the earnings-per-share equation from the previous chapter, we see that the EPS for MarCor Industries in 1995 was:

$$\text{EPS} = \frac{\text{net profit after taxes} - \text{preferred dividends}}{\text{number of common shares outstanding}}$$

$$\text{For MarCor} = \frac{\$18,005 - \$0}{3,800} = \underline{\underline{\$4.74}}$$

In this case, the company's profits of $18 million translate into earnings of $4.74 for *each share* of outstanding common stock. Given this EPS figure and the stock's current market price (assume it is currently trading at 48½), we can use Equation 6.14 to determine the P/E ratio for MarCor Industries:

$$\text{P/E} = \frac{\$48.50}{\$4.74} = \underline{\underline{10.2}}$$

In effect, the stock is currently selling at a multiple of about 10 times its 1995 earnings. Price/earnings multiples are widely quoted in the financial press and are an essential part of many stock valuation models.

Dividends per Share   The principle here is the same as for EPS: to translate total common stock dividends paid by the company into a per share figure. (*Note*: If it is not on the income statement, the amount of dividends paid to common stock can be found on the statement of cash flows—Table 6.5.) *Dividends per share* is measured as follows:

Equation 6.15 $$\text{Dividends per share} = \frac{\text{annual dividends paid to common stock}}{\text{number of common shares outstanding}}$$

$$\text{For MarCor} = \frac{\$8,626}{3,800} = \underline{\underline{\$2.27}}$$

For fiscal 1995 MarCor Industries paid out dividends of $2.27 per share—at a quarterly rate of about 57 cents per share. As we saw in the preceding chapter, we can relate dividends per share to the market price of the stock to determine its present *dividend yield*: $2.27 ÷ $48.50 = 4.7%.

Payout Ratio   Another important dividend measure is the dividend *payout ratio*. It indicates the amount of earnings paid out to stockholders in the form of dividends. Well-managed companies try to maintain *target payout ratios*. Thus, if earnings are going up over time, so will dividends. The payout ratio is calculated as follows:

Equation 6.16 $$\text{Payout ratio} = \frac{\text{dividends per share}}{\text{earnings per share}}$$

$$\text{For MarCor} = \frac{\$2.27}{\$4.74} = \underline{\underline{.48}}$$

For MarCor Industries in 1995, dividends accounted for about 48 percent of earnings. This is fairly typical, for most companies that pay dividends tend to pay out somewhere between 40 and 60 percent of earnings. Paying out much more than that is often a sign of trouble. Indeed, once the payout ratio reaches 70 to 80 percent of earnings, extra care should be taken. A payout ratio that high is often an indication that the company will not be able to maintain its current level of dividends—and if there's one thing the market doesn't like, it's cuts in dividends.

Book Value per Share   The last common stock ratio is *book value per share*, a measure that deals with stockholders' equity. Actually, book value is simply another term for equity (or net worth); it represents the difference between total assets and total liabilities. Book value per share is computed as follows:

Equation 6.17

$$\text{Book value per share} = \frac{\text{stockholders' equity}}{\text{number of common shares outstanding}}$$

$$\text{For MarCor} = \frac{\$169,951}{3,800} = \underline{\underline{\$44.72}}$$

Presumably, a stock should sell for *more* than its book value (as MarCor does). If not, it could be an indication that something is seriously wrong with the company's outlook and profitability.

A convenient way to relate the book value of a company to the market price of its stock is to compute the *price-to-book-value ratio*:

Equation 6.18

$$\text{Price-to-book-value} = \frac{\text{market price of common stock}}{\text{book value per share}}$$

$$\text{For MarCor} = \frac{\$48.50}{\$44.72} = \underline{\underline{1.08}}$$

Widely used by investors, this ratio shows how aggressively the stock is being priced. Most stocks have a price-to-book-value of more than 1.0—which simply indicates that the stock is selling for more than its book value. In fact, in strong bull markets, it's not uncommon to find stocks trading at two or three times their book values. On the other hand, a price-to-book ratio of only 1.08, like MarCor's, is often viewed as a positive sign (especially by so-called value investors) that the stock is reasonably priced relative to its underlying asset base.

INTERPRETING THE NUMBERS

Rather than compute all the financial ratios themselves, most investors rely on published reports for such information. Many large brokerage houses and a variety of financial services publish such reports, an example of which is given in Figure 6.3. These reports provide a good deal of vital information in a convenient and easy-to-read format, and they relieve investors of the chore of computing the financial ratios themselves. (Similar information is also available from some of the computer on-line services, as well as from various software providers—like the *AAII Stock Software disk* that's available with this book.) Even so, investors must be able to evaluate this published information. To do that, they need not only a basic understanding of financial ratios but also some standard of performance, or benchmark, against which they can assess trends in company performance.

Basically, two types of performance standards are used in financial statement analysis: historical and industry. With *historical standards*, various financial ratios and measures are run on the company for a period of three to five years (or longer) in order to assess developing trends in the company's operations and financial condition. That is, are they improving or deterio-

Figure 6.3 An Example of a Published Analytical Report with Financial Statistics
This and similar reports are widely available to investors and play an important part in the security analysis process. (Source: Standard & Poor's *NYSE Reports*, August 23, 1994.)

Liz Claiborne

NYSE Symbol LIZ Options on CBOE In S&P 500

Price	Range	P–E Ratio	Dividend	Yield	S&P Ranking	Beta
Aug. 16'94	1994					
21	26⅝–19¼	17	0.45	2.1%	A	1.24

Summary

This designer of women's and men's clothing and related items made by independent suppliers in the U.S. and overseas sells its "better apparel" through department and specialty stores in the U.S., Canada and abroad. In 1992, LIZ enhanced its product offerings by acquiring several well-known brands from Russ Togs. Earnings, which have declined since the fourth quarter of 1992 because of soft retail conditions, are expected to continue under pressure in 1994, but could rebound in 1995, although they are estimated to be substantially lower than 1992's profits.

Current Outlook

Share earnings for 1994 are projected at $1.50, down slightly from 1993's depressed $1.54 (which excluded a $0.02 accounting credit). Earnings could rebound to $1.75 a share in 1995.

The dividend should continue at $0.11¼ quarterly.

Sales for 1994 should be flat, reflecting lower volume for the company's core sportswear products due to the weak retail environment. However, LIZ does not expect to lose any market share and is planning to sell the majority of this type of clothing in the second half of the year at full prices. Sales of the Russ Togs, Crazy Horse and Villager brands should continue to rise. Unlike LIZ's other lines, these brands are distributed through value-oriented retailers. Overseas sales are also expected to increase, partly reflecting expansion in Japan and China. Retail sales should also rise on an increase in First Issue store openings. Sales of Dana Buchman and fragrances and accessories should continue to be strong, as well as men's wear and women's dresses and evening wear. Margins should rebound somewhat in the second half of the year, reflecting elimination of excess inventories. Share earnings will benefit from fewer outstanding shares, reflecting an ongoing stock-buyback program.

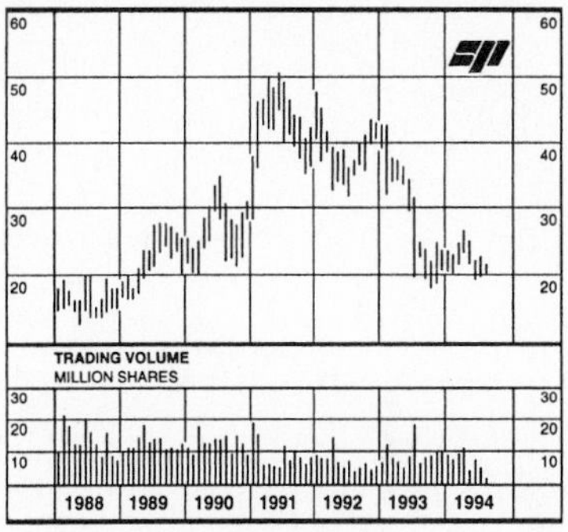

Net Sales (Million $)

13 Weeks:	1994	1993	1992	1991
Mar.	[4]541	531	557	502
Jun.	490	507	473	416
Sep.	---	622	618	558
Dec.	---	544	546	531
	---	2,204	2,194	2,007

Sales for the first half of 1994 were down fractionally, year to year, and net income fell 40%, to $0.55 a share (based on 4.2% fewer shares), from $0.88 (excluding a $0.02 accounting credit).

Common Share Earnings ($)

13 Weeks:	1994	1993	1992	1991
Mar.	[4]0.35	0.50	0.74	0.72
Jun.	0.20	0.38	0.47	0.46
Sep.	E0.50	0.47	0.77	0.77
Dec.	E0.45	0.19	0.63	0.66
	E1.50	1.54	2.61	2.61

Important Developments

Jul. '94— LIZ attributed the margin erosion in the first half 1994 to the continued liquidation at distressed prices of excess inventory manufactured in 1993. However, virtually all of this inventory was eliminated by the end of the second quarter. Separately, LIZ noted that as of July 22, 1994, it had bought back about 12.8 million of its shares for approximately $375 million.

Next earnings report expected in late October.

Per Share Data ($)

Yr. End Dec. 31	1993	1992	1991	1990	1989	[1]1988	1987	1986	1985	1984
Tangible Bk. Val.	[2]12.41	[2]12.05	10.67	8.39	6.94	5.22	4.10	2.86	1.90	1.23
Cash Flow	1.93	2.95	2.92	2.62	2.05	1.40	1.38	1.05	0.75	0.52
Earnings[3]	1.54	2.61	2.61	2.37	1.87	1.26	1.32	1.00	0.71	0.50
Dividends	0.438	0.388	0.325	0.238	0.194	0.175	0.162	0.116	0.081	0.047
Payout Ratio	28%	15%	12%	10%	10%	14%	12%	12%	12%	9%
Prices—High	42⅞	47⅞	50¾	35	27¾	20	39⅛	24¼	12⅜	6⅝
Low	18	31⅞	28¼	20¼	16½	12¾	12¼	11⅞	5⅞	3⅛
P/E Ratio—	28–12	18–12	19–11	15–9	15–9	16–10	30–9	24–12	17–8	13–6

Data as orig. reptd. Adj. for stk. divs. of 100% Jun. 1987, 100% Apr. 1986, 100% Dec. 1984. **1.** Refl. acctg. change. **2.** Incl. intangibles. **3.** Bef. spec. item of +0.02 in 1993. **4.** 14 wks. E-Estimated.

Standard NYSE Stock Reports
Vol. 61/No. 163/Sec. 16

August 23, 1994
Copyright © 1994 McGraw-Hill, Inc. All Rights Reserved

Standard & Poor's
25 Broadway, NY, NY 10004

rating, and where do the company's strengths and weaknesses lie? *Industry standards*, in contrast, enable the investor to compare the financial ratios of the company with comparable firms, or the average results for the industry as a whole. Here, attention centers on determining the relative strength of the firm with respect to its competitors. Using MarCor Industries, we'll see how both of these standards of performance can be used to evaluate and interpret financial ratios.

Take a look at Table 6.6 (on page 264). It provides a summary of historical data and average industry figures (for the latest year) for most of the ratios discussed above.

Table 6.6 Comparative Historical and Industry Ratios

	Historical Figures for MarCor Industries				Industry Averages for the Apparel Industry in 1995
	1992	1993	1994	1995	
Liquidity measures:					
Current ratio	3.05	2.86	3.10	3.29	2.87
Activity measures:					
Receivables turnover	5.22	4.87	5.52	5.76	8.00
Inventory turnover	3.10	2.98	3.57	3.69	3.75
Total asset turnover	1.75	1.65	1.67	1.79	1.42
Leverage measures:					
Debt-equity ratio	.52	.56	.58	.49	.89
Times interest earned	4.65	4.50	4.75	5.50	3.35
Profitability measures:					
Net profit margin	3.6%	3.0%	2.7%	2.9%	2.5%
Return on assets	6.3%	4.9%	4.6%	5.3%	3.9%
Return on equity	11.8%	8.6%	9.8%	10.6%	8.9%
Common stock measures:					
Earnings per share	$4.67	$ 4.15	$ 4.08	$ 4.74	$ 2.86
Price/earnings ratio	9.50	10.90	11.20	10.20	10.10
Dividend yield	4.90%	4.20%	4.20%	4.70%	3.9%
Payout ratio	47.0%	46.0%	47.0%	48.0%	45.5%
Price-to-book-value	1.07	1.15	1.09	1.08	1.05

Now, based on the comparative financial ratios contained in Table 6.6, here are some observations we can make about MarCor:

1. We see a modest improvement in MarCor's already strong *liquidity position*: The current ratio remains well above the industry standard.

2. The *activity measures* show that although receivables and inventory turnover are improving, they still remain below industry standards: Accounts receivable turnover appears to be especially out of line—almost 40 percent below normal. Unless there is an operating or economic explanation for this, a lot of excess (nonproductive) resources seem to be tied up in accounts receivable, costing the firm millions of dollars a year in profits. The inventory position, in contrast, has improved. Although still a bit below average, it certainly does not appear to be much of a problem. Finally, total asset turnover is up from last year and continues well above average.

3. The *leverage position* of MarCor Industries seems well controlled: The company tends to use a lot less debt in its financial structure than the average firm in the apparel industry. The payoff for this judicious use of debt comes in the form of a coverage ratio that is well above average.

4. The *profitability picture* for MarCor is equally attractive, as the profit margin, return on assets, and ROE are all improving and remain well above the industry norm.

In summary, our analysis suggests that this firm is, with the possible exception of accounts receivable, fairly well managed and highly profitable. The results of this are reflected in *common stock ratios* that are consistently equal or superior to industry averages.

In addition to looking at a company historically and relative to *average performance* for the industry, it's also advisable to evaluate the firm relative to two or three of its major competitors. A lot can be gained by seeing how a company stacks up against its competitors and by determining if it is, in fact, well positioned to take advantage of unfolding developments. Table 6.7 does just that by providing an array of comparative financial statistics for MarCor and three of its major competitors. (This type of firm-specific data can generally be obtained from industry surveys similar to those put out by S&P and others—or, again, from various software providers.)

As the data show, MarCor Industries is fully capable of holding its own against other leading producers in the industry. Indeed, in just about every category MarCor's numbers are about equal or superior to any one of its three major competitors. It may be smaller than a couple of the firms, but it outperforms them in terms of profit margins and growth rates. Equally important, MarCor is a lot less leveraged than the other manufacturers—which is a real plus in a highly volatile industry. Yet even with its low financial leverage, it is still able to maintain a highly attractive ROE. In all, Tables 6.6 and 6.7 suggest that MarCor Industries is a solid, up-and-coming business that's been able to make a real name for itself in a highly competitive industry; the company has certainly done well in the past and appears to be well managed today. Our major concern at this point (and the topic of the first part of Chapter 8) is whether MarCor will continue to produce above-average returns to investors.

Table 6.7   Comparative Financial Statistics: MarCor Industries and Its Major Competitors
(All figures are for year-end 1995 or for the 5-year period ending in 1995; $ in Millions)

Financial Measure	MarCor Industries	Regatta Group	Holbrook Industries	Bellwood, Inc.
Total assets	$338.6	$568.6	$231.9	$469.4
Long-term debt	$ 53.7	$124.8	$ 41.5	$128.1
Stockholders' equity	$170.0	$196.9	$103.7	$200.2
Stockholders' equity as a % of total assets	50.2%	34.6%	44.7%	42.6%
Total revenues	$614.9	$807.5	$505.9	$808.0
Net earnings	$ 18.0	$ 14.5	$ 10.6	$ 12.4
Net profit margin	2.9%	1.8%	2.1%	1.5%
5-year growth rates in:				
Total assets	8.9%	10.2%	8.6%	5.6%
Total revenues	8.8%	9.5%	9.0%	3.5%
Net earnings	32.0%	18.0%	7.5%	2.5%
Dividends	10.8%	N/A	8.0%	6.0%
Total asset turnover	1.79×	1.42×	2.18×	1.73×
Debt-equity ratio	0.49	0.74	0.60	0.84
Times interest earned	5.50×	2.65×	4.67×	2.26×
ROA	5.30%	4.10%	5.20%	4.50%
ROE	10.60%	6.70%	8.50%	9.20%
Price/earnings ratio	10.20×	10.20×	13.60×	12.90×
Payout ratio	48.00%	N/A	58.80%	67.00%
Dividend yield	4.70%	N/A	4.30%	6.25%
Price-to-book-value	1.08	1.07	0.95	1.17

CONCEPTS *in Review*

6.12 What is *fundamental analysis?* Does the performance of a company have any bearing on the value of its stock? Explain.

6.13 Why do investors bother to look at the historical performance of a company when future behavior is what really counts? Explain.

6.14 What is *ratio analysis?* Describe the role and contribution of ratio analysis to the study of a company's financial condition and operating results.

6.15 Contrast historical standards of performance with industry standards. Briefly note the role of each in analyzing the financial condition and operating results of a company.

On Track with STOCK-TRAK®

Selling Stocks Short with STOCK-TRAK®

STOCK-TRAK® allows investors to short sell shares of companies that have poor financial ratios and show little financial vitality. When investors sell shares they don't own, they are said to be *short selling* the stock. STOCK-TRAK® lends users the shares to be sold short. Short sellers do not have access to the proceeds—in fact, they must deposit 50 percent of the market value of the stock as margin (or collateral). When users buy the shares, they cover their short position; STOCK-TRAK® provides access to the investment proceeds and frees the margin. Consistent with stock market rules requiring that short sales be made on up-ticks, STOCK-TRAK® *prohibits short selling on days when the price of the stock in questions declines.*

SUMMARY

LG 1 Discuss the security analysis process, including its goals and the functions it performs. Success in buying common stocks is largely a function of careful security selection and investment timing. Security analysis helps the investor make the crucial selection decision by determining the intrinsic value (or underlying worth) of a stock; security analysis consists of economic, industry, and fundamental (company) analyses.

LG 2 Gain an appreciation of the purpose and contribution of economic analysis to the stock valuation process. Economic analysis evaluates the general state of the economy and its potential effects on security returns. In essence, economic analysis tries to identify the kind of future economic environment the investor will be facing, and it is used to set the tone for the security analysis process.

LG 3 Describe industry analysis and note the role it plays in stock valuation. In industry analysis, the investor focuses attention on the activities of one or more industries. Especially important are how the competitive position of a particular industry stacks up against others and which companies within an industry hold particular promise. Industry analysis studies the makeup and basic characteristics of an industry and key economic and operating variables that are important in defining industry performance, and, ultimately, in developing an industry outlook.

LG 4 Gain a basic understanding of how fundamental analysis fits into the stock valuation process and why company analysis is used to assess the financial condition and operating results of the firm. Fundamental analysis is conducted on the premise that the value of a stock is influenced in part by the performance of the company that issued the stock. Such analysis looks at the fundamentals of the company—at its competitive position, its sales and profit margins, its asset mix, its capital structure, and, eventually, its future prospects. A key aspect of this analytical process is company analysis, which involves an in-depth study of the actual financial condition and operating results of the company. The purpose is to provide the investor with insights into what drives the company's sales and profits—which, in turn, will help the investor formulate expectations about the future growth and profitability of the company.

LG 5 Calculate a variety of financial ratios and describe how financial statement analysis can be used to determine the financial vitality of a company. The company's balance sheet, income statement, and statement of cash flows are all used in company analysis. An essential part of such analysis is financial ratios, which expand the perspective and information content of financial statements. There are five broad categories of financial ratios—liquidity, activity, leverage, profitability, and market (common stock) ratios—all of which involve the study of relationships among and between various financial accounts.

LG 6 Use various financial measures to compare a company's recent performance with its own past and with other companies in the same industry, and explain how the insights derived from such analysis form the basic input for the valuation process. In order to evaluate financial ratios properly, it is necessary to base the analysis on historical and industry standards of performance. Whereas historical standards are used to assess developing trends in the company, industry benchmarks enable the investor to see how the firm stacks up against competitors.

DISCUSSION QUESTIONS

1. Economic analysis is generally viewed as being an integral part of the "top-down" security analysis process. In this context, identify each of the following and note how each would probably behave in a strong economy:
   a. Fiscal policy
   b. Interest rates
   c. Industrial production
   d. Retail sales
   e. Producer prices

2. As an investor, what kind(s) of economic information would you look for if you were thinking about investing in the following?
   a. An airline stock
   b. A cyclical stock
   c. An electrical utility stock
   d. A building materials stock
   e. An aerospace firm, with heavy exposure in the defense industry

3. Match the specific ratios from the left-hand column with the ratio categories listed in the right-hand column:

   a. Inventory turnover   1. Profitability ratios
   b. Debt-equity ratio   2. Activity ratios
   c. Current ratio   3. Liquidity ratios
   d. Net profit margin   4. Leverage ratios
   e. Return on assets   5. Common stock ratios
   f. Total asset turnover
   g. Price/earnings ratio
   h. Times interest earned
   i. Price-to-book-value
   j. Payout ratio

4. Annual stockholders' reports are loaded with information about the company, its operations, financial condition, product lines, manufacturing sites, and so on. To help you learn more about these reports and what you can expect to find in them, we're about to go on an "annual report scavenger hunt." Look in the *Investor's Resource Manual* that accompanies this book, and you'll find the 1994 Annual Report for Tootsie Roll Industries. Use that annual report to answer as many of the following questions as you can. Good luck!

    a. When did the company start selling candy, and, in addition to Tootsie Roll, what other brands of candy does the company sell?

    b. Who's the president of this company? Who is its CEO?

    c. Who was recently appointed by President Clinton to the *President's Export Council?* (*Hint:* See the "Operating Report.")

    d. Where is the stock traded, when did it start trading there, and what is its symbol?

    e. How much of a *stock dividend* was paid in 1994, and for how many years has a stock dividend been paid?

    f. What was the stock's high price in the second quarter of 1993?

    g. Between 1990 and 1994, what happened to the company's long-term debt? Over the same period, did the company's current ratio improve or deteriorate?

    h. In what quarter does the company normally make the most profit?

    i. Identify four of the company's *Corporate Principles*.

    j. Did EPS go up or down over the past five years (i.e., 1990–1994)? How about the net profit margin?

    k. According to the *Statement of Cash Flows,* how much net cash was provided by operating activities in 1994?

    l. What company did Tootsie Roll acquire in 1993?

    m. How much in sales *and* earnings did the company generate in Mexico and Canada in 1994?

PROBLEMS   **LG 5**

1. Assume you're given the following abbreviated financial statements:

	($ in Millions)
Current assets	$150.0
Fixed and other assets	200.0
Total assets	$350.0
Current liabilities	$100.0
Long-term debt	50.0
Stockholders' equity	200.0
	$350.0
Common shares outstanding	10 million shares
Total revenues	$500.0
Total operating costs and expenses	435.0
Interest expense	10.0
Income taxes	20.0
Net profits	$ 35.0
Dividends paid to common stockholders	$ 10.0

Based on the above information, calculate as many liquidity, activity, leverage, profitability, and common stock measures as you can. (*Note:* Assume the current market price of the common stock is $75/share.)

 LG 6

2. The Amherst Company has net profits of $10 million, sales of $150 million, and 2.5 million shares of common stock outstanding. The company has total assets of $75 million and total stockholders' equity of $45 million; it pays $1 per share in common dividends and the stock trades at $20 per share. Given this information, determine:

a. Amherst's earnings per share (EPS)
b. Amherst's book value per share *and* price-to-book-value
c. The firm's price/earnings (P/E) ratio
d. The company's net profit margin
e. The stock dividend payout ratio *and* its dividend yield

 3. Sunbelt Solar Products produces $2 million in profits from $28 million in sales and has total assets of $15 million.

a. Calculate SSP's total asset turnover and compute its net profit margin.
b. Find the company's ROA, ROE, and book value per share, given that SSP has a total net worth of $6 million and 500,000 shares of common stock out-standing.

 4. Financial Learning Systems has 2.5 million shares of common stock outstanding and 100,000 shares of preferred stock (the preferred pays annual cash dividends of $5 a share and the common pays annual cash dividends of 25 cents a share). Last year, the company generated net profits (after taxes) of $6,850,000. The company's balance sheet shows total assets of $78 million, total liabilities of $32 million, and $5 million in pre-ferred stock. The firm's common stock is currently trading in the market at $45 a share.

a. Given the preceding information, find the stock's earnings per share, price/earnings ratio, and book value per share.
b. What would happen to the price of the stock if earnings per share rise to $3.75 and the P/E ratio stays where it is? What will happen if EPS *drops* to $1.50 and the P/E ratio doesn't change?
c. What will happen to the price of the stock if EPS rises to $3.75 and the P/E ratio jumps to 25 times earnings?
d. What will happen if *both* EPS and the P/E ratio drop—to $1.50 and 10 times earnings, respectively?
e. Comment on the effect that EPS and the P/E ratio have on the market price of the stock.

 5. The Shasta Flower Farm has total assets of $10 million, an asset turnover of 2.0 times, and a net profit margin of 15 percent.

a. What is Shasta's return on assets?
b. Find Shasta's ROE, given that 40 percent of the assets are financed with stockholders' equity.

 6. Find the EPS, P/E ratio, and dividend yield of a company that has 5 million shares of common stock outstanding (the shares trade in the market at $25), earns 10 percent after taxes on annual sales of $150 million, and has a dividend payout ratio of 35 percent.

 7. Using the resources available at your campus or public library, select any common stock you like and determine as many of the profitability, activity, liquidity, leverage, and market ratios as you can; compute the ratios for the latest available fiscal year. (*Note:* Show your work for all calculations.)

 8. Listed below are six pairs of stocks. Pick one of these pairs and then, using the resources available at your campus or public library, comparatively analyze the two stocks to determine which one is fundamentally stronger and holds more promise for the future. Compute (or obtain) as many ratios as you see fit. As part of your analysis, obtain the latest S&P and/or *Value Line* reports on both stocks, and use them for added insights about the firms and their stocks.

a. Wal-Mart versus Kmart
b. J. M. Smucker versus Campbell Soup
c. IBM versus Intel
d. H&R Block versus Crown Cork & Seal
e. Liz Claiborne versus Hartmarx
f. General Dynamics versus Weyerhaeuser

9. Listed below are the 1992 and 1993 financial statements for Tootsie Roll Industries, the makers of those well-known chocolate treats:

Balance Sheets ($ in thousands)

Assets

	December 31,	
	1993	1992
Current assets:		
Cash and cash equivalents	$ 56,203	$ 88,942
Accounts receivable, net of allowances	20,656	12,889
Inventories	29,294	24,845
Prepaid expenses	5,761	6,536
Total current assets	$111,914	$133,212
Property, plant and equipment, at cost	137,273	85,024
Less: Accumulated depreciation and amortization	(50,574)	(44,767)
Net fixed assets	$ 86,699	$ 40,257
Other assets:	105,327	51,001
	$303,940	$224,470

Liabilities and Shareholders' Equity

Current liabilities:		
Notes and accounts payable	28,860	4,927
Dividends payable	1,026	791
Accrued liabilities	20,976	16,780
Total current liabilities	$ 50,862	$ 22,498
Noncurrent liabilities:		
Long-term debt	$ 40,735	$ 20,268
Shareholders' equity:		
Common stock	7,315	7,103
Capital in excess of par value	111,108	86,162
Retained earnings	93,920	88,439
Total shareholders' equity	$212,343	$181,704
	$303,940	$224,470
Average number of common shares outstanding	10,848,000	10,848,000

Income Statements ($ in thousands)

	For the Year Ended December 31,	
	1993	1992
Net sales	$259,593	$245,424
Cost of goods sold	133,978	127,123
Gross margin	$125,615	$118,301
Operating expenses:	72,098	70,368
Earnings from operations	$ 53,517	47,933
Other income (expense), net	4,193	3,989
Earnings before income taxes	$ 57,710	$ 51,922
Provision for income taxes	22,268	19,890
Net earnings	$ 35,442	$ 32,032
Cash dividends ($.35 and $.27 per share)	3,769	2,947
Average price per share of common stock (in the 4th Quarter of the year)	$ 74.25	$ 80.75

a. Based on the information provided, calculate the following financial ratios for 1992 and 1993:

| | Tootsie Roll | | Industry Averages |
	1992	1993	(for 1993)
Current ratio	1587	1587	2.36
Total asset turnover			1.27
Debt-equity ratio			10.00
Net profit margin			9.30
ROA			15.87
ROE			19.21
EPS			1.59
P/E ratio			19.87
Cash dividend yield			.44
Payout ratio			.26
Price-to-book-value			6.65

b. Based on the financial ratios you computed, along with the industry averages, how would you characterize the financial condition of Tootsie Roll Industries? Explain.

10. The following summary financial statistics were obtained from the 1989 Tootsie Roll annual report:

	1989 ($ in millions)
Net sales	$179.3
Total assets	$136.3
Net earnings	$ 20.2
Shareholders' equity	$109.6

a. Use the profit margin and asset turnover to compute the 1989 ROA for Tootsie Roll. Now introduce the equity multiplier to find ROE.
b. Obtain the same summary financial information from the *1993* Tootsie Roll financial statements (see problem 9 above), and use it to compute the 1993 ROA and ROE. Use the same procedures to calculate these measures as you did in (a) above.
c. Based on your calculations, describe how *each* of the components contributed to the change in Tootsie Roll's ROA and ROE between 1989 and 1993. Which component(s) contributed the most to the change in ROA? Which contributed the most to the change in ROE?
d. Generally speaking, do you think that these changes are fundamentally healthy for the company?

CASE PROBLEMS   **6.1 SOME FINANCIAL RATIOS ARE REAL EYE-OPENERS**

Jack Simms is a resident of Brownfield, Texas, where he is a prosperous rancher and businessman. He has also built up a sizable portfolio of common stock, which, he believes, is due to the fact that he thoroughly evaluates each stock he invests in. As Jack says, "Y'all can't be too careful about these things! Anytime I'm fixin' to invest in a stock, you can bet I'm gonna learn as much as I can about the company." Jack prefers to compute his own ratios even though he could easily obtain various types of analytical reports from his broker at no cost. (In fact, Billy Bob Smith, his broker, has been volunteering such services for years.)

Recently, Jack has been keeping an eye on a small chemical issue. This firm, South Plains Chemical Company, is big in the fertilizer business—which, not by coincidence, is something Jack knows a lot about. Not long ago, he received a copy of the company's latest financial statements (summarized below) and decided to take a closer look at the company.

Balance Sheet
($ Thousands)

Cash	$ 1,250		
Accounts receivable	8,000	Current liabilities	$10,000
Inventory	12,000	Long-term debt	8,000
Current assets	$21,250	Stockholders' equity	12,000
Fixed and other assets	8,750	Total	$30,000
Total	$30,000		

Income Statement
($ Thousands)

Sales	$50,000
Cost of goods sold	25,000
Operating expenses	15,000
Operating profit	$10,000
Interest expense	2,500
Taxes	2,500
Net profit	$ 5,000

Notes:	Dividends paid to common stockholders (dollars in thousands)	$1,250
	Number of common shares outstanding	5 million
	Recent market price of the common stock	$25

Questions

1. Compute the following ratios, using the South Plains Chemical Company figures:

	Latest Industry Averages			Latest Industry Averages
Liquidity			*Common Stock Ratios*	
a. Net working capital	N/A		l. Earnings per share	$2.00
b. Current ratio	1.95		m. Price/earnings ratio	20.0
			n. Dividends per share	$1.00
Activity			o. Dividend yield	2.5%
c. Receivables turnover	5.95		p. Payout ratio	50.0%
d. Inventory turnover	4.50		q. Book value per share	$6.25
e. Total asset turnover	2.65		r. Price-to-book-value	6.4
Leverage				
f. Debt-equity ratio	0.45			
g. Times interest earned	6.75			
Profitability				
h. Operating ratio	85.0%			
i. Net profit margin	8.5%			
j. Return on assets	22.5%			
k. ROE	32.2%			

2. Compare the company ratios you prepared to the industry figures. What are the company's strengths? What are its weaknesses?

3. What is your overall assessment of South Plains Chemical? Do you think Simms should continue with his evaluation of the stock? Explain.

6.2 DORIS LOOKS AT AN AUTO ISSUE

Doris Wise is a young career woman; she lives in Chicago, where she owns and operates a highly successful modeling agency. Doris manages her modest but rapidly growing investment portfolio, made up mostly of high-grade common stocks. Because she's young and single and has no pressing family requirements, Doris has invested primarily in stocks that offer attractive capital gains potential. Her broker recently recommended one of the auto issues and sent her some literature and analytical reports to study. Among the reports was one prepared by the brokerage house she deals with; it provided an up-to-date look at the economy, an extensive study of the auto industry, and an equally extensive review of several auto companies (including the one her broker recommended). She feels strongly about the merits of security analysis and believes it is important to spend time studying a stock before making an investment decision.

Questions

1. Doris tries to stay informed about the economy on a regular basis. At the present time, most economists agree that the economy, now well into the third year of a recovery, is healthy, with industrial activity remaining strong. What other information about the economy do you think Doris would find helpful in evaluating an auto stock? Prepare a list—and be specific. Which three items of economic information (from your list) do you feel are most important? Explain.

2. In relation to a study of the auto industry, briefly note the importance of each of the following:
   a. Auto imports
   b. The United Auto Workers union
   c. Interest rates
   d. The price of a gallon of gas

3. A variety of financial ratios and measures are provided about one of the auto companies and its stock; however, these are a bit incomplete, so some additional information will have to be computed. Specifically, we know that:

Net profit margin is	15%
Total assets are	$25 billion
Earnings per share are	$3.00
Total asset turnover is	1.5
Net working capital is	$3.4 billion
Payout ratio is	40%
Current liabilities are	$5 billion
Price/earnings ratio is	12.5

Given this information, calculate the following:
   a. Sales
   b. Net profits after taxes
   c. Current ratio
   d. Market price of the stock
   e. Dividend yield

CHAPTER 7

STOCK VALUATION AND
INVESTMENT DECISIONS

LEARNING GOALS

After studying this chapter, you should be able to:

LG 1 Explain the role that a company's future plays in the stock valuation process and develop a forecast of a stock's expected cash flow, including future dividends and anticipated price behavior.

LG 2 Discuss the concepts of intrinsic value and required rates of return and note how they are used as standards of performance in judging investment suitability.

LG 3 Determine the underlying value of a stock using the dividend valuation model, as well as other present-value-based stock valuation models that account for both expected return and potential risk.

LG 4 Understand the central role that the price/earnings ratio plays in defining a stock's price behavior and how the P/E multiple can be used in the stock valuation process.

LG 5 Describe the key attributes of technical analysis, including some popular measures and procedures used to assess the market, and the role technical analysis plays in selecting stocks.

LG 6 Discuss the idea of random walks and efficient markets and note the challenges these theories hold for the stock valuation process.

"An equity analyst's job is very intense," says Morgan Stanley software analyst Charles Phillips. "There's never enough time to read all the articles, attend all the meetings, visit the companies I follow, write reports, and respond to clients and the firm's sales force." As a "sell-side" analyst for an investment banking firm, Phillips develops stock research reports and recommendations by talking directly to industry and company sources. Formerly a "buy-side" analyst (one employed by an institutional investor such as an insurance company, bank, or mutual fund), he describes the difference between the two: "The goal is the same—to pick stocks that appreciate in value. Buy-side analysts are usually generalists, following many companies, whereas their sell-side counterparts tend to be industry specialists. Buy-siders have less time to evaluate companies, may not be as close to a company they invest in, and may focus on a particular investing approach such as growth, high dividend yield, or price/earnings ratios. They combine firsthand information from sell-side analysts with their own analysis to make recommendations to their portfolio managers."

Most commonly, sell-side analysts prepare reports on the 15 to 20 companies they follow: They gather as much information as possible from a variety of sources, form a conclusion about the company, and make recommendations—buy, hold, or sell. "I'm like a detective, looking for unique information not generally known to the public—although most is available if you dig hard enough—to identify the most attractive companies in my industry," Phillips says.

Phillips cautions investors not to focus too heavily on historical information. "Stocks move on *anticipated events*. It's more important to figure out what may happen in the next 6 to 12 months than to analyze what happened in the past. Change is a given, especially in high-tech industries like software." He looks for what drives revenue growth, because sales are the most important—and the least predictable—element. To do this, he evaluates each company, its products, competition, and industry trends in great depth.

The most difficult part of the analyst's job is putting together all the empirical and financial information to develop earnings forecasts. Phillips considers such factors as new products, distribution channels, competition, and market penetration, and he then converts these qualitative, market-oriented factors to financial information. "Once you have the earnings, the valuation process is relatively straightforward," he explains. "Most analysts today use

> **STOCKS MOVE ON ANTICIPATED EVENTS. IT'S MORE IMPORTANT TO FIGURE OUT WHAT MAY HAPPEN IN THE NEXT 6 TO 12 MONTHS THAN TO ANALYZE WHAT HAPPENED IN THE PAST.**

some type of earnings acceleration model to value stocks. The tougher decision is whether you believe the earnings forecast. It's an imprecise process at best, requiring judgment and experience."

Charles Phillips received his B.S. in computer science from the U.S. Air Force Academy, his MBA from Hampton University, and his J.D. from New York Law School. From 1986 to 1989, he was a buy-side analyst at Bank of New York. He moved to the sell-side in 1989, working for Soundview Financial until 1992 and Kidder, Peabody & Co. from 1992 to 1994, when he became a principal at Morgan Stanley & Co.

How much would you be willing to pay for a share of stock? That's a tough question and one investors have been wrestling with for about as long as common stocks have been traded. The answer, of course, depends on the kind of return you expect to receive and the amount of risk involved in the transaction. This chapter looks at the question of a stock's worth in detail: at how we can estimate the company's future prospects, value the stock, and make the investment decision.

VALUATION: OBTAINING A STANDARD OF PERFORMANCE

stock valuation
the process by which the underlying value of a stock is established, as based on future risk and return performance of the security.

Obtaining a standard of performance that can be used to judge the investment merits of a share of stock is the underlying purpose of **stock valuation**. A stock's intrinsic value furnishes such a standard since it indicates the future risk and return performance of a security. The question of whether and to what extent a stock is under- or overvalued is resolved by comparing its current market price to its intrinsic value. At any given point in time, the price of a share of common stock depends on investor expectations about the future behavior of the security. If the outlook for the company and its stock is good, the price will probably be bid up. If conditions deteriorate, the price of the stock will probably go down. Let's look now at the single most important issue in the stock valuation process: *the future*.

THE COMPANY AND ITS FUTURE

In Chapter 6 we examined several aspects of security analysis, including economic and industry analysis, as well as the historical (company) phase of fundamental analysis. It should be clear, however, that it's *not the past* that's important but *the future*. The primary reason for looking at past performance is to gain insight about the future direction of the firm and its profitability. Granted, past performance provides no guarantees about future returns, but it can give us a good idea of company strengths and weaknesses. For example, it can tell us how the company's products have done in the marketplace, how the company's fiscal health shapes up, and how management tends to respond to difficult situations. In short, the past can reveal how well the company is positioned to take advantage of the things that may occur in the future.

Because *the value of a stock is a function of its future returns*, the investor's task at hand is to use available historical data to project key financial variables into the future. In this way, the investor can assess the future prospects of the company and the expected returns from its stock. We are especially interested in dividends and price behavior.

Forecasted Sales and Profits

The key to our forecast is, of course, the future behavior of the *company,* and the most important aspects to consider in this regard are the outlook for sales and the trend in the net profit margin. One way to develop a sales forecast is to assume that the company will continue to perform as it has in the past, and simply extend the historical trend. For example, if a firm's sales have been growing at the rate of 10 percent per year, then assume they will continue at that rate of growth. Of course, if there is some evidence about the economy, industry, or company that suggests a faster or slower rate of growth, the forecast should be adjusted accordingly. More often than not, this "naive" approach will be about as effective as more complex techniques.

Once the sales forecast has been generated, we can shift our attention to the net profit margin. We want to know what kind of return on sales we can expect. A naive estimate can be obtained simply by using the average profit margin that has prevailed for the past few years; again, this should be adjusted to account for any unusual industry or company developments. For most individual investors, valuable insight about future revenues and earnings can be obtained from industry or company reports put out by brokerage houses, advisory services (e.g., *Value Line*), and the financial media (e.g., *Forbes*).

Given a satisfactory sales forecast and estimate of the future net profit margin, we can combine these two pieces of information to arrive at future earnings:

Equation 7.1

$$\begin{array}{c}\text{Future after-tax}\\\text{earnings in year } t\end{array} = \begin{array}{c}\text{estimated sales}\\\text{for year } t\end{array} \times \begin{array}{c}\text{net profit margin}\\\text{expected in year } t\end{array}$$

The "year t" notation in the equation simply denotes a given calendar or fiscal year in the future. It can be next year, the year after that, or any other year in which we are interested. Let's say that in the year just completed, a company reported sales of $100 million, and it is estimated that revenues will grow at an 8 percent annual rate, while the net profit margin should amount to about 6 percent. Thus, estimated sales next year will equal $108 million ($100 million $\times$ 1.08), and with a 6 percent profit margin, we should see earnings next year of:

$$\begin{array}{c}\text{Future after-tax}\\\text{earnings next year}\end{array} = \$108 \text{ million} \times .06 = \underline{\underline{\$6.5 \text{ million}}}$$

Using this same process, we would then estimate sales and earnings *for all other years* in our forecast period.

Forecasted Dividends and Prices

At this point, we have an idea of the future earnings performance of the company—assuming, of course, that our expectations and assumptions hold up. We are now ready to evaluate the effects of this performance on returns to common stock investors. Given a corporate earnings forecast, we need three additional pieces of information:

1. An estimate of future dividend payout ratios
2. The number of common shares that will be outstanding over the forecast period
3. A future price/earnings (P/E) ratio

For the first two variables, unless we have evidence to the contrary, we can assume that these estimates will hold for the forecast period and simply project recent experience into the future. Payout ratios are usually fairly stable, so there is little risk in using a recent average figure. (Or, if a company follows a fixed dividend policy, we could use the latest dividend rate in our forecast.) At the same time, it is generally safe to assume that the number of common shares outstanding will hold at the latest level.

The only really thorny issue is defining the future P/E ratio. This figure is important, since it has considerable bearing on the future price behavior of the stock. Generally speaking, the P/E ratio is a function of several variables, including:

1. The growth rate in earnings
2. The general state of the market outlook
3. The amount of debt in a company's capital structure
4. The current and projected rate of inflation
5. The level of dividends

As a rule, higher P/E ratios can be expected with higher growth rates in earnings, an optimistic market outlook, and lower debt levels (since less debt means less financial risk).

The link between the inflation rate and P/E multiples is a bit more complex: Generally speaking, as inflation rates rise, so do bond interest rates, which, in turn, causes required returns on stocks to rise (in order for stock returns to remain competitive with bond returns)—and higher required returns on stocks mean lower stock prices and lower P/E multiples. On the other hand, declining inflation (and interest) rates normally translate into higher P/E ratios and stock prices. We can also argue that a high P/E ratio should be expected with high dividend payouts. In practice, however, most companies with high P/E ratios have *low dividend payouts*. The reason: Earnings growth tends to be more valuable than dividends, especially in companies with high rates of return on equity.

A useful starting point for evaluating the P/E ratio is the *average market multiple*, which is simply the average P/E ratio of stocks in the marketplace. The average market multiple indicates the general state of the market and gives us an idea of how aggressively the market in general is pricing stocks. Other things being equal, the higher the P/E ratio, the more optimistic the market. Table 7.1 lists S&P price/earnings multiples for the past 34 years and shows that market multiples do tend to move over a fairly wide range.

Table 7.1 Average Market P/E Multiples 1961–1994

Year	Market Multiples (Average S&P P/E Ratio)	Year	Market Multiples (Average S&P P/E Ratio)
1961	22.4	1978	8.3
1962	17.2	1979	7.4
1963	18.7	1980	9.1
1964	18.6	1981	8.1
1965	17.8	1982	10.2
1966	14.8	1983	12.4
1967	17.7	1984	10.0
1968	18.1	1985	13.7
1969	15.1	1986	16.3
1970	16.7	1987	15.1
1971	18.3	1988	12.2
1972	19.1	1989	15.6
1973	12.2	1990	15.5
1974	7.3	1991	26.2
1975	11.7	1992	22.8
1976	11.0	1993	21.3
1977	8.8	1994	18.9

Source: Average year-end multiples derived from Standard & Poor's *Index of 500 Stocks* and its *Statistical Service—Security Price Index Record,* various issues. Listed P/Es are all year-end (December) figures, except 1994, which is as of the end of the third quarter.

relative P/E multiple
the measure of how a stock's P/E behaves relative to the average market multiple.

With the market multiple as a benchmark, the investor can then evaluate a stock's P/E performance relative to the market. That is, you can calculate a **relative P/E multiple** by dividing a stock's P/E by the market multiple. For example, if a stock currently has a P/E of 25 while the market multiple is 15, the stock's relative P/E would be 25/15 = 1.67 times. Looking at the relative P/E, the investor can quickly get a feel for how aggressively the stock has been priced in the market and what kind of relative P/E is normal for the stock. Other things being equal, a high relative P/E is desirable, since the higher this measure, the higher the stock will be priced in the market. But watch out for the downside: High relative P/E multiples can also mean more price volatility. (Similarly, we can also use average *industry* multiples to get a feel for the kind of P/E multiples that are standard for a given industry, and then use that information, along with market multiples, to assess or project the P/E for a particular stock.)

Given the above, we can now generate a forecast of what the stock's *future* P/E will be over the anticipated *investment horizon*—that is, the period of time over which we expect to hold the stock. For example, using the existing P/E multiple as a base, an *increase* might be justified if you believe the *market multiple* will increase (as the market tone becomes more bullish) and the *relative P/E* also is likely to increase. Armed with an estimate for the dividend payout ratio, the number of shares outstanding, and the price/earnings multiple, we can now forecast earnings per share:

Equation 7.2
$$\frac{\text{Estimated EPS}}{\text{in year } t} = \frac{\text{future after-tax earnings in year } t}{\text{number of shares of common stock outstanding in year } t}$$

Rather than projecting *aggregate* sales and earnings to obtain forecasted EPS, as we did above, some investors prefer to *concentrate on earnings from a per share basis right from the start*. That can be done by looking at the major forces that drive earnings per share—namely, ROE and book value. Quite simply, by employing these two variables, we can define earnings per share, as follows:

Equation 7.3   EPS = ROE × book value per share

This formula will produce exactly the same results as the standard EPS equation first shown in Chapter 5 (Equation 5.1) and then again in Chapter 6. The major advantage of this form of the equation is that it allows the investor to assess the extent to which EPS is influenced by the company's book value position and (especially) its ROE. As we saw in the previous chapter, ROE is a key financial measure, because it captures the amount of success the firm is having in managing its assets, operations, and capital structure. And as we see here, not only is ROE important in defining overall corporate profitability, it also plays a crucial role in defining a stock's EPS.

To produce an estimated EPS using Equation 7.3, the individual investor would go directly to the two basic components of the formula and try to get a handle on their future behavior. In particular, what kind of growth is expected in the firm's book value per share, *and* what's likely to happen to the company's ROE? In the vast majority of cases, ROE is really the driving force. Thus, it's important to produce a good estimate of that variable. Investors will often do that by breaking ROE into its component parts—margin, turnover, and equity multiplier. Once the investor has projected ROE and book value per share figures, they can be plugged into Equation 7.3 to produce estimated EPS. The bottom line is that, one way or another (using the approach imbedded in Equation 7.2 or that captured by Equation 7.3), the investor has to arrive at a forecasted EPS number that he or she is comfortable with. Given that's been done, it's a pretty simple matter to use the forecasted payout ratio to estimate dividends per share, as follows:

Equation 7.4
$$\text{Estimated dividends per share in year } t = \text{estimated EPS in year } t \times \text{estimated payout ratio}$$

The last item is the future price of the stock, which can be determined as:

Equation 7.5
$$\text{Estimated share price at end of year } t = \text{estimated EPS in year } t \times \text{estimated P/E ratio}$$

For example, using the aggregate sales and earnings approach, if the company had 2 million shares of common stock outstanding and that number was expected to hold in the future, then given the estimated earnings of $6.5 million that we computed earlier, the firm should generate earnings per share (EPS) next year of:

$$\text{Estimated EPS next year} = \frac{\$6.5 \text{ million}}{2 \text{ million}} = \underline{\underline{\$3.25}}$$

This result, of course, would be equivalent to the firm having a projected ROE of, say, 15 percent and an estimated book value per share of $21.67. According to Equation 7.3, those conditions would also produce an estimated EPS of $3.25 (i.e., .15 × $21.67). Anyway, using this EPS figure, along with an estimated payout ratio of 40 percent, we see that dividends per share next year should equal:

$$\text{Estimated dividends per share next year} = \$3.25 \times .40 = \underline{\underline{\$1.30}}$$

Of course, if the firm adheres to a *fixed-dividend policy*, this estimate may have to be adjusted to reflect the level of dividends being paid. For example, if the company has been paying annual dividends at the rate of $1.25 per share *and is expected to continue doing so for the near future*, then estimated dividends should be adjusted accordingly (i.e., use $1.25/share). Finally, if it has been estimated that the stock should sell at 17.5 times earnings, then a share of stock in this company should be trading at a price of about 56⅞ by the *end* of next year:

$$\text{Estimated share price at the end of next year} = \$3.25 \times 17.5 = \underline{\underline{\$56.88}}$$

Actually, we are interested in the price of the stock at the end of our anticipated investment horizon. Thus, if we had a one-year horizon, the 56⅞ figure would be appropriate. However, if we had a three-year holding period, we would have to extend the EPS figure for two more years and repeat our calculations with the new data. As we shall see, *estimated share price is important because it has embedded in it the capital gains portion of the stock's total return.*

DEVELOPING AN ESTIMATE
OF FUTURE BEHAVIOR

Using MarCor Industries, we can now illustrate this forecasting process. Recall from Chapter 6 that an assessment of the economy and the apparel industry was positive, and that the company's operating results and financial condition looked strong, both historically and relative to industry standards. Because everything looks favorable for MarCor, we decide to take a look at the future of the company and its stock. Assume we have chosen a three-year investment horizon, based on our belief (formulated from earlier studies of economic and industry factors) that the economy and the market for apparel stocks will start running out of steam sometime near the end of 1998 or early 1999.

Selected historical financial data are provided in Table 7.2. They cover a six-year period (ending with the latest, 1995, fiscal year) and will provide the basis for much of our forecast. The data in the table reveal that except for 1990 (which was an "off" year for MarCor), the company has performed at a fairly steady pace and has been able to maintain a respectable rate of growth. Our economic analysis suggests that the economy is about to pick up, and our research (from Chapter 6) indicates that the industry and company are well situated to take advantage of the upswing. Therefore, we conclude that the rate of growth in sales should pick up in 1996 to about 9.5 percent. After a modest amount of pent-up demand is worked off, the rate of growth in sales should then drop to about 9 percent in 1997 and stay there through 1998.

The essential elements of the financial forecast for 1996, 1997, and 1998 are provided in Table 7.3. Highlights of the key assumptions and the reasoning behind them are as follows:

- *Net profit margin.* Since various published industry and company reports suggest a comfortable improvement in earnings, we decide to use a profit margin of 3.0 percent in 1996, followed by an even better 3.2 percent in 1997. Finally, because of some capacity problems prominently mentioned in one of the reports, we show a drop in the margin in 1998 back to 3.0 percent.

Table 7.2   Selected Historical Financial Data, MarCor Industries

	1990	1991	1992	1993	1994	1995
Total assets (millions)	$220.9	$240.7	$274.3	$318.2	$340.5	$338.6
Debt-equity ratio	53%	51%	52%	56%	58%	49%
Total asset turnover	1.72×	1.81×	1.75×	1.65×	1.67×	1.79×
Net sales (millions)	$397.9	$435.6	$480.0	$525.0	$568.0	$606.6
Annual rate of growth in sales*	− 5.7%	9.5%	10.2%	9.4%	8.2%	6.8%
Interest and other income (millions)	$ 6.3	$ 6.0	$ 6.8	$ 7.7	$ 7.1	$ 8.3
Net profit margin	1.1%	2.0%	3.6%	3.0%	2.7%	2.9%
Payout ratio	97.0%	45.0%	47.0%	46.0%	47.0%	48.0%
Price/earnings ratio	8.3×	12.8×	9.5×	10.9×	11.2×	10.2×
Number of common shares outstanding (millions)	3.2	3.2	3.7	3.8	3.8	3.8

*Annual rate of growth in sales = change in sales from one year to the next divided by the level of sales in the base (or earliest) year; for 1991, the annual rate of growth in sales equaled 9.5% = (1991 sales − 1990 sales)/1990 sales = ($435.6 − $397.9)/$397.9 =.095.

Table 7.3   Summary Forecast Statistics, MarCor Industries

	Latest Actual Figures (Fiscal 1995)	Average for the Past 5 Years (1991–1995)	Forecasted Figures		
			1996	1997	1998
Annual rate of growth in sales	6.8%	8.8%	9.5%	9.0%	9.0%
Net sales (millions)	$606.6	N/A*	$664.2**	$724.0**	$789.2**
+ Interest and other income (millions)	$ 8.3	$ 7.2	$ 7.2	$ 7.2	$ 7.2
= Total revenue (millions)	$614.9	N/A	$671.4	$731.2	$796.4
× Net profit margin	2.9%	2.8%	3.0%	3.2%	3.0%
= Net after-tax earnings (millions)	$ 18.0	N/A	$ 20.1	$ 23.4	$ 24.0
÷ Common shares outstanding (millions)	3.8	3.7	3.8	3.8	3.8
= Earnings per share	$ 4.74	N/A	$ 5.29	$ 6.16	$ 6.32
× Payout ratio	48.0%	39.0%	50.0%	50.0%	55.0%
= Dividends per share	$ 2.27	$ 1.75	$ 2.65	$ 3.08	$ 3.48
Earnings per share	$ 4.74	N/A	$ 5.29	$ 6.16	$ 6.32
× P/E ratio	10.20	10.92	10.50	10.75	11.00
= Share price at year end	$ 48.50	N/A	$ 55.50	$ 66.25	$ 69.50

*N/A: Not applicable.

**Forecasted sales figures: Sales from *preceding* year x growth rate in sales = growth in sales; then: growth in sales + sales from preceding year = forecast sales for the year. For example, for 1997: $664.2 ×.09 = $59.5 + $664.2 = $724.0 million.

- *Common shares outstanding.* Our assessment indicates the company will be able to handle the growth in assets and meet financing needs without issuing any new common stock. Therefore, the common shares outstanding remain at 3.8 million throughout the forecast.

- *Payout ratio.* We assume that the dividend payout ratio will hold at around 50 percent of earnings, as it has for most of the recent past—with the notable exception of 1990.

- *P/E ratio.* Based primarily on expectations of improved growth in revenues and earnings, we are projecting a P/E multiple that will gradually rise from its present level of 10 times earnings to roughly 11 times earnings in 1998. Although this is a fairly conservative increase in the P/E, when coupled with the hefty growth in EPS, the net effect will be a big jump in the projected price of MarCor stock.

Table 7.3 also shows the sequence involved in arriving at forecasted dividends and price behavior. The sequence is as follows:

1. The company dimensions of the forecast are handled first. These include sales and revenue estimates, net profit margins, net earnings, and amount of outstanding stock. Note that after-tax earnings are derived according to the procedure described earlier in this chapter.

2. Next, earnings per share are estimated, following the procedures established earlier.

3. The bottom line of the forecast is, of course, the dividends and capital gains returns the investor can expect from a share of MarCor stock, given that

the assumptions about net sales, profit margins, earnings per share, and so forth, hold up. We see in Table 7.3 that dividends should go up by about $1.21 per share over the next three years (from $2.27 to an expected $3.48) and that the price of a share of stock should appreciate in value by more than 40 percent, rising from its latest price of $48.50 to $69.50 in 1998.

We now have the figures on what the future cash flows of the investment are likely to be and are in a position to establish an intrinsic value for MarCor Industries stock.

THE VALUATION PROCESS

valuation
process by which an investor determines the worth of a security using risk and return concepts.

Valuation is a process by which an investor determines the worth of a security using the risk and return concepts introduced in Chapter 4. This formal process can be applied to any asset that produces a stream of cash flow—be it a share of stock, a bond, a piece of real estate, or an oil well. In order to establish the value of an asset, the investor must determine certain key inputs, including the amount of future cash flows, the timing of these cash flows, and the rate of return required on the investment. In terms of common stock, the essence of valuation is to determine what the stock *ought to be worth*, given estimated returns to stockholders (future dividends and price behavior) and the amount of potential risk exposure. Toward this end, we employ various types of stock valuation models, the end product of which represent the elusive intrinsic value we have been seeking. That is, the stock valuation models determine either an *expected rate of return* or the *intrinsic worth of a share of stock*, which in effect represents the stock's "justified price." In this way, we obtain a standard of performance, based on future stock behavior, that can be used to judge the investment merits of a particular security.

If the computed rate of return equals or exceeds the yield the investor feels is warranted or if the justified price (intrinsic worth) is equal to or greater than the current market price, the stock under consideration is considered a worthwhile investment candidate. Note especially that a security is considered acceptable even if its yield simply *equals* the required rate of return or if its intrinsic value simply *equals* the current market price of the stock. There is nothing irrational about such behavior, since in either case, the security meets the minimum standards you've established (i.e., the security is giving you the required rate of return you wanted).

However, remember this about the valuation process: That is, even though valuation plays an important part in the investment process, there is *absolutely no assurance* that the actual outcome will be even remotely similar to the forecasted behavior. The stock is still subject to economic, industry, company, and market risks that could well negate *all* your assumptions about the future. Security analysis and stock valuation models are used not to guarantee success but to help investors better understand the return and risk dimensions of a proposed transaction.

Required Rate of Return

required rate of return
the return necessary to compensate an investor for the risk involved in an investment.

One of the key elements in the stock valuation process is the **required rate of return**. Generally speaking, the amount of return required by an investor should be related to the level of risk that must be assumed in order to generate that return. In essence, the required return provides a mechanism whereby the investor establishes a level of compensation that is compatible with the amount of risk involved in an investment. Such a standard helps the investor determine whether the expected return on a stock (or any other security) is satisfactory. Since we don't know for sure what the cash flow of an investment will be, we should expect to earn a rate of return that reflects this uncertainty. Thus, the greater the perceived risk, the more return we should expect to earn. As we saw in Chapter 4, this is basically the notion behind the *capital asset pricing model* (CAPM).

Recall that using the CAPM, we define a stock's required return as:

Equation 7.6

$$\begin{matrix} \text{Required} \\ \text{rate of return} \end{matrix} = \begin{matrix} \text{risk-free} \\ \text{rate} \end{matrix} + \left[\begin{matrix} \text{stock's} \\ \text{beta} \end{matrix} \times \left(\begin{matrix} \text{market} \\ \text{return} \end{matrix} - \begin{matrix} \text{risk-free} \\ \text{rate} \end{matrix} \right) \right]$$

The required input for this equation is readily available: You can obtain a stock's beta from *Value Line* or S&P's *Stock Reports,* the risk-free rate is basically the average return on Treasury bills for the past year or so, and a good proxy for the market return is the average stock returns over the past 10 to 15 years (like the data reported in Table 5.1).

In the CAPM, the risk of a stock is captured by its beta. For that reason, the required return on a stock will increase (or decrease) with increases (or decreases) in its beta. As an illustration of the CAPM at work, consider MarCor's stock, which has a beta of 1.10. Given the risk-free rate is, say, 5 percent and the market return is 13 percent, this stock would have a required return of:

Required return = 5% + [1.10 × (13% – 5%)] = 13.8%

This return—let's round it to 14 percent—can now be used in a stock valuation model to assess the investment merits of a share of stock.

As an alternative, or in conjunction with the CAPM, we could take a more subjective approach to finding required return. For example, if our assessment of the historical performance of the company had uncovered wide swings in sales and earnings, we could conclude that the stock is subject to a good deal of business risk. Also important is market risk, as measured by a stock's beta. A valuable reference point in arriving at a measure of risk is the rate of return available on less risky but competitive investment vehicles. For example, we can use the rate of return on long-term Treasury bonds or high-grade corporate issues as a starting point in defining our desired rate of return. That is, starting with yields on long-term, low-risk bonds, we can adjust such returns for the levels of business and market risk to which we believe the common stock is exposed.

To see how these elements make up the desired rate of return, let's return to the case of MarCor Industries. Assume it is now early 1996 and rates on Treasury bonds are hovering around 8 percent. Given that our analysis thus far has indicated that the apparel industry in general and MarCor in particular are subject to a "fair" amount of business risk, we would want to adjust that figure upward—probably by around 2 or 3 points. In addition, with its beta of 1.10, we can conclude that the stock carries some market risk. Thus, we should increase our base rate of return even more—say, by another 3 points. That is, starting from a base (Treasury bond) rate of 8 percent, we tack on 3 percent for the company's added business risk and another 3 percent for the stock's market risk. We conclude that an appropriate required rate of return should be around 14 percent for an investment in MarCor Industries common stock. Note that this figure of 14 percent is almost the same as what we would obtain from the CAPM, using a beta of 1.1, a risk-free rate of 5 percent, and a market return of 13 percent (as in Equation 7.6). The fact that the two numbers are so close shouldn't be surprising: If they're carefully (and honestly) done, you'd expect the two procedures—the CAPM and the subjective approach—to yield similar results. Whichever procedure is used, the required rate of return stipulates the minimum return we would expect to receive from an investment. To accept anything less means we'll fail to be fully compensated for the risk we must assume.

CONCEPTS *in Review*

7.1   What is the purpose of stock valuation? What role does intrinsic value play in the stock valuation process?

7.2   Are the expected future earnings of the firm important in determining a stock's investment suitability? Discuss how these and other future estimates fit into the stock valuation framework.

7.3   Can the growth prospects of a company affect its price/earnings multiple? Explain. How about the amount of debt a firm uses? Are there other variables that affect the level of a firm's P/E ratio?

7.4   What is the *market multiple,* and how can it help in evaluating a stock's P/E? Is a stock's relative P/E the same thing as the market multiple? Explain.

7.5   In the stock valuation framework, how can you tell if a particular security is a worthwhile investment candidate? What roles does the required rate of return play in this process? Would you invest in a stock if all you could earn was a rate of return that equaled your required return? Explain. ▬

STOCK VALUATION MODELS

Take a look in the market and you'll discover that investors employ a number of different stock valuation models. While they all may ultimately be aimed at the future cash benefits of the security, their approaches to valuation are nonetheless considerably different. Take, for example, those investors who search for value in a company's financials—by keying in on such factors as book value, debt load, return on equity, and cash flow. These are the so-called *value investors*, who rely as much on historical performance as on earnings projections to identify undervalued stock. Then there are the *growth investors*, who concentrate solely on growth in earnings. To them, though past growth is important, the real key lies in projected earnings—that is, in finding companies that are going to produce big earnings, along with big price/earnings multiples, in the future. Whereas value investors tend to buy and hold for the long haul, growth investors do not hesitate to dump their holdings at the first sign of trouble. The value and growth approaches to stock valuation are popular with many individual as well as institutional investors. And more often than not, investors tend to prefer one approach over the other. That is, they tend to be *either* value investors *or* growth investors. For while there are some similarities in these two approaches, as the *Investor Insights* box on the next page suggests, there are also some real differences.

INVESTOR INSIGHTS: *Investing in Action*

Value or Growth: Which Will It Be?

Value and growth—wouldn't any investor consider these desirable characteristics for an investment? However, these terms also refer to specific—and very different—equity investment styles. The *value investor* buys less expensive stocks the market has ignored and waits for them to bounce back. The *growth investor* pays premium prices for companies based on strong earnings growth forecasts. Investors in each camp argue long and hard that theirs is the better approach.

A *value stock* is one whose prices are low compared to its fundamentals: earnings, book value per share, cash flow, asset values, dividend yield, or similar quantitative measures. However, those factors alone don't tell the whole story. Value investors identify *why* the company's valuation is low and then buy if they expect a "catalyst" (e.g., new management, sale of assets, corporate takeover, regulatory change, or reassessment by Wall Street analysts) to push up the stock price. Value investors are contrarians; they seek out companies they hope are (temporarily) out of favor, perhaps due to poor earnings or industry factors, like IBM in the early to middle 1990s. They expect them to gain popularity when investors discover their hidden values. Investors following this approach need to be patient; it may be hard to predict when the tide will turn in your favor. Value stocks are often in staid, cyclical industries like automobiles, chemicals, financial services, and steel. They shine when interest rates are low and the economy is recovering (e.g., 1992–1994), and they peak when economic growth slows.

It's at that point when *growth stocks*, whose earnings can grow regardless of the economic cycle, often take off. The theory behind growth investing is that stock prices of companies with above-average growth in earnings—say, over 15 percent a year—should ultimately yield higher returns. Growth stocks may be large companies like Home Depot, Johnson & Johnson, and PepsiCo or small companies in high-growth industries like biotechnology and software. These stocks tend to have high prices and price/earnings ratios and pay little or no dividends.

On the face of it, growth investing certainly makes sense. However, it carries more risk because these stocks rise faster—and fall harder—than the S&P 500. There's no guarantee that stocks with high projected earnings growth will live up to their forecasts, and choosing growth stocks can be tricky. Some investors focus on whether a company can sustain its growth rate; others buy only if a stock's price/earnings multiple is below the company's growth rate. Growth investors need to monitor both a company's performance and its industry carefully. Waiting too long to buy or sell may wipe out the rewards of taking on greater risk.

How does the performance of value and growth stocks compare? These investment strategies run in cycles; growth may be "in" in one season; value, the next. The S&P/BARRA index divides the S&P 500 into growth or value indexes based on price-to-book-value ratio. From 1982 to 1992, the value index outperformed the growth index in five years, and growth outperformed value in six years. What's more, even the categories change: Today's growth stock may be tomorrow's value stock. About 20 percent of the companies on the S&P/BARRA indexes change in any year. Thus, it would seem prudent for both types of investors to reevaluate their stocks regularly. Given the differences between the two investment philosophies, perhaps both value and growth stocks belong in your portfolio.

Sources: William P. Barrett, "The New Growth Stocks," *Smart Money*, September 1994, pp. 81–89; Jeff Laderman, "Growth vs. Value: Tips for the Intrepid Investor," *Business Week*, June 15, 1992, pp. 136–37; Derrick Niederman, "Getting Your Money's Worth from Growth Stocks," *Worth Online: Derrick's Daily Commentary*, America Online/© Capital Publishing Company, June 17, 1994, and "Value Stocks (Is There Any Other Kind?)," *Worth Online: Derrick's Daily Commentary*, America Online/© Capital Publishing Company, June 16, 1994; and Ken Sheets, "Stocks Only a Contrarian Could Love," *Kiplinger's Personal Finance Magazine*, March 1994, pp. 133–36.

There are still other models that use variables like dividend yield, price-to-sales ratios, abnormally low P/E multiples, and even company size as key elements in the decision-making process. For purposes of our discussion here, we'll focus on several stock valuation models that are both theoretically sound and widely used by investment professionals. In one form or another, these models use the required rate of return, along with expected cash flows from dividends and/or the future price of the stock, to derive the intrinsic value of an investment. Let's begin with a procedure known as the dividend valuation model.

THE DIVIDEND VALUATION MODEL

In the valuation process, the intrinsic value of any investment equals the *present value of the expected cash benefits*. For common stock, the intrinsic value amounts to the cash dividends received each year plus the future sale price of the stock. Another way to view the cash flow benefits from common stock is to assume that the dividends will be received over an infinite time horizon—an assumption that is appropriate so long as the firm is considered a "going concern." Seen from this perspective, *the value of a share of stock is equal to the present value of all the future dividends it is expected to provide over an infinite time horizon.*

Although by selling stock at a price which is above that originally paid, a stockholder can earn capital gains in addition to dividends, from a strictly theoretical point of view, what is really being sold is the right to all remaining future dividends. Thus, just as the *current* value of a share of stock is a function of future dividends, the *future* price of the stock is also a function of future dividends. In this framework, the *future* price of the stock will rise or fall as the outlook for dividends (and the required rate of return) changes. This approach, which holds that the value of a share of stock is a function of its future dividends, has come to be known as the **dividend valuation model** (DVM).

dividend valuation model (DVM)
a model that values a share of stock on the basis of the future dividend stream it is expected to produce; its three versions are zero-growth, constant-growth, and variable-growth.

There are three versions of the dividend valuation model, each based on different assumptions about the future rate of growth in dividends: (1) *the zero-growth model*, which assumes that dividends will not grow over time; (2) *the constant-growth model*, which is the basic version of the dividend valuation model and assumes that dividends will grow by a fixed/constant rate over time; and (3) *the variable-growth model*, in which the rate of growth in dividends varies over time.

Zero Growth

The simplest way to picture the dividend valuation model is to assume that you're dealing with a stock that has a fixed stream of dividends. In other words, dividends stay the same year in and year out, and they're expected to stay that way in the future. Under such conditions, the value of a zero-growth stock is simply *the capitalized value of its annual dividends*. To find the capitalized value, just divide annual dividends by the required rate of return, which in effect acts as the capitalization rate. That is:

Equation 7.7
$$\frac{\text{Value of a}}{\text{share of stock}} = \frac{\text{annual dividends}}{\text{required rate of return}}$$

For example, if a stock paid a (constant) dividend of $3 a share and you wanted to earn 10 percent on your investment, you would value the stock at $30 a share (i.e., $3/.10 = $30).

As you can see, the only cash flow variable that's used in this model is the fixed annual dividend. Since the annual dividend on this stock never changes, does that mean the price of the stock never changes? Absolutely not! For as the capitalization rate—that is, the required rate of return—changes, so will the price of the stock. Thus, if the capitalization rate goes up—to, say, 15 percent—the price of the stock will fall, to $20 ($3/.15). Although this may be a very simplified view of the valuation model, it's actually not as far-fetched as it may appear: As we'll see in Chapter 10, this is basically the procedure used to price *preferred stocks* in the marketplace.

Constant Growth

The zero-growth model is a good beginning, but it does not take into account a growing stream of dividends, which is more likely to be the case in the real world. That is, rather than assume no growth in dividends, the standard and more widely recognized version of the dividend valuation model assumes that dividends will grow over time at a specified rate. Under this variation of the model, the value of a share of stock is still considered to be a function of its future dividends, but in this case such dividends are expected to grow forever (to infinity) at a constant rate of growth, *g*. Accordingly, the value of a share of stock can be found as follows:

Equation 7.8
$$\frac{\text{Value of a}}{\text{share of stock}} = \frac{\text{next year's dividends}}{\text{required rate} - \text{constant rate of}}$$
$$\frac{}{\text{of return} \quad \text{growth in dividends}}$$

Equation 7.8a
$$V = \frac{D_1}{k - g}$$

where:

D_1 = annual dividends expected to be paid *next* year (the first year in the forecast period).

k = the discount rate, or capitalization rate (which defines the required rate of return on the investment).

g = the annual rate of growth in dividends, which is expected to hold constant to infinity.

This model succinctly captures the essence of stock valuation: *Increase* the cash flow (through *D* or *g*) and/or *decrease* the required rate of return (*k*), and the value of the stock will *increase*.

The constant-growth DVM should not be used with just any stock. Rather, *it is best suited to the valuation of mature companies* that hold established market positions—companies with strong track records that have reached the "mature" stage of growth. This means that you're very likely dealing with large-cap—or perhaps even some mature mid-cap—companies that have demonstrated an ability to generate steady rates of growth year in and year out. The growth rates may *not be identical* from year to year, but they tend to move within such a small range that they are seldom or never far off the average rate. These are companies that have established dividend policies, particularly with regard to the payout ratio, and fairly predictable growth rates in earnings and dividends. Thus, to use the constant growth DVM on such companies, all that's required is some basic information about the stock's *current* level of dividends and the expected rate of growth in dividends, g.

One popular and fairly simple way to find the dividend growth rate is to look at the *historical* behavior of dividends and, if they are in fact growing at a relatively constant rate, then assume that they'll continue to grow at (or near) that average rate into the future. You can find historical dividend data in a company's annual report, from on-line computer services, or from publications like *Value Line*. Given this stream of dividends, you can use basic present-value arithmetic to find the average rate of growth. Here's how: Take the level of dividends, say, ten years ago, and divide that amount by the level of dividends paid today. You'll end up with a present-value interest factor (PVIF). Now look in Table A.3 for the discount rate that's linked to the interest factor you just computed. In this case, the *discount rate is the average rate of growth in dividends*. (See Chapter 4 for a detailed discussion of how to use present value to find growth rates.)

Once we've determined the dividend growth rate, g, we can find next year's dividend, D_1, as: $D_0 \times (1 + g)$, where D_0 equals the actual (current) level of dividends. Let's say that in the latest year Sweatmore Industries paid \$2.50 a share in dividends. If we expect these dividends to grow at the rate of 6 percent a year, we can find next year's dividends as follows: $D_1 = D_0(1 + g)$ = \$2.50 (1 + .06) = \$2.50 (1.06) = \$2.65. The only other information we need is the capitalization rate, or required rate of return, k. (Note in the constant-growth model that k must be greater than g in order for the model to be mathematically operative.)

To see this dividend valuation model at work, let's consider a stock that currently pays an annual dividend of \$1.75 a share. Let's say that by using the present-value approach described above, you find that dividends are growing at a rate of 8 percent a year and you expect they will continue to do so into the future. In addition, you feel that because of the risks involved, the investment should carry a required rate of return of 12 percent. Given this information, we can use Equation 7.8 to price the stock. That is, given $D_0 = \$1.75$, $g = .08$, and $k = .12$, it follows that:

$$\text{Value of a share of stock} = \frac{D_0(1+g)}{k-g} = \frac{\$1.75(1.08)}{.12-.08} = \frac{\$1.89}{.04} = \underline{\underline{\$47.25}}$$

If the investor wants to earn a 12 percent return on this investment, then according to the constant growth dividend valuation model, he or she should pay no more than \$47.25 a share for the stock.

Note that with this version of the DVM, *the price of the stock will increase over time* so long as k and g don't change. This occurs because the cash flow from the investment will increase with time as dividends grow. To see how this happens, let's carry our example further: Recall that $D_0 = \$1.75$, $g = 8\%$, and $k = 12\%$; based on this information, we found the current value of the stock to be \$47.25. Now look what happens to the price of this stock if k and g don't change:

Year	Dividend	Stock Price*
(Current year) 0	$1.75	$47.25
1	1.89	51.00
2	2.04	55.00
3	2.20	59.50
4	2.38	64.25
5	2.57	69.50

*As determined by the dividend valuation model, given $g = .08$, $k = 12$, and D_0 = dividend level for any given year.

As you can see in the above table, the price of the stock *in the future* can also be found by using the standard dividend valuation model. To do this, we simply redefine the appropriate level of dividends. For example, to find the price of the stock in year 3, we use the expected dividend in the third year, $2.20, and increase it by the factor $(1 + g)$; thus, the stock price in year 3 $= D_3 \times (1 + g)/(k - g) = \$2.20 \times (1 + .08)/(.12 - .08) = \$2.38/.04 = \$59.50$. Of course, if future expectations about k or g do change, the *future price* of the stock will change accordingly. Should that occur, an investor could then use the new information to decide whether to continue to hold the stock.

Variable Growth

Although the constant-growth dividend valuation model is an improvement over the zero-growth model, it still has some shortcomings, one of the most obvious of which is the fact that it does not allow for any changes in expected growth rates. To overcome this problem, there's a form of the DVM that allows for *variable rates of growth* over time. Essentially, the *variable-growth dividend valuation model* uses two stages to derive a value based on future dividends and the future price of the stock (which price is a function of all future dividends to infinity). The variable-growth version of the model finds the value of a share of stock as follows:

Equation 7.9

$$\text{Value of a share of stock} = \begin{array}{c}\text{present value of} \\ \text{future dividends} \\ \text{during the initial} \\ \text{variable-growth period}\end{array} + \begin{array}{c}\text{present value of the price} \\ \text{of the stock at the end of} \\ \text{the variable-growth period}\end{array}$$

Equation 7.9a

$$V = (D_1 \times PVIF_1) + (D_2 \times PVIF_2) + \cdots$$

$$+ (D_v \times PVIF_v) + \left(PVIF_v \times \frac{D_v (1 + g)}{k - g} \right)$$

where:

D_1, D_2, etc. = future annual dividends

$PVIF_t$ = present value interest factor, as specified by the required rate of return for a given year t (use Table A.3 in the appendix)

v = number of years in the initial variable-growth period

Note that the last element in this equation is the standard constant-growth dividend valuation model, which is used to find the price of the stock at the end of the initial growth period.

This form of the DVM is appropriate for companies that are expected to experience variable rates of growth for a period of time—perhaps for the first three to five years, or more—and then settle down to a constant (average) growth rate thereafter. This, in fact, is the growth pattern of many companies, and therefore the model has considerable application in practice. Finding the value of a stock using Equation 7.9 is actually a lot easier than it looks. All you need do is follow these steps:

1. Estimate annual dividends during the initial variable-growth period and then specify the constant rate, g, at which dividends will grow after the initial period.

2. Find the present value of the dividends expected during the initial variable-growth period.

3. Using the constant-growth DVM, find the price of the stock at the end of the initial growth period.

4. Find the present value of the price of the stock (as determined in step 3, above); note that the price of the stock is discounted at the same PVIF as the last dividend payment in the initial growth period, since the stock is being priced (per step 3) at the end of this initial period.

5. Add the two present-value components (from steps 2 and 4, above) to find the value of a stock.

To see how this works, let's apply the variable-growth model to MarCor Industries. Let's assume that dividends will grow at a variable rate for the first three years (1996, 1997, and 1998); after that, the annual rate of growth in dividends is expected to settle down to 8 percent and stay there for the foreseeable future. We can use the dividend projections we prepared (for 1996–1998) in Table 7.3, along with our required rate of return (formulated earlier) of 14 percent. Table 7.4 (on the next page) shows the variable-growth DVM in action. As we can see in the table, the value of MarCor stock, according to the variable-growth DVM, is just under $49.25 a share. In essence, that's the maximum price an investor should be willing to pay for the stock if he or she wants to earn a 14 percent rate of return.

Finding the Growth Rate

Mechanically, application of the DVM is really quite simple, as it relies on just three key pieces of information: future dividends, future growth in dividends, and a required rate of return. But this model is not without its difficulties: That is, one of the most important and most difficult aspects of the DVM is *specifying the appropriate growth rate, g, over an extended period of time.* For the fact is, whether an investor is using the constant-growth or the variable-growth version of the dividend valuation model, the growth rate, g, is a crucial element in the DVM and has an enormous impact on the value derived from the model. Indeed, the DVM is *very sensitive* to the growth rate being used, because it affects both the model's numerator and its denominator. As such, considerable attention should be directed toward coming up with the proper growth rate.

Table 7.4 Using the Variable-Growth DVM to Value MarCor Stock

Step

1. Projected annual dividends: 1996 $2.65
   (see Table 7.3)   1997 $3.08
                               1998 $3.48

   Estimated annual rate of growth in dividends, g, for 1999 and beyond: 8%

2. Present value of dividends—using a required rate of return, k, of 14%—during the initial variable growth period:

Year	Dividends	$\times$	PVIF $(k = 14\%)$	$=$	Present Value
1996	$2.65		.877		$2.32
1997	3.08		.769		2.37
1998	3.48		.675		2.35
				Total	$7.04 (to step 5)

3. Price of the stock at the end of the initial growth period:

$$P_{1998} = \frac{D_{1999}}{k - g} = \frac{D_{1998} \times (1 + g)}{k - g} = \frac{\$3.48 \times (1.08)}{.14 - .08} = \frac{\$3.75}{.06} = \$62.50$$

4. Discount the price of the stock (as computed above) back to its present value, at $k = 14\%$:

$$PV(P_{1998}) = \$62.50 \times PVIF_{14\%, \, 3 \, yrs} = \$62.50 \times .675 = \underline{\$42.19} \text{ (to step 5)}$$

5. Add the present value of the initial dividend stream (step 2) to the present value of the price of the stock at the end of the initial growth period (step 4):

   Value of MarCor stock = $7.04 + $42.19 = $49.23

As we saw earlier in this chapter, we can choose the growth rate from a strictly historical perspective—by using present value to find the past rate of growth and then use it (or something close) in the DVM. Although that technique might work fine with the constant-growth model, it has some obvious shortcomings for use with the variable-growth DVM. One procedure that's widely used in practice is to define the growth rate, g, according to the following equation:

Equation 7.10 g = ROE $\times$ the firm's retention rate, rr

where:

       rr = 1 − dividend payout ratio

Both variables in Equation 7.10 (ROE and rr) are *directly related to the firm's rate of growth*, and both play key roles in defining a firm's future growth. The *retention rate* represents the percentage of the firm's profits that are plowed back into the company. Thus, if the firm pays out 35 percent of its earnings in dividends (i.e., it has a dividend payout ratio of 35 percent), it has a retention rate of 65 percent: rr = 1 − .35 = .65. The retention rate, in effect, is an indication of the amount of capital that's flowing into the company to finance its growth. Other things being equal, the more money that's being retained in the company, the higher the rate of growth. The other component of Equation 7.10 is the familiar return on equity. Clearly, the more the company can earn on its retained capital, the higher the growth rate.

Let's look at some numbers to see how this actually works: For example, if a company retained, on average, about 80 percent of its earnings and generated an ROE of around 15 percent, you'd expect it to have a growth rate of:

$$g = \text{ROE} \times rr = .15 \times .80 = \underline{12\%}$$

Actually, the growth rate will probably be a bit more than 12 percent, since Equation 7.10 ignores financial leverage, which in itself will magnify growth. But at least the equation gives you a good idea of what to expect. Or it can serve as a starting point in assessing past and future growth. That is, you can use Equation 7.10 to compute expected growth, then assess the two key components of the formula (ROE and rr) to see if they're likely to undergo major changes in the future. If so, then what impact is the change in ROE and/or rr likely to have on the growth rate, g? The idea is to take the time to study the forces (ROE and rr) that drive the growth rate, because the DVM itself is so sensitive to the rate of growth being used. Employ a growth rate that's too high and you'll end up with an intrinsic value that's way too high also. The downside to that, of course, is that you may end up buying a stock that you really shouldn't.

ALTERNATIVES TO THE DVM

The variable-growth approach to stock valuation is fairly compatible with the way most people invest. That is, unlike the underlying assumptions in the standard dividend valuation model (which employs an infinite investment horizon), most investors have a holding period that seldom exceeds five to seven years. Under such circumstances, *the relevant cash flows are future dividends and the future selling price of the stock.*

There are some alternatives to the DVM that use comparable cash flow streams to value stock. One is the so-called *dividends-and-earnings approach,* which in many respects is quite similar to the variable-growth DVM. Another is the *P/E approach,* which builds the stock valuation process around the stock's price/earnings ratio. Let's now take a closer look at both of these, as well as a technique that arrives at the expected return on the stock (in percentage terms) rather than a (dollar-based) "justified price."

A Dividends-and-Earnings Approach

As we saw in the variable-growth DVM, the value of a share of stock is a function of the amount and timing of future cash flows and the level of risk that must be taken on to generate that return. A stock valuation model has been developed that conveniently captures the essential elements of expected risk and return, and does so in a present-value context. The model is as follows:

Equation 7.11

$$\begin{array}{l}\text{Present value of} \\ \text{a share of stock}\end{array} = \begin{array}{l}\text{present value of} \\ \text{future dividends}\end{array} + \begin{array}{l}\text{present value of} \\ \text{the price of the stock} \\ \text{at date of sale}\end{array}$$

Equation 7.11a

$$V = (D_1 \times PVIF_1) + (D_2 \times PVIF_2) + \cdots$$
$$+ (D_N \times PVIF_N) + (SP_N \times PVIF_N)$$

where:

$$D_t = \text{future annual dividend in year } t$$

$$PVIF_t = \text{present-value interest factor, specified at the required rate of return (from Table A.3 in the appendix)}$$

$$SP_N = \text{estimated share price of the stock at date of sale, year } N$$

$$N = \text{number of years in the investment horizon}$$

dividends-and-earnings (D&E) approach
stock valuation approach that uses projected dividends, EPS, and P/E multiples to value a share of stock.

This is the so-called **dividends-and-earnings (D&E) approach** to stock valuation. Note its similarities to the variable-growth DVM: It's also present-value-based, and its value is also derived from future dividends and the expected selling price of the stock. The big difference between the two procedures revolves around how the future price of the stock is determined. That is, whereas the variable-growth approach uses future dividends to price the stock, the D&E approach employs projected earnings per share and estimated P/E multiples—the same two variables that drive the price of the stock in the market. Its major advantages are that it is a bit more flexible than the DVM and is a lot easier to understand and apply. Using the D&E valuation approach, the investor's attention is directed toward projecting future dividends and share price behavior over a defined, finite investment horizon, much as we did for MarCor in Table 7.3.

Especially important in the D&E approach is finding a viable P/E multiple that can be used to project the future price of the stock. This is a critical part of this stock valuation process, because of the major role that capital gains (and therefore the estimated price of the stock at its projected date of sale) play in defining the level of security returns. Using market or industry P/Es as benchmarks, the investor will try to establish a multiple that he or she feels the stock will trade at in the future. Couple this number with projected earnings per share and you have an estimate of what the stock should sell for in the future. Like the growth rate, g, in the DVM, the P/E multiple is the single most important (and most difficult) variable to project in the present-value model. Using this input, along with estimated future dividends, the present-value-based stock valuation model generates a *justified price* based on estimated returns. Basically, this intrinsic value represents the price we should be willing to pay for the stock given its expected dividend and price behavior, and assuming we want to realize a return that is equal to or greater than our required rate of return (as found by using the CAPM or some other more subjective approach).

To see how this procedure works, consider once again the case of MarCor Industries. Let's return to our original three-year investment horizon. Given the forecasted annual dividends and share price from Table 7.3, along with a 14 percent required rate of return, we can see from the computations below that the value of MarCor stock is:

Present value of a share = ($2.65 × .877) + ($3.08 × .769) + ($3.48 × .675)
of MarCor stock   + ($69.50 × .675)

= $2.32 + $2.37 + $2.35 + $46.92

= $53.96

You'll note that, as compared to the variable-growth DVM, this model produces a slightly higher intrinsic value ($53.96 vs. $49.23, as computed in Table 7.4). This difference, of course, is due to the higher share price we're projecting here ($69.50), compared to the one we ended up with in the DVM ($62.50). All the other variables are basically the same. In any event, the present-value figure computed here means that with the projected dividend and share price behavior, we would realize our desired rate of return *only* if we were able to buy the stock at around $54 a share. Because MarCor Industries is currently trading at $48.50, we can conclude that the stock at present is an attractive investment vehicle. That is, since we can buy the stock at something less than its computed intrinsic value, we'll be able to earn our required rate of return— so long as dividends, EPS, and P/E projections hold up.

Determining Expected Return

Sometimes investors find it more convenient to deal in terms of expected return than a dollar-based justified price. Fortunately, this is no problem; nor is it necessary to sacrifice the present-value dimension of the stock valuation model to achieve such an end. For the *approximate yield* measure, first introduced in Chapter 4 (as Equation 4.10), can easily be used with common stocks to find a present-value-based rate of return. This approach to stock valuation uses forecasted dividend and price behavior, along with the *current market price* of the stock, to arrive at the fully compounded rate of return you can expect to earn from a given long-term investment.

To see how a stock's expected return is computed, let's look once more at MarCor Industries. Using the 1996–1998 information from Table 7.3, along with the stock's current price of $48.50, we find MarCor's expected return as follows:

$$\text{Expected return} = \frac{\$3.07 + \dfrac{\$69.50 - \$48.50}{3}}{\dfrac{\$69.50 + \$48.50}{2}}$$

$$= \frac{\$3.07 + \$7.00}{\$59.00}$$

$$= \underline{\underline{17.1\%}}$$

As seen here, MarCor can be expected to earn an annual return of around 17 percent, assuming the stock can be bought at $48.50, is held for three years (during which time annual dividends will average about $3.07 per share), and is then sold for $69.50 per share. Note that in this version of the stock valuation model, it is the *average annual dividend* that is used rather than the specific dividends. For MarCor Industries, dividends will average $3.07 per share over each of the next three years—that is, ($2.65 + $3.08 + $3.48)/3 = $3.07. When compared to the 14 percent required rate of return, the 17.1 percent expected return this investment offers is clearly more than adequate.

Expected return can also be found by using the present-value-based *internal rate of return (IRR)* procedure (see Chapter 4, pages 150–153). We use the same input as we did above, but in this case, we want to find the discount rate that equates the future stream of benefits from the investment (i.e., the future annual dividends and future price of the stock) to its current market price. In other words, find the discount rate that produces a present value of future benefits equal to the price of the stock and you have the IRR, or expected return on that stock. Here's how it works: Using the MarCor example, on page 295, we know that the stock is expected to pay per share dividends of $2.65, $3.08, and $3.48, respectively, over each of the next three years. At the end of that time, we hope to sell the stock for $69.50. Given that the stock is currently trading at $48.50, we're looking for the discount rate that will produce a present value (of the future annual dividends and stock price) equal to $48.50. That is:

$$(\$2.65 \times PVIF_1) + (\$3.08 \times PVIF_2) + (\$3.48 \times PVIF_3) + (\$69.50 \times PVIF_3) = \$48.50$$

We need to solve for the discount rate—or the present-value interest factors (PVIFs)—in the above equation. Through a process of "hit and miss" (hopefully with the help of a personal computer or hand-held calculator), you'll find that if you use an interest factor of 18.3 percent, the present value of the future cash benefits from this investment will equal exactly $48.50. That, of course, is our expected return. Note that this result varies a bit from our expected return calculation above. This is due to the fact that whereas our first calculation employed an approximate yield procedure, the IRR produces a more precise measure of return.

The Price/Earnings (P/E) Approach

One of the problems with the stock valuation procedures that we've looked at above is that they are fairly mechanical (i.e., mathematical) and involve a good deal of "number crunching." Although such an approach is fine with a lot of stocks, it just doesn't work well with others. Fortunately, an alternative is available that is more intuitive in approach. That alternative is the **price/earnings (or P/E) approach** to stock valuation.

price/earnings (P/E) approach
stock valuation approach that tries to find the P/E ratio that's most appropriate for the stock, which along with estimated EPS, is used to determine a reasonable stock price.

The P/E approach is a favorite of professional security analysts and, along with the dividend valuation model, is widely used in practice. It's relatively simple to use (mechanically, anyway), as it's based on the standard P/E formula first introduced in Chapter 6 (Equation 6.14). There we showed that a stock's P/E is equal to its market price divided by the stock's EPS. Using this equation and solving for the market price of the stock, we have:

Equation 7.12   Stock price = EPS × P/E ratio

Equation 7.12 basically captures the P/E approach to stock valuation: That is, given an estimated EPS figure, you *decide on a P/E ratio that you feel is appropriate for the stock; then use it in Equation 7.12 to see what kind of price you come up with and how that compares to the stock's current price.*

Actually, this approach is no different from what's used in the market every day. It shows what investors are willing to pay for one dollar of earnings: The higher the multiple, the better investors feel about the company and its future prospects. Look at the stock quotes in the *Wall Street Journal*; they include the stock's P/E and show what investors are willing to pay for earnings. Essentially, the *Journal* relates the company's earnings per share for the *last* 12 months (known as *trailing earnings*) to the latest price of the stock, to find the P/E ratio. In practice, however, investors buy stocks not for their past earnings but for their *expected future earnings*. Thus, in Equation 7.12, it's customary to *use forecasted EPS for next year*. Once that's done, the investor's attention is directed toward coming up with an appropriate P/E ratio.

As you might expect when using this approach to stock valuation, the key concern of the investor is the stock's P/E ratio. Indeed, a good deal of the investor's time is spent in determining that number. Fortunately, though, it's not as big a problem as it may at first appear, for the P/E ratio can be derived directly from the constant-growth dividend valuation model. That is, by dividing both sides of the constant-growth DVM by expected earnings per share for next year, E_1, we get an equation that defines a stock's P/E:

Equation 7.13

$$\text{Price/earnings ratio} = \frac{\text{next year's (expected) dividend payout ratio}}{\text{required rate of return} - \text{the expected rate of growth in dividends}}$$

Equation 7.13a

$$P_0/E_1 = \frac{D_1/E_1}{k - g}$$

It is important to note that in Equation 7.13, the P/E ratio is defined as the *current* price of the stock, P_0, relative *to next year's* expected EPS, or E_1. This is a common way of looking at the P/E ratio—and is, in fact, the standard for the P/E stock valuation approach. Also, note that we are using the *dividend payout ratio* (D_1/E_1) in the numerator of the equation. Of course, since both the dividends and earnings variables are next year's estimates, we are using the *expected payout ratio*, rather than the current dividend payout. Which is fine, because just as the standard dividend valuation model uses an estimate of next year's dividend, it's only appropriate that the P/E version of the model use an estimate of next year's dividend payout ratio.

According to Equation 7.13, we can see that a stock's P/E ratio is determined by three factors: (1) the investor's required rate of return, k; (2) the expected rate of growth in dividends (or earnings), g; and (3) the expected dividend payout ratio. Recall in the basic stock valuation models that the required return variable, k, varies with the perceived riskiness of the investment. Thus, this variable is used in Equation 7.13 *to capture the level of risk embedded in the stock*. Estimates of all of these variables are important, but the P/E ratio, and consequently the forecasted stock price, is perhaps most sensitive to the first two.

Let's take an example. Assume that the appropriate required rate of return is 12 percent, earnings (and dividends) are expected to grow at a 6 percent rate for the foreseeable future, and the firm is expected to pay out 60 percent of its earnings as dividends. According to Equation 7.13, this should result in a P/E of around 10 times earnings. That is:

$$P/E = \frac{0.60}{0.12 - 0.06} = \frac{0.60}{0.06} = \underline{\underline{10}}$$

Using an expected EPS of $3.50 results in a stock price of $3.50 × 10 = $35 a share. Now look what happens when the growth rate drops to 4 percent:

$$P/E = \frac{0.60}{0.12 - 0.04} = \frac{0.60}{0.08} = \underline{\underline{7.5}}$$

Or when the required return increases to 14 percent:

$$P/E = \frac{0.60}{0.14 - 0.06} = \frac{0.60}{0.08} = \underline{\underline{7.5}}$$

In either case, the P/E drops to 7.5 times earnings, and the price of the stock also drops, to $3.50 \times 7.5 = 26.25. Thus, if the growth rate is expected to drop or if the required return goes up (with higher perceived risk), the net effect is a *lower P/E* and therefore a *lower stock price*. Such behavior is totally predictable, however, since you'd expect the price of a stock (and therefore its P/E ratio) to have strong ties to earnings growth and the (perceived) riskiness of the investment.

To implement the P/E approach, the first thing the investor has to do is come up with a forecasted EPS. In the early part of this chapter, we saw how this might be done (see, e.g., Equation 7.3). Given the forecasted EPS, the next task is to evaluate the variables that drive the P/E ratio. Most of that assessment is intuitive. For example, as we saw above, the investor would try to determine the stock's expected payout ratio, required rate of return (potential risk exposure), and rate of growth in earnings or dividends (perhaps by using something like Equation 7.10). The P/E ratio so obtained might then be adjusted a bit to account for the perceived state of the market and/or anticipated changes in the rate of inflation. Along with estimated EPS, we now have the P/E we need to compute (via Equation 7.12) the price at which the stock should be trading. By comparing that targeted price to the current market price of the stock, we can decide whether the stock is a good buy. For example, we would consider the stock undervalued and therefore a good buy if the computed price of the stock is more than its market price.

An alternative way of using this stock valuation approach is to isolate the stock's latest P_0/E_1 ratio and look at the expectations that are embedded in that ratio. For example, given an *estimated* EPS and the *current* market price of the stock, what kind of growth rate, payout ratio, and so on, are implied by the latest P_0/E_1 ratio? If, on the whole, these estimates seem reasonable, then the stock is probably being fairly valued in the market and should be considered a viable investment candidate.

CONCEPTS *in Review*

7.6   Briefly describe the *dividend valuation model* and the three different ways this model can be used. Explain how CAPM fits into the *variable-growth DVM*.

7.7   What is the difference between the variable-growth dividend valuation model and the dividends-and-earnings approach to stock valuation? Which of these two would you prefer? Explain.

7.8   How would you go about finding the expected return on a stock? Note how such information would be used in the stock selection process.

7.9   Briefly describe the *P/E approach* to stock valuation and note how this approach differs from the variable-growth DVM.

7.10   Explain how risk fits into the stock valuation process. Note especially its relationship to the investment return of a security.

TECHNICAL ANALYSIS

technical analysis
the study of the various forces at work in the marketplace and their effect on stock prices.

How many times have you turned on the TV or radio and in the course of the day's news heard a reporter say, "The market was up 17 points today" or "The market remained sluggish in a day of light trading"? Such comments reflect the importance of the stock market itself. And rightly so, for as we will see, the market is important because of the role it plays in determining the price behavior of common stocks. In fact, some experts believe the market is so important that studying it should be the major, if not the only, ingredient in the stock selection process. These experts argue that much of what is done in security analysis is useless because it is the *market* that matters and not individual companies. Others argue that studying the stock market is only one element in the security analysis process and is useful in helping the investor time decisions.

Analyzing the stock market is known as **technical analysis,** and it involves a study of the various forces at work in the marketplace itself. For some investors, it's another piece of information to use when deciding whether to buy, hold, or sell a stock; for others, it's the only input they use in their investment decisions; and for still others, technical analysis, like fundamental analysis, is regarded as just a waste of time. Here we will assume that technical analysis does have some role to play in the investment decision process. Accordingly, in the pages that follow, we will examine the major principles of market analysis, as well as some of the techniques used to assess market behavior.

PRINCIPLES OF MARKET ANALYSIS

Analyzing market behavior dates back to the 1800s, when there was no such thing as industry or company analysis. Detailed financial information simply was not made available to stockholders, let alone the general public. There were no industry figures, balance sheets, or income statements to study, no sales forecasts to make, and no earnings-per-share data or price/earnings multiples. About the only thing investors could study was the market itself. Some analysts used detailed charts in an attempt to monitor what large market operators were doing. These charts were intended to show when major buyers were moving into or out of particular stocks and to provide information that could be used to make profitable buy-and-sell decisions. The charts centered on stock price movements, because it was believed that these movements produced certain "formations" that indicated when the time was right to buy or sell a particular stock. The same principle is still applied today: Technical analysts argue that internal market factors, such as trading volume and price movements, often reveal the market's future direction long before the cause is evident in financial statistics.

If the behavior of stock prices were completely independent of market movements, market studies and technical analysis would be useless. But we have ample evidence that there is some connection: In fact, stock prices do tend to move with the market. Studies of stock betas have shown that, as a rule, anywhere from 20 to 50 percent of the price behavior of a stock can be traced to market forces. When the market is bullish, stock prices in general can be expected to behave accordingly. When the market turns bearish, most issues will feel the brunt to some extent.

Stock prices, in essence, react to various supply and demand forces that are at work in the market: After all, it's the *demand* for securities and the *supply* of funds in the market that determine whether we're in a bull or a bear market. So long as a given supply and demand relationship holds, the market will remain strong (or weak). When the balance begins to shift, however, future prices can be expected to change as the market itself changes. Thus, more than anything else, technical analysis is intended to monitor the pulse of the supply and demand forces in the market and to detect any shifts in this important relationship.

MEASURING THE MARKET

If assessing the market is a worthwhile endeavor, it follows that some sort of tool or measure is needed to do it. Charts are popular with many investors because they provide a visual summary of the behavior of the market and the price movements of individual stocks. As an alternative or supplement to *charting*, however, some investors prefer to study various market statistics, such as the volume of trading, the amount of short selling, and the buying and selling patterns of small investors (odd-lot transactions). This approach is based on the idea that by assessing some of the key elements of market behavior, investors can gain valuable insights about the general condition of the market and, perhaps, where it's headed over the next few months. Normally, several of these measures would be used together, either in an informal way or more formally as a series of complex ratios and measures, like 200-day moving averages or buy-sell ratios. Although there are many market measures—or *technical indicators,* as they are called—we will confine our discussion to the most closely followed technical indicators: (1) market volume, (2) breadth of the market, (3) short interest, (4) odd-lot trading, and (5) relative price levels. After we've discussed each of these, we'll take a look at charting.

Market Volume

Market volume is an obvious reflection of the amount of investor interest. Volume is a function of the supply of and demand for stocks and indicates underlying market strengths and weaknesses. The market is considered to be *strong* when volume goes up in a rising market or drops off during market declines. In contrast, it is considered *weak* when volume rises during a decline or drops off during rallies. For instance, the market would be considered strong if the Dow Jones Industrial Average went up by, say, 48 points while market volume was heavy. Investor eagerness to buy or sell is felt to be captured by market volume figures. The financial press regularly publishes volume data, so investors can conveniently watch this important technical indicator. An example of this and other vital market information is shown in Figure 7.1.

Breadth of the Market

Each trading day, some stocks go up in price and others go down; in market terminology, some stocks *advance* and others *decline*. The breadth-of-the-

Figure 7.1 Some Market Statistics
Individual investors can obtain all sorts of technical information, at little or no cost, from brokerage houses, investment services, and the popular financial media. Here, for example, is a sample of information from the *Wall Street Journal.* Note that a variety of information about market volume, new highs and lows, number of advancing and declining stocks, and market averages is available from just this one source. (Source: *Wall Street Journal,* January 24, 1995.)

STOCK MARKET DATA BANK 1/24/95

MAJOR INDEXES

HIGH	LOW (†365 DAY)		CLOSE	NET CHG	% CHG	†365 DAY CHG	% CHG	FROM 12/31	% CHG
DOW JONES AVERAGES									
3978.36	3593.35	30 Industrials	3862.70	− 4.71	− 0.12	− 32.64	− 0.84	+ 28.26	+ 0.74
1862.29	1371.89	20 Transportation	1517.91	− 10.24	− 0.67	− 290.73	− 16.07	+ 62.88	+ 4.32
226.01	173.94	15 Utilities	188.77	+ 0.59	+ 0.31	− 29.20	− 13.40	+ 7.25	+ 3.99
1447.06	1224.18	65 Composite	1303.39	− 3.06	− 0.23	− 107.77	− 7.64	+ 28.98	+ 2.27
456.27	416.31	Equity Mkt. Index	439.39	+ 0.20	+ 0.05	− 6.13	− 1.38	+ 6.32	+ 1.46
NEW YORK STOCK EXCHANGE									
267.71	243.14	Composite	253.70	+ 0.23	+ 0.09	− 7.43	− 2.85	+ 2.76	+ 1.10
327.93	298.30	Industrials	320.04	+ 0.06	+ 0.02	− 0.31	− 0.10	+ 1.94	+ 0.61
230.70	197.30	Utilities	202.42	+ 1.06	+ 0.53	− 19.53	− 8.80	+ 4.01	+ 2.02
285.03	212.94	Transportation	230.42	− 0.56	− 0.24	− 47.61	− 17.12	+ 7.96	+ 3.58
224.90	190.17	Finance	200.45	+ 0.27	+ 0.13	− 17.36	− 7.97	+ 4.65	+ 2.37
STANDARD & POOR'S INDEXES									
482.00	438.92	500 Index	465.86	+ 0.05	+ 0.01	− 5.06	− 1.07	+ 6.59	+ 1.43
184.79	162.44	400 MidCap	172.03	+ 1.19	+ 0.70	− 6.22	− 3.49	+ 2.59	+ 1.53
104.45	88.14	600 SmallCap	93.83	+ 0.51	+ 0.55	− 6.72	− 6.68	− 0.34	− 0.36
NASDAQ									
803.93	693.79	Composite	763.20	+ 3.69	+ 0.49	− 23.19	− 2.95	+ 11.24	+ 1.49
851.80	703.27	Industrials	758.46	+ 4.60	+ 0.61	− 66.18	− 8.03	+ 4.65	+ 0.62
960.18	858.96	Insurance	957.09	+ 7.65	+ 0.81	+ 39.55	+ 4.31	+ 31.22	+ 3.37
787.92	662.57	Banks	725.39	+ 2.20	+ 0.30	+ 31.85	+ 4.59	+ 28.32	+ 4.06
356.61	307.55	Nat. Mkt. Comp.	340.38	+ 1.69	+ 0.50	− 7.73	− 2.22	+ 5.14	+ 1.53
342.72	282.87	Nat. Mkt. Indus.	308.01	+ 1.97	+ 0.64	− 22.75	− 6.88	+ 1.97	+ 0.64
OTHERS									
487.89	420.23	Amex	437.40	+ 0.49	+ 0.11	− 43.19	− 8.99	+ 3.73	+ 0.86
258.31	235.50	Russell 1000	248.38	+ 0.30	+ 0.12	− 3.76	− 1.49	+ 3.74	+ 1.53
271.08	235.16	Russell 2000	248.94	+ 0.87	+ 0.35	− 13.11	− 5.00	− 1.42	− 0.57
278.44	254.01	Russell 3000	266.89	+ 0.38	+ 0.14	− 4.98	− 1.83	+ 3.45	+ 1.31
305.87	266.56	Value-Line(geom.)	279.20	+ 1.00	+ 0.36	− 19.26	− 6.45	+ 1.68	+ 0.61
4804.31	4373.58	Wilshire 5000	4602.44	+ 8.47	+ 0.18	− 89.03	− 1.90	+ 61.82	+ 1.36

†-Based on comparable trading day in preceding year.

MOST ACTIVE ISSUES

NYSE	VOLUME	CLOSE	CHANGE
PlgrmPrm rt	11,327,000	5/64	......
TelefMex	8,795,500	35	− ¾
Citicorp	7,116,700	40¼	+ ¼
FordMotor	6,511,000	x25¾	− ⅛
Wellcome	5,238,500	15¼	+ ⅛
SantaFePac	4,165,700	18	......
IBM	3,176,600	74	− ¼
RJR Nabisco	3,171,000	5⅞	......
CitzUtil A	3,127,900	13⅜	......
AT&T Cp	2,382,700	48⅝	+ ¼
Chrysler	2,273,500	46¾	− ⅝
PepsiCo	2,271,900	35	+ ¼
ChaseManh	2,231,400	33¼	− ¼
GrpTelevADR	2,211,000	22⅜	− ⅜
Merck	2,194,000	37¾	− ⅛
NASDAQ			
Intel	6,916,000	71½	+ 1⅛
Aldila	4,275,900	5	+ ⅛
MCI Comm	4,194,800	18	− ¼
DSC Comm	4,097,600	35½	− ½
CiscoSys	3,903,600	35⅞	+ 15/16
BayNtwrk	3,344,000	31¼	+ 1
Novell	2,703,600	18½	......
Microsoft	2,296,200	62 1/64	− 51/64
ImmunResp	2,286,300	6⅜	− ⅛
CyrixCp	2,151,300	26	......
AppleCptr	1,947,300	41⅝	− ⅝
SunMicrsys	1,871,500	33	+ 13/16
Qualcomm	1,844,900	27½	+ 2¼
AMEX			
Viacom rt	1,048,400	1 15/16	......
ViacomB	1,027,800	44⅜	+ ⅛
CheynSftwr	991,400	15⅞	+ ⅜
IvaxCp	861,200	22¼	+ ⅝
ViacomVar rt	626,200	13/16	− 1/16

DIARIES

NYSE	TUE	MON	WK AGO
Issues traded	2,937	2,917	2,955
Advances	1,265	826	1,303
Declines	936	1,399	948
Unchanged	736	692	704
New highs	29	20	53
New lows	41	81	28
zAdv vol (000)	146,919	132,958	171,299
zDecl vol (000)	103,660	146,617	119,208
zTotal vol (000)	325,162	325,812	330,898
Closing tick[1]	−32	+147	+655
Closing Arms[2] (trin)	.95	.65	.96
zBlock trades	6,885	7,315	7,762
NASDAQ			
Issues traded	5,119	5,115	5,112
Advances	1,809	1,222	1,794
Declines	1,485	2,049	1,476
Unchanged	1,825	1,844	1,842
New highs	74	45	119
New lows	81	94	77
Adv vol (000)	158,135	102,674	187,532
Decl vol (000)	100,420	141,686	117,744
Total vol (000)	298,330	276,417	337,328
Block trades	5,479	5,026	6,268
AMEX			
Issues traded	746	756	761
Advances	257	227	288
Declines	249	298	243
Unchanged	240	231	230
New highs	5	11	22
New lows	21	24	10
zAdv vol (000)	7,895	6,748	7,780
zDecl vol (000)	4,935	6,485	6,456
zTotal vol (000)	15,926	16,796	17,664
Comp vol (000)	19,537	20,546	21,225
zBlock trades	n.a.	312	297

← Arms Index

market indicator deals with these advances and declines. The idea behind it is actually quite simple: So long as the number of stocks that advance in price on a given day exceeds the number that decline, the market is considered strong. The extent of that strength depends on the spread between the number of advances and declines. For example, if the spread narrows so that the number of declines starts to approach the number of advances, market strength is said to be deteriorating. Similarly, the market is considered weak when the number of declines repeatedly exceeds the number of advances. The principle behind this indicator is that the number of advances and declines reflects the underlying sentiment of investors. When the mood is optimistic, for example, look for advances to outnumber declines. Again, information on advances and declines is published daily in the financial press.

A market measure that attempts to capture both the *number* of advancing and declining stocks and the *volume* of shares rising or falling is the *Arms index*, named after the person who created the measure. The index is computed by relating the ratio of the number of advancing and declining issues to the ratio of the volume of shares going up and down. Sounds confusing, doesn't it? Nonetheless, this index is widely quoted in the financial media—it's in Figure 7.1—and is supposed to indicate the amount of buying or selling pressure in the market. An Arms index of less than 1.00 signals buying pressure.

Short Interest

short interest
the number of stocks sold short in the market at any given time; a technical indicator believed to indicate future market demand.

When investors anticipate a market decline, they will sometimes sell a stock short—that is, they will sell borrowed stock. The number of stocks sold short in the market at any given point in time is known as the **short interest**. The more stocks that are sold short, the higher the short interest. Since all short sales must eventually be "covered" (the borrowed shares must be returned), a short sale in effect ensures future demand for the stock. Thus, the market is viewed optimistically when the level of short interest becomes relatively high by historical standards. The logic is that as shares are bought back to cover outstanding short sales, the additional demand will push prices up. The amount of short interest on the NYSE, AMEX, and Nasdaq's National Market is published monthly in the *Wall Street Journal* and *Barron's*. Figure 7.2 shows the type of information that's available.

Keeping track of the level of short interest can indicate future market demand, but it can also reveal *present* market optimism or pessimism. Short selling is usually done by knowledgeable investors, and a significant buildup or decline in the level of short interest is thought to reveal the sentiment of sophisticated investors about the current state of the market or a company. For example, a significant shift upward in short interest is believed to indicate pessimism concerning the *current* state of the market, even though it may signal optimism with regard to *future* levels of demand.

Odd-Lot Trading

A rather cynical saying on Wall Street suggests that the best thing to do is just the opposite of whatever the small investor is doing. The reasoning behind this is that as a group, small investors are notoriously wrong in their timing of investment decisions: The investing public usually does not come into the market in force until after a bull market has pretty much run its course, and it does not get out until late in a bear market. Although its validity is debatable,

Figure 7.2 Short Interest in the NYSE and AMEX
The amount of short selling being done in the market is closely watched by many investment professionals and individual investors. The summary report shown here provides an overview of the extent to which stocks are being shorted in the NYSE and the AMEX. In addition to summary statistics, this monthly report also lists all stocks that have been sold short and the number of shares shorted. (Source: *Wall Street Journal*, September 22, 1994.)

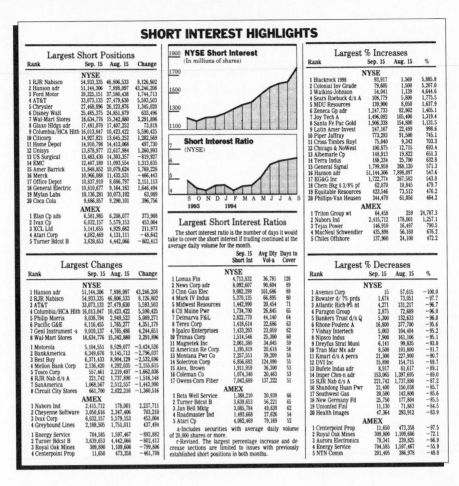

theory of contrary opinion
a technical indicator that uses the amount and type of odd-lot trading as an indicator of the current state of the market and pending changes.

this view is the premise behind a widely followed technical indicator and the basis for the **theory of contrary opinion**. This theory uses the amount and type of odd-lot trading as an indicator of the current state of the market and pending changes. Because many individual investors deal in transactions of less than 100 shares, the combined sentiments of this type of investor are supposedly captured in the odd-lot figures. The idea is to see what odd-lot investors are doing "on balance." So long as there is little or no difference in the spread between the volume of odd-lot purchases and sales, the theory of contrary opinion concludes that the market will probably continue pretty much along its current line (either up or down). But when the balance of odd-lot purchases and sales begins to change dramatically, it may be a signal that a bull or bear market is about to end. For example, if the amount of odd-lot purchases starts to exceed odd-lot sales by an ever widening margin, it may suggest that speculation on the part of small investors is starting to get out of control—an ominous signal that the final stages of a bull market may be at hand.

Relative Price Levels

While market volume, short-interest positions, and odd-lot trading are of interest to many investors, others are concerned more about market prices in general. To them, the question is not so much what's driving the market as how pricey the market is getting. Many professional traders track prices in the market by jointly monitoring three measures of overall market performance: (1) the *market P/E multiple,* (2) the *market's price-to-book-value ratio,* and (3) its *dividend yield.* In a sense, these measures provide yardsticks about *the relative value* of stocks and, as such, capture underlying price pressures in the market. For example, a large upward move in overall market prices will cause the market P/E and price-to-book ratios to move up and the dividend yield to move down. The idea is that if prices are going up, they should be doing so because of a healthy growth in corporate earnings, stockholders' equity, and dividends—not because of unbridled investor speculation.

Using these three measures, technical analysts have developed historical standards of performance that are felt to reflect normal market behavior. These standards are not designed to pinpoint market swings or indicate how deep or how long a bear (or bull) market will last. However, they do offer signals that historically have pointed out zones of extreme over- or undervaluation. That is, these relative price measures point out when the market is moving into danger zones (on the upside) or significant buying opportunities (on the downside). As a rule, it's felt that the market is starting to overheat and prices, in general, are getting too high when the market P/E (on the S&P 500) moves above 18 to 20 times earnings, the market's average price-to-book goes above 2 to 2.5, and the average dividend yield drops below 3 percent. On the other hand, it's felt that stocks have proved to be bargains when the market P/E drops to 10 or less, the price-to-book starts getting close to 1.0, and dividend yield rises above 6 percent. Keeping track of the market's P/E, price-to-book, and dividend yield is fairly easy, since this information is regularly reported in the *Wall Street Journal, Barron's,* and a number of other sources.

USING TECHNICAL ANALYSIS

Investors have a wide range of choices with respect to technical analysis. They can use the charts and complex ratios of the technical analysts, or they can, more informally, use technical analysis just to get a general sense of the market. In the latter case, it's not market behavior per se that is important so much as the implications such market behavior can have on the price performance of a particular common stock. Thus, technical analysis might be used in conjunction with fundamental analysis to determine the proper time to add a particular investment candidate to one's portfolio. Some investors and professional money managers, in fact, look at the technical side of a stock *before* doing any fundamental analysis. If the stock is found to be technically sound, then they'll spend the time to look at its fundamentals; if not, they'll look for another stock. For these investors, the concerns of technical analysis are still the same: *Do the technical factors indicate that this might be a good stock to buy?*

Most investors rely on published sources, such as those put out by brokerage firms, to obtain necessary technical insights, and they often find it helpful to use several different approaches. For example, an investor might follow market P/Es, dividend yields, and price-to-book values, and at the same time keep track of information on market volume and breadth of the market. All of this information, which is derived directly from and therefore describes the market itself, provides the individual investor with a convenient and low-cost way of staying abreast of the market. Certainly, trying to determine the right (or best) time to get into the market is a principal objective of technical analysis—and one of the major pastimes of many investors. But as the accompanying *Investor Insights* box (on page 306) suggests, over the long run, finding the right time to invest may not be as all-important as it's cracked up to be.

CHARTING

charting
the activity of charting price behavior and other market information and then using the patterns these charts form to make investment decisions.

Charting is perhaps the best-known activity of the technical analyst. Technicians—analysts who believe it is chiefly (or solely) supply and demand forces that establish stock prices—use various types of charts to plot the behavior of everything from the Dow Jones Industrial Average to the share price movements of individual listed and OTC stocks. Also, just about every kind of technical indicator is charted in one form or another. Figure 7.3 shows a typical stock chart; in this case, the price behavior of Liz Claiborne has been plotted,

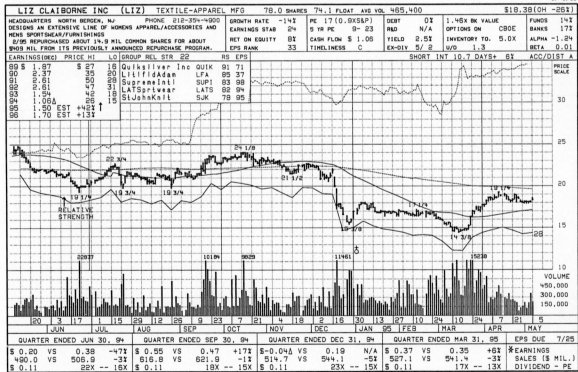

Figure 7.3   A Stock Chart
This chart for Liz Claiborne contains information about the daily price behavior of the stock, along with the stock's relative strength, its trading volume, and several other pieces of supplementary data. (Source: "A Stock Chart—Liz Claiborne." Courtesy of Daily Graphs. Graph reprinted with permission from Daily Graphs, Inc., 12655 Beatrice Street, Los Angeles, CA. 90066. Phone: 800-472-7479 or 310-448-6843)

INVESTOR INSIGHTS: *Conflicting Viewpoints*

A Nightmare on Wall Street: Buying at the Top?

It's every investor's dream: buying a stock at its low and riding it to the top of the bull market, then selling at its peak. Obviously, if it were easy, more people would make that dream come true. Many investors worry about whether it's the right time to buy. A falling market might drop more; a rising market may start to fall just after you buy.

Accurately predicting the market's ups and downs is no easy task, and even the experts don't always agree. Over the years, market timing has not proved itself as a successful investment strategy. Still, many tout its virtues and claim to have a system to spot market highs and lows, so you can sell when the market drops and buy when it's rising. Their results are not encouraging: Only 2 percent of market-timing newsletters beat the Wilshire 5000 for most of the 1980s. Also, moving in and out of the market several times a year runs up transaction costs.

Admittedly, it's hard to sit tight when the market starts to drop. Investors get scared and sell equities—often at a loss—in favor of money market funds, CDs, and savings accounts. By doing so, they risk being out of the market when stocks rise again. As painful as it is to go through a bear market, investors will be rewarded if they hold firm and stick to their investment plan. History shows that investing for the long term pays off: From 1926 to 1993, annualized returns on large-company stocks were 10.3 percent, even though the market dropped in 25 percent of those years.

No investor always times the market right. But what if you did? Several studies have tracked portfolios based on just that premise. Investment firm Piper Jaffray compared two hypothetical investors who in 1960 began investing $1,000 in the S&P 500 Index each year. One timed the market perfectly, buying on the lowest day each year, and by 1993 (34 years later) earned a 10.6 percent annualized return. Surprisingly, the hapless investor who bought at the annual high earned almost as much— 10.4 percent! In another study, an investor who put $5,000 into the S&P 500 index on the *peak day* in each year from 1974 to 1993 earned a compounded annual return of 13.7 percent, and the $100,000 total investment grew to $465,397. Because the odds of *always* buying at the worst possible time are nil, your own portfolio would have done even better.

In fact, *when you buy* really shouldn't matter all that much as long as you invest for the long term, rather than try to react to every blip in the market. Trying to outsmart the market rarely works. You're more likely to miss the bull market than avoid the bear. Market timing is one of the least important factors affecting portfolio performance, accounting for only 2 percent return. Learn to live with market corrections, and don't let emotions rule your investing strategy. As Hugh Johnson, chief investment officer of First Albany Corp., says, "It's time in the market, not timing the market, that's the key to success."

Sources: Stephen T. Goldberg, "Buying at the Top," *Kiplinger's Personal Finance Magazine,* July 1994, pp. 40–43; Jonathan D. Pond, "The Harsh Reality of Market Timing," *Worth,* July/August 1994, pp. 117–18; and Gerald Pettit, "Overcoming the Bear Market Blues," *Worth,* July/August, 1994, pp. 107–8.

---

along with a variety of supplementary information. Charts are popular because they provide a visual summary of activity over time and, perhaps more importantly, because (in the eyes of technicians, at least) they contain valuable information about developing trends and the future behavior of the market and/or individual stocks. Chartists believe price patterns evolve into *chart formations* that provide signals about the future course of the market or a stock. We will now briefly review the practice of charting, including popular types of charts, chart formations, and investor uses of charts.

Bar Charts

bar chart
the simplest kind of chart on which share price is plotted on the vertical axis and time on the horizontal axis; stock prices are recorded as vertical bars showing high, low, and closing prices.

The simplest and probably most widely used type of chart is the **bar chart**. Market or share prices are plotted on the vertical axis, and time is plotted on the horizontal axis. This type of chart derives its name from the fact that prices are recorded as vertical bars that depict high, low, and closing prices. A typical bar chart is illustrated in Figure 7.4. Note that on December 31, this particular stock had a high price of 29, a low of 27, and it closed at 27½. Because these charts contain a time element, technicians frequently plot a variety of other pertinent information on them. For example, volume is often put at the base of most bar charts (see the Liz Claiborne chart in Figure 7.3).

Point-and-Figure Charts

point-and-figure charts
charts used to keep track of emerging price patterns by plotting significant price changes with Xs and Os but with no time dimension used.

Point-and-figure charts are used strictly to keep track of emerging price patterns. Because there is no time dimension on them, they are *not* used for plotting technical measures. In addition to the time feature, point-and-figure charts are unique in two other ways: First, only *significant* price changes are recorded on these charts; that is, prices have to move by a certain minimum amount—usually at least a point or two—before a new price level is recognized. Second, price *reversals* show up only after a predetermined change in direction occurs. Normally, only closing prices are charted, though some point-and-figure charts use all price changes during the day. An *X* is used to denote an increase in price, and an *O* a decrease.

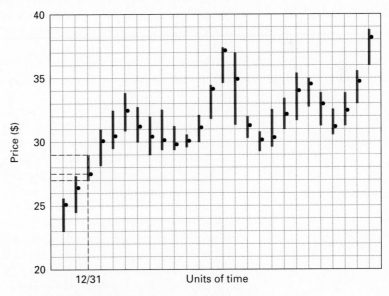

Key
← High price (for the day, week, month, or year).
← Closing price (for the day or other unit of time).
← Low price (for the day or other unit of time).

Figure 7.4   A Bar Chart
Bar charts are widely used to track stock prices, market averages, and numerous other technical measures.

Figure 7.5 A Point-and-Figure Chart
Point-and-figure charts are unusual because they have no time dimension. Rather, a column of *X*s is used to reflect a general upward drift in prices, and a column of *O*s is used when prices are drifting downward.

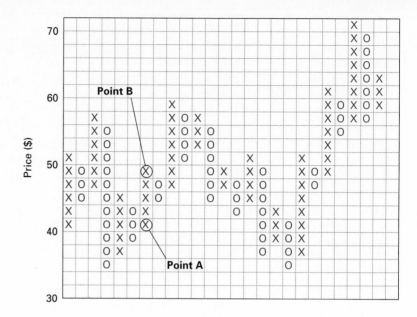

Figure 7.5 shows a common point-and-figure chart. In this case, the chart employs a 2-point box, which means that the stock must move by a minimum of 2 points before any changes are recorded. The chart could cover a span of one year or less, if the stock is highly active. Or it could cover a number of years, if the stock is not very active. As a rule, low-priced stocks will be charted with 1-point boxes, moderately priced shares will use increments of 2 to 3 points, and high-priced securities will appear on charts with 3- to 5-point boxes.

Here is how point-and-figure charts work: Suppose we are at point A on the chart in Figure 7.5, where the stock has been hovering around the $40–$41 mark for some time. Assume, now, that it just closed at 42. Because the minimum 2-point movement has been met, the chartist would place an X in the box immediately *above* point A. The chartist would remain with this new box as long as the price moved (up or down) within the 2-point range of 42 to 43⅞. Although the chartist follows *daily* prices, a new entry is made on the chart only after the price has changed by a certain minimum amount and moved into a new 2-point box. We see that from point A, the price generally moved up over time to nearly $50 a share. At that point (indicated as point B on the chart), things began to change as a reversal set in: That is, the price of the stock began to drift downward and in time moved out of the $48–$50 box. This reversal prompts the chartist to change columns and symbols, by moving one column to the right and recording the new price level with an O in the $46–$48 box. The chartist will continue to use Os as long as the stock continues to close on a generally lower note.

Chart Formations

The information that charts supposedly contain about the future course of the market (or a stock) is thought by some to be revealed in chart *formations*. That is, in response to certain supply and demand forces, chartists believe that emerging price patterns will result in various types of formations that historically have indicated that certain types of market behavior are imminent. If you know how to interpret charts (which, by the way, is no easy task), you can see formations building and recognize buy and sell signals. These formations are often given some pretty exotic names. For example, terms like *head and shoulders, falling wedge, scallop and saucer, ascending triangle,* and *island reversal* all describe chart formations.

Figure 7.6 shows four formations. The patterns form "support levels" and "resistance lines" that, when combined with the basic formations, yield buy and sell signals. Panel A is an example of a *buy* signal, which occurs when prices break out above a resistance line after a particular pattern has been formed. In contrast, when prices break out below a support level, as they do at the end of the formation in panel B, a *sell* signal is said to occur. Supposedly, a sell signal means everything is in place for a major drop in the market (or in the price of a share of stock), and a buy signal indicates that the opposite is about to occur. Unfortunately, one of the major problems with charting is that the formations rarely appear as neatly and cleanly as those in Figure 7.6. Rather, their identification and interpretation often require considerable imagination on the part of the chartist.

Investor Uses

Charts are nothing more than tools used by market analysts and technicians to assess conditions in the market and/or the price behavior of individual stocks. Unlike other types of technical measures, charting is seldom done on

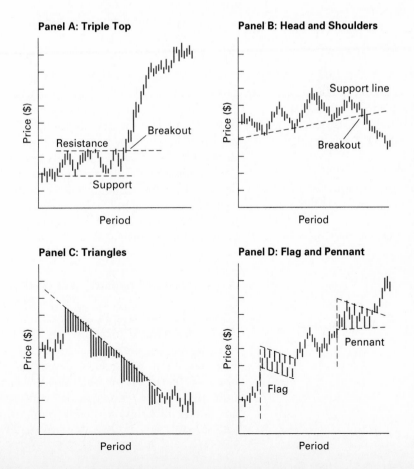

Figure 7.6 Some Popular Chart Formations
To chartists, each of these formations has meaning about the future course of events.

an informal basis. You either chart because you believe in its value, or you don't chart at all. A chart by itself tells you little more than where the market or a stock has been. But to a chartist, those price patterns yield formations that, along with things like resistance lines, support levels, and breakouts, tell what to expect in the future. Chartists believe that history repeats itself, so they study the historical reactions of stocks (or the market) to various formations and devise trading rules based on these observations. It makes no difference to chartists whether they are following the market or an individual stock, because *it is the formation that matters*, not the issue being plotted. The value of charts lies in knowing how to "read" them and how to respond to the signals they are said to give about the future. A long-standing debate (some would call it a feud) still rages on Wall Street regarding the merits of charting. Although it may be scoffed at by a large segment of investors and investment professionals, to avid chartists, charting is no laughing matter.

CONCEPTS *in Review*

7.11   What is the purpose of technical analysis? Explain how and why it is used by technicians; note how it can be helpful in timing investment decisions.

7.12   Can the market really have a measurable effect on the price behavior of individual securities? Explain.

7.13   What is a stock chart? What kind of information can be put on charts, and what is the purpose of charting?
   a.   What is the difference between a *bar chart* and a *point-and-figure chart*?
   b.   What are chart formations, and why are they important?

RANDOM WALKS AND EFFICIENT MARKETS

random walk hypothesis
the theory that stock price movements are unpredictable and there's thus little way of knowing where future prices are headed.

If a drunk were abandoned in an open field at night, where would you begin to search for him the next morning? The answer, of course, is the spot where the drunk was left the night before, since there's no way to predict where the drunk will go. To some analysts, stock prices seem to wander about in a similar fashion. Observations of such erratic movements have led to a body of evidence called the **random walk hypothesis**. Its followers believe that price movements are unpredictable and therefore security analysis will not help to predict future market behavior. This hypothesis obviously has serious implications for much of what we have discussed in the last two chapters.

A BRIEF HISTORICAL OVERVIEW

To describe stock prices as a random walk suggests that price movements cannot be expected to follow any type of pattern or, put another way, that price movements are independent of one another. In order to find a theory for such behavior, researchers developed the concept of efficient markets. Basically, the idea behind an efficient market is that the market price of securities always fully reflects available information and therefore it is difficult, if not impossible, to consistently outperform the market by picking "undervalued" stocks.

Random Walks

The first evidence of random price movements dates back to the early 1900s. During that period, statisticians noticed that commodity prices seemed to follow a "fair game" pattern: That is, prices seemed to move up and down randomly, giving no advantage to any particular trading strategy. Although a few studies on the subject appeared in the 1930s, thorough examination of the randomness in stock prices did not begin until 1959. From that point on, particularly through the decade of the 1960s, the random walk issue was one of the most keenly debated topics in stock market literature. The development of high-speed computers has helped researchers compile convincing evidence that stock prices do, in fact, come very close to a random walk.

Efficient Markets

Given the extensive random walk evidence, market researchers were faced with another question: What sort of market would produce prices that seem to fluctuate randomly? Such behavior could be the result of investors who are irrational and make investment decisions on whim. However, it has been argued much more convincingly that investors are not irrational; rather, random price movements are evidence of highly efficient markets.

efficient market
a market in which securities reflect all possible information quickly and accurately.

An **efficient market** is one in which securities fully reflect all possible information quickly and accurately. The concept states that investors will incorporate all available information into their decisions on the price at which they are willing to buy or sell. At any point in time, then, the current price of a security incorporates all information. Additionally, the current price not only reflects past information, such as might be found in company reports, financial newspapers, and magazine articles, but also includes information about events that have been announced but haven't occurred yet, like a forthcoming dividend payment. Furthermore, the current price also reflects *predictions* about future information: Investors, in their zeal to beat the competition, actively forecast important events and incorporate those forecasts into their estimate of the correct price. Obviously, because of the keen competition among investors, when new information becomes known, the price of the security adjusts quickly. This adjustment is not always perfect. Sometimes it is too large and at other times too small, but on average it balances out and is correct. The new price, in effect, is set after investors have fully assessed the new information.

WHY SHOULD MARKETS BE EFFICIENT?

Active markets, such as the New York Stock Exchange, are efficient—they are made up of many rational, highly competitive investors who react quickly and objectively to new information. Investors, searching for stock market profits, compete vigorously for new information and do extremely thorough analyses. The **efficient markets hypothesis (EMH)**, which is the basic theory describing the behavior of such a market, specifically states:

efficient markets hypothesis (EMH)
basic theory of the behavior of efficient markets, in which there are a large number of knowledgeable investors, information is widely available to all investors, and they react quickly to new information, causing securities prices to adjust quickly and accurately.

1. Many knowledgeable investors are actively analyzing, valuing, and trading any particular security. No one of these individual traders alone can affect the price of any security.

2. Information is widely available to all investors at approximately the same time, and this information is practically "free."
3. Information on events, such as labor strikes, industrial accidents, and changes in product demand, tends to occur randomly.
4. Investors react quickly and accurately to new information, causing prices to adjust quickly, and on average, accurately.

For the most part, the securities markets do, in fact, exhibit these characteristics.

LEVELS OF MARKET EFFICIENCY

The EMH is concerned with information—not only the type and source of information but also the quality and speed with which it is disseminated among investors. In considering the EMH, it is convenient to discuss three cumulative categories of information: past prices only, past prices *plus* all other public data, and, finally, past prices and public data *plus* private information. Together, these three types of information flows in the market represent three forms of the EMH: the weak, semi-strong, and strong forms.

Weak Form

weak form (EMH)
form of the EMH holding that past data on stock prices are of no use in predicting future prices.

The **weak form of the EMH** holds that past data on stock prices are of no use in predicting future price changes. If prices follow a random walk, price changes over time are random. Today's price change is unrelated to yesterday's, or that of any other day. If new information arrives randomly, then prices will change randomly. Each step by a drunkard is unrelated to previous steps.

A number of people have asserted that it is possible to profit from "runs" in a stock's price. They contend that when a stock's price starts moving up, it will continue to move up for a period of time, developing a momentum. If you can spot a run, then you can develop a trading strategy that will produce a profit, based on past prices alone. The results from much careful research suggest that, indeed, momentum in stock prices does exist, and if investors quickly trade at the beginning of the run, large profits can be made. But there's a problem: In addition to spotting a run right off the bat (no easy task), an investor would have to make numerous trades, and when commissions are factored in, the only person that makes a profit is the broker. Many other trading rules have been tested to determine if profits can be made by examining past stock price movements, and there is very little, if any, evidence that a trading rule *based solely on past price data* can outperform a simple buy-and-hold strategy.

Semi-Strong Form

semi-strong form (EMH)
form of the EMH holding that abnormally large profits cannot be consistently earned using publicly available information.

The **semi-strong form of the EMH** holds that abnormally large profits cannot be consistently earned using publicly available information. This information includes not only past price and volume data but also data such as corporate earnings, dividends, inflation, and stock splits. The semi-strong information set includes all of the information publicly considered in the weak form, *as well as all other information publicly available*. Tests of the semi-strong form of the EMH are basically concerned with the speed at which information is disseminated to investors. The overall conclusions of research tests support the position that stock prices adjust very rapidly to new information and therefore support the semi-strong form of the EMH—but there are still some unanswered questions.

Most tests of semi-strong efficiency have examined how a stock price changes in response to an economic or financial event. A famous early study involved stock splits. A stock split does not change the value of a company, and so the value of the stock should not be affected by a stock split. Although the research indicated that there are sharp increases in the price of a stock *before* a stock split, the changes after the split are random. Investors cannot gain by purchasing stocks on or after the announcement of a split; they would have to purchase before the split to earn abnormal profits. By the time the stock split is announced, the market has already incorporated any favorable information associated with the split into the price.

Other studies have examined the impact of major events on stock prices. The overwhelming evidence indicates that stock prices react within minutes, if not seconds, to any important new information. Certainly, by the time an investor reads about the event in the newspaper, the stock price has almost completely adjusted to the news. Even hearing about the event on radio or television usually allows too little time to react and complete the transaction to make an abnormal profit.

Strong Form

strong form (EMH)
form of the EMH that holds that there is no information, public or private, that allows investors to consistently earn abnormal profits.

The **strong form of the EMH** holds that there is no information, public or private, that allows investors to consistently earn abnormal profits. It states that stock prices immediately adjust to any information, even if it isn't available to every investor. This extreme form of the EMH has not received universal support.

One type of private information is the kind obtained by corporate insiders, such as officers, directors, or other privileged individuals within a corporation. They have access to valuable information about major strategic and tactical decisions that are planned by the company. They also have detailed information about the financial state of the firm that may not be available to other shareholders. Corporate insiders may legally trade shares of stock in their own company, if they report the transactions to the Securities and Exchange Commission (SEC) each month. This information is then made public, usually within several weeks. It should not be surprising to learn that most studies of corporate insiders find that they consistently earn abnormally large profits when they sell their company stock. They are able to sell their stock holdings before major announcements are made to the public and can thereby profit from the stock price adjustment that comes quickly after important news is released.

Other market participants occasionally have inside—nonpublic—information they obtained *illegally*. With this information, they can gain an unfair advantage that permits them to earn an excess return. Clearly, those who trade securities based on illegal inside information have an unfair and illegal advantage. Empirical research has confirmed that those with such inside information do indeed have an opportunity to earn an excess return.

POSSIBLE IMPLICATIONS

The concept of an efficient market holds serious implications for investors. In particular, it could have considerable bearing on traditional security analysis and stock valuation procedures and on the way stocks are selected for investment. In fact, some people contend that investors should spend less time trying to beat the market by analyzing securities and more time on such matters as reducing taxes and transaction costs, eliminating unnecessary risk, and constructing a widely diversified portfolio that is compatible with the investor's risk temperament. Make no mistake about it, though: *Even in an efficient market, all sorts of return opportunities are available.* To proponents of efficient markets, however, the only way to increase returns is to invest in a portfolio of higher-risk securities.

Implications for Technical Analysis

The most serious challenge the random walk evidence presents is to technical analysis. If price fluctuations are purely random, charts of past prices are unlikely to produce significant trading profits. In a highly efficient market, shifts in supply and demand occur so rapidly that technical indicators simply measure after-the-fact events, with no implications for the future. If markets are less than perfectly efficient, however, information may be absorbed slowly, producing gradual shifts in supply and demand conditions—and profit opportunities for those who recognize the shifts early. Although the great bulk of evidence supports a random walk, many investors follow a technical approach because they believe it improves their investment results.

Implications for Fundamental Analysis

Many strict fundamental analysts were at first pleased by the random walk attack on technical analysis. Further development of the efficient markets concept, however, was not so well received: In an efficient market, it's argued, prices react so quickly to new information that not even security analysis will enable investors to realize consistently superior returns on their investments. Because of the extreme competition among investors, security prices are seldom far above or below their justified levels, and fundamental analysis thus loses much of its value. The problem is not that fundamental analysis is poorly done; on the contrary, it is done all too well! As a result, so many investors, competing so vigorously for profit opportunities, simply eliminate the opportunities before other investors can capitalize upon them.

SO WHO IS RIGHT?

Some type of fundamental analysis probably has a role in the stock selection process. Even in an efficient market, there is no question that stock prices reflect a company's profit performance. Some companies are fundamentally strong and others fundamentally weak, and investors must be able to distinguish between the two. Thus, it can be a profitable activity to evaluate a company and its stock to determine not whether it is undervalued but whether it is fundamentally strong.

The level of investor return, however, is more than a function of the fundamental condition of the company; the level of risk exposure is also important. We saw earlier that fundamental analysis can help assess potential risk exposure and identify securities that possess risk commensurate with the return they offer. The extent to which the markets are efficient is still subject to considerable debate. At present, there seems to be a growing consensus that though the markets may not be *perfectly* efficient, evidence suggests that they are, at the least, *reasonably* efficient.

In the final analysis, it is the individual investor who must decide on the merits of fundamental and technical analysis. Certainly, a large segment of the investing public believes in security analysis, even in a market that may be efficient. What is more, the principles of stock valuation—that promised return should be commensurate with exposure to risk—are valid in any type of market setting.

CONCEPTS *in Review*

7.14 What is the *random walk hypothesis,* and how does it apply to stocks? What is an *efficient market?* How can a market be efficient if its prices behave in a random fashion?

7.15 Explain why it is difficult, if not impossible, to consistently outperform an efficient market.

    a. Does that mean that high rates of return are not available in the stock market?

    b. How can an investor earn a high rate of return in an efficient market?

7.16 What are the implications of random walks and efficient markets for technical analysis? For fundamental analysis? Do random walks and efficient markets mean that technical analysis and fundamental analysis are useless? Explain.

On Track with STOCK-TRAK®

Transaction Costs Assessed by STOCK-TRAK®

STOCK-TRAK®'s transaction cost schedule highlights the importance of considering these expenses when you evaluate possible gains in fundamental and technical analysis. STOCK-TRAK®'s brokerage commission, charged on all transactions, parallels that charged by a discount broker.

The commission is calculated as $50 plus $5 per 100 shares. Buying 100 shares would entail a commission of $55 [$50 + ($5 × 1)], and 1,000 shares would result in a commission of $100 [$50 + ($5 × 10)]. Stated another way, the more shares you buy, the smaller the transaction cost will be on a per share basis.

For example, if you buy 100 shares of XYZ Corporation at $20, the commission is $55 and the total cost is $2,055. Let's assume the stock goes up $1, to $21, and you decide to sell. In that case, the commission is $55 and your proceeds will be $2,045—for a loss of $10. Compare that to purchasing 1,000 shares of XYZ Corporation at $2,000: The total cost is $20,100. When you sell at $21 per share, the commission is $100, your proceeds will be $29,900, and you gain $800!

SUMMARY

 Explain the role a company's future plays in the stock valuation process and develop a forecast of a stock's expected cash flow, including future dividends and anticipated price behavior. The final phase of security analysis involves an assessment of the investment merits of a specific company and its stock. The focus here is on formulating expectations about the company's future prospects and the potential risk and return behavior of the stock. In stock valuation, it's not the past but the future that's important. In particular, as potential investors, we would like to get some idea of what the stock's future earnings, dividends, and share prices look like, because that's ultimately the basis of our return.

LG 2 **Discuss the concepts of intrinsic value and required rates of return and note how they are used as standards of performance in judging investment suitability.** Information such as projected sales, forecasted earnings, and estimated dividends are important in establishing the intrinsic value of a stock—which is a measure of what the stock ought to be worth, based on expected return performance and risk exposure. A key element is the investor's required rate of return, which is used to define the amount of return that should be earned on the investment given the stock's perceived exposure to risk. The more risk in the investment, the more return one should require. Under these conditions, a stock would be viewed as a worthwhile investment candidate if it offered a rate of return that equaled or exceeded the required rate of return—or if its computed intrinsic value equaled or exceeded the prevailing market price of the stock.

LG 3 **Determine the underlying value of a stock using the dividend valuation model, as well as other present-value-based stock valuation models that account for both expected return and potential risk.** A number of stock valuation procedures are in use today, including the dividend valuation model, which derives the value of a share of stock from the stock's future growth in dividends and the appropriate market capitalization rate. Another popular valuation procedure is the dividends-and-earnings approach, which is similar to the variable-growth DVM but uses a finite investment horizon to derive a present-value-based "justified price." Sometimes investors find it more convenient to deal in terms of expected returns than in dollar-based justified prices; that's no problem, since it's easy to find the fully compounded rate of return by adopting the approximate yield (or holding period return) to the stock valuation process.

LG 4 **Understand the central role that the price/earnings ratio plays in defining a stock's price behavior and how the P/E multiple can be used in the stock valuation process.** The price/earnings (P/E) multiple is one of the most important determinants of stock performance. It has a direct bearing on the price behavior of a share of stock: Other things being equal, as the P/E ratio moves up (or down), so will the price of the stock. It's a key variable in determining the amount of capital gains a stock is capable of producing and, as a result, has a substantial impact on defining a stock's return potential. Because it is so important, the P/E multiple plays a critical role in several stock valuation models (such as the dividends-and-earnings approach and the expected return model). In fact, it's the centerpiece of the so-called P/E approach, which uses a stock's price/earnings ratio, per se, to determine whether the stock is fairly valued.

LG 5 **Describe the key attributes of technical analysis, including some popular measures and procedures used to assess the market, and the role technical analysis plays in selecting stocks.** Technical analysis is another phase of the analytical process; it deals with the behavior of the stock market itself and the various economic forces at work in the marketplace. Some investors use technical analysis as their principle valuation tool; others use technical analysis, along with fundamental analysis, primarily as a way to help them time their investment decisions. A number of tools can be used to assess the state of the market, including market measures like volume of trading, breadth of the market, short-interest positions, odd-lot trading, and relative price levels. In contrast, other investors like to use charting to assess the condition of everything from the overall market to specific stocks.

 Discuss the idea of random walks and efficient markets and note the challenges these theories hold for the stock valuation process. In recent years, the whole notion of both technical and fundamental analysis has been seriously challenged by the random walk and efficient market hypotheses. Indeed, considerable evidence indicates that stock prices do move in a random fashion. The efficient market hypothesis is an attempt to explain *why* prices behave randomly. The idea behind an efficient market is that available information about the company and/or its stock is always fully reflected in the price of securities, and therefore investors should *not* expect to consistently outperform the market. Although few investors believe the market is *perfectly* efficient, a good deal of evidence suggests that it is, at the very least, *reasonably* efficient.

DISCUSSION QUESTIONS

1. Using the resources available at your campus or public library, select a company from *Value Line* that would be of interest to you. (*Hint*: Pick a company that's been publicly traded for at least 10 to 15 years, and avoid public utilities, banks, and other financial institutions.) Obtain a copy of the latest *Value Line* report on your chosen company. Using the historical and forecasted data reported in *Value Line*, along with one of the valuation techniques described in this chapter, calculate the maximum (i.e., justified) price you'd be willing to pay for this stock. (*Note*: You might want to use the *IMD Disk* to perform these calculations.) Use the CAPM to find the required rate of return on your stock. (For the purposes of this problem, use a market rate of return of, say, 12 percent, and for the risk-free rate, use the latest 3-month Treasury bill rate.)

   a. How does the justified price you computed above compare to the latest market price of the stock?

   b. Would you consider the stock you've valued to be a worthwhile investment candidate? Explain.

2. Briefly define each of the following, and note the conditions that would suggest the market is technically strong:

   a. Breadth of the market

   b. Short interest

   c. The market's price-to-book ratio

   d. Theory of contrary opinion

   e. Head and shoulders

3. A lot has been written and said about the concept of an *efficient market*. Although you may or may not believe the markets are efficient, it's probably safe to say that there are some of your classmates who believe the markets may be efficient and others who believe they are not. So, let's have a debate to see if we can resolve this issue (at least among ourselves). Pick a side, either for or against efficient markets, and then develop your "ammunition." Be prepared to discuss these three aspects:

   a. Exactly what is an efficient market, and do such markets really exist?

   b. Are stock prices always (or nearly always) correctly set in the market? If so, does that mean there's little opportunity to find undervalued stocks?

   c. Can you find any reason(s) to use fundamental and/or technical analysis in your stock selection process? If not, how would you go about selecting stocks?

PROBLEMS

1. An investor estimates that next year's sales for Gilt Edge Products should amount to about $75 million. The company has 2.5 million shares outstanding, generates a net profit margin of about 5 percent, and has a payout ratio of 50 percent. All figures are expected to hold for next year. Given this information, compute:

   a. Estimated net earnings for next year
   b. Next year's dividends per share
   c. The expected price of the stock (assuming the P/E ratio is 12.5 times earnings)
   d. The expected holding period return (latest stock price: $15/share)

2. Charlene Lewis is thinking about buying some shares of Education, Inc., at $50 per share. She expects the price of the stock to rise to $75 over the next 3 years, during which time she also expects to receive annual dividends of $5 per share.

   a. What is the intrinsic worth of this stock, given a 10 percent required rate of return?
   b. What is its approximate expected return?

3. Amalgamated Something-or-Other, Inc., is expected to pay a dividend of $1.50 in the coming year. The required rate of return is 16 percent, and dividends are expected to grow at 7 percent per year. Using the dividend valuation model, find the intrinsic value of the company's common shares.

4. Assume you've generated the following information about the stock of Bufford's Burger Barns: The company's latest dividends of $4 a share are expected to grow to $4.32 next year, to $4.67 the year after that, and to $5.04 in year 3. In addition, the price of the stock is expected to rise to $77.75 in 3 years.

   a. Use the dividends-and-earnings model and a required rate of return of 15 percent to find the value of the stock.
   b. Use the approximate yield formula to find the stock's expected return; now use the IRR procedure to find expected return.
   c. Given that dividends are expected to grow indefinitely at 8 percent, use a 15 percent required rate of return and the dividend valuation model to find the value of the stock.
   d. Assume dividends in year 3 actually amount to $5.04, the dividend growth rate stays at 8 percent, and the required rate of return stays at 15 percent. Use the dividend valuation model to find the price of the stock at the end of year 3. [*Hint*: In this case, the value of the stock will depend on 4, which equals $D_3 \times (1 + g)$.] Do you note any similarity between your answer here and the forecasted price of the stock ($77.75) given in the problem? Explain.

5. Let's assume that you're thinking about buying some stock in U.S. Electronics. So far in your analysis, you've uncovered the following information: The stock pays annual dividends of $2.50 a share (and that's not expected to change within the next few years—*nor are any of the other variables*); it trades at a P/E of 12 times earnings and has a beta of 1.15; in addition, you plan on using a risk-free rate of 7 percent in the CAPM, along with a market return of 14 percent. You would like to hold the stock for 3 years, at the end of which time you think EPS will peak out at about $7 a share. Given the stock presently trades at $55, use the approximate yield formula to find this security's expected return. Now use the present-value (dividends-and-earnings) model to put a price on this stock. Does this look like a good investment? Explain.

6. The price of Consolidated Everything is now $75, and the company pays no dividends. Ms. Bossard expects the price 3 years from now to be $100 per share. Should Ms. B. buy Consolidated E. if she desires a 10 percent rate of return? Explain.

 7. This year, Southwest Light and Gas (SWL&G) paid its stockholders an annual dividend of $3 a share. A major brokerage firm recently put out a report on SWL&G stating that, in its opinion, the company's annual dividends should grow at the rate of 10 percent per year for each of the next 5 years and then level off and grow at the rate of 6 percent a year thereafter.

    a. Use the variable-growth DVM and a required rate of return of 12 percent to find the maximum price you should be willing to pay for this stock.

    b. Redo the SWL&G problem in (a), except this time, assume that after year 5, dividends stop growing altogether (i.e., for year 6 and beyond, $g = 0$). Use all other information as given above to find the stock's intrinsic value.

    c. Contrast your two answers and comment on your findings. How important is growth to this valuation model?

 8. Assume there are three companies that in the past year paid exactly the same annual dividend of $2.25 a share. In addition, the future annual rate of growth in dividends for each of the three companies has been estimated as follows:

Buggies-Are-Us	Steady Freddie, Inc.	Gang Buster Group	
$g = 0\%$	$g = 6\%$	Year 1	$2.53
(i.e., dividends	(for the	2	$2.85
are expected	foreseeable	3	$3.20
to remain at	future)	4	$3.60
$2.25/share)		Year 5 and beyond: $g = 6\%$	

Assume also that due to a strange set of circumstances, these three companies all have the same required rate of return ($k = 10\%$).

    a. Use the appropriate DVM to value each of these companies.

    b. Comment briefly on the comparative values of these three companies. What's the major cause of the differences in these three valuations?

 9. Drabble Company's stock sells at a P/E ratio of 14 times earnings; it is expected to pay dividends of $2 per share in each of the next 5 years and generate an EPS of $5 per share in year 5. Using the dividends-and-earnings model and a 12 percent discount rate, compute the stock's justified price.

 10. A particular company currently has sales of $250 million; these are expected to grow by 20 percent next year (year 1). For the year after next (year 2), the growth rate in sales is expected to equal 10 percent. Over each of the next 2 years, the company is expected to have a net profit margin of 8 percent and a payout ratio of 50 percent and to maintain the number of shares of common stock outstanding at 15 million shares. The stock always trades at a P/E ratio of 15 times earnings, and the investor has a required rate of return of 20 percent. Given this information:

    a. Find the stock's intrinsic value (its justified price).

    b. Determine its expected return, given that the stock is currently trading at $15 per share. (*Note*: Use the IRR procedure to find expected return.)

    c. Find the holding period returns for year 1 and for year 2.

11. Assume a major investment service has just given Oasis Electronics its highest investment rating, along with a strong buy recommendation. So you decide to take a closer look for yourself and to place a value on the company's stock. Here's what you find: This year, Oasis paid its stockholders an annual dividend of $3 a share, but because of its high rate of growth in earnings, its dividends are expected to grow at the rate of 12 percent a year for the next 4 years and then level out at 9 percent a year thereafter. So far, you've learned that the stock has a beta of 1.80, the risk-free rate of return is 6 percent, and the expected return on the market is 11 percent. Using the CAPM to find the required rate of return, put a value on this stock.

12. Consolidated Software presently doesn't pay any dividends but is expected to start paying dividends in 4 years. That is, Consolidated will go 3 more years without paying any dividends, then it's expected to pay its first dividend (of $3 per share) in the fourth year. Once the company starts paying dividends, it's expected to continue to do so. The company is expected to have a dividend payout ratio of 40 percent and to maintain a return on equity of 20 percent. Given a required rate of return of 15 percent, what is the maximum price you should be willing to pay for this stock today?

13. Assume you obtain the following information about a certain company:

Total assets	$50,000,000
Total equity	$25,000,000
Net income	$ 3,750,000
EPS	$5.00 per share
Dividend payout ratio	40 percent
Required return	12 percent

Use the constant-growth DVM to place a value on this company's stock.

14. You're thinking about buying some stock in Astro Corporation and want to use the P/E approach to value the shares. So far, you've estimated that next year's earnings should come in at about $4.00 a share and that the company should pay dividends of $2.40 a share next year. The company has been experiencing growth in earnings (and dividends) of about 6 percent per year, and this is expected to hold for the foreseeable future.

    a. Given that you feel a 12 percent required rate of return is appropriate for this stock, what's the maximum price you should be willing to pay for this stock?

    b. Given the information supplied above, if this stock is currently trading at $48 a share, what is its P_0/E_1 ratio? Given a 12 percent required rate of return and a 60 percent payout ratio, what growth rate is embedded in this P_0/E_1 ratio? Do you think it's reasonable, given the past growth rates noted in the problem? Explain.

15. AviBank Plastics has an ROE of 16 percent, its book value per share *next year* is expected to rise to $20 per share, it has a dividend payout ratio of 40 percent (which is expected to hold in the future), and the stock has a 12 percent required rate of return. Use the P/E approach to set a value on this stock.

CASE PROBLEMS   **7.1 CHRIS LOOKS FOR A WAY TO INVEST HIS NEWFOUND WEALTH**

Chris Norton is a young Hollywood writer who is well on his way to television super-stardom. After writing several successful television specials, he was recently named the head writer for the top rated TV sitcom *Sad About You*. Chris fully realizes that his business is a fickle one and, on the advice of his dad and manager, has decided to set up an investment program. Chris will earn about a half-million dollars this year. Because of his age, income level, and desire to get as big a bang as possible from his investment dollars, he has decided to invest in speculative, high-growth stocks.

Chris is presently working with a respected Beverly Hills broker and is in the process of building up a diversified portfolio of speculative stocks. The broker recently sent him information on a hot new issue. She suggested Chris study the numbers and, if he likes them, buy as many as 1,000 shares of the stock. In particular, the broker forecasts corporate sales for the next 3 years at:

Year	Sales (in millions)
1	$22.5
2	35.0
3	50.0

The firm has 1.2 million shares of common stock outstanding (they are currently being traded at 62½ and pay no dividends). It has been running a phenomenal net profit rate of 20 percent, and its stock has been trading at a P/E ratio of around 25 times earnings (which is a bit on the high side). All these operating characteristics are expected to hold in the future.

Questions

1. Looking first at the stock:

    a. Compute the company's net profits and EPS for each of the next 3 years.

    b. Compute the price of the stock 3 years from now.

    c. Assuming all expectations hold up and that Chris buys the stock at 62½, determine the expected return on this investment.

    d. What risks is he facing by buying this stock? Be specific.

    e. Should he consider the stock to be a worthwhile investment candidate? Explain.

2. Now, looking at his investment program in general:

    a. What do you think of his investment program? What do you see as its strengths and weaknesses?

    b. Are there any suggestions you would make?

    c. Do you think Chris should consider adding foreign stocks to his portfolio? Explain.

LG 3   LG 5   **7.2 AN ANALYSIS OF A HIGH-FLYING STOCK**

Glenn Wilt is a recent university graduate and a security analyst with the Kansas City brokerage firm of Lippman, Brickbats, and Shaft. Wilt has been following one of the hottest issues on Wall Street, C&I Construction Supplies, a company that has turned in an outstanding performance lately and, even more importantly, has exhibited excellent growth potential. It has 5 million shares outstanding and pays a nominal annual dividend of 25 cents per share. Wilt has decided to take a closer look at C&I to see whether or not it still has any investment play left. Assume the company's sales for the past 5 years have been:

Year	Sales (in millions)
1991	$10.0
1992	12.5
1993	16.2
1994	22.0
1995	28.5

Wilt is concerned with the future prospects of the company, not its past. As a result, he pores over the numbers laboriously and generates the following estimates of future performance:

Expected net profit margin	12%
Estimated annual dividends per share	25¢
Number of common shares outstanding	No change
P/E ratio at the end of 1996	35
P/E ratio at the end of 1997	50

Questions

1. Determine the average annual rate of growth in sales over the past 5 years.
   a. Use this average growth rate to forecast revenues for next year (1996) and the year after that (1997).
   b. Now determine the company's net earnings and EPS for each of the next 2 years (1996 and 1997).
   c. Finally, determine the expected future price of the stock at the end of this 2-year period.

2. Because of several intrinsic and market factors, Wilt feels that 20 percent is a viable figure to use for a desired rate of return.
   a. Using the 20 percent rate of return and the forecasted figures you came up with above, compute the stock's justified price.
   b. If C&I is presently trading at $25 per share, should Wilt consider the stock a worthwhile investment candidate? Explain.

3. The stock is actively traded on the AMEX and enjoys considerable market interest. Recent closing prices are listed below.
   a. Prepare a point-and-figure chart of these prices (use a 1-point system—i.e., make each box worth $1).

b. Discuss how these and similar charts are used by technical analysts.
c. Cite several other types of technical measures, and note how they might be used in the analysis of this stock.

Recent Price Behavior: C&I Construction Supplies

14 (8/15/95)	18½	20	17½
14¼	17½	20¼	18½
14⅞	17½	20¼	19¾
15½	17¼	20⅛	19½
16	17	20	19¼
16	16¾	20¼	20
16½	16½	20½	20⅞
17	16½	20¾	21
17¼	16⅛	20½	21¾
17½	16¾	20	22½
18	17⅛	20¼	23¼
18 (9/30/95)	17¼	20	24
18½	17¼	19½	24¼
18½	17¼ (10/31/95)	19¼	24⅛
18¾	17¾	18¼ (11/30/95)	24¾
19	18¼	17½	25
19⅛	19¼	16¾	25½
18⅞	20½	17	25½ (12/31/95)

PART THREE

INVESTING IN FIXED-INCOME SECURITIES

CHAPTER 8
BOND INVESTMENTS

CHAPTER 9
BOND VALUATION AND ANALYSIS

CHAPTER 10
PREFERRED STOCK AND CONVERTIBLE SECURITIES

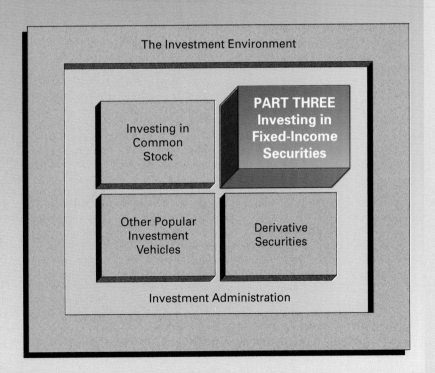

The Investment Environment

Investing in Common Stock

PART THREE
Investing in Fixed-Income Securities

Other Popular Investment Vehicles

Derivative Securities

Investment Administration

CHAPTER 8

BOND INVESTMENTS

LEARNING GOALS

After studying this chapter, you should be able to:

LG 1 Explain the basic investment attributes of bonds and discuss the appeal these securities hold as investment vehicles.

LG 2 Describe the essential features of a bond and be able to distinguish between different types of call, refunding, and sinking fund provisions.

LG 3 Describe the relationship between bond prices and market interest rates and, in general, explain why some bonds are more volatile than others.

LG 4 Identify the different types of bonds and the kinds of investment objectives these fixed-income securities can fulfill.

LG 5 Gain an appreciation of how the bond market is becoming more global in nature and discuss the difference between dollar-denominated and non-dollar-denominated foreign bonds.

LG 6 Describe the role bond ratings play in the market and the quotation system that's used with various types of bonds.

Investing comes naturally to Renée Barnow, who was raised in a household where investing was highly valued and the *Wall Street Journal* was considered the only newspaper worth reading. Her first stock was a gift received when she was 12 years old, and she began investing on her own when she graduated from college and married. At first, her investment goals were undefined. She liked playing the investment game—and did so in an undisciplined and eclectic way. "In those days," she recounts, "I invested money based on friends' hot tips—stocks, speculative ventures—without fully understanding the risks or doing enough investigation of my own. As a result, I lost money."

Renée's subsequent investment behavior has been shaped in part by two factors: a divorce and not having children. Although this independence has given her more freedom to take investment risks, it has also made her aware that she alone is responsible for taking care of her future financial security. Based on this realization, she began adding bonds to her portfolio of stocks, mutual funds, and savings accounts. She bought tax-free municipal bonds and zero-coupon bonds (bonds sold at a deep discount that pay no current interest and are worth more than their initial value at maturity) for her regular account and a corporate bond for her Individual Retirement Account (IRA). She bases her selections on brokers' recommendations (she maintains several accounts), bond ratings (A or better), rates of return (at least 7½ percent, tolerating slightly lower rates for zero-coupon bonds), and maturity (most are long term and of varying duration, staggered to coincide with various retirement dates).

Renée invests in bonds because they make her save, offer tax advantages, and provide steady income to reinvest in her retirement accounts. She follows a "buy and hold" approach rather than trading, which involves many variables and greater risk. After her stock market losses, she wanted the forced discipline that bonds brought to her portfolio. However, she watches interest rates carefully. In spring 1992, when interest rates dropped, Renée stopped buying bonds and returned to equity investing. When interest rates rose in 1994, she again turned to fixed-income investments, buying short- and intermediate-term Treasury bonds yielding 6½ to 7¾ percent.

In the fall of 1994, Renée, then in her mid-forties, reviewed her portfolio with a financial planner. Realizing that she was about halfway through her career, she thought about changing the portfolio, which was invested 20 percent in cash and cash equivalents, 30 percent in fixed-income instruments, and 50 percent in equities. The planner suggested

> AS MUCH AS I LOVE THE THRILL OF PLAYING THE STOCK MARKET, I RECOGNIZE THAT HOLDING BONDS GIVES MY PORTFOLIO THE BALANCE IT NEEDS.

that Renée reduce the percentage in cash, increase the fixed-income portion by that amount, and maintain the same percentage in stocks. However, Renée is concerned about erosion of bond principal by inflation and looks to her equity investments to provide growth. "As much as I love the thrill of playing the stock market," Renée says, "I recognize that holding bonds gives my portfolio the balance it needs."

Renée Barnow is a public affairs and publications director for a small federal agency in Washington, D.C. She also writes feature magazine articles and is a consultant in technical writing, editing, and marketing communication.

bonds
publicly traded long-term debt securities, whereby the issuer agrees to pay a fixed amount of interest over a specified period of time and to repay a fixed amount of principal at maturity.

For many years, bonds were viewed as rather dull investments that produced current income and little else. No longer is this true; instead, bonds today are viewed as highly competitive investment vehicles that offer the potential for attractive returns. **Bonds** are publicly traded, long-term debt securities; they are issued in convenient denominations and by a variety of borrowing organizations, including the U.S. Treasury, various agencies of the U.S. government, state and local governments, and corporations. Bonds are often referred to as *fixed-income securities* because the debt-service obligations of the issuers are fixed. That is, the issuing organization agrees to pay a fixed amount of interest periodically and to repay a fixed amount of principal at maturity.

This is the first of three chapters dealing with various types of fixed-income securities. In this chapter, we will examine bonds as an investment vehicle and look at some of the basic features of fixed-income securities. In Chapter 9, we will shift our attention to bond valuation and the various ways these securities can be used by investors. Finally, in Chapter 10, we'll examine two hybrid types of fixed-income securities—preferred stocks and convertible bonds. When we complete these three chapters, you too, like Renée Barnow, may recognize that holding bonds can help balance an investment portfolio.

WHY INVEST IN BONDS?

Like any other type of investment vehicle, bonds provide investors with two kinds of income: (1) They provide a generous amount of current income, and (2) they can often be used to generate substantial amounts of capital gains. The current income, of course, is derived from the interest payments received over the life of the issue. Capital gains, in contrast, are earned whenever market interest rates fall. A basic trading rule in the bond market is that *interest rates and bond prices move in opposite directions*. When interest rates rise, bond prices fall; when rates drop, bond prices move up. Thus, it is possible to buy bonds at one price and to sell them later at a higher price. Of course, it is also possible to incur a capital loss, should market rates move against you. Taken together, the current income and capital gains earned from bonds can lead to attractive and highly competitive investor returns.

In addition to their returns, bonds are also a versatile investment outlet. They can be used conservatively by those who primarily (or exclusively) seek high current income, or they can be used aggressively by those who go after capital gains. While bonds have long been considered attractive investments for those seeking current income, it's only been since the advent of high and volatile interest rates that they have also been recognized as outstanding trading vehicles. Given the relation of bond prices to interest rates, investors found that the number of profitable trading opportunities increased substantially as wider and more frequent swings in interest rates began to occur.

In addition, certain types of bonds can be used for tax shelter: Municipal obligations are perhaps the best known in this regard, but as we'll see later in this chapter, Treasury and federal agency issues also offer some tax advantages. Finally, due to the general high quality of many bond issues, they can also be used for the preservation and long-term accumulation of capital. With quality issues, not only do investors have a high degree of assurance that they'll get their money back at maturity, but the stream of interest income is also highly dependable.

PUTTING BOND MARKET PERFORMANCE IN PERSPECTIVE

The bond market is driven by interest rates. In fact, *the behavior of interest rates is the single most important force in the bond market.* These rates determine not only the amount of current income investors will make but also the amount of capital gains (or losses) bondholders will incur. It's not surprising, therefore, that interest rates are so closely followed by bond market participants, and that bond market performance is generally portrayed in terms of market interest rates.

Figure 8.1 provides a look at bond interest rates over the 33-year period from 1961 to 1994. It shows that from a state of relative stability, interest rates took off in the latter half of the 1960s, and over the course of the next 15 years, the rates paid on high-grade bonds almost tripled. Indeed, interest rates rose from the 4 to 5 percent range in the early 1960s to over 16 percent by 1982. But then things began to change, as rates dropped sharply, and by 1986, they were back to the single-digit range once again. Thus, after a protracted bear market, bonds abruptly reversed course, and the strongest bull market on record occurred from 1982 to early 1987 (the bond market is considered *bearish* when market interest rates are high or rising, and *bullish* when rates are low or falling). Even though interest rates did move back up for a short time in 1987–1988, they quickly retreated, and by 1993 interest rates were down to a level not seen in over a quarter-century! In fact, by 1993, short-term securities, like Treasury bills and bank certificates of deposit, were yielding *less than 3 percent*, and long Treasury bonds were down to *under 6 percent*. Unfortunately, rates bottomed out in late 1993 and rose sharply in 1994, as the economy started to move into high gear.

As with stocks, *total returns* in the bond market are also made up of current income and capital gains (or losses). Not surprisingly, because rising rates mean falling prices, the drawn-out bear market in bonds meant depressing returns for bondholders. Granted, for investors just entering the market, the higher market yields were welcomed, because they meant higher levels of

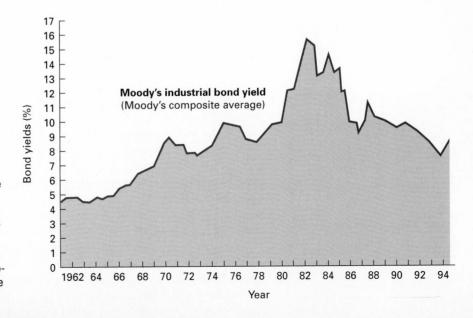

Figure 8.1 The Behavior of Interest Rates Over Time From an era of relative stability, bond interest rates rose dramatically and became far more volatile. The net result was that bond yields not only became highly competitive with the returns offered by other securities, they also provided investors with attractive capital gains opportunities.

Table 8.1 Historical Annual Yields and Returns in the Bond Market: 1955–1994
(Yields and returns based on performance of high-grade corporate bonds)

Year	Year-End Bond Yields*	Total Rates of Return**	Year	Year-End Bond Yields*	Total Rates of Return**
1994	8.64%	−7.76%	1974	8.89	−3.06
1993	7.31	13.19	1973	7.79	1.14
1992	8.34	9.39	1972	7.41	7.26
1991	8.58	19.91	1971	6.48	11.01
1990	9.61	6.86	1970	6.85	18.37
1989	9.18	16.23	1969	7.83	−8.09
1988	9.81	10.70	1968	6.62	2.57
1987	10.33	−0.27	1967	6.30	−4.95
1986	9.02	19.85	1966	5.55	0.20
1985	10.63	30.90	1965	4.79	−0.46
1984	12.05	16.39	1964	4.46	4.77
1983	12.76	4.70	1963	4.46	2.19
1982	11.55	43.80	1962	4.34	7.95
1981	14.98	−0.96	1961	4.56	4.82
1980	13.15	−2.62	1960	4.52	9.07
1979	10.87	−4.18	1959	4.68	−0.97
1978	9.32	−0.07	1958	4.19	−2.22
1977	8.50	1.71	1957	4.07	8.71
1976	8.14	18.65	1956	3.90	−6.81
1975	8.97	14.64	1955	3.24	0.48

*Year-end bond yields are for (S&P) AA-rated corporate (industrial and utility) bonds.

**Total return figures are based on interest income as well as capital gains (or losses).

Sources: Annual yields derived from Standard & Poor's S&P *Trade and Security Statistics*; total return figures from Ibbotson and Sinquefield, *Stocks, Bonds, Bills, and Inflation: Historical Returns (1926–1992).*

interest income. *But for those already holding bonds*, the implications were much different, as returns fell way *below* expectations and, in many cases, resulted in outright losses.

Table 8.1 shows year-end market yields and total annual returns for high-grade corporate bonds for the 40-year period from 1955 through 1994. Note how bond returns started to slip in 1965, as market yields began to climb; in fact, from 1965 to 1981, there were no fewer than 8 years when average returns were negative. In contrast, look what happened over the 12-year period from 1982–1993, when rates were in a general state of decline: A negative return occurred only once (in 1987), whereas double-digit returns (of 10.7 percent to 43.8 percent) occurred in no less than 8 of the 12 years. Clearly, the 1982–1993 period was not a bad time for bonds.

To see how market yields and bond returns have interacted over time, compare these two columns in Table 8.1. Note that when yields go one way, returns go the other. For example, in 1980, market yields went way up, but total returns fell to −2.62 percent. In contrast, two years later, in 1982, it was market yields that plunged, and total returns were a whopping 43.8 percent—providing a standard of performance that holds up well even against stocks.

Table 8.2 contains return performance over various holding periods of 5 to 40 years. These figures demonstrate the type of long-term returns possible from bonds, and they show that *average annual returns of around 8 to 10 percent on high-grade issues are not out of the question.* Although such performance may lag behind that of stocks (which it should, in light of the reduced

Table 8.2   Holding Period Returns in the Bond Market: 1955–1994

		Average Annual Returns*	Cumulative Total Returns	Amount to Which a $10,000 Investment Will Grow over Holding Period
5 years:	1990–94	7.9%	46.3%	$ 14,634.05
10 years:	1985–94	11.4	194.6	29,460.06
15 years:	1980–94	11.3	397.9	49,790.53
25 years:	1970–94	9.3	830.3	93,036.20
40 years:	1955–94	6.1	982.9	108,294.22
The 1960s:	1960–69	1.7	18.1	11,809.13
The 1970s:	1970–79	6.2	83.1	18,305.73
The 1980s:	1980–89	13.0	240.2	34,022.87

*Average annual return figures are fully compounded returns and are based on interest income as well as capital gains (or losses).

Sources: Annual yields derived from Standard & Poor's *S&P Trade and Security Statistics*; total return figures from Ibbotson and Sinquefield, *Stocks, Bonds, and Inflation: Historical Returns (1926–1992)*.

exposure to risk), it really isn't all that bad. The big question facing bond investors, however, is, What kind of returns will they be able to produce over the next 10 to 12 years? The 1980s and early 1990s were very good for bond investors. But that market was driven by falling interest rates, which in turn produced hefty capital gains and outsize returns. Whether or not market interest rates will (or even can) continue on that path is doubtful. Most market observers, in fact, caution against expecting abnormally high (double-digit) rates of return over the next 10 or so years. Indeed, as seen in the *Investor Insights* box on page 332, some market pros even go so far as to question whether bonds should have *any place at all* in an investment portfolio. They reason that if interest rates have bottomed out, then bonds won't have much to offer investors (other than relatively low returns). But that view ignores one of the key roles of bonds—*the element of stability they introduce to a portfolio*. Besides, what's so bad about generating fully compounded returns of 8 or 9 percent, over extended periods of time, from a traditionally low-risk investment vehicle?

EXPOSURE TO RISK

Like any other type of investment vehicle, fixed-income securities should also be viewed in terms of their risk and return. Generally speaking, bonds are exposed to five major types of risks: interest rate risk, purchasing power risk, business/financial risk, liquidity risk, and call risk.

- **Interest Rate Risk.** Interest rate risk is the number one source of risk to fixed-income investors, because *it's the major cause of price volatility in the bond market*. In the case of bonds, interest rate risk translates into market risk: The behavior of interest rates, in general, affects *all* bonds and cuts across *all* sectors of the market—even the U.S. Treasury market. When market interest rates rise, bond prices fall, and vice versa. And as interest rates become more volatile, so do bond prices.

INVESTOR INSIGHTS: *Conflicting Viewpoints*

Is There a Future for Bonds?

Being a bond investor from 1981 to 1993 really paid off: Moderating inflation and declining interest rates pushed annual returns on long-term government bonds to 14.1 percent, compared to historical returns of 5 percent, and corporate bondholders reaped similar rewards. By year-end 1993, however, interest rates were so low that they could only go up, which they did in 1994 when the Federal Reserve Bank raised interest rates, ending the bull market in bonds. From January through October 1994, prices on long-term Treasuries fell 20 percent—the worst bond market loss ever. Many economists think the bond market will not experience a similar bull market anytime soon. In light of these bond market changes, should investors rethink the role of bonds in their portfolios?

Tradition dictates that bonds or bond funds belong in every investor's portfolio. They provide fixed income from interest payments and are a lower-risk investment than common stock. Also, historically bonds have risen as stocks declined, helping to balance portfolio returns. In 1994, however, the markets were erratic and both stocks and bonds plunged. As a result, some Wall Street advisers believed that portfolios of stocks and cash, with no or few bonds, would produce higher returns. Although cash returns are below bond returns, the risk is less, so an investor can hold more stocks with growth potential. Also, inflation erodes the value of fixed-income investments. Because bonds have no growth element, these advisers rate stocks a better buy for the long term, and they suggest that investors who want fixed income, such as retirees, should devote less of their portfolio to bonds and buy dividend-paying stocks instead.

In November 1994, interest rates started to fall again. Other strategists believed that the bond market could again head upward and that the time was right to take advantage of attractive bond yields. They urged investors, especially those who get nervous riding the stock market's ups and downs, to devote 30 to 50 percent of their portfolios to bonds.

Well, if even the experts disagree, then what's an individual investor to do? To begin with, it's important to pick securities that meet your investment goals and strategies. Although bond returns probably won't soon regain the highs of the past ten years, bonds may still belong in your portfolio. With bonds, you can lock in a fixed return, so if you hold the bond until it matures, bonds could be good investments for the future. However, you should educate yourself before buying bonds. If you must sell and interest rates are higher than when you bought, you'll lose part of your principal. Maturities are another consideration, as are interest rate and inflation forecasts. If you think interest rates won't rise much and you plan to hold the bond to maturity, you may want long-term bonds. Shorter maturities lower your interest rate risk. Remember to take inflation into account to calculate the real income flow, reassess bond holdings periodically, and, as with other securities, diversify your holdings.

Sources: Jonathan Clements, "Stocks, Bonds, or Cash: Which to Choose?" *Wall Street Journal*, November 10, 1994, pp. C1, C18; Jerry Edgerton, "Who Needs Bonds?" *Money*, September 1994, pp. 120–24; Christopher Farrell, "These Are the Good Old Days for Bonds," *Business Week*, December 6, 1993, p. 154; and Terence P. Paré, "How Investors Can Profit from the Increase in Interest Rates," *Fortune*, December 12, 1994, pp. 45–46.

• **Purchasing Power Risk.** Purchasing power risk accompanies inflation. During periods of mild inflation, bonds do pretty well, because their returns tend to outstrip inflation rates. Purchasing power risk really heats up when inflation takes off, the way it did in the late 1970s; when that happens, bond yields start to lag behind inflation rates. The reason: You have a fixed coupon rate on your bond, so even though market yields are rising with inflation, your return is locked in for the long haul.

- **Business/Financial Risk.** This is basically the risk that the *issuer will default on interest and/or principal payments.* Business/financial risk has to do with the quality and financial integrity of the issuer; the stronger the issuer, the less business/financial risk there is to worry about. This risk doesn't even exist for some securities (e.g., U.S. Treasuries), whereas for others (corporate and municipal bonds), it's a very important consideration.

- **Liquidity Risk.** Liquidity risk is the risk that a bond will be difficult to unload if you want or have to sell it. Actually, this is a major problem in certain sectors of the market—far bigger than a lot of investors realize. For even though the U.S. bond market is enormous, the market is chiefly over-the-counter in nature, and much of the activity occurs in the primary/new issue market. Therefore, with the exception of the Treasury market and a good deal of the agency market, little trading is done in the secondary markets, particularly with corporates and municipals.

- **Call Risk.** Call risk is the risk that a bond will be "called"—that is, retired—long before its scheduled maturity date. Issuers are often given the opportunity to prepay their bonds, and they do so by calling them in for prepayment. (We'll examine call features later in this chapter.) When issuers call their bonds, the bondholders end up getting cashed out of the deal and have to find another place for their investment funds—and there's the problem. Because bonds are nearly always called for prepayment after interest rates have taken a big fall, comparable investment vehicles just aren't available. Thus, the investor has to replace a high-yielding bond with a much lower-yielding issue. Being able to prepay a bond might be great for the issuer, but from the bondholder's perspective, a called bond means not only a disruption in the investor's cash flow but also a sharply reduced rate of return.

ESSENTIAL FEATURES OF A BOND

A *bond* is a negotiable, long-term debt instrument that carries certain obligations (including the payment of interest and the repayment of principal) on the part of the issuer. Bondholders, unlike the holders of common stock, have no ownership or equity position in the organization that issues the bond. Because bonds are debt and because, in a roundabout way, bondholders are only lending money to the issuer, they are not entitled to an ownership position or any of the rights and privileges that go along with it.

Bond Interest and Principal

In the absence of any trading, a bond investor's return is limited to fixed interest and principal payments. That's because bonds involve a fixed claim on the issuer's income (as defined by the size of the periodic interest payments) and a fixed claim on the assets of the issuer (equal to the repayment of principal at maturity). As a rule, bonds pay interest every six months. There are exceptions, however; some issues carry interest payment intervals as short as a month, and a few as long as a year. The amount of interest due is a function of the **coupon**, which defines the annual interest income that will be paid by the issuer to the bondholder. For instance, a $1,000 bond with an 8 percent coupon would pay $80 in interest annually—generally in the form of two $40

coupon
feature on a bond that defines the amount of annual interest income.

principal
on a bond, the amount of capital that must be paid at maturity.

semiannual payments. The **principal** amount of a bond, also known as an issue's *par value*, specifies the amount of capital that must be repaid at maturity. For example, there is $1,000 of principal in a $1,000 bond.

Of course, debt securities regularly trade at market prices that differ from their principal (or par) values. This occurs whenever an issue's coupon differs from the prevailing market rate of interest. That is, the price of the issue will change inversely with interest rates until its yield is compatible with the prevailing market yield. Such behavior explains why a 7 percent issue will carry a market price of only $825 in a 9 percent market. The drop in price from its par value of $1,000 is necessary to raise the yield on this bond from 7 to 9 percent. In essence, the new, higher yield is produced in part from annual coupons and in part from capital gains, as the price of the issue moves from $825 back to $1,000 at maturity.

Maturity Date

maturity date
the date on which a bond matures and the principal must be repaid.

Unlike common stock, all debt securities have limited lives and will expire on a given date in the future, the issue's **maturity date**. Although a bond carries a series of specific interest payment dates, the principal is repaid only once: on or before maturity. Because the maturity date is fixed (and never changes), it not only defines the life of a new issue but also denotes the amount of time remaining for older, outstanding bonds. Such a life span is known as an issue's *term to maturity*. For example, a new issue may come out as a 25-year bond; 5 years later, it will have only 20 years remaining to maturity.

term bond
a bond that has a single, fairly lengthy maturity date.

serial bond
a bond that has a series of different maturity dates.

note
a debt security originally issued with a maturity of from 2 to 10 years.

Two types of bonds can be distinguished on the basis of maturity: term and serial issues. A **term bond** has a single, fairly lengthy maturity date and is the most common type of issue. A **serial bond,** in contrast, has a series of different maturity dates, perhaps as many as 15 or 20, within a single issue. For example, a 20-year term bond issued in 1995 would have a single maturity date of 2015, but that same issue as a serial bond might have 20 annual maturity dates that extend from 1996 through 2015. At each of these annual maturity dates, a certain portion of the issue would come due and be paid off. Maturity is also used to distinguish a *note* from a *bond*. That is, a debt security that's originally issued with a maturity of 2 to 10 years is known as a **note,** whereas a *bond* technically has an initial term to maturity of more than 10 years. In practice, notes are often issued with maturities of 5 to 7 years, whereas bonds will normally carry maturities of 20 to 30 years or more.

Call Features—Let the Buyer Beware!

call feature
feature that specifies whether and under what conditions the issuer can retire a bond prior to maturity.

Consider the following situation: You've just made an investment in a high-yielding, 25-year bond. Now all you have to do is sit back and let the cash flow in, right? Well, perhaps. Certainly, that will happen for the first several years. However, if market interest rates drop, it's also likely that you'll receive a notice from the issuer that the bond is being *called*. This means that the issue is being retired before its maturity date. There's really nothing you can do but turn in the bond and invest your money elsewhere. It's all perfectly legal because every bond is issued with a **call feature**, which stipulates whether or not and under what conditions a bond can be called in for retirement prior to maturity.

Basically, there are three types of call features:

1. A bond can be *freely callable,* which means that the issuer can prematurely retire the bond at any time.

2. A bond can be *noncallable,* meaning that the issuer is prohibited from retiring the bond prior to maturity.

3. The issue could carry a *deferred call,* which means that the issue cannot be called until after a certain length of time has passed from the date of issue. In essence, the issue is noncallable during the deferment period and then becomes freely callable.

Obviously, in our illustration above, either the high-yielding bond was issued as a freely callable security or it became freely callable with the end of its call deferment period.

Call features are placed on bonds *for the benefit of the issuers.* They're used most often to replace an issue with one that carries a lower coupon; the issuer benefits by being able to realize a reduction in annual interest cost. Thus, when market interest rates undergo a sharp decline, as they did in 1982–1986 and again in 1991–1993, bond issuers will retire their high-yielding bonds (by calling them in) and replace them with lower-yielding obligations. *The net result is that the investor is left with a much lower rate of return than anticipated.*

In a halfhearted attempt to compensate investors who find their bonds called out from under them, a **call premium** is tacked onto a bond and paid to investors, along with the issue's par value, at the time the bond is called. The sum of the par value plus call premium represents the issue's **call price,** which is the amount the issuer must pay to retire the bond prematurely. As a general rule, call premiums usually equal about one year's interest at the earliest date of call and then become systematically smaller as the issue nears maturity. Using this rule, the initial call price of a 9 percent bond would be around $1,090, with $90 representing the call premium.

In addition to call features, some bonds may also carry **refunding provisions,** which are much like call features except that they prohibit just one thing: the premature retirement of an issue from the proceeds of a lower-coupon refunding bond. For example, a bond could come out as freely callable but *nonrefundable* for five years; in this case, the bond would probably be sold by brokers as a *deferred refunding issue,* with little or nothing said about its call feature. The distinction is important, however, since it means that a nonrefunding or deferred refunding issue *can still be called and prematurely retired for any reason other than refunding.* Thus, an investor could face a call on a high-yielding (nonrefundable) issue if the issuer has the cash to retire the bond prematurely.

Sinking Funds

Another provision that's important to investors is the **sinking fund,** which stipulates how a bond will be paid off over time. This provision applies only to term bonds, of course, since serial issues already have a predetermined method of repayment. Not all (term) bonds have sinking fund requirements, but for those that do, a sinking fund specifies the annual repayment schedule that will be used to pay off the issue; it indicates how much principal will be retired

call premium
the amount added to a bond's par value and paid to investors when a bond is retired prematurely.

call price
the price the issuer must pay to retire a bond prematurely; equal to par value plus the call premium.

refunding provisions
provisions that prohibit the premature retirement of an issue from the proceeds of a lower-coupon refunding bond.

sinking fund
a provision that stipulates the amount of principal that will be retired annually over the life of a bond.

each year. Sinking fund requirements generally begin one to five years after the date of issue and continue annually thereafter until all or most of the issue is paid off. Any amount not repaid (which might equal 10 to 25 percent of the issue) would then be retired with a single "balloon" payment at maturity. Unlike a call or refunding provision, generally no call premium exists with sinking fund calls; instead, bonds are normally called for sinking fund purposes at par.

Secured or Unsecured Debt

A single issuer may have many different bonds outstanding at any given point in time. In addition to coupon and maturity, one bond can be differentiated from another by the type of collateral behind the issue. Issues can be either junior or senior. **Senior bonds** are secured obligations, which are backed by a legal claim on some specific property of the issuer. Such issues would include **mortgage bonds,** which are secured by real estate; **collateral trust bonds,** which are backed by financial assets owned by the issuer but held in trust by a third party; **equipment trust certificates,** which are secured by specific pieces of equipment (e.g., boxcars and airplanes) and are popular with railroads and airlines; and **first and refunding bonds,** which are basically a *combination* of first mortgage and junior lien bonds (i.e., the bonds are secured in part by a first mortgage on some of the issuer's property and in part by second or third mortgages on other properties). (Note that first and refunding bonds are *less secure* than and should *not* be confused with straight first-mortgage bonds.)

---

senior bonds
secured debt obligations, backed by a legal claim on specific property of the issuer.

mortgage bonds
senior bonds secured by real estate.

collateral trust bonds
senior bonds backed by securities owned by the issuer but held in trust by a third party.

equipment trust certificates
senior bonds secured by specific pieces of equipment; popular with transportation companies such as airlines.

first and refunding bonds
bonds secured in part with both first and second mortgages.

Figure 8.2 Announcement of a New Corporate Bond Issue This two-part, $400 million bond was issued by The New York Times Company (the newspaper publisher) and is secured by nothing more than the good name of the company. The (unsecured) notes carry a 10-year maturity, and the unsecured debenture bonds have 30-year maturities. During the first 10 years, the company will pay nearly $315 million in interest, and it will make another $248 million in interest payments during the last 20 years. Indeed, by the time the second bond matures, the company will have paid over a half-billion dollars in interest on this issue. (Source: *Wall Street Journal,* March 3, 1995, p. C17.)

This announcement is neither an offer to sell nor a solicitation of offers to buy any of these securities. The offering is made only by the Prospectus and the related Prospectus Supplement.

NEW ISSUES   March 24, 1995

$400,000,000

THE NEW YORK TIMES COMPANY

$250,000,000 7⅝% Notes Due March 15, 2005
Price 99.781%
plus accrued interest, if any, from March 29, 1995

$150,000,000 8¼% Debentures Due March 15, 2025
Price 99.269%
plus accrued interest, if any, from March 29, 1995

Copies of the Prospectus and the related Prospectus Supplement may be obtained in any State in which this announcement is circulated only from such of the undersigned as may legally offer these securities in such State. The Debentures are redeemable prior to maturity as set forth in the Prospectus and the related Prospectus Supplement.

CS First Boston

J.P. Morgan Securities Inc.

Morgan Stanley & Co.
Incorporated

junior bonds
debt obligations backed only by the promise of the issuer to pay interest and principal on a timely basis.

debenture
an unsecured (junior) bond.

subordinated debentures
unsecured bonds whose claim is secondary to other debentures.

income bonds
unsecured bonds requiring that interest be paid only after a specified amount of income is earned.

Junior bonds, on the other hand, are backed only by the promise of the issuer to pay interest and principal on a timely basis. There are several classes of unsecured bonds, the most popular of which is known as a **debenture.** Figure 8.2 shows the announcement of a debenture bond that was issued in 1995. Note that even though no collateral backed up this obligation, the issuer—The New York Times Company—was able to sell $400 million worth of these securities. In addition, **subordinated debentures** are also used; these issues have a claim on income secondary to other debenture bonds. **Income bonds,** the most junior of all, are unsecured debts requiring that interest be paid only after a certain amount of income is earned. With these bonds, there is no legally binding requirement to meet interest payments on a timely or regular basis so long as a specified amount of income has not been earned. These issues are similar in many respects to *revenue bonds* found in the municipal market.

PRINCIPLES OF BOND PRICE BEHAVIOR

The price of a bond is a function of its coupon, its maturity, and the movement of market interest rates. The relationship of bond prices to market interest rates is captured in Figure 8.3. Basically, the graph reinforces the *inverse relationship* between bond prices and market rates: *Lower* rates lead to *higher* bond prices. Figure 8.3 also shows the difference between premium and discount bonds. A **premium bond** is one that sells for more than its par value. A premium results whenever market interest rates drop below the coupon rate on the bond. A **discount bond,** in contrast, sells for less than par and is the result of market rates being greater than the issue's coupon rate. Thus, the 10 percent bond in our illustration traded as a premium bond when market rates were at 8 percent, but as a discount bond when rates stood at 12 percent.

When a bond is first issued, it is usually sold to the public at a price that equals or is very close to its par value. Likewise, when the bond matures—

premium bond
a bond with a market value in excess of par; occurs when interest rates drop below the coupon rate.

discount bond
a bond with a market value lower than par; occurs when market rates are greater than the coupon rate.

Figure 8.3 The Price Behavior of a Bond
A bond will sell at its par value so long as the prevailing market interest rate remains the same as the bond's coupon—in this case, 10 percent. However, when market rates drop (or rise), bond prices move up (or down). As a bond approaches its maturity, the price of the issue will move toward its par value, *regardless* of the level of prevailing interest rates.

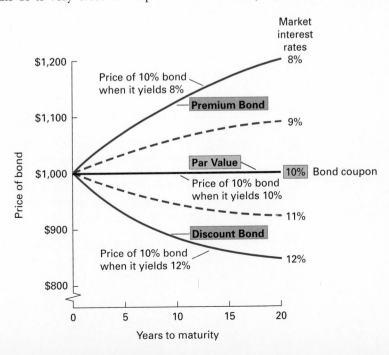

some 15, 20, or 30 years later—it will once again be priced at its par value. But what happens to the price of the bond in between is of considerable interest to most bond investors. In this regard, we know that the extent to which bond prices move depends not only on the *direction* of change in interest rates but also on the *magnitude* of such changes; the greater the moves in interest rates, the greater the swings in bond prices.

However, bond price volatility also varies according to the coupon and maturity of an issue. That is, bonds with *lower coupons* and/or *longer maturities* will respond more vigorously to changes in market rates and will therefore undergo sharper price swings. (Note in Figure 8.3 that for a given change in interest rates—e.g., from 10 to 8 percent—the largest change in price occurs when the bond has the greatest number of years to maturity.) Therefore, if a *decline* in interest rates is anticipated, an investor should seek lower coupons and longer maturities (since this would produce maximum amounts of capital gains). When interest rates move *up*, the investor should do just the opposite: seek high coupons with short maturities. This choice will cause minimal price variation and act to preserve as much capital as possible.

Actually, of the two variables, the *maturity* of an issue has the bigger impact on price volatility. For example, look what happens to the price of an 8 percent bond when market interest rates rise by 1, 2, or 3 percentage points:

Bond Maturity	Change in the Price of an 8% Bond When Interest Rates Rise by:		
	1 Percentage Point	2 Percentage Points	3 Percentage Points
5 years	− 4.0%	−7.7%	− 11.2%
25 years	− 9.9%	− 18.2%	− 25.3%

For purposes of this illustration, we assume the interest rate changes occur "instantaneously," so the maturities remain fixed, at 5 or 25 years. Given the computed price changes, it's clear that the shorter (5-year) bond offers a lot more price stability. Such a behavioral trait is universal with all fixed-income securities. This is a very important feature, because it means that if you want to reduce your exposure to capital loss or, more to the point, if you want to lower the amount of price volatility in your bond holdings, then just *shorten your maturities*.

CONCEPTS *in Review*

8.1   What appeal do bonds hold for individual investors? Give several reasons why bonds make attractive investment outlets.

8.2   How would you describe the behavior of market interest rates and bond returns over the last 40 years? Do swings in market interest rates have any bearing on bond returns? Explain.

8.3   Identify and briefly describe the five types of risk to which bonds are exposed. What is the most important source of risk for bonds in general? Explain.

8.4   Can issue characteristics (e.g., coupon and call features) affect the yield and price behavior of bonds? Explain.

8.5   What is the difference between a *call feature* and a *sinking fund provision*? Briefly describe the three different types of call features. Can a bond be freely callable but nonrefundable?

8.6   What is the difference between a *premium bond* and a *discount bond*? What three attributes are most important in determining an issue's price volatility?

THE MARKET FOR DEBT SECURITIES

Thus far, our discussion has dealt with basic bond features; we now shift our attention to a review of the market in which these securities are traded. The bond market is chiefly over-the-counter in nature, since listed bonds represent only a small portion of total outstanding obligations. And in comparison to the stock market, the bond market is far more price-stable. Granted, interest rates (and therefore bond prices) do move up and down and have been volatile in recent times, but when bond price activity is measured on a daily basis, it is remarkably stable. There are two things about the bond market that stand out—it's big, and it has been growing at a rapid clip. From a $250 billion market in 1950, it has grown to the point where the bonds outstanding in this country (in 1993) totaled $7.1 *trillion*. That makes the bond market about *50 percent bigger* than the U.S. stock market.

MAJOR MARKET SEGMENTS

There are issues available in today's bond market to meet almost any investment objective and to suit just about any type of investor. As a matter of convenience, the bond market is normally separated into four major segments, according to type of issuer: Treasury, agency, municipal, and corporate. As we will see below, each sector has developed its own issue and operating features, as well as its own trading characteristics.

Treasury Bonds

"Treasuries" (or "governments," as they are sometimes called) are a dominant force in the fixed-income market, and if not the most popular type of bond, they certainly are the best known. The U.S. Treasury issues bonds, notes, and other types of debt securities (e.g., Treasury bills) as a way of meeting the ever increasing needs of our federal government. All Treasury obligations are of the highest quality because they are all backed by the "full faith and credit" of the U.S. government. This feature, along with their liquidity, makes them very popular with individual and institutional investors, both here and abroad. Indeed, the market for U.S. Treasury securities is the biggest and most active in the world. *Every day,* more than $125 billion worth of Treasury obligations change hands, as these securities are traded in all the major markets of the world, from New York to London to Tokyo. That's three-quarters of a *trillion* dollars in bond trades *every week*. To put that number into perspective, in an average week the NYSE trades about $45 to $50 billion worth of stock.

Treasury notes carry maturities of 2 to 10 years, whereas **Treasury bonds** have maturities of more than 10 years and up to 30 years. Treasury notes and bonds are sold in $1,000 denominations (except 2- to 3-year notes, which are

Treasury notes
U.S. Treasury debt securities that are issued by the U.S. Treasury with maturities of 10 years or less.

Treasury bonds
U.S. Treasury debt securities that are issued with maturities of more than 10 years—usually 20 years or more.

sold in $5,000 minimums). Interest income is subject to normal federal income tax but *is exempt from state and local taxes*. The Treasury issues its notes and bonds at regularly scheduled auctions, the results of which are widely reported by the financial media (see Figure 8.4). It's through this auction process that the Treasury establishes the initial yields and coupons on the securities it issues. All government notes and bonds today are issued as *noncallable* securities. In fact, the last time the U.S. Treasury issued callable bonds was in 1984; until then, most Treasury bonds carried long-term call deferments, under which the bonds became freely callable during the last 5 years of the issue's life. There are still some deferred call Treasuries outstanding, but they're easy to pick out, because the deferred call features are a specific part of the bond listing system. For example, the 10 percent issue of 2005–10 signifies that this Treasury bond has a maturity date of 2010 and a deferred call feature that extends through 2005.

Agency Bonds

agency bonds
debt securities issued by various agencies and organizations of the U.S. government.

Agency bonds are debt securities issued by various agencies and organizations of the U.S. government—such as the Resolution Trust Corp., the Federal Farm Credit Banks, and the Government National Mortgage Association. For the most part, though these securities are the closest things to Treasuries, they are not obligations of the U.S. Treasury and technically should not be considered the same as a Treasury bond. An important feature of agency bonds is that they usually provide yields that are comfortably above the market rates for Treasuries; as such, they offer investors a way to increase returns with little or no real difference in risk.

Agency issues are of two types: government-sponsored and federal agencies. Although there are only six government-sponsored organizations, the number of federal agencies exceeds two dozen. To overcome some of the

Figure 8.4 The Reported Results of a Treasury Note Auction
Treasury auctions are closely followed by the financial media; here, the results of a three-year Treasury note auction are reported. These auctions are highly competitive; the amount of bids submitted generally far exceeds the size of the issue, and as a result, the spread between the highest and lowest bid is quite small: Here, it amounts to just 2 basis points, or 2/100 of 1 percent (7.09 percent to 7.07 percent). (Source: *Wall Street Journal*.)

Here are details of yesterday's three-year note auction:
Rates are determined by the difference between the purchase price and face value. Thus, higher bidding narrows the investor's return while lower bidding widens it.

Three-Year Notes

Applications	$33,801,230,000
Accepted bids	$13,559,645,000
Accepted at low price	59%
Accepted noncompetitively	$1,080,000,000
Average price (rate)	99.761 (7.09%)
High price (rate)	99.814 (7.07%)
Low price (rate)	99.761 (7.09%)
Interest rate	7%
CUSIP number	912827A77

The amount of bids submitted

Size of the issue— the amount of bids accepted

The amount of noncompetitive bids submitted (and accepted)

The average, high, and low ($) price and yield (rate) on the issue

The coupon that the issue will carry, which is set after the auction

Table 8.3   Characteristics of Popular Agency Issues

Type of Issue	Minimum Denomination	Initial Maturity	Tax Status* Federal	State	Local
Federal Farm Credit Banks	$ 1,000	13 months to 15 years	T	E	E
Federal Intermediate Credit Banks	5,000	9 months to 4 years	T	E	E
Federal Home Loan Bank	10,000	1 to 20 years	T	E	E
Federal Land Banks	1,000	1 to 10 years	T	E	E
Farmers Home Administration	25,000	1 to 25 years	T	T	T
Federal Housing Administration	50,000	1 to 40 years	T	T	T
Federal Home Loan Mortgage Corp.** ("Freddie Macs")	25,000	18 to 30 years	T	T	T
Federal National Mortgage Association** ("Fannie Maes")	25,000	1 to 30 years	T	T	T
Government National Mortgage Association** (GNMA—"Ginnie Maes")	25,000	12 to 40 years	T	T	T
Student Loan Marketing Association	10,000	3 to 10 years	T	E	E
Tennessee Valley Authority (TVA)	1,000	5 to 50 years	T	E	E
U.S. Postal Service	10,000	25 years	T	E	E
Federal Financing Bank	1,000	1 to 20 years	T	E	E

*T = taxable; E = tax-exempt
**Mortgage-backed securities.

problems in the marketing of many relatively small federal agency securities, Congress established the Federal Financing Bank to consolidate the financing activities of all federal agencies. (As a rule, the generic term *agency* is used to denote both government-sponsored and federal agency obligations.)

Selected characteristics of some of the more popular agency bonds are presented in Table 8.3. As the list of issuers in the table indicates, most of the government agencies that exist today were created to support either agriculture or housing. Although agency issues are not direct liabilities of the U.S. government, a few of them actually do carry government guarantees and therefore effectively represent the full faith and credit of the U.S. Treasury. But even those issues that do not carry such guarantees are highly regarded in the marketplace, since they are all viewed as *moral obligations* of the U.S. government—meaning it's highly unlikely that Congress would ever allow one to default. Also, like Treasury securities, agency issues are normally noncallable or carry lengthy call deferment features. One final point: Since 1986, *all new agency (and Treasury) securities* have been issued in *book entry form*. This means that no certificate of ownership is issued to the buyer of the bonds; rather, the buyer receives a "confirmation" of the transaction, and his or her name is entered in a computerized logbook, where it remains as long as the security is owned. Many experts believe that in the not-too-distant future, all security transactions will be handled in this way.

Municipal Bonds

municipal bonds
debt securities issued by states, counties, cities, and other political subdivisions; most of these bonds are tax-exempt (free of federal income tax on interest income).

Municipal bonds are the issues of states, counties, cities, and other political subdivisions, such as school districts and water and sewer districts. This is a trillion-dollar market today, and it's the only segment of the bond market that's dominated by individual investors: About two-thirds of all municipal bonds are held by individuals. (There are few tax incentives for institutional investors to hold these securities.) These bonds are often issued as *serial*

general obligation bonds
municipal bonds backed by the full faith, credit, and taxing power of the issuer.

revenue bonds
municipal bonds that require payment of principal and interest only if sufficient revenue is generated by the issuer.

municipal bond guarantees
guarantees from a party other than the issuer that principal and interest payments will be made in a prompt and timely manner.

obligations, meaning that the issue is broken into a series of smaller bonds, each with its own maturity date and coupon.

Municipal bonds ("munis") are brought to the market as either general obligation or revenue bonds. **General obligation bonds** are backed by the full faith, credit, and taxing power of the issuer. **Revenue bonds,** in contrast, are serviced by the income generated from specific income-producing projects (e.g., toll roads). Although general obligations dominated the municipal market prior to the mid-1970s, the vast majority of munis today come out as revenue bonds (accounting for about 65 to 70 percent of the new issue volume).

The distinction between a general obligation and a revenue bond is important for a bondholder, since the issuer of a revenue bond is obligated to pay principal and interest *only if a sufficient level of revenue is generated*. (If the funds aren't there, the issuer does not have to make payment on the bond.) General obligation bonds, however, are required to be serviced in a prompt and timely fashion irrespective of the level of tax income generated by the municipality. Obviously, revenue bonds involve a lot more risk than general obligations, and because of that, they provide higher yields. Regardless of the type, municipal bonds are customarily issued in $5,000 denominations.

A somewhat unusual aspect of municipal bonds is the widespread use of **municipal bond guarantees.** With these guarantees, a party other than the issuer assures the bondholder that principal and interest payments will be made in a prompt and timely manner. The third party, in essence, provides an additional source of collateral in the form of insurance placed on the bond, at the date of issue, which is nonrevocable over the life of the obligation. As a result, bond quality is improved. The three principal insurers are the Municipal Bond Investors Assurance Corporation (MBIA), the American Municipal Bond Assurance Corporation (AMBAC), and the Financial Guaranty Insurance Co. (FGIC). All of these guarantors will insure any general obligation or revenue bond as long as it carries an S&P rating of triple-B or better. Municipal bond insurance results in higher ratings (usually triple-A) and improved liquidity, as these bonds are generally more actively traded in the secondary markets. About a third of all municipal bonds issued today are insured. They're especially common in the revenue market and, as such, put a whole new light on these issues. That is, whereas an uninsured revenue bond lacks certainty of payment, a guaranteed issue is very much like a general obligation bond because the investor knows principal and interest payments will be made on time.

Without a doubt, the thing that makes municipal securities unique is the fact that, in most cases, their interest income is immune from federal income taxes. This is the reason these issues are known as *tax-free*, or *tax-exempt*, bonds. Normally, the obligations are also exempt from state and local taxes *in the state in which they were issued*. For example, a California issue would be free of California tax if the bondholder lived in California, but its interest income would be subject to state tax if the investor resided in Arizona. Note, however, that in contrast to interest income, *capital gains on municipal bonds are not exempt from taxes*.

Individual investors are the biggest buyers of municipal bonds, and tax-free yield is certainly a major draw. To put this yield in perspective, Table 8.4 shows what a taxable bond would have to yield to equal the net yield of a tax-free bond. *It demonstrates how the yield attractiveness of municipals varies*

Table 8.4 Taxable Equivalent Yields for Various Tax-Exempt Returns

Taxable Income*			Tax-Free Yield							
Joint Returns ($000)	Individual Returns ($000)	Federal Tax Bracket	5%	6%	7%	8%	9%	10%	12%	14%
$ 0–$38	$ 0–$22.75	15%	5.88	7.06	8.24	9.41	10.59	11.76	14.12	16.47
$38–$91.85	$22.75–$55.1	28	6.94	8.33	9.72	11.11	12.50	13.89	16.67	19.44
$91.85–$140	$55.1–$115	31	7.25	8.70	10.15	11.59	13.04	14.49	17.39	20.29
$140–$250	$115–$250	36	7.81	9.38	10.94	12.50	14.06	15.63	18.75	21.88
$250 and above	$250 and above	39.6	8.28	9.93	11.59	13.25	14.90	16.56	19.87	23.18

*Taxable income and federal tax rates effective January 1, 1994.

taxable equivalent yield
the return a fully taxable bond would have to provide to match the after-tax return of a lower-yielding, tax-free municipal bond.

with an investor's income level. Clearly, the higher the individual's tax bracket, the more attractive municipal bonds become. Generally speaking, an investor has to be in one of the higher federal tax brackets (i.e., 31 to 39.6 percent) before municipal bonds offer yields that are truly competitive with fully taxable issues. This is because municipal yields are substantially lower than those available from fully taxable issues (such as corporates); and unless the tax effect is sufficient to raise the yield on a municipal to a figure that equals or surpasses taxable rates, it obviously doesn't make much sense to buy municipal bonds.

We can determine the level of return a fully taxable bond would have to provide in order to match the after-tax return of a lower-yielding, tax-free issue by computing what is known as a municipal's **taxable equivalent yield.** This measure can be calculated according to the following simple formula:

Equation 8.1

$$\text{Taxable equivalent yield} = \frac{\text{yield of municipal bond}}{1 - \text{federal tax rate}}$$

For example, if a certain municipal offered a yield of 6.5 percent, then an individual in the 39.6 percent tax bracket would have to find a fully taxable bond with a yield of 10.76 percent (i.e., 6.5%/.604 = 10.76%) in order to reap the same after-tax returns as the municipal.

Note, however, that Equation 8.1 considers *federal taxes only.* As a result, the computed taxable equivalent yield would apply only to certain situations: (1) to states that have no state income tax, (2) to situations where the investor is looking at an out-of-state bond (which would be taxable by the investor's state of residence), or (3) where the investor is comparing a municipal bond to a Treasury (or agency) bond—in which case *both* the Treasury and municipal bonds are free from state income tax. Under any of these conditions, the only tax that's relevant is federal income tax, and therefore use of Equation 8.1 is appropriate.

But what if the investor is comparing an in-state bond to, say, a corporate bond? In this case, the in-state bond would be free from both federal and state taxes, but the corporate bond would not. As a result, Equation 8.1 could not be used. Instead, the investor should use a form of the equivalent yield formula that considers *both* federal and state income taxes:

Equation 8.2

$$\text{Taxable equivalent yield for both federal and state taxes} = \frac{\text{municipal bond yield}}{1 - \left[\frac{\text{federal}}{\text{tax rate}} + \frac{\text{state}}{\text{tax rate}}\left(1 - \frac{\text{federal}}{\text{tax rate}}\right)\right]}$$

When both federal and state taxes are included in the calculations, the net effect is to *increase* the taxable equivalent yield. Of course, the size of the increase depends on the level of state income taxes; in a high-tax state like California, for example, the impact can be substantial. Return to the 6.5 percent municipal bond introduced above: If a California resident in the maximum federal and state tax brackets (of 39.6 and 11 percent, respectively) were considering a corporate issue, she would have to get a yield of 12.09 percent on the corporate in order to match the 6.5 percent yield on the California bond:

$$\text{Taxable equivalent yield for both federal and state taxes} = \frac{6.5}{1 - [.396 + .11(1 - .3960]}$$

$$= \frac{6.5}{1 - [.396 + .066]}$$

$$= \underline{\underline{12.09\%}}$$

This yield compares to a taxable equivalent yield of 10.76 percent when only federal taxes were included in the calculation. That's a difference of more than one full percentage point, certainly *not* an insignificant amount.

Corporate Bonds

The major nongovernmental issuers of bonds are corporations. The market for corporate bonds is customarily subdivided into four segments: industrials (the most diverse of the groups), public utilities (the dominant group in terms of volume of new issues), rail and transportation bonds, and financial issues (banks, finance companies, etc.). Not only is there a full range of bond quality available in the corporate market, but there's also a wide assortment of different types of bonds, ranging from first-mortgage obligations to convertible bonds (which we'll examine in Chapter 10), debentures, subordinated debentures, senior subordinated issues, capital notes (a type of unsecured debt issued by banks and other financial institutions), and income bonds. Interest on corporate bonds is paid semiannually, and sinking funds are fairly common. The bonds usually come in $1,000 denominations and are issued on a term basis with a single maturity date. Maturities usually range from 25 to 40 years or more, and many corporates, especially the longer ones, carry call deferment provisions that prohibit prepayment for the first 5 to 10 years. Corporate issues are popular with individuals because of their relatively attractive yields.

Although most corporates fit the general description above, one that does not is the *equipment trust certificate,* which is a security issued by railroads, airlines, and other transportation concerns. The proceeds from equipment trust certificates are used to purchase equipment (e.g., jumbo jets and railroad engines) that serves as the collateral for the issue. These bonds are usually issued in serial form and carry uniform annual installments throughout. They normally carry maturities that range from 1 year to a maximum that seldom exceeds 15 to 17 years. An attractive feature of equipment trust certificates is that despite a near-perfect payment record that dates back to pre-Depression days, these issues generally offer above-average yields to investors.

SPECIALTY ISSUES

In addition to the basic bond vehicles described above, investors can also choose from a number of *specialty issues*—bonds that possess unusual issue characteristics. For the most part, these bonds have coupon or repayment provisions that are out of the ordinary. Most are issued by corporations, although they are being used increasingly by other issuers as well. Three of the most actively traded specialty issues today are zero-coupon bonds, mortgage-backed securities (including collateralized mortgage obligations, or CMOs), and high-yield junk bonds. All three of these are not only actively traded but also rank as some of the most popular bonds on Wall Street. Let's now take a closer look at each of these specialty issues.

Zero-Coupon Bonds

zero-coupon bonds
bonds with no coupons that are sold at a deep discount from par value.

As the name implies, **zero-coupon bonds** have no coupons. Rather, these securities are sold at a deep discount from their par values and then increase in value over time at a compound rate of return so that at maturity, they are worth much more than their initial investment. Other things being equal, the cheaper the zero-coupon bond, the greater the return an investor can earn: For example, a 6 percent bond might cost $420, whereas an issue with a 10 percent yield will cost only $240.

Because they don't have coupons, these bonds do not pay interest semiannually; in fact, they pay *nothing* to the investor until the issue matures. As strange as it might seem, this feature is the main attraction of zero-coupon bonds. Because there are no interest payments, investors do not have to worry about reinvesting coupon income twice a year. Instead, the fully compounded rate of return on a zero-coupon bond is virtually guaranteed at the rate stated when the issue was purchased. For example, in late 1994, U.S. Treasury zero-coupon bonds with 20-year maturities were available at yields of around 8.4 percent. Thus, for just $200, you could buy a bond that would be worth five times that amount, or $1,000, at maturity in 20 years. Best of all, you would be *locking in* an 8.4 percent compound rate of return on your investment for the full 20-year life of the issue.

The foregoing advantages notwithstanding, zeros also have some serious disadvantages. One is that if rates do move up over time, you won't be able to participate in the higher return (since you'll have no coupon income to reinvest). In addition, zero-coupon bonds are subject to tremendous price volatility: If market rates climb, you'll experience a sizable capital loss as the prices of zero-coupons plunge. (Of course, if interest rates *drop*, you'll reap enormous capital gains if you hold long-term zeros; indeed, such issues are unsurpassed in capital gains potential.) A final disadvantage is that the IRS has ruled that zero-coupon bondholders must report interest as it is accrued, even though no interest is actually received. For this reason, most fully taxable zero-coupon bonds should either be used in tax-sheltered investments, such as Individual Retirement Accounts (IRAs), or be held by minor children who are 14 or older and likely to be taxed at the lowest rate, if at all.

Treasury Strips (Strip-Ts)
zero-coupon bonds sold by the U.S. Treasury.

Zeros are issued by corporations, municipalities, and federal agencies. You can even buy U.S. Treasury notes and bonds in the form of zero-coupon securities—they're known as **Treasury Strips**, or **Strip-Ts**, for short. Actually, the Treasury does *not* issue zero-coupon bonds but, instead, *allows government securities dealers to take regular coupon-bearing notes and bonds in stripped form*, which can then be sold to the public as zero-coupon securities. Essentially, the coupons are stripped from the bond, repackaged, and then sold separately as zero-coupon bonds. For example, a 20-year Treasury bond has 40 semiannual coupon payments, plus one principal payment; each of these 41 cash flows can be repackaged and sold as 41 different zero-coupon securities, with maturities that range from 6 months to 20 years. Because they sell at such large discounts, Treasury Strips are often sold in minimum denominations (par values) of $10,000—but with their big discounts, that means you probably will pay only $2,100 or $2,200 for $10,000 worth of 20-year Strip-Ts, depending on their yields. Because there's an active secondary market for Treasury Strips, investors can get in and out of these securities with ease just about anytime they want. Strip-Ts offer the maximum in issue quality, a full array of different maturities, and an active secondary market—all of which goes to explain why these securities are so popular.

Mortgage-Backed Securities

mortgage-backed bond
a debt issue secured by a pool of home mortgages; issued primarily by federal agencies.

Simply put, a **mortgage-backed bond** is a debt issue that is secured by a pool of residential mortgages. An issuer, such as the Government National Mortgage Association (GNMA), puts together a pool of home mortgages and then issues securities in the amount of the total mortgage pool. These securities, known as *pass-through securities* or *participation certificates*, are usually sold in minimum denominations of $25,000. Though their maturities can go out as far as 30 years, the average life of one of these issues is generally much shorter (perhaps as short as 8 to 10 years), because so many of the pooled mortgages are paid off early. (Technically, the *average life* of a mortgage-backed security (MBS) is the weighted-average time to full principal repayment. It does *not* mean the bond will be fully paid off in that period of time; indeed, only about half of the bond will have been paid off by the time it reaches its average life, so it will still have a number of years to go before it's fully retired.)

As an investor in one of these securities, you hold an undivided interest in the pool of mortgages. When a homeowner makes a monthly mortgage payment, that payment is essentially passed through to you, the bondholder, to pay off the mortgage-backed bond you hold. Although these securities come with normal coupons, *the interest is paid monthly rather than semiannually*. Actually, the monthly payments received by bondholders are, like mortgage payments, made up of both principal and interest. Since the principal portion of the payment represents return of capital, it is considered tax-free. Not so with interest income, however, which is subject to ordinary state and federal income taxes.

Mortgage-backed securities are issued primarily by three federal agencies. Although there are some state and private issuers—mainly big banks and S&Ls—agency issues dominate the market and account for 90 to 95 percent of the activity. The major agency issuers of mortgage-backed securities (MBSs) are:

• *Government National Mortgage Association (GNMA).* Known as Ginnie Mae, it is the oldest and largest issuer of MBSs.

- *Federal Home Loan Mortgage Corporation (FHLMC).* Known as Freddie Mac, it was the first to issue pools containing conventional mortgages. Stock in FHLMC is publicly owned and traded on the NYSE.

- *Federal National Mortgage Association (FNMA).* Known as Fannie Mae, it's the newest agency player and is the leader in the marketing of seasoned/older mortgages. Its stock also is publicly owned and traded on the NYSE.

One of the problems with mortgage-backed securities is that they are *self-liquidating investments*, since a portion of the monthly cash flow to the investor is repayment of principal. Thus, the investor is always receiving back part of the original investment capital, so that at maturity there is *no* big principal payment. To counter this problem, a number of *mutual funds* were formed that invest in mortgage-backed securities *but* automatically and continually reinvest the capital/principal portion of the cash flows. Mutual fund investors therefore receive only the interest from their investments and are thus able to preserve their capital.

collateralized mortgage obligation (CMO)
mortgage-backed bond whose holders are divided into classes based on the length of investment desired; principal is channeled to investors in order of maturity, with short-term classes first.

Loan prepayments are another problem with mortgage-backed securities. In fact, it was in part an effort to defuse some of the prepayment uncertainty in standard mortgage-backed securities that led to the creation of **collateralized mortgage obligations**, or **CMOs**. Normally, as pooled mortgages are prepaid, *all* bondholders receive a prorated share of the prepayments. The net effect is to sharply reduce the life of the bond. A CMO, in contrast, divides investors into classes (formally called "tranches," which is French for "slice"), depending on whether they want a short-term, intermediate-term, or long-term investment. Now, while interest is paid to all bondholders, *all principal payments* go first to the shortest class, until it is fully retired; then the next class (tranche) in the sequence becomes the sole recipient of principal; and so on, until the last tranche is retired.

Basically, CMOs are *derivative securities* created from traditional mortgage-backed bonds, which are placed in a trust; participation in this trust is then sold to the investing public in the form of CMOs. The net effect of this transformation is that CMOs look and behave very much like any other bond: They offer predictable (monthly) interest payments and have predictable maturities. However, although they carry the same triple-A ratings and implicit U.S. government backing as the mortgage-backed bonds that underlie them, CMOs represent a quantum leap in complexity. Some types of CMOs can be as simple and safe as Treasury bonds, but others can be far more volatile—and risky—than the standard MBSs they're made from. That's because when putting CMOs together, Wall Street performs the financial equivalent of gene splicing: Investment bankers isolate the interest and principal payments from the underlying MBSs and then rechannel them to a number of different tranches. It's not issue quality or risk of default that's the problem here, but rather, prepayment, or call, risk—all the bonds will be paid off; it's just a matter of when. Different types of CMO tranches have different levels of prepayment risk. Since the overall risk in a CMO cannot exceed that of the underlying mortgage-backed bonds, it follows that in order to have some CMO tranches with very little (or no) prepayment risk, others have to endure a lot more. The net effect is that while some CMO tranches are low in risk, others are extremely volatile. Unfortunately, CMOs had become so complex and so exotic, that nobody, not even professional money managers, knew what they were getting into. So, when market interest rates shot way up in 1994, CMO investors took huge losses and, in the process, lost much of their appetite for these securities. Of course, the mortgage market still exists today, but investors are no longer interested in the "exotics"; instead, their attention has shifted back to plain vanilla MBSs or to simpler, less exotic (i.e., less risky) CMOs.

The creation of mortgage-backed securities and CMOs quickly led to the development of a new market technology—the process of **securitization**, whereby various bank lending vehicles are transformed into marketable securities, much like a mortgage-backed security. Investment bankers are now selling billions of dollars of pass-through securities, known as **asset-backed securities** (or **ABS**, for short), which are backed by pools of auto loans and credit card bills (the two principal types of collateral that back these securities), as well as computer leases, hospital receivables, home-equity loans, or just about anything else that can be securitized. For example, GMAC, the financing arm of General Motors, is a regular issuer of collateralized auto loan securities. Similarly, MasterCard and Visa receivables are regularly used as collateral on credit-card-backed securities. These obligations are just like mortgage-backed securities, except they have much shorter maturities (generally, only about three to five years) and they're backed by a pool of auto loans or credit-card receivables, rather than home mortgages.

Junk Bonds

Junk bonds, or *high-yield bonds*, as they're also called, are highly speculative securities that have received low, sub-investment-grade ratings (typically Ba or B) from such organizations as Moody's and Standard & Poor's. These bonds are issued primarily by corporations and, increasingly, by municipalities as well. Junk bonds generally take the form of *subordinated debentures*, meaning the debt is unsecured and has a low claim on assets. These bonds are called "junk" because of the high risk of loss associated with them: The companies that issue them use excessive amounts of debt in their capital structures, and their ability to service that debt is subject to considerable doubt. Probably the most unusual type of junk bond is something called a **PIK-bond**. PIK stands for *payment in kind* and means that rather than paying the bond's coupon in cash, annual interest payments can be made in the form of additional debt. This "financial printing press" usually goes on for five or six years, after which time the issuer is supposed to start making interest payments in real money.

Traditionally, the term *junk bond* was applied to the issues of troubled companies, which might have been well rated when first issued but slid to low ratings through corporate mismanagement, heavy competition, or other factors. That all changed during the 1980s, when the vast majority of junk bonds originated not with troubled companies but with a growing number of mature (fairly well-known) firms that used enormous amounts of debt to finance takeovers and buyouts. These companies would change overnight from investment-grade firms to junk as they piled on debt to finance a takeover—or the threat of one. (Wall Street refers to these firms as "fallen angels.")

So, why would any rational investor be drawn to junk bonds? The answer is simple: They offer very high yields. Indeed, in a typical market, relative to investment-grade bonds, investors can expect to pick up anywhere from 2.5 to 5 percentage points in added yield. In late 1994, for example, investors were

securitization
the process of transforming bank lending vehicles such as mortgages into marketable securities.

asset-backed securities (ABS)
securities similar to mortgage-backed securities that are backed by a pool of bank loans, leases, and other assets (mostly auto loans and credit cards).

junk bonds
high-risk securities that have low ratings but produce high yields.

PIK-bond
a payment-in-kind junk bond, which makes annual interest payments in new bonds rather than in cash.

getting around 11 or 12 percent yields on junk bonds, compared to 8 or 9 per-cent on investment-grade corporates. Obviously, *such yields are available only because of the correspondingly higher exposure to risk*. However, as we saw earlier in this chapter, there's more to bond returns than yield alone: The *returns* you end up with don't always correspond to the *yields* you went in with. Junk bonds are subject to a good deal of risk, and their prices are unstable. Indeed, unlike investment-grade bonds, whose prices are closely linked to the behavior of market interest rates, junk bonds tend to behave more like stocks. As a result, the returns you actually end up with are highly unpredictable. Accordingly, only investors who are thoroughly familiar with the risks involved and, equally as important, who are comfortable with such risk exposure should use these securities.

A GLOBAL VIEW OF THE BOND MARKET

Globalization has hit the bond market, just as it has the stock market, and investors who are taking advantage of it are loving it. Foreign bonds are catching on with American investors because of their high yields and attrac-tive returns. Indeed, as more of these securities find their way to the portfolios of U.S. investors, some market observers feel that foreign bonds will be to the 1990s what junk bonds were to the 1980s. There are risks with foreign bonds, of course, but high risk of default (which is so prevalent with junk bonds) is *not* one of them. Instead, the big risk with foreign bonds has to do with the impact that currency fluctuations can have on returns in U.S. dollars.

By year-end 1992, the total value of the world bond market reached some $15 trillion. The United States has the biggest debt market, accounting for about 46 percent of the total. Far behind us is Japan, with about 18 percent of the world market, followed by Germany (at 8 percent), then France, Italy, the United Kingdom, and Canada. Together, these seven countries account for nearly 90 percent of the world bond market.

Although the United States today accounts for just under half of the avail-able fixed-income securities, that percentage is sure to decline in the future as foreign markets continue to expand. Therefore, by investing solely in the U.S. fixed-income markets, an investor is excluding not only half of the investment possibilities worldwide but, more importantly, the faster growing half. Also, as Table 8.5 reveals, investors in U.S. bonds are missing out on some pretty attractive returns. (The results reported in the table are *total returns in U.S. dollars* and include coupon income, capital gains or losses, and the effects of changes in currency exchange rates.) In fact, over the 15-year period from 1980 through 1994, the U.S. market provided the highest annual return only once (in 1982). A lot of the difference between U.S. and foreign returns in the bond market is due, of course, to the impact of currency exchange rates. Still, the fact remains that from an international perspective, better returns to U.S. investors are usually available to those willing to go offshore.

U.S.-Pay Versus Foreign-Pay Bonds

There are several different ways to invest in foreign bonds (*excluding* foreign bond mutual funds, which we'll examine in Chapter 11). From the perspective of a U.S. investor, foreign bonds can be divided into two broad categories on

Table 8.5   Comparative Annual Returns in the World's Major Bond Markets

	Australia	Belgium	Canada	France	Germany	Italy	Japan	U.K.	U.S. (Rank)*	
					Annual Total Returns (in U.S. Dollars)					
1994	6.2%	11.2%	−9.9%	4.6%	9.1%	2.1%	8.5%	−1.7%	−7.8%	(8th)
1993	16.2	5.6	11.4	13.1	7.3	14.0	27.1	19.5	13.2	(5th)
1992	−0.1	8.2	−0.5	4.6	6.2	−14.4	11.3	−3.9	9.4	(2nd)
1991	24.3	12.0	21.5	13.4	9.8	15.1	23.4	12.8	19.9	(5th)
1990	16.3	25.3	7.2	22.4	14.8	28.8	7.2	31.3	6.9	(7th)
1989	5.1	6.7	16.1	8.9	5.6	15.5	−14.6	−3.7	16.2	(3rd)
1988	29.8	−3.8	18.9	2.2	−6.6	−1.0	2.6	2.5	10.7	(3rd)
1987	29.1	33.0	10.4	27.6	28.6	14.2	41.4	47.7	−0.3	(9th)
1986	17.1	45.8	19.5	34.4	38.4	88.6	36.4	13.8	19.8	(7th)
1985	−13.2	55.5	34.0	53.1	41.8	37.5	36.8	38.6	30.9	(7th)
1984	4.9	0.7	1.1	6.6	1.4	21.9	2.3	−12.4	16.4	(2nd)
1983	0.5	0.8	1.9	−0.4	−7.7	15.1	12.3	8.1	4.7	(5th)
1982	15.0	−1.4	1.4	5.3	16.5	11.5	3.6	28.8	43.8	(1st)
1981	−7.1	−12.7	−4.7	−18.8	−8.8	−25.0	8.4	−18.8	−0.9	(3rd)
1980	−19.0	−8.9	−1.6	−11.0	−10.3	−11.8	24.0	31.2	−2.6	(5th)

					Average Annual Returns Over Extended Holding Periods					
5 years:										
1980–84	−1.8%	−4.5%	−0.4%	−4.2%	−2.3%	0.7%	9.9%	5.4%	11.1%	
1985–89	12.4	25.4	19.5	23.9	20.0	27.6	18.3	18.1	14.9	
1990–94	12.3	12.2	5.4	11.4	9.4	8.1	15.2	10.8	7.9	
10 years:										
1985–94	12.3	18.6	12.2	17.5	14.6	17.5	16.7	14.4	11.4	
15 years:										
1980–94	7.4	10.4	7.9	9.8	8.7	11.6	14.4	11.3	11.3	

Note: Total return = coupon income + capital gain (or loss) + profit (or loss) from changes in currency exchange rates.

*Parenthetical rank shows how U.S. returns rank among the listed major markets—for example, in 1991, U.S. ranked fifth out of the 9 markets listed in the table.

Source: International returns obtained from Ibbotson Associates and Templeton International; U.S. returns from Ibbotson and Sinquefield.

Yankee bonds
bonds issued by foreign governments or corporations but denominated in dollars and registered with the SEC.

the basis of the currency in which the bond is denominated: *U.S.-pay* (or dollar-denominated) bonds and *foreign-pay* (or non-dollar-denominated) bonds. All the cash flows—including purchase price, maturity value, and coupon income—from dollar-denominated foreign bonds are in U.S. dollars, whereas the cash flows from nondollar bonds are designated in a foreign currency or in a basket of foreign currencies, such as the European Currency Unit (ECU).

Dollar-denominated foreign bonds are of two types: Yankee bonds and Eurodollar bonds. **Yankee bonds** are issued by foreign governments or corporations or by so-called supernational agencies, like the World Bank and the InterAmerican Bank. These bonds are issued and traded in the United States; they're registered with the SEC, and all transactions are in U.S. dollars. Buying a Yankee bond, then, is really no different from buying any other U.S. bond: These bonds are traded on U.S. exchanges and our OTC market, and *because* *everything's in dollars, there's no currency exchange risk to deal with.* The bonds are generally very high in quality (which is not surprising, given the quality of the issuers) and offer highly competitive yields to investors.

Eurodollar bonds, in contrast, are issued and traded outside the United States. They are denominated in U.S. dollars, but they are not registered with the SEC, which means underwriters are legally prohibited from selling new issues to the U.S. public. (Only "seasoned" Eurodollar issues can be sold in this country.) The Eurodollar market today is dominated by foreign-based investors (though that is changing) and is primarily aimed at institutional investors.

Eurodollar bonds
foreign bonds denominated in dollars but not registered with the SEC, thus restricting sales of new issues.

From the standpoint of U.S. investors, foreign-pay international bonds encompass all those issues denominated in some currency other than dollars. These bonds are issued and traded overseas and are not registered with the SEC. Examples are German government bonds, which are payable in deutsche marks; Japanese bonds, issued in yen; and so forth. When we speak of *foreign bonds,* it's this segment of the market that most investors are thinking of. *These bonds are subject to changes in currency exchange rates,* which in turn can dramatically affect total returns to U.S. investors. The fact is, the returns on foreign-pay bonds are a function of three things: (1) the level of coupon (interest) income earned on the bonds; (2) the change in market interest rates, which determine the level of capital gains (or losses); and (3) the behavior of currency exchange rates. The first two variables are the same as those that drive bond returns in this country and are, of course, just as important to foreign bonds as they are to domestic bonds. Thus, if you're investing overseas, you still want to know where yields are today and where they're headed; it's really the third variable that separates the return behavior of dollar-denominated from foreign-pay bonds.

We can assess returns from foreign-pay bonds by employing the same (modified) holding period return formula first introduced in our discussion of foreign stock returns. (See Equation 5.6, page 221.) For example, assume an American investor purchased a German government bond, in large part because of the attractive 10 percent coupon it carried. If the bond was bought at par and market rates fell over the course of the year, the security itself would have provided a return in excess of 10 percent, because the decline in rates would have provided some capital gains to the investor. However, if the deutsche mark fell relative to the dollar, the total return (in U.S. dollars) could have actually ended up at a lot less than 10 percent, depending on what happened to the U.S. $/D-mark exchange rate. To find out exactly how this investment turned out, all we'd have to do is use Equation 5.6 and make a few (very minor) modifications to it (e.g., use interest income in place of dividends received). Like foreign stocks, foreign-pay bonds can pay off from both the behavior of the security and the behavior of the currency. As Table 8.5 shows, that combination, in many cases, means superior returns to U.S. investors. Knowledgeable investors find these bonds attractive not only because of their competitive returns but also because of the positive diversification effects they have on bond portfolios. Because the United States is the only country with a well-developed, actively traded corporate bond market, the foreign-pay markets are dominated by foreign government issues: It's estimated that about 80 percent, or more, of the non-dollar-denominated market is made up of foreign government bonds.

CONCEPTS *in Review*

8.7 Briefly describe each of the following types of bonds: (a) *Treasury bonds*, (b) *agency issues*, (c) *municipal securities*, and (d) *corporate bonds*. Note some of the major advantages and disadvantages of each.

8.8 Briefly define each of the following and briefly note how they might be used by fixed-income investors: (a) *zero-coupon bonds*, (b) *CMOs*, (c) *junk bonds*, and (d) *Yankee bonds*.

8.9 What are the special tax features of (a) Treasury securities, (b) agency issues, and (c) municipal bonds?

8.10 Identify the seven biggest bond markets in the world. How important is the U.S. bond market relative to the rest of the world?

8.11 What's the difference between dollar-denominated and non-dollar-denominated foreign bonds? Briefly describe the two major types of U.S.-pay bonds. Can currency exchange rates affect the total return of U.S.-pay bonds? Of foreign-pay bonds? Explain.

TRADING BONDS

Due in large part to the perceived safety and stability of bonds, many individual investors view bond investing as a relatively simple process. Such thinking, however, can often lead to unsatisfactory results, even losses. The fact is that not all bonds are alike, and picking the right security for the time is just as important for bond investors as it is for stock investors. Indeed, success in the bond market demands a thorough understanding not only of the different types of bonds but also of the many technical factors that drive bond yields, prices, and returns—things like call features, refunding provisions, and the impact that coupon and maturity have on bond price volatility. Also, because bond ratings are so important to a smooth-running bond market, investors should become thoroughly familiar with them. So let's now take a look at these ratings, as well as the quotation system used for bonds.

BOND RATINGS

bond ratings
letter grades that designate investment quality and are assigned to a bond issue by rating agencies.

Bond ratings are like grades: A letter grade is assigned to an issue on the basis of extensive, professionally conducted financial analysis that designates its investment quality. Ratings are widely used and are an important part of the municipal and corporate bond markets, where issues are regularly evaluated and rated by one or more of the rating agencies. Even some agency issues, like the Tennessee Valley Authority (TVA), are rated, although they always receive ratings that confirm the obvious—that the issues are prime grade. The two largest and best-known rating agencies are Moody's and Standard & Poor's; two lesser known but still important bond rating agencies are Fitch Investors Service and Duff & Phelps.

How Ratings Work

Every time a large new issue comes to the market, it is analyzed by a staff of professional bond analysts to determine default risk exposure and investment quality. (A fee, usually ranging from $1,000 to $15,000 and paid by the issuer or the underwriter of the securities being rated, is charged for rating each corporate bond.) The financial records of the issuing organization are thoroughly worked over and its future prospects assessed. Although the specifics of the actual credit analysis conducted by the rating agencies change with each issue, several major factors enter into most bond ratings. With a corporate issue, for example, these factors would include an analysis of the issue's indenture provisions, an in-depth study of the firm's earning power (including the stability of its earnings), a look at the company's liquidity and how it is managed, a study of the company's relative debt burden, and an in-depth exploration of its coverage ratios to determine how well it can service both existing debt and any new bonds that are being contemplated or proposed. As you might expect, the financial strength and stability of the firm is very important in determining the appropriate bond rating. Indeed, while there is far more to setting a rating than cranking out a few financial ratios, a strong relationship nevertheless does exist between the operating results and financial condition of the firm and the rating its bonds receive. Generally, the higher ratings are associated with more profitable companies that rely *less* on debt as a form of financing, are more liquid, have stronger cash flows, and have no trouble servicing their debt in a prompt and timely fashion.

Table 8.6 lists the various ratings assigned to bonds by each of the two major services. In addition to the standard rating categories noted in the table, Moody's uses numerical modifiers (1, 2, or 3) on bonds rated double-A to B,

Table 8.6   Bond Ratings

Moody's	S&P	Definition
Aaa	AAA	*High-grade investment bonds.* The highest rating assigned, denoting extremely strong capacity to pay principal and interest. Often called "gilt edge" securities.
Aa	AA	*High-grade investment bonds.* High quality by all standards but rated lower primarily because the margins of protection are not quite as strong.
A	A	*Medium-grade investment bonds.* Many favorable investment attributes, but elements may be present that suggest susceptibility to adverse economic changes.
Baa	BBB	*Medium-grade investment bonds.* Adequate capacity to pay principal and interest but possibly lacking certain protective elements against adverse economic conditions.
Ba	BB	*Speculative issues.* Only moderate protection of principal and interest in varied economic times. (This is one of the ratings carried by junk bonds.)
B	B	*Speculative issues.* Generally lacking desirable characteristics of investment bonds. Assurance of principal and interest may be small; this is another junk-bond rating.
Caa	CCC	*Default.* Poor-quality issues that may be in default or in danger of default.
Ca	CC	*Default.* Highly speculative issues, often in default or possessing other market shortcomings.
C		*Default.* These issues may be regarded as extremely poor in investment quality.
	C	*Default.* Rating given to income bonds on which no interest is paid.
	D	*Default.* Issues actually in default, with principal or interest in arrears.

Source: Moody's *Bond Record* and Standard & Poor's *Bond Guide.*

and S&P uses plus (+) or minus (−) signs on the same rating classes to show relative standing within a major rating category. For example, an A+ (or A1) means a strong, high A rating, whereas an A− (or A3) indicates the issue is on the low end of the A rating scale. Except for slight variations in designations (Aaa vs. AAA), the meanings and interpretations are basically the same. Note that the top four ratings (Aaa through Baa, or AAA through BBB) designate *investment-grade* bonds. Such ratings are highly coveted by issuers, since they indicate financially strong, well-run companies. The next two ratings (Ba/B or BB/B) are reserved for junk bonds. These ratings mean that although *the principal and interest payments on the bonds are still being met in a prompt and timely fashion*, the risk of default is relatively high, because the issuers generally lack the financial strength found with investment-grade issues. (Sometimes the Caa1/CCC+ category will be counted as part of the junk category, although technically the C rating class is meant to designate bonds that are already in default, or getting very close to it.) Most of the time, Moody's and S&P assign identical ratings. Sometimes, however, an issue will carry two different ratings. These are known as **split ratings** and are viewed simply as "shading" the quality of an issue one way or another. For example, an issue might be rated Aa by Moody's but A or A+ by S&P.

Also, just because a bond is given a certain rating at the time of issue doesn't mean it will keep that rating for the rest of its life. Ratings will change as the financial condition of the issuer changes. In fact, all rated issues are reviewed on a regular basis to ensure that the assigned rating is still valid. While many issues will carry a single rating to maturity, it is not uncommon for some ratings to be revised up or down during the life of the issue. As you might expect, the market responds to rating revisions by adjusting bond yields accordingly. For example, an upward revision (e.g., from A to AA) will cause the market yield on the bond to drop, as a reflection of the bond's improved quality. One final point: Although it may appear that the firm is receiving the rating, it is actually the *issue* that receives it. As a result, a firm can have different ratings assigned to different issues: The senior securities, for example, might carry one rating and the junior issues another, lower rating.

What Ratings Mean

Most bond investors pay close attention to agency ratings, since they can affect not only potential market behavior but comparative market yields as well. Specifically, the higher the rating, the lower the yield of an obligation, other things being equal. For example, whereas an A-rated bond might offer an 8½ percent yield, a comparable triple-A issue would probably yield something like 8 percent. Furthermore, investment-grade securities are far more interest-sensitive and tend to exhibit more uniform price behavior than junk bonds and other lower-rated issues. Perhaps most important, *bond ratings serve to relieve individual investors from the drudgery of evaluating the investment quality of an issue on their own*. Large institutional investors often have their own staff of credit analysts who independently assess the creditworthiness of various corporate and municipal issuers; individual investors, in contrast, have little if anything to gain from conducting their own credit analysis. After all, the credit analysis process is time-consuming and costly, and it involves a good deal more expertise than the average individual investor possesses. Most importantly, the ratings are closely adhered to by a large segment

split ratings
different ratings given to a bond issue by the two major rating agencies.

INVESTOR FACTS

HERE'S A CLUB THAT'S REALLY EXCLUSIVE—The cream of corporate America continues to thin. Although more than a thousand companies have publicly traded bonds outstanding, just a handful belong to the exclusive (and elusive) Triple-A Club. In fact, only about a dozen industrial companies have bonds rated triple-A by *both* Moody's and Standard & Poor's. Some of the members of this ultraexclusive club include American Home Products, GE, Kellogg, and Merck.

of the bond investment community, in large part because it's been shown that *the rating agencies themselves do a remarkably good job of assessing bond quality.* Thus, individual investors can depend on assigned agency ratings as a viable measure of the creditworthiness of the issuer and an issue's risk of default. A word of caution is in order, however: Bear in mind that bond ratings are intended as a measure of an issue's *default risk* only, which has no bearing whatsoever on an issue's exposure to *market risk.* Thus, if interest rates increase, even the highest-quality issues can (and will) go down in price, subjecting investors to capital loss and market risk.

READING THE QUOTES

One thing you quickly learn in the bond market is that transactions are not always as easy to conduct as they may seem. In the first place, many bonds have relatively "thin" markets, meaning that not a lot of trading goes on; indeed, some issues may trade only five or ten bonds a week, and many have no secondary market at all. There are, of course, numerous high-volume issues, but even so, investors should pay particularly close attention to an issue's trading volume—especially if they are looking for lots of price action and need prompt order executions. In addition, market information sometimes is simply not available: As the *Investor Insights* box (on page 357) reveals, it's not always easy to obtain current information on bond prices and other market developments. Finally, investors often have to look to both brokers and bankers to complete transactions. The reason is that most brokerage houses tend to confine their activities to new issues and to secondary market transactions of listed Treasury obligations, agency issues, and corporate bonds; commercial banks, in contrast, are still the major dealers in municipal bonds and are active in Treasury and agency securities as well.

Except for municipal issues (which are usually quoted in terms of the yield they offer), all other bonds are quoted on the basis of their dollar prices. Such quotes are always interpreted as a *percent of par.* Thus, a quote of 97½ does not mean $97.50 but, instead, means that the issue is trading at 97.5 percent of the par value of the obligation. In the bond market, it's assumed we're dealing with bonds that have par values of $1,000—or some multiple thereof. Accordingly, a quote of 97½ translates into a dollar price of $975. (With bond quotes, 1 point = $10, and ⅛ of a point = $1.25.) As can be seen in the bond quotes in Figure 8.5, one quotation system is used for corporate bonds and another for governments. (Treasuries and agencies are quoted the same.)

To understand the system used with corporate bonds, look at the AT&T issue highlighted in Figure 8.5. The group of numbers immediately following the company name (which is often highly abbreviated) gives the coupon and the year in which the bond matures; thus, the "8⅛ 24" means that this particular bond carries an 8⅛ percent annual coupon and will mature in the year 2024. The next column, labeled "Curr Yld," provides the *current yield*—in this case, 8.6 percent—being offered by the issue at its *current market price.* **Current yield** is a measure of the amount of annual interest income a bond provides relative to its prevailing market price. It is found by dividing annual coupon income by the closing price of the issue. In many respects, it is equivalent to the dividend yield measure used with stocks. We'll look at this bond valuation measure in more detail in Chapter 9.

current yield
measure of the annual interest income a bond provides relative to its current market price.

Figure 8.5 Price Quotations for Corporate and Government Bonds
While both corporate and Treasury bonds are quoted as a percent of their par values, note that corporate bonds are quoted in eighths of a point, whereas Treasuries are quoted in thirty-seconds. Also observe that both coupon and maturity play vital roles in the quotation system. (Source: *Wall Street Journal*, October 7, 1994.)

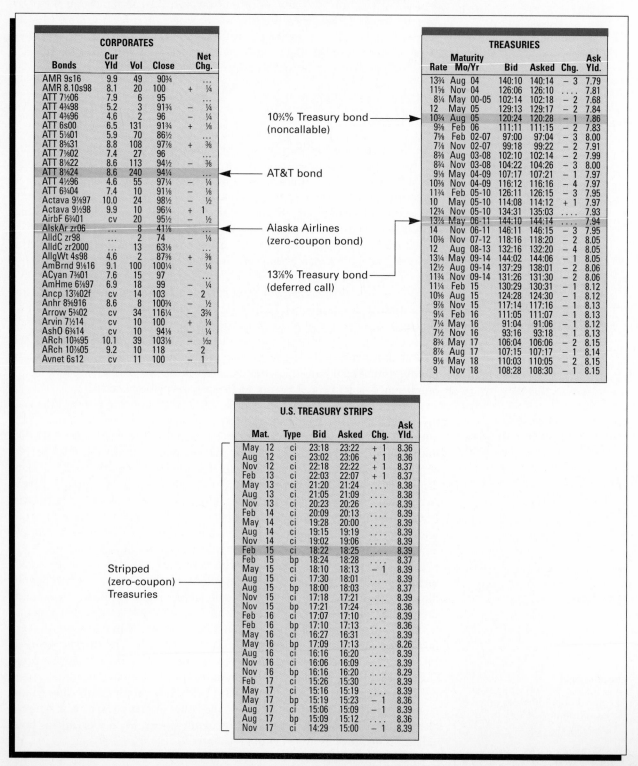

CORPORATES

Bonds	Cur Yld	Vol	Close	Net Chg.
AMR 9s16	9.9	49	90¾	...
AMR 8.10s98	8.1	20	100	+ ¼
ATT 7½06	7.9	6	95	...
ATT 4¾98	5.2	3	91¾	− ¼
ATT 4⅜96	4.6	2	96	− ¼
ATT 6s00	6.5	131	91¾	+ ⅛
ATT 5⅛01	5.9	70	86½	...
ATT 8⅝31	8.8	108	97⅞	+ ⅜
ATT 7⅛02	7.4	27	96	...
ATT 8⅛22	8.6	113	94½	− ⅜
ATT 8⅛24	8.6	240	94¼	...
ATT 4½96	4.6	55	97¼	− ¼
ATT 6¾04	7.4	10	91⅛	− ⅛
Actava 9⅞97	10.0	24	98½	− ½
Actava 9½98	9.9	10	96¼	+ 1
AirbF 6¾01	cv	20	95½	− ½
AlskAr zr06	...	8	41⅛	...
AlldC zr98	...	2	74	− ¼
AlldC zr2000	...	13	63⅛	...
AllgWt 4s98	4.6	2	87⅜	+ ⅜
AmBrnd 9⅛16	9.1	100	100¼	− ¼
ACyan 7⅜01	7.6	15	97	...
AmHme 6⅞97	6.9	18	99	− ¼
Ancp 13⅞02f	cv	14	103	− 2
Anhr 8⅝916	8.6	8	100¾	− ½
Arrow 5¾02	cv	34	116¼	− 3¾
Arvin 7½14	cv	10	100	+ ¼
AshO 6¾14	cv	10	94⅛	− ¼
ARch 10⅜95	10.1	39	103⅛	− 1/32
ARch 10⅞05	9.2	10	118	− 2
Avnet 6s12	cv	11	100	− 1

AT&T bond

Alaska Airlines (zero-coupon bond)

10¾% Treasury bond (noncallable)

13⅞% Treasury bond (deferred call)

TREASURIES

Rate	Maturity Mo/Yr	Bid	Asked	Chg.	Ask Yld.
13¾	Aug 04	140:10	140:14	− 3	7.79
11⅝	Nov 04	126:06	126:10	....	7.81
8¼	May 00-05	102:14	102:18	− 2	7.68
12	May 05	129:13	129:17	− 2	7.84
10¾	Aug 05	120:24	120:28	− 1	7.86
9⅜	Feb 06	111:11	111:15	− 2	7.83
7⅝	Feb 02-07	97:00	97:04	− 3	8.00
7⅞	Nov 02-07	99:18	99:22	− 2	7.91
8⅜	Aug 03-08	102:10	102:14	− 2	7.99
8¾	Nov 03-08	104:22	104:26	− 3	8.00
9⅛	May 04-09	107:17	107:21	− 1	7.97
10⅜	Nov 04-09	116:12	116:16	− 4	7.97
11¾	Feb 05-10	126:11	126:15	− 3	7.95
10	May 05-10	114:08	114:12	+ 1	7.97
12¾	Nov 05-10	134:31	135:03	....	7.93
13⅞	May 06-11	144:10	144:14	....	7.94
14	Nov 06-11	146:11	146:15	− 3	7.95
10⅜	Nov 07-12	118:16	118:20	− 2	8.05
12	Aug 08-13	132:16	132:20	− 4	8.05
13¼	May 09-14	144:02	144:06	− 1	8.05
12½	Aug 09-14	137:29	138:01	− 2	8.06
11¾	Nov 09-14	131:26	131:30	− 2	8.06
11¼	Feb 15	130:29	130:31	− 1	8.12
10⅝	Aug 15	124:28	124:30	− 1	8.12
9⅞	Nov 15	117:14	117:16	− 1	8.13
9¼	Feb 16	111:05	111:07	− 1	8.13
7¼	May 16	91:04	91:06	− 1	8.12
7½	Nov 16	93:16	93:18	− 1	8.13
8¾	May 17	106:04	106:06	− 2	8.15
8⅞	Aug 17	107:15	107:17	− 1	8.14
9⅛	May 18	110:03	110:05	− 2	8.15
9	Nov 18	108:28	108:30	− 1	8.15

U.S. TREASURY STRIPS

Stripped (zero-coupon) Treasuries

Mat.	Type	Bid	Asked	Chg.	Ask Yld.
May 12	ci	23:18	23:22	+ 1	8.36
Aug 12	ci	23:02	23:06	+ 1	8.36
Nov 12	ci	22:18	22:22	+ 1	8.37
Feb 13	ci	22:03	22:07	+ 1	8.37
May 13	ci	21:20	21:24	....	8.38
Aug 13	ci	21:05	21:09	....	8.38
Nov 13	ci	20:23	20:26	....	8.39
Feb 14	ci	20:09	20:13	....	8.39
May 14	ci	19:28	20:00	....	8.39
Aug 14	ci	19:15	19:19	....	8.39
Nov 14	ci	19:02	19:06	....	8.39
Feb 15	ci	18:22	18:25	....	8.39
Feb 15	bp	18:24	18:28	....	8.37
May 15	ci	18:10	18:13	− 1	8.39
Aug 15	ci	17:30	18:01	....	8.39
Aug 15	bp	18:00	18:03	....	8.37
Nov 15	ci	17:18	17:21	....	8.39
Nov 15	bp	17:21	17:24	....	8.36
Feb 16	ci	17:07	17:10	....	8.39
Feb 16	bp	17:10	17:13	....	8.36
May 16	ci	16:27	16:31	....	8.39
May 16	bp	17:09	17:13	....	8.26
Aug 16	ci	16:16	16:20	....	8.39
Nov 16	ci	16:06	16:09	....	8.39
Nov 16	bp	16:16	16:20	....	8.29
Feb 17	ci	15:26	15:30	....	8.39
May 17	ci	15:16	15:19	....	8.39
May 17	bp	15:19	15:23	− 1	8.36
Aug 17	ci	15:06	15:09	− 1	8.39
Aug 17	bp	15:09	15:12	....	8.36
Nov 17	ci	14:29	15:00	− 1	8.39

INVESTOR INSIGHTS: *Investing in Action*

Trading in the Dark: Real Bond Prices Are Hard to Come By

When market vibrations cause investors to worry about how their favorite stocks are holding up, all they have to do is check the closing prices in the business section of their newspaper. For those whose portfolios include fixed-income securities, however, particularly corporate or municipal bonds, keeping track isn't so simple. The financial pages provide little information on general bond market activity and even less on particular securities. Indeed, daily price quotes are widely available on only a few of the hundreds of thousands of publicly traded corporate and muni bonds.

Why? One reason is that most bonds are traded over-the-counter, not on centralized exchanges. Bond people, noting that the institutions dominate the bond market, imply that they are sophisticated enough to get whatever information they need. And, they argue, an individual can usually get a price quote or trade a bond through his or her broker.

However, these apologists ignore some pertinent facts about the bond market and the motivations of its participants. While the price an individual gets through his or her broker for a corporate or municipal bond might reflect the current market, it is likely also to be influenced by how many of those bonds the brokerage has in its inventory and whether the firm regularly makes a market in the security. Because most individual investors have only one brokerage account, they cannot easily confirm that the price quoted is the best one available.

Perhaps most significantly, the current framework motivates those with the information to keep it from those who don't. Most bonds trade over-the-counter through a dealer, a firm that makes a market in a particular bond. The dealer, as intermediary, makes a profit by buying from the seller at one price and selling to the buyer at a higher one. Therein lies the problem—obviously, it's in the dealer's interest to keep the playing field uneven by controlling the flow of information.

The fact is, the OTC market for most bonds is vastly different from that for stocks. There is no unified system such as Nasdaq to post quotes to all market makers. Nor must a market maker in bonds post a verifiable price. Often a firm makes a market simply because a customer has a large order to execute. The dilemma for individual investors is obvious. To determine the market for a given bond, an individual's broker usually must call his or her firm's bond trading desk. If the bond isn't one of that day's most active issues, the trader might have to call several other market makers to get the best available price.

Of the three major bond markets—government (i.e., Treasuries and agencies), corporate, and municipal—information is most widely available on government securities prices. However, individuals probably won't be able to trade at the bond prices quoted in the paper, because those prices are based on transactions of $1 million or more. Despite its faults, compared to public information on corporate and municipal bonds, the government bond arena looks like the Library of Congress. In the corporate and muni markets, some services offer trading data and prices on select bonds; however, quotes on the vast majority of issues simply aren't attainable. Thus, in these markets, individual investors truly are "trading in the dark."

Source: Adapted from Edward A. Wyatt, "Trading in the Dark," *Barron's,* November 6, 1989, pp. 15, 43, 46–47.

The next entry in the AT&T quote in Figure 8.5 is the "Vol" column, which shows the actual number of bonds traded. In this case, 240 bonds were traded on the day of the quotes. The last two columns provide the bond's closing price for the day and the net change in the closing price. Note that corporate bonds are usually quoted in eighths of a point (95⅞). In contrast, government bonds (Treasuries and agencies) are listed in thirty-seconds of a point. With government bonds, the figures to the right of the colon (:) indicate the number of thirty-seconds in the fractional bid or ask price. For example, look at the bid price of the highlighted 10¾ percent Treasury issue; observe that it's being quoted at 120:24 (bid). Translated, that means the bond's being quoted at 120²⁴⁄₃₂, or 120.75 percent of par. Thus, an investor who wants to buy, say, $15,000 worth of this issue can expect to pay $18,112.50 (i.e., $15,000 × 1.2075). Actually, the amount would be more than that after dealer spreads and other transaction costs are tacked on.

Treasury (and agency) bond quotes include not only the coupon (see the "Rate" column of the Treasury quotes) but also the year and *month* of maturity. Note also that when there's more than one date in the maturity column (e.g., see the 13⅞ percent Treasury bond, which shows a maturity of 2006–11), it's the *second* figure that indicates the issue's maturity date; the first one shows when the bond becomes freely callable. Thus, the 13⅞ percent bond matures in May 2011, and it carries a call deferment provision that extends through May 2006. In contrast, a Treasury note or bond with a single maturity date, such as the 10¾ percent bond of August 2005, indicates that the issue is *noncallable*. Unlike corporates, these bonds are quoted in bid/ask terms, where the bid price signifies what the bond dealers are willing to pay for the securities (which is how much you can sell them for), and the ask price is what the dealers will sell the bonds for (which is what you have to pay to buy them). Again, keep in mind that these bid/ask prices ignore transaction costs. When transaction costs are factored in, you'll end up getting *less* than the quoted price when you sell and pay *more* than the quoted price when you buy. This is especially true in the Treasury, agency, and municipal markets, where (secondary market) trades of, say, $25,000 or less can involve transactions costs of as much as *1 to 5 percent* of the amount traded. Finally, note that the "Yld" column with Treasuries is not the current yield of the issue but, rather, the bond's *promised yield-to-maturity*. Promised yield-to-maturity is basically a fully compounded measure of return that captures both current income and capital gains or losses. (We'll examine yield-to-maturity in Chapter 9.)

Also highlighted in both the corporate and Treasury quotes are some zero-coupon bonds. Look at Alaska Airlines ("AlskAr") in the corporate column, which has a zero-coupon bond outstanding. Such bonds are identified by a *zr* in place of their coupons. For instance, with the Alaska Airlines bonds, the *zr06* means that the issue is a zero-coupon bond that matures in 2006. Zeros are even easier to pick out in the Treasury quotes, because they're all listed under the heading "U.S. Treasury Strips." As we discussed earlier in this chapter, the Treasury basically creates these securities by "stripping" the coupons from their bond issues and selling them separately from the principal. By doing so, the principal and interest *cash flows* can be sold on their own. (Look at the Strips quotes: A *ci* behind the maturity date means the issue is made up of coupon/interest cash flow, whereas a *bp* means it is made up of bond principal.) Regardless of whether they're corporates or stripped Treasuries, the prices of most zeros are quite low compared to regular coupon bonds; this is particularly true for longer maturities. Thus, the quoted price of 41⅛ for the Alaska Airlines issue is *not* a misprint; rather, it means you could buy this bond for $411.25 (or 41.125 percent of par) and in the year 2006 receive $1,000 in return. Likewise, you could buy the Feb–15 stripped Treasury for just $187.81 (18²⁵⁄₃₂ of par) and in 2015 receive a payment of $1,000 on your investment—providing you with a fully compounded return of 8.39 percent.

CONCEPTS *in Review*

8.12 What are *bond ratings*, and how can they affect investor returns? What are *split ratings*?

8.13 From the perspective of an individual investor, what good are bond ratings? Do bond ratings provide any indication of the amount of market risk imbedded in a bond? Explain.

8.14 Bonds are said to be quoted "as a percent of par"; what does that mean? What is 1 point worth in the bond market?

8.15 Why should an aggressive bond trader be concerned with the trading volume of a particular issue?

On Track with STOCK-TRAK®

Making Bond Investments Through STOCK-TRAK®

STOCK-TRAK® account holders can trade a variety of corporate and Treasury bonds. The specific choices are listed in the registration materials. The "ticker symbol"—in this case, a symbol assigned to the bond issue by STOCK-TRAK®—is given first in the listing; STOCK-TRAK® uses these symbols to improve record-keeping accuracy. Next, the issue itself is listed. There is a relationship between the issue and the ticker symbol assigned it. For example, "B-T99" is the July 1999 Treasury bond, and "B-EK" is the Eastman Kodak corporate bond. Bond prices are shown in the third column, the way of reading the price in the fourth column, par value in the fifth column, and the resulting price in the sixth column. For instance, a Treasury bond priced at 103.16 is worth $103\frac{16}{32}$ percent of par. Because Treasury and corporate bonds have $1,000 par values, the price of this T-bond is 1.035 × $1,000, or $1,035.

SUMMARY

LG 1 **Explain the basic investment attributes of bonds and discuss the appeal these securities hold as investment vehicles.** Bonds are publicly traded debt securities that provide investors with two types of income: (1) current income and (2) capital gains. Current income is derived from the coupon (interest) payments received over the life of the issue, whereas capital gains can be earned whenever market interest rates fall. Investor interest in bonds has increased substantially in recent years as higher and more volatile interest rates have attracted both income- and capital-gains-oriented investors to the bond market. In addition to their yields and returns, bonds can also be used to shelter income from taxes and for the preservation and long-term accumulation of capital.

LG 2 **Describe the essential features of a bond and be able to distinguish between different types of call, refunding, and sinking fund provisions.** All bonds carry some type of coupon, which specifies the annual rate of interest to be paid by the issuer; most bonds carry coupon rates that remain fixed for the life of the issue. In addition, bonds have predetermined maturity dates—some bonds will carry a single maturity date (e.g., term bonds), and others have a series of maturity dates (e.g., a serial issue). Every bond is issued with some type of call feature, be it freely callable, noncallable, or deferred callable. Basically, call features spell out whether or not an issue can be prematurely retired, and if so, when. Some bonds will (temporarily) prohibit the issuer from paying off one bond with the proceeds from another by including a refunding provision, and others will be issued with sinking fund provisions, which specify how a bond will be paid off over time.

LG 3 **Describe the relationship between bond prices and market interest rates, and, in general, explain why some bonds are more volatile than others.** The price behavior of a bond depends on the issue's coupon and maturity and on the movement in market interest rates. When interest rates go down, bond prices go up, and vice versa. However, the extent to which bond prices move up or down depends on the coupon and maturity of an issue. Bonds with lower coupons and/or longer maturities generate larger price swings.

LG 4 **Identify the different types of bonds and the kinds of investment objectives these fixed-income securities can fulfill.** Basically, the bond market is divided into four major segments: Treasuries, agencies, municipals, and corporates. Treasury (or government) bonds are issued by the U.S. Treasury and are considered to be virtually default-free. Agency bonds are issued by various political subdivisions of the U.S. government and make up an increasingly important segment of the bond market. Municipal bonds are issued by state and local governments in the form of either general obligation or revenue bonds. Corporate bonds make up the major nongovernment sector of the market and are backed by the assets and profitability of the issuing companies. Generally speaking, Treasuries are attractive because of their high quality; agencies and corporates, because of the added returns they provide; and munies, because of the tax shelter they offer.

LG 5 **Gain an appreciation of how the bond market is becoming more global in nature and discuss the difference between dollar-denominated and non-dollar-denominated foreign bonds.** In addition to the securities issued in this country, there's growing investor interest in foreign bonds—particularly foreign-pay securities—because of the highly competitive yields and returns they offer. Foreign-pay bonds cover all those issues that are denominated in some currency other than dollars (sometimes referred to as non-dollar-denominated bonds). These bonds have an added source of return: currency exchange rates. In addition, there are also dollar-denominated foreign bonds—Yankee bonds and Eurodollar bonds—which have no currency exchange risk because they are issued in U.S. dollars.

LG 6 **Describe the role bond ratings play in the market and the quotation system that's used with various types of bonds.** Municipal and corporate issues are regularly rated for bond quality by independent rating agencies. A rating of Aaa indicates an impeccable record; lower ratings, such as A or Baa, indicate less protection for the investor. As with all investments, the returns required of lower-quality instruments generally are higher than those required of high-quality bonds. Just as the bond market has its own rating system, it also has its quotation system. Generally speaking, bonds are quoted as a percent of par and as such, one point in the bond market represents $10, not $1 as in the stock market. Furthermore, while corporate bonds are quoted in eighths of a point, Treasuries and agencies are quoted in thirty-seconds.

DISCUSSION QUESTIONS

1. Using the bond returns in Tables 8.1 and 8.2 as a basis of discussion:
   a. Compare the returns during the 1970s versus those produced in the 1980s. How do you explain the differences?
   b. What do you think would be a fair rate of return to expect from bonds in the future? Explain.

2. Identify and briefly describe each of the following types of bonds:
    a. Agency bonds   d. Junk bonds
    b. Municipal bonds   e. Foreign bonds
    c. Zero-coupon bonds   f. Collateralized mortgage obligations (CMOs)

Looking at these six different kinds of bonds, what type of investor do you think would be most attracted to each?

3. "Treasury securities are guaranteed by the U.S. government; therefore, there is no risk in the ownership of such bonds." Briefly discuss the wisdom (or folly) of this statement.

4. Select a security from the left-hand column that best fits the investor needs described in the right-hand column.
    a. 5-year Treasury note   1. Lock in a high coupon yield.
    b. A bond with a low coupon   2. Accumulate capital over a long period
        and long maturity   of time.
    c. Yankee bond   3. Generate a monthly income.
    d. Insured revenue bond   4. Avoid a lot of price volatility.
    e. Long-term Treasury Strips   5. Generate tax-free income.
    f. Noncallable bond   6. Invest in a foreign bond.
    g. CMO   7. Go for the highest yield available.
    h. Junk bond   8. Invest in a pool of credit-card receivables.
    i. ABS   9. Go for maximum price appreciation.

5. Using the quotes in Figure 8.5, answer the following questions:
    a. What's the dollar (bid) price of the Feb–17 Treasury Strip bond, and when does it mature?
    b. What's the current yield on the Feb–17 Treasury Strip issue?
    c. Which is higher priced: the AT&T 7⅛–02 or the 7½ percent U.S. Treasury of Nov–16? (Use ask prices.) If the Treasury bond is a higher-quality issue, why doesn't it sell for more than the AT&T issue?
    d. What's the dollar (ask) price of the 14 percent U.S. Treasury of Nov 06–11? Why is that issue priced so high? When does it mature?
    e. Contrast the call feature on the 12½ percent Aug 09–14 Treasury bond with the 9¼ percent Feb–16 Treasury issue.
    f. Which bond was more actively traded: the AT&T 8⅛–22 or the Atlantic Richfield (ARch) 10⅞–05?
    g. Which of the following bonds has the highest current yield: the AMR 9s16, the U.S. Treasury 13¾ percent of Aug–04, or the U.S. Treasury Strip of Nov–17? Which one has the lowest current yield? Which one would produce the most dollar amount of annual interest income (per $1,000 par bond)?

PROBLEMS   1. A 6 percent, 15-year bond has 3 years remaining on a deferred call feature (call premium is equal to 1 year's interest). The bond is currently priced in the market at $850. What is the issue's current yield?

   2. An investor is in the 28 percent tax bracket and lives in a state with no income tax. He is trying to decide which of two bonds to purchase: One is a 7½ percent corporate bond that is selling at par, and the other is a municipal bond with a 5¼ percent coupon that is also selling at par. If all other features of these two bonds are comparable, which should the investor select? Why? Would your answer change if this were an *in-state* municipal bond and the investor lived in a place with high state income taxes? Explain.

3. Sara Thomas is a wealthy investor who's looking for a tax shelter. Sara's in the maximum (39.6 percent) federal tax bracket, and she lives in a state with a very high state income tax (she pays the maximum of 11½ percent in state income tax). Sara is currently looking at two municipal bonds, both of which are selling at par: One's a double-A-rated in-state bond that carries a coupon of 6⅜ percent, and the other is a double-A-rated out-of-state bond that carries a 7⅛ percent coupon. Her broker has informed her that comparable fully taxable corporate bonds are currently available with yields of 9¾ percent; alternatively, long Treasuries are now available at yields of 9 percent. She has $100,000 to invest, and since all the bonds are high-quality issues, she wants to select the one that will give her maximum after-tax returns.

     a. Which one of the four bonds should she buy?

     b. Rank the four bonds (from best to worst) in terms of their taxable equivalent yields.

4. Which of the following three bonds offers the highest current yield?

     a. A 9½ percent, 20-year bond quoted at 97¾

     b. A 16 percent, 15-year bond quoted at 164⅝

     c. A 5¼ percent, 18-year bond quoted at 54

5. Assume that an investor pays $850 for a long-term bond that carries a 7½ percent coupon. Over the course of the next 12 months, interest rates drop sharply, and as a result, the investor sells the bond at a price of $962.50. Given this information:

     a. Find the current yield that existed on this bond at the beginning of the year. What was it by the end of the one-year holding period?

     b. Determine the holding period return on this investment. (See Chapter 4 for the HPR formula.)

6. In early January 1989, an investor purchased $30,000 worth of some single-A-rated corporate bonds; the bonds carried a coupon of 8⅞ percent and mature in 2008. The investor paid 94⅛ when she bought the bonds, and over the five-year period from 1989 through 1993, the bonds were priced in the market as follows:

	Quoted Prices		
Year	Beginning of the Year	End of the Year	Year-End Bond Yields
1989	94⅛	100⅝	8.82%
1990	100⅝	102	8.70
1991	102	104⅝	8.48
1992	104⅝	110¼	8.05
1993	110¼	121⅛	7.33

Coupon payments were made on schedule throughout the five-year period.

     a. Based on this information, find the annual holding period returns for 1989 through 1993. (See Chapter 4 for the HPR formula.)

     b. Use the return information in Table 8.1 to evaluate the investment performance of this bond. How do you think it stacks up against the market? Explain.

7. Georgette Robbins is an aggressive bond investor and is currently thinking about investing in a foreign (non-dollar-denominated) government bond. In particular, she's looking at a German government bond that matures in 15 years and carries a 9½ percent coupon. The bond has a par value of 10,000 D-marks and is currently trading at 110 (i.e., at 110 percent of par).

Georgette plans to hold the bond for a period of one year, at which time she thinks it will be trading at 117½—she's anticipating a sharp decline in German interest rates, which explains why she expects bond prices to move up. The current exchange rate is 1.58 D-marks/U.S. $, but she expects that to fall to 1.25 D-marks/U.S. $. Use the foreign investment return formula introduced in Chapter 5 (Equation 5.6) to answer the questions below.

    a. *Ignoring the currency effect*, find the bond's total return (in its local currency).

    b. Now find the total return on this bond *in U.S. dollars*. Did currency exchange rates affect the return in any way? Do you think this bond would make a good investment? Explain.

CASE PROBLEMS

8.1 FRANK AND LUCILLE DEVELOP A BOND INVESTMENT PROGRAM

Frank and Lucille Leadbetter, along with their two teenage sons, Lou and Lamar, live in Jenks, Oklahoma. Frank works as an electronics salesman, and Lucille is a personnel officer at a local bank; together they earn an annual income of around $75,000. Frank has just learned that his recently departed rich uncle has named him in his will to the tune of some $250,000 after taxes. Needless to say, the Leadbetters are elated. Frank intends to spend $50,000 of his inheritance on a number of long-overdue family items (e.g., some badly needed remodeling of their kitchen and family room, a new Nissan 300ZX, and braces to correct Lamar's overbite); he wants to invest the remaining $200,000 in various types of fixed-income securities.

Frank and Lucille have no unusual income requirements, health problems, or the like. Their only investment objectives are that they want to achieve some capital appreciation and they want to keep their funds fully invested for a period of at least 20 years; they would rather not have to rely on their investments as a source of current income but want to maintain some liquidity in their portfolio just in case.

Questions

1. Describe the type of bond investment program you think the Leadbetters should follow. In answering this question, give appropriate consideration to both return and risk factors.

2. List several different types of bonds that you would recommend for their portfolio, and briefly indicate why you would recommend each.

3. Using a recent issue of the *Wall Street Journal* or *Barron's*, construct a $200,000 bond portfolio for the Leadbetters. Use real securities and select any eight bonds (or notes) you like, given the following ground rules:

    a. The portfolio must include at least one Treasury, one agency, and one corporate bond.

    b. No more than 5 percent of the portfolio can be in short-term U.S. Treasury bills.

   c. Ignore all transaction costs (i.e., invest the full $200,000) and assume all securities have par values of $1,000 (though they can be trading in the market at something other than par).

   d. Use the latest available quotes to determine how many bonds/notes/bills you can buy.

4. Prepare a schedule listing all the securities in your recommended portfolio. Use a form like the one below and include the following information on each security in the portfolio:

Security Issuer-Coupon-Maturity	Latest Quoted Price	Number of Bonds Purchased	Amount Invested	Annual Coupon Income	Current Yield
Example: U.S. Treas - 8½%-'05	96⁸⁄₃₂	25	$ 24,062	$ 2,125	8.83%
1.					
2.					
3.					
4.					
5.					
6.					
7.					
8.					
Totals	—		$200,000	$	%

5. *In one brief paragraph*, note the key investment attributes of your recommended portfolio and the investment objectives you hope to obtain with it.

LG 6   **8.2 THE CASE OF THE MISSING BOND RATINGS**

While a lot goes into a bond rating, it's probably safe to say that there's nothing more important in determining a bond's rating than the underlying financial condition and operating results of the company issuing the bonds. Generally speaking, a variety of financial ratios are used to assess the financial health of a firm, and just as financial ratios can be used in the analysis of common stocks, so too can they be used in the analysis of bonds—a process which we refer to as *credit analysis*. In credit analysis, attention is directed toward the basic liquidity and profitability of the firm, the extent to which the firm employs debt, and the ability of the firm to service its debt.

    The following financial ratios are often helpful in carrying out such analysis: (1) current ratio, (2) quick ratio, (3) net profit margin, (4) return on total capital, (5) long-term debt to total capital, (6) owners' equity ratio, (7) pretax interest coverage, and (8) cash flow to total debt. The first two ratios measure the liquidity of the firm; the next two, its profitability; the following two, the debt load; and the final two, the ability of the firm to service its debt load. (For ratio 5, the *lower* the ratio, the better; for all the others, the *higher* the ratio, the better.) The following table lists each of these ratios for six different companies.

A Table of Financial Ratios
(All ratios are real and pertain to real companies)

Financial Ratio	Company 1	Company 2	Company 3	Company 4	Company 5	Company 6
1. Current ratio	1.13 ×	1.39 ×	1.78 ×	1.32 ×	1.03 ×	1.41 ×
2. Quick ratio	0.48 ×	0.84 ×	0.93 ×	0.33 ×	0.50 ×	0.75 ×
3. Net profit margin	4.6%	12.9%	14.5%	2.8%	5.9%	10.0%
4. Return on total capital	15.0%	25.9%	29.4%	11.5%	16.8%	28.4%
5. Long term debt to total capital	63.3%	52.7%	23.9%	97.0%	88.6%	42.1%
6. Owners' equity ratio	18.6%	18.9%	44.1%	1.5%	5.1%	21.2%
7. Pretax interest coverage	2.3 ×	4.5 ×	8.9 ×	1.7 ×	2.4 ×	6.4%
8. Cash flow to total debt	34.7%	48.8%	71.2%	20.4%	30.2%	42.7%

Notes: Ratio (2)—Whereas the current ratio relates current assets to current liabilities, the quick ratio considers only the most liquid current assets (cash, short-term securities, and accounts receivable) and relates them to current liabilities.
Ratio (4)—Relates pre-tax profit to the total capital structure (long-term debt + equity) of the firm.
Ratio (6)—Shows the amount of stockholders' equity used to finance the firm (stockholders' equity ÷ total assets).
Ratio (8)—Looks at the amount of corporate cash flow (from net profits + depreciation) relative to the total (current + long-term) debt of the firm.
The other four ratios are as described in Chapter 6.

Questions

1. Three of these companies have bonds that carry investment-grade ratings, and the other three companies carry junk-bond ratings. Based on the information in the table, which three companies have the investment-grade bonds and which three the junk bonds? Briefly explain your selections.

2. One of these six companies is a AAA-rated firm and one is B-rated. Pick out those two companies. Briefly explain your selection.

3. Of the remaining four companies, one carries a AA rating, one an A rating, and two are BB-rated. Which ones are they?

CHAPTER 9

BOND VALUATION AND ANALYSIS

LEARNING GOALS

After studying this chapter, you should be able to:

LG 1 Explain the behavior of market interest rates and identify the forces that cause interest rates to move.

LG 2 Describe the term structure of interest rates and note how these so-called yield curves can be used by investors.

LG 3 Gain an understanding of how bonds are valued in the marketplace.

LG 4 Describe the various measures of yield and return, and explain how these standards of performance are used in the bond valuation process.

LG 5 Understand the basic concept of duration, how it can be measured, and its use in the management of bond portfolios.

LG 6 Discuss various bond investment strategies and the different ways these securities can be used by investors.

Until the early to mid–1980s, most bond investors followed a buy-and-hold strategy," explains bond analyst Linda Carter. "Since then, bond markets have become more trading oriented, as investors realized that, like equities, fixed-income securities can be mispriced. My job is to identify such securities, thus earning higher returns for John Hancock's bond funds." She attributes the change in investment strategy to several factors. One of these factors, she believes, is the Federal Reserve Board's increased willingness to raise interest rates to control inflation, thereby increasing interest rate volatility. Also, since 1980, financial markets and the business environment have become increasingly complex and dynamic. For many years, insurance companies and banks were the major institutional bond investors; now, mutual funds make bond investments on behalf of individual investors. "Institutional investors don't expect to hold bonds to maturity; they take a value approach and seek bonds that may trade at lower prices than comparable issues, to benefit from capital appreciation," Carter says.

Finding undervalued bonds with good potential for capital appreciation is a complex process that takes into account both the issuer's creditworthiness and economic factors. Carter analyzes the issuing company, its financial condition, and industry trends. Her analysis focuses on the firm's ability to generate sufficient earnings before interest and taxes (EBIT) to repay its fixed obligations. Carter then looks at economic factors, particularly anticipated interest rate movements and inflation expectations. "Our goal is to structure our bond portfolios to take advantage of the economic forecast. We look at the economy and where it's headed, and then select bonds in industries that do well in given scenarios." For example, when the Federal Reserve raised interest rates in 1994 to slow the economy, the funds adjusted their strategy: They reduced exposure to cyclically sensitive industries like automobiles, increased holdings in consumer nondurables such as drugs and supermarkets, and shortened maturities to reduce interest rate risk.

"Bond markets tend to be biased in favor of large institutional investors, who can diversify across industries and maturities to reduce risk," Carter explains. "Anything under $1 million is considered an odd lot, and price quotes aren't easy to obtain." However, informed investors who have carefully considered both credit and economic issues when valuing bonds have benefited from

INFORMED INVESTORS WHO HAVE CAREFULLY CONSIDERED BOTH CREDIT AND ECONOMIC ISSUES WHEN VALUING BONDS HAVE BENEFITED FROM HAVING BONDS IN THEIR PORTFOLIOS.

having bonds in their portfolios. As with any investment, the key is a thorough understanding of the forces that influence bond values.

A chartered financial analyst specializing in fixed-income securities for the telecommunications, retail, food, and tobacco industries, Linda Carter joined John Hancock Funds as senior research officer in 1994. For the previous seven years she was first an investment officer and then a vice-president at Allmerica Financial in Worcester, Massachusetts. She has a B.S. in management from the University of Massachusetts and an M.S. in finance from Boston College.

As the interview with Linda Carter indicates, investing in bonds for capital appreciation can be a daunting task for the individual investor with limited funds to invest. However, when you get right down to it, a bond is pretty much like any other investment product: It provides a future cash flow to the investor, and, depending on the amount and certainty of that cash flow, it has a given market value. The problem the investor faces is deciding whether the value as established in the marketplace will provide the kind of return he or she is looking for. This chapter addresses such concerns, as it deals with bond valuation and analysis. Here we will examine how bonds are valued and how they can be used to fulfill certain investor objectives. In particular, we'll look into the pricing of bonds and various measures of yield and return. In addition, we'll discuss a key measure of bond price volatility—duration—and see how it can be used to "immunize" bond portfolios from market and interest rate risks. We'll then close with a review of various investment strategies and bond management techniques. But first, because of the crucial role that they play in the bond market, let's begin this discussion with a look at interest rates and the market forces that drive them.

THE BEHAVIOR OF MARKET INTEREST RATES

You will recall from Chapter 4 that rational investors will try to earn a return that fully compensates them for risk. In the case of bondholders, that required return (r_i), called the *market interest rate*, has three components—the real rate of return (r^*), an expected inflation premium (IP), and a risk premium (RP). It is expressed by this equation:

Equation 9.1
$$r_i = r^* + IP + RP$$

The real rate of return plus the inflation premium are external economic factors and together equal the risk-free rate (R_F). To get the required return, we must add to the risk-free rate the risk premium that relates to the particular bond issue and its issuer. Key issue and issuer characteristics include such variables as the type of bond (secured or unsecured, convertible, etc.), maturity, call features, and bond rating. These three components $(r^*, IP,$ and $RP)$ determine interest rate levels at a given point in time.

Because interest rates have such a significant bearing on bond prices and yields, they are closely monitored by both conservative and aggressive investors. Interest rates are important to conservative investors because one of their major objectives is to lock in high yields. Aggressive traders also have a stake in interest rates because their investment programs are often built on the capital gains opportunities that accompany major swings in rates.

KEEPING TABS ON MARKET INTEREST RATES

Just as there is no single bond market but a series of different market sectors, so too there is no single interest rate that applies to all segments of the market. Rather, each segment has its own, unique level of interest rates. Granted, the various rates do tend to drift in the same direction over time and to follow the same general pattern of behavior, but it's also common for **yield spreads** (or interest rate differentials) to exist in the various market sectors. We can summarize some of the more important market yields and yield spreads as follows:

yield spreads
differences in interest rates that exist in various sectors of the market.

1. Municipal bonds usually carry the lowest market rates because of the tax-exempt feature of these obligations. As a rule, their market yields are about two-thirds those of corporates. In the taxable sector, Treasuries have the lowest yields (because they have the least risk), followed by agencies and then corporates, which provide the highest returns.

2. Those issues that normally carry bond ratings (e.g., municipals or corporates) generally display the same behavior: The lower the rating, the higher the yield.

3. There is generally a direct relationship between the coupon an issue carries and its yield: Discount (low-coupon) bonds yield the least, and premium (high-coupon) bonds yield the most.

4. In the municipal sector, revenue bonds yield more than general obligation bonds.

5. Bonds that are freely callable generally provide the highest returns, at least at date of issue; these are followed by deferred call obligations and then by noncallable bonds, which yield the least.

6. As a rule, bonds with long maturities tend to yield more than short issues. However, this rule does not hold all the time; sometimes, such as in early 1989, short-term yields exceed the yields on long-term bonds.

The preceding list can be used as a general guide to the higher-yielding segments of the bond market. For example, income-oriented municipal bond investors might do well to consider certain high-quality revenue bonds as a way to increase yields; or, agency bonds, rather than Treasuries, might be selected for the same reason by investors who like to stick to high-quality issues.

Investors should pay close attention to interest rates and yield spreads, and try to stay abreast not only of the current state of the market but also of the *future direction in market rates*. If a conservative (income-oriented) bond investor thinks, for example, that rates have just about peaked, that should be a clue to try to lock in the prevailing high yields with some form of call protection (e.g., buying bonds—like Treasuries or double-A-rated utilities—that are noncallable or still have lengthy call deferments). In contrast, if an aggressive bond trader thinks rates have peaked (and are about to drop), that should be a signal to buy bonds that offer maximum price appreciation potential (e.g., low-coupon bonds that still have a long time before they mature). Clearly, in either case, the *future direction of interest rates is important!*

But how does a bond investor formulate such expectations? Unless the investor has considerable training in economics, he or she will have to rely on various published sources. Fortunately, a wealth of such information is available. One's broker is an excellent source for such reports, as are investor services such as Moody's and Standard & Poor's. Finally, there are widely circulated business and financial publications—like the *Wall Street Journal*, *Forbes*, *Business Week*, and *Fortune*—that regularly address the current state and future direction of market interest rates. One of the best of these is illustrated in Figure 9.1. Make no mistakes about it, predicting the future direction of interest rates is not an easy task. However, by taking the time to regularly and carefully read some of these publications and reports, investors can keep track of the behavior of interest rates and at least get a handle on what experts predict is likely to occur in the near future—say, over the next 6 to 12 months, perhaps longer.

Figure 9.1 A Popular Source of Information About Interest Rates and the Credit Markets The "Credit Markets" column, which appears every day in the the *Wall Street Journal,* provides a capsule view of current conditions and future prospects in the bond market. Note that on this particular day, a good deal of the article was devoted to foreign bonds and the growing importance of global bond issues. (Source: *Wall Street Journal*, October 20, 1994.)

Argentina and Chinese Holding Company Find Buyers Eager for Their Emerging-Markets Debt

CREDIT
MARKETS

By Thomas T. Vogel Jr.
Staff Reporter of The Wall Street Journal

NEW YORK — Call it the return of the emerging-markets debt issuers.

Yesterday two favorites of investors in developing-nation debt, Argentina and **China International Trust & Investment Corp.**, a government-owned investment holding company, returned to the U.S. markets for the first time this year.

Citic sold $200 million of 12-year notes while Argentina launched a global offering of $500 million of five-year notes.

Both issuers seemed to succeed in attracting strong investor interest, but the market for emerging-markets debt is a different animal these days. Gone are the days when investors would pile onto a debt issue without hesitation because they figured the bond markets would just keep rallying.

After the Federal Reserve raised rates in February for the first time in nearly five years, bond prices plunged world-wide and some of the hardest-hit credits were those from developing nations, like China and Argentina.

"The market is certainly not as good as last year," said Ton Gardeniers, a vice president of capital markets at J.P. Morgan Securities Inc., which was the lead manager for the Citic offering.

"I wouldn't call the difference day and night, but there is a clear difference between this year's market and last year's," said Mr. Gardeniers. Investors are more picky this year, he said, though demand remains fairly strong for Chinese bond

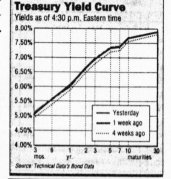

Treasury Yield Curve
Yields as of 4:30 p.m. Eastern time

— Yesterday
— 1 week ago
⋯⋯ 4 weeks ago

Source: Technical Data's Bond Data

YIELD COMPARISONS

Based on Merrill Lynch Bond Indexes, priced as of midafternoon Eastern time.

			—52 Week—	
	10/19	10/18	High	Low
Corp.-Govt. Master	7.51%	7.47%	7.60%	5.24%
Treasury 1-10yr	6.95	6.91	7.04	4.29
10+ yr	8.10	8.06	8.18	6.06
Agencies 1-10yr	7.37	7.34	7.49	5.03
10+ yr	8.26	8.22	8.34	6.44
Corporate				
1-10 yr High Qlty	7.75	7.70	7.85	5.39
Med Qlty	8.06	8.01	8.14	5.81
10+yr High Qlty	8.57	8.53	8.64	6.96
Med Qlty	8.98	8.94	9.04	7.32
Yankee bonds(1)	8.28	8.24	8.37	6.34
Current-coupon mortgages (2)				
GNMA 8.50%	8.69	8.69	8.87	6.13
FNMA 8.50%	8.59	8.59	8.81	6.13
FHLMC8.50%	8.62	8.62	8.84	6.12
High-yield corporates	10.87	10.87	10.91	9.25
New tax-exempts				
7-12-yr G.O. (AA)	5.62	5.62	5.97	4.60
12-22-yr G.O. (AA)	6.06	6.04	6.69	4.91
22+yr revenue (A)	6.33	6.31	6.71	5.31

Note: High quality rated AAA-AA; medium quality A-BBB/Baa; high yield, BB/Ba-C.
(1) Dollar-denominated, SEC-registered bonds of foreign issuers sold in the U.S. (2) Reflects the 52-week high and low of mortgage-backed securities indexes rather than the individual securities shown.

would account for part of the wider gap.

Yesterday the 10-year Treasury note

nage points in order to attract enough U.S. and European institutional investors to "clear the deal," one underwriter said.

"It is very fairly priced and gives investors a real incentive to get back into the market," said one underwriter. "The republic wanted to re-establish its name in the marketplace."

While China and Argentina are both considered emerging-markets issuers, their credit ratings are very different. The Citic issue is rated single-A-3 by Moody's Investors Service Inc. and triple-B by Standard & Poor's Ratings Group, both low investment-grade ratings. The long-term debt rating of Argentina, on the other hand, is single-B-1 from Moody's and double-B-minus from S&P, both subinvestment-grade, or junk, ratings.

Citic, sold 9% coupon noncallable 12-year Yankee bonds at a price of 99.501 to yield 9.07%. Yankee bonds are securities sold by foreign issuers in the U.S. and are usually denominated in dollars. According to J.P. Morgan, "proceeds from the offering will be used to finance offshore oil development projects of **China National Offshore Oil** Corp., China's state-owend offshore oil-exploration and development company."

"We've seen a number of first-time Yankee buyers," with this issue, said John Massad, a vice president at J.P. Morgan. A number of state pension funds and other public-sector pension funds have begun buying Yankee issues after hiring analysts and getting foreign securities approved by their boards of directors, he said.

Citic debt isn't directly guaranteed by the People's Republic of China, but Citic can borrow from the central bank and it has the same rating as the country.

WHAT CAUSES INTEREST RATES TO MOVE?

Although the subject of interest rates is a complex economic issue, we do know that certain forces are especially important in influencing the general behavior of market rates. Serious bond investors should make it a point to become familiar with the major determinants of interest rates and try to monitor those variables—at least informally.

And in that regard, perhaps no variable is more important than *inflation.* Changes in the inflation rate (or even expectations about the future course of inflation) have a direct and pronounced effect on market interest rates, and have been a leading cause of wide swings in interest rates. Clearly, if expectations are for inflation to slow down, then market interest rates should fall as well. To gain an appreciation of the extent to which interest rates are linked to inflation, refer to Figure 9.2. Note that as inflation drifts up, so too do interest rates. On the other hand, a drop in inflation is matched by a similar decline in interest rates.

In addition to inflation, there are at least five other important economic variables that can significantly affect the level of interest rates:

1. *Changes in the money supply.* An increase in the money supply pushes rates down (as it makes more funds available for loans), and vice versa. This is true only up to a point, however: If the growth in the money supply becomes excessive, it can lead to inflation which, of course, means higher interest rates.

2. *The size of the federal budget deficit.* When the U.S. Treasury must borrow large amounts to cover the budget deficit, the increased demand for funds exerts an upward pressure on interest rates.

3. *The level of economic activity.* Businesses need more capital when the economy expands. This need increases the demand for funds, and rates tend to rise. During a recession, economic activity contracts, and rates typically fall.

4. *Policies of the Federal Reserve.* Actions of the Federal Reserve to control inflation also have a major effect on market interest rates. For example, when the Fed wants to slow real (or perceived) inflation, it usually does so by driving up interest rates, as it did seven times during 1994. Unfortunately, such actions can also have the nasty side effect of slowing down business activity as well.

5. *The level of interest rates in major foreign markets.* Today, investors look beyond national borders for investment opportunities. If rates in major foreign markets rise, rates in the United States will have to rise to attract investors; if not, investors will dump dollars, as they did in 1992, to buy high-yielding foreign securities.

Figure 9.2 The Impact of Inflation on the Behavior of Interest Rates
The behavior of interest rates has always been closely tied to movements in the rate of inflation. What changed in the early 1980s, however, was the spread between inflation and interest rates. Whereas a spread of roughly 3 points was common in the past, it has held at about 5 to 6 percentage points since 1982.

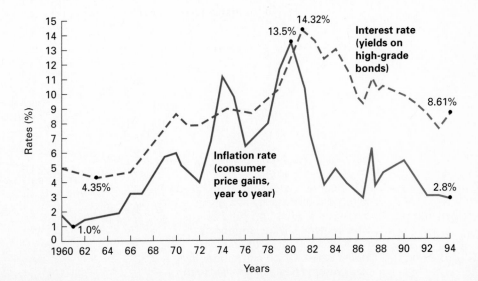

THE TERM STRUCTURE OF INTEREST RATES AND YIELD CURVES

Although many factors affect the behavior of market interest rates, one of the most popular and widely studied is *bond maturity*. The relationship between the interest rates (yield) and time to maturity for any class of similar-risk securities is called the **term structure of interest rates**. This relationship can be depicted graphically by a **yield curve**, which relates a bond's *term* to maturity to its *yield* to maturity at a given point in time. A particular yield curve exists for only a short period of time; as market conditions change, so do the yield curve's shape and location.

Types of Yield Curves

Two different types of yield curves are illustrated in Figure 9.3. By far, the most common type is curve 1, the *upward-sloping*, or normal, curve. It indicates that yields tend to increase with longer maturities. The longer a bond has to go to maturity, the greater the potential for price volatility and the risk of loss. Investors, therefore, require higher risk premiums to induce them to buy the longer, riskier bonds. Occasionally, the yield curve takes the *inverted*, or downward-sloping, shape shown in curve 2, where short-term rates are higher than long-term rates. This generally results from actions by the Federal Reserve to curtail inflation by driving short-term interest rates way up. Two other yield curves also appear from time to time: the *flat* yield curve, when rates for short- and long-term debt are essentially similar, and the *humped* yield curve, when intermediate-term rates are the highest.

Plotting Your Own Curves

Yield curves are constructed by plotting the yields for a group of bonds that are similar in all respects except maturity. Treasury securities (bills, notes, and bonds) are typically used to draw yield curves, for several reasons: Their yields are easily found in financial publications, they have no risk of default, and they are homogeneous with regard to quality and other issue characteristics. Investors can also construct yield curves for other classes of debt securities

term structure of interest rates
the relationship between the interest rate or rate of return (yield) on a bond and its time to maturity.

yield curve
a graph that represents the relationship between a bond's term to maturity and its yield at a given point in time.

Figure 9.3 Two Types of Yield Curves
A yield curve relates term to maturity to yield-to-maturity at a given point in time. Although yield curves come in many shapes and forms, the most common is the *upward-sloping curve*, which shows that investor returns (yields) increase with longer maturities.

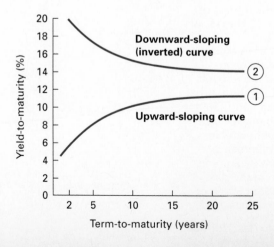

Figure 9.4 Yield Curves on U.S. Treasury Issues
Here we see two yield curves constructed from actual market data (quotes). Note that although the general shape is about the same, curve 1 is a lot steeper than curve 2, because there's a wider spread between short-term and long-term interest rates.

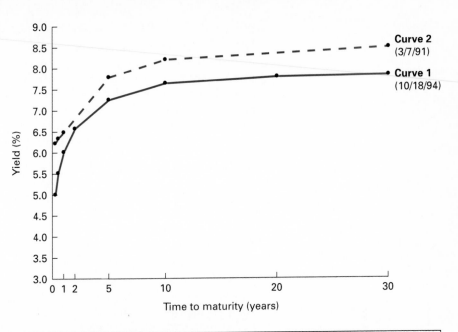

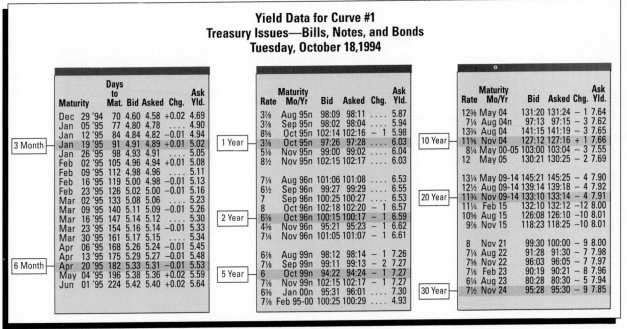

Yield Data for Curve #1
Treasury Issues—Bills, Notes, and Bonds
Tuesday, October 18,1994

	Maturity	Days to Mat.	Bid	Asked	Chg.	Ask Yld.
	Dec 29 '94	70	4.60	4.58	+0.02	4.69
	Jan 05 '95	77	4.80	4.78	....	4.90
	Jan 12 '95	84	4.84	4.82	−0.01	4.94
3 Month	Jan 19 '95	91	4.91	4.89	+0.01	5.02
	Jan 26 '95	98	4.93	4.91	....	5.05
	Feb 02 '95	105	4.96	4.94	+0.01	5.08
	Feb 09 '95	112	4.98	4.96	....	5.11
	Feb 16 '95	119	5.00	4.98	−0.01	5.13
	Feb 23 '95	126	5.02	5.00	−0.01	5.16
	Mar 02 '95	133	5.08	5.06	....	5.23
	Mar 09 '95	140	5.11	5.09	−0.01	5.26
	Mar 16 '95	147	5.14	5.12	....	5.30
	Mar 23 '95	154	5.16	5.14	−0.01	5.33
	Mar 30 '95	161	5.17	5.15	....	5.34
	Apr 06 '95	168	5.26	5.24	−0.01	5.45
	Apr 13 '95	175	5.29	5.27	−0.01	5.48
6 Month	Apr 20 '95	182	5.33	5.31	−0.01	5.53
	May 04 '95	196	5.38	5.36	+0.02	5.59
	Jun 01 '95	224	5.42	5.40	+0.02	5.64

	Rate	Maturity Mo/Yr	Bid	Asked	Chg.	Ask Yld.
	3⅞	Aug 95n	98:09	98:11	....	5.87
	3⅞	Sep 95n	98:02	98:04	....	5.94
	8⅝	Oct 95n	102:14	102:16	− 1	5.98
1 Year	3⅞	Oct 95n	97:26	97:28	....	6.03
	5⅛	Nov 95n	99:00	99:02	....	6.04
	8½	Nov 95n	102:15	102:17	....	6.03
	7¼	Aug 96n	101:06	101:08	....	6.53
	6½	Sep 96n	99:27	99:29	....	6.55
	7	Sep 96n	100:25	100:27	....	6.53
	8	Oct 96n	102:18	102:20	− 1	6.57
2 Year	6⅞	Oct 96n	100:15	100:17	− 1	6.59
	4⅜	Nov 96n	95:21	95:23	− 1	6.62
	7¼	Nov 96n	101:05	101:07	− 1	6.61
	6⅞	Aug 99n	98:12	98:14	− 1	7.26
	7⅛	Sep 99n	99:11	99:13	− 2	7.27
5 Year	6	Oct 99n	94:22	94:24	− 1	7.27
	7⅞	Nov 99n	102:15	102:17	− 1	7.27
	6⅜	Jan 00n	95:31	96:01	....	7.30
	7⅞	Feb 95-00	100:25	100:29	....	4.93

	Rate	Maturity Mo/Yr	Bid	Asked	Chg.	Ask Yld.
	12⅜	May 04	131:20	131:24	− 1	7.64
	7¼	Aug 04n	97:13	97:15	− 3	7.62
	13¾	Aug 04	141:15	141:19	− 3	7.65
10 Year	11⅝	Nov 04	127:12	127:16	+ 1	7.66
	8¼	May 00-05	103:00	103:04	− 3	7.55
	12	May 05	130:21	130:25	− 2	7.69
	13¼	May 09-14	145:21	145:25	− 4	7.90
	12½	Aug 09-14	139:14	139:18	− 4	7.92
20 Year	11¾	Nov 09-14	133:10	133:14	− 4	7.91
	11¼	Feb 15	132:10	132:12	−12	8.00
	10⅝	Aug 15	126:08	126:10	−10	8.01
	9⅞	Nov 15	118:23	118:25	−10	8.01
	8	Nov 21	99:30	100:00	− 9	8.00
	7¼	Aug 22	91:28	91:30	− 7	7.98
	7⅝	Nov 22	96:03	96:05	− 7	7.97
	7⅛	Feb 23	90:19	90:21	− 8	7.96
	6¼	Aug 23	80:28	80:30	− 5	7.94
30 Year	7½	Nov 24	95:28	95:30	− 9	7.85

with similar characteristics, such as A-rated municipal bonds, Aa-rated corporate bonds, or even certificates of deposit.

Figure 9.4 shows the yield curves for Treasury securities on two dates—March 7, 1991, and October 18, 1994. To draw these curves, you need Treasury quotes from the *Wall Street Journal*—note that actual quoted yields for Curve #1 are provided in the boxed information right below the graph. Given the required quotes, select the yields for the Treasury bills, notes, and bonds maturing in approximately 3 months, 6 months, and 1, 2, 5, 10, 20, and 30 years. The yields used for this curve are highlighted. (You could include more points, but they would not have much effect on the shape of the curve.) Next, plot the points on a graph whose horizontal (x) axis represents time to maturity in years and whose vertical (y) axis represents yield to maturity. Connect the points to create the curves shown in Figure 9.4. Note that in both cases the pattern is upward-sloping, which historically has been the "normal" pattern.

Explanations of the Term Structure of Interest Rates

As noted earlier, the shape of the yield curve changes over time. Three commonly cited theories—the expectations hypothesis, the liquidity preference theory, and the market segmentation theory—explain more fully the reasons for the general shape of the yield curve.

expectations hypothesis
theory that the shape of the yield curve reflects investor expectations of future interest rates.

Expectations Hypothesis   The **expectations hypothesis** suggests that the yield curve reflects investor expectations about the future behavior of (short-term) interest rates. The relationship between rates today and rates expected in the future is due primarily to investor expectations regarding inflation: If investors anticipate higher rates of inflation in the future, they will require higher long-term interest rates today, and vice versa. To see how this explanation of the term structure can be applied in practice, consider the behavior of U.S. Treasury securities.

Because Treasury securities are considered essentially risk-free, only two components determine their yield: the real rate of interest and inflation expectations. Because the real interest rate is the same for all maturities, variations in yields are caused by differing inflation expectations associated with different maturities. This hypothesis can be illustrated using the October 18, 1994, yields for four of the Treasury maturities in Figure 9.4. If we assume that the real rate of interest is 3 percent, the inflation expectation during the period to maturity can be calculated for each maturity and is shown in column 3 of the following table:

Maturity	(1) Oct. 18, 1994 Yield	(2) Real Rate of Interest	(3) Inflation Expectation [(1) − (2)]
3 months	5.02%	3.00%	2.02%
1 year	6.03	3.00	3.03
5 years	7.27	3.00	4.27
30 years	7.85	3.00	4.85

Therefore, it appears that on October 18, 1994, investors were indeed expecting inflation to heat up in the future; as a result, the yield curve was upward-sloping, as shown in Figure 9.4.

Generally, under the expectations hypothesis, an increasing inflation expectation results in an upward-sloping yield curve, a decreasing inflation expectation results in a downward-sloping yield curve, and a stable inflation expectation results in a flat yield curve. Although, as we'll see below, other theories do exist, the observed strong relationship between inflation and interest rates lends considerable credence to this widely accepted theory.

Liquidity Preference Theory   More often than not, yield curves are upward-sloping. One explanation for the frequency of such yield curves is the

liquidity preference theory
theory that investors tend to prefer the greater liquidity of short-term securities and therefore require a premium to invest in long-term securities.

liquidity preference theory. This theory states that, intuitively, long-term bond rates should be higher than short-term rates because of the added risks involved with the longer securities. In other words, because of the risk differential (real or perceived) between long- and short-term debt securities, rational investors will prefer the less risky short-term obligations *unless they can be motivated, via higher interest rates, to invest in the longer bonds.*

Actually, there are a number of reasons why rational investors should prefer short-term securities. To begin with, they are more liquid (i.e., more easily converted to cash) and less sensitive to changing market rates, which means there is less risk of loss of principal. For a given change in market rates, the prices of longer-term bonds will show considerably more movement than the prices of short-term bonds. Simply put, uncertainty increases over time, and investors therefore require a premium to invest in long maturities. In addition, investors tend to require a premium for tying up funds for longer periods, whereas borrowers will pay a premium in order to obtain long-term funds. Borrowers thus assure themselves that funds will be available and they can avoid having to roll over short-term debt at unknown and possibly unfavorable rates. All of these preferences and market forces explain why higher rates of interest should be associated with longer maturities and why it's perfectly rational to expect upward-sloping yield curves.

market segmentation theory
theory that the market for debt is segmented based on maturity, that supply and demand within each segment determines the prevailing interest rate, and that the slope of the yield curve depends on the relationship between the prevailing rates in each segment.

Market Segmentation Theory   Another often-cited theory, the **market segmentation theory**, suggests that the market for debt is segmented based on the maturity preferences of different types of financial institutions and investors. According to this theory, the yield curve changes as the supply and demand for funds within each maturity segment determines its prevailing interest rate. The equilibrium between the financial institutions that supply the funds for short-term maturities (e.g., banks) and the borrowers of those short-term funds (e.g., businesses with seasonal loan requirements) establishes interest rates in the short-term markets. Similarly, the equilibrium between suppliers and demanders in such long-term markets as life insurance and real estate determines the prevailing long-term interest rates. The shape of the yield curve could be either upward- or downward-sloping, as determined by the general relationship between rates in each market segment. When supply outstrips demand for short-term loans, short-term rates would be relatively low. If, at the same time, the demand for long-term loans is higher than the available supply of funds, long-term rates would be high, and the yield curve would slope upward. Simply stated, low rates in the short-term segment and high rates in the long-term segment cause an upward-sloping yield curve, and vice versa.

Which Theory?   It is clear that all three theories of the term structure of interest rates have merit in explaining the shape of the yield curve. From them, we can conclude that at any time, the slope of the yield curve is affected by (1) inflationary expectations, (2) liquidity preferences, and (3) the supply and demand conditions in the short- and long-term market segments. Upward-sloping yield curves result from higher future inflation expectations, lender preferences for shorter-maturity loans, and greater supply of short- as opposed to long-term loans relative to the respective demand in each market segment. The opposite behavior, of course, results in a downward-sloping yield curve. At any point in time, the interaction of these forces determines the prevailing slope of the yield curve.

Using the Yield Curve in Investment Decisions

Bond investors often use yield curves in making investment decisions. As noted earlier, yield curves change in accordance with market conditions. Analyzing the changes in yield curves over time provides investors with information about future interest rate movements and how they can affect price behavior and comparative returns. For example, if the yield curve begins to rise sharply, it usually means that inflation is starting to heat up or is expected to do so in the near future; as such, investors can expect that interest rates, too, will rise. Under these conditions, most seasoned bond investors will turn to short or intermediate (3 to 5 years) maturities, which provide reasonable returns and at the same time minimize exposure to capital loss when interest rates go up (and bond prices fall). A downward-sloping yield curve, though unusual, generally results from actions of the Federal Reserve to reduce inflation. As suggested by the expectations hypothesis, this would signal that rates have peaked and are about to fall.

Another factor to consider is the difference in yields on different maturities at a particular point in time, or the "steepness" of the curve. For example, a steep yield curve—that is, one where long rates are *much higher* than short rates—is often seen as an indication that long-term rates may be near their peak and are about to fall, thereby narrowing the spread between long and short rates. Steep yield curves are generally viewed as a bullish sign. For aggressive bond investors, they could be the signal to start moving into long-term securities. Flatter yield curves, on the other hand, sharply reduce the incentive for going long-term. For example, look at curve 2 in Figure 9.4. Notice that the difference in yield between the 10- and 30-year maturities is almost nonexistent (it's only 16 basis points, or less than a quarter of 1 percent). As a result, a lot of investors would tend to favor the 10-year security, because they would not gain enough (only 16 basis points) to justify the much greater risk of the 30-year maturity. However, if the spread were, say, 75 basis points, the investor would have to consider his or her own risk tolerance to determine whether this risk premium was sufficient for the additional risk of buying the longer-term security.

CONCEPTS *in Review*

9.1   Is there a single market rate of interest applicable to all segments of the bond market, or is there a series of market yields that exists? Explain and note the investment implication of such a market environment.

9.2   Explain why interest rates are important to both conservative and aggressive bond investors. What causes interest rates to move, and how can individual investors monitor such movements?

9.3   What is the *term structure of interest rates*, and how does it relate to the *yield curve*? What information is required to plot a yield curve? Describe an upward-sloping yield curve and explain what it has to say about the behavior of interest rates.

9.4   How might you, as a bond investor, use information on the term structure of interest rates and yield curves when making investment decisions?   ▬

THE PRICING OF BONDS

If there's one common denominator in the bond market, it's the way bonds are priced. No matter who the issuer is, what kind of bond it is, or whether it's fully taxable or tax-free, all bonds are priced pretty much the same. In particular, all bonds (including *notes* with maturities of more than a year) are priced according to the *present value of their future cash flow* streams. Indeed, once the prevailing or expected market yield is known, the whole process becomes rather mechanical. Even so, mechanical or not, this system is very effective, and it is the process through which the market value of a bond is established.

Bond prices are driven by market yields. That's because in the marketplace, the *appropriate yield at which the bond should sell is determined first*, and then that yield is used to find the price (or market value) of the bond. The appropriate yield on a bond is a function of certain market and economic forces (e.g., the risk-free rate of return and inflation), as well as key issue and issuer characteristics—such as the number of years to maturity and the agency rating assigned to the bond. Together, these forces combine to form the *required rate of return*—which is the (expected) rate of return the investor would like to earn in order to justify an investment in a given fixed-income security. In the bond market, required return is market driven and is generally considered the issue's market yield. That is, the required return defines the yield at which the bond should be trading and serves as the *discount rate* in the bond valuation process.

Basically, bond investors are entitled to two distinct types of cash flows: (1) the periodic receipt of coupon income over the life of the bond and (2) the recovery of principal (or par value) at the end of the bond's life. Thus, in valuing a bond, you're dealing with an *annuity* of coupon payments plus a large *single cash flow*, as represented by the recovery of principal at maturity. These cash flows, along with the required rate of return on the investment, are then used in a present-value-based bond valuation model to find the dollar price of a bond. We'll demonstrate the bond valuation process in two ways. First, we'll use *annual compounding*—i.e., because of its computational simplicity, we'll assume we're dealing with annual coupons that are paid once a year. Second, we'll examine bond valuation under conditions of *semiannual compounding*, which is more like the way most bonds actually pay their coupons.

ANNUAL COMPOUNDING

Along with a table of present-value interest factors (see Appendix A, Tables A.3 and A.4), the following information is needed to value a bond: (1) the annual coupon payment, (2) the bond's par value, and (3) the number of years remaining to maturity. The prevailing market yield (or an estimate of future market rates) is then used as the discount rate to compute the price of a bond as follows:

Equation 9.2

$$\text{Bond price} = \frac{\text{present value of the annuity}}{\text{of annual interest income}} + \frac{\text{present value of the}}{\text{bond's par value}}$$

Equation 9.2a

$$BP = (I \times PVIFA) + (PV \times PVIF)$$

where:

I = amount of annual interest income

$PVIFA$ = present-value interest factor for an *annuity* (Appendix A, Table A.4)

PV = par value of the bond, which is assumed to be $1,000

$PVIF$ = present-value interest factor for a *single cash flow* (Appendix A, Table A.3)

To illustrate the bond price formula in action, consider a 20-year, 9½ percent bond that's being priced to yield 10 percent. From this, we know the bond pays an annual coupon of 9½ percent (or $95), has 20 years left to maturity, and should be priced to provide a market yield of 10 percent. As we saw in Chapter 4, the maturity and market yield information is used to find the appropriate present-value interest factors (in Appendix A, Tables A.3 and A.4). Given these interest factors, we can now use Equation 9.2 to find the price of our bond as follows:

Bond price = ($95 × *PVIFA* for 10% and 20 years) + ($1,000 × *PVIF* for 10% and 20 years)

= ($95 × 8.514) + ($1,000 × .149) = $957.83

Note that since this is a coupon-bearing bond, we have an annuity of coupon payments of $95 a year for 20 years, plus a single cash flow of $1,000 that occurs at the end of year 20. Thus, in bond valuation, we first find the present value of the coupon annuity and then add that amount to the present value of the recovery of principal at maturity. In this particular case, around $958 is what we should be willing to pay for this bond so long as we're satisfied with earning 10 percent on our money.

SEMIANNUAL COMPOUNDING

In practice, most bonds pay interest every 6 months, and as a result, semiannual compounding is used in the valuation of bonds. Although using annual compounding, as we did above, simplifies the valuation process a bit, it's not the way bonds are actually valued in the marketplace. Fortunately, it's relatively easy to go from annual to semiannual compounding: All you need do is cut the annual coupon payment in half and make two minor modifications to the present-value interest factors. Given these changes, finding the price of a bond under conditions of semiannual compounding is much like pricing a bond using annual compounding. That is:

Equation 9.3

Bond price (with semiannual compounding) = present value of an annuity of *semiannual* coupon payments + present value of the bond's par value

Equation 9.3a

$$BP = (I/2 × PVIFA^*) + (PV × PVIF^*)$$

where:

$PVIFA^*$ = present-value interest factor for an annuity, with required return and years-to-maturity adjusted for *semiannual compounding* (Appendix A, Table A.4)

$PVIF^*$ = present-value interest factor for a single cash flow, with required return and years-to-maturity adjusted for *semiannual compounding* (Appendix A, Table A.3)

I, PV = as described above

Note that in Equation 9.3, the present-value interest factors (both *PVIFA* and *PVIF*) are adjusted to accommodate semiannual compounding. To do so, *simply cut the required return in half and double the number of years to maturity.* By making that modification, we are, in effect, dealing with a semiannual return and the number of 6-month periods to maturity (rather than *years* to maturity). For example, in our bond illustration above, we wanted to price a 20-year bond to yield 10 percent. With semiannual compounding, we would be dealing with a semiannual return of 10%/2 = 5%, and with 20 × 2 = 40 semiannual periods to maturity. Thus, we'd find the present-value interest factors for 5% and 40 periods from Table A.4 (for *PVIFA**) and from Table A.3 (for *PVIF**). Also note that we adjust the present-value interest factor for the $1,000 par value, since that too will be subject to semiannual compounding, even though the cash flow will be received in one lump sum.

To see how this all fits together in the bond valuation process, consider once again the 20-year, 9½ percent bond, except this time, assume it's being priced to yield 10 percent, compounded semiannually. Using Equation 9.3, we'd have:

$$\text{Bond price (with semiannual compounding)} = (\$95/2 \times PVIFA^* \text{ for 5\% and 40 periods}) + (\$1,000 \times PVIF^* \text{ for 5\% and 40 periods})$$

$$= (\$47.50 \times 17.159) + (\$1,000 \times .142) = \$957.02$$

The price of the bond in this case ($957.02) is slightly less than the price we obtained with annual compounding ($957.83). Clearly, the use of annual versus semiannual compounding doesn't make all that much difference, though the differences do tend to increase a bit with lower coupons and shorter maturities.

CONCEPTS *in Review*

9.5 Explain how market yield affects the price of a bond. Could you value (price) a bond without knowing its market yield? Explain.

9.6 Why are bonds usually priced using semiannual compounding? Does it make much difference if you use annual compounding? ▬▬

MEASURES OF YIELD AND RETURN

As surprising as it may seem, in the bond market, investment decisions are made more on the basis of a bond's yield than its dollar price. Not only does yield affect the price at which a bond trades, but also it serves as an important measure of return. To use yield as a measure of return, we simply *reverse the bond valuation process* described above and solve for the yield on a bond, rather than its price. Actually, there are two widely used measures of yield: current yield and yield-to-maturity. We'll look at both of them here, along with a variation of yield-to-maturity, known as *expected return*, which measures the expected (or actual) rate of return earned over a specific holding period.

CURRENT YIELD

current yield
return measure that indicates the amount of current income a bond provides relative to its market price.

Current yield is the simplest of all return measures but also has the most limited application. This measure looks at just one source of return: *a bond's interest income*. In particular, it indicates the amount of current income a bond provides relative to its prevailing market price. It is calculated as follows:

Equation 9.4

$$\text{Current yield} = \frac{\text{annual interest}}{\text{current market price of the bond}}$$

For example, an 8 percent bond would pay $80 per year in interest for every $1,000 of principal. However, if the bond were currently priced at $800, it would have a current yield of 10 percent ($80/$800 = .10). Current yield is a measure of a bond's annual coupon income and as such, it would be of interest to investors seeking high levels of current income.

YIELD-TO-MATURITY

yield-to-maturity (YTM)
the fully compounded rate of return earned by an investor over the life of a bond, including interest income and price appreciation.

promised yield
same as yield-to-maturity.

Yield-to-maturity (YTM) is the most important and widely used bond valuation measure. It evaluates both interest income and price appreciation and considers total cash flow received over the life of an issue. Also known as **promised yield**, it indicates the fully compounded rate of return earned by an investor, given the bond is held to maturity and all principal and interest payments are made in a prompt and timely fashion. This measure of yield is used not only to gauge the return on a single issue but also to track the behavior of the market in general. In other words, market interest rates are nothing more than a reflection of the average promised yields that exist in a given segment of the market. Promised yield provides valuable insight about an issue's investment merits and is used to assess the attractiveness of alternative investment vehicles. Other things being equal, the higher the promised yield of an issue, the more attractive it is.

Although there are several ways to compute promised yield, the simplest is to use a procedure first introduced in Chapter 4, known as the *approximate yield method*:

Equation 9.5

$$\text{Approximate yield-to-maturity} = \frac{\text{annual interest income} + \dfrac{\$1,000 - \text{current market price}}{\text{years remaining until maturity}}}{\dfrac{\$1,000 + \text{current market price}}{2}}$$

Equation 9.5a

$$\text{YTM} = \frac{I + \dfrac{\$1,000 - P}{N}}{\dfrac{\$1,000 + P}{2}}$$

As it now stands, we an example, consider the following hypothetical situation: Assume a 7½ percent bond with a par value of $1,000 has 15 years remaining to maturity and is currently priced at $809.50. Using this information, we see that the approximate yield-to-maturity on this bond is:

$$\text{Approximate yield-to-maturity} = \frac{\$75 + \dfrac{\$1,000 - \$809.50}{15}}{\dfrac{\$1,000 + \$809.50}{2}} = \frac{\$75 + \$12.70}{\$904.75} = 9.69\%$$

In this case, if an investor pays $809.50 for the bond and holds it to maturity, he or she can expect to earn a yield of approximately 9.69 percent. Now there's no doubt that promised yield—whether computed using the approximate procedure or a more precise measure (which we'll introduce below)—is an important measure of performance. However, as discussed in the *Investor Insights* box on page 382, this measure provides only part of the story.

A More Precise Measure of Yield

Although approximate yield, as obtained from Equation 9.5, may be appropriate for many investment decisions, one big drawback is its lack of precision. This could be a problem for some investors. If it is, then use a more precise measure—one that's derived directly from the bond valuation model described above. In particular, assuming annual compounding, we can use Equation 9.2 to find the yield-to-maturity on a bond. Except in this case we know the current price of the bond and are trying to solve for the discount rate that equates the present value of the bond's cash flow (its coupon and principal payments) to its current market price. This procedure may sound familiar: It's just like the *internal rate of return* measure described in Chapter 4. Indeed, we're basically looking for the internal rate of return on a bond; find that and we have the bond's yield-to-maturity.

Unfortunately, unless you have a hand-held calculator or computer software that will do the calculations for you, finding the precise yield-to-maturity is a matter of trial and error. Here's how it's done: Let's say we want to find the yield-to-maturity on the 7½ percent, 15-year bond we introduced above. From Equation 9.2, we know that:

Bond price = (*I* × *PVIFA*) + (*PV* × *PVIF*)

As it now stands, we know the current market price of the bond ($809.50), the amount of annual interest/coupon income (7½% = $75), the par value of the bond ($1,000), and the number of years to maturity (15). To compute yield-to-maturity, we need to find the discount rate (in the present-value interest factors) that produces a bond price of $809.50.

Here's what we have so far:

Bond price = (*I* × *PVIFA*) + (*PV* × *PVIF*)

$809.50 = ($75 × *PVIFA* for 15 years and a discount rate of ?%)
          + ($1,000 × *PVIF* for 15 years and a discount rate of ?%)

INVESTOR INSIGHTS: *Investing in Action*

There's More to Bond Returns Than Yield Alone

When individuals choose bond investments, they usually focus on yields, in the belief that higher yields generate better returns. But yields and returns are two different things, and investors who blindly chase higher yields can end up regretting it. The fact is, yield is only part of the story: It tells you what you can expect going into an investment, *not* what you'll actually end up earning on the deal. Indeed, yield is often a poor proxy for return, and confusing the two can be damaging to your wealth.

Total return for fixed-income investments is made up of not only the initial yield but also (1) interest on reinvested interest and (2) price change. In essence, return is a measure of actual performance over a given investment period. Only in the case of short-term investments, such as one-year CDs or Treasury bills, is yield a good gauge of return. For long-term bonds and bonds purchased at prices far above or below face value, other factors often dwarf yield in determining returns. That's true even when the bonds are of triple-A quality and are noncallable.

For instance, interest-on-interest easily becomes the biggest factor in returns for buy-and-hold investors in long-term bonds, especially if interest rates rise during the life of the bond. If you bought a 30-year Treasury bond yielding 7.9 percent today and interest rates subsequently rose so that your average reinvestment rate was 9 percent over the life of the bond, almost 80 percent of your total return at maturity would come from income on reinvested interest. On the other hand, while interest-on-interest dominates bond returns for long holding periods, price change dominates return for short-term investors. In either case, future interest rate changes are the major concern for investors who want to safeguard their total returns.

The starting yield on a bond becomes a bigger boon or burden to investors the longer the bond's maturity—which makes total returns on longer-term bonds much more sensitive to interest rate swings. For instance, in the 1950s,

1960s, and 1970s, long-term Treasury bonds actually had lower total returns than money market funds, despite their persistently higher yields. Unfortunately, steadily rising interest rates erased an average of 2.5 percent a year from the value of long-term bond portfolios in the 1950–1980 period—more than wiping out the bonds' yield advantage over T-bills. In the 1980s, by contrast, a steady decline in interest rates meant long-term bonds put on a much better showing than yields would have indicated. Rising bond prices, caused by falling market rates, pushed total returns on Treasury bonds up to an average of 12.6 percent a year—beating T-bill returns by 3.7 percentage points.

Of course, no one really knows where interest rates will go—and trying to predict them has proved a fruitless exercise. But investors can get a handle on the risks they face in the short run by considering how total returns on different investments might react to interest rate changes over, say, the next 12 months. For example, if interest rates were to fall 1 percentage point over the next 12 months, a typical portfolio of long-term bonds (with lives of more than 10 years) would generate an estimated total return of about 13 percent. But if interest rates were to rise by 1 percentage point, the total return would shrink to about 1 percent—making a money fund return look good by comparison. Looking at the problem this way tells the investor how much rates would have to rise before the returns on long-term bonds are reduced to the level of, say, bank CDs or some other short-term benchmark. Clearly, the farther rates have to rise, the more cushion you have and the more secure your investments. The old adage "you can't tell a book by its cover" certainly does apply to the bond market: Just because a bond promises a *yield* of x percent doesn't mean that's the *return* you'll actually end up with.

Source: Adapted from Barbara Donnelly, "Bond Investors Who Fixate Too Much on Yields Risk Missing the Big Picture," *Wall Street Journal*, March 13, 1992, p. C1.

Right now there's only one thing we know about the yield on this bond—it has to be more than 7½ percent. (Why? Because this is a discount bond, the yield-to-maturity must exceed the coupon rate.) To get even closer to the required solving rate, we can compute the approximate yield—recall that this was found to be 9.69 percent.

There are two properties of the approximate yield procedure that will prove helpful at this point. They are: (1) On a discount bond, the approximate yield will always be less than the true yield, and (2) on premium bonds, the approximate yield will always be more than the true yield. Therefore, because we're dealing with a discount bond, we know not only that the yield has to be more than the coupon but, more importantly, that the promised yield on this issue has to be more than its approximate yield of 9.69 percent. It's pretty obvious, therefore, that we should start our trial-and-error process with a discount rate of 10 percent:

$$\text{Bond price} = (\$75 \times PVIFA \text{ for 15 years and 10\%})$$
$$+ (\$1,000 \times PVIFA \text{ for 15 years and 10\%})$$
$$= (\$75 \times 7.606) + (\$1,000 \times .239)$$
$$= \underline{\underline{\$809.45}}$$

The computed price of $809.45 is reasonably close to the bond's current market price of $809.50. As a result, the solving rate of 10 percent is the true yield-to-maturity (or promised yield) on this bond.

Given some fairly simple modifications, it's also possible to find *yield-to-maturity using semiannual compounding*. To do so, we cut the annual coupon in half, double the number of years (periods) to maturity, and use the bond valuation model in Equation 9.3. Returning to our 7½ percent, 15-year bond, let's see what happens when we try a discount rate of 10 percent. In this case, with semiannual compounding, we'd use a discount rate of 5 percent (i.e., 10% ÷ 2); using this discount rate and 30 six-month periods to maturity (i.e., 15 × 2) to specify the present-value interest factor, we have:

$$\text{Bond price} = (\$75/2 \times PVIFA^* \text{ for 5\% and 30 periods})$$
$$+ (\$1,000 \times PVIFA \text{ for 5\% and 30 periods})$$
$$= (\$37.50 \times 15.373) + (\$1,000 \times .231) = \underline{\underline{\$807.49}}$$

As we can see, a semiannual discount rate of 5 percent results in a computed bond value that's a bit short of our target price of $809.50. Given the inverse relationship between price and yield, it follows that if we need a higher price, we'll have to try a lower yield (discount rate). Therefore, we know the semiannual yield on this bond has to be something less than 5 percent. Through interpolation, we find that a semiannual discount rate of 4.90 percent gives us a computed bond value of $809.50.

At this point, since we're dealing with semiannual cash flows, to be technically accurate we should find the bond's "effective" annual yield. However, that's not the way it's done in practice. Rather, *market convention is to simply state the annual yield as twice the semiannual yield*. This practice produces what the market refers to as the **bond-equivalent yield**. Returning to the bond yield problem we started above, we know that the issue has a semiannual yield of 4.90 percent. According to the bond-equivalent yield convention, all we

bond-equivalent yield
the annual yield on a bond, calculated as twice the semiannual yield.

have to do now is *double the solving rate in order to obtain the annual rate of return on this bond*. Doing this gives us a yield-to-maturity (or promised yield) of 4.90% × 2 = 9.80%, which is the annual rate of return we'll earn on this bond if we hold it to maturity.

Actually, in addition to holding the bond to maturity, there are a couple of other critical assumptions embedded in any yield-to-maturity figure. The computed promised yield measure—whether found with annual or semiannual compounding, or even the approximate method—is based on present-value concepts and therefore contains important reinvestment assumptions. That is, the yield-to-maturity figure itself is the *minimum required reinvestment rate the investor must subsequently earn on each of the interim coupon receipts* to actually generate a return equal to or greater than promised yield. In essence, the calculated yield-to-maturity figure is only the return "promised" so long as the issuer meets all interest and principal obligations on a timely basis *and* the investor reinvests all coupon income (from the date of receipt to maturity) at an average rate equal to or greater than the computed promised yield. In our example above, the investor would have to reinvest (to maturity) each of the coupons received over the next 15 years at a rate of about 10 percent. *Failure to do so would result in a realized yield of less than the 10 percent promised*. In fact, if the worst did occur and the investor made no attempt to reinvest any of the coupons, he or she would earn a realized yield over the 15-year investment horizon of just over 6½ percent—far short of the 10 percent promised return. Clearly, unless it's a zero-coupon bond, a significant portion of a bond's total return over time is derived from the *reinvestment of coupons*.

Finding the Yield on a Zero

The same promised yield procedures described above—Equation 9.2 with annual compounding or Equation 9.3 with semiannual compounding—can also be used to find the yield-to-maturity on a zero-coupon bond. The only difference is that the coupon portion of the equation can be ignored, since it will, of course, equal zero. All you have to do to find the promised yield on a zero is to divide the current market price of the bond by $1,000 and then look for the computed interest factor in the present-value Table A.3 (in Appendix A).

To illustrate, consider a 15-year zero-coupon issue that can be purchased today for $315. Dividing this amount by the bond's par value of $1,000, we obtain an interest factor of $315/$1,000 = .315. Now, using annual compounding, look in Table A.3 (the table of present-value interest factors for single cash flows); go down the first column to year 15 and then look across that row until you find an interest factor that equals (or is very close to) .315. Once you've found the factor, look up the column to the "Interest Rate" heading and you've got the promised yield of the issue. Using this approach, we see that the bond in our example has a promised yield of 8 percent, because that rate gives us the interest factor we're looking for. Had we been using semi-annual compounding, we'd do exactly the same thing, except we'd go down to "year 30" and start the process there.

EXPECTED RETURN

Rather than buying a bond and holding it to maturity (as presumed in the promised yield formulas), many investors will trade in and out of bonds long before they mature. These investors have short anticipated holding periods and have no intention of holding the bonds to maturity. As a result, yield-to-maturity has relatively little meaning for them, other than providing an indication of the rate of return used to price the bond. These investors obviously need an alternative measure of return that can be used to assess the investment appeal of those bonds they intend to trade. Such an alternative measure is **expected return**, which indicates the rate of return an investor can expect to earn by holding a bond over a period of time that's less (and in many cases, substantially less) than the life of the issue. (Expected return is also known as **realized yield**, because it shows the return an investor would realize by trading in and out of bonds over short holding periods.)

expected return
the rate of return an investor can expect to earn by holding a bond over a period of time that's less than the life of the issue.

realized yield
same as expected return.

Expected return lacks the precision of yield-to-maturity, because the major cash flow variables are largely the product of investor estimates. In particular, going into the investment, both the length of the holding period and the future selling prices of the bond are pure estimates and therefore subject to varying degrees of uncertainty. For this reason, the approximate yield method is often used to measure expected return. With some modifications to the standard approximate yield formula, we can use the following equation to measure expected return:

Equation 9.6
$$\text{Expected return} = \frac{\text{annual interest income} + \dfrac{\text{expected future price} - \text{current market price}}{\text{years in the holding period}}}{\dfrac{\text{expected future price} + \text{current market price}}{2}}$$

Equation 9.6a
$$ER = \frac{I + \dfrac{FP - P}{n}}{\dfrac{FP + P}{2}}$$

Note that, in this case, the *expected future price* of the bond is used in place of par value ($1,000), and the *length of the holding period* is used in place of term to maturity. As noted above, the *future price* of the bond has to be determined when computing expected realized yield; this is done by using the standard bond price formula, as described above. The most difficult part of deriving a reliable future price is, of course, coming up with future market interest rates that you feel will exist when the bond is sold. Based on an analysis of market interest rates, *the investor estimates a promised yield that the issue is expected to carry at the date of sale and then uses that yield to figure the bond's future price.*

To illustrate, take one more look at our 7½ percent, 15-year bond. This time, let's assume the bond is trading at a discount but the investor feels the price will rise sharply as interest rates fall over the next few years. In particular, assume the bond is currently priced at $810 (to yield 10 percent) and that the investor anticipates holding the bond for 3 years. Over that time, he or she expects market rates to drop so that the price of the bond should rise to around $960 by the end of the 3-year holding period. (Actually, we found the future price of the bond—$960—by assuming interest rates will fall to 8 percent in 3 years; we then used the standard bond price formula—in this case Equation 9.2—to find the value of a 7½ percent, 12-year obligation, which is how many years to maturity a 15-year bond will have at the end of a 3-year holding period.) Thus, we are assuming that an investor will buy the bond today at a market price of $810 and sell the issue 3 years later—after interest rates have declined to 8 percent—at a price of $960. Given these assumptions, the expected return (realized yield) on this bond would be:

$$\text{Expected return} = \frac{\$75 + \dfrac{\$960 - \$810}{3}}{\dfrac{\$960 + \$810}{2}} = 14.12\%$$

The better than 14 percent return on this investment is fairly substantial, but keep in mind that this is a measure of *expected return* only. It is, of course, subject to variation if things do not turn out as anticipated, particularly with regard to the market yield expected to prevail at the end of the holding period. (*Note:* If the anticipated investment horizon is one year or less, Equation 9.6 can be used to measure expected return over such a short holding period. Alternatively, an investor could just as easily use a simple *holding period return* measure, e.g., the one described in Chapter 4. There would be a slight difference in computed returns, but it wouldn't be all that much.)

VALUING A BOND

Depending on investor objectives, the value of a bond can be determined by either its promised yield or its expected return. Conservative, income-oriented investors will employ *promised yield* as the way to value bonds. Coupon income over extended periods of time is the principal objective of these investors, and promised yield provides a viable measure of return under these circumstances. More aggressive bond traders, on the other hand, will use *expected return* to value bonds. The capital gains that can be earned by buying and selling bonds over relatively short holding periods is a chief concern of these investors, and expected return is more important to them than the promised yield that exists at the time the bond is purchased.

In either case, promised or expected yield provides a *measure of return* that can be used to determine the relative attractiveness of fixed-income securities. But to do so, the appropriate measure of return should be evaluated in light of the amount of *risk* involved in the investment. Bonds are no different from stocks in that the amount of promised or expected return should be sufficient to cover the investor's exposure to risk. Thus, the greater the amount of perceived risk, the greater the amount of return the bond should generate. If the bond meets this hurdle, it can then be compared to other potential investments outlets. If you find it difficult to do better in a risk-return sense, then the bond under evaluation should be given serious consideration as an investment outlet.

CONCEPTS *in Review*

9.7   What's the difference between *current yield* and *yield-to-maturity*? Between *promised yield* and *realized yield*?

9.8   Briefly describe the term *bond-equivalent yield*. Is there any real difference between promised yield and bond-equivalent yield? Explain.

9.9   Why is the reinvestment of interest income so important to bond investors?

DURATION AND IMMUNIZATION

One of the problems with yield-to-maturity (YTM) is that it assumes you can reinvest the bond's periodic coupon payments at the same rate over time. But, if you reinvest this interest income at a lower rate (or if you spend it), your real return will be much lower than that indicated by YTM. The assumption that interest rates will remain constant is a key weakness of YTM. Another flaw is that YTM assumes the issuer will make all payments on time and won't call the bonds before maturity, as often happens when interest rates drop. For bonds that are not held to maturity, prices will reflect prevailing interest rates, which are likely to differ from YTM. If rates have moved up since a bond was purchased, the bond will sell at a discount. If interest rates have dropped, it will sell at a premium. The sales price will obviously have a big impact on the total return earned.

The problem with yield-to-maturity, in effect, is that it fails to take into account the effects of reinvestment risk and price (or market) risk. To see how reinvestment and price risks behave relative to one another, consider a situation in which market interest rates have undergone a sharp decline. Under such conditions, many investors might be tempted to cash out their holdings and take some gains (i.e., do a little "profit taking"). The fact is that selling before maturity is the only way to take advantage of falling interest rates, since a bond will pay its par value at maturity, regardless of prevailing interest rates. The problem is that when interest rates fall, so too do opportunities to invest at high rates. Therefore, although you gain on the price side, you lose on the reinvestment side. Even if you don't sell out, you are faced with increased reinvestment risk, because in order to earn the YTM promised on your bonds, you have to be able to reinvest each coupon payment at the same YTM rate. Obviously, as rates fall, you'll find it increasingly difficult to reinvest the stream of coupon payments at or above the YTM rate. When market rates rise, just the opposite happens: The price of the bond falls, but your reinvestment opportunities improve.

What is needed is a yardstick or measure of performance that overcomes these deficiencies and takes into account both price and reinvestment risks. Such a yardstick is provided by something called **duration**, which captures in a single measure the extent to which the price of a bond will react to different interest rate environments. Because duration gauges the price volatility of a bond, it gives you a better idea of how likely you are to earn the return (YTM) you expect. That in turn will help you tailor your holdings to match your expectations of interest rate movements.

duration
a measure of bond price volatility, which captures both price and reinvestment risks, and which is used to indicate how a bond will react to different interest rate environments.

THE CONCEPT OF DURATION

The concept of duration was first outlined in 1938 by actuary Frederick Macaulay to help insurance companies match their cash inflows with payments. When applied to bonds, duration recognizes that the amount and frequency of the interest payments, yield-to-maturity, and time to maturity all affect the "time dimension" of a bond. The time to maturity is important because it influences how much a bond's price rises or falls as interest rates change. In general, bonds with longer maturities fluctuate more than shorter-term issues when rates move. However, maturity alone isn't a sufficient measure of the time dimension of bonds. Maturity tells you only when the last payment will be made; it doesn't say anything about interim payments. The amount of reinvestment risk is also directly related to the size of a bond's coupons: Bonds paying high coupons have greater reinvestment risk simply because there's more to reinvest.

Any change in interest rates will cause price risk and reinvestment risk to push and pull bonds in opposite directions. An increase in rates will produce a drop in price but will lessen reinvestment risk by making it easier to reinvest coupon payments at or above the YTM rate. Declining rates, in contrast, will boost prices but increase reinvestment risk. At some point in time, these two forces should exactly offset each other. *That point in time is the bond's duration.*

In general, bond duration possesses the following properties:

- Higher coupons result in shorter durations.
- Longer maturities mean longer durations.
- Higher yields (YTMs) lead to shorter durations.

Together, a bond's coupon, maturity, and yield interact with one another to produce the issue's measure of duration. Knowing a bond's duration is helpful because it combines price and reinvestment risks in such a way that it captures the underlying *volatility* of a bond. *A bond's duration and volatility are directly related: The shorter the duration, the less volatility there is in the bond.*

 MEASURING DURATION

Duration is a measure of the effective, as opposed to actual, maturity of a fixed-income security. As we will see, only those bonds promising a single payment to be received at maturity (i.e., no yearly coupons) have durations equal to their actual years to maturity. Zero-coupon bonds are such bonds. For all others, *duration measures are always less than their actual maturities.*

Although a bond's term to maturity is certainly a useful concept, it falls short of being a reliable measure of a bond's effective life, because it does not consider all the bond's cash flows or the time value of money. Duration is a far superior measure of the effective timing of a bond's cash flows, since it explicitly considers both the time value of money and the bond's coupon and principal payments. Duration may be thought of as the *weighted-average life of a bond,* where the weights are the relative future cash flows of the bond, all of which are discounted to their present values. Mathematically, we can find the duration of a bond as follows:

Equation 9.7
$$\text{Duration} = \sum_{t=1}^{T} \left[\frac{PV(C_t)}{P_{\text{bond}}} \times t \right]$$

where:

$PV(C_t)$ = present value of a future coupon or principal payment

P_{bond} = current market price of the bond

t = year in which the cash flow (coupon or principal) payment is received

T = the remaining life of the bond, in years

The duration measure obtained from the equation above is often referred to as *Macaulay duration*—named after the actuary who developed the concept.

Although duration can be (and often is) computed using semiannual compounding, Equation 9.7 uses *annual coupons and annual compounding* in order to keep the ensuing discussion and calculations as simple as possible. But even then, the formula may still look more formidable than it actually is. For the fact is, if you just follow a few basic steps, as noted below, you'll find that duration is really not all that tough to calculate after all. Here are the steps involved:

Step 1.   Find the present value of each annual coupon or principal payment $[PV(C_t)]$. *Use the prevailing YTM on the bond as the discount rate.*

Step 2.   Divide this present value by the current market price of the bond (P_{bond}).

Step 3.   Multiply this relative value by the year in which the cash flow is to be received (t).

Step 4.   Repeat steps 1 through 3 for each year in the life of the bond, and then *add up* the values computed in step 3.

Table 9.1 illustrates this procedure, as it presents the duration calculation for a 7½ percent, 15-year bond priced (at $957) to yield 8 percent. Note that this particular 15-year bond has a duration of less than 9½ years—9.36 years, to be exact. Here's how we found that value: Along with the current market price of the bond ($957), the first three columns of Table 9.1 provide the basic input data: Column (1) is the year (t) of the cash flow, column (2) is the amount of the annual cash flows (from coupons and principal), and column (3) is the appropriate present-value interest factors, given an 8 percent discount rate (which is equal to the prevailing YTM on the bond). The first thing

Table 9.1   Duration Calculation for a 7½%, 15-year Bond Priced to Yield 8%

(1) Year (t)	(2) Annual Cash Flow (C_t)	(3) PVIF (@8%)	(4) Present Value of Annual Cash Flows [$PV(C_t)$] (2) × (3)	(5) $PV(C_t)$ Divided by Current Market Price of the Bond* (4) ÷ $957	(6) Time-Weighted Relative Cash Flow (1) × (5)
1	$ 75	.926	$ 69.45	.0726	.0726
2	75	.857	64.27	.0672	.1343
3	75	.794	59.55	.0622	.1867
4	75	.735	55.12	.0576	.2304
5	75	.681	51.08	.0534	.2668
6	75	.630	47.25	.0494	.2962
7	75	.583	43.72	.0457	.3198
8	75	.540	40.50	.0423	.3386
9	75	.500	37.50	.0392	.3527
10	75	.463	34.72	.0363	.3628
11	75	.429	32.18	.0336	.3698
12	75	.397	29.78	.0311	.3734
13	75	.368	27.60	.0288	.3749
14	75	.340	25.50	.0266	.3730
15	1075	.315	338.62	.3538	5.3076
					Duration: 9.36 yrs.

*If this bond is priced to yield 8%, it would be quoted in the market at $957.

we do—Step 1—is to find the present value of each of the annual cash flows (column 4), and then—Step 2—divide each of these present values by the current market price of the bond (column 5). Finally, multiplying the relative cash flows from column (5) by the year (*t*) in which the cash flow occurs—Step 3— results in a time-weighted value for each of the annual cash flow streams (column 6). When we add up all the values in column (6)—Step 4—we have the duration of the bond. As you can see, the duration of this bond is a lot less than its maturity—a condition that would exist with any coupon-bearing bond. In addition, keep in mind that *the duration on any bond will change over time* as YTM and term to maturity change. For example, the duration on this 7½ percent, 15-year bond will fall as the bond nears maturity and/or as the market yield (YTM) on the bond increases.

Duration is not merely a single security concept; it also applies to whole portfolios of fixed-income securities. The duration of an entire portfolio is actually fairly easy to calculate—all that's required are the durations of the individual securities in the portfolio and the proportion that each security contributes to the overall value of the portfolio. Given this, *the duration of a portfolio is simply the weighted average of the durations of each security in the portfolio,* where the weights are the wealth proportions of each of the individual securities. For example, consider a five-bond portfolio made up as follows:

Bond	Amount Invested*	Weight	×	Bond Duration	=	Portfolio Duration
Government bonds	$ 270,000	0.15		6.25		0.9375
Aaa corporates	180,000	0.10		8.90		0.8900
Aa utilities	450,000	0.25		10.61		2.6525
Agency issues	360,000	0.20		11.03		2.2060
Baa industrials	540,000	0.30		12.55		3.7650
	$1,800,000	1.00				10.4510

*Amount invested = current market price times the par value of the bonds. That is, if the government bonds are quoted at 90 and the investor holds $300,000 in these bonds, then .90 × $300,000 = $270,000.

In this case, the $1.8 million bond *portfolio* has an average duration of approximately 10.5 years. Obviously, if you want to change the duration of the portfolio, you can do so by either (1) changing the asset mix of the portfolio (shift the weight of the portfolio to longer- or shorter-duration bonds, as desired) and/or (2) adding new bonds to the portfolio with the desired duration characteristics. As we will see below, such information is used in a bond portfolio strategy known as *bond immunization.*

BOND DURATION AND PRICE VOLATILITY

A bond's price volatility is, in part, a function of its term to maturity and, in part, of its coupon yield. Unfortunately, there is no exact relationship between bond maturities and bond price volatilities with respect to interest rate changes. There is, however, a fairly close relationship between bond duration and price volatility—at least, so long as the market doesn't experience wide swings in yield. That is, duration can be used as a viable predictor of price volatility *so long as the yield swings are relatively small* (no more than 100 basis points or so). The problem is, because the price-yield relationship of a bond is convex in form (but duration is not), when the market (or bond) undergoes a *big change* in yield, duration will *understate* price appreciation when rates fall and *overstate* the price decline when rates rise. Assuming that's not the case (i.e., that we're dealing with relatively small changes in market yield) then multiplying a bond's duration value by −1 results in its price elasticity with respect to interest rate changes. Thus, by calculating a bond's duration, we can obtain a fairly accurate measure of how much its price will change relative to a given (reasonably small) change in market interest rates.

The mathematical link between bond price and interest rate changes involves the concept of *modified duration*. To find modified duration, we simply take the (Macaulay) duration for a bond—as found from Equation 9.7—and adjust it for the bond's yield to maturity. That is:

Equation 9.8
$$\text{Modified duration} = \frac{\text{(Macaulay) duration in years}}{1 + \text{yield to maturity}}$$

Thus, the modified duration for the 15-year bond discussed above is as follows:

$$\text{Modified duration} = \frac{9.36}{1 + 0.08} = \underline{\underline{8.67}}$$

Note that here we use the bond's computed (Macaulay) duration of 9.36 years and the same YTM we used to compute duration in Equation 9.7; in this case, the bond was priced to yield 8 percent, so we use a yield-to-maturity of 8 percent.

To determine this bond's percentage price change resulting from an increase in market interest rates from, say, 8 to 8½ percent, the modified duration value calculated above is first multiplied by −1 (due to the inverse relationship between bond prices and interest rates) and then by the change in the level of the market interest rates. That is:

Equation 9.9
$$\frac{\text{Percent change}}{\text{in bond price}} = -1 \times \text{modified duration} \times \text{change in interest rates}$$

$$= -1 \times 8.67 \times 0.5\% = \underline{\underline{-4.33\%}}$$

Thus, a 50-basis-point (or ½ of 1%) change in market interest rates will lead to almost a 4½ percent drop in the price of this 15-year bond. Such information is useful to bond investors seeking—or trying to avoid—price volatility.

USES OF BOND DURATION MEASURES

Bond investors have learned to use duration analysis in many ways. One use, for example, is, as we saw above, to use modified duration to measure the potential price volatility of a particular issue. Another, perhaps more important use of duration is in the *structuring of bond portfolios*. For example, if a bond investor believes that interest rates are about to increase, he or she could calculate the expected percentage decrease in the value of the portfolio, given a certain change in market interest rates, and then reduce the overall duration of the portfolio by selling higher-duration bonds and buying those of shorter duration. Such a strategy would prove profitable, since short-duration instruments do not decline in value to the same degree as longer bonds. Of course, if the investor believed that interest rates were about to decrease, the opposite strategy would be optimal.

Although active, short-term investors frequently use duration analysis in their day-to-day operations, longer-term investors have also employed duration analysis in planning their investment decisions. Indeed, a strategy known as *bond portfolio immunization* represents one of the most important uses of duration.

Bond Immunization

Some investors holding portfolios of bonds do not actively attempt to "beat the market" but, rather, they seek to accumulate a specified level of wealth by the end of a given investment horizon. For these investors, bond portfolio immunization often proves to be of great value. Immunization allows an investor to derive a specified rate of return from bond investments over a given investment interval *regardless of what happens to market interest rates over the course of the holding period.* In essence, an investor is able to "immunize" his or her portfolio from the effects of changes in market interest rates over a given investment horizon.

To understand how and why bond portfolio immunization is possible, one needs to understand that changes in market interest rates lead to two distinct and opposite changes in bond valuation: The first effect, known as the *price effect*, results in portfolio valuation changes when interest rates change before the end of the desired investment horizon. This is true because interest rate decreases lead to bond price increases, and vice versa. The second effect, known as the *reinvestment effect*, arises because the yield-to-maturity calculation assumes that all of a bond's coupon payments will be reinvested at the prevailing yield-to-maturity on the bond when it was purchased. If interest rates increase, however, the coupons may be reinvested at a higher rate than that expected by the investor, leading to increases in investor wealth. Of course, the opposite is true when interest rates decrease. Thus, whereas an increase in rates has a negative effect on a bond's price, it has a positive effect on the reinvestment of coupons: Taken together, when interest rate changes do occur, the price and reinvestment effects work against each other from the standpoint of the investor's wealth.

When do these counteracting effects exactly offset each other and leave the investor's wealth position unchanged? You guessed it: when the average duration of the portfolio just equals the investment horizon of the investor. This should not come as much of a surprise, since such a property is already imbedded in and fundamental to duration itself. Accordingly, if it applies to a single bond, it should also apply to the *weighted-average duration of a bond portfolio.* Such a condition (of offsetting price and reinvestment effects) is said to exist when a bond portfolio *is immunized.* More specifically, an investor's wealth position is immunized from the effects of interest rate changes *when the weighted-average duration of the bond portfolio exactly equals the desired investment horizon.* Table 9.2 provides an example of bond immunization using a 10-year, 8 percent coupon bond with a duration of 8 years; here, we assume the investor's desired investment horizon is also 8 years in length.

The example provided in Table 9.2 assumes that the investor originally purchased the 8 percent coupon bond when issued at par. It further assumes

Table 9.2 Bond Immunization

Year	Cash Flow from Bond							Terminal Value of Reinvested Cash Flow
1	$80	×	$(1.08)^4$	×	$(1.06)^3$	=		$ 129.63
2	80	×	$(1.08)^3$	×	$(1.06)^3$	=		120.03
3	80	×	$(1.08)^2$	×	$(1.06)^3$	=		111.14
4	80	×	(1.08)	×	$(1.06)^3$	=		102.90
5	80	×	$(1.06)^3$			=		95.28
6	80	×	$(1.06)^2$			=		89.89
7	80	×	(1.06)			=		84.80
8	80	×				=		80.00
8	$1,036.64*	×				=		1,036.64

Total		$1,850.31
Investor's required wealth at 8%		$1,850.90
Difference		$ .59

*The bond could be sold at a market price of $l,036.64, which is the value of an 8 percent bond with 2 years to maturity priced to yield 6 percent.
Note: Bond interest coupons are assumed to be paid at year-end. Therefore, there are 4 years of reinvestment at 8 percent and 3 years at 6 percent for the first year's $80 coupon.

that market interest rates for bonds of this quality change from 8 to 6 percent at the end of the fifth year. Since the investor had an investment horizon of exactly 8 years and desires to lock in an interest rate return of exactly 8 percent, he or she expects to have a terminal wealth value of $1,850.90 [i.e., $1,000 invested at 8 percent for 8 years = $1,000 × $(1.08)^8$ = $1,850.90], regardless of interest rate changes in the interim. As can be seen from the bottom-line results presented in Table 9.2, the immunization strategy netted the investor a total of $1,850.31—just 59 cents short of the desired goal. This remarkable result clearly demonstrates the power of bond immunization and the versatility of bond duration. Even though the table uses a single bond for purposes of illustration, the same results—that is, achieving a desired terminal value/rate of return—could be obtained from a bond *portfolio* that is maintained at the *proper weighted-average duration.*

Although bond immunization is a powerful investment tool, it is clearly not a passive investment strategy. It requires *continual portfolio rebalancing* on the part of the investor in order to maintain a fully immunized portfolio. Indeed, every time interest rates change, the duration of a portfolio will change. Since effective immunization requires that the portfolio have a duration value equal in length to the investor's remaining investment horizon, the composition of the investor's portfolio must be rebalanced each time interest rates change. Further, even in the absence of interest rate changes, a bond's duration declines more slowly than its term to maturity. This, of course, means that the mere passage of time will dictate changes in portfolio composition. Such changes will ensure that the duration of the portfolio continues to match the remaining time in the investment horizon. In summary, portfolio immunization strategies can be extremely effective bond management tools. At the same time, it is important to realize that immunization is not a totally passive strategy and is not without potential problems—the most notable of which are those associated with portfolio rebalancing.

CONCEPTS *in Review*

9.10 What does the term *duration* mean to bond investors, and how does the duration on a bond differ from its maturity? What is *modified duration*, and how is it used?

9.11 Describe the process of *bond portfolio immunization* and explain why an investor would want to immunize a portfolio. Would you consider portfolio immunization to be a passive investment strategy, comparable to, say, a buy-and-hold approach? Explain.

BOND INVESTMENT STRATEGIES

Generally, bond investors tend to follow one of three kinds of investment programs. First, there are those who live off the income—the conservative, quality-conscious, income-oriented investors who seek to maximize current income. Second are speculators (bond traders) who have a considerably different investment objective: to maximize capital gains, often within a short time span. This investment approach requires considerable expertise, as it is based almost entirely on estimates of the future course of interest rates. Finally, there are the serious long-term investors, whose objective is to maximize *total return*—from both current income and capital gains—over fairly long holding periods.

In order to achieve the objectives of any one of these three programs, an investor needs to adopt a strategy that will be compatible with his or her goals. Professional money managers use a variety of techniques to manage the multimillion-dollar bond portfolios under their direction. These vary from passive approaches, to semiactive strategies, to active, fully managed strategies using interest rate forecasting and yield spread analysis. Most of these strategies are fairly complex and require substantial computer support. Even so, we can look briefly at some of the more basic strategies to at least gain an appreciation of the different ways fixed-income securities can be used to reach different investment objectives.

PASSIVE STRATEGIES

The bond immunization strategies discussed above are considered to be primarily *passive* in nature; investors using these tools typically are *not* attempting to beat the market. Rather, these investors immunize their portfolios in an effort to lock in specified rates of return (or terminal values) they deem acceptable, given the risks involved. Generally, passive investment strategies are characterized by a lack of input regarding investor expectations of interest rate and/or bond price changes. Further, these strategies typically do not generate significant transaction costs. A *buy-and-hold* strategy is perhaps the most passive of all investment strategies: All that is required is that the investor replace bonds that have deteriorating credit ratings, have matured, or have been called. Although buy-and-hold investors restrict their ability to earn above-average returns, they also minimize the dead-weight losses represented by transaction costs.

One approach that is a bit more active than buy-and-hold and is popular with many individual and institutional investors is the use of so-called **bond ladders.** In this strategy, an equal amount is invested in a *series* of bonds with staggered maturities. Here's how a bond ladder works: Suppose an individual

bond ladders
an investment strategy wherein an equal amount of money is invested in a series of bonds with staggered maturities.

wants to confine his or her investing to fixed-income securities with maturities of 10 years or less; the investor could set up a ladder by investing in (roughly) equal amounts of, say, 3-, 5-, 7-, and 10-year issues. Then, when the 3-year issue matures, the money from it (along with any new capital) would be put into a new 10-year note. The process would continue rolling over like this so that eventually the investor would hold a full ladder of staggered 10-year notes. By rolling into new 10-year issues every 2 or 3 years, the investor can do a kind of dollar-cost averaging and thereby lessen the impact of swings in market rates. Actually, the laddered approach is a safe, simple, and almost automatic way of investing for the long haul—indeed, once the ladder is set up, it's followed in a fairly routine manner. A key ingredient of this or any other passive strategy is, of course, the use of high-quality investment vehicles that possess attractive features, maturities, and yields.

TRADING ON FORECASTED INTEREST RATE BEHAVIOR

The *forecasted interest rate* approach to bond investing is highly risky, because it relies on the imperfect forecast of future interest rates. It seeks attractive capital gains when interest rates are expected to decline and the preservation of capital when an increase in interest rates is anticipated. The idea is to increase the return on a bond portfolio by making strategic moves in anticipation of interest rate changes. Such a strategy is essentially *market timing* and, as a result, carries with it some definite risks and costs. An unusual feature of this tactic is that most of the trading is done with *investment-grade securities*, since a high degree of interest rate sensitivity is required to capture the maximum amount of price behavior. Once interest rate expectations have been specified, this strategy rests largely on technical matters. For example, when a decline in rates is anticipated, aggressive bond investors will often seek to lengthen the maturity (or duration) of their bonds (or bond portfolios). The reason: Longer-term bonds rise more in price in response to a given drop in rates than their shorter-term counterparts do. At the same time, investors look for low-coupon and/or moderately discounted bonds, which add to duration and increase the amount of potential price volatility. These interest swings are usually short-lived, so bond traders try to earn as much as possible in as short a time as possible. (Margin trading—the use of borrowed money to buy bonds—is also used as a way of magnifying returns when rate declines are expected.) When rates start to level off and move up, these investors begin to shift their money out of long, discounted bonds and into high-yielding issues with short maturities. In other words, they do a complete reversal. During these periods when bond prices are dropping, investors try to earn high yields and protect their money from capital losses. Thus, they tend to use such short-term obligations as Treasury bills, money funds, short-term (2 to 5 years) notes, or even variable rate notes.

BOND SWAPS

bond swap
an investment strategy wherein an investor liquidates one current bond holding and simultaneously buys a different issue in its place.

In a **bond swap**, an investor simply liquidates one position and simultaneously buys a different issue in its place. Swaps can be executed to increase current yield or yield-to-maturity, to take advantage of shifts in interest rates, to improve the quality of a portfolio, or for tax purposes. Although some swaps

INVESTOR INSIGHTS: *Investing in Action*

Swapping Taxes for Returns

As interest rates climbed and bond prices fell during 1994, investors who purchased bonds in late 1993 were faced with a difficult decision: Should they keep the bonds, waiting for the market to improve, or should they cut their losses and sell? Sometimes taking a loss on your investments can work to your advantage by reducing your tax bill. With a *tax swap*, you not only sell your bond but immediately replace it with a similar—but not identical—issue. Depending on market conditions, you may be able to buy a similar bond with a higher coupon than the one you sold.

The loss on your original bond offsets taxes on either capital gains from the sale of stocks or bonds or ordinary income in the current or future tax years. There is no limit on the amount of capital gains you can offset, but you can deduct up to only $3,000 of ordinary income per year on a joint return. Any unused portion of your loss can be carried forward to reduce your tax liability in subsequent years. Typically, investors consider tax swaps at year-end, when they review their portfolio's gains and losses. However, it may not be a good idea to wait. Finding suitable replacement bonds gets harder as more investors turn to tax swaps late in the year.

Here's how a bond swap works: Suppose that in November 1993, you bought a $10,000, 6½ percent coupon, 10-year Wal-Mart bond for $10,469. A year later, it had dropped in price to $8,855. However, during the year, you had made a profit of $1,250 on a stock investment. You decide to sell the bond and purchase a $10,000, 6.75 percent coupon, 10-year AT&T bond for a slightly higher price, $9,111. On your tax return, you can use the $1,614 loss as follows: $1,250 will offset your capital gain on the stock transaction, and $364 is deducted from ordinary income. Because both corporate bonds are of similar credit quality, your portfolio maintains its balance. If your bond investments are in mutual funds, you can still use the swap strategy: just buy a similar fund from a different fund family.

Deciding whether to swap and what bonds to swap can be complicated. Bond prices and commissions vary from dealer to dealer. Do your research and calculations carefully to be sure transaction costs don't eliminate tax savings. It's not uncommon to find high price markups on bonds, particularly tax-free issues. Be aware of the IRS *wash-sale rule*, which disallows tax losses if the swap involves essentially identical securities. Therefore, to qualify as a tax swap, at least two of the following features must be different: issuer, coupon rate, maturity, or call feature. Also, don't let tax considerations govern your investment decisions, regardless of how attractive the tax savings are. Many people place too much focus on tax savings and ignore the overall impact on their portfolio of selling the security.

Sources: Tom Herman, "Swapping May Be Way to Save Face and Taxes on Long-Term Bond Losers," *Wall Street Journal,* October 11, 1994, pp. C1, 12; "Swapping Your Investment Losses for Tax Savings," *On Retirement* (PaineWebber), Fall 1994, pp. 10–11; and "The Best Year-End Investment Moves," *Smart Money,* December 1994, pp. 111–12.

are highly sophisticated, most are fairly simple transactions. They go by a variety of colorful names, such as "profit takeout," "substitution swap," and "tax swap," but they are all used for one basic reason: *to seek portfolio improvement.* We will briefly review two types of bond swaps that are fairly simple and hold considerable appeal for investors: the yield pickup swap and the tax swap.

In a **yield pickup swap,** an investor switches out of a low-coupon bond into a comparable higher-coupon issue in order to realize an automatic and instantaneous pickup of current yield and yield-to-maturity. For example, you would be executing a yield pickup swap if you sold the 20-year, A-rated, 6½ percent bonds you held (which were yielding 8 percent at the time) and replaced them

yield pickup swap
replacement of a low-coupon bond for a comparable higher-coupon bond in order to realize an increase in current yield and yield-to-maturity.

with an equal amount of 20-year, A-rated, 7 percent bonds that were priced to yield 8½ percent. By executing the swap, you would improve your current yield (by moving from coupon income of $65 a year to $70 a year), as well as your yield-to-maturity (from 8 to 8½ percent). Basically, such swap opportunities arise because of the *yield spreads* that normally exist between, say, industrial and public utility bonds. The mechanics are fairly simple, and any investor can execute such swaps simply by watching for swap candidates and/or by asking a broker to do so. In fact, the only thing you have to be careful of is that commissions and transaction costs do not eat up all the profits.

tax swap
replacement of a bond that has a capital loss for a similar security; used to offset a gain generated in another part of an investor's portfolio.

The other type of swap that's popular with many investors is the **tax swap**, which is also relatively simple and involves few risks. The technique, which is more fully explained in the *Investor Insights* box on page 396, can be used whenever an investor has a substantial tax liability that has come about as a result of selling some security holdings at a profit. The objective is to execute a bond swap in such a way that the tax liability accompanying the capital gains can be *eliminated* or *substantially reduced*. This is done by selling an issue that has undergone a capital loss and replacing it with a comparable obligation. The only precaution that should be kept in mind is that *identical issues cannot be used* in such swap transactions, since the IRS would consider this a "wash sale" (see Chapter 3) and therefore disallow the loss. Moreover, the capital loss must occur in the same taxable year as the capital gain. These are the only limitations and explain why this technique is so popular with knowledgeable investors, particularly at year-end, when tax loss sales and tax swaps multiply as investors hurry to establish capital losses.

CONCEPTS *in Review*

9.12 Briefly describe a *bond ladder* and note how and why an investor would use this investment strategy. What is a *tax swap*, and why would it be used?

9.13 What strategy would you expect an aggressive bond investor (i.e., someone who's looking for capital gains) to employ?

9.14 Why is interest sensitivity so important to bond speculators? Does the need for interest sensitivity explain why active bond traders tend to use high-grade issues? Explain.

On Track with STOCK-TRAK®

STOCK-TRAK®'s Bond-Trading Procedures

STOCK-TRAK® simulates actual bond market trading in several ways. First, bonds are quoted as a percentage of par. Second, bond par values are normally $1,000. Third, transaction costs are low; incremental transaction cost is $5.00 per bond, or 0.5 percent on a $1,000 bond. Fourth, accrued interest is paid to the seller when the bonds are traded between coupon payment dates. For instance, the buyer of a 6 percent bond (0.5 percent per month) would have to pay $5.00 ($1,000 × .005) per month in accrued interest for each month that has passed since the last interest payment. The accrued interest is recovered at the next interest payment date or portfolio valuation date, because STOCK-TRAK® includes interest receivable in portfolio value calculations.

SUMMARY

LG 1   **Explain the behavior of market interest rates and identify the forces that cause interest rates to move.** The behavior of interest rates is the single most important force in the bond market, because it determines not only the amount of current income an investor will receive but also the amount of capital gains (or losses) an investor will earn. Indeed, changes in market interest rates can have a dramatic impact on the total annual returns actually obtained from bonds over time.

LG 2   **Describe the term structure of interest rates and note how these so-called yield curves can be used by investors.** There are many forces that drive the behavior of interest rates over time, including inflation, the cost and availability of funds, the size of the federal deficit, and the level of interest rates in major foreign markets. One force that's particularly important and is very closely followed is the term structure of interest rates, which relates yield-to-maturity to term to maturity.

LG 3   **Gain an understanding of how bonds are valued in the marketplace.** Bonds are valued (priced) in the marketplace on the basis of their required rates of return (or market yields). Indeed, the whole process of pricing a bond begins with the yield it should provide. Once that important piece of information is known (or estimated), the bond valuation process becomes rather mechanical: A standard, present-value-based model is used to find the dollar price of a bond.

LG 4   **Describe the various measures of yield and return, and explain how these standards of performance are used in the bond valuation process.** Three types of yields are important to investors: current yield, promised yield, and expected yield (or return). Promised yield (also known as yield-to-maturity) is the most important and widely used bond valuation measure and captures both the current income and the price appreciation of an issue. Expected return, in contrast, is a valuation measure that's used by aggressive bond traders to show the total return that can be earned from trading in and out of a bond long before it matures.

LG 5   **Understand the basic concept of duration, how it can be measured, and its use in the management of bond portfolios.** Bond duration is one of the most important concepts in bond valuation and investing. Basically, duration takes into account the effects of both reinvestment and price (or market) risks. It captures, in a single measure, the extent to which the price of a bond will react to different interest rate environments. Equally important, duration can be used to immunize whole bond portfolios from the often devastating forces of changing market interest rates.

LG 6   **Discuss various bond investment strategies and the different ways these securities can be used by investors.** As investment vehicles, bonds can be used as a source of income, as a way to seek capital gains by speculating on the movement in interest rates, or as a way to earn attractive long-term returns. To achieve these objectives, investors will often employ one or more of the following bond investment strategies: passive strategies like buy-and-hold, bond ladders, and portfolio immunization; bond trading based on forecasted interest rate behavior; and bond swaps.

DISCUSSION QUESTIONS

1. Describe briefly each of the following theories of the term structure of interest rates:

    a. Expectations hypothesis
    b. Liquidity preference theory
    c. Market segmentation theory

According to these theories, what conditions would result in a downward-sloping yield curve? What conditions would result in an upward-sloping yield curve? Which theory do you think is most valid, and why?

2. Using a recent copy of the *Wall Street Journal* or *Barron's*, find bond yields for Treasury securities with the following maturities: 3 months, 6 months, 1 year, 3 years, 5 years, 10 years, 15 years, 20 years, and 30 years. Construct a yield curve based on these reported yields, putting term to maturity on the horizontal (*x*) axis and yield-to-maturity on the vertical (*y*) axis. Briefly discuss the general shape of your yield curve. What conclusions might you draw about interest rate movements from this yield curve?

3. Briefly explain what will happen to a bond's duration measure if the following events occur:

   a. The yield-to-maturity on the bond falls from 8½ to 8 percent.
   b. The bond gets one year closer to its maturity.
   c. Market interest rates go from 8 to 9 percent.
   d. The bond's *modified* duration falls by half-a-year.

4. Assume that an investor comes to you looking for investment advice. She has $200,000 to invest and wants to put it all into bonds.

   a. If she considers herself to be a fairly aggressive investor, willing to take the risks necessary to generate the big returns, what kind of investment strategy (or strategies) would you suggest? Be specific.
   b. What kind of investment strategies would you recommend if your client were a very conservative investor, who could not tolerate market losses?
   c. What kind of investor do you think would be most likely to use:
      (1) An immunized bond portfolio?
      (2) A yield pickup swap?
      (3) A bond ladder?
      (4) A long-term zero-coupon bond when interest rates fall?

5. Using the resources available at your campus or public library, select any six bonds you like, consisting of *two* Treasury bonds, *two* corporate bonds, and *two* agency issues. Determine the latest current yield and promised yield for each. (For promised yield, use the precise method, with annual compounding.) In addition, find the duration and modified duration for each bond. (*Note:* You might want to use the IMD disk to compute the various yield and duration measures.)

   a. Now, assuming that you put an equal amount into each of the six bonds you selected, find the duration for this six-bond portfolio.
   b. What would happen to your bond portfolio if market interest rates fell by 100 basis points?
   c. Assuming that you have $100,000 to invest, use at least four of these bonds to develop a bond portfolio that emphasizes either the potential for capital gains or preservation of capital. Briefly explain your logic.

PROBLEMS   **LG 3**   1. Two bonds have par values of $1,000; one is a 5 percent, 15-year bond priced to yield 8 percent, and the other is a 7½ percent, 20-year bond priced to yield 6 percent. Which of these two has the lower price? (Assume annual compounding in both cases.)

 LG 4   2. Using semiannual compounding, find the prices of the following bonds:
   a. A 10½ percent, 15-year bond priced to yield 8 percent
   b. A 7 percent, 10-year bond priced to yield 8 percent
   c. A 12 percent, 20-year bond priced at 10 percent

Repeat the problem using annual compounding. Then comment on the differences you found in the prices of the bonds.

LG 3 3. An investor is considering the purchase of an 8 percent, 18-year corporate bond that's being priced to yield 10 percent. She thinks that in a year, this same bond will be priced in the market to yield 9 percent. Using annual compounding, find the price of the bond today and in one year. Next, find the holding period return on this investment, assuming the investor's expectations hold up. (If necessary, see Chapter 4 for the holding period return formula.)

LG 4 4. Compute the current yield of a 10 percent, 25-year bond that is currently priced in the market at $1,200. Use the approximate method to find the promised yield on this bond. Repeat the promised yield calculation, but this time use semiannual compounding to find the precise yield-to-maturity.

LG 4 5. A 25-year, zero-coupon bond was recently being quoted at 11⅝. Find the current yield *and* the promised yield of this issue, given that the bond has a par value of $1,000. Using annual compounding, how much would an investor have to pay for this bond if it were priced to yield 12 percent?

LG 4 6. Assume that an investor pays $800 for a long-term bond that carries an 8 percent coupon. In 3 years, she hopes to sell the issue for $850. If her expectations come true, what realized yield would this investor earn? What would her holding period return be if she were able to sell the bond (at $850) after only 6 months?

LG 4 7. Using annual compounding, find the yield-to-maturity for each of the following bonds:

     a. A 9½ percent, 20-year bond priced at $957.43
     b. A 16 percent, 15-year bond priced at $1,684.76
     c. A 5½ percent, 18-year bond priced at $510.65

LG 5 8. Find the Macaulay duration and modified duration of a 20-year, 10 percent corporate bond that's being priced to yield 8 percent. According to the modified duration of this bond, how much of a price change would this bond incur if market yields rose to 9 percent in one year? Using annual compounding, calculate the price of this bond in one year if rates do rise to 9 percent. How does this price change compare to that predicted by the modified duration? Explain the difference.

LG 5 9. Which *one* of the following bonds would you select if you thought market interest rates were going to fall by 50 basis points over the next 6 months?

     a. A bond with a Macaulay duration of 8.46 years that's currently being priced to yield 7½ percent
     b. A bond with a Macaulay duration of 9.30 years that's priced to yield 10 percent
     c. A bond with a Macaulay duration of 8.75 years that's priced to yield 5¾ percent

LG 5 **LG 6** 10. Arlene Darling is an aggressive bond trader who likes to speculate on interest rate swings. Market interest rates are presently at 9 percent, but she expects they will fall to 7 percent within a year. As a result, Arlene is thinking about buying one of the following issues: a 25-year, zero-coupon bond, or a 20-year, 7½ percent bond. (Both bonds have $1,000 par values and carry the same agency rating.) Assuming Arlene wants to maximize capital gains, which one of the two issues should she select? What if she wants to maximize the total return (interest income and capital gains) from her investment? Why did one issue provide better capital gains than the other? Based on the duration of each bond, which one should be more price volatile?

11. Bill Peters is a 35-year-old bank executive who's just inherited a large sum of money. Having spent several years in the bank's investments department, he's well aware of the concept of duration and decides to apply it to his bond portfolio. In particular, Bill intends to use $1 million of his inheritance to purchase four U.S. Treasury bonds:

1. An 8½ percent, 13-year bond that's priced at $1,045 to yield 7.47 percent
2. A 7⅞ percent, 15-year bond that's priced at $1,020 to yield 7.60 percent
3. A 20-year stripped Treasury that's priced at $202 to yield 8.22 percent
4. A 24-year, 7½ percent bond that's priced at $955 to yield 7.90 percent

   a. Find the duration and modified duration of each bond.
   b. Find the duration of the whole bond portfolio if Bill puts $250,000 into each of the four U.S. Treasury bonds.
   c. Find the duration of the portfolio if Bill puts $360,000 each into bonds 1 and 3 and $140,000 each into bonds 2 and 4.
   d. Which portfolio—(b) or (c)—should Bill select if he thinks rates are about to head up and he wants to avoid as much price volatility as possible? Explain. From which portfolio does he stand to make more in annual interest income? Which portfolio would you recommend, and why?

CASE PROBLEMS   ### 9.1 THE BOND INVESTMENT DECISIONS OF ROB AND KATHY JOBST

Rob and Kathy Jobst live in the Boston area, where Rob has a successful orthodontics practice. The Jobsts have built up a sizable investment portfolio and have always had a major portion of their investments in fixed-income securities. They adhere to a fairly aggressive investment posture and actively go after both attractive current income and substantial capital gains. Assume that it is now 1996 and Rob is currently evaluating two investment decisions: One involves an addition to their portfolio, and the other a revision to it.

The Jobsts' first investment decision involves a short-term trading opportunity. In particular, Rob has a chance to buy a 7½ percent, 25-year bond that is currently priced at $852 to yield 9 percent; he feels that in 2 years the promised yield of the issue should drop to 8 percent.

The second is a bond swap; the Jobsts hold some Beta Corporation 7 percent, 2011 bonds that are currently priced at $785. They want to improve both current income and yield-to-maturity, and they are considering one of three issues as a possible swap candidate: (a) Dental Floss, Inc., 7½ percent, 2011, currently priced at $780; (b) Root Canal Products of America, 6½ percent, 2009, selling at $885; and (c) Kansas City Dental Insurance, 8 percent, 2013, priced at $950. All of the swap candidates are of comparable quality and have comparable issue characteristics.

Questions

1. Regarding the short-term trading opportunity:

    a. What basic trading principle is involved in this situation?
    b. If Rob's expectations are correct, what will the price of this bond be in two years?
    c. What is the expected return on this investment?
    d. Should this investment be made? Why?

2. Regarding the bond swap opportunity:

    a. Compute the current yield and promised yield (use semiannual compounding) of the bond the Jobsts currently hold and each of the three swap candidates.
    b. Do any of the three swap candidates provide better current income and/or current yield than the Beta Corporation bond the Jobsts now hold? If so, which one(s)?
    c. Do you see any reason why Rob should switch from his present bond holding into one of the other three issues? If so, which swap candidate would be the best choice? Why?

 ## 9.2 CONNIE DECIDES TO IMMUNIZE HER PORTFOLIO

Connie Moore is the owner of an extremely successful dress boutique in midtown Manhattan. Although high fashion is Connie's first love, she's also very interested in investments, particularly bonds and other fixed-income securities. She actively manages her own investments and over time has built up a substantial portfolio of securities. She's well versed on the latest investment techniques and is not afraid to apply those procedures to her own investments.

Connie's been playing with the idea of trying to immunize a big chunk of her bond portfolio. She'd like to cash out this part of her portfolio in 7 years and use the proceeds to buy a vacation home on the South Carolina seashore. To do this, she intends to use the $200,000 she now has invested in the following four corporate bonds (she currently has $50,000 invested in each one):

1. A 12-year, 7½ percent bond that's currently priced at $895
2. A 10-year, zero-coupon bond priced at $405
3. A 10-year, 10 percent bond priced at $1,080
4. A 15-year, 9¾ percent bond priced at $980

(*Note:* These are all noncallable, investment-grade, nonconvertible/straight bonds.)

 Questions

1. Given the information provided above, find the current yield and the promised yield for each bond in the portfolio. (Use the precise method with annual compounding.)

2. Calculate the Macaulay and modified durations of each bond in the portfolio, and indicate how the price of each bond would change if interest rates were to rise by 75 basis points. How would the price change if interest rates were to fall by 75 basis points?

3. Find the duration of the current four-bond portfolio. Given the 7-year target that Connie has, would you consider this to be an immunized portfolio? Explain.

4. How could you lengthen or shorten the duration of this portfolio? What's the shortest portfolio duration you can achieve? What's the longest?

5. Using one or more of the four bonds described above, is it possible to come up with a $200,000 bond portfolio that will exhibit the duration characteristics Connie is looking for? Explain.

6. Using one or more of the four bonds, put together a $200,000 immunized portfolio for Connie. Since this portfolio will now be immunized, will Connie be able to treat it as a buy-and-hold portfolio—one she can put away and forget about? Explain.

CHAPTER 10

PREFERRED STOCK AND CONVERTIBLE SECURITIES

LEARNING GOALS

After studying this chapter, you should be able to:

LG 1 Describe the basic features of preferred stock, including sources of value and exposure to risk.

LG 2 Discuss the rights and claims of preferred stockholders and note some of the popular issue characteristics that are often found with these securities.

LG 3 Develop an understanding of the various measures of investment worth and identify several investment strategies that can be used with preferred stocks.

LG 4 Identify the fundamental characteristics of convertible securities and explain the nature of the underlying conversion privilege.

LG 5 Describe the advantages and disadvantages of investing in convertible securities, including the risk and return attributes of these investment vehicles.

LG 6 Measure the value of a convertible security and explain how these securities can be used to meet different investment objectives.

Harry Payton became serious about investing in the early 1980s, when his law firm's profit sharing plan grew to significant proportions. Until then, he'd entrusted his investment decisions to a major Wall Street broker. "After several sad experiences—no profits and mostly losses—I decided to rely on my own resources for investment selections and began reading *Barron's* and The *Wall Street Journal*. Nevertheless, I made my early security selections without good information," Harry says. He then subscribed to *Value Line Investment Survey* and in 1986 found a good broker to provide information and, more importantly, act as a "conscience" to keep him from making investment mistakes.

Harry continues to read many investment and finance publications. "I've learned that successful securities investing takes patience, discipline, adherence to a philosophy of investing, some luck, and accepting losses as part of the overall program. I also recognized that hitting consecutive singles will produce the results I seek, with less risk of striking out," he explains. "However, losses seem to take place at a much more rapid pace than gains do!"

Over the years, Harry has built a diversified portfolio that currently consists of mortgages (20 percent), cash (10 percent), corporate bonds and mortgage-backed securities (15 percent), convertible securities (5 percent), common stock (20 percent), and preferred stock (30 percent). The composition changes with the economy. When he thinks interest rates are close to their highest point in the economic cycle, he adds fixed-income securities, typically with a maximum time horizon of ten years, to capture appreciation as interest rates decline further along in the economic cycle. Investment-grade preferred stock with generous dividends—recent purchases included Chase Manhattan, Salomon Brothers, and Household Finance, each yielding over 9 percent—provide good cash flow and also appreciate when interest rates decline.

Convertible securities have been part of Harry's portfolio for over ten years. He finds investment-grade convertible bonds attractive because he receives a healthy interest payment while waiting for the stock to grow in value. He selects convertible preferred stocks based on quality and yield, keeping in mind the longer-term outlook for the stock and interest rates. When a convertible bond he owns is called for redemption, he bases the decision to redeem or convert on the outlook for the stock, the conversion value at the time, and the availability of other investment alternatives. For example, he converted National Semiconductor bonds and has profited nicely from the stock appreciation. However, he sold Seagate Technology bonds before the con-

> **I'VE LEARNED THAT SUCCESSFUL SECURITIES INVESTING TAKES PATIENCE, DISCIPLINE, ADHERENCE TO A PHILOSOPHY OF INVESTING, SOME LUCK, AND ACCEPTING LOSSES AS PART OF THE OVERALL PROGRAM.**

version date, due to a weakening industry outlook.

Harry would invest in more convertible securities if more investment-grade offerings were available. Another factor is their complexity: "Even though I read *Value Line Convertibles* and *Investor's Business Daily*, I find it harder to get good information on convertibles than on common stocks. I struggle to analyze them and to fully understand the conversion features and dynamics of valuation," Harry admits. "And I just don't have enough time to analyze every convertible that interests me."

Attorney Harry A. Payton, 55, is an attorney in private practice specializing in commercial litigation. He resides in Coral Gables, Florida; is married; and has three children.

What would you think of a stock that promised to pay you a fixed annual dividend for life—nothing more, nothing less? If you're an income-oriented investor, the offer might sound pretty good. But where would you find such an investment? Right on the NYSE or AMEX, where hundreds of these securities trade every day, in the form of *preferred stock*—a type of security that looks like a stock but doesn't behave like one. Well, if preferreds don't interest you, how about a bond that lets you participate in the price behavior of the company's stock? Does an investment that gives you the security of a bond and the price behavior of a stock sound too good to be true? It's not—such securities actually do exist. Called *convertible debentures,* they too are actively traded on the New York and American exchanges, and they truly are bonds that behave like stocks. Investing in preferred stock and convertible securities has paid off for Harry Payton, and you may want to consider them for your portfolio as well.

Both preferreds and convertibles are corporate securities, and both are considered to be *fixed-income securities* (even though preferreds are actually a form of equity ownership). Convertible securities, usually issued as bonds, are subsequently convertible into shares of the issuing firm's common stock. Indeed, the investment merits of these securities are based principally on the *equity kicker* they provide: That is, the tendency for the market price of these issues to behave much like the common stock into which they can be converted. Preferred stocks, in contrast, are issued as equity and remain as equity; however, like bonds, they too produce a fixed income. In fact, preferred stocks derive their name in part from the *preferred claim* on income they hold: All preferred dividends must be paid before any payments can be made to holders of common stock. In many respects, these two issues represent *hybrid securities* since there's is a bit of debt and equity in both of them. Let's now take a closer look at each, starting with preferred stocks.

PREFERRED STOCKS

preferred stock
a stock that has a prior claim (ahead of common) on the income and assets of the issuing firm.

Preferred stocks carry fixed dividends that are paid quarterly and are expressed either in dollar terms or as a percentage of the stock's par (or stated) value. They're used by companies that need the funds but don't want to raise debt to get it; in effect, preferred stocks are widely viewed by issuers as an alternative to debt. Companies like to issue preferreds because they don't count as common stock (and, therefore, don't effect EPS). Yet being a form of equity, they don't count as debt, either—and therefore don't add to the company's debt load. There are today about a thousand OTC and listed preferred stocks outstanding, many of which are issued by public utilities, although the number of industrial, financial, and insurance issues is rapidly increasing.

PREFERRED STOCKS AS INVESTMENT VEHICLES

Preferred stocks are available in a wide range of quality ratings, from investment-grade issues to highly speculative stocks. Table 10.1 provides a representative sample of some actively traded preferred stocks. It shows the types of annual dividends and dividend yields these securities were providing in November 1994. Note especially the variety of different types of issuers, and how the market price of a preferred tends to vary with the size of the annual dividend.

Table 10.1   A Sample of Some High-Yielding Preferred Stock

S&P Rating	Issuer	Annual Dividend	Market Price	Dividend Yield
B−	Citicorp	$6.00	$71.50	8.4%
B+	DuPont	3.50	48.25	7.3
BBB	General Motors	1.98	22.25	8.9
BBB+	GTE	2.00	46.50	4.3
B	IL Power	2.36	24.13	9.8
B	Sears	2.22	25.00	8.9
B−	Tenneco	2.36	38.63	6.1
NR	USX	3.87	49.88	7.8
B−	Bank Boston	3.00	44.00	6.8
B	Bank America	3.25	42.88	7.6
C	Digital Equipment	2.22	22.25	10.0
A−	Duke Power	1.95	38.50	5.1
BBB+	First Chicago	3.50	47.75	7.3
B+	JP Morgan	5.00	62.63	8.0

Note: All of these issues are straight (nonconvertible) preferred stocks traded on the NYSE. All the information that appears in this table was obtained in November 1994.

Advantages and Disadvantages

Investors are attracted to preferred stocks because of the current income they provide. Moreover, such dividend income is highly predictable, even though it can, under certain circumstances, be temporarily discontinued. Figure 10.1 illustrates the average yields on preferred stocks and shows how they compare to high-grade bond returns. Note the tendency for preferreds to generate yields that are slightly *less* than those on high-grade bonds. This is due to the fact that 70 percent of the preferred dividends *received by a corporation* are exempt from federal income taxes; the net effect of this favorable tax treatment is, of course, reduced preferred dividend yields. Safety is another desirable feature of preferreds: Despite a few well-publicized incidents, *high-grade* preferred stocks have an excellent record of meeting dividend payments in a

Figure 10.1   Average High-Grade Preferred Stock Yields Versus Average Market Yields on AA-Rated Corporate Bonds
Note that preferred stock yields tend to move in concert with the market behavior of bond returns—and that they tend to stay *below* bond yields. Source: Standard & Poor's *Trade and Securities Statistics*.

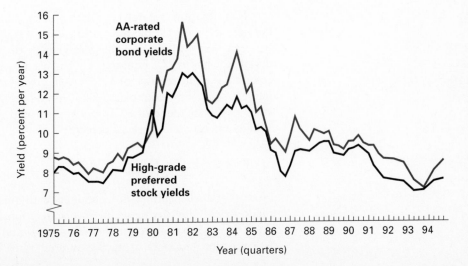

prompt and timely manner. A final advantage of preferred stocks is the low unit cost of many of the issues, which gives even small investors the opportunity to participate actively in preferreds.

A major disadvantage of preferred stocks is their susceptibility to inflation and high interest rates. Like many other fixed-income securities, preferred stocks simply have not proved to be satisfactory long-term hedges against inflation. Another disadvantage is that preferred dividends may be suspended, or "passed," if the earnings of the corporate issuer drop off. Thus, unlike coupon payments on a bond, dividends on preferreds have no legal backing, and failure to pay them does not lead to default. Still another drawback is that most preferreds lack substantial capital gains potential. Although it is possible to enjoy fairly attractive capital gains from preferred stocks when interest rates decline dramatically, these amounts generally do not match the price performances of common stocks. But, perhaps the biggest disadvantage of preferreds is the *yield give-up* they incur relative to bonds. In essence, there is virtually nothing a preferred has to offer that can't be obtained from a comparably rated corporate bond—and *at less risk and more return than can be earned from a preferred.*

Sources of Value

With the exception of convertible preferreds, the value of high-grade preferred stocks is a function of the dividend yields they provide. More specifically, the value (or market price) of a preferred stock is closely related to prevailing market rates: As the general level of interest rates moves up, so too do the yields of preferreds, and, as such, their prices decline. When interest rates drift downward, so will the yields on preferreds, as their prices rise. Just like a bond, therefore, *the price behavior of a high-grade preferred stock is inversely related to market interest rates.* Moreover, its price is directly linked to the issue's level of income. That is, other things being equal, the higher the dividend payment, the higher the market price of an issue. Therefore, the price of a preferred can be defined as follows:

Equation 10.1 $$\text{Price of a preferred stock} = \frac{\text{annual dividend income}}{\text{prevailing market yield}}$$

This equation is simply a variation of the standard dividend yield formula, but here we solve for the price of the issue. (You might also detect a similarity between this formula and the zero-growth dividend valuation model introduced in Chapter 7.) Equation 10.1 is used to price preferred stocks and to compute the future price of a preferred, given an estimate of expected market interest rates. For example, a $2.50 preferred stock (which implies that the stock pays a dividend of $2.50 per year) would be priced at $20.83 if the prevailing market yield were 12 percent:

$$\text{Price} = \frac{\$2.50}{.12} = \underline{\underline{\$20.83}}$$

Note that higher prices are obtained with this formula by decreasing the market yield, thus giving us the inverse relationship between price and yield.

The yield that a preferred stock offers—and therefore its market value—is a function not only of market interest rates but also of the issue's credit quality: That is, *the lower the quality of a preferred, the higher its yield*. Such behavior is, of course, compatible with the risk-return tradeoffs that usually exist in the marketplace. Fortunately, preferred stocks are rated, much like bonds, by Moody's and Standard & Poor's. Finally, the value of a preferred is affected by issue characteristics such as call features and sinking fund provisions. For example, freely callable preferreds will normally provide higher yields to investors than noncallable issues, due to the greater call risk inherent in the former type of security. Quality and issue features, however, have only slight effects on price behavior over time, and they certainly do not compare in importance with the movement of market yields.

Risk Exposure

Preferred stock investors are exposed to both business and interest rate risks. Business risk is important with preferreds, because these securities are a form of equity ownership and as such, lack many of the legal protections of bonds. Annual operating costs and corporate financial strength, therefore, are of concern to preferred stockholders. Preferred stock ratings (discussed later in this chapter) can be used to assess the amount of business risk embedded in an issue; higher-quality/higher-rated issues are believed to possess less business risk. Because of the fixed-income nature of these securities and the way they're valued in the market, interest rate risk is also important to preferred stockholders. That is, when market interest rates move up, the value of these securities (like bonds) falls. Indeed, such risk exposure can be very damaging if interest rates move against the investor in a big way.

Market Transactions

Preferred stocks are subject to the same transaction costs as shares of common stock: Their brokerage fees and transfer taxes are identical. In addition, preferred investors use the same types of orders (market, limit, and stop-loss) and operate under the same margin requirements. Even the quotes of preferred stock are commingled with those of common. Fortunately, preferreds are easy to pick out in the financial pages; simply look for the letters *pf* or *pr* after the name of the company. (Technically, the *pf* denotes *regular preferred stock*, and the *pr* stands for *prior preferred*, or *preference*, shares. The differences will be explained below.)

Quotes for preferred stock are interpreted exactly like those for common stock, except that the price/earnings ratios are not listed. Note also that the preferreds are always listed right after the company's common stock. In the quotes in Figure 10.2, we see that there are four issues of preferred stocks listed for Ohio Edison (OhioEd). Actually, the company could have other issues outstanding, but if they did not trade on the day of the quotes, they would not be listed. These preferreds pay annual dividends of anywhere from $1.94 to $8.20 per share. (Note that the higher the annual dividend, the higher the price of the stock.) At quoted market prices, these preferreds were providing current yields of 8.8 to 9.4 percent. Observe also the relatively low unit cost of the stock: One of the preferreds is priced at under $25 a share, another at about $45 a share, and the other two are moderately priced at around $80 to $90 a share.

Figure 10.2 Published Quotes for Preferred Stocks
Preferred stock quotes are listed right along with the company's common stock. They are identified by the two-letter initials *pf* or *pr* that appear after the name of the company. (Source: *Wall Street Journal*, November 2, 1994.)

52 Weeks Hi	Lo	Stock	Sym	Div	Yld %	PE	Vol 100s	Hi	Lo	Close	Net Chg
22⅜	15⅛	OcciPete	OXY	1.00	4.7	dd	12272	21¾	21	21⅛	− ¾
n 50½	39⅞	OcciPete pf		3.00	6.0	...	54	50½	50	50⅛	− ⅛
17½	11	OceanrgInt	OII		...	22	678	12⅞	12⅝	12¾	− ⅛
s 27	18⅞	OffcDepot	ODP		...	40	2882	24¾	24	24½	− ½
22½	13½	OffshrPipe	OFP		...	14	720	20½	20⅛	20⅛	− ¼
50⅜	37	OffshrPipe pf		2.25	5.0	...	1	44¾	44¾	44¾	− ¼
25⅜	19⅞	Ogden	OG	1.25	5.8	14	379	21⅝	21⅜	21⅜	...
18	14⅝	OgdenProj	OPI		...	12	115	17⅝	17⅜	17⅝	+ ⅛
24⅛	16½	OhioEd	OEC	1.50	7.9	cc	1289	19⅛	18¾	18⅞	− ⅜
59	44¼	OhioEd pfA		3.90	8.8	...	1	44¼	44¼	44¼	− ¼
100	77⅝	OhioEd pfE		7.24	9.1	...	3	80	79½	79½	−1
103	84⅜	OhioEd pfH		8.20	9.2	...	1	89	89	89	...
26⅛	20¼	OhioEd pfM		1.94	9.4	...	35	20¾	20⅝	20⅝	+ ⅛
23⅜	17⅜	OilDriAmer	ODC	.32f	1.7	13	15	18¾	18½	18⅝	...
37¼	29⅜	OklaGE	OGE	2.66	7.9	12	645	33⅞	33⅜	33¾	...
▼ 14¾	10¼	OklaGE pf		.80	7.8	...	z1140	10¼	9¾	10¼	...
25⅛	20⅛	OldRepublic	ORI	.48	2.4	7	1224	20⅝	20¼	20⅝	...
27¾	24⅞	OldRepublic pf		2.19	8.7	...	6	25¼	25⅛	25¼	+ ⅛
60⅛	44⅞	Olin	OLN	2.20	4.1	dd	2294	54⅞	53¾	54	− ⅛
52¼	45⅜	Olin pfA		3.64	7.1	...	752	51⅜	51¼	51¼	− ¼
26½	22⅜	OmegaHlthcr	OHI	2.32	9.6	...	175	24¼	24⅛	24¼	...
41¼	23½	Omnicare	OCR	.18	.5	35	472	37½	36¼	37½	+1

} Ohio Edison's preferred stocks

ISSUE CHARACTERISTICS

Preferred stocks possess features that not only distinguish them from other types of securities but also help differentiate one preferred from another. For example, preferred stocks may be issued as convertible or nonconvertible, although the majority fall into the nonconvertible category. A **conversion feature** allows the holder to convert the preferred stock into a specified number of shares of the issuing company's common stock. Because convertible preferreds are, for all intents and purposes, very much like convertible bonds, a thorough examination of them will be deferred to later in this chapter. At this point, we'll concentrate on *nonconvertible issues*, although many of the features we are about to discuss apply equally to convertible preferreds. In addition to convertibility, investors should be aware of several other important preferred stock features; they include the rights of preferred stockholders and the special provisions (such as those pertaining to passed dividends or call features) that are built into preferred stock issues.

conversion feature
allows the holder of a convertible preferred to convert to a specified number of shares of the issuing company's common stock.

Rights of Preferred Stockholders

The contractual agreement of a preferred stock specifies the rights and privileges of preferred stockholders. The most important of these deal with the level of annual dividends, the claim on income, voting rights, and the claim on assets. The issuing company agrees that it will pay preferred stockholders a (minimum) fixed level of quarterly dividends and that such payments *will take priority over common stock dividends*. The only condition is that the firm generate income sufficient to meet the preferred dividend requirements. However, the firm is not legally bound to pay dividends. Of course, it cannot pass dividends on preferred stock and then pay dividends on common stock, because that would clearly violate the preferreds' prior claim on income. Although most preferred stocks are issued with dividend rates that remain fixed for the life of the issue, in the early 1980s some preferreds began to appear with floating dividend rates. Known as **adjustable** (or **floating**) **rate preferreds**, these issues adjust dividends periodically in line with yields on specific Treasury issues, although minimum and maximum dividend rates are usually established as a safeguard for investors.

Even though they hold an ownership position in the firm, preferred stockholders normally have no voting rights. However, if conditions deteriorate to the point that the firm needs to pass one or more consecutive quarterly dividends, preferred shareholders are usually given the right to elect a certain number of corporate directors so that their views can be represented. And if liquidation becomes necessary, the holders of preferreds are given a prior claim on assets. These preferred claims, limited to the par or stated value of the stock, must be satisfied before the claims of the common stockholders. Of course, this obligation does not always mean that the full par or stated value of the preferred will be recovered, because the claims of senior securities, like bonds, must be met first. That is, all bonds—including convertible bonds—have a higher claim on assets (and income) than preferred stock, whereas preferreds have a higher claim than common stock. Thus, preferred shareholders have a claim that's somewhere between that of bondholders and common stockholders.

Finally, when a company has more than one issue of preferred stock outstanding, it will sometimes issue **preference** (or **prior preferred**) **stock**. Essentially, this stock has seniority over other preferred stock in its right to receive dividends and in its claim on assets in the event of liquidation. Therefore, preference stocks should be viewed as senior preferreds. They're usually easy to pick out in the financial pages as they use the letters *pr* instead of *pf* in their quotes.

Preferred Stock Provisions

There are three preferred stock provisions that investors should be well aware of *before* making an investment in a preferred security. Especially important is the obligation of the issuer in case any dividends are missed. In addition, the investor should determine whether or not the stock has a call feature and/or a sinking fund provision. Let's start by looking at how passed dividends are handled, which is determined by whether the preferred stock is issued on a cumulative or noncumulative basis.

Fortunately for investors, most preferred stocks are issued on a **cumulative** basis. This means that any preferred dividends that have been passed *must be made up in full* before dividends can be restored to common stockholders. As long as dividends on preferred stocks remain **in arrears**—which means that there are outstanding unfulfilled preferred dividend obligations—a corporation will not be able to make dividend payments on common shares. Assume, for example, that a firm normally pays a $1 quarterly dividend on its preferred stock but has missed the dividend for three quarters in a row. In this case, the firm has preferred dividends in arrears of $3 a share, which it is obligated to meet, along with the next quarterly dividend payment, before it can pay dividends to common shareholders. The firm could fulfill this obligation by paying, say, $2 per share to the preferred stockholders at the next quarterly dividend date, and $3 per share at the following one (with the $3 covering the remaining $2 in arrears and the current $1 quarterly payment). If the preferred stock had carried a **noncumulative provision**—as some do—the issuing company would be under no obligation to make up any of the passed dividends. Of course, the firm could not make dividend payments on common stock either, but all it would have to do to resume such payments would be to meet the next quarterly preferred dividend. Other things being equal, a cumulative preferred stock should be more highly valued than an issue without such a provision—that is, it should increase the price (and in so doing, lower the yield) of these issues.

noncumulative provision
a provision found on some preferred stocks excusing the issuing firm from having to make up any passed dividends.

Since the early 1970s, it has become increasingly popular to issue preferred stocks with call features. Today, a large number of preferreds carry this provision, which gives the firm the right to call the preferred for retirement. Callable preferreds are usually issued on a *deferred-call basis*, meaning they cannot be retired for a certain number of years after the date of issue. After the deferral period, which often extends for five to seven years, the preferreds become freely callable. Of course, such issues are then susceptible to call if the market rate for preferreds declines dramatically, which explains why the yields on freely callable preferreds should be higher than those on noncallable issues. As with bonds, the call price of a preferred is made up of the par value of the issue and a call premium that may amount to as much as one year's dividends.

Another preferred stock feature that has become popular in the past ten years or so is the *sinking fund provision*, which denotes how (all or a part of) an issue will be paid off—amortized—over time. Such sinking fund preferreds actually have *implied* maturity dates. They are used by firms to reduce the cost of financing, since sinking fund issues generally have *lower* yields than non-sinking fund preferreds. A typical sinking fund preferred might require the firm to retire half the issue over a ten-year period by retiring, say, 5 percent of the issue each year. Unfortunately, the investor has no control over which shares are called for sinking fund purposes.

CONCEPTS *in Review*

10.1 Define a *preferred stock*. What types of prior claims do preferred stockholders enjoy?

10.2 In what ways is a preferred stock like equity? In what ways is it like a bond?

10.3 Distinguish a *cumulative* preferred from a *callable* preferred. Do cumulative dividend provisions and call features affect the investment merits of preferred issues? Explain.

10.4 What are the advantages and the disadvantages of investing in preferreds?

VALUING AND INVESTING IN PREFERREDS

LG 3

As we just saw, while preferred stocks may be a form of equity, they behave in the market more like a bond than a stock. Therefore, it seems logical that preferreds should be *valued* much like bonds, with market interest rates and investment quality playing key roles. Similarly, when it comes to investing in preferreds, you would expect to find interest rates—that is, either the level of market interest rates or the movements therein—playing key roles in preferred stock investment strategies. In fact, that's exactly what you do find: The two most widely used preferred investment strategies involve either going after high levels of current income or seeking capital gains when market rates are falling.

PUTTING A VALUE ON PREFERREDS

Evaluating the investment suitability of preferreds involves assessing comparative return opportunities. Let's look now at some of the return measures that are important to preferred stockholders, and then at the role that agency ratings play in the valuation process.

Dividend Yield: A Critical Measure of Value

Dividend yield is the key variable in determining the price and return behavior of most preferred stocks. It is computed according to the following simple formula:

Equation 10.2

$$\text{Dividend yield} = \frac{\text{annual dividend income}}{\text{current market price of the preferred stock}}$$

dividend yield
a measure of the amount of return earned on annual dividends.

Dividend yield is a measure of the amount of return earned on annual dividends, and is the basis upon which comparative preferred investment opportunities are evaluated. (It is basically the same as the *dividend yield* used in Chapter 6 with common stocks and is comparable to the *current yield* measure used with bonds, as described in Chapter 9.)

Here is how dividend yield works: Suppose an 8 percent preferred stock has a par value of $25 and is currently trading at a price of $21 per share. The annual dividend on this stock is $2—that is, for preferreds whose dividends are denoted as a percent of par (or stated) value, the dollar value of the annual dividend is found by multiplying the dividend rate (in this case, 8 percent) by the par value (here it's $25). The dividend yield in this example is:

$$\text{Dividend yield} = \frac{\$2}{\$21} = 9\tfrac{1}{2}\%$$

As we can see, at $21 a share, this particular preferred is yielding 9½ percent to investors. If the price moves up (to, say, $27 a share), the dividend yield would drop (in this case, to a little less than 7½ percent). In practice, we would expect investors to compute or have available a current dividend yield measure for each preferred under consideration, and then to make a choice by comparing the yields of the alternative preferreds—along with, of course, the risk and issue characteristics of each.

Long-term investors consider dividend yield to be a critical factor in their investment decisions. Short-term traders, in contrast, generally focus on anticipated price behavior and the expected return from buying and selling an issue over a short period of time. Thus, the expected future price of a preferred is important to short-term traders. It is found by first forecasting future market interest rates and then using that information to determine expected future price. To illustrate, suppose a preferred stock pays $3 in dividends and its yield is expected to decline to 6 percent within the next two years. If such market rates prevail, then two years from now, the issue would have a market price of $50 (using Equation 10.1, annual dividend ÷ yield = $3 ÷ .06 = $50). This forecasted price, along with the current market price and level of annual dividends, would then be used in either the approximate yield or holding period return (HPR) formula (both of which were first introduced in Chapter 4) to compute the expected return from the transaction.

To continue with our example above, if the stock were currently priced at $28 a share, the expected return on the stock (over the two-year investment horizon) would be an attractive 35.9 percent:

Equation 10.3

$$\text{Expected return} = \frac{\text{annual dividend} + \dfrac{\text{expected future selling price} - \text{current market price}}{\text{years in holding period}}}{\dfrac{\text{expected future selling price} + \text{current market price}}{2}}$$

$$= \frac{\$3 + \dfrac{\$50 - \$28}{2}}{\dfrac{\$50 + \$28}{2}} = \frac{\$3 + \$11}{\$39} = \underline{35.9\%}$$

Note that in our illustration here, we use the approximate yield version of expected return (Equation 10.3). Such return information is used to judge the relative attractiveness of preferred stock. In general, the higher the expected return figure, the more appealing the investment.

Book Value

book value (net asset value)
a measure of the amount of debt-free assets supporting each share of preferred stock.

The **book value** (or **net asset value**) of a preferred stock is simply a measure of the amount of debt-free assets supporting each share of preferred stock. Book value per share is found by subtracting all the liabilities of the firm from its total assets and dividing the difference by the number of preferred shares outstanding. It reflects the quality of an issue with regard to the preferred's *claim on assets*. Obviously, a preferred with a book value of $150 per share enjoys generous asset support and more than adequately secures a par value of, say, $25 a share. Net asset value is most relevant when it is used relative to an issue's par, or stated, value. Other things being equal, *the quality of an issue improves as the margin by which book value exceeds par value increases.*

Fixed Charge Coverage

fixed charge coverage
a measure of how well a firm is able to cover its preferred stock dividends.

Fixed charge coverage is a measure of how well a firm is able to cover its preferred dividends; attention centers on the firm's ability to service the dividends on its preferred stock and live up to the preferred's preferential *claim on income*. Therefore, fixed charge coverage is an important ingredient in determining the quality of a preferred issue. Fixed charge coverage is computed as follows:

Equation 10.4

$$\text{Fixed charge coverage} = \frac{\text{earnings before interest and taxes (EBIT)}}{\text{interest expense} + \dfrac{\text{preferred dividends}}{.66}}$$

Note in this equation that preferred dividends are adjusted by a factor of .66 (equivalent to multiplying dividends by 1.5) to take into account the maximum corporate tax rate (of 34 percent), all of which is necessary to place preferred dividends on the same basis as interest paid on bonds. (Recall that bond interest is tax deductible, whereas preferred dividends are not.) *Normally, the higher the fixed charge coverage, the greater the margin of safety*. A ratio of 1.0 means the company is generating just enough earnings to meet its preferred dividend payments—not a very healthy situation. A coverage ratio of 0.7 would suggest the potential for some real problems, whereas a coverage of, say, 7.0 would indicate that the preferred dividends are fairly secure.

Agency Ratings

Standard & Poor's has long rated the investment quality of preferred stocks and, since 1973, so has Moody's. S&P uses basically the same rating system as it does for bonds; Moody's uses a slightly different system. Figure 10.3 shows Moody's system and indicates why the various ratings are assigned. These two agencies assign ratings largely on the basis of their judgment regarding the relative safety of dividends. The greater the likelihood that the issuer will be able to service the preferred in a prompt and timely fashion, the higher the rating. Much like bonds, the top four ratings designate *investment-grade* (high-quality) preferreds. Although preferreds come in a full range of agency ratings, most tend to fall in the medium-grade categories (a and baa) or lower. Generally speaking, higher agency ratings reduce the market yield of

Figure 10.3 Moody's Preferred Stock Ratings These agency ratings indicate the quality of the issue and are based largely on an assessment of the firm's ability to pay preferred dividends in a prompt and timely fashion. (*Source:* Moody's Investors Service, Inc.)

Rating Symbol	Definition
aaa	Indicates a "top quality" issue which provides good asset protection and the least risk of dividend impairment.
aa	A "high grade" issue with reasonable assurance that earnings will be relatively well-protected in the near future.
a	"Upper medium grade." Somewhat greater risk than *aa* and *aaa*, but dividends are still considered adequately protected.
baa	"Lower medium grade." Earnings protection adequate at present, but may be questionable in the future.
ba	A "speculative" type issue, its future earnings may be moderate and not well safeguarded. Uncertainty of position is common for this class.
b	Generally lacking in desirable investment quality, this class may have little assurance of future dividends.
caa–c	Likely to already be in arrears on dividend payments. These categories are reserved for securities that offer little or no likelihood of eventual payment.

Note: Preferred stock ratings should not be compared with bond ratings as they are not equivalent; preferreds occupy a position junior to the bonds.

an issue and increase its interest sensitivity. Agency ratings are important to serious, long-term investors as well as to those who use preferreds for short-term trading. Not only do they eliminate much of the need for fundamental analysis, but they also help investors get a handle on the yield and potential price behavior of an issue.

INVESTMENT STRATEGIES

There are several investment strategies that can be followed by preferred stockholders. Each is useful in meeting a different investment objective, and each offers a different level of return and exposure to risk.

Using Preferreds to Obtain Attractive Yields

This strategy represents perhaps the most popular use of preferred stocks and is ideally suited for serious long-term investors. High current income is the objective, and the procedure basically involves seeking out those preferreds with the most attractive yields. Of course, consideration must also be given to such features as the quality of the issue, whether or not the dividends are cumulative, and the existence of any call or sinking fund provisions.

Certainty of income and safety are important in this strategy, since yields are attractive only as long as dividends are paid. Some investors may never buy anything but the highest-quality preferreds. Others may sacrifice quality in return for higher yields when the economy is strong, and use higher-quality issues only during periods of economic distress. Whenever you leave one of the top four agency ratings, you should recognize the speculative position you are assuming and the implications it holds for your investment portfolio. This is especially so with preferreds, since their dividends lack legal enforcement. Individual investors should also keep in mind that this investment strategy will likely involve a yield give-up relative to what could be obtained from comparably rated corporate bonds: As we saw in Figure 10.1, preferreds usually generate somewhat lower yields than bonds, even though they are less secure and may be subject to a bit more risk.

Trading on Interest Rate Swings

Rather than assuming a "safe" buy-and-hold position, the investor who trades on movements in interest rates adopts an aggressive short-term trading posture. This is done for one major reason: *capital gains*. Of course, although a high level of return may be possible with this approach, it is not without the burden of higher risk exposure. Because preferreds are fixed-income securities, the market behavior of *investment-grade issues* is closely linked to the movements in interest rates. If market interest rates are expected to decline substantially, attractive capital gains opportunities may be realized from preferred stocks. Indeed, this is precisely what happened in the mid-1980s, and again in the early 90s, when market interest rates dropped sharply. During this period, it was not uncommon to find preferreds generating *annual* returns of 20 to 30 percent, or more.

As is probably clear by now, this strategy is identical to that used by bond investors. In fact, many of the same principles used with bonds apply equally well to preferred stocks. For example, it is important to select high-grade preferred stocks, since interest sensitivity is an essential ingredient of this investment strategy. Moreover, margin trading is often used as a way to magnify short-term holding period returns. A basic difference is that the very high leverage rates of bonds are not available with preferreds, because they fall under the same, less generous margin requirements as common stocks. The investment selection process is simplified somewhat as well, because neither maturity nor the size of the annual preferred dividend (which is equivalent to a bond's coupon) has an effect on the *rate of price volatility*. That is, a $2 preferred will appreciate just as much (in percentage terms) as an $8 preferred for a given change in market yields.

Speculating on Turnarounds

This speculative investment strategy can prove profitable if you're nimble enough to catch a trading opportunity before everyone else does. The idea is to find preferred stocks whose dividends have gone into arrears and whose rating has tumbled to one of the speculative categories. The price of the issue, of course, would be depressed to reflect the corporate problems of the issuer. There is more to this strategy, however, than simply finding a speculative-grade preferred stock. The difficult part is to uncover a speculative issue whose fortunes, for one reason or another, *are about to undergo a substantial turnaround*. This strategy requires a good deal of fundamental analysis and is, in many respects, akin to investing in speculative common stock.

In essence, the investor is betting that the firm will undergo a turnaround and will once again be able to service its preferred dividend obligations easily—a set of conditions that obviously involves a fair amount of risk. Unfortunately, although the rewards from this kind of high-risk investing can be substantial, they are somewhat limited. For example, if the turnaround candidate is expected to recover to a single-a rating, we would expect its capital gains potential to be limited by the price level of other a-rated preferreds. This condition is depicted in Figure 10.4. As can be seen, although price per-

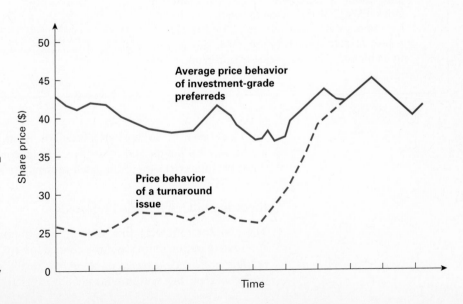

Figure 10.4 Price Pattern of a Hypothetical Preferred Turnaround Candidate
Although a turnaround issue will seek the price level of other preferreds of comparable quality and dividend payout, this level also acts as a type of price cap and clearly limits capital appreciation.

INVESTOR INSIGHTS: *Investing in Action*

Here's a Preferred That Might PERC Up Returns

Because it's difficult to predict how interest rates will move, income investors would be wise to have two types of securities in their portfolios: those that gain value during periods of stable or falling interest rates—for instance, bonds and utility stocks—and, for balance, some that aren't as vulnerable when rates rise, like *preferred equity redemption cumulative stock (PERCs)*. Pioneered in 1988 by Morgan Stanley & Co., PERCs convert to shares of common stock *at a specified conversion price on the maturity date*. Although their dividend rate is considerably above that paid on the common stock of the issuing company, *the potential for capital gains is limited to the conversion price set on the PERCs.*

Suppose you bought Sears PERCs that have an annual dividend of $3.75 (paid quarterly) and a $59 conversion price. At maturity, if Sears common stock is trading at $59 or more, for each of your PERCs shares you'll get $59 worth of common stock. If you bought the PERCs at $52 a year before they matured, your total one-year return from capital appreciation and dividends would be about 14 percent.

Although this return is indeed attractive, investors need to weigh the advantages and disadvantages of PERCs before investing. One obvious benefit is the higher dividends. For example, Sears PERCs pay $3.75 in dividends and yield about 7 percent, compared to $1.60 and about 3.3 percent for Sears common stock. PERCS also provide protection in declining interest rate environments. Preferred stock is less volatile than common stock, due in part to its higher dividend. It doesn't drop as fast or

as far in a bear market; of course, it also doesn't rise as much as in a bull market. Finally, the conversion feature allows investors to share in the company's upside potential.

On the downside, however, an investor may lose principal if the actual stock price is below the conversion price at maturity. If Sears common stock sold for $45 at the maturity date of the PERCs, each PERCs share would convert into a share of stock worth only $45, for a $7 per share *loss* on the $52 PERC purchase price. And any future price appreciation is capped at the stated conversion price. If Sears traded at $65 on the maturity date, you would get only $59 worth of stock for each share, since that's the stated conversion price on the PERCs. The tradeoff is a limit on your upside in exchange for the higher dividend.

Investors considering PERCs should ask themselves several questions before buying: First, what is the outlook for the company's common stock? The PERCs investor takes most of the same risks as the common shareholder. You should carefully evaluate the risk of principal loss at the time of conversion. Also, does the higher dividend adequately compensate you for the risk of putting a limit on your potential gain? For growth investors looking for high rates of capital appreciation, the answer may be no. Other investors may find PERCs to their liking.

Sources: Randall Smith, "Preferreds: Perennial Wallflower Blooms for Investors," *Wall Street Journal*, December 6, 1991, p. C1; and William Stern, "Another Option," *Forbes*, July 19, 1993.

---

formance may be somewhat limited, it is still substantial and can readily amount to holding period returns of 50 percent or more. However, in view of the substantial risks involved, such returns are certainly not out of line.

Investing in Convertible Preferreds

The investor following this strategy uses the conversion feature to go after speculative opportunities and the chance for attractive returns. The use of *convertible preferreds* is based on their link to the company's common stock and the belief that they will provide generous price appreciation. Convertibles will be reviewed in detail below; at this point, suffice it to say that as the price of the underlying common stock appreciates in value, so will the market price of a convertible preferred. This strategy can offer handsome returns, but remember that investors who employ it are actually speculating on the common stock dimension of the security. There is a type of preferred, however, that does allow investors to "bet" on the future price performance of the company's common stock without giving up much, if anything, in dividend yield. Known as **PERCs**, these securities not only carry conversion privileges but also offer attractive dividend returns as well. However, there's a catch: As explained in the *Investor Insights* box on page 418, there is a cap on the capital appreciation potential of these securities.

PERCs
preferred equity redemption cumulative stock; preferred securities that carry conversion privileges and offer attractive dividend returns.

CONCEPTS *in Review*

10.5 Describe how high-grade preferred stocks are priced in the market. What roles does dividend yield play in the valuation of preferred stocks? Could you use the zero-growth dividend valuation model to value a preferred stock? Explain.

10.6 Discuss why dividend yield is critical in evaluating the investment merits of high-grade preferred stocks during periods when market yields are expected to decline.

10.7 Identify several investment uses of preferred stocks. Would preferreds be suitable for both conservative and aggressive investors? Explain. ▬▬

CONVERTIBLE SECURITIES

convertible securities
fixed-income obligations that have a feature permitting the holder to convert the security into a specified number of shares of the issuing company's common stock.

Convertible securities, more popularly known simply as "convertibles," represent still another type of fixed-income security. Usually issued as debenture bonds, these securities are subsequently convertible into shares of the issuing firm's common stock. Although it possesses the features and performance characteristics of both a fixed-income security and equity, a convertible should be viewed primarily *as a form of equity*. That's because most investors commit their capital to such obligations not for the attractive yields they provide but, rather, for the potential price performance the stock side of the issue offers. In fact, it is always a good idea *to determine whether a corporation has convertible issues outstanding whenever you are considering a common stock investment*, for in some circumstances, the convertible may be a better investment than the firm's common stock.

CONVERTIBLES AS INVESTMENT OUTLETS

equity kicker
another name for the conversion feature, giving the holder of a convertible security a deferred claim on the issuer's common stock.

Convertible securities are popular with investors because of their **equity kicker**—that is, the tendency for the market price of the convertible to behave much like the price of the firm's common stock. They are used by all types of corporations and are issued either as convertible *bonds* (by far, the most common type of convertible) or as convertible *preferreds*. Companies like to issue convertibles principally because *they enable firms to raise equity capital at fairly attractive prices*. That is, when a company issues stock the normal way (by simply selling more shares in the company), it does so by setting a price on the stock that's *below* prevailing market prices. For example, it might be able to get $25 for a stock that's currently priced in the market at, say, $30 a share. In contrast, when it issues the stock indirectly through a convertible issue, a firm can set a price that's *above* the prevailing market—that is, it might be able to get $35 for the same stock. As a result, the company can raise the *same amount of money* by issuing a lot less stock through a convertible than by selling it directly in the market. Thus, companies issue convertibles *not* as a way of raising debt capital but, rather, as a way of raising equity. Because they are supposed to eventually be converted into shares of the issuing company's common stock, convertible securities are usually viewed as a form of **deferred equity**.

deferred equity
securities issued in one form and later redeemed or converted into shares of common stock.

Not surprisingly, whenever the stock market is strong, convertibles tend to be strong; when the market softens, so does interest in convertibles. Convertible bonds and convertible preferreds are both linked to the equity position of the firm, and therefore they are usually considered interchangeable for investment purposes. Except for a few peculiarities (e.g., the fact that preferreds pay *dividends* rather than interest, and do so on a quarterly basis rather than semiannually), convertible bonds and convertible preferreds are evaluated in much the same way. Our discussion therefore will be mostly in terms of bonds, but the information and implications apply equally well to convertible preferreds.

Convertible Bonds

Convertible bonds are usually issued as debentures (long-term, unsecured corporate debt), but carry the provision that within a stipulated time period, *the bond may be converted into a certain number of shares of the issuing company's common stock*. Generally, there is little or no cash involved at the time of conversion; the investor merely trades in the convertible bond for a stipulated number of shares of common stock. Figure 10.5 provides some specifics about a convertible bond recently issued by Argosy Gaming Co. Note that this obligation originally was issued as a 12 percent subordinated note, but in time each $1,000 bond can be converted into Argosy stock at $17.70 a share. Thus, *regardless of what happens to the market price of the stock*, the convertible investor can redeem each bond for 56.5 shares of the company's stock (i.e., $1,000 ÷ $17.70 = 56.5 shares). If at the time of conversion, Argosy stock is trading in the market at, say, $35 a share, then the investor would have just converted a $1,000 bond into $1,977.50 worth of stock (i.e., 56.5 × $35 = $1,977.50).

forced conversion
the calling in of convertible bonds by the issuing firm.

The *bondholder* has the right to convert the bond at any time, but more commonly, the issuing firm will initiate conversion by calling the bonds—a practice known as **forced conversion**. To provide the corporation with the flexibility to retire the debt and force conversion, most convertibles come out as freely callable issues, or they carry *very short* call deferment periods. To force conversion, the corporation would call for the retirement of the bond and give the bondholder one of two options: to convert the bond into common stock or to redeem the bond for cash at the stipulated call price (which, in the case of convertibles, contains very little call premium). So long as the convertible is called when the market value of the stock exceeds the call price of the

Figure 10.5 A New Convertible Bond Issue
Holders of this Argosy bond can convert it into the company's common stock at the stated price of $17.70 per share. As a result, they would receive 56.5 shares of stock for each $1,000 convertible bond owned. Prior to conversion, the bondholder will receive annual interest income of $120 for each bond—which, in the context of 1994 market interest rates, clearly makes it a high-yield bond. (Source: *Wall Street Journal*, June 9, 1994.)

This announcement is neither an offer to sell, nor a solicitation of an offer to buy, any of these securities. The offer is made only by the Prospectus. Neither the Illinois Gaming Board nor any other State regulatory body has passed upon the adequacy or accuracy of the Prospectus.

New Issue   June 9, 1994

$115,000,000

12% Convertible Subordinated Notes Due 2001

The Notes are convertible into Common Stock of the Company at any time at or prior to maturity at a conversion price of $17.70 per share (equivalent to a conversion rate of 56.50 shares per $1,000 principal amount of Notes), subject to adjustment under certain circumstances.

Price 100%

Copies of the Prospectus may be obtained in any State from such of the undersigned as may legally offer these securities in compliance with the securities laws of such State.

Donaldson, Lufkin & Jenrette
Securities Corporation

C.J. Lawrence/Deutsche Bank
Securities Corporation

Montgomery Securities

issue (which is almost always the case), seasoned investors would never choose the second option. Instead, they would opt to convert the bond, as the firm wants them to. After the conversion is complete, the bonds no longer exist; instead, there is additional common stock in their place.

Conversion Privilege

conversion privilege
the conditions and specific nature of the conversion feature of convertible securities.

conversion period
the time period during which a convertible issue can be converted.

The key element of any convertible is its **conversion privilege**, which stipulates the conditions and specific nature of the conversion feature. To begin with, it states exactly when the debenture can be converted. With some issues, there may be an initial waiting period of six months to perhaps two years after the date of issue, during which time the security cannot be converted. The **conversion period** then begins, after which the issue can be converted at any time. Although the conversion period typically extends for the remaining life of the debenture, it may exist for only a certain number of years. This is done to provide the issuing firm with more control over its capital structure. If the issue has not been converted by the end of its conversion period, it then reverts to a straight debt issue with *no* conversion privileges.

conversion ratio
the number of shares of common stock into which a convertible issue can be converted.

conversion price
the stated price per share at which common stock will be delivered to the investor in exchange for a convertible issue.

From the investor's point of view, the most important piece of information is the *conversion price* or the *conversion ratio*. These terms are used interchangeably and specify the number of shares into which the bond can be converted. **Conversion ratio** denotes the number of common shares into which the bond can be converted; **conversion price** indicates the stated value per share at which the common stock will be delivered to the investor in exchange for the bond. When you stop to think about these two measures, it becomes clear that a given conversion ratio implies a certain conversion price, and vice versa. For example, a $1,000 convertible bond might stipulate a conversion ratio of 20, meaning that the bond can be converted into 20 shares of common stock. This same privilege could also be stated in terms of a conversion price—that the $1,000 bond may be used to acquire stock in the corporation at a "price" of $50 per share (here, the conversion ratio of 20 signifies a conversion price of $50). Note that the Argosy convertible depicted in Figure 10.5 uses both conversion price ($17.70 per share) and conversion ratio (of 56.5 shares) to describe its conversion feature. (One basic difference between a convertible debenture and a convertible preferred is that whereas the conversion ratio of a debenture generally deals with large multiples of common stock, such as 15, 20, or 30 shares, the conversion ratio of a preferred is generally very small, often less than 1 share of common and seldom more than 2 or 3 shares.)

The conversion ratio is generally fixed over the conversion period, although some convertibles are issued with variable ratios/prices. In such cases, the conversion ratio decreases (while the conversion price increases) over the life of the conversion period, to reflect the supposedly higher value of the equity. The conversion ratio is also normally adjusted for stock splits and significant stock dividends, to maintain the conversion rights of the investor. As a result, if a firm declares, say, a 2-for-1 stock split, the conversion ratio of any of its outstanding convertible issues would also double. And when the ratio includes a fraction, such as 33⅓ shares of common, the conversion privilege will specify how any fractional shares are to be handled. Usually, the investor can either put up the additional funds necessary to purchase another full share of stock at the conversion price or receive the cash equivalent of the fractional share (at the conversion price). Table 10.2 lists some basic features for a number of actively traded convertible bonds and preferreds, and reveals a variety of conversion privileges.

SOURCES OF VALUE

Because convertibles are fixed-income securities linked to the equity position of the firm, they are normally valued in terms of *both the stock and the bond dimensions* of the issue. In fact, it is ultimately the stock and the bond dimensions of the convertible that give the security its value. This, of course, explains why it is so important to analyze the underlying common stock *and* to formulate interest rate expectations when considering convertibles as an investment outlet. Let's look first at the stock dimension.

Convertible securities will trade much like common stock—in effect, they will deliver their values from the common stock—whenever the market price of the stock is equal to or greater than the stated conversion price. This means that whenever a convertible trades near its par value ($1,000) or above, it will exhibit price behavior that closely matches that of the underlying common

Table 10.2   Features of Some Actively Traded Convertible Securities

Convertible Bonds	S&P Rating	Conversion Ratio	Market Price of Convertible	Yield*	Conversion Premium
Avnet 6.0 2012	A−	23.26	$1,010.00	5.94%	18.2%
Champion Int'l 6.5 2011	BBB−	28.78	$1,060.00	5.39%	6.0%
Chock Full O' Nuts 7.0 2012	B−	118.01	$ 860.00	9.07%	16.6%
Chubb 6.0 1998	AA	11.63	$1,015.00	5.91%	13.2%
Hasbro 6.0 1998	A−	34.09	$1,050.00	5.71%	7.1%
Home Depot 4.5 1997	A−	25.81	$1,200.00	3.75%	1.4%
Interface Inc. 8.0 2013	B+	59.13	$ 890.00	8.94%	36.8%
Mediq Inc 7.25 2006	CCC+	94.79	$ 640.00	12.78%	28.0%
Price Co. 5.5 2012	BBB	42.07	$ 805.00	7.01%	28.6%
Potomac Electric 7.0 2018	A	37.04	$ 900.00	7.65%	28.7%
Waban Inc. 6.5 2002	BB−	40.40	$ 920.00	8.00%	34.9%
Wendy's Int'l 7.0 2006	BBB	81.30	$1,290.00	4.03%	7.6%
Convertible Preferreds					
Amax Gold Inc. $3.75 pfd	BB	6.06	$53.00	7.1%	29.6%
Bethlehem Steel $2.50 pfd	B−	0.84	$27.38	9.1%	70.4%
Cooper Industries $1.60 pfd	BBB+	0.55	$31.63	7.0%	53.9%
Ford Motor Co. $4.20 pfd	A−	3.27	$96.75	4.3%	0.3%
GATX $3.87 pfd	BBB−	1.15	$52.88	7.3%	9.1%
B.F. Goodrich $3.50 pfd	BBB−	0.91	$50.13	7.0%	22.7%
James River $3.38 pfd	BB+	1.23	$39.75	8.5%	41.3%
Magma Copper $2.81 pfd	BB+	3.45	$66.50	4.2%	7.8%
Norwest Corp. $3.50 pfd	A	2.74	$66.75	5.1%	−0.6%
Republic New York $3.38 pfd	A+	1.04	$53.25	6.3%	11.9%
Stone Container Co. $1.75 pfd	C	0.72	$18.38	—	52.4%
USF & G $5.00 pfd	BB−	4.16	$57.50	8.7%	1.4%

*Yield-to-maturity for convertible bonds; current yield for convertible preferreds; all prices and yields as of December 1994.

stock: If the stock goes up in price, so will the convertible, and vice versa. In fact, the price change of the convertible will exceed that of the common, since the conversion ratio will define the convertible's rate of price change. For example, if a convertible carries a conversion ratio of, say, 20, then for every point the common stock goes up (or down) in price, the price of the convertible will move *in the same direction* by roughly that same multiple (in this instance, 20). In essence, whenever a convertible trades as a stock, its market price will approximate a multiple of the share price of the common, with the size of the multiple being defined by the conversion ratio.

When the price of the common is depressed, so that its trading price is well below the conversion price, the convertible will lose its tie to the underlying common stock and will begin to trade as a bond. The issue should then trade according to prevailing bond yields. At that point, an investor should focus attention on *market rates of interest*. However, because of the equity kicker and their relatively low agency ratings, *convertibles generally do not possess high interest rate sensitivity*. Gaining more than a rough idea of what the prevailing yield of the convertible obligation ought to be is often difficult. For example, if the issue is rated Baa and if the market rate for this quality range is 9 percent, the convertible should be priced to yield *something around* 9 percent, plus or minus perhaps as much as half a percentage point or so.

conversion premium
the amount by which the market price of a convertible exceeds its conversion value.

The bond feature will also establish a *price floor* for the convertible, which tends to parallel interest rates and is independent of the behavior of common share prices.

ADVANTAGES AND DISADVANTAGES OF INVESTING IN CONVERTIBLES

The major advantage of a convertible issue is that it reduces downside risk (via the issue's bond value or price floor) and at the same time provides an upward price potential comparable to that of the firm's common stock. This two-sided feature is critical with convertibles and is impossible to match with straight common stock or straight debt. Another benefit is that the current income from bond interest normally exceeds the income from dividends that would be paid with a *comparable investment* in the underlying common stock. For example, let's say you had the choice of investing $1,000 in a new 8 percent convertible or investing the same amount in the company's common stock, presently trading at $42.50 a share. (As is customary with new convertibles, the stock price is a bit *below* the bond's conversion price—of $50 a share.) Under these circumstances, the investor could buy *one* convertible or 23½ *shares* of common stock (i.e., $1,000/$42.50 = 23.5). If the stock paid $2 a share in annual dividends, a $1,000 investment in the stocks would yield $47 a year in dividends. In contrast, the investor could collect substantially more by putting the same amount into the company's convertible bond, where he or she would receive $80 a year in interest income. Thus, it is possible with convertibles to reap the advantages of common stock (in the form of potential upward price appreciation) and yet generate improved current income.

On the negative side, buying the convertible instead of directly owning the underlying common stock means the investor has to give up some potential profits. Consider the example in the preceding paragraph: Put $1,000 directly into the common stock and you can buy 23½ shares; put the same $1,000 into the company's convertible bond and you end up with a claim on only 20 shares of stock. Thus, the convertible bond investor is left with a *shortfall* of 3½ shares of stock—which in turn represent potential price appreciation the convertible investor will never enjoy. In effect, it's a *give-up* that the investor has to take in exchange for the convertible's higher current income and safety. Looked at from another angle, this is basically what **conversion premium** is all about. That is, unless the market price of the stock is very high and exceeds the conversion price by a wide margin, a convertible will almost always trade at a price that is above its true value. The amount of this excess price is conversion premium, and it has the unfortunate side effect of diluting the price appreciation potential of a convertible. What's more, an investor who truly wants to hold bonds can almost certainly find better current and promised yields from straight debt obligations.

So if improved returns are normally available from the direct investment in either straight debt and/or straight equity, why buy a convertible? The answer is simple: Convertibles provide a great way to achieve attractive risk-return tradeoffs. In particular, by combining the characteristics of both stocks and bonds into one security, convertibles offer some risk protection and at the same time considerable—although perhaps not maximum—upward price potential. Thus, although the return may not be the most in absolute terms, neither is the risk.

Figure 10.6 Listed Quotes for Convertible Bonds
Convertible bonds (of which there are six in this figure) are listed right along with other corporate issues and are identified by the letters *cv* in the "Cur Yld" column. Except for this distinguishing feature, they are quoted like any other corporate bond. (Source: *Wall Street Journal*, November 9, 1994.)

Bonds	Cur Yld	Vol	Close	Net Chg.
GnDyn 9.95s18	9.2	29	108	+2⅞
GEICap 7⅞06	8.1	10	97⅜	+ ⅜
GHost 11½02	13.2	48	87¼	− ⅛
GHost 8s02	cv	85	73½	+1¼
GnSgnl 5¾02	cv	10	104	−1
Gene 10⅜03	13.8	40	75	− ⅞
GaPw 6⅛99	6.6	5	92⅛	...
Hallwd 7s00	11.3	97	62⅛	+1⅝
HlthsoR 5s01	cv	25	109¼	−4½
HlthsoR 9½01	9.9	41	96¼	− ¼
Hlttrst 10¾02	9.9	20	108¼	...
Hlttrst 8¾05	9.1	136	96	+ ⅜
HomeDp 4½97	cv	80	122	+ ⅛
HorMan 6½99	cv	80	93¼	− ½
HospFrn 4½99	cv	1	96⅝	− ⅞
HostM 10⅝00	10.5	45	101	+ ⅛
HostM 9⅛00	9.3	35	98	+ ⅜
HostM 9⅞01	10.0	50	98⅝	− ⅜

Home Depot convertible bond

EXECUTING TRADES

Convertible bonds are subject to the same brokerage fees and transfer taxes as straight corporate debt, and convertible preferreds trade at the same costs as straight preferreds and common stock. Any market or limit order that can be used with bonds or stocks can also be used with convertibles.

Convertible debentures are listed along with corporate bonds; they are distinguished from straight debt issues by the letters *cv* in the "Cur Yld" column of the bond quotes, as illustrated in Figure 10.6. Note that it's not unusual for some convertibles (e.g., the Home Depot 4½ percent issue of 1997) to trade at fairly high prices. These situations are justified by the correspondingly high values attained by the underlying common stock. Convertible preferreds, in contrast, normally are not isolated from other preferreds. They are listed with a *pf* annotation, but they carry no other distinguishing symbols. As a result, the investor must turn to some other source to find out whether a preferred is convertible. One national business newspaper that *does* identify convertible preferreds is *Investor's Business Daily;* it provides a separate list of preferred stocks traded on the NYSE and AMEX and uses boldface type to highlight the convertible issues.

CONCEPTS *in Review*

10.8 What is a *convertible debenture*? How does a *convertible bond* differ from a *convertible preferred*?

10.9 Identify the *equity kicker* of a convertible security and explain how it affects the value and price behavior of convertibles.

10.10 Explain why it is necessary to examine both the bond and the stock properties of a convertible debenture when determining its investment appeal.

10.11 What are the investment attributes of convertible debentures? What are the disadvantages of such vehicles?

VALUING AND INVESTING IN CONVERTIBLES

Basically, investing in convertibles can take two different forms: Either the investor uses convertibles as a type of deferred equity investment, in which case he or she is looking at the stock value of the security, or the investor uses convertibles as a high-yield, fixed-income investment, where it's the bond value that's important. Regardless of which approach you follow, to get the most from your investment program, you need a good understanding of the normal price and investment behavior of convertible securities. Of course, you also have to know how to value a convertible. So let's take a look now at the valuation concepts used with convertible bonds and then at a couple of convertible bond investment strategies.

 ### MEASURING THE VALUE OF A CONVERTIBLE

In order to evaluate the investment merits of convertible securities, you must consider both the bond and stock dimensions of the issue. Fundamental security analysis of the equity position is, of course, especially important in light of the key role the equity kicker plays in defining the price behavior of a convertible. Agency ratings are helpful and are widely used in evaluating the bond side of the issue. And, just like other types of bonds, yield-to-maturity and current yield are important measures of return. But there's more: For in addition to analyzing the bond and stock dimensions of the issue, it is essential to evaluate the conversion feature itself. The two critical areas in this regard are conversion value and investment value. These measures have a vital bearing on a convertible's price behavior and therefore can have a dramatic effect on an issue's holding period return.

Conversion Value

conversion value
an indication of what a convertible issue should trade for if it were priced to sell on the basis of its stock value.

Equation 10.5

In essence, **conversion value** indicates what a convertible issue should trade for if it were priced to sell on the basis of its stock value. Conversion value is easy to find:

$$\text{Conversion value} = \text{conversion ratio} \times \text{current market price of the stock}$$

conversion equivalent (conversion parity)
the price at which the common stock would have to sell in order to make the convertible security worth its present market price.

Equation 10.6

For example, a convertible that carries a conversion ratio of 20 would have a conversion value of $1,200 if the firm's stock traded at a current market price of $60 per share (20 × $60 = $1,200). Sometimes an alternative measure is used, and the **conversion equivalent**, or what is also known as **conversion parity**, may be computed. The conversion equivalent indicates the price at which the common stock would have to sell in order to make the convertible security worth its present market price. Conversion equivalent is calculated as follows:

$$\text{Conversion equivalent} = \frac{\text{current market price of the convertible bond}}{\text{conversion ratio}}$$

Thus, if a convertible is trading at $1,400 and has a conversion ratio of 20, the conversion equivalent of the common stock would be $70 per share ($1,400 ÷ 20 = $70). In effect, we would expect the current market price of the common stock in this example to be at or near $70 per share in order to support a convertible trading at $1,400.

Unfortunately, convertible issues *seldom* trade precisely at their conversion values. Rather, as noted earlier, they trade at a conversion premium. The absolute size of an issue's conversion premium is determined by taking the difference between the convertible's market price and its conversion value (per Equation 10.5). To place the premium on a relative basis, simply divide the dollar amount of the conversion premium by the issue's conversion value. That is:

Equation 10.7

$$\text{Conversion premium (in \$)} = \frac{\text{current market price}}{\text{of the convertible bond}} - \frac{\text{conversion}}{\text{value}}$$

where conversion value is found according to Equation 10.5. Then:

Equation 10.8

$$\text{Conversion premium (in \%)} = \frac{\text{conversion premium (in \$)}}{\text{conversion value}}$$

To illustrate, if a convertible trades at $1,400 and its conversion value equals $1,200, it would have a conversion premium of $200 ($1,400 − $1,200 = $200). In relation to what the convertible should be trading at, this $200 differential would amount to a conversion premium of 16.7 percent ($200/$1,200 = .167). Conversion premiums are common in the market (refer back to Table 10.2) and can often amount to as much as 25 to 30 percent (or more) of an issue's true conversion value.

Investors are willing to pay a premium primarily because of the added current income a convertible provides relative to the underlying common stock. An investor has two ways of recovering this premium: either through the added income the convertible provides or by subsequently selling the issue at a premium equal to or greater than that which existed at the time of purchase. Unfortunately, the latter source of recovery is tough to come by, since conversion premiums tend to fade away as the price of the convertible goes up. Thus, if a convertible is bought for its potential price appreciation (which many are), all or a major portion of this price premium will probably disappear as the convertible appreciates and moves closer to its true conversion value.

The size of the conversion premium can obviously have a big impact on investor return, so when picking convertibles, one of the major questions you should ask is whether the premium is justified. One way to assess conversion premium is to compute the issue's payback period. Basically, the **payback period** is a measure of the length of time it takes for the buyer to recover the conversion premium from the *extra* interest income earned on the convertible. Since this added income is a principal reason for the conversion premium, it makes sense to use it to assess the premium. The payback period can be found as follows:

payback period
the length of time it takes for the buyer of a convertible to recover the conversion premium from the extra current income earned on the convertible.

Equation 10.9

$$\text{Payback period} = \frac{\text{conversion premium (in \$)}}{\begin{array}{c}\text{annual interest} \\ \text{income from convertible} \\ \text{bond}\end{array} - \begin{array}{c}\text{annual dividend} \\ \text{income from underlying} \\ \text{common stocks}\end{array}}$$

where *annual dividends are found by multiplying the stock's latest annual dividends per share by the bond's conversion ratio.*

For example, in the illustration above, the bond had a conversion premium of $200. Now let's say this bond (which carries a conversion ratio of 20) has an 8 percent coupon and the underlying stock paid dividends this past year of 50 cents a share. Given this information, we can use Equation 10.9 to find the payback period:

$$\text{Payback period} = \frac{\$200}{\$85 - (20 \times \$0.50)}$$

$$= \frac{\$200}{\$85 - (\$10.00)} = \underline{\underline{2.7 \text{ years}}}$$

In essence, the investor in this case will recover the premium in 2.7 years (a fairly decent payback period). As a rule, everything else being equal, *the shorter the payback period, the better*. Also, watch out for excessively high premiums (of 50 percent or more), as you may have real difficulty ever recovering such astronomical premiums. Indeed, to avoid such premiums, most experts recommend that you stick to convertibles that have payback periods of 4 years or less. The bottom line is, in order to get the most from these investments, take the time to fully evaluate a bond's conversion premium before investing.

Investment Value

investment value
the price at which a convertible would trade if it were nonconvertible and priced at or near the prevailing market yields of comparable nonconvertible issues.

The price floor of a convertible is defined by its bond properties and is the object of the investment value measure. It's the point within the valuation process where attention is centered on current and expected market interest rates. **Investment value** is the price at which the bond would trade if it were nonconvertible and if it were priced at or near the prevailing market yields of comparable nonconvertible bonds. The same bond price formula given in Chapter 9 is used to compute investment value—see Equation 9.2. Since the coupon and maturity are known, the only additional piece of information needed is the market yield-to-maturity of comparably rated issues. For example, if comparable nonconvertible bonds are trading at 9 percent yields and if a particular 20-year convertible carries a 6 percent coupon, its investment value would be roughly $725. (*Note:* This value was calculated using techniques discussed in Chapter 9.) This figure indicates how far the convertible will have to fall before it hits its price floor and begins trading as a straight debt instrument. Other things being equal, the greater the distance between the current market price of a convertible and its investment value, the farther the issue can fall in price before it hits its bond floor, and as a result, the greater the downside risk exposure.

INVESTMENT STRATEGIES

Convertible securities offer some rewarding investment opportunities, as they can be used to meet several different investor objectives: Some investors buy them because of the underlying stock; others, because of the attractive yields they offer as fixed-income securities. For the more savvy and adventuresome investors, there are even *zero-coupon convertibles*. These securities, with their deep discounted prices, not only carry conversion features but many of them also give holders the right to periodically cash in their bonds. As more fully discussed in the *Investor Insights* box on page 429, these securities combine

INVESTOR INSIGHTS: *Market Innovations*

Are LYONs All They're Cracked Up to Be?

Take a zero-coupon bond, add a conversion feature, throw in a put option, and what do you have? Why, a LYON, of course! Also known as "zero-coupon accreters," these bonds are convertible, at a *fixed* conversion ratio, for the life of the issue. They can also be "put" back to the issuer, usually every three or five years, at specified values reflecting the accretion of the implied interest return. These put features reduce downside risk because they give bondholders the right (or option) to redeem their bonds at prespecified prices. Thus, investors know they can get out of these securities, at set prices, if things move against them. There are two types of put options: so-called "hard" puts, which are payable only in cash, and "soft" puts, which are the most common and may be paid in cash, common stock, notes, or some combination thereof. Merrill Lynch created these zero-coupon convertibles six years ago and called them LYONs—liquid yield option notes. Now, most zero-coupon convertibles come out with the features of a LYON, though they may be called something else.

What's their attraction? The conversion factor lets you participate in stock market gains while keeping a solid hedge against loss of principal through the put option. Issuers like

them because they enhance cash flow: The implied interest is deducted from taxable income, but no cash is actually paid out. Of course, for the investor, the implied interest reflected in annual price accretion is subject to taxes, so these convertibles should be used only for tax-deferred accounts. Otherwise, the investor will be paying out cash in taxes without getting any cash return. Remember too that convertibles can be as volatile as the common stock itself, so investors shouldn't take the plunge unless they plan to hold for a long time. They must also watch those conversion and put terms, which vary widely, to know what the issuer can use to pay off the put. The payoff may be in cash, but sometimes it can be stock or a new bond—not always what you might want. One other thing: Because the conversion ratio is fixed while the underlying accreted value of the bond keeps increasing, the net effect is that the conversion price on the stock will keep getting higher over time. Thus, the market price of the stock had better go up by more than the rate of appreciation of the bond or you'll never be able to convert your LYON into a roaring success.

Source: Adapted from Ben Weberman, "Double-Edge Play in the Convert Market," *Forbes*, April 29, 1991, p. 343.

the steady appreciation of zero-coupon bonds with the capital gains potential of common stocks. However, they also have some serious drawbacks and therefore may not be suitable for all investors.

An Overview of Price and Investment Behavior

The price behavior of a convertible security is influenced by both the equity and the fixed-income elements of the obligation. The variables that play key roles in defining the market value of a typical convertible therefore include: (1) the potential price behavior of the underlying common stock and (2) expectations regarding the pattern of future market yields and interest rates.

The typical price behavior of a convertible issue is depicted in Figure 10.7. In the top panel are the three market elements of a convertible bond: the bond value, or price floor; the stock (conversion) value of the issue; and the actual market price of the convertible. The figure reveals the customary relationship among these three important elements and shows that conversion premium is a common occurrence with these securities. Note especially that the conversion premium tends to diminish as the price of the stock increases. The top panel of Figure 10.7 is somewhat simplified, however, because of the steady price floor (which unrealistically assumes no variation in market interest rates) and the steady upswing in the stock's value. The lower panel of the figure relaxes these conditions, although for simplicity, we ignore conversion premium. The figure illustrates how the market value of a convertible will approximate the price behavior of the underlying stock *so long as stock value is greater than bond value*. When the stock value drops below the bond value floor, as it does in the shaded areas of the illustration, the market value of the convertible becomes linked to the bond portion of the obligation, and it continues to move as a debt security until the price of the underlying stock picks up again and approaches or equals this price floor.

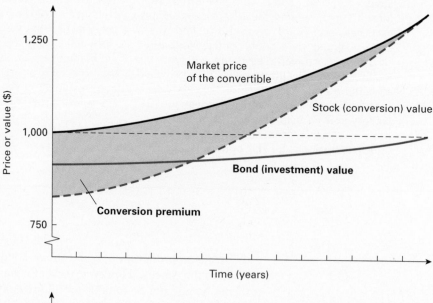

Figure 10.7 Typical Price Behavior of a Convertible Bond
The price behavior of a convertible security is tied to the stock or the bond dimension of the issue: When the price of the underlying stock is up, the convertible will trade much like the stock; when the price of the stock falls, the bond value will act as a price floor for the convertible.

Convertibles as Deferred Equity Investments

Convertible securities—even zero-coupon convertibles—are purchased most often because of the *equity attributes* they offer to investors. Using convertibles as an alternative to a company's common stock, investors may be able to match (or possibly even exceed) the return from the common, but with less exposure to risk. Also, compared to stocks, convertibles generally offer improved current income. Convertibles can be profitably used as alternative equity investments whenever one feels that the underlying stock offers desired capital gains opportunities. In order to achieve maximum price appreciation under such circumstances, the investor would want assurance that the convertible is trading in concert with its stock value and that it does not have an inordinate amount of conversion premium. If these necessary conditions do in fact exist, investor attention should logically center on the potential market behavior of the underlying stock. To assess such behavior, it is necessary to evaluate both current and expected conversion value.

For example, assume a 7 percent convertible bond carries a conversion ratio of 25 and is presently trading in the market at $900. In addition, assume the stock (which pays no dividends) is currently trading at $32 and the convertible is trading at a conversion premium of $100, or 12.5 percent. The formulation of future interest rates also comes into play with this trading strategy, as the investor will want to assess the bond price floor and the extent of downward risk exposure: Using the same approach as discussed in Chapter 9, he or she would forecast future interest rates, which would then be used to determine the possible bond price behavior of the issue. Generally speaking, a drop in interest rates would be viewed positively by convertible bond investors, as such behavior would signal a rise in the price floor of the convertible issue and therefore a reduction in downside risk exposure. That is, should the common stock not perform as expected, the price of the convertible could still go up as the (bond) price floor rises—or at the least, it would reduce any drop in the price of the convertible issue.

But most of the attention is centered not on the bond price floor but on the anticipated behavior of the common stock and the conversion premium. To continue our example, assume the investor expects the price of the stock to rise to $60 per share within the next two years. A conversion ratio of 25 would then yield a future conversion value of $1,500. If an expected conversion premium of 6 to 7 percent (or about $100) is added on, it means the market price of the convertible should rise to about $1,600 by the end of the two-year investment horizon. This expected future price of the convertible, along with its annual coupon payment and current market price, would then be used to determine the issue's expected return. That is:

$$\text{Expected return} = \frac{\$70 + \dfrac{\$1,600 - \$900}{2}}{\dfrac{\$1,600 + \$900}{2}} = \frac{\$70 + \$350}{\$1,250} = \underline{\underline{33.6\%}}$$

The expected return equation above is identical to the one used with straight bonds and preferred stocks. It is really nothing more than the approximate yield formula first introduced in Chapter 4 (Equation 4.10).

Although this 33.6 percent rate of return may indeed appear attractive, the investor should be sure of several points before committing capital to this security, in particular, that this approach is in fact superior to a direct investment in the issuer's common stock (at least from a risk-return point of view) and that there is no better rate of return (with commensurate risk exposure) available from some other investment vehicle. To the extent that these conditions are met, investing in a convertible may be a suitable course of action, especially if (1) the price of the underlying common stock is under strong upward pressure, (2) bond interest rates are falling off sharply, and (3) there is little or no conversion premium in the price of the convertible. The first attribute means conversion value should move up, leading to appreciation in the price of the convertible. The second means that the bond value (price floor) should also move up, thereby reducing exposure to risk. And the third feature means the investor should be able to capture all or most of the price appreciation of the underlying common stock rather than lose a chunk of it to the inevitable drop in conversion premium. Although it would be nice if all three of these attributes were available with a single security, the fact is rarely is that the case. So investors normally have to settle for only one or two of these features and then assess the costs that the missing one(s) has on potential returns. Hopefully, the bottom line is the convertible will still be an attractive investment vehicle.

Convertibles as High-Yield Fixed-Income Investments

Another common use of convertibles is to buy them for the attractive fixed-income returns they offer. The key element in this strategy is the issue's bond dimension. Many convertible securities provide current yields and yields-to-maturity that are safe and highly competitive with straight debt obligations. Investors should make certain, however, that the high yields are not a function of low (speculative) ratings. Normally, such investors would seek discount issues, particularly those that are trading close to their bond price floor. Otherwise, the issue would be trading at a premium price, which would certainly involve a yield give-up, and perhaps a substantial one. Most investors who use this strategy view convertibles as ideal for locking in high rates of return. They are not widely used for speculating on interest rates, however, because even investment-grade convertibles often lack the needed interest sensitivity (due to the equity kicker of the issue). Yet for those who use convertibles to seek high, safe yields, the equity kicker can provide an added source of return if the underlying stock does indeed take off. The investor then has a bond that offers a handsome rate of return, plus an equity kicker to boot.

CONCEPTS *in Review*

10.12 What is the difference between *conversion parity* and *conversion value*? How would you describe the *payback period* on a convertible? What is the bond *investment value* of a convertible, and what does it reveal?

10.13 What is a LYON? Describe the key features of a LYON; note the similarities and differences between a LYON and a regular convertible debenture.

10.14 Discuss the various investment uses of convertible debentures. What are the three major attributes investors should look for when using convertibles as deferred equity investments?

On Track with STOCK-TRAK®

"Trading" Preferred Stock and Convertible Bonds Through STOCK-TRAK®

As of the writing of this textbook, STOCK-TRAK® does not include preferred stock as an investment option. Nor are any convertible securities found among the eligible bonds listed in the registration materials. Trading of preferred stock and convertible bonds will probably be added to STOCK-TRAK®'s opportunity set over time.

One way for STOCK-TRAK® investors to simulate the purchase of preferred stock or convertible bonds is to purchase mutual funds that invest primarily in preferred stock or convertible bonds. Several funds offer investors the security of the "guaranteed" current income that convertibles offer with the added potential of benefiting from an increase in common stock prices. STOCK-TRAK® does not limit selection of mutual funds, and so investors should be able to find some that offer the investment advantages of preferred stock or convertible bonds.

SUMMARY

LG 1 Describe the basic features of preferred stock, including sources of value and exposure to risk. Preferred stocks are hybrid securities—combining features of both debt and equity—that offer investors potentially rewarding investment opportunities. Although a form of equity, preferred stocks are considered senior to common stocks because they have a higher claim on the income and assets of the issuing company; among other things, that means that preferred dividends have to be paid before the company can pay dividends to its common stockholders. As investment vehicles, preferreds provide attractive dividend yields and, when interest rates decline, will produce capital gains as well.

LG 2 Discuss the rights and claims of preferred stockholders and note some of the popular issue characteristics that are often found with these securities. Preferreds are considered less risky than common stock because their shareholders enjoy a senior position with regard to dividend payments and asset claims. From a practical perspective, the most important feature of a preferred stock is its preferential claim on dividends. In addition, investors should be aware of several preferred stock provisions—the obligations of the issuer in case any dividends are missed (i.e., whether the stock is issued with cumulative or noncumulative provisions), whether the stock is callable, and whether it carries sinking fund provisions.

LG 3 Develop an understanding of the various measures of investment worth and identify several investment strategies that can be used with preferred stocks. Except for convertible preferreds, the value of a preferred stock is generally linked to the dividend yield it provides to investors. Indeed, the price behavior of a preferred stock is inversely related to market interest rates. The principal purpose for holding preferreds is their yield. In addition, preferreds can be held for capital gains purposes by investors willing to trade on interest rate behavior or on turnaround situations.

LG 4 Identify the fundamental characteristics of convertible securities and explain the nature of the underlying conversion privilege. Convertible securities are initially issued as bonds (or preferreds), but they can subsequently be converted into shares of common stock. These securities are highly attractive because they offer investors a generous stream of fixed income (in the form of annual coupon payments), plus an equity kicker.

LG 5 Describe the advantages and disadvantages of investing in convertible securities, including the risk and return attributes of these investment vehicles. From an investment perspective, convertibles provide a combination of both good upside potential (from the equity feature of the issue) and good downside protection (through the fixed-income characteristics of the issue). This risk-return tradeoff, combined with the relatively high current income of convertibles, is unmatched by any other type of security.

LG 6 Measure the value of a convertible security and explain how these securities can be used to meet different investment objectives. Because convertible securities can be converted into common stock, the value of a convertible depends largely on the price behavior of the underlying common. This is captured in the security's conversion value, which represents the worth of a convertible if it were converted into common stock. Investors use convertible securities primarily as a form of deferred equity, where the investment is made as a way to capture the capital gains potential of the underlying common stock. In addition, convertibles are sometimes used as high-yielding fixed-income securities, when the investor principally goes after the higher current income of the bond (and the equity kicker is viewed as little more than a pleasant by-product).

DISCUSSION QUESTIONS

1. Briefly describe each of the following, and note how each differs from a "regular" preferred stock:
   a. Convertible preferreds
   b. Floating rate preferreds
   c. Prior preferred stocks
   d. PERCs

As an investor, why would you choose a *convertible preferred* over a regular preferred? Why would you choose a *floating rate preferred* over a regular preferred? Finally, instead of investing in a regular preferred, why not just invest in a common stock?

2. Is it possible for a firm to pass (miss) dividends on preferred stocks, even if it earns enough to pay them? Explain. What usually happens when a company passes (misses) a dividend on a cumulative preferred stock? Are common stock dividends affected in any way?

3. Why do companies like to issue convertible securities—i.e., what's in it for them? What about preferred stocks—why do companies like to issue them?

4. Using the resources available at your campus or public library, find the information requested below. (*Note*: You might want to use the IMD disk to perform the calculations.)
   a. Select any two *convertible debentures* and determine the conversion ratio, conversion parity, conversion value, conversion premium, and payback period for each.
   b. Select any two *convertible preferreds* and determine the conversion ratio, conversion parity, conversion value, conversion premium, and payback period for each.
   c. Comparing the two convertible bonds you selected (above) with the two convertible preferreds, in what way(s) are these two securities similar to one another? Are there any differences? Explain.

PROBLEMS **LG 3**

1. An adjustable rate preferred is currently selling at a dividend yield of 9 percent; assume the dividend rate on the stock is adjusted once a year, and it's presently paying an annual dividend of $5.40 a share. Because of major changes that have occurred in the market, it's anticipated that annual dividends will drop to $4.50 a share on the next

dividend adjustment date, which is just around the corner. What would the new dividend yield on this issue be if its market price does not change? What would the new market price on the issue be if the stock's dividend yield holds at 9 percent? What would it be if the yield drops to 7 percent?

LG 3   2.   The Danzer Company has 500,000 shares of $2 preferred stock outstanding; it generates an EBIT of $40 million and has annual interest payments of $2 million. Given the above information, determine the fixed charge coverage of the preferred stock.

LG 3   3.   Select one of the preferred stocks listed in Table 10.1. Using the resources available at your campus or public library, determine the following:
   a.   Latest market price
   b.   Dividend yield
   c.   Fixed charge coverage
   d.   Book value per share
   e.   The preferred's stated par value
Now, briefly comment on the issue's yield and the quality of its claim on income and assets.

LG 1   4.   DuPont has a preferred stock outstanding that pays annual dividends of $3.50 a share. At what price would this stock be trading if market yields were 7½ percent? Now, use one of the dividend valuation models (from Chapter 7) to price this stock, assuming you have a 7½ percent required rate of return. Are there any similarities between the two prices? Explain.

LG 3   5.   Charlene Weaver likes to speculate with preferred stock by trading on movements in market interest rates. Right now, she thinks the market is poised for a big drop in rates. Accordingly, she is thinking seriously about investing in a certain preferred stock that pays $7 in annual dividends and is currently trading at $75 per share. What rate of return would she realize on this investment if the market yield on the preferred drops to 6½ percent within 2 years? What if the drop in rates takes place in *1 year*?

LG 6   6.   A certain 6 percent convertible bond (maturing in 20 years) is convertible at the holder's option into 20 shares of common stock. The bond is currently trading at $800, and the stock (which pays 75¢ a share in annual dividends) is currently priced in the market at $35 a share.
   a.   What is the current yield of the convertible bond?
   b.   What is the conversion price?
   c.   What is the conversion ratio?
   d.   What is the conversion value of this issue? What is its conversion parity?
   e.   What is the conversion premium, in dollars and as a percentage?
   f.   What is the bond's payback period?
   g.   What is the approximate yield-to-maturity of the convertible bond?
   h.   If comparably rated nonconvertible bonds sell to yield 8 percent, what is the investment value of the convertible?

LG 6   7.   An 8 percent convertible bond carries a par value of $1,000 and a conversion ratio of 20. Assume that an investor has $5,000 to invest and that the convertible sells at a price of $1,000 (which includes a 25 percent conversion premium). How much total income (coupon plus capital gains) would this investment offer if, over the course of the next 12 months, the price of the stock moves to $75 per share and the convertible trades at a price that includes a conversion premium of 10 percent? What is the holding period return on this investment? Finally, given the information in the problem, what is the underlying common stock currently selling for?

8. Assume you just paid $1,200 for a convertible bond that carries a 7½ percent coupon and has 15 years to maturity. The bond can be converted into 24 shares of stock, which are now trading at $50 a share. Find the bond investment value of this issue, given that comparable nonconvertible bonds are presently selling to yield 9 percent.

 9. Find the conversion value of a *convertible preferred stock* that carries a conversion ratio of 1.8, given that the market price of the underlying common stock is $40 a share. Would there be any conversion premium if the convertible preferred were selling at $90 a share? If so, how much (in dollar and in percentage terms)? Also, explain the concept of conversion parity, and then find the conversion parity of this issue, given that the preferred trades at $90 per share.

CASE PROBLEMS   **10.1   PENNI SHOWS A PREFERENCE FOR PREFERREDS**

Kathleen "Penni" Jock is a young career woman who has built up a substantial investment portfolio. Most of her holdings are preferred stocks—a situation she does not want to change. Penni is now considering the purchase of $4,800 worth of LaRamie Mine's $5 preferred, which is currently trading at $48 per share. Penni's stockbroker has told her that he feels the market yield on preferreds like LaRamie should drop to 8 percent within the next 2 years and that these preferreds would make a sound investment. Instead of buying the LaRamie preferred, Penni has an alternative investment (with comparable risk exposure) that she is confident can produce earnings of about 10 percent over each of the next 2 years.

Questions

 1. If preferred yields behave as Penni's stockbroker thinks they will, what will be the price of the LaRamie $5 preferred in 2 years?

 2. What return would this investment offer over the 2-year holding period if all the expectations about it come true (particularly with regard to the price it is supposed to reach)? How much profit (in dollars) will Penni make from her investment?

3. Would you recommend that she buy the LaRamie preferred? Why?

4. What are the investment merits of this transaction? What are its risks?

10.2   DAVE AND MARLENE CONSIDER CONVERTIBLES

Dave and Marlene Jenkins live in Irvine, California, where she manages a bridal shop and he runs an industrial supply firm. Their annual income is usually in the middle to upper nineties; they have no children and maintain a "comfortable" lifestyle. Recently, they came into some money and are eager to invest it in some high-yielding fixed-income security. Although not aggressive investors, they like to maximize the return on every investment dollar they have. For this reason, they like the high yields and added equity kicker of convertible bonds, and are now looking at such an issue as a way to invest their recent windfall. In particular, Dave and Marlene have their eyes on the convertible debentures of Maria Pottery, Inc. They have heard that the price of the stock is on the way up, and after some in-depth analysis of their own, they feel the company's prospects are indeed bright. They've also looked at market interest rates, and based on economic reports obtained from their broker, they expect interest rates to decline sharply.

The details on the convertible they're looking at are as follows: It's a 20-year, $1,000 par value issue that carries a 7½ percent coupon and is at present trading at $800. The issue is convertible into 15 shares of stock, and the stock, which pays no dividends, was recently quoted at $49.50 per share.

Questions

1. Ignoring conversion premium, find the price of the convertible if the stock goes up to $66.67 per share. What if it goes up to $75 per share? To $100 per share? Repeat the computations, assuming the convertible will trade at a 5 percent conversion premium.

2. Find the approximate promised yield of the convertible. (*Hint*: Use the same approach as we did with straight bonds in Chapter 9.)
   a. Now find the bond value of the convertible if, within 2 years, interest rates drop to 8 percent. (Remember: In 2 years, the security will have only 18 years remaining to maturity.) What if they drop to 6 percent?
   b. What implication does the drop in interest rates hold as far as the investment appeal of the convertible is concerned?

3. Given expected future stock prices and interest rate levels (as stated above), find the minimum and maximum expected yield this investment offers over the 2-year holding period.
   a. What is the worst return Dave and Marlene can expect over their 2-year holding period if the price of the stock drops to $40 per share and interest rates drop to 9 percent? What if the price of the stock drops to $40 and interest rates rise to 11 percent? (Assume a zero conversion premium in both cases.)

4. Should Dave and Marlene invest in the Maria convertibles? Discuss the pros and cons of the investment.

PART FOUR

OTHER POPULAR INVESTMENT VEHICLES

CHAPTER 11
MUTUAL FUNDS: AN INDIRECT ROUTE TO THE MARKET

CHAPTER 12
REAL ESTATE AND OTHER TANGIBLE INVESTMENTS

CHAPTER 13
TAX-ADVANTAGED INVESTMENTS

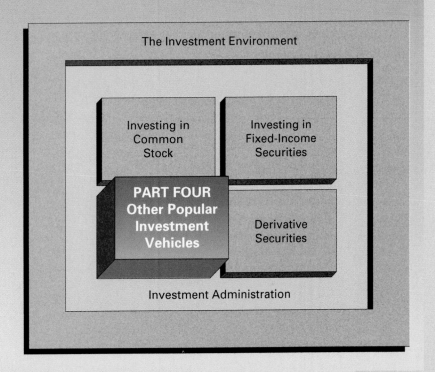

CHAPTER 11

MUTUAL FUNDS: AN INDIRECT ROUTE TO THE MARKET

LEARNING GOALS

After studying this chapter, you should be able to:

LG 1 Describe the basic features of a mutual fund, and explain how diversification and professional management are the cornerstones of the industry.

LG 2 Describe essential fund characteristics, including the difference between open- and closed-end mutual funds, and discuss the various types of fund loads, fees, and charges.

LG 3 Discuss the types of funds available and the variety of investment objectives these funds seek to fulfill.

LG 4 Identify and discuss the different kinds of investor services offered by mutual funds and how these services can fit into an investment program.

LG 5 Gain an appreciation of the investor uses of mutual funds, along with the variables that should be considered when assessing and selecting funds for investment purposes.

LG 6 Identify the sources of return and compute the rate of return earned on an investment in a mutual fund.

INVESTOR INTERVIEW

Noted investment adviser Louis Rukeyser describes Elizabeth Bramwell, with her 25 years' experience in securities analysis and portfolio management, as "the most experienced rookie in the mutual fund business." Before forming Bramwell Capital Management, Inc. in early 1994 and launching Bramwell Growth Fund in August 1994, Bramwell managed Gabelli Growth Fund from its inception in 1987. Under her expert guidance, the fund earned an impressive average annual return of 16.6 percent.

With no sales charges and low investment requirements (minimum initial investment of $1,000 and incremental investments of $100), Bramwell Growth Fund was designed to appeal to a wide range of investors. The fund began with 30 to 50 stocks and is expected to grow to no more than 100. Its initial focus was companies with $1 to $5 billion capitalization. The fund invests up to 25 percent in foreign securities, including closed-end country funds, which Bramwell considers an efficient way for a small fund to get international exposure. She also uses U.S. firms with large overseas operations, such as Coca-Cola, Gillette, and Dow Chemical, to achieve international diversification.

Bramwell's investment strategy is to build a diversified fund (no more than 25 percent in one industry) of both large- and small-cap stocks. Fundamental research and primary research—going directly to company management—are the basis of her stock selection. She looks for large-cap stocks with growth of around 10 to 11 percent, at least a 3 percent dividend yield, and a relatively low price/earnings multiple—about 11 to 12, based on next year's earnings. She also likes companies whose price/earnings multiples are less than 80 percent of their long-term growth rates. Industry sectors she finds attractive include manufacturing (worldwide), consumer products, and productivity-enhancing companies. "We look for companies that, over the long term, will benefit from research and development, capital spending, and market expansion," Bramwell explains. "Generally, we will look at companies from the bottom up and make forecasts of their earnings. Then macroeconomic factors—projections or expectations on interest rates, inflation, currency rates, and political conditions—provide a framework to evaluate individual stocks in terms of economic and political world events."

Bramwell's new fund takes a long-term approach. "It's not really geared toward big 'pops' in the next quarter, but rather toward companies that are really going to move in the next 12 months or so. Historically, I've tried to take a lower-risk profile: This means companies with growth rates in the 10 to 20 percent, rather than the 20 to 50 percent, range." The fund sells stocks when their price/earnings ratios rise above their growth rates as fundamentals deteriorate.

> **DIVERSIFICATION IS IMPORTANT. INVESTORS COULD EASILY HOLD FIVE DIFFERENT FUNDS, INCLUDING MORE THAN ONE GROWTH FUND. STAY ON TOP OF THEM, AND KEEP AN EYE ON THE ONE-, THREE-, AND FIVE-YEAR PERFORMANCE RECORDS.**

For example, Bramwell looks carefully at a stock with a long-term growth rates of 12 percent that's selling at over 20 times earnings.

Bramwell offers the following advice to individual investors: "Diversification is important. Investors could easily hold five different funds, including more than one growth fund. Stay on top of them, and keep an eye on the one-, three-, and five-year performance records. And be sure you know who's running the funds and what stocks they own."

Sources: Adapted from "Aiming for Another Bull's-Eye," Louis Rukeyser's Mutual Funds, October 1994, pp. 4–5; "Booming Economy Predicted for 1995," Pensions & Investments, December 26, 1994, pp. 3, 13–21; and "Interview with Elizabeth Bramwell," Value Line Mutual Fund Advisor, August 23, 1994, pp. 4–6.

Questions of which stock or bond to select, when to buy, and when to sell have plagued investors for as long as there have been organized capital markets. Such concerns lie at the very heart of the mutual fund concept, and explain, in large part, the growth mutual funds have experienced. Many investors lack the time, know-how, or commitment to manage their own portfolios and, as a result, they turn to others. That's why increasing numbers of investors are letting professional investment managers like Elizabeth Bramwell decide which stocks to buy and when to sell.

THE MUTUAL FUND PHENOMENON

mutual fund
an investment company that invests its shareholders' money in a diversified portfolio of securities.

Basically, a **mutual fund** is a type of financial service organization that receives money from its shareholders and then invests those funds on their behalf in a diversified portfolio of securities. Mutual funds have been a part of our investment landscape for more than 70 years. The first one was started in Boston in 1924—and it's still in business today. By 1940, the number of mutual funds had grown to 68, and by 1980, to 564 funds. But that was only the beginning: The next dozen or so years saw unprecedented growth in the mutual fund industry, as assets under management grew from less than $100 billion in 1980 to *over $2 trillion* in 1994. Indeed, by 1994 *there were more than 6,000 publicly traded mutual funds in existence*. The fund industry has grown so much, in fact, that it is now the second largest financial intermediary, behind only commercial banks—but not by much. Finally, although we tend to think of mutual funds as an American phenomenon, the fact is that mutual funds, in one form or another, are found in all the major markets of the world. In 1994, there was $2 trillion in assets under management in foreign funds, an amount nearly equivalent to the assets in U.S. funds.

What caused the extraordinary growth of mutual funds? Basically, three things: First, money market mutual funds experienced explosive growth. Second, the introduction of self-directed individual retirement accounts (IRAs) created a strong demand for mutual fund products. Third, the stock and bond markets experienced record-breaking performances (resulting from a number of factors, including sharply reduced inflation). Investors in unprecedented numbers flocked to those markets, and the mutual fund industry responded by developing new products and new funds. So many new products were created, in fact, that there are now more mutual funds in existence than there are stocks on the *New York and American stock exchanges combined!*

AN OVERVIEW OF MUTUAL FUNDS

Mutual fund investors come from all walks of life and all income levels. They range from highly inexperienced to highly experienced investors who all share a common view: Each has decided, for one reason or another, to turn over at least a part of his or her investment management activities to professionals. Mutual funds are popular because they offer not only a variety of interesting investment opportunities but also a wide array of services that many investors find appealing. Indeed, there are mutual funds available today to meet just about any investor need. Individuals who invest in mutual funds are considered shareholders of the fund. In the final analysis, however, an investment in a mutual fund really represents *an ownership position in a professionally managed portfolio of securities*. When you buy shares in a mutual fund, you become a part owner of a portfolio of securities.

Pooled Diversification

The mutual fund concept is based on the simple idea of turning the problems of security selection and portfolio management over to professional money managers. In essence, a mutual fund combines the investment capital of many people who have similar investment goals, and it invests the funds for those individuals in a wide variety of securities. (In an abstract sense, you can think of a mutual fund as the *financial product* that's sold to the public by an investment company. That is, the investment company builds and manages a portfolio of securities and then sells ownership interests—shares of stock—in that portfolio through a vehicle known as a mutual fund.)

Investors in mutual funds are able to enjoy much wider investment diversification than they could otherwise achieve. To appreciate the extent of such diversification, take a look at Figure 11.1. It provides a partial list of the securities held in the portfolio of a major mutual fund (actually, just one page of a

Figure 11.1 A Partial List of Portfolio Holdings
The list of holdings in this one fund alone goes on for another 15 pages and includes stocks in hundreds of different companies. Certainly, this is far more diversification than most individual investors could ever hope to achieve. (Source: Fidelity Growth Company.)

Common Stocks – continued	Shares	Value (000s)
HOLDING COMPANIES – 0.4%		
Granite Industries BHD (a)	790,000	$ 1,855
Grupo Carso SA de CV Class A-1 (a)	893,800	10,052
Grupo Sidek SA de CV Class B Ord. (a)	155,500	664
		12,571
INDUSTRIAL MACHINERY & EQUIPMENT – 3.6%		
Electrical Equipment – 2.3%		
American Power Conversion Corp. (a)	105,600	1,703
General Electric Co.	1,268,300	58,342
Ortel Corp. (a)	4,900	127
Scientific-Atlanta, Inc.	223,800	4,420
Sensormatic Electronics Corp.	110,300	3,557
Star Paging International Holdings Ltd. (warrants) (a)	1,356,800	61
		68,210
Industrial Machinery & Equipment – 0.9%		
Case Corp.	200,600	3,937
Caterpillar, Inc.	318,900	17,220
PRI Automation, Inc. (a)	127,700	2,139
Ultratech Stepper, Inc.	94,100	3,670
Veeco Instruments, Inc. (a)	48,800	537
		27,503
Pollution Control – 0.4%		
Browning-Ferris Industries, Inc.	114,400	3,089
WMX Technologies, Inc.	338,200	8,708
		11,797
TOTAL INDUSTRIAL MACHINERY & EQUIPMENT		107,510
MEDIA & LEISURE – 3.0%		
Broadcasting – 1.4%		
Comcast Corp. Class A (Special)	158,200	2,511
Emmis Broadcasting Corp. Class A (a)	21,300	312
Infinity Broadcasting Corp. (a)	114,400	3,432
Tele-Communications, Inc. Class A (a)	417,600	9,866

16-page list of security holdings). Observe that in November 1994, this fund owned anywhere from 4,900 shares of one company (Ortel Corp.) to nearly 1.4 *million* shares of another (GE). Furthermore, note that within each industry segment, the fund diversified its holdings across a number of different stocks. Clearly, this is far more diversification than most investors could ever hope to attain. Yet each investor who owns shares in this fund is, in effect, a part owner of this diversified portfolio of securities.

Of course, not all funds are as big or as diversified as the one depicted in Figure 11.1. But whatever the size of the fund, as the securities held by it move up and down in price, the market value of the mutual fund shares moves accordingly. When dividend and interest payments are received by the fund, they are passed on to the mutual fund shareholders and distributed on the basis of prorated ownership. For example, if you own 1,000 shares of stock in a mutual fund and that represents 10 percent of all shares outstanding, you will receive 10 percent of the dividends paid by the fund. When a security held by the fund is sold for a profit, the capital gain is also passed on to fund shareholders. The whole mutual fund idea, in fact, rests on the concept of **pooled diversification**, which works very much like health insurance, whereby individuals pool their resources for the collective benefit of all the contributors.

pooled diversification
a process whereby investors buy into a diversified portfolio of securities for the collective benefit of the individual investors.

Attractions and Drawbacks of Mutual Fund Ownership

The attractions of mutual fund ownership are numerous. One of the most important is *diversification*; it benefits mutual fund shareholders by spreading out holdings over a wide variety of industries and companies, thus reducing the risk inherent in any one investment. Another appeal of mutual funds is full-time professional management, which removes much of the day-to-day management and record-keeping chores from the shoulders of investors. What's more, the fund may be able to offer better investment talents than individual investors can provide. Still another advantage is that most (but not all) mutual fund investments can be started with a modest capital outlay. Sometimes, there is no minimum investment required at all, and after the initial investment has been made, additional shares can usually be purchased in small amounts. The services mutual funds offer also make them appealing to many investors: These include automatic reinvestment of dividends, withdrawal plans, exchange privileges, and the like. Finally, mutual funds offer convenience. They are relatively easy to acquire; the funds handle the paperwork and record keeping; their prices are widely quoted; and it is possible to deal in fractional shares.

There are, of course, some major drawbacks to mutual fund ownership. One of the biggest disadvantages is that mutual funds in general can be costly and involve substantial transaction costs. Many funds carry sizable commission charges (or what are known as "load charges"). In addition, a **management fee** is levied annually for the professional services provided, and it is deducted right off the top, regardless of whether the fund has had a good or a bad year. Yet, even in spite of all the professional management and advice, it seems that mutual fund performance over the long haul is at best about equal to what you would expect from the market as a whole. There are some notable exceptions, of course, but most funds do little more than just keep up with the market—and in many cases, don't even do that. Take a look at Figure 11.2; it

management fee
a fee levied annually for professional mutual fund services provided; paid regardless of the performance of the portfolio.

Figure 11.2   The Comparative Performance of Mutual Funds Versus the Market
As shown here, even with the services of professional money managers, it's tough to outperform the market. In this case, the average performance of 9 out of the 12 fund categories failed to meet the market's standard of return. (Source: Data developed from *Morningstar's Mutual Fund Performance Report*, December 1994.)

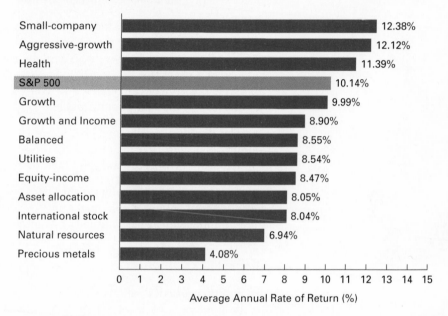

Average Annual Rate of Return (%)

Small-company	12.38%
Aggressive-growth	12.12%
Health	11.39%
S&P 500	10.14%
Growth	9.99%
Growth and Income	8.90%
Balanced	8.55%
Utilities	8.54%
Equity-income	8.47%
Asset allocation	8.05%
International stock	8.04%
Natural resources	6.94%
Precious metals	4.08%

shows the investment performance for 12 different types of equity (or equity-oriented) funds over the five-year period from 1990 to 1994. (*Note:* These 12 categories represent more than 90 percent of assets under management by equity-oriented funds.) The reported returns are average, fully compounded annual rates of return, and they assume that all dividends and capital gains distributions are reinvested into additional shares of stock. Note that when compared to the S&P 500, only *three* fund categories outperformed the market, whereas a number of them fell far short of the mark. The message is clear: *Consistently beating the market is no easy task*—even for professional money managers. Although a handful of funds have given investors above-average and even spectacular rates of return, most mutual funds simply do not meet these levels of performance. This is not to say that the long-term returns from mutual funds are substandard or that they fail to equal what you could achieve by putting your money in, say, a savings account or some similar risk-free investment outlet. Quite the contrary: The long-term returns from mutual funds have been substantial, but most of these returns can be traced to strong market conditions and/or to the reinvestment of dividends and capital gains.

How Mutual Funds Are Organized and Run

Although it's tempting to think of a mutual fund as a single large entity, that view is not really accurate. Various functions—investing, record keeping, safe-keeping, and others—are split among two or more companies. Besides the fund itself, organized as a separate corporation or trust, there are several other main players:

• The *management company* runs the fund's daily operations. Management companies are the firms we know as Fidelity, Kemper, IDS, Dreyfus, Oppenheimer, and so forth; they are the ones that create the funds in the first place. Usually, the management firm also serves as investment adviser.

• The *investment adviser* buys and sells stocks or bonds and otherwise oversees the portfolio. Usually, three parties participate in this phase of the operation: (1) the *money manager*, who actually runs the portfolio and makes the buy and sell decisions; (2) *security analysts*, who analyze securities and look for viable investment candidates; and (3) *traders*, who buy and sell big blocks of securities at the best possible price.

• The *distributor* sells fund shares, either directly to the public or through authorized dealers (like major brokerage houses and commercial banks). When you request a prospectus and sales literature, you deal with the distributor.

• The *custodian* physically safeguards the securities and other assets of the fund, without taking a role in the investment decisions. To discourage foul play, an independent party, usually a bank, serves in this capacity.

• The *transfer agent* keeps track of purchase and redemption requests from shareholders and maintains other shareholder records.

Each of these parties collects a fee for its services. However, actual ownership of the fund rests with its shareholders. Given some of the problems experienced by a number of financial institutions (from banks and S&Ls to life insurance companies) during the 1980s, one might wonder if the same thing could happen to the mutual fund industry as well. Or more to the point, we might ask: Are mutual funds really all that safe? The answer: Yes! For while there are no guarantees that you'll always *make money* on your investments (the value of your mutual fund shares will go up and down with the market), the chance of you ever losing money *from a mutual fund collapse* is, as the accompanying *Investor Insights* box reveals, really quite low—almost non-existent.

Mutual Fund Regulations

Although securities regulations were discussed in Chapter 2, it might be helpful to review briefly some of the major regulatory provisions that apply to mutual funds. To begin with, the *Securities Act of 1933* requires the filing of full information about a mutual fund with the SEC. This act also requires the fund to provide potential investors with a current prospectus, disclosing the fund's management, its investment policies and objectives, and other essential data. In addition, the purchase and sale of mutual fund shares are subject to the antifraud provisions of the *Securities Exchange Act of 1934*, and the *Investment Advisers Act of 1940* regulates the activities of the investment advisers that work for mutual funds. Most importantly, in order to qualify for investment company status, a fund must comply with the provisions of the *Investment Company Act of 1940*. That comprehensive piece of legislation provides the foundation for the regulation of the mutual fund industry and,

INVESTOR INSIGHTS: *Investing in Action*

Could Your Mutual Fund Go Under?

When historians look back at the 1990s, they'll remember it for traumatizing the nation's financial services industry. One domino that didn't fall, however, was the mutual fund sector. The business remains generally healthy and, more to the point, offers a different set of protections for investors. Obviously, you can lose money if your fund's stock or bond holdings decline in price. But there's little chance of loss stemming from fraud, scandal, or bankruptcy involving the management company itself. That's a key distinction: By transferring investment risk to shareholders, mutual fund companies have been able to sidestep many of the problems currently plaguing their financial cousins.

A regular, open-end mutual fund is a separate corporation or trust that's owned by its shareholders, not by the firm that runs it. The only formal link with the management company is through a contract that must be renewed on a regular basis. Consequently, the fund's assets—stocks, bonds, and cash in the portfolio—are not kept in the drawers of the management company. Rather, they're placed in the custody of an independent third party, typically a trust or custodial bank. "We do not have easy access to our shareholders' money," says Charles J. Tennes, a vice-president with the GIT Investment Funds in Arlington, Virginia. "We have authority to buy and sell securities on their behalf, but the assets are held by someone else."

As another safeguard, each fund features a board of directors or trustees who are charged with keeping tabs on the management company and renewing its contract. According to federal regulations, at least 40 percent of a fund's board members must be independent of the management company. The directors are elected by shareholders, are paid with shareholder money, and can be sued for ignoring their fiduciary duties.

As further protection, the management company and other affiliated parties can't engage in certain types of transactions with a fund. For example, the investment adviser can't dump its own stock and bond holdings by selling them to the fund. Nor can an adviser with a brokerage arm charge the fund excessive commissions for conducting trades.

Bob Pozen, general counsel and managing director of Fidelity Investments in Boston, believes more fundamental reasons explain the lack of scandal in the industry. First, he says, funds must stand ready to redeem investor shares upon demand. That forces them to stick with assets for which there's a liquid market. Second, funds must value their holdings every day, a process known as *marking-to-market*. "I feel one of the big problems with insurance companies was that they didn't mark-to-market their assets daily. They were able to go a long time before anybody realized they had a problem," Pozen says.

In over 70 years, there has not been a major crisis or scandal like what has happened in other parts of the financial services industry. Tight regulations and structural firewalls have helped, as has the fact that shareholders bear the investment risks.

Source: Adapted from Russ Wiles, "Checks and Balances: How Funds Are Organized," *Personal Investor*, September 1991, pp. 28–30.

among other things, establishes standards of income distribution, fee structures, and diversification of assets. Finally, from a tax perspective, a mutual fund can be treated as an essentially tax-exempt organization (and thereby avoid the double taxation of dividends and income) so long as it qualifies under *Subchapter M* of the Internal Revenue Code of 1954. Briefly, to operate as a regulated investment company and enjoy the attendant tax benefits, a fund must annually distribute to its shareholders all of its realized capital gains and at least 90 percent of its interest and dividend income. That way, the fund will pay *no* taxes on any of its earnings, whether they're derived from current income or from capital gains.

ESSENTIAL CHARACTERISTICS

Although investing in mutual funds has been made as simple and as painless as possible, investors nevertheless should have a clear understanding of what they're getting into. For not only are there many different types of mutual funds available, there are also some significant differences in organizational structure that you should be aware of—and there's a wide array of fees and charges that you should become familiar with.

Open-End Investment Companies

open-end investment company
a type of investment company in which investors buy shares from and sell them back to the mutual fund itself, with no limit on the number of shares the fund can issue.

The term *mutual fund* is commonly used to describe an open-end investment company. In an **open-end investment company**, investors buy their shares from and sell them back to the mutual fund itself. When an investor buys shares in an open-end fund, the fund issues new shares of stock and fills the purchase order with those new shares. There is no limit, other than investor demand, to the number of shares the fund can issue. (Occasionally, funds will *temporarily* close themselves to new investors—meaning they won't open any new accounts—in an attempt to keep fund growth in check.) All open-end mutual funds stand behind their shares and buy them back when investors decide to sell. Thus, there is never any trading between individuals. Mutual funds are the dominant type of open-end investment company and account for well over 90 percent of the assets under management. Many of these funds are very large and hold hundreds of millions of dollars' worth of securities. Indeed, in 1994, the typical stock or bond fund held an average portfolio of some $400 million, and there were more than 250 billion-dollar funds.

net asset value (NAV)
the underlying value of a share of stock in a particular mutual fund.

Both buy and sell transactions in mutual funds are carried out at prices based on the current market value of all the securities held in the fund's portfolio. (Technically, this would also include the book value of any other assets, such as cash and receivables from securities transactions, that the fund might hold at the time—though, for all practical purposes, these other assets generally account for only a tiny fraction of the fund's total portfolio.) Known as the fund's **net asset value** (**NAV**), this current market value is calculated at least once a day and represents the underlying value of a share of stock in a particular mutual fund. NAV is found by taking the total market value of all securities (and other assets) held by the fund, less any liabilities, and dividing this amount by the number of fund shares outstanding. For example, if the market value of all the securities (and other assets) held by the XYZ mutual fund on a given day equaled $10 million, and if XYZ on that particular day had 500,000 shares outstanding, the fund's net asset value per share would amount to $20 ($10,000,000 ÷ 500,000 = $20). This figure, as we'll see below, is then used to derive the price at which the fund shares are bought and sold.

Closed-End Investment Companies

closed-end investment companies
a type of investment company that operates with a fixed number of shares outstanding.

Whereas the term *mutual fund* is supposed to be used only with open-end funds, it is, as a common practice, regularly used to refer to closed-end investment companies as well. Basically, **closed-end investment companies** operate with a fixed number of shares outstanding and do not regularly issue new shares of stock. In effect, they have a capital structure like that of any other corporation, except that the corporation's business happens to be investing in marketable securities. Shares in closed-end investment companies are actively traded in the secondary market, like those of any other common stock. But unlike open-end funds, *all trading in closed-end funds is done between investors in the open market*. The fund itself plays no role in either buy or sell transactions; once the shares are issued, the fund is out of the picture. By far, most closed-end investment companies are traded on the New York Stock Exchange, a few are on the American Exchange, and occasionally some are traded in the OTC market or on some other exchange. As Figure 11.3 shows, the shares of closed-end companies are listed right along with shares of other common stocks. In this case, Adams Express (one of the larger closed-end investment companies) is quoted on the NYSE.

Many of the investment advisers that run closed-end funds (like Putnam, Dean Witter, Kemper, Nuveen, MFS, Scudder, and Templeton) also manage open-end funds, often with similar investment objectives. Why do they do that? They do it because the funds are two different investment products. For while it may not appear so on first glance, there are some major differences between open- and closed-end funds. To begin with, because closed-end funds have a fixed amount of capital to work with, they don't have to worry about stock redemptions or new money coming into the fund. Therefore, they don't have to be concerned about keeping cash on hand (or readily available) to meet redemptions. Equally important, because there will be no pressure on portfolio managers to cash in these securities at inopportune times, they can be more aggressive in their investment styles by investing in obscure yet attractive securities that may not be actively traded. Also, because they don't have new money flowing in all the time, portfolio managers don't have to worry about finding new investments but can instead concentrate on a set portfolio

Figure 11.3 Stock Quotations for Closed-End Investment Companies
The quotes for closed-end investment companies are listed right along with those of other common stocks. Except for the lack of a P/E ratio, their quotes are pretty much the same. (Source: *Wall Street Journal*, December 12, 1994.)

52 Weeks					Yld		Vol				Net
Hi	Lo	Stock	Sym	Div	%	PE	100s	Hi	Lo	Close	Chg
▼ 27⅜	20⅝	ATT Cap	TCC	.40f	1.9	10	122	20¾	20⅜	20¾	...
57⅛	47¼	AT&T Cp	T	1.32	2.7	16	30920	49¼	48⅝	49⅛	+ ½
33	25⅜	AbbotLab	ABT	.76	2.4	17	9220	31⅝	31	31⅝	+ ⅛
8¼	2⅞	Abex	ABE		...	10	124	7⅛	7	7⅛	– ⅛
15¼	11¼	Abitibi g	ABY		...	...	282	13⅜	13⅛	13¼	...
18	11⅛♣	AcceptIns	AIF		...	10	28	13¾	13½	13½	– ¼
31¼	20¾	ACE Ltd	ACL	.44	2.0	dd	760	22¼	22	22¼	– ⅛
15½	8¾	AcmeCleve	AMT	.44	3.9	12	113	11⅜	11⅜	11⅜	– ⅛
14	6½	AcmeElec	ACE		...	dd	124	12½	12¼	12¼	– ½
30	23 ♣	Acordia	ACO	.60	2.0	15	15	30	29¾	29¾	– ⅛
13¾	5¾	ActavaGp	ACT	.09j	...	dd	168	9	8⅞	8⅞	...
18⅜	11¼	Acuson	ACN		...	25	343	15½	15¼	15½	...
18⅜	15½	AdamsExp	ADX	1.60e	10.3	...	412	15⅝	15½	15½	...
n 19⅛	18⅛	PensnProvdSA ADR	PVD		...	...	366	19⅛	18¾	19⅛	+ ⅝
31¾	16¾	AdvMicro	AMD		...	8	6231	24⅛	23⅛	23¾	+ ¼
64	46½	AdvMicro pf		3.00	5.7	...	8	52½	51½	52½	+ ¾
6⅞	5	Advest	ADV		...	15	106	5¼	5¼	5¼	...
20	15	Advo	AD	.10	.6	15	116	16½	16	16	– ¾

of securities. But that also puts added pressures on the money managers, since their investment styles and fund portfolios are closely monitored and judged by the market. That is, the share prices of closed-end companies are determined not only by their net asset values but also by general supply and demand conditions in the stock market. As a result, depending on the market outlook and investor expectations, closed-end companies generally trade at a discount or premium to NAV. Share price discounts and premiums can at times become quite large. For example, it's not unusual for such spreads to amount to as much as 25 to 30 percent of net asset value—occasionally more—depending on market judgments and expectations. Table 11.1 lists some actively traded closed-end funds, along with prevailing premiums (+) and discounts (−).

Unit Investment Trusts

unit investment trust
a type of investment vehicle whereby the trust sponsors put together a fixed/unmanaged portfolio of securities and then sell ownership units in the portfolio to individual investors.

A **unit investment trust** represents little more than an interest in an unmanaged pool of investments. In essence, a portfolio of securities is simply held in safekeeping for investors under conditions set down in a trust agreement. The portfolios usually consist of corporate, government, or municipal bonds, with tax-free municipal bonds and mortgage-backed securities being the most popular types of investment vehicles. Because there is no trading in the portfolios, the returns, or yields, are fixed and usually predictable—at least for the short term. Unit trusts are like second cousins to mutual funds: Whereas in conventional mutual funds securities are actively traded, in a unit trust, the sponsor simply puts together a portfolio of securities, and that's it. After the securities are deposited with a trustee, no new securities are added and, with rare exceptions, none are sold.

Various sponsoring brokerage houses put together these diversified pools of securities and then sell units of the pool to investors (each unit being like a share in a mutual fund). For example, a brokerage house might put together a diversified pool of corporate bonds that amounts to, say, $100 million. The sponsoring firm would then sell units in this pool to the investing public at a price of $1,000 per unit (a common price for these securities). The sponsoring organization does little more than routine recordkeeping, and it services the investments by collecting coupons and distributing the income (often on a monthly basis) to the holders of the trust units. Trusts appeal primarily to income-oriented investors who are looking for monthly (rather than semiannual) income. These investments do have their dark sides, though. For one thing, they tend to be very costly and involve substantial up-front transaction costs. For another, various strategies may be used to pump up yields artificially and make returns look better than they are. Also, contrary to what many investors believe (or are told), you *can* lose money on these things if premium-priced bonds in the trust are called for prepayment.

Load and No-Load Funds

load fund
a mutual fund that charges a commission when shares are bought; also known as *front-end load fund*.

The question of whether a fund is "load" or "no-load" is a matter of concern only to investors in *open-end* funds. (Recall from our discussion above that closed-end funds trade on listed or OTC markets and thus are subject to the same commission and transactions costs as any other share of common stock.) The load charge on an open-end fund is the commission the investor pays when buying shares in a fund. Generally speaking, the term **load fund** is used

Table 11.1 Some Actively Traded Closed-End Mutual Funds

Fund Name	Stock Exch	NAV	Market Price	Prem /Disc	52-week Market Return
General Equity Funds					
Adams Express	N	17.63	15½	−12.1	− 5.7
Alliance All-Mkt	N	18.46	16⅝	− 9.9	N/A
Baker Fentress	N	16.83	13⅞	−17.6	− 6.4
Bergstrom Cap	A	92.74	83⅛	−10.4	− 5.0
Blue Chip Value	N	7.36	6½	−11.7	−16.4
Central Secs	A	16.25	15⅞	− 2.3	10.1
Charles Allmon	N	10.39	9⅜	− 9.8	− 6.2
Engex	A	N/A	6½	N/A	−41.6
Equus II -a	A	19.69	13½	−31.4	1.3
Gabelli Equity -a	N	9.17	9⅝	+ 5.0	− 1.5
General American	N	21.48	19⅛	−11.0	− 7.1
Inefficient Mkt	A	11.33	9⅛	−19.5	−11.0
Jundt Growth	N	13.86	13	− 6.2	0.7
Liberty All-Star	N	8.99	8¼	− 8.2	−14.8
Morgan FunShares -c	O	7.16	7	− 2.3	N/A
Morgan Gr Sm Cap	N	10.75	9⅜	−12.8	− 9.6
NAIC Growth -c	C	11.10	9½	−14.4	1.0
Royce Value	N	12.91	11⅞	− 8.0	− 6.2
Salomon SBF	N	12.60	10⅞	−13.7	− 1.8
Source Capital	N	37.25	37½	+ 0.7	− 7.6
Spectra	O	17.34	14½	−16.4	4.3
Tri-Continental	N	23.22	20¼	−12.8	− 3.9
Z-Seven	O	16.40	16	− 2.4	− 1.8
Zweig	N	10.23	10½	+ 2.6	−14.6
Specialized Equity Funds					
Alliance Gl Env	N	10.84	8¾	−19.3	−11.4
C&S Realty	A	8.01	8	− 0.1	− 8.6
C&S Total Rtn -a	N	11.96	12	+ 0.3	− 9.5
Centrl Fd Canada -c	A	4.60	4¾	+ 3.3	− 7.1
Counsellors Tand	N	14.06	12⅝	−10.2	− 9.0
Delaware Gr Div	N	12.53	11½	− 8.2	−10.6
Delaware Grp Gl	N	12.95	11¾	− 9.3	N/A
Dover Reg Fincl	O	6.73	N/A	N/A	N/A
Duff&Ph Util Inc	N	7.34	8	+ 9.0	−13.3
Emer Mkts Infra	N	13.90	11⅛	−20.0	N/A
Emer Mkts Tel	N	21.71	19½	−10.2	−13.7
First Financial	N	13.61	12⅛	−10.9	5.9
Gabelli Gl Media	N	7.49	7⅛	− 4.9	N/A
Global Health	N	11.84	9⅜	−20.8	−13.0
Global Privat	N	14.09	11¾	−16.6	N/A
H&Q Health Inv	N	15.39	13	−15.5	−22.5
H&Q Life Sci Inv	N	10.16	8⅛	−20.0	−29.6
J Hancock Bank	N	18.64	16⅛	−13.5	N/A

Source: Wall Street Journal, December 12, 1994.

no-load fund
a mutual fund that does not charge a commission when shares are bought.

to describe a mutual fund that charges a commission when shares are bought (such charges are also known as *front-end loads*). A **no-load fund**, in contrast, means that no sales charges are levied. Load charges can be fairly substantial and can amount to as much as 7¼ percent of the *purchase price* of the shares. Although there may be little or no difference in the performance of load and no-load funds, *the cost savings with no-load funds tend to give investors a head start in achieving superior rates of return.* Unfortunately, the true no-load fund is becoming harder to find, as more and more no-loads are becoming *12(b)-1 funds.* Although such funds do not directly charge commissions at the time of purchase, they assess what are known as 12(b)-1 charges *annually* to make up for any lost commissions (these charges are more fully described below). Overall, less than 30 percent of the funds sold today are pure no-loads; the rest charge some type of load or fee.

Fortunately, the quotation system used with mutual funds distinguishes the no-load from the load funds. That is, all open-end mutual funds are priced according to their net asset values, which—as you can see in the first column in Figure 11.4—are part of the standard mutual fund quotations. The "NAV" (net asset value) column is the price the mutual fund will pay to buy back the fund shares (or, from the investor's point of view, the price at which the shares can be sold); it's also the price you pay when you buy *no-load* funds. Unfortunately, the price you have to pay to buy *load* funds is not included in the *Wall Street Journal* quotes. It's not even in the quotes for Monday through Thursday, since all they consist of are NAV, net change, and year-to-date return. To find the so-called *offer price* of a fund—the price you pay to *buy shares*—you'd have to either call the fund itself to get a quote or estimate it using the NAV price (you may also be able to get it directly from your local paper, as some big city newspapers include offer prices in their fund quotes).

To estimate the offer price from the NAV, simply factor in the initial load charge (which is listed in the next-to-last column in Figure 11.4—see the column headed "Maximum Initial Charge"). That is, if you take the quoted NAV and multiply it by *one plus the initial load charge,* you'll end up with a fairly close approximation of the load fund's offer price (it's an approximation because the load charge is stated relative to the fund's offer price, not the lower net asset value). Thus, for the FPA Paramount Fund, which has a quoted NAV in Figure 11.4 of $15.05 and an initial load charge of 6.5 percent, you'd have an approximate offer price of: $15.05 \times 1.065 = 16.03 (the actual offer price was $16.09). The difference between the NAV and the offer price represents the front-end load charge. For the FPA Paramount Fund, the stated load charge of $6\frac{1}{2}$ percent is relative to the fund's offer price. However, the load rate is actually *more* when the commission is related to a more appropriate base—the NAV of the fund. When stated as a percentage of NAV, the load charge for this fund is closer to 7 percent. Relative to what it costs to buy and sell common stocks, that's a pretty hefty charge, even after taking into account the fact that you normally don't have to pay a commission on the *sale* of most funds. While the *maximum* load charge is $7\frac{1}{4}$ percent of the purchase price, few funds charge the maximum. Rather, many funds charge commissions of only 2 or 3 percent—such funds are known as **low-load funds**. There is a commission to pay on low-load funds, but it's relatively small.

Occasionally, a fund will have a **back-end load**, which means commissions are levied when shares are sold. These loads may amount to as much as $7\frac{1}{4}$ percent of the value of the shares sold, although back-end loads tend to decline over time and usually disappear altogether after five or six years. The stated purpose of back-end loads is to enhance fund stability by discouraging investors from trading in and out of the funds over short investment horizons. In addition, a substantial (and growing) number of funds charge something called a **12(b)-1 fee**—a fee that's assessed annually for as long as you own the fund. Known appropriately as *hidden loads,* these fees have been allowed since

low-load fund
a mutual fund that charges a small commission (2 to 3 percent) when shares are bought.

back-end load
a commission charged on the *sale* of shares in a mutual fund.

12(b)-1 fee
a fee levied by some mutual funds to cover management and other operating costs; amounts to as much as 1 percent annually on the average net assets.

Figure 11.4 Mutual Fund Quotations, Showing Load and No-Load Funds

Open-end mutual funds are listed separately from other securities, and they have their own quotation system, as shown here in the *Friday* quotes of the *Wall Street Journal*. For one thing, these securities are quoted in dollars and cents (most other securities are listed in eighths or thirty-seconds). Also, the type of load charge, if any, is indicated as part of the quote. (Source: *Wall Street Journal*, September 15, 1995.)

The price you get when you SELL shares, or what you pay when you BUY no-load funds

The Monday through Thursday quotes in the *Wall Street Journal* consist only of the name of the fund, its NAV, net change, and YTD return.

Emerald Small Cap Fund

Enterprise Capital Appreciation

FBL Blue Chip

FPA Paramount

Federated Fortress Bond Fund

Federated Fortress Municipal Income Fund

MUTUAL FUND QUOTATIONS

NAV	Net Chg.	Fund Name	Inv. Obj.	YTD %chg	4Wk %chg	Total Return 1Yr-R	3Yr-R	5Yr-R	Max Init Chrg.	Exp Ratio
		Eaton V Traditional:								
14.61	+0.11	China p	IL + 5.3	+ 3.8	− 7.7 D	NS ..	NS ..	4.75	2.121	
10.93	+0.04	GovtObl p	IG +10.5	+ 2.3	+10.1 D	5.8 B +	8.5 B	3.75	1.731	
8.63	+0.02	Growth p	GR +25.0	+ 5.0	+21.6 D	7.7 E +	11.7 E	4.75	0.951	
7.97	+0.01	Inc Bos p	HC+11.9k	+0.5k	+11.2kD+	9.5k C +	14.2k C	3.75	1.04	
7.65	−0.14	India p	IL −22.3	− 6.5	−32.5 E	NS ..	NS ..	4.75	2.461	
8.14	+0.03	Invest p	MP +23.6	+ 3.8	+22.1 A	11.0 B +	12.6 C	4.75	0.911	
9.89	+0.01	MunBond p	GM +12.0	+ 2.9	+ 8.8 D	6.1 C +	8.9 B	3.75	0.80	
8.43	...	Spec Eq p	GR +22.5	+ 4.1	+19.0 E +	7.0 E +	14.2 D	4.75	1.021	
60.36	+0.04	ST Trsy p	SB + 4.9	+ 0.6	+ 6.3 D +	3.8 E	NS ..	0.00	0.60	
13.68	+0.07	Stock p	GI +27.5	+ 5.0	+22.7 C +	9.2 E +	11.7 E	4.75	0.981	
8.61	+0.08	Tot Rtn p	SE +16.0	+ 3.5	+20.2 B +	4.8 E +	10.2 D	4.75	1.181	
		Emerald Funds:								
11.88	+0.05	Balinst	MP +25.6	+ 3.4	+23.5 A	NS ..	NS ..	0.00	0.28	
14.58	+0.04	EqA	GR +34.9	+ 3.7	+29.2 B +	11.1 D	NS ..	4.50	1.07	
14.60	+0.04	Eqinst	GR +35.2	+ 3.6	+29.7 B	NS ..	NS ..	0.00	0.79	
10.89	+0.04	FLTxEA	SS +11.5	+ 3.7	+ 8.7 D +	6.4 C	NS ..	4.50	0.96	
10.89	+0.04	FLTxEI	SS +11.7	+ 3.6	+ 9.0 C	NS ..	NS ..	0.00	0.71	
10.38	+0.05	MgdBdl	AB +14.2	+ 3.1	+14.0 B	NS ..	NS ..	0.00	0.27	
13.23	−0.02	SmCapl	SC +33.5	+ 4.8	+31.8 C	NS ..	NS ..	0.00	1.29	
10.32	+0.03	USGovA	IG +11.0	+ 1.9	+10.1 D +	5.5 B	NS ..	4.50	0.98	
10.29	+0.02	USGovl	IG +11.1	+ 1.9	+10.3 C	NS ..	NS ..	0.00	0.68	
17.75	+0.01	EmpBld	SS +10.3	+ 3.2	+ 8.5 D +	6.1 D +	7.8 E	0.00	0.93	
18.45	+0.10	Endow	GI +20.9	+ 3.1	+19.0 E +	11.5 D +	14.5 D	0.00	0.73	
		Enterprise Group:								
37.82	+0.10	CapA p	CP +32.5	+ 5.2	+28.4 C +	12.4 D +	19.6 B	4.75	1.66	
11.63	+0.03	GvSec A p	LG +14.8	+ 3.1	+13.7 B +	5.7 C +	8.5 C	4.75	1.30	
10.28	+0.01	Gwth A p	GR +32.5	+ 1.2	+29.6 B +	15.3 B +	18.3 B	4.75	1.60	
20.21	+0.14	GrIncA p	GI +24.5	+ 5.1	+19.9 D +	13.1 C +	14.0 D	4.75	1.50	
11.38	+0.04	HYBd A p	HC +13.0	+ 0.9	+13.2 B +	10.6 B +	13.3 C	4.75	1.30	
16.03	+0.02	IntlGr A p	IL + 9.0	+ 1.0	+ 3.6 B +	12.5 C +	8.5 B	4.75	2.00	
6.54	+0.03	Magd A	MP +33.2	+ 4.0	NS ..	NS ..	NS ..	NA	NA	
6.52	+0.02	Magd B	MP NA	NA	NA ..	NA ..	NA ..	NA	NA	
5.88	+0.01	SmCo A	SC +13.7	+ 2.8	+ 9.2 E	NS ..	NS ..	4.75	1.75	
13.82	+0.01	TE Inc p	GM +11.7	+ 2.9	+ 9.3 C +	5.6 E +	7.6 E	4.75	1.25	
		Excelsior Instl:								
7.95	+0.02	Balanced	MP +20.1	+ 2.8	+17.0 C	NS ..	NS ..	0.00	0.12	
8.56	+0.02	EqGrowth	GR +21.1	+ 2.6	+16.8 E	NS ..	NS ..	0.00	0.12	
9.14	+0.08	EqIndex	GI +29.3	+ 4.5	+27.7 A	NS ..	NS ..	0.00	0.12	
7.36	+0.03	Income	AB NS	+ 2.2	NS ..	NS ..	NS ..	NA	NA	
7.53	+0.04	ToRtnBd	AB NS	+ 2.8	NS ..	NS ..	NS ..	NA	NA	
7.48	+0.01	ExcHY p	HC +13.9	+ 0.4	+13.0 B +	9.8 C +	12.9 D	4.75	1.33	
25.33	+0.08	FAM Val	GI +20.4	+ 5.4	+25.4 B +	14.7 B +	18.9 A	0.00	1.39	
		FBL Series Fund:								
23.47	+0.24	BlChip t	GI +24.9	+ 4.4	+23.2 C +	12.6 D +	13.8 D	0.00	1.83	
14.01	+0.05	Growth t	GI +20.5	+ 4.2	+15.1 E +	13.7 C +	14.0 D	0.00	1.60	
10.31	+0.02	HIGrBd t	AB + 9.9	+ 1.3	+10.0 E	NA ..+	8.7 E	0.00	1.90	
10.02	...	HIYldBd t	HC +10.2	+ 0.5	+ 9.1 E	NA ..+	10.7 E	0.00	2.00	
12.69	+0.09	Managed t	MP +19.5	+ 3.7	+15.5 D	NA ..+	11.9 D	0.00	1.96	
14.50	+0.07	FBPBalanced	MP +21.4	+ 3.1	NA ..	NA ..+	14.4 B	0.00	1.17	
10.85	...	FFBNJ	SS +12.0	+ 2.9	+ 9.7 B +	6.4 C	NS ..	4.50	0.25	
		FPA Funds:								
28.60	+0.02	Capit	GR +43.9	+ 3.3	+47.1 A +	29.9 A +	30.2 A	6.50	0.96	
11.06	+0.02	NwInc	GT +11.6	+ 1.3	+11.3 C +	8.3 A +	11.7 B	4.50	0.74	
15.05	+0.02	Parmt	GI +14.7	+ 5.2	+12.1 E +	15.6 A +	16.0 B	6.50	0.90	
22.00	+0.13	Peren	GI +15.4	+ 3.6	+14.8 E +	7.8 E +	11.9 E	6.50	1.12	
30.41	−0.08	Fairmt	CP +26.4	+ 5.3	+19.1 D +	19.6 B +	20.5 B	6.50	1.74	
21.83	+0.07	Fasciano	MC +27.1	+ 3.9	+28.5 C	NA ..+	16.7 D	0.00	1.70	
		Federated Fortress:								
9.54	+0.01	AdjRt t	MG + 6.3	+ 0.8	+ 6.1 D +	3.4 D	NS ..	0.00	1.02	
17.97	+0.12	AmLdrFs	GI +27.5	+ 4.5	NA ..	NS ..	NS ..	1.00	1.27	
9.73	+0.03	BondFdF r	AB +14.6	+ 2.2	+14.5 B +	9.0 A +	14.0 A	1.00	1.05	
10.21	+0.02	CAmuFS t	SS +14.6	+ 3.0	+ 9.5 C	NS ..	NS ..	1.00	1.25	
13.12	+0.07	EqIncFS t	EI +24.5	+ 4.3	+19.0 C	NS ..	NS ..	1.00	1.24	
8.81	+0.03	GISl r	MG +11.1	+ 1.9	+10.7 C +	4.7 C +	7.4 E	1.00	0.97	
9.82	...	LtdMuFS t	SM + 7.0	+ 0.9	NA ..	NS ..	NS ..	1.00	0.44	
9.93	+0.04	LtdTmFS t	SB + 9.0	+ 1.4	NA ..	NS ..	NS ..	1.00	0.99	
10.76	+0.02	Muninc t	GM +12.4	+ 2.7	+ 9.7 B +	5.8 D +	7.9 D	1.00	1.09	
10.23	+0.02	NYmunFS t	SS +14.3	+ 3.3	+ 8.7 D	NS ..	NS ..	1.00	0.39	
11.36	+0.02	OHmunFS p	SS +12.9	+ 3.0	+ 9.9 B +	6.5 B	NS ..	1.00	0.90	
13.06	+0.10	UtilFd r	SE +14.8	+ 2.9	+12.6 D +	7.9 D +	12.5 C	1.00	1.11	

◄ A true no-load fund

◄ A load fund that also charges a 12(b)-1 fee (p)

◄ A fund with no initial load charge, but with both a redemption fee and a 12(b)-1 fee (t)

◄ A load fund that has a 6½% front-end load

◄ A low-load fund with a redemption fee (r)

A fund with a little of everything: a front-end load, a redemption fee, and a 12(b)-1 fee (t)

1980 and were originally designed to help funds (particularly the no-loads) cover their distribution and marketing costs. The 12(b)-1 fees can amount to as much as 1 percent per year of assets under management. In good markets and bad, these fees are paid right off the top, and that can take its toll. Consider, for instance, $10,000 in a fund that charges a 1 percent 12(b)-1 fee: That translates into a charge of $100 a year—certainly not an insignificant amount of money.

The latest trend in mutual fund fees is the so-called *multiple-class sales charge*. You'll find such arrangements at firms like American Capital, Dreyfus, Merrill Lynch, MFS, Keystone, Smith Barney, and Prudential. The way the multiple-class sales charge works is that the mutual fund will issue different classes of stocks on the same fund or portfolio of securities. Thus, rather than having just one class of stock outstanding, there might be three: Class A shares might have normal (relatively high) front-end loads, Class B shares might have no front-end loads but substantial back-end loads along with a modest annual 12(b)-1 fee, and Class C shares might carry maximum 12(b)-1 fees and nothing else. In other words, you choose your own poison.

To try to bring some semblance of order to fund charges and fees, in 1992 the SEC instituted a series of caps on mutual fund fees. Under the 1992 rules, a mutual fund cannot charge more than 8½ percent in *total sales charges and fees*, including front- and back-end loads as well as 12(b)-1 fees. Thus, if a fund charges a 5 percent front-end load and a 1 percent 12(b)-1 fee, it can charge a maximum of only 2½ percent in back-end load charges without violating the 8½ percent cap. In addition, the SEC set a 1 percent cap on annual 12(b)-1 fees and, perhaps more significantly, stated that true no-load funds cannot charge more than 0.25 percent in annual 12(b)-1 fees. If they do, they have to drop the no-load label in their sales and promotional material.

Other Fees and Costs

Another cost of owning mutual funds is the *management fee,* the compensation paid to the professional managers who administer the fund's portfolio. It must be paid regardless of whether a fund is load or no-load, or whether it is open- or closed-end. Unlike load charges, which are one-time costs, management fees and 12(b)-1 charges, if imposed, are levied annually and are paid regardless of the portfolio's performance. In addition, there are the administrative costs of operating the fund. These are fairly modest and represent the normal cost of doing business (e.g., the commissions paid when the fund buys and sells securities).

The various fees that funds charge generally range from less than 0.5 percent to as much as 2.5 percent of average assets under management. Total expense ratios bear watching, since high expenses will take their toll on performance. As a point of reference, in 1994 domestic stock funds had average expense ratios of around 1.35 percent, foreign stock funds around 1.85 percent, and domestic bond funds about 0.85 percent. Expense ratios for individual funds are quite easy to monitor because they are published each Friday in the *Wall Street Journal*. Take another look at Figure 11.4. The last column in the exhibit, "Exp Ratio," shows the fund's total expense ratio, which represents the latest administrative, management, and 12(b)-1 fees levied by the fund in question. Note in Figure 11.4 that the Enterprise Capital Appreciation fund has an annual expense ratio of 1.66 percent of assets under management, whereas FFB Lexicon's Capital Appreciation fund has a ratio of only 0.55 percent. Why the big difference? Probably, in large part, because Enterprise has an annual 12(b)-1 charge, while FFB Lexicon does not.

A final cost of mutual funds is the taxes paid on security transactions. In order to avoid double taxation, nearly all mutual funds operate as *regulated investment companies*. This means that all (or nearly all) of the dividend and interest income is passed on to the investor, as are any capital gains realized when securities are sold. The mutual fund therefore pays no taxes but instead passes the tax liability on to its shareholders. This holds true regardless of whether such distributions are reinvested in the company (in the form of additional mutual fund shares) or paid out in cash. Mutual funds annually provide each stockholder with a summary report on the amount of dividends and capital gains received and the amount of taxable income earned (and to be reported) by the fund shareholder.

Keeping Track of Fund Fees and Loads

Critics of the mutual fund industry have come down hard on the proliferation of fund fees and charges. Indeed, some argue that the different charges and fees are really meant to do one thing: confuse the investor. The fact is that a lot of funds were going to great lengths—lowering a cost here, tacking on a fee there, hiding a charge somewhere else—to make themselves look like something they weren't. The funds were following the letter of the law, and indeed they were fully disclosing all their expenses and fees. The trouble was that the funds were able to hide all but the most conspicuous charges in a bunch of legalese. Fortunately, steps have been taken to bring fund fees and loads out into the open.

For one thing, fund charges are now more fully reported by the financial press. You don't have to look any further than the mutual fund quotations found in the *Wall Street Journal* and most other major papers. For example, refer back to the quotations in Figure 11.4; notice the use of the letters *r*, *p*, and *t* behind the name of the fund. An *r* behind a fund's name means that the fund charges some type of redemption fee, or back-end load, when you sell your shares. This is the case, for example, with the Federated Fortress Bond Fund. A *p* in the quotes means that the fund levies a 12(b)-1 fee, which you'll have to pay, for example, if you invest in the Enterprise Capital Appreciation Fund. Finally, a *t* indicates funds that charge both redemption fees and 12(b)-1 fees. Notice, for example, that the Federated Fortress Municipal Income Fund is one such fund. In fact, if you look closely at the quotations, you'll see that this municipal income fund not only levies redemption and 12(b)-1 fees but also has a front-end load—as indicated by the difference in its NAV and offer price. The point is this: Don't be surprised to find load funds that also charge redemption and/or 12(b)-1 fees. The same goes for no-load funds, which are allowed to charge annual 12(b)-1 fees of 0.25 percent and still call themselves "no-load" funds. The quotations, of course, tell you only the *kinds* of fees charged by the funds; they do not tell you how much is charged. To get the specifics on the amount charged, you'll have to turn to the fund itself.

All (open-end) mutual funds are required *to fully disclose* all of their expenses in a standardized, easy-to-understand format. Every fund prospectus

Table 11.2 Mutual Fund Expense Disclosure Table

Expenses and Costs of Investing in the Fund

The following information is provided in order to assist investors in understanding the transaction costs and annual expenses associated with investing in the Fund.

A. Shareholder Transaction Costs

Sales load on purchases 2%
Sales load on reinvested dividends ....None
Redemption fees or deferred sales charges..None
Exchange (or conversion) fees ....None

B. Annual Fund Operating Expenses (as a percentage
    of average net assets)

Management fees 0.40%
12(b)-1 fees ....None
Other expenses (estimated) 0.32%

C. Example of Fund Expenses over Time

You would pay the following total expenses over time on a $1,000 investment assuming a 5 percent annual return, and a complete redemption of the investment at the end of each indicated time period:

1 year	3 years	5 years	10 years
$27	$43	$59	$108

must contain, up front, a fairly detailed *fee table*, much like the one illustrated in Table 11.2. on page 456. Notice that this table has three parts: The first specifies all *shareholder transaction costs*. In effect, this tells you what it's going to cost to buy and sell shares in the mutual fund. The next section lists the *annual operating expenses* of the fund. Showing these expenses as a percentage of average net assets, the fund must break out management fees, those elusive 12(b)-1 fees, and any other expenses. The third section provides a rundown of the *total cost over time* of buying, selling, and owning the fund. This part of the table contains both transaction and operating expenses and shows what the total costs would be over hypothetical 1-, 3-, 5-, and 10-year holding periods. To ensure consistency and comparability, the funds must follow a rigid set of guidelines when constructing the illustrative costs.

CONCEPTS *in Review*

11.1 What is a *mutual fund*? Discuss the mutual fund concept, including the importance of diversification and professional management.

11.2 What are the attractions and drawbacks of mutual fund ownership?

11.3 Briefly describe how a mutual fund is organized. Who are the key players in a typical mutual fund organization?

11.4 Define each of the following:
    a. Open-end investment company
    b. Closed-end investment company
    c. Unit investment trust

11.5   What is the difference between a *load fund* and *no-load fund*? What are the advantages of each type? What is a 12(b)-1 fund? Can such a fund operate as a no-load fund?

11.6   Describe a *back-end load*, a *low load*, and a *hidden load*. How can you tell what kind of fees and charges a fund has?

TYPES OF FUNDS AND SERVICES

Some mutual funds specialize in stocks, others in bonds. Some have maximum capital gains as an investment objective, and some seek high current income. Some funds appeal to speculators, whereas others are of interest primarily to income-oriented investors. Every fund has a particular investment objective. Common objectives are growth (or capital gains), current income, tax-exempt income, preservation of capital, or some combination thereof. Disclosure of a fund's investment objective is required by the SEC, and each fund is expected to do its best to conform to its stated investment policy and objective. Categorizing funds according to their investment policies and objectives is widely practiced in the mutual fund industry, as it tends to reflect similarities not only in how the funds manage their money, but also in their risk and return characteristics. Some of the more popular types of mutual funds include growth, aggressive growth, equity-income, balanced, growth-and-income, bond, money market, index, sector, socially responsible, asset allocation, and international funds. Let's look now at these various types of mutual funds to see what they are and how they operate.

TYPES OF MUTUAL FUNDS

Growth Funds

growth fund
a mutual fund whose primary goals are capital gains and long-term growth.

The objective of a **growth fund** is simple: capital appreciation. Long-term growth and capital gains are the primary goals of such funds. Therefore, growth funds invest principally in well-established, large- or mid-cap companies that have above-average growth potential but offer little (if anything) in the way of dividends and current income. Because of the uncertain nature of their investment income, growth funds may involve a fair amount of risk exposure. They are usually viewed as long-term investment vehicles most suitable for the more aggressive investor who wants to build up capital and has little interest in current income.

Aggressive Growth Funds

aggressive growth fund
a highly speculative mutual fund that seeks large profits from capital gains.

Aggressive growth funds are the so-called performance funds that tend to increase in popularity when markets heat up. **Aggressive growth funds** are highly speculative investment vehicles that seek large profits from capital gains. In many respects, they are an extension of the growth fund concept. Also known as *capital appreciation* or *small-cap* funds, many are fairly small, and their portfolios consist mainly of high-flying common stocks. These funds often buy stocks of small, unseasoned companies; stocks with relatively high price/earnings multiples; and common stocks whose prices are highly volatile. They seem to be especially fond of turnaround situations and may even use leverage in their portfolios (i.e., buy stocks on margin); they also use options very aggressively, various hedging techniques, and perhaps even short selling. These techniques are designed, of course, to yield big returns. But aggressive funds are also highly speculative and are among the most volatile of all mutual funds. When the markets are good, aggressive growth funds do well; when the markets are bad, these funds often experience substantial losses.

Equity-Income Funds

equity-income fund
a mutual fund that emphasizes current income and capital preservation and invests primarily in high-yielding common stocks.

Equity-income funds emphasize current income, and they do so by investing primarily in high-yielding common stocks. Capital preservation is also important, and so are capital gains, although capital appreciation is not a primary objective of equity-income funds. These funds invest heavily in high-grade common stocks, some convertible securities and preferred stocks, and occasionally even junk bonds or certain types of high-grade foreign bonds. As far as their stock holdings are concerned, they lean heavily toward blue chips (including perhaps even "baby blues"), public utilities, and financial shares. They like securities that generate hefty dividend yields but also consider potential price appreciation over the longer haul. In general, because of their emphasis on dividends and current income, these funds tend to hold higher-quality securities that are subject to less price volatility than the market as a whole. They're generally viewed as a fairly low-risk way of investing in stocks.

Balanced Funds

balanced fund
a mutual fund whose objective is to generate a balanced return of both current income and long-term capital gains.

Balanced funds are so named because they tend to hold a balanced portfolio of both stocks and bonds, and they do so for the purpose of generating a well-balanced return of both current income and long-term capital gains. In many respects, they're much like equity-income funds, except that balanced funds usually put more into fixed-income securities; generally, they keep at least 25 to 50 percent of their portfolios—and sometimes more—in bonds. The bonds are used principally to provide current income, and stocks are selected mainly for their long-term growth potential.

The funds can, of course, shift the emphasis in their security holdings one way or the other. Clearly, the more the fund leans toward fixed-income securities, the more income oriented it will be. For the most part, balanced funds tend to confine their investing to high-grade securities, including growth-oriented blue-chip stocks, high-quality income shares, and high-yielding investment-grade bonds. Therefore, they're usually considered to be a relatively safe form of investing, in which you can earn a competitive rate of return without having to endure a lot of price volatility.

Growth-and-Income Funds

growth-and-income fund
a mutual fund that seeks both long-term growth and current income, with primary emphasis on capital gains.

Growth-and-income funds also seek a balanced return made up of both current income and long-term capital gains, but they place a greater emphasis on growth of capital. Moreover, unlike balanced funds, growth-and-income funds put most of their money into equities. Indeed, it's not unusual for these funds to have 80 to 90 percent of their capital in common stocks. They tend to confine most of their investing to quality issues, so you can expect to find growth-oriented blue-chip stocks in their portfolios, along with a fair amount of high-quality income stocks. One of the big appeals of these funds is the fairly substantial returns many of them have been able to generate over the long haul. Of course, these funds do involve a fair amount of risk, if for no other reason than the emphasis they place on stocks and capital gains. Thus, growth-and-income funds are most suitable for those investors who can tolerate the risk and price volatility.

Bond Funds

bond fund
a mutual fund that invests in various kinds and grades of bonds, with income as the primary objective.

As the name implies, **bond funds** invest exclusively in various kinds and grades of bonds—from Treasury and agency bonds to corporates and municipals. Income is the primary investment objective, although capital gains is not ignored. There are three important advantages to buying shares in bond funds, rather than investing directly in bonds. First, the bond funds are generally more liquid than is true of direct investments in bonds. Second, they offer a cost-effective way of achieving a high degree of diversification in an otherwise expensive investment vehicle (most bonds carry minimum denominations of $1,000 to $5,000 or more). Third, bond funds will automatically reinvest interest and other income, thereby allowing the investor to earn fully compounded rates of return.

Bond funds, generally considered to be a fairly conservative form of investment, are not without risk, since *the prices of the bonds held in the fund's portfolio will fluctuate with changing interest rates*. While many bond funds are managed pretty conservatively, a growing number are becoming increasingly aggressive. In fact, much of the growth that bond funds have experienced recently can be attributed to a more aggressive investment attitude. In today's market, investors can find everything from high-grade government bond funds to highly speculative funds that invest in nothing but junk bonds, or even in highly volatile derivative securities. Indeed, exotic derivative securities became a real problem in 1993–1994, when many of the bond funds that had large positions in derivatives experienced eye-popping losses. But there was a good side to these losses as they taught investors a valuable lesson: Watch out for funds with heavy exposure to exotic derivative securities, or at the least, recognize that if the fund is heavily invested in such securities, you may be in for a very bumpy ride. Despite all this, however, bond funds remain a sound investment (because the vast majority of bond funds have steered clear of derivatives), and continue to be popular with investors looking for a relatively conservative investment outlet. With that in mind, here's a list of the different types of bond funds available today:

• *Government bond funds*, which invest in U.S. Treasury and agency securities.

• *Mortgage-backed bond funds*, which put their money into various types of mortgage-backed securities of the U.S. government (e.g., GNMA issues). These funds appeal to investors for several reasons: (1) They provide diversification, (2) they are an affordable way to get into mortgage-backed securities, and (3) they have a provision that allows investors (if they so choose) to reinvest the principal portion of the monthly cash flow, thereby enabling investors to preserve rather than consume their capital.

• *High-grade corporate bond funds*, which invest chiefly in investment-grade securities rated triple-B or better.

- *High-yield corporate bond funds*, which are risky investments that buy junk bonds for the yields they offer.

- *Convertible bond funds*, which invest primarily in securities (domestic and possibly foreign) that can be converted or exchanged into common stocks. By investing in convertible bonds and preferreds, the funds offer investors some of the price stability of bonds, along with the capital appreciation potential of stocks.

- *Municipal bond funds*, which invest in tax-exempt securities and are suitable for investors looking for tax-free income. Like their corporate counterparts, municipals can also come out as either high-grade or high-yield funds. A special type of municipal bond fund is the so-called *single-state fund*, which invests in the municipal issues of only one state, thus producing (for residents of that state) interest income that is *fully exempt* from both federal and state taxes (and possibly even local/city taxes as well).

- *Intermediate-term bond funds*, which invest in bonds with maturities of 7 to 10 years or less and offer not only attractive yields but relatively low price volatility as well. The shorter (2- to 5-year) intermediate-term funds are often used as substitutes for money market investments by investors looking for higher returns on their money, especially when short-term rates are way down.

Clearly, no matter what you're looking for in a fixed-income security, you're likely to find a bond fund that fits the bill. The number and variety of such funds have skyrocketed in the past 10 years or so, with the net results being that by 1994, there were roughly 2,100 publicly traded bond funds that had more than $750 billion worth of bonds under management.

Money Market Funds

money market mutual fund (money fund)
a mutual fund that pools the capital of a number of investors and uses it to invest in short-term money market instruments.

The first **money market mutual fund**, or **money fund** for short, was set up in November 1972 with just $100,000 in total assets. It was a new idea that applied the mutual fund concept to the buying and selling of short-term money market instruments—bank certificates of deposit, U.S. Treasury bills, and the like. For the first time, investors with modest amounts of capital were given access to the high-yielding money market, where many instruments require minimum investments of $100,000 or more. (Money funds, along with other short-term investment vehicles, were discussed in detail in Chapter 3.) The idea caught on quickly, and the growth in money funds was nothing short of phenomenal. That growth temporarily peaked in 1982, however, when the introduction of money market deposit accounts by banks and S&Ls caused money fund assets to level off and eventually decline. It didn't take long for the industry to recover, and by 1994 there were some 900 money funds that together held nearly $600 billion in assets—which accounted for about *30 percent of all the assets held by mutual funds.*

Actually, there are several different kinds of money market mutual funds:

- *General purpose money funds*, which invest in any and all types of money market investment vehicles, from Treasury bills and bank CDs to corporate commercial paper. The vast majority of money funds are of this type. They invest their money wherever they can find attractive short-term yields.

- *Government securities money funds*, which were established as a way to meet investor concerns for safety. They effectively eliminate any risk of default by confining their investments to Treasury bills and other short-term securities of the U.S. government or its agencies.

- *Tax-exempt money funds*, which limit their investing to very short (30-day to 90-day) tax-exempt municipal securities. Because their income is free from federal income taxes, they appeal predominantly to investors in high tax brackets. The yields on these funds are about 25 to 35 percent below the returns on other types of money funds, so you need to be in a high enough tax bracket to produce a competitive after-tax return. Some tax-exempt funds confine their investing to the securities of a single state, so that residents of high-tax states can enjoy income that's free from both federal and state taxes.

Just about every major brokerage firm has at least one or two money funds of its own, and hundreds more are sold by independent fund distributors. Most require minimum investments of $1,000 (although $2,500 to $5,000 minimum requirements are not uncommon). Because the maximum average maturity of fund holdings can not exceed 90 days, money funds are highly liquid investment vehicles. They're also very low in risk and virtually immune to capital loss, because at least 95 percent of the fund's assets must be invested in top-rated/prime-grade securities. However, the interest income produced by the funds is not so secure, because it tends to follow general interest rate conditions. As a result, the returns to shareholders are subject to the ups and downs of market interest rates. Even with their variability, though, the yields on money funds are highly competitive with those of other short-term securities. And with the check-writing privileges they offer, money funds are just as liquid as checking or savings accounts. They are viewed by many investors as a convenient, safe, and profitable way to accumulate capital and temporarily store idle funds.

Index Funds

index fund
a mutual fund that buys and holds a portfolio of stocks (or bonds) equivalent to those in a specific market index.

"If you can't beat 'em, join 'em." That saying pretty much describes the idea behind index funds. Essentially, an **index fund** is a type of mutual fund that buys and holds a portfolio of stocks (or bonds) equivalent to those in a market index like the S&P 500 Index. An index fund that's trying to match the S&P 500, for example, would hold the same 500 stocks that are held in that index, in exactly (or very nearly) the same proportion. Rather than trying to beat the market, as most actively managed funds do, *index funds simply try to match the market*—that is, to match the performance of the index on which the fund is based. They do this through low-cost investment management; in fact, in most cases, the whole portfolio is run almost entirely by a computer that matches the fund's holdings with those of the targeted index.

The approach of index funds is strictly buy-and-hold. Indeed, about the only time an index-fund portfolio changes is when the targeted market index alters its "market basket" of securities. (Occasionally an index will drop a few securities and replace them with new ones.) A pleasant by-product of this buy-and-hold approach is that the funds have extremely low portfolio turnover rates and, therefore, very little in *realized* capital gains. As a result, they produce very little taxable income from year to year, causing some high-income investors to view these funds as a type of tax-sheltered investment.

But, in addition to their tax shelter, these funds provide something else: That is, as boring as the whole idea may sound, by simply trying to match the market, index funds actually produce *highly competitive returns* to investors! The fact is that it's very tough to outperform the market, whether you are a professional money manager or an amateur individual investor. Most stock-index funds, in fact, outperform the vast majority of all other types of stock funds. Indeed, historical data show that only about 20 percent of stock funds outperform the market. Since a (true) index fund will pretty much match the market, these funds tend to produce better returns than 75 to 80 percent of competing stock funds.

Besides the S&P 500, which is the most popular index, a number of other market indexes are used: the S&P Midcap 400, the Russell 2000 Small Stock, and the Wilshire 5000 indexes, as well as value-stock indexes, growth-stock indexes, international-stock indexes, and even bond indexes. When picking index funds, be sure to avoid high-cost funds, as such fees significantly *reduce* the chance that the fund will be able to even match the market. Also, avoid index funds that use gimmicks as a way to "enhance" yields: That is, rather than follow the index, these funds will "tilt" their portfolios in an attempt to not only match the market but outperform it. Your best bet is to buy a *true* index fund—one that has no added "bells and whistles"—and a low-cost one at that.

Sector Funds

sector fund
a mutual fund that restricts its investments to a particular segment of the market.

One of the hottest products on Wall Street is the so-called **sector fund**, a mutual fund that restricts its investments to a particular sector, or segment, of the market. In effect, these funds concentrate their investment holdings in one or more industries that make up the sector being aimed at. For example, a health care sector fund would focus on such industries as drug companies, hospital management firms, medical suppliers, and biotech concerns. The portfolio of a sector fund would then consist of promising growth stocks from these particular industries. Among the more popular sector funds are those that concentrate their investments in aerospace and defense, energy, financial services, gold and precious metals, leisure and entertainment, natural resources, electronics, chemicals, computers, telecommunications, utilities, and, of course, health care—basically, all the "glamour" industries.

The underlying investment objective of a sector fund is *capital gains*. In many respects, a sector fund is similar to a growth fund and should be considered speculative in nature. The sector fund concept is that the really attractive returns come from small segments of the market; so rather than diversifying your portfolio across the market, put your money where the action is! It's an interesting notion that warrants consideration by aggressive investors willing to take on the added risks that often accompany these funds.

Socially Responsible Funds

For some, investing is far more than just cranking out financial ratios and calculating investment results. To these investors, the security selection process doesn't end with bottom lines, P/E ratios, growth rates, and betas. Rather, it also includes the *active, explicit consideration of moral, ethical, and environmental issues.* The idea is that social concerns should play just as big a role in investment decisions as do profits and other financial matters. Not surprisingly, there are a number of funds today that cater to such investors: Known as **socially responsible funds,** they actively and directly incorporate ethics and morality into the investment decision. Thus, as far as these funds are concerned, their investment decisions revolve around *both* morality and profitability.

socially responsible fund
a mutual fund that actively and directly incorporates ethics and morality into the investment decision.

Socially responsible funds consider only certain companies for inclusion in their portfolios; if a company doesn't meet the fund's moral, ethical, or environmental tests, fund managers simply won't consider buying the stock, no matter how good the bottom line looks. Generally speaking, these funds abstain from investing in companies that derive revenues from tobacco, alcohol, or gambling; that are weapons contractors; or that operate nuclear power plants. (South Africa used to be a primary screen, but it has pretty much been dropped from consideration, as the politics there have changed.) In addition, the funds tend to favor firms that produce "responsible" products or services, that have strong employee relations and positive environmental records, and that are socially responsive to the communities in which they operate. Although these screens may seem to eliminate a lot of stocks from consideration, these funds (most of which are fairly small) still have plenty of securities to choose from, so it's not all that difficult for them to keep their portfolios fully invested. As far as performance is concerned, the general perception is that there's a price to pay, in the form of lower average returns, for socially responsible investing. That's not too surprising, however, for as you add more investment hurdles, you're likely to reduce return potential. But, those who truly believe in socially responsible investing apparently are willing to put their money where their mouths are!

Asset Allocation Funds

Studies have shown that the most important decision an investor can make is to decide where to allocate his or her investment assets. This is known as *asset allocation,* and it basically involves deciding how you're going to divide up your investments among different types of securities. For example, what portion of your money do you want to devote to money market securities, what portion to stocks, and what portion to bonds? Asset allocation deals in broad terms (types of securities) and does not address individual security selection. Strange as it may sound, asset allocation has been found to be a far more important determinant of total returns on a portfolio than individual security selection.

asset allocation fund
a mutual fund that spreads investors' money across stocks, bonds, and money market securities.

Because many individual investors have a tough time making asset allocation decisions, the mutual fund industry has, not surprisingly, created a product to do the job for them. Known as **asset allocation funds,** these funds spread investors' money across different types of markets. That is, whereas most mutual funds concentrate on one type of investment—whether stocks, bonds, or money market securities—asset allocation funds put money into all these markets. Many of them also include foreign securities in the asset allocation scheme, and some even include inflation-resistant investments, such as gold or real estate. These funds are designed for people who want to hire fund managers not only to select individual securities for them but also to make the strategic decision of how to allocate money among the various markets.

international fund
a mutual fund that does all or most of its investing in foreign securities.

Here's how a typical asset allocation fund works. The money manger will establish a desired allocation mix, which might look something like this: 50 percent of the portfolio goes to U.S. stocks, 30 percent to bonds, 10 percent to foreign securities, and 10 percent to money market securities. Securities are then purchased for the fund in these proportions, and the overall portfolio maintains the desired mix. Actually, each segment of the fund is managed almost as a separate portfolio. Thus, securities within, say, the stock portion are bought, sold, and held as the market dictates.

What really separates asset allocation funds from the rest of the pack is that *as market conditions change over time, the asset allocation mix will change as well*. For example, if the U.S. stock market starts to soften, funds will be moved out of stocks to some other area; as a result, the stock portion of the portfolio might drop to, say, 35 percent and the foreign securities portion might increase to 25 percent. Of course, there's no assurance that the money manager will make the right moves at the right time, but the expectation with these funds is that he or she will. (It's interesting to note that *balanced funds* are really a form of asset allocation fund, except they tend to follow a *fixed-mix* approach to asset allocation—say, put 60 percent of their portfolio into stocks and 40 percent into bonds—and then pretty much stick to that mix, no matter what the markets are doing.)

Asset allocation funds are supposed to provide investors with one-stop shopping. That is, you just find an asset allocation fund (or two) that fits your needs and invest in it (or them), rather than buying a couple of stock funds, a couple of bond funds, and so on. The success of these funds rests not only on how well the money manager picks securities but also on how well he or she times the market and moves funds among different segments of the market. Investors have plenty of asset allocation funds to choose from: In 1994, there were over 90 asset allocation funds in operation, with nearly $36 billion in assets under management.

International Funds

In their search for higher yields and better returns, U.S. investors have shown a growing interest in foreign securities. Sensing an opportunity, the mutual fund industry was quick to respond with a proliferation of so-called **international funds**—a type of mutual fund that does all or most of its investing in foreign securities. Just look at the number of international funds around today versus a few years ago: In 1985, there were only about 40 of these funds; by 1994, the number had grown to over 350. The fact is that a lot of people would like to invest in foreign securities but simply don't have the experience or know-how to do so. International funds may be just the vehicle for such investors, *provided they have at least a basic appreciation of international economics*. Since these funds deal with the international economy, balance of trade positions, and currency valuations, investors should have a fundamental understanding of what these issues are and how they can affect fund returns.

Technically, the term *international fund* describes a type of fund that invests *exclusively in foreign securities*, often confining its activities to specific geographic regions (e.g., Mexico, Australia, Europe, or the Pacific Rim). In addition, there's a special class of international funds, known as *global funds*, that invest not only in foreign securities but also in U.S. companies—usually multinational firms. As a rule, global funds provide more diversity and, with access to both foreign and domestic markets, can go where the action is.

Regardless of whether they're global or international (from here on out, we'll use the term *international* to apply to both), you'll find just about any type of fund you could possibly want in the international sector. There are international stock funds, international bond funds, even international money market funds. In addition, there are aggressive growth funds, balanced funds, long-term growth funds, high-grade bond funds, and so forth. Furthermore, there are funds that confine their investing to large, established markets (Japan, Germany, Australia, etc.) and others that stick to the more exotic (and risky) emerging markets (e.g., such as Thailand, Mexico, Chile, or even former Communist countries like Poland). Thus, no matter what your investment philosophy or objective, you're likely to find what you're looking for in the international area.

Basically, these funds attempt to take advantage of international economic developments in two ways: (1) by capitalizing on changing market conditions and (2) by positioning themselves to benefit from devaluation of the dollar. They do so because they can make money from rising share prices in a foreign market and, perhaps just as important, from a falling dollar (which in itself produces capital gains for American investors in international funds). Many of these funds, however, attempt to protect their investors from currency exchange risks by using various types of *hedging strategies*. That is, by using foreign currency options and futures (or some other type of derivative product), the fund will try to eliminate (or reduce) the effects of currency exchange rates. Some funds, in fact, do this on a permanent basis: In essence, these funds hedge away exchange risk so that they concentrate on the higher returns offered by the foreign securities themselves. Others are only occasional users of currency hedges and will employ them only if they feel there's a real chance of a substantial swing in currency values. But even with currency hedging, international funds are still considered to be fairly high-risk investments and should be used only by investors who understand and are able to tolerate such risks. This warning is especially true for funds that invest narrowly in *a single developing country* (like Mexico or India), where diversification is so limited that if something goes wrong in the host country (as it did in Mexico in 1994), the whole fund suffers—often in a big way.

INVESTOR SERVICES

Ask most investors why they buy a particular mutual fund and they'll probably tell you that the fund provides the kind of income and return they're looking for. Now, no one would question the importance of return in the investment decision, but there are some other important reasons for investing in mutual funds, not the least of which are the services they provide. Indeed, many investors find these services so valuable that they often buy the funds as much for their services as for their returns. Some of the most sought-after *mutual fund services* include automatic investment and reinvestment plans, regular income programs, conversion and phone-switching privileges, and retirement programs.

Automatic Investment Plans

It takes money to make money, and for an investor, that means being able to accumulate the capital to put into the market. Unfortunately, that's not always

automatic investment plan
a mutual fund service that allows shareholders automatically to send fixed amounts of money from their paychecks or bank accounts into the fund.

the easiest thing to do. Enter mutual funds, which have come up with a program that makes savings and capital accumulation as painless as possible. The program is the **automatic investment plan**, which allows fund shareholders to funnel fixed amounts of money *from their paychecks or bank accounts* automatically into a mutual fund. It's much like a payroll deduction plan, where investments to your mutual fund are automatically deducted from your paycheck or bank account.

This fund service has become very popular, because it enables shareholders to invest on a regular basis without having to think about it. Just about every fund group offers some kind of automatic investment plan for virtually all of its stock and bond funds. To enroll, you simply fill out a form authorizing the fund to siphon a set amount (usually a minimum of $25 to $100 per period) from your bank account or paycheck at regular intervals—typically, monthly or quarterly. Once enrolled, you'll be buying more shares in the fund(s) of your choice every month or quarter (most funds deal in fractional shares). Of course, if it's a load fund, you'll still have to pay normal sales charges on your periodic investments. To remain diversified, you can divide your money among as many funds (within a given fund family) as you like. Finally, you can get out of the program anytime you like, without penalty, by simply calling the fund. Although convenience is perhaps the chief advantage of automatic investment plans, they also make solid investment sense: One of the best ways of building up a sizable amount of capital is to add funds to your investment program systematically over time. The importance of making regular contributions to your investment program cannot be overstated; it ranks right up there with compound interest.

Automatic Reinvestment Plans

automatic reinvestment plan
a mutual fund service that enables shareholders automatically to buy additional shares in the fund through reinvestment of dividends and capital gains income.

An automatic reinvestment plan is one of the real draws of mutual funds and is a service offered by just about every open-ended fund. Whereas the automatic investment plans we discussed above deal with money the shareholder is putting into a fund, automatic *re*investment plans deal with the dividends the funds pay to their shareholders. A lot like the dividend reinvestment plans we looked at with stocks (in Chapter 5), the **automatic reinvestment plans** of mutual funds enable you to keep your capital fully employed. Through this service, dividend and/or capital gains income is automatically used to buy additional shares in the fund. Most funds deal in fractional shares, and such purchases are often commission-free. Keep in mind, however, that even though an investor may reinvest all dividends and capital gains distributions, the IRS will treat them as cash receipts and, as such, will tax them as investment income in the year in which they were paid.

Automatic reinvestment plans are especially attractive since they enable investors to earn fully compounded rates of return. That is, by plowing back profits, the investor can essentially put his or her profits to work in generating even more earnings. Indeed, the effects of these plans on total accumulated capital over the long run can be substantial. Figure 11.5 shows the long-term impact of one such plan. (These are the actual performance numbers for a *real* mutual fund—the Mutual Shares Fund.) In the illustration, we assume the investor starts with $10,000 and, except for the reinvestment of dividends and capital gains, *adds no new capital over time*. Even so, note that the initial investment of $10,000 grew to more than $168,000 over a nearly 18-year period (which amounts to a compounded rate of return of about 17½ percent). Of course, not all periods will match this performance; nor will all mutual funds be able to perform as well, even in strong markets. The point is, though, that as long as care is taken in selecting an appropriate fund, *attractive benefits can be derived from the systematic accumulation of capital offered by automatic reinvestment plans.* Clearly, investors should seriously consider the idea of incorporating these plans into their mutual fund investment program.

Regular Income

systematic withdrawal plan
a mutual fund service that enables shareholders to automatically receive a predetermined amount of money every month or quarter.

Although automatic investment and reinvestment plans are great for the long-term investor, what about the investor who's looking for a steady stream of income? Once again, mutual funds have a service to meet this kind of need. It's called a **systematic withdrawal plan**, and it's offered by most open-ended funds. Once enrolled in one of these plans, an investor will automatically receive a predetermined amount of money every month or quarter. Usually, the funds require a minimum investment of $5,000 or more in order to participate in such plans, and the size of the minimum payment must normally be $50 or more per period (with no limit on the maximum). The funds will pay out the monthly or quarterly income first from dividends and realized capital gains. If this source proves to be inadequate and the shareholder so authorizes, the

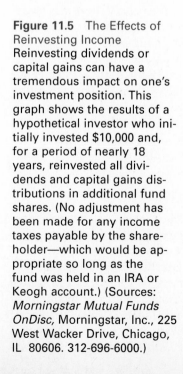

Figure 11.5 The Effects of Reinvesting Income Reinvesting dividends or capital gains can have a tremendous impact on one's investment position. This graph shows the results of a hypothetical investor who initially invested $10,000 and, for a period of nearly 18 years, reinvested all dividends and capital gains distributions in additional fund shares. (No adjustment has been made for any income taxes payable by the shareholder—which would be appropriate so long as the fund was held in an IRA or Keogh account.) (Sources: *Morningstar Mutual Funds OnDisc,* Morningstar, Inc., 225 West Wacker Drive, Chicago, IL 80606. 312-696-6000.)

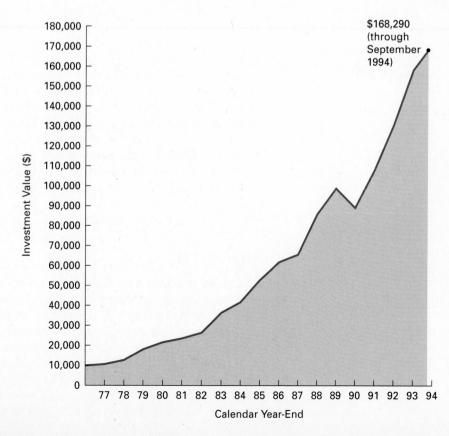

fund can then tap the principal or original paid-in capital in the account to meet the required periodic payments.

Conversion Privileges and Phone Switching

Sometimes investors find it necessary, for one reason or another, to switch out of one fund and into another. The investor's investment objectives or the investment climate itself may have changed. **Conversion** (or **exchange**) **privileges** were devised to meet the needs of such investors in a convenient and economical manner. Investment management companies that offer a number of different funds—known as **fund families**—often provide conversion privileges that enable shareholders to move easily from one fund to another, usually by phone. Indeed, with *phone switching*, an investor can simply pick up the phone to move money among funds—the only constraint being that the switches must be confined to the same *family* of funds. For example, an investor can switch from a Dreyfus growth fund to a Dreyfus money fund, or to its income fund, or to any other fund managed by Dreyfus. With some fund families, the alternatives open to investors seem almost without limit; indeed, some of the larger families offer 20 or 30 funds (or more). One investment company (Fidelity) has over 200 different funds in its family—everything from high-performance stock funds to bond funds, tax-exempt funds, a couple dozen sector funds, and a couple dozen money funds. More than 100 fund families are in operation today. They all provide low-cost conversion/phone-switching privileges and some even provide these privileges free, although most families that offer free exchanges have limits on the number of times such switches can occur each year. Fifteen of the largest fund families are listed in Table 11.3. Note that, together, these 15 families have nearly $1.2 *trillion* in assets under management and offer over 1,250 different mutual funds to the investing public.

Conversion privileges are usually considered beneficial from the shareholder's point of view, because they allow investors to meet their ever changing long-term investment goals. In addition, they permit investors to manage their mutual fund holdings more aggressively by allowing them to move in and out of funds as the investment environment changes. Unfortunately, there is one major drawback: For tax purposes, the exchange of shares from one fund to another is regarded as a sale transaction followed by a subsequent purchase of a new security. As a result, if any capital gains exist at the time of the exchange, the investor is liable for the taxes on that profit, even though the holdings were not truly liquidated.

Retirement Programs

As a result of government legislation, self-employed individuals are permitted to divert a portion of their pretax income into self-directed retirement plans. Also, all working Americans, whether or not they are self-employed, are allowed to establish individual retirement accounts (IRAs). (Even after the provisions for IRAs changed with the Tax Reform Act of 1986, they can still be set up by anyone who is gainfully employed, although the tax deductibility of IRA *contributions* is now limited to certain individuals.) Today all mutual funds provide a special service that allows individuals to set up tax-deferred retirement programs as either IRA or Keogh accounts—or, through their place

Table 11.3   Fifteen of the Biggest Fund Families

Fund Families	Asset Base ($ Billions)	Number of Stock/Bond Funds	Number of Money Funds	Total Number of Funds
Fidelity Distributors	$278.6	169	41	210
Vanguard Group	137.5	83	7	90
Merrill Lynch Funds	125.4	106	22	128
Capital Research and Management	112.1	32	2	34
Franklin/Templeton	90.3	93	17	110
Putnam Financial Services	63.0	80	4	84
Federated Investors	62.4	101	58	159
Dean Witter Reynolds	58.1	89	5	94
Smith Barney	55.0	57	6	63
Prudential-Bache	52.1	47	13	60
IDS Financial Services	47.1	33	2	35
T. Rowe Price Associates	39.9	77	7	84
Kemper Financial Services	39.4	26	4	30
Scudder	33.2	31	5	36
Oppenheimer Fund Management	29.3	36	2	38

*Number of funds in existence as of late 1994/early 1995; all these fund families offer conversion privileges.

Source: Asset base, *Investment Company Institute*; number of funds, from various sources, including the funds themselves.

of employment, to participate in a qualified tax-sheltered retirement plan, such as a 401(k). The funds set up the plans and handle all the administrative details so that the shareholder can easily take full advantage of available tax savings.

CONCEPTS *in Review*

11.7 Briefly describe each of the following types of mutual funds:
   a. Aggressive growth funds
   b. Equity-income funds
   c. Growth-and-income funds
   d. Bond funds
   e. Sector funds
   f. Socially responsible funds

11.8 What is an *asset allocation fund*, and how does such a fund differ from other types of mutual funds?

11.9 If growth, income, and capital preservation are the primary objectives of mutual funds, why do we bother to categorize them by type? Do you think such classifications are helpful in the fund selection process? Explain.

11.10 What are *fund families*? What advantages do fund families offer investors? Are there any disadvantages?

11.11 Briefly describe some of the investor services provided by mutual funds. What are *automatic reinvestment plans*, and how do they differ from *automatic investment plans*? What is phone switching, and why would an investor want to use this type of service?

**INVESTING IN
MUTUAL FUNDS**

Suppose you are confronted with the following situation: You have money to invest and are trying to select the right place to put it. You obviously want to pick a security that meets your idea of acceptable risk and will generate an attractive rate of return. The problem is that you have to make the selection from a list of over 6,000 securities. Sound like a "mission impossible"? Well, that's basically what the investor is up against when trying to select a suitable mutual fund. However, if the problem is approached systematically, it may not be so formidable a task. As we will see, it is possible to whittle down the list of alternatives by matching one's investment needs with the investment objectives of the funds. Before doing that, though, it might be helpful to examine more closely the various investor uses of mutual funds. With this background, we can then look at the selection process and at several measures of return that can be used to assess performance.

INVESTOR USES OF MUTUAL FUNDS

Mutual funds can be used by individual investors in a variety of ways. For instance, performance funds can serve as a vehicle for capital appreciation, whereas bond funds can provide current income. Regardless of the kind of income a mutual fund provides, individuals tend to use these investment vehicles for one of three reasons: (1) as a way to accumulate wealth, (2) as a storehouse of value, and (3) as a speculative vehicle for achieving high rates of return.

Accumulation of Wealth

Accumulation of wealth is probably the most common reason for using mutual funds. Basically, the investor uses mutual funds over the long haul to build up investment capital. Depending upon the investor's personality, a modest amount of risk may be acceptable, but usually preservation of capital and capital stability are considered important. The whole idea is to form a "partnership" with the mutual fund in building up as big a capital pool as possible: You provide the capital by systematically investing and reinvesting in the fund, and the fund provides the return by doing its best to invest your resources wisely.

Storehouse of Value

Investors may also use mutual funds as a storehouse of value. The idea here is to find a place where investment capital can be fairly secure and relatively free from deterioration yet still generate a relatively attractive rate of return. Short- and intermediate-term bond funds are logical choices for such purposes, and so are money funds. Capital preservation and income over the long term are very important to some investors, while others might seek storage of value only for the short term, using money funds as a way to "sit it out" until a more attractive opportunity comes along.

Speculation and Short-Term Trading

Speculation is not a common use of mutual funds; the reason, of course, is that most mutual funds are long-term in nature and thus not really meant to be used as aggressive trading vehicles. However, a growing number of funds (e.g., sector funds) now cater to speculators, and some investors find that mutual funds are indeed attractive outlets for speculation and short-term trading. One way to do this is to trade in and out of funds aggressively as the investment climate changes. Load charges can be avoided (or reduced) by dealing in families of funds offering low-cost conversion privileges and/or by dealing only in no-load funds. Some investors might choose to invest in funds for the long run but still seek extraordinarily high rates of return by investing in aggressive mutual funds. A number of funds follow very aggressive trading strategies, which may well appeal to investors who are willing to accept substantial risk exposure. These aggressive funds are usually the fairly specialized smaller funds: Sophisticated enhanced-yield funds, leverage funds, option funds, emerging-market funds, small-cap aggressive growth funds, and sector funds are examples. In essence, such investors are simply applying the basic mutual fund concept to their investment needs by letting professional money managers handle their accounts in a way they would like to see them handled: *aggressively*.

THE SELECTION PROCESS

When it comes to mutual funds, one question every investor has to answer is: Why invest in a mutual fund to begin with—why not just go it alone by buying individual stocks and bonds directly? For beginning investors or investors with little capital, the answer is pretty simple: With mutual funds, investors get far more diversification than they could ever get on their own, plus they get the help of professional money managers, and at a very reasonable cost to boot. For more seasoned, wealthier investors, the answers are probably a bit more involved. Certainly, diversification and professional money management come into play, but there are other reasons as well. The competitive returns offered by mutual funds are a factor with many investors, as are the services they provide. Many well-to-do investors have simply decided they can get better returns over the long haul by carefully selecting mutual funds than by investing on their own. As a result, they put all or a big chunk of their money into funds. Many of these investors will use part of their capital to buy and sell individual securities on their own, and the rest will be used *to buy mutual funds that invest in areas they don't fully understand or don't feel well informed about.* For example, they'll use mutual funds to get into foreign markets, to buy mortgage-backed securities, to buy junk bonds (where diversification is so very important), or to buy value funds (because that's such a tricky and time-consuming way to invest).

Once the decision to use mutual funds has been made, the investor will then have to decide which fund(s) to buy. In many respects, the selection process is the critical dimension in defining the amount of success one will have with mutual funds. It means putting into action all you know about funds, in order to gain as much return as possible from an acceptable level of risk. The selection process begins with an assessment of your own investment needs; this sets the tone of the investment program. Obviously, what you want to do is select from those 6,000 or so funds the one or two (or three or four) that will best meet your total investment needs.

Objectives and Motives for Using Funds

Selecting the right investment means finding those funds that are most suitable to your investment needs. The place to start is with your own investment objectives. In other words, why do you want to invest in a mutual fund, and what are you looking for in a fund? Obviously, an attractive rate of return would be desirable, but there is also the matter of a tolerable amount of risk exposure. Face it: Some investors are more willing to take risks than others. Most likely, when you look at your own risk temperament in relation to the various types of mutual funds available, you will discover that certain types of funds are more appealing to you than others. For instance, aggressive growth or sector funds will probably *not* be attractive to individuals who wish to avoid high exposure to risk.

Another important factor in the selection process is the intended use of the mutual fund. That is, do you want to invest in mutual funds as a means of accumulating wealth, as a storehouse of value, or to speculate for high rates of return? This is useful information, since it puts into clearer focus the question of exactly what you are trying to do with your investment dollars. Finally, there is the matter of the types of services provided by the fund. If you are particularly interested in certain services, you should be sure to look for them in the funds you select. Having assessed what you are looking for in a fund, you now want to look at what the funds have to offer.

What Funds Offer

The ideal mutual fund would achieve maximum capital growth when security prices rise, provide complete protection against capital loss when prices decline, and achieve high levels of current income at all times. Unfortunately, this fund does not exist. Instead, just as each individual has a set of investment needs, each fund has its own *investment objective*, its own *manner of operation*, and its own *range of services*. These three parameters are useful in helping you to assess investment alternatives. But where does the investor look for such information? One obvious place is the fund's prospectus (or its "Statement of Additional Information"), where detailed information on investment objectives, portfolio composition, management, and past performance can be obtained. (*Note:* There may soon be another, even more useful source of information, as the SEC is currently conducting a one-year (1995–96) test of a new, slimmed-down prospectus—tentatively called a *fund profile*—which is meant to provide, on one page and in simple, straightforward language, key information about a fund.) In addition, publications such as the *Wall Street Journal, Barron's, Money, Fortune,* and *Forbes* offer useful information about mutual funds. These sources provide a wealth of operating and performance statistics in a convenient and easy-to-read format. For instance, each year *Forbes* rates over 2,000 mutual funds, and every quarter *Barron's* publishes an extensive mutual fund performance report.

There are also a number of reporting services that provide background information and assessments on a wide range of funds. Among the best in this category are *Morningstar Mutual Funds* (an excerpt of which is shown in Figure 11.6), Wiesenberger's *Investment Companies* (an annual publication with quarterly updates), Donoghue's *Mutual Funds Almanac* (a low-cost, annual publication that provides a variety of operating and performance

Figure 11.6 Some Relevant Information About Specific Mutual Funds
Investors who want in-depth information about the operating characteristics, investment holdings, and market behavior of specific mutual funds, such as this one for AIM Constellation, can usually find what they are looking for in periodicals like *Morningstar Mutual Funds*. (Source: Morningstar, Inc., *Morningstar Mutual Funds*, 1994.)

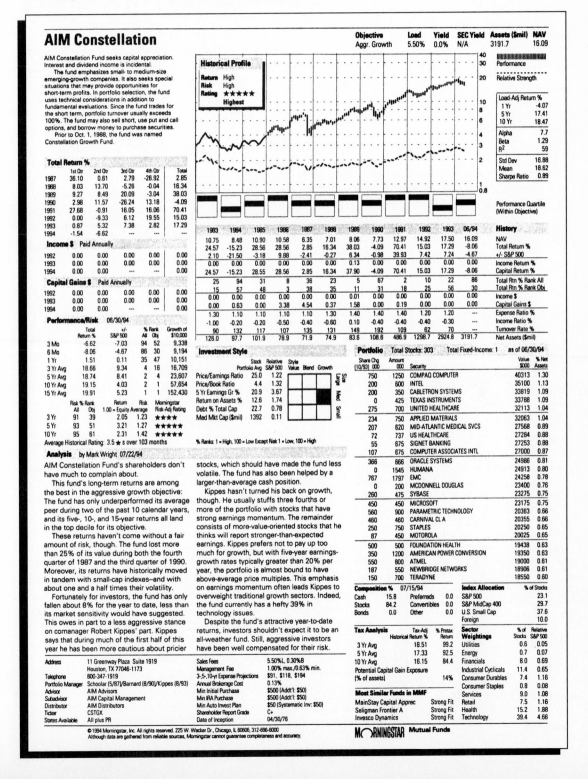

statistics), *Value Line* (which produces a mutual funds report similar to its stock report), and Kiplinger's individual *Mutual Fund Reports* (reports on chosen companies that can be obtained at any time via a toll-free number). In addition, computer databases provide all sorts of performance statistics on disks for easy use on home computers. For example, such quarterly or annually updated software is available, at very low cost, from Morningstar or from the American Association of Individual Investors (AAII). Using sources like these, investors can obtain information on such things as investment objectives, load charges and annual expense rates, summary portfolio analyses, services offered, historical statistics, and reviews of past performance.

Whittling Down the Alternatives

At this point, fund selection becomes a process of elimination as investor needs are weighed against the types of funds available. Large numbers of funds can be eliminated from consideration simply because they fail to meet stated needs. Some funds may be too risky; others may be unsuitable as a storehouse of value. Thus, rather than trying to evaluate 6,000 different funds, you can narrow down the list to two or three *types* of funds that best match your investment needs. From here, you can whittle down the list a bit more by introducing other constraints. For example, because of cost considerations, you may want to deal only in no-load or low-load funds (more on this topic below), or you may be seeking certain services that are important to your investment goals.

Now we introduce the final (but certainly not the least important) element in the selection process: *the fund's investment performance*. Useful information includes (1) how the fund has performed over the past five to seven years, (2) the type of return it has generated in good markets as well as bad, (3) the level of dividend and capital gains distributions, and (4) the type of investment stability the fund has enjoyed over time (or put another way, the amount of volatility/risk in the fund's return). By evaluating such information, you can identify some of the more successful mutual funds—the ones that not only offer the investment objectives and services you seek but also provide the best payoffs. While you're looking at performance, it probably wouldn't hurt to check out the fund's *fee structure*. Be on guard for funds that charge abnormally high management fees, as they can really hurt returns over time.

Note that in this decision process, considerable weight is given to *past performance*. As a rule, the past is given little or no attention in the investment decision—after all, it's the future that matters. Although the *future performance* of a mutual fund is still the variable that holds the key to success, a good deal of time should be spent looking at past investment results, in order to see how successful the fund's investment managers have been. In essence, the success of a mutual fund rests in large part on the *investment skills of the fund managers*. Therefore, when investing in a mutual fund, look for consistently good performance, in up as well as down markets, over *extended* periods of time (five years or more). Most importantly, check to see if the same key people are still running the fund. Although past success is certainly no guarantee of future performance, a strong team of money managers can have a significant bearing on the level of fund returns.

Stick with No-Loads or Low-Loads

There's a long-standing "debate" in the mutual fund industry regarding load funds and no-load funds. The question is: Do load funds add value? And if not, then why pay the load charges? As it turns out, the results generally don't support the idea that load funds provide added value. Indeed, load fund returns, in general, don't seem to be any better than—and certainly not superior to—the returns from no-load funds. In fact, in many cases, the funds with abnormally high loads and 12(b)-1 charges often produce returns that are far less than what you can get from no-load funds. In addition, because of compounding, the differential returns tend to widen with longer holding periods. But that should come as no surprise, since big load charges and/or 12(b)-1 fees do nothing more than reduce your investable capital—and therefore reduce the amount of money you have working for you. In fact, the only way a load fund can overcome this handicap is to produce *superior returns*—which is no easy thing to do, year in and year out. Granted, a handful of load funds have produced very attractive returns over extended periods of time, but they are the exception rather than the rule.

Obviously, it's in your best interest to pay close attention to load charges (and other fees) whenever you're considering an investment in a mutual fund. As a rule, to maximize returns, you should *seriously consider sticking to no-load funds or to low-loads* (funds that have total load charges, including 12(b)-1 fees, of 3 percent or less). Or at the very minimum, you should consider a more expensive load fund *only* if it has a much better performance record (and offers more return potential) than a less expensive fund. There may well be times when the higher costs are justified, but far more often than not, you're better off trying to minimize load charges. That shouldn't be difficult to do, however: There are around a thousand no-load and low-load funds to choose from, and they come in all different types and sizes. What's more, most of the top-performing funds are found in the universe of no-loads or low-loads. So why would you even want to look anywhere else?

INVESTING IN CLOSED-END FUNDS

A closed-end fund is, in many respects, both a stock and an investment company. As the original form of investment company, closed-end funds have enjoyed a long, although not always illustrious, history that dates back to nineteenth-century England and Scotland. In the United States, closed-end funds were actively traded during the 1920s bull market, when they far outnumbered their open-end relatives. During that freewheeling era, however, they were highly leveraged and consequently were hit hard during the Crash of 1929, earning a bad reputation with investors. They remained something of an oddity for decades afterward, and it wasn't until the bull market of the 1980s that closed-end funds came back into fashion.

Today, the assets of closed-end funds (CEFs) represent only a tiny fraction of the more than $2 trillion invested in open-end funds. Indeed, as we can see in Table 11.4, at the end of the 1994 there were 526 CEFs, with total net assets of $127.9 billion. As is true of open-end funds, CEFs come in a variety of different types and styles, including funds that specialize in municipal bonds,

Table 11.4   The Closed-End Fund Universe

Fund Category	Number of Funds*	Total Net Assets* ($ in billions)
Municipal Bond	226	$ 55.6
Taxable Bond	122	33.0
Hybrid	50	9.1
Domestic Equity	41	12.0
World International Equity	21	4.3
Regional International Equity	26	4.6
Single-Country International Equity	40	8.4
Total	526	$127.9

*As of December 31, 1994.

Source: Morningstar Closed-End Funds, Morningstar, Inc.

taxable bonds, various types of equity securities, and international securities, as well as regional and single-country funds. Both taxable and tax-free bonds dominate the CEF universe, although municipal bonds, which enjoyed considerable popularity during the late 1980s and early 1990s, today account for over 40 percent of CEF assets. In addition to bonds, many closed-end funds target foreign stock markets. For example, regional funds focus on a group of countries within a broad geographic area, such as Europe or Latin America. In contrast, single-country funds will target either *emerging markets,* such as Brazil, China, the Czech Republic, India, Indonesia, Mexico, the Philippines, and Turkey, or *developed markets,* such as France, Germany, Japan, and the United Kingdom.

 ## Some Key Differences Between Closed-End and Open-End Funds

Because closed-end funds trade like stocks, you must deal with a broker to buy or sell shares; as such, the usual brokerage commissions apply. Open-end funds, in contrast, are bought from and sold to the fund operators themselves, many of which carry no sales charge at all (i.e., no-load funds). Another important difference between open- and closed-end funds is their liquidity. You can buy and sell relatively large dollar amounts of an open-end mutual fund at its NAV without worrying about affecting the price. However, a relatively large buy or sell order for a CEF could easily bump your price up or down. Thus, the greater liquidity of open-end funds gives them a distinct advantage. At the same time, just like open-end funds, most CEFs offer dividend reinvestment plans, but in many cases, that's about it. CEFs simply don't provide the full range of services mutual fund investors are accustomed to—such as automatic investment plans, telephone switching, and systematic withdrawal plans. In addition, unlike open-end funds, CEFs typically have a relatively constant capitalization; that is, unless there is an additional offering of new stock, investors don't continually buy new shares of stock from the fund, as they do with open-end funds. On the other hand, if you happen to hold a CEF that's going through a stock offering, you'll find that the new shares are sold through the use of *stock rights.* Any CEF investor should have at least a basic understanding of these offerings, if for no other reason than the fact that they are becoming so common today. Toward that end, the accompanying *Investor Insights* box provides some helpful information about *CEF rights offerings.*

INVESTOR INSIGHTS: *Market Innovations*

The Ins and Outs of Rights Offerings on Closed-End Mutual Funds

Unlike open-end mutual funds, closed-end funds do not have a continual flow of cash from the sale of new shares. Instead, CEFs use stock rights to raise money from existing shareholders at what management feels is an appropriate time, commonly—but not always—during a bull market. Shareholders are usually issued one right for each share held, and the rights can be used to purchase additional shares at a predetermined subscription price, commonly 5 to 10 percent *below* the fund's market price (or average price) as of a particular time. As a rule, several rights—typically, three or more—are needed to acquire each new share. Most closed-end rights offerings enable shareholders to exercise their option within several weeks; when the rights expire, they are worthless.

Although rights offerings enable CEFs to raise fresh capital, they do have a nasty side effect: They dilute the positions of shareholders who do not participate. This dilution is especially bothersome *when the fund trades at a discount*. In effect, the size of the pie (total assets) grows, but its slices (net asset value per share) shrink, because there are more shares. It's important to recognize that the dilution affects only those shareholders who don't exercise their rights—or sell them if they are transferable. Many closed-end rights offerings, however, are *nontransferable*; that is, the rights cannot be sold separately from the stock in the open market. Conversely, *transferable* rights can be sold in the secondary market during the "ex-rights" period by shareholders who choose not to exercise the rights. If the rights are transferable, sell them quickly, because the stock price typically declines during the offering period.

Critics have called nontransferable rights offerings coercive, because shareholders may not realize that they need not add to their holdings to realize their value. But shareholders who don't want to increase their investment can still derive the value from nontransferable rights. To begin with, never let a rights offering catch you off guard. When you receive a prospectus describing an upcoming rights offering, take the time to read it carefully. The worst scenario is to do nothing. One way to be prepared is to have a reserve of liquid assets sufficient to participate, if you feel the conditions are right for adding to your investment. But suppose you're strapped for cash or you simply don't want to increase your dollar commitment to the fund because you feel it's not the best time to do so. Or perhaps your fund is held in an IRA and you can't invest more. You nevertheless can capture at least some of the value of nontransferable rights. Here's how: Assume you own 3,600 shares of a fund that has a nontransferable rights offering. The subscription ratio (the number of rights needed to buy one new share of stock) is 3:1, so your 3,600 shares will allow you to subscribe to 1,200 new ones. You could simply sell 1,200 of your shares on the open market, at, say, $9.75, and then exercise your rights and purchase 1,200 new shares for the subscription price, which we'll assume is $9. The neat thing here is that (ignoring commissions) you end up making $900 [1,200 × ($9.75 − $9)] on the deal, and you still hold 3,600 shares of the fund!

All CEF investors should understand rights offerings, even if they've never invested in a fund that has had one, because their usage has increased dramatically in the past few years. Also, if your shares are held in street name, be sure that your broker contacts you about the offering; some may not. And finally, when it comes to CEF rights offerings, remember: *Inaction is the biggest mistake you can make.*

Source: Adapted from Albert J. Fredman, "A Close Look at the Subtleties of Closed-End Fund Rights Offerings, " *AAII Journal*, September 1994, pp. 8–11.

But all things considered, probably the most important difference (because it *directly affects* investor costs and returns) is the way these funds are priced in the marketplace. In particular, while open-end funds can be bought and sold at NAV (plus any front-end load or minus any redemption charge), CEFs have *two values*—a market value, or stock price, and net asset value (NAV). The two are rarely the same, since CEFs typically trade at either a premium or a discount. Premiums and discounts are reported weekly in *Barron's*, the *Wall Street Journal*, and other newspapers. The premium or discount is calculated as follows:

Equation 11.1   Premium (or discount) = (share price − NAV) / NAV

Suppose Fund A has a NAV of $10. If its share price is $8, it will sell at a 20 percent discount. That is:

$$\text{Premium (or discount)} = (\$8 - \$10)/\$10$$
$$= -\$2/\$10 = -.20 = \underline{\underline{-20\%}}$$

Since the answer above ended up negative, the fund is trading at a *discount*. On the other hand, if this same fund were priced at $12 per share, it would be trading at a *premium* of 20 percent—that is, ($12 − $10) / $10 = $2/$10 = .20. Because the value is positive, the fund is trading at a premium.

What to Look For in a Closed-End Fund

If you know what to look for and your timing and selection are good, you may find that some deeply discounted CEFs provide a great way to earn attractive returns. For example, if a fund trades at a 20 percent discount, you pay only 80 cents for each dollar's worth of assets. At certain times, the market offers the opportunity to pick up funds at attractive prices—which could well be the case when double-digit discounts exist. At other times, discounts may be too narrow to represent any special value. If you can buy a fund at an abnormally wide discount and sell it when the discount narrows or turns to a premium, you can enhance your overall return. In fact, even if the discount does not narrow, your return will be improved, because the yield on your investment is higher than it would be with an otherwise equivalent open-end fund. The reason: You're investing less money. Here's a simple example. Suppose a CEF trades at $8, a 20 percent discount from its NAV of $10. If the fund distributes $1 in dividends for the year, it would yield 12.5 percent ($1 divided by its $8 price). However, if it was a no-load, open-end fund, it would be trading at its higher NAV and therefore would yield only 10 percent ($1 divided by its $10 NAV). Thus, when investing in CEFs, be sure to pay close attention to the size of the premium and discount; in particular, keep your eyes open for funds trading at deep discounts, because that feature alone can enhance potential returns.

For the most part, except for the premium or discount, a CEF should be analyzed just like any other mutual fund. That is, pay close attention to the expense ratio, portfolio turnover rate, past performance, cash position, and so on. In addition, study the past history of the discount. Generally, other things being equal, the time to buy is when a fund's discount is, say, 5 percentage points wider than its past average. Suppose a domestic equity fund had been selling at an average discount of 10 percent over the past six months and now its discount has widened to 15 percent. This change could signal a buying opportunity—but also be sure to compare a fund's discount with those of its peers. Information on closed-end funds can be found in such publications as *Morningstar Closed-End Funds*, Standard & Poor's *Stock Reports*, and *Value*

Line Investment Survey. Also, keep in mind that with CEFs, you usually won't get a prospectus (as you would with open-end funds), because they do not continuously offer shares to incoming investors.

One final point to keep in mind when developing a closed-end fund investment program: Stay clear of new issues (IPOs) of closed-end funds and funds that sell at steep *premiums.* Never buy new CEFs when they are brought to the market as IPOs. Why? Because IPOs are always brought to the market at *hefty premiums* and the investor therefore faces the almost inevitable risk of losing money as the shares fall to a discount within a month or two. This drop in price occurs because the IPO funds have to be offered at a premium just to cover the amount of the underwriting spread. You also want to avoid funds that are trading at premiums—especially at steep premiums, such as volatile single-country portfolios. That too can lead to built-in losses when, if sentiment sours, these premiums quickly turn to discounts. And, of course, the higher the premium, the greater the risk of loss.

MEASURING PERFORMANCE

Like any investment decision, return performance is a major dimension in the mutual fund selection process. The level of dividends paid by the fund, its capital gains, and growth in capital are all important aspects of return. Such return information enables the investor to judge the investment behavior of the fund and to appraise its performance in relation to other funds and investment vehicles. Here, we will look at different measures that can be used by mutual fund investors to assess return. Also, because risk is so important in defining the investment behavior of a fund, we will examine mutual fund risk as well.

Sources of Return

An open-end fund has three potential sources of return: (1) dividend income, (2) capital gains distribution, and (3) change in the price (or net asset value) of the fund. Depending on the type of fund, some mutual funds will derive more income from one source than another. For example, we would normally expect income-oriented funds to have much higher dividend income than capital gains distributions. Open-end mutual funds regularly publish reports that recap investment performance. One such report is the *Summary of Income and Capital Changes,* an example of which is provided in Table 11.5. This statement, which is found in the fund's prospectus or annual report, gives a brief overview of the fund's investment activity, including expense ratios and portfolio turnover rates. Of interest here is the top part of the report (which runs from "Investment income" to "NAV at the end of the year"—lines 1 to 9); this part reveals the amount of dividend income and capital gains distributed to the shareholders, along with any change in the fund's net asset value.

dividend income
income derived from the dividend and interest income earned on the security holdings of a mutual fund.

Dividend income is derived from the dividend and interest income earned on the security holdings of the mutual fund. It's paid out of the *net investment income* that's left after all operating expenses have been met. When the fund

capital gains distributions
payments made to mutual fund shareholders that come from the profits that a fund makes from the sale of its securities.

receives dividend or interest payments, it passes these on to shareholders in the form of dividend payments. The fund accumulates all of the current income it has received for the period and then pays it out on a prorated basis. If a fund earned, say, $2 million in dividends and interest in a given year and if that fund had 1 million shares outstanding, each share would receive an annual dividend payment of $2. **Capital gains distributions** work on the same principle, except that these payments are derived from the capital gains earned by the fund. It works like this: Suppose the fund bought some stock a year ago for $50 and sold that stock in the current period for $75 per share. Clearly, the fund has achieved capital gains of $25 per share. If it held 50,000 shares of this stock, it would have realized a total capital gain of $1,250,000 ($25 × 50,000 = $1,250,000). Given that the fund has 1 million shares outstanding, each share is entitled to $1.25 in the form of a capital gains distribution. Note that this capital gains distribution applies only to *realized* capital gains—that is, the security holdings actually sold and the capital gains actually earned.

unrealized capital gains (paper profits)
a capital gain made only "on paper," that is, not realized until the fund's holdings are sold.

Unrealized **capital gains** (or **paper profits**) are what make up the third and final element of a mutual fund's return. When the fund's holdings go up or down in price, the net asset value of the fund moves accordingly. Suppose an investor buys into a fund at $10 per share and sometime later the fund is quoted at $12.50. The difference of $2.50 per share is the unrealized capital gains contained in the fund's security holdings. It represents the profit share-

Table 11.5 A Report of Mutual Fund Income and Capital Changes
(For a share outstanding throughout the year)

			1995	1994	1993
		Income and Expenses			
	1.	Investment income	$ .76	$ .88	$ .67
	2.	Less expenses	.16	.22	.17
	3.	Net investment income	$ .60	$ .66	$ .50
Dividend Income→	4.	Dividends from net investment income	(.55)	(.64)	(.50)
		Capital Changes			
	5.	Net realized and unrealized gains (or losses) on security transactions	6.37	(1.74)	3.79
Capital Gains Distribution→	6.	Distributions from realized gains	(1.75)	(.84)	(1.02)
Change in NAV→	7.	Net increase (decrease) in NAV*	$ 4.67	($ 2.56)	$ 2.77
	8.	NAV at beginning of year	24.47	27.03	24.26
	9.	NAV at end of year	$29.14	$24.47	$27.03
	10.	Ratio of operating expenses to average net assets	1.04%	.85%	.94%
	11.	Ratio of net investment income to average net assets	1.47%	2.56%	2.39%
	12.	Portfolio turnover rate**	85%	144%	74%
	13.	Shares outstanding at end of year (000s omitted)	10,568	6,268	4,029

*Net increase (decrease) in NAV, line 7 = line 3 − line 4 + line 5 − line 6. For example, the 1995 net increase in NAV was found as $.60 − .55 + 6.37 − 1.75 = $4.67

**Portfolio turnover rate relates the number of shares bought and sold by the fund to the total number of shares held in the fund's portfolio. A high turnover rate (e.g., in excess of 100 percent) would mean the fund has been doing a lot of trading.

gains), and—for closed-end funds—the change in premium or discount. Holding period returns and approximate yields recognize these elements and provide simple yet effective ways of measuring the annual rate of return from a mutual fund. Return is important to mutual fund investors, but so is risk. Although a fund's extensive diversification may protect investors from business and financial risks, considerable market risk still remains because most funds tend to perform much like the market, or at least that segment of the market in which they specialize.

DISCUSSION QUESTIONS

1. Contrast *mutual fund ownership* with the *direct investment in stocks and bonds.* Assume your class is going to debate the merits of investing through mutual funds versus investing directly in stocks and bonds. Develop some arguments, pro and con, on each side of this debate and be prepared to discuss them in class. If you had to choose one side to be on, which would it be? Why?

2. Using the mutual fund quotes in Figure 11.4, answer the questions listed below for each of the following 5 funds:
   (1) Fairmont Fund (Fairmt)
   (2) FPA Capital Fund (Capit)
   (3) Enterprise Tax-Exempt Income Fund (TE Inc)
   (4) Federated Fortress Utility Fund (UtilFd)
   (5) FBL High Yield Bond Fund (HiYlBd)

   a. How much would you have to pay to buy each of the funds?

   b. How much would you pay (in dollars and percentage) in front-end load charges with each of the funds?

   c. How much would you receive for each if you were selling the funds?

   d. Which of the five listed funds have 12(b)-1 fees?

   e. Which funds have redemption fees?

   f. Are any of the funds no-loads?

   g. Which fund has the highest year-to-date return? Which has the lowest?

   h. Which fund has the highest expense ratio? Which has the lowest?

3. For each pair of funds listed below, select the one that is likely to be the *least* risky. Briefly explain your answer.

   a. Growth versus growth-and-income funds

   b. Equity-income versus high-grade corporate bond funds

   c. Balanced versus sector funds

   d. Global versus aggressive growth funds

   e. Intermediate-term bonds versus high-yield municipal bond funds

4. Imagine that you've just inherited $20,000 from a rich relative. Now you're faced with the "problem" of how to spend it. You could make a down payment on a condo, or you could buy that sports car you've always wanted. Or, you could build a mutual fund portfolio. After some soul-searching, you decide to do the latter: build a $20,000 mutual fund portfolio. Using actual mutual funds and actual quoted prices, come up with a plan to invest as much of the $20,000 as you can in a portfolio of mutual funds. Be specific! Briefly describe your planned portfolio, including the investment objectives you are trying to achieve.

PROBLEMS

1. A year ago, an investor bought 200 shares of a mutual fund at $8.50 per share; over the past year, the fund has paid dividends of 90 cents per share and had a capital gains distribution of 75 cents per share.
   a. Find the investor's holding period return, given that this no-load fund now has a net asset value of $9.10.
   b. Find the holding period return assuming all the dividends and capital gains distributions are reinvested into additional shares of the fund at an average price of $8.75 per share.

2. A year ago, the Really Big Growth Fund was being quoted at a NAV of $21.50 and an offer price of $23.35; today, it's being quoted at $23.04 (NAV) and $25.04 (offer). What is the holding period return on this load fund, given that it was purchased a year ago and its dividends and capital gains distributions over the year have totaled $1.05 per share?

3. The All State Mutual Fund has the following five-year record of performance:

	1995	1994	1993	1992	1991
Net investment income	$ .98	$ .85	$ .84	$ .75	$ .64
Dividends from net investment income	(.95)	(.85)	(.85)	(.75)	(.60)
Net realized and unrealized gains (or losses) on security transactions	4.22	5.08	(2.18)	2.65	(1.05)
Distributions from realized gains	(1.05)	(1.00)	—	(1.00)	—
Net increase (decrease) in NAV	$ 3.20	$ 4.08	($ 2.19)	$ 1.65	($ 1.01)
NAV at beginning of year	12.53	8.45	10.64	.99	10.00
NAV at end of year	$15.73	$12.53	$ 8.45	$10.64	$ 8.99

Find this no-load fund's 5-year (1991–1995) average annual compound rate of return; also find its 3-year (1993–1995) average annual compound rate of return. If an investor bought the fund in 1991 at $10.00 a share and sold it 5 years later (in 1995) at $15.73, how much total profit per share would she have made over the 5-year holding period?

4. You've uncovered the following per-share information about a certain mutual fund:

	1993	1994	1995
Ending share prices:			
Offer	$46.20	$64.68	$61.78
NAV	43.20	60.47	57.75
Dividend income	2.10	2.84	2.61
Capital gains distribution	1.83	6.26	4.32
Beginning share prices:			
Offer	55.00	46.20	64.68
NAV	51.42	43.20	60.47

Based on this information, find the fund's holding period return for 1993, 1994, and 1995. (In all three cases, assume you buy the fund at the beginning of the year and sell it at the end each year.) In addition, find the fund's average annual compound rate of return over the 3-year period, 1993—1995. What would the 1994 holding period return have been if the investor had initially bought 500 shares of stock and reinvested both dividends and capital gains distributions into additional shares of the fund, at an average price of $52.50 per share?

 5. Listed below is the 10-year, per-share performance record of Larry, Moe, & Curly's Growth Fund, as obtained from the fund's May 30, 1995, prospectus:

	Years Ended March 31									
	1995	1994	1993	1992	1991	1990	1989	1988	1987	1986
1. Investment income	$ 1.98	$ 1.90	$ 1.64	$ 1.17	$ .81	$ .76	$ 1.11	$ .63	$ .44	$ .61
2. Expenses	.59	.55	.55	.54	.39	.27	.32	.26	.11	.23
3. Investment income—net	$ 1.39	$ 1.35	$ 1.09	$ .63	$ .42	$ .49	$ .79	$ .37	$ .33	$ .38
4. Dividends from investment income—net	(.83)	(1.24)	(.90)	(.72)	(.46)	(.65)	(.37)	(.26)	(.33)	(.58)
5. Realized and unrealized gain (loss) on investments—net	8.10	9.39	8.63	(6.64)	11.39	19.59	5.75	2.73	15.80	(.02)
6. Distributions from realized gain on investments—net	(2.42)	(3.82)	—	(9.02)	(6.84)	(1.78)	(3.69)	(1.88)	(1.23)	(9.92)
7. Net increase (decrease) in net asset value	$ 6.24	$ 5.68	$ 8.82	($15.75)	$ 4.51	$17.65	$ 2.48	$ .96	$14.57	($10.14)
Net asset value:										
8. Beginning of year	8.60	52.92	44.10	59.85	55.34	37.69	35.21	34.25	19.68	29.82
9. End of year	$64.84	$58.60	$52.92	$44.10	$59.85	$55.34	$37.69	$35.21	$34.25	$19.68

Use the information above to find LM&C's holding period return in 1995 and 1992. Also, find the fund's average annual rate of return over the 5-year period 1991–1995, and the 10-year period, 1986–1995. Finally, rework the four return figures assuming the LM&C fund has a front-end load charge of 3 percent (of NAV). Comment on the impact load charges have on the return behavior of mutual funds.

 6. Using the resources available at your campus or public library, select five mutual funds—a growth fund, an equity-income fund, an international (stock) fund, a sector fund, and a high-yield corporate bond fund—that you feel would make good investments. Briefly explain why you selected these funds. List the funds' holding period returns for the past year and their annual compound rates of return for the past 3 years. (Use a schedule like the one in Table 11.5 to show relevant performance figures.)

 7. One year ago, Super Star Closed-End Fund had a NAV of $10.40 and was selling at an 18 percent discount; today, its NAV is $11.69 and it's priced at a 4 percent premium. During the year, Super Star paid net dividend income of 40 cents and had a capital gains distribution of 95 cents. Based on the above information, calculate each of the following:
   a. Super Star's NAV-based holding period return for the year
   b. Super Star's market-based holding period return for the year. Did the market premium/discount hurt or add value to the investor's return? Explain.

c. Repeat the market-based holding period return calculation, except this time assume the fund started the year at an 18 percent *premium* and ended it at a 4 percent *discount*. (Assume the beginning and ending NAVs remain at $10.40 and $11.69, respectively.) Is there any change in this measure of return? Why?

CASE PROBLEMS   **11.1   REVEREND ROBIN PONDERS MUTUAL FUNDS**

Reverend Robin is the minister of a church in the San Antonio area. He is married, has one young child, and earns a "modest income." Since religious organizations are not notorious for their generous retirement programs, the reverend has decided he should do some investing on his own. He would like to set up a program that enables him to supplement the church's retirement program and at the same time provide some funds for his child's college education (which is still some 12 years away). He is not out to break any investment records, but feels he needs some backup in order to provide for the long-run needs of his family.

Although his income is meager, Reverend Robin feels that, with careful planning, he could probably invest about $250 a quarter (and, with luck, maybe increase this amount over time). He currently has about $15,000 in a passbook savings account that he would be willing to use to begin this program. In view of his investment objectives, he is not interested in taking a lot of risk. Because his knowledge of investments extends to savings accounts, Series EE savings bonds, and a little bit about mutual funds, he approaches you for some investment advice.

Questions

1. In light of Reverend Robin's long-term investment goals, do you think mutual funds are an appropriate investment vehicle for him?

2. Do you think he should use his $15,000 savings to start off a mutual fund investment program?

3. What type of mutual fund investment program would you set up for the reverend? Include in your answer some discussion of the types of funds you would consider, the investment objectives you would set, and any investment services (e.g., withdrawal plans) you would seek. Would taxes be an important consideration in your investment advice? Explain.

11.2 TOM LASNICKA SEEKS THE GOOD LIFE

Tom Lasnicka is a widower who recently retired after a long career with a major midwestern manufacturer. Beginning as a skilled craftsman, he worked his way up to the level of shop supervisor over a period of more than 30 years with the firm. Tom receives Social Security benefits and a generous company pension; together, these two sources amount to over $2,500 per month (part of which is tax-free). The Lasnickas had no children, so he lives alone. Tom owns a two-bedroom rental house that is next to his home, with the rental income from it covering the mortgage payments for both the rental and his house.

Over the years, Tom and his late wife, Camille, always tried to put a little money aside each month. The results have been nothing short of phenomenal, as the value of Tom's liquid investments (all held in bank CDs and passbook savings accounts) runs well into the six figures. Up to now, Tom has just let his money grow and has not used any of his savings to supplement his Social Security, pension, and rental income. But things are about to change. Tom has decided, "What the heck, it's time I start living the good life!" Tom wants to travel and, in effect, start reaping the benefits of his labors. He has therefore decided to move $100,000 from one of his savings accounts to one or two high-yielding mutual funds. He would like to receive $1,000 a month from the fund(s) for as long as possible, since he plans to be around for a long time.

Questions

1. Given Tom's financial resources and investment objectives, what kinds of mutual funds do you think he should consider?

2. Are there any factors in Tom's situation that should be taken into consideration in the fund selection process? If so, how might these affect Tom's course of action?

3. What types of services do you think he should look for in a mutual fund?

4. Assume Tom invests in a mutual fund that earns about 10 percent annually from dividend income and capital gains. Given that Tom wants to receive $1,000 a month from his mutual fund, what would be the size of his investment account 5 years from now? How large would the account be if the fund could earn 16 percent on average and everything else remains the same? How important is the fund's rate of return to Tom's investment situation? Explain.

CHAPTER 12

REAL ESTATE AND OTHER TANGIBLE INVESTMENTS

LEARNING GOALS

After studying this chapter, you should be able to:

LG 1 Describe how real estate investment objectives are set, how real estate features are analyzed, and what determines real estate value.

LG 2 Discuss the valuation techniques commonly used to estimate the market value of real estate.

LG 3 Understand the procedures involved in performing real estate investment analysis.

LG 4 Demonstrate the framework used to value a prospective real estate investment, and evaluate results in light of the stated investment objectives.

LG 5 Describe the structure and investment appeal of real estate investment trusts (REITs) and real estate limited partnerships (RELPs).

LG 6 Review the investment characteristics and suitability of investing in tangibles such as gold and other precious metals, gemstones, and collectibles.

I started investing as soon as I started working, by saving about $50 a week—not easy when I made only $300 before taxes!" notes Gene Polley. "But I'd been taught to 'save for a rainy day,' so it was a priority." He and his wife, Diane Strum, each manage their own investments but share an investment goal: to have the resources for a comfortable retirement, to travel, and to enjoy life without worrying about money.

Gene's portfolio is 75 percent investment real estate, 20 percent domestic stocks and mutual funds, and 5 percent international equities. The couple also owns a house that has appreciated nicely as well. "I believe in diversification, but I focus on real estate for its profit potential. Diane's portfolio is in stocks, mutual funds, and bonds, so our combined investments are pretty well diversified. When income rather than growth becomes important, I'll add bonds to my portfolio too," comments Gene. As a long-term investor, he doesn't worry about year-to-year performance: "Over time, I want to earn 10 percent or more annually, so that my capital doubles every seven years and I stay ahead of inflation. As I get older, I invest more conservatively and listen less to people with 'hot tips.'"

Gene and a partner own two apartment buildings, with a total of 62 units, in central San Diego County. "Income-producing real estate is best chosen dispassionately," Gene advises. "Buy a house because you love it, but buy investment real estate based on the numbers. I value property based on its growth potential from both the income stream and its intrinsic value—mostly appearance, but also how I can improve it." He uses net present value (NPV) calculations not just when acquiring property but also when determining whether a proposed improvement will increase cash flow from higher rents and thus boost return. Unless the numbers work out, he doesn't make the improvement.

Because Gene likes to maintain control of his real estate investments, he invests in property directly rather than through limited partnerships or real estate investment trusts (REITs). In Gene's opinion, "If somebody else controls the investment, they may sell when it's convenient for them, not for me, creating capital gains in a year when I don't want additional income." On the other hand, he acknowledges that most people don't want the hassles of actively managing a property, and for them, REITs work well—as long as they understand the nature of the investment. "Real estate is illiquid. It is also cyclical; like stocks, real estate values can increase as a result of market forces as well as specific property characteristics and performance. Periods of high growth are followed by periods

> **BUY A HOUSE BECAUSE YOU LOVE IT, BUT BUY INVESTMENT REAL ESTATE BASED ON THE NUMBERS.**

when real estate is out of favor. No matter what form your real estate investment takes, you should be in it for the long haul."

For Gene, the challenge of real estate investing is also its appeal. "It was tough during the recession, but we got through it. Now, the California economy is recovering and people are moving here again," he says. "There has been almost no new apartment construction in southern California for five years, and once the vacancy rate drops below 5 percent, owners can raise rents. This increases both profits and the building's value. We should start seeing dramatic returns in rental properties—and I'm certainly looking forward to that time!"

Before starting his own management consulting firm, Gene Polley was a marketing specialist for several software and aerospace firms. He and his wife, both 47, live in San Diego, California.

real estate
entities such as residential homes, raw land, and income property.

tangibles
investment assets, other than real estate, which can be seen or touched.

Wh at do warehouses, silver bars, and Pez containers have in common? They are all investment vehicles—yes, even the Pez containers—chosen by investors who want to put their money in something that can be seen and felt. Real estate and other tangible investments, such as gold, gemstones, and collectibles, offer attractive ways to diversify a portfolio. As noted in Chapter 1, **real estate** includes entities such as residential homes, raw land, and a variety of forms of income property, including warehouses, office and apartment buildings, condominiums, and cooperatives (co-ops). **Tangibles** are investment assets, other than real estate, which can be seen or touched. Ownership of real estate and tangibles differs from ownership of security investments in one primary way: It involves an asset you can see and touch rather than a security that evidences a financial claim. Particularly appealing are the favorable risk-return tradeoffs resulting from the uniqueness of real estate and other tangible assets and the relatively inefficient markets in which they are traded. In addition, certain types of real estate investments offer attractive tax benefits that may enhance their returns.

In this chapter we first consider the important aspects of real estate investment. In that discussion we provide an analytical framework intended to do two things: (1) help you decide what price to pay for a property and (2) guide you through the many operating decisions you will need to make if you choose to own real estate. Like Gene Polley, you can maximize real estate returns only when you consider both types of decisions. The chapter concludes with a brief look at some of the other popular forms of tangible investments.

INVESTING IN REAL ESTATE

In addition to the fact that real estate is a tangible asset, it differs from security investments in yet another way: Managerial decisions about real estate greatly affect the returns earned from investing in it. In real estate, you must answer questions such as, What rents should be charged? How much should be spent on maintenance and repairs? What media should be selected to advertise the availability of the real estate for rent or for sale? What purchase, lease, or sales contract provisions should be used to transfer certain rights to the property? Along with market forces, it is the answers to such questions that determine whether or not you will earn the desired return on a real estate investment.

Like other investment markets, the real estate market changes over time. For example, the national real estate market was generally strong through the 1970s and 1980s, but beginning in 1989, it began to collapse and remained weak through the early 1990s. The strong market during the 1970–1989 period was driven by generally prosperous economic times with high income growth. Market strength was also supported by the demand of large numbers of foreign investors, particularly from Japan and Europe, for U.S. commercial and residential real estate. The collapse of the real estate market resulted from a variety of factors, including tax-law changes that eliminated important tax benefits for investments in real estate, the collapse of oil prices, a slowing economy, the S&L crisis, and an excessive inventory of commercial real estate. Not only do real estate markets change over time; they also differ from region to region. Regional economic differences can result in significantly different real estate markets. For example, the national collapse of the real estate market in the late 1980s hit particularly hard the "oil patch" in Texas,

Oklahoma, Louisiana, and Colorado, most of New England, and California. Today real estate values in some areas of the country, such as the Midwest and Southeast, are currently appreciating, while values in other areas, such as New England and California, are recovering slowly due to the existence of large inventories of distressed, unoccupied, and unsold properties. For today's real estate investors, the lessons are clear: Macro issues such as the economic outlook, the demand for new space, the current supply of space, and regional considerations are of major importance.

As recent history demonstrates, investing in real estate means more than just "buying right" or "selling right." It also means choosing the right properties for your investment needs and managing them right. Here we begin by considering investor objectives, analysis of important features, and determinants of real estate value.

INVESTOR OBJECTIVES

Setting objectives involves two steps. First, you should consider differences in the investment characteristics of real estate. Second, you should establish investment constraints and goals.

Investment Characteristics

Individual real estate investments differ in their characteristics even more than individual people differ in theirs. So, just as you wouldn't marry without thinking long and hard about the type of person you'd be happy with, you shouldn't select an investment property without some feeling for whether or not it is the right one for you. To select wisely, you need to consider the available types of properties and whether you want an equity or a debt position.

In this chapter we discuss real estate investment primarily from the standpoint of equity. Individuals can also invest in instruments of real estate debt, such as mortgages and deeds of trust. Usually, these instruments provide a fairly safe rate of return if the borrowers are required to maintain at least a 20 percent equity position in the mortgaged property (no more than an 80 percent loan-to-value ratio). This owner equity position gives the real estate lender a margin of safety should foreclosure have to be initiated.

income property
leased-out residential or commercial real estate that is expected to provide returns primarily from periodic rental income.

speculative property
raw land and real estate investment properties that are expected to provide returns primarily from appreciation in value.

We can classify real estate into two investment categories: income properties and speculative properties. **Income property** includes residential and commercial properties that are leased out and expected to provide returns primarily from periodic rental income. *Residential properties* include single-family properties (houses, condominiums, cooperatives, and townhouses) and multifamily properties (apartment complexes and buildings). *Commercial properties* include office buildings, shopping centers, warehouses, and factories. **Speculative property** typically includes raw land and investment properties that are expected to provide returns primarily from appreciation in value due to location, scarcity, and so forth, rather than from periodic rental income.

Income properties are subject to a number of sources of risk and return. Losses can result from tenant carelessness, excessive supply of competing rental units, or poor management. On the profit side, however, income properties can provide increasing rental incomes, appreciation in the value of the property, and possibly even some shelter from taxes.

Speculative properties, as the name implies, give their owners a chance to make a financial killing but also the chance for heavy loss due to high uncertainty. For instance, rumors may start that a new multimillion-dollar plant is going to be built on the edge of town. Land buyers would jump into the market, and prices soon would be bid up. The right buy-sell timing could yield returns of several hundred percent or more. But people who bought into the market late or those who failed to sell before the market turned might lose the major part of their investment. Before investing in real estate, you should determine the risks various types of properties present and then decide which risks you will accept and can afford.

Constraints and Goals

When setting your real estate investment objectives, in addition to considering investment characteristics, you need to set both financial and nonfinancial constraints and goals. One financial constraint is the risk-return relationship you find acceptable. In addition, you must consider how much money you want to allocate to the real estate portion of your portfolio. Furthermore, you should define a quantifiable financial objective. Often this financial goal is stated in terms of *discounted cash flow* (also referred to as *net present value*) or approximate yield. Later in this chapter we will show how various constraints and goals can be applied to real estate investing.

Although you probably will want to invest in real estate for its financial rewards, you also need to consider how your technical skills, temperament, repair skills, and managerial talents fit a potential investment. Do you want a prestigious, trouble-free property? Or would you prefer a fix-up special on which you can release your imagination and workmanship? Would you enjoy living in the same building as your tenants, or would you prefer as little contact with them as possible? Just as you wouldn't choose a career solely on the basis of money, neither should you buy a property just for the money.

ANALYSIS OF IMPORTANT FEATURES

The analytical framework suggested in this chapter can guide you in estimating a property's investment potential. Yet first you must consider four general features relating to real estate investment:

1. *Physical property*. When buying real estate, make sure you are getting both the quantity and the quality of property you think you are. Problems can arise if you fail to obtain a site survey, an accurate square-footage measurement of the buildings, or an inspection for building or site defects. When signing a contract to buy a property, make sure it accurately identifies the real estate and lists all items of personal property (e.g., refrigerator and curtains) you expect to receive.

2. *Property rights*. Strange as it may seem, when buying real estate, what you buy is a bundle of legal rights that fall under concepts in law such as deeds, titles, easements, liens, and encumbrances. When investing in real estate, make sure that along with various physical inspections, you also get a legal inspection from a qualified attorney. Real estate sale and lease agreements should not be the work of amateurs.

3. *Time horizon*. Like a roller coaster, real estate prices go up and down. Sometimes market forces pull them up slowly but surely; in other periods, prices can fall so fast that they take an investor's breath away. Before judging whether a prospective real estate investment will appreciate or depreciate, you must decide what time period is relevant. The short-term investor might count on a quick drop in mortgage interest rates and buoyant market expectations, whereas the long-term investor might look more closely at population growth potential.

4. *Geographic area*. Real estate is a spatial commodity, which means that its value is directly linked to what is going on around it. With some properties, the area of greatest concern consists of a few square blocks; in other instances, an area of hundreds or even thousands of miles serves as the relevant market area. As a result, you must decide what spatial boundaries are important for your investment before you can productively analyze real estate demand and supply.

DETERMINANTS OF VALUE

When analyzing real estate investment, value generally serves as the central concept. Will a property increase in value? Will it produce increasing amounts of cash flows? To address these questions, you need to evaluate the four major determinants of real estate value: demand, supply, the property, and the property transfer process.

Demand

demand
in real estate, people's willingness to buy or rent a given property.

In valuing real estate, **demand** refers to people's willingness to buy or rent a given property. In part, demand stems from a market area's economic base. In most real estate markets, the source of buying power comes from jobs. Property values follow an upward path when employment is increasing, and values typically fall when employers begin to lay off personnel. Therefore, the first questions you should ask about demand are, What is the outlook for jobs in the relevant market area? Are schools, colleges, and universities gaining enrollment? Are major companies planning expansion? Are wholesalers, retailers, and financial institutions increasing their sales and services? Upward trends in these indicators often signal a rising demand for real estate.

demographics
measurable characteristics of an area's population, such as household size, age structure, occupation, gender, and marital status.

psychographics
characteristics that describe people's mental dispositions, such as personality, lifestyle, and self-concept.

Population characteristics also influence demand. To analyze demand for a specific property, you should look at an area's population demographics and psychographics. **Demographics** refers to measurable characteristics, such as household size, age structure, occupation, gender, and marital status. **Psychographics** pertains to those characteristics that describe people's mental dispositions, such as personality, lifestyle, and self-concept. By comparing demographic and psychographic trends to the features of a property, you can judge whether it is likely to gain or lose favor among potential buyers or tenants. For example, if an area's population is made up of a large number of sports-minded, highly social 25- to 35-year-old singles, the presence of nearby or on-site health club facilities may be important to a property's success.

Mortgage financing is also a key factor. Tight money can choke off the demand for real estate. As investors saw in the early 1980s, rising interest rates and the relative unavailability of mortgages caused inventories of unsold properties to grow and real estate prices to fall. Conversely, as mortgage interest rates fell, beginning in late 1982 and early 1983 and continuing through 1988, real estate sales and refinancing activity in many cities throughout the United States rapidly expanded. Although interest rates rose slightly in 1989 and 1990, their steady decline from 1991 through 1995 failed to stimulate real estate activity due to generally poor economic conditions, a lack of attractive tax incentives, and, most importantly, the low expected returns caused by a large surplus of investment properties. The rise in mortgage interest rates in early 1994 tended to dampen what at that time appeared to be the beginning of a modest recovery in real estate activity and values.

Supply

supply
in real estate, the potential competitors available in the market.

Analyzing **supply** really means sizing up the competition. Nobody wants to pay you more for a property than the price he or she can pay your competitor; nor when you're buying (or renting) should you pay more than the prices asked for other similar properties. As a result, an integral part of value analysis requires that you identify sources of potential competition and then inventory them by price and features. In general, people in real estate think of competitors in terms of similar properties. If you are trying to sell a house, then it seems natural to see your competition as other similar houses for sale in the same neighborhood.

principle of substitution
the principle that people do not really buy or rent real estate per se but, instead, judge properties as different sets of benefits and costs.

For longer-term investment decisions, however, you should expand your concept of supply. That is, you should identify competitors through the **principle of substitution**. This principle holds that people do not really buy or rent real estate per se. Instead, they judge properties as different sets of benefits and costs. Properties fill people's needs, and it is really these needs that create demand. Thus, an analysis of supply should not limit potential competitors to geographically and physically similar properties. In some markets, for example, low-priced single-family houses might compete with condominium units, manufactured homes ("mobile homes"), and even rental apartments. Before investing in any property, you should decide what market that property appeals to and then define its competitors as other properties that its buyers or tenants might also typically choose from.

After identifying all relevant competitors, you should inventory these properties in terms of features and respective prices. In other words, look for the relative pros and cons of each property. Many large real estate investors hire professional market consultants to do the research that the analysis of demand and supply requires.

The Property

We've seen that a property's value is influenced by demand and supply. The price people will pay is governed by their needs and the relative prices of the properties available to meet those needs. Yet in real estate, the property itself is also a key ingredient. To try to develop a property's competitive edge, an investor should consider five items: (1) restrictions on use, (2) location, (3) site, (4) improvements, and (5) property management.

Restrictions on Use   In today's highly regulated society, both state and local laws and private contracts limit the rights of all property owners. Government restrictions derive from zoning laws, building and occupancy codes, and health and sanitation requirements. Private restrictions include deeds, leases, and condominium bylaws and operating rules. Because of all these restrictions, you should not invest in a property until you or your lawyer determines that what you want to do with the property *fits within* applicable laws, rules, and contract provisions.

Location   You may have heard the adage "The three most important factors in real estate value are location, location, and location." Of course, location is not the only factor that affects value, yet a good location unquestionably increases a property's investment potential. With that said, how can you tell a bad location from a good one? A good location rates highly on two key dimensions: convenience and environment.

convenience
in real estate, the accessibility of a property to the places the people in a target market frequently need to go.

Convenience refers to how accessible a property is to the places the people in a target market frequently need to go. Any selected residential or commercial market segment will have a set of preferred places its tenants or buyers will want to be close to. Another element of convenience is transportation facilities. Proximity to highways, buses, taxis, subways, and commuter trains is of concern to both tenants and buyers of commercial and residential property. Commercial properties need to be readily accessible to their customers and vice versa.

environment
in real estate, the natural as well as aesthetic, socioeconomic, legal, and fiscal surroundings of a property.

In the analysis of real estate, the term **environment** has broader meaning than trees, rivers, lakes, and air quality. When you invest in real estate, even more important than its natural surroundings are its aesthetic, socioeconomic, legal, and fiscal surroundings. Neighborhoods with an *aesthetic environment* are those where buildings and landscaping are well executed and well maintained. There is no intrusion of noise, sight, or air pollution, and encroaching unharmonious land uses are not evident. The *socioeconomic environment* refers to the demographics and lifestyles of the people who live or work in nearby properties. The *legal environment* relates to the restrictions on use that apply to nearby properties. And last, you need to consider a property's *fiscal environment*: the amount of property taxes and municipal assessments you will be required to pay and the government services you will be entitled to receive (police, fire, schools, parks, water, sewer, trash collection, libraries). Property taxes are a two-sided coin. On the one side, they pose a cost, but on the other, they give a property's users the right to services that may be of substantial benefit.

Site   One of the most important features of a property site is its size. For residential properties, such as houses, condominiums, and apartments, some people want a large yard for a garden or for children to play in; others may prefer virtually no yard at all. For commercial properties, such as office buildings and shopping centers, adequate parking space is necessary. Also, with respect to site size, if you are planning a later addition of space, make sure the site is large enough to accommodate it, both physically and legally. Site quality such as soil fertility, topography, elevation, and drainage capacity is also important. For example, sites with relatively low elevation may be subject to flooding.

improvements
in real estate, the additions to a site, such as buildings, sidewalks, and various on-site amenities.

Improvements   In real estate, the term **improvements** refers to the additions to a site, such as buildings, sidewalks, and various on-site amenities. Typically, building size is measured and expressed in terms of square footage. Because square footage is so important in building and unit comparison, you should get accurate square-footage measures on any properties you consider investing in.

Another measure of building size is room count and floor plan. For example, a well-designed 750-square-foot apartment unit might in fact be more livable and therefore easier to rent and at a higher price than a poorly designed one of 850 square feet. You should make sure that floor plans are logical; that traffic flows through a building will pose no inconveniences; that there is sufficient closet, cabinet, and other storage space; and that the right mix of rooms exists. For example, in an office building you should not have to cross through other offices to get to the building's only restroom facilities; small merchants in a shopping center should not be placed in locations where they do not receive the pedestrian traffic generated by the larger (anchor) tenants.

Attention should also be given to amenities, style, and construction quality. Amenities such as air conditioning, swimming pools, and elevators can significantly affect the value of investment property. In addition, the architectural style and quality of construction materials and workmanship are important factors influencing property value.

Property Management   In recent years, real estate owners and investors have increasingly recognized that investment properties (apartments, office buildings, shopping centers, etc.) do not earn maximum cash flows by themselves. They need to be guided toward that objective, and skilled property management can help. Without effective property management, no real estate investment can produce maximum benefits for its users and owners.

Today, property management requires you or a hired manager to run the entire operation as well as to perform day-to-day chores. The property manager will segment buyers, improve a property's site and structure, keep tabs on competitors, and develop a marketing campaign. The property manager also assumes responsibility for the maintenance and repair of buildings and their physical systems (electrical, heating, air conditioning, and plumbing) and for the keeping of revenue and expense records. In addition, property managers decide the best ways to protect properties against loss from perils such as fire, flood, theft, storms, and negligence. In its broadest sense, **property management** means finding the optimal level of benefits for a property and providing them at the lowest costs. Of course, for speculative investments such as raw land, the managerial task is not so pronounced and the manager has less control over the profit picture.

property management
in real estate, finding the optimal level of benefits for a property and providing them at the lowest costs.

Property Transfer Process

In Chapter 7 we introduced the concept of efficient markets, in which information flows so quickly among buyers and sellers that it is virtually impossible for an investor to outperform the average systematically. As soon as something good (an exciting new product) or something bad (a multimillion-dollar product liability suit) occurs, the price of the affected company's stock adjusts to reflect its current potential for earnings or losses. Some people accept the premise that securities markets are efficient, while others do not. But one thing is sure: *No one believes real estate markets are efficient*. What this means is that real estate market research pays off. Skillfully conducted analysis can help you beat the averages.

The reason real estate markets differ from securities markets is that no good system exists for complete information exchange among buyers and sellers and among tenants and lessors. There is no central marketplace, like the NYSE, where transactions are conveniently made by equally well-informed investors who share similar objectives. Instead, real estate is traded in generally *illiquid markets* that are regional or local in nature and where transactions are made to achieve investors' often unique investment objectives.

property transfer process
the process of promotion and negotiation of real estate, which can significantly influence the cash flows a property will earn.

In the **property transfer process** itself, the inefficiency of the market means that how you collect and disseminate information will affect your results. The cash flows a property will earn can be influenced significantly through promotion and negotiation. *Promotion* refers to the task of getting information about a property to its buyer segment. You can't sell or rent a property quickly and for top dollar unless you can reach the people you want to reach in a cost-effective way. Among the major ways to promote a property are advertising, publicity, sales gimmicks, and personal selling. *Negotiation* of price is just as important. Seldom does the minimum price a seller is willing to accept just equal the maximum price a buyer is willing to pay; often some overlap occurs. In real estate, the asking price for a property may be anywhere from 5 to 60 percent *above* the price that a seller (or lessor) will accept. Therefore, the negotiating skills of each party determine the final transaction price.

CONCEPTS *in Review*

12.1 Define and differentiate between *real estate* and *tangibles.* Give examples of each of these forms of investment.

12.2 How does real estate investment differ from securities investment? Why might adding real estate to your investment portfolio decrease your overall risk? Explain.

12.3 Describe the two steps involved in setting objectives in real estate investing. Define and differentiate between *income property* and *speculative property.* Differentiate between and give examples of residential and commercial income properties.

12.4 Briefly describe the following important features to consider when making a real estate investment:
   a. Physical property
   b. Property rights
   c. Time horizon
   d. Geographic area

12.5 What role do demand and supply play in determining the value of real estate? What are *demographics* and *psychographics,* and how do they relate to demand? How does the *principle of substitution* affect the analysis of supply?

12.6 How do restrictions on use, location, site, improvements, and property management each affect a property's competitive edge?

12.7 Are real estate markets *efficient?* Why or why not? How does the efficiency or inefficiency of these markets affect both promotion and negotiation as parts of the property transfer process?

REAL ESTATE VALUATION

market value
in real estate, the actual worth of a property; indicates the price at which it would sell under current market conditions.

In real estate, **market value** is a property's actual worth, which indicates the price at which it would sell under current market conditions. This concept is interpreted differently from its meaning in stocks and bonds. This difference arises for a number of reasons: (1) Each property is unique; (2) terms and conditions of sale may vary widely; (3) market information is imperfect; (4) properties may need substantial time for market exposure, time that may not be available to any given seller; and (5) buyers too sometimes need to act quickly. All these factors mean that no one can tell for sure what a property's "true" market value is. As a result, many properties sell for prices significantly above or below their estimated market values. To offset such inequities, many real estate investors forecast investment returns to evaluate potential property investments. Here we first look at procedures for estimating the market value of a piece of real estate and then consider the role and procedures used to perform investment analysis.

ESTIMATING MARKET VALUE

appraisal
in real estate, the process for estimating the current market value of a piece of property.

In real estate, estimating the current market value of a piece of property is done through a process known as a real estate **appraisal**. Using certain techniques, an appraiser will set the value on a piece of property that he or she feels represents the current market value of the property. Even so, if you are told that a property has an appraised market value of, say, $150,000, you should interpret that value a little skeptically. Because of both technical and informational shortcomings, this estimate can be subject to substantial error.

Although you can arrive at the market values of frequently traded stocks simply by looking at current quotes, in real estate, appraisers and investors typically must use three complex techniques and then correlate results to come up with one best estimate. These three imperfect approaches to real estate market value are (1) the cost approach, (2) the comparative sales approach, and (3) the income approach.

The Cost Approach

cost approach
a real estate valuation approach based on the idea that an investor should not pay more for a property than it would cost to rebuild it at today's prices.

The **cost approach** is based on the idea that an investor should not pay more for a property than it would cost to rebuild it at today's prices for land, labor, and construction materials. This approach to estimating value generally works well for new or relatively new buildings. The cost approach is more difficult to apply to older properties, however. To value these older properties, you would have to subtract from the replacement cost estimates some amount for physical and functional depreciation. Most experts agree that the cost approach is a good method to use as a check against a price estimate, but rarely should it be used exclusively.

The Comparative Sales Approach

comparative sales approach
a real estate valuation approach that uses as the basic input the sales prices of properties that are similar to the subject property.

The **comparative sales approach** uses as the basic input the sales prices of properties that are similar to the subject property. This method is based on the idea that the value of a given property is about the same as the prices for which other similar properties have recently sold. Of course, the catch here is that all properties are unique in some respect. Therefore, the price that a subject property could be expected to bring must be adjusted upward or downward to reflect its superiority or inferiority to comparable properties. Nevertheless, because the comparable sales approach is based on *selling* prices, not asking prices, it can give you a good feel for the market. As a practical matter, if you can find at least one sold property slightly better than the one you're looking at, and one slightly worse, their recent sales prices can serve to bracket an estimated market value for a subject property.

The Income Approach

income approach
a real estate valuation approach that calculates a property's value as the present value of all its future income.

Under the **income approach,** a property's value is viewed as the present value of all its future income. The most popular income approach is called *direct capitalization*. This approach is represented by the formula in Equation 12.1. It is similar in logic and form to the zero growth dividend valuation model presented in Chapter 7 for common stock (see Equation 7.7 on page 287).

Equation 12.1

$$\text{Market value} = \frac{\text{annual net operating income}}{\text{market capitalization rate}}$$

Equation 12.1a

$$V = \frac{\text{NOI}}{R}$$

net operating income (NOI)
the amount left after subtracting vacancy and collection losses and property operating expenses from an income property's *gross potential* rental income.

market capitalization rate
the rate used to convert an income stream to a present value; used to estimate the value of real estate under the *income approach.*

Annual **net operating income (NOI)** is calculated by subtracting vacancy and collection losses and property operating expenses, including property insurance and property taxes, from an income property's *gross potential* rental income. An estimated **market capitalization rate** is obtained by looking at recent market sales figures to determine the rate of return currently required by investors. Technically, the market capitalization rate means the rate used to convert an income stream to a present value. By dividing the annual net operating income by the appropriate market capitalization rate, you get an income property's estimated market value. An example of the application of the income approach is given in Table 12.1.

Table 12.1   Applying the Income Approach

Comparable Property	(1) NOI	(2) Sale Price	(3) (1) ÷ (2) Market Capitalization Rate (*R*)
2301 Maple Avenue	$16,250	$182,500	.0890
4037 Armstrong Street	15,400	167,600	.0919
8240 Ludwell Street	19,200	198,430	.0968
7392 Grant Boulevard	17,930	189,750	.0945
Subject property	$18,480	?	?

From this market-derived information, an appraiser would work through Equation 12.1a, to determine the subject property's value as follows:

$$V = \frac{\text{NOI}}{R}$$

$$V = \frac{\$18,480}{R}$$

$$V = \frac{\$18,480}{.093*}$$

$$V = \$198,710$$

*Based on an analysis of the relative similarities of the comparables and the subject property, the appraiser decided the appropriate *R* equals .093.

Using an Expert

Real estate valuation is a complex and technical procedure. It requires reliable information about the features of comparable properties, their selling prices, and applicable terms of financing. It also involves some subjective judgments, as was the case in the example in Table 12.1. As a result, rather than relying exclusively on their own judgment, many investors hire a real estate agent or a professional real estate appraiser to advise them about the market value of a property. As a form of insurance against overpaying, the use of an expert can be well worth the cost.

PERFORMING INVESTMENT ANALYSIS

investment analysis
approach to real estate valuation that not only considers what similar properties have sold for but also looks at the underlying determinants of value.

Estimates of market value play an integral role in real estate decision making. Yet today, more and more investors supplement their market value appraisals with **investment analysis**. This form of real estate valuation not only considers what similar properties have sold for but also looks at the underlying determinants of value. It is an extension of the traditional valuation approaches (cost, comparative sales, and income) that gives investors a better picture of whether a selected property is likely to satisfy their investment objectives.

Market Value Versus Investment Analysis

The concept of market value differs from investment analysis in four important ways: (1) retrospective versus prospective, (2) impersonal versus personal, (3) unleveraged versus leveraged, and (4) net operating income (NOI) versus after-tax cash flows.

Retrospective Versus Prospective Market value appraisals look backward; they attempt to estimate the price a property will sell for by looking at the sales prices of similar properties in the recent past. Under static market conditions, such a technique can be reasonable. But if, say, interest rates, population, or buyer expectations are changing rapidly, past sales prices may not accurately indicate the current value or the future value of a subject property. An investment analysis tries to forecast and incorporate in the valuation process such factors as economic base, population demographics and psychographics, availability and cost of mortgage financing, and potential sources of competition.

Impersonal Versus Personal A market value estimate represents the price a property will sell for under certain specified conditions—in other words, a sort of market average. But in fact, each buyer and seller has a unique set of needs, and each real estate transaction can be structured to meet those needs. So an investment analysis looks beyond what may constitute a "typical" transaction and attempts to evaluate a subject property's terms and conditions of sale (or rent) as they correspond to a given investor's constraints and goals.

For example, a market value appraisal might show that with normal financing and conditions of sale, a property is worth $180,000. Yet because of personal tax consequences, it might be better for a seller to ask a higher price for the property and offer owner financing at a below-market interest rate.

leverage
in real estate, the use of debt financing to purchase a piece of property and thereby affect its risk-return parameters.

positive leverage
a position in which, if a property's return is in excess of its debt cost, the investor's return will be increased to a level well above what could have been earned from an all-cash deal.

negative leverage
a position in which, if a property's return is below its debt cost, the investor's return will be less than from an all-cash deal.

Unleveraged Versus Leveraged   The returns a real estate investment offers will be influenced by the amount of the purchase price that is financed with debt. But simple income capitalization $[V = (NOI/R)]$ does not incorporate alternative financing plans that might be available. It assumes either a cash or an unleveraged purchase.

The use of debt financing, or **leverage,** gives differing risk-return parameters to a real estate investment. Leverage automatically increases investment risk because borrowed funds must be repaid. Failure to repay a mortgage loan results in foreclosure and possible property loss. Alternatively, leverage may also increase return. If a property can earn a return in excess of the cost of the borrowed funds (i.e., debt cost), the investor's return will be increased to a level well above what could have been earned from an all-cash deal. This is known as **positive leverage.** Conversely, if the return is below the debt cost, the return on invested equity will be less than from an all-cash deal. This is called **negative leverage.** The following example shows how leverage affects return and provides insight into the possible associated risks.

Assume an investor purchases a parcel of land for $20,000. The investor has two financing choices: Choice A is all cash; that is, no leverage is employed. Choice B involves 80 percent financing (20 percent down payment) at 12 percent interest. With leverage (choice B), the investor signs a $16,000 note (.80 × $20,000) at 12 percent interest, with the entire principal balance due and payable at the end of one year. Now suppose the land appreciates during the year to $30,000. (A comparative analysis of this occurrence is presented in Table 12.2.) Had the investor chosen the all-cash deal, the one-year return on the investor's initial equity would have been 50 percent. The use of leverage magnifies that return, no matter how much the property appreciated. The leveraged alternative (choice B) involved only a $4,000 investment in personal initial equity, with the balance financed by borrowing at 12 percent interest. The property sells for $30,000, of which $4,000 represents the recovery of the initial equity investment, $16,000 goes to repay the principal balance on the debt, and another $1,920 of gain is used to pay interest ($16,000 × .12). The balance of the proceeds, $8,080, represents the

Table 12.2   The Effect of Positive Leverage on Return: An Example*

Purchase price: $20,000
Sale price: $30,000
Holding period: One year

Item Number	Item	Choice A No Leverage	Choice B 80% Financing
1	Initial equity	$20,000	$ 4,000
2	Loan principal	0	16,000
3	Sale price	30,000	30,000
4	Capital gain [(3) − (1) − (2)]	10,000	10,000
5	Interest cost [.12 × (2)]	0	1,920
6	Net return [(4) − (5)]	10,000	8,080
	Return on investor's equity [(6) ÷ (1)]	$\frac{\$10,000}{\$20,000} = +50\%$	$\frac{\$8,080}{\$4,000} = +202\%$

*To simplify this example, all values are presented on a *before-tax* basis. To get the true return, taxes on the capital gain and the interest expense would be considered.

investor's return. The return on the investor's initial equity is 202 percent—over four times that provided by the no-leverage alternative, choice A.

We used 12 percent in the above example, but it is important to understand that the cost of money has surprisingly little effect on comparative (leveraged vs. unleveraged) returns. For example, using 6 percent interest, the return on investor's equity rises to 226 percent, still way above the unleveraged alternative. Granted, using a lower interest cost does improve return, but other things being equal, what really drives return on equity is the *amount* of leverage being used.

There is another side to the coin, however: No matter what the eventual outcome, risk is *always* inherent in leverage; it can easily turn a bad deal into a disaster. Suppose the $20,000 property discussed above dropped in value by 25 percent during the one-year holding period. The comparative results are presented in Table 12.3. The unleveraged investment would have resulted in a negative return of 25 percent. This is not large, however, compared to the leveraged position in which the investor loses not only the entire initial investment of $4,000 but an additional $2,920 ($1,000 additional principal on the debt + $1,920 interest). The total loss of $6,920 on the original $4,000 of equity results in a (negative) return of 173 percent. Thus the loss in the leverage case is nearly seven times the loss experienced in the unleveraged situation.

NOI Versus After-Tax Cash Flows   Recall that to estimate market value, the income approach capitalizes net operating income (NOI). To most investors, though, the NOI figure holds little meaning. The reason is that the majority of real estate investors finance their purchases. In addition, few investors today can ignore the effect of federal income tax law on their investment decisions. Investors want to know how much cash they will be required to put into a transaction and how much cash they are likely to get out. The concept of NOI does not address these questions. Thus, in investment analysis we instead use **after-tax cash flows (ATCFs)**, which are the annual cash flows earned on a real estate investment, net of all expenses, debt payments, and

after-tax cash flows (ATCFs)
the annual cash flows earned on a real estate investment, net of all expenses, debt payments, and taxes.

Table 12.3   The Effect of Negative Leverage on Return: An Example*

Purchase price:	$20,000		
Sale price:	$15,000		
Holding period:	One year		

Item Number	Item	Choice A No Leverage	Choice B 80% Financing
1	Initial equity	$20,000	$ 4,000
2	Loan principal	0	16,000
3	Sale price	15,000	15,000
4	Capital loss [(3) − (1) − (2)]	5,000	5,000
5	Interest cost [.12 × (2)]	0	1,920
6	Net loss [(4) − (5)]	5,000	6,920
	Return on investor's equity [(6) ÷ (1)]	$\dfrac{-\$\,5,000}{\$20,000} = -25\%$	$\dfrac{-\$6,920}{\$4,000} = -173\%$

*To simplify this example, all values are presented on a *before-tax* basis. To get the true return, taxes on the capital gain and the interest expense would be considered.

taxes. To them we apply the familiar finance measure of investment return—discounted cash flow—as a prime criterion for selecting real estate investments. (Sometimes approximate yield is used instead to assess the suitability of a prospective real estate investment.)

Calculating Discounted Cash Flow

discounted cash flow
use of present-value techniques to find *net present value (NPV)*.

Calculating **discounted cash flow** involves the techniques of present value as discussed in Chapter 4; in addition, you need to learn how to calculate annual after-tax cash flows and the after-tax net proceeds of sale. With this knowledge, you can discount the cash flows an investment is expected to earn over a specified holding period. This figure in turn gives you the present value of the cash flows. Next, you find the **net present value (NPV)**—the difference between the present value of the cash flows and the amount of equity required to make the investment. The resulting difference tells you whether the proposed investment looks good (a positive net present value) or bad (a negative net present value).

net present value (NPV)
the difference between the present value of the cash flows and the amount of equity required to make an investment.

This process of discounting cash flows to calculate the net present value (NPV) of an investment can be represented by the following equation:

Equation 12.2

$$NPV = \left[\frac{CF_1}{(1 + r)^1} + \frac{CF_2}{(1 + r)^2} + \cdots + \frac{CF_{n-1}}{(1 + r)^{n-1}} + \frac{CF_n + CF_{R_n}}{(1 + r)^n} \right] - I_0$$

where:

I_0 = the original required investment

CF_i = annual after-tax cash flow for year i

CF_{R_n} = the after-tax net proceeds from sale (reversionary after-tax cash flow) occurring in year n

r = the discount rate and $[1/(1 + r)^i]$ is the present-value interest factor for \$1 received in year i using an r percent discount rate.

In this equation, the annual after-tax cash flows, *CFs*, may be either inflows to investors or outflows from them. Inflows would be preceded by a plus (+) sign, and outflows by a minus (−) sign.

Calculating Approximate Yield

approximate yield
procedure for assessing investment suitability that recognizes the time value of money in its estimation of the rate of return (yield) on an investment.

An alternative way of assessing investment suitability would be to calculate the **approximate yield**, which was first presented as Equation 4.10 in Chapter 4. Restating the formula in terms of the variables defined above, we have:

Equation 12.3

$$\text{Approximate yield} = \frac{\overline{CF} + \dfrac{CF_{R_n} - I_0}{n}}{\dfrac{CF_{R_n} + I_0}{2}}$$

where

Equation 12.4

$$\overline{CF} = \begin{array}{c}\text{average annual}\\\text{after-tax}\\\text{cash flow}\end{array} = \frac{CF_1 + CF_2 + \cdots + CF_{n-1} + CF_n}{n}$$

If the calculated approximate yield is greater than the discount rate appropriate for the given investment, the investment would be acceptable. In that case, the net present value would be positive.

When consistently applied, the net present value and approximate yield approaches will always give the same recommendation for accepting or rejecting a proposed real estate investment. In the next section we'll show how all of the elements discussed so far in this chapter can be applied to a real estate investment decision.

CONCEPTS *in Review*

12.8 What is the *market value* of a property? What is real estate *appraisal?* Comment on the following statement: "Market value is always the price at which a property sells."

12.9 Briefly describe each of the following approaches to real estate market value:
     a. Cost approach
     b. Comparative sales approach
     c. Income approach

12.10 What is real estate *investment analysis?* How does it differ from the concept of market value?

12.11 What is *leverage,* and what role does it play in real estate investment? How does it affect the risk-return parameters of a real estate investment?

12.12 What is *net operating income (NOI)?* What are *after-tax cash flows (ATCFs)?* Why do real estate investors prefer to use ATCFs?

12.13 What is the *net present value (NPV)?* What is the *approximate yield?* How are the NPV and approximate yield used to make real estate investment decisions?

AN EXAMPLE OF REAL ESTATE VALUATION

Assume that Jack Wilson is deciding whether to buy the Academic Arms Apartments. To improve his real estate investment decision making, Jack follows a systematic procedure. He designs a schematic framework of analysis that corresponds closely to the topics we've discussed. Following this framework (Figure 12.1), Jack (1) sets out his investment objectives, (2) analyzes important features of the property, (3) investigates the determinants of the property's value, (4) performs an investment analysis, and (5) synthesizes and interprets the results of his analysis.

INVESTOR OBJECTIVES

Jack is a tenured associate professor of management at Finley College. He's single, age 40, and earns an income of $80,000 per year from salary, consulting fees, stock dividends, and book royalties. His applicable tax rate on ordinary income is 31 percent. Jack wants to further diversify his investment

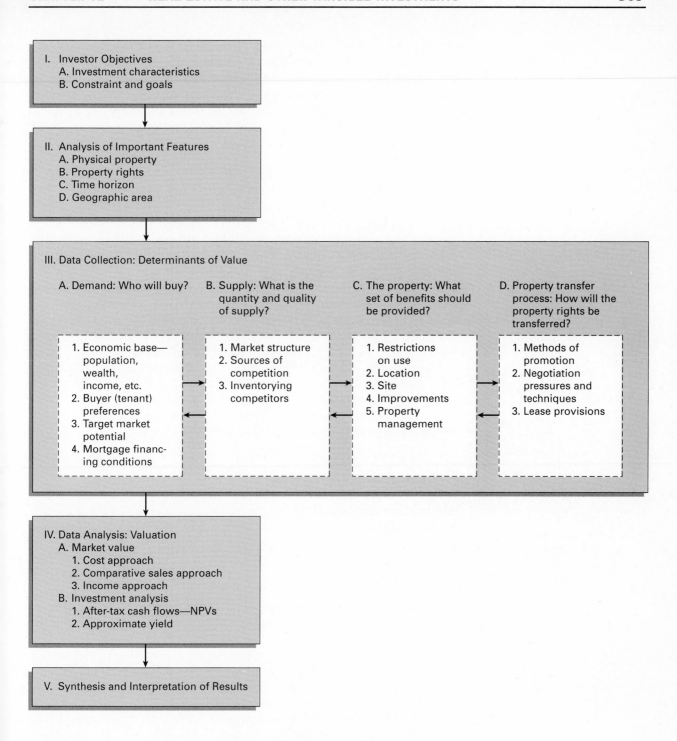

Figure 12.1   Framework for Real Estate Investment Analysis
This framework depicts a logical approach for analyzing potential investment
properties to assess whether or not they are acceptable investments that might
be included in one's investment portfolio. (Source: Adapted from Gary W. Elred,
Real Estate: Analysis and Strategy, New York: Harper & Row, 1987, p. 18.)

portfolio. He would like to add a real estate investment that has good appreciation potential and also provides a positive yearly after-tax cash flow. For convenience, Jack requires the property to be close to his office, and he feels his talents and personality suit him for ownership of apartments. Jack has $60,000 of cash to invest. On this amount, he would like to earn a 13 percent rate of return. Jack has his eye on a small apartment building, the Academic Arms Apartments.

ANALYSIS OF IMPORTANT FEATURES

The Academic Arms building is located six blocks from the Finley College Student Union. The building contains eight 2-bedroom, 2-bath units of 1,100 square feet each. It was built in 1980, and all systems and building components appear to be in good condition. The present owner gave Jack an income statement reflecting the property's 1995 income and expenses. The owner has further assured Jack that no adverse easements or encumbrances affect the building's title. Of course, if Jack decides to buy Academic Arms, he would have a lawyer verify the quality of the property rights associated with the property. For now, though, he accepts the owner's word.

Jack considers a 5-year holding period reasonable. At present, he's happy at Finley and thinks he will stay there at least until age 45. Jack defines the market for the property as a one-mile radius from campus. He reasons that students who walk to campus (the target market) would limit their choice of apartments to those that fall within that geographic area.

DETERMINANTS OF VALUE

Once Jack has analyzed the important features, he next thinks about the factors that will determine the property's investment potential: (1) demand, (2) supply, (3) the property, and (4) the property transfer process.

Demand

Finley College is the lifeblood institution in the market area. The base of demand for the Academic Arms Apartments will grow (or decline) with the size of the college's employment and student enrollment. On this basis, Jack judges the prospects for the area to be in the range of good to excellent. During the coming 5 years, major funding (due to a $25 million gift) will increase Finley's faculty by 15 percent, and expected along with faculty growth is a rise in the student population from 3,200 to 3,700 full-time students. Jack estimates that 70 percent of the *new* students will live away from home. In the past, Finley largely served the local market, but with its new affluence—and the resources this affluence can buy—the college will draw students from a wider geographic area. Furthermore, because Finley is a private college with relatively high tuition, the majority of students come from upper-middle-income families. Parental support can thus be expected to heighten students' ability to pay. Overall, then, Jack believes the major indicators of demand for the market area look promising.

Supply

Jack realizes that even strong demand cannot yield profits if a market suffers from oversupply. Fortunately, Jack thinks that Academic Arms is well insulated from competing units. Most important is the fact that the designated market area is fully built up, and as much as 80 percent of the area is zoned single-family residential. Any efforts to change the zoning would be strongly opposed by neighborhood residents. The only potential problem Jack sees is that the college might build more student housing on campus. Though the school administration has discussed this possibility, no funds have yet been allocated to such a project. In sum, Jack concludes that the risk of oversupply in the Academic Arms market area is low—especially during the next 5 years.

The Property

Now the question becomes, Will the Academic Arms Apartments appeal to the desired market segment? On this issue, Jack concludes the answer is yes. The property already is zoned multifamily, and its present (and intended) use complies with all pertinent ordinances and housing codes. Of major importance, though, is the property's location. Not only does the site have good accessibility to the campus, but it is also three blocks from the Campus Town shopping district. In addition, the aesthetic, socioeconomic, legal, and fiscal environments of the property are compatible with student preferences.

On the negative side, the on-site parking has space for only six cars. Still, the building itself is attractive, and the relatively large two-bedroom, two-bath units are ideal for roommates. Although Jack has no experience managing apartments, he feels that if he studies several books on property management and applies his formal business education, he can succeed.

Property Transfer Process

As noted earlier, real estate markets are *not efficient*. Thus, before a property's sale price or rental income can reach its potential, an effective means to get information to buyers or tenants must be developed. Here, of course, Jack has great advantage. Notices on campus bulletin boards and an occasional ad in the school newspaper should be all he needs to keep the property rented. Although he might experience some vacancy during the summer months, Jack feels he can overcome this problem by requiring 12-month leases but then granting tenants the right to sublet as long as the sublessees meet his tenant-selection criteria.

INVESTMENT ANALYSIS

Real estate cash flows depend on the underlying characteristics of the property and the market. That is why we have devoted so much attention to analyzing the determinants of value. Often real estate investors lose money because they "run the numbers" without sufficient research. Jack decided to use the determinants of value to perform an investment analysis, which should allow him to assess the property's value relative to his investment objectives. He may

Table 12.4 Income Statement, Academic Arms Apartments, 1995

Gross rental income		
(8 × $335 × 12)		$32,160
Operating expenses:		
Utilities	$2,830	
Trash collection	675	
Repairs and maintenance	500	
Promotion and advertising	150	
Property insurance	840	
Property taxes	3,200	
Less: Total operating expenses		8,195
Net operating income (NOI)		$23,965

later use an appraisal of market value as confirmation. As we go through Jack's investment analysis calculations, remember that the numbers coming out will be no better than the numbers going in.

The Numbers

At present, Mrs. Bowker, the owner of Academic Arms Apartments, is asking $260,000 for the property. To assist in the sale, she is willing to offer owner financing to a qualified buyer. The terms would be 20 percent down, 11.5 percent interest, and full amortization of the outstanding mortgage balance over 30 years. The owner's income statement for 1995 is shown in Table 12.4. After talking with Mrs. Bowker, Jack believes she would probably accept an offer of $60,000 down, a price of $245,000, and a 30-year mortgage at 11 percent. On this basis, Jack prepares his investment calculations.

Cash Flow Analysis

As a first step in cash flow analysis, Jack reconstructs the owner's income statement (as shown in Table 12.5). This reconstruction reflects higher rent levels, higher expenses, and a lower net operating income. Jack believes that due to poor owner management and deferred maintenance, the present owner is not getting as much in rents as the market could support. In addition, how-

Table 12.5 Reconstructed Income Statement, Academic Arms Apartments, 1996

Gross potential rental income	$37,800	
Less: Vacancy and collection losses at 4%	1,512	
Effective gross income (EGI)		$36,288
Operating expenses:		
Management at 5% of EGI	$ 1,814	
Utilities	3,100	
Trash collection	750	
Repairs and maintenance	2,400	
Promotion and advertising	150	
Property insurance	960	
Property taxes	4,292	
Less: Total operating expenses		13,466
Net operating income (NOI)		$22,822

ever, her expenses understate those he is likely to incur. For one thing, a management expense should be deducted. Jack wants to separate what is rightfully a return on labor from his return on capital. Also, once the property is sold, a higher property tax assessment will be levied against it. Except for promotion and advertising, other expenses have been increased to adjust for inflation and a more extensive maintenance program. With these adjustments, the expected NOI for Academic Arms during 1996 is estimated at $22,822.

To move from NOI to after-tax cash flows (ATCFs), we need to perform the calculations shown in Table 12.6. From this table, you can see that to calculate ATCF, Jack must first compute the income tax savings or income taxes he would incur as a result of property ownership. In this case, potential tax savings accrue during the first 3 years because the allowable tax deductions of interest and depreciation exceed the property's net operating income; in the final 2 years, income exceeds deductions and, therefore, taxes are due.

The "magic" of simultaneously losing and making money is caused by **depreciation**. Tax statutes incorporate this tax deduction, which is based on the original cost of the building, to reflect its declining economic life. However, because this deduction does not actually require a current cash outflow by the property owner, it acts as a *noncash expenditure* that reduces taxes and increases cash flow. In other words, in the 1996–1998 period, the property ownership provides Jack with a tax shelter; that is, Jack uses the income tax losses sustained on the property to offset the taxable income he receives from salary, consulting fees, stock dividends, and book royalties. (We'll consider tax shelters in more detail in Chapter 13.)

depreciation
in real estate investing, a tax deduction based upon the original cost of a building and used to reflect its declining economic life.

Table 12.6 Cash Flow Analysis, Academic Arms Apartments, 1996–2000

	1996	1997	1998	1999	2000
	Income Tax Computations				
Tax savings (+) or taxes (−)	$22,822	$24,419	$26,128	$27,957	$29,914
− Interest*	20,350	20,259	20,146	20,022	19,877
− Depreciation**	6,545	6,545	6,545	6,545	6,545
Taxable income (loss)	($ 4,073)	($ 2,385)	($ 563)	$ 1,390	$ 3,492
Marginal tax rate	.31	.31	.31	.31	.31
Tax savings (+) or taxes (−)	+$ 1,263	+$ 739	+$ 175	−$ 431	−$ 1,083
	After-Tax Cash Flow (ATCF) Computations				
NOI	$22,822	$24,419	$26,128	$27,957	$29,914
− Mortgage payment	21,280	21,280	21,280	21,280	21,280
Before-tax cash flow	$ 1,542	$ 3,139	$ 4,848	$ 6,677	$ 8,634
Tax savings (+) or taxes(−)	+ 1,263	+ 739	+ 175	− 431	− 1,083
After-tax cash flow (ATCF)	$ 2,805	$ 3,878	$ 5,023	$ 6,246	$ 7,551

Average annual after-tax cash flow $(\overline{CF})$*** $= \dfrac{\$2,805 + \$3,878 + \$5,023 + \$6,246 + \$7,551}{5} = \underline{\$5,101}$

*Based on a $185,000 mortgage at 11 percent, compounded annually. Some rounding has been used.

**Based on straight-line depreciation over 27.5 years and a depreciable basis of $180,000. Land value is assumed to equal $65,000.

***Found by substituting values for ATCF into Equation 12.4.

Once the amount of tax savings (or taxes) is known, it is added to (or subtracted from) the before-tax cash flow. Because Jack qualifies as an "active manager" of the property (an important provision of the Tax Reform Act of 1986, discussed more fully in Chapter 13) and because his income is low enough (also discussed in Chapter 13), he can use the real estate losses to reduce his other income. It is important to recognize that under the Tax Reform Act of 1986, the amount of tax losses that can be applied to other taxable income is limited. *It is therefore important to consult a tax expert about the tax consequences of expected income tax losses when calculating ATCFs from real estate investments.*

 ### Proceeds from Sale

Jack must now estimate the net proceeds he will receive when he sells the property. For purposes of this analysis, Jack has assumed a 5-year holding period. Now he must forecast a selling price for the property. From that amount he will subtract selling expenses, the outstanding balance on the mortgage, and applicable federal income taxes. The remainder equals Jack's after-tax net proceeds from sale. These calculations are shown in Table 12.7. (Note that although Jack's ordinary income is subject to a 31 percent tax rate, the maximum rate of 28 percent is applicable to the capital gain expected on the sale of the property.)

Jack wants to estimate his net proceeds from sale conservatively. He believes that at a minimum, market forces will push up the selling price of the property at the rate of 5 percent per year beyond his assumed purchase price of $245,000. Thus, he estimates that the selling price in 5 years will be $312,620. (He obtained this amount by multiplying the $245,000 purchase price by the future-value interest factor of 1.276 from Appendix A, Table A.1, for 5 percent and 5 years, that is, $245,000 × 1.276 = $312,620.) Making the indicated deductions from the forecasted selling price, Jack computes after-tax net proceeds from the sale equal to $89,514.

Table 12.7 Estimated After-Tax Net Proceeds from Sale, Academic Arms Apartments, 2000

Income Tax Computations	
Forecasted selling price (at 5% annual appreciation)	$312,620
− Selling expenses at 7%	21,883
− Book value (purchase price less accumulated depreciation)	212,275
Gain on sale	$ 78,462
× Tax rate on gain*	28%
Taxes payable	$ 21,969
Computation of After-Tax Net Proceeds	
Forecasted selling price	$312,620
− Selling expenses	21,883
− Mortgage balance outstanding	179,254
Net proceeds before taxes	$111,483
− Taxes payable (calculated above)	21,969
After-tax net proceeds from sale ($CF_{R_{2000}}$)	$ 89,514

*Although Jack's ordinary income is taxed at a 31 percent rate, under the Tax Reform Act of 1986 this gain would be taxed at the 28 percent maximum rate applicable to capital gains.

Table 12.8   Net Present Value, Academic Arms Apartments*

$$NPV = \left[\frac{CF_1}{(1+r)^1} + \frac{CF_2}{(1+r)^2} + \frac{CF_3}{(1+r)^3} + \frac{CF_4}{(1+r)^4} + \frac{CF_5 + CF_{R5}}{(1+r)^5} \right] - I_0$$

$$NPV = \left[\frac{\$2,805}{(1+.13)^1} + \frac{\$3,878}{(1+.13)^2} + \frac{\$5,023}{(1+.13)^3} + \frac{\$6,246}{(1+.13)^4} + \frac{\$97,065^{**}}{(1+.13)^5} \right] - 60,000$$

$$NPV = \$2,483 + \$3,037 + \$3,481 + \$3,829 + \$52,707 - \$60,000^{***}$$

$$NPV = \$65,537 - \$60,000$$

$$NPV = +\underline{\$5,537}$$

*All inflows are assumed to be end-of-period receipts.

**Includes both the fifth-year annual after-tax cash flow of $7,551 and the after-tax net proceeds from sale of $89,514.

***Calculated using present-value interest factors from Appendix A, Table A.3.

Discounted Cash Flow

In this step, Jack discounts the projected cash flows to find their present value, and he subtracts the amount of his equity investment from their total to get net present value (NPV). In making this calculation (see Table 12.8), Jack finds that at his required rate of return of 13 percent, the NPV of these flows equals $5,537. Looked at another way, the present value of the amounts Jack forecasts he will receive exceeds the amount of his initial equity investment by about $5,500. The investment therefore meets (and exceeds) his acceptance criterion.

Approximate Yield

Alternatively, Jack could apply the approximate yield formula using the initial equity, I_0, of $60,000, along with the average annual after-tax cash flow, $\overline{CF}$, of $5,101 (calculated at the bottom of Table 12.6) and the after-tax net proceeds from sale, CF_{R2000}, of $89,514 (calculated in Table 12.7). Substituting these values into the approximate yield formula presented in Equation 12.3, Jack gets:

$$\text{Approximate yield} = \frac{\$5,101 + \dfrac{\$89,514 - \$60,000}{5}}{\dfrac{\$89,514 + \$60,000}{2}} = \frac{\$5,101 + \$5,903}{\$74,757}$$

$$= \frac{\$11,004}{\$74,757} = \underline{14.7\%}$$

Because the approximate yield of 14.7 percent is in excess of Jack's required rate of return of 13 percent, the investment meets (and exceeds) his acceptance criterion. Although we have merely approximated his return here, this technique, when consistently applied, should always result in the same conclusion as to acceptability as that obtained using net present value.

SYNTHESIS AND INTERPRETATION

Now Jack reviews his work: He evaluates his analysis for important features and determinants of the property's value, checks all the facts and figures in the investment analysis calculations, and then evaluates the results in light of his stated investment objectives. He asks himself, "All things considered, is the expected payoff worth the risk?" In this case, he decides it is.

Even a positive finding, however, does not necessarily mean Jack should buy this property. He might still want to shop around to see if he can locate an even better investment. Furthermore, he might be wise to hire a real estate appraiser to confirm that the price he is willing to pay seems reasonable with respect to the recent sales prices of similar properties in the market area. Nevertheless, Jack realizes that any problem can be studied to death; no one can ever obtain all the information that will bear on a decision. He gives himself a week to investigate other properties and talk to a professional appraiser. If nothing turns up to cause him second thoughts, he decides that he will offer to buy the Academic Arms Apartments. On the terms presented, he is willing to pay up to a maximum price of $245,000.

CONCEPTS *in Review*

12.14 List and briefly describe the five steps in the framework for real estate investment analysis shown in Figure 12.1.

12.15 Define *depreciation* from a tax viewpoint. Explain why it is said to offer tax shelter potential. What real estate investments provide this benefit? Explain.

12.16 Explain why, despite its being acceptable based on NPV or on approximate yield, a real estate investment still might not be acceptable to a given investor.

REAL ESTATE INVESTMENT SECURITIES

The most popular ways to invest in real estate are through individual ownership (as we've just seen), real estate investment trusts (REITs), and real estate limited partnerships (RELPs). (Due to adverse tax consequences, real estate investors typically have avoided the corporate form of ownership.) Individual ownership of investment real estate is most common among wealthy individuals, professional real estate investors, and financial institutions. The strongest advantage of individual ownership is personal control, and the strongest drawback is that it requires a relatively large amount of capital. Although thus far we have emphasized active, individual real estate investment, it is likely that most individuals will invest in real estate by purchasing shares of either a real estate investment trust or a limited partnership. Here we will examine each of these investment alternatives.

REAL ESTATE INVESTMENT TRUSTS (REITs)

real estate investment trust (REIT)
a type of closed-end investment company that sells shares to investors and invests the proceeds in various types of real estate and real estate mortgages.

A **real estate investment trust (REIT)** is a type of closed-end investment company (see Chapter 11) that invests money, obtained through the sale of its shares to investors, in various types of real estate and real estate mortgages. REITs were established with the passage of the Real Estate Investment Trust

Act of 1960, which set forth requirements for forming a REIT, as well as rules and procedures for making investments and distributing income. The appeal of REITs lies in their ability to allow small investors to receive both the capital appreciation and the income returns of real estate ownership without the headaches of property management.

REITs were quite popular until the mid–1970s, when the bottom fell out of the real estate market as a result of many bad loans and an excess supply of property. In the early 1980s, however, both the real estate market and REITs began to make a comeback. Indeed, by 1995 there were about 240 such investment companies. Revived interest in REITs has been attributed to generally lower mortgage interest rates and the greatly diminished appeal of real estate limited partnerships (described later) resulting from the efforts of the IRS to reduce their tax advantages. (The efforts of the IRS in fact culminated in passage of the Tax Reform Act of 1986.) As a result, REITs are popular forms of real estate investment that at times have earned attractive annual rates of return of 10 to 20 percent or more. Of course, REIT returns vary over time. For example, the average annual rate of return on publicly traded REITs was −17.4 percent in 1990, 35.7 percent in 1991, 12.2 percent in 1992, 18.6 percent in 1993, and 0.8 percent in 1994.

Basic Structure

REITs sell shares of stock to the investing public and use the proceeds, along with borrowed funds, to invest in a portfolio of real estate investments. The investor therefore owns part of the real estate portfolio held by the real estate investment trust. Typically, REITs yield a return at least 1 to 2 percentage points above money market funds and about the same return as high-grade corporate bonds. REITs are required by law to pay out 95 percent of their income as dividends, which leaves little to invest in new acquisitions. Furthermore, they must keep at least 75 percent of their assets in real estate investments, earn at least 75 percent of their income from real estate, and hold each investment for at least four years.

Like any investment fund, each REIT has certain stated investment objectives, which should be carefully considered before acquiring shares. There are three basic types of REITs:

- *Equity REITs.* These invest in properties such as apartments, office buildings, shopping centers, and hotels. They are by far the most common type.
- *Mortgage REITs.* These make both construction and mortgage loans to real estate investors.
- *Hybrid REITs.* These invest both in properties and in construction and real estate mortgage loans.

Equity REITs are by far the most common types. The shares of REITs are traded on organized exchanges such as the NYSE and AMEX as well as in the over-the-counter (OTC) market. Some of the better-known REITs include Avalon Properties, Federal Realty Investment Trust, National Health Investment Trust, Property Trust America, and Weingarten Realty.

Investing in REITs

REITs provide an attractive mechanism for real estate investment by individual investors. They also provide professional management, thereby allowing the investor to assume a passive role. In addition, because their shares can be traded in the securities markets, investors can conveniently purchase and sell shares with the assistance of a retail or discount broker. Investors in REITs can reap tax benefits by placing their shares in a Keogh plan, an individual retirement arrangement (IRA), or some other tax-deferring vehicle.

The most direct way to investigate REITs before you buy is to get the names of those that interest you and then call or write the headquarters of each for information on the properties and/or mortgages it holds, its management, its future plans, and its track record. Additional information on REIT investments can be obtained from the National Association of Real Estate Investment Trusts, 1129 Twentieth Street NW, Suite 305, Washington, DC 20036 (202–785–8717).

The evaluation process will, of course, depend upon the type of REIT you are considering. Equity REITs tend to be most popular because they share directly in real estate growth. If a property's rent goes up, so will the dividend distribution, and share prices may also rise to reflect property appreciation. These REITs can be analyzed by applying the same basic procedures described in Chapters 6 and 7 for common stock valuation. Because mortgage REITs earn most of their income as interest on real estate loans, they tend to trade like bonds; therefore, many of the techniques for analyzing bond investments presented in Chapters 8 and 9 can be used to evaluate them. Hybrid REITs have the characteristics of both property and mortgages and should therefore be evaluated accordingly.

Regardless of type, you should review the REIT's investment objective and performance in a fashion similar to that used in mutual fund investing (see Chapter 11). Carefully check the types of properties and/or mortgages held by the REIT. Be sure to look at the REIT's dividend yield and capital gain potential. Above all, as with any investment, select the REIT that is consistent with your investment risk and return objectives. The *Investor Insights* box on page 519 discusses REITs that have captured recent investor interest and offers guidelines for selecting a REIT that's right for you.

REAL ESTATE LIMITED PARTNERSHIPS (RELPs)

real estate limited partnership (RELP)

a professionally managed real estate syndicate that invests in various types of real estate; the managers take the role of general partner, with unlimited liability, and other investors are limited partners, with liability limited to the amount of their investment.

A **real estate limited partnership (RELP)** is a professionally managed real estate syndicate that invests in various types of real estate. Some RELPs are set up to speculate in raw land; others invest in income-producing properties like apartments, office buildings, and shopping centers; and still others invest in various types of mortgages (the so-called *debt partnerships,* as opposed to the *equity partnerships* that own land and buildings). Managers of RELPs assume the role of general partner, meaning their liability is unlimited, while other investors are limited partners, meaning they are legally liable for only the amount of their investment. Most limited partnerships require a minimum investment of between $2,500 and $10,000. Because of the limited liability, along with the potentially high returns provided by these arrangements, they often appeal to the individual investor wishing to buy real estate. (A detailed discussion of the structure and operation of limited partnerships is presented in Chapter 13.) Investment in a limited partnership can be made directly through ads in the financial news, through stockbrokers or financial planners, or with the assistance of a commercial real estate broker.

INVESTOR INSIGHTS: *Investing in Action*

Real Estate Rides Again

Want to own a golf course? Or perhaps a factory outlet shopping center would be more your style? The new breed of real estate investment trusts (REITs) makes it easy to choose. Unlike earlier REITs that bought a variety of properties and made speculative loans on new construction, today's REITs are niche players that typically focus on one geographic area and specialize in one property type—apartments, factory outlet malls, shopping centers, office buildings, mobile home parks, even golf courses. This investment strategy has paid off: According to a ten-year study by Kemper Securities, specialized REITs averaged returns of 19 percent per year, compared to 3 percent for broadly diversified REITs.

Attracted by high returns, low volatility, growth, and the inflation hedge provided by the underlying asset, investors flocked to REITs in 1994 as the stock and bond markets faltered. This capital influx doubled the REIT market to an estimated $40 billion in about 18 months. REIT share prices fell as these new offerings created a glut on the market, luring even more investors with promises of 8 percent returns and future total annual returns in the 15 to 20 percent range. Today, individual investors are the main source of real estate capital, replacing institutional investors who cut back on real estate investments after the real estate market collapsed in the early 1990s.

Many financial advisers recommend putting 5 to 10 percent of your portfolio in real estate. If you find REITs attractive, advisers recommend buying several types of them to diversify both geographically and in terms of property type, because each type of REIT performs differently.

Choosing a REIT can be difficult; the fundamental research is harder than stock analysis.

You must evaluate not only the types and merits of property owned, plus regional and local economic factors, but also the structure of the REIT itself (ownership, management, debt, etc.). Finally, you must take general stock market dynamics into account. Study the prospectus carefully, concentrating on the following areas:

- *Management.* Look for a track record of five or more years of buying, selling, and managing properties before going public. Management should also own 10 to 15 percent of the REIT, so that its interests are the same as yours.

- *Leverage.* This should be under 40 percent and mostly fixed-rate, amortized, long-term debt, rather than short-term variable rate, which leaves the REIT vulnerable to interest rate changes.

- *Assets.* Analyze the quality of assets, consistency by geographic region or type of asset, and demographic and economic characteristics of the locations.

Still confused about which REITs to buy? Buy shares in a real estate mutual fund that invests in REITs and let professional managers choose the best REITs.

Sources: Adapted from Lynn Asinoff, "REITs: A Smart Investment or a Sucker's Bet?" *Wall Street Journal*, June 3, 1994, p. C1; Jack Egan, "Best Real Estate Deal on the Block?" *U.S. News & World Report*, November 21, 1994, p. 98; Stephanie Anderson Forest, "Now Dividend Hunters Are Stalking REITs," *Business Week*, June 6, 1994, pp. 120–21; and Gordon Williams, "They're Baaaaaaack," *Financial World*, May 24, 1994, pp. 80–83.

Types of Syndicates

There are two basic types of real estate limited partnerships: single property and blind pool syndicates. The **single property syndicate** is established to raise money to purchase a specific piece (or pieces) of property. For example, 50 units of a partnership can be sold at $7,500 each to buy a piece of property for $1 million. A "unit" in a limited partnership is like a share of stock in a

single property syndicate
a type of RELP established to raise money to purchase a specific property (or properties).

company and represents an ownership position in the partnership. In this case, a total of $375,000 (50 units × $7,500) would come from the partners, and the remaining $625,000 would be borrowed.

blind pool syndicate
a type of RELP formed by a syndicator—often well known—to raise a given amount of money to be invested at the syndicator's discretion.

The **blind pool syndicate,** on the other hand, is formed by a syndicator—often well known—to raise a given amount of money to be invested at his or her discretion, though the general partner often has some or all of the properties already picked out. The blind pool syndicator takes a specified percentage of all income generated as a management fee. Large real estate brokerage firms commonly arrange these types of syndicates.

Investing in RELPs

Prior to the Tax Reform Act of 1986, much of the appeal of real estate limited partnerships came from the tax-sheltered income these investments provided. However, that is no longer the case. Instead, like other forms of real estate, these limited partnerships are considered to be *passive* investments. As such, the amount of write-offs that can be taken on them is limited to the amount of income they generate. This means that such write-offs cannot be used to shelter ordinary income from taxes. Although limited partnerships have lost some of their appeal, they remain a popular way to invest in real estate, especially for those with limited investment capital. Today, rather than emphasizing the tax-sheltered nature of their income, many of the real estate limited partnerships are less leveraged (some use no debt at all) and are structured to provide attractive current income (from rents, etc.) and/or capital gains. In essence, they are now being promoted for their underlying investment merits and not on the basis of some artificial tax motive. Certainly for an individual with as little as $2,500 to $5,000 to invest, a carefully selected limited partnership may be a sensible way to invest in real estate.

master limited partnerships (MLPs)
limited partnerships that are publicly traded on major stock exchanges.

One of the key drawbacks of RELPs is that it's always been difficult to get out of them, because there is no organized market for limited partnership units. A number of years ago, it appeared that **master limited partnerships (MLPs)**—partnerships that are publicly traded on major stock exchanges—would improve partnership liquidity. However, recent tax-law changes have greatly reduced their attractiveness.

The annual return on RELPs *in the past* typically ranged between 5 and 15 percent of the amount invested. (There is, of course, *no* insurance that such returns will continue in the future.) The emphasis with respect to the type of return generated differs from one syndicate to another. Most real estate limited partnerships today place major emphasis on producing attractive levels of current income for their investors; some, however, still emphasize capital gains. Of course, the goals of the syndicate, the quality of its management, and the specific properties involved should be carefully evaluated *before* purchasing, in order to estimate the expected risk and return. Information useful in analyzing RELPs can be obtained from the syndicator in the form of a *prospectus*. Of course, before purchasing a RELP, make sure that it is the best vehicle for meeting your investment objectives.

CONCEPTS *in Review*

12.17 Briefly describe the basic structure and investment considerations associated with a *real estate investment trust (REIT)*. Describe the basic types of REITs.

12.18 Briefly describe the basic structure and investment considerations associated with a *real estate limited partnership (RELP)*. Differentiate between a single property syndicate and a blind pool syndicate. What is a *master limited partnership (MLP)?*

OTHER TANGIBLE INVESTMENTS

Although real estate investing is much more popular, some individuals find *tangibles*—investment assets, other than real estate, that can be seen or touched—to be attractive investment vehicles. Common types of tangibles (sometimes referred to as "other tangible investments" because real estate is a tangible asset) include precious metals, gemstones, coins, stamps, artwork, antiques, and other so-called hard assets. During the 1970s, particularly in 1978 and 1979, tangibles soared in popularity, for several reasons: First, the 1970s was a period of high inflation. Double-digit inflation rates became commonplace. These high inflation rates made investors nervous about holding cash or securities like bonds, stocks, and mutual funds. Their nervousness was heightened by the poor returns securities offered in those years. As a result, they turned to investments offering returns that exceeded the rate of inflation—in other words, tangibles.

In 1981 and 1982, things began to change, however, as interest in tangibles waned and their prices underwent substantial declines. For example, in the 12-month period from June 1981 to June 1982, the price of gold dropped 34 percent, silver plunged 45 percent, and U.S. coins fell almost 30 percent in value. With a few exceptions, the investment returns on tangibles continued at a substandard pace through the rest of the 1980s and into the 1990s. Such performance, of course, is precisely what you would have expected: These investment vehicles tend to perform nicely during periods of high inflation, but they don't do nearly so well when inflation drops off—as it has since 1982. Indeed, as Table 12.9 reveals, the investment performance of tangibles from 1972 to 1982 stands in stark contrast to the returns on these same investments from 1982 to 1992. Note especially how stocks and bonds performed in the latest period compared to the decade of the 1970s. There's no doubt that securities today are more lucrative investments than most tangibles. Even so, because

Table 12.9 Comparative Rates of Return for Various Investment Vehicles

10 Years, 6/72–6/82		10 Years, 6/82–6/92	
Vehicle	Return*	Vehicle	Return*
Stamps	21.9%	Stocks	18.4%
Gold	18.6	Bonds	15.2
Chinese ceramics	15.3	Old Master paintings	13.3
Silver	13.6	Chinese ceramics	8.5
Diamonds	13.3	3-month Treasury bills	7.6
Real estate	9.9	Diamonds	6.4
Old Master paintings	9.0	Foreign exchange	4.5
Stocks	3.8	Housing	4.0
Bonds	3.6	Gold	0.6

*Investment returns are measured in terms of average annual fully compounded rates of return. They represent the effective annual yields from these investments; annual returns do not include taxes or transaction costs.

Source: Salomon Bros., Inc.

there's still a lot of interest in tangibles as investment vehicles, we'll take a brief look at these unusual and at times highly profitable investment vehicles.

TANGIBLES AS INVESTMENT OUTLETS

You can hold a gold coin, look at a work of art, or sit in an antique car. Some tangibles, such as gold and diamonds, are easily transported and stored; others, such as art and antiques, usually are not. These differences can affect the price behavior of tangibles. Art and antiques, for example, tend to appreciate fairly rapidly during periods of high inflation and relatively stable international conditions. Gold, on the other hand, is preferred during periods of unstable international conditions, in part because it is portable. Investors appear to believe that if international conditions deteriorate past the crisis point, at least they can "take their gold and run."

The market for tangibles varies widely and therefore so too does the *liquidity* of these investments. On the one hand, we have gold and silver, which can be purchased in a variety of forms and which are generally viewed as being fairly liquid to the extent that it's relatively easy to buy and sell these metals. (To a degree, platinum also falls into this category.) On the other hand, we have all the other forms of tangibles, which are highly *illiquid*: They are bought and sold in rather fragmented markets, where transaction costs are high and where selling an item is often a time-consuming and laborious process.

The tangibles market is dominated by three forms of investments:

- Gold and other precious metals (silver and platinum)
- Gemstones (diamonds, rubies, emeralds, sapphires)
- Collectibles (everything from coins and stamps to artworks and antiques)

These are the tangibles that are likely to be of interest to so-called collector-investors. As the *Investor Insights* box on page 523 indicates, interest in collectibles has exploded lately as our consumer culture has churned out even more products deemed collectible.

Investment Merits

The only source of return from investing in tangibles comes in the form of *appreciation in value*—capital gains, in other words. There's no current income (interest or dividends) from holding tangibles. Instead, investors may be facing substantial *opportunity costs*, in the form of lost income that could have been earned on the capital, if their tangibles do not appreciate rapidly in value. Another factor to consider is that most tangibles have *storage* and/or *insurance costs* that require regular cash outlays.

The future prices and therefore the potential returns on tangibles tend to be affected by one or more of the following key factors:

- Rate of inflation
- Scarcity (supply-demand relationship) of the assets
- Domestic and international instability

Because future prices are linked to inflation as well as to the changing supply-demand relationship of these assets, investments in tangibles tend to be some-

INVESTOR INSIGHTS: *Conflicting Viewpoints*

Treasure or Trash?

No longer is the world of collectibles the exclusive domain of the rich, cultured, and famous. Today's collectors are as likely to save comic books, snow domes, a Soviet space suit, and autographed baseballs as Old Master paintings, rare books, and antiques. "Miscellany"— a catchall category ranging from costly jewelry, to vintage clothes, sports, and entertainment memorabilia, to mundane things like comic books and Pez candy dispensers—is now a major category at leading auction houses.

Collecting has captured the fancy of "baby boomers" (those born between 1946 and 1964) and of "baby busters" (the children of the baby boomers), whose eclectic tastes are changing the collectibles markets. Popular culture reigns supreme; a first edition of Dashiell Hammett's *Maltese Falcon* now outprices a rarer seventeenth-century first edition of Milton's *Paradise Lost*. Experts predict that the new treasures will be relics of the twentieth-century technology revolution—old televisions and computers—and things boomers and busters remember from childhood—Barbie and G.I. Joe dolls, comic books, typed manuscripts, Princess telephones, and entertainment memorabilia from favorite TV shows and movies.

What's behind the broadened popularity of collecting? Many like the sheer fun and the thrill of the hunt. There's always the chance you'll find hidden treasure, but it's rare that anyone makes a killing in "junk collectibles." Figuring out what will become next year's hottest collectible is difficult. Karen Keane, managing director of Skinner, Inc., a Boston auction house, recommends things that represent their time period. Who could guess that a 1900-era electric fan would sell for $13,200 or a Barbie no. 1 doll would fetch $4,000 in 1994

(with an expected $8,000 by 2004)? Also, collectibles run in cycles, and today's fad may be out tomorrow: For example, the market for old computers didn't exist in 1989 but was hot in 1994; baseball cards were hot in the early 1990s but cooled off during the prolonged 1994–1995 baseball strike.

To identify future prize collectibles, look for museum demand for a certain historical period, a cultlike group of collectors (*Star Trek* fans, for example), an oversold market, and limited availability. Don't expect mass-market items or manufactured collectibles like Hummels and so-called limited-edition collector's plates and coins to appreciate much. Veteran collectors advise novices to pick a field that interests you, so that you also get pleasure from what you own. You're also more likely to find underpriced items if you know something about the field. In addition to contacting auction house experts to ask if an item has value, you can get advice and even find buyers on-line; CompuServe and the Internet have collecting forums.

What's ahead for collectors? Some possible collectibles for the late 1990s and beyond are psychedelic 1960s record album covers, cigarette memorabilia, fast-food premiums like Happy Meal favors, old PCs, Vietnam memorabilia, slide rules, and metal roller skates. Only time will tell, however, if any of these become treasure or just trash.

Sources: Adapted from Edward Baig, "Collectibles: How Do You Tell Trash from Treasure?" *Business Week*, June 27, 1994, pp. 106, E2–E4; Christie Brown, "Revenge of the Philistines," *Forbes*, December 6, 1993, pp. 149–54; and Alexandra Peers, "Keep Everything," *Wall Street Journal*, December 9, 1994, p. R8.

what risky. A slowdown in inflation or a sizable increase in the supply of the asset relative to the demand for it can unfavorably affect its market price. On the other hand, increasing inflation and continued scarcity can favorably influence the return. Another factor that tends to affect the market value—and therefore the return—of tangible investments, especially precious metals and gemstones, is the domestic and/or international political environment. In favorable times, these forms of investing are not especially popular, whereas in times of turmoil, their demand tends to rise due to their tangible (and portable) nature.

INVESTING IN TANGIBLES

To some extent, investing in tangibles is no different from investing in securities. Selection and timing are important in both cases and play a key role in determining the rate of return on invested capital. Yet when investing in tangibles, you have to be careful to separate the economics of the decision from the pleasure of owning these assets. Let's face it, many people gain a lot of pleasure from wearing a diamond, owning a piece of fine art, or driving a rare automobile. There's certainly nothing wrong with that, but when you're buying tangible assets for their *investment merits*, there's only one thing that matters—the economic payoff from the investment.

As a serious investor in tangibles, you must consider expected price appreciation, anticipated holding period, and potential sources of risk. In addition, you should carefully weigh the insurance and storage costs of holding such assets, as well as the potential impact that a lack of a good resale market can have on return. Perhaps most importantly, *don't start a serious tangibles investment program until you really know what you're doing*. Know what to look for when buying a diamond, a rare coin, or a piece of fine art, and know what separates the good diamonds, rare coins, or artwork from the rest. In the material that follows, we look at tangibles strictly as *investment vehicles*.

Gold and Other Precious Metals

precious metals
tangibles—like gold, silver, and platinum—that concentrate a great deal of value in a small amount of weight and volume.

Precious metals are tangibles that concentrate a great deal of value in a small amount of weight and volume. In other words, just a small piece of a precious metal is worth a lot of money. Three kinds of precious metals command the most investor attention: gold, silver, and platinum. Of these three, silver (at about $5.30 per ounce in late 1995) is the cheapest. It is far less expensive than either gold (about $385.00 per ounce) or platinum (about $430.00 per ounce), which were also priced in late 1995. Gold is, by far, the most popular. Thus, we'll use gold here as the principal vehicle to discuss precious metals.

For thousands of years, people have been fascinated with gold. Records from the age of the pharaohs in Egypt show a desire to own gold. Today, ownership of gold is still regarded as a necessity by many investors, although its price has dropped considerably since the January 1980 peak of $875 per ounce. Actually, Americans are relatively recent gold investors, due to the legal prohibition on gold ownership, except in jewelry form, that existed from the mid-1930s until January 1, 1975. Like other forms of precious metals, gold is a highly speculative investment vehicle whose price has fluctuated widely in recent years (see Figure 12.2). Many investors hold at least a part—and at times, a substantial part—of their portfolios in gold as a hedge against inflation or a world economic or political disaster.

Gold can be purchased as coins, bullion, or jewelry (all of which can be physically held); it can also be purchased though gold-mining stocks and mutual funds, gold futures (and futures options), and gold certificates. Here's a brief rundown of the different ways gold can be held as a form of investing:

Figure 12.2 The Price of Gold, 1974–1995
The price of gold is highly volatile and can pave the way to big returns or, just as easily, subject the investor to large losses.

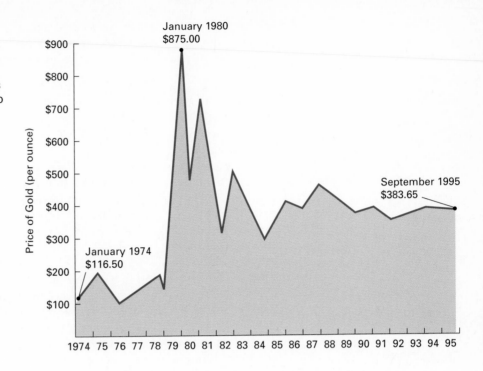

- *Gold coins.* Gold coins have little or no collector value; rather, their value is determined primarily by the quality and amount of gold in the coins. Popular gold coins include the American Eagle, the Canadian Maple Leaf, the Mexican 50-Peso, and the Chinese Panda.

- *Gold bullion.* Gold bullion is gold in its basic ingot (bar) form. Bullion ranges in weight from 5- to 400-gram bars; the kilo bar (which weighs 32.15 troy ounces) is probably the most popular size.

- *Gold jewelry.* Jewelry is a popular way to own gold, but it's not a very good way to invest in gold, because gold jewelry usually sells for a substantial premium over its underlying gold value (to reflect artisan costs, retail markups, and other factors). Moreover, most jewelry is not pure 24-carat gold but a 14- or 18-carat *blend* of gold and other, nonprecious metals.

- *Gold stocks and mutual funds.* Many investors prefer to purchase shares of gold-mining companies or mutual funds that invest in *gold stocks.* The prices of gold-mining stocks tend to move in direct relationship to the price of gold. Thus, if gold rises in value, these stocks usually move up too. It is also possible to purchase shares in mutual funds that invest primarily in gold-mining stocks. Gold funds offer not only professional management but a much higher level of portfolio diversification; the shares of gold-oriented mutual funds also tend to fluctuate along with the price of gold.

- *Gold futures.* A popular way of investing in the short-term price volatility of gold is through futures contracts or futures options.

- *Gold certificates.* A convenient and safe way to own gold is to purchase a gold certificate through a bank or broker. The certificate represents ownership of a specific quantity of gold that is stored in a bank vault. In this way, investors do not have to be concerned about the safety that taking physical possession of gold entails; also, by purchasing gold certificates, investors can avoid state sales taxes (which may be imposed on coin or bullion purchases).

Like gold, silver and platinum can also be bought in a variety of forms. Silver can be purchased as bags of silver coins, bars or ingots, silver-mining stocks, futures contracts, or futures options. Similarly, platinum can be bought in the form of coins, of plates and ingots, of platinum-mining stocks, and of futures contracts.

Transaction costs in precious metals vary widely, depending on the investment form chosen. At one extreme, an investor buying one Canadian Maple Leaf coin might pay 5 percent commission, 7 percent dealer markup, and 4 percent gross excise tax (sales tax). In contrast, the purchase of a gold certificate would entail only a 2 percent total commission and markup, with no sales tax. Storage costs vary as well. Gold coins and bars can easily be stored in a safe-deposit box that costs perhaps $25 per year. Gold purchased via gold certificates usually is subject to a storage fee of less than 1 percent per year. Gold coins, bullion, and jewelry can be easily stolen, so it is imperative that these items be stored in a safe-deposit box at a bank or other depository. Except for transaction costs, the other expenses of buying and holding gold can be avoided when investments are made in gold-mining stocks and mutual funds and in gold futures.

Gemstones

gemstones
diamonds and colored precious stones (rubies, sapphires, and emeralds).

By definition, **gemstones** consist of diamonds and the so-called colored precious stones (rubies, sapphires, and emeralds). Precious stones offer their owners beauty and are often purchased for aesthetic pleasure. However, diamonds and colored stones also serve as a viable form of investing. Along with gold, they are among the oldest of investment vehicles, providing a source of real wealth, as well as a hedge against political and economic uncertainties. However, diamonds and colored stones are very much a specialist's domain. Generally, standards of value are fully appreciated only by experienced personnel at fine stores, dealers, cutters, and an occasional connoisseur-collector. In diamonds, the value depends on the whiteness of the stone and the purity of crystallization. A key factor, therefore, is for the purchaser to understand the determinants of quality. Precious stones will vary enormously in price, depending on how close they come to gem color and purity.

Investment diamonds and colored stones can be purchased through registered gem dealers. Depending on quality and grade, commissions and dealer markups can range from 20 to 100 percent. Due to the difficulty in valuing gemstones, it is imperative to select only dealers with impeccable reputations. As investment vehicles, diamonds and colored stones offer no current income, but their prices are *highly* susceptible to changing market conditions. For example, the peak price of the best-quality, flawless one-carat diamond, a popular investment diamond, was about $60,000 in early 1980. By late 1982, this stone was worth only about $20,000—a drop of 67 percent in just over two years. Since then, prices have fluctuated a bit but still remain at about $20,000 in early 1995.

The big difficulty in precious stone investments, aside from the expertise needed in deciding what is in fact gem quality, is the relative *illiquidity* of the

A real estate market and financial consultant has estimated that Marilyn could buy the office building for $200,000. In addition, this consultant analyzed the property's rental potential with respect to trends in demand and supply. He discussed the following items with Marilyn: (1) The office building was occupied by two tenants, who each had 3 years remaining on their leases, and (2) it was only 4 years old, was in excellent condition, and was located near a number of major thoroughfares. For her purposes, Marilyn decided the building should be analyzed on the basis of a 3-year holding period. The gross rents in the most recent year were $32,000, and operating expenses were $15,000. The consultant pointed out that the leases had built-in 10 percent per year rent escalation clauses and that he expected operating expenses to increase by 8 percent per year. He further expected no vacancy or collection loss, because both tenants were excellent credit risks.

Marilyn's accountant estimated that annual tax depreciation would be $5,100 in each of the next 3 years. To finance the purchase of the building, Marilyn has considered a variety of alternatives, one of which would involve assuming the existing $120,000 mortgage. Upon the advice of a close friend, a finance professor at the local university, Marilyn decided to arrange a $150,000, 10.5 percent, 25-year mortgage from the bank at which she maintains her business account. The annual loan payment would total $17,000. Of this, the following breakdown between interest and principal would apply in each of the first 3 years:

Year	Interest	Principal	Total
1	$15,750	$1,250	$17,000
2	15,620	1,380	17,000
3	15,470	1,530	17,000

The loan balance at the end of the 3 years would be $145,840. The consultant expects the property to appreciate by about 9 percent per year to $260,000 at the end of 3 years. Marilyn will incur a 5 percent sales commission expense on this assumed sale price. The building's book value at the end of 3 years would be $184,700. The net proceeds on the sale would be taxed at Marilyn's capital gains tax rate of 28 percent.

Questions

1. What is the expected annual after-tax cash flow (ATCF) for each of the 3 years (assuming Marilyn has other passive income that can be used to offset any losses from this property)?

2. At a 15 percent required rate of return, will this investment produce a positive net present value?

3. What rate of return does the approximate yield formula show for this proposed investment?

4. Could Marilyn increase her returns by assuming the existing mortgage at a 9.75 percent interest rate, rather than arranging a new loan? What measure of return do you believe Marilyn should use to make this comparison?

5. Do you believe Marilyn has thought about her real estate investment objectives enough? Why or why not?

CHAPTER 13

TAX-ADVANTAGED INVESTMENTS

LEARNING GOALS

After studying this chapter, you should be able to:

LG 1 Understand what is meant by taxable income and the basic procedures involved in its calculation.

LG 2 Define tax avoidance and tax deferral and the characteristics of tax shelters.

LG 3 Explain how investors can earn tax-favored income, with particular emphasis on income excluded from taxation, strategies that defer tax liabilities to the next year, programs that defer tax liabilities to retirement, strategies that trade current income for capital gains, and tax swaps.

LG 4 Summarize the characteristics of deferred annuities—use in retirement plans, fixed versus variable, and their appeal as investment vehicles—and single-premium life insurance.

LG 5 Describe the tax status of limited partnerships and how they work.

LG 6 Discuss popular forms of limited partnerships, partnership structure, and their essential investment considerations—leverage, risk and return, and investment suitability.

"Taxes affect my investment decisions, but they are not my primary concern," states Bill Josephs. "I would much rather pay 40 percent in federal and state capital gains taxes than take a loss!" Bill incorporates tax planning into his overall investment strategies as he builds a nest egg for his son's college education and retirement. An "information junkie" who finds the capital markets fascinating, Bill focuses primarily on stocks and stock mutual funds. Recognizing that he doesn't have the information resources, time, or capital to trade effectively in and out of the market, he's building a solid portfolio of dividend-paying stocks with long-term growth potential. "I also own some speculative stocks, but I do a lot of digging before buying them," Bill comments. "I fully understand the chance for total loss as well as big gains. Certainly, since my son was born, I direct a larger percentage of my portfolio into more conservative investments." He also owns a few publicly traded oil and gas limited partnerships. His selection criteria include high income and a good track record of making capital distributions.

Bill uses a variety of strategies to lower his tax liability. He and his wife, Jane, start with some basic tactics: They put as much as possible into their 401(k) plans and IRAs, whose income is tax deferred. They also use before-tax dollars to the extent possible for medical and dental plan contributions and child care. To avoid federal taxes on their cash reserve fund, they use a government securities fund. Investing in growth stocks is also a good idea tax-wise, because gains come from price appreciation that is not taxed until they sell, and when it is taxed, it is at the capital gains rate, which may be lower than what they pay on regular income.

> **NO ONE LIKES TAXES, SO I DERIVE A PARTICULARLY INTENSE FORM OF GLEE WHEN I MAKE THEM WORK FOR ME!**

Careful timing of securities sales is another way Bill manages tax payments. "If I am holding an appreciated security I want to sell, I wait and sell it in January rather than in December. This pushes the final cash tax impact out 15 months." He also found himself with large tax-loss carryforwards because of some bad investments—penny stocks he bought years ago. (Tax-loss carryforwards arise when you have more than $3,000 in tax losses in excess of capital gains; because you can deduct only $3,000 of these losses per year, the undeducted balance is carried over to the next year.) The tax loss can be used only to offset capital gains, so by investing in securities that provide capital gains rather than dividends, he reduces his tax liability.

A final tax consideration is tax-loss selling. In December, investors typically sell stocks that show a loss, to offset any sales that resulted in capital gains. Bill reviews his portfolio each September or October and takes his losses then. Not only do the losses offset any capital gains, but they provide cash to buy any end-of-year bargains. "I look for stocks that have been beaten down by the broad tax-loss selling that typically occurs in the market at year-end. No one likes taxes, so I derive a particularly intense form of glee when I make them work for me!"

Bill Josephs (not his real name) received his first stock when he was 12 but lost interest in investing until 15 years later. Now 38, he's an active investor. He and his family live in northern California, where Bill is a systems analyst for Chevron.

It is often said that the necessities of life include food, clothing, and shelter. Shelter is important because it protects us from the elements—rain, wind, snow, extreme heat or cold—in the physical environment. In a similar fashion, investors need shelter from the taxes charged on income, for without adequate protection, the returns earned by an investor can be greatly reduced by the ravages of the tax code. Thus, in making investment decisions, we must assess not only risk and return but also the tax effects associated with a given investment vehicle or strategy. Because the tax effects depend on one's "tax bracket," it is important to choose investment vehicles that provide the maximum after-tax return for a given risk. Making such choices is part of **tax planning**, which involves the formation of strategies that will exclude, defer, or reduce the taxes to be paid. Like Bill Josephs, you should make tax planning an essential part of your investment strategy. An awareness of **tax-advantaged investments**, which are various vehicles and associated strategies for legally reducing one's tax liability, and an understanding of the role they can play in a portfolio are fundamental to obtaining the highest after-tax returns for a given level of risk. We will begin by looking at tax fundamentals.

tax planning
the formulation of strategies that will exclude, defer, or reduce the taxes to be paid.

tax-advantaged investments
various vehicles and associated strategies for legally reducing one's tax liability.

TAX FUNDAMENTALS

As currently structured, federal income tax law imposes a higher tax burden on higher taxable income. This is done through a progressive rate structure that taxes income at one of five rates—15, 28, 31, 36, or 39.6 percent. As discussed in Chapter 3, taxpayers filing *individual* returns must follow one tax rate structure and those filing *joint* returns must follow another. Table 13.1 shows the tax rates and income brackets for these two major filing categories. Notice that you pay not only more taxes as your taxable income increases but also *progressively* more if your taxable income rises into a higher bracket.

TAXABLE INCOME

taxable income
the income to which tax rates are applied; equals adjusted gross income minus itemized deductions and exemptions.

Taxable income, as its name implies, is the income to which tax rates are applied. From an investments perspective, this includes such items as cash dividends, interest, profits from a sole proprietorship or share in a partnership,

Table 13.1 Tax Rates and Income Brackets for Individual and Joint Returns (1994)

Tax Rates	Taxable Income	
	Individual Returns	Joint Returns
15%	$0 to $22,750	$0 to $38,000
28%	$22,751 to $55,100	$38,001 to $91,850
31%	$55,101 to $115,000	$91,851 to $140,000
36%	$115,001 to $250,000	$140,001 to $250,000
39.6%	Over $250,000	Over $250,000

and gains from the sale of securities or other assets. As we saw in Chapter 3, federal tax law makes an important distinction between ordinary income and capital gains (and losses).

To review, *ordinary income* broadly refers to any compensation received for labor services (active income) or from invested capital (portfolio or passive income). The form in which the income is received is immaterial. For example, if you owe a debt to someone and that person forgives the debt (excuses you from repaying it), the amount could wind up as income taxable to you, depending on how the debt was initially created and treated for tax purposes in previous periods. As a general rule, *any event that increases your net worth is income, and unless it is specifically excluded from taxable income or considered a capital gain, it is ordinary income.*

The tax law as revised by the Tax Reform Act of 1986 treats gains or losses resulting from the sale of capital assets as ordinary income. A **capital asset** is defined as anything you own and use for personal reasons, pleasure, or investment. A house and a car are capital assets; so are shares of common stock, bonds, and stamp collections. Your **basis** in a capital asset usually means what you paid for it, including commissions and other costs related to the purchase. If an asset is sold for a price greater than its basis, a *capital gain* is the result; if the reverse is true, then you have a *capital loss*. All capital gains are included in full as a part of ordinary income. As for capital losses, a maximum of $3,000 of losses in excess of capital gains can be claimed in any one year. Any losses that cannot be applied in the current year can be carried forward to future years and then deducted. (Timing the sale of securities to optimize the tax treatment of capital losses is an important part of tax planning and is treated more thoroughly later in this chapter.)

capital asset
any asset owned and used for personal reasons, pleasure, or investment.

basis
the amount paid for a capital asset, including commissions and other costs related to the purchase.

DETERMINING TAXABLE INCOME

Determining taxable income involves a series of steps. Because these are illustrated more clearly with an example, let us consider the 1994 income tax situation of the Edward and Martha Meyer family, a family of three. In 1994, the family had the following income items:

1.	Wages and salaries	
	Edward	$26,000
	Martha	12,000
2.	Interest on tax-free municipal bonds	400
3.	Interest on savings accounts	900
4.	Dividends on common stock (owned jointly)	600
5.	Capital gains on securities	1,500

The family also had the following deductions in 1994:

1.	Deductible contribution to IRA account	$1,800
2.	Interest on home mortgage	7,500
3.	Charitable contributions	1,000

The Meyers' income tax due for 1994 was $3,503, as determined in Table 13.2 and explained below.

Table 13.2   Determining 1994 Federal Income Tax Due for the Edward and Martha Meyer Family

I.	**GROSS INCOME**	
	1. Wages and salaries ($26,000 + $12,000)	$38,000
	2. Interest on savings accounts	900
	3. Dividends	600
	4. Capital gains	1,500
	Gross income	$41,000
II.	**ADJUSTMENTS TO GROSS INCOME**	
	Deductible IRA contribution	$ 1,800
III.	**ADJUSTED GROSS INCOME** (I − II) = ($41,000 −$1,800)	$39,200
IV.	**ITEMIZED DEDUCTIONS**	
	1. Mortgage interest	$ 7,500
	2. Charitable contributions	1,000
	Total itemized deductions	$ 8,500
V.	**EXEMPTIONS**	
	Edward, Martha, and one child (3 × $2,450)	$ 7,350
VI.	**TAXABLE INCOME** (III − IV − V) = ($39,200 − $8,500 − $7,350)	$23,350
VII.	**FEDERAL INCOME TAX** (per rate schedule, Table 13.1)	
	(.15 × $23,350)	$ 3,503
VIII.	**TAX CREDITS**	$ 0
IX.	**TAX DUE** (VII − VIII) = ($3,503 − $0)	$ 3,503

Gross Income

gross income
all includable income for federal income tax purposes.

Gross income begins with all includable income but then allows certain exclusions that are provided in the tax law. Table 13.2 shows that in the Meyers' case, all income is included except interest on the tax-free municipal bonds, which is not subject to federal income tax. Notice that interest on savings accounts and dividend income *is* included. In addition, all capital gains are included in gross income, although the maximum tax rate applied to certain capital gains is 28 percent.

Adjustments to Gross Income

Adjustments to gross income reflect the intent of Congress to favor certain activities. The only one shown for the Meyers is their allowable IRA contribution (discussed later) of $1,800, which was determined using a formula provided under the prevailing tax law. You should note the tax-sheltering quality of the IRA; without it, the Meyers would have paid taxes on an additional $1,800 of income in 1994.

Adjusted Gross Income

adjusted gross income
gross income less the total allowable adjustments for tax purposes.

Subtracting the adjustments from gross income provides **adjusted gross income.** This figure is necessary in calculating certain deductions (e.g, medical and dental expenses, charitable contributions, job and other expenses, and the amount of allowable real estate losses) not illustrated in our example. The Meyers' adjusted gross income is $39,200.

Itemized Deductions

Taxpayers can elect to take a **standard deduction,** which is indexed to the cost of living. The standard deduction amounts for 1994 ranged from $3,800 to $9,150 depending on filing status, age, and vision. (There are specific deductions for blind taxpayers.) The standard deduction for the Meyers, if they choose to take it, is $6,350.

If they don't wish to take the standard deduction, taxpayers can choose to *itemize deductions.* Taxpayers with itemized deductions in excess of the applicable standard deduction will prefer to itemize. This group will typically include those individuals who own a mortgaged primary and/or second home. Such was the case for the Meyers, because their itemized deductions of $8,500 exceeded the $6,350 standard deduction.

A number of personal living and family expenses qualify as **itemized deductions,** the most common of which are residential mortgage interest and charitable contributions. All other things being equal, there is a tax advantage to ownership of a principal (as well as a second) residence, because interest on the associated mortgage loans is tax deductible. Consumer interest is *not* tax deductible, whereas investment interest—interest paid on funds borrowed for personal investment purposes—is deductible, subject to certain limitations. Clearly, allowable interest deductions are less expensive on an after-tax basis.

Exemptions

The tax law allows a deduction, called an **exemption,** for each qualifying dependent. It was $2,450 in 1994 ($2,500 in 1995). When taxpayers have adjusted gross income above specified values, their allowable exemptions are reduced by formula. Specific rules determine who qualifies as a dependent. These should be reviewed if the potential dependent is not your child or an immediate member of your family residing in your home. Table 13.2 shows that the Meyers claimed three exemptions.

Taxable Income

Subtracting itemized deductions and exemptions from adjusted gross income leaves *taxable income*; in the Meyers' case, this amount is $23,350. Although the Meyers have none, certain *miscellaneous expenses*, which include union dues, safe-deposit box rental, investment advice, membership dues for professional organizations, and the cost of business publications, generally can be deducted only to the extent that they exceed 2 percent of adjusted gross income. In addition, certain *unreimbursed employee expenses,* such as 50 percent of entertainment bills, 100 percent of travel expenses, and 50 percent of meal expenses, are deductible if substantiated by receipts.

You can use Table 13.1 to calculate the tax due for the Meyers. Their taxable income of $23,350 puts them in the 15 percent income bracket. Thus, their tax, as calculated in the table, is $3,503. The Meyers pay a 15 percent **marginal tax rate,** which means the tax rate on additional income up to $38,000 is 15 percent. *It is the marginal tax rate that should be considered when evaluating the tax implications of an investment strategy.*

By all means, do not confuse the marginal rate with the average rate. The **average tax rate** is simply taxes due divided by taxable income. In the Meyers' case, because they are in the lower tax bracket, this rate also equals 15 percent ($3,503 ÷ $23,350). Of course, for taxpayers in the 28, 31, 36, or 39.6 percent tax brackets, the marginal rate will exceed the average tax rate. The average tax rate has absolutely no relevance to the Meyers' investment decision making.

Tax Credits

tax credits
tax reductions allowed by the IRS on a dollar-for-dollar basis under certain specified conditions.

A number of **tax credits** are available. These are particularly attractive because they reduce taxes on a dollar-for-dollar basis, in contrast to a *deduction*, which reduces taxes only by an amount determined by the marginal tax rate. A frequently used tax credit is for child care and dependent care expenses. Other common tax credits include the credit for the elderly or disabled, foreign tax credit, minimum tax credit, mortgage interest credit, and electric vehicle credit. The Meyers, as is true for most taxpayers under the Tax Reform Act of 1986, were not eligible for any tax credits.

Taxes Due or Refundable

The final amount of tax due is determined by subtracting any tax credits from the income tax. The Meyers' tax due is $3,503. They now compare this amount to the total of tax withheld (indicated on their year-end withholding statements) and any estimated taxes they may have paid during 1994. If these two add up to more than $3,503, then they are entitled to a refund of the difference; if the total is less than $3,503, they must pay the difference when they file their 1994 federal income tax return.

The Alternative Minimum Tax

alternative minimum tax (AMT)
a tax passed by Congress to ensure that all individuals pay at least some federal income tax.

As a result of many taxpayers effectively using tax shelters (tax-favored investments) to reduce their taxable incomes to near zero, Congress in 1978 introduced the **alternative minimum tax (AMT)**. The purpose of this law is to raise additional revenue by making sure that all individuals pay at least some tax. The AMT rate is 26 percent of the first $175,000 of the alternative minimum tax base and 28 percent of the excess. The AMT base is determined by making adjustments to the individual's regular taxable income. The procedures for determining the alternative minimum tax base and the alternative minimum tax are quite complicated. A tax expert should be consulted if you feel the alternative minimum tax might apply in your situation.

CONCEPTS *in Review*

13.1 What is *tax planning*? Describe the current tax rate structure and explain why it is considered progressive.

13.2 What is a *capital asset?* Explain how capital asset transactions are taxed and compare their treatment to that of ordinary income.

13.3 Describe the steps involved in calculating a person's taxable income. How do any tax credits differ from tax deductions?

TAX STRATEGIES

A comprehensive tax strategy attempts to maximize the total after-tax income of an investor over his or her lifetime. The goal is to either avoid taxable income altogether or defer it to another period when it may receive more favorable tax treatment. Even when deferral does not reduce one's taxes, it still gives the investor the use of saved tax dollars during the deferral period.

TAX AVOIDANCE AND TAX DEFERRAL

tax evasion
illegal activities designed to avoid paying taxes by omitting income or overstating deductions.

tax avoidance
reducing or eliminating taxes in *legal ways.*

Tax avoidance is quite different from **tax evasion,** which consists of illegal activities such as omitting income or overstating deductions. **Tax avoidance** is concerned with *legal ways* of reducing or eliminating taxes. As we have already noted in the Meyers' example, the most popular form of tax avoidance is investing in securities offering tax-favored income (to be explained in greater detail in the next section). Another broad approach to avoiding taxes is to distribute income-producing assets to family members (usually children) who either pay no taxes at all or pay them at much lower rates. Because this is also a highly specialized area of the tax law, we do not pursue it further in this text. Again, you should seek professional counsel whenever a tax strategy of this type is contemplated.

tax deferral
the strategy of delaying taxes by shifting income subject to tax into a later period.

    Tax deferral deals with means of delaying taxes and can be accomplished in a number of ways. Frequently, taxes are deferred for only one year as part of a year-end tax strategy to shift income from one year to the next when it is known that taxable income or tax rates will be lower. A simple way to defer taxes is to use vehicles specifically designed to accomplish this objective. Included would be certain retirement plans—401(k)s, Keoghs, and IRAs—and annuities. The role of each of these vehicles is described later in this chapter.

TAX SHELTERS

tax shelter
an investment vehicle that offers potential reductions of taxable income.

A **tax shelter** is any investment vehicle that offers potential reductions of taxable income. Usually, you must own the vehicle directly, rather than indirectly. For example, if the Meyers had a tax-deductible loss of $1,000 on investment property directly owned by them, it could have provided a tax shelter. Had they instead set up a corporation to own this property, the net loss of $1,000 would have been the corporation's, not theirs. Thus, they could not have claimed that tax deduction and the related tax savings on their individual tax return. Similarly, when publicly owned corporations show huge losses, those losses are of no immediate tax benefit to the shareholders. Although the market price of the stock probably falls, which means you could sell it at a tax loss, such a capital loss is limited to only $3,000 a year (in excess of capital gains). If you owned a large amount of stock, your loss might be many times that amount and yet be of no immediate use in reducing your taxes.

    Thus, there is a tax advantage in organizing certain activities as sole proprietorships or partnerships, and even more specifically, as limited partnerships. The majority of these business forms can pass on losses resulting from certain deductions—depreciation, depletion, and amortization—directly to individual owners. The amount, if any, of such losses that can be deducted when calculating taxable income is currently limited by law. The few remaining tax shelters and the structure of the limited partnerships that are commonly used to organize them are explained later in this chapter. Now, however, let us turn our attention to those vehicles that offer tax-favored income.

CONCEPTS *in Review*

13.4 How does *tax avoidance* differ from *tax deferral?* Explain whether either of these is a form of tax evasion.

13.5 What is a *tax shelter?* What is the tax advantage of organizing certain business activities as a sole proprietorship or a partnership rather than as a corporation?

TAX-FAVORED INCOME

tax-favored income
an investment return that is not taxable, is taxed at a rate less than that on other similar investments, defers the payment of tax to a later period, or trades current income for capital gains.

An investment is said to offer **tax-favored income** if it has any of the following results:

1. Offers a return that is not taxable
2. Offers a return that is taxed at a rate less than that on other similar investments
3. Defers the payment of tax to the next year or to retirement
4. Trades current for capital gain income

These tax "favors" have been written into the tax law to foster or promote certain activities as well as to provide convenient tax-reporting procedures. So far in this book, we have examined in detail how real estate can provide shelter from taxes for certain investors (see Chapter 12). Below, we will briefly examine a number of other noteworthy tax-sheltered vehicles and strategies; later in the chapter, we'll look at two other vehicles—deferred annuities and single-premium life insurance.

INCOME EXCLUDED FROM TAXATION

Some items are simply *excluded from taxation*, either totally or partially. These include interest earned on tax-free municipals and on Treasury and government agency issues, as well as certain proceeds from the sale of a personal residence. Tax exclusion was written into the tax code for these vehicles in order to encourage investment in them. (If Congress decides otherwise, the tax exclusions on these investment vehicles could be removed.)

Tax-Free Municipal Bond Interest

Municipal bonds were described in Chapter 8. All interest received from the most common form—tax-free municipals—is free of federal income tax. In fact, this income is not even reported on the return. However, any gains or losses resulting from the sale of municipal bonds must be included as capital gains or losses. In addition, interest paid on money borrowed to purchase municipal bonds is *not* tax-deductible.

Treasury and Government Agency Issues

Treasury and government agency issues were also discussed in Chapter 8. Although interest on these securities is included as income on the federal tax return, it is excluded for state and local income tax purposes. The rationale for this prohibition on the states and localities taxing interest income derived from federal government debt is to make it easier and less expensive for the federal government to borrow to finance its operations. Because combined state and local income tax rates can be as high as 20 percent in some parts of the country, individuals in high tax brackets may find such exclusions worthwhile.

Sale of Personal Residence

A capital gain results if you sell your personal residence for a price greater than its basis (the price originally paid for it). However, two provisions in the tax law aimed at stimulating home ownership soften the tax impact and actually make investment in a home an excellent tax shelter: First, if a gain exists from the sale of your home, it can be deferred from taxation if you purchase another home at a price equal to or greater than the price of the home you sold—as long as you buy the other home within 24 months. The second, and more important, tax implication is that you have a one-time exclusion of $125,000 of gain from gross income from the sale of a personal residence. On a joint return, one spouse must be age 55 or older and must meet certain other conditions to be eligible for this exclusion. This is a major tax break for most people and certainly enhances the investment appeal of the personal residence.

STRATEGIES THAT DEFER TAX LIABILITIES TO THE NEXT YEAR

Very often, an investor may enjoy sizable gains in a security's value within a relatively short period of time. Suppose you bought 100 shares of XYZ common stock in mid-1995; by year-end 1996, your investment would have increased in value by 50 percent, because the price of this stock increased from $30 a share to around $45 over that period. Assume that at year-end 1996, you believe the stock price has just about peaked and you wish to sell it and invest the $4,500 elsewhere. In such a case, you would be taxed on a capital gain of $1,500 ($4,500 sale price − $3,000 cost). Assuming a 28 percent tax bracket, you would owe income taxes for 1996 of $420 on the sale. However, because you believe tax rates may be lower next year or merely to benefit from the time value of money, you wish to defer the tax on this transaction to the following year (1997). Three available strategies for preserving a gain while deferring tax to the following year are (1) the short sale against the box, (2) the put hedge, and (3) the deep-in-the-money call option.

shorting-against-the-box
a technique used to lock in a security profit and defer the taxes on it to the following tax year by short selling a number of shares equal to those already owned.

Short Sale Against the Box

The shorting-against-the-box technique can be used to lock in a profit and defer the taxes on the profit to the following tax year. By **shorting-against-the-box**—selling short a number of shares equal to what you already own—you lock in an existing profit and thus eliminate any risk of a price decline. You also give up any future increases in price, but this should not be of concern, because you believe the current price is relatively high. For example, to lock in and defer the $1,500 capital gain on the XYZ transaction, prior to year-end you would sell short 100 shares of XYZ. No matter what happens to the price of the stock after that date, you are guaranteed $1,500. You would then have two positions—one long and one short—both involving an equal number of XYZ shares. After year-end, you would use the 100 shares held long to close out the short position, thereby realizing the $1,500 capital gain.

Put Hedge

put hedge
the purchase of a put option on shares currently owned, to lock in a profit and defer taxes on the profit to the next taxable year.

put
an *option* that enables its holder to sell the underlying security at a specified price over a set period of time.

The put hedge can be used to lock in a profit and defer the taxes on the profit to the next tax year. It can accomplish the same objectives as the short sale against the box without losing the potential for additional price appreciation. Essentially, a **put hedge** involves buying a **put**, which is an *option* that enables its holder to sell the underlying security at a specified price over a set period of time, on shares currently owned. (Options are discussed more fully in Chapter 14.) If the price of the stock falls, your losses on the shares are offset by the profit on the put option. For example, suppose that when XYZ was trading at $45, you purchased for $150 a six-month put option with a contractual sale price of $45. By doing this, you locked in a price of $45: If the price fell to, say, $40 a share, your $500 loss on the stock would be offset exactly by a $500 profit on the option. However, you would still be out the $150 cost of the option. At a closing price of $40, your ending after-tax position would be:

1. Initial cost of 100 shares		$3,000
2. Profit on 100 shares [100 × ($40 − $30)]		1,000
3. Profit on the put option	$ 500	
4. Cost of the put option	− 150	
5. Taxable gain on put option [(3) − (4)]		350
6. Total tax on transaction		
Profit on stock (2)	$1,000	
Plus taxable gain on put (5)	+ 350	
Total gain	$1,350	
Times tax rate	× .28	
Total tax		378
7. After-tax position [(1) + (2) + (5) − (6)]		$3,972

The final after-tax position in this example is about the same as if you had simply held the stock while its price declined to around $43.50 a share. However, keep in mind two important points: (1) The put hedge locks in this position regardless of how low the price might fall, whereas simply holding the stock does not, and (2) any price appreciation will be enjoyed with either approach. (Notice that with the put hedge, you do not give up this advantage, as you do when shorting-against-the-box.) Put hedges are discussed in more detail in the next chapter.

deep-in-the-money call option
a tax-deferral strategy that involves selling a call option on shares currently owned, locking in a price equal to the amount received from the sale of the call option but giving up future price appreciation.

Deep-in-the-Money Call Option

call
an *option* that gives its holder the right to buy the underlying security at a specified price over a set period of time.

Selling a **deep-in-the-money call option** is a strategy similar to the put hedge, but there are important differences: In this case, you give up any potential future price increases, and you lock in a price only to the extent of the amount you receive from the sale of the **call**, which is an *option* that gives its holder the right to buy the underlying security at a specified price over a set period of time.

To illustrate, suppose that call options on XYZ with a $40 contractual buy price and six-month maturity were traded at $600 ($6 per share) when XYZ was selling for $45. If six months later XYZ closed at $40, it would result in this ending after-tax position:

1. Initial cost of 100 shares		$3,000
2. Profit on 100 shares [100 × ($40 − $30)]		1,000
3. Profit on the sale of the option; because the stock closed at the contractual buy price of $40, profit is the total amount received		600
4. Total tax on transaction		
Profit on stock (2)	$1,000	
Plus profit on option (3)	+ 600	
Total gain	$1,600	
Times tax rate	× .28	
Total tax		448
5. After-tax position [(1) + (2) + (3) − (4)]		$4,152

This final after-tax position is better than with the put hedge, but it closes off any price appreciation. In effect, when you sell the call option, you are agreeing to deliver your shares at the option's contractual buy price. If the price of XYZ increases to, say, $50 or beyond, you do not benefit, because you have agreed to sell your shares at $40. Furthermore, your downside protection extends only to the amount received for the option—$6 per share. Therefore, if XYZ's price went to $35, you would lose $4 a share before taxes [$45 − ($35 + $6)].

Summary of the Strategies

As you can see, deferring tax liabilities to the next year is a potentially rewarding activity, requiring the analysis of a number of available techniques. The choice can be simplified by considering which method works best given one's expectation of the future price behavior of the stock. Table 13.3 summarizes how each strategy performs under different expectations of future

Table 13.3 Ranking of Strategies to Defer Tax Liabilities to the Next Year Given Different Expectations About the Future Price of the Stock

Strategy	Price Will Vary by a Small Amount Above or Below Current Price	Price Will Vary by a Large Amount Above or Below Current Price	Future Price Will Be Higher than Current Price	Future Price Will Be Lower than Current Price
Do nothing—hold into next tax year	2	4	1	4
Short sale against the box	3+	2+	4	1
Put hedge	3+	1	2	2
Sell deep-in-the-money call option	1	2+	3	3

Note: Ranking: 1, best; 4, worst.

price behavior. To complete the analysis, you would have to consider commission costs—something we have omitted. Although these costs can be somewhat high in absolute dollars, they are usually a minor part of the total dollars involved if the potential savings is as large as the ones we have been considering in our examples. However, if the savings is relatively small—say, under $500—then commissions may be disproportionately large in relation to the tax savings and/or deferral. Clearly, you need to work out the specific figures for each situation.

PROGRAMS THAT DEFER TAX LIABILITIES TO RETIREMENT

As noted in Chapter 3, accumulating funds for retirement is the *single most important reason for investing*. A large part of the retirement income of many people comes from Social Security and basic employer-sponsored programs. Such programs may be totally funded by the employer, may require employee contributions, or may involve a combination of employer and employee contributions. Here we focus on arrangements that give the employee (or self-employed person) an option to contribute to a retirement program that provides tax shelter by deferring taxes to retirement. The three programs are 401(k) plans, Keogh plans, and individual retirement arrangements (IRAs).

401(k)Plans

401(k) plans
retirement programs that allow employees to divert a portion of salary to a company-sponsored tax-sheltered savings account, thus deferring taxes until retirement.

Many employers offer their employees *salary reduction plans* known as **401(k) plans.** [Although our discussion here will center on 401(k) plans, similar programs are also available for employees of public, nonprofit organizations; known as *403(b) plans*, they offer many of the same features and tax shelter provisions as 401(k) plans.] Basically, a 401(k) plan gives you, as an employee, the option to divert a portion of your salary or wages to a company-sponsored tax-sheltered savings account. Taxes on both the salary (wages) placed in the savings plan and the investment earnings accumulated are deferred until the funds are withdrawn.

Generally, participants in 401(k) plans are offered several options for investing their contributions—typically, a money market fund, company stock, one or more equity funds, or a guaranteed investment contract (GIC). About 60 percent of all 401(k) plan investments are made in **guaranteed investment contracts (GICs)**, which are portfolios of fixed-income securities with guaranteed competitive rates of return that are backed and sold by insurance companies. A firm's pension plan manager buys large GIC contracts and invests employees' 401(k) contributions in them.

guaranteed investment contracts (GICs)
portfolios of fixed-income securities with guaranteed competitive rates of return that are backed and sold by an insurance company.

Of course, *taxes will have to be paid on 401(k) funds eventually, but not until you start drawing down the account at retirement*. At that point, presumably, you are in a lower tax bracket. A special attraction of most 401(k) plans is that the firms offering them often "sweeten the pot" by matching all or part of an employee's contribution (up to a set limit). Currently, about 85 percent of the companies that offer 401(k) plans have some type of matching contribution program, often putting up 50 cents (or more) for each $1 contributed by the employee. Such matching programs provide both tax and savings incentives to individuals and clearly enhance the appeal of 401(k) plans.

In 1994, an individual employee could put as much as $9,240 (depending on his or her salary) into a tax-deferred 401(k) plan. The annual dollar cap increases yearly, because it is indexed to the rate of inflation. [The contribution limits for 403(b) plans are currently set at a maximum of $9,500 per year, and that amount won't be indexed to inflation until the 401(k) contribution limit attains parity.] To encourage savings for retirement, such contributions are "locked up" until the employee turns 59½ or leaves the company. A major exception to this rule lets employees tap their accounts, without penalty, in the event of any of a number of clearly defined "financial hardships."

To see how such tax-deferred plans work, consider an individual who earned, say, $50,000 in 1994 and who would like to contribute the maximum allowable ($9,240) to the 401(k) plan where she works. Doing so would reduce her taxable income to $40,760 and enable her to lower her federal tax bill by over $2,587 (i.e., .28 × $9,240). Such tax savings will offset a good portion of her contribution. In effect, she will add $9,240 to her retirement program with only $6,653 of her own money; the rest will come from the IRS via a reduced tax bill. What's more, all the *earnings* on her savings account will accumulate tax-free as well. Remember, the taxes on both the earnings placed in the 401(k) plan and the investment earnings accumulated on them are deferred until retirement. The *Investor Insights* box on page 548 provides some tips from professionals on managing your 401(k) plan.

Keogh Plans

Keogh plans
programs that allow self-
employed individuals to establish self-directed, tax-deferred
retirement plans for themselves
and their employees.

Keogh plans allow *self-employed individuals* to establish tax-deferred retirement plans for themselves and their employees. Like contributions to 401(k) plans, payments to Keogh accounts may be taken as deductions from taxable income. As a result, they reduce the tax bill of self-employed individuals. The maximum contribution to this tax-deferred retirement plan is $30,000 per year or 20 percent of earned income, whichever is less. Any individual who is self-employed, either full- or part-time, is eligible to set up a Keogh account. Keoghs can be used not only by the self-employed businessperson or professional but also by individuals who hold full-time jobs *and* "moonlight" on a part-time basis—for example, the engineer who has a small consulting business on the side or the accountant who does tax returns in the evenings and on weekends. Take the engineer, for example: If he earns $10,000 a year from his part-time consulting business, he can contribute 20 percent of that income ($2,000) to his Keogh account and in so doing reduce both his taxable income and the amount he pays in taxes. Also, he is eligible to receive full retirement benefits from his full-time job.

Keogh accounts can be opened at banks, insurance companies, brokerage firms, mutual funds, and other financial institutions. Annual contributions must be made at the time the respective tax return is filed, or by April 15 of the following calendar year (e.g., you have until April 15, 1996, to make the contribution to your Keogh for 1995). Although a designated financial institution acts as custodian of all the funds held in a Keogh account, *the actual investments held in the account are under the complete direction of the individual contributor*. Unlike 401(k) plans, these are self-directed retirement programs, and thus the *individual* decides which investments to buy and sell (subject to a few basic restrictions). The income earned from the investments in a Keogh plan must be plowed back into the account, and it too accrues tax-free.

INVESTOR INSIGHTS: *Investing in Action*

Don't Ignore Your 401(k) Plan

Traditional pension plans—funded by employers and managed by professionals—are on the decline. Therefore, chances are that you'll have to manage your own defined-contribution plan—401(k)s at private firms and the similar 403(b)s for public, nonprofit employees. How much retirement money you'll have depends on how much you invest and how well you manage the funds. If you worry about choosing the right investments for your 401(k) plan, you're not alone. By 1997, these plans will account for 43 percent of all retirement assets.

Until recently, the average 401(k) plan offered limited options—perhaps a guaranteed investment contract (GIC), the company's stock, and a mutual fund. Some offered only GICs. But new regulations protect companies against lawsuits over poor 401(k) performance if they meet certain conditions: They must offer at least three different investment options in addition to company stock, provide information about investment options so that participants can choose based on risk-return features, report performance frequently, and allow more frequent changes to employees' plans. Experts predict that soon about half of major company 401(k) plans will offer ten or more fund choices. Good news, in a way, except that as your investment choices increase, so does your confusion about selecting the right retirement plan investments.

A trap many fall into, according to investment advisers, is being too conservative with their 401(k) investments. The average 401(k) investor chooses GICs and low-yielding money market funds, focusing more on the safety of his or her capital than on the way inflation erodes returns. Jonathan Pond, president of Financial Planning Information of Boston, notes that a *professional* pension fund manager who invested this way would be grossly negligent of his or her responsibilities.

The typical pension plan holds about 60 percent equities for dividend growth, capital appreciation, and an inflation hedge. Another common mistake of those who manage their own pension plans is buying too much company stock. It's too risky to invest in one stock, especially when you also work for the company. Advisers typically suggest limiting company stock to 10 to 25 percent of your 401(k).

What do financial planning experts suggest as an ideal 401(k) plan? Obviously, this depends on your age, circumstances, retirement goals, and plan offerings. They recommend following the lead of the pension funds and investing heavily in common stock; the percentage and type of equities should change as you move through life cycle stages. You should also coordinate your 401(k) plan with your other investments so that you have an appropriate balance overall. Are you now in your twenties? Start your plan now and save whatever you can—especially if your employer matches contributions—even if you can't contribute the maximum. Concentrate on growth-oriented equities, up to 100 percent of your plan, while you're young. As you move through your thirties, diversify into international equities and move a portion—say, 30 percent—into fixed-income investments. During your forties and fifties, shift into more conservative equity and fixed-income investments as you near retirement. However, many advisers recommend keeping a reasonably high portion in equities to hedge against inflation even after you retire, because today's longer life expectancy means you'll probably live for quite a while past 65.

Sources: Jane Bryant Quinn, "Is Your 401(k) OK?" *Newsweek,* September 19, 1994, pp. 44–45; Ruth Simon, "We Have Some Bad News About Your 401(k)," *Money,* May 1994, pp. 94–102; Penelope Wang, "ABC's of 401(k) Investing," *Money,* February 1995, pp. 144–45; and Gordon Williams, "Fiddling with 401(k)s," *Financial World,* February 1, 1994, pp. 64–68.

All Keogh contributions and investment earnings must remain in the account until the individual turns 59½, unless the individual becomes seriously ill or disabled. However, you are not *required* to start withdrawing the funds at age 59½. Rather, they can stay in the account and continue to earn tax-free income until you turn 70½, at which time you have the remainder of your life to liquidate the account. In fact, as long as the self-employment income continues, an individual can continue to make tax-deferred contributions to a Keogh account, up to the maximum age of 70½. Of course, once an individual starts withdrawing funds from a Keogh account (at age 59½ or after), all such withdrawals are treated as active income and are subject to the payment of ordinary income taxes. *Thus, the taxes on all contributions to and earnings from a Keogh account are deferred to retirement, when they will have to be paid.*

A program that's similar in many respects to the Keogh account is something called a *Simplified Employee Pension Plan (SEP-IRA)*. It's aimed at small-business owners, particularly those with *no employees*, who want a plan that is simple to set up and administer. SEP-IRAs *can be used in place of Keoghs*. Although they are simpler to administer and have the same annual dollar contribution cap ($30,000), their contribution *rate* is less generous: You can put in only 15 percent of earned income for a SEP-IRA, versus 20 percent for a Keogh.

Individual Retirement Arrangements (IRAs)

individual retirement arrangements (IRAs)
self-directed, tax-deferred retirement programs available to any gainfully employed individual, who can make up to a specified maximum annual contribution.

Individual retirement arrangements (IRAs) are virtually the same as any other investment account you open with a bank, savings and loan, credit union, stockbroker, mutual fund, or insurance company, with one exception: IRAs are self-directed, tax-deferred retirement programs that are *available to any gainfully employed individual*. The form you complete to open the account designates the account as an IRA and makes the institution its trustee. The maximum annual IRA contribution is $2,000 for an individual and $2,250 for an individual and a nonworking spouse. If both spouses work, each can contribute up to $2,000 to his or her own IRA.

To be able to use your annual IRA contributions as a tax deduction, *one* of the following two conditions has to be met:

1. Neither you nor your spouse (if filing a joint return) can be covered by a company-sponsored pension plan.

2. Your adjusted gross income has to be less than $40,000 (for married couples) or $25,000 (for singles).

Translated, this means your IRA contributions *would fully qualify* as a tax deduction if you were covered by a company-sponsored pension plan but your adjusted gross income fell below the specified amounts ($40,000 for joint filers or $25,000 for singles) *or* if you (or your spouse) weren't covered by a company-sponsored pension plan, no matter how much your adjusted gross income was. [Note that the income ceilings are phased out, so that people with adjusted gross incomes of $40,000 to $50,000 (or $25,000 to $35,000) who are covered by employer pension plans are still entitled to prorated *partial deductions*.] If the contributions qualify as tax deductions (per the two conditions noted above), then the amount of the IRA contributions can be shown on the tax return as a deduction from taxable income—which, of course, will also reduce the amount of taxes that have to be paid. As with 401(k) and Keogh plans, the taxes on all the *earnings* from an IRA account are deferred until you start drawing down the funds.

Even if you don't qualify for a tax deduction, you can *still contribute up to the maximum of $2,000 a year to an IRA account,* but you will be making these nondeductible contributions with after-tax income. *The earnings you generate from the investments you hold in your IRA account are tax deferred: They accumulate tax-free until you withdraw funds from your IRA*, at which point taxes are due. This provision applies regardless of your income or whether you're already covered by a pension plan at your place of employment. You can deposit as much or as little as you want up to the applicable limit, and there are no percentage-of-income contribution limitations. For example, if your earned income is only $1,800, then you can contribute *all* of it to your IRA.

IRAs are *self-directed accounts*—that is, you are free, within limits, to make whatever investment decisions you wish with the capital held or deposited in your IRA. Of course, your investment options are limited by the types of products offered by financial institutions. Banks and thrift institutions push their savings vehicles, insurance companies have their annuities, and brokerage houses offer everything from mutual funds to stocks, bonds, and annuities. Except for serious illness, any withdrawals from an IRA prior to age 59½ are subject to a 10 percent penalty on top of the regular tax on the withdrawal itself.

Bear in mind that IRAs, along with all other retirement plans permitting contributions on a pretax basis, *defer* but do not *eliminate* taxes. When you receive the income (contributions and investment earnings) in retirement, it is then taxed, at the then prevailing tax rates. Even so, the impact of tax deferral is substantial. Table 13.4 compares the results of investments in IRA and non-IRA accounts—both of which earn an annual rate of return of 8 percent. This example assumes that you invest $1,000 of earned income each year. If you choose an IRA, you shelter from taxes both the $1,000 initial investment and its subsequent earnings, so that at the end of the first year, for example, you have accumulated $1,080. If you select the same investment vehicle but do not make it an IRA, you must first pay $280 in taxes (assuming a 28 percent tax rate), leaving only $720 to invest. The subsequent earnings of $58 (.08 × $720) are also taxed at 28 percent, leaving after-tax income of only $42 [$58 − (.28 × $58) = $58 − $16 = $42]. Thus, the first-year accumulation is just $762. As the table indicates, after about 25 years, accumulated funds in an

Table 13.4 Accumulated Funds from a $1,000-a-Year Investment in an IRA and from a Fully Taxable (Non-IRA) Account*

Years Held	IRA	Non-IRA
1	$ 1,080	$ 762
5	6,335	4,272
10	15,645	9,926
15	29,323	17,405
20	49,421	27,359
25	78,951	40,471
30	122,341	57,821
35	186,097	80,778
40	279,774	111,153
45	417,417	159,502

*Contributions and earnings are taxed at 28 percent in the non-IRA account but are tax-free in the IRA; an annual rate of return of 8 percent is assumed in both cases.

IRA are about twice as great as for a non-IRA; after 45 years, the funds are nearly 2.6 times as great ($417,417 vs. $159,502).

Funding Keoghs and IRAs

As with any investment, an individual can be conservative or aggressive when choosing securities for a Keogh or IRA, though the nature of these retirement programs generally favors a more conservative approach. In fact, conventional wisdom favors funding your Keogh and IRA with *income-producing assets*. This strategy would also suggest that if you are looking for capital gains, it is best to do so *outside of* your retirement account. The reasons for this are twofold: (1) Growth-oriented securities are by nature *more risky*, and (2) you cannot write off losses from the sale of securities held in a Keogh or IRA account. This does *not* mean it would be altogether inappropriate to place a good-quality growth stock or mutual fund in a Keogh or IRA—in fact, many advisers contend that growth investments should always have a place in your retirement account. The reason is their *performance*: Such investments may pay off handsomely, because they can appreciate totally free of taxes. In the end, *it is how much you have in your retirement account that matters, rather than how your earnings were made along the way.*

Although very few types of investments are prohibited outright, some should be avoided simply because they are inappropriate for such accounts. For example, with tax-free municipal securities, the tax shelter from a Keogh or IRA would be redundant because their income is tax-exempt anyway. In addition to most long-term securities, money market accounts—both bank deposits (MMDAs) and mutual funds (MMMFs)—also appeal to Keogh and IRA investors, especially those who view short-term securities as one way to capture volatile market rates. Not surprisingly, as the size of an account begins to build up, an investor will often use more than one kind of security to diversify the portfolio.

Remember that although Keoghs and IRAs offer attractive tax advantages, they in no way affect the underlying risks of the securities held in these accounts. Also, regardless of what types of investment vehicles are used, keep in mind that once money is put into a Keogh or IRA, it's meant to stay there for the long haul.

STRATEGIES THAT TRADE CURRENT INCOME FOR CAPITAL GAINS

Whereas ordinary income is taxed in the year it's received, capital gains are not taxed until they are actually realized. This means that *unrealized* capital gains are not taxed. For example, the receipt of $100 in cash dividends on a stock in the current year would be taxed at the assumed 28 percent rate, leaving $72 of after-tax income. On the other hand, if the price of a stock that pays no dividend rises by $100 during the current year, *no tax would be due until the stock is actually sold*. Sooner or later, you'll pay taxes on your income, but at least with capital gains, you defer the taxes until the profit is actually realized, which could be years away. Therefore, if the market price of the stock is stable or increasing, earning capital gains may achieve a tax-deferred buildup of funds. From a strict tax viewpoint, investment vehicles that provide such a tax-deferred buildup of value may be more attractive than those that provide annual taxable income. Some of the more common methods for trading current income for capital gains are described below.

Growth Versus Income Stocks

Choosing growth rather than income stocks is a simple yet basic way to earn capital gains income. Companies that pay out a low percentage of earnings as dividends usually reinvest the retained earnings to take advantage of growth opportunities. If you select a company that pays dividends amounting to a 10 percent current return on your investment, your after-tax return will be 7.2 percent, assuming you are in the 28 percent tax bracket. In comparison, a company that pays no dividends but is expected to experience 10 percent annual growth in its share price from reinvestment of earnings will also offer an after-tax rate of return of 7.2 percent [$(1.00 - 0.28) \times .10$], but in this case the taxes will not have to be paid until the stock is actually sold and the gain realized. At that point, the hope is that you will be in a lower tax bracket or that the tax rate will be lower. If neither, at least in the interim you've been able to keep invested the funds that you otherwise would have paid out in taxes. The deferral of tax payment is, of course, appealing as long as the stock price continues to increase in value.

Deep Discount Bonds

deep discount bond
a bond selling at a price far below its par value.

Purchasing a **deep discount bond**—one that is selling at a price far below its par value—also offers a capital gain opportunity. To illustrate, suppose you have the choice of buying two different bonds: ABC's bond, which has a coupon rate of 5 percent and is selling for $700 in the market, or DEF's bond, with a coupon of 10 percent selling at par. Which would you prefer if both mature to a $1,000 par value at the end of 10 years? With the ABC bond, you will earn interest of $50 a year taxed as ordinary income. At the end of 10 years, you will have a $300 capital gain, which will also be taxed as ordinary income. With the DEF bond, all of your return—that is, the $100 you receive each year—is ordinary income. From a strict tax perspective, the ABC bond is clearly the better of the two, *because the portion of the return represented by the capital gain is not taxed until it's realized at maturity.* (Remember, though, that the higher-coupon bond is giving you a higher return earlier, and that adds to its attractiveness.)

To choose between the two bonds, a rate of return analysis could be performed, assuming an equal number of dollars is invested in each bond. For example, an investment of $7,000 would purchase 10 ABC bonds or 7 DEF bonds. Total annual interest on the ABC bonds would be $500; on the DEF bonds, it would be $700. To an investor in the 28 percent tax bracket, the after-tax advantage of the DEF bonds is $144 (.72 $\times$ $200) a year. However, the ABC bonds will be worth $10,000 at maturity, whereas the DEF bonds will be worth only their current value of $7,000. On an after-tax basis, the additional $3,000 is worth $2,160 [$3,000 $-$ (.28 $\times$ $3,000)]. The choice boils down to whether you prefer $144 of additional income each year for the next 10 years or an additional $2,160 at the *end* of 10 years. Using the future value techniques developed in Chapter 4, you would arrive at the conclusion that it would take about a 9 percent rate of return to make you indifferent between the two bonds. That is, if you invest $144 a year for 10 years at 9 percent, it accumulates to around $2,160 at the end of 10 years. Interpreting this answer, if you can invest at an after-tax rate greater than 9 percent, you should select the DEF bonds; if you feel your after-tax reinvestment rate will be lower, then you should select the ABC bonds.

Income Property Depreciation

Federal tax law, as noted in Chapter 12, permits the *depreciation* of income property such as apartment houses and similar structures. Essentially, a specified amount of annual depreciation can be deducted from ordinary pretax income. The depreciable life of residential rental property (apartments) is 27.5 years. Nonresidential property (office buildings and shopping centers) placed in service after May 13, 1993, has a depreciable life of 39 years. In both cases, straight-line depreciation is used. When a property is sold, any amount received in excess of its book value is treated as a capital gain and is taxed at the same rate as ordinary income. For example, assume you buy a four-unit apartment building for $100,000 and hold it for 3 years, taking $2,900 in depreciation each year. Now, suppose at the end of the third year you sell it for its original $100,000 purchase price. The depreciation you took reduced ordinary income each year by $2,900 and was worth, assuming a 28 percent tax bracket, $812 (.28 × $2,900). Your gain on the sale is $8,700 (3 years × $2,900 per year), which results in a tax of $2,436 (.28 × $8,700). There is no tax savings in this situation; however, you received a tax deferral because the tax savings of $812 in each of the first 3 years did not have to be paid back until the property was sold at the end of the third year. (Of course, if the property were sold for less than its original purchase price, full repayment would not occur.)

The use of the depreciation deduction (which does not involve any actual cash payment) results in a type of interest-free loan. The deduction reduces taxes during the property's holding period and delays the repayment of those taxes until the property is sold. *This tax deferral is the primary tax benefit provided by depreciation.* In our example, the tax deferral of $812 in each of the first 3 years (i.e., 3 × $812 = $2,436), which is repaid as $2,436 of taxes at the end of the third year, represents a loan at a 0 percent rate of interest. However, very restrictive limits on the use of tax losses resulting from real estate investments established by the Tax Reform Act of 1986 may severely limit an investor's ability to take advantage of these depreciation tax benefits. As a result, as noted in Chapter 12, the appeal of real estate investment no longer lies in its potential tax shelter value; rather, it lies in its ability to earn a profit from annual rents and/or price appreciation.

TAX SWAPS: A STRATEGY THAT REDUCES OR ELIMINATES A TAX LIABILITY

Thus far, we have considered several short-term strategies aimed at affecting an investor's tax liability in one way or another: (1) ways to exclude income from taxation, (2) ways to defer taxes from one tax year to the next, (3) programs that defer tax liabilities to retirement, and (4) techniques that trade

tax swap
selling one security that has a capital loss and replacing it with another, similar security to offset, partially or fully, a capital gain that has been *realized* in another part of the portfolio.

current income for capital gains. We will now look at a strategy that essentially reduces or eliminates a tax liability altogether. This procedure, called a tax swap, is extremely popular at year-end among knowledgeable stock and bond investors. A **tax swap** is simply the replacement of one security that has a capital loss with another to offset, partially or fully, a capital gain that has been *realized* in another part of the portfolio. Of course, because we are trying to offset a gain, the security that is sold in the tax swap would be one that has *lost* money for the investor. Because we are selling one security that has experienced a capital loss and replacing it with another, similar security, the investor's stock or bond position remains essentially unchanged, although his or her tax liability has been reduced—and perhaps substantially so.

A tax swap works like this: Suppose that during the current year, you realized a capital gain of $1,100 on the sale of bonds. Assume that in your portfolio you held 100 shares of International Oil Corporation common stock, purchased 20 months earlier for $38 per share and currently selling for $28 per share. Although you wish to maintain an oil stock in your portfolio, it does not matter to you whether you hold International Oil or one of the other multinational oils. To realize the $10 per share capital loss on International Oil while not altering your portfolio, you sell the 100 shares of International Oil and buy 100 shares of World Petroleum, which is also selling for $28 per share. The result is a *realized* capital loss of $1,000 [100 × ($28 − $38)], which can be used to offset all but $100 of the $1,100 capital gain realized on the earlier bond sale. Clearly, the tax swap is an effective way of reducing and possibly eliminating a tax liability without altering one's portfolio.

Swaps of common stock are an important part of year-end tax planning. Even more popular are bond swaps, because it is usually far easier to find a substitute bond for the one held. Most full-service brokerage houses publish a list of recommended year-end swaps for both stocks and bonds. You might be wondering why it wouldn't make sense just to sell the security for tax purposes and then immediately buy it back. This procedure is called a **wash sale** and is disallowed under the tax law. A sold security cannot be repurchased within 30 days before or after its sale *without losing the tax deduction*.

wash sale
the procedure of selling securities on which capital losses can be realized and then immediately buying them back; disallowed under the tax law.

CONCEPTS *in Review*

13.6 What is *tax-favored income*? Briefly describe the following forms of income excluded from taxation:
   a. Tax-free municipal bond interest
   b. Treasury and government agency issues
   c. Sale of a personal residence

13.7 Explain conditions that favor the following strategies for deferring tax liabilities to the next year:
   a. A short sale against the box
   b. A put hedge
   c. Selling a deep-in-the-money call option
When is it best simply to hold the stock and do nothing?

13.8 Briefly describe each of the following programs for deferring taxes to retirement:

a. 401(k) plans
b. Keogh plans
c. Individual retirement arrangements (IRAs)

13.9 What are *guaranteed investment contracts (GICs),* and what role do they play in 401(k) plans? What investment vehicles might be suitable for funding a Keogh or IRA?

13.10 Briefly describe each of the following strategies that trade current for capital gains income:
a. Growth stocks
b. Deep discount bonds
c. Income property depreciation

13.11 Describe how a *tax swap* can be used to reduce or eliminate a tax liability without significantly altering the composition of one's portfolio.   ▬▬

DEFERRED ANNUITIES AND SINGLE-PREMIUM LIFE INSURANCE

As noted in the discussions of tax-favored income, effective tax strategy seeks to defer taxable income for extended periods of time. The earnings on investment are therefore available for reinvestment during the period of deferment. The additional earnings resulting from investment of pretax rather than after-tax dollars over long periods of time can be large. Put in proper perspective, a tax-deferred annuity may be worth more to an individual investor than any other single tax strategy. That is why it is important to understand the topic thoroughly. In addition, a somewhat similar but generally less attractive product is single-premium life insurance.

annuity
a series of payments guaranteed for a number of years or over a lifetime.

single-premium annuity
an annuity contract purchased with a single lump-sum payment.

installment annuity
an annuity contract acquired by making payments over time; at a specified future date, the installment payments, plus interest earned on them, are used to purchase an annuity contract.

annuitant
the person to whom the future payments on an annuity contract are directed.

immediate annuity
an annuity contract under which payments to the annuitant begin as soon as it is purchased.

deferred annuity
an annuity contract in which the payments to the annuitant begin at some future date.

ANNUITIES: AN OVERVIEW

An **annuity** is a series of payments guaranteed for a number of years or over a lifetime. The two types of annuities are classified by their purchase provisions. The **single-premium annuity** is a contract purchased with a single lump-sum payment. The purchaser pays a certain amount and receives a series of payments that begins either immediately or at some future date. The second type of contract, the **installment annuity,** is acquired by making payments over time; at a specified future date, the installment payments, plus interest earned on them, are used to purchase an annuity contract. The person to whom the future payments are directed is called the **annuitant.** Annuities of many types are issued by hundreds of insurance companies.

An **immediate annuity** is a contract under which payments to the annuitant begin as soon as it is purchased. The amount of the payment is based on statistical analyses performed by the insurance company and depends on the annuitant's gender and age; the payment is a function of how long the insurance company expects the annuitant to live. A **deferred annuity,** in contrast, is one in which the payments to the annuitant begin at some future date. The date is specified in the contract or at the annuitant's option. The amount the annuitant will periodically receive depends on his or her contributions, the interest earned on them, the annuitant's gender, and the annuitant's age when payments begin.

accumulation period
under an annuity contract, the period of time between when payments to the insurance company are made and when payments to the annuitant begin.

distribution period
under an annuity contract, the period of time over which payments are made to the annuitant.

The period of time between when payments are made to the insurance company and when the insurance company begins to pay the annuitant is the **accumulation period.** All interest earned on the accumulated payments during this period is tax deferred: Because no payment is made to the purchaser, no tax liability is created. The period of time over which payments are made to the annuitant is the **distribution period.** Earnings on the annuity during the accumulation and distribution periods become taxable to the annuitant when received.

CHARACTERISTICS OF DEFERRED ANNUITIES

current interest rate
for an annuity contract, the yearly return the insurance company is currently paying on accumulated deposits.

The growth in popularity of deferred annuities stems from the competitive interest rates paid on these contracts. An annuity contract's **current interest rate** is the yearly return the insurance company is now paying on accumulated deposits. The current interest rate fluctuates with market rates over time and is not guaranteed by the insurance company. However, some contracts have a "bailout" provision that allows an annuity holder to withdraw the contract value—principal and all earned interest—if the insurance company fails to pay a specified minimum return. The minimum is typically a return that is 1 percent or more below the initial rate.

minimum guaranteed interest rate
for a deferred annuity purchase contract, the minimum interest rate on contributions that the insurance company will guarantee over the full accumulation period.

The deferred annuity purchase contract specifies a **minimum guaranteed interest rate** on contributions. The insurance company will guarantee this rate over the full accumulation period. The minimum rate is usually substantially less than the current interest rate. However, you should study a prospectus or contract and remember that *the minimum rate is all you are guaranteed.* (Very often, the promotional literature provided by the company emphasizes the high *current* interest rate.)

Special Tax Features

Deferred annuities, both single-premium and installment, have several advantageous tax shelter features. First, interest earned on the purchaser's contributions is not subject to income tax until it is actually paid to her by the insurance company. Suppose that $10,000 is invested in a 7 percent single-premium deferred annuity. During the first year the contract is in effect, the account earns $700 in interest. If none of this interest is withdrawn, no income tax is due. Thus, for an investor in the 28 percent tax bracket, the first year's tax savings is $196. The tax-deferral privilege permits the investor to accumulate substantial sums of compound interest that can be used to help provide a comfortable retirement income. However, it is important to note that the Tax Reform Act of 1986 provides that this tax-favored treatment is available only on annuity contracts held by individuals, trusts, or other entities, such as a decedent's estate, a qualified employer plan, a qualified annuity plan, or an IRA. In all other cases, the income on the annuity is taxed when earned.

tax-sheltered annuity
an annuity contract that allows employees of certain institutions to make a *tax-free contribution* from current income to purchase a deferred annuity.

Certain employees of institutions such as schools, universities, governments, and not-for-profit organizations may qualify for the **tax-sheltered annuity.** A special provision in the income tax laws allows these employees to make a *tax-free contribution* from current income to purchase a deferred annuity. The interest earned on these contributions is tax deferred as well. The maximum amount that can be contributed is limited. Purchasers of these annuities do not have to pay any income tax on contributions or interest earnings until they actually receive annuity payments in future years. The expectation is that, if timed to coincide with retirement, the deferred income will be taxed at a lower rate than current income would be. Thus, the tax-sheltered annuity is attractive because it can save income taxes today as well as provide a higher level of retirement income later.

Investment Payout

payout
the investment return provided by an annuity contract; it is realized when the distribution period begins.

straight annuity
an annuity contract that provides for a series of payments for the rest of the annuitant's life.

The investment return, or **payout,** provided by an annuity contract is realized when the distribution period begins. The annuitant can choose a **straight annuity,** which is a series of payments for the rest of his or her life. Most companies also offer a variety of other payout options, including a contract specifying payments for both annuitant and spouse for the rest of both their lives, as well as a contract specifying rapid payout of accumulated payments with interest over a short period of time. The amount an annuitant receives depends on the amount accumulated in the account and the payout plan chosen. It is important to choose the program that provides the highest return for the desired payout plan. Such a plan will probably have a relatively high interest rate and relatively low (or no) sales charges and administration fees.

Sales Charges and Administration Fees

Many annuities are sold by salespersons who must be compensated for their services. Some annuities, called "no-load," have no sales charges paid by the purchaser; in this case, the insurance company pays the salesperson directly. Other annuities require the purchaser to pay commissions of up to 10 percent. Administration fees for management, yearly maintenance, and one-time "setup charges" may also be levied. The key item for a prospective purchaser to analyze is the *actual return on investment after all sales charges and administration fees are deducted.*

DEFERRED ANNUITIES AND RETIREMENT PLANS

Many investors tie the purchase of deferred annuities to their overall retirement plans. Because Keogh plans and individual retirement arrangements (IRAs) are somewhat similar to deferred annuities, they should be evaluated with them. If you are not fully using any allowable IRA exclusion each year, you may prefer adding to it as a part of your retirement plan, rather than purchasing a tax-deferred annuity. Far greater benefit results from deducting from taxable income the full amount of the allowable IRA payment. With an annuity, unless you're in one of the qualified professional fields noted above, you cannot deduct its purchase price but can only defer earned income.

Although both IRA and deferred annuity withdrawals prior to age 59½ are subject to a 10 percent additional tax, it is important to recognize that income withdrawn from a deferred annuity will be taxed in the year it is withdrawn. Moreover, any annuity withdrawal is first viewed for tax purposes as income; once all income is withdrawn, subsequent withdrawals are treated as a return of principal, so any partial withdrawal will most likely be fully taxable.

FIXED VERSUS VARIABLE ANNUITY

fixed annuity
an annuity contract that pays an unchanging amount of monthly income during the distribution period.

variable annuity
an annuity contract that adjusts the monthly income it pays during the distribution period according to the investment experience (and sometimes the mortality experience) of the insurer.

The annuity payout during the distribution period can be either fixed or variable. Most contracts are written as **fixed annuities**: Once a payment schedule is selected, the amount of monthly income does not change. In contrast, a growing number of annuity plans adjust the monthly income according to the actual investment experience (and sometimes the mortality experience) of the insurer. These latter contracts are called **variable annuities.** The advantage of a fixed annuity is that the dollar amount of monthly income is guaranteed to the annuitant regardless of how poorly or well the insurer's investments perform. A major disadvantage, however, is that in periods of inflation, the purchasing power of the dollar erodes. For example, with a 5 percent annual inflation rate, $1 of purchasing power is reduced to 78 cents in just 5 years.

To overcome the lack of inflation protection provided by fixed-dollar annuities, the variable annuity was developed. With this plan, annuitants face a different risk, however. They cannot be certain how well the insurer's investments—which may consist of common stocks, bonds, or money market funds—will do. Annuitants therefore take a chance that they will receive an even lower monthly income, in absolute dollars, than a fixed-dollar contract would provide. Most people who participate in variable annuity plans, of course, anticipate that they will be able to at least keep up with the cost of living. Unfortunately, variable annuity values and inflation, often measured by the consumer price index (CPI), do not always perform the same.

Some people invest in a variable annuity during the accumulation period and then switch to a fixed annuity at retirement. In this manner, they participate in the growth of the economy over their working careers but guard against short-term recessions that may occur during retirement years.

ANNUITIES AS INVESTMENT VEHICLES

Annuities have several potential uses in an investment program. An immediate annuity can provide a safe and predictable source of income for the balance of one's life. A deferred annuity offers tax shelter and safety features and in addition can provide a convenient method for accumulating funds. When considering the purchase of a deferred annuity, the investor needs to assess its investment suitability and understand the purchase procedures.

Investment Suitability

The principal positive feature of deferred annuities is that they allow an investor to accumulate tax-deferred earnings. The tax-deferral feature allows interest to accumulate more quickly than would be the case if earnings were taxed. For those qualifying for a tax-sheltered annuity, current income tax on premium payments can be deferred as well. Furthermore, annuities are a low-risk type of investment.

On the negative side, deferred annuities can be faulted for two reasons: (1) lack of inflation protection and (2) high sales charges and administration fees. Most variable annuities, despite providing a fluctuating interest rate during the accumulation period, do not provide an annual interest rate in excess of the rate of inflation. Thus, they are not an inflation hedge. The second negative aspect of annuities—relatively high sales charges and administration fees—is due largely to the fact that sales commissions, whether paid by the purchaser or the insurance company, are generous and tend to lower the purchaser's return. In addition, insurance companies have high overheads that must be met from annuity proceeds. In general, then, although annuities can play an important role in an investment portfolio, they should not be the only vehicle held. Other vehicles providing higher returns (and probably carrying higher risk) are available.

Buying Annuities

Annuities are sold by licensed salespersons and many stockbrokers. There are probably 50 or more annuity plans available through these outlets in a given community. Before you invest in a particular annuity, you should obtain a prospectus and any other available literature on a number of them. Then carefully compare these materials. The annuity you choose should be one that contains features consistent with your investment objectives and also offers the highest actual return on investment after all charges and fees are deducted. Just as important, because *the annuity is only as good as the insurance company that stands behind it*, check to see how the company is rated in *Best's Insurance Reports*. These ratings are much like those found in the bond market and reflect the *financial strength* of the insurance company. Letter grades (ranging from A+ down to C) are assigned on the principle that the stronger the company, the lower the risk of loss. Accordingly, if security is important to you, stick with insurers that carry A+ or A ratings. If you're considering a *variable annuity*, go over it much the same way you would a traditional mutual fund: Look for superior past performance, proven management talents, moderate expenses, and the availability of attractive investment alternatives that you can switch in and out of. The *Investor Insights* box on page 560 provides some guidelines about whether a variable annuity is right for your portfolio.

SINGLE-PREMIUM LIFE INSURANCE (SPLI)

Since 1982, tax legislation has reduced the tax shelter appeal of single-premium deferred annuities (SPDAs). Currently, a 10 percent federal tax penalty is charged on withdrawals made prior to age 59½, regardless of how long the annuity has been held. In addition, most insurers charge withdrawal penalties—typically, on withdrawals of 10 percent or more during the first seven to ten years. Clearly, these restrictions limit the tax shelter appeal of SPDAs.

As a result of the limitations placed on single-premium deferred annuities by the Tax Reform Act of 1986, the **single-premium life insurance (SPLI) policy** emerged as a popular alternative investment vehicle. These policies, in addition to offering the features of SPDAs, provided a mechanism for making tax-sheltered withdrawals prior to age 59½. Generally, the policyholder paid a large premium, often $15,000 or more, to purchase *whole life insurance* (see Chapter 3). Whole life provided a stated death benefit (that passed tax-free to beneficiaries) and earned a competitive interest rate on the cash value buildup,

single-premium life insurance (SPLI) policy
an investment vehicle for which the policyholder purchases a whole life insurance policy that provides a stated death benefit and earns interest on the cash value buildup, which occurs over time on a tax-free basis.

INVESTOR INSIGHTS: *Conflicting Viewpoints*

Should You Buy a Variable Annuity?

Although variable annuities have been around for over 40 years, investors have just recently rediscovered them, pouring a record $43 billion into them in 1993. Sold by insurance companies, mutual funds, and banks, these investments combine an insurance contract with various portfolios, called subaccounts, that resemble mutual funds. Because insurance investments are shielded from taxes, the annuity's income, like that of a 401(k) or IRA, grows tax-free.

What's the current attraction of variable annuities? Unlike 401(k) and IRA plans, variable annuities carry no limit on investments and no requirement to start withdrawing funds at age 70½. They are also appealing because they allow the annuitant to select among subaccounts and fund managers. The average fund contains eight subaccounts, which may include several types of stock funds, from small-caps to international; several fixed-income accounts; and even some asset allocation funds. An annuity may have multiple fund managers; for example, American Skandia offers 35 in its Advisors Choice annuity. Recent annuity performance has been competitive with that of mutual funds. In short, variable annuities provide a flexible way to manage diversified assets tax deferred.

What are the drawbacks? For one thing, annuity deposits are not tax deductible, as are 401(k) and some IRA contributions. As with any tax-deferred investment, you owe ordinary income taxes plus a 10 percent penalty on funds withdrawn before age 59½. Also, their high fees can erode investment returns. These fees typically include an insurance charge averaging 1.3 percent per year, a management fee of 0.5 to 1.5 percent, and an annual contract fee of about $30. Total annuity fees can top 2 percent per year—about .75 to 1 percent more than the average mutual fund you'd buy for your 401(k) or IRA. Most have surrender charges that start at 7 to 10 percent and decline over seven years. Together, tax penalties and surrender charges could cancel out tax benefits.

If you decide to investigate annuities, look first at the number of subaccounts—the more categories and funds within each category, the better. Make sure the subaccounts match your investment style and goals; for example, not all annuities offer broad diversification or specialty funds. Next, evaluate performance. A wide selection of funds does you no good if the funds perform poorly. Growth-oriented funds have performed best, providing the high returns needed to cover expenses. Weigh fees against performance, but look twice before investing in an annuity that charges over 2.1 percent. Seek out those with solid performance, low expense ratios, and no front-end or surrender charges. Several annuities may offer the same fund portfolios, so check Morningstar's monthly *Variable Annuity/Life Performance Report* to find the lowest-cost annuity with that subaccount.

Are annuities right for you? Because of their high fees, investing in variable annuities makes sense only if you've maxed out contributions to other tax-deferred plans and can leave the money in place for 10 to 15 years. So look at your overall retirement program and choose these long-term investments carefully if you decide to proceed.

Sources: Adapted from Kristin Davis, "Annuities: Picking Your Way Through the Jungle, *Kiplinger's Personal Finance Magazine,* October 1994, pp. 55–63; Amey Stone, "Variable Annuities. More Choices, More Fans," *Business Week,* June 27, 1994, pp. 104–105; and Walter L. Updegrave, "The Best Variable Annuities," *Money,* January 1994, pp. 118–28.

which occurred over time on a tax-free basis. As with any whole life policy, the policyholder could cancel the policy and withdraw its cash value. In such a case, taxes would be due on any gains above the amount originally invested.

The most attractive feature of SPLI policies was the ability they afforded the policyholder to *make tax-free cash withdrawals at any time, using a policy loan.* However, in 1988 Congress closed the loophole in the tax law that allowed tax-free policy loans. Today's SPLI policies preserve the principal and usually guarantee returns for the first year or so. After that, rates of return are changed periodically to reflect prevailing money market rates; however, rates normally cannot fall below a certain minimum level (usually around 4 to 6 percent), as specified in the policy. Single-premium *variable life insurance* policies (see Chapter 3) let policyholders put their money in a number of investment choices, ranging from stocks and bonds to mutual funds and money market instruments. However, these policies *do not guarantee preservation of principal or a minimum return*. Substantial investment losses can result.

The rate of return on investment in SPLI policies is frequently below the return on tax-exempt municipal bonds, and the value of SPLI as life insurance is not as great as that available from term insurance. Like all forms of whole life insurance, SPLIs' only tax shelter appeals are the tax-free buildup of value and the tax-free passage of death benefits to beneficiaries. Because SPDAs are vehicles for retirement, whereas SPLI policies provide greatest benefits when held until death, interest rates on SPDAs are usually one-half percentage point higher than on SPLIs. (Universal and variable life insurance, as discussed in Chapter 3, also enable policyholders to accumulate earnings on a tax-free basis; as such, they are also viewed—by some, at least—as viable tax shelter investments. However, it should be understood that often these vehicles too suffer from relatively low earnings rates over the long haul.) Despite the aggressive and often tempting sales pitches, today most experts agree that this product is *not* well suited for young, moderate-income families, because it is neither an especially attractive tax-sheltered investment nor a very effective form of life insurance.

CONCEPTS *in Review*

13.12 Define an annuity, explain the role it might play in an investment portfolio, and differentiate between:
   a. Single-premium and installment annuities
   b. Immediate and deferred annuities
   c. Fixed and variable annuities

13.13 Define the following terms as they relate to deferred annuities:
   a. Current interest rate
   b. Minimum guaranteed interest rate
   c. Payout

13.14 Explain how a deferred annuity works as a tax shelter. How does a *tax-sheltered annuity* work, and who is eligible to purchase one? Discuss whether a deferred annuity is a better tax shelter than an IRA.

13.15 Discuss the investment suitability of a deferred annuity, particularly its positive and negative features. Briefly describe the procedures for buying annuities.

13.16 What is a *single-premium life insurance (SPLI) policy*? Describe the basic features of an SPLI policy, compare it to the single-premium deferred annuity (SPDA), and explain why the popularity of SPLI policies has diminished since 1988.

USING LIMITED PARTNERSHIPS (LPS)

limited partnership (LP)
vehicle in which the investor can passively invest with limited liability, receive the benefit of active professional management, and apply the resulting profit or loss (subject to limits) to his or her tax liability.

passive activity
an investment in which the investor does not "materially participate" in its management or activity.

The **limited partnership (LP)** is a vehicle in which you can passively invest with limited liability, receive the benefit of active professional management, and apply the resulting profit or loss (subject to limits) to your tax liability. The Tax Reform Act of 1986 in effect eliminated the tax-sheltering appeal of LPs. It limited the tax deductions for net losses generated by passive activities to the amount of net income earned by the taxpayer on all passive activities. Generally, a **passive activity** is one in which the investor does not "materially participate" in its management or activity. Rental investments involving real estate, equipment, and other property are treated as passive activities regardless of whether or not the taxpayer materially participates.

An important exception exists for taxpayers actively participating in real estate rental activities. If more than half of an investor's personal service and at least 750 hours in a year are spent in active participation in a real estate rental activity, the passive loss restrictions do *not* apply. Investors who actively participate, but at lower levels, may deduct up to $25,000 of net losses if their adjusted gross income (AGI) is less than $100,000. The deduction is gradually phased out for AGI between $100,000 and $150,000; taxpayers with AGI above $150,000 cannot apply such losses. Another exception applies to oil and gas properties, if the form of ownership does *not* limit the taxpayer's liability.

While the value of LPs for tax shelters is no longer significant, this form of ownership is widely used to structure profit-making, cash-flow-generating investments. Like any investment, limited partnerships should be purchased *on their investment merits* only after considering both risk and return. It is therefore important to first understand why LPs are used and how they work.

POOLING OF CAPITAL AND SHARING OF RISKS

syndicate
a joint venture–general partnership, corporation, or limited partnership–in which investors pool their resources.

general partnership
a joint venture in which all partners have management rights and all assume unlimited liability for any debts or obligations the partnership incurs.

corporation
a form of organization that provides a limited-liability benefit to shareholder investors and that has an indefinite life.

In an effort to obtain economies of scale and diversify risk, investors often pool their resources and form joint ventures. These joint ventures, frequently called **syndicates,** can take several forms: general partnerships, corporations, or limited partnerships. In a **general partnership,** all partners have management rights, and all assume unlimited liability for any debts or obligations the partnership incurs. Obviously, the unlimited-liability feature can be disadvantageous to passive investors (those who do not wish to participate actively in the partnership's operation).

The corporate form of syndication—that is, a **corporation**—provides a limited-liability benefit to shareholder investors. Additionally, corporations have an indefinite life and do not cease to exist if a stockholder dies (whereas a partnership could end if a general partner dies). However, the corporate form of syndication has a significant disadvantage: Its profits and losses cannot be passed directly to its stockholders. The partnership form of syndication, on the other hand, provides for the flow-through of profits and losses. The *limited partnership* combines the favorable investment features of both the corporation and the general partnership: It provides an investor with a limited-liability vehicle that allows profits and losses to flow through to each partner's tax return.

HOW LIMITED PARTNERSHIPS WORK

Legal Structure

A limited partnership (LP) is a legal arrangement governed principally by state law. State laws vary, of course, but typically they require that various written documents be filed with a county or state official prior to the commencement of the limited partnership's business. Additionally, the limited partnership is normally structured to conform to IRS regulations; this is done to ensure that any tax benefits generated can be used by the partners. Limited partnerships can be utilized to invest in many things, and their size and scope vary widely. However, all have one common characteristic: They must have at least one general partner and at least one limited partner.

Figure 13.1 illustrates a typical limited partnership arrangement. The **general partner**—the active manager of the operation—runs the business and assumes unlimited liability. (Often, to mitigate the unlimited liability, the general partner is a corporation.) The general partner's major contribution to the enterprise is frequently in the form of management expertise, not capital. Most of the capital is usually supplied by the limited partners, who do little else. They cannot participate in the management of the enterprise or they will lose their limited-liability protection. Furthermore, a limited partner's liability normally does not exceed his or her capital contribution, an amount specified in the partnership agreement. **Limited partners,** then, are the suppliers of capital whose role in the venture is passive. Usually, the only power limited partners have is to fire the general partner and/or to sell their partnership investment. A person considering investment in a limited partnership should carefully analyze the general partner's management capabilities because the success of the partnership is literally "riding on" them.

general partner
the managing partner who accepts unlimited liability and uses his expertise to manage the partnership.

limited partners
the passive investors in a partnership, who supply most of the capital and have liability limited to the amount of their investment.

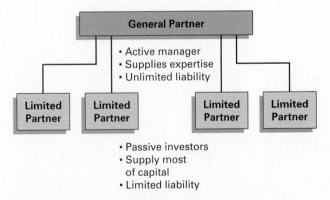

Figure 13.1   The Limited Partnership Structure
In a limited partnership, the general partner is an active manager who typically provides management expertise and accepts all liability. The limited partners are passive investors who supply most of the capital and accept liability limited only to the amount of their investment.

Return to Investors

An investor can realize a return from a limited partnership investment in two basic ways—through cash flow and through price appreciation. Investors in a limited partnership receive periodic cash payments as the investment generates income. These periodic returns are the partnership's *cash flow*. Limited partners receive a share of this cash flow, prorated to the size of their investment. Cash distributions may be made monthly, quarterly, or yearly, and these returns are taxable to the limited partners as ordinary income. The general partner's management fee is normally paid prior to the distribution of cash flow. However, frequently the general partner will take only a small fee until the limited partners have fully recovered their initial investment. Then the general partner's share of additional cash distributions will become commensurately larger.

The other source of investment return for limited partners is *price appreciation,* resulting from an increase in the value of the investment. The general partner may earn a portion of the realized price appreciation as well. Investments, such as real estate, that increase in value due to inflation and other factors are often sources of appreciated value for limited partnership investors. Like the appreciation experienced on any investment vehicle, this form of return may be realized or unrealized (as an actual return of dollars or as a "paper" return). Of course, realized capital gains are taxable to the partners.

POPULAR FORMS OF LIMITED PARTNERSHIPS

Limited partnerships have been used to invest in many different types of assets. They are most often formed to invest in opportunities requiring sizable outlays and professional management. Limited partnerships vary in risk, from a conservative one formed to own a fully rented office building with long-term leases to a risky one formed to own the sperm bank of a famous thoroughbred horse that has never sired a winning offspring. Here we focus on three principal areas: real estate, energy resources, and equipment leasing. Other popular areas include livestock feeding or breeding programs, research and development programs, major movie or play production programs, cable TV programs, and real estate mortgage programs.

Real Estate

Depending upon property type, a periodic cash flow, price appreciation, and/or tax shelter can be realized from investing in real estate. Raw land is normally purchased for its price appreciation potential. Apartment buildings, shopping centers, office buildings, and the like can provide cash flow as well as price appreciation. Very often, these types of properties are syndicated and bought by limited partnerships. The typical real estate limited partnership consists of a general partner who manages the investment and the limited partners who provide most or all of the capital. As noted earlier, limited tax shelter may be available only to those *actively* participating in real estate investment.

There are two major types of real estate syndicates: The *blind pool syndicate* is formed by a syndicator to raise a given amount of money to be invested at his or her discretion, though the general partner often has some or all of the properties already picked out. The *single property syndicate*, on the other hand, is established to raise money to purchase specific properties. Very often, the large, multiproperty limited partnership syndicates with many investors are blind pools. Single property syndicates are generally smaller in scope.

Energy Resources

The United States depends heavily on energy for its economic well-being, so the federal government has provided tax incentives to encourage people to invest in the search for energy. Limited partnerships are a popular vehicle used to pool capital with which to finance exploration for oil, natural gas, coal, and geothermal steam. The most popular energy-related limited partnerships are oil and gas investments.

There are three basic types of oil and gas limited partnerships: *Exploratory programs*, also known as "wildcats," drill in areas where oil or gas is believed to exist but has not yet been discovered. *Developmental programs* finance the drilling of wells in areas of known and proven oil and gas reserves. (They often drill wells that are near already producing oil or gas finds.) *Income programs* buy existing wells with proven reserves.

The oil and gas business is risky due to the high degree of uncertainty associated with it. Even the most knowledgeable geologists and petroleum engineers are never quite sure how much oil or gas is in a particular well or field. Oil and gas limited partnership investments are therefore risky. The degree of risk, of course, depends on the type of program an investor purchases. Exploratory programs carry the highest risk of the three types and, correspondingly, offer the highest potential return.

Equipment Leasing

Another popular limited partnership investment deals with various types of leasable property—airplanes, railroad cars, machinery, computers, trucks, and automobiles. The limited partnership buys the equipment, such as a computer, and then leases it to another party. As the lessor of the equipment, the partnership can depreciate the item. Additionally, the partnership may use borrowed capital to increase potential return. The business of leasing property requires a great deal of knowledge and skill. The key to investment success in leasing is a competent general partner. Computers and various types of industrial machinery, for example, often have a high obsolescence risk.

PARTNERSHIP STRUCTURE: PRIVATE OR PUBLIC

private partnership
a limited partnership that has a limited number of investors and is not registered with a public agency.

public partnership
a limited partnership that is registered with state and/or federal regulators and usually has 35 or more investors.

The size and scope of limited partnerships vary considerably. For example, three friends might establish a limited partnership to buy a six-unit apartment building. In contrast, large partnerships involving thousands of investors and tens of millions of dollars are frequently formed to acquire producing oil and gas properties. There are two distinct types of limited partnerships: The **private partnership** has a limited number of investors and is not registered with a public agency such as a state securities commission or the SEC. The **public**

partnership is registered with the appropriate state and/or federal regulators and usually has 35 or more investors. State and federal laws regulate offerings of all limited partnership programs.

Private Partnerships

Private limited partnerships are often assembled by a local real estate broker or an attorney; they tend to be more for the well-to-do and to *take more risks* than public partnerships. Often the investors know one another personally. Potential investors in the partnership are commonly given a *private placement memorandum*, a document describing the property to be purchased, management fees, and other financial details. It usually also contains the limited partnership agreement.

Private partnerships have several advantages: First, because they do not have to be registered with a public agency, they usually carry lower transaction and legal costs than public partnerships. (Legal fees in connection with registration of securities are costly and are paid indirectly by the limited partners.) Another advantage of the private partnership is that it may be easier to obtain firsthand knowledge about the general partner. A good source of information on a general partner is other limited partners who have previously invested in his or her partnerships.

Public Partnerships

Public limited partnership syndications must be registered with state and sometimes federal regulatory authorities. Interstate sales of limited partnership interests must comply with federal as well as state laws. Offerings sold only within one state, however, need comply only with that state's laws. Public partnerships are sold by stockbrokers and other licensed securities dealers, and transaction costs are high. The brokerage commission on a typical oil and gas limited partnership is about 8 percent. Limited partnership interests, both private and public, are relatively illiquid, and sometimes the interest cannot be sold without the approval of the state authority. A potential buyer of a public limited partnership must be given a *prospectus*, a detailed statement containing the financial data, management information, and transaction and legal costs associated with the offering. Most public partnerships are large in scope and usually contain over $1 million in assets. An investor in a public partnership may find that his or her shares represent an investment in a *diversified* portfolio of real estate or energy resource properties. Geographic diversity may be easier to obtain by investing in public partnerships.

ESSENTIAL INVESTMENT CONSIDERATIONS

Limited partnership promoters sometimes concoct unbelievable schemes for earning significant returns. They advertise that you can earn a sizable return on an investment as a result of the general partner's unique situation or expertise. Although this is possible, it is certainly not without risk, and generally the actual amount earned, if any, is far less than the amount suggested. For each potential investment in a limited partnership, you should review its leverage, its risk and return, and its investment suitability.

Leverage

In limited partnerships the presence of *leverage* indicates that the underlying business activity utilizes borrowed funds—perhaps in substantial amounts. An equipment-leasing venture, for example, might involve 80 to 90 percent of debt financing. This means your initial investment dollar buys more assets than would be the case were leverage not used. For example, suppose a limited partnership raises $100,000, borrows $900,000 for which the partners have shared liability, and then buys computer equipment for $1,000,000 to lease to a business over a ten-year period. Suppose further that the partnership earns $50,000 in the first year. If you own 5 percent of the partnership (you invested $5,000), in the first year your earnings are $2,500. Your total first-year recovery is therefore equal to 50 percent of your total investment. Had the partnership not used leverage, you would have had to invest $50,000 to own 5 percent (.05 × $1,000,000) of the investment. In such a case, your return would have been only 5 percent on your initial investment ($2,500 ÷ $50,000). Clearly, the use of leverage enhances your return.

However, you must also bear in mind that you are legally liable for your share of the loan, which is $45,000 or (.05 × $900,000). If the loan is with some type of captive finance company that is willing to forgive the debt if the partnership goes under, or if you do not have legal liability for your portion of the debt, the whole deal may (except in the case of real estate partnerships) be considered a sham by the Internal Revenue Service. In such a case, you could be subject to tax penalties. Remember that leverage can increase returns, but to do so, it almost always carries more risk.

Risk and Return

Evaluating the risk and return of a limited partnership investment depends on the property involved. There are two general factors to consider: First, you should carefully *study the general partner*. Again, read the private placement memorandum or prospectus carefully. Find out how much the promoters (general partner and associates) are taking off the top in commissions, legal fees, and management fees. The more they take, the less of your money is invested in the project and the less likely it is that you will receive a high return.

A second factor to recognize is that *most limited partnerships are not very liquid*. In fact, depending on state law, they may not be salable prior to their disbandment. In other words, your interest may be difficult or impossible to resell. Two vehicles are available for enhancing the marketability of LP shares. One is the *master limited partnership (MLP)*, which is a limited partnership that is publicly traded on a major stock exchange. The stock represents a marketable claim on a group of limited partnership interests that are acquired by the MLP in any of a number of ways. Although when they were first introduced it appeared that the MLPs would indeed improve partnership liquidity, subsequent tax-law changes have greatly diminished their attractiveness. The second outlet for LP shares is the emerging secondary market for them. For better-known public limited partnerships, established market makers provide quotes. Private deals and smaller public deals remain quite illiquid, however. Of course, sizable commissions must be paid on these LP transactions, and the general lack of LP liquidity tends to increase the risk associated with investment in them.

Investment Suitability

As you have probably concluded by now, limited partnerships are not for everyone. They tend to be risky and illiquid and thus are usually not suitable for conservative investors primarily interested in the preservation of capital. A private placement memorandum or prospectus will often contain a statement limiting purchase to investors with a minimum net worth (e.g., $100,000) and in the 31, 36, or 39.6 percent tax bracket. This rule excluding certain types of investors is called a **suitability rule.** Its purpose is to allow only investors who can bear a high amount of risk to participate. Additionally, there may be a statement in the prospectus that says, "The securities offered herewith are very high risk." Believe this statement: *If the regulatory authorities require it, it must be a high-risk investment.* Suitability rules vary, depending on applicable state and federal laws. The rules are intended to prevent the sale of high-risk projects to investors who cannot sustain the loss financially. Suitability rules are also usually fairly rigid for public limited partnerships (offerings registered with securities regulators).

suitability rule
a rule excluding investors who cannot bear a high amount of risk from buying limited partnership interests.

CONCEPTS *in Review*

13.17 How does a *limited partnership (LP)* differ from a *general partnership* and a *corporation?* What are the functions of the general and limited partners? How did the Tax Reform Act of 1986 affect the popularity of LPs as tax shelters? Explain.

13.18 In which two ways can an investor earn a return from a limited partnership? Explain.

13.19 What are the popular forms of limited partnerships? Differentiate between *private partnerships* and *public partnerships*.

13.20 How does leverage affect the return and risk of a limited partnership? What are *suitability rules,* and why must they be met by limited partnership investors?

On Track with STOCK-TRAK®

Trading Tax-Advantaged Investments Through STOCK-TRAK®

STOCK-TRAK® does not consider taxes in calculating total portfolio value; nor is tax deferral a consideration, given the short-term, semester-long time horizon for this investment simulation. Nevertheless, several instruments offering tax-favored income are available through STOCK-TRAK®. Many mutual funds, for instance, invest solely in tax-free municipal bonds. Examples are Nuveen Municipal Value Fund, which invests in the state and local issues of many states and is traded on the New York Stock Exchange, and the ACM Government Income Fund, a NYSE-listed fund that invests in U.S. Treasury bonds.

Additionally, investors seeking to make direct investment in the Treasury market can select from a wide variety of Treasury offerings available through STOCK-TRAK®. As interest rates decline and the likelihood of higher taxes increases, the value of these investments often increases.

SUMMARY   **LG 1**   **Understand what is meant by taxable income and the basic procedures involved in its calculation.** As taxable income increases, so do tax burdens imposed by federal tax law. Taxable income can be either ordinary income—active, portfolio, or passive—or capital gains or losses. Both ordinary income and capital gains are subject to the same schedule of tax rates. Taxable income is calculated first by finding gross income, which includes all forms of income, with some exceptions. After subtracting certain adjustments to gross income, adjusted gross income results. Subtracting itemized deductions and exemptions results in taxable income, from which federal income taxes are calculated. Taxes due are found by subtracting any eligible tax credits from the federal income tax.

LG 2   **Define tax avoidance and tax deferral and the characteristics of tax shelters.** Tax-avoidance strategies attempt to earn tax-favored income, which is essentially income not subject to taxes. Tax-deferral strategies attempt to defer taxes from current periods to later periods. A tax shelter is an investment vehicle that earns a portion of its return by offering potential offsets to the investor's other taxable income.

LG 3   **Explain how investors can earn tax-favored income, with particular emphasis on income excluded from taxation, strategies that defer tax liabilities to the next year, programs that defer tax liabilities to retirement, strategies that trade current income for capital gains, and tax swaps.** Tax-favored income excluded from taxation includes tax-free municipal bond interest, Treasury and government agency issues (free of state and local income taxes), and the sale of a personal residence. Strategies that defer tax liabilities to the next year include a short sale against the box, a put hedge, and selling a deep-in-the-money call option. Each strategy has relative advantages and disadvantages, depending on the assumed future movement of the stock's price.

Programs that defer tax liabilities to retirement include 401(k) plans, Keogh plans, and individual retirement arrangements (IRAs). Popular strategies that trade current income for capital gains include buying growth rather than income stocks, buying deep discount bonds, and investing in income property. Tax swaps are a strategy that can be used to reduce or eliminate a tax liability without altering the basic portfolio.

LG 4   **Summarize the characteristics of deferred annuities—use in retirement plans, fixed versus variable, and their appeal as investment vehicles—and single-premium life insurance.** Because they pay relatively high market rates of interest and allow for tax-free reinvestment, deferred annuities have some appeal as a tax-deferral vehicle. Tax-sheltered annuities can be purchased by employees of certain institutions by making limited tax-free contributions from current income. Annuity payouts can be either fixed or variable; the payouts on variable annuities depend on the insurer's actual investment performance.

Deferred annuities are relatively low-risk vehicles that may not produce earnings on a par with inflation rates; therefore, investors should determine by analysis whether they are suitable. The single-premium life insurance policy, in the past a popular alternative to the deferred annuity, has diminished in popularity since 1988, due to tax-law changes that virtually eliminated the ability to use policy loans to make tax-free withdrawals.

LG 5   **Describe the tax status of limited partnerships and how they work.** A limited partnership is an organizational form that allows an individual to invest with limited liability, receive the benefit of professional management, and apply the resulting profit or loss (subject to limits) when calculating his or her tax liability. The general partner actively runs the business, while the limited partners supply the capital and take a passive role in the venture. The return from a limited partnership comes from either cash flow or price appreciation.

Discuss popular forms of limited partnerships, partnership structure, and their essential investment considerations—leverage, risk and return, and investment suitability. Limited partnerships have been formed to acquire many different kinds of assets; the most common are real estate, energy resources, and equipment for leasing purposes. Limited partnerships can be structured as private or public partnerships. Leverage can increase the potential earnings as well as the risk in a limited partnership. Potential investors should study the private placement memorandum or prospectus for a limited partnership to carefully examine the investment's risk-return characteristics and hence its suitability. Often investors themselves must meet certain suitability rules prior to investing in a limited partnership.

DISCUSSION QUESTIONS

1. Obtain a copy of the most recent year's Form 1040 (*U.S. Individual Income Tax Return*), along with Schedules A (*Itemized Deductions*), B (*Interest and Dividend Income*), and D (*Capital Gains and Losses*) and instructions for preparing the return. Use your actual (or forecast) data to prepare your return for the most recent year. If you earn no or very low income, instead use data provided by a family member.
   a. Discuss the exemptions claimed and their effect on taxable income.
   b. Study Schedule A and discuss how each of the following are treated:
      (1) Medical and dental expenses
      (2) Mortgage interest
      (3) Job expenses
   c. Discuss the key factor affecting whether to itemize deductions or take the standard deduction.
   d. Describe how the total tax was calculated. What top tax bracket applied?
   e. What, if any, recommendation would you give with regard to actions that might be advantageous from a tax standpoint?

2. Assume you have a sizable gain on 200 shares of stock that you bought 2 years ago for $22 per share and that is now (December 15) selling for $50 per share. Given a just announced tax rate cut, effective next calendar year, you want to delay realizing the gain until next year, but you are concerned that the stock's price might decline in the interim. To defer the tax liability to next year, you are considering (1) shorting-against-the-box, (2) using a put hedge, or (3) selling deep-in-the-money call options.
   a. Contact a stockbroker and obtain the approximate cost of implementing each of these strategies.
   b. Compare and contrast the brokerage cost associated with each strategy. Which strategy is cheapest in terms of these costs?
   c. What, if any, impact should these costs have on the selection of the best strategy? (Be sure to measure these costs on a *per share* basis.)
   d. For the cheapest strategy, by approximately how much will the brokerage costs reduce the unrealized gain on the stock?

3. Imagine that, given your current age and marital status, you have decided to make the maximum contribution to an individual retirement arrangement (IRA) each year from now until age 65. (Assume that the current maximum contribution rate will remain unchanged over this period.) You expect to earn a 10 percent annual rate of return on IRA investments and are subject to a 30 percent tax rate.
   a. How much would you have in the IRA account at age 65 if you can earn 10 percent on IRA investments and IRA contributions are:
      (1) Deductible?
      (2) Nondeductible?

b. How much better off would you be as a result of having a deductible rather than a nondeductible IRA? What, if any, tax benefit does a nondeductible IRA offer?

c. Describe and justify the overall investment strategy you would employ on your IRA investments.

d. What specific types of vehicles would you include in your IRA investment portfolio? Justify your choices.

e. Compare and contrast the deductible IRA to a (1) 401(k) plan and (2) a Keogh plan. If you could contribute to any of these plans, which would be preferable? Why?

4. Obtain from a licensed salesperson or stockbroker a prospectus and any other available literature on a popular deferred annuity. Analyze the terms, and answer the following questions.

a. What is the *current interest rate*? How does it compare to T-bill rates? To AAA bond yields?

b. What is the *minimum guaranteed interest rate* on contributions? How does it compare to T-bill rates? To AAA bond yields?

c. What, if any, *tax benefit* does it offer the investor?

d. What *payout options* does it offer? Is it a *fixed* or *variable annuity*? Which payout option do you find most appealing?

e. What sales charges and administrative fees are levied on this annuity? How does it compare to other annuities?

f. What is the rating of the financial strength of the insurer given in *Best's Insurance Reports*?

g. What are the pros and cons of purchasing this annuity?

5. Ask a stockbroker for the prospectus of a currently popular public limited partnership real estate investment. Carefully analyze the prospectus, and answer the following questions.

a. What are the *suitability rules* for investing in this partnership?

b. What is the partnership's investment objective? Does it seem achievable?

c. Is this partnership a *blind pool* or a *single property syndicate*? In general, what kind of properties are being acquired?

d. What is the background of the general partner? Does it seem appropriate/acceptable?

e. Is *leverage* being used by the partnership? What effect does it have on risk?

f. What are the potential risk-return factors of this investment? What other important factors should be considered when evaluating this partnership? Would you recommend investing in this partnership?

PROBLEMS   1. Using Table 13.1, calculate Ed Robinson's income tax due on his $35,000 taxable income, assuming he files as a single taxpayer. After you make the calculation, explain to Ed what his marginal tax rate is and why it is important in making investment decisions.

    2. During the year just ended, Jean Sanchez's taxable income of $48,000 was twice as large as her younger sister Rachel's taxable income of $24,000. Use the tax rate schedule in Table 13.1 to answer the following questions with regard to the Sanchez sisters, who are both single.

a. Calculate each sister's tax liability.

b. Determine the (1) marginal tax rate and (2) average tax rate for each sister.

c. Do your findings in (b) demonstrate the progressive nature of income taxes? Explain.

 LG 1 3. Sheila and Jim Mendez reported the following income tax items in 1996:

Salaries and wages	$38,000
Interest on bonds	1,100*
Dividends (jointly owned stocks)	1,000
Capital gains on securities	1,500
Deductible IRA contribution	2,000
Itemized deductions	8,000

*$400 of this total was received from tax-free municipal bonds.

If Sheila and Jim claim three dependents and file a joint return for 1996, calculate their income tax due. (Use Table 13.1 and assume an exemption of $2,450 for each qualifying dependent.)

LG 1 4. The Akais just finished calculating their taxable income for their 1996 joint federal income tax return. It totaled $58,750 and showed no tax credits. Just prior to filing their return, the Akais realized they had treated a $1,000 outlay as an itemized deduction, rather than correctly treating it as a $1,000 tax credit.

a. Use the tax rate schedule in Table 13.1 to calculate the Akais' tax liability and tax due based on their original $58,750 estimate of taxable income.

b. How much taxable income would the Akais have if they correctly treat the $1,000 as a tax credit rather than a tax deduction?

c. Use your finding in (a) to calculate the Akais' tax liability and tax due after converting the $1,000 tax deduction to a tax credit.

d. Compare and contrast your findings in (a) and (c). Which would you prefer— a tax deduction or an equal-dollar-amount tax credit? Why?

LG 3 5. Shawn Healy bought 300 shares of Apple Computer common stock at $32 a share. Fifteen months later, in December, Apple was up to $47 a share and Shawn was considering selling her shares, because she believed Apple's price could drop as low as $42 within the next several months. What advice would you offer Shawn for locking in the gain and deferring the tax to the following year? Explain.

LG 3 6. Karen Jones purchased 200 shares of Mex Inc. common stock for $10 per share exactly 2 years ago, in December 1994. Today, December 15, 1996, the stock is selling for $18 per share. Because Karen strongly believes that the stock is fully valued in the market, she wishes to sell it and invest the proceeds in the stock of an attractive emerging company. Karen, who is in the 28 percent tax bracket, realizes that if she sells the stock prior to year-end, the capital gain of $1,600 [200 shares × ($18 sale price − $10 purchase price)] would result in taxes for 1996 of $448 (.28 × $1,600). Because Karen would like to lock in her $1,600 profit but defer the tax on it until 1997, she plans to investigate the strategies available for accomplishing this objective.

a. How can Karen use shorting-against-the-box to accomplish her objective? Will she be able to benefit from any future increases in Mex Inc.'s stock price if she uses the shorting-against-the-box strategy?

b. If Karen can purchase two put options on Mex Inc.'s stock at a contractual sale price of $18 for a total cost of $180 ($90 per 100-share option), what would be her after-tax position if the stock price declined to $16 per share? Will Karen be able to benefit from any future increases in Mex Inc.'s stock price using this put hedge strategy?

   c. If Karen can sell two call options on Mex Inc.'s stock with a $16 contractual
       buy price and 6-month maturity for $480 ($240 per 100-share option) when
       the stock is selling for $18 per share, what would be her after-tax position if
       the stock price declined to $16 per share? Will Karen be able to benefit from
       any future increases in Mex Inc.'s stock price using this deep-in-the-money
       call option strategy? Is the price of $18 fully locked in using this strategy?
   d. Use your findings in (a), (b), and (c) to compare and contrast the three strate-
       gies. Then recommend a strategy to Karen, assuming the stock price *does*
       drop below the current price.

 7. Juan Gonzalez, a single person working for Harla, Inc., earned $48,000 in 1996
       and is considering contributing $7,000 to the firm's 401(k) plan. If Juan is in the 28
       percent tax bracket, what will his taxable income be? How much tax savings will
       result, and how much did it cost Juan on an after-tax basis to make the $7,000 contri-
       bution?

CASE PROBLEMS   ### 13.1   TAX PLANNING FOR THE WILSONS

Hal and Terri Wilson had most of their funds invested in common stock in the spring
of 1995. The Wilsons didn't really do very much investment planning, and they had
practically no background or understanding of how income taxes might affect their
investment decisions. Their holdings consisted exclusively of common stocks, selected
primarily on the advice of their stockbroker, Sid Nichols. Despite a relatively lackluster
market, they did experience some nice capital gains, even though several of their holdings showed losses from their original purchase prices. A summary of their holdings on
December 20, 1995, appears below.

Stock	Date Purchased	Original Cost	Current Market Value
Consolidated Power and Light	2/10/93	$10,000	$16,000
Cargon Industries	7/7/95	3,000	8,000
PYT Corporation	6/29/95	7,000	6,000
Amalgamated Iron & Steel	8/9/94	8,000	5,000
Jones Building Supplies	3/6/91	4,500	4,700

   Hal feels this might be a good time to revise their portfolio. He favors selling all
their holdings and reinvesting the funds in several growth-oriented mutual funds and
perhaps several real estate limited partnerships. Terri agrees their portfolio could use
some revision, but she is reluctant to sell everything. For one thing, she is concerned
that federal income taxes might take a sizable share of their profits. In addition, she
strongly believes Amalgamated Iron & Steel will make a significant recovery, as will all
steel stocks, in 1996.
   After some discussion, the Wilsons decided to consult their friend, Elaine Byer, who
was a CPA for a major public accounting firm. Byer indicated that she was not an
expert in the investment field and therefore couldn't tell the Wilsons which securities
to buy or sell from that perspective. From a tax point of view, however, she did not recommend selling everything in the 1995 tax year. Instead, she said that Consolidated
Power and Light, PYT Corporation, Amalgamated Iron & Steel, and Jones Building
Supplies should be sold in December 1995, but that Cargon Industries should be carried into 1996 and sold then—if that was what the Wilsons wanted to do.
   Hal and Terri were grateful for Byer's advice, but they had two major concerns.
First, they were concerned about waiting to sell Cargon Industries, because it had

showed such a sizable gain and they were afraid its price might decline sharply in a stock market sell-off. Second, they were reluctant to sell Amalgamated Iron & Steel despite the benefit of its tax loss, because they wanted to remain invested in the steel industry over the long run. As a final step, they contacted Nichols, their stockbroker, who agreed with Byer's advice; he said not to worry about the Cargon situation. The stock was selling at $80 a share, and he would put in a short against the box for them, which would enable them to deliver the shares whenever they wanted. He also explained that they could use a tax swap to get the tax benefit of the loss on Amalgamated Iron & Steel while staying invested in the steel industry. He suggested United States Iron as a swap candidate, because it was selling for about the same price as Amalgamated.

Questions

1. Assuming the Wilsons are in the 28 percent tax bracket, calculate the resulting federal income tax (a) if they sold all their securities in 1995 at their current market values, and (b) if they sold Consolidated Power and Light, PYT Corporation, Amalgamated Iron & Steel, and Jones Building Supplies at their respective market values in 1995, and then sold Cargon Industries at its current market value on January 2, 1996. What do you conclude from your calculations?

2. As noted, Nichols suggested a short sale against the box for Cargon. Explain his reasoning about the future price of this stock.

3. Suppose you thought Cargon had a good possibility for further price increases in 1996, but you were equally concerned that its price could fall sharply. Would you then agree with the strategy Nichols recommended, or would you prefer a different strategy? Explain your answer.

4. Discuss the tax swap suggested by Nichols. Does this strategy allow the Wilsons to minimize taxes while retaining their position in the steel industry? Explain.

5. What overall strategies would you recommend to the Wilsons, given their investment objectives and tax status? Explain.

13.2   DO OIL AND FRED CRANSTON MIX?

Fred Cranston, age 36, is the West Coast marketing manager and vice-president of a major auto parts supply firm. His salary reflects his success in his job: $90,000 per year. Additionally, his firm provides him with a car, an excellent pension and profit sharing plan, superior life and medical insurance coverage, and company stock options. Fred owns his home, which is located in the exclusive Marin County, California, area.

In addition to Fred's house and his pension and profit sharing plans, he has a stock portfolio worth about $75,000, a tax-free municipal bond portfolio valued at $150,000, and about $100,000 in a highly liquid money market mutual fund. Fred would like to make more risky investments to increase his returns. He is considering taking $50,000 out of the money market mutual fund and investing in some limited partnerships. His broker, Marie Bell, has proposed that he invest $50,000 divided among five oil and gas limited partnerships. Marie's specific recommendation is to buy two developmental and three income programs, each for $10,000. She explained to Fred that this $50,000 investment could potentially increase his income by $20,000 per year. Marie has also pointed out that if the expected rise in oil prices occurs, Fred could expect to receive even larger cash returns in future years. Fred meets the suitability rules required for such investments as prescribed by the securities commission of California. Being a relatively conservative individual, he is trying to justify in his mind the reasonableness of his broker's recommendations.

Questions

1. What do you think of Marie Bell's investment recommendations for Fred? Are developmental programs too risky? Should Fred buy five different oil and gas programs, or should he invest the entire $50,000 in one program? Explain.

2. How would you describe the legal structure of a limited partnership to Fred? What should Fred know about the general partner in each of these programs?

3. In general, does investment in oil and gas development and income programs make sense to you? Why or why not?

4. What other forms of limited partnerships might you suggest that Fred consider? Discuss the leverage and risk-return tradeoffs involved in them.

PART FIVE

DERIVATIVE SECURITIES

CHAPTER 14
OPTIONS: PUTS AND CALLS, RIGHTS, AND WARRANTS

CHAPTER 15
COMMODITIES AND FINANCIAL FUTURES

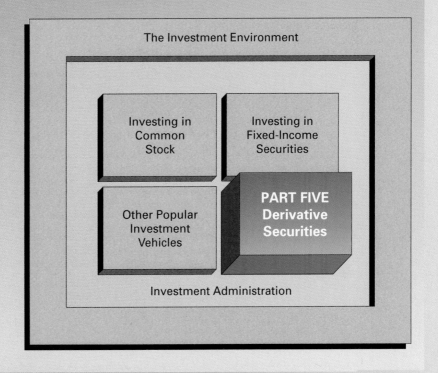

CHAPTER 14

OPTIONS: PUTS AND CALLS, RIGHTS, AND WARRANTS

LEARNING GOALS

After studying this chapter, you should be able to:

LG 1 Discuss the basic nature of options in general and puts and calls in particular, and gain an understanding of how these investment vehicles work.

LG 2 Explain how put and call options are valued and the forces that drive options prices in the marketplace.

LG 3 Describe the profit potential of puts and calls, as well as the risk and return behavior of various put and call investment strategies.

LG 4 Describe market index options, puts and calls on foreign currencies, and LEAPS, and note how these securities can be used by investors.

LG 5 Describe the basic features and fundamental investment attributes of stock rights.

LG 6 Discuss the basic investment characteristics of stock warrants and describe the trading strategies that can be used to gain maximum benefits from this investment vehicle.

Soon after Craig Berman began investing, his broker introduced him to the options market. "Rather than buy stock, for the same money I could buy options and use leverage to increase my profits. The first few trades I did were profitable beyond my wildest dreams!" Craig recalls. "I was hooked and learned as much as I could about options. I was single and willing to take the higher risk of options for the chance of significantly bigger rewards. With options, I could reach my investment goals—in the early days, a sports car; now, a house with a pool—much faster. Later, I discovered market index options." Now that he is married, Craig continues to trade options, but weekly rather than daily, and for lesser amounts.

Craig invests in U.S. equity options and three market indexes: the S&P 100, S&P 500, and XMI (Major Market Index). He hedges with options to protect equity positions, particularly in retirement accounts. For example, one stock in his IRA rose sharply until mid-1994. Because he liked the company and its management and didn't want to sell, he bought puts to ensure against a downtrend. When the price did fall, the puts gained in value and protected his profits. Index options are speculative and allow him to profit from the changing value of the whole market without having to buy each stock. "If I think the market's rising, I own calls or sell a put spread. If the reverse is true, I own puts or sell a call spread. A *spread* sometimes involves simultaneously buying an option and selling a higher-priced option of the same type—say, *selling* a March 430 S&P 500 call for $10 and *buying* a March 440 call for $3. If the market should fall, the spread between the two options narrows, providing profit," Craig explains. "But if the market rises, the call spread caps my losses. Therefore, I'm protected from a rapid decline in my investment but still have an opportunity to profit."

Options trading can be very frustrating, and as with any investment, it's hard to avoid looking back. For example, in January 1995 Berman paid $9,000 for 100 contracts of America Online February 60 calls and sold them for $33,700. "Sounds great, right? A week later, they sold for $94,000!" he says ruefully.

Craig counsels investors to use options as insurance against the vagaries of market movement. "Conservative investors can use covered options (on stocks they own) to protect profits and increase yield. Index options are for only the most daring; you're playing directly against professionals. Unless you're absolutely right, you'll lose big in short order," he cautions. He recommends first getting free options market information offered by the Chicago Board of Trade (800-OPTIONS) and then "paper trading" for a while until you feel you know what you're doing. Pick a company and "invest" on paper a reasonable amount—not a million dollars but what you'd actually invest—in options. Follow the stock daily, find a broker who really understands options, and learn how options markets work and how changing stock prices affect options prices. Then start small. "See how you react to playing with real money," Craig advises. "Gauge your risk tolerance, nervousness, and, of course, your results. Stick with things you know before you go exploring the wider world of options trading."

CONSERVATIVE INVESTORS CAN USE OPTIONS TO PROTECT PROFITS AND INCREASE YIELD.

Craig Berman was fortunate to turn his options investing "hobby" into a career. Today, he invests in options for both his own and his clients' accounts at Gruntal & Co., a New York City brokerage firm where he has been an account executive since 1988. He is 38, is married, and lives in New York City.

When investors buy shares of common or preferred stock, they become the registered owners of the securities and are entitled to all the rights and privileges of ownership. Investors who acquire bonds or convertible issues are also entitled to the benefits of ownership. However, options are another matter: *Investors who buy options acquire nothing more than the right to subsequently buy or sell other, related securities*. That is, an **option** gives the holder the right to buy or sell a certain amount of an underlying security at a specified price over a specified period of time. As Craig Berman discovered, the world of options opens up whole new investment opportunities, whether investors are conservative and want to protect stocks they own or are aggressive risk takers who speculate on stock and market movements.

There are three basic kinds of options: (1) puts and calls, (2) rights, and (3) warrants. Although rights hold little investment appeal for the average individual investor, the other two types of options—and especially puts and calls—enjoy considerable popularity today as attractive trading vehicles. All of these securities are a bit unusual, and their use requires special investor know-how. The focus of this chapter, therefore, is to explain the essential characteristics and investment merits of these securities and to demonstrate how they can be used in various types of investment programs. We begin our discussion with a rather detailed examination of put and call options. After that, we'll move on briefly to stock rights and then to warrants. You'll find that most of this chapter is devoted to puts and calls, since they are, by far, the dominant type of options security and certainly the most actively traded.

option
a security that gives the holder the right to buy or sell a certain amount of an underlying financial asset at a specified price for a specified period of time.

PUT AND CALL OPTIONS

Stocks, bonds, and convertibles are all examples of *financial assets*. They represent financial claims on the issuing corporation or organization, and they entitle the holders of such securities to certain rights, privileges, and claims (on the income and assets of the issuer). In contrast, options are *contractual instruments*, whereby two parties enter into an agreement (or "contract") to give something of value to the other. In particular, an options contract gives the buyer the right to buy or sell a certain amount of some underlying asset, for a given period of time, at a price that's fixed at the time of the contract. The option seller, on the other hand, stands ready to buy or sell the underlying asset according to the terms of the contract—for which the seller is paid a certain amount of money. Thus, as in any contract, each party grants something of value to the other. The buyer pays the seller a fee (the option's price), in return for which the seller grants the buyer the right (but not the obligation) to buy or sell some underlying asset at a fixed price.

DEFINITIONS AND CHARACTERISTICS

One of the market phenomenas of the 1970s was the remarkable performance and investment popularity of stock options—particularly, puts and calls on common stock. By the early 1980s, the interest in options spilled over to other kinds of financial assets, so that, today, investors can trade puts and calls on:

- Common stock
- Stock indexes
- Debt instruments
- Foreign currencies
- Commodities and financial futures

As we will see, although the underlying financial assets may vary, the basic features and behavioral characteristics of these securities are much the same. Regardless of the type of option, much of the popularity of options stems from the fact that investors can buy a lot of price action with a limited amount of capital, while nearly always enjoying limited exposure to risk.

A Negotiable Contract

Puts and calls are negotiable instruments, issued in bearer form, that allow the holder to buy or sell a specified amount of a specified security at a specified price. For example, a put or a call on common stock covers 100 shares of stock in a specific company. A **put** enables the holder to sell the underlying security at the specified price (known as the *exercise* or *strike* price) over a set period of time. A **call**, in contrast, gives the holder the right to buy the securities at the stated (strike) price within a certain time period. As with any option, there are no voting rights, no privileges of ownership, and no interest or dividend income. Instead, puts and calls possess value to the extent that they allow the holder to participate in the price behavior of the underlying financial asset.

Because puts and calls derive their value from the price behavior of some other real or financial asset, they are known as **derivative securities**. Rights and warrants, as well as futures contracts (which we'll study in Chapter 15), are also derivative securities, as they too derive their value from an underlying security or asset. The fact is that many different types of derivative securities are available in the market today, from puts and calls to structured CDs to exotic debt instruments, like collateralized mortgage obligations (CMOs). Although certain segments of this market are for big institutional investors only, there are plenty of these securities that are sold to individual investors. Derivative securities received a lot of attention in 1993 and 1994, as they caused some real serious problems for investors—namely, some big-time losses. But as the accompanying *Investor Insights* box discusses, these securities have both a good side and a bad side. So, you be the judge: Are derivative securities as bad as some would have you believe?

Puts and calls are traded on listed exchanges and, on a *much smaller scale*, in the over-the-counter market. They provide attractive leverage opportunities because they carry low prices relative to the market price of the underlying financial assets. To illustrate, consider a call on a common stock that gives the holder the right to buy 100 shares of a $50 stock at a (strike) price of $45 a share. The stock would be priced at $50, but the call would trade at an effective price of only $5 a share (or the difference between the market price of the common and the price it can be purchased at as specified on the call). However, since a single stock option always involves 100 shares of stock, the actual market price of our $5 call would be $500 (i.e., $5 × 100 shares = $500).

put
a negotiable instrument that enables the holder to sell the underlying security at a specified price over a set period of time.

call
a negotiable instrument that gives the holder the right to buy securities at a stated price within a certain time period.

derivative securities
securities, such as puts, calls, and other options, that derive their value from the price behavior of an underlying real or financial asset.

INVESTOR INSIGHTS: *Conflicting Viewpoints*

Derivative Securities: There Are Two Sides to Every Story

Derivatives—they're an $18 trillion market that some investors shun at all costs and others use as a route to big returns: Individual investors buy puts and calls to limit their downside risk on stocks they own; risk takers use them to speculate on stock price movements. Even if you don't personally use them, the corporations, financial institutions, and mutual funds in which you invest use them to manage risk efficiently and to increase investment returns. How can you determine the effect that will have on the profitability of a company or a mutual fund in which you invest?

Derivatives vary tremendously in complexity and risk. Traditional, "conservative" derivatives like put and call options and futures are used all the time by companies and mutual funds as a type of insurance to limit risk. Recently, however, investment bankers have created increasingly complex and "toxic" synthetic derivatives. Examples include an *interest strip* (in which a bond's interest stream—the derivative—is separated from the bond and provides *only interest payments* on the underlying security), *collateralized mortgage obligations* (derived from mortgage-backed securities, themselves created from pools of home mortgages), *interest rate swaps* (in which two parties exchange fixed rates for variable rate interest payments), and even *swaptions* (options to enter into a swap).

In many cases, derivatives are the least expensive way to protect against sharp movements in currency values, commodity prices, or interest rates. Many sophisticated corporate treasurers and fund managers use them successfully to stabilize earnings and lower risk, and funds that use derivatives often earn higher returns than those that don't. Hedging with currency forwards and futures reduces the risk of fluctuating currency prices for mutual funds holding foreign securities and companies wishing to protect foreign revenues, prices on imported products, and raw materials purchased abroad. On the other hand, betting on market movements is speculative and very risky. Even experienced, sophisticated investors can lose big; in 1994, Procter & Gamble lost $157 million pretax when it misjudged the direction of interest rates.

Should you panic if you find such derivatives as forwards, futures, and CMOs lurking in the financial reports of a corporation or mutual fund you own? Probably not, but you will need to ask some questions: How experienced is the person who's investing in derivatives? Are the derivatives used appropriately for the company or fund (i.e., to *hedge* currency exposure rather than to *speculate* on market movements)? Once you know the answers, you can judge if the derivatives are good or bad for the organization's—and your portfolio's—financial health.

Sources: Adapted from Lee Berton, "Understanding the Complex World of Derivatives," *Wall Street Journal*, June 14, 1994, pp. C1, C17; Rita Koselka, "Safe When Used Properly," *Forbes*, August 15, 1994, pp. 47–48; Lililana Nealon, "Derivatives and the Bogey Monster," *Worth*, October 1994, p. 107–8; and Maria Crawford Scott, "A Look at Derivatives and Their Use in Mutual Fund Portfolios," *AAII Journal*, September 1994, pp. 12–15.

American or European Options

American option
an option that can be exercised on any business day the option is traded, on or before the option's expiration date.

European option
an option that can be exercised only on the date of expiration.

Put and call options can be issued in either *American* or *European* form. Actually, these terms have absolutely nothing to do with where the options are traded but, rather, with when the options can be exercised. Specifically, an **American option** can be exercised on any business day on which the option is traded, on or before the option's expiration date. In contrast, a **European option** can be exercised only on the date of expiration. Put another way, an American option can be exercised prior to expiration; a European option cannot. The vast majority of puts and calls traded in the United States are American options. For example, all listed stock options are of the American form. European options, on the other hand, are not as common and are found mostly on stock-index and foreign currency options.

Although it's true that, other things being equal, American options should be more valuable than European options because they give you more exercise dates, the fact is that for all practical purposes, most investors couldn't care less whether an option is American or European. The reasons? First, only a tiny fraction of options are ever exercised, so it doesn't make much difference when they can be cashed in. Second, and more importantly, just because an option can't be exercised prior to maturity doesn't mean you have to hold it to expiration date. Any option—American or European—can be sold at any time. (For purposes of this and the next chapter, we'll assume that we're dealing with American options throughout.)

Maker Versus Buyer

option maker (writer)
the individual or institution that writes/creates put and call options.

Puts and calls are a unique type of security because they are *not* issued by the organizations that issue the underlying stock or financial asset. Instead, puts and calls *are created by investors*. It works like this: Suppose one individual wants to sell to another the right to buy 100 shares of common stock. This individual would "write a call." The individual or institution writing the option is known as the **option maker** or **writer**. The maker who writes and sells an option is entitled to receive the price paid for the put or call (less modest commissions and other transaction costs). The put or call option is now a full-fledged financial asset and trades in the open market much like any other security.

Puts and calls are both written (sold) and purchased through security brokers and dealers, and they are actively bought and sold in the secondary market. The writer stands behind the option, as it is the *writer* who must buy or deliver the stocks or other financial assets according to the terms of the option. (*Note*: Unlike the holders/buyers of put or call options, the writers or makers of these securities *do have a legally binding obligation* to stand behind the terms of the contracts they have written. The buyer can just walk away from the deal if it turns sour; the writer cannot.) Puts and calls are written for a variety of reasons, most of which we will explore below. At this point, suffice it to say that writing options can be a viable investment strategy and can be a profitable course of action since, more often than not, *options expire worthless*.

How Puts and Calls Work

Using the *buyer's* point of view, let us now briefly examine how puts and calls work and how they derive their value. To understand the mechanics of puts and calls, it is best to look at their profit-making potential. For example, using stock options as a basis of discussion, consider a stock currently priced at $50 a share. Assume you can buy a call on the stock for $500, which enables you to purchase 100 shares of the stock at a fixed price of $50 each. A rise in the price of the underlying security (in this case, common stock) is what you, as an investor, hope for. With that in mind, what is the profit potential from this transaction if the price of the stock does indeed move up to, say, $75 by the expiration date on the call? The answer is that you will earn $25 ($75 − $50) on each of the 100 shares of stock in the call, for a total gross profit of some

$2,500—and all from a $500 investment. This is so since you can buy 100 shares of the stock—from the option writer—at a price of $50 each and immediately turn around and sell them in the market for $75 a share. You could have made the same profit by investing directly in the common stock, but because you would have had to invest $5,000 (100 shares × $50 per share), your rate of return would have been much lower. Obviously, there is considerable difference between the profit potential of common stocks and calls, and it is this difference that attracts investors and speculators to calls whenever the price outlook for the underlying financial asset is upward. (Note that although our illustration is couched in terms of common stock, this same valuation principle applies to *any* of the other financial assets that may underlie call options, such as market indexes, foreign currencies, or futures contracts.)

A similar situation can also be worked out for puts. Assume that for the same $50 stock you could pay $500 and buy a put to sell 100 shares of the stock at a strike price of $50 each. As the buyer of a put, you want the price of the stock to *drop*. Assume your expectations are correct and the price of the stock does indeed drop, to $25 a share. Here again, you would realize a gross profit of $25 for each of the 100 shares in the put. You can do this by going to the market and buying 100 shares of the stock at a price of $25 a share, and immediately turning around and selling them to the writer of the put at a price of $50 per share.

Fortunately, put and call investors do *not* have to exercise these options and make simultaneous buy and sell transactions in order to receive their profit, because *options do have value and can be traded in the secondary market*. In fact, the value of both puts and calls is directly linked to the market price of the underlying financial asset. That is, the *value of a call* increases as the market price of the underlying security *rises*, whereas the *value of a put* increases as the price of the security *declines*. Thus, *investors can get their money out of options by selling them in the open market*, just as with any other security.

Advantages and Disadvantages

The major advantage of investing in puts and calls is the leverage they offer. This feature also carries the advantage of limiting the investor's exposure to risk, because only a set amount of money (the purchase price of the option) can be lost. Also appealing is the fact that puts and calls can be used profitably when the price of the underlying security goes up *or* down.

A major disadvantage of puts and calls is that the holder enjoys neither interest or dividend income nor any other ownership benefit. Moreover, because the instruments have limited lives, the investor has a limited time frame in which to capture desired price behavior. Another disadvantage is that puts and calls themselves are a bit unusual, and many of their trading strategies are complex. Thus, investors must possess special knowledge and fully understand the subtleties of this trading vehicle.

OPTIONS MARKETS

Although the concept of options can be traced back to the writings of Aristotle, options trading in the United States did not begin until the late 1700s. And even then, up to the early seventies, this market remained fairly small, largely unorganized, and the almost private domain of a handful of specialists and traders. All of this changed, however, on April 26, 1973, when a new securities market was created with the opening of the Chicago Board Options Exchange (CBOE).

Conventional Options

Prior to the creation of the CBOE, put and call options trading was conducted in the over-the-counter market through a handful of specialized dealers. Investors who wished to purchase puts and calls dealt with these options dealers via their own brokers, and the dealers would find individuals (or institutions) willing to write the options. If the buyer wished to exercise an option, he or she did so with the writer and no one else—a system that largely prohibited any secondary trading. On the other hand, there were virtually no limits to what could be written, so long as the buyer was willing to pay the price. Put and call options were written on New York and American stocks, as well as on regional and over-the-counter securities, for as short as 30 days and as long as a year. Over-the-counter options, known today as **conventional options**, were hard hit by the CBOE and other options exchanges. The conventional market still exists, although on a greatly reduced scale.

Listed Options

The creation of the CBOE signaled the birth of so-called **listed options**, a term used to describe put and call options traded on organized exchanges, rather than over-the-counter. The CBOE launched trading in calls on just 16 firms. From these rather humble beginnings, there evolved in a relatively short period of time a large and active market for listed options. Today, trading in listed options is done in both puts and calls and takes place on five exchanges, the largest of which is the CBOE. Options are also traded on the AMEX, the NYSE, the Philadelphia Exchange, and the Pacific Stock Exchange. In total, *put and call options are now traded on over 1,200 different stocks*. Although many of these options are written on large, well-known NYSE companies, the list also includes a number of AMEX and OTC stocks, both large and small. In addition to stocks, listed options are also available on stock indexes, debt securities, foreign currencies, and even commodities and financial futures.

Listed options not only provided a convenient market for the trading of puts and calls but also standardized the expiration dates and exercise prices. The listed options exchanges created a clearinghouse organization that eliminated direct ties between buyers and writers of options and reduced the cost of executing put and call transactions. They also developed an active secondary market, with wide distribution of price information. As a result, it is now as easy to trade a listed option as a listed stock.

STOCK OPTIONS

The advent of the CBOE and other listed option exchanges had a quick and dramatic impact on the trading volume of puts and calls. Indeed, the level of activity in listed stock options grew rapidly—so much so, in fact, that it took only eight years for the annual volume of contracts traded to pass the 100 million

strike price
the price contract between the buyer of an option and the writer; the stated price at which you can buy a security with a call or sell a security with a put.

expiration date
the date at which an option expires.

mark. Although contract volume fell off after 1987, it has started inching up again and is now back up to over 150 million contracts a year.

The creation and continued expansion of listed options exchanges have unquestionably given the field of investments a whole new dimension. In order to avoid serious (and possibly expensive) mistakes with these securities, however, investors must fully understand their basic features. In the sections that follow, we will look closely at the investment attributes and trading strategies that can be used with stock options. Later, we'll explore stock-index options and then briefly look at other types of puts and calls, including interest rate and currency options, and long-term options. (Futures options will be taken up in Chapter 15, after we study futures contracts.)

Stock Option Provisions

Because of their low unit cost, stock options (or *equity options*, as they're also called) are very popular with individual investors. Except for the underlying financial asset, they are like any other type of put or call, subject to the same kinds of contract provisions and market forces. As far as options contracts are concerned, there are two provisions that are especially important and to which investors should pay particular attention: (1) the price—known as the *strike price*—at which the stock (or other financial asset) can be bought or sold and (2) the amount of time remaining until expiration. As we'll see below, both the strike price and the time remaining to expiration have a significant bearing on the valuation and pricing of options.

Strike Price   The **strike price**, as specified on the option, represents the price contract between the buyer of the option and the writer. For a call, the strike price specifies the price at which each of the 100 shares of stock can be bought. For a put, it represents the price at which the stock can be sold to the writer. With conventional (OTC) options, there are no constraints on strike price, although it is usually specified at or near the prevailing market price of the stock at the time the option is written. With listed options, however, strike prices are *standardized*: stocks selling for less than $25 per share carry strike prices that are set in 2½ dollar increments ($7½, $10, $12½, $15, etc.). The increment jumps to $5 for stocks selling between $25 and $200 per share. Finally, for stocks that trade at prices greater than $200 a share, the strike price is set in $10 increments. And, of course, the strike price of both conventional and listed options is adjusted for substantial stock dividends and stock splits.

Expiration Date   The **expiration date** is also an important provision, because it specifies the life of the option, just as the maturity date indicates the life of a bond. The expiration date, in effect, specifies the length of the contract between the holder and the writer of the option. Thus, if you hold a six-month call on Sears, that option would give you the right to buy 100 shares of Sears common stock at a strike price of, say, $40 per share at any time over the next six months. Now, *no matter what happens to the market price of the stock,* you can use your call option to buy 100 shares of Sears at $40 a share for the next six months. If the price of the stock moves up, you stand to make money; if it goes down, you'll be out the cost of the option.

Expiration dates for options in the conventional market can fall on any working day of the month. In contrast, expiration dates are standardized in the *listed* options market. The exchanges initially created three expiration cycles for all listed options, and each issue was (and still is) assigned to one of these three cycles. One cycle is January, April, July, and October; another is February, May, August, and November; and the third is March, June, September, and December. This system has been modified a bit to include *both* the current month and the following month, *plus* the next two months in the regular expiration cycle. The exchanges still use the *same three expiration cycles*, but they've been altered so that investors are always able to trade in the two near-term months plus the next two closest months in the option's regular expiration cycle. For reasons that are pretty obvious, this is sometimes referred to as a *two-plus-two* schedule.

Take, for example, the January cycle—you would find the following options available in January: January, February, April, and July. Thus, we'd have the two current months (January and February), plus the next two months in the cycle (April and July). Then, in February, the available contracts would be February, March, April, and July, and so on, as the expiration dates continue rolling over like this during the course of the year. Given the month of expiration, the actual day of expiration is always the same: the Saturday following the third Friday of each expiration month. Thus, for all practical purposes, listed options always expire on the third Friday of the month of expiration.

Put and Call Transactions

Option traders are subject to commission and transaction costs whenever they buy or sell an option or whenever an option is written. The writing of puts and calls is subject to normal transaction costs, because it effectively represents remuneration to the broker or dealer for *selling* the option. Listed options have their own marketplace and quotation system. Finding the price (or *premium*, as it's called) of a listed stock option is fairly easy, as the options quotations in Figure 14.1 indicate. Note that quotes are provided for calls and puts separately, and for each option, quotes are listed for various combinations of strike prices and expiration dates. Because there are so many options, a substantial number of which are rarely traded, financial publications like the *Wall Street Journal* generally list quotes for only the most actively traded options. Also, the quotes listed are only for the options that actually traded on the day in question. For example, in Figure 14.1, there may be many other options available on Philip Morris, but only the ones that actually traded (on Wednesday, January 25, 1995) are listed.

The quotes are standardized and read as follows: The name of the company and the closing price of the underlying stock are listed first; note that Philip Morris stock ("PhMor") closed at 58⅜. The strike price is listed next, followed by the expiration date; then the closing prices of the call (and/or put) options are quoted relative to their strike prices and expiration dates. For example, a Philip Morris March *call* with a strike price of $55 is quoted at 4½ (which translates into a dollar price of $450, because stock options trade in 100-share lots). In contrast, a Philip Morris *put* with a $60 strike price and June expiration date is trading at 4⅛ (or $412.50).

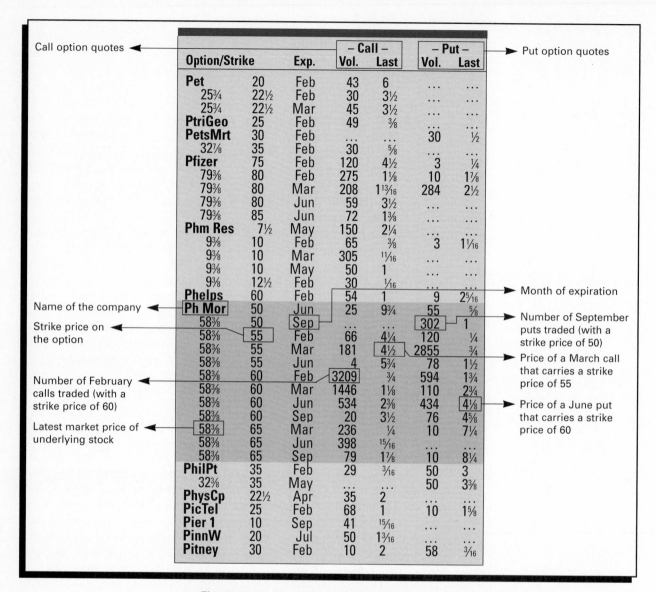

Call option quotes ◄

Put option quotes ►

Option/Strike		Exp.	– Call –		– Put –	
			Vol.	Last	Vol.	Last
Pet	20	Feb	43	6	...	...
25¾	22½	Feb	30	3½	...	...
25¾	22½	Mar	45	3½	...	...
PtriGeo	25	Feb	49	⅜	...	...
PetsMrt	30	Feb	...	...	30	½
32⅛	35	Feb	30	⅝	...	...
Pfizer	75	Feb	120	4½	3	¼
79⅜	80	Feb	275	1⅛	10	1⅞
79⅜	80	Mar	208	1¹³⁄₁₆	284	2½
79⅜	80	Jun	59	3½	...	...
79⅜	85	Jun	72	1⅜	...	...
Phm Res	7½	May	150	2¼	...	...
9⅜	10	Feb	65	⅜	3	1¹⁄₁₆
9⅜	10	Mar	305	¹¹⁄₁₆	...	...
9⅜	10	May	50	1	...	...
9⅜	12½	Feb	30	¹⁄₁₆	...	...
Phelps	60	Feb	54	1	9	2⁵⁄₁₆
Ph Mor	50	Jun	25	9¾	55	⅝
58⅜	50	Sep	...	...	302	1
58⅜	55	Feb	66	4¼	120	¼
58⅜	55	Mar	181	4½	2855	¾
58⅜	55	Jun	4	5¾	78	1½
58⅜	60	Feb	3209	¾	594	1¾
58⅜	60	Mar	1446	1⅛	110	2¾
58⅜	60	Jun	534	2⅜	434	4⅛
58⅜	60	Sep	20	3½	76	4⅝
58⅜	65	Mar	236	¼	10	7¼
58⅜	65	Jun	398	¹⁵⁄₁₆	...	...
58⅜	65	Sep	79	1⅞	10	8¼
PhilPt	35	Feb	29	³⁄₁₆	50	3
32⅜	35	May	...	...	50	3⅜
PhysCp	22½	Apr	35	2	...	...
PicTel	25	Feb	68	1	10	1⅝
Pier 1	10	Sep	41	¹⁵⁄₁₆	...	...
PinnW	20	Jul	50	1³⁄₁₆	...	...
Pitney	30	Feb	10	2	58	³⁄₁₆

Month of expiration ►

Name of the company ◄

Strike price on the option ◄

Number of February calls traded (with a strike price of 60) ◄

Latest market price of underlying stock ◄

Number of September puts traded (with a strike price of 50) ►

Price of a March call that carries a strike price of 55 ►

Price of a June put that carries a strike price of 60 ►

Figure 14.1 Listed Options Quotations
As seen here, the quotes for puts and calls are listed side by side. In addition to the closing price of the option, the latest price of the underlying security is also shown, along with the strike price on the option. (Source: *Wall Street Journal.*)

CONCEPTS *in Review*

14.1 Describe *put* and *call* options. Are they issued like other corporate securities? Explain.

14.2 What are *listed options*, and how do they differ from *conventional options*? What's the difference between an *American option* and a *European option*?

14.3   What are the main investment attractions of put and call options? What are the risks?

14.4   What is a *stock option*? What is the difference between a stock option and a *derivative security*? Describe a derivative security and give several examples.

14.5   What's a *strike price*? How does it differ from the market price of the stock? Do both puts and calls have strike prices? Explain.

14.6   Why do put and call options have expiration dates? Is there a market for options that have passed their expiration dates? Explain.   ▬▬

OPTIONS PRICING AND TRADING

The value of a put or call depends to a large extent on the market behavior of the common stock (or other financial asset) that underlies the option. Getting a firm grip on the current and expected future value of a put or call is extremely important to options-traders and investors. Similarly, to get the most from any options trading program, it's imperative that investors understand how options are priced in the market. *Continuing to use stock options as a basis of discussion,* let's look now at the basic principles of options valuation and pricing, starting with a brief review of how profits are derived from puts and calls; then we'll take a look at several ways these options can be used by investors.

THE PROFIT POTENTIAL OF PUTS AND CALLS

Although the quoted market price of a put or call is affected by such factors as time to expiration, stock volatility, market interest rates, and supply and demand conditions, by far the most important variable is the *price behavior of the underlying common stock*. This is the variable that drives any significant moves in the price of the option and that in turn determines the option's profit (return) potential. Thus, when the underlying stock moves *up* in price, *calls do well*; when the price of the underlying stock *drops*, *puts do well*. Such performance also explains why it's important to get a good handle on the expected future price behavior of a stock *before* an option is bought or sold (written).

The typical price behavior of an option is illustrated graphically in Figure 14.2. The diagram on the left depicts a call; the one on the right, a put. The *call* diagram is constructed assuming you pay $500 for a call that carries a strike price of $50; likewise, the *put* diagram assumes you can buy a put for $500 and obtain the right to sell the underlying stock at $50 a share. With the call, the diagram shows what happens to the value of the option when the price of the stock increases; with the put, it shows what happens when the price of the stock falls. Observe that a call does not gain in value until the price of the stock *advances past the stated exercise price* ($50). Also, because it costs $500 to buy the call, the stock has to move up another 5 points (from $50 to $55) in order for the option investor to recover the premium and thereby reach a break-even point. So long as the stock continues to rise in price, everything from there on out is profit. Once the premium is recouped, the profit from the call position is really only limited by the extent to which the stock price increases over the remaining life of the contract.

Figure 14.2 The Valuation Properties of Put and Call Options
The value of a put or call is a reflection of the price behavior of its underlying common stock (or other financial asset). Therefore, once the cost of the option has been recovered (which occurs when the option passes its break-even point), the profit potential of a put or call is limited only by the price behavior of the underlying financial asset.

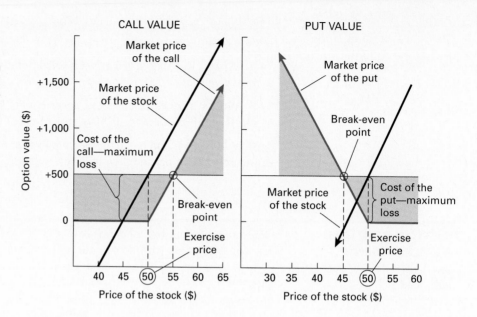

Similarly, the value of a put is also derived from the price of the underlying stock, except that their respective market prices move in opposite directions. Note in Figure 14.2 that the value of the put remains constant until the market price of the corresponding stock *drops to the exercise price* ($50) on the put. Then, as the price of the stock continues to fall, the value of the option increases accordingly. Again, note that since the put cost $500, the investor doesn't start making money on the investment until the price of the stock drops below the break-even point of $45 a share. Beyond that point, the profit from the put is defined by the extent to which the price of the underlying stock continues to fall over the remaining life of the option.

FUNDAMENTAL VALUE

As we saw above, the fundamental value of a put or call depends ultimately on the exercise price stated on the option, as well as on the prevailing market price of the underlying common stock. More specifically, the *value of a call* is determined according to the following simple formula:

Equation 14.1

$$\text{Fundamental value of a call} = \left(\begin{array}{ccc} \text{market price of} & & \text{strike price} \\ \text{underlying} & - & \text{on} \\ \text{common stock} & & \text{the call} \end{array} \right) \times 100$$

$$V = (MP - SPC) \times 100$$

In other words, the fundamental or intrinsic value of a call is nothing more than the difference between market price and strike price. As implied in Equation 14.1, a call has value whenever the market price of the underlying stock (or financial asset) exceeds the strike price stipulated on the call. A simple illustration will show that a call carrying a strike price of $50 on a stock currently trading at $60 has a value of $1,000; that is: ($60 − $50) × 100 = $10 × 100 = $1,000.

A put, on the other hand, cannot be valued in the same way, because puts and calls allow the holder to do different things. To find the *value of a put*, we simply reverse the order of the equation a bit, so that:

Equation 14.2
$$\text{Fundamental value of a put} = \begin{pmatrix} \text{strike price} & & \text{market price of} \\ \text{on} & - & \text{underlying} \\ \text{the put} & & \text{common stock} \end{pmatrix} \times 100$$

$$V = (SPP - MP) \times 100$$

In this case, a put has value so long as the market price of the underlying stock (or financial asset) *is less than* the strike price stipulated on the put.

In-the-Money/Out-of-the-Money

in-the-money
a call option with a strike price less than the market price of the underlying security; a put option whose strike price is greater than the market price of the underlying security.

out-of-the-money
a call option with no real value because the strike price exceeds the market price of the stock; a put option whose market price exceeds the strike price.

When written, options do not necessarily have to carry strike prices at the pre-vailing market prices of the underlying common stocks. Also, as an option subsequently trades on the listed exchanges, the price of the option will move in response to moves in the price of the underlying common stock. When a call has a strike price that is less than the market price of the underlying common stock, it has a positive intrinsic value and is known as an **in-the-money** option. A major portion of the option price in this case is based on (or derived from) the fundamental or intrinsic value of the call. When the strike price exceeds the market price of the stock, the call has no "real" value and is known as an **out-of-the-money** option. Since the option has no intrinsic value, its price is made up solely of investment premium. These terms are much more than convenient, exotic names given to options. As we will see below, they characterize the investment behavior of options and can affect return and risk. A put option, by the way, is in-the-money when its strike price is greater than the market price of the stock; it is out-of-the-money when the market price of the stock exceeds the strike price.

Option Prices and Premiums

option premium
the quoted price the investor pays to buy a listed put or call option.

Put and call values, as found according to Equations 14.1 and 14.2, denote what the options *should* be valued and trading at. This rarely occurs, however, as these securities almost always trade at prices that exceed their intrinsic or fundamental values, especially for options that still have a long time to run. That is, puts and calls nearly always trade at premium prices. Therefore, the term **option premium** is used to describe the market price of listed put and call options. Technically, option premium is the (quoted) price the buyer pays for the *right* to buy or sell a certain amount of the underlying common stock (or other financial asset) at a specified price for a specified period of time. The option seller, on the other hand, receives the premium and gets to keep it whether or not the option is exercised. To the option seller, the option premium represents compensation for agreeing to fulfill certain *obligations* of the contract. As we'll see below, the term *premium* is also used to denote the extent to which the market price of an option exceeds its fundamental or intrinsic value. Thus, to avoid confusion and keep matters as simple as possible, we'll use the word *price* in the usual way: to describe the amount it takes to buy an option in the market.

WHAT DRIVES OPTIONS PRICES?

Option prices can be reduced to two separate components. The first is the *fundamental* (or *intrinsic*) value of the option, which is driven by the current market price of the underlying common stock. That is, as we saw in Equations 14.1 and 14.2, the greater the difference between the market price of the stock and the strike price on the option, the greater the value of the put or call. The second component of an option price is customarily referred to as the **time premium,** which represents, in effect, the excess value imbedded in the option price. That is, time premium is *the amount by which the option price exceeds the option's fundamental value.* Table 14.1 lists some quoted prices for an actively traded call option. These quoted prices (Panel A) are then separated into fundamental value (Panel B) and time premium (Panel C). Note that three strike prices are used—$65, $70, and $75. Relative to the market price of the stock ($71.75), one strike price ($65) is well below market—this is an in-the-money call. One ($70) is fairly near the market. The third ($75) is well above the market—this is an out-of-the-money call. Notice the considerable difference in the makeup of the options prices, as we move from an in-the-money call to an out-of-the-money call.

Panel B in the table lists the fundamental values of the call options, as determined by Equation 14.1. For example, note that while the March 65 call (the call with the March expiration date and $65 strike price) is trading at 7¾, its intrinsic value is only 6¾. The difference, essentially, is how much the option is trading in-the-money. Thus, while most of the price of the March 65 call is made up of fundamental value, certainly not all of it is. Even better, look at the calls with the $75 strike price: None of these has any fundamental value; they're all out-of-the-money, as their prices are made up solely of time premium. Basically, the value of these options is determined entirely by the *belief* that the price of the underlying stock could rise to over $75 a share before the

time premium
the amount by which the option price exceeds the option's fundamental value.

Table 14.1   Option Price Components for an Actively Traded Call Option

Stock Price	Strike Price	Expiration Months		
		Feb.	Mar.	June
Panel A: Quoted Options Prices				
71¾	65	s	7¾	9¾
71¾	70	2¼	3⅞	6¾
71¾	75	³⁄₁₆	1½	3⅞
Panel B: Underlying Fundamental Values				
71¾	65		6¾	6¾
71¾	70	1¾	1¾	1¾
71¾	75	neg.	neg.	neg.
Panel C: Time Premiums				
71¾	65		1	3
71¾	70	½	2⅛	5
71¾	75	³⁄₁₆	1½	3⅞

Note: s = No option available at that strike price and expiration date.
          neg. = Options have negative intrinsic/fundamental values.

options expire. Panel C shows the amount of time premium imbedded in the call prices, which represents the difference in the quoted call prices (Panel A) and the call's fundamental value (Panel B). It shows that the price of every traded option contains at least some premium. Indeed, unless the options are about to expire, you'd expect them to be trading at a premium. Also, note that with all three strike prices, *the longer the time to expiration, the greater the size of the premium.*

As you might expect, *time to expiration* is an important element in explaining the size of the price premium in Panel C. However, a couple of other variables also have a bearing on the behavior of this premium. One is the *price volatility of the underlying common stock.* Other things being equal, the more volatile the stock, the more it enhances the speculative appeal of the option—and therefore the bigger the time premium. In addition, the size of the premium is *directly related to the level of interest rates.* That is, the amount of premium imbedded in a call option will generally increase along with interest rates. In addition, other, less important variables include the dividend yield on the underlying common stock, the trading volume of the option, and the exchange on which the option is listed. For the most part, however, there are four major forces that drive the price of an option. They are, in descending order of importance, (1) the price behavior of the underlying common stock (or other financial asset), (2) the amount of time remaining to expiration, (3) the amount of price volatility in the underlying common stock (or financial asset), and (4) the general level of interest rates.

Option Pricing Models

Financial economists, notably Professors Fisher Black and Myron Scholes, have developed option pricing formulas that are capable of valuing call options (and, with minor modifications, put options) within a few cents of their fair values. Many active market traders use these formulas, which are most suitable for use with preprogrammed personal computers (or even some hand-held calculators), to identify and trade over- and undervalued options.

It is not surprising that the parameter values required to implement these models follow directly from those variables identified above. For example, the five parameters used by the Black-Scholes option pricing model are (1) the risk-free rate of interest, (2) the price volatility of the underlying stock, (3) the current price of the underlying stock, (4) the strike price of the option, and (5) the option's time to expiration. Using these variables in a computer or pre-programmed calculator, an investor can obtain fair market values for the options in question within seconds. Options with market prices above those produced by the formula are considered overvalued, and vice versa. (*Note*: A more detailed discussion of the Black-Scholes option pricing model, including the basic equations used in the model, is provided in Appendix B of this textbook.)

TRADING STRATEGIES

For the most part, stock options can be used in three types of trading strategies: (1) buying puts and calls for speculation, (2) hedging with puts and calls, and (3) option writing and spreading.

Buying for Speculation

Buying for speculation is the simplest and most straightforward use of puts and calls. Basically, it is just like buying stock ("buy low, sell high") and, in fact, represents an alternative to investing in stock. For example, if an investor feels the market price of a particular stock is going to move up, one way of capturing that price appreciation is to buy a call on the stock. In contrast, if an investor feels the stock is about to drop in price, a put could convert the price decline into a profitable situation. In essence, investors buy options rather than stock whenever the options are likely to yield a greater return. The principle here, of course, is to get the biggest return from one's investment dollar—something that can often be done with puts and calls, due to the added leverage they offer. Plus, options offer downside protection—the most you can lose is the cost of the option, which is always less than the cost of the under-lying stock. Thus, by using options as a vehicle for speculation, the investor can put a cap on losses and still get almost as much profit potential as with the underlying stock.

To illustrate the essentials of speculating with options, imagine that you have uncovered a stock you feel will move up in price over the next six months. What you would like to find out at this point is what would happen if you were to buy a call on this stock rather than investing directly in the firm's common. To find out, let's see what the numbers show: Assume the price of the stock is now $49, and you anticipate that within six months, it will rise to about $65. In order to determine the relative merits of your investment alternatives, you need to determine the expected return associated with each course of action. Because call options have short lives, holding period return can be used to measure yield (see Chapter 4). Thus, if your expectations about the stock are correct, it should go up by $16 and in so doing provide stock-holders with a 33 percent holding period return [($65 − $49) ÷ $49 = $16 ÷ $49 = .33]. But there are also some listed options available on this stock; let's see how they would do. For illustrative purposes, we will use two six-month calls that carry $40 and $50 striking prices, respectively. A recap of these two call alternatives, relative to the behavior of the underlying common stock, is summarized in Table 14.2. Clearly, from a holding period return per-spective, either call option represents a superior investment to buying the stock itself. The dollar amount of profit may be a bit more with the stock, but notice that the size of the required investment ($4,900) is a lot more too—thus, it has the lowest HPR.

Observe that one of the calls is an in-the-money option (the one with the $40 striking price) and the other is out-of-the-money. The difference in returns generated by these calls is rather typical; that is, investors are usually able to generate much better rates of return with lower-priced (out-of-the-money) options and also enjoy less exposure to loss. Of course, the major drawback of out-of-the-money options is that their price is made up solely of investment premium—a sunk cost that will be lost if the stock does not move in price.

To see how investors can speculate in puts, consider the following situa-tion: Assume that the price of your stock is now $51, but you anticipate a drop in price to about $35 per share within the next six months. If that occurs, you could sell the stock short and make a profit of $16 per share. (See Chapter 2 for a discussion of short selling.) Alternatively, an out-of-the-money put (with a striking price of $50) can be purchased for, say, $300. Again, if the price of the underlying stock does indeed drop, investors will make money with the

Table 14.2   Speculating with Call Options

	100 Shares of Underlying Common Stock	6-Month Call Options on the Stock	
		$40 Strike Price	$50 Strike Price
Today			
Market value of stock (at $49/share)	$4,900		
Market price of calls*		$1,100	$ 400
6 Months Later			
Expected value of stock (at $65/share)	$6,500		
Expected price of calls*		$2,500	$1,500
Profit	$1,600	$1,400	$1,100
Holding period return**	33%	127%	275%

*The price of the calls was computed according to Equation 14.1 and includes some investment premium in the purchase price, but *none* in the expected sales price.

**Holding period return (HPR) = (ending price of the stock or option − beginning price of the stock or option)/beginning price of the stock or option.

put. The profit and rate of return on the put are summarized below, along with the comparative returns from short selling the stock:

	Buy 1 Put	Sell Short 100 Shares of Stock
Purchase price (today)	$ 300	
Selling price (6 months later)	1,500	
Short sell (today)		$5,100
Cover (6 months later)		3,500
Profit	$1,200	$1,600
Holding period return	400%	63%*

*Assumes the short sale was made with a required margin deposit of 50 percent.

Once again, in terms of holding period return, the stock option is the superior investment vehicle by a wide margin. Of course, not all option investments perform as well as the ones in our examples; success in this strategy rests on picking the right underlying common stock. Thus, *security analysis and proper stock selection are critical dimensions of this technique.* It is a highly risky investment strategy, but it may be well suited for the more speculatively inclined investor.

Hedging

hedge
a combination of two or more securities into a single investment position for the purpose of reducing or eliminating risk.

A **hedge** is simply a combination of two or more securities into a single investment position for the purpose of reducing risk. This strategy might involve, for example, buying stock and simultaneously buying a put on that same stock; or it might consist of selling some stock short and then buying a call. There are many types of hedges, some of which are very sophisticated and others very simple. They are all used for the same basic reason: to earn or protect a profit without exposing the investor to excessive loss. For example, an options hedge may be appropriate if you have generated a profit from an earlier common stock investment and wish to protect that profit. Or it may be appropriate if you are about to enter into a common stock investment and wish to protect your money by limiting potential capital loss. If you hold a stock that has gone up in price, the purchase of a put would provide the type of downside protection you need; the purchase of a call, in contrast, would provide protection to a short seller of common stock. Thus, option hedging always involves two transactions: (1) the initial common stock position (long or short) and (2) the simultaneous or subsequent purchase of the option.

Let's examine a simple options hedge in which a put is used to limit capital loss or protect profit. Assume that you want to buy 100 shares of stock. Being a bit apprehensive about the stock's outlook, you decide to use an option hedge to protect your capital against loss. You simultaneously buy the stock and a put on the stock (which fully covers the 100 shares owned); this type of hedge is known as a *protective put*. Preferably, the put would be a low-priced option with a strike price at or near the current market price of the stock. Suppose you purchase the common at $25 and pay $150 for a put with a $25 strike price. Now, no matter what happens to the price of the stock over the life of the put, you can lose no more than $150; at the same time, there's no limit on the gains. If the stock does not move, you will be out the cost of a put. If it drops in price, then whatever is lost on the stock will be made up with the put. The bottom line? The most you can lose is the cost of the put ($150, in this case). However, if the price of the stock goes up (as hoped), the put becomes useless, and you will earn the capital gains on the stock (less the cost of the put, of course). The essentials of this option hedge are shown in Table 14.3. The $150 paid for the put is sunk cost, and that's lost no matter what happens to the price of the stock; in effect, it is the price paid for the hedge. Moreover, this hedge is good only for the life of the put. When this put

Table 14.3   Limiting Capital Loss with a Put Hedge

		Stock	Put*
Today			
Purchase price of the stock		$25	
Purchase price of the put			$ 1½
Sometime Later			
A. Price of common goes *up* to:		$50	
Value of put			$ 0
Profit:			
100 shares of stock ($50 − $25)	$2,500		
Less: Cost of put	− 150		
Profit:	$2,350		
B. Price of common goes *down* to:		$10	
Value of put**			$15
Profit:			
100 shares of stock (loss: $10 − $25)	−$1,500		
Value of put (profit)	+ 1,500		
Less: Cost of put	− 150		
Loss:	$ 150		

*Put is purchased simultaneously and carries a strike price of $25.
**See Equation 14.2.

Table 14.4 Protecting Profits with a Put Hedge

	Stock	3-Month Put with a $75 Strike Price
Purchase price of the stock (some time ago)	$ 35	
Today		
Market price of the stock	$ 75	
Market price of the put		$ 2½
3 Months Later		
A. Price of common goes *up* to:	$100	
Value of put		$ 0
Profit:		
100 shares of stock ($100 − $35) $6,500		
Less: Cost of put − 250		
Profit: $6,250		
B. Price of common goes *down* to:	$ 50	
Value of put*		$25
Profit:		
100 shares of stock ($50 − $35) $1,500		
Value of put (profit) 2,500		
Less: Cost of put − 250		
Profit: $3,750		

*See Equation 14.2.

expires, you will have to replace it with another put or forget about hedging your capital.

The other basic use of an option hedge involves entering into the options position *after* a profit has been made on the underlying stock. This could be done because of investment uncertainty or for tax purposes (to carry over a profit to the next taxable year). For example, if you bought 100 shares of stock at $35 and it moved to $75, there would be a profit of $40 per share to protect. The profit could be protected with an option hedge by buying a put; assume you decide to put such a hedge into place and you do so by buying a three-month put with a $75 strike price at a cost of $250. Now, regardless of what happens to the stock over the life of the put, you are guaranteed a minimum profit of $3,750 (the $4,000 profit in the stock made so far, less the $250 cost of the put). This can be seen in Table 14.4. Notice that if the price of the stock should fall, the worst that can happen is a guaranteed minimum profit of $3,750. And there is still *no limit on how much profit can be made*: As long as the stock continues to go up, you will reap the benefits. (*Note*: Although this discussion pertains to put hedges, it should be clear that call hedges can also be set up to limit the loss or protect a profit on a short sale. For example, when a stock is sold short, a call can be purchased to protect the short seller against a rise in the price of the stock—with the same basic results as outlined above.)

Option Writing and Spreading

The advent of listed options has led to many intriguing options-trading strategies. Yet, despite the apparent appeal of these exotic techniques, there is one important point that all the experts agree on: *Such specialized trading strategies should be left to experienced investors who fully understand their subtleties.* Our goal at this point is not to master these specialized strategies but to learn in general terms what they are and how they operate. There are two types of specialized options strategies: (1) writing options and (2) spreading options.

Writing Options   Generally, investors write options because they feel the price of the underlying stock is going to move in their favor. That is, it is not going to rise as much as the buyer of a call expects; nor will it fall as much as the buyer of a put hopes. *And, more often than not, the option writer is right*; that is, he or she is going to make money far more often than the buyer of the put or call. Such favorable odds explain, in part, the underlying economic motivation for writing put and call options. Options writing represents an investment transaction to the writers, since they receive the full option premium (less normal transaction costs, of course) in exchange for agreeing to live up to the terms of the option.

naked options
options written on securities not owned by the writer.

Investors can write options in one of two ways. One is to write **naked options**, which involves writing options on stock not owned by the writer. The investor simply writes the put or call, collects the option premium, and hopes the price of the underlying stock does not move against him or her. If successful, naked writing can be highly profitable due to the modest amount of capital required. One thing to keep in mind, however, is that the amount of return to the writer is always limited to the amount of option premium received. On the other hand, there is really *no limit to loss exposure*. And that's the catch: The price of the underlying stock can rise or fall by just about any amount over the life of the option, and in so doing can deal a real blow to the writer of the naked put or call.

covered options
options written against stock owned (or short sold) by the writer.

Such risk exposure can be partially offset by writing **covered options**, in which case the options are written against stocks the investor (writer) already owns or has a position in. For example, an investor could write a call against stock she owns or write a put against stock she has short sold. In this way, she can use the long or short position to meet the terms of the option. Such a strategy represents a fairly conservative way to generate attractive rates of return. The object is to write a slightly out-of-the-money option, pocket the option premium, and hope the price of the underlying stock will move up or down to (but not exceed) the option's striking price. In effect, what an investor is doing is adding option premium to the other usual sources of return that accompany stock ownership or short sales (dividends and/or capital gains). But there's more: While the option premium adds to the return, it also reduces risk, since it can be used to cushion a loss if the price of the stock moves against the investor. There is a hitch to all this, of course, and that is the amount of return the covered option investor can realize is limited. For once the price of the underlying common stock begins to exceed the striking price on the option, the option becomes valuable. When that happens, the investor starts *to lose* money on the options. From this point on, for every dollar the investor makes on the stock position, she loses an equal amount on the option position. That's a major risk of writing covered call options—if the price of the underlying stock takes off, you'll miss out on the added profits.

To illustrate the ins and outs of covered call writing, let's assume you own 100 shares of PFP, Inc.—an actively traded, high-yielding common stock. The stock is currently trading at 73½ and pays *quarterly* dividends of $1 a share.

You decide to write a three-month call on PFP, giving the buyer the right to take the stock off your hands at $80 a share (i.e., the call carries a strike price of 80). Such options are trading in the market at 2½, so you receive $250 for writing the call. Now, if you're like most covered call writers, you fully intend to hold on to the stock, so you'd like to see the price of PFP stock rise to no more than 80 by the expiration date on the call. If that happens, not only do you earn the dividends and capital gains on the stock, but you also get to pocket the $250 you received when you wrote the call, since it (the call option) will expire worthless. Basically, you've just *added* $250 to the quarterly return on your stock.

Table 14.5 summarizes the profit and loss characteristics of this covered call position. Notice that the maximum profit on this transaction occurs *when the market price of the stock equals the strike price on the call*. If the price of the stock keeps going up, you miss out on the added profits. Even so, the

Table 14.5 Covered Call Writing

	Stock	3-Month Call with an $80 Strike Price
Current market price of the stock	$73½	
Current market price of the put		$ 2½
3 Months Later		
A. Price of the stock is *unchanged:*	$73½	
Value of the call		$ 0
Profit:		
Quarterly dividends received $ 100		
Proceeds from sale of call 250		
Total profit: $ 350		
B. Price of the stock goes *up* to:	$80 ←	Price Where Maximum Profit Occurs
Value of the call		$ 0
Profit:		
Quarterly dividends received $ 100		
Proceeds from sale of call 250		
Capital gains on stock ($80 − $73½) 650		
Total profit: $1,000		
C. Price of the stock goes *up* to:	$90	
Value of the call*		$10
Profit:		
Quarterly dividends received $100		
Proceeds from sale of call $250		
Capital gains on stock ($90 − $73½) $1,650		
Less: Loss on call ($1,000)		
Net profit: $1,000		
D. Price of the stock *drops* to:	$71 ←	Break-Even Price
Value of the call*		$ 0
Profit:		
Capital loss on stock ($71 − $73½) ($ 250)⎱ $0 profit or loss		
Proceeds from sale of call 250 ⎰		
Quarterly dividends 100		
Net profit: $ 100		

*See Equation 14.1

$1,000 profit that's earned at a stock price of 80 or above translates into a (three-month) holding period return of a very respectable 13.6 percent (i.e., $1,000/$7,350)—which represents an *annualized* return of nearly 55 percent. With this kind of return potential, it's not difficult to see why covered call writing is so popular. Plus, as we see in Situation D in the table, covered call writing also adds a little cushion to losses: The price of the stock has to drop more than 2½ points (which is what you received when you wrote/sold the call) before you start losing money.

option spreading
combining two or more options with different strike prices and/or expiration dates into a single transaction.

Spreading Options   Option spreading is nothing more than combining two or more options into a single transaction. We could create an options spread, for example, by simultaneously buying and writing options on the same underlying stock. These cannot be identical options, however; they must differ with respect to strike price and/or expiration date. Spreads are a very popular use of listed options, and they account for a substantial amount of the trading activity on the listed options exchanges. These spreads go by a variety of exotic names, such as *bull spreads, bear spreads, money spreads, vertical spreads,* and *butterfly spreads.* Each is different, constructed to meet a certain type of investment goal.

Consider, for example, a *vertical spread,* which would be set up by *buying* a call at one strike price and then *writing* a call (on the same stock and for the same expiration date) at a different—higher—strike price. For instance, you could buy a February call on XYZ at a strike price of, say, 30 and simultaneously sell (write) a February call on XYZ at a strike price of 35. Strange as it may sound, such a position would generate a hefty return if the price of the underlying stock goes up by just a few points. Other spreads are used to profit from a falling market, and still others try to make money when the price of the underlying stock moves either way, up *or* down. Whatever the objective, most spreads are created to take advantage of differences in prevailing option prices and premiums. The payoff from spreading is usually substantial, but *so is the risk.* In fact, some spreads that seem to involve almost no risk may end up with devastating results if the market and the "spread" (or difference) between option premiums move against the investor.

option straddle
the simultaneous purchase (or sale) of a put and a call on the same underlying common stock (or financial asset).

A variation of this theme involves an **option straddle**, the simultaneous purchase (or sale) of *both* a put *and* a call on the same underlying common stock. Unlike spreads, straddles will normally involve the same strike price and expiration date. Here, the object is to earn a profit from *either* an increase *or* a decrease in the price of the underlying stock. Otherwise, the principles of straddles are much like those for spreads: to build an investment position with combinations of options that will enable an investor to capture the benefits of certain types of stock price behavior. But keep in mind that if the prices of the underlying stock and/or the option premiums do not behave in the anticipated manner, the investor loses. *Spreads and straddles are extremely tricky and should be used only by knowledgeable investors.*

CONCEPTS *in Review*

14.7 Briefly explain how you would make money on (a) a call option and (b) a put option. Do you have to exercise the option in order to capture the profit? Explain.

14.8 How do you find the intrinsic value of a call? Of a put? Does an *out-of-the-money option* have intrinsic value? Explain.

14.9 Name at least four variables that have an impact on the price behavior of listed options, and briefly explain how each affects prices. How important are fundamental (intrinsic) value and time value to in-the-money options? To out-of-the-money options?

14.10 Describe at least three different ways stock options can be used by investors.

14.11 What's the most that can be made from writing calls? Why would an investor want to write *covered calls?* Can you reduce the risk on the underlying common stock by writing covered calls? Explain.

STOCK-INDEX AND OTHER TYPES OF OPTIONS

Imagine being able to buy or sell a major stock market index like the S&P 500—and at a reasonable cost. Think of what you could do: If you felt the market was heading up, you could invest in a security that tracks the price behavior of the S&P 500 index and make money when the market goes up. No longer would you have to go through the often haphazardous process of selecting specific stocks that you hope will capture the market's performance. Rather, you could play the market *as a whole.* Well, that's exactly what investors can do with *stock-index options*—puts and calls that are written on major stock market indexes. Index options have been around since 1983 and have become immensely popular with both individual and institutional investors. Let's now take a closer look at these popular and often highly profitable investment vehicles.

STOCK-INDEX OPTIONS: CONTRACT PROVISIONS

stock-index option
a put or call option written on a specific stock market index, such as the S&P 500.

Basically, a **stock-index option** is nothing more than a put or a call written on a specific stock market index, like the S&P 500. The underlying security in this case is the specific market index. Thus, when the market index moves in one direction or another, the value of the index option moves accordingly. Since there are no stocks or other financial assets backing these options, settlement is defined in terms of cash. Specifically, the cash value of an *index option* is equal to 100 times the published market index that underlies the option. For example, if the S&P 500 is at 610, the cash value of an S&P 500 index option is $100 \times 610 = \$61,000$; if the underlying index moves up or down in the market, so will the cash value of the option.

In early 1995, there were some 26 stock market index options available, including options on major U.S. market indexes (like the S&P 500, Russell 2000, or S&P MidCap 400), options on foreign market indexes (Mexico, Israel, Japan, and Hong Kong), and options on different segments of the market (like pharmaceutical, bank, and utility indexes). Many of these stock-index options, however, are very thinly traded and really don't amount to much of a market. Actually, there are eight indexes that dominate the stock-index options market and account for the vast majority of trading activity; they are:

- The S&P 500 Index (traded on the CBOE)
- The S&P 100 Index (CBOE)
- The Value Line Index (Philadelphia Exchange)
- The Major Market Index (AMEX)
- The Institutional Index (AMEX)
- The S&P MidCap Index (AMEX)
- The Nasdaq 100 Index (CBOE)
- The Russell 2000 Index (CBOE)

Among these eight actively traded index options, you'll find contracts not only on the popular S&P indexes (including the S&P MidCap, which tracks the market behavior of 400 midsize companies) but also on the Value Line Index (of the roughly 1,700 companies tracked by Value Line) and an index of the 75 stocks that are most favored by big institutional investors (the Institutional Index). There's even an index (the Russell 2000) that tracks the behavior of small-cap stocks. Although the most popular index of them all— the Dow Jones Industrial Average—has refused to let itself be the basis of an index option, the AMEX has come up with an index (the Major Market Index) designed to imitate the Dow; this index is made up of 20 stocks, 17 of which are part of the DJIA. The S&P 100 and S&P 500 are, by far, the most popular index options. There's more trading in these two contracts than all the 24 other index options combined; in fact, these two are *the most actively traded of all listed options*, regardless of type.

Both puts and calls are available on index options. They are valued and have issue characteristics like any other put or call. That is, a put lets a holder profit from a drop in the market (when the underlying market index goes down, the value of a put goes up); a call enables the holder to profit from a market that's going up. As seen in Figure 14.3, these options even have a quotation system that is very similar to that used for puts and calls on stocks.

 ### Putting a Value on Stock-Index Options

Like equity options, the market price of index options is a function of the difference in the strike price on the option (which is stated in terms of the underlying index) and the latest published stock market index. To illustrate, consider the highly popular S&P 100 Index, traded on the CBOE. As the index option quotes in Figure 14.3 reveal, this index recently closed at 433.90 (see the highlighted "closing values for the underlying indexes" at the bottom of the exhibit); at the same time, there was a March call on this index that carried a striking price of 430. Given that a stock-index *call* will have a value so long as the underlying index exceeds the index striking price (just the opposite for puts), the intrinsic value of this call was 433.90 − 430 = 3.90. As we can see in the quotes, this call was trading at 9¾ (or 9.75), some 5.85 points *above* the call's underlying fundamental value. This difference, of course, was the *time premium*. Just like stock options, the amount of premium in an index option tends to *increase with longer options* and with *more volatile market conditions*. If the S&P 100 Index in our example were to go up to 460 by late March (the expiration date on the call), this option would be quoted at 460 − 430 = 30; as a result, because all index options are valued in multiples of

$100, this option would be worth $3,000. If an investor had purchased the option when it was trading at 9¾ (9.75), it would have cost $975 and in a little over two months would have generated a profit of $3,000 − $975 = $2,025. The investor would, in effect, have more than tripled his or her money. From this example, it should be clear that because they're a form of derivative security, stock-index options are valued according to how the market (i.e., the market index) performs. Thus, *calls should be more highly valued if the market is expected to go up in the future*, whereas *puts should be more highly valued in falling markets*.

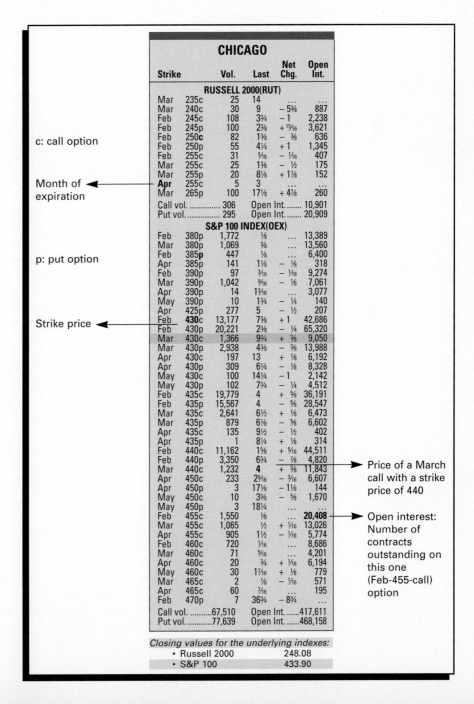

Figure 14.3 Quotations on Index Options
The quotation system used with index options is a lot like that used with stock options—that is, strike prices and expiration dates are shown along with closing option prices. The biggest differences are that put (*p*) and call (*c*) quotes are mixed together and the closing values for the *underlying indexes* are shown separately. (Source: *Wall Street Journal*.)

INVESTMENT USES

Although they can be used in spreads and straddles, index options are used most often for speculating or for hedging. As a speculative vehicle, they provide investors with the opportunity to play the market with a relatively small amount of capital. Like any other put or call, *index options provide attractive leverage opportunities and at the same time limit exposure to loss to the price paid for the option.*

Index options are equally effective as *hedging vehicles*. In fact, hedging is a major use of index options and accounts for a good deal of the trading in these securities. To see how these options can be used for hedging, consider an investor who holds a diversified portfolio of common stocks. One way to protect the whole portfolio against an adverse market is to buy puts on one of the market indexes. If you hold a portfolio of, say, a dozen different stocks and you think the market is heading down, you can protect your capital by selling all of your stocks. However, that could become expensive, especially if you plan to get back into the market after it drops. Fortunately, there is a way to "have your cake and eat it too," and that is to hedge your stock portfolio with a stock index put. In this way, if the market does go down, you'll make money on your puts, which can then be used to buy more stocks at the lower, "bargain" prices. On the other hand, if the market doesn't retreat but continues to go up, you'll be out *only the cost of the puts*—which could well be recovered from the increased value of your stock holdings. The principles of hedging with stock-index options are exactly the same as those for hedging with stock options; the only difference is that with stock-index options, you're trying to protect a *whole portfolio* of stocks rather than *individual* stocks.

There is one important consideration to keep in mind, however: The amount of profit you make or the protection you obtain depends in large part on how closely the behavior of your stock portfolio is matched by the behavior of the stock-index option you employ in the hedge. *There is no guarantee that the two will behave in the same way.* You should therefore select an index option that closely reflects the nature of the stocks in your portfolio. If, for example, you hold a number of mid-cap stocks, you might be well advised to select something like the S&P MidCap Index as the hedging vehicle. If you hold mostly blue chips, you might choose the Major Market Index. While you probably can't get dollar-for-dollar portfolio protection, at least you should try to get as close a match as possible. After all, the closer the match, the greater your chances of offsetting any portfolio losses with gains from the index options. Another factor that's important in portfolio hedging is the cost of the underlying hedge vehicle itself. This and other considerations are discussed in the accompanying *Investor Insights* box, which deals with the use of index options in portfolio hedging.

Given their effectiveness for either speculating or hedging the entire market, it's little wonder that index options have become so popular with investors. But a word of caution is in order: Although trading index options appears simple and seems to provide high rates of return, these vehicles involve *high risk* and are subject to considerable price volatility. They should not be used by amateurs. True, there's only so much you can lose with these options; the trouble is that it's very easy to lose that amount. Attractive profits are indeed available from these securities, but they're not investments you can buy and then forget about until they expire. With the wide market swings that are so common today, *these securities must be closely monitored on a daily basis.*

INVESTOR **I**NSIGHTS: *Investing in Action*

Using Index Options to Protect a Whole Portfolio

When the stock market heads down, investors begin to worry about protecting the value of their portfolios. But simply liquidating their stock holdings and putting the proceeds into a money market fund is too drastic a step for most people. Not only would they incur substantial brokerage commissions and capital gains taxes, but also they would lose out if the market rallies. A far less drastic—and less costly—way for investors to shield their portfolios from the possibility of a sustained sell-off is to buy "insurance" in the form of stock-index put options.

These options offer a simple method of insuring the value of an entire portfolio with a single trade. That can be especially helpful because many issues in an investor's portfolio may not have individual put options traded on them. Such portfolio protection is similar to any other kind of insurance. The more protection investors want and the less risk they are willing to bear, the more the insurance costs. For example, suppose an investor wants to hedge a $100,000 stock portfolio and, after examining the characteristics of the major stock indexes, concludes that the S&P 100 best matches the portfolio. With the S&P 100 Index standing at, say, 372 in February, the market value of the S&P 100 Index would be $37,200. So the investor would buy three puts to approximate the $100,000 portfolio value.

The investor might buy three "May 360" puts that expire in three months (i.e., in May) with a strike price of 360 and a price of about 4. To turn that into dollars, an investor multiplies by 100; the puts would cost about $400 each—$1,200 for all three—or 1.2 percent of the $100,000 portfolio. If the market retreats about 15 percent from current levels, bringing the S&P 100 down to about 318, each May 360 put would be worth a minimum of 42 points (360 − 318), or $4,200. After paying their cost, the investor would have a profit on the puts of $11,400 ($4,200 − $400 = $3,800 × 3), offsetting a substantial portion of the $15,000 the portfolio would have lost in a 15 percent decline.

By purchasing puts with strike prices that are 12 points below the current level of the S&P Index, the investor effectively insures the portfolio against any losses that occur *after* the market has fallen 12 points, or 3.2 percent, to 360. An investor willing to bear more market risk could reduce the insurance cost even further by purchasing puts with even lower strike prices. On the other hand, to be fully insured, an investor might have bought puts with a higher strike price, but that would have raised the cost of the insurance. May 370 puts, for instance, would have cost 7¼, or $725 each. Harrison Roth, an options strategist, says the basic question for investors is, "Do you want to hedge against any and all declines, or do you simply want protection against catastrophic moves?" He believes most investors are in the second camp.

Even with relatively low-cost puts such as the May 360s, the cost of put option hedges can add up if the insurance goes unused. Buying three-month puts like these four times a year would cost the equivalent of 4.8 percent of a $100,000 portfolio. One way to reduce the cost is to sell the put options before they expire. Put options lose most of their value in the final few weeks before their expiration if they have strike prices below the current price of the underlying securities. For this reason, some market advisers recommend that investors hold their options only for a month, sell them, and then buy the next month out. This strategy recovers most of the options' value, significantly reducing the cost to hedge, even after incurring the higher commissions.

Source: Adapted from Stanley W. Angrist, "Put Options Can Help Protect Portfolios," *Wall Street Journal*, February 28, 1989, p. C1.

OTHER TYPES OF OPTIONS

Although options on stocks and stock indexes account for most of the market activity in listed options, put and call options can also be obtained on debt instruments and foreign currencies. In addition to these securities, you can also buy puts and calls with extended expiration dates—these options are known as *LEAPS*. Let's now take a brief look at these other kinds of options, starting with interest rate options.

Interest Rate Options

interest rate options
put and call options written on fixed-income (debt) securities.

Puts and calls on fixed-income (debt) securities are known as **interest rate options**. Treasury securities with 5-, 10-, and 30-year maturities underlie these options, and as the prices of these bonds go up or down in the market, the puts and calls respond accordingly: Calls become more valuable as interest rates drop (and bond prices rise), whereas puts increase in value as rates rise (and bond prices fall). Unfortunately, the market for interest rate options never took hold and to this day, it remains very small. In an effort to beef up volume, the CBOE in mid-1989 introduced two new trading vehicles: an option on *short-term interest rates* and an option on *long-term interest rates*. But even these vehicles didn't seem to help much, as trading volume continues to be weak. Trading in interest rate options has all but dried up (and could well disappear altogether in the near future) since most professional investors don't seem to bother with these securities. Instead, they use interest rate futures contracts or options on these futures contracts (both of which will be examined in Chapter 15) for hedging or other investment purposes.

Currency Options

currency options
put and call options written on foreign currencies.

Foreign exchange options, or just **currency options** as they're more commonly called, provide a way for investors to speculate on foreign exchange rates or to hedge foreign currency or foreign security holdings. Currency options are available on the currencies of most of the countries with which we have strong trading ties. These options are traded on the Philadelphia Exchange and include the following currencies:

- British pound
- Swiss franc
- German mark
- Canadian dollar
- Japanese yen
- Australian dollar

In essence, puts and calls on these currencies give the holders the right to sell or buy large amounts of the specified foreign currency. However, in contrast to the standardized contracts used with stock and stock-index options, the specific unit of trading in this market varies with the particular underlying currency, the details of which are spelled out in Table 14.6. Currency options are traded in full or fractional cents per unit of the underlying currency, relative to the amount of foreign currency involved. Thus, if a put or call on the British pound were quoted at, say, 6.40 (which is read as "6.4 cents"), it would be valued at $2,000, because there are 31,250 British pounds that underlie this option—that is, $31,250 \times .064 = \$2,000$.

The value of a currency option is linked to the exchange rate between the U.S. dollar and the underlying foreign currency. For example, if the Canadian

Table 14.6 Foreign Currency Option Contracts on the Philadelphia Exchange

Underlying Currency*	Size of Contracts
British pound	31,250 pounds
Swiss franc	62,500 francs
German mark	62,500 marks
Canadian dollar	50,000 dollars
Japanese yen	6,250,000 yen
Australian dollar	50,000 dollars

*The British pound, Swiss franc, German mark, Canadian dollar, and Australian dollar are all quoted in full cents; the Japanese yen is quoted in one-hundredths of a cent.

dollar becomes stronger *relative to the U.S. dollar*, causing the exchange rates to go up, the price of a *call* option on the Canadian dollar will increase, and the price of a *put* will decline. (*Note*: Some cross-currency options are available in the market, but such options/trading techniques are beyond the scope of this book; thus, our discussion will focus solely on foreign currency options [or futures] that are linked to U.S. dollars.)

To understand how you can make money with currency options, consider a situation in which an investor wants to speculate on exchange rates. The strike price of a currency option is stated in terms of *exchange rates*. Thus, a strike price of 150, for example, implies each unit of the foreign currency (such as one British pound) is worth 150 cents, or $1.50, in U.S. money. If an investor held a 150 call on this foreign currency, he or she would make money if *the foreign currency strengthened relative to the U.S. dollar* so that the exchange rate rose—say, to 155. In contrast, if the investor held a 150 put, he or she would profit from a decline in the exchange rate—say, to 145. Success in forecasting movements in foreign exchange rates is obviously essential to a profitable foreign currency options program.

LEAPS

LEAPS
long-term options.

They look like regular puts and calls, they behave pretty much like regular puts and calls, but they're not—they're different. We're talking about **LEAPS**, which are puts and calls with lengthy expiration dates. Basically, LEAPS are long-term options. Whereas standard options have maturities of eight months or less, LEAPS have expiration dates that extend out as far as two years. Known formally as *Long-term Equity AnticiPation Securities*, they are listed on all five of the major options exchanges. LEAPS are available on over 100 different stocks and several stock indexes, including the S&P 100, S&P 500, and Major Market indexes.

Aside from their time frame, LEAPS work like any other equity or index option. For example, a single (equity) LEAPS contract gives the holder the right to buy or sell 100 shares of stock at a predetermined price on or before the specified expiration date. LEAPS give investors more time to be right about their bets on the direction of a stock or stock index, and they give hedgers more time to protect their positions. But there's a price for all this extra time: You can expect to pay a lot more for a LEAPS than you would for a regular (short-term) option. For example, in early 1995, a three-month call on Merck (with a strike price of 35) was trading at 3½; the same call with a two-year expiration date was trading at 7¼. The difference should come as no surprise, because LEAPS, being nothing more than long-term options, are loaded with *time premium*. As we saw earlier in this chapter, other things being equal, *the more time an option has to expiration, the higher the quoted price.*

CONCEPTS *in Review*

14.12 Briefly describe the differences and similarities in *stock-index options* and *stock options*. Do the same for *foreign currency options* and stock options.

14.13 Identify and briefly discuss two different ways to use stock-index options. Do the same for foreign currency options.

14.14 Why would an investor want to use index options to hedge a portfolio of common stock? If the investor thinks the market is in for a fall, why not just sell the stock?

14.15 What are *LEAPS*? Why would an investor want to use a LEAPS option rather than a regular listed option?

RIGHTS

 LG 5

right
an option to buy shares of a new issue of common stock at a specified price, over a specified, fairly short period of time.

A **right** is a special type of option that has a short market life, usually existing for no more than a few weeks. Essentially, rights originate when corporations raise money by issuing new shares of common stock. From an investor's perspective, a right enables a stockholder to buy shares of the new issue at a specified price, over a specified, fairly short time period. Although not specifically designed for speculation or for use as trading vehicles, *rights do have value*, and they should never be lightly discarded. Instead, unwanted rights should be sold in the open market.

CHARACTERISTICS

Let's assume that a firm has one million shares of common stock outstanding and that it has decided to issue another 250,000 shares. This might well be done through a *rights offering*: Rather than directly issuing the new shares of common stock, the firm would instead issue *stock rights* to the existing shareholders. These rights can then be used by their holders to purchase the new issue of stock. Existing stockholders are sometimes given the right to maintain their proportionate share of ownership in a firm, a privilege known as a **preemptive right**. Since each stockholder receives, without charge, one right for each share of stock currently owned, the company in our example above would issue one million rights, and it would take four rights to buy one new share of common.

preemptive right
the right of existing stockholders to maintain their proportionate share of ownership in a firm.

Rights and Privileges

exercise (subscription) price
with rights, the price at which a new share of common stock can be bought.

Because most stock rights allow their holders to purchase only a fractional share of the new common stock, two or more rights are usually needed to buy a single new share. The price of the new stock—known as the **exercise** (or subscription) price—is spelled out in the right; it is always set below the prevailing market price of the stock. For each new share of common stock purchased, the investor has to *redeem a specified number of rights* and *pay the stipulated subscription price in cash*. Rights not used by their expiration date *lose all value* and simply cease to exist. Unfortunately, many investors allow their rights to expire and thereby lose money.

The Value of a Right

rights-on
a condition when a firm's common stock is trading with a stock right attached to it.

rights-off (ex-rights)
a condition when a firm's common stock and its rights are trading in separate markets, separate from each other.

Technically, the precise measure of a right's value depends on whether the security is trading "rights-on" or "rights-off." **Rights-on** indicates that the common stock is trading with the right attached to it; an investor who buys a share of stock during such a period also receives the attached stock right. When issues are trading **rights-off**, or **ex-rights**, the company's stock and its rights are trading in separate markets and are distinct from one another. Regardless of whether a security is trading rights-on or rights-off, however, we can use the following formula to approximate the value of a right:

Equation 14.3

$$\text{Value of a right} = \frac{\text{market price of old stock} - \text{subscription price of new stock}}{\text{number of rights needed to buy one new share}}$$

As an example of how Equation 14.3 works, let's continue with the illustration we began above. Assume the prevailing market price of the old stock is $50 and the new shares carry a subscription price of $40 per share. Remember that it takes four rights and $40 to buy one new share of stock. We thus find the approximate value of a right as follows:

$$\text{Value of a right} = \frac{\$50 - \$40}{4} = \frac{\$10}{4} = \$2.50$$

Each right in our hypothetical example will have a market value of about $2.50 (as long as the price of the stock remains at $50). This is the price at which each right could be sold in the market if the investor chooses not to exercise them.

INVESTMENT MERITS

The major investment attribute of a stock right is that it lets the holder acquire the stock at a reduced price. It also enables the holder to acquire additional shares of stock *without paying the customary commission fees*. Although the savings may not be enormous, the opportunity to execute commission-free transactions should not be overlooked. However, except for the commission savings, the cost of buying the stock *will be the same whether the shares are bought outright or through the use of rights*. That is, the cost of the rights plus the subscription price of the stock should just about equal the market price of the common. Unfortunately, stock rights hold little opportunity for profitable trading. The life of these securities is simply too short and the range of price activity too narrow to allow for any significant trading profits. Thus, the role of stock rights is limited in most individual's portfolios to selling unwanted rights or to buying or using them to reduce the commissions on subsequent stock transactions.

CONCEPTS *in Review*

14.16 Describe a *stock right* and note how such rights are tied to the *preemptive rights* of investors. How would a stock right be used by an investor? Why does it have limited investment appeal?

WARRANTS

warrant
a long-lived option that gives the holder the right to buy stock in a company at a price specified in the warrant itself.

A **warrant** is a type of long-term option that enables the holder to acquire common stock. Like rights, warrants are found in the corporate sector of the market. Occasionally, warrants can be used to purchase preferred stock or even bonds, but common stock is the leading redemption vehicle.

GENERAL ATTRIBUTES

Of the various types of options, warrants normally have the longest lives, with maturities that extend to 5, 10, or even 20 years or more. Indeed, some warrants have no maturity date at all. They have no voting rights, pay no dividends, and have no claim on the assets of the company. What the warrant does offer is a chance to participate indirectly in the market behavior of the issuing firm's common stock and, in so doing, to generate capital gains. Warrants are perhaps most closely related to *call LEAPS*, or long-term *call* options. There are a couple of important differences, however. First, whereas a call LEAPS covers 100 shares of stock, a warrant usually covers just one or two shares of the underlying stock (or some fraction thereof). The second big difference involves the issuer of the instruments: Whereas warrants are issued by the same company that issues the underlying stock, LEAPS are not—they can be written by anybody or any institution.

Warrants are created as "sweeteners" to bond issues. To make a bond more attractive, the issuing corporation will sometimes attach warrants, which give the holder the right to purchase a stipulated number of stocks at a stipulated price anytime within a stipulated period. A single warrant usually allows the holder to buy one full share of stock, although some involve more than one share per warrant and a few involve fractional shares. The life of a warrant is specified by its *expiration date*, and the stock purchase price stipulated on the warrant is known as the *exercise price*.

Because warrants are a type of equity issue, they can be margined at the same rate as common stock. They are purchased through brokers and are subject to commission and transaction costs similar to those for common stock. Warrants are usually listed with the common stock of the issuer, but their quotes are easy to pick out, since the letters *wt* appear next to the name of the company. For example, the quote for the Magna Copper warrant is highlighted in Figure 14.4. Notice that the market information for warrants is listed just like any other common stock, except, of course, there's no dividend, dividend yield, or price/earnings ratio.

ADVANTAGES AND DISADVANTAGES

Warrants offer several advantages to investors, one of which is their tendency to exhibit price behavior much like the common stock to which they are linked—which is just what you'd expect since this is, after all, a type of (call)

52 Weeks		Stock	Sym	Div	Yld %	PE	Vol 100s	Hi	Lo	Close	Net Chg
Hi	Lo										
41¼	23¼	Madeco	MAD	.66e	2.5	...	44	26¼	26¼	26¼	+ ⅛
34¾	21	MaderasSintet	MYS	.51e	2.4	...	181	21⅛	21⅛	21⅛	...
18¾	13¼	MagmaCopper	MCU		...	16	1571	17⅜	17	17⅛	− ⅛
69⅞	54½	MagmaCopper	pfD	2.81	4.5	...	3	62⅜	62¼	62¼	− ⅛
10⅝	6⅛	MagmaCopper wt			...	...	4	9	9	9	...
54	31⅛	Magnalnt g	MGA	1.08	...	...	1930	38⅝	38⅛	38⅜	+ ⅛
16¾	12⅜♣	MagneTek	MAG		...	54	164	13¼	12⅞	13	− ⅛
n 17½	13	MalanRlty	MAL	1.70	11.8	...	55	14⅜	14¼	14⅜	...
s 22¾	14⅝	MalaysaFd	MF	1.91e	12.1	...	372	15⅞	15½	15¾	...

Figure 14.4 Stock Quotations Showing Market Information for a Warrant
Warrants are listed right along with common stocks, but they're easy to pick out—just look for the letters *wt* behind the company's name. (Source: *Wall Street Journal.*)

leverage
the ability to obtain a given equity position at a reduced capital investment, thereby magnifying returns.

option. Warrants thus provide the investor with an alternative way of achieving capital gains from an equity issue; that is, instead of buying the stock, the investor can purchase warrants on the stock. Indeed, such a tactic may even be more rewarding than investing directly in the stock.

Another advantage is the relatively low unit cost of warrants and the attractive leverage potential that accompanies this low unit cost. The concept of **leverage** rests on the principle of reducing the level of required capital in a given investment position without affecting the payoff or capital appreciation of that investment. Put another way, an investor can use warrants to obtain a given equity position at a substantially reduced capital investment. In so doing, the investor can *magnify returns*, because the warrant provides roughly the same capital appreciation potential as the more costly common stock. For example, note in Figure 14.4 that the Magna Copper warrants are trading at 9, while shares of Magna common stock are trading at 17½.

A final advantage of warrants is that their low unit cost also leads to reduced downside risk exposure. In essence, the lower unit cost simply means there is less to lose if the investment goes sour. For example, a $50 stock can drop to $25 if the market falls, but there is no way the same company's $10 warrants can drop by the same amount.

However, warrants do have some disadvantages. For one thing, warrants pay no dividends, which means that investors sacrifice current income. Second, because these issues usually carry an expiration date, there is only a certain period of time during which an investor can capture the type of price behavior sought. Although this may not be much of a problem with long-term warrants, it can prove to be a burden for those issues—like the Magna Copper warrants—with fairly short lives (of perhaps one to two years, or less).

PUTTING A VALUE ON WARRANTS

A warrant, like any option, is a type of *derivative security*, since it derives its value from some underlying stock (or other financial asset). For example, the Magna Copper warrants noted above are directly linked to the price behavior of Magna's common stock. Thus, under the right conditions, when Magna

Copper stock goes up (or down) in price, the warrants will too. Actually, warrants possess value whenever the market price of the underlying common equals or exceeds the exercise price on the warrant. This so-called *fundamental value* is determined as follows:

Equation 14.4   Fundamental value of a warrant = $(M - E) \times N$

where

M = prevailing market price of the common stock

E = exercise price stipulated on the warrant

N = number of shares of stock that can be acquired with one warrant (if one warrant entitles the holder to buy one share of stock, $N = 1$; however, if two warrants are required to buy one share of stock, $N = .5$, etc.)

The formula shows fundamental value and therefore what the market value of a warrant *should be*, given the respective market and exercise prices of the common and the number of shares of stock that can be acquired with one warrant. As an example, consider a warrant that carries an exercise price of $40 per share and enables the holder to purchase one share of stock per warrant. If the common stock has a current market price of $50 a share, then the warrants would be valued at $10 each:

Fundamental value of a warrant = ($50 − $40) × 1 = ($10) × 1 = $10

Obviously, the greater the spread between the market and exercise prices, the greater the fundamental value of a warrant. *So long as the market price of the stock equals or exceeds the exercise price of the warrant*, and the redemption provision carries a 1-to-1 ratio (meaning one share of common can be bought with each warrant), the value of a warrant will be directly linked to the price behavior of the common stock.

Premium Prices

Equation 14.4 indicates how warrants should be valued, but they are seldom priced exactly that way in the marketplace. Instead, the market price of a warrant usually *exceeds* its fundamental value. This happens when warrants with negative values trade at prices greater than zero. It also occurs when warrants with positive fundamental values trade at even higher market prices (e.g., when a warrant that's valued at $10 trades at $15). This discrepancy is known as **warrant premium**, and it exists because warrants possess speculative value. As a rule, the amount of premium embedded in the market price of a warrant is directly related to the option's time to expiration and the volatility of the underlying common stock. On the other hand, the amount of premium does tend to diminish as the underlying (fundamental) value of a warrant increases. This can be seen in Figure 14.5, which shows the typical behavior of warrant premiums.

The premium on a warrant is easy to measure: Just take the difference between the value of a warrant (as computed according to the formula above) and its market price. For instance, a warrant has $5 in premium if it has a value of $10 but is trading at $15. The amount of premium can also be expressed on a relative (percentage) basis by dividing the dollar premium by

warrant premium
the difference between the true value of a warrant and its market price.

Figure 14.5 The Normal Price Behavior of Warrant Premiums
Observe that as the price of the underlying common stock increases, the amount of premium in the market price of the warrant tends to decrease—though it never totally disappears.

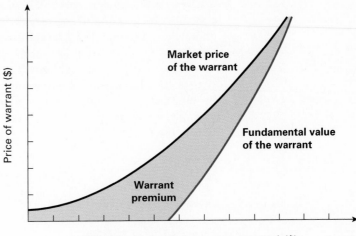

Price/share of underlying common stock ($)

the warrant's fundamental value. For example, there is a 50 percent premium embedded in the price of the $15 warrant cited above (i.e., the dollar premium ÷ the fundamental value of the warrant = $5 ÷ $10 = .50). Premiums on warrants can at times become fairly substantial. Indeed, premiums of 20 to 30 percent or more are not uncommon.

TRADING STRATEGIES

Because their attraction to investors rests primarily with the capital gains opportunities they provide, warrants are used chiefly as alternatives to common stock investments. Let's now look at some warrant trading strategies and the basic ways in which these securities can be profitably employed by investors.

 ### The Basic Price Behavior of Warrants

Since warrants carry relatively low unit costs, they possess much greater *price volatility* and the potential for generating substantially higher *rates of return* than a direct investment in the underlying common stock. Consider the following illustration, which involves the common shares and warrants of the same company. Assume the price of the common is now $50 per share and the warrant, which carries a one-to-one redemption provision, has a $40 exercise price. (We will ignore premium in this illustration.) Observe below what happens when the price of the stock increases by $10:

	Common Stock	Warrant
Issue price *before* increase	$50	$10
Increase in price of common	$10	—
Issue price *after* increase	$60	$20
Increase in market value	$10	$10
Holding period return (increase in value/beginning issue price)	20%	100%

The reason the warrants provide a rate of return five times greater than the common stock is due to the fact that the two issues move parallel to one another, even though the warrant carries a much lower unit cost.

As in our illustration above, the standard holding period return formula would be used to assess the payoff when the investment horizon equals one year or less. In contrast, a variation of the approximate yield formula would be used when the investment horizon amounts to more than a year. For example, if we assume a three-year investment horizon, we could find the return on the investment by using this version of the approximate yield formula:

Equation 14.5

$$\text{Approximate yield} = \frac{\dfrac{\text{sale price of warrant} - \text{purchase price of warrant}}{\text{number of years in investment horizon}}}{\dfrac{\text{sale price} + \text{purchase price}}{2}}$$

$$= \frac{\dfrac{\$20 - \$10}{3}}{\dfrac{\$20 + \$10}{2}} = \frac{\$3.33}{\$15} = \underline{\underline{22.2\%}}$$

Note in this case that we can ignore the dividend component of the standard approximate yield formula, because there are no dividends on warrants. Instead, the return in Equation 14.5 is based solely on the average annual capital gains produced from the investment.

Trading with Warrants

Warrant trading generally follows one of two approaches: (1) The leverage embedded in warrants is used to magnify dollar returns, or (2) their low unit cost is used to reduce the amount of invested capital and limit losses. The first approach is the more aggressive, and the second has considerable merit as a conservative strategy.

Our comparative illustration above can be used to demonstrate the first technique, which seeks to magnify returns. If an investor wishes to make a $5,000 equity investment and if price appreciation is the main objective, he or she would be better off committing such a sum to the warrants. The reason is that a $5,000 investment in the common stock will buy 100 shares of stock ($5,000 ÷ $50 = 100 shares), which will generate only $1,000 in capital gains ($10 profits per share × 100 shares). That same $5,000 invested in the lower-priced warrants will buy 500 of these securities ($5,000 ÷ $10 = 500 warrants) and will result in $5,000 in profits ($10 in profits per warrant × 500 warrants). The common stock thus provides a 20 percent HPR, whereas the warrants yield 100 percent. The biggest risk in this investment is the potential loss exposure. Observe that if the price of the stock in our example decreases by $10, the warrant holder is virtually wiped out (Actually, the warrant will probably retain some value greater than zero, but not much.) In contrast, the price of the stock drops to "only" $40, and the stockholder will still have $4,000 in capital left.

One way to limit this exposure to loss is to follow the second, more conservative trading approach. In this strategy, the investor buys only enough warrants to realize the same level of capital gains as available from the common stock. In our illustration, since we are dealing with options that carry one-to-one redemption provisions, the investor would need to acquire only 100 warrants to obtain the same price behavior as 100 shares of stock. Thus, rather than buying $5,000 worth of stock, the investor would purchase only $1,000 worth of the warrants to realize the same capital gains. If the stock performs as expected, the warrant investor will realize a 100 percent holding period return (as computed above) by generating the same amount of capital gains as the stock—$1,000. But since this will be done with substantially less capital, the yield with the warrants will be greater *and* the loss exposure will be less. In this case, if the price of the stock drops by 10 points, the most the warrant holder can lose is $1,000. On the other hand, if the price of the stock drops by *more* than $10 a share, the warrant holder still will lose no more than $1,000, whereas the stockholder can lose a lot more, depending on the extent of the drop in share price.

CONCEPTS *in Review*

14.17 What is a *warrant* and what is its chief attraction? Describe the leverage features of a warrant and note why leverage is so attractive to investors.

14.18 What factors are important in determining the investment appeal of warrants? Why is the price of the warrant itself so important in the investment decision?

On Track with *STOCK-TRAK*®

Trading Options Through *STOCK-TRAK*®

STOCK-TRAK® options choices include any stock option, the Standard & Poor's 100 Index option, and the Standard & Poor's 500 Index option. For clerical precision, STOCK-TRAK® uses a unique stock option symbol. The first component of the symbol is the stock's ticker symbol, such as *CPQ* for Compaq Computers. Next comes a letter that signifies whether the option is a call or a put and the expiration month; for example, the letter *R* represents June puts. The final component of the options symbol is a letter that signifies the strike price, such as *W* for $17.50. The complete set of expiration month codes and strike price codes is presented in a table in the STOCK-TRAK® registration materials.

The registration materials also illustrate the pricing of stock-index options: Index prices are multiplied by 100 to calculate contract values. The margin requirement is at 15 percent for stock options and 5 percent for index options.

SUMMARY

LG 1 Discuss the basic nature of options in general and puts and calls in particular, and gain an understanding of how these investment vehicles work. An option gives the holder the right (but not the obligation) to buy or sell a certain amount of some real or financial asset at a set price for a set period of time. Puts and calls are by far the most popular and widely used type of option; these derivative securities offer attractive value and considerable leverage potential. A put enables the holder to *sell* a certain amount of a specified security at a specified price over a specified time period. A call, in contrast, gives the holder the right to *buy* the same security at a specified price over a specified period of time. The three basic features of puts and calls are (1) strike price, (2) expiration date, and (3) the purchase price of the option itself.

LG 2 Explain how put and call options are valued and the forces that drive options prices in the marketplace. The value of a call is measured by the market price of the underlying security less the strike price designated on the call. The value of a put is its strike price less the market price of the security. Although the value of an option is driven by the current market price of the underlying asset, most puts and calls sell at premium prices. The size of the premium depends on the length of the option contract (the so-called time premium), the speculative appeal and amount of price volatility in the underlying financial asset, and the general level of interest rates.

LG 3 Describe the profit potential of puts and calls, as well as the risk and return behavior of various put and call investment strategies. Investors who hold puts make money when the value of the underlying asset goes down over time (i.e., prior to the expiration date on the option); in contrast, call investors make money when the underlying asset moves up in price. Aggressive investors will use puts and calls either for speculation or in highly specialized writing and spreading programs. Conservative investors are attracted to puts and calls because of their low unit costs and the limited risk they offer in absolute dollar terms. Often, conservative investors will use options in covered call writing programs or to form hedge positions in combination with other securities.

LG 4 Describe market index options, puts and calls on foreign currencies, and LEAPS, and note how these securities can be used by investors. In addition to the 1,200 or so listed stock options, standardized put and call options are also available on a couple dozen stock-market indexes, like the S&P 500 (index options), and a number of foreign currencies (currency options). And then there are LEAPS, which are listed options that carry lengthy expiration dates (of as long as two years). While these securities can be used just like stock options, the index and currency options tend to be used primarily for speculation or to develop hedge positions.

LG 5 Describe the basic features and fundamental investment attributes of stock rights. A right is a short-lived financial instrument (option) that enables the holder to purchase a new issue of common stock at a subscription price that's set below the prevailing market price of existing stock. Because of their short lives and the way they're linked to new issues of common stock, rights offer very little in the way of profitable trading opportunities (other than being able to buy stocks at sharply lower transaction costs).

LG 6 Discuss the basic investment characteristics of stock warrants and describe the trading strategies that can be used to gain maximum benefits from this investment vehicle. A warrant is similar to a call option, but its maturity is much longer. Attached to bond issues as "sweeteners," warrants allow the holder to purchase common stock at a set exercise price on or before a stipulated expiration date. Trading in warrants is done primarily as a substitute for common stock investing and is based on the magnified capital gains warrants offer. The value of a warrant changes directly with and by approximately the same amount as the underlying common stock; but because a warrant's unit cost is often much lower than that of the common stock, the same dollar change in price represents a considerably larger percentage yield.

DISCUSSION QUESTIONS

1. Using the stock or index option quotations in Figures 14.1 and 14.3, respectively, find the option premium, the time premium, and the stock or index break-even point for the following puts and calls:
    a. The June Pfizer *call* with the $80 strike price
    b. The March Philip Morris *put* with the $65 strike price
    c. The March Pet *call* with the strike price of 22½
    d. The April S&P 100 *call* with the strike price of 430
    e. The March Russell 2000 *put* with the strike price of 255

2. Prepare a schedule similar to the one in Table 14.1 for the February, March, and April S&P 100 *calls*. (Use the ones with strike prices of 430, 435, and 440.) Do the same for the February, March, and April S&P 100 *puts*. (Use strike prices of 430, 435, and 440.) Briefly explain your findings.

3. Assume an investor holds a well-balanced portfolio of common stocks. Under what conditions might he or she want to use a stock-index option to hedge the portfolio?
    a. Briefly explain how such options could be used to hedge a portfolio against a drop in the market.
    b. Discuss what would happen if the market does, in fact, go down.
    c. What happens if the market instead goes up?

PROBLEMS

1. A 6-month call on a certain common stock carries a strike price of $60; it can be purchased at a cost of $600. Assume that the underlying stock rises to $75 per share by the expiration date of the option. How much profit would this option generate over the 6-month holding period, and (using HPR) what is the rate of return?

2. Dorothy Cappel does a lot of investing in the stock market and is a frequent user of stock-index options. She is convinced that the market is about to undergo a broad retreat, and has decided to buy a put on the S&P 100 Index. The put carries a strike price of 390 and is quoted in the financial press at 4½. Although the S&P Index of 100 stocks is currently at 386.45, Dorothy thinks it will drop to 365 by the expiration date on the option. How much profit will she make, and what will be her holding period return if she is right? How much will she lose if the S&P 100 goes up (rather than down) by 25 points and reaches 415 by the date of expiration?

3. Bill Brickshooter holds 600 shares of Lubbock Gas and Light. He bought the stock several years ago at 48½, and the shares are now trading at 75. Bill's concerned that the market's beginning to soften; he doesn't want to sell the stock, but he would like to be able to protect the profit he's made. He decides to hedge his position by buying 6 puts on Lubbock G&L; the 3-month puts carry a strike price of 75 and are currently trading at 2½.
    a. How much profit or loss will Bill make on this deal if the price of Lubbock G&L does indeed drop—to $60 a share—by the expiration date on the puts?
    b. How would he do if the stock kept going up in price and reached $90 a share by the expiration date?
    c. What do you see as the major advantages to using puts as hedge vehicles?
    d. Would Bill have been better off using in-the-money puts—that is, puts with an $85 strike price that are trading at 10½? How about using out-of-the-money puts—say, those with a $70 strike price, trading at 1? Explain.

4. Dave Bentley just purchased 500 shares of AT&E at 61½, and he's decided to write covered calls against these stocks. Accordingly, he sells 5 AT&E calls at their current market price of 5¾; the calls have 3 months to expiration and carry a strike price of 65. Given that the stock pays a quarterly dividend of 80 cents a share:
    a. Determine the total profit and holding period return Bentley will generate if the stock rises to $65 a share by the expiration date on the calls.
    b. What happens to Bentley's profit (and return) if the price of the stock rises to more than $65 a share?
    c. Does this covered call position offer any protection (or cushion) against a drop in the price of the stock? Explain.

5. Assume a company has 1 million shares of common stock outstanding and intends to issue another 200,000 shares via a rights offering; the rights will carry a subscription price of $48½. If the current market price of the stock is $53, what is the value of 1 right?

6. Assume that 1 warrant gives the holder the right to buy 1 share of stock at an exercise price of $40. What is the value of this warrant if the current market price of the stock is $44? At what premium (in dollars and as a percentage) would the warrants be trading if they were quoted in the market at a price of $5?

7. A warrant carries an exercise price of $20; assume it takes 3 warrants to buy 1 share of stock. At what price would the warrant be trading if it sold at a 20 percent premium, while the market price of the stock was $35 per share? What holding period return would an investor make if he or she buys these warrants (at a 20 percent premium) when the stock is trading at $35 and sells them sometime later, when the stock is at $48½ and the premium on the warrants has dropped to 15 percent?

CASE PROBLEMS

14.1   THE SLATERS' INVESTMENT OPTIONS

Phil Slater is a successful businessman in Atlanta. The box manufacturing firm he and his wife, Judy, founded several years ago has prospered. Because he is self-employed, Phil is building his own retirement fund. So far, he has accumulated a substantial sum in his investment account, mostly by following an aggressive investment posture; he does this because, as he puts it, "you never know when the bottom's gonna fall out in this business." Phil has been following the stock of Rembrandt Paper Products (RPP), and after conducting extensive analysis, he feels the stock is about ready to move. Specifically, he believes that within the next 6 months, RPP could go to about $80 per share, from its current level of $57.50. The stock pays annual dividends of $2.40 per share, and Phil figures he would receive two quarterly dividend payments over his 6-month investment horizon.

In studying the company, Phil has learned that it has some warrants outstanding (they mature in 8 years and carry an exercise price of $45); also, it has 6-month call options (with $50 and $60 striking prices) listed on the CBOE. Each warrant is good for 1 share of stock, and they are currently trading at $15; the CBOE calls are quoted at $8 for the options with $50 strike prices and at $5 for the $60 options.

Questions

1. How many alternative investment vehicles does Phil have if he wants to invest in RPP for no more than 6 months? What if he has a 2-year investment horizon?

2. Using a 6-month holding period and assuming the stock does indeed rise to $80 over this time frame:
    a. Find the market price of the warrants at the end of the holding period, given that they then trade at a premium of 10 percent.
    b. Find the value of both calls, given that at the end of the holding period neither contains any investment premium.
    c. Determine the holding period return for each of the four investment alternatives open to Phil Slater.

3. Which course of action would you recommend if Phil simply wants to maximize profit? Would your answer change if other factors (e.g., comparative risk exposure) were considered along with return? Explain.

     14.2   FRED'S QUANDARY—TO HEDGE OR NOT TO HEDGE

A little more than 10 months ago, Fred Weaver, a mortgage banker in Phoenix, bought 300 shares of stock at $40 per share. Since then, the price of the stock has risen to $75 per share. It is now near the end of the year, and the market is starting to weaken; Fred feels there is still plenty of play left in the stock but is afraid the tone of the market will be detrimental to his position. His wife, Denise, is taking an adult education course on the stock market and has just learned about put and call hedges. She suggests that he use puts to hedge his position. Fred is intrigued with the idea, which he discusses with his broker—who advises him that the needed puts are indeed available on his stock. Specifically, he can buy 3-month puts, with $75 strike prices, at a cost of $550 each (quoted at 5½).

Questions

1. Given the circumstances surrounding Fred's current investment position, what benefits could be derived from using the puts as a hedge device? What would be the major drawback?

2. What would Fred's minimum profit be if he buys three puts at the indicated option price? How much would he make if he did not hedge but instead sold his stock immediately at a price of $75 per share?

3. Assuming Fred uses three puts to hedge his position, indicate the amount of profit he would generate if the stock moves to $100 by the expiration date of the puts. What if the stock drops to $50 per share?

4. Should Fred use the puts as a hedge? Explain. Under what conditions would you urge him *not* to use the puts as a hedge?

CHAPTER 15

COMMODITIES AND FINANCIAL FUTURES

LEARNING GOALS

After studying this chapter, you should be able to:

LG 1 Describe the essential features of a futures contract, as well as the basic operating characteristics of the futures market.

LG 2 Explain the role hedgers and speculators play in the futures market, including how profits are made and lost.

LG 3 Describe the commodities segment of the futures market and the basic characteristics of these investment vehicles.

LG 4 Discuss the various investment strategies and trading techniques that investors can use with commodities, and explain how investment returns can be measured.

LG 5 Know the difference between a physical commodity and a financial future, and gain an appreciation of the growing role that financial futures play in the market today.

LG 6 Discuss the trading techniques that can be used with financial futures and note how these securities can be used in conjunction with other investment vehicles (like stocks, bonds, and foreign securities).

INVESTOR INTERVIEW

An inheritance gave Charles Stone the funds to start investing, and, like many new investors, he began with mutual funds. "I lost almost $500 in a month," he recalls. "Although everyone said it was a long-term investment and not to worry, I wanted more immediate results so I could have a sizable portfolio when I retire from the Air Force in about ten years." He soon discovered that futures trading suited him. "I'm impatient; I like the excitement and going for quick profits. And because futures trading is done on margin, I get the benefits—plus the greater risk—of leverage."

Although a substantial amount of his current portfolio—42 percent—is in futures, the rest is conservatively invested in savings, a CD, and an equity mutual fund to which he adds regularly. "Speculating in futures is an emotional—and financial—roller coaster, but I can handle the above-average risk," he says. "For example, from June 1994 to March 1995, my initial $5,000—the minimum to open a commodities account—grew to $13,000, dropped to $2,000, and then rose to $9,600! I learned a lot during that losing streak. Many trades turned into winners soon after I exited. Now, I may stay with a losing position longer, to wait for a turnaround."

He cites an example: "I buy a contract (5,000 bushels) of December wheat in July, when the supply is high, at $3.25 per bushel—a total of $16,250. On margin that contract costs me only $500. In grains, 1 cent equals $50; a 50 cent increase in the price of wheat in December, when supply is low, results in $2,500 profit ($0.50 × 5,000 bushels) on my $500 in five months! If news of a good harvest in Russia reduces exports and the price drops 25 cents to $3 in September, there will be a margin call, and I have to cover my position with $1,250 in reserves from my account. I can either ride it out, if I think that the price will rise again, or cut my losses and sell."

Charles invests mainly in cattle and wheat futures. "We were weekend cattle ranchers in east Texas," he explains. "Wheat is easy to understand (plant, grow, harvest, sell), the margin is low, and the market typically has bull and bear cycles during the year. I also look for other opportunities; I traded federal funds futures when it was clear the Fed would raise inter-

> **FUTURES TRADING HAS A BIG LEARNING CURVE. YOU USUALLY LOSE MONEY BEFORE YOU LEARN HOW THE MARKETS WORK.**

est rates in early 1995." He prefers to spread the risk over many small, short-term trades rather than a few large ones. His trading strategy uses both fundamentals, such as seasonal tendencies of agricultural commodities, and technical analysis, such as price movements, charting, and statistics.

"Futures trading has a big learning curve. You usually lose money before you learn how the markets work," Charles states. "It condenses the time aspect of stock trading from years to months. You need a strong stomach and time to follow your trades daily or even hourly; you can't forget a trade." He also recommends finding a good broker, hedging to lock in profits, and following market trends. A commodities market moves in a particular direction for a reason, and the small trader may not be privy to this information," he notes.

A United States Air Force staff sergeant, Charles Stone is 29 years old and lives with his wife in Phoenix, Arizona.

Psst, wanna buy some copper? How about some coffee, or pork bellies, or propane? Maybe the Japanese yen or Swiss franc strikes your fancy. Sound a bit unusual? Perhaps, but all these items have one thing in common: They represent investment vehicles that are popular with millions of investors. This is the more exotic side of investing—the market for commodities and financial futures—and it often involves a considerable amount of speculation. In fact, the risks are enormous, but with a little luck, the payoffs can be phenomenal, too. Even more important than luck, however, is the need for patience and know-how. Because *these are specialized investment products that require specialized investor skills,* they should never be used by investors who are unsure of what they're doing. As Charles Stone discovered, you may have beginner's luck and earn quick profits right away, but you can easily have a losing streak soon after, until you learn how the markets work.

In this chapter we will take a brief look at these investment vehicles, to see not only what they are but also, in very general terms, how they can be used in various types of investment programs. First, we will examine the futures market in general. Then we will look at investing in commodities, and after that, at financial futures and how they can be used by investors.

THE FUTURES MARKET

The amount of futures trading in the United States has mushroomed over the past 20 or 25 years as an increasing number of investors have turned to futures trading as a way to earn attractive, highly competitive rates of return. But it's *not* the traditional commodities contracts that have drawn many of these investors; rather, it's the new investment vehicles that are being offered. Indeed, a major reason behind the growth in the volume of futures trading has been *the big jump in the number and variety of contracts available for trading.* Thus, today we find that in addition to the traditional primary commodities, such as grains and metals, markets also exist for live animals, processed commodities, crude oil and gasoline, foreign currencies, money market securities, U.S. Treasury notes and bonds, Eurodollar securities, and common stocks (via stock market indexes). In fact, you can even buy listed put and call *options* on just about any actively traded futures contract. All these commodities and financial assets are traded in what is known as the *futures market.*

MARKET STRUCTURE

cash market
a market where a product or commodity changes hands in exchange for a cash price paid when the transaction is completed.

futures market
the organized market for the trading of futures contracts.

When a bushel of wheat is sold, the transaction takes place in the **cash market;** in other words, the bushel changes hands in exchange for a cash price paid to the seller. The transaction occurs at that point in time and for all practical purposes is completed then and there. Most traditional securities are traded in this type of market. However, a bushel of wheat could also be sold in the **futures market,** the organized market for the trading of futures contracts. In this market, the seller would not actually deliver the wheat until some mutually agreed-upon date in the future. As a result, the transaction would not be completed for some time: The seller would receive partial payment for the bushel of wheat at the time the agreement was entered into, and the balance on delivery. The buyer, in turn, would own a highly liquid futures contract that could be held (and presented for delivery of the bushel of wheat) or traded in the futures market. No matter what the buyer does with the contract, as long as it is outstanding, the seller has a *legally binding obligation to make delivery* of the stated quantity of wheat on a specified date in the future, and the buyer/holder has a similar *obligation to take delivery* of the underlying commodity.

Futures Contracts

futures contract
a commitment to deliver a certain amount of some specified item at some specified date in the future.

delivery month
the time when a commodity must be delivered; defines the life of a futures contract.

A **futures contract** is a commitment to deliver a certain amount of a specified item at a specified date at a price agreed upon at the time the contract is sold. The seller of the contract agrees to make the specified future delivery, and the buyer agrees to accept it. Each market establishes its own contract specifications, which include not only the quantity and quality of the item but the delivery procedure and delivery month as well. The **delivery month** for a futures contract is much like the expiration date used on put and call options; it specifies when the commodity or item must be delivered and thus defines the life of the contract. For example, the Chicago Board of Trade specifies that each of its soybean contracts will involve 5,000 bushels of USDA Grade 2 yellow soybeans; delivery months are January, March, May, July, August, September, and November. In addition, futures contracts have *their own trading hours*. Unlike listed stocks and bonds, which begin and end trading at the same time, normal trading hours for commodities and financial futures vary widely. For example, oats trade from 9:30 A.M. to 1:15 P.M. (Central); silver, from 7:25 A.M. to 1:40 P.M.; live cattle, from 9:05 A.M. to 1:15 P.M.; U.S. Treasury bills, from 7:20 A.M. to 2:15 P.M.; and S&P 500 stock-index contracts, from 8:30 A.M. to 3:15 P.M. It may sound a bit confusing, but it seems to work.

Table 15.1 lists a cross-section of 12 different commodities and financial futures. As you can see, the typical futures contract covers a large quantity of the underlying product or financial instrument. However, although the value of a single contract is normally quite large, the actual amount of investor capital required to deal in these vehicles is relatively small, because *all trading in this market is done on a margin basis*.

Table 15.1   Futures Contract Dimensions

Contract	Size of a Contract*	Recent Market Value of a Single Contract**
Corn	5,000 bu	$ 11,475
Wheat	5,000 bu	18,500
Live cattle	40,000 lb	29,740
Pork bellies	40,000 lb	17,520
Coffee	37,500 lb	58,312
Cotton	50,000 lb	46,750
Gold	100 troy oz	37,540
Copper	25,000 lb	34,450
Japanese yen	12.5 million yen	126,250
Treasury bills	$1 million	940,500
Treasury bonds	$100,000	101,500
S&P 500 Stock Index	$500 times the index	236,100

*The size of some contracts may vary by exchange.

**Contract values are representative of those that existed in early 1995.

Options Versus Futures Contracts   In many respects, futures contracts are closely related to the call options we studied in Chapter 14. Both involve the future delivery of an item at an agreed-upon price. But there is a *significant difference* between a futures contract and an options contract: A futures contract *obligates* a person to buy or sell a specified amount of a given commodity on or before a stated date, unless the contract is canceled or liquidated before it expires. In contrast, an option gives the holder the *right* to buy or sell a specific amount of a real or financial asset at a specific price over a specified period of time. In addition, whereas *price* (i.e., strike price) is one of the specified variables on a call option, it is *not* stated anywhere on a futures contract. Instead, the price on a futures contract is established through trading on the floor of a commodities exchange—meaning that the delivery price is set by supply and demand at whatever price the contract sells for. Equally important, the risk of loss with an option is limited to the price paid for it, whereas a futures contract has *no such limit on exposure to loss.*

Futures Contracts Versus Forward Contracts   In addition to futures contracts, there are also forward contracts. Basically, a **forward contract** is an agreement whereby a seller agrees to deliver a specific commodity or product to a buyer sometime in the future, *at a price specified in the contract itself.* Actually, forward contracts are widely used in practice and are common in real estate leases, fixed-rate loans, credit cards, mortgage loans, even magazine subscriptions. In all these cases, two parties agree that a product or service will be delivered sometime in the future at some set price. For example, when home buyers apply for a mortgage, they can "lock in" an interest rate at the time they start the loan application process, rather than having to wait until the deal closes—which could be two or three months later. When they lock in the rate, they are effectively entering into a forward contract with the mortgage lender, with regard to the rate of interest that will be charged on the mortgage (assuming, of course, that the buyers qualify for the loan). Without forward contracts, it would be impossible for buyers and sellers to agree on anything, and prices would have to be constantly renegotiated.

    Although futures and forward contracts may appear to be the same, there are some real differences between them. The most obvious, perhaps, has to do with price: Whereas price is specified on a forward contract, it is set through trading on a futures contract. Moreover, in contrast to futures contracts, prices and contract terms on forward contracts are *not standardized.* As a result, forward contracts *are not actively traded on organized exchanges*; there *is* a forward market for some types of contracts, but there are no organized exchanges. Because there are no exchanges, there are no central clearinghouses in the forward market. Consequently, there is a risk that one or both of the parties won't be able to hold up its end of the bargain. In sharp contrast, certain financial constraints prevent this type of situation from occurring in the futures market.

Major Exchanges

Although futures contracts can be traced back to biblical times, their use (on an organized basis) in this country did not occur until the mid–1800s. They originated in the agricultural segment of the economy, where individuals who produced, owned, and/or processed foodstuffs sought a way to protect themselves against adverse price movements. Later, futures contracts came to be

forward contract
agreement whereby a seller agrees to deliver a specific commodity or product to a buyer sometime in the future, at a price specified in the contract itself.

traded by individuals who were not necessarily connected with agriculture but who wanted to make money with commodities by speculating on their price swings.

The first organized commodities exchange in this country was the Chicago Board of Trade, which opened its doors in 1848. Over time, additional markets opened, so that today no fewer than 12 exchanges deal in listed futures contracts. The Chicago Board of Trade (CBT) is the largest and most active U.S. exchange. (In fact, it's the largest commodities exchange in the world.) The CBT is followed in size by the Chicago Mercantile Exchange (CME), the New York Mercantile Exchange (NYMerc), and the Commodity Exchange of New York (COMEX). Together, these four exchanges account for more than 80 percent of all the trading volume conducted on American futures exchanges. All totalled, trading activity on the 12 U.S. commodities exchanges has reached the point where the futures market today is a *trillion-dollar* institution that in many respects rivals the stock market.

Most exchanges deal in a number of different commodities or financial assets, and many commodities and financial futures are traded on more than one exchange. Although the exchanges are highly efficient and annual volume has surpassed the trillion-dollar mark, futures trading is still conducted by **open outcry auction:** As shown in Figure 15.1, actual trading on the floors of these exchanges is conducted through a series of shouts, body motions, and hand signals.

open outcry auction
in futures trading, an auction in which trading is done through a series of shouts, body motions, and hand signals.

TRADING IN THE FUTURES MARKET

Basically, the futures market contains two types of traders: hedgers and speculators. The market simply could not exist and operate efficiently without either one. The **hedgers** are commodities producers and processors (which today include financial institutions and corporate money managers) who use futures contracts as a way to protect their interest in the underlying commodity or financial instrument. For example, if a rancher thinks the price of cattle will drop in the near future, he will hedge his position by selling a futures contract on cattle in the hope of locking in as high a price as possible for his herd. In effect, the hedgers provide the underlying strength of the futures market and represent the very reason for its existence. *Speculators*, in contrast, give the market liquidity; they are the ones who trade futures contracts not because of a need to protect a position in the underlying commodity but simply to earn a profit on expected swings in the price of a futures contract. They are the risk takers, the investors who have no inherent interest in the commodity or financial future other than the price action and potential capital gains it can produce.

hedgers
producers and processors who use futures contracts to protect their interest in an underlying commodity or financial instrument.

Trading Mechanics

Once futures contracts are created by the hedgers and speculators, they can readily be traded in the market. Like common stocks and other traditional investment vehicles, futures contracts are bought and sold through local brokerage offices. Most firms have at least one or two people in each office who specialize in futures contracts. In addition, a number of commodity firms that deal only in futures contracts stand ready to help individuals with their investment needs. Except for setting up a special commodities trading account, there

Figure 15.1 The Auction Market at Work on the Floor of the Chicago Board of Trade
Traders employ a system of open outcry and hand signals to indicate whether they wish to buy or sell and the price at which they wish to do so. Fingers held *vertically* indicate the number of contracts a trader wants to buy or sell. Fingers held *horizontally* indicate the fraction of a cent above or below the last traded full-cent price at which the trader will buy or sell. (Source: Chicago Board of Trade.)

is really no difference between trading futures and dealing in stocks or bonds. The same types of orders are used, and the use of margin is the standard way of trading futures. Any investor can buy or sell any contract, with any delivery month, at any time, so long as it is currently being traded on one of the exchanges.

Buying a contract is referred to as taking a *long position*, whereas selling one is termed taking a *short position*. It is exactly like going long or short with stocks and has the same connotation: The investor who is long wants the price to rise, and the short seller wants it to drop. Both long and short positions can be liquidated simply by executing an offsetting transaction. The short seller, for example, would cover his or her position by buying an equal amount of the contract. In general, less than 1 percent of all futures contracts are settled by delivery; the rest are offset prior to the delivery month. All trades are subject to normal transaction costs, which include **round-trip commissions** of about $60 to $90 for each contract traded. (A round-trip commission includes the commission costs on both ends of the transaction—to buy and to sell a contract.) The exact size of the commission depends on the number and type of contracts being traded.

round-trip commissions
the commission costs on both ends (buying and selling) of a securities transaction.

Margin Trading

Buying on margin means putting up only a fraction of the total price in cash; margin, in effect, is the *amount of equity* that goes into the deal. Margin trading plays a crucial role in futures transactions because *all futures contracts are traded on a margin basis*. The margin required usually ranges from about 2 to 10 percent of the value of the contract, which, when compared to the margin required for stocks and most other types of securities, is very low. Furthermore, there is *no borrowing* required on the part of the investor to finance the balance of the contract; the margin, or **margin deposit,** as it is called with futures, exists simply as a way to guarantee fulfillment of the contract. The margin deposit is not a partial payment for the commodity or financial instrument; nor is it in any way related to the value of the product or item underlying the contract. Rather, it represents security to cover any loss in the market value of the contract that may result from adverse price movements.

margin deposit
amount deposited with a broker to cover any loss in the market value of a futures contract that may result from adverse price movements.

The size of the required margin deposit is specified as a dollar amount and varies according to the type of contract (i.e., the amount of price volatility in the underlying commodity or financial asset) and, in some cases, the exchange on which the commodity is traded. Table 15.2 gives the margin requirements for the same 12 commodities and financial instruments listed in Table 15.1, on page 623. Compared to the size and value of futures contracts, margin requirements are very low. The **initial deposit** noted in Table 15.2 is the amount of investor capital that must be deposited with the broker when the transaction is initiated and represents the amount of money required to make a given investment.

initial deposit
the amount of investor capital that must be deposited with a broker at the time of a commodity transaction.

After the investment is made, the market value of a contract will, of course, rise and fall as the quoted price of the underlying commodity or financial instrument goes up or down. Such market behavior will cause the amount of margin on deposit to change. To be sure that an adequate margin is always on hand, investors are required to meet a second type of margin requirement, the **maintenance deposit.** This deposit is slightly less than the initial deposit and establishes the minimum amount of margin that must be kept in the account at

maintenance deposit
the minimum amount of margin that must be kept in a margin account at all times.

Table 15.2   Margin Requirements for a Sample of Commodities and Financial Futures

	Initial Margin Deposit	Maintenance Margin Deposit
Corn	$1,000	$ 750
Wheat	1,000	750
Live cattle	1,000	750
Pork bellies	1,000	750
Coffee	2,500	1,875
Cotton	1,000	750
Gold	900	675
Copper	1,000	750
Japanese yen	1,600	1,200
Treasury bills	1,000	750
Treasury bonds	2,700	2,000
S&P 500 Stock Index	10,000	7,500

Note: These margin requirements were specified by a major full-service brokerage firm in early 1995; they may exceed the minimums established by the various exchanges. They are meant to be typical of the ongoing requirements that customers are expected to live up to. Depending upon the volatility of the market, exchange-minimum margin requirements are changed frequently, and thus the requirements in this table are also subject to change on short notice.

all times. For instance, if the initial deposit on a commodity is $1,000 per contract, its maintenance margin might be $750. So long as the market value of the contract does not fall by more than $250 (the difference between the contract's initial and maintenance margins), the investor has no problem. But if the market moves against the investor and the value of the contract drops by more than the allowed amount, the investor will receive a *margin call*. He or she must then immediately deposit enough cash to bring the position back to the initial margin level. An investor's margin position is checked daily via a procedure known as **mark-to-the-market**. That is, the gain or loss in a contract's value is determined at the end of each session, at which time the broker debits or credits the trader's account accordingly. In a falling market, an investor may receive a number of margin calls and be required to make additional margin payments (perhaps on a daily basis) in order to keep the position above the maintenance margin level. Failure to do so will mean that the broker has no choice but to close out the position—that is, sell the contract.

mark-to-the-market
a daily check of an investor's margin position, determined at the end of each session, at which time the broker debits or credits the account as needed.

CONCEPTS *in Review*

15.1   What is a *futures contract*? Briefly explain how it is used as an investment vehicle.

15.2   Discuss the difference between a *cash market* and a *futures market*.
    a. List some of the reasons why the futures market has become popular.
    b. What is the difference between a futures contract and a *forward contract*?

15.3   What is the major source of return to commodities speculators? How important is current income from dividends and interest to these investors?

15.4 Why are both hedgers and speculators important to the efficient operation of a futures market?

15.5 Explain how margin trading is conducted in the futures market.
   a. What is the difference between an *initial deposit* and a *maintenance deposit*?
   b. Are investors ever required to put up additional margin? If so, when?

COMMODITIES

Physical commodities like grains, metals, wood, and meat make up a major portion of the futures market. They have been actively traded in this country for well over a century and still account for a good deal of the trading activity. The text material that follows focuses on *commodities trading* and begins with a review of the basic characteristics and investment merits of these vehicles.

BASIC CHARACTERISTICS

Various types of physical commodities are found on nearly all of the 12 U.S. futures exchanges (in fact, three of them deal only in commodities). The market for commodity contracts is divided into four major segments: grains and oilseeds, livestock and meat, food and fiber, and metals and petroleum. Such segmentation does not affect trading mechanics and procedures but provides a convenient way of categorizing commodities into groups based on similar underlying characteristics. Table 15.3 shows the diversity of the commodities market and the variety of contracts available. Although the list changes yearly, we can see from the table that investors had nearly three dozen different commodities to choose from in 1995, and a number of these (e.g., soybeans, wheat, and sugar) are available in several different forms or grades.

Table 15.3 Major Classes of Commodities

Grains and Oilseeds	Metals and Petroleum
Corn	Aluminum
Oats	Copper
Soybeans	Gold
Soybean meal	Platinum
Soybean oil	Silver
Wheat	Palladium
Barley	Gasoline
Canola	Heating oil
Flaxseed	Crude oil
Rice	Gas oil
	Propane
	Natural gas
Livestock and Meat	**Food and Fiber**
Cattle—live	Cocoa
Cattle—feeder	Coffee
Hogs	Cotton
Pork bellies	Orange juice
	Sugar

A Commodities Contract

Every commodity has its own specifications regarding the amounts and quality of the product being traded. Figure 15.2 is an excerpt from the "Futures Prices" section of the *Wall Street Journal* and shows the contract and quotation system used with commodities. Each commodity quote is made up of the same five parts, and all prices are quoted in an identical fashion. In particular, every commodities contract or quote specifies: (1) the product; (2) the exchange on which the contract is traded; (3) the size of the contract (in bushels, pounds, tons, etc.); (4) the method of valuing the contract, or pricing unit (e.g., cents per pound or dollars per ton); and (5) the delivery month. Using a corn contract as an illustration, we can see each of these parts in the following illustration:

KEY
1 the product
2 the exchange
3 the size of the contract
4 the pricing unit
5 the delivery months

		Open	High	Low	Settle	Change	Lifetime High	Lifetime Low	Open Interest
1 **2** **3** **4**									
Corn (CBT)—5,000 bu.; cents per bu.									
5	May	253½	253¾	252¼	252½	–1¾	286½	230½	42,796
	July	258	258	256½	256¾	–1¾	288	233	60,477
	Sept.	260	260½	259	259	–1½	263	236	7,760
	Dec.	263½	264	262½	263	–1¼	267¼	244	41,638
	Mar. 97	271¾	272	270½	271	–1¼	276	254¾	11,098
	May	277¼	278	276¼	277	–1	281	273¼	1,326

The quotation system used for commodities is based on the size of the contract and the pricing unit. The financial media generally report the open, high, low, and closing prices for each delivery month. With commodities, the last price of the day, or the closing price, is known as the **settle price**. Also reported, at least by the *Wall Street Journal*, is the amount of **open interest** in each contract—that is, the number of contracts currently outstanding. Note in the above illustration that the settle price for May corn was quoted at 252½. Since the pricing system is cents per bushel, this means that the contract was being traded at $2.52½ per bushel, and that the market value of the contract was $12,625 (each contract involves 5,000 bushels and each bushel is worth $2.52½; thus, 5,000 × $2.525 = $12,625).

settle price
the closing price (last price of the day) for commodities and financial futures.

open interest
the number of contracts currently outstanding on a commodity or financial future.

Price Behavior

Commodity prices react to a unique set of economic, political, and international pressures—as well as to the weather. Although the explanation of why commodity prices change is beyond the scope of this book, it should be clear that they do move up and down just like any other investment vehicle—which is precisely what speculators want. However, because we are dealing in such large trading units (5,000 bushels of this or 40,000 pounds of that), even a modest price change can have an enormous impact on the market value of a contract and therefore on investor returns or losses. For example, if the price of corn goes up or down by just 20 cents per bushel, the value of a *single contract* will change by $1,000. Since a corn contract can be bought with a $750 initial margin deposit, it is easy to see the effect this kind of price behavior can have on investor return.

Figure 15.2 Quotations on Actively Traded Commodity Futures Contracts These quotes reveal at a glance key information about the various commodities, including the latest high, low, and closing ("settle") prices, as well as the lifetime high and low prices for each contract. (Source: *Wall Street Journal*, February 1, 1995.)

FUTURES PRICES

Tuesday, January 31, 1995

Open Interest Reflects Previous Trading Day

GRAINS AND OILSEEDS

	Open	High	Low	Settle	Change	Lifetime High	Lifetime Low	Open Interest
CORN (CBT) 5,000 bu.; cents per bu.								
Mar	229¼	230½	229	229½	....	282½	220½	103,345
May	236¾	237¾	236½	236¾	− ¼	285	228	65,985
July	242	243	241½	242¼	....	285½	232½	63,006
Sept	247½	248	247¼	247¾	....	270½	238	10,032
Dec	252¾	253¼	252¼	253	....	263	235¼	48,547
Mr96	258¾	259½	258¾	259½	+ ¼	260¼	249½	5,783
May	262¾	263½	262¾	263½	+ ¼	264¼	259½	149
July	264¾	265½	264¾	265½	+ ¼	267	254	2,906
Dec	253¾	254	253¾	254	+ ¼	257	239	1,108
Est vol 29,000; vol Mon 77,762; open int 300,873, −3,930.								
OATS (CBT) 5,000 bu.; cents per bu.								
Mar	121	122	120½	121¼	+ ¼	152¼	116½	7,499
May	125½	126¼	125¼	126¼	+ ¼	151	122¼	3,427
July	130¼	131½	130¼	131½	+ ½	142½	127½	2,018
Sept	134½	134½	134½	135½	+ ½	142½	132	115
Est vol 500; vol Mon 356; open int 13,081, −24.								
SOYBEANS (CBT) 5,000 bu.; cents per bu.								
Mar	548	550¾	547¼	547½	− 1½	705	547¼	59,416
May	557½	559¼	556	556¼	− 1¼	705½	556	31,894
July	563	565	562	562¼	− ¾	706½	561½	30,089
Aug	565	567	564½	564½	− 1½	612	564½	3,564
Sept	567¼	569	567	567	− 1¼	615	566¼	2,660
Nov	576¼	578	575	575¼	− 1	645	574½	16,398
Ja96	585	586½	583½	583½	− 1	616	583½	865
July	602	602	601	601	− ¼	636¼	599½	244
Nov	587	588	587	587	− ½	611	585	478
Est vol 24,000; vol Mon 30,406; open int 145,660, +2,931.								
SOYBEAN MEAL (CBT) 100 tons; $ per ton.								
Mar	157.00	157.40	156.10	156.20	− .90	207.50	155.90	35,363
May	159.10	160.00	159.00	159.10	− .50	207.00	159.00	22,766
July	163.20	163.70	162.50	162.60	− .90	206.00	162.50	17,747
Aug	165.20	165.50	164.70	164.70	− .60	182.60	164.70	5,550
Sept	167.30	167.50	166.70	166.80	− .30	182.70	165.40	3,975
Oct	168.50	169.20	168.50	168.70	+ .30	181.90	168.50	6,916
Dec	171.50	172.20	171.30	171.70	....	185.20	171.30	6,311
Ja96				173.20	....	185.50	173.10	119
Est vol 12,000; vol Mon 11,561; open int 98,747, +827.								
SOYBEAN OIL (CBT) 60,000 lbs.; cents per lb.								
Mar	26.86	26.99	26.69	26.70	− .20	28.45	22.91	36,988
May	25.81	25.94	25.69	25.70	− .20	28.05	22.85	24,616
July	25.33	25.42	25.16	25.20	− .19	27.85	22.76	15,075
Aug	25.05	25.10	24.90	24.93	− .12	27.20	22.73	4,020
Sept	24.75	24.77	24.65	24.66	− .13	25.70	22.75	4,766
Oct	24.53	24.56	24.45	24.47	− .07	25.35	22.75	5,417
Dec	24.20	24.32	24.10	24.13	− .10	25.05	22.80	7,373
Ja96	23.95	23.95	23.95	23.95	− .10	24.85	23.20	136
Mar				23.90	− .20	24.50	23.85	134
Est vol 15,000; vol Mon 10,399; open int 98,525, +256.								
WHEAT (CBT) 5,000 bu.; cents per bu.								
Mar	368¼	374	368¼	373½	+ 5	426¾	327	36,032
May	355	359½	355	358¾	+ 3¼	398½	325	11,610
July	337	338¾	336	337¼	....	363¾	311½	19,306
Sept	342¼	343	341½	343	− ¾	365	339	1,286
Dec	352¼	354	352¼	352½	− ¾	375	349	828
Est vol 11,000; vol Mon 9,608; open int 69,092, +121.								
WHEAT (KC) 5,000 bu.; cents per bu.								
Mar	369¼	375	369¼	374¾	+ 5¼	427¼	326½	20,036
May	356½	361	356½	360	+ 2¾	403	321½	6,945
July	339	342	339	340¼	+ ¾	368¼	316½	6,991
Sept	342½	345	342½	343½	+ ½	377	329	357
Dec	351½	352	351	351	+ ½	369½	336½	281
Est vol 4,916; vol Mon 4,114; open int 34,610, −283.								
WHEAT (MPLS) 5,000 bu.; cents per bu.								
Mar	363½	368	363½	365¾	+ 1¾	431	325¼	10,499
May	365½	369½	365½	368½	+ 1	419¼	332½	3,919
July	356	358½	356	357½	+ 2½	386	324½	527
Sept	347¾	349	347	347	+ ½	366	345	461
Est vol 2,619; vol Mon 2,024; open int 15,445, −67.								
BARLEY (WPG) 20 metric tons; Can. $ per ton								
Feb	119.00	119.90	119.00	119.90	− .20	126.50	90.80	260
May	121.70	122.80	121.70	122.80	+ .90	126.70	93.80	5,540
Aug	119.00	119.50	119.50	119.00	− .30	126.70	99.00	1,496
Nov	113.00	113.00	113.00	113.00	+ .40	115.00	111.60	1,727
Est vol 375; vol Mon 683; open int 9,028, +67.								
CANOLA (WPG) 20 metric tons; Can. $ per ton								
Mar	431.50	432.80	431.10	431.60	− 1.10	452.80	331.00	21,016
June	439.00	440.00	438.60	439.00	− 1.50	457.20	346.50	15,958
Aug	418.00	418.20	417.70	418.00	− .50	435.20	362.00	837
Sept	400.00	401.10	400.00	401.10	+ 1.20	405.00	350.00	1,342
Nov	399.00	401.00	398.80	399.80	+ .80	405.00	331.00	8,283
Ja96				403.10	+ .30	404.00	402.80	100
Est vol 2,015; vol Mon 2,549; open int 47,556, +167.								

	Open	High	Low	Settle	Change	Lifetime High	Lifetime Low	Open Interest
Nov	22.21	22.21	22.20	22.21	+ .01	22.27	21.80	2,075
Ja96	21.95	21.99	21.97	21.98	+ .08	22.03	21.80	236
Mar				21.92	+ .02	21.98	21.90	462
Est vol 345; vol Mon 713; open int 14,813, −119.								
COTTON (CTN) 50,000 lbs.; cents per lb.								
Mar	93.90	94.30	93.40	93.47	− .88	94.70	64.00	26,509
May	92.10	92.15	91.25	91.33	− 1.02	92.75	64.00	16,972
July	89.90	90.00	89.25	89.27	− .91	91.39	69.30	12,420
Oct	80.10	80.30	79.90	80.00	− .30	81.45	66.80	4,047
Dec	74.20	74.50	74.20	74.39	− .06	74.96	66.25	14,148
Mr96	75.35	75.55	75.35	75.44	− .02	75.90	68.80	1,024
Est vol 9,000; vol Mon 9,364; open int 75,188, +1,960.								
ORANGE JUICE (CTN) 15,000 lbs.; cents per lb.								
Mar	103.00	103.70	101.80	102.80	+ .10	124.25	93.00	18,815
May	106.75	107.60	106.00	106.80	+ .55	126.50	97.50	3,535
July	109.60	110.10	109.60	110.30	+ .75	128.70	100.50	1,001
Sept	113.65	114.25	113.50	114.00	+ 1.15	131.50	102.50	2,653
Nov	113.00	113.00	113.00	113.75	+ .95	129.00	109.00	2,031
Ja96	113.50	113.50	113.25	113.75	+ 1.00	129.00	105.50	809
Est vol 2,300; vol Mon 1,668; open int 28,937, −28.								

METALS AND PETROLEUM

	Open	High	Low	Settle	Change	Lifetime High	Lifetime Low	Open Interest
COPPER-HIGH (CMX) 25,000 lbs.; cents per lb.								
Feb	138.10	138.10	137.80	137.80	− 1.25	143.30	87.85	1,586
Mar	138.20	139.25	135.60	136.30	− 1.30	142.90	76.30	29,782
Apr	137.30	137.30	135.15	135.15	− 1.20	140.50	90.10	1,025
May	135.10	135.75	132.70	133.45	− 1.00	138.60	76.85	6,370
June				131.65	− .95	134.75	106.30	597
July	131.70	132.20	129.90	129.75	− .95	134.00	78.00	4,267
Aug				127.75	− .90	130.00	111.40	403
Sept	127.60	127.60	125.00	125.75	− .85	129.20	79.10	2,629
Oct				124.55	− .80	126.90	113.00	321
Nov				123.50	− 1.20	125.50	113.95	127
Dec	123.50	123.50	123.00	122.10	− .80	124.35	88.00	3,661
Jan				121.00	− .75	122.80	88.50	121
Mar	120.00	120.00	120.00	118.70	− .70	120.80	99.20	824
May				116.30	− .70	118.50	107.00	188
July	117.00	117.00	116.80	116.10	− .70	117.00	105.50	108
Est vol 9,000; vol Mon 8,290; open int 52,060, −991.								
GOLD (CMX) 100 troy oz.; $ per troy oz.								
Feb	376.20	376.50	374.50	375.40	− 1.40	411.00	363.50	12,357
Apr				376.00	− 1.70	385.50	378.50	4
Apr	378.90	379.00	376.80	377.70	− 1.70	425.00	375.60	62,225
June	382.20	382.80	380.20	381.20	− 1.70	430.00	351.00	28,037
Aug	385.10	385.10	384.50	385.20	− 1.70	414.50	380.50	15,479
Oct				389.30	− 1.70	419.20	390.00	4,701
Dec	393.80	393.80	393.50	393.50	− 1.70	439.50	358.00	13,315
Fb96				397.80	− 1.60	424.50	398.50	5,843
Apr				402.30	− 1.60	430.20	418.30	2,818
June				406.70	− 1.60	447.00	370.90	6,260
Aug				411.00	− 1.60	423.00	423.00	549
Dec				420.10	− 1.60	447.50	379.60	3,878
Ju97				433.90	− 1.60	456.00	436.00	2,932
Dec	448.00	448.00	448.00	447.70	− 1.60	477.00	402.00	2,873
Ju98				461.70	− 1.60	489.50	464.50	1,946
Dec				475.90	− 1.60	505.00	468.00	3,282
Ju99				490.10	− 1.60	520.00	497.50	4,043
Dec				504.60	− 1.60			943
Est vol 34,000; vol Mon 44,264; open int 171,500, −3,996.								
PLATINUM (NYM) 50 troy oz.; $ per troy oz.								
Apr	na	419.50	414.50	415.80	− 2.90	439.00	390.00	17,080
July	423.50	423.50	423.50	419.40	− 3.10	439.00	409.50	4,091
Oct				423.60	− 3.10	441.30	413.00	1,125
Ja96				427.30	− 3.10	454.50	418.10	170
Est vol 1,794; vol Mon 1,817; open int 22,466, −619.								
PALLADIUM (NYM) 100 troy oz.; $ per troy oz.								
Mar	158.65	159.75	158.25	158.75	+ .05	164.50	134.00	5,525
June	161.00	161.00	160.25	160.25	+ .05	166.00	152.00	1,913
Sept				161.25	+ .05	163.00	157.10	276
Est vol 236; vol Mon 473; open int 7,767, −129.								
SILVER (CMX) 5,000 troy oz.; cents per troy oz.								
Feb	465.5	465.5	465.5	464.9	− 6.5	480.0	465.5	3
Mar	469.5	470.5	458.0	466.3	− 6.7	604.0	416.5	64,710
May	475.5	476.5	463.5	471.6	− 6.8	606.5	418.0	14,129
July	480.5	481.5	469.0	477.3	− 6.9	610.0	403.0	7,916
Sept	484.0	487.0	474.5	483.0	− 7.0	615.0	474.5	10,172
Dec	496.5	498.0	484.5	492.1	− 7.2	628.0	434.0	15,333
Mr96	506.5	506.5	498.5	501.6	− 7.4	622.0	498.0	8,565
May	506.0	506.0	506.0	508.1	− 7.5	599.0	499.0	4,102
July	512.0	512.0	512.0	514.7	− 7.8	630.0	512.0	2,552
Sept				521.6	− 8.0	534.0	534.0	304
Dec	530.0	530.0	530.0	531.7	− 8.2	670.0	454.0	1,865
Jl97	550.0	550.5	550.0	556.4	− 8.8	655.0	550.0	537
Dec				575.5	− 9.2	695.0	502.0	308
Dc98				623.2	− 10.2	734.0	628.0	113
Est vol 28,000; vol Mon 12,158; open int 132,018, −993.								

But do commodity prices really move all that much? Judge for yourself: The price change columns in Figure 15.2 show some excellent examples of sizable price changes that occur from one day to the next. Note, for example, that March wheat rose $262.50, May cotton fell $510, and March copper dropped $325. Now, keep in mind that these are *daily* price swings that occurred on *single* contracts. These are sizable changes, even by themselves; but when you look at them relative to the (very small) original investment required ($1,000 for each of the three contracts), they quickly add up to serious returns (or losses)! And they occur not because of the volatility of the underlying prices, but because of the sheer magnitude of the commodities contracts themselves.

Clearly, this kind of price behavior is one of the magnets that draw investors to commodities. The exchanges recognize the volatile nature of commodities contracts and try to put lids on price fluctuations by imposing daily price limits and maximum daily price ranges. (Similar limits are also put on financial futures.) The **daily price limit** restricts the interday change in the price of the underlying commodity. For example, the price of corn can change by no more than 10 cents per bushel from one day to the next, and the daily limit on copper is 3 cents per pound. Such limits, however, still leave plenty of room to turn a quick profit. For example, the daily limits on corn and copper translate into per-day changes of $500 for one corn contract and $750 for a copper contract. The **maximum daily price range**, in contrast, limits the amount the price can change *during* the day and is usually equal to twice the daily limit restrictions. For example, the daily price limit on corn is 10 cents per bushel and its maximum daily range is 20 cents per bushel.

daily price limit
restriction on the day-to-day change in the price of an underlying commodity.

maximum daily price range
the amount a commodity price can change during a day; usually equal to twice the daily price limit.

return on invested capital
return to investors based on the amount of money actually invested in a security, rather than the value of the contract itself.

Return on Invested Capital

Futures contracts have only one source of return: the capital gains that can be earned when prices move in a favorable direction. There is no current income of any kind. The volatile price behavior of futures contracts is one reason high returns are possible; the other is leverage. That is, because all futures trading is done on margin, it takes only a small amount of money to control a large investment position and to participate in the large price swings that accompany many futures contracts. Of course, the use of leverage also means that it is possible for an investment to be wiped out with just one or two bad days.

Investment return can be measured by calculating **return on invested capital**. This is simply a variation of the standard holding period return formula that bases return on the *amount of money actually invested in the contract*, rather than on the value of the contract itself. It is used because of the generous amount of leverage (margin) used in commodities trading. The return on invested capital for a commodities position can be determined according to the following simple formula:

Equation 15.1

$$\text{Return on invested capital} = \frac{\text{selling price of commodity contract} - \text{purchase price of commodity contract}}{\text{amount of margin deposit}}$$

Equation 15.1 can be used for both long and short transactions. To see how it works, assume you just bought two September corn contracts at 245 ($2.45 per bushel) by depositing the required initial margin of $2,000 ($1,000 for each contract). Your investment amounts to only $2,000, but you control

10,000 bushels of corn worth $24,500 at the time they were purchased. Now, assume that September corn has just closed at 259, so you decide to sell out and take your profit. Your return on invested capital would be as follows:

$$\text{Return on invested capital} = \frac{\$25,900 - \$24,500}{\$2,000}$$

$$= \frac{\$1,400}{\$2,000} = \underline{\underline{70.0\%}}$$

Clearly, this high rate of return was due not only to an increase in the price of the commodity but also—and perhaps more importantly—to the fact that you were using very low margin. (The initial margin in this particular transaction equaled just 6 percent of the underlying value of the contract.)

TRADING COMMODITIES

Investing in commodities takes one of three forms. The first, *speculating*, is popular with investors who use commodities as a way to generate capital gains. In essence, speculators try to capitalize on the wide price swings that are characteristic of so many commodities. Figure 15.3 provides weekly futures prices (in cents per pound) for cotton contracts over the six-year period from 1989 through 1994, and graphically illustrates the volatile behavior of commodity prices. Although such price movements may be appealing to speculators, they frighten many other investors. Some of these more cautious investors turn to *spreading*, the second form of commodities investing. Futures investors use this trading technique much like the spreading that's done with put and call options, as a way to capture some of the benefits of volatile commodities prices but without all the exposure to loss.

Finally, commodities futures can be used as *hedging* vehicles. A hedge in the commodities market is more of a technical strategy and is used almost exclusively by producers and processors to protect a position in a product or commodity. For example, a producer or grower would use a commodity hedge to obtain as *high a price* as possible for the goods he or she sells. The processor or manufacturer who uses the commodity, however, would use a hedge for the opposite reason: to obtain the goods at as *low a price* as possible. A successful hedge, in effect, means added income to producers and lower costs to processors.

We'll now look briefly at the two trading strategies that are used mostly by individual investors—speculating and spreading—not only to see what they are but also to gain a better understanding of how commodities can be used as investment vehicles.

Speculating

Speculators are in the market for one reason: They expect the price of a commodity to go up or down, and they hope to capitalize on it by going long or short. To see why a speculator would go long when prices are expected to rise, consider an individual who buys a March silver contract at 533½ (i.e., $5.33½ an ounce) by depositing the required initial margin of $1,300. Since one silver contract involves 5,000 troy ounces, it has a market value of $26,675. If silver goes up, the investor makes money. Assume that it does, and that by February

Figure 15.3 The Behavior of Commodity Prices over Time (1989–1994)
This graph shows the volatile nature of commodity prices and underscores the need for investor know-how when dealing in commodities. (Source: Courtesy of *Commodity Price Charts,* Cedar Falls, Iowa (800-635-3931).

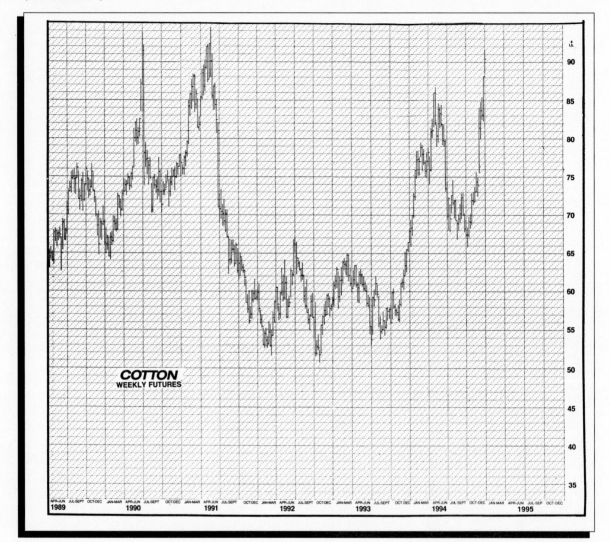

(one month before the contract expires), the price of the contract rises to 552. The speculator then liquidates the contract and makes a profit of 18½ cents per ounce (552 − 533½). That means a $925 profit from an investment of just $1,300—which translates into a return on invested capital of 71.2 percent.

Of course, instead of rising, the price of silver could have dropped by 18½ cents per ounce. In this case, the investor would have lost most of his original investment ($1,300 − $925 leaves only $375, out of which would have to come a round-trip commission of $60 or $70). But to a *short seller,* the drop in price would be just what she was after, for she could profit from such a turn of events. Here's how: She sells—"shorts"—the March silver at 533½ and buys it back sometime later at 515. Clearly, the difference between her selling price and purchase price is the same 18½ cents, but in this case it is *profit,* since the selling price exceeds the purchase price. (See Chapter 2 for a review of short selling.)

Spreading

Instead of attempting to speculate on the price behavior of a futures contract, an investor might choose to follow the more conservative tactic of *spreading*. Much like spreading with put and call options, the idea is to combine two or more different contracts into one investment position that offers the potential for generating a modest amount of profit while restricting exposure to loss. One very important reason for spreading in the commodities market is that, unlike options, *there is no limit to the amount of loss that can occur with a futures contract*. An investor will set up a spread by buying one contract and simultaneously selling another. Although one side of the transaction will lead to a loss, the investor obviously hopes that the profit earned from the other side will be more than enough compensation and that the net result will be at least a modest amount of profit. If the investor is wrong, the spread will serve to limit (but not eliminate) any losses. Here is a simple version of how a spread might work: Suppose you buy Contract A at 533½ and at the same time short sell Contract B for 575½. Sometime later, you close out your interest in Contract A by selling it at 542 and simultaneously cover your short position in B by purchasing a contract at 579. Although you made a profit of 8½ points on the long position, Contract A (542 − 533½), you lost 3½ points on the contract you shorted, B (575½ − 579). The net effect, however, is a profit of 5 points, which, if you were dealing in cents per pound, would mean a profit of $250 on a 5,000-pound contract. All sorts of commodity spreads can be set up for almost any type of investment situation. Most are highly sophisticated and require specialized skills.

COMMODITIES AND THE INDIVIDUAL INVESTOR

Commodities appeal to investors because of the high rates of return they offer and their ability to act as inflation hedges during periods of rapidly rising consumer prices. When sustained high rates of inflation become a problem, traditional investment outlets just do not seem to be able to provide the type of return necessary to keep investors ahead of the game. That is, more often than not, in periods of high inflation investors lose more in purchasing power than they gain from after-tax returns. Under such circumstances, investors can be expected to seek outlets that provide better protection against inflation, which explains why the interest in commodities tends to pick up with inflation.

Commodities can play an important role in a portfolio so long *as the investor understands the risks involved and is well versed in the principles and mechanics of commodities trading*. Despite what the successes of certain well-known commodities investors might lead you to believe, making money in the commodities market is an extremely tough thing to do! Very, very few investors—even the most experienced—can turn $1,000 into $100,000 by trading cattle futures or any other futures contract. Indeed, for most people, the quickest way to lose money in commodities is to jump in without knowing what they are doing. Because there is the potential for a lot of price volatility and because commodity trading is done on a very low margin, the potential for loss is enormous. Accordingly, most experts recommend that only a portion of an individual's investment capital be committed to commodities. The specific amount would, of course, be a function of investor aversion to risk and the amount of resources available. An investor has to be prepared men-

INVESTOR INSIGHTS: *Investing in Action*

Investing in Commodities Through Mutual Funds

The time may be right to add commodity investments to your portfolio. Industry experts consider commodities cheap, compared to historical levels. They predict that prices in commodities markets, which jumped 11.3 percent in 1993 after a 12-year bear market, should continue to rise as the world economy improves and the demand for physical commodities—raw materials like agricultural products, oil, and metals—increases. Because commodities can also provide an inflation hedge for your portfolio, some financial advisers recommend putting 5 percent of your investment portfolio in commodities. But speculating in commodities is risky: An estimated 75 to 90 percent of small investors lose money in the futures markets.

If betting that India might reduce cotton exports, thus pushing cotton prices up, doesn't get your investment juices flowing, you may prefer *commodity-oriented mutual funds.* These funds invest in companies that produce commodities, rather than in the actual commodities themselves. Although the performance of these funds won't duplicate the results you'd get from buying futures, they are run by professional managers who decide which commodity firms to buy and when. (Such funds are distinct from *managed futures* funds and pools that invest directly in futures markets. They have high expenses and require a large initial investment.)

As with other mutual funds, commodity-based funds provide a simple, affordable way to diversify commodity holdings and spread risk. Some take a conservative approach and invest in many commodity-based corpora-

tions. For example, T. Rowe Price's New Era Fund invests in a broad group of natural resource companies; it earned annual returns of 5.2 percent in 1994 and 7.4 percent from 1992 to 1994. This conservative, no-load fund has about 72 percent of its holdings in energy, gold mining, industrial metals, forest products, and real estate; the remainder is in consumer, service, and technology stocks. More aggressive funds focus on three or four commodities. An example is the Fidelity Select Industrial Materials Fund, which invests in oil, aluminum, chemical, and paper stocks. Its annual return was 8.2 percent in 1994 and averaged 13.8 percent from 1992 to 1994. The riskiest funds invest in just one commodity; examples include the no-load Vanguard Specialized Energy Fund and the Invesco Strategic Energy Fund. Although Vanguard earned a 9.4 percent annual return from 1992 to 1994, its 1994 return was −1.6 percent. Clearly, a single-commodity fund is more volatile than a diversified one. Yet another option is a contrarian fund like Robertson Stephens Contrarian Fund, which has half its assets in gold and commodity stocks. And some major asset-allocation funds—Fidelity Asset Manager, for example—include commodities in their asset mix. Regardless of which type of fund you use to add commodities to your portfolio, you'll be positioned to benefit if commodity prices rise in the years to come.

Source: Adapted from Earl C. Gottschalk, Jr., "Commodity Mutual Funds Add Diversity," *Wall Street Journal,* June 28, 1994, pp. C1, C18; "Mutual Fund Scoreboard," *Business Week,* February 6, 1995, pp. 114–40; and Amey Stone, "Futures: Dare You Defy the Odds?" *Business Week,* February 28, 1994, pp. 112–13.

tally and should be in a position financially to absorb losses—perhaps a number of them. And not only should an adequate cash reserve be kept on hand (to absorb losses or to meet margin calls), but it's also a good idea to maintain a diversified holding of commodities in order to spread your risks.

Individuals can invest directly in the commodities market, or they can buy put and call options on a number of the actively traded futures contracts. Alternatively, they can invest in limited partnership *commodity pools.* These pools, which are a lot like mutual funds, might be used by individuals who wish to invest in the commodities market but lack the time or expertise to manage their own investments. Still another alternative is to consider investing in *commodity-oriented mutual funds*. As more fully explained in the accompanying *Investor Insights* box, these funds usually don't invest in actual commodities contracts but instead buy stocks whose business it is to produce those commodities. Thus, they offer some of the results of commodities trading but are viewed as a much safer way to play the game.

CONCEPTS *in Review*

15.6   List and briefly define the five essential parts of a commodity contract. Which parts have a direct bearing on the price behavior of the contract?

15.7   Briefly define each of the following:
   a. Settle price
   b. Daily price limit
   c. Open interest
   d. Maximum daily price range
   e. Delivery month

15.8   Note several approaches to investing in commodities and explain the investment objectives of each.

15.9   Explain why it is important for individuals to be well versed in the behavior and investment characteristics of commodities futures when investing in this market. Why should futures holdings be well diversified?

FINANCIAL FUTURES

financial futures
a type of futures contract in which the underlying "commodity" is a financial asset, such as debt securities, foreign currencies, or market baskets of common stocks.

Another dimension of the futures market is **financial futures,** a segment of the market in which futures contracts are traded on a variety of financial instruments. Actually, financial futures are little more than an extension of the commodities concept. They were created for much the same reason as commodity futures, they are traded in the same market, their prices behave much like those of commodities, and they have similar investment merits. Yet despite all these similarities, financial futures are a unique type of investment vehicle. Let's now look more closely at these instruments and how they can be used by investors.

THE FINANCIAL FUTURES MARKET

Even though the financial futures market has been around for only 20 years or so, it is today a dominant force in the whole futures market. Its level of trading far surpasses that of the traditional commodities market. Indeed, many of the best-selling futures contracts today are financial futures—like U.S. Treasury bonds, S&P 500, or Eurodollar contracts. Much of the current interest in financial futures is due to hedgers and big institutional investors who use these contracts as portfolio- and debt-management tools. But individual investors can also find plenty of opportunities here. For example, financial futures offer yet another way to speculate on the behavior of interest rates. They can also be used by investors who wish to speculate in the stock market. They even offer a convenient way to speculate in the highly specialized, and often highly profitable, foreign currency markets.

The financial futures market was established in response to the economic turmoil the United States had been experiencing during the 1970s. The dollar had become unstable on the world market and was causing serious problems for multinational firms. Closer to home, interest rates had begun to behave in a volatile manner, which caused severe difficulties for corporate treasurers, financial institutions, and money managers in general. All these parties needed a way to protect themselves from the ravages of wide fluctuations in the value of the dollar and interest rates, and so a market for financial futures was born. Hedging provided the economic rationale for the market in financial futures, but speculators were quick to respond as they found the price volatility of these instruments attractive and at times highly profitable. At present, most of the financial futures trading in this country occurs on just three exchanges—the Chicago Board of Trade, the MidAmerica Commodity Exchange, and the Chicago Mercantile Exchange—as well as on several foreign exchanges, the most noteworthy of which is the London International Financial Futures Exchanges. The three basic types of financial futures include foreign currencies, debt securities, and stock indexes.

Foreign Currencies, Interest Rates, and Stock Indexes

currency futures
futures contracts on foreign currencies, traded much like commodities.

The financial futures market started rather inconspicuously in May 1972, with the listing of a handful of foreign currency contracts. Known as **currency futures**, they have become a major hedging vehicle as international trade to and from this country has mushroomed. Most of the currency trading today is conducted in the following six foreign currencies:

- British pound
- German mark
- Swiss franc
- Canadian dollar
- Japanese yen
- Australian dollar

All of these currencies involve countries with which the United States has strong international trade and exchange ties.

interest rate futures
futures contracts on debt securities.

In October 1975, the first futures contract on debt securities, or **interest rate futures,** as they are more commonly known, was established when trading started in GNMA pass-through certificates (a special type of mortgage-backed bond issued by an agency of the U.S. government). In time, other issues were added, so that today trading is carried out in a variety of U.S. and foreign debt securities and interest rates, including:

- U.S. Treasury bills
- U.S. Treasury notes
- U.S. Treasury bonds
- 30-day interest rates
- 90-day Euromarket deposits (e.g., Eurodollar deposits, Euromark deposits, etc.)
- Various foreign government bonds (e.g., bonds issued by the British, German, and Canadian governments)

stock-index futures
futures contracts written on broad based measures of stock market performance (e.g., the S&P 500 Stock Index), allowing investors to participate in the general movements of the stock market.

Interest rate futures were immediately successful. Their popularity has grown rapidly and continues to grow today.

In February 1982, a new trading vehicle was introduced: the stock-index futures contract. **Stock-index futures,** as they are called, are contracts pegged to broad-based measures of stock market performance. At present, trading is done in five U.S. stock-index futures:

- The S&P 500 Stock Index
- The NYSE Composite Stock Index
- The Value Line Composite Stock Index
- The Major Market Index (which is intended to track the DJIA)
- The S&P MidCap 400 Index

In addition to these U.S. indexes, investors can also trade stock-index futures contracts based on the London, Tokyo, Paris, Sydney, and Toronto stock exchanges. Stock-index futures—which are similar to the stock-index options we discussed in Chapter 14—allow investors to participate in the general movements of the entire stock market. These index futures (and other futures contracts) represent a type of *derivative security* because they, like options, derive their value from the price behavior of the assets that underlie them. In the case of stock-index futures, they are supposed to reflect the general performance of the stock market as a whole, as measured by a particular index like the S&P 500. Thus, when the market, as measured by the S&P 500, goes up, the value of an S&P 500 futures contract should go up as well. Accordingly, investors can use stock-index futures as a way to buy the market—or a reasonable proxy thereof—and thereby participate in broad market moves.

Contract Specifications

In principle, financial futures contracts are like the commodities contracts we examined above. They control large sums of the underlying financial instrument and are issued with a variety of delivery months. All this can be seen in Figure 15.4, which lists quotes for several foreign currency, interest rate, and stock-index futures contracts. Looking first at currency futures, we see that the contracts entitle the holders to a certain position in a specified foreign currency; in effect, the owner of a currency future holds a claim on a certain amount of foreign money. The precise amount ranges from 62,500 British pounds to 12.5 million Japanese yen. Similarly, holders of interest rate futures have a claim on a certain amount of the underlying debt security. This claim is also quite large, as it amounts to $100,000 worth of Treasury notes and bonds, $1 million worth of Eurodollar deposits and Treasury bills, and $5 million in 30-day interest rate contracts.

Stock-index futures, however, are a bit different because the seller of one of these contracts is *not* obligated to deliver the *underlying stocks* at expiration date. Instead, ultimate delivery is in the form of cash (which is fortunate, since it would indeed be a task to make delivery of the roughly 1,700 stocks that compose the Value Line Index, or the 500 issues in the S&P Index). The commodity underlying stock-index futures, therefore, is *cash*. Basically, the amount of underlying cash is set at 500 times the value of the stock index. For example, if the S&P 500 Index stood at 470, the amount of cash underlying a single S&P 500 stock-index futures contract would be $500 × 470 = $235,000. Again, the amount is substantial. In terms of delivery months, the lives of financial futures contracts run from about 12 months or less for stock-index and currency futures to about 3 years or less for interest rate instruments.

Figure 15.4 Quotations on Selected Actively Traded Financial Futures
The trading exchange, size of the trading unit, pricing unit, and delivery months are all vital pieces of information included as part of the quotation system used with financial futures. (Source: *Wall Street Journal*, February 1, 1995.)

CURRENCY

	Open	High	Low	Settle	Change	Lifetime High	Lifetime Low	Open Interest
JAPAN YEN (CME) – 12.5 million yen; $ per yen (.00)								
Mar	1.0211	1.0211	1.0067	1.0075	– .0132	1.0560	.9680	75,810
June	1.0290	1.0310	1.0185	1.0188	– .0135	1.0670	.9915	7,495
Sept	1.0333	1.0333	1.0320	1.0311	– .0138	1.0775	1.0175	568
Dec	1.0500	1.0500	1.0460	1.0438	– .0141	1.0760	1.0300	191

Est vol 35,993; vol Mon 30,247; open int 84,156, –272.

DEUTSCHEMARK (CME) – 125,000 marks; $ per mark

Mar	.6653	.6666	.6545	.6566	– .0087	.6744	.5798	81,260
June	.6650	.6668	.6565	.6587	– .0088	.6747	.5980	2,970
Sept	....	....	.6625	.6613	– .0088	.6770	.6290	215

Est vol 43,609; vol Mon 30,301; open int 84,478, +1,313.

CANADIAN DOLLAR (CME) – 100,000 dlrs.; $ per Can $

Mar	.7035	.7098	.7021	.7086	+ .0056	.7605	.6983	52,002
June	.6998	.7065	.6998	.7065	+ .0057	.7600	.6948	2,268
Sept	.6988	.7043	.6988	.7038	+ .0058	.7438	.6920	1,733
Dec	.6970	.7025	.6970	.7019	+ .0059	.7400	.6895	587
Mr96	....	....	.7001	.7001	+ .0060	.7325	.6900	192

Est vol 10,374; vol Mon 5,422; open int 56,795, +1,087.

BRITISH POUND (CME) – 62,500 pds.; $ per pound

Mar	1.5938	1.5964	1.5770	1.5796	– .0118	1.6440	1.4530	38,179
June	1.5848	1.5858	1.5770	1.5776	– .0118	1.6380	1.5330	1,330

Est vol 15,220; vol Mon 17,543; open int 39,515, –7,149.

INTEREST RATE

TREASURY BONDS (CBT) – $100,000; pts. 32nds of 100%

	Open	High	Low	Settle	Change	Lifetime High	Lifetime Low	Open Interest
Mar	101-00	101-19	100-25	101-15	+ 15	116-20	95-13	348,474
June	100-19	101-04	100-11	101-00	+ 16	113-15	94-27	26,699
Sept	100-12	100-24	100-01	100-22	+ 15	112-15	94-10	4,192
Dec	99-28	100-15	99-25	100-13	+ 14	111-23	93-27	436

Est vol 375,000; vol Mon 267,836; op int 379,936, –17,114.

Mar	101-15	101-23	101-07	101-22	+ 7	111-07	98-11	260,898
June	100-30	101-08	100-24	101-07	+ 7	105-22	97-27	18,632
Sept	100-18	100-26	100-12	100-26	+ 7	100-26	97-11	3,856
Dec	100-07	100-15	100-00	100-15	+ 7	100-15	96-30	29

Est vol 105,105; vol Mon 81,652; open int 283,415, –9,087.

5 YR TREAS NOTES (CBT) – $100,000; pts. 32nds of 100%

Mar	01-105	101-15	101-04	101-12	+ 1.5	103-09	99-15	209,456
June	100-30	101-02	00-255	01-005	+ 1.5	101-02	99-06	5,799
Sept	....	....	00-255	+ 1.5	100-24	99-07	1

Est vol 57,500; vol Mon 48,783; open int 215,256, –6,053.

2 YR TREAS NOTES (CBT) – $200,000, pts. 32nds of 100%

Mar	01-005	101-03	00-287	00-315	– 2	01-03	99-252	45,075

Est vol 4,000; vol Mon 1,470; open int 45,117, –369.

TREASURY BILLS (CME) – $1 mil.; pts. of 100%

	Open	High	Low	Settle	Chg	Discount Settle	Discount Chg	Open Interest
Mar	94.06	94.08	94.02	94.05	....	5.95	....	9,624
June	93.43	93.48	93.37	93.42	....	6.58	....	9,173
Sept	93.12	93.15	93.07	93.11	– .02	6.89	+ .02	3,491

Est vol 3,791; vol Mon 4,570; open int 23,367, +1,311.

INDEX

S&P 500 INDEX (CME) $500 times index

	Open	High	Low	Settle	Chg	High	Low	Open Interest
Mar	469.85	472.90	469.40	472.20	+ 2.25	484.10	441.45	195,261
June	474.40	476.80	473.50	476.15	+ 2.30	487.40	449.50	13,791
Sept	481.30	481.30	480.80	481.00	+ 2.35	487.40	456.55	2,940
Dec	....	....	486.15	+ 2.30	486.80	474.50	722

Est vol 74,900; vol Mon 60,808; open int 212,714, –2,079.
Indx prelim High 471.03; Low 468.18; Close 470.42 +1.91

S&P MIDCAP 400 (CME) $500 times index

Mar	170.80	172.30	170.55	172.00	+ 1.00	188.25	163.50	13,495

Est vol 665; vol Mon 690; open int 13,559, –22.
The index: High 171.46; Low 170.24; Close 170.96 +.60

Prices and Profits

There are three basic types of financial futures and, not surprisingly, the price of each type of contract is quoted somewhat differently:

- *Foreign currency futures.* All currency futures are quoted in dollars or cents per unit of the underlying foreign currency (e.g., in dollars per British pound or cents per Japanese yen). Thus, according to the closing ("settle") prices in Figure 15.4, one June British pound contract was worth $98,600 (62,500 pounds × $1.5776), and a December Japanese yen contract was valued at $130,475 (because a quote of 1.0438 cents per yen amounts to 12,500,000 yen × $0.010438).

- *Interest rate futures.* Except for the quotes on Treasury bills and other short-term securities, which we'll examine in the next section, interest-rate futures contracts are priced as a percentage of the par value of the underlying debt instrument (e.g., Treasury notes or Treasury bonds). Since these instruments are quoted in increments of 1/32 of 1 percent, a quote of 101–22 for the settle price of the March ('96) Treasury bonds (in Figure 15.4) translates into 101 22/32—which (when you divide 22 by 32) converts into a quote of 101.6875 percent of par. Applying this rate to the par value of the underlying securities, we see that this March Treasury bond contract is worth $101,687.50 (i.e., $100,000 × 1.016875).

- *Stock-index futures.* Stock-index futures are quoted in terms of the actual underlying index but, as noted above, they carry a face value of $500 times the index.

The value of an interest rate futures contract responds to interest rates exactly like the debt instrument that underlies the contract. That is, when interest rates go up, the value of an interest rate futures contract goes down, and vice versa. However, the quote system for interest rate as well as currency and stock-index futures is set up to reflect the *market value of the contract* itself. Thus, when the price or quote of a financial futures contract increases, the investor who is long makes money. In contrast, when the price decreases, the short seller makes money. Price behavior is the only source of return to speculators; for even though stocks and debt securities are involved in some financial futures, such contracts have no claim on the dividend and interest income of the underlying issues. Even so, huge profits (or losses) are possible with financial futures due to the equally large size of the contracts. For instance, if the price of Swiss francs goes up by just 2 cents against the dollar, the investor is ahead $2,500, because one futures contract covers 125,000 Swiss francs. Likewise, a 3-point drop in the NYSE Composite Index means a $1,500 loss to an investor (3 × $500). When related to the relatively small initial margin deposit required to make transactions in the financial futures markets, such price activity can mean very high rates of return—or very high risk of a total wipeout.

Pricing Futures on Treasury Bills and Other Short-Term Securities

Because Treasury bills and other short-term securities are normally traded in the money market on what is known as a discount basis, it was necessary to devise a special pricing system that would reflect the actual price movements

index price
technique used to price T-bill and other short-term securities futures contracts, by subtracting current yield from an index of 100.

of these futures contracts. To accomplish this, an **index price** system was developed whereby the yield is subtracted from an index of 100. Thus, when the yield on an underlying security, such as a Treasury bill or Eurodollar deposits, is 5.25 percent, the contract would be quoted at an index of 94.75 (100.00 − 5.25). Under such a system, when someone buys, say, a T-bill future and the index goes up, that individual has made money; when the index goes down, a short seller has made money. Note also that the 30-day interest rate futures, as well as 90-day T-bill and Eurodollar/Euromarket contracts, are all quoted in *basis points*, where 1 basis point equals 1/100 of 1 percent. Thus, a quote of 94.05 (which was the settle price on the March T-bill contract in Figure 15.4) translates into a T-bill yield of 5.95 percent (i.e., 100.00 − 94.05).

The index price system traces only the price behavior of the futures contract. To find the *actual price* or *value* of a 90-day T-bill or Eurodollar contract (two of the more actively traded short-term contracts), we use the following formula:

Equation 15.2

$$\text{Price of a 90-day futures contract} = \$1,000,000 - \left(\frac{\text{security's yield} \times 90 \times \$10,000}{360} \right)$$

A similar formula would be used to find the price of a 30-day interest rate contract, except that a value of 30 would be used in the formula's numerator, in place of the 90; everything else would be handled exactly the same as shown in Equation 15.2.

Notice that this price formula is based not on the quoted price index but on the *yield of the security itself*, which can be determined by subtracting the price index quote from 100. To see how it works, consider a 90-day T-bill futures contract quoted at 94.05; recall that this T-bill futures contract is priced to yield 5.95 percent. Now, using Equation 15.2, we can see that the price (or value) of this futures contract is:

$$\text{Price of a 90-day futures contract} = \$1,000,000 - \left(\frac{5.95 \times 90 \times \$10,000}{360} \right)$$

$$= \$1,000,000 - \$14,875$$

$$= \underline{\underline{\$985,125}}$$

A handy shortcut for *tracking the price behavior* of T-bill or Eurodollar/Euromarket futures contracts is to remember that the price of a 90-day contract will change by $25 for every one basis point change in yield. Thus, when the yield on the underlying 90-day security moves from, say, 5.95 to 6.10 percent, it goes up by 15 basis points and causes the price of the futures contract to drop by 15 × $25 = $375.

TRADING TECHNIQUES

Financial futures can be used for three purposes: hedging, spreading, and speculating. Multinational companies and firms that are active in international trade might consider *hedging* with currency or Euromarket futures, whereas various financial institutions and corporate money managers often use interest rate futures for hedging purposes. In either case, the objectives are the same: to lock in the best monetary exchange or interest rate possible. In addition, individual investors and portfolio managers use stock-index futures for hedging purposes in order to protect their security holdings against temporary market declines. Financial futures can also be used for *spreading*. This tactic is popular with investors who adopt strategies of simultaneously buying and selling combinations of two or more contracts to form a desired investment position. One type of futures spread is described in the *Investor Insights* box nearby; note in this case that the spread is set up to capture profits from the "January effect" in the stock market. Finally, financial futures are widely used for *speculation*. As this brief review suggests, although the instruments may differ, the trading techniques used with financial futures are virtually identical to those used with commodities.

Although all three techniques are widely employed by investors, we will focus primarily on the use of financial futures by speculators and hedgers. (The *Investor Insights* box on page 644 is our only look at the use of financial futures for spreading.) We will first examine speculating in currency and interest rate futures and then look at how these contracts can be used to hedge investments in stocks, bonds, and foreign securities.

Speculating in Financial Futures

Speculators are especially interested in financial futures because of the large size of the futures contracts. For instance, in early 1995, Canadian dollar contracts were worth over $70,000, Treasury notes were going for over $100,000, and Treasury bill contracts were being quoted at close to $1 million. With contracts of this size, it obviously does not take much movement in the underlying asset to produce big price swings—and therefore big profits. Currency or interest rate futures can be used for just about any speculative purpose. For example, an investor who expects the dollar to be devalued relative to the German mark would buy mark currency futures, because the contracts should go up in value. A speculator who anticipates a rise in interest rates might consider going short (selling) interest rate futures, since they should go down in value. Because margin is used and financial futures have the same source of return as commodities (appreciation in the price of the futures contract), return on invested capital is used to measure the profitability of financial futures.

Let's look at an example of a foreign currency contract. Suppose an individual investor believes that the Japanese yen is about to appreciate in value relative to the dollar. This investor decides to buy three September yen contracts at 1.0311. Each contract is worth $128,887.50 (12,500,000 yen × $0.010311), and the total market value of three contracts would be $386,662.50. Even so, the investor has to deposit only $6,000 to acquire this position. (Recall from Table 15.2 that the required initial margin for Japanese yen is $2,000 per contract.) Now, if the price of a yen moves up just a fraction—say, about half a cent, from 1.0311 to 1.080—the value of the three contracts will rise to $405,000, and the investor, in a matter of months, will have made a profit of $18,337. Using Equation 15.1, for return on invested capital, we find that such a profit translates into an enormous 306 percent rate of return. Of course, an even smaller fractional change in the other direction would have wiped out this investment, so it should be clear that these *high returns are not without equally high risk.*

Now consider an investment in an interest rate future. Assume the investor is anticipating a sharp rise in long-term rates. Because a rise in rates means that interest rate futures will drop in value, the investor decides to short

INVESTOR INSIGHTS: *Market Innovations*

Playing the "January Effect" with Stock-Index Futures

In an efficient market, an investor should not be able to consistently outperform the market. Yet we know that certain market anomalies do exist, and that knowledgeable investors can take advantage of unusual price patterns that seem to appear with some degree of regularity. One of the most widely known market anomalies is the so-called *January effect*, in which small stocks typically begin to rally each December, outpacing big stocks, in a phenomenon that extends into January. This rally occurs after tax-related selling beats prices to bargain-basement levels. But trying to profit from the January effect is dicey at best. That's because playing this price pattern in the most obvious ways (buying and selling small stocks) isn't always easy. For example, if investors buy just a few small stocks, they might select ones that perform poorly. Also, when they buy, they frequently pay the highest going price, the "asked price," and usually receive the lower "bid price" when they sell. Obviously, this bid-ask penalty can put a real dent in January-effect profits. Then throw in commissions, and investors are lucky if there's any profit left.

One way small investors can play the January effect and minimize transaction costs is to use the futures markets to create a *spread*. The Value Line futures contract on the Kansas City Board of Trade is based on an index of 1,665 stocks; of these, 66 percent have a market value of less than $1 billion. Only about 30 percent of the stocks in the Standard & Poor's 500 Stock Index have market values below $1 billion. Other indexes top-weighted with big stocks are the New York Stock Exchange Composite Index and the Major Market Index. The difference in composition means the January effect can be exploited by buying Value Line futures and simultaneously selling futures contracts based on an index with more big stocks, such as the S&P 500. This kind of futures trade is known as a *spread*.

For instance, if the market does rally and the January effect works, the Value Line contracts should move up more than the S&P 500 contracts. If the market falls, the Value Line contracts should fall less than the big stock index futures. Either scenario would produce a profit for investors holding a spread that consisted of long, or purchased, Value Line futures and short positions in futures based on a big stock index. (With a spread, if the market goes up, you'll make money on the long position but lose on the short—the object, of course, is to net out more profit than loss.)

Since 1982, when stock-index futures started trading, this futures strategy has produced a theoretical profit each year the Value Line contract was used as a proxy for small stocks and the S&P 500 represented big stocks. In each case, it was assumed that the trade was initiated, using March futures contracts, on December 15 and closed out on the following January 15. The largest profit was $2,750 per spread (one contract purchased and one sold short) closed out in January 1991, and the smallest was $275 for a trade closed in 1989, and again in 1992. The average profit was about $1,500. That's not bad—especially when you consider that the minimum capital needed to execute this spread is only $9,500. With commissions at a discount broker of only $30 to $50, plenty of profit is left. Of course, there's no guarantee that the January effect will occur each year. But it's clear that the futures spread described here puts you in a pretty good position to make a nice profit when it does.

Source: Adapted from Stanley W. Angrist, "Futures Offer Cheap Play on Small Stocks' Annual Rally," *Wall Street Journal*, December 13, 1990, p. C1.

---

sell two June T-bond contracts at 101–00, which means that the contracts are trading at 101 percent of par. Thus, the two contracts are worth $202,000 ($100,000 × 1.01 × 2), but the amount of money required to make the investment is only $5,400 (the initial margin deposit is $2,700 per contract). Assume that interest rates do, in fact, move up, and as a result, the price on Treasury bond contracts drops to 92-16 (or 92½). Under such circumstances, the investor would buy back the two December T-bond contracts (in order to cover the short position) and in the process make a profit of $17,000. (The investor originally sold the two contracts at $202,000 and then bought them back sometime later at $185,000; as with any investment, the difference between what you pay for a security and what you sell it for is profit.) In this case, the return on invested capital amounts to 315 percent. Again, however, this kind of return is due in no small part to the *enormous risk of loss* the investor assumes.

Trading Stock-Index Futures

Most investors use stock-index futures for speculation or hedging. (Stock-index futures are similar to the *index options* introduced in Chapter 14; therefore, much of the discussion that follows also applies to index options.) Whether speculating or hedging, the key to success is *predicting the future course of the stock market*. Because investors are "buying the market" with stock-index futures, it is important to get a handle on the future direction of the market via technical analysis (as discussed in Chapter 7) or some other technique. Once an investor has a feel for the market's direction, he or she can formulate a stock-index futures trading or hedging strategy. For example, an investor who feels strongly that the market is headed up would want to go long (buy stock-index futures); in contrast, if the investor's analysis of the market suggests a sharp drop in equity values, he or she could make money by going short (selling stock-index futures). Speculating in this way could prove profitable, if the investor's expectations about the market actually materialize.

Assume, for instance, that you believe the market is undervalued and therefore a move up is imminent. You can try to identify one or a handful of stocks that should go up with the market (and assume the stock selection risks that go along with this approach), or you can buy an S&P 500 stock-index future currently trading at, say, 474.45. To execute this speculative transaction, you need to deposit an initial margin of only $10,000. Now, if your expectations are correct and the market does rise so that the S&P 500 Index moves to 490.95 by the expiration of the futures contract, you will earn a profit of $8,250 [(490.95 − 474.45) × $500 = $8,250]. Given that this was earned on a $10,000 investment, your return on invested capital would amount to a very respectable 82.5 percent. Of course, keep in mind that if the market drops by only 20 points (or just 4.2 percent), the investment will be a *total loss*.

Stock-index futures also make excellent hedging vehicles in that they provide investors with a highly effective way of protecting stock holdings in a declining market. Although this tactic is not perfect, it does enable investors to obtain desired protection against a decline in market value without disturbing their equity holdings. Here's how a so-called *short hedge* would work: Assume that an investor holds a total of 2,000 shares of stock in a dozen different companies and that the market value of this portfolio is around $135,000. If the investor thinks the market is about to undergo a temporary sharp decline, he or she can do one of three things: sell his or her shares, short sell all stock holdings against the box, or buy puts on each of the stocks. Clearly, these alternatives are cumbersome and/or costly and therefore undesirable for protecting a widely diversified portfolio. The desired results could also be achieved, however, by *short selling stock-index futures*. (Note that basically the same pro-

INVESTOR **F**ACTS

THE NOTIONAL VALUE OF FINANCIAL FUTURES— Financial futures just don't get the respect they deserve, because most investors don't realize how big this market is. To get an idea of its size, consider the *notional value* of these securities—the value of the assets that underlie these agreements. In effect, the notional value represents the amount of financial futures contracts outstanding at any given point in time. In mid-year 1994, that amount was estimated to be some *$6.6 trillion*. And that's for exchange-traded futures only— i.e., futures contracts traded on listed exchanges, like the CBT or LIFFE. More than 95 percent of this value is centered in interest rate futures (notional value of $6.4 trillion), followed by stock-index futures ($150 billion), and finally, currency futures (about $30 billion). What was the biggest contract of all? The Eurodollar futures contract, traded on the Chicago Mercantile Exchange, which alone accounted for more than $2.5 trillion in notional value.

(Source: *Wall Street Journal*, August 24, 1994, p. A4.)

tection can be obtained in this hedging situation by turning to options and buying a *stock-index put*.)

Suppose the investor short sells one NYSE stock-index futures contract at 268.75. Such a contract would provide a close match to the current value of the investor's portfolio (it would be valued at $134,375), and yet the stock-index futures contract would require an initial margin deposit of only $5,000. (Margin deposits are lower for hedgers than for speculators.) Now, if the NYSE Composite Index does drop to, say, 248.00, the investor will make a profit from the short-sale transaction of some $10,000. That is, because the index fell 20.75 points (268.75 − 248.00), the total profit will be $10,375 (20.75 × $500). Ignoring taxes, this profit can be added to the portfolio (additional shares of stock can be purchased at their new lower prices), with the net result being a new portfolio position that will approximate the one that existed prior to the decline in the market. How well the "before" and "after" portfolio positions match will depend on how far the portfolio dropped in value. If the average price dropped about $5 per share in our example, the positions will closely match. However, this does not always happen; the price of some stocks will change more than others, and therefore the amount of protection provided by this type of short hedge depends on how sensitive the stock portfolio is to movements in the market. Thus, the type of stocks held in the portfolio is an important consideration in structuring the stock-index short hedge. OTC and highly volatile stocks will probably require more protection than stocks that are relatively more price-stable or have betas closer to 1.0. In any event, hedging with stock-index futures can be a low-cost yet effective way of obtaining protection against loss in a declining stock market.

Hedging Other Securities

Just as stock-index futures can be used to hedge stock portfolios, so too can *interest rate futures* be used to hedge bond portfolios, and *foreign currency futures* be used with foreign securities as a way to protect against foreign exchange risk. Let's consider an interest rate hedge: If an investor holds a substantial portfolio of bonds, the last thing he or she wants to see is a big jump in interest rates, which could cause a sharp decline in the value of the portfolio. Assume this investor holds nearly $300,000 worth of Treasury and agency issues, with an average (approximate) maturity of around 18 years. If he strongly believes that market rates are headed up, he could hedge his bond portfolio by short selling three U.S. Treasury bond futures contracts (since each T-bond futures contract is worth about $100,000, it would take three of them to cover a $300,000 portfolio). Now, if rates do head up, the portfolio will be protected against loss—though, as we noted with stocks above, the exact amount of protection will depend on how well the T-bond futures contracts parallel the price behavior of this particular bond portfolio.

There is, of course, a downside to all this: *If market interest rates go down*, rather than up, *the investor will miss out on potential profits as long as the short hedge position remains in place*. This is so because all or most of the profits being made in the portfolio will be offset by losses from the futures contracts. Actually, this will occur with any type of portfolio (stocks, bonds, or anything else) that's tied to an offsetting short hedge, because when the short hedge is created, it essentially *locks in a position at that point*. Although you don't lose anything when the market falls, you also don't make anything when the market goes up. In either case, the profits you make from one position are offset by losses from the other.

To see how futures contracts can be used to hedge foreign exchange risk, let's assume that an investor just purchased $150,000 worth of German government one-year notes. (The investor did this because higher yields were available on the German notes than on comparable U.S. Treasury securities.) Now, since these notes are denominated in *marks*, this investment is subject to loss if currency exchange rates move against the investor (i.e., if the value of the dollar rises relative to the mark). If all the investor wanted was the higher yield offered by the German note, he or she could basically eliminate the currency exchange risk (or, at least, most of it) by setting up a currency hedge. Here's how it's done: Let's say that at the current exchange rate, one U.S. dollar will "buy" 1.65 marks, meaning marks are worth about 60 cents (i.e., $1/1.65 marks = $0.60). If currency contracts on German marks were trading at around $0.60 a mark, our investor would have to *sell* two contracts in order to protect the $150,000 investment: Each mark contract covers 125,000 marks, so if they're being quoted at .6000, then each contract is worth $0.60 × 125,000 = $75,000.

Assume that one year later, the value of the dollar has, in fact, increased, relative to the mark, so that one U.S. dollar will now "buy" 1.725 marks. Under such conditions, a German mark futures contract would be quoted at around .5800 (i.e., $1/1.725 = $0.58). At this price, each futures contract would be worth $72,500 (125,000 × $0.58). Each contract, in effect, would be worth $2,500 less than it was a year ago, but because the contract was sold short when the hedge was set up, the hedger will make a profit of $2,500 per contract—for a total profit of $5,000 on the two contracts. Unfortunately, that's not *net profit*, because this profit will offset the loss the investor will incur on the German note investment. In very simple terms, when the investor sent $150,000 overseas to buy the German notes, the money was worth 250,000 marks; however, when the investor brought the money back one year later, those 250,000 marks purchased only 145,000 American dollars. So the investor is out $5,000 on his or her original investment. Were it not for the currency hedge, the investor would be out the full $5,000, and the return on this investment would be a lot lower. But the hedge covered the loss and the net effect was that the investor was able to enjoy the added yield of the German note, without having to worry about any potential loss from currency exchange rates.

FINANCIAL FUTURES AND THE INDIVIDUAL INVESTOR

Financial futures can play an important role in an investor's portfolio so long as the individual: (1) thoroughly understands these investment vehicles, (2) clearly recognizes the tremendous risk exposure of such vehicles, and (3) is fully prepared (financially and emotionally) to absorb some losses. Financial futures are highly volatile securities that have enormous potential for profit and for loss. For instance, in 1994, during an eight-month period of time, the March (1995) S&P 500 futures contract fluctuated in price from a low of 441.45 to a high of 484.10. This range of nearly 43 points for a single contract translates into a *potential* profit—or loss—of some $21,300, and all from an initial investment of only $10,000. Investment diversification is obviously essential as a means of reducing the potentially devastating impact of price volatility. Financial futures are exotic investment vehicles, but, if properly used, they can provide generous returns.

OPTIONS ON FUTURES

futures options
options that give the holders the right to buy or sell a single standardized futures contract for a specified period of time at a specified striking price.

The evolution that began with listed stock options and financial futures spread, over time, to interest rate options and stock-index futures. Eventually, it led to the merger of options and futures and to the creation of the ultimate leverage vehicle: *options on futures contracts*. Known as **futures options**, they represent listed puts and calls on actively traded futures contracts. In essence, they give the holders the right to buy (with calls) or sell (with puts) a single standardized futures contract for a specific period of time at a specified strike price. Table 15.4 lists the futures options available in early 1995; note that such options are available on both commodities and financial futures. These puts and calls cover the same amount of assets as the underlying futures contracts—for example, 112,000 pounds of sugar, 100 ounces of gold, 62,500 British pounds, or $100,000 in Treasury bonds. Accordingly, they also involve the same amount of price activity as is normally found with commodities and financial futures.

Table 15.4   Futures Options: Puts and Calls on Futures Contracts

Commodities	Financial Futures
Corn	British pound
Soybeans	German mark
Soybean meal	Swiss franc
Soybean oil	Japanese yen
Heating oil	Canadian dollar
Gasoline	U.S. dollar index
Cotton	Eurodollar deposits
Sugar	Euromark deposits
Live cattle	Treasury bills
Live hogs	Treasury notes
Feeder cattle	Treasury bonds
Pork bellies	NYSE Composite Index
Lumber	S&P 500 Stock Index
Orange juice	London 1-month bank rates
Cocoa	British government bonds
Coffee	German government bonds
Wheat	
Oats	
Rice	
Platinum	
Copper	
Gold	
Silver	
Crude oil	
Natural gas	
Gas oil	

Futures options have the same standardized strike prices, expiration dates, and quotation system as other listed options. Depending on the strike price on the option and the market value of the underlying futures contract, these options can also be in-the-money and out-of-the-money. Futures options are valued like other puts and calls—by the difference between the option's strike price and the market price of the underlying futures contract (see Chapter 14). Moreover, they can also be used like any other listed option—that is, for speculating or hedging, in options writing programs, or for spreading.

The biggest difference between a futures option and a futures contract is that *the option limits the loss exposure* to the price of the option. The most you can lose is the price paid for the put or call, whereas there is no real limit to the amount of loss a futures investor can incur. To see how futures options work, assume that you want to trade some gold contracts. You believe that the price of gold will increase over the next nine months from its present level of $355 an ounce to around $400 an ounce. You can buy a futures contract at 364.50 by depositing the required initial margin of $1,300, or you can buy a futures call option with a $350 per ounce strike price that is currently being quoted at, say, 10.75. (Because the underlying futures contract covers 100 ounces of gold, the total cost of this option would be $10.75 × 100 = $1,075.) The call is an in-the-money option, because the market price of gold exceeds the exercise price on the option. The figures below summarize what happens to both investments if the price of gold reaches $400 per ounce by the expiration date and, in addition, what happens if the price of gold drops by $45 to $310 an ounce:

	Futures Contract		Futures Option	
	Dollar Profit (or Loss)	Return on Invested Capital	Dollar Profit (or Loss)	Return on Invested Capital
If price of gold *increases* by $45 an ounce	$3,550	273.1%	$3,925	365.1%
If price of gold *decreases* by $45 an ounce	($5,450)	—	($ 650)	—

Clearly, the futures option provides not only a much higher rate of return but also a reduced exposure to loss. Futures options offer interesting investment opportunities, but, as always, they *should be used only by knowledgeable commodities and financial futures investors.*

CONCEPTS *in Review*

15.10 What is the difference between physical *commodities* and *financial futures*? What are their similarities?

15.11 Describe a *currency future* and contrast it with an *interest rate future*. What is a *stock-index future*, and how can it be used by investors?

15.12 Discuss how stock-index futures can be used for speculation and for hedging. What advantages are there to speculating with stock-index futures rather than specific issues of common stock?

15.13 What are *futures options*? Explain how they can be used by speculators. Why, for example, would an investor want to use an option on an interest rate futures contract rather than the futures contract itself?

On Track with STOCK-TRAK®

Trading Futures Contracts Through STOCK-TRAK®

STOCK-TRAK® offers a wide assortment of futures contracts for potential investment. Stock-index futures include the Standard & Poor's 500 and Japan's Nikkei 225 contracts. Commodity futures include contracts on agricultural commodities such as corn, lumber, and coffee; precious metals futures on gold and silver; and energy futures on crude oil and natural gas. Foreign currency futures contracts may be bought on the Canadian dollar, the German mark, and the British pound; in addition, futures options on these foreign currencies can also be traded. Financial futures on Treasury bills, notes, and bonds are also available.

Alphanumeric symbols are used to indicate the expiration month of futures contracts (see the registration materials). Contract sizes vary, ranging from 50 ounces of platinum, to 40,000 pounds of pork bellies, to 12.5 million Japanese yen. For simplicity, STOCK-TRAK® has set a margin requirement of $2,000 per contract, which jumps to $10,000 for index futures.

SUMMARY

LG 1   **Describe the essential features of a futures contract, as well as the basic operating characteristics of the futures market.** Commodities and financial futures are traded in the futures market, a market that has its roots in the agricultural segment of our economy. Today, there are numerous U.S. and foreign exchanges that deal in futures contracts, which are commitments to make (or take) delivery of a certain amount of some real or financial asset at a specified date in the future.

LG 2   **Explain the role hedgers and speculators play in the futures market, including how profits are made and lost.** From the investor's point of view, the key fact about futures contracts is that they control large amounts of the underlying commodity or financial instrument and, as a result, can produce wide price swings and very attractive rates of return (or very unattractive losses). Such returns (or losses) are further magnified because all trading in the futures market is done on margin. Whereas a speculator's profit is derived directly from the wide price fluctuations that occur in the market, hedgers derive their profit from the protection they gain against adverse price movements.

LG 3   **Describe the commodities segment of the futures market and the basic characteristics of these investment vehicles.** Commodities like grains, metals, and meat make up the traditional (commodities) segment of the futures market. While a large portion of this market is concentrated in the agricultural segment of our economy, there's also a very active market for various metals and petroleum products. As the prices of commodities go up and down in the market, the respective futures contracts will behave in much the same way; thus, if the price of corn goes up, the value of corn futures contracts will rise as well. Being on the right side of the transaction (i.e., buyer or seller of the contract) will decide whether the investor is going to make money or lose it.

LG 4   **Discuss the various investment strategies and trading techniques that investors can use with commodities, and explain how investment returns can be measured.** A variety of trading strategies can be used with commodities contracts—that is, commodities can be used for speculating, spreading, or hedging. Irrespective of whether investors are in a long or a short position, they have only one source of return from commodities and financial futures: appreciation (or depreciation) in the price of the contract. Investors use the rate of return on invested capital to assess the actual or potential profitability of a futures transaction.

LG 5   **Know the difference between a physical commodity and a financial future, and gain an appreciation of the growing role that financial futures play in the market today.** Whereas commodities deal with physical assets, such as agricultural and petroleum products, financial futures deal with financial assets, such as stocks, bonds, and currencies. Even though the nature of the underlying assets may differ, both are traded in the same place: the futures market. Financial futures are the newcomers (they've been around only since the early 1970s), but even so, this segment of the market has grown to the point where the volume of trading in financial futures now far exceeds that of commodities.

LG 6   **Discuss the trading techniques that can be used with financial futures and note how these securities can be used in conjunction with other investment vehicles (like stocks, bonds, and foreign securities).** There are three types of financial futures: currency futures, interest rate futures, and stock-index futures. The first type deals in several different kinds of foreign currencies. Interest rate futures, in contrast, involve various types of short- and long-term debt instruments, such as Treasury bonds and Treasury bills. Stock-index futures are contracts pegged to broad movements in the stock market, as measured by such indexes as the S&P 500 or the NYSE Composite Index. These securities can be used just like commodities for speculating, spreading, or hedging. They hold a special appeal to investors who use them to hedge other security positions; for example, interest rate futures contracts are widely used to protect bond portfolios against a big jump in market interest rates, and currency futures are used to hedge the foreign currency exposure that accompanies investments in foreign securities.

DISCUSSION QUESTIONS

1.   Four of the biggest U.S. commodities exchanges—the CBT, CME, NYMerc, and COMEX—were identified in this chapter. They are just four out of a dozen American exchanges, plus there are several Canadian commodities exchanges that are closely followed here in the United States. Obtain a recent copy of the *Wall Street Journal* and look in the "Commodities/Futures Prices" section of the paper for the futures quotes. As noted in this chapter, futures quotes include the name of the exchange on which a particular contract is traded.

   a.   Using these quotes, how many more U.S. *commodities exchanges* can you identify? List them.
   b.   Are quotes from foreign exchanges listed in the *Wall Street Journal*? If so, list them, too.
   c.   For each U.S. and foreign exchange you found in parts (a) and (b) above, give an example of one or two contracts traded on that exchange. For example: CBT—Chicago Board of Trade: oats and Treasury bonds.

2.   Using settle prices from Figures 15.2 and 15.4, find the value of the following commodity and financial futures contracts:

   a.   July cotton
   b.   May 1996 silver
   c.   September soybeans
   d.   June deutsche mark
   e.   March 5-year Treasury notes
   f.   June S&P 500 Index

3. Listed below are a variety of futures transactions. Based on the information provided, indicate how much profit or loss you would make in each of the transactions. (*Hint:* You might want to refer to Figures 15.2 and 15.4 for the size of the contract, pricing unit, etc.)

   a. You buy 3 yen contracts at a quote of 1.0180 and sell them a few months later at 1.0365.
   b. The price of orange juice goes up 60 cents a pound, and you hold 3 contracts.
   c. You short sell 2 copper contracts at $1.30 a pound, and the price of copper drops to $1.05 a pound.
   d. You recently purchased a 90-day Treasury bill contract at 94.15, and T-bill interest rates rise to 6.60 percent.
   e. You short sell S&P MidCap 400 contracts when the index is at 196.55 and cover when the index moves to 171.95.
   f. You short 3 corn contracts at $2.34 a bushel, and the price of corn goes to $2.49½ a bushel.

PROBLEMS

1. Kirk O'Malley considers himself to be a shrewd commodities investor. For instance, not long ago he bought 1 July cotton contract at 54 cents a pound and recently sold it at 58 cents a pound. How much profit did he make? What was his return on invested capital if he had to put up a $1,500 initial deposit?

2. Shirley Ledbetter is a regular commodities speculator; she is presently considering a short position in July oats, which are now trading at 148. Her analysis suggests that July oats should be trading at about 140 in a couple of months. Assuming her expectations hold up, what kind of return on invested capital would she make if she shorts 3 July oats contracts (with each contract covering 5,000 bushels of oats) by depositing an initial margin of $500 per contract?

3. Walt Benaski is thinking about doing some speculating in interest rates; he thinks rates will fall and, in response, the price of Treasury bond futures should move from 92–15, their present quote, to a level of about 98. Given a required margin deposit of $2,000 per contract, what would Walt's return on invested capital be if prices behave as he expects?

4. Judi Jordan has been an avid stock market investor for years; she manages her portfolio fairly aggressively and likes to short sell whenever the opportunity presents itself. Recently, she has become fascinated with stock-index futures, especially the idea of being able to play the market as a whole. At the present time, Judi thinks the market is headed down, and she decides to short sell some NYSE Composite stock-index futures. Assume she shorts 3 contracts at 287.95 and has to make a margin deposit of $6,000 for each contract. How much profit will she make, and what will her return on invested capital be if the market does indeed drop so that the NYSE contracts are trading at 265.00 by the time they expire?

5. A wealthy investor holds $500,000 worth of U.S. Treasury bonds; these bonds are currently being quoted at par (100). The investor is concerned, however, that rates are headed up over the next 6 months, and he would like to do something to protect this bond portfolio. His broker advises him to set up a hedge using T-bond futures contracts; assume these contracts are now trading at 101–06.

   a. Briefly describe how the investor would set up this hedge—would he go long or short, and how many contracts would he need?
   b. It's now 6 months later, and rates have indeed gone up. The investor's Treasury bonds are now being quoted at 91½, and the T-bond futures con-

tract used in the hedge are now trading at 94–00. Show what has happened to the value of the bond portfolio and the profit (or loss) made on the futures hedge.

   c. Was this a successful hedge? Explain.

LG 6

6. Not long ago, Joan Atwood sold the company she founded for several million dollars (after taxes); she took some of that money and put it into the stock market. Today, Joan's portfolio of blue-chip stocks is worth $2.3 million. Joan wants to keep her portfolio intact, but she's concerned about a developing weakness in the market for blue chips. She decides, therefore, to hedge her position with 6-month futures contracts on the Major Market Index (MMI), which is currently trading at 460.

   a. Why would she choose to hedge her portfolio with the Major Market Index rather than the S&P 500?

   b. Given that Joan wants to cover the full $2.3 million in her portfolio, describe how she would go about setting up this hedge.

   c. If each contract required a margin deposit of $7,500, how much money would she need to set up this hedge?

   d. Assume that over the next 6 months stock prices do fall, and the value of Joan's portfolio drops to $2.0 million. If MMI futures contracts are trading at 391, how much will she make (or lose) on the futures hedge? Is it enough to offset the loss in her portfolio—that is, what's her net profit or loss on the hedge?

   e. Will she now get her margin deposit back, or is that a "sunk cost"—gone forever?

LG 6

7. An American currency speculator feels strongly that the value of the Canadian dollar is going to fall relative to the U.S. dollar over the short run. If he wants to profit from these expectations, what kind of position (long or short) would he take in Canadian dollar futures contracts? How much money would he make from each contract if Canadian dollar futures contracts moved from an initial quote of .8775 to an ending quote of .8250?

LG 6

8. With regard to futures options, how much profit would an investor make if she bought a call option on gold at 7.20 when gold was trading at $482 an ounce, given that the price of gold went up to $525 an ounce by the expiration date on the call? (*Note:* Assume the call carried a strike price of 480.)

CASE PROBLEMS   **LG 5** **LG 6**   **15.1   T.J.'S FAST TRACK INVESTMENTS: INTEREST RATE FUTURES**

T.J. Patrick is a successful industrial designer in Portland, Oregon, who enjoys the excitement of commodities speculation. Although only 29 years old, T.J. has been dabbling in commodities since he was a teenager. He was introduced to it by his dad, who is a grain buyer for one of the leading food processors. T.J. recognizes the enormous risks involved in commodities speculating but feels that since he's still single, now is the perfect time to take chances. And he can well afford to: As a principal in a thriving industrial design firm, T.J. earns an income that ranges between $60,000 and $75,000 per year—enough to allow him to enjoy some of the finer things in life. Even so, he does follow a well-disciplined investment program and annually adds $10,000 to $15,000 to his portfolio.

   Recently, T.J. has started playing with financial futures—interest rate futures, to be exact. He admits he is no expert in interest rates, but he likes the price action these investment vehicles offer. This all started several months ago, when T.J. met Vinnie

Banano, a broker who specializes in financial futures, at a party. T.J. liked what Vinnie had to say (mostly how you couldn't go wrong with interest-rate futures) and soon set up a trading account with Vinnie's firm, Banano's of Portland.

The other day, Vinnie called T.J. and suggested he get into T-bill futures. As Vinnie saw it, interest rates were going to continue to head up at a brisk pace, and T.J. should short sell some 90-day T-bill futures. In particular, he thinks that rates on T-bills should go up by another half-point (moving from about 5½ up to 6 percent), and he recommends that T.J. short 4 contracts. This would be a $4,000 investment, because each contract requires an initial margin deposit of $1,000.

Questions

1. Assume 90-day T-bill futures are now being quoted at 94.35.
   a. Determine the current price (underlying value) of this T-bill futures contract.
   b. What would this futures contract be quoted at if Vinnie is right and the yield goes up by ½ of 1 percent?

2. How much profit would T.J. make if he shorts 4 contracts at 94.35 and T-bill yields do go up by ½ of 1 percent—that is, if T.J. covers his short position when T-bill futures contracts are quoted at 93.85? Also, calculate the return on invested capital from this transaction.

3. What happens if rates go down? For example, how much would T. J. make if the yield on T-bill futures goes down by just ¼ of 1 percent?

4. What risks do you see in the recommended short-sale transaction? What is your assessment of T. J.'s new interest in financial futures; how do you think it compares to his established commodities investment program?

LG 5 LG 6   ### 15.2 JIM AND POLLY PARKER TRY HEDGING WITH STOCK-INDEX FUTURES

Jim Parker and his wife, Polly, live in Birmingham, Alabama. Like many young couples today, the Parkers are a two-income family; Jim and Polly are both college graduates and hold well-paying jobs. Jim has been an avid investor in the stock market for a number of years and over time has built up a portfolio that is currently worth nearly $115,000. The Parkers' portfolio is well balanced: It contains quality growth stocks, some high-income utilities, and a small amount of moderately speculative stock. The Parkers reinvest all dividends and regularly add investment capital to their portfolio. Up to now, they have avoided short selling and do only a modest amount of margin trading.

Their portfolio has undergone a substantial amount of capital appreciation in the last 18 months or so, and Jim is eager to protect the profit they have earned. And that's the problem, because Jim feels the market has pretty much run its course and is about to enter a period of decline. He has studied the market and economic news very carefully and does not believe the retreat will be of a major magnitude or cover an especially long period of time. He feels fairly certain, however, that most, if not all, of the stocks in his portfolio will be adversely affected by these market conditions—though they certainly won't all be affected to the same degree (some will drop more in price than others). Jim has been following stock-index futures for some time and feels he knows the ins and outs of these securities pretty well. After careful deliberation, Jim and Polly decide to use stock-index futures—in particular, the NYSE Composite futures contract—as a way to protect (hedge) their portfolio of common stocks.

Questions

1. Explain why the Parkers would want to use stock-index futures to hedge their stock portfolio, and note how Jim would go about setting up such a hedge. Be specific.
    a. What alternatives does Jim have to protect the capital value of his portfolio?
    b. What are the benefits and risks of using stock-index futures for such purposes (as hedging vehicles)?

2. Assume that NYSE Composite futures contracts are presently being quoted at 225.60. How many contracts would the Parkers have to buy (or sell) to set up the hedge?
    a. If the value of the Parker portfolio dropped 12 percent over the course of the market retreat, to what price must the stock-index futures contract move in order to cover that loss?
    b. Given that a $6,000 margin deposit is required to buy or sell a single NYSE futures contract, what would be the Parkers' return on invested capital if the price of the futures contract changes by the amount computed in part 2(a)?

3. Assume that the value of the Parker portfolio declined by $12,000, while the price of a NYSE Composite futures contract moved from 225.60 to 207.60. (Assume that Jim short sold 1 futures contract to set up the hedge.)
    a. Add the profit from the hedge transaction to the new (depreciated) value of the stock portfolio. How does this amount compare to the $115,000 portfolio that existed just before the market started its retreat?
    b. Why did the stock-index futures hedge fail to give complete protection to the Parker portfolio? Is it possible to obtain *perfect* (dollar-for-dollar) protection from these types of hedges? Explain.

4. What if, instead of hedging with futures contracts, Parker decides to set up the hedge by using *futures options*? Suppose a put on a NYSE Composite futures contract (strike price = 225) is currently quoted at 5.80, and a comparable call is quoted at 2.35. Use the same portfolio and futures price conditions as set out in question 3 above to determine how well the portfolio would be protected. (*Hint*: Add the net profit from the hedge to the new depreciated value of the stock portfolio.) What are the advantages and disadvantages of using futures options to hedge a stock portfolio, rather than the stock-index futures contract itself?

PART SIX

INVESTMENT ADMINISTRATION

CHAPTER 16
PORTFOLIO CONSTRUCTION

CHAPTER 17
PORTFOLIO MANAGEMENT AND CONTROL

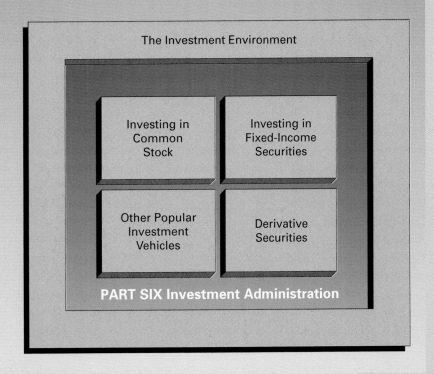

The Investment Environment

Investing in Common Stock

Investing in Fixed-Income Securities

Other Popular Investment Vehicles

Derivative Securities

PART SIX Investment Administration

CHAPTER 16

PORTFOLIO CONSTRUCTION

LEARNING GOALS

After studying this chapter, you should be able to:

LG 1 Understand the objectives of portfolio management and the procedures used to calculate the return and standard deviation of a portfolio.

LG 2 Discuss the concepts of correlation and diversification, their impact on portfolio risk and return, and the effectiveness, methods, and benefits of international diversification.

LG 3 Review the two basic approaches to portfolio management—traditional management versus the modern approach—and reconcile them.

LG 4 Describe the role of investor characteristics, investor objectives, and portfolio objectives and policies in planning and constructing an investment portfolio.

LG 5 Summarize the motives and various approaches involved in using an asset allocation scheme to construct an investment portfolio consistent with the investor's objectives.

LG 6 Relate investor objectives to the asset allocations and risk-return profiles reflected in various types of portfolios.

"I've followed the stock market for over 20 years, focusing on blue chip and California-based companies," says Lynn Rice (a pseudonym). "I'd majored in economics in college and enjoyed investing, so I started building our family's portfolio in 1982. My goal was to provide extras for our children, now 18 and 15—from braces and extracurricular activities to private college tuition."

Because interest rates were high and stock prices were low in 1982, Lynn put 30 percent of her initial portfolio in two-year Treasury bills and the rest into individual stocks. After researching various approaches to building a portfolio, she decided a conservative, value-oriented strategy suited her best. "I look for large companies with at least $100 million in sales, products and markets I understand, and management ownership of stock," Lynn explains. "Other criteria include price/earnings ratios of 10 or less, book value close to price (except in groups like drugs, utilities, and biotechnology), low debt-to-asset ratio, dividend yield of 5 percent or more, and a beta near 1. I like stocks that have been clobbered by the media and suffered as a result—Phillip Morris and the drug industry are two recent examples. I buy when the price is near a ten-year low and considerable price appreciation is expected in the next three to five years."

Macroeconomics influences Lynn's portfolio strategies. "My asset allocation choices depend on where the economy is going," Lynn says. "Are interest rates going higher or falling? Is the government encouraging research and development? Are production and overall capacity high or low?" She also looks at overall levels of the stock market and at dividend yield. When interest rates are high, dividend yields low, and the market high, Lynn sells stocks to take profits and invests in short-term Treasuries. "I make sure I have enough cash in reserve to take advantage of market corrections and individual stock lows. Usually, I am better at buying at or near a low than selling at the absolute high," Lynn notes. "I've learned from studying the market history that it's better not to be too greedy; when the market heads south, the decline can be immediate and drastic."

Lynn's typical portfolio is 80 to 90 percent stocks, with the rest in cash. She likes to hold 15 to 20 stocks—mainly cyclicals, drugs, utilities, and technology—to spread the risk over companies and industries. When the market is high and dividend yields low, as in spring 1995, she increases cash. Recently, she put her portfolio on *Street Smart*, a computer program that saves her money through electronic trading and tracks transactions and price history.

> **LYNN'S TYPICAL PORTFOLIO IS 80 TO 90 PERCENT STOCKS, WITH THE REST IN CASH. SHE LIKES TO HOLD 15 TO 20 STOCKS . . .**

Lynn holds most of her stocks for at least two years. "I've owned both extreme winners and losers: I bought Seagrams at $15 and sold at $65; Johnson and Johnson, at $38 and sold at $57 (only to see it go higher!). Pan Am and International Harvester were losers for me—let's forget those numbers! Fortunately, winners have far outnumbered the losers, and my average annual portfolio return has been about 15 percent."

Lynn Rice, 42, manages her investments in San Diego, where she lives with husband, Duane, and two teenagers. Her son, Mike, attends college on the East Coast—with tuition paid from investment profits—and her daughter, Kate, is a high school sophomore.

Investors benefit from holding portfolios of investments rather than single investment vehicles. *Without sacrificing returns, investors who hold portfolios can reduce risk, often to a level below that of any of the investments held in isolation.* In other words, when it comes to risk, $1 + 1 < 1$.

To achieve his or her investment objectives, an investor needs to plan and construct a portfolio that exhibits the desired risk-return behavior. The input to the portfolio is the expected risk-return characteristics of the individual investment vehicles; its output is the portfolio's actual risk and return. Selecting investment vehicles for a portfolio is best accomplished using certain analytical procedures. The body of knowledge on how to create portfolios that provide the best risk-return tradeoffs is based on complex mathematical concepts, many of which are beyond the scope of an introductory investments text. However, like Lynn Rice, you can develop a profitable portfolio strategy through solid research and by following the criteria for stock selection that best fit your own investment style. In this chapter we will emphasize general principles and simple approaches that allow an investor to plan and construct a portfolio consistent with his or her objectives. To demonstrate, we will analyze four typical portfolios.

PRINCIPLES OF PORTFOLIO PLANNING

growth-oriented portfolio
a portfolio whose primary objective is long-term price appreciation.

income-oriented portfolio
a portfolio that stresses current dividend and interest returns.

As defined in Chapter 1, a *portfolio* is a collection of investment vehicles assembled to meet a common investment goal. Of course, different investors will have different objectives for their portfolios: The primary goal of a **growth-oriented portfolio** is long-term price appreciation. An **income-oriented portfolio** stresses current dividend and interest returns. The *Investor Insights* box on page 664 offers some basic portfolio tips for the novice investor.

PORTFOLIO OBJECTIVES

Setting portfolio objectives involves definite tradeoffs: tradeoffs between risk and return, between potential price appreciation and current income, and between varying risk levels in the portfolio. These will depend on the investor's income tax bracket, current income needs, and ability to bear risk. The key point is that the portfolio objectives must be established *before* beginning to invest.

efficient portfolio
a portfolio that provides the highest return for a given level of risk or that has the lowest risk for a given level of return.

The ultimate goal of an investor is an **efficient portfolio**, one that provides the highest return for a given level of risk or that has the lowest risk for a given level of return. Such portfolios aren't necessarily obvious: Investors usually must search out reasonable investment alternatives to get the best combinations of risk and return. Thus, when given the choice between two equally risky investments offering different returns, the investor would be expected to choose the alternative with the higher return. Likewise, given two investment vehicles offering the same returns but differing in risk, the *risk-averse* investor would prefer the vehicle with the lower risk. In trying to create an efficient portfolio, the investor should be able to put together the best portfolio possible given his or her disposition toward risk and the alternative investment vehicles available.

PORTFOLIO RETURN AND STANDARD DEVIATION

The *return on a portfolio* is calculated as a weighted average of returns on the assets (investment vehicles) from which it is formed. The portfolio return, r_p, can be found by using Equation 16.1:

Equation 16.1

$$\begin{matrix}\text{Return} \\ \text{on} \\ \text{portfolio}\end{matrix} = \begin{pmatrix}\text{proportion of} \\ \text{portfolio's total} \\ \text{dollar value} \\ \text{represented by} \\ \text{Asset 1}\end{pmatrix} \times \begin{matrix}\text{return} \\ \text{on Asset} \\ 1\end{matrix} + \begin{pmatrix}\text{proportion of} \\ \text{portfolio's total} \\ \text{dollar value} \\ \text{represented by} \\ \text{Asset 2}\end{pmatrix} \times \begin{matrix}\text{return} \\ \text{on Asset} \\ 2\end{matrix} + \cdots +$$

$$\begin{pmatrix}\text{proportion of} \\ \text{portfolio's total} \\ \text{dollar value} \\ \text{represented by} \\ \text{Asset } n\end{pmatrix} \times \begin{matrix}\text{return} \\ \text{on Asset} \\ n\end{matrix} = \sum_{j=1}^{n} \begin{pmatrix}\text{proportion of} \\ \text{portfolio's total} \\ \text{dollar value} \\ \text{represented by} \\ \text{Asset } j\end{pmatrix} \times \begin{matrix}\text{return} \\ \text{on Asset} \\ j\end{matrix}$$

Equation 16.1a

$$r_p = (w_1 \times r_1) + (w_2 \times r_2) + \cdots + (w_n \times r_n) = \sum_{j=1}^{n}(w_j \times r_j)$$

Of course, $\sum_{j=1}^{n} w_j = 1$, which means that 100 percent of the portfolio's assets must be included in this computation.

The *standard deviation of a portfolio's returns* is found by applying Equation 4.12, the formula used in Chapter 4 to find the standard deviation of a single asset. Assume that we wish to determine the return and standard deviation of returns for Portfolio XY, created by combining equal portions (50 percent) of Assets X and Y. The expected returns of Assets X and Y for each of the next five years (1997–2001) are given in Columns 1 and 2, respectively, in Part A of Table 16.1. In Columns 3 and 4, the weights of 50 percent for both assets X and Y, along with their respective returns from columns 1 and 2, are substituted into Equation 16.1 to get an expected portfolio return of 12 percent for each year, 1997 to 2001. Furthermore, as shown in Part B of Table 16.1, the average expected portfolio return, $\bar{r}_p$, over the five-year period is also 12 percent. Substituting into Equation 4.12, Portfolio XY's standard deviation, s_p, of 0 percent is calculated in Part C of Table 16.1. This value should not be surprising, because the expected return each year is the same—12 percent. Therefore, no variability is exhibited in the expected returns from year to year shown in Column 4 of Part A of the table.

CORRELATION AND DIVERSIFICATION

As noted in Chapter 1, *diversification* involves the inclusion of a number of different investment vehicles in a portfolio. It is an important aspect of creating an efficient portfolio. Underlying the intuitive appeal of diversification is the statistical concept of *correlation*. An understanding of the concepts of correlation and diversification and their relationship to a portfolio's total risk and return is a central part of effective portfolio planning. Here we take a closer look at these key concepts and their interrelationships.

Table 16.1 Expected Return, Average Return, and Standard Deviation of Returns for Portfolio XY

A. Expected Portfolio Returns

	(1)	(2)	(3)	(4)
	Expected Return			Expected Portfolio
Year	Asset X	Asset Y	Portfolio Return Calculation[*]	Return, r_p
1997	8%	16%	$(.50 \times 8\%) + (.50 \times 16\%) =$	12%
1998	10	14	$(.50 \times 10\ ) + (.50 \times 14\ ) =$	12
1999	12	12	$(.50 \times 12\ ) + (.50 \times 12\ ) =$	12
2000	14	10	$(.50 \times 14\ ) + (.50 \times 10\ ) =$	12
2001	16	8	$(.50 \times 16\ ) + (.50 \times 8\ ) =$	12

B. Average Expected Portfolio Return, 1997–2001

$$\bar{r}_p = \frac{12\% + 12\% + 12\% + 12\% + 12\%}{5} = \frac{60\%}{5} = \underline{\underline{12\%}}$$

C. Standard Deviation of Expected Portfolio Returns[**]

$$s_p = \sqrt{\frac{(12\% - 12\%)^2 + (12\% - 12\%)^2 + (12\% - 12\%)^2 + (12\% - 12\%)^2 + (12\% - 12\%)^2}{5 - 1}}$$

$$= \sqrt{\frac{0\% + 0\% + 0\% + 0\% + 0\%}{4}} = \sqrt{\frac{0\%}{4}} = \underline{\underline{0\%}}$$

[*]Using Equation 16.1.

[**]Using Equation 4.12 presented in Chapter 4.

Correlation

correlation
a statistical measure of the relationship, if any, between series of numbers representing data of any kind.

positively correlated
describes two series that move in the same direction.

negatively correlated
describes two series that move in opposite directions.

correlation coefficient
a measure of the degree of correlation between two series.

perfectly positively correlated
describes two positively correlated series that have a correlation coefficient of +1.

perfectly negatively correlated
describes two negatively correlated series that have a correlation coefficient of −1.

Correlation is a statistical measure of the relationship, if any, between series of numbers representing data of any kind. If two series move in the same direction, they are **positively correlated**. If the series move in opposite directions, they are **negatively correlated**.

The degree of correlation—whether positive or negative—is measured by the **correlation coefficient**. The coefficient ranges from +1 for **perfectly positively correlated** series to −1 for **perfectly negatively correlated** series. These two extremes are depicted in Figure 16.1 for Series M and N. The perfectly positively correlated series move exactly together, whereas the perfectly negatively correlated series move in exactly opposite directions.

Diversification

To reduce overall risk in a portfolio, it is best to combine assets that have a negative (or a low-positive) correlation. Combining negatively correlated assets can reduce the overall variability of returns, or risk, s. Figure 16.2 shows that a portfolio containing the negatively correlated assets F and G, both having the same average expected return, $\bar{r}$, also has the same return, $\bar{r}$, but has less risk (variability) than either of the individual assets. Even if assets are not negatively correlated, the lower the positive correlation between them, the lower the resulting risk.

Figure 16.1 The Correlation Between Series M and N
The perfectly positively correlated series M and N in the left graph move exactly together. The perfectly negatively correlated series M and N in the right graph move in exactly opposite directions.

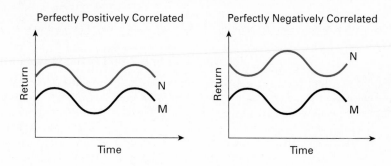

uncorrelated
describes two series that lack any relationship or interaction and therefore have a correlation coefficient close to zero.

Some assets are **uncorrelated**: They are completely unrelated, with no interaction between their returns. Combining uncorrelated assets can reduce risk—not as effectively as combining negatively correlated assets, but more effectively than combining positively correlated assets. The correlation coefficient for uncorrelated assets is close to zero and acts as the midpoint between perfect positive and perfect negative correlation.

Correlation is important to reducing risk, but it can do only so much. A portfolio of two assets having perfectly positively correlated returns *cannot* reduce the portfolio's overall risk below the risk of the least risky asset. However, a portfolio combining two assets with less than perfectly positive correlation *can* reduce total risk to a level below that of either of the components, which in certain situations may be zero. For example, assume you own the stock of a machine tool manufacturer that is very *cyclical*, having high earnings when the economy is expanding and low earnings during a recession. If you bought stock in another machine tool company, which would have earnings positively correlated with those of the stock you already own, the combined earnings would continue to be cyclical. As a result, risk would remain the same. As an alternative, however, you could buy stock in a sewing machine manufacturer, which is *countercyclical*, having low earnings during economic expansion and high earnings during recession (because consumers are more likely to make their own clothes and clothing repairs at such a time). Combining the machine tool stock and the sewing machine stock, which have negatively correlated earnings, should reduce risk: The low machine tool earnings during a recession would be balanced out by high sewing machine earnings, and vice versa.

Figure 16.2 Combining Negatively Correlated Assets to Diversify Risk
The risks or variability of returns, resulting from combining negatively correlated Assets F and G, both having the same expected return, $\bar{r}$, results in a portfolio (shown in the right-hand graph) with the same level of expected return but less risk.

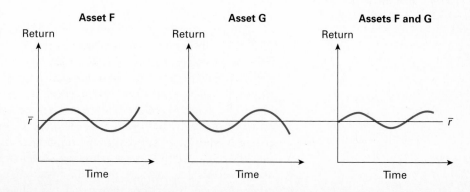

INVESTOR INSIGHTS: *Investing in Action*

Portfolio-Building Tips for the Novice Investor

You've just received a $2,000 bonus check at work and you're ready to invest. Where do you start? And what if you have less to invest—say, a few hundred dollars?

Before you spend a penny, be sure to put aside a cash reserve fund for emergencies and other liquidity needs and develop a long-term investment strategy, with a mix of assets geared to your overall goals. Stick to this framework as you build your portfolio; otherwise, you could end up with investments that don't fit your needs. With limited funds, you can't fully implement your game plan right away but you can work toward it: Start with your largest asset category and then add the others as you have more funds to invest.

A small investor can take many routes to build a portfolio. One conservative approach that appeals to many novices starts with a balanced or asset allocation mutual fund with stocks, bonds, and cash. This one investment gives you instant diversification among asset classes. You add to this fund regularly until you build up more money—and investment confidence—to move into specific fund categories or individual stocks. If you are more aggressive, you can buy a stock-index fund that, with its focus on large-cap stocks, forms the core of your portfolio's equity portion. You need a greater risk tolerance to start with full commitment to stocks, but the index fund is fairly conservative.

With either strategy, as more money becomes available, you diversify into other investment categories to meet allocation goals. If you own a balanced fund, buying a stock fund next moves you closer to your target equity percentage. With the stock-index fund approach, buying an intermediate bond fund would create your own balanced fund. Or you might buy a small-cap or international fund. Don't agonize if you vary a few percentage points from your plan; your target percentages are a general guide.

Building a portfolio of individual stocks takes more time and discipline than buying a fund. One good way for an investor with limited funds to get started and also keep expenses down is with dividend reinvestment plans (DRIPs), offered by over 800 companies. After you own the stock—all you need is one share—you can reinvest dividends in more shares and buy stock directly from the company, usually without a fee. Do your homework by studying shareholder information packages and DRIP prospectuses from companies that interest you. Diversify: Buy shares in a variety of industries and economic sectors, and include growth, value, and income stocks. Work up to about 10 to 20 companies, focusing on quality, not quantity; 4 good stocks are better than 10 bad ones!

Finally, *invest regularly in your funds or stocks*—every month or pay period, if possible. And be patient; plan to hold your investments for a while, or transaction costs and taxes can wipe out profits.

Sources: Adapted from Steven T. Goldberg, "An Investing Plan for a Lifetime," *Kiplinger's Personal Finance Magazine,* August 1994, pp. 32–40; Ellen C. Schultz, "How to Build a Stock Portfolio, Even If You Aren't a Moneybags," *Wall Street Journal,* April 14, 1992, p. C1; and Maria Crawford Scott, "How to Implement Your Strategy If You Are Starting from Scratch," *AAII Journal,* February 1995, pp. 18–20.

A numeric example will provide a better understanding of the role of correlation in the diversification process. Table 16.2 presents the expected returns from three different assets—X, Y, and Z—over the next five years, along with their average returns and standard deviations. Each of the assets has an expected value of return of 12 percent and a standard deviation of 3.16 percent. The assets therefore have equal return and equal risk, although their return patterns are not necessarily identical. Comparing the return patterns of Assets X and Y, we see that they are perfectly negatively correlated, because they move in exactly opposite directions over time. A comparison of Assets X and Z shows that they are perfectly positively correlated: They move in precisely the same direction. (Note that the returns for X and Z are identical,

Table 16.2 Expected Returns, Average Returns, and Standard Deviations for Assets X, Y, and Z and Portfolios XY and XZ

	Assets			Portfolios	
				XY*	XZ**
Year	X	Y	Z	(50%X + 50%Y)	(50%X + 50%Z)
1997	8%	16%	8%	12%	8%
1998	10	14	10	12	10
1999	12	12	12	12	12
2000	14	10	14	12	14
2001	16	8	16	12	16
Statistics:					
Average returns[†]	12%	12%	12%	12%	12%
Standard deviation[‡]	3.16%	3.16%	3.16%	0%	3.16%

*Portfolio XY illustrates *perfect negative correlation*, because these two return streams behave in completely opposite fashion over the five-year period. The return values shown here were calculated in Part A of Table 16.1.

**Portfolio XZ illustrates *perfect positive correlation*, because these two return streams behave identically over the five-year period. These return values were calculated using the same method demonstrated for Portfolio XY in Part A of Table 16.1.

[†]The average return for each asset is calculated as the arithmetic average found by dividing the sum of the returns for the years 1997–2001 by 5—the number of years considered.

[‡]Equation 4.12 was used to calculate the standard deviation. Calculation of the average return and standard deviation for Portfolio XY is demonstrated in Parts B and C, respectively, of Table 16.1. The portfolio standard deviation can be directly calculated from the standard deviation of the component assets using the following formula:

$$s_p = \sqrt{w_1^2 s_1^2 + w_2^2 s_2^2 + 2w_1 w_2 p_{1,2} s_1 s_2}$$

where w_1 and w_2 are the proportions of the component assets 1 and 2; s_1 and s_2 are the standard deviations of the component assets 1 and 2; and $p_{1,2}$ is the correlation coefficient between the returns of component assets 1 and 2.

although it is not necessary for return streams to be identical in order for them to be perfectly positively correlated.)

Portfolio XY (shown in Table 16.2) is created by combining equal portions of Assets X and Y—the perfectly negatively correlated assets. Calculation of Portfolio XY's annual expected returns, average expected return, and the standard deviation of expected portfolio returns is demonstrated in Table 16.1. The risk of the portfolio created by this combination, as reflected in the standard deviation, is reduced to 0 percent, while its average return remains at 12 percent. Because both assets have the same average return, are combined in equal parts, and are perfectly negatively correlated, the combination results in the complete elimination of risk. Whenever assets are perfectly negatively correlated, an optimum combination (similar to the 50-50 mix in the case of Assets X and Y) exists for which the resulting standard deviation will equal 0.

Portfolio XZ (shown in Table 16.2) is created by combining equal portions of Assets X and Z—the perfectly positively correlated assets. The risk of this portfolio, reflected by its standard deviation, which remains at 3.16 percent, is unaffected by this combination, and the average return remains at 12 percent. Whenever perfectly positively correlated assets such as X and Z are combined, the standard deviation of the resulting portfolio cannot be reduced below that of the least risky asset; the maximum portfolio standard deviation will be that of the riskiest asset. Because Assets X and Z have the same standard deviation (3.16 percent), the minimum and maximum standard deviations are both 3.16 percent, which is the only value that could be taken on by a combination of these assets.

Impact on Risk and Return

In general, the lower (less positive and more negative) the correlation between asset returns, the greater the potential diversification of risk. For each pair of assets, there is a combination that will result in the lowest risk (standard deviation) possible. *The amount of potential risk reduction for this combination depends on the degree of correlation of the two assets.* This concept is a bit difficult to grasp, because many potential combinations could be made, given the expected return for each of two assets, the standard deviation for each asset, and the correlation coefficient. However, only one combination of the infinite number of possibilities will minimize risk.

Three possible correlations—perfect positive, uncorrelated, and perfect negative—illustrate the effect of correlation on the diversification of risk and return. Table 16.3 summarizes the impact of correlation on the range of return and risk for various two-asset portfolio combinations. The table shows that, as we move from perfect positive correlation to uncorrelated assets to perfect negative correlation, the ability to reduce risk is improved. Note that in no case will creating portfolios of assets result in risk greater than that of the riskiest asset included in the portfolio. To demonstrate, assume that a firm has carefully calculated the average return, $\bar{r}$, and risk, s, for each of two assets— A and B—as summarized below:

Asset	Average Return, $\bar{r}$	Risk (Standard Deviation), s
A	6%	3%
B	8%	8%

From these data, we can see that Asset A is clearly a lower-risk, lower-return asset than Asset B.

To evaluate possible combinations, we consider three possible correlations—perfect positive, uncorrelated, and perfect negative. The results of the analysis are shown in Figure 16.3. The ranges of return and risk exhibited are consistent with those noted in Table 16.3. In all cases, the return will range between the 6 percent return of A and the 8 percent return of B. The risk, on the other hand, ranges between the individual risks of A and B (from 3 to 8 percent) in the case of perfect positive correlation; from below 3 percent (the risk of A), but greater than 0, to 8 percent (the risk of B) in the uncorrelated case; and between 0 and 8 percent (the risk of B) in the perfectly negatively correlated case. Note that *only in the case of perfect negative correlation can*

Table 16.3 Correlation, Return, and Risk for Various Two-Asset Portfolio Combinations

Correlation Coefficient	Range of Return	Range of Risk
+1 (perfect positive)	Between returns of two assets held in isolation	Between risk of two assets held in isolation
0 (uncorrelated)	Between returns of two assets held in isolation	Between risk of most risky asset and less than risk of least risky asset, but greater than 0
−1 (perfect negative)	Between returns of two assets held in isolation	Between risk of most risky asset and 0

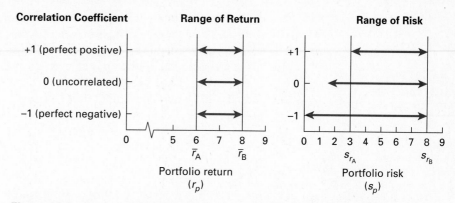

Figure 16.3 Range of Portfolio Return (r_p) and Risk (s_p) for Combinations of Assets A and B for Various Correlation Coefficients
The range of a portfolio's return is between that of the lowest and highest component asset returns and is unaffected by the degree of asset correlations. Portfolio risk, on the other hand, can be reduced below the risk of the least risky asset as the asset correlation moves from perfectly positive to uncorrelated to perfectly negative, where it can be reduced to zero by combining assets in the proper proportion.

the risk be reduced to 0. As the correlation becomes less positive and more negative (moving from the top of the figure down), the ability to reduce risk improves. Keep in mind that the amount of risk reduction achieved also depends on the proportions in which the assets are combined. Although determining the risk-minimizing combination is beyond the scope of this discussion, you should know that it is an important issue in developing portfolios of assets.

INTERNATIONAL DIVERSIFICATION

Diversification is clearly a primary consideration when constructing an investment portfolio for the risk-averse investor. Thus far, the focus and examples have been basically domestic. However, as noted in several earlier discussions in this book, numerous opportunities for international diversification are now available to the investor. Here we consider three aspects of international diversification: effectiveness, methods, and benefits.

Effectiveness of International Diversification

Investing internationally obviously offers greater diversification than investing only domestically. That is true for American investors. It is even truer for investors from countries with capital markets that offer much more limited diversification opportunities than are available in the United States.

However, does the diversification international investment offers actually reduce risk, particularly the variability of rates of return? Two recent studies overwhelmingly support the argument that well-structured international diversification does indeed reduce the variability (or risk) of a portfolio and increases the return on portfolios of comparable risk. For example, one study based upon an investor diversifying in 12 European countries in 7 different industries between 1978 and 1992 demonstrated that an investor could actually reduce the risk of a portfolio much more by diversifying internationally *in the same industry* than by diversifying across industries within one country. If the investor diversified both across countries and across industries, the opportunities for risk reduction would be even greater.

Another study examined the risk versus return performance between January 1984 and November 1994 of diversified stock portfolios: the S&P 500 in the United States and Morgan Stanley's Europe, Australasia, and Far East (EAFE) Index. It found that a 100 percent EAFE portfolio offered a much greater return than a 100 percent S&P 500 portfolio did—but at much greater risk. However, by creating a portfolio composed of various combinations of the two indexes, an investor realizes both lower risk and a higher return than for the 100 percent S&P 500 portfolio, and less risk and a moderately lower return for the 100 percent EAFE portfolio. For the American investor, a portfolio consisting of 70 percent S&P 500 coupled with 30 percent EAFE would have reduced risk by about 5 percent and increased return by about 7 percent (from around 14 percent to more than 15 percent). Or for the same degree of risk, an investor could have increased return by about 18 percent (from around 14 percent to more than 16.5 percent).

Methods of International Diversification

In earlier chapters we examined a wide range of alternatives for international portfolio diversification. Investments in bond and other debt instruments can be made abroad in either U.S. dollars in the Euromarket or in foreign currencies—either directly or via foreign mutual funds. Foreign currency investment, however, brings the risk (and potential benefit) of foreign exchange risk. This risk can be hedged using various contracts, most commonly currency forwards, futures, and options.

Investing abroad, even if there is little or no foreign exchange risk, is generally less convenient, more expensive, and riskier than investing domestically. When making direct investments abroad, the investor should have a clear idea of the benefits being sought, should be knowledgeable, and should have the time to monitor foreign markets.

International diversification can also be achieved domestically in the United States. Several hundred foreign companies list and sell their stocks on American exchanges or over-the-counter; most of them are Canadian companies. Also, many foreign issuers, both corporate and government, sell their bonds (called *Yankee bonds*) in the United States. The stocks of more than 1,100 foreign companies trade in the United States in the form of American Depositary Receipts. ADRs are available for companies from almost 50 countries. Finally, country, global, and other international mutual funds (e.g., EAFE or the Japan Fund) provide investors with a broad range of foreign investment opportunities. These domestic alternatives offer the advantages of convenience and cost, often with less risk than investments made directly abroad.

Benefits of International Diversification

Can greater returns be found overseas than in the United States? Yes! Can a portfolio's risk be reduced by including foreign investments? Yes! Is international diversification desirable for an individual investor? We don't know! A successful global investment strategy depends on many things, just as a purely domestic strategy does. Included are factors such as the resources, goals, sophistication, and psychology of the investor.

In general, investors should avoid investing directly in foreign-currency-denominated instruments. Unless the magnitude of each foreign investment is in hundreds of thousands of dollars, the transactions costs will tend to be expensive—not just when buying and selling, but especially when dividends or interest are paid. Therefore, for most investors who are sophisticated enough to seek international diversification, the optimal vehicles are available in the United States. International mutual funds are available for those who seek diversified foreign investments, coupled with the professional investment expertise of fund managers. ADRs can be used by those wishing to make foreign investments in individual stocks. With either mutual funds or ADRs, the investment enjoys low cost, convenience, transactions in U.S. dollars, protection under American security laws, and (usually) attractive markets (although some ADRs have thin markets).

CONCEPTS *in Review*

16.1 What is a *portfolio*? What is an *efficient portfolio*, and what role should such a portfolio play in investing?

16.2 How can the return and standard deviation of a portfolio be determined? Compare the portfolio standard deviation calculation to that used for a single asset.

16.3 What is *correlation*, and why is it important with respect to asset returns? Describe the characteristics of returns that are (a) positively correlated, (b) negatively correlated, and (c) uncorrelated. Define and differentiate between *perfect positive correlation* and *perfect negative correlation*.

16.4 What is *diversification*? How does the diversification of risk in the asset selection process allow the investor to combine risky assets so that the risk of the portfolio is less than that of the individual assets it contains?

16.5 Discuss how the amount of correlation between asset returns affects the risk and return behavior of the resulting portfolio. Describe the potential range of risk and return when the correlation between two assets is (a) perfectly positive, (b) uncorrelated, and (c) perfectly negative.

16.6 What, if any, benefit does international diversification offer the individual investor? Compare and contrast the methods of achieving international diversification by investing abroad versus investing domestically. Which method is probably better? Why?

TRADITIONAL VERSUS MODERN PORTFOLIO THEORY

Two approaches are currently used by portfolio managers to plan and construct their portfolios. The *traditional approach* refers to the less quantitative methods that money managers have been using since the evolution of the public securities markets. *Modern portfolio theory (MPT)* is a more mathematical, more recent development that has been refined over the past 25 or so years and continues to grow in popularity and acceptance. Some MPT concepts are indirectly used by practitioners of the traditional approach, yet there are major differences between the two.

THE TRADITIONAL APPROACH

Traditional portfolio management emphasizes "balancing" the portfolio by assembling a wide variety of stocks and/or bonds. The typical emphasis is interindustry diversification, which means that the portfolio contains securities of companies from a broad cross-section of industries. Most institutional portfolio managers utilize the security analysis techniques discussed in Chapters 6 and 7 when they select individual securities for the traditional portfolio.

Table 16.4 presents the industry groupings and percentages invested in them by a typical mutual fund that is managed by professionals using the traditional approach. This fund, the Zweig Appreciation Fund, is an open-end mutual fund with a 5.5 percent maximum initial load. The portfolio's value at December 31, 1994, was approximately $353 million. Its objective is to provide investors with long-term capital appreciation through investment primarily in small-company stocks, consistent with preservation of capital and reduction of portfolio exposure to market risk. The Zweig Appreciation Fund holds shares of 561 different stocks from 73 industries, as well as short-term obligations, repurchase agreements, and other assets.

Analyzing the stock portion of the Zweig Appreciation Fund, which accounts for about 64 percent of the fund's total assets, we can observe the traditional approach to portfolio management at work. This fund holds numerous stocks from a diverse cross-section of the total universe of available stocks, although its stocks represent only small companies. By far the largest industry group is banks, with 10.98 percent of the total portfolio. The fund's largest individual holding is Equitable Iowa Companies, an insurance company, which accounts for only .51 percent of the total portfolio. Citicorp, one of the nation's leading banks, ranks second, at .43 percent. The third largest holding—.37 percent—is Bank of Boston Corp., another major bank. Although most of the fund's 561 stocks are those of small companies, it does include the stocks of some major companies such as Citicorp and Bank of Boston Corp.

Traditional portfolio managers want to invest in well-known companies for three reasons. First, because these companies have been and probably will continue to be successful business enterprises, investing in them is perceived as less risky than investing in lesser known firms. Second, professional managers prefer to invest in large companies because the securities of these firms are more liquid and are available in large quantities. Managers of large portfolios invest substantial sums of money and need to acquire securities in large quantities to achieve an efficient order size. Third, traditional portfolio managers also prefer well-known companies because it is easier to convince clients to invest in well-known corporations. *Window dressing*, a Wall Street term, refers to the practice of many investment managers to load up portfolios with well-known stocks, thus making it easier to sell their services to clients.

MODERN PORTFOLIO THEORY

During the 1950s, Harry Markowitz, a trained mathematician, first developed the theories that form the basis of modern portfolio theory. Many other scholars and investment experts have contributed to the theory in the intervening years. **Modern portfolio theory (MPT)** utilizes several basic statistical

Table 16.4 Portfolio of Zweig Appreciation Fund, December 31, 1994

The Zweig Appreciation Fund appears to adhere to the traditional approach to portfolio management. Its total portfolio value is about $353 million, of which over 64 percent ($227 million) is common stock, including 561 different stocks in 73 industry groupings, plus about 21 percent ($74 million) in short-term obligations, about 12 percent ($42 million) in repurchase agreements, and about 3 percent ($10 million) in other assets.

Zweig Appreciation Fund
Investments by Industry Group
as of December 31, 1994

Industry Group	Percentage	Industry Group	Percentage
Common Stocks	**64.39%**	Home building and land development	.49%
Advertising	.12	Hospital and health care	.97
Aerospace	.80	Hotels and resorts	.04
Air freight	.37	Household furniture	.25
Aircraft manufacturing	.16	Industrial products, services, and machinery	1.83
Airlines	.53	Insurance	2.91
Apparel	.60	Investment banking and brokerage	.90
Automobiles	.79	Manufacturing	.58
Automobile aftermarket	.54	Marine transportation	.27
Automobile parts and equipment	.75	Medical instruments specialities and distribution	.58
Banks	10.98	Metal fabrication	.73
Broadcasting and entertainment	.01	Metals and steels	1.86
Building materials and products	1.15	Natural gas	1.01
Casino operators	.32	Office automation and equipment	.49
Catalog distribution	.19	Oil and gas	3.12
Cellular communications	.11	Pharmaceuticals	.01
Chemicals	.90	Precision instruments	.53
Commercial services	.50	Printing and forms	1.02
Computer/music electronics chains	.32	Publishing	.75
Computers and software	.16	Railroads	.10
Conglomerates	1.24	Real estate development	.02
Construction equipment	1.61	Real estate investment trusts	.10
Consumer electronics	.57	Recreational products	.89
Consumer products and services	.18	Rental and leasing	1.44
Containers and packaging	.17	Restaurants	.37
Data processing systems	2.16	Retail trade	1.56
Electrical products	.74	Savings and loan associations	.96
Electronics	3.20	Semiconductors	1.55
Engineering	.26	Telecommunications	.36
Entertainment	.10	Textiles	.35
Environmental services	.13	Tobacco	.08
Farming and milling	.22	Trucking	.63
Finance	1.20	Utilities—electric	1.49
Fluid controls	.22	Water supply	.10
Food chains and distributors	.93	Wholesale distributors	.46
Food and beverages	2.34	**Short-Term Obligations**	**21.02**
Footwear chains and manufacturing	.36	**Repurchase Agreements**	**11.92**
Forest and paper products	.50	**Other Assets (net)**	**2.67**
Health care and hospital management	.16		

Source: Zweig Series Trust, *1994 Annual Report*, December 31, 1994.

measures to develop a portfolio plan. Included are *expected returns* and *standard deviations* of returns for both securities and portfolios and the *correlation* between returns. According to MPT, diversification is achieved by combining securities in a portfolio *so that individual securities have negative (or low positive) correlations between each other's rates of return.* Thus, the statistical diversification is the deciding factor in choosing securities for an

MPT portfolio. Two important aspects of MPT are the *efficient frontier* and *beta*. As we'll see below, the efficient frontier is a more theoretical but less practical tool than beta is.

The Efficient Frontier

At any point in time, an investor is faced with virtually hundreds of investment vehicles from which to choose. Using some or all of these vehicles, the investor can form a large number of possible portfolios. In fact, using only, say, ten of the vehicles, hundreds of portfolios could be created by changing the weights, w_j, which represent the proportion of the portfolio's dollar value represented by each asset j. As noted earlier, each portfolio formed would have an expected return, r_p, and risk as measured by its standard deviation, s_p. Clearly, unless the securities included in a given portfolio are *perfectly positively correlated*, some risk reduction would result from the diversification achieved by the portfolio.

If we were to create all possible portfolios, calculate the return (r_p) and risk (s_p) of each, and plot each risk-return combination on a set of risk-return (s_p-r_p) axes, we would have the *feasible* or *attainable set* of all possible portfolios. This set is represented by the shaded area in Figure 16.4. It is the area bounded by ABYOZCDEF. As defined earlier, an *efficient portfolio* is a portfolio that provides the highest return for a given level of risk or provides minimum risk for a given level of return. For example, let's compare Portfolio T to Portfolios B and Y depicted in Figure 16.4. It appears that Portfolio Y is preferable to Portfolio T because it has a higher return for the same level of risk. Portfolio B also dominates Portfolio T because it has lower risk for the same level of return. The boundary BYOZC of the feasible or attainable set of portfolios, called the **efficient frontier**, represents *all efficient portfolios*—those that provide the best tradeoff between risk and return. All portfolios on the efficient frontier are preferable to all other portfolios in the feasible or attainable set. Any portfolios that would fall to the left of the efficient frontier are *not available* for investment, because they fall outside of the feasible or attainable set. Portfolios that fall to the right of the efficient frontier are *not desirable,* because their risk-return tradeoffs are inferior to those of portfolios on the efficient frontier.

efficient frontier
the leftmost boundary of the feasible (attainable) set of portfolios that includes all efficient portfolios—those providing the best attainable tradeoff between risk (measured by the standard deviation) and return.

The efficient frontier can, in theory, be used with an *investor's utility function* or *risk-indifference curves*, which indicate for a given level of utility (satisfaction) the set of risk-return combinations for which an investor would be indifferent. These curves, labeled I_1, I_2, and I_3 in Figure 16.4, reflect increasing utility (satisfaction) as we move from I_1 to I_2 to I_3. The optimal portfolio, O, is the point at which indifference curve I_2 meets the efficient frontier. This portfolio reflects the highest level of satisfaction the investor can achieve given the available set of portfolios. The higher utility provided by I_3 cannot be achieved given the best available portfolios represented by the efficient frontier.

When coupled with a risk-free asset, the efficient frontier can be used to develop the *capital asset pricing model* (introduced in Chapter 4) in terms of portfolio risk (measured by the standard deviation, s_p) and return (r_p). Rather than focus further on theory, we will shift our attention to the more practical aspects of the efficient frontier and its extensions. To do so, we revisit *beta*, the risk measure introduced in Chapter 4, and consider its use in a portfolio context.

Figure 16.4 The Feasible or Attainable Set and the Efficient Frontier
The *feasible* or *attainable set* (shaded area) represents the risk-return combinations attainable with all possible portfolios; the *efficient frontier* is the locus of all efficient portfolios. The point O where the investor's highest possible indifference curve is tangent to the efficient frontier is the optimal portfolio. It represents the highest level of satisfaction the investor can achieve given the available set of portfolios.

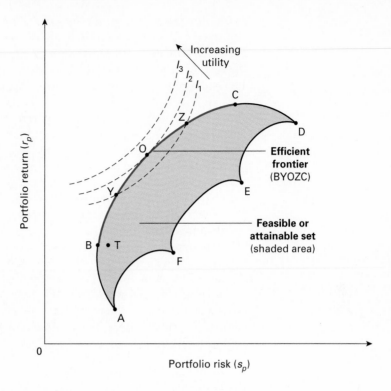

Portfolio Betas

As noted above, investors strive to diversify their portfolios by including a variety of noncomplementary investment vehicles, to reduce the risk of loss while meeting their return objectives. Remember from Chapter 4 that investment vehicles possess two basic types of risk: (1) *diversifiable risk*, the risk unique to a particular investment vehicle, and (2) *nondiversifiable risk*, the risk possessed by every investment vehicle.

A great deal of research has been conducted on the topic of risk as it relates to security investments. As noted in Chapter 4, the results show that, in general, investors *earn higher rates of return by buying riskier investments*; that is, *to earn more return, one must bear more risk*. More startling, however, are research results showing that only with nondiversifiable risk is there a positive risk-return relationship. High levels of *diversifiable risk* do not result in correspondingly high levels of return. Because there is no reward for bearing diversifiable risk, an investor should minimize this form of risk by diversifying the portfolio so that only nondiversifiable risk remains.

Risk Diversification   As we've seen, diversification minimizes diversifiable risk because of a balancing effort that tends to cause the poor return on one vehicle to be offset by the good return on another. Minimizing diversifiable risk through careful selection of investment vehicles requires that the vehicles chosen for the portfolio come from a wide range of industries.

To understand better the effect of diversification on the basic types of risk, let's consider what happens when we begin with a single asset (security) in a portfolio and then expand the portfolio by randomly selecting additional securities from, say, the population of all actively traded securities. Using the standard deviation, s_p, to measure the portfolio's *total risk*, we can depict the behavior of the total portfolio risk (y-axis) as more securities are added (x-axis), as done in Figure 16.5. As securities are added, the total portfolio risk declines, due to the effects of diversification (explained earlier), and it tends to approach a limit. Research has shown that, on average, most of the benefits of diversification, in terms of risk reduction, can be gained by forming portfolios containing 8 to 15 randomly selected securities. Unfortunately, because an investor holds but one of a large number of possible x-security portfolios, it is unlikely that he or she will experience the average outcome. As a consequence, some researchers suggest that the individual investor needs to hold about 40 different stocks to achieve efficient diversification. This suggestion tends to support the popularity of investment in mutual funds by individual investors.

Because, as noted in Chapter 4, any investor can create a portfolio of assets that will eliminate all, or virtually all, diversifiable risk, the only **relevant risk** is that which is nondiversifiable. Any investor must therefore be concerned solely with nondiversifiable risk, which reflects the contribution of an asset to the risk of the portfolio. The measurement of nondiversifiable risk is thus of primary importance in selecting those assets possessing the most desired risk-return characteristics.

relevant risk
risk that is nondiversifiable.

Calculating Portfolio Betas The *nondiversifiable* or *relevant risk* of a security can be measured using *beta*, a measure that was defined, derived, and

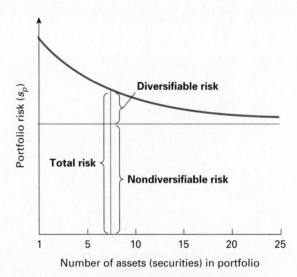

Figure 16.5 Portfolio Risk and Diversification As randomly selected assets (securities) are combined to create a portfolio, the total risk of the portfolio (measured by its standard deviation, s_p) declines. The portion of the risk eliminated is the *diversifiable risk*, and the remaining portion is the *nondiversifiable* or *relevant risk*. On average, most of the benefits of diversification result from forming portfolios containing 8 to 15 randomly selected securities.

demonstrated in Chapter 4. Betas can be positive (return changes in same direction as market) or negative (return changes in opposite direction as market). Most betas are positive. The beta for the market is equal to 1.0. Securities with betas greater than 1.0 are more risky than the market, and those with betas below 1.0 are less risky than the market. The beta for the risk-free asset is 0.0. Betas for a broad range of securities can be readily obtained from brokerage firms and subscription services such as Value Line.

The **portfolio beta**, b_p, is merely the weighted average of the betas of the individual assets it includes. It can be easily estimated using the betas of the component assets. To find the portfolio beta, b_p, we can use Equation 16.2:

portfolio beta, b_p
the beta of a portfolio; calculated as the weighted average of the betas of the individual assets the portfolio includes.

Equation 16.2

$$\text{Portfolio beta} = \begin{pmatrix} \text{proportion of} \\ \text{portfolio's total} \\ \text{dollar value} \\ \text{represented by} \\ \text{Asset 1} \end{pmatrix} \times \begin{matrix} \text{beta} \\ \text{for} \\ \text{Asset 1} \end{matrix} + \begin{pmatrix} \text{proportion of} \\ \text{portfolio's total} \\ \text{dollar value} \\ \text{represented by} \\ \text{Asset 2} \end{pmatrix} \times \begin{matrix} \text{beta} \\ \text{for} \\ \text{Asset 2} \end{matrix} + \cdots +$$

$$\begin{pmatrix} \text{proportion of} \\ \text{portfolio's total} \\ \text{dollar value} \\ \text{represented by} \\ \text{Asset } n \end{pmatrix} \times \begin{matrix} \text{beta} \\ \text{for} \\ \text{Asset } n \end{matrix} = \sum_{j=1}^{n} \begin{pmatrix} \text{proportion of} \\ \text{portfolio's total} \\ \text{dollar value} \\ \text{represented by} \\ \text{Asset } j \end{pmatrix} \times \begin{matrix} \text{beta} \\ \text{for} \\ \text{Asset } j \end{matrix}$$

Equation 16.2a

$$b_p = (w_1 \times b_1) + (w_2 \times b_2) + \cdots + (w_n \times b_n) = \sum_{j=1}^{n} (w_j \times b_j)$$

Of course $\sum_{j=1}^{n} w_j = 1$, which means that 100 percent of the portfolio's assets must be included in this computation.

Portfolio betas are interpreted in exactly the same way as individual asset betas. They indicate the degree of responsiveness of the portfolio's return to changes in the market return. For example, when the market return increases by 10 percent, a portfolio with a beta of .75 will experience a 7.5 percent increase in its return (.75 × 10%), whereas a portfolio with a beta of 1.25 will experience a 12.5 percent increase in its return (1.25 × 10%). Low-beta portfolios are less responsive and therefore less risky than high-beta portfolios. Clearly, a portfolio containing mostly low-beta assets will have a low beta, and vice versa.

To demonstrate, consider the Austin Fund, a large investment company that wishes to assess the risk of two portfolios—V and W. Both portfolios contain five assets, with the proportions and betas shown in Table 16.5. The

Table 16.5 Austin Fund's Portfolios V and W

Asset	Portfolio V Proportion	Portfolio V Beta	Portfolio W Proportion	Portfolio W Beta
1	.10	1.65	.10	.80
2	.30	1.00	.10	1.00
3	.20	1.30	.20	.65
4	.20	1.10	.10	.75
5	.20	1.25	.50	1.05
Total	1.00		1.00	

betas for Portfolios V and W, b_v and b_w, can be calculated by substituting the appropriate data from the table into Equation 16.2, as follows:

$$b_v = (.10 \times 1.65) + (.30 \times 1.00) + (.20 \times 1.30) + (.20 \times 1.10) + (.20 \times 1.25)$$
$$= .165 + .300 + .260 + .220 + .250 = 1.195 \approx \underline{\underline{1.20}}$$
$$b_w = (.10 \times .80) + (.10 \times 1.00) + (.20 \times .65) + (.10 \times .75) + (.50 \times 1.05)$$
$$= .080 + .100 + .130 + .075 + .525 = \underline{\underline{.91}}$$

Portfolio V's beta is 1.20, and Portfolio W's is .91. These values make sense because Portfolio V contains relatively high-beta assets and Portfolio W contains relatively low-beta assets. Clearly, Portfolio V's returns are more responsive to changes in market returns—and therefore more risky—than Portfolio W's.

Using Portfolio Betas The usefulness of beta depends on how well it explains relative return fluctuations. The *coefficient of determination (R²)* can be used to statistically evaluate a beta coefficient. That is, it indicates the percentage of the change in the return on an individual security that is explained by its relationship with the market return. R^2 can range from 0 to 1.0. If a regression equation has an R^2 of 0, none (0 percent) of the variation in the security's return is explained by its relationship with the market. An R^2 of 1.0 indicates the existence of perfect correlation (100 percent) between a security and the market.

Beta is much more useful in explaining a portfolio's return fluctuations than a security's return fluctuations. A well-diversified stock portfolio will have a beta equation R^2 of around .90. This means that 90 percent of the stock portfolio's fluctuations are related to changes in the stock market as a whole. Individual security betas have a wide range of R^2s but tend to be in the .20 to .50 range. Other factors (diversifiable risk, in particular) also cause individual security prices to fluctuate. When securities are combined in a well-diversified portfolio, most of the fluctuation in that portfolio's return is caused by the movement of the entire stock market.

Interpreting Portfolio Betas If a portfolio has a beta of +1.0, the portfolio experiences changes in its rate of return equal to changes in the market's rate of return. This means the +1.0 beta portfolio would tend to experience a 10 percent increase in return if the stock market as a whole experienced a 10 percent increase in return. Conversely, if the market return fell by 6 percent, the return on the +1.0 beta portfolio would also fall by 6 percent.

Table 16.6 lists the expected returns for three portfolio betas in two situations: an increase in market return of 10 percent and a decrease in market return of 10 percent. The 2.0 beta portfolio is twice as volatile as the market. When the market return increases by 10 percent, the portfolio return increases by 20 percent. Conversely, the portfolio's return will fall by 20 percent when the market has a decline in return of 10 percent. This portfolio would be considered a relatively high-risk, high-return portfolio. The middle, .5 beta portfolio is considered a relatively low-risk, low-return portfolio—a conservative portfolio for investors who wish to maintain a low-risk investment posture. The .5 beta portfolio is half as volatile as the market. A portfolio with a beta of −1.0 moves opposite the direction of the market. A bearish investor would probably want to own a negative-beta portfolio, because this type of invest-

Table 16.6 Portfolio Betas and Associated Changes in Returns

Portfolio Beta	Change in Return on Market	Change in Expected Return on Portfolio
+2.0	+10.0%	+20.0%
	−10.0	−20.0
+ .5	+10.0	+5.0
	−10.0	−5.0
−1.0	+10.0	−10.0
	−10.0	+10.0

ment tends to rise in value when the stock market declines, and vice versa. Finding securities with negative betas is difficult, however. Most securities have positive betas, because they tend to experience return movements in the same direction as changes in the stock market.

The Risk-Return Tradeoff: Some Closing Comments

Another valuable outgrowth of modern portfolio theory is the specific delineation between nondiversifiable risk and investment return. The basic premise is that an investor must have a portfolio of relatively risky investments to earn a relatively high rate of return. That relationship is illustrated in Figure 16.6. The upward-sloping line shows the **risk-return tradeoff**. The point where the risk-return line crosses the return axis is called the **risk-free rate,** R_F. This is the return an investor can earn on a risk-free investment such as a U.S. Treasury bill or an insured money market account. As we proceed upward along the line, portfolios of risky investments appear. For example, four investment portfolios, A through D, are depicted. Portfolios A and B are investment opportunities that provide a level of return commensurate with their respective risk levels. Portfolio C provides a high return at a relatively low risk level—and therefore would be an excellent investment. Portfolio D, in contrast, offers high risk but low return—an investment to avoid.

risk-return tradeoff
the positive relationship between the risk associated with a given investment and its expected return.

risk-free rate, R_F
the return an investor can earn on a risk-free investment such as a U.S. Treasury bill or an insured money market account.

Figure 16.6 The Portfolio Risk-Return Tradeoff
As the risk of an investment portfolio increases from zero, the return provided should increase above the risk-free rate, R_F. Portfolios A and B offer returns commensurate with their risk, Portfolio C provides a high return at a low-risk level, and Portfolio D provides a low return for high risk. Portfolio C is highly desirable; Portfolio D should be avoided.

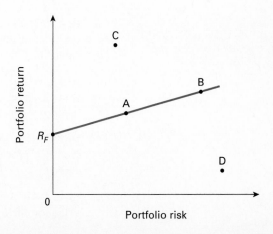

RECONCILING THE TRADITIONAL APPROACH AND MPT

We have reviewed two fairly different approaches to portfolio management—the traditional approach and MPT. The question that naturally arises is, Which technique should be used by the individual investor? There is no definite answer; the question must be resolved by the judgment of each investor. However, we can offer a few useful ideas. The average individual investor does not have the resources, computers, and mathematical acumen to implement an MPT portfolio strategy. Although most individual investors find total MPT portfolio management impractical, they can extract and use ideas from *both* MPT and the traditional approach. The traditional approach stresses security selection using fundamental and technical analysis. It also emphasizes diversification of the portfolio across industry lines. MPT stresses negative correlations between rates of return for the security issues within the portfolio. This approach calls for diversification, to minimize diversifiable risk. So, following either strategy, diversification must be accomplished to ensure satisfactory performance.

Beta is a useful tool for determining the level of a portfolio's nondiversifiable risk and should be part of the decision-making process. We recommend the following portfolio management policy:

- Determine how much risk you are willing to bear.
- Seek diversification among different types of securities and across industry lines, and pay attention to how the return from one security is related to another.
- Consider how a security responds to the market, and use beta in diversifying your portfolio as a way to keep the portfolio in line with your acceptable level of risk.
- Evaluate alternative portfolios to make sure that the portfolio selected provides the highest return for the given level of acceptable risk.

CONCEPTS *in Review*

16.7 Describe *traditional portfolio management*. Give three reasons why traditional portfolio managers like to invest in well-established companies. Explain each reason.

16.8 What is *modern portfolio theory (MPT)*? What is the feasible or attainable set of all possible portfolios? How is it derived for a given group of investment vehicles?

16.9 What is the *efficient frontier*? How does it relate to the feasible or attainable set of all possible portfolios? How can it be used with an investor's utility function or risk-indifference curves to find the optimal portfolio?

16.10 Define and differentiate between the diversifiable, nondiversifiable, and total risk of a portfolio. Which is considered the *relevant risk*? How is it measured?

16.11 Define beta. How can you find the beta of a portfolio when you know the betas for each of the assets included within it?

16.12 What does the coefficient of determination (R^2) for the regression equation used to derive a beta coefficient indicate? Would this statistic indicate that beta is more useful in explaining the return fluctuations of individual assets than of portfolios?

16.13 Are there any particular techniques an investor can use as part of a portfolio strategy? Explain how traditional and modern portfolio approaches can be reconciled.

CONSTRUCTING A PORTFOLIO USING AN ASSET ALLOCATION SCHEME

In this section we will examine the criteria that can be used to construct a portfolio. We will look at investor characteristics and objectives and at portfolio objectives and policies. We then will use these factors to develop a plan for allocating assets in various investment categories. This plan provides a basic, useful framework for selecting individual investment vehicles for the portfolio. In attempting to weave the concepts of risk and diversification into a solid portfolio policy, we will rely on both traditional and modern approaches to plan and construct an investment portfolio.

INVESTOR CHARACTERISTICS AND OBJECTIVES

An investor's financial and family situations are important inputs in determining portfolio policy. The following are vital determinants: level and stability of income, family factors, net worth, investor experience and age, and disposition toward risk. The portfolio strategy of an individual investor obviously must be tailored to meet that person's needs. The types of investments in the portfolio depend upon relative income needs and ability to bear risk: A young investor might have an aggressive investment policy, whereas a married investor with young children would probably not be seeking high-risk investments until some measure of financial security had been provided for the family, whereupon more risky ventures could be undertaken. Simply stated, *an investor's risk exposure should not exceed that person's ability to bear risk.*

The size of income and the certainty of an investor's employment also bear on portfolio strategy. An investor with a secure job is more likely to embark on a risk-oriented investment program than one who has a less secure position. Income taxes bear on the investment decision as well. The higher an investor's income, the more important the tax ramifications of an investment program become. An individual's investment experience also influences the appropriate investment strategy. It normally is best to "get one's feet wet" in the investment market by slipping into it gradually rather than leaping in headfirst. Very often, investors who make risky initial investments suffer heavy losses, damaging the long-run potential of their entire investment program. A cautiously developed investment program is likely to provide more favorable long-run results than an impulsive, risky one.

Once an investor has developed a personal financial profile, the next question is, "What do I want from my portfolio?" An investor must usually choose between earning a high current income from an investment portfolio or obtaining significant capital appreciation from it. It is difficult to have both. The price of having high appreciation potential in the portfolio is often low current income potential.

The investor's needs may determine which avenue is chosen. For instance, a retired investor whose income depends on his or her portfolio will probably choose a lower-risk, current-income-oriented approach. In contrast, a high-income, financially secure investor (e.g., a physician) may be much more willing to take on risky investments in the hope of improving net worth. Thus, it should be clear that a portfolio must be built around the individual's needs, which depend on income, responsibilities, financial resources, age, retirement plans, and ability to bear risk.

PORTFOLIO OBJECTIVES AND POLICIES

Constructing a portfolio is a logical activity and is best done after careful analysis of the investor's needs and of the available investment vehicles. The following objectives should be considered when planning and constructing a portfolio: current income needs, capital preservation, capital growth, tax considerations, and risk.

Any one or more of these factors will play an influential role in defining the desirable type of portfolio for an investor. For convenience, these factors can be tied together as follows: The first two items, current income and capital preservation, are portfolio objectives synonymous with a low-risk, conservative investment strategy. Normally, a portfolio with this orientation contains low-beta (low-risk) securities. A capital growth objective (the third item) implies increased risk and a reduced level of current income. Higher-risk growth stocks, real estate, gold, options, futures, and other more speculative investments may be suitable for this investor. An investor's tax bracket (the fourth item) will influence investment strategy. A high-income investor probably wishes to defer taxes and earn investment returns in the form of capital gains. This implies a strategy of higher-risk investments and a longer holding period. Lower-bracket investors are less concerned with how they earn the income, and they may wish to invest in higher current income vehicles. The most important item an investor must decide upon is risk (the final item). The risk-return tradeoff should be considered *in all investment decisions*.

DEVELOPING AN ASSET ALLOCATION SCHEME

Once an investor's needs are converted into specific portfolio objectives, a portfolio designed to achieve these goals can be constructed. Before buying any investment vehicles, however, the investor must develop an *asset allocation scheme*. **Asset allocation** involves dividing one's portfolio into various asset classes, such as U.S. stocks, U.S. bonds, foreign securities, short-term securities, and other vehicles like tangibles (especially gold) and real estate. The emphasis of asset allocation is on *preservation of capital*—protecting against negative developments while still taking advantage of positive developments. Asset allocation, although similar to diversification in its objective, is a bit different: Its focus is on *investment in various asset classes*, whereas diversification tends to focus more on investing in various vehicles *within* an asset class.

Asset allocation is based upon the belief that the total return of a portfolio is influenced more by the division of investments into asset classes than by the

asset allocation
a scheme that involves dividing one's portfolio into various asset classes to preserve capital by protecting against negative developments and taking advantage of positive ones.

actual investments. In fact, studies have shown that as much as 90 percent or more of a portfolio's *return* comes from asset allocation. Therefore, less than 10 percent can be attributed to the actual security selection. Furthermore, researchers have found that asset allocation has a much greater impact on reducing *total risk* than selecting the best investment vehicle in any single asset category does. Clearly, asset allocation is an important aspect of portfolio management.

Approaches to Asset Allocation

There are three basic approaches to asset allocation. The first two—fixed weightings and flexible weightings—differ with respect to the proportions of each asset category maintained in the portfolio. The third—tactical asset allocation—is a more exotic technique frequently used by sophisticated institutional portfolio managers.

fixed-weightings approach
asset allocation plan in which a fixed percentage of the portfolio is allocated to each asset category.

Fixed Weightings   Under the **fixed-weightings approach,** a fixed percentage of the portfolio is allocated to each of the asset categories, of which there typically are three to five. Assuming four categories—common stocks, bonds, foreign securities, and short-term securities—a fixed allocation might be:

Category	Allocation
Common stock	30%
Bonds	50
Foreign securities	15
Short-term securities	5
Total portfolio	100%

Generally, the fixed weightings do not change over time. Because of shifting market values, the portfolio may have to be adjusted annually or after major market moves to maintain the desired fixed-percentage allocations.

Fixed weights may or may not represent equal percentage allocations to each category. One could, for example, allocate 25 percent to each of the four categories above. Research has shown that over the 1967–1988 period, equal (20 percent) allocations to U.S. stocks, foreign stocks, long-term bonds, cash, and real estate resulted in a portfolio that outperformed the S&P 500 in terms of both return and risk. These findings add further support to the importance of even a somewhat naive "buy and hold" asset allocation strategy.

flexible weightings approach
asset allocation plan in which weights for each asset category are adjusted periodically based on market or technical analysis.

Flexible Weightings   The **flexible weightings approach** involves the periodic adjustment of the weights for each asset category based either on market analysis or on technical analysis (i.e., market timing). The use of a flexible weighting scheme is often called *strategic asset allocation.* For example, the initial and new allocation based on a flexible weighting scheme may be:

Category	Initial Allocation	New Allocation
Common stock	30%	45%
Bonds	40	40
Foreign securities	15	10
Short-term securities	15	5
Total portfolio	100%	100%

tactical asset allocation
asset allocation plan that uses stock-index futures and bond futures to change a portfolio's asset allocation.

The new allocation may have resulted from an expectation of lower inflation, which was expected to result in increased domestic stock and bond prices and a decline in foreign and short-term security returns. The weightings were therefore changed to capture greater returns in a changing market.

Tactical Asset Allocation   The third approach, **tactical asset allocation**, uses stock-index futures and bond futures (see Chapter 15) to change a portfolio's asset allocation. When stocks seem less attractive than bonds, this strategy involves selling stock-index futures and buying bond futures. Conversely, when bonds seem less attractive than stocks, the strategy results in buying stock-index futures and selling bond futures. Because this sophisticated technique relies on a large portfolio and the use of quantitative models for cues, it is generally appropriate only for large institutional investors.

Asset Allocation Alternatives

Assuming the use of a fixed-weight asset allocation plan and using, say, four asset categories—common stock, bonds, foreign securities, and short-term securities—we can demonstrate three asset allocations. Table 16.7 shows allocations in each of the categories for a conservative (low-return–low-risk), moderate (average-return–average-risk), and aggressive (high-return–high-risk) portfolio. The conservative allocation relies heavily on bonds and short-term securities to provide predictable returns. The moderate allocation includes mostly common stock and bonds and more foreign securities and fewer short-term securities than the conservative allocation. Its moderate return-risk behavior reflects a move away from safe short-term securities to a larger dose of common stock and foreign securities than under the conservative allocation. Finally, as we move to the aggressive portfolio, more dollars are allocated to common stock, fewer to bonds, and more to foreign securities, thereby generally increasing the expected portfolio return and risk.

Applying Asset Allocation

An asset allocation plan should consider the economic outlook and the individual's investments, savings and spending patterns, tax situation, return expectations, risk tolerance, and so forth. Such plans must be formulated for the long run, stress capital preservation, and provide for periodic revision to maintain consistency with changing investment goals. As your portfolio

Table 16.7 Alternative Asset Allocations

	Allocation Alternative		
Category	Conservative (low-return–low-risk)	Moderate (average-return–average-risk)	Aggressive (high-return–high-risk)
Common stock	15%	30%	40%
Bonds	45	40	30
Foreign securities	5	15	25
Short-term securities	35	15	5
Total portfolio	100%	100%	100%

INVESTOR INSIGHTS: *Investing in Action*

Taming the Portfolio Monster

As your portfolio grows in number and type of investments, it's easy to become overwhelmed and confused by the paperwork you accumulate. Before long, you might lose control of your investments or lose track of important details, such as why you bought that stock in the first place! Says Roger Gibson, author of *Asset Allocation: Balancing Financial Risk*, "People tend to build portfolios the way they pick up seashells on the beach . . . based on whatever catches a person's eye." As a result, many investors don't know if the parts of their portfolio make sense when taken together.

A good place to start is by taking stock of your financial assets. That means sorting through stacks of paper: mutual fund "welcome" kits, prospectuses, annual and quarterly reports on companies whose securities you own, and brokerage firm and mutual fund statements. St. Cloud, Minnesota, financial planner Sandra Johnson suggests dividing the documents based on statements you get. For example, all statements from the brokerage firm where you have several stocks and bonds go in one pile, with the most recent on top. Always keep your original transaction confirmations. You can throw out items you no longer need, such as welcome kits, old annual reports, and monthly or quarterly statements whose information is included in your annual statement. Then file each set of documents in individual file folders or in a three-ring binder.

Next, set up tables by asset categories, such as cash/cash equivalents, domestic bonds, international bonds, domestic stocks, international stocks, mutual funds, real estate, and precious metals, and list each bond, stock, or mutual fund within its category. If one invest-

ment falls into two or more categories—such as a 401(k) retirement plan with both bond and stock investments or an asset allocation fund—divide it accordingly. Your tables should include columns for *total value* (based on current share price or fund net asset value), *interest rate* or *total return*, *maturity date* (for bonds; for a bond fund, use its average weighted maturity), *yield*, and the *investment's purpose*. Be sure to include all your assets; don't forget employee retirement funds or IRAs.

With your record-keeping system in place, you can more easily control your portfolio and see which investments are profitable and which are not. You may discover that you have many small, similar investments that can be consolidated to simplify your portfolio while still achieving your objectives. Do you really need three stockbrokers, or can you combine your accounts at one firm? The same goes for mutual funds. You may want to concentrate on one or two large fund families with many fund choices. Your lists also make it easy to compare your performance to market indexes or other measures and to quickly see how your actual asset allocation compares with your target weights. And at tax time, your records will provide the necessary details about securities you sold during the year, such as the purchase and sales dates, the number of shares you bought/sold, and the purchase and sale prices.

Sources: Adapted from William Giese, "Get Tough with Your Portfolio," *Kiplinger's Personal Finance Magazine*, April 1994, pp. 83–88; and Steven T. Goldberg, "An Investing Plan for a Lifetime," *Kiplinger's Personal Finance Magazine*, August 1994, p. 40.

grows, and over the long run, you'll find it extremely useful to keep good records of your transactions, as the *Investor Insights* box above describes.

Generally, to decide on the appropriate asset mix, investors must evaluate each asset category relative to current return, growth potential, safety, liquidity, transactions costs (brokerage fees), and potential tax savings. Many investors use mutual funds (see Chapter 11) as part of their asset allocation activities, to diversify within each asset category. As an alternative to constructing your own portfolio, however, you can buy shares in an **asset allocation fund**—a mutual fund that seeks to reduce variability of returns by

asset allocation fund
a mutual fund that seeks to reduce the variability of returns by investing in the right assets at the right time; emphasizes diversification and relatively consistent performance rather than the potential for spectacular gains.

investing in the right assets at the right time. These funds, like all asset allocation schemes, emphasize diversification and perform at a relatively consistent level by passing up the potential for spectacular gains in favor of predictability. Some asset allocation funds use fixed weightings, whereas others have flexible weights that change within prescribed limits. As a rule, investors with more than about $50,000 to invest and adequate time can justify do-it-yourself asset allocation, those with between $5,000 and $50,000 and adequate time can use mutual funds to create a workable asset allocation, and those with less than $5,000 or with limited time may find asset allocation funds most attractive. Major Wall Street firms now offer individual investors asset allocation advice. Their approaches and recommendations may differ, however.

Most importantly, you should recognize that to be effective, an asset allocation scheme *must be designed for the long haul*. Develop an asset allocation scheme you can live with for at least seven to ten years, and perhaps longer. Once you have it set, stick with it. The key to success involves remaining faithful to your asset allocation; that means fighting the temptation to wander.

CONCEPTS *in Review*

16.14 What role, if any, do an investor's personal characteristics play in determining portfolio policy? Explain.

16.15 What role do an investor's portfolio objectives play in constructing a portfolio?

16.16 What is *asset allocation*? How does it differ from diversification? What role does asset allocation play in constructing an investment portfolio?

16.17 Briefly describe the three basic approaches to asset allocation: (a) fixed weightings, (b) flexible weightings, and (c) tactical asset allocation.

16.18 Describe the procedures used to apply asset allocation. What role could an *asset allocation fund* play in this process?

PORTFOLIO PLANNING IN ACTION

In this section we will analyze four portfolios that have been developed to meet four different investment objectives. The principles and ideas discussed throughout this book will be applied to these four situations.

In each of the analyses that follow, the objectives and the portfolios are real, although the investors' and securities' names are fictitious. When possible, asset allocation weights are given. The specific reasons why a stock or bond is included in the portfolio are also given (the portfolios include only stocks and bonds). As a useful exercise, you might want to consider each situation and develop your own recommendations using current investment information.

The four cases have different risk-return profiles because the investors for whom the portfolios are designed have different incomes and lifestyles. Each portfolio relies heavily on the *traditional approach*, with the following exceptions: First, the number of securities in each portfolio is *below the normal number* the traditional portfolio manager would be likely to recommend. In line with MPT, it is assumed that the proper interindustry diversification can be achieved with the careful selection of 8 to 12 securities in a $100,000 portfolio. A larger portfolio might have more securities, but it would probably also have fewer securities than a traditionalist might recommend. Second, beta is utilized to quantify risk in the all-equity portfolios. Thus, these examples blend elements of modern portfolio theory (MPT) with the traditional approach to portfolio management.

Dara Yasakawa: Woman Wonder

At age 28, Dara Yasakawa has done well for herself. She has built a $300,000 investment portfolio consisting of investment real estate in Honolulu, Hawaii, with a current market value of $240,000, and $60,000 in short-term investments. Her current asset allocation is therefore 80 percent real estate ($240,000 ÷ $300,000) and 20 percent short-term investments ($60,000 ÷ $300,000). Ms. Yasakawa is currently employed as the controller of Kamehameha Management, a real estate management firm in Honolulu. She is a CPA, and her income from salary and property rentals is $75,000 per year, putting her in a 35 percent marginal income tax bracket (federal and Hawaii state income tax combined). Ms. Yasakawa is single, and her only debts are secured by her properties.

Dara Yasakawa has decided to diversify her portfolio. Most of her net worth consists of rental condominiums located in the Waikiki area of Honolulu. Clearly, diversification is needed to reduce her risk exposure and to increase her overall investment return. The Hawaii real estate market is somewhat unpredictable, and Ms. Yasakawa wishes to lessen her risk exposure in that market. She asked her investment adviser, Marjorie Wong, to help her diversify into common stock. Marjorie recommended selling one of Dara's properties for $60,000 and selling $15,000 in short-term securities to obtain $75,000 to invest in common stock. The resulting asset allocation would be 60 percent real estate ($180,000 ÷ $300,000), 25 percent common stock ($75,000 ÷ $300,000), and 15 percent short-term securities ($45,000 ÷ $300,000). Because of her relatively young age and her strong future earning capacity, Ms. Yasakawa can bear the risks of a speculative investment program. Her portfolio of stocks will emphasize issues that have a strong price appreciation potential.

Ms. Yasakawa's common stock portfolio is presented in Table 16.8. It consists of eight stocks, all of which have above-average risk-return potential. The betas of the issues range from 1.13 to 2.31; the portfolio's beta (calculated using Equation 16.2) is approximately 1.59, indicating an above-average risk exposure. The portfolio is diversified across industry lines, with a fairly wide mix of securities. All are selected for their above-average price appreciation potential. Altuna Airlines, an interisland carrier in Hawaii, was chosen because of the expected increase in the number of visitors to Hawaii. Betta Computer is a fast growing personal computer manufacturer. Easy Work, Inc., is a growing retailer that services the do-it-yourself home improvement market. Gomez Industries is a rapidly expanding glass manufacturer and photo processor. Hercules is a growing brewer. Jama Motor, based in Japan, provides a measure of international diversification for the portfolio. Karl

Table 16.8   Dara Yasakawa's Common Stock Portfolio

		Objective: Speculative Growth (High-Risk, High-Return Potential)					
Number of Shares	Company	Dividend per Share	Dividend Income	Price per Share	Total Cost (including commission)	Beta	Dividend Yield
1,200	Altuna Airlines	$ —	$ —	$ 7	$ 8,480	1.75	—%
300	Betta Computer	—	—	30	9,090	1.87	—
400	Easy Work, Inc.	—	—	25	10,090	1.59	—
300	Gomez Industries	0.36	108	30	9,090	1.19	1.2
300	Hercules Brewing	0.80	240	32	9,700	1.27	2.5
300	Jama Motor ADR	0.35	105	33	10,000	1.13	1.1
500	Karl Lewis Enterprises	—	—	20	10,100	1.79	—
1,300	Ranch Petroleum	—	—	6	7,880	2.31	—
	Total		$453		$74,430		0.6%

Portfolio beta = 1.59

Lewis Enterprises is an expanding fast-food operator based in California. Ranch Petroleum is a small oil company with refining and oil-production interests.

Most of the securities Ms. Wong selected for Ms. Yasakawa are not "household names." Rather, they are firms with exciting growth potential. Given the portfolio's beta, Dara's holdings should fluctuate in value at a rate approximately 1.6 times greater than the stock market as a whole. The dividend yield on the portfolio is a relatively low 0.6 percent. Most of the return Ms. Yasakawa anticipates from this portfolio is in the form of price appreciation. She plans to hold the stocks for at least three to five years to realize this anticipated appreciation. Given Ms. Yasakawa's relatively high marginal income tax bracket, it seems preferable for her to defer taxes and earn returns in the form of capital gains.

BOB AND GAIL WEISS: LOTTERY WINNERS

Bob Weiss, a professor of political science at the University of West Bay City in Michigan, and his wife, Gail, are lucky people. After buying a $1 Michigan State Lottery ticket, Professor Weiss won $275,000. After paying income taxes on the prize and after spending a small amount for personal needs, Bob and Gail had $210,000 remaining. Because of their philosophy of saving any wind-falls and not spending accumulated capital on day-to-day living expenses, they chose to invest these funds (in contrast with many lottery winners, who simply blow their winnings on fast living).

The Weisses have two young children. Bob Weiss is 37 years of age and has a secure teaching position. His salary is approximately $60,000 per year. In addition, he earns approximately $15,000 per year from his book publishing royalties and from several other small sources. Professor Weiss's tax bracket (federal and state) is approximately 30 percent. His life insurance protection of approximately $90,000 is provided by the university. Bob's wife, Gail, is a librarian. She currently is at home with their children and is not expected to be a source of steady income for another several years. The Weiss family owns (free and clear) their home in Bay City. In addition, they have about $40,000 in a money market mutual fund. Therefore, their asset allocation prior to the lottery windfall was 100 percent money funds ($40,000 ÷ $40,000). They have no outstanding debts.

Professor Weiss asked his investment adviser, Gene Bowles, to develop an investment portfolio for them. Together, they decided on the following strategy: First, the professor and his wife tend to be somewhat risk-averse; that is, they do not wish to bear inordinate amounts of risk of loss. In addition, the Weisses indicated they would welcome some increase in spendable income. Given these facts, Mr. Bowles suggested the portfolio presented in Table 16.9. With this portfolio their asset allocation would become about 84 percent common stock ($210,000 ÷ $250,000) and 16 percent money funds ($40,000 ÷ $250,000). The emphasis in the portfolio is long-term growth at an average risk level, with a moderate dividend return. The portfolio consists of nine issues, which appears to be sufficient diversification. The portfolio's beta is 1.04, indicating a level of nondiversifiable risk that approximately equals that of the stock market as a whole. The portfolio's dividend yield is about 4.9 percent, which approximates the average dividend return for the entire stock market. The betas of individual securities in the portfolio vary somewhat. However, the portfolio's overall risk is moderate.

The Weiss portfolio consists of stocks from a wide range of American business. All the companies have above-average growth potential, and none is engaged in high-risk businesses that could face technological obsolescence or heavy foreign competition. Two banking stocks are included, Bancorp West, Inc., and Florida Southcoast Banks. The former is a well-managed bank holding company that owns the largest bank in California. The latter is a growing bank holding company located on the south coast of Florida. Both regions are experiencing rapid population and economic growth. BST, Inc., appears to be well positioned in the growing communications industry. Kings is a food processor with a solid future. Light Newspapers is a large chain with many Sunbelt papers. Miller Foods is expanding as well, helped by the 1995 acquisition of Denton Companies, a superbly managed supermarket chain.

Table 16.9   Bob and Gail Weiss's Common Stock Portfolio

	Objective: Long-Term Growth (Average Risk, Moderate Dividends)						
Number of Shares	Company	Dividend per Share	Dividend Income	Price per Share	Total Cost (including commission)	Beta	Dividend Yield
1,000	Bancorp West, Inc.	$1.20	$ 1,200	$22	$ 22,200	.86	5.4%
600	BST, Inc.	2.80	1,680	40	24,200	1.00	6.9
1,000	Florida Southcoast Banks	1.20	1,200	23	23,200	.84	5.2
1,000	Kings	1.60	1,600	25	25,300	.88	6.3
500	Light Newspapers	0.92	460	46	23,200	1.12	2.0
600	Miller Foods	1.88	1,128	37	22,400	1.07	5.0
800	State Oil of California	1.00	800	27	21,800	1.30	3.7
600	Vornox	2.28	1,368	40	24,200	1.04	5.7
600	Woodstock	1.30	780	36	21,800	1.32	3.6
	Total		$10,216		$208,300		4.9%

Portfolio beta = 1.04

The portfolio has two natural resource stocks, State Oil and Woodstock. These companies are well positioned in their respective industries. Vornox is a major drug firm that should benefit from America's aging demographic mix. All of the stocks in the Weisses' portfolio are securities of well-managed companies. With this portfolio, the Weisses will have potential price appreciation coupled with a steady dividend income.

JULIO AND GINA VITELLO: RETIREES

Having just sold their family business and liquidated their real estate investment property, Julio and Gina Vitello are eager to begin their retirement. At age 60, both have worked hard for 35 years building the successful business they recently sold. In addition, they have made some successful real estate investments over the years. The sale of their business and real estate holdings has netted them $600,000 after taxes. They wish to invest these funds and have asked their investment adviser, Jane Tuttle, to develop a portfolio for them. The relevant financial information about the Vitellos is as follows: They own their home free and clear and have a $300,000 bond portfolio that yields yearly income of $30,000. In addition, they have $100,000 in short-term securities that they wish to hold as a ready cash reserve. Their most recent asset allocation is therefore 60 percent business and real estate investments ($600,000 ÷ $1,000,000), 30 percent bonds ($300,000 ÷ $1,000,000), and 10 percent short-term securities ($100,000 ÷ $1,000,000). Mr. Vitello has a $200,000 whole life insurance policy on his life, with Mrs. Vitello the designated beneficiary.

Now that they are retired, neither of the Vitellos plans to seek employment. They do have a small pension plan that will begin paying an income of $6,000 per year in five years. However, their main source of income will be their investment portfolio. During their last few working years, their combined yearly income was approximately $90,000. Their standard of living is rather high, and they do not wish to significantly change their lifestyle. They do not plan to spend any of their investment capital on living expenses, because they wish to keep their estate intact for their two children. Thus, the Vitellos' basic investment objective is current income with some capital appreciation potential. The Vitellos do not wish to reinvest in real estate but, rather, have asked Ms. Tuttle to develop a $600,000 securities portfolio for them. (They will leave their $300,000 bond portfolio and $100,000 in short-term securities undisturbed.) Their resulting asset allocation would shift to 60 percent common stock, 30 percent bonds, and 10 percent short-term securities.

The portfolio developed for the Vitellos is shown in Table 16.10. It contains nine stocks with approximately $65,000 invested in each issue. The emphasis is on quality, with low-risk, high-yield issues, and diversification. The portfolio's beta is approximately .80—a risk level that is below that of the general stock market. It is expected that a large portion of the portfolio's total return (dividends plus price appreciation) will be in the form of dividend income. The portfolio has a current dividend yield of approximately 8.7 percent, an above-average dividend yield. Dividend income totals over $52,000, which, added to the bond income and the short-term securities' interest, will provide the Vitellos with a gross income of about $90,000. The Vitellos' after-

Table 16.10   Julio and Gina Vitello's Common Stock Portfolio

Number of Shares	Company	Dividend per Share	Dividend Income	Price per Share	Total Cost (including commission)	Beta	Dividend Yield
		Objective: Current Income (Low Risk, High Yield)					
3,000	Alaska Bancorp, Inc.	$1.20	$ 3,600	$22	$ 66,600	.86	5.4%
2,000	Dallas National Corporation	2.40	4,800	30	60,600	.81	7.9
2,500	Energon	3.00	7,500	27	68,100	1.01	11.0
2,000	Findly Power and Light	3.36	6,720	32	64,600	.63	10.4
2,000	Geoco	2.80	5,600	35	70,700	1.13	7.9
2,500	Gulf Gas and Electric	3.00	7,500	28	70,700	.53	10.6
4,000	Public Power Company	1.76	7,040	16	64,600	.72	10.9
2,500	Smith, Roberts & Company	1.36	3,400	27	68,100	.92	5.0
3,000	Southwest Utilities	2.04	6,120	21	63,600	.60	9.6
	Total		$52,280		$597,600		8.7%

Portfolio beta = .80

tax income will equal their working years' income; thus, they will not have to alter their lifestyle.

Analyzing the individual issues in the Vitellos' portfolio, we can see that four public utility stocks are included. Utility stocks are often suitable for low-risk, current-income-oriented portfolios. High-quality electric and natural gas concerns tend to have moderate growth in earnings and dividends. The four issues in the portfolio, Findly Power and Light, Gulf Gas and Electric, Public Power Company, and Southwest Utilities, have growing service areas and records of profit and dividend increases. The stocks of two large American companies, Energon and Smith, Roberts & Company, are included in the portfolio. Energon is a large U.S. energy company that offers a high dividend yield. Smith, Roberts is one of the largest retailers, and the company is now diversifying into information services. Two bank holding company stocks were also selected, Alaska Bancorp and Dallas National. Alaska Bancorp offers a top-quality vehicle to participate in Alaska's growth. Dallas National was selected because of its above-average dividend yield and because the firm is well positioned in the Dallas market. Additionally, the company has raised its dividend several times in recent years, and future dividend increases are expected. Geoco is a large company with chemical and other diversified operations. All the issues in the Vitellos' portfolio are well-known, relatively large corporations. Stability, low risk, and a relatively high dividend yield with some potential for increase characterize the stocks in this portfolio.

LUCILLE HATCH: WIDOW

Most retirees have less money to invest than the Vitellos in the preceding example. Lucille Hatch, age 70, was recently widowed. Between the estate of her late husband, her personal assets, and their jointly owned assets, Lucille has approximately $350,000 in liquid assets, all of it in savings and money market accounts (short-term investments). Her current asset allocation is therefore 100 percent short-term investments ($350,000 ÷ $350,000). Lucille owns her home free and clear. Other than the interest on her savings, her income consists of $700 per month from Social Security. Unfortunately, her husband's employer did not have a pension plan. She has turned to her investment adviser, Charles Puckett, to discuss strategy and to develop an investment policy.

Between Social Security and interest earned on her short-term investments, Mrs. Hatch's current income is approximately $35,000 annually. She wishes to increase that income, if possible, while only minimally raising her risk exposure. Mr. Puckett recommended the investment portfolio presented in Table 16.11. The portfolio's objective is to maximize current income while keeping risk at a low level. All of the money was invested in fixed-income securities, with approximately $296,000 going to high-quality corporate bonds and the balance ($54,000) retained in short-term investments to provide a substantial contingency reserve. The resulting asset allocation is about 85 percent bonds ($296,000 ÷ $350,000) and 15 percent short-term investments ($54,000 ÷ $350,000). By investing in the bond portfolio, Mrs. Hatch's yearly income will rise from approximately $35,000 to about $49,100 ($8,400 Social Security, $4,100 earnings on short-term investments, and $36,600 bond interest). This puts Mrs. Hatch in a 30 percent marginal tax bracket (federal and state tax combined). Taxable corporate bonds were recommended over tax-free municipal bonds because her after-tax rate of return would be greater with the former.

Turning to the portfolio, we see that there are six corporate bond issues that cost about $50,000 each. Each issuer is a high-quality company with a low risk of default. Mrs. Hatch's portfolio is diversified in several ways: First, it contains a mix of industrial, utility, railroad, and financial issues. The two

Table 16.11   Lucille Hatch's Bond Portfolio

			Objective: Maximize Current Income (Minimal Risk)				
Par Value	Issue	Standard & Poor's Bond Rating	Interest Income	Price	Total Cost	Yield to Maturity	Current Yield
$50,000	Boise Northern 12⅞% due 2017	A	$ 6,437.50	100	$ 50,000	12.875%	12.875%
50,000	Dalston Company 11½% due 2001	A	5,750.00	98	49,000	11.900	11.700
50,000	Maryland-Pacific 10.70% due 1999	A	5,350.00	97	48,500	11.600	11.000
50,000	Pacific Utilities 12⅞% due 2025	AA	6,437.50	100	50,000	12.875	12.875
50,000	Trans-States Telephone 12.70% due 2031	A	6,350.00	97	48,500	13.200	13.100
50,000	Urban Life 12½% due 2002	AA	6,250.00	100	50,000	12.500	12.500
	Total		$36,575.00		$296,000	12.500%	12.400%

utility bond issues are Pacific Utilities and Trans-States Telephone. Both companies are large and financially secure. The two industrial concerns, Dalston and Maryland-Pacific, are large as well. Boise Northern is a financially solid railroad, and Urban Life is a large, secure insurance company. A second added measure of diversification is attained by staggering the bonds' maturities. They mature in six different years: 1999, 2001, 2002, 2017, 2025, and 2031. The shorter-term bonds will provide ready cash when they mature, and they generally will fluctuate less in price than the longer-term ones. The portfolio has been diversified to keep the risk of loss low. By switching funds out of her short-term investments into bonds, Mrs. Hatch was able to increase her current income substantially while experiencing only a minimal increase in risk.

CONCEPTS *in Review*

16.19 Describe and contrast the expected portfolios for each of the following investors:

    a. A retired investor in need of income

    b. A high-income, financially secure investor

    c. A young investor with a secure job and no dependents

On Track with *STOCK-TRAK*®

Measuring Standard Deviation with STOCK-TRAK®

STOCK-TRAK® portfolio statements include the data necessary to calculate holding period returns and standard deviations. For the portfolio, the first holding period return is calculated by dividing the difference between the total portfolio value (found at the bottom of the first biweekly statement) and the original allocation by the original dollar allocation. That is:

$$\text{First HPR} = \frac{\text{total portfolio value} - \text{original dollar allocation}}{\text{original dollar allocation}}$$

The holding period return for the next two weeks would be the change in total portfolio value during that period divided by the first statement's ending total portfolio value. Applying this technique to data from each report results in multiple two-week holding period returns. Then, following the procedure outlined in the text, the portfolio's standard deviation can be easily calculated. (If the simulation is run for longer than three months, you may want to use monthly holding periods.) Note that standard deviation is calculated across time periods, not across individual securities.

SUMMARY Understand the objectives of portfolio management and the procedures used to calculate the return and standard deviation of a portfolio. A portfolio is a collection of investment vehicles assembled to achieve a common investment goal. It involves a tradeoff between risk and return, potential price appreciation and current income, and varying risk levels in the portfolio. The return on a portfolio is calculated as a weighted average of the returns of the assets from which it is formed. The standard deviation of a portfolio's returns is found by applying the same formula that is used to find the standard deviation of a single asset.

LG 2   **Discuss the concepts of correlation and diversification, their impact on portfolio risk and return, and the effectiveness, methods, and benefits of international diversification.** Correlation is a statistic used to measure the relationship, if any, between the returns on assets. To diversify, it is best to add assets with negatively correlated returns. In general, the less positive and more negative the correlation between asset returns, the more effectively a portfolio can be diversified to reduce its risk. Through diversification, the risk (standard deviation) of a portfolio can be reduced below the risk of the least risky asset (and sometimes to zero); however, the return of the resulting portfolio will be no lower than the smallest return of its component assets. International diversification may allow an investor to reduce portfolio risk without experiencing corresponding reduction in return. It can be achieved by investing abroad or through domestic investment in foreign companies or funds. The use of ADRs or international mutual funds available in the United States is generally preferable.

LG 3   **Review the two basic approaches to portfolio management—traditional management versus the modern approach—and reconcile them.** Under the traditional approach, portfolios are constructed by combining a large number of securities issued by companies from a broad cross-section of industries. Modern portfolio theory (MPT) uses statistical diversification to develop efficient portfolios. Theoretically, to determine the optimal portfolio, MPT finds the efficient frontier and couples it with an investor's utility function or risk-indifference curves. In practice, portfolio betas can be used to develop efficient portfolios consistent with the investor's risk-return preferences. Generally, investors use elements of both the traditional approach and MPT to create portfolios.

LG 4   **Describe the role of investor characteristics, investor objectives, and portfolio objectives and policies in planning and constructing an investment portfolio.** To construct a portfolio, the investor should consider characteristics such as level and stability of income, family factors, net worth, experience and age, and disposition toward risk. After an investor has developed a personal financial profile, he or she should specify objectives and plan and construct a portfolio consistent with them. Commonly considered portfolio objectives include current income, capital preservation, capital growth, tax considerations, and level of risk.

LG 5   **Summarize the motives and various approaches involved in using an asset allocation scheme to construct an investment portfolio consistent with the investor's objectives.** Asset allocation involves dividing one's portfolio into various asset classes, such as U.S. stocks, U.S. bonds, foreign securities, short-term securities, and other vehicles, in order to preserve capital. Similar to diversification, asset allocation aims to protect against negative developments while taking advantage of positive developments. The basic approaches to asset allocation involve the use of fixed weightings, flexible weightings, or tactical asset allocation—a sophisticated approach that uses futures contracts. Asset allocation can be achieved on a do-it-yourself basis, with the use of mutual funds, or by merely buying shares in an asset allocation fund.

LG 6   **Relate investor objectives to the asset allocations and risk-return profiles reflected in various types of portfolios.** An investor's objectives determine the asset allocations and risk-return profile reflected in his or her portfolio. A single investor who wants to build wealth quickly will tend to allocate funds to more risky assets that have high growth potential; a retired couple who needs income to meet their living expenses will allocate funds to conservative, low-risk investment vehicles that provide periodic income in the form of dividends or interest. The asset classes, their weightings, and the specific vehicles included in an investor's portfolio should be consistent with his or her personal financial and family characteristics and investment and portfolio objectives.

1.   State your portfolio objectives. Then construct a 10-stock portfolio (of companies that have been public for at least 5 years) that you feel is consistent with your objectives. Obtain annual dividend and price data on the stocks you've chosen for each of the past 5 years.

   a.   Calculate the historical return for each stock for each year.
   b.   Calculate the historical portfolio return for each of the 5 years, using your findings in part (a).
   c.   Use your findings in part (b) to calculate the average portfolio return over the 5 years.
   d.   Use your findings in parts (b) and (c) to find the standard deviation of the portfolio's returns over the 5-year period.
   e.   Use the historical average return from part (c) and standard deviation from part (d) to evaluate the portfolio's return and risk in light of your stated portfolio objectives.

2.   Choose, according to the following guidelines, the stocks—A, B, and C—of three firms that have been public for at least 10 years. Stock A should be one you are interested in buying. Stock B should be a stock, possibly in the same line of business or industry, you feel will have high positive return correlation with stock A. Finally, Stock C should be one you feel will have high negative return correlation with Stock A.

   a.   Calculate the annual rates of return for each of the past 10 years for each stock.
   b.   Plot the 10 annual return values for each stock on the same set of year (x-axis)–annual return in percentage terms (y-axis) axes.
   c.   Join the points for the returns for each stock on the graph. Evaluate and describe the returns of Stocks A and B in the graph. Do they exhibit the expected positive correlation? Why or why not?
   d.   Evaluate and describe the relationship between the returns of Stocks A and C in the graph. Do they exhibit the expected negative correlation? Why or why not?
   e.   Compare and contrast your findings in parts (c) and (d) to the expected relationships among Stocks A, B, and C. Discuss your findings.

3.   Obtain a prospectus for a major mutual fund that includes some international securities. Carefully read the prospectus and study the portfolio's composition in light of the fund's stated objectives.

   a.   Assess the fund manager's investment approach. Does the fund use a traditional approach, modern portfolio theory (MPT), or a combination of the two?
   b.   Evaluate the amount of diversification and the types of industries and companies held. Is the portfolio well diversified?
   c.   Assess the degree of international diversification achieved. Does management consciously include international securities to improve the fund's risk-return outcome?
   d.   Overall, how well does management seem to be managing the portfolio in light of the fund's stated objectives with regard to diversification?

4.   Use *Value Line* or some other source to select 6 stocks with betas ranging from about .5 to 1.5. Record the current market prices of each of these stocks. Assume you wish to create a portfolio that combines all 6 stocks in such a way that the resulting portfolio beta is about 1.1.

   a.   Through trial and error, use all 6 stocks to create a portfolio with the target beta of 1.1.

b. If you have $100,000 to invest in this portfolio, based on the weightings determined in part (a), how much in dollars would you invest in each stock?

c. Approximately how many shares of each of the 6 stocks would you buy given the dollar amounts calculated in part (b)?

d. Repeat parts (a), (b), and (c) above with a different set of weightings that still result in a portfolio beta of 1.1. Can only one unique portfolio with a given beta be created from a given set of stocks?

e. Why might the use of beta to measure the risk of the portfolios created in parts (a) and (d) not be an accurate measure of risk in this case? Explain.

5. List your personal characteristics and then state your investment objectives in light of them. Use these objectives as a basis for developing and stating your portfolio objectives and policies. Assume that you plan to create a portfolio aimed at achieving your stated objectives. The portfolio will be constructed by allocating your money to any of the following asset classes: common stock, bonds, foreign securities, short-term securities, and real estate.

a. Determine and justify an asset allocation to the 5 classes in light of your stated portfolio objectives and policies.

b. Describe the types of investments you would choose for each of the asset classes.

c. Assume that after making the asset allocations specified in part (a), you receive a sizable inheritance that causes your portfolio objectives to change to a much more aggressive posture. Describe the changes from those in part (a) that you would make in your asset allocations.

d. Describe other asset classes you might consider when developing your asset allocation scheme.

PROBLEMS 1. Assume you are considering a portfolio containing two assets, L and M. Asset L will represent 40 percent of the dollar value of the portfolio, and Asset M will account for the other 60 percent. The expected returns over the next 6 years, 1997–2002, for each of these assets, are summarized in the following table.

	Expected Return (%)	
Year	Asset L	Asset M
1997	14	20
1998	14	18
1999	16	16
2000	17	14
2001	17	12
2002	19	10

a. Calculate the expected portfolio return, r_p, for each of the 6 years.

b. Calculate the average expected portfolio return, $\bar{r}_p$, over the 6-year period.

c. Calculate the standard deviation of expected portfolio returns, s_p, over the 6-year period.

d. How would you characterize the correlation of returns of the two assets L and M?

e. Discuss any benefits of diversification achieved through creation of the portfolio.

2. You have been given the following return data on three assets—F, G, and H—over the period 1997–2000:

	Expected Return (%)		
Year	Asset F	Asset G	Asset H
1997	16	17	14
1998	17	16	15
1999	18	15	16
2000	19	14	17

Using these assets, you have isolated three investment alternatives:

Alternative	Investment
1	100% of Asset F
2	50% of Asset F and 50% of Asset G
3	50% of Asset F and 50% of Asset H

a. Calculate the portfolio return over the 4-year period for each of the three alternatives.
b. Calculate the standard deviation of returns over the 4-year period for each of the three alternatives.
c. Based on your findings above, which of the three investment alternatives would you recommend? Why?

3. You have been asked for your advice in selecting a portfolio of assets and have been supplied with the following data:

	Expected Return (%)		
Year	Asset A	Asset B	Asset C
1997	12	16	12
1998	14	14	14
1999	16	12	16

You have been told that you can create two portfolios—one consisting of Assets A and B and the other consisting of Assets A and C—by investing equal proportions (i.e., 50 percent) in each of the two component assets.

a. What is the average expected return, $\bar{r}$, for each asset over the 3-year period
b. What is the standard deviation, s, for each asset's expected return?
c. What is the average expected return, $\bar{r}_p$, for each of the two portfolios?
d. How would you characterize the correlations of returns of the two assets making up each of the two portfolios identified in part (c)?
e. What is the standard deviation of expected returns, s_p, for each portfolio?
f. Which portfolio do you recommend? Why?

4. Assume you wish to evaluate the risk and return behaviors associated with various combinations of Assets V and W under three assumed degrees of correlation—perfect positive, uncorrelated, and perfect negative. The following average return and risk values were calculated for each of the assets:

Asset	Average Return, $\bar{r}$ (%)	Risk (Standard Deviation), s (%)
V	8	5
W	13	10

a. If the returns of Assets V and W are *perfectly positively correlated* (correlation coefficient = +1), describe the *range* of (1) return and (2) risk associated with all possible portfolio combinations.

b. If the returns of Assets V and W are *uncorrelated* (correlation coefficient = 0), describe the *approximate range* of (1) return and (2) risk associated with all possible portfolio combinations.

c. If the returns of Assets V and W are *perfectly negatively correlated* (correlation coefficient = −1), describe the *range* of (1) return and (2) risk associated with all possible portfolio combinations.

5. Portfolios A through J, listed in the following table along with their returns (r_p) and risk (measured by the standard deviation, s_p), represent all currently available portfolios in the feasible or attainable set:

Portfolio	Return (r_p)	Risk (s_p)
A	9%	8%
B	3	3
C	14	10
D	12	14
E	7	11
F	11	6
G	10	12
H	16	16
I	5	7
J	8	4

a. Plot the *feasible or attainable set* represented by the data above on a set of portfolio risk, s_p (x-axis)–portfolio return, r_p (y-axis) axes.

b. Draw the *efficient frontier* on the graph in part (a).

c. Which portfolios lie on the efficient frontier? Why do these portfolios dominate all others in the feasible or attainable set?

d. How would an investor's *utility function* or *risk-indifference curves* be used with the efficient frontier to find the optimal portfolio?

6. For his portfolio, David Finney randomly selected securities from all those listed on the New York Stock Exchange. He began with one security and added securities one by one until a total of 20 securities were held in the portfolio. After each security was added, David calculated the portfolio standard deviation, s_p. The calculated values are given at the top of page 697:

Number of Securities	Portfolio Risk, s_p (%)	Number of Securities	Portfolio Risk, s_p (%)
1	14.50	11	7.00
2	13.30	12	6.80
3	12.20	13	6.70
4	11.20	14	6.65
5	10.30	15	6.60
6	9.50	16	6.56
7	8.80	17	6.52
8	8.20	18	6.50
9	7.70	19	6.48
10	7.30	20	6.47

a. On a set of axes showing number of securities in portfolio (*x*-axis) and portfolio risk, s_p (*y*-axis), plot the portfolio risk data given in the preceding table.

b. Divide the total portfolio risk in the graph into its *nondiversifiable* and *diversifiable* risk components and label each of these on the graph.

c. Describe which of the two risk components is the *relevant risk* and explain why it is relevant. How much of this risk exists in David Finney's portfolio?

LG 3 7. If Portfolio A has a beta of +1.5 and Portfolio Z has a beta of −1.5, what do the two values indicate? If the return on the market rises by 20 percent, what impact, if any, would this have on the returns from Portfolios A and Z? Explain.

LG 3 8. Stock A has a beta of 0.80, Stock B has a beta of 1.40, and Stock C has a beta of −0.30.

a. Rank these stocks from the most risky to the least risky.

b. If the return on the market portfolio increases by 12 percent, what change in the return for each of the stocks would you expect?

c. If the return on the market portfolio declines by 5 percent, what change in the return for each of the stocks would you expect?

d. If you felt the stock market was just ready to experience a significant decline, which stock would you most likely add to your portfolio? Why?

e. If you anticipated a major stock market rally, which stock would you most likely add to your portfolio? Why?

LG 3 9. Rose Berry is attempting to evaluate two possible portfolios—both consisting of the same 5 assets but held in different proportions. She is particularly interested in using beta to compare the risk of the portfolios and, in this regard, has gathered the following data:

Asset	Asset Beta	Portfolio Weights (%) Portfolio A	Portfolio B
1	1.30	10	30
2	.70	30	10
3	1.25	10	20
4	1.10	10	20
5	.90	40	20
Total		100	100

a. Calculate the betas for Portfolios A and B.

b. Compare the risk of each portfolio to the market as well as to each other. Which portfolio is more risky?

CASE PROBLEMS

16.1   TRADITIONAL VERSUS MODERN PORTFOLIO THEORY: WHO'S RIGHT?

Walt Davies and Shane O'Brien are district managers for Lee, Inc. Over the years, as they moved through the firm's sales organization, they became, and still remain, close friends. Walt, who is 33 years old, currently lives in Newark, New Jersey; Shane, who is 35, lives in Houston, Texas. Recently, at the national sales meeting, they were discussing various company matters, as well as bringing each other up to date on their families, when the subject of investments came up. Each of them had always been fascinated by the stock market, and now that they had achieved some degree of financial success, they had begun actively investing. As they discussed their investments, Walt indicated that he felt the only way an individual who does not have hundreds of thousands of dollars can invest safely is to buy mutual fund shares. He emphasized that to be safe, a person needs to hold a broadly diversified portfolio and that only those with a lot of money and time can achieve the needed diversification that can be readily obtained by purchasing mutual fund shares.

Shane totally disagreed. He said, "Diversification! Who needs it?" He felt that what one must do is to look carefully at stocks possessing desired risk-return characteristics and then invest all one's money in that one best stock. Walt told him he was crazy. He said, "There is no way to conveniently measure risk—you're just gambling." Shane disagreed. He explained how his stockbroker had acquainted him with beta, which is a measure of risk. Shane said that the higher the beta, the more risky the stock, and therefore the higher its return. By looking up the betas for potential stock investments in his broker's beta book, he can pick stocks having an acceptable risk level for him. Shane explained that with beta, one does not need to diversify; one merely needs to be willing to accept the risk reflected by beta and then hope for the best. The conversation continued, with Walt indicating that although he knew nothing about beta, he didn't believe one could safely invest in a single stock. Shane continued to argue that his broker had explained to him that betas can be calculated not just for a single stock but also for a portfolio of stocks, such as a mutual fund. He said, "What's the difference between a stock with a beta of, say, 1.20 and a mutual fund with a beta of 1.20? They both have the same risk and should therefore provide similar returns."

As Walt and Shane continued to discuss their differing opinions relative to investment strategy, they began to get angry with each other. Neither was able to convince the other that he was right. The level of their voices now raised, they attracted the attention of the company vice-president of finance, Elinor Green, who was standing nearby. She came over and indicated she had overheard their argument about investments and thought that, given her expertise on financial matters, she might be able to resolve their disagreement. She asked them to explain the crux of their disagreement, and each reviewed his own viewpoint. After hearing their views, Elinor responded, "I have some good news and some bad news for each of you. There is some validity to what each of you says, but there also are some errors in each of your explanations. Walt tends to support the traditional approach to portfolio management; Shane's views are more supportive of modern portfolio theory." Just then, the company president interrupted them, needing to talk to Elinor immediately. Elinor apologized for having to leave and made an arrangement to continue their discussion later that evening.

Questions

1. Analyze Walt's argument and explain why a mutual fund investment may be over-diversified. Also explain why one does not necessarily have to have hundreds of thousands of dollars to diversify adequately.

2. Analyze Shane's argument and explain the major error in his logic relative to the use of beta as a substitute for diversification. Explain the key assumption underlying the use of beta as a risk measure.

3. Briefly describe the traditional approach to portfolio management and relate it to the approaches supported by Walt and Shane.

4. Briefly describe modern portfolio theory (MPT) and relate it to the approaches supported by Walt and Shane. Be sure to mention diversifiable, nondiversifiable, and total risk, along with the role of beta.

5. Explain how the traditional approach and modern portfolio theory can be blended into an approach to portfolio management that might prove useful to the individual investor. Relate this to reconciling Walt's and Shane's differing points of view.

16.2   SUSAN LUSSIER'S INHERITED PORTFOLIO: DOES IT MEET HER NEEDS?

Susan Lussier is a 35-year-old divorcée currently employed as a tax attorney for a major oil and gas exploration company. She has no children and earns nearly $90,000 per year from her salary and from participation in the company's drilling activities. Divorced only one year, Susan has found being single quite exciting. An expert on oil and gas taxation, she does not concern herself with job security—she is content with her income and finds it adequate to allow her to buy and do whatever she wishes. Her current philosophy is to live each day to its fullest, not concerning herself with retirement, which is too far in the future to require her current attention.

A month ago, Susan's only surviving parent, her father, was killed in a sailing accident. He had retired in La Jolla, California, 2 years earlier and had spent most of his time sailing. Prior to retirement he owned a children's clothing manufacturing firm in South Carolina. Upon retirement he sold the firm and invested the proceeds in a security portfolio that provided him with retirement income of over $30,000 per year. In his will, which incidentally had been drafted by Susan a number of years earlier, he left his entire estate to her. The estate was structured in such a way that, in addition to a few family heirlooms, Susan received a security portfolio having a market value of nearly $350,000 and about $10,000 in cash. The portfolio contained 10 securities—5 bonds, 2 common stocks, and 3 mutual funds. A table listing the securities and key characteristics is given on page 700. The 2 common stocks were issued by large, mature, well-known firms that had exhibited continuing patterns of dividend payment over the past 5 years. The stocks offered only moderate growth potential—probably no more than 2 to 3 percent appreciation per year. The 3 mutual funds in the portfolio were income funds invested in diversified portfolios of income-oriented stocks and bonds. They provided stable streams of dividend income but little opportunity for capital appreciation.

Case 16.2　Susan Lussier's Inherited Securities Portfolio

Bonds

Par Value	Issue	S&P Rating	Interest Income	Price	Total Cost	Current Yield
$40,000	Delta Power and Light 10⅛% due 2014	AA	$ 4,050	$ 98	$ 39,200	10.33%
30,000	Mountain Water 9¾% due 2006	A	2,925	102	30,600	9.56
50,000	California Gas 9½% due 2001	AAA	4,750	97	48,500	9.79
20,000	Trans-Pacific Gas 10% due 2012	AAA	2,000	99	19,800	10.10
20,000	Public Service 9⅞% due 2002	AA	1,975	100	20,000	9.88

Common Stocks

Number of Shares	Company	Dividend per Share	Dividend Income	Price per Share	Total Cost	Beta	Dividend Yield
2,000	International Supply	$2.40	$ 4,800	$ 22	$ 44,900	.97	10.91%
3,000	Black Motor	1.50	4,500	17	52,000	.85	8.82

Mutual Funds

Number of Shares	Fund	Dividend per Share	Dividend Income	Price per Share	Total Cost	Beta	Dividend Yield
2,000	International Capital Income A Fund	$ .80	$ 1,600	$ 10	$ 20,000	1.02	8.00%
1,000	Grimner Special Income Fund	2.00	2,000	15	15,000	1.10	7.50
4,000	Ellis Diversified Income Fund	1.20	4,800	12	48,000	.90	10.00
	Total annual income: $33,400			Portfolio value: $338,000			Portfolio current yield: 9.88%

7Now that Susan owns the portfolio, she wishes to determine whether it is suitable for her situation. She realizes that the high level of income provided by the portfolio will be taxed at a rate (federal plus state) in excess of 35 percent. Because she does not currently need it, Susan plans to invest the after-tax income in tax-deferred real estate, oil and gas partnerships, and/or common stocks offering high capital gain potential. She clearly needs to shelter taxable income. (Susan is already paying out a sizable portion of her current income in taxes.) She feels fortunate to have received the portfolio and wants to make certain it provides her with the maximum benefits, given her financial situation. The $10,000 cash left to her will be especially useful in paying broker's commissions associated with making portfolio adjustments.

Questions

1. Briefly assess Susan's financial situation and develop a portfolio objective for her that's consistent with her needs.

2. Evaluate the portfolio left to Susan by her father. Assess its apparent objective and evaluate how well it may be doing in fulfilling this objective. Use the total cost values to describe the asset allocation scheme reflected in the portfolio. Comment on the risk, return, and tax implications of this portfolio.

3. If Susan decided to invest in a security portfolio consistent with her needs—indicated in response to question 1—describe the nature and mix, if any, of securities you would recommend she purchase. What asset allocation scheme would result from your recommendation? Discuss the risk, return, and tax implications of such a portfolio.

4. Compare the nature of the security portfolio inherited by Susan (from the response to question 2) with what you believe would be an appropriate security portfolio for her (from the response to question 3).

5. What recommendations would you give Susan about the inherited portfolio? Explain the steps she should take to adjust the portfolio to her needs.

CHAPTER 17

PORTFOLIO MANAGEMENT AND CONTROL

LEARNING GOALS

After studying this chapter, you should be able to:

LG 1 Discuss sources of needed data and common indexes used to evaluate the performance of investments.

LG 2 Describe the techniques used to measure the performance of individual investment vehicles, and compare performance to investment goals.

LG 3 Understand the techniques used to measure income, capital gains, and total portfolio return relative to the amount of money invested in a portfolio.

LG 4 Use the Sharpe, Treynor, and Jensen measures to compare a portfolio's return with a risk-adjusted, market-adjusted rate of return, and discuss portfolio revision.

LG 5 Describe the role of formula plans and the logic of dollar-cost averaging, constant-dollar plans, constant-ratio plans, and variable-ratio plans.

LG 6 Explain the role of limit and stop-loss orders in investment timing, the warehousing of liquidity, and the key factors in timing investment sales to achieve investment goals.

Mary Bechmann developed her investing style when she joined a private venture capital fund in 1987. "I invest in companies or industries I know well, where I believe I know something the market doesn't and the time is ripe for the stock to move," she explains. "I often invest in 'fallen angels'—neglected companies or industries that are not well followed on Wall Street or ones where investors have reacted strongly to bad news. These are stocks that are close to the bottom based on the company's intrinsic or cash liquidation value. It's worked well for me; my returns have been above 20 percent compounded annually."

Mary built her growth- and capital-appreciation-oriented portfolio using a balanced approach. Current allocations are 15 percent cash, 28 percent U.S. stocks, 10 percent bonds, 10 percent mutual funds, and 37 percent private venture capital types of deals. "As a venture capitalist, I'm comfortable with more risk than many investors, and at 37, I'm young enough to take that risk," she says. "Also, I get opportunities to personally invest in high-risk—but good-quality—venture capital deals."

Like many new investors, Mary at first lost money. "It's a tough lesson," she notes, "but I've become a wiser investor, with better control of my portfolio. I keep a diary of past mistakes—why I think I made them, the flaw in my judgment or thought process—so I won't repeat them. It works! I also record the specific attributes I seek in a stock or a management team, to help me identify future opportunities." Her most painful mistake was blindly following a friend's advice to invest in a computer manufacturer she didn't know well. "I didn't check out management for myself and lost a bundle. So I learned to *always* listen to my instincts and *never* invest without doing my homework."

A patient investor, Mary carefully follows an industry or company before investing, waiting until a stock with the right mix of upside potential and limited downside risk gets down to a target price. "I have to personally believe in the company's long-term prospects, core value, and long-term competitive position before I'll invest," she says. "That way, I don't lose on hot tips or highfliers. I can take what seems like higher risks on my hand-picked stocks."

She actively manages her portfolio, monitoring prices daily and measuring overall performance quarterly. She sets a target sell price and usually sticks to it. Once the price rises, she may sell some shares to recoup part of her original investment. Mary sells the rest only when she's convinced

> **SHE ACTIVELY MANAGES HER PORTFOLIO, MONITORING PRICES DAILY AND MEASURING OVERALL PERFORMANCE QUARTERLY.**

there's been a fundamental, dramatic change in the company or industry—for example, a new CEO, new government regulations affecting the industry, too many competitors, or declining margins. "For me, the buy-or-sell decision usually boils down to quality of management," Mary says. "I worry less about timing and more about fundamental value, to separate the 'diamond in the rough' from what's merely carbon."

Mary Bechmann, a venture capitalist and private equity investor since 1985, was the first woman partner ever in a major Wall Street leveraged buyout (LBO) fund. Since 1992, she has been one of three partners in Baccharis Capital, a venture capital fund in Menlo Park, California.

Imagine one of your most important personal goals is to accumulate $15,000 of savings three years from now in order to have enough money to purchase your first home. Based on your projections, the desired home will cost $100,000, and the $15,000 will be sufficient to make a 10 percent down payment and pay the associated closing costs. Your calculations indicate this goal can be achieved by investing existing savings plus an additional $200 per month over the next three years in a vehicle earning 12 percent per year. Projections of your earnings over the three-year period indicate you should just be able to set aside the needed $200 per month. You consult with an investment adviser, Cliff Orbit, who leads you to believe that, under his management, the 12 percent return can be achieved.

It seems simple: Give Cliff your existing savings, send him $200 each month over the next 36 months, and at the end of that period, you will have the $15,000 needed to purchase the home. Unfortunately, there are many uncertainties involved. For example, what if your income proves inadequate to set aside $200 each month? What if Cliff fails to earn the needed 12 percent annual return? What if in three years the desired house costs more than $100,000? Clearly, you must do more than simply devise what appears to be a feasible plan for achieving a future goal. You must also periodically assess progress toward the goal, to improve the chances it will be met. For example, had you found that your earnings were not adequate to permit the $200 per month investment, you might have found a new, higher-paying job. Or were the required 12 percent return not being earned on your funds, you might have sought a new investment adviser. As actual outcomes occur, you must compare them to the *planned* outcomes and make any necessary alterations in your plans. If such changes do not permit you to achieve your goal, you may have to adjust the goal and/or its timing.

The final and most important aspect of the personal investment process involves continuously managing and controlling the portfolio in order to keep moving toward the achievement of financial goals. Mary Bechmann clearly incorporates this activity into her investment program. This chapter describes the key aspects of portfolio management and control, which includes assessing actual performance, comparing it to planned performance, revising and making needed adjustments, and timing these adjustments to achieve maximum benefit.

EVALUATING THE PERFORMANCE OF INDIVIDUAL INVESTMENTS

Investment vehicles are typically selected for a portfolio on the basis of expected returns, associated risks, and certain tax considerations that may affect the returns. Because the actual outcomes may not coincide with those expected, investors must measure and compare actual performance with anticipated performance. Here we will emphasize developing measures suitable for analyzing investment performance. We begin with sources of data.

OBTAINING NEEDED DATA

The first step in analyzing investment returns is gathering data that reflect the actual performance of each investment. As pointed out in Chapter 3, a broad range of sources of investment information is available. The *Wall Street*

Journal and *Barron's*, for example, contain numerous items of information that is useful in assessing the performance of securities. The same type of information used to make an investment decision is used to evaluate the performance of investments. Two key areas to stay informed about are (1) returns on owned investments and (2) economic and market activity.

Return Data

The basic ingredient in analyzing investment returns is current market information. Many publications provide daily price quotations for securities such as stocks and bonds. Investors often maintain logs that contain the cost of each investment, as well as dividends, interest, and other sources of income received. By regularly recording price and return data, an investor can create an ongoing record of price fluctuations and cumulative returns. The investor should also monitor corporate earnings and dividends, because a company's earnings and dividends will affect its stock price. The two sources of investment return—current income and capital gains—must, of course, be combined to determine total return. The combination of return components using the techniques presented in Chapter 4 will be illustrated for some of the more popular investment vehicles later in this chapter.

Economic and Market Activity

Changes in the economy and market will affect returns—both the level of current income and the market value of an investment vehicle. The astute investor will keep abreast of international, national, and local economic and market developments. By following economic and market changes, an investor should be able to assess their potential impact on returns. As economic and market conditions change, an investor must be prepared to make revisions in the portfolio. In essence, a knowledgeable investor improves his or her chances of generating a profit (or avoiding a loss).

INDEXES OF INVESTMENT PERFORMANCE

In measuring investment performance, it is often worthwhile to compare the investor's returns with appropriate, broad-based market measures. Indexes useful for the analysis of common stock include the Dow Jones Industrial Average (DJIA), the Standard & Poor's 500 stock composite index (S&P 500), and the New York Stock Exchange composite index (NYSE index). (Detailed discussions of these averages and indexes can be found in Chapter 3.) Although the DJIA is widely cited by the news media, it is *not* considered the most appropriate comparative gauge of stock price movement, because of its narrow coverage and its exclusion of many types of stocks. If an investor's portfolio is composed of a broad range of common stocks, the NYSE composite index is probably a more appropriate tool. This index consists of stocks that constitute more than 50 percent of all publicly traded stocks, based upon dollar market value.

A number of indicators are also available for assessing the general behavior of the bond markets. These indicators consider either bond price behavior or bond yield. The Dow Jones composite bond average, based on the closing prices of ten utility and ten industrial bonds, is a popular measure of bond price behavior. Like bond quotations, this average reflects the average percentage of face value at which the bonds sell. Other sources of bond yield data, which reflect the rate of return one would earn on a bond purchased today and held to maturity, are also available. *Barron's*, Standard & Poor's, Moody's Investor Services, and the Federal Reserve are examples. Indexes of bond price and bond yield performance can be obtained for specific types of bonds (industrial, utility, and municipal), as well as on a composite basis. In addition, these and other indexes are sometimes reported in terms of *total returns*—that is, dividend/interest income is combined with price behavior (capital gain or loss) to reflect total return. Such indexes are available for both stocks and bonds.

There are a few other indexes that cover listed options and futures; there are no widely publicized indexes/averages for mutual funds or tangibles. Nor is there a broad index of real estate returns, because such returns tend to be localized. Thus, real estate investors should compare their returns with those earned by other local real estate investors. In addition, it might be wise to compare the investor's real estate returns with the consumer price index and with the NYSE composite index. The former will serve as a useful comparative measure of real estate's effectiveness as an inflation hedge. The latter is useful in comparing the relative return on a diversified stock portfolio with that from real estate investment. Similar approaches can be used in assessing other forms of property investment.

MEASURING THE PERFORMANCE OF INVESTMENT VEHICLES

Reliable techniques for consistently measuring the performance of each investment vehicle are needed to monitor an investment portfolio. In particular, the holding period return (HPR) measure, first presented in Chapter 4, is also used to determine *actual* return performance from stocks, bonds, mutual funds, real estate, tangibles, and other investments. Investment holdings need to be evaluated periodically over time—at least once a year. HPR is an excellent way to assess actual return behavior, because it captures *total return* performance; it is most appropriate for holding or assessment periods of one year or less. Total return, in this context, includes the periodic cash income from the investment as well as price appreciation or loss, whether realized or unrealized. Clearly, as noted in Chapter 4, the calculation of returns for periods of more than a year should be made using *yield* (internal rate of return), because it recognizes the time value of money; yield can easily be estimated with the *approximate yield formula*. Because the following discussions center on the annual assessment of return, HPR will be used as the measure of return. The formula for HPR, presented in Chapter 4 (Equation 4.8) and applied throughout this chapter, is restated in Equation 17.1:

Equation 17.1

$$\text{Holding period return} = \frac{\substack{\text{current income} \\ \text{during period}} + \substack{\text{current gain (or loss)} \\ \text{during period}}}{\text{beginning investment value}}$$

Equation 17.1a

$$\text{HPR} = \frac{C + CG}{V_0}$$

where

Equation 17.2   Capital gain (or loss) = ending investment value − beginning investment value
                            during period

Equation 17.2a $CG = V_n - V_0$

Stocks and Bonds

There are several measures of investment return for stocks and bonds. Dividend yield, for instance, measures the current yearly dividend return earned from a stock investment. It is calculated by dividing a stock's yearly cash dividend by its price. This measure of investment return was discussed in Chapter 5. The current yield and promised yield (yield-to-maturity) for bonds were analyzed in Chapter 9. These measures of investment return capture various components of an investor's return but do not reflect actual total return. The holding period return method provides a measure of total return. *Holding period return (HPR) measures the total return (income plus change in value) actually earned on an investment over a given investment period.* We will use a holding period of approximately one year in the illustrations that follow.

Stocks   The HPR for common and preferred stocks includes both cash dividends received and any price change in the security during the period of ownership. Table 17.1 illustrates the HPR calculation as applied to the actual performance of a common stock. The investor purchased 1,000 shares of Dallas National Corporation in May 1995 at a cost of $27,312 (including commissions). After holding the stock for just over one year, the stock was sold, with proceeds to the investor of $32,040. The investor received $2,000 in cash dividends during the period of ownership. In addition, a $4,728 capital gain was realized on the sale. Thus, the calculated HPR is 24.63 percent.

The HPR found above was calculated without consideration for income taxes paid on the dividends and capital gain. Because many investors are concerned with both pretax and after-tax rates of return, it is useful to calculate an after-tax HPR. We assume, for simplicity, that the investor in this example is in the 30 percent tax bracket (federal and state combined); we also assume that, for federal and state tax purposes, capital gains are taxed at the full marginal tax rate. Thus, dividend and capital gain income to this investor is taxed

Table 17.1   Calculation of Pretax HPR on a Common Stock

Security: Dallas National Corporation common stock
Date of purchase: May 1, 1995
Purchase cost: $27,312
Date of sale: May 7, 1996
Sale proceeds: $32,040
Dividends received (May 1995 to May 1996): $2,000

$$\text{Holding period return} = \frac{\$2,000 + (\$32,040 - \$27,312)}{\$27,312}$$

$$= +24.63\%$$

Table 17.2   Calculation of Pretax HPR on a Bond

Security: Phoenix Brewing Company 10% bonds
Date of Purchase: June 2, 1995
Purchase cost: $10,000
Date of sale: June 5, 1996
Sale proceeds: $9,704
Interest earned (June 1995 to June 1996): $1,000

$$\text{Holding period return} = \frac{\$1,000 + (\$9,704 - \$10,000)}{\$10,000}$$

$$= \underline{\underline{+7.04\%}}$$

at a 30 percent rate. Income taxes reduce the after-tax dividend income to $1,400 [(1 − .30) × $2,000] and the after-tax capital gain to $3,310 [(1 − .30) × ($32,040 − $27,312)]. The after-tax HPR is therefore 17.25 percent [($1,400 + $3,310) ÷ $27,312], a reduction of 7.38 percentage points. It should be clear that both pretax HPR and after-tax HPR are useful gauges of return.

Bonds   The HPR for a bond investment is similar to that for stocks. The calculation holds for both straight debt and convertible issues. It includes the two components of a bond investor's return: interest income and capital gain or loss. Calculation of the HPR on a bond investment is illustrated in Table 17.2. The investor purchased the Phoenix Brewing Company bonds for $10,000, held them for just over one year, and then realized $9,704 at sale. In addition, the investor earned $1,000 in interest during the period of ownership. Thus, the HPR of this investment is 7.04 percent. The HPR is lower than the bond's current yield of 10 percent ($1,000 interest ÷ $10,000 purchase price) because the bonds were sold at a capital loss. Assuming a 30 percent tax bracket, the after-tax HPR is 4.93 percent: {[(1 − .30) × $1,000] + [(1 − .30) × ($9,704 − $10,000)]} ÷ $10,000—about 2 percentage points less than the pretax HPR.

Mutual Funds

There are two basic components of return from a mutual fund investment: dividend income (including any capital gains distribution) and any change in value. The basic HPR equation for mutual funds is identical to that for stocks. Table 17.3 presents a holding period return calculation for a no-load mutual fund. The investor purchased 1,000 shares of the fund in July 1995 at an NAV of $10.40 per share. Because it is a no-load fund, no commission was charged, so the investor's cost was $10,400. During the one-year period of ownership, the Pebble Falls Mutual Fund distributed investment income dividends totaling $270 and capital gains dividends of $320. The investor redeemed (sold) this fund at an NAV of $10.79 per share, thereby realizing $10,790. As seen in Table 17.3, the pretax holding period return on this investment is 9.42 percent. Assuming a 30 percent tax bracket, the after-tax

Table 17.3 Calculation of Pretax HPR on a Mutual Fund

Security: Pebble Falls Mutual Fund
Date of purchase: July 1, 1995
Purchase cost: $10,400
Date of redemption: July 3, 1996
Sale proceeds: $10,790
Distributions received (July 1995 to July 1996)
    Investment income dividends: $270
    Capital gains dividends: $320

$$\text{Holding period return} = \frac{(\$270 + \$320) + (\$10,790 - \$10,400)}{\$10,400}$$

$$= +9.42\%$$

HPR for the fund is 6.60 percent: $\{[(1 - .30) \times (\$270 + \$320)] + [(1 - .30) \times (\$10,790 - \$10,400)]\} \div \$10,400$—nearly 3 percentage points below the pretax return.

Real Estate

The two basic components of an investor's return from real estate are the yearly after-tax cash flow and the change in property value that is likely to occur. (For a more expanded analysis of real estate investments, see Chapter 12.)

An investor who purchases raw land is interested only in capital appreciation because there is normally no positive cash flow from such an investment. Carrying costs associated with a raw land investment may include property taxes, special assessments, and interest costs if financing is used. An investor's return from a raw land investment is normally realized when the land is sold. **Reversion,** the after-tax net proceeds received upon disposition of real property, is calculated by subtracting from the property's realized selling price all selling costs (commissions plus closing costs), any mortgage principal balances that are paid upon sale, and all income taxes paid on realized capital gains from the sale. Reversion, then, represents the after-tax dollars an investor puts in his or her pocket when the property is sold.

An income property investment provides return in two forms: yearly after-tax cash flow and reversion. A property's yearly after-tax cash flow is basically its rental income minus operating expenses, mortgage payments, and income taxes. In other words, after-tax cash flow is the yearly net cash return an investor receives from rental properties. Both yearly after-tax cash flow and reversion are included when calculating an investor's total return from a rental property.

To provide some insight into the calculation of real estate investment returns, we demonstrate in Table 17.4 the calculation of the after-tax holding period return on an apartment property. (*Note:* Due to the complex nature of real estate taxation, only the after-tax HPR calculation is illustrated.) The Maitland Apartments were acquired one year ago with a $100,000 equity investment by an investor who is in the 30 percent tax bracket. If the investor

reversion
the after-tax net proceeds received upon disposition of real property.

Table 17.4   Cash Flow, Tax Statement, and After-Tax HPR
Calculation for Maitland Apartments (Past year)

Real Estate Cash Flow Statement	
Gross potential rental income	$51,000
Less: Vacancy and collection losses	−1,500
Effective gross income (EGI)	$49,500
Less: Total operating expenses	−20,000
Net operating income (NOI)	$29,500
Less: Mortgage payment	−20,500
Before-tax cash flow	$ 9,000
Less: Owner's income tax (from below)	−2,250
After-tax cash flow (ATCF)	$ 6,750
Owner's Income Tax Statement	
Net operating income	$29,500
Less: Interest	−17,000
Less: Depreciation	−5,000
Taxable income	$ 7,500
Owner's income tax (tax rate=.30)	$ 2,250
After-Tax HPR Calculation	

$$\text{After-Tax HPR} = \frac{\$6,750 + (\$110,000 - \$100,000)}{\$100,000}$$

$$= +16.75\%$$

sold the property today, she would realize reversion of $110,000 after all sales expenses, mortgage repayments, and taxes. The holding period return analysis in Table 17.4 contains the proper real estate cash flow statement, the owner's tax statement for the past year of ownership, and the HPR calculation. The investor received $6,750 in after-tax cash flow plus $10,000 ($110,000 − $100,000) in after-tax capital appreciation, resulting in an after-tax HPR of 16.75 percent. An investor seeking to compare the return on a security with the return on real estate or other property investments should find the HPR calculation illustrated in Table 17.4 a useful analytical tool.

Other Investment Vehicles

The only source of return on other investment vehicles (e.g., tangibles, options, and futures) is capital gains. To calculate a holding period return for an investment in gold, for instance, the basic HPR formula is used (but current income is set equal to zero). If an investor purchased 10 ounces of gold for $425 per ounce and sold the gold one year later for $500 per ounce, the pretax holding period return would be 17.65 percent. This is simply sales proceeds ($5,000) minus cost ($4,250) divided by cost. Assuming a 30 percent tax rate, the after-tax HPR would be 12.35 percent, which is the after-tax gain of $525 [$750 − (.30 × $750)] divided by cost ($4,250). The HPRs of options and futures are calculated in a similar fashion. Because the return is in the form of capital gains only, the HPR analysis can be applied to any investment on a pretax or an after-tax basis. (The same basic procedure would be used for securities that are sold short.)

COMPARING PERFORMANCE TO INVESTMENT GOALS

After computing an HPR (or yield) on an investment, the investor must compare it to his or her investment goal. Keeping track of an investment's performance by periodically computing its return will help you decide which investments you should continue to hold and which have become possible candidates for sale. Clearly, an investment would be a candidate for sale if (1) it failed to perform up to expectations and no real change in performance is anticipated, (2) it has met the original investment objective, or (3) more attractive uses of your funds (better investment outlets) are currently available.

Comparing Risk and Return

In this book, we have frequently discussed the basic tradeoff between investment risk and return. The relationship is fundamentally as follows: To earn more return, you must take more risk. In analyzing an investment, the key question is, "Am I getting the proper return for the amount of investment risk I am taking?"

Nongovernment security and property investments are by nature riskier than U.S. government bonds or insured money market deposit accounts. This implies that *a rational investor should invest in these riskier vehicles only when the expected rate of return is well in excess of what could have been earned from a low-risk investment.* Thus, one benchmark against which to compare investment returns is the rate of return on low-risk investments. If one's risky investments are outperforming low-risk investments, they are obtaining extra return for taking extra risk. If they are not outperforming low-risk investments, a careful examination of the investment strategy is in order.

Isolating Problem Investments

A *problem investment* is one that has not lived up to expectations. It may be a loss situation or an investment that has provided a return less than the investor expected. Many investors try to forget about problem investments, hoping the problem will go away or the investment will turn itself around. This is obviously a mistake: Problem investments require immediate attention, not neglect. In studying a problem investment, the key question is, "Should I take my loss and get out, or should I hang on and hope it turns around?" Some investors do not like to realize losses on their investments. They hold on to mediocre ones in the hope that they can eventually be sold for a profit. Such a strategy can result in a portfolio of poorly performing investments.

It is best to analyze each investment in a portfolio periodically. For each, two questions should be considered: First, has it performed in a manner that could reasonably be expected? Second, if the investment were not currently in the portfolio, would you buy it today? If the answers to both are negative, then the investment probably should be sold. A negative answer to one of the questions qualifies the investment for the "problem list." It should then be watched closely. In general, maintaining a portfolio of investments requires constant attention and analysis to ensure the best chance of satisfactory returns. Problem investments need special attention and work.

CONCEPTS *in Review*

17.1 Why is it important for an investor to continuously manage and control his or her portfolio? Explain.

17.2 What role does current market information play in analyzing investment returns? How do changes in economic and market activity affect investment returns? Explain.

17.3 Which indexes can an investor use to compare his or her investment performance to general market returns? Briefly explain each of these indexes.

17.4 What are indicators of bond market behavior, and how are they different from stock market indicators? Name three sources of bond yield data.

17.5 Aside from comparing returns on real estate investment with those of local real estate investors, why would a real estate investor also compare returns with the consumer price index and with the New York Stock Exchange composite index? Explain.

17.6 Briefly discuss dividend yield and holding period return (HPR) as measures of investment return. Are they equivalent? Explain.

17.7 Distinguish between the types of dividend distributions mutual funds make. Are these dividends the only source of return for a mutual fund investor? Explain.

17.8 What are the two basic components of an investor's return from real estate investment? What is meant by *reversion*, and how is it calculated? Explain.

17.9 Under what three conditions would an investment holding be a candidate for sale? What must be true about the expected return on a risky investment when compared with the return on a low-risk investment to cause a rational investor to acquire the risky investment? Explain.

17.10 What is a problem investment? What two questions should be considered when analyzing an investment portfolio? Explain.

ASSESSING PORTFOLIO PERFORMANCE

active portfolio management
building a portfolio using traditional and modern approaches and managing and controlling it to achieve its objectives; a worthwhile activity that can result in superior returns.

A portfolio can be either passively or actively built and managed. A *passive portfolio* results from random selection of securities that are held over the given investment horizon. An *active portfolio* is built using the traditional and modern approaches presented in Chapter 16; it is managed and controlled in order to achieve, at minimum, its stated objectives. While passive portfolios may outperform equally risky active portfolios, evidence suggests that despite efficient market arguments (see Chapter 7), **active portfolio management** is a worthwhile activity that can result in superior returns (although from an investor's point of view returns can rarely—if ever—be too great). Many of the ideas presented in this text are consistent with the belief that active portfolio management will improve the investor's chance of earning superior (excess) returns.

Once a portfolio is built, the first step in active portfolio management is to assess performance on a regular basis and to use that information to revise the portfolio. Calculating the portfolio return can be tricky, as discussed in the *Investor Insights* box on page 714. The procedures used to assess portfolio performance are based on many of the concepts presented earlier in this chapter. Here we will demonstrate the assessment of portfolio performance, using a hypothetical securities portfolio over a one-year holding period. We will examine each of three measures that can be used to compare a portfolio's return with a risk-adjusted, market-adjusted rate of return.

MEASURING PORTFOLIO RETURN

Table 17.5 presents the investment portfolio, as of January 1, 1996, of Robert K. Hathaway. Mr. Hathaway is a 50-year-old widower, and his children are married. His income is $60,000 per year. His primary investment objective is long-term growth with a moderate dividend return. He selects stocks with two criteria in mind: quality and growth potential. On January 1, 1996, his portfolio consisted of ten issues, all of good quality. Mr. Hathaway has been fortunate in his selection process: He has approximately $74,000 in unrealized price appreciation in his portfolio. During 1996, he decided to make a change in the portfolio. On May 7, he sold 1,000 shares of Dallas National Corporation for $32,040. Mr. Hathaway's holding period return for that issue was discussed earlier in this chapter (see Table 17.1). Using funds from the Dallas National sale, he acquired an additional 1,000 shares of Florida Southcoast Banks on May 10, because he liked the prospects for the Florida bank holding. Florida Southcoast is based in one of the fastest growing counties in the country.

Measuring the Amount Invested

Every investor would be well advised to list periodically his or her holdings, as done in Table 17.5. The table shows number of shares, acquisition date, cost, and current value for each issue. These data aid in continually formulating strategy decisions; the cost data, for example, are used to determine the

Table 17.5   Robert K. Hathaway's Portfolio (January 1, 1996)

Number of Shares	Company	Date Acquired	Cost (including commission)	Cost per Share	Current Price per Share	Current Value
1,000	Bancorp West, Inc.	1/16/94	$ 21,610	$21.61	$30	$ 30,000
1,000	Dallas National Corporation	5/ 1/95	27,312	27.31	29	29,000
1,000	Dator Companies, Inc.	4/13/90	13,704	13.70	27	27,000
500	Excelsior Industries	8/16/93	40,571	81.14	54	27,000
1,000	Florida Southcoast Banks	12/16/93	17,460	17.46	30	30,000
1,000	Maryland-Pacific	9/27/93	22,540	22.54	26	26,000
1,000	Moronson	2/27/93	19,100	19.10	47	47,000
500	Northwest Mining and Mfg.	4/17/94	25,504	51.00	62	31,000
1,000	Rawland Petroleum	3/12/94	24,903	24.90	30	30,000
1,000	Vornox	4/16/94	37,120	37.12	47	47,000
	Total		$249,824			$324,000

INVESTOR INSIGHTS: *Investing in Action*

Portfolio Return Is Tough to Calculate

Most investors have a pretty good idea of how major market benchmarks like Standard & Poor's 500 stock index did in any year, or they can easily look them up. But when it comes to the return on their own portfolios, most people have only the roughest notion. And there aren't any easy answers in year-end brokerage and mutual fund statements.

Although securities firms have added more information to their statements in recent years, these still don't show an overall performance figure that can be compared with, say, last year's total return on the S&P 500. Unless investors do the frequently daunting calculations for themselves, they generally have no way of knowing how their investments stack up.

Mutual fund investors don't have it much better. Fund companies do report total return figures for each fund, but that's often only part of the answer. People who moved their money around—say, shifting some dollars between a money market fund and a stock fund—are still left groping in the dark. Nor does a stock fund's annual return "tell you how you did if you bought at the highs and sold at the lows," or the reverse.

Investors can, of course, calculate their own portfolio returns. But unless they have only a few investment accounts and don't add or subtract money over the course of the year, they'll need lots of records and a strong stomach for math.

Take a simple case first. Say a family has a single brokerage account valued at $50,000 at the beginning of the year and no funds were added or withdrawn during the year. All income—including stock dividends, bond interest, and mutual fund distributions—was reinvested within the account. The total annual return would simply be the percentage difference between the value at year-end and the value at the beginning of the year. That would tell the family the average return, including both price change and income, on dollars invested as of the beginning of the year.

The equation gets tricky, however, if the family added money or subtracted money at some time during the year. Say they added $15,000 from an inheritance. Depending on when the new money came in, it may have contributed in a big way—or not at all—to the gains or losses in the portfolio. So, contrary to first impressions, you can't just add the net inflow of new funds to the original balance and measure the percentage change over the year. Investors should add up asset values quarterly or, ideally, monthly; calculate average returns for short time periods; and then combine them for an annual figure.

Investors should also be careful when selecting appropriate benchmarks to measure their portfolios against. One financial adviser suggests constructing a customized index that represents a hypothetical portfolio that has an investment mix similar to that of the investor.

Say that a family had about 50 percent of its investment dollars in common stocks, 30 percent in corporate and government bonds, and 20 percent in money market funds. Take the total return each category of investment produced last year—for instance, by using the S&P 500 index, Merrill Lynch & Co.'s corporate and government bond master index, and the average taxable money fund return reported by the Donoghue Organization (Holliston, Massachusetts). Then multiply each of those return percentages by the percentage of the portfolio they represent. Add up the results for a weighted average return representative of that particular asset mix. This return is a customized benchmark that the family can measure its portfolio against.

Source: Adapted from Karen Slater, "Portfolio Return Is Tough Figure to Find," *Wall Street Journal*, January 22, 1990, p. C1.

amount invested. Mr. Hathaway's portfolio does not utilize the leverage of a margin account. Were leverage present, all return calculations would be based on the investor's *equity* in the account. (Recall from Chapter 2 that an investor's equity in a margin account equals the total value of all the securities in the account minus any margin debt.)

To measure Mr. Hathaway's return on his invested capital, we need to perform a one-year holding period return analysis. His invested capital as of January 1, 1996, is $324,000. No new additions of capital were made in the portfolio during 1996, although he sold one stock, Dallas National, and used the proceeds to buy another, Florida Southcoast Banks.

Measuring Income

There are two sources of return from a portfolio of common stocks: income and capital gains. Current income is realized from dividends or, for a portfolio of bonds, is earned in the form of interest. Investors must report taxable dividends and interest on federal and state income tax returns. Companies are required to furnish income reports (Form 1099-DIV for dividends and Form 1099-INT for interest) to stockholders and bondholders. Many investors maintain logs to keep track of dividend and interest income as it is received. Table 17.6 lists Mr. Hathaway's dividends for 1996. He received two quarterly dividends of 45 cents per share before he sold the Dallas National stock, and he received two 32-cent-per-share quarterly dividends on the additional Florida Southcoast Banks shares he acquired. His total dividend income for 1996 was $10,935.

Measuring Capital Gains

Table 17.7 shows the unrealized gains in value for each of the issues in the Hathaway portfolio. The January 1, 1996, and December 31, 1996, values are listed for each issue except the additional shares of Florida Southcoast Banks.

Table 17.6   Dividend Income on Hathaway's Portfolio
(Calendar year 1996)

Number of Shares	Company	Annual Dividend per Share	Dividends Received
1,000	Bancorp West, Inc.	$1.20	$ 1,200
1,000	Dallas National Corporation*	1.80	900
1,000	Dator Companies, Inc.	1.12	1,120
500	Excelsior Industries	2.00	1,000
2,000	Florida Southcoast Banks**	1.28	1,920
1,000	Maryland-Pacific	1.10	1,100
1,000	Moronson	—	—
500	Northwest Mining and Mfg.	2.05	1,025
1,000	Rawland Petroleum	1.20	1,200
1,000	Vornox	1.47	1,470
	Total		$10,935

*Sold May 7, 1996.
**1,000 shares acquired on May 10, 1996.

Table 17.7 Unrealized Gains in Value of Hathaway's Portfolio
(January 1, 1996, to December 31, 1996)

Number of Shares	Company	Market Value (1/1/96)	Market Price (12/31/96)	Market Value (12/31/96)	Unrealized Gain (Loss)	Percentage Change
1,000	Bancorp West, Inc.	$ 30,000	$27	$ 27,000	($ 3,000)	−10.0%
1,000	Dator Companies, Inc.	27,000	36	36,000	9,000	+33.3
500	Excelsior Industries	27,000	66	33,000	6,000	+22.2
2,000	Florida Southcoast Banks*	62,040	35	70,000	7,960	+12.8
1,000	Maryland-Pacific	26,000	26	26,000	—	—
1,000	Moronson	47,000	55	55,000	8,000	+17.0
500	Northwest Mining and Mfg.	31,000	60	30,000	(1,000)	− 3.2
1,000	Rawland Petroleum	30,000	36	36,000	6,000	+20.0
1,000	Vornox	47,000	43	43,000	(4,000)	−8.5
	Total	$327,040**		$356,000	$28,960	+8.9%

*1,000 additional shares acquired on May 10, 1996, at a cost of $32,040. The value listed is the cost plus the market value of the previously owned shares as of January 1, 1996.

**This total includes the $324,000 market value of the portfolio on January 1, 1996 (from Table 17.5) plus the $3,040 *realized* gain on the sale of the Dallas National Corporation stock on May 7, 1996. The inclusion of the realized gain in this total is necessary to calculate the *unrealized* gain on the portfolio during 1996.

The amounts listed for Florida Southcoast Banks reflect the fact that 1,000 additional shares of the stock were acquired on May 10, 1996, at a cost of $32,040. Mr. Hathaway's current holdings had beginning-of-the-year values of $327,040 (including the additional Florida Southcoast Banks shares at the date of purchase) and are worth $356,000 at year-end.

During 1996, the portfolio increased in value by 8.9 percent, or $28,960, in unrealized capital gains. In addition, Mr. Hathaway realized a capital gain in 1996 by selling his Dallas National holding. From January 1, 1996, until its sale on May 7, 1996, the Dallas National holding rose in value from $29,000 to $32,040. This was the only sale in 1996; thus, the total *realized* gain was $3,040. During 1996, the portfolio had both a realized gain of $3,040 and an unrealized gain of $28,960. The total gain in value equals the sum of the two: $32,000. Put another way, because no capital was added to or withdrawn from the portfolio over the year, the total capital gain is simply the difference between the year-end market value (of $356,000, from Table 17.7) and the value on January 1 (of $324,000, from Table 17.5). This, of course, amounts to $32,000, of which, for tax purposes, only $3,040 is considered realized.

Measuring the Portfolio's Holding Period Return

We use the holding period return (HPR) to measure the total return on the Hathaway portfolio during 1996. The basic one-year HPR formula for portfolios is:

Equation 17.3

$$\text{Holding period return for a portfolio} = \frac{\text{dividends and interest received} + \text{realized gain} + \text{unrealized gain}}{\text{initial equity investment} + \left(\text{new funds} \times \frac{\text{number of months in portfolio}}{12}\right) - \left(\text{withdrawn funds} \times \frac{\text{number of months withdrawn from portfolio}}{12}\right)}$$

Equation 17.3a
$$HPR_p = \frac{C + RG + UG}{E_0 + \left(NF \times \dfrac{ip}{12}\right) - \left(WF \times \dfrac{wp}{12}\right)}$$

This formula includes both the realized gains (income plus capital gains) and the unrealized yearly gains of the portfolio. Portfolio additions and deletions are time-weighted for the number of months they are in the portfolio.

Table 17.7 analyzes in detail the portfolio's change in value: All the issues that are in the portfolio as of December 31, 1996, are listed, and the unrealized gain during the year is calculated. The beginning and year-end values are included for comparison purposes. The crux of the analysis is the HPR calculation for the year, presented in Table 17.8. All the elements of a portfolio's return are included. Dividends total $10,935 (from Table 17.6). The realized gain of $3,040 represents the increment in value of the Dallas National holding from January 1, 1996, until its sale. During 1996, the portfolio had a $28,960 unrealized gain (from Table 17.7). There were no additions of new funds, and no funds were withdrawn. Utilizing Equation 17.3 for HPR, we find that the portfolio had a total return of 13.25 percent in 1996.

COMPARISON OF RETURN WITH OVERALL MARKET MEASURES

The HPR figure derived from the calculation above should be utilized in a risk-adjusted, market-adjusted rate of return comparison. This type of comparative study is useful because it can provide some idea of how the portfolio is doing in comparison to the stock market as a whole. The S&P 500 stock composite index or the NYSE composite index are acceptable indexes for this type of analysis, because they are broadly based and appear to represent the

Table 17.8 Holding Period Return Calculation on Hathaway's Portfolio (January 1, 1996, to December 31, 1996, holding period)

Data	
Portfolio value (1/1/96):	$324,000
Portfolio value (12/31/96):	$356,000
Realized appreciation (1/1/96 to 5/7/96 when Dallas National was sold):	$ 3,040
Unrealized appreciation (1/1/96 to 12/31/96):	$ 28,960
Dividends received:	$ 10,935
New funds invested or withdrawn:	None

Portfolio HPR Calculation

$$HPR_p = \frac{\$10,935 + \$3,040 + \$28,960}{\$324,000}$$

$$= +13.25\%$$

stock market as a whole. Assume that during 1996, the return on the S&P 500 index was +10.75 percent; this return includes both dividends and capital gains. The return from Mr. Hathaway's portfolio, as calculated above, was +13.25 percent. His results compare very favorably with the broadly based index: The Hathaway portfolio performed about 23 percent better than this broad indicator of stock market return.

Although such a comparison tends to factor out the influences of general market movements, it fails to consider risk. Clearly, a raw return figure, such as the +13.25 percent above, requires further analysis because an investor needs to know how the portfolio *has performed in relation to other portfolios and in relation to the market in general*. A number of risk-adjusted, market-adjusted rate of return measures are available for use in assessing portfolio performance. Here we'll discuss three of the most popular—Sharpe's measure, Treynor's measure, and Jensen's measure—and demonstrate their application to Hathaway's portfolio.

Sharpe's Measure

Sharpe's measure of portfolio performance, developed by William F. Sharpe, compares the risk premium on a portfolio to the portfolio's standard deviation of return. The risk premium on a portfolio is the total portfolio return minus the risk-free rate. Sharpe's measure can be expressed as the following formula:

Equation 17.4

$$\text{Sharpe's measure} = \frac{\text{total portfolio return} - \text{risk-free rate}}{\text{portfolio standard deviation}}$$

Equation 17.4a

$$SM = \frac{r_p - R_F}{s_p}$$

Sharpe's measure
a measure of portfolio performance that measures the risk premium of a portfolio per unit of total risk, which is measured by the portfolio's standard deviation of return.

This measure allows the investor to assess the risk premium per unit of total risk, which is measured by the portfolio standard deviation. Assume the risk-free rate, R_F, is 7.50 percent and the standard deviation of Hathaway's portfolio, s_p, is 16 percent. The total portfolio return, r_p, which is the HPR for Hathaway's portfolio calculated in Table 17.8, is 13.25 percent. Substituting those values into Equation 17.4, we get Sharpe's measure, SM:

$$SM = \frac{13.25\% - 7.50\%}{16\%} = \frac{5.75\%}{16\%} = \underline{\underline{.36}}$$

Sharpe's measure is meaningful when compared either to other portfolios or to the market. In general, the higher Sharpe's measure, the better—the higher the risk premium per unit of risk. If we assume the market return, r_m, is currently 10.75 percent and the standard deviation for the market portfolio, s_{p_m}, is 11.25 percent, Sharpe's measure for the market, SM_m, would be:

$$SM_m = \frac{10.75\% - 7.5\%}{11.25\%} = \frac{3.25\%}{11.25\%} = \underline{\underline{.29}}$$

Because Sharpe's measure for Hathaway's portfolio of .36 is greater than the measure of .29 for the market portfolio, Hathaway's portfolio exhibits superior performance—its risk premium per unit of risk is above that of the market. Of course, had Sharpe's measure for Hathaway's portfolio been below that of the market (i.e., below .29), the portfolio's performance would be considered inferior to the market performance.

Treynor's Measure

Jack L. Treynor developed a portfolio performance measure that is similar to Sharpe's measure. Like Sharpe's, **Treynor's measure** measures the risk premium per unit of risk, but it differs in its portfolio risk measure. Treynor's measure uses the portfolio beta to measure risk; Sharpe's uses the portfolio standard deviation. Treynor therefore focuses only on *nondiversifiable risk*, assuming that the portfolio has been built in a fashion that diversifies away all diversifiable risk; Sharpe, on the other hand, uses total risk. Treynor's measure is calculated as shown in Equation 17.5:

Equation 17.5

$$\text{Treynor's measure} = \frac{\text{total portfolio return} - \text{risk-free rate}}{\text{portfolio beta}}$$

Equation 17.5a

$$TM = \frac{r_p - R_F}{b_p}$$

This measure gives the risk premium per unit of nondiversifiable risk, which is measured by the portfolio beta. Using the data for the Hathaway portfolio presented earlier and assuming that the beta for Hathaway's portfolio, b_p, is 1.20, we can substitute into Equation 17.5 to get Treynor's measure, TM, for Hathaway's portfolio:

$$TM = \frac{13.25\% - 7.50\%}{1.20} = \frac{5.75\%}{1.20} = \underline{\underline{4.79\%}}$$

Treynor's measure, like Sharpe's, is useful when compared either to other portfolios or to the market. Generally, the higher the value of Treynor's measure, the better—the greater the risk premium per unit of nondiversifiable risk. Again assuming the market return, r_m, is 10.75 percent, and recognizing that, by definition (see Chapter 4), the beta for the market portfolio, b_{p_m}, is 1.00, we can use Equation 17.5 to find Treynor's measure for the market, TM_m:

$$TM_m = \frac{10.75\% - 7.50\%}{1.00} = \frac{3.25\%}{1.00} = \underline{\underline{3.25\%}}$$

The fact that Treynor's measure of 4.79 percent for Hathaway's portfolio is greater than the measure of 3.25 percent for the market portfolio indicates that Hathaway's portfolio exhibits superior performance—its risk premium per unit of nondiversifiable risk is above that of the market. Conversely, had Treynor's measure for Hathaway's portfolio been below that of the market (i.e., below 3.25 percent), the portfolio's performance would be viewed as inferior to that of the market.

Jensen's Measure (Jensen's Alpha)

Michael C. Jensen developed a portfolio performance measure that seems quite different from the measures of Sharpe and Treynor yet is theoretically consistent with Treynor's measure. **Jensen's measure**, also called **Jensen's alpha**, is based on the *capital asset pricing model (CAPM)*, which was developed in Chapter 4 (see Equation 4.14). It calculates the portfolio's *excess return*—the amount by which the portfolio's actual return deviates from its required return, which is determined using its beta and CAPM. The value of the excess return may be positive, zero, or negative. Like Treynor's measure,

Jensen's measure focuses only on the nondiversifiable or relevant risk, by using beta and CAPM; it assumes that the portfolio has been adequately diversified. Jensen's measure is calculated as shown in Equation 17.6:

Equation 17.6

Jensen's measure = (total portfolio return − risk-free rate) − [portfolio beta × (market return − risk-free rate)]

Equation 17.6a

$$JM = (r_p - R_F) - [b_p \times (r_m - R_F)]$$

Jensen's measure indicates the difference between the portfolio's actual return and its required return. Positive values are preferred; they indicate the portfolio earned a return in excess of its risk-adjusted, market-adjusted required return. A value of zero indicates the portfolio earned *exactly* its required return; negative values indicate the portfolio failed to earn its required return.

Using the data for Hathaway's portfolio presented earlier, we can substitute into Equation 17.6 to get Jensen's measure, *JM*, for Hathaway's portfolio:

$$JM = (13.25\% - 7.50\%) - [1.20 \times (10.75\% - 7.50\%)]$$
$$= 5.75\% - (1.20 \times 3.25\%) = 5.75\% - 3.90\% = \underline{1.85\%}$$

The 1.85 percent value for Jensen's measure indicates that Hathaway's portfolio earned an *excess return* 1.85 percentage points above its required return, given its nondiversifiable risk as measured by beta. Clearly, Hathaway's portfolio has outperformed the market on a risk-adjusted basis. Note that unlike the Sharpe and Treynor measures, Jensen's measure, through its use of CAPM, automatically adjusts for the market return. Therefore, there is no need to make a separate market comparison. In general, the higher Jensen's measure, the better the portfolio has performed; only those portfolios with positive Jensen measures have outperformed the market on a risk-adjusted basis. Because of its computational simplicity, its reliance only on nondiversifiable risk, and its inclusion of both risk and market adjustments, Jensen's measure (alpha) tends to be preferred over those of Sharpe and Treynor when assessing portfolio performance.

PORTFOLIO REVISION

In the Hathaway portfolio discussed above, one transaction occurred during 1996. The reason for this transaction was that Mr. Hathaway believed the Florida Southcoast Banks stock had more return potential than the Dallas National stock. An investor should periodically analyze the portfolio with one basic question in mind: "Does this portfolio continue to meet my needs?" In other words, does the portfolio contain those issues that are best suited to the investor's risk-return needs? Investors who systematically study the issues in their portfolios will find an occasional need to sell certain issues and to purchase new securities. This process is commonly called **portfolio revision**. As the economy evolves, certain industries and stocks become either less or more attractive as investments. In today's stock market, timeliness is the essence of profitability.

INVESTOR FACTS

TIME TO REVISE YOUR PORTFOLIO?—Over time, you will need to review your portfolio to ensure it reflects the right risk-return characteristics for your goals and needs. Here are four good reasons to perform this task:
• A major life event—marriage, birth of a child, job loss, illness, loss of a spouse, children finish college—changes your investment objectives.
• The proportion of one asset class increases or decreases substantially.
• You expect to reach a specific goal within two years.
• The percentage in an asset class varies from your original allocation by 10 percent or more.

(Source: *Fidelity Focus*, Winter 1994, p. 15.)

---

portfolio revision
the process of selling certain issues in a portfolio and of purchasing new ones.

Given the dynamics of the investment world, periodic reallocation and rebalancing of the portfolio are a necessity. Many circumstances require such changes. In Chapter 16 we noted that as an investor nears retirement, the portfolio's emphasis normally evolves from a strategy that stresses growth/capital appreciation to one that seeks to preserve capital. For an investor approaching retirement, an appropriate strategy might be to switch gradually from growth issues into low-risk, high-yield securities. Changing a portfolio's emphasis normally occurs as an evolutionary process rather than an overnight switch. Individual issues in the portfolio often change in risk-return characteristics. As this occurs, an investor would be wise to eliminate those issues that do not meet his or her objectives. In addition, the need for diversification is constant. As issues rise or fall in value, their diversification effect may be lessened. Thus, portfolio revision may be needed to maintain diversification in the portfolio. The *Investor Insights* box on page 722 offers some tips on knowing when and what to sell.

CONCEPTS *in Review*

17.11 What is *active portfolio management*? How does evidence with regard to it conflict with efficient market arguments? Explain.

17.12 Describe the steps involved in measuring portfolio return. Explain the role of the portfolio's HPR in this process and explain why one must differentiate between realized and unrealized gains.

17.13 Why is it important to utilize a portfolio's HPR in a risk-adjusted, market-adjusted rate of return comparison? Why is comparing a portfolio's return to the return on a broad market index generally inadequate? Explain.

17.14 Briefly describe each of the following risk-adjusted, market-adjusted return measures available for assessing portfolio performance, and explain how they are used.
  a. Sharpe's measure
  b. Treynor's measure
  c. Jensen's measure (Jensen's alpha)

17.15 How is Jensen's measure similar to Treynor's measure? Why is Jensen's measure (alpha) generally preferred over the measures of Sharpe and Treynor when assessing portfolio performance? Explain.

17.16 Briefly define and discuss *portfolio revision*. Explain its role in the process of managing and controlling a portfolio. ▬▬

TIMING TRANSACTIONS

The essence of timing is to "buy low and sell high." This is the dream of all investors. Although there is no tried-and-true way to achieve such a goal, there are several methods you can utilize to time purchases and sales. First, there are formula plans, discussed below. Investors can also use limit and stop-loss orders as a timing aid, can follow procedures for warehousing liquidity, and can take into consideration other aspects of timing when selling their investments.

INVESTOR INSIGHTS: *Investing in Action*

Knowing When to Hold and When to Fold

One of your stocks is up 20 percent in value, another is off 15 percent. Should you sell either one? Selling a winner is hard: It may go even higher. Nor is it easy to admit you made a mistake and dump a loser: It may bounce back. Then again, it may not: One EuroDisney investor who couldn't bear to sell watched $27,000 he earned working part-time during high school and college dwindle to $6,000. Or maybe you need cash for a new car or your child's college tuition and don't know what to sell. Selling the wrong securities can throw your whole portfolio out of balance or increase your taxes.

Developing your own selling strategy is good discipline. It provides an opportunity to fine-tune your portfolio by reassessing both your individual investments and your asset allocation. Following rules helps avoid emotional decisions for each stock. Some general guidelines include selling when the reason you bought a stock is no longer valid, when your investment goals change, or when you have a more attractive investment opportunity.

Beyond the basic rules, however, your criteria should reflect your investing style. If you're a value investor, set a target price at a certain percentage over the purchase price. When it's reached, reevaluate the stock to see if you'd buy today at that price; if not, sell. Likewise, set a target price/earnings ratio; noted money manager David Dreiman sells when a stock's P/E ratio approaches the overall market P/E. Sell cyclicals when P/E ratios are in the single digits, which usually means earnings are peaking. Growth investors let their stocks ride up and pay premium prices for companies with strong earnings growth. One key guideline is

the relationship of the next year's P/E ratio to the company's projected three- to five-year growth rate. Conservative growth fund managers sell when the P/E ratio equals the growth rate; others will tolerate a 1.25 or greater ratio between P/E and growth. Your choice depends on your risk tolerance. Another sell signal is earnings that don't meet expectations.

But what do you sell if you need to raise money? Your asset allocation strategy can guide what to sell—whatever helps your balance—as well as what to buy. If you start your portfolio with 70 percent stocks and 30 percent bonds and your equity portion appreciates to 85 percent, selling stocks brings your asset mix back in line. To choose what particular securities to sell, use some of the above criteria. Also, rank your investments based on your personal needs, risk tolerance, and performance. For example, if you're trying to build your portfolio quickly, don't sell growth stocks; if you need current income, don't sell bonds. An investment that's earning lower returns than its peers may be a sell candidate. Or follow the lead of many professional money managers who sell a bit of everything. Picking just one investment causes the risk of choosing the wrong one. One last factor is taxes, which can help you decide between two equal choices. Sell whatever results in the lowest tax, either by offsetting a capital gain with a loss or by selling an investment with a high cost basis.

Sources: Adapted from Manuel Schiffres, "When to Sell a Stock," *Kiplinger's Personal Finance Magazine*, February 1994, pp. 98–104, and "When to Hold and When to Fold," *Kiplinger's Personal Finance Magazine*, November 1994, pp. 121–22.

FORMULA PLANS

formula plans
mechanical methods of portfolio management that try to take advantage of price changes in securities that result from cyclical price movements.

Formula plans are mechanical methods of portfolio management that try to take advantage of price changes in securities that result from cyclical price movements. Formula plans are not set up to provide unusually high returns; rather, they are conservative strategies that are primarily oriented toward investors who do not wish to bear a high level of risk. Four popular formula plans are discussed here: dollar-cost averaging; the constant-dollar plan; the constant-ratio plan; and the variable-ratio plan.

Dollar-Cost Averaging

dollar-cost averaging
a formula plan for timing invest-ment transactions, in which a fixed dollar amount is invested in a security at fixed intervals.

Dollar-cost averaging is a formula plan in which a fixed dollar amount is invested in a security at fixed intervals. In this passive buy-and-hold strategy, the periodic dollar investment is held constant. The investor must have the dis-cipline to invest on a regular basis to make the plan work. The goal of a dollar-cost averaging program is growth in the value of the security to which the funds are allocated. The price of the investment security will probably fluc-tuate over time. If the price declines, more shares are purchased per period; conversely, if the price rises, fewer shares are purchased per period.

In the example of dollar-cost averaging shown in Table 17.9, the investor is investing $500 per month in the Wolverine Mutual Fund, a growth-oriented, no-load mutual fund. During one year's time, the investor has placed $6,000 in the mutual fund shares. Because this is a no-load fund, shares are purchased at net asset value. Purchases were made at NAVs ranging from a low of $24.16 to a high of $30.19. At year-end, the investor's holdings in the fund were valued at slightly less than $6,900. Dollar-cost averaging is a passive strategy; other formula plans are more active.

Constant-Dollar Plan

constant-dollar plan
a formula plan for timing invest-ment transactions, in which the investor establishes a target dollar amount for the specula-tive portion of the portfolio and transfers funds to or from the conservative portion as needed to maintain the target dollar amount.

A **constant-dollar plan** consists of a portfolio that is divided into two parts, speculative and conservative. The speculative portion is invested in securities having high promise of capital gains. The conservative portion consists of low-risk investments such as bonds or a money market account. The target dollar amount for the speculative portion is constant, and the investor establishes trigger points (upward or downward movement in the speculative portion) at

Table 17.9 Dollar-Cost Averaging
($500 per month, Wolverine Mutual Fund shares)

	Transactions	
Month	Net Asset Value (NAV) Month-End	Number of Shares Purchased
January	$26.00	19.23
February	27.46	18.21
March	27.02	18.50
April	24.19	20.67
May	26.99	18.53
June	25.63	19.51
July	24.70	20.24
August	24.16	20.70
September	25.27	19.79
October	26.15	19.12
November	29.60	16.89
December	30.19	16.56
	Annual Summary	

Total investment: $6,000.00
Total number of shares purchased: 227.95
Average cost per share: $26.32
Year-end portfolio value: $6,881.81

which funds are removed from or added to that portion. The constant-dollar plan basically skims off profits from the speculative portion of the portfolio if it rises a certain percentage or amount in value. These funds are then added to the conservative portion of the portfolio. If the speculative portion of the portfolio declines by a specific percentage or amount, funds are added to it from the conservative portion.

Table 17.10 illustrates a constant-dollar plan over time. The beginning $20,000 portfolio consists of $10,000 invested in a high-beta, no-load mutual fund and $10,000 deposited in a money market account. The investor has decided to rebalance the portfolio every time the speculative portion is worth $2,000 more or $2,000 less than its initial value of $10,000: If the speculative portion of the portfolio equals or exceeds $12,000, sufficient shares of the fund are sold to bring its value down to $10,000. The proceeds from the sale are added to the conservative portion. If the speculative portion declines in value to $8,000 or less, funds are taken from the conservative portion and used to purchase sufficient shares to raise the value of the speculative portion to $10,000.

Two portfolio rebalancing actions are taken in the time sequence illustrated in Table 17.10. Initially, $10,000 is allocated to each portion of the portfolio. When the mutual fund's NAV rises to $12.00, at which point the speculative portion is worth $12,000, the investor sells 166.67 shares valued at $2,000 and the proceeds are added to the money market account. Later, the mutual fund's NAV declines to $9.50 per share, causing the value of the speculative portion to drop below $8,000. This change triggers the purchase of sufficient shares to raise the value of the speculative portion to $10,000. Over the long run, if the speculative investment of the constant-dollar plan rises in value, the conservative component of the portfolio will increase in dollar value as profits are transferred into it.

Constant-Ratio Plan

constant-ratio plan
a formula plan for timing investment transactions, in which a desired fixed *ratio* of the speculative to the conservative portion of the portfolio is established; when the actual ratio differs by a predetermined amount from the desired ratio, transactions are made to rebalance the portfolio to achieve the desired ratio.

The **constant-ratio plan** is similar to the constant-dollar plan except that it establishes a desired fixed *ratio* of the speculative to the conservative portion of the portfolio. When the actual ratio of the two differs by a predetermined amount from the desired ratio, rebalancing occurs. At that point, transactions

Table 17.10 Constant-Dollar Plan

Mutual Fund NAV	Value of Speculative Portion	Value of Conservative Portion	Total Portfolio Value	Transactions	Number of Shares in Speculative Portion
$10.00	$10,000.00	$10,000.00	$20,000.00		1,000
11.00	11,000.00	10,000.00	21,000.00		1,000
12.00	12,000.00	10,000.00	22,000.00		1,000
→ 12.00	10,000.00	12,000.00	22,000.00	Sold 166.67 shares	833.33
11.00	9,166.63	12,000.00	21,166.63		833.33
9.50	7,916.64	12,000.00	19,916.64		833.33
→ 9.50	10,000.00	9,916.64	19,916.64	Purchased 219.30 shares	1,052.63
10.00	10,526.30	9,916.64	20,442.94		1,052.63

are made to bring the actual ratio back to the desired ratio. An investor using the constant-ratio plan must decide on the appropriate apportionment of the portfolio between speculative and conservative investments. Then, a decision must be made regarding the ratio trigger point at which transactions occur.

A constant-ratio plan for an initial portfolio of $20,000 is illustrated in Table 17.11. The investor has decided to allocate 50 percent of the portfolio to the speculative high-beta mutual fund and 50 percent to a money market account. Rebalancing will occur when the ratio of the speculative portion to the conservative portion is greater than or equal to 1.20 or less than or equal to .80. A sequence of net asset value changes is listed in Table 17.11. Initially, $10,000 is allocated to each portion of the portfolio. When the fund NAV reaches $12, the 1.20 ratio triggers the sale of 83.33 shares. Then, the portfolio is back to its desired 50-50 ratio. Later, the fund NAV declines to $9, lowering the value of the speculative portion to $8,250. The ratio of the speculative portion to the conservative portion is then .75, which is below the .80 trigger point. A total of 152.78 shares is purchased to bring the desired ratio back up to the 50-50 level.

The long-run expectation under a constant-ratio plan is that the speculative securities will rise in value. When this occurs, sales of the securities will be undertaken to reapportion the portfolio and increase the value of the conservative portion. This philosophy is similar to the constant-dollar plan, except that a *ratio* is utilized as a trigger point.

variable-ratio plan
a formula plan for timing investment transactions, in which the ratio of the speculative portion to the total portfolio varies depending upon the movement in value of the speculative securities; when the ratio rises or falls by a predetermined amount, the amount committed to the speculative portion of the portfolio is reduced or increased, respectively.

Variable-Ratio Plan

The **variable-ratio plan** is the most aggressive of these four fairly passive investment strategies. It attempts to turn stock market movements to the investor's advantage by timing the market; that is, it tries to "buy low and sell high." The ratio of the speculative portion to the total portfolio varies depending upon the movement in value of the speculative securities. When the ratio rises a certain predetermined amount, the amount committed to the speculative portion of the portfolio is reduced. Conversely, if the value of the speculative portion declines so that it drops significantly in proportion to the

Table 17.11   Constant-Ratio Plan

Mutual Fund NAV	Value of Speculative Portion	Value of Conservative Portion	Total Portfolio Value	Ratio of Speculative Portion to Conservative Portion	Transactions	Number of Shares in Speculative Portion
$10.00	$10,000.00	$10,000.00	$20,000.00	1.000		1,000
11.00	11,000.00	10,000.00	21,000.00	1.100		1,000
12.00	12,000.00	10,000.00	22,000.00	1.200		1,000
→ 12.00	11,000.00	11,000.00	22,000.00	1.000	Sold 83.33 shares	916.67
11.00	10,083.00	11,000.00	21,083.00	0.917		916.67
10.00	9,166.70	11,000.00	20,166.70	0.833		916.67
9.00	8,250.00	11,000.00	19,250.00	0.750		916.67
→ 9.00	9,625.00	9,625.00	19,250.00	1.000	Purchased 152.78 shares	1,069.44
10.00	10,694.40	9,625.00	20,319.40	1.110		1,069.44

whole portfolio, the amount committed to the speculative portion of the portfolio is increased.

When implementing the variable-ratio plan, an investor has several decisions to make. First, he or she has to determine the initial allocation between the speculative and conservative portions of the portfolio. Next, the investor must choose trigger points to initiate buy or sell activity. These points are a function of the ratio between the value of the speculative portion and the value of the portfolio. Finally, the investor must set adjustments in that ratio at each trigger point.

An example of a variable-ratio plan is shown in Table 17.12. Initially, the portfolio is divided equally between the speculative and the conservative portions. The former consists of a high-beta (around 2.0) mutual fund, and the latter is a money market account. The investor decided that when the speculative portion reached 60 percent of the total portfolio, its proportion would be reduced to 45 percent. If the speculative portion of the portfolio dropped to 40 percent of the total portfolio, then its proportion would be raised to 55 percent. The logic behind this strategy is an attempt to time the cyclical movements in the mutual fund's value. When the fund moves up in value, profits are taken and the proportion invested in the no-risk money market account is increased. When the fund declines markedly in value, the proportion of capital committed to it is increased.

A sequence of transactions is depicted in Table 17.12. When the fund NAV climbs to $15, the 60 percent ratio trigger point is reached, and 250 shares of the fund are sold. The proceeds are placed in the money market account, which causes the speculative portion to then represent 45 percent of the value of the portfolio. Later the fund NAV declines to $10, causing the speculative portion of the portfolio to drop to 35 percent. This triggers a portfolio rebalancing, and 418.75 shares are purchased, moving the speculative portion to 55 percent. When the fund NAV then moves to $12, the total portfolio is worth in excess of $23,500. In comparison, had the initial investment of $20,000 been allocated equally and no rebalancing been done between the mutual fund and the money market account, the portfolio's value at this time would have been only $22,000 ($12 × 1,000 = $12,000 in the speculative portion plus $10,000 in the money market account).

Table 17.12   Variable-Ratio Plan

Mutual Fund NAV	Value of Speculative Portion	Value of Conservative Portion	Total Portfolio Value	Ratio of Speculative Portion to Conservative Portion	Transactions	Number of Shares in Speculative Portion
$10.00	$10,000.00	$10,000.00	$20,000.00	0.50		1,000
15.00	15,000.00	10,000.00	25,000.00	0.60		1,000
→ 15.00	11,250.00	13,750.00	25,000.00	0.45	Sold 250 shares	750
10.00	7,500.00	13,750.00	21,250.00	0.35		750
→ 10.00	11,687.50	9,562.50	21,250.00	0.55	Purchased 418.75 shares	1,168.75
12.00	14,025.00	9,562.50	23,587.50	0.41		1,168.75

USING LIMIT AND STOP-LOSS ORDERS

In Chapter 2 we discussed the market order, the limit order, and the stop-loss order. (See Chapter 2, pages 53–55, for a review of these types of orders.) Here we will see how the limit and stop-loss orders can be employed to rebalance a portfolio. These types of security orders, if properly used, can increase an investor's return by lowering transaction costs.

Limit Orders

There are many ways an investor can use limit orders when securities are bought or sold. For instance, if an investor has decided to add a stock to the portfolio, a limit buy order will ensure that the investor buys only at the desired purchase price or below. An investor using a limit *good-'till-canceled (GTC)* order to buy has the broker trying to buy stock until the entire order is filled. The primary risk in using limit instead of market orders is that the order may not be executed. For example, if an investor placed a GTC order to buy 100 shares of State Oil of California at $27 per share and the stock never traded at $27 per share or less, the order would never be executed. Thus, an investor must weigh the need for immediate execution (market order) versus the possibility of a better price with a limit order.

Limit orders, of course, can increase an investor's return if they enable the investor to buy a security at a lower cost or sell at a higher price. During a typical trading day, a stock will fluctuate up and down over a normal trading range. For example, suppose the common shares of Jama Motor traded ten times in the following sequence: 36, 35⅞, 35¾, 35⅞, 35½, 35⅝, 35¾, 36, 36⅛, 36. A market order to sell could have been executed at somewhere between 35½ (the low) and 36⅛ (the high). A limit order to sell at 36 would have been executed at 36. Thus, a half-point per share (50 cents) might have been gained by using a limit order.

Stop-Loss Orders

Stop-loss orders can be used to limit the downside loss exposure of an investment. For example, assume an investor purchases 500 shares of Easy Work at 26 and has set a specific goal to sell the stock if it reaches 32 or drops to 23. To implement this goal, a GTC stop order to sell is entered with a price limit of 32, and another stop order is entered at a price of 23. If the issue trades at 23 or less, the stop-loss order becomes a market order, and the stock is sold at the best price available. Conversely, if the issue trades at 32 or higher, the broker will sell the stock. In the first situation, the investor is trying to reduce his losses, and in the second, he's trying to protect a profit.

whipsawing
the situation where a stock temporarily drops in price and then bounces back upward.

The principal risk in using stop-loss orders is **whipsawing**—a situation where a stock temporarily drops in price and then bounces back upward. If Easy Work dropped to 23, then 22½, and then rallied back to 26, the investor who placed the stop-loss at 23 would have been sold out at a price between 23 and 22½. For this reason, limit orders, including stop-loss orders, require careful analysis before they are placed. An investor must consider the stock's probable fluctuations as well as the need to purchase or sell the stock when choosing between a market, a limit, and a stop-loss order.

WAREHOUSING LIQUIDITY

Investing in risky stocks or in property offers probable returns in excess of money market deposit accounts or bonds. However, stocks and property are risky investments. One recommendation for an efficient portfolio is to keep a portion of it in a low-risk, highly liquid investment to protect against total loss. The low-risk asset acts as a buffer against possible investment adversity. A second reason for maintaining funds in a low-risk asset is the possibility of future opportunities. When opportunity strikes, an investor who has the extra cash available will be able to take advantage of the situation. A sudden market dip, an attractive real estate deal, and a valuable painting available at a low price are all examples of situations in which an investor with cash to invest immediately may benefit. An investor who has set aside funds in a highly liquid investment need not disturb the existing portfolio.

There are two primary media for warehousing liquidity: money market deposit accounts at financial institutions and money market mutual funds. The money market deposit as well as some NOW accounts at banks and savings and loan associations provide relatively easy access to funds and furnish returns competitive with (but somewhat lower than) money market mutual funds. Over time, the products offered by financial institutions are expected to become more competitive with those offered by mutual funds and stock brokerage firms. (See Chapter 3 for a detailed discussion of the role of and vehicles available for warehousing liquidity.)

TIMING INVESTMENT SALES

One of the more difficult decisions an investor must make concerns the appropriate time to sell an investment. Knowing when to sell a stock is as important as deciding which stock to buy. Periodically, an investor must review the portfolio and consider possible sales and new purchases. Here we discuss two items relevant to the sale decision: tax consequences and achieving investment goals.

Tax Consequences

Taxes affect nearly all investment actions. All investors can and should understand certain basics. The treatment of capital losses is important: *A maximum of $3,000 of losses in excess of capital gains can be applied in any one year*. If an investor has a loss position in an investment and has concluded that it would be wise to sell it, the best time to sell is when a capital gain is available against which the loss can be applied. Clearly, the tax consequences of investment sales should be carefully considered prior to taking action.

Achieving Investment Goals

Every investor would enjoy buying an investment at its lowest price and selling it at its top price. At a more practical level, an investment should be sold when it no longer meets the needs of the portfolio's owner. In particular, if an investment has become either more or less risky than is desired, or if it has not met its return objective, it should be sold. The tax consequences mentioned above help to determine the appropriate time to sell. However, *taxes are not the foremost consideration in a sale decision*: The dual concepts of risk and return should be the overriding concerns.

Each investment should be examined periodically in light of its return performance and relative risk. The investor should sell any investment that no longer belongs in the portfolio and should buy vehicles that are more suitable. Finally, an investor should not hold out for every nickel of profit. Very often, those who hold out for the top price watch the value of their holdings plummet downward. If an investment looks ripe to sell, an investor should sell it, take the profit, reinvest it in an appropriate vehicle, and enjoy his or her good fortune. An investor, in sum, should set realistic goals and criteria, and stick with them.

CONCEPTS *in Review*

17.17 Explain the role *formula plans* can play in timing security transactions. Describe the logic underlying the use of these plans.

17.18 Briefly describe and differentiate among each of the following plans:
   a. Dollar-cost averaging
   b. Constant-dollar plan
   c. Constant-ratio plan
   d. Variable-ratio plan

17.19 Describe how a limit order can be used when securities are bought or sold. How can a stop-loss order be used to reduce losses? To protect profit?

17.20 Give two reasons why an investor might want to maintain funds in a low-risk, highly liquid investment.

17.21 Describe the two items an investor should consider before reaching a decision to sell an investment vehicle.

On Track with STOCK-TRAK®

Comparing Portfolio and Market Returns Using STOCK-TRAK®

STOCK-TRAK®'s summary reports, which are sent to your professor, include all of the data needed to compare portfolio performance with market benchmarks. The most important information is in the "Equity" column, where one can find the value of the individual's account, a quasi-risk-free "Interest Only" account, and Standard & Poor's 500 account on the statement date.

Use of account value changes across multiple summary reports makes it possible to estimate standard deviation and Sharpe's measure. Tracking the simultaneous changes in the investor accounts and the S&P 500 account values makes it possible to estimate beta and the Treynor measure. Using the text symbols, Jensen's measure requires the actual return on the investor's portfolio (r_p), the return on the "Interest Only" account (R_F), the return on the S&P 500 (r_m), and the beta of the investor's portfolio (b_p).

SUMMARY

LG 1   **Discuss sources of needed data and common indexes used to evaluate the performance of investments.** To analyze the performance of individual investments, the investor must gather current market information and stay abreast of international, national, and local economic and market developments. Indexes of investment performance such as the Dow Jones Industrial Average (DJIA) and bond market indicators are available for use in assessing market behavior.

LG 2   **Describe the techniques used to measure the performance of individual investment vehicles, and compare performance to investment goals.** The performance of individual investment vehicles, including stocks, bonds, mutual funds, real estate, and other investment vehicles (tangibles, options, and futures), can be measured on both a pretax and an after-tax basis using the holding period return (HPR). HPR measures the total return (income plus change in value) actually earned on the investment during the investment period. HPR can be compared to investment goals to assess whether the proper return is being earned for the risk involved and to isolate and act on any problem investments.

LG 3   **Understand the techniques used to measure income, capital gains, and total portfolio return relative to the amount of money invested in a portfolio.** To measure portfolio return, the investor must estimate the amount invested, the income earned, and any capital gains—both realized and unrealized—over the relevant current time period. Using these values, along with information about any new funds added or funds withdrawn during the period, the investor can calculate the portfolio's holding period return (HPR) by dividing the total returns by the amount of investment during the period. Comparison of the portfolio's HPR to overall market measures can provide some insight with regard to the portfolio's performance relative to the market.

LG 4   **Use the Sharpe, Treynor, and Jensen measures to compare a portfolio's return with a risk-adjusted, market-adjusted rate of return, and discuss portfolio revision.** A risk-adjusted, market-adjusted comparison of a portfolio's return can be made using Sharpe's measure, Treynor's measure, or Jensen's measure. Sharpe's and Treynor's measures find the risk premium per unit of risk, which can be compared to similar market measures to assess the portfolio's performance relative to the market. Jensen's measure, which is theoretically consistent with Treynor's, calculates the portfolio's excess return using beta and CAPM. Because it is relatively easy to calculate and directly makes both risk and market adjustments, Jensen's measure tends to be preferred over Sharpe's and Treynor's. Portfolio revision—selling certain issues and purchasing new ones—should take place when returns are unacceptable or when the portfolio fails to meet the investor's objectives.

LG 5   **Describe the role of formula plans and the logic of dollar-cost averaging, constant-dollar plans, constant-ratio plans, and variable-ratio plans.** Formula plans are used to time purchase and sale decisions to take advantage of price changes that result from cyclical price movements. The four commonly used formula plans are dollar-cost averaging, the constant-dollar plan, the constant-ratio plan, and the variable-ratio plan. All of them have certain decision rules or triggers that signal a purchase and/or sale action.

LG 6   **Explain the role of limit and stop-loss orders in investment timing, the warehousing of liquidity, and the key factors in timing investment sales to achieve investment goals.** Limit and stop-loss orders can be used to trigger the rebalancing of a portfolio to contribute toward improved portfolio returns. Low-risk, highly liquid investment vehicles such as money market deposit accounts (and some NOWs) and money market mutual funds can warehouse liquidity. Such liquidity can protect against total loss and allow the investor to quickly seize attractive future investment opportunities. Investment sales should be timed to obtain maximum tax benefits (or minimum tax consequences) and to contribute to the achievement of the investor's goals.

DISCUSSION QUESTIONS

1. Choose an established local (or nearby) company that has its stock listed and actively traded on a major exchange. Find the stock's closing price at the end of each of the preceding 6 years and the amount of dividends paid in each of the preceding 5 years. Also, obtain the value of the Dow Jones Industrial Average (DJIA) at the end of each of the preceding 6 years.

   a. Use Equation 17.1 to calculate the pretax holding period return (HPR) on the stock for each of the preceding 5 years.

   b. Learn and discuss the international, national, and local economic and market developments that occurred during the preceding 5 years.

   c. Compare the stock's returns to the DJIA for each year over the 5-year period of concern.

   d. Discuss the stock's returns in light of the economic and market developments noted in part (b) and the behavior of the DJIA as noted in part (c) over the 5 preceding years. How well did the stock perform in light of these factors?

2. Assume that you are in the 35 percent tax bracket (federal and state combined). Select a major stock, bond, and mutual fund in which you are interested in investing. For each of them, gather data for each of the past 3 years on the annual dividends or interest paid and the capital gain (or loss) that would have resulted had they been purchased at the start of each year and sold at the end of each year. For the mutual fund, be sure to separate any dividends paid into investment income dividends and capital gains dividends.

   a. For each of the three investment vehicles, calculate the pretax and after-tax HPR for each of the 3 years.

   b. Use your annual HPR findings in part (a) to calculate the average after-tax HPR for each of the investment vehicles over the 3-year period.

   c. Compare the average returns found in part (b) for each of the investment vehicles. Discuss the relative risks in view of these returns and the characteristics of each vehicle.

3. Choose six actively traded stocks for inclusion in your investment portfolio. Assume the portfolio was created 3 years earlier by purchasing 200 shares of each of the six stocks. Find the acquisition price of each stock, the annual dividend paid by each stock, and the year-end prices for the 3 calendar years. Record for each stock its total cost, cost per share, current price per share, and total current value for each of the 3 calendar years.

   a. For each of the 3 years, find the amount invested in the portfolio.

   b. For each of the 3 years, measure the annual income from the portfolio.

   c. For each of the 3 years, determine the unrealized capital gains from the portfolio.

   d. For each of the 3 years, calculate, using the values in parts (a), (b), and (c), the portfolio's HPR.

   e. Use your findings in part (d) to calculate the average HPR for the portfolio over the 3-year period. Discuss your finding.

4. Find five actively traded stocks and record their prices at the start and the end of the most recent calendar year. Also, find the amount of dividends paid on each stock during that year and each stock's beta at the end of the year. Assume that the five stocks were held during the year in an equal-dollar-weighted portfolio (i.e., 20 percent in each stock) created at the start of the year. Also find the current risk-free rate, R_F, and the market return, r_m, for the given year. Assume the standard deviation for the portfolio of the five stocks is 14.25 percent and the standard deviation for the market portfolio is 10.80 percent.

   a. Use the formula presented in Chapter 16 (Equation 16.1) to find the portfolio return, r_p, for the year under consideration.

    b. Calculate Sharpe's measure for both the portfolio and the market. Compare and discuss these values. Based on this measure, is the portfolio's performance inferior or superior? Explain.

    c. Calculate Treynor's measure for both the portfolio and the market. Compare and discuss these values. Based on this measure, is the portfolio performance inferior or superior? Explain.

    d. Calculate Jensen's measure (Jensen's alpha) for both the portfolio and the market. Compare and discuss these values. Based on this measure, is the portfolio performance inferior or superior? Explain.

    e. Compare, contrast, and discuss your analysis using the three measures in parts (b), (c), and (d). Is the portfolio a good one?

5. Choose a high-growth mutual fund and a money market mutual fund. Find and record their closing net asset values (NAVs) at the end of each *week* for the immediate past year. Assume that you wish to invest $10,400.

    a. If you use dollar-cost averaging to buy shares in both the high-growth and the money market funds by purchasing $100 of each of them at the end of each week—a total investment of $10,400 (52 weeks × $200/week), how many shares would you have purchased in each fund by year-end? What are the total number of shares, the average cost per share, and the year-end portfolio value of each fund? Total the year-end fund values and compare them to the total that would have resulted from investing $5,200 in each fund at the end of the first week.

    b. Assume you use a constant-dollar plan with 50 percent invested in the high-growth fund (speculative portion) and 50 percent invested in the money market fund (conservative portion). If the portfolio is rebalanced every time the speculative portion is worth $500 more or $500 less than its initial value of $5,200, what would be the total portfolio value and number of shares in the speculative portion at year-end?

    c. Assume that, as in part (b), you initially invest 50 percent in the speculative portion and 50 percent in the conservative portion. But in this case you use a constant-ratio plan under which rebalancing to the 50-50 mix occurs whenever the ratio of the speculative to the conservative portion is greater than or equal to 1.25 or less than or equal to .75. What would be the total portfolio value and number of shares in the speculative portion at year-end?

    d. Compare and contrast the year-end values of the total portfolio under each of the plans in parts (a), (b), and (c) above. Which plan would have been best in light of these findings? Explain.

PROBLEMS   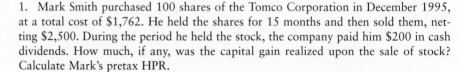

1. Mark Smith purchased 100 shares of the Tomco Corporation in December 1995, at a total cost of $1,762. He held the shares for 15 months and then sold them, netting $2,500. During the period he held the stock, the company paid him $200 in cash dividends. How much, if any, was the capital gain realized upon the sale of stock? Calculate Mark's pretax HPR.

2. Jill Clark invested $25,000 in the bonds of Industrial Aromatics, Inc. She held them for 13 months, at the end of which she sold them for $26,746. During the period of ownership, she earned $2,000 interest. Calculate the pretax and after-tax HPR on Jill's investment. Assume she is in the 31 percent tax bracket.

3. Charlotte Smidt bought 2,000 shares of the balanced no-load LaJolla Fund exactly 1 year ago for an NAV of $8.60 per share. During the year, the fund distributed investment income dividends of 32 cents per share and capital gains dividends of 38 cents per share. At the end of the year, Charlotte, who is in the 35 percent tax bracket

(federal and state combined), realized $8.75 per share on the sale of all 2,000 shares. Calculate Charlotte's pretax and after-tax HPR on this transaction.

4. Peter Hancock bought a parcel of land in Red Woods 1 year ago for $55,000. He sold the property this year for $63,000, and his reversion from the sale was $61,000 after deducting $2,000 in closing costs and income taxes. Estimate Peter's after-tax holding period return on the investment.

5. Marilyn Gore, who is in a 33 percent tax bracket (federal and state combined), purchased 10 ounces of gold for $4,000 exactly 1 year ago. Due to the release of a large amount of gold onto the market by a major South African mining company, Marilyn netted only $370 per ounce upon the sale of her 10 ounces of gold today. What are Marilyn's pretax and after-tax HPRs on this transaction?

6. On January 1, 1996, Simon Love's portfolio of 15 common stocks, completely equity-financed, had a market value of $264,000. At the end of May 1996, Simon sold 1 of the stocks, which had a beginning-of-year value of $26,300, for $31,500. He did not reinvest those or any other funds in the portfolio during the year. He received total dividends from stocks in his portfolio of $12,500 during the year. On December 31, 1996, Simon's portfolio had a market value of $250,000. Find the HPR on Simon's portfolio during the year ended December 31, 1996. (Measure the amount of withdrawn funds at their beginning-of-year value.)

7. Niki Malone's portfolio earned a return of 11.8 percent during the year just ended. The portfolio's standard deviation of return was 14.1 percent. The risk-free rate is currently 6.2 percent. During the year, the return on the market portfolio was 9.0 percent and its standard deviation was 9.4 percent.
   a. Calculate Sharpe's measure for Niki Malone's portfolio for the year just ended.
   b. Compare the performance of Niki's portfolio found in part (a) to that of Hector Smith's portfolio, which has Sharpe's measure of .43. Which portfolio performed better? Why?
   c. Calculate Sharpe's measure for the market portfolio for the year just ended.
   d. Use your findings in part (c) to discuss the performance of Niki's portfolio relative to the market during the year just ended.

8. During the year just ended, Anna Schultz's portfolio, which has a beta of .90, earned a return of 8.6 percent. The risk-free rate is currently 7.3 percent, and the return on the market portfolio during the year just ended was 9.2 percent.
   a. Calculate Treynor's measure for Anna's portfolio for the year just ended.
   b. Compare the performance of Anna's portfolio found in part (a) to that of Stacey Quant's portfolio, which has Treynor's measure of 1.25 percent. Which portfolio performed better? Explain.
   c. Calculate Treynor's measure for the market portfolio for the year just ended.
   d. Use your findings in part (c) to discuss the performance of Anna's portfolio relative to the market during the year just ended.

9. Chee Chew's portfolio has a beta of 1.3 and earned a return of 12.9 percent during the year just ended. The risk-free rate is currently 7.8 percent, and the return on the market portfolio during the year just ended was 11.0 percent.
   a. Calculate Jensen's measure (Jensen's alpha) for Chee's portfolio for the year just ended.
   b. Compare the performance of Chee's portfolio found in part (a) to that of Carri Uhl's portfolio, which has Jensen's measure of −0.24. Which portfolio performed better? Explain.

c. Use your findings in part (a) to discuss the performance of Chee's portfolio relative to the market during the period just ended.

 10. The risk-free rate is currently 8.1 percent. Use the data in the following table for the Fio family's portfolio and the market portfolio during the year just ended to answer the questions below.

Data Item	Fios' Portfolio	Market Portfolio
Rate of return	12.8%	11.2%
Standard deviation of return	13.5%	9.6%
Beta	1.10	1.00

a. Calculate Sharpe's measure for the portfolio and the market, compare them, and assess the performance of the Fios' portfolio during the year just ended.
b. Calculate Treynor's measure for the portfolio and the market, compare them, and assess the performance of the Fios' portfolio during the year just ended.
c. Calculate Jensen's measure (Jensen's alpha), and use it to assess the performance of the Fios' portfolio during the year just ended.
d. Based on your findings in parts (a), (b), and (c), assess the performance of the Fios' portfolio during the year just ended.

 11. Over the past 2 years, Jonas Cone has used a dollar-cost averaging formula to purchase $300 worth of FCI common stock each month. The price per share paid each month over the 2 years is given in the following table. Assume Jonas paid no brokerage commissions on these transactions.

| Month | Price per Share of FCI | |
	Year 1	Year 2
January	11⅝	11⅜
February	11½	11¾
March	11½	12
April	11	12
May	11¾	12⅛
June	12	12½
July	12⅜	12¾
August	12½	13
September	12¼	13¼
October	12½	13
November	11⅞	13⅜
December	11½	13½

a. How much was Jonas's total investment over the 2-year period?
b. How many shares did Jonas purchase over the 2-year period?
c. Use your findings in parts (a) and (b) to calculate Jonas's average cost per share of FCI.
d. What was the value of Jonas's holdings in FCI at the end of the second year?

CASE PROBLEMS

17.1   ASSESSING THE STALCHECKS' PORTFOLIO PERFORMANCE

The Stalchecks, Mary and Nick, have an investment portfolio containing four vehicles. It was developed to provide them with a balance between current income and capital appreciation. Rather than acquire mutual fund shares or diversify within a given class of investment vehicle, they developed their portfolio with the idea of diversifying across various types of vehicles. The portfolio currently contains common stock, industrial bonds, mutual fund shares, and a real estate investment. They acquired each of these vehicles during the past 3 years, and they plan to invest in gold and other vehicles sometime in the future.

Currently, the Stalchecks are interested in measuring the return on their investment and assessing how well they have done relative to the market. They hope that the return earned over the past calendar year is in excess of what they would have earned by investing in a portfolio consisting of the S&P 500 stock composite index. Their investigation has indicated that the risk-free rate was 7.2 percent and the (before-tax) return on the S&P stock portfolio was 10.1 percent during the past year. With the aid of a friend, they have been able to estimate the beta of their portfolio, which was 1.20. In their analysis, they have planned to ignore taxes, because they feel their earnings have been adequately sheltered. Because they did not make any portfolio transactions during the past year, the Stalchecks would have to consider only unrealized capital gains, if any. To make the necessary calculations, the Stalchecks have gathered the following information on each of the four vehicles in their portfolio:

Common stock. They own 400 shares of KJ Enterprises common stock. KJ is a diversified manufacturer of metal pipe and is known for its unbroken stream of dividends. Over the past few years, it has entered new markets and, as a result, has offered moderate capital appreciation potential. Its share price has risen from 17¼ at the start of the last calendar year to 18¾ at the end of the year. During the year, quarterly cash dividends of 20, 20, 25, and 25 cents were paid.

Industrial bonds. The Stalchecks own 8 Cal Industries bonds. The bonds have a $1,000 par value, have a 9¾ percent coupon, and are due in 2006. They are A-rated by Moody's. The bond was quoted at 97 at the beginning of the year and ended the calendar year at 96⅜.

Mutual fund. The Stalchecks hold 500 shares in the Holt Fund, a balanced, no-load mutual fund. The dividend distributions on the fund during the year consisted of 60 cents in investment income and 50 cents in capital gains. The fund's NAV at the beginning of the calendar year was $19.45, and it ended the year at $20.02.

Real estate. The Stalchecks own a parcel of raw land that had an appraised value of $26,000 at the beginning of the calendar year. Although they did not have it appraised at year-end, they were offered $30,500 for it at that time. Because the offer was made through a realtor, they would have had to pay nearly $1,500 in sales commissions and fees to make the sale at that price.

Questions

1. Calculate the holding period return on a before-tax basis for each of the four investment vehicles described above.

2. Assuming that the Stalchecks' ordinary income is currently being taxed at a combined (state and federal) tax rate of 38 percent, determine the after-tax HPR for each of their four investment vehicles.

3. Recognizing that all gains on the Stalchecks' investments were unrealized, calculate the before-tax portfolio HPR for their four-vehicle portfolio during the past calendar year. Evaluate this return relative to its current income and capital gain components.

4. Use the HPR calculated in question 3 to calculate Jensen's measure (Jensen's alpha) to analyze the performance of the Stalcheck's portfolio on a risk-adjusted, market-adjusted basis. Comment on your finding. Is it reasonable to use Jensen's measure to evaluate a four-vehicle portfolio? Why or why not?

5. Based upon your analysis in questions 1, 3, and 4, what, if any, recommendations might you offer the Stalchecks relative to the revision of their portfolio? Explain your recommendations.

17.2   EVALUATING FORMULA PLANS: CHARLES SPURGE'S APPROACH

Charles Spurge, a mathematician with Ansco Petroleum Company, wishes to develop a rational basis for timing his portfolio transactions. He currently holds a security portfolio with a market value of nearly $100,000, divided equally between a very conservative, low-beta common stock, ConCam United, and a highly speculative, high-beta stock, Fleck Enterprises. Based upon his reading of the investments literature, Charles does not believe it is necessary to diversity one's portfolio across 8 to 15 securities. His own feeling, based on his independent mathematical analysis, is that one can achieve the same results by holding a 2-security portfolio in which one security is very conservative and the other is highly speculative. His feelings on this point will not be altered; he plans to continue to hold such a 2-security portfolio until he finds that his theory does not work. During the past couple of years, he has earned a rate of return in excess of the risk-adjusted, market-adjusted rate expected on such a portfolio.

Charles's current interest centers on investigating and possibly developing his own formula plan for timing portfolio transactions. The current stage of his analysis focuses on the evaluation of four commonly used formula plans in order to isolate the desirable features of each. The four plans being considered are (1) dollar-cost averaging, (2) the constant-dollar plan, (3) the constant-ratio plan, and (4) the variable-ratio plan. Charles's analysis of the plans will involve the use of two types of data. Because dollar-cost averaging is a passive buy-and-hold strategy in which the periodic investment is held constant, whereas the other plans are more active in that they involve periodic purchases and sales within the portfolio, differing data are needed to evaluate each of them.

For evaluating the dollar-cost averaging plan, Charles decided he would assume an investment of $500 at the end of each 45-day period. He chose to use 45-day time intervals to achieve certain brokerage fee savings that would be available by making larger transactions. The $500 per 45 days totaled $4,000 for the year and equaled the total amount Charles invested during the past year. (*Note:* For convenience, the returns earned on the portions of the $4,000 that remain uninvested during the year are ignored.) In evaluating this plan, he would assume that half ($250) was invested in the conservative stock (ConCam United) and the other half in the speculative stock (Fleck Enterprises). The share prices for each of the stocks at the end of the eight 45-day periods when purchases were to be made are given below.

Period	Price per Share	
	ConCam	Fleck
1	22⅛	22⅛
2	21⅞	24½
3	21⅞	25⅜
4	22	28½
5	22¼	21⅞
6	22⅛	19¼
7	22	21½
8	22¼	23⅝

To evaluate the three other plans, Charles decided to begin with a $4,000 portfolio evenly split between the 2 stocks. He chose to use $4,000, because that amount would correspond to the total amount invested in the 2 stocks over 1 year using dollar-cost averaging. He planned to use the same eight points in time given earlier to assess and make, if required, transfers within the portfolio. For each of the three plans evaluated using these data, he established the triggering points given below.

Constant-dollar plan. Each time the speculative portion of the portfolio is worth 13 percent more or less than its initial value of $2,000, the portfolio is rebalanced to bring the speculative portion back to its initial $2,000 value.

Constant-ratio plan. Each time the ratio of the value of the speculative portion of the portfolio to the value of the conservative portion is (a) greater than or equal to 1.15 or (b) less than or equal to .84, the portfolio is rebalanced through sale or purchase, respectively, to bring the ratio back to its initial value of 1.0.

Variable-ratio plan. Each time the value of the speculative portion of the portfolio rises above 54 percent of the total value of the portfolio, its proportion is reduced to 46 percent. Each time the value of the speculative portion of the portfolio drops below 38 percent of the total value of the portfolio, its proportion would be raised to 50 percent.

Questions

1.   Under the dollar-cost averaging plan, determine the total number of shares purchased, the average cost per share, and the year-end portfolio value expressed both in dollars and as a percentage of the amount invested for (a) the conservative stock, (b) the speculative stock, and (c) the total portfolio.

2.   Using the constant-dollar plan, determine the year-end portfolio value expressed both in dollars and as a percentage of the amount initially invested for (a) the conservative portion, (b) the speculative portion, and (c) the total portfolio.

3.   Repeat question 2 for the constant-ratio plan. Be sure to answer all parts.

4.   Repeat question 2 for the variable-ratio plan. Be sure to answer all parts.

5.   Compare and contrast your results from questions 1 through 4. You may want to summarize them in tabular form. Which plan would appear to have been most beneficial in timing Charles's portfolio activities during the past year? Explain.

Appendixes

APPENDIX A
FINANCIAL TABLES

Table A.1 Future-Value Interest Factors for One Dollar, *FVIF*

					Interest Rate					
Period	1%	2%	3%	4%	5%	6%	7%	8%	9%	10%
1	1.010	1.020	1.030	1.040	1.050	1.060	1.070	1.080	1.090	1.100
2	1.020	1.040	1.061	1.082	1.102	1.124	1.145	1.166	1.188	1.210
3	1.030	1.061	1.093	1.125	1.158	1.191	1.225	1.260	1.295	1.331
4	1.041	1.082	1.126	1.170	1.216	1.262	1.311	1.360	1.412	1.464
5	1.051	1.104	1.159	1.217	1.276	1.338	1.403	1.469	1.539	1.611
6	1.062	1.126	1.194	1.265	1.340	1.419	1.501	1.587	1.677	1.772
7	1.072	1.149	1.230	1.316	1.407	1.504	1.606	1.714	1.828	1.949
8	1.083	1.172	1.267	1.369	1.477	1.594	1.718	1.851	1.993	2.144
9	1.094	1.195	1.305	1.423	1.551	1.689	1.838	1.999	2.172	2.358
10	1.105	1.219	1.344	1.480	1.629	1.791	1.967	2.159	2.367	2.594
11	1.116	1.243	1.384	1.539	1.710	1.898	2.105	2.332	2.580	2.853
12	1.127	1.268	1.426	1.601	1.796	2.012	2.252	2.518	2.813	3.138
13	1.138	1.294	1.469	1.665	1.886	2.133	2.410	2.720	3.066	3.452
14	1.149	1.319	1.513	1.732	1.980	2.261	2.579	2.937	3.342	3.797
15	1.161	1.346	1.558	1.801	2.079	2.397	2.759	3.172	3.642	4.177
16	1.173	1.373	1.605	1.873	2.183	2.540	2.952	3.426	3.970	4.595
17	1.184	1.400	1.653	1.948	2.292	2.693	3.159	3.700	4.328	5.054
18	1.196	1.428	1.702	2.026	2.407	2.854	3.380	3.996	4.717	5.560
19	1.208	1.457	1.753	2.107	2.527	3.026	3.616	4.316	5.142	6.116
20	1.220	1.486	1.806	2.191	2.653	3.207	3.870	4.661	5.604	6.727
21	1.232	1.516	1.860	2.279	2.786	3.399	4.140	5.034	6.109	7.400
22	1.245	1.546	1.916	2.370	2.925	3.603	4.430	5.436	6.658	8.140
23	1.257	1.577	1.974	2.465	3.071	3.820	4.740	5.871	7.258	8.954
24	1.270	1.608	2.033	2.563	3.225	4.049	5.072	6.341	7.911	9.850
25	1.282	1.641	2.094	2.666	3.386	4.292	5.427	6.848	8.623	10.834
30	1.348	1.811	2.427	3.243	4.322	5.743	7.612	10.062	13.267	17.449
35	1.417	2.000	2.814	3.946	5.516	7.686	10.676	14.785	20.413	28.102
40	1.489	2.208	3.262	4.801	7.040	10.285	14.974	21.724	31.408	45.258
45	1.565	2.438	3.781	5.841	8.985	13.764	21.002	31.920	48.325	72.888
50	1.645	2.691	4.384	7.106	11.467	18.419	29.456	46.900	74.354	117.386

Table A.1 Future-Value Interest Factors for One Dollar, *FVIF (Continued)*

Interest Rate

Period	11%	12%	13%	14%	15%	16%	17%	18%	19%	20%
1	1.110	1.120	1.130	1.140	1.150	1.160	1.170	1.180	1.190	1.200
2	1.232	1.254	1.277	1.300	1.322	1.346	1.369	1.392	1.416	1.440
3	1.368	1.405	1.443	1.482	1.521	1.561	1.602	1.643	1.685	1.728
4	1.518	1.574	1.630	1.689	1.749	1.811	1.874	1.939	2.005	2.074
5	1.685	1.762	1.842	1.925	2.011	2.100	2.192	2.288	2.386	2.488
6	1.870	1.974	2.082	2.195	2.313	2.436	2.565	2.700	2.840	2.986
7	2.076	2.211	2.353	2.502	2.660	2.826	3.001	3.185	3.379	3.583
8	2.305	2.476	2.658	2.853	3.059	3.278	3.511	3.759	4.021	4.300
9	2.558	2.773	3.004	3.252	3.518	3.803	4.108	4.435	4.785	5.160
10	2.839	3.106	3.395	3.707	4.046	4.411	4.807	5.234	5.695	6.192
11	3.152	3.479	3.836	4.226	4.652	5.117	5.624	6.176	6.777	7.430
12	3.498	3.896	4.334	4.818	5.350	5.936	6.580	7.288	8.064	8.916
13	3.883	4.363	4.898	5.492	6.153	6.886	7.699	8.599	9.596	10.699
14	4.310	4.887	5.535	6.261	7.076	7.987	9.007	10.147	11.420	12.839
15	4.785	5.474	6.254	7.138	8.137	9.265	10.539	11.974	13.589	15.407
16	5.311	6.130	7.067	8.137	9.358	10.748	12.330	14.129	16.171	18.488
17	5.895	6.866	7.986	9.276	10.761	12.468	14.426	16.672	19.244	22.186
18	6.543	7.690	9.024	10.575	12.375	14.462	16.879	19.673	22.900	26.623
19	7.263	8.613	10.197	12.055	14.232	16.776	19.748	23.214	27.251	31.948
20	8.062	9.646	11.523	13.743	16.366	19.461	23.105	27.393	32.429	38.337
21	8.949	10.804	13.021	15.667	18.821	22.574	27.033	32.323	38.591	46.005
22	9.933	12.100	14.713	17.861	21.644	26.186	31.629	38.141	45.923	55.205
23	11.026	13.552	16.626	20.361	24.891	30.376	37.005	45.007	54.648	66.247
24	12.239	15.178	18.788	23.212	28.625	35.236	43.296	53.108	65.031	79.496
25	13.585	17.000	21.230	26.461	32.918	40.874	50.656	62.667	77.387	95.395
30	22.892	29.960	39.115	50.949	66.210	85.849	111.061	143.367	184.672	237.373
35	38.574	52.799	72.066	98.097	133.172	180.311	243.495	327.988	440.691	590.657
40	64.999	93.049	132.776	188.876	267.856	378.715	533.846	750.353	1051.642	1469.740
45	109.527	163.985	244.629	363.662	538.752	795.429	1170.425	1716.619	2509.583	3657.176
50	184.559	288.996	450.711	700.197	1083.619	1670.669	2566.080	3927.189	5988.730	9100.191

Table A.1 Future-Value Interest Factors for One Dollar, *FVIF (Continued)*

Period	21%	22%	23%	24%	25%	30%	35%	40%	45%	50%
1	1.210	1.220	1.230	1.240	1.250	1.300	1.350	1.400	1.450	1.500
2	1.464	1.488	1.513	1.538	1.562	1.690	1.822	1.960	2.102	2.250
3	1.772	1.816	1.861	1.907	1.953	2.197	2.460	2.744	3.049	3.375
4	2.144	2.215	2.289	2.364	2.441	2.856	3.321	3.842	4.421	5.063
5	2.594	2.703	2.815	2.932	3.052	3.713	4.484	5.378	6.410	7.594
6	3.138	3.297	3.463	3.635	3.815	4.827	6.053	7.530	9.294	11.391
7	3.797	4.023	4.259	4.508	4.768	6.275	8.172	10.541	13.476	17.086
8	4.595	4.908	5.239	5.589	5.960	8.157	11.032	14.758	19.541	25.629
9	5.560	5.987	6.444	6.931	7.451	10.604	14.894	20.661	28.334	38.443
10	6.727	7.305	7.926	8.594	9.313	13.786	20.106	28.925	41.085	57.665
11	8.140	8.912	9.749	10.657	11.642	17.921	27.144	40.495	59.573	86.498
12	9.850	10.872	11.991	13.215	14.552	23.298	36.644	56.694	86.380	129.746
13	11.918	13.264	14.749	16.386	18.190	30.287	49.469	79.371	125.251	194.620
14	14.421	16.182	18.141	20.319	22.737	39.373	66.784	111.119	181.614	291.929
15	17.449	19.742	22.314	25.195	28.422	51.185	90.158	155.567	263.341	437.894
16	21.113	24.085	27.446	31.242	35.527	66.541	121.713	217.793	381.844	656.841
17	25.547	29.384	33.758	38.740	44.409	86.503	164.312	304.911	553.674	985.261
18	30.912	35.848	41.523	48.038	55.511	112.454	221.822	426.875	802.826	1477.892
19	37.404	43.735	51.073	59.567	69.389	146.190	299.459	597.625	1164.098	2216.838
20	45.258	53.357	62.820	73.863	86.736	190.047	404.270	836.674	1687.942	3325.257
21	54.762	65.095	77.268	91.591	108.420	247.061	545.764	1171.343	2247.515	4987.883
22	66.262	79.416	95.040	113.572	135.525	321.178	736.781	1639.878	3548.896	7481.824
23	80.178	96.887	116.899	140.829	169.407	417.531	994.653	2295.829	5145.898	11222.738
24	97.015	118.203	143.786	174.628	211.758	542.791	1342.781	3214.158	7461.547	16834.109
25	117.388	144.207	176.857	216.539	264.698	705.627	1812.754	4499.816	10819.242	25251.164
30	304.471	389.748	497.904	634.810	807.793	2619.936	8128.426	24201.043	69348.375	*
35	789.716	1053.370	1401.749	1861.020	2465.189	9727.598	36448.051	*	*	*
40	2048.309	2846.941	3946.340	5455.797	7523.156	36117.754	*	*	*	*
45	5312.758	7694.418	11110.121	15994.316	22958.844	*	*	*	*	*
50	13779.844	20795.680	31278.301	46889.207	70064.812	*	*	*	*	*

*FVIF > 99,999.

Table A.2 Future-Value Interest Factors for a One-Dollar Annuity, *FVIFA*

Interest Rate

Period	1%	2%	3%	4%	5%	6%	7%	8%	9%	10%
1	1.000	1.000	1.000	1.000	1.000	1.000	1.000	1.000	1.000	1.000
2	2.010	2.020	2.030	2.040	2.050	2.060	2.070	2.080	2.090	2.100
3	3.030	3.060	3.091	3.122	3.152	3.184	3.215	3.246	3.278	3.310
4	4.060	4.122	4.184	4.246	4.310	4.375	4.440	4.506	4.573	4.641
5	5.101	5.204	5.309	5.416	5.526	5.637	5.751	5.867	5.985	6.105
6	6.152	6.308	6.468	6.633	6.802	6.975	7.153	7.336	7.523	7.716
7	7.214	7.434	7.662	7.898	8.142	8.394	8.654	8.923	9.200	9.487
8	8.286	8.583	8.892	9.214	9.549	9.897	10.260	10.637	11.028	11.436
9	9.368	9.755	10.159	10.583	11.027	11.491	11.978	12.488	13.021	13.579
10	10.462	10.950	11.464	12.006	12.578	13.181	13.816	14.487	15.193	15.937
11	11.567	12.169	12.808	13.486	14.207	14.972	15.784	16.645	17.560	18.531
12	12.682	13.412	14.192	15.026	15.917	16.870	17.888	18.977	20.141	21.384
13	13.809	14.680	15.618	16.627	17.713	18.882	20.141	21.495	22.953	24.523
14	14.947	15.974	17.086	18.292	19.598	21.015	22.550	24.215	26.019	27.975
15	16.097	17.293	18.599	20.023	21.578	23.276	25.129	27.152	29.361	31.772
16	17.258	18.639	20.157	21.824	23.657	25.672	27.888	30.324	33.003	35.949
17	18.430	20.012	21.761	23.697	25.840	28.213	30.840	33.750	36.973	40.544
18	19.614	21.412	23.414	25.645	28.132	30.905	33.999	37.450	41.301	45.599
19	20.811	22.840	25.117	27.671	30.539	33.760	37.379	41.446	46.018	51.158
20	22.019	24.297	26.870	29.778	33.066	36.785	40.995	45.762	51.159	57.274
21	23.239	25.783	28.676	31.969	35.719	39.992	44.865	50.422	56.764	64.002
22	24.471	27.299	30.536	34.248	38.505	43.392	49.005	55.456	62.872	71.402
23	25.716	28.845	32.452	36.618	41.430	46.995	53.435	60.893	69.531	79.542
24	26.973	30.421	34.426	39.082	44.501	50.815	58.176	66.764	76.789	88.496
25	28.243	32.030	36.459	41.645	47.726	54.864	63.248	73.105	84.699	98.346
30	34.784	40.567	47.575	56.084	66.438	79.057	94.459	113.282	136.305	164.491
35	41.659	49.994	60.461	73.651	90.318	111.432	138.234	172.314	215.705	271.018
40	48.885	60.401	75.400	95.024	120.797	154.758	199.630	259.052	337.872	442.580
45	56.479	71.891	92.718	121.027	159.695	212.737	285.741	386.497	525.840	718.881
50	64.461	84.577	112.794	152.664	209.341	290.325	406.516	573.756	815.051	1163.865

Table A.2 Future-Value Interest Factors for a One-Dollar Annuity, FVIFA *(Continued)*

					Interest Rate					
Period	11%	12%	13%	14%	15%	16%	17%	18%	19%	20%
1	1.000	1.000	1.000	1.000	1.000	1.000	1.000	1.000	1.000	1.000
2	2.110	2.120	2.130	2.140	2.150	2.160	2.170	2.180	2.190	2.200
3	3.342	3.374	3.407	3.440	3.472	3.506	3.539	3.572	3.606	3.640
4	4.710	4.779	4.850	4.921	4.993	5.066	5.141	5.215	5.291	5.368
5	6.228	6.353	6.480	6.610	6.742	6.877	7.014	7.154	7.297	7.442
6	7.913	8.115	8.323	8.535	8.754	8.977	9.207	9.442	9.683	9.930
7	9.783	10.089	10.405	10.730	11.067	11.414	11.772	12.141	12.523	12.916
8	11.859	12.300	12.757	13.233	13.727	14.240	14.773	15.327	15.902	16.499
9	14.164	14.776	15.416	16.085	16.786	17.518	18.285	19.086	19.923	20.799
10	16.722	17.549	18.420	19.337	20.304	21.321	22.393	23.521	24.709	25.959
11	19.561	20.655	21.814	23.044	24.349	25.733	27.200	28.755	30.403	32.150
12	22.713	24.133	25.650	27.271	29.001	30.850	32.824	34.931	37.180	39.580
13	26.211	28.029	29.984	32.088	34.352	36.786	39.404	42.218	45.244	48.496
14	30.095	32.392	34.882	37.581	40.504	43.672	47.102	50.818	54.841	59.196
15	34.405	37.280	40.417	43.842	47.580	51.659	56.109	60.965	66.260	72.035
16	39.190	42.753	46.671	50.980	55.717	60.925	66.648	72.938	79.850	87.442
17	44.500	48.883	53.738	59.117	65.075	71.673	78.978	87.067	96.021	105.930
18	50.396	55.749	61.724	68.393	75.836	84.140	93.404	103.739	115.265	128.116
19	56.939	63.439	70.748	78.968	88.211	98.603	110.283	123.412	138.165	154.739
20	64.202	72.052	80.946	91.024	102.443	115.379	130.031	146.626	165.417	186.687
21	72.264	81.698	92.468	104.767	118.809	134.840	153.136	174.019	197.846	225.024
22	81.213	92.502	105.489	120.434	137.630	157.414	180.169	206.342	236.436	271.028
23	91.147	104.602	120.203	138.295	159.274	183.600	211.798	244.483	282.359	326.234
24	102.173	118.154	136.829	158.656	184.166	213.976	248.803	289.490	337.007	392.480
25	114.412	133.333	155.616	181.867	212.790	249.212	292.099	342.598	402.038	471.976
30	199.018	241.330	293.192	356.778	434.738	530.306	647.423	790.932	966.698	1181.865
35	341.583	431.658	546.663	693.552	881.152	1120.699	1426.448	1816.607	2314.173	2948.294
40	581.812	767.080	1013.667	1341.979	1779.048	2360.724	3134.412	4163.094	5529.711	7343.715
45	986.613	1358.208	1874.086	2590.464	3585.031	4965.191	6879.008	9531.258	13203.105	18280.914
50	1668.723	2399.975	3459.344	4994.301	7217.488	10435.449	15088.805	21812.273	31514.492	45496.094

Table A.2 Future-Value Interest Factors for a One-Dollar Annuity, *FVIFA (Continued)*

					Interest Rate						
Period	21%	22%	23%	24%	25%	30%	35%	40%	45%	50%
1	1.000	1.000	1.000	1.000	1.000	1.000	1.000	1.000	1.000	1.000
2	2.210	2.220	2.230	2.240	2.250	2.300	2.350	2.400	2.450	2.500
3	3.674	3.708	3.743	3.778	3.813	3.990	4.172	4.360	4.552	4.750
4	5.446	5.524	5.604	5.684	5.766	6.187	6.633	7.104	7.601	8.125
5	7.589	7.740	7.893	8.048	8.207	9.043	9.954	10.946	12.022	13.188
6	10.183	10.442	10.708	10.980	11.259	12.756	14.438	16.324	18.431	20.781
7	13.321	13.740	14.171	14.615	15.073	17.583	20.492	23.853	27.725	32.172
8	17.119	17.762	18.430	19.123	19.842	23.858	28.664	34.395	41.202	49.258
9	21.714	22.670	23.669	24.712	25.802	32.015	39.696	49.152	60.743	74.887
10	27.274	28.657	30.113	31.643	33.253	42.619	54.590	69.813	89.077	113.330
11	34.001	35.962	38.039	40.238	42.566	56.405	74.696	98.739	130.161	170.995
12	42.141	44.873	47.787	50.895	54.208	74.326	101.840	139.234	189.734	257.493
13	51.991	55.745	59.778	64.109	68.760	97.624	138.484	195.928	276.114	387.239
14	63.909	69.009	74.528	80.496	86.949	127.912	187.953	275.299	401.365	581.858
15	78.330	85.191	92.669	100.815	109.687	167.285	254.737	386.418	582.980	873.788
16	95.779	104.933	114.983	126.010	138.109	218.470	344.895	541.985	846.321	1311.681
17	116.892	129.019	142.428	157.252	173.636	285.011	466.608	759.778	1228.165	1968.522
18	142.439	158.403	176.187	195.993	218.045	371.514	630.920	1064.689	1781.838	2953.783
19	173.351	194.251	217.710	244.031	273.556	483.968	852.741	1491.563	2584.665	4431.672
20	210.755	237.986	268.783	303.598	342.945	630.157	1152.200	2089.188	3748.763	6648.508
21	256.013	291.343	331.603	377.461	429.681	820.204	1556.470	2925.862	5436.703	9973.762
22	310.775	356.438	408.871	469.052	538.101	1067.265	2102.234	4097.203	7884.215	14961.645
23	377.038	435.854	503.911	582.624	673.626	1388.443	2839.014	5737.078	11433.109	22443.469
24	457.215	532.741	620.810	723.453	843.032	1805.975	3833.667	8032.906	16579.008	33666.207
25	554.230	650.944	764.596	898.082	1054.791	2348.765	5176.445	11247.062	24040.555	50500.316
30	1445.111	1767.044	2160.459	2640.881	3227.172	8729.805	23221.258	60500.207	*	*
35	3755.814	4783.520	6090.227	7750.094	9856.746	32422.090	*	*	*	*
40	9749.141	12936.141	17153.691	22728.367	30088.621	*	*	*	*	*
45	25294.223	34970.230	48300.660	66638.937	91831.312	*	*	*	*	*
50	65617.202	94525.279	*	*	*	*	*	*	*	*

*FVIFA > 99,999.

A-9

Table A.3 Present-Value Interest Factors for One Dollar, *PVIF*

Period	Discount (Interest) Rate									
	1%	2%	3%	4%	5%	6%	7%	8%	9%	10%
1	.990	.980	.971	.962	.952	.943	.935	.926	.917	.909
2	.980	.961	.943	.925	.907	.890	.873	.857	.842	.826
3	.971	.942	.915	.889	.864	.840	.816	.794	.772	.751
4	.961	.924	.888	.855	.823	.792	.763	.735	.708	.683
5	.951	.906	.863	.822	.784	.747	.713	.681	.650	.621
6	.942	.888	.837	.790	.746	.705	.666	.630	.596	.564
7	.933	.871	.813	.760	.711	.665	.623	.583	.547	.513
8	.923	.853	.789	.731	.677	.627	.582	.540	.502	.467
9	.914	.837	.766	.703	.645	.592	.544	.500	.460	.424
10	.905	.820	.744	.676	.614	.558	.508	.463	.422	.386
11	.896	.804	.722	.650	.585	.527	.475	.429	.388	.350
12	.887	.789	.701	.625	.557	.497	.444	.397	.356	.319
13	.879	.773	.681	.601	.530	.469	.415	.368	.326	.290
14	.870	.758	.661	.577	.505	.442	.388	.340	.299	.263
15	.861	.743	.642	.555	.481	.417	.362	.315	.275	.239
16	.853	.728	.623	.534	.458	.394	.339	.292	.252	.218
17	.844	.714	.605	.513	.436	.371	.317	.270	.231	.198
18	.836	.700	.587	.494	.416	.350	.296	.250	.212	.180
19	.828	.686	.570	.475	.396	.331	.277	.232	.194	.164
20	.820	.673	.554	.456	.377	.312	.258	.215	.178	.149
21	.811	.660	.538	.439	.359	.294	.242	.199	.164	.135
22	.803	.647	.522	.422	.342	.278	.226	.184	.150	.123
23	.795	.634	.507	.406	.326	.262	.211	.170	.138	.112
24	.788	.622	.492	.390	.310	.247	.197	.158	.126	.102
25	.780	.610	.478	.375	.295	.233	.184	.146	.116	.092
30	.742	.552	.412	.308	.231	.174	.131	.099	.075	.057
35	.706	.500	.355	.253	.181	.130	.094	.068	.049	.036
40	.672	.453	.307	.208	.142	.097	.067	.046	.032	.022
45	.639	.410	.264	.171	.111	.073	.048	.031	.021	.014
50	.608	.372	.228	.141	.087	.054	.034	.021	.013	.009

Table A.3 Present-Value Interest Factors for One Dollar, *PVIF (Continued)*

					Discount (Interest) Rate					
Period	11%	12%	13%	14%	15%	16%	17%	18%	19%	20%
1	.901	.893	.885	.877	.870	.862	.855	.847	.840	.833
2	.812	.797	.783	.769	.756	.743	.731	.718	.706	.694
3	.731	.712	.693	.675	.658	.641	.624	.609	.593	.579
4	.659	.636	.613	.592	.572	.552	.534	.516	.499	.482
5	.593	.567	.543	.519	.497	.476	.456	.437	.419	.402
6	.535	.507	.480	.456	.432	.410	.390	.370	.352	.335
7	.482	.452	.425	.400	.376	.354	.333	.314	.296	.279
8	.434	.404	.376	.351	.327	.305	.285	.266	.249	.233
9	.391	.361	.333	.308	.284	.263	.243	.225	.209	.194
10	.352	.322	.295	.270	.247	.227	.208	.191	.176	.162
11	.317	.287	.261	.237	.215	.195	.178	.162	.148	.135
12	.286	.257	.231	.208	.187	.168	.152	.137	.124	.112
13	.258	.229	.204	.182	.163	.145	.130	.116	.104	.093
14	.232	.205	.181	.160	.141	.125	.111	.099	.088	.078
15	.209	.183	.160	.140	.123	.108	.095	.084	.074	.065
16	.188	.163	.141	.123	.107	.093	.081	.071	.062	.054
17	.170	.146	.125	.108	.093	.080	.069	.060	.052	.045
18	.153	.130	.111	.095	.081	.069	.059	.051	.044	.038
19	.138	.116	.098	.083	.070	.060	.051	.043	.037	.031
20	.124	.104	.087	.073	.061	.051	.043	.037	.031	.026
21	.112	.093	.077	.064	.053	.044	.037	.031	.026	.022
22	.101	.083	.068	.056	.046	.038	.032	.026	.022	.018
23	.091	.074	.060	.049	.040	.033	.027	.022	.018	.015
24	.082	.066	.053	.043	.035	.028	.023	.019	.015	.013
25	.074	.059	.047	.038	.030	.024	.020	.016	.013	.010
30	.044	.033	.026	.020	.015	.012	.009	.007	.005	.004
35	.026	.019	.014	.010	.008	.006	.004	.003	.002	.002
40	.015	.011	.008	.005	.004	.003	.002	.001	.001	.001
45	.009	.006	.004	.003	.002	.001	.001	.001	*	*
50	.005	.003	.002	.001	.001	.001	*	*	*	*

*PVIF = .000 when rounded to three decimal places.

Table A.3 Present-Value Interest Factors for One Dollar, *PVIF (Continued)*

Period	Discount (Interest) Rate										
	21%	22%	23%	24%	25%	30%	35%	40%	45%	50%
1	.826	.820	.813	.806	.800	.769	.741	.714	.690	.667
2	.683	.672	.661	.650	.640	.592	.549	.510	.476	.444
3	.564	.551	.537	.524	.512	.455	.406	.364	.328	.296
4	.467	.451	.437	.423	.410	.350	.301	.260	.226	.198
5	.386	.370	.355	.341	.328	.269	.223	.186	.156	.132
6	.319	.303	.289	.275	.262	.207	.165	.133	.108	.088
7	.263	.249	.235	.222	.210	.159	.122	.095	.074	.059
8	.218	.204	.191	.179	.168	.123	.091	.068	.051	.039
9	.180	.167	.155	.144	.134	.094	.067	.048	.035	.026
10	.149	.137	.126	.116	.107	.073	.050	.035	.024	.017
11	.123	.112	.103	.094	.086	.056	.037	.025	.017	.012
12	.102	.092	.083	.076	.069	.043	.027	.018	.012	.008
13	.084	.075	.068	.061	.055	.033	.020	.013	.008	.005
14	.069	.062	.055	.049	.044	.025	.015	.009	.006	.003
15	.057	.051	.045	.040	.035	.020	.011	.006	.004	.002
16	.047	.042	.036	.032	.028	.015	.008	.005	.003	.002
17	.039	.034	.030	.026	.023	.012	.006	.003	.002	.001
18	.032	.028	.024	.021	.018	.009	.005	.002	.001	.001
19	.027	.023	.020	.017	.014	.007	.003	.002	.001	*
20	.022	.019	.016	.014	.012	.005	.002	.001	.001	*
21	.018	.015	.013	.011	.009	.004	.002	.001	*	*
22	.015	.013	.011	.009	.007	.003	.001	.001	*	*
23	.012	.010	.009	.007	.006	.002	.001	*	*	*
24	.010	.008	.007	.006	.005	.002	.001	*	*	*
25	.009	.007	.006	.005	.004	.001	.001	*	*	*
30	.003	.003	.002	.002	.001	*	*	*	*	*
35	.001	.001	.001	.001	*	*	*	*	*	*
40	*	*	*	*	*	*	*	*	*	*
45	*	*	*	*	*	*	*	*	*	*
50	*	*	*	*	*	*	*	*	*	*

*PVIF = .000 when rounded to three decimal places.

Table A.4 Present-Value Interest Factors for a One-Dollar Annuity, *PVIFA*

Period		Discount (Interest) Rate								
	1%	2%	3%	4%	5%	6%	7%	8%	9%	10%
1	.990	.980	.971	.962	.952	.943	.935	.926	.917	.909
2	1.970	1.942	1.913	1.886	1.859	1.833	1.808	1.783	1.759	1.736
3	2.941	2.884	2.829	2.775	2.723	2.673	2.624	2.577	2.531	2.487
4	3.902	3.808	3.717	3.630	3.546	3.465	3.387	3.312	3.240	3.170
5	4.853	4.713	4.580	4.452	4.329	4.212	4.100	3.993	3.890	3.791
6	5.795	5.601	5.417	5.242	5.076	4.917	4.767	4.623	4.486	4.355
7	6.728	6.472	6.230	6.002	5.786	5.582	5.389	5.206	5.033	4.868
8	7.652	7.326	7.020	6.733	6.463	6.210	5.971	5.747	5.535	5.335
9	8.566	8.162	7.786	7.435	7.108	6.802	6.515	6.247	5.995	5.759
10	9.471	8.983	8.530	8.111	7.722	7.360	7.024	6.710	6.418	6.145
11	10.368	9.787	9.253	8.760	8.306	7.887	7.499	7.139	6.805	6.495
12	11.255	10.575	9.954	9.385	8.863	8.384	7.943	7.536	7.161	6.814
13	12.134	11.348	10.635	9.986	9.394	8.853	8.358	7.904	7.487	7.103
14	13.004	12.106	11.296	10.563	9.899	9.295	8.746	8.244	7.786	7.367
15	13.865	12.849	11.938	11.118	10.380	9.712	9.108	8.560	8.061	7.606
16	14.718	13.578	12.561	11.652	10.838	10.106	9.447	8.851	8.313	7.824
17	15.562	14.292	13.166	12.166	11.274	10.477	9.763	9.122	8.544	8.022
18	16.398	14.992	13.754	12.659	11.690	10.828	10.059	9.372	8.756	8.201
19	17.226	15.679	14.324	13.134	12.085	11.158	10.336	9.604	8.950	8.365
20	18.046	16.352	14.878	13.590	12.462	11.470	10.594	9.818	9.129	8.514
21	18.857	17.011	15.415	14.029	12.821	11.764	10.836	10.017	9.292	8.649
22	19.661	17.658	15.937	14.451	13.163	12.042	11.061	10.201	9.442	8.772
23	20.456	18.292	16.444	14.857	13.489	12.303	11.272	10.371	9.580	8.883
24	21.244	18.914	16.936	15.247	13.799	12.550	11.469	10.529	9.707	8.985
25	22.023	19.524	17.413	15.622	14.094	12.783	11.654	10.675	9.823	9.077
30	25.808	22.397	19.601	17.292	15.373	13.765	12.409	11.258	10.274	9.427
35	29.409	24.999	21.487	18.665	16.374	14.498	12.948	11.655	10.567	9.644
40	32.835	27.356	23.115	19.793	17.159	15.046	13.332	11.925	10.757	9.779
45	36.095	29.490	24.519	20.720	17.774	15.456	13.606	12.108	10.881	9.863
50	39.197	31.424	25.730	21.482	18.256	15.762	13.801	12.234	10.962	9.915

Table A.4 Present-Value Interest Factors for a One-Dollar Annuity, *PVIFA (Continued)*

Period				Discount (Interest) Rate						
	11%	12%	13%	14%	15%	16%	17%	18%	19%	20%
1	.901	.893	.885	.877	.870	.862	.855	.847	.840	.833
2	1.713	1.690	1.668	1.647	1.626	1.605	1.585	1.566	1.547	1.528
3	2.444	2.402	2.361	2.322	2.283	2.246	2.210	2.174	2.140	2.106
4	3.102	3.037	2.974	2.914	2.855	2.798	2.743	2.690	2.639	2.589
5	3.696	3.605	3.517	3.433	3.352	3.274	3.199	3.127	3.058	2.991
6	4.231	4.111	3.998	3.889	3.784	3.685	3.589	3.498	3.410	3.326
7	4.712	4.564	4.423	4.288	4.160	4.039	3.922	3.812	3.706	3.605
8	5.146	4.968	4.799	4.639	4.487	4.344	4.207	4.078	3.954	3.837
9	5.537	5.328	5.132	4.946	4.772	4.607	4.451	4.303	4.163	4.031
10	5.889	5.650	5.426	5.216	5.019	4.833	4.659	4.494	4.339	4.192
11	6.207	5.938	5.687	5.453	5.234	5.029	4.836	4.656	4.487	4.327
12	6.492	6.194	5.918	5.660	5.421	5.197	4.988	4.793	4.611	4.439
13	6.750	6.424	6.122	5.842	5.583	5.342	5.118	4.910	4.715	4.533
14	6.982	6.628	6.303	6.002	5.724	5.468	5.229	5.008	4.802	4.611
15	7.191	6.811	6.462	6.142	5.847	5.575	5.324	5.092	4.876	4.675
16	7.379	6.974	6.604	6.265	5.954	5.669	5.405	5.162	4.938	4.730
17	7.549	7.120	6.729	6.373	6.047	5.749	5.475	5.222	4.990	4.775
18	7.702	7.250	6.840	6.467	6.128	5.818	5.534	5.273	5.033	4.812
19	7.839	7.366	6.938	6.550	6.198	5.877	5.585	5.316	5.070	4.843
20	7.963	7.469	7.025	6.623	6.259	5.929	5.628	5.353	5.101	4.870
21	8.075	7.562	7.102	6.687	6.312	5.973	5.665	5.384	5.127	4.891
22	8.176	7.645	7.170	6.743	6.359	6.011	5.696	5.410	5.149	4.909
23	8.266	7.718	7.230	6.792	6.399	6.044	5.723	5.432	5.167	4.925
24	8.348	7.784	7.283	6.835	6.434	6.073	5.747	5.451	5.182	4.937
25	8.422	7.843	7.330	6.873	6.464	6.097	5.766	5.467	5.195	4.948
30	8.694	8.055	7.496	7.003	6.566	6.177	5.829	5.517	5.235	4.979
35	8.855	8.176	7.586	7.070	6.617	6.215	5.858	5.539	5.251	4.992
40	8.951	8.244	7.634	7.105	6.642	6.233	5.871	5.548	5.258	4.997
45	9.008	8.283	7.661	7.123	6.654	6.242	5.877	5.552	5.261	4.999
50	9.042	8.305	7.675	7.133	6.661	6.246	5.880	5.554	5.262	4.999

Table A.4 Present-Value Interest Factors for a One-Dollar Annuity, *PVIFA (Continued)*

						Discount (Interest) Rate						
Period	21%	22%	23%	24%	25%	30%	35%	40%	45%	50%
1	.826	.820	.813	.806	.800	.769	.741	.714	.690	.667
2	1.509	1.492	1.474	1.457	1.440	1.361	1.289	1.224	1.165	1.111
3	2.074	2.042	2.011	1.981	1.952	1.816	1.696	1.589	1.493	1.407
4	2.540	2.494	2.448	2.404	2.362	2.166	1.997	1.849	1.720	1.605
5	2.926	2.864	2.803	2.745	2.689	2.436	2.220	2.035	1.876	1.737
6	3.245	3.167	3.092	3.020	2.951	2.643	2.385	2.168	1.983	1.824
7	3.508	3.416	3.327	3.242	3.161	2.802	2.508	2.263	2.057	1.883
8	3.726	3.619	3.518	3.421	3.329	2.925	2.598	2.331	2.109	1.922
9	3.905	3.786	3.673	3.566	3.463	3.019	2.665	2.379	2.144	1.948
10	4.054	3.923	3.799	3.682	3.570	3.092	2.715	2.414	2.168	1.965
11	4.177	4.035	3.902	3.776	3.656	3.147	2.752	2.438	2.185	1.977
12	4.278	4.127	3.985	3.851	3.725	3.190	2.779	2.456	2.196	1.985
13	4.362	4.203	4.053	3.912	3.780	3.223	2.799	2.469	2.204	1.990
14	4.432	4.265	4.108	3.962	3.824	3.249	2.814	2.477	2.210	1.993
15	4.489	4.315	4.153	4.001	3.859	3.268	2.825	2.484	2.214	1.995
16	4.536	4.357	4.189	4.033	3.887	3.283	2.834	2.489	2.216	1.997
17	4.576	4.391	4.219	4.059	3.910	3.295	2.840	2.492	2.218	1.998
18	4.608	4.419	4.243	4.080	3.928	3.304	2.844	2.494	2.219	1.999
19	4.635	4.442	4.263	4.097	3.942	3.311	2.848	2.496	2.220	1.999
20	4.657	4.460	4.279	4.110	3.954	3.316	2.850	2.497	2.221	1.999
21	4.675	4.476	4.292	4.121	3.963	3.320	2.852	2.498	2.221	2.000
22	4.690	4.488	4.302	4.130	3.970	3.323	2.853	2.498	2.222	2.000
23	4.703	4.499	4.311	4.137	3.976	3.325	2.854	2.499	2.222	2.000
24	4.713	4.507	4.318	4.143	3.981	3.327	2.855	2.499	2.222	2.000
25	4.721	4.514	4.323	4.147	3.985	3.329	2.856	2.499	2.222	2.000
30	4.746	4.534	4.339	4.160	3.995	3.332	2.857	2.500	2.222	2.000
35	4.756	4.541	4.345	4.164	3.998	3.333	2.857	2.500	2.222	2.000
40	4.760	4.544	4.347	4.166	3.999	3.333	2.857	2.500	2.222	2.000
45	4.761	4.545	4.347	4.166	4.000	3.333	2.857	2.500	2.222	2.000
50	4.762	4.545	4.348	4.167	4.000	3.333	2.857	2.500	2.222	2.000

APPENDIX B
THE BLACK-SCHOLES OPTION PRICING MODEL

One of the best-known and most widely used formulas in finance is the Black-Scholes option pricing model (OPM). It was originally developed in 1973 by two professors, Fischer Black and Myron Scholes. They designed the model to calculate the price of a European-style call option on non-dividend-paying stocks. (Recall that a European option is one that can be exercised only on the expiration date, not before, as opposed to an American option, which can be executed anytime before the expiration date.) Options traders and others who make their living in the market quickly learned to use the Black-Scholes model to determine the correct price for options and to help them adjust their complicated stock and options combinations. The model can be modified to apply to American options, puts, and options on stocks that pay dividends, as well as to options on other underlying securities such as futures and indexes.

THE BLACK-SCHOLES OPTION PRICING MODEL

Understanding the basic Black-Scholes model is fundamental to understanding both the theory of option pricing and the strategies of profitable trading. The mathematical concepts that underlie the model are advanced and complex, but the application of the model is relatively simple, especially with calculators or computers. For the first course in investments, rather than try to derive the option pricing model, it's beneficial simply to explain the concept and show how to use the model to price options.

The foundation of the model rests on the construction of a hypothetical risk-free portfolio, consisting of long call options and short positions in the underlying stock. With proper selection of the number of call options held and the number of stocks sold, the investor can lock in a certain amount of profit. Since this profit is certain, or risk free, the investor earns the risk-free rate on the portfolio. The model uses four directly observable variables (the market price of the stock, the exercise price on the call, the time remaining until expiration on the call, and the risk-free interest rate) and one variable that is fairly easy to estimate (the standard deviation of the stock's returns). With the five variables, the basic Black-Scholes option pricing model calculates the *price of a call option* as follows:

Equation B.1
$$C = (S)[N(d_1)] - (X)(\exp^{-rt})[N(d_2)]$$

B-1

where

C = the price of the call, or the call premium

S = the price of the underlying asset, such as a stock price

X = the exercise price or the strike price of the call

r = the continuously compounded annual risk-free interest rate

t = the time (in fractions of 1 year) to the option's maturity

exp = approximately 2.718292; it is included as a function key (sometimes labeled e^x) on most financial calculators

$N(d_1)$ and $N(d_2)$ = probabilities from the cumulative standard normal distribution (see Table B.1)

Table B.1 Standard Normal Distribution Function

t	0	1	2	3	4	5	6	7	8	9
− 2.9	.0019	.0018	.0018	.0017	.0017	.0016	.0015	.0015	.0014	.0014
− 2.8	.0026	.0025	.0024	.0023	.0023	.0022	.0021	.0021	.0020	.0019
− 2.7	.0035	.0034	.0033	.0032	.0031	.0030	.0029	.0028	.0027	.0026
− 2.6	.0047	.0045	.0044	.0043	.0041	.0040	.0039	.0038	.0037	.0036
− 2.5	.0062	.0060	.0059	.0057	.0055	.0054	.0052	.0051	.0049	.0048
− 2.4	.0082	.0080	.0078	.0075	.0073	.0071	.0069	.0068	.0066	.0064
− 2.3	.0107	.0104	.0102	.0099	.0096	.0094	.0091	.0089	.0087	.0084
− 2.2	.0139	.0136	.0132	.0129	.0125	.0122	.0119	.0116	.0113	.0110
− 2.1	.0179	.0174	.0170	.0166	.0162	.0158	.0154	.0150	.0146	.0143
− 2.0	.0228	.0222	.0217	.0212	.0207	.0202	.0197	.0192	.0188	.0183
− 1.9	.0287	.0281	.0275	.0268	.0262	.0256	.0250	.0244	.0239	.0233
− 1.8	.0359	.0351	.0344	.0336	.0329	.0322	.0314	.0307	.0300	.0294
− 1.7	.0446	.0436	.0427	.0418	.0409	.0401	.0392	.0384	.0375	.0367
− 1.6	.0548	.0537	.0526	.0516	.0505	.0495	.0485	.0475	.0465	.0455
− 1.5	.0668	.0655	.0643	.0630	.0618	.0606	.0594	.0582	.0571	.0560
− 1.4	.0808	.0793	.0778	.0764	.0750	.0735	.0721	.0708	.0694	.0681
− 1.3	.0968	.0951	.0934	.0918	.0901	.0885	.0869	.0853	.0838	.0823
− 1.2	.1151	.1131	.1112	.1093	.1075	.1056	.1038	.1020	.1003	.0985
− 1.1	.1357	.1335	.1314	.1292	.1271	.1251	.1230	.1210	.1190	.1170
− 1.0	.1587	.1562	.1539	.1515	.1492	.1469	.1446	.1423	.1401	.1379
− .9	.1841	.1814	.1788	.1762	.1736	.1711	.1685	.1660	.1635	.1611
− .8	.2119	.2090	.2061	.2033	.2005	.1977	.1949	.1921	.1894	.1867
− .7	.2420	.2389	.2358	.2327	.2296	.2266	.2236	.2206	.2177	.2148
− .6	.2743	.2709	.2676	.2643	.2611	.2578	.2546	.2514	.2483	.2451
− .5	.3085	.3050	.3015	.2981	.2946	.2912	.2877	.2843	.2810	.2776
− .4	.3446	.3400	.3372	.3336	.3300	.3264	.3228	.3192	.3156	.3121
− .3	.3821	.3783	.3745	.3707	.3669	.3632	.3594	.3557	.3520	.3483
− .2	.4207	.4168	.4129	.4090	.4052	.4013	.3974	.3936	.3897	.3859
− .1	.4602	.4562	.4522	.4483	.4443	.4404	.4364	.4325	.4286	.4247
− .0	.5000	.4960	.4920	.4880	.4840	.4801	.4761	.4721	.4681	.4641

Let's look at this equation before we try to use it. It begins by stating that in calculating the price of a call, the difference between the stock price and the exercise price is very important. In fact, at expiration, either the price of a call will be zero, if it is out-of-the-money (i.e., if the stock price is less than the strike price), or it will be equal to the difference between the stock price and the strike price, if it is in-the-money. Because we are trying to price the call at a point in time before expiration, we explicitly capture the time value of money by finding the present value of the exercise price. This continuous discounting process is performed by $\exp^{-rt}$.

Also, since we do not know what the stock price will be by the expiration date, we must use a probability distribution to adjust the call premium for the uncertainty involved. The variables $N(d_1)$ and $N(d_2)$ are probabilities of the stock price being at a certain price relative to where it is now. The values for d_1 and d_2 are used to calculate the probabilities that the stock price at expiration

Table B.1   Standard Normal Distribution Function *(Continued)*

t	0	1	2	3	4	5	6	7	8	9
.0	.5000	.5040	.5080	.5120	.5160	.5199	.5239	.5279	.5319	.5359
.1	.5398	.5438	.5478	.5517	.5557	.5596	.5636	.5675	.5714	.5753
.2	.5793	.5832	.5871	.5910	.5948	.5987	.6026	.6064	.6103	.6141
.3	.6179	.6217	.6255	.6293	.6331	.6368	.6406	.6443	.6480	.6517
.4	.6554	.6592	.6628	.6664	.6700	.6736	.6772	.6808	.6844	.6880
.5	.6915	.6950	.6985	.7019	.7054	.7088	.7123	.7157	.7190	.7224
.6	.7257	.7291	.7324	.7357	.7389	.7422	.7454	.7486	.7517	.7549
.7	.7580	.7611	.7642	.7673	.7704	.7734	.7764	.7794	.7823	.7852
.8	.7881	.7910	.7939	.7967	.7995	.8023	.8051	.8078	.8106	.8133
.9	.8159	.8186	.8212	.8238	.8264	.8289	.8315	.8340	.8365	.8389
1.0	.8413	.8438	.8461	.8485	.8508	.8531	.8554	.8577	.8599	.8621
1.1	.8643	.8665	.8686	.8708	.8729	.8749	.8770	.8790	.8810	.8830
1.2	.8849	.8870	.8888	.8907	.8925	.8944	.8962	.8980	.8997	.9015
1.3	.9032	.9049	.9066	.9082	.9099	.9115	.9131	.9147	.9162	.9177
1.4	.9192	.9207	.9222	.9236	.9251	.9265	.9279	.9292	.9306	.9319
1.5	.9332	.9345	.9357	.9370	.9382	.9394	.9406	.9418	.9429	.9441
1.6	.9452	.9463	.9474	.9484	.9495	.9505	.9515	.9525	.9535	.9545
1.7	.9554	.9564	.9573	.9582	.9591	.9599	.9608	.9616	.9625	.9633
1.8	.9641	.9649	.9656	.9664	.9671	.9678	.9686	.9693	.9700	.9706
1.9	.9713	.9719	.9726	.9732	.9738	.9744	.9750	.9756	.9761	.9767
2.0	.9772	.9778	.9783	.9788	.9793	.9798	.9803	.9808	.9812	.9817
2.1	.9821	.9826	.9830	.9834	.9838	.9842	.9846	.9850	.9854	.9857
2.2	.9861	.9864	.9868	.9871	.9875	.9878	.9881	.9884	.9887	.9890
2.3	.9893	.9896	.9898	.9901	.9904	.9906	.9909	.9911	.9913	.9916
2.4	.9918	.9920	.9922	.9925	.9927	.9929	.9931	.9932	.9934	.9936
2.5	.9938	.9940	.9941	.9943	.9945	.9946	.9948	.9949	.9951	.9952
2.6	.9953	.9955	.9956	.9957	.9959	.9960	.9961	.9962	.9963	.9964
2.7	.9965	.9966	.9967	.9968	.9969	.9970	.9971	.9972	.9973	.9974
2.8	.9974	.9975	.9976	.9977	.9977	.9978	.9979	.9979	.9980	.9981
2.9	.9981	.9982	.9982	.9983	.9984	.9984	.9985	.9985	.9986	.9987
3.	.9987									

Value for $d_1(.73)$ → .7 row

Value for $d_2(.57)$ → .5 row

will be a certain number of standard deviations above or below the standardized mean (i.e., 0). Their formulas are:

Equation B.2

$$d_1 = \frac{\ln(S/X) + (r + .5\sigma^2)t}{\sigma\sqrt{t}}$$

Equation B.3

$$d_2 = d_1 - \sigma\sqrt{t}$$

Notice that in the calculation of d_1, *ln* refers to the natural logarithm of the ratio of the stock price and exercise price. This function too is included on most financial calculators. Also note that the equation uses both the standard deviation, σ, and the variance, σ^2, of the stock's returns. The variable t is included as a fraction of a 365-day year, and r is the risk-free interest rate in decimal form.

Although you will most often want to use the Black-Scholes option pricing formula on a preprogrammed calculator or computer, it is useful to work through an application to see how the model works. Assume that you want to earn income by writing a call option on Gogol MegaCorp stock, which you think will decrease in value. The current stock price is $32 5/8, and you want to write a call with a strike price of $30, to expire in 85 days. The risk-free rate is currently 7%, and you estimate that the volatility of the stock's returns has a standard deviation of .32.

To value this call, we must first compute d_1 and d_2; that is:

$$d_1 = \frac{\ln(S/X) + (r + .5\sigma^2)t}{\sigma\sqrt{t}}$$

$$= \frac{\ln\left(\dfrac{32.625}{30}\right) + (.07 + .5[.32^2])\left(\dfrac{85}{365}\right)}{.32\sqrt{\dfrac{85}{365}}}$$

$$= \frac{\ln(1.0875) + (.1212)(.2329)}{.32\sqrt{.2329}} = \frac{.0839 + .0282}{.1544} = \underline{\underline{.7260}}$$

Now for d_2:

$$d_2 = d_1 - \sigma\sqrt{t}$$
$$= .7260 - .1544 = \underline{\underline{.5716}}$$

Next, we take these numbers to the cumulative standard normal table to find the associated probabilities. These values are given in Table B.1. To use it, we need to first round d_1 and d_2 to two decimal places. This gives $d_1 = .73$ and $d_2 = .57$. Looking these values up in the table, we find the respective probabilities of $N(d_1) = .7673$ and $N(d_2) = .7157$.

We can now complete the OPM by calculating the call price:

$$C = (S)N(d_1) - (X)(\exp^{-rt})[N(d_2)]$$
$$= 32.625(.7673) - 30\exp^{(-0.07)(.2329)}(.7157)$$
$$= 25.03 - 30(.9838)(.7157)$$

$$= 25.03 - 21.12$$

$$= \underline{\underline{\$3.91}}$$

Computer solutions may give slightly different answers, due to rounding and the accuracy involved in using the standard normal table. Also, the solution provided by the Black-Scholes model will not always exactly equal the price at which the option is trading. This basic model ignores the fact that the stock could pay a dividend and that the option is American, not European. Even so, the option price provided by the model (especially by the more complicated extensions of the model) is usually very close to the actual price; *if it is not, then a trading opportunity may exist.* A number of empirical studies have attempted to test the accuracy of various versions of the option pricing model. Most find that the model gives fairly accurate results.

A change in any of the five variables of the option pricing model will result in a change in the call premium—that is, in the price of the option. A summary of the direction of change is given in Table B.2. Most of these changes can be observed by looking at a quotation of options prices and observing the option premiums over a period of time.

A simple extension of the Black-Scholes model can be made to incorporate dividend information. The annual dividend yield of the stock is the expected annual dividend divided by the current stock price. Instead of using the stock price directly in the formulas, the following substitution should be made:

Equation B.4 $S' = S(\exp^{-Dt})$

where D is the annual dividend yield. For example, suppose Gogal MegaCorp is expected to pay $2 per share in dividends in the coming year. This means that the dividend yield is about 6.13% (2 ÷ 32.625). If we use $S' = 32.16$ instead of $S' = 32.625$, we get an option price of about $3.50. This result makes intuitive sense: the lower the stock price (S), the lower will be the price of the call (C).

The option pricing model also gives another useful number besides the option price. The variable $N(d_1)$ is called the **hedge ratio,** or the **delta,** for the call option. The hedge ratio tells how much the option price will change when the underlying stock price changes by some small amount. For example, our option for Gogal MegaCorp had a hedge ratio of about .77. This means that if the price of Gogal increased (or decreased) by one dollar per share, the price of the call option would increase (or decrease) by about $0.77. This information is very useful for option traders who are trying to combine stocks and options into portfolios that will have offsetting movements. The number of call contracts or stocks held can be adjusted using the hedge ratio to produce protected portfolios. Remember, though, that the hedge ratio will change

Table B.2   Determinants of the Call Premium

An Increase in . . .	Will Cause the Call Premium to . . .
Stock price	Increase
Exercise price	Decrease
Time to expiration	Increase
Volatility of returns	Increase
Risk-free rate	Increase

whenever the stock price changes and also as the time to maturity decreases. Thus, the information provided by the hedge ratio is good for only small stock price changes, and for only a short period of time.

PROBLEMS

1. Using the Black-Scholes option pricing formula, calculate the value of a call option given the following information:

Stock price = $50

Exercise price = $45

Interest rate = 6%

Time to expiration = 90 days

Standard deviation = 0.4

2. Using the above information, recalculate the call price if the stock paid a $1.50 annual dividend.

3. Using the information in problem 1, determine how much the call price changes if all values stay the same except:
    a. The interest rate doubles to 12%.
    b. The standard deviation doubles to 0.8.
    c. What do your answers tell you about the relative importance of the interest rate and the standard deviation?

APPENDIX C
KEY EQUATIONS AND
DISK ROUTINES

Topic	Equation Number	On Disk	Page Number
Stocks			
Chapter 5			
Book value per share		🖫	202
Earnings per share (EPS)	5.1	🖫	205
Dividend yield	5.2	🖫	208
Dividend payout ratio	5.3	🖫	208
Total return from foreign investment, in U.S. dollars	5.4, 5.5, 5.6	🖫	221
Chapter 6		🖫	
Current ratio	6.1	🖫	255
Current working capital	6.2	🖫	255
Accounts receivable turnover	6.3	🖫	256
Inventory turnover	6.4	🖫	256
Total asset turnover	6.5	🖫	256
Debt-equity ratio	6.6	🖫	257
Times interest earned	6.7	🖫	257
Net profit margin	6.8	🖫	258
Return on assets (ROA)	6.9, 6.11	🖫	258
Return on equity (ROE)	6.10, 6.12, 6.13	🖫	258
Price/earnings (P/E) ratio	6.14	🖫	260
Earnings per share	6.14a	🖫	261
Dividends per share	6.15	🖫	261
Dividend yield		🖫	260
Dividend payout ratio	6.16	🖫	261
Book value per share	6.17	🖫	262
Price-to-book-value	6.18	🖫	262
Summary of all financial ratios		🖫	264
Chapter 7			
Estimated after-tax earnings	7.1	🖫	276
Estimated earnings per share	7.2, 7.3	🖫	279
Estimated dividends per share	7.4	🖫	280
Estimated share price	7.5	🖫	280
Estimated cash flow stream (summary)		🖫	281
Required rate of return	7.6	🖫	284
Zero growth dividend valuation model	7.7	🖫	287
Constant growth dividend valuation model	7.8	🖫	288
Variable growth dividend valuation model	7.9	🖫	290
Growth rate	7.10		292
Present value of a share of stock	7.11	🖫	293
Stock price, P/E approach	7.12	🖫	296
Price/earnings ratio	7.13	🖫	297
Chapter 8			
Taxable equivalent yield on municipal bonds, federal taxes only	8.1	🖫	341
Taxable equivalent yield of municipal bonds, federal and state taxes	8.2	🖫	343
Current yield		🖫	355
Chapter 9			
Pricing bonds with annual compounding	9.2	🖫	377

APPENDIX D
USING STOCK INVESTOR:
THE STUDENT VERSION

Stock Investor: The Student Version is a simplified version of the American Association of Individual Investors' (AAII's) popular *Stock Investor* program. Created by AAII specifically for users of HarperCollins finance textbooks, it is a basic screening and analysis program with fundamental information on 1,000 publicly traded companies and 60 (broadly defined) industry groups. The software includes a stand-alone, menu-driven program that allows you to look up, analyze, and screen for companies meeting specific criteria. *Stock Investor: The Student Version* enables students of investing to practice their investment skills by selecting a manageable number of companies for further analysis.

The AAII-HarperCollins partnership demonstrates a shared commitment to bringing the latest investment tools, at affordable prices, to students of investing. (*Note*: Throughout the remainder of this appendix, *Stock Investor: The Student Version* will be referred to simply as *Stock Investor*.)

HOW TO USE THIS APPENDIX

This appendix is divided into four parts. The first part describes the features of *Stock Investor*. The second part provides instructions and examples for using the program. The third part of this appendix includes chapter-by-chapter applications (including questions) keyed to *Fundamentals of Investing*. The final part provides information about AAII.

ABOUT STOCK INVESTOR

Stock Investor provides detailed historical, fundamental, and price data from Media General on hundreds of securities. These include stocks, closed-end funds, and REITs listed on the New York Stock Exchange, American Stock Exchange, Nasdaq National Market, and Nasdaq Small Cap Market. The program includes over 200 data elements for *each* security; the data are organized into financial statements.

SYSTEM REQUIREMENTS

The database size and powerful screening capabilities require an IBM-compatible 386 microprocessor or higher with 3 megabytes of available RAM and 30 megabytes of available hard disk space.

INFORMATION CONTAINED IN THE DATA SET

The data set includes the following categories of information: basic company information, current and historical market multiples, quarterly income statement data, annual income statement data, I/B/E/S earnings estimates, balance sheet data, ratios, price and share data, valuation models, and dividend reinvestment plan details.

Basic Company Information   Basic company information includes company name, address, phone, ticker symbol, and exchange; broad and narrow industry groupings; and a brief description of the company's business.

Current and Historical Market Multiples   Current and historical market multiples include price/earnings (P/E) ratio, five-year average of price/earnings ratio, price-to-book value ratio, price-to-sales ratio, price-to-cash-flow ratio, and dividend yield. Multiples are also provided for both broad and narrow industry groups to help make meaningful judgments and comparisons.

Quarterly Income Statement Data   Quarterly data covering the last two years are provided for basic income statement items, such as earnings per share from total operations.

Annual Income Statement Data   Five years' worth of annual income statement data is provided, including sales, cost of goods sold, gross operating income, net income, gross profit margin, net profit margin, total earnings per share, earnings per share for continuing operations, cash flow per share, dividends per share, and number of shares outstanding.

I/B/E/S Earnings Estimates   Consensus earnings for the current fiscal year and the next fiscal year and for the long-term earnings are provided.

Balance Sheet Data   This category includes three years' worth of information, including current assets, net fixed assets, other noncurrent assets, total assets, current liabilities, long-term debt, other noncurrent liabilities, preferred stock, common stock equity, total liabilities and equity, and total capitalization.

Ratios   Ratios to measure the profitability, liquidity, leverage, and asset management of the firm are provided, along with industry information to help the user make meaningful comparisons. Ratios provided include those for gross profit margin, net profit margin, return on assets, return on equity, current ratio, ratio of liabilities to assets, ratio of debt to capital, and asset turnover.

Price and Share Data   The program provides closing stock prices for each of the last five quarters, high/low/close prices for each of the last five calendar years, 52-week high and low price, 200-day moving average, relative strength versus all stocks for the last 52 weeks, beta, average volume for the last 52 weeks, market capitalization, and percentage of shares held by institutions.

Valuation Models   A series of basic valuation models help examine the stock price supported by current and historical price/earnings ratios, dividend yields, price-to-book-value ratios, and price-to-sales ratios.

Dividend Reinvestment Plan Details   The program includes information on firms that offer dividend reinvestment plans providing a low-cost way of investing directly with the company. The category covers areas such as program availability, investment requirements and limits, fees and discounts, and contact information.

HOW TO USE STOCK INVESTOR

In this section, we provide instructions and examples for using the screening function and working with a portfolio.

SCREENING FUNCTION

The screening function lets you scan for stocks that meet any criteria you desire. *Stock Investor* makes it easy for you to locate stocks with low price/earnings ratios, earnings momentum, profitability above industry averages, and even relative strength. The function is flexible and lets you use any of the included data fields or fields you design yourself (User-Defined Fields, or UDFs).

So that you don't waste time reentering the same criteria, *Stock Investor* lets you save your filters for later use. It is easy to save the set of companies that pass though a screen in a custom portfolio by following the directions when the "Create Portfolio" command is displayed at the bottom of the Screening Editor.

To screen the database, do the following:

1. Select **Screen** from the menu bar (**Alt-S**).
2. Select **New** (type **N**), which will open up the Screening Editor.
3. Choose **Add** (type **A**) from the Edit Criteria to set up your screening criterion. (A criterion is a comparison of two values, and you will need to include at least one criterion in a screen.) *Note:* DOS users omit this step.
4. Press **Choose_Field** (type **F**).
5. Choose a **Field Category** from the list and press **Select**. (Use the arrow keys to scroll, or press the first letter of a category and press **Enter.**)
6. Choose a **Field** from the list and press **Select**. (The Field listing will be triggered by the Field Category that you chose.) You can get a brief description of a field by highlighting it and pressing the F2 key.
7. Select a comparison operator from the middle box. (Use the mouse to open up the pop-up box by clicking on the arrow and selecting **operand.** If you are using the keyboard, use the arrow keys to highlight **operand** and press the **Tab** key to move to the next dialogue.)

8. Select a criterion to compare the first value. The right-hand box presents three choices: value, field, or industry. (Use the arrow keys to highlight an option, and then press the **Spacebar** to select.)
   - Value is a fixed value.
   - Field is a data field. Data fields used in a specified criterion must be of the same type.
   - Industry is the industry average of the data field chosen for comparison.
9. Press **OK** (**Alt-O,** or use the **Tab** key to move to the button and press **Enter**).

After you have entered all of the screening criteria:

1. Select **How Many** (type **H**) to determine how many companies match the criteria. Press **OK** (type **O**). A window will display the number of companies that match the screening criteria.
2. Select **Browse** (type **B**); then press **OK** (type **O**). Choose **Standard** (type **S**) to display a list of companies that match the screening criterion.
3. After you have reviewed the companies that match the screen, press **Enter.**

Other Screening Editor options include *Change* (modifies the screening criterion), *Delete* (removes a criterion from a screen), *Reset* (deletes all of the criteria currently in the screening filter); and *Or* (sets up a screen to find stocks that pass one of two sets of criteria).

A Screening Example

Sample assignment: *Develop a screening filter that incorporates a few of the criteria used to select Shadow Stocks (companies with a market value between $20 million and $100 million and with positive earnings per share for the two most recent years).*

1. Select **Screen** from the menu bar and then select **New.**
2. Select **Add** to define the first criterion.
3. Define the first criterion as Market_Cap > 20. To do this:
   - Press the **Choose_Field** button.
   - Choose the Price & Share Data category and press **Select.**
   - Choose the Market Cap field and press **Select.**
   - Choose the ">" operand.
   - Choose the value option and type in **20.**
   - Press **OK.**
4. Define the second criterion as Market_Cap < 100. To do this:
   - Select **Add.**
   - Press the **Choose_Field** button.
   - Choose the Price & Share Data category and press **Select.**
   - Choose the Market Cap field and press **Select.**
   - Choose the " < " operand.
   - Choose the value option and type in **100.**
   - Press **OK.**
5. Define the third criterion as EPS Y1 > 0. To do this:
   - Select **Add.**
   - Press the **Choose_Field** button.

- Choose the Income Statement–Ann'l category and press **Select.**
- Choose the EPS Y1 field and press **Select.**
- Choose the ">" operand.
- Choose the value option and type in **0.**
- Press **OK.**

6. Define the fourth criterion as EPS Y2 > 0. To do this:
   - Select **Add.**
   - Press the **Choose_Field** button.
   - Choose the Income Statement–Ann'l category and press **Select.**
   - Choose the EPS Y2 field and press **Select.**
   - Choose the ">" operand.
   - Choose the value option and type in **0.**
   - Press **OK.**

7. Define the fifth criterion as EPS 12M > 0. To do this:
   - Select **Add.**
   - Press the **Choose_Field** button.
   - Choose the Income Statement–Ann'l category and then press **Select.**
   - Choose the EPS 12M field and press **Select.**
   - Choose the ">" operand.
   - Choose the value option and type in **0.**
   - Press **OK.**

8. Save your work. Name this screen Small Cap.

9. Load the screen. (This makes the active set the companies that pass through this screen.) You can then browse through the financial summary sheets, perform additional screens, develop reports, and so forth.

DEFINING PORTFOLIOS

You can define groups of stocks into portfolios and work with these groups over time. You can create portfolios manually or define them by screening. *Stock Investor* includes a number of predefined portfolios that cover the major market indexes. With *Stock Investor*, you can create any number of portfolios using your own or your instructor's criteria. To define portfolios:

1. Select **Portfolio** from the menu bar (**Alt-P**).
2. Select **New** (type **N**).
3. To create a new portfolio, search through the database by either Ticker or Name for the company to be added to the portfolio (use the **Tab** key to move to the search button). Choose a stock by typing in the company Ticker or Name or by scrolling through the company listing (using the arrow keys). Press **Enter** to select. Press **Add** (type **A**).
4. Continue this process until your portfolio selections are complete. Next, select **Save.** (Use the **Tab** key to move to the **Save** button and then press **Enter**). A window will prompt you for a name and description of the portfolio.

After you have saved the portfolio, the program will ask if you want to load it. If you reply "no," you return to the main menu. If you reply "yes," your portfolio will be loaded and will become the *active* set. "Active set" describes the group of stocks that the program uses when you perform an action. Once a portfolio is loaded, screens and reports may be run on that portfolio. However, if you try to load another portfolio while one is running, the program will automatically unload the previous portfolio and load the current one.

To load a saved portfolio, do the following:

1. Select **Portfolio** from the menu bar (**Alt-P**).
2. Select **Load** (type **L**).
3. Choose a portfolio and press **Select.** (Use the arrow keys to highlight Portfolio and use the **Tab** key to move to the **Select** button. Press **Enter.**)
4. A window displays information on the current active set. Press **Enter** to acknowledge that the correct information appears.
5. Choose one of the following:
   • Select **Lookup** to browse the financial summary windows.
   • Select **File** and **Print** for reports.
   • Select **Rank** to order the Portfolio companies.
   • Select **Screen** to perform screening functions.

A Portfolio Example

Sample assignment: *Create a small portfolio of hotels, motels, and resorts.*

1. Select **Portfolio** from the menu bar.
2. Select **New.**
3. Press **Search by Name.** (Use the **Tab** key to highlight and then press **Enter.**)
4. Choose Hilton Hotels and press **Enter.**
5. Press **Add.**
6. Press **Search by Ticker** (Use the **Tab** key to highlight and press **Enter.**)
7. Choose RIOH for Rio Hotel Casino and then press **Enter.**
8. Press **Add.**
9. Press **Search by Name.**
10. Choose Showboat Inc. and press **Enter.**
11. Press **Add.**
12. Press the **Save** button and a window will prompt you to enter the name and an optional description. Name the portfolio Hotels, Motels, and Resorts. Press **OK.**
13. Select **Yes** when the program asks if you want to load the portfolio. The three companies that constitute your portfolio will become the active set. When you have finished working with this portfolio, select **Portfolio,** followed by **Unload,** and the entire database will become the active set again.

ADDITIONAL FEATURES OF STOCK INVESTOR

Sorting   You can alter the order in which companies are sorted. You may sort on any field in the program, including your own custom-defined fields.

Reports   *Stock Investor* includes a number of predefined reports containing detailed information for a single company or summary information for groups of securities or industries. You can also define your own reports and export those reports to a number of file formats, including several popular spreadsheet programs.

Documentation   *Stock Investor* users are provided with a short manual that includes detailed program information as well as a tutorial for beginners.

CHAPTER-BY-CHAPTER APPLICATIONS FOR STOCK INVESTOR

CHAPTER 1—DIVIDENDS

Stock Investor enables the investor to select a manageable number of companies for further analysis. Dividends are discussed in Chapter 1. What is the highest dividend payment during the past 12-month period and who made it? Also, how many companies paid an annual dividend exceeding $4.00 ($1.00/quarter)?

Note: The line below the assignment provides those field definitions that you should use to solve the assignment. The field definitions for the Chapter 1 assignment are:
[DIV_12M]

CHAPTER 2—DOMESTIC AND FOREIGN EXCHANGES

Following up on Chapter 2's discussion of global investment markets, which firms included in *Stock Investor* are headquartered in Canada (State Code = CN) and Mexico (State Code = MX)? How many firms are traded on the New York Stock Exchange and American Stock Exchange?
[STATE, EXCHANGE: N,A]

CHAPTER 3—CAPITAL LOSSES

Capital losses occur when the firm's proceeds from the sale of an asset are less than its initial cost. Investors experience capital losses when share prices decline. How many firms experienced a capital loss during the past 12 months? Which firm had the most negative earnings per share over the past 12 months? Furthermore, how many firms experienced a decline in share price since the end of the last full calendar year?
[EPS_12M, PRICE_LAST, PRICE_Y1]

CHAPTER 4—GROWTH RATES

An important variable in valuing shares is the dividend growth rate. Use *Stock Investor* to screen for the average compound increase or decrease in dividends over the most recent 5-year period. How many firms offer dividend growth rates exceeding 6 percent? Which firms have growth rates exceeding 10 percent?
[DIV_GR]

CHAPTER 5—BOOK VALUE

Book value is a measure of share price based upon the firm's balance sheet. Use *Stock Investor* to screen for the number of firms with a negative book value per share. Next, screen the database for the number of shares with a most recent stock price that is less than the book value per share. List five of these firms. [BV_PER_SHR, PRICE_LAST]

CHAPTER 6—RATIO ANALYSIS

Chapter 6 covers key fundamental ratios that include the current ratio, total asset turnover ratio, and return on assets. What is the mean value of these ratios for those firms included in the data set that produce specialty chemicals? How do these values vary for firms in the trucking industry? [CURR_R_Y1, TA_TRN_Y1, ROA, IND_3_DIG]

CHAPTER 7—VALUATION

Stock Investor data set valuation estimates based on sales use information on the latest 12-month sales, sales growth rates, and the price-to-sales ratio. How many firms have share prices below their sales-based estimates? In another fundamental valuation procedure, *Stock Investor* uses the latest 12 months' total EPS, earnings growth rate, and the P/E ratio. How many firms have share prices below the earnings-based valuation estimate? List ten firms from each undervalued group. [SPS_VALTN, EPS_VALTN, PRICE_LAST]

CHAPTER 8—GROSS OPERATING MARGINS

Bond ratings, discussed in Chapter 8, are related to firm profitability. Firms with a negative gross profit margin are not earning enough to cover operating costs, regardless of financing costs. How many firms in the data set had a negative gross operating margin in the prior 12 months? Are more of these firms in the health industry or publishing industry? Which firms are included? [GPM_12M, IND_2_DIG]

CHAPTER 9—LONG-TERM DEBT

To get a feel for the level of bond financing, screen the data set for the median level of long-term debt as a percentage of the total capital. Identify the number of firms with a long-term debt ratio of zero, indicating that the firm has not issued any bonds. List ten of these firms, if available. [LTD_TC_Y1]

CHAPTER 10—PREFERRED STOCK FINANCING

Not all firms issue preferred stock, covered in Chapter 10. How many companies in the data set reported preferred stock on their balance sheet at the end of the last full fiscal year? Has the frequency of issuing preferred stock increased from the end of the prior year? Has there been a trend toward more usage of preferred stock by firms in the data set over the past 3 years?
[PREFSTK_Y1, PREFSTK_Y2, PREFSTK_Y3]

CHAPTER 11—CLOSED-END MUTUAL FUNDS

Closed-end mutual funds are covered in Chapter 11. United Asset Management is a holding company of several closed-end mutual funds. What is the latest price for United Asset Management, which has a ticker symbol of UAM? What is UAM's telephone number, in the event that you want to obtain additional information about the company?
[TICKER, PRICE_LAST, PHONE]

CHAPTER 12—REAL ESTATE INVESTMENT TRUSTS

Equity real estate investment trusts and mortgage real estate investment trusts are included in the data set. How many firms within each group appear in the data set? Which type of trust (equity or mortgage real estate investment) experienced the greater increase in annual income growth rates recently?
[NETINC_GR, IND_3_DIG]

CHAPTER 13—SHORT SALE AGAINST THE BOX

A short sale against the box protects profits while allowing the investor to defer taxes. Determine the frequency of instances where this technique would have been useful. First, screen for those firms that had a higher price at the end of the last full calendar year than at the end of the prior year. Within this subset, how many firms had a recent price below that of the close of the last year? List five of these candidates for shorting-against-the-box.
[PRICE_Y1, PRICE_Y2, PRICE_LAST]

CHAPTER 14—OPTIONABLE SHARES

Options are not available on all shares. How many firms in the data set have listed options available on them? Find 10 companies in the data set that list options available. Are listed options traded on COMPAQ and TECO energy?
[SI_CI.OPTIONS, COMPANY]

CHAPTER 15—SUGAR PRODUCERS AND USERS

Sugar is one of the commodities on which futures contracts are written. Sugar producers may sell futures contracts in the futures market to hedge risk arising from sales price volatility, while confectioners may buy futures contracts to hedge their costs. How many hedgers in the confectioners industry had sales during the last full fiscal year that exceeded $1 billion?
[SALES_Y1, IND_3_DIG]

CHAPTER 16—BETA

Countercyclical price performance, discussed in Chapter 16, can be studied through an examination of betas. How many firms in the data set have negative betas? Are most of these firms on the New York Stock Exchange, American Stock Exchange, or Nasdaq markets? Provide a list of firms with negative betas and those with betas that exceed 2.0.
[BETA]

CHAPTER 17—ACCELERATING GROWTH APPROACH TO PORTFOLIO DEVELOPMENT

The American Association of Individual Investors presents several screens for growth companies in its *User's Manual*. In the accelerating growth search, AAII proposes that one seek firms with increasing and positive earnings per share from continuing operations for each quarter over the most recent four quarters. Form a portfolio that meets these criteria and find the beta and expected dividend yield for this portfolio.
[EPSCON_Q1, EPSCON_Q2, EPSCON_Q3, EPSCON_Q4, BETA, YIELD]

ABOUT THE AMERICAN ASSOCIATION OF INDIVIDUAL INVESTORS (AAII)

The American Association of Individual Investors (AAII) is an independent, nonprofit organization that was formed in 1978 to help individuals become effective managers of their own assets. AAII achieves this goal through publications, seminars, home-study books, an educational video, and local chapters that focus on investing and investment techniques.

MEMBERSHIP IN AAII

Members of AAII are entitled to a year's subscription to the *AAII Journal*, a how-to publication that centers on providing investors with investment information and fundamentals; *The Individual Investor's Guide to Low-Load Mutual Funds*, a reference book that provides data on over 800 no-load and low-load mutual funds; a yearly tax-planning guide (a mid-November publication that helps you plan for April 15); and a member's discount on its many seminars and books. The current annual membership fee is $49.

If you want more information about becoming a member of AAII, call or write:

American Association of Individual Investors
625 North Michigan Avenue
Chicago, IL 60611
(312)280–0170

STOCK INVESTOR—THE COMPLETE VERSION

If you are interested in subscribing to the full-blown *Stock Investor* program, contact AAII at the above address. The subscription includes quarterly updates on the over 8,100 companies and 200 industries included in the program.

GLOSSARY

Numbers in parentheses indicate the chapter in which the term is discussed in detail.

12(b)-1 fee (11)   a fee levied by some mutual funds to cover management and other operating costs; amounts to as much as 1 percent annually on the average net assets.

401(k) plans (13)   retirement programs that allow employees to divert a portion of salary to a company-sponsored tax-sheltered savings account, thus deferring taxes until retirement.

accrual-type securities (3)   securities for which interest is paid when the bond is cashed, on or before maturity, rather than periodically over the life of the bond.

accumulation period (13)   under an annuity contract, the period of time between when payments to the insurance company are made and when payments to the annuitant begin.

active portfolio management (17)   building a portfolio using traditional and modern approaches and managing and controlling it to achieve its objectives; a worthwhile activity that can result in superior returns.

activity ratios (6)   financial ratios that are used to measure how well a firm is managing its assets.

adjustable (floating) rate preferreds (10)   preferred stock whose dividends are adjusted periodically in line with yields on certain Treasury issues.

adjusted gross income (13)   gross income less the total allowable adjustments for tax purposes.

after-tax cash flows (ATCFs) (12)   the annual cash flows earned on a real estate investment, net of all expenses, debt payments, and taxes.

agency bonds (8)   debt securities issued by various agencies and organizations of the U.S. government.

aggressive growth fund (11)   a highly speculative mutual fund that seeks large profits from capital gains.

alternative minimum tax (AMT) (13)   a tax passed by Congress to ensure that all individuals pay at least some federal income tax.

American Depositary Receipts (ADRs) (2)   dollar-denominated negotiable receipts for the stocks of foreign companies that are held in the vaults of banks in the companies' home countries.

American option (14)   an option that can be exercised on any business day the option is traded, on or before the option's expiration date.

AMEX index (3)   measure of the current price behavior of the stocks listed on the AMEX.

analytical information (3)   available current data in conjunction with projections and recommendations about potential investments.

annuitant (13)   the person to whom the future payments on an annuity contract are directed.

annuity (4, 13)   a stream of equal cash flows that occur in equal intervals over time; *also* a series of payments guaranteed for a number of years or over a lifetime.

appraisal (12)   in real estate, the process for estimating the current market value of a piece of property.

approximate yield (12)   procedure for assessing investment suitability that recognizes the time value of money in its estimation of the rate of return (yield) on an investment.

arbitration (2)   a dispute resolution process in which a customer and a broker present their argument before a panel, which then decides the case.

ask price (2)   the lowest price at which a dealer is willing to sell a givensecurity.

asset allocation (16)   a scheme that involves dividing one's portfolio into various asset classes to preserve capital by protecting against negative developments and taking advantage of positive ones.

asset allocation fund (11, 16)   a mutual fund that seeks to reduce the variability of returns by investing in the right assets at the right time; emphasizes diversification and relatively consistent performance rather than the potential for spectacular gains.

asset-backed securities (ABS) (8)   securities similar to mortgage-backed securities that are backed by a pool of bank loans, leases, and other assets (mostly auto loans and credit cards).

automatic investment plan (11)   a mutual fund service that allows shareholders automatically to send fixed amounts of money from their paychecks or bank accounts into the fund.

automatic reinvestment plan (11)   a mutual fund service that enables shareholders automatically to buy additional shares in the fund through reinvestment of dividends and capital gains income.

average tax rate (13)   taxes due divided by taxable income; different from the marginal tax rate.

averages (3)   numbers used to measure the general behavior of stock prices by reflecting the arithmetic average price behavior of a representative group of stocks at a given point in time.

back-end load (11)   a commission charged on the *sale* of shares in a mutual fund.

back-office research reports (3)   brokerage firm's analyses of and recommendations on investment prospects; made available on request at no cost to existing and potential clients.

balance sheet (6)   a financial summary of a firm's assets, liabilities, and share-holders' equity at a single point in time.

balanced fund (11)   a mutual fund whose objective is to generate a balanced return of both current income and long-term capital gains.

bank discount yield (BDY) (3)   the rate at which T-bills are quoted in the *Wall Street Journal* and other financial media; represents the annualized percentage discount (redemption value − 2 current price) at which the T-bill can be currently purchased.

banker's acceptances (3)   short-term, low-risk investment vehicles arising from bank guarantees of business transactions; are sold at a discount from their face value and provide yields generally slightly below those of CDs and commercial paper.

bar chart (7)   the simplest kind of chart on which share price is plotted on the vertical axis and time on the horizontal axis; stock prices are recorded as vertical bars showing high, low, and closing prices.

Barron's **(3)**   a weekly business newspaper; a popular source of financial news.

basis (13)   the amount paid for a capital asset, including commissions and other costs related to the purchase.

bear markets (2)   unfavorable markets normally associated with falling prices, investor pessimism, economic slowdowns, and government restraint.

beta (4)   a measure of *nondiversifiable risk* that indicates how the price of a security responds to market forces; found by relating the historical returns on a security with the historical returns for the market.

bid price (2)   the highest price offered by a dealer to purchase a given security.

blind pool syndicate (12)   a type of RELP formed by a syndicator—often well known—to raise a given amount of money to be invested at the syndicator's discretion.

bond equivalent yield (BEY) (3)   the annual percentage rate that would be earned by an investor in a short-term security sold at a discount were it purchased today at its current price and held to its maturity.

bond fund (11)   a mutual fund that invests in various kinds and grades of bonds, with income as the primary objective.

bond ladders (9)   an investment strategy wherein an equal amount of money is invested in a series of bonds with staggered maturities.

bond ratings (8)   letter grades that designate investment quality and are assigned to a bond issue by rating agencies.

bond swap (9)   an investment strategy wherein an investor liquidates one current bond holding and simultaneously buys a different issue in its place.

bond yield (3)   summary measure of the return an investor would receive on a bond if it were purchased at its current price and held to maturity; reported as an annual rate of return.

bonds (1, 8)   long-term debt instruments (IOUs), issued by corporations and governments, that offer a known interest return plus return of the bond's face value at maturity; the issuer agrees to pay a fixed amount of interest over a specified period of time and to repay a fixed amount of principal at maturity.

book value (5) the amount of stockholders' equity in a firm; equals the amount of the firm's assets minus the firm's liabilities and preferred stock.

book value (net asset value) (10) a measure of the amount of debt-free assets supporting each share of preferred stock.

brokered CDs (3) certificates of deposit sold by stockbrokers; offer slightly higher yields than other CDs and typically can be sold prior to maturity without incurring a penalty.

bull markets (2) favorable markets normally associated with rising prices, investor optimism, economic recovery, and governmental stimulus.

business cycle (6) an indication of the current state of the economy, reflecting changes in total economic activity over time.

business risk (4) the degree of uncertainty associated with an investment's earnings and the investment's ability to pay investors the returns owed them.

call (13, 14) an *option* that gives its holder the right to buy the underlying security at a specified price over a set period of time.

call feature (8) feature that specifies whether and under what conditions the issuer can retire a bond prior to maturity.

capital asset pricing model (CAPM) (4) model that uses beta, the risk-free rate, and the market return to help investors define the required return on an investment; it formally links together the notions of risk and return.

capital gain (1, 3) the amount by which the proceeds from the sale of a capital asset exceed its original purchase price.

capital gains distributions (11) payments made to mutual fund shareholders that come from the profits that a fund makes from the sale of its securities.

capital loss (3) the amount by which the proceeds from the sale of a capital asset are *less than* its original purchase price.

capital market (2) market in which long-term securities such as stocks and bonds are bought and sold.

cash account (2) a brokerage account in which a customer can make only cash transactions.

cash dividend (5) payment of a dividend in the form of cash.

cash market (15) a market where a product or commodity changes hands in exchange for a cash price paid when the transaction is completed.

cash value (3) the amount of money set aside by an insurer to provide for the payment of the death benefit.

central asset account (3) a comprehensive deposit account that combines checking, investing, and borrowing activities; it automatically "sweeps" excess balances into short-term investments and borrows to meet shortages.

certificates of deposit (CDs) (3) savings instruments in which funds must remain on deposit for a specified period; withdrawals prior to maturity incur interest penalties.

charting (7) the activity of charting price behavior and other market information and then using the patterns these charts form to make investment decisions.

churning (2) an illegal and unethical act by a broker to increase commissions by causing excessive trading of clients' accounts.

classified common stock (5) common stock issued in different classes, each of which offers different privileges and benefits to its holders.

closed-end investment companies (11) a type of investment company that operates with a fixed number of shares outstanding.

coefficient of variation, CV (4) a statistic used to measure the *relative* dispersion of an asset's returns; it is useful in comparing the risk of assets with differing average or expected returns.

collateral trust bonds (8) senior bonds backed by securities owned by the issuer but held in trust by a third party.

collateralized mortgage obligation (CMO) (8) mortgage-backed bond whose holders are divided into classes based on the length of investment desired; principal is channeled to investors in order of maturity, with short-term classes first.

collectibles (12) items that have value because of their attractiveness to collectors and because of their relative scarcity and historical significance.

commercial paper (3) short-term, unsecured promissory notes (IOUs) issued by corporations with very high credit standings.

common stock (1) equity investment representing ownership in a corporation; each share represents a fractional ownership interest in the firm.

common stock (market) ratios (6) financial ratios that convert key information about a firm to a per share basis.

comparative sales approach (12) a real estate valuation approach that uses as the basic input the sales prices of properties that are similar to the subject property.

compound interest (4) interest paid not only on the initial deposit but also on any interest accumulated from one period to the next.

constant-dollar plan (17) a formula plan for timing investment transactions, in which the investor establishes a target dollar amount for the speculative portion of the portfolio and transfers funds to or from the conservative portion as needed to maintain the target dollar amount.

constant-ratio plan (17) a formula plan for timing investment transactions, in which a desired fixed *ratio* of the speculative to the conservative portion of the portfolio is established; when the actual ratio differs by a predetermined amount from the desired ratio, transactions are made to rebalance the portfolio to achieve the desired ratio.

continuous compounding (4) interest calculation in which interest is compounded over the smallest possible interval of time.

convenience (12) in real estate, the accessibility of a property to the places the people in a target market frequently need to go.

conventional options (14) put and call options sold over-the-counter.

conversion (exchange) privilege (11) feature of a mutual fund that allows shareholders to move money from one fund to another, within the same family of funds.

conversion equivalent (conversion parity) (10) the price at which the common stock would have to sell in order to make the convertible security worth its present market price.

conversion feature (10) allows the holder of a convertible preferred to convert to a specified number of shares of the issuing company's common stock.

conversion period (10) the time period during which a convertible issue can be converted.

conversion premium (10) the amount by which the market price of a convertible exceeds its conversion value.

conversion price (10) the stated price per share at which common stock will be delivered to the investor in exchange for a convertible issue.

conversion privilege (10) the conditions and specific nature of the conversion feature of convertible securities.

conversion ratio (10) the number of shares of common stock into which a convertible issue can be converted.

conversion value (10) an indication of what a convertible issue should trade for if it were priced to sell on the basis of its stock value.

convertible securities (1, 10) fixed-income obligations that have a feature permitting the holder to convert the security into a specified number of shares of the issuing company's common stock.

corporation (13) a form of organization that provides a limited-liability benefit to shareholder investors and that has an indefinite life.

correlation (16) a statistical measure of the relationship, if any, between series of numbers representing data of any kind.

correlation coefficient (16) a measure of the degree of correlation between two series.

cost approach (12) a real estate valuation approach based on the idea that an investor should not pay more for a property than it would cost to rebuild it at today's prices.

coupon (8) feature on a bond that defines the amount of annual interest income.

covered options (14) options written against stock owned (or short sold) by the writer.

cumulative provision (10) a provision requiring that any preferred dividends that have been passed must be paid in full before dividends can be restored to common stockholders.

currency futures (15) futures contracts on foreign currencies, traded much like commodities.

currency options (14) put and call options written on foreign currencies.

current income (4) usually cash or near-cash that is periodically received as a result of owning an investment.

current interest rate (13) for an annuity contract, the yearly return the insurance company is currently paying on accumulated deposits.

current yield (8, 9) measure of the annual interest income a bond provides relative to its current market price.

custodial account (2) the brokerage account of a minor; requires a parent or guardian to be part of all transactions.

daily price limit (15) restriction on the day-to-day change in the price of an underlying commodity.

date of record (5) the date on which an investor must be a registered shareholder of a firm to be entitled to receive a dividend.

de-listed (2) removed from listing on an organized stock exchange.

dealers (2) traders who "make markets" by offering to buy or sell certain over-the-counter securities at stated prices.

debenture (8) an unsecured (junior) bond.

debit balance (2) the amount of money being borrowed; the size of a margin loan.

debt (1) funds loaned in exchange for the receipt of interest income and the promised repayment of the loan at a given future date.

deep discount bond (13) a bond selling at a price far below its par value.

deep-in-the-money call option (13) a tax-deferral strategy that involves selling a call option on shares currently owned, locking in a price equal to the amount received from the sale of the call option but giving up future price appreciation.

deferred annuity (13) an annuity contract in which the payments to the annuitant begin at some future date.

deferred equity (10) securities issued in one form and later redeemed or converted into shares of common stock.

deflation (4) a period of generally declining prices.

delivery month (15) the time when a commodity must be delivered; defines the life of a futures contract.

demand (12) in real estate, people's willingness to buy or rent a given property.

demographics (12) measurable characteristics of an area's population, such as household size, age structure, occupation, gender, and marital status.

depreciation (12) in real estate investing, a tax deduction based upon the original cost of a building and used to reflect its declining economic life.

derivative securities (1, 14) securities, such as puts, calls, and futures that derive their value from the price behavior of an underlying real or financial asset.

descriptive information (3) factual data on the past behavior of the economy, the market, the industry, the company, or a given investment vehicle.

direct investment (1) investment in which an investor directly acquires a claim on a security or property.

discount basis (3) a method of earning interest on a security by purchasing it at a price below its redemption value; the difference is the interest earned.

discount bond (8) a bond with a market value lower than par; occurs when market rates are greater than the coupon rate.

discount broker (2) broker who charges low commissions to make transactions for customers but provides little or no research information or investment advice.

discount rate (4) the annual rate of return that could be earned currently on a similar investment; used when finding present value; also called *opportunity cost*.

discounted cash flow (12) use of present-value techniques to find *net present value (NPV)*.

distribution period (13)   under an annuity contract, the period of time over which payments are made to the annuitant.

diversifiable (unsystematic) risk (4)   the portion of an investment's risk resulting from uncontrollable or random events that can be eliminated through diversification; also called *unsystematic risk*.

diversification (1, 3)   the inclusion of a number of different investment vehicles in a portfolio, to increase returns or incur less risk.

dividend income (11)   income derived from the dividend and interest income earned on the security holdings of a mutual fund.

dividend payout ratio (5)   the portion of earnings per share (EPS) that a firm pays out as dividends.

dividend reinvestment plans (DRIPs) (5)   plans in which shareholders have cash dividends automatically reinvested in additional shares of the firm's common stock.

dividend valuation model (DVM) (7)   a model that values a share of stock on the basis of the future dividend stream it is expected to produce; its three versions are zero-growth, constant-growth, and variable-growth.

dividend yield (5, 10)   a measure that relates dividends to share price and puts common stock dividends on a relative (percentage) rather than absolute (dollar) basis; measures the amount of return earned on annual dividends.

dividends (1)   periodic payments made by firms to their stockholders.

dividends-and-earnings (D&E) approach (7)   stock valuation approach that uses projected dividends, EPS, and P/E multiples to value a share of stock.

dollar-cost averaging (17)   a formula plan for timing investment transactions, in which a fixed dollar amount is invested in a security at fixed intervals.

domestic investments (1)   debt, equity, and derivative securities and property of U.S.-based companies.

Dow Jones bond averages (3)   mathematical averages of the closing prices for groups of utility, industrial, and composite bonds.

Dow Jones Industrial Average (DJIA) (3)   a stock market average made up of 30 high-quality industrial stocks selected for total market value and for broad public ownership and believed to reflect overall market activity.

dual listing (2)   listing of a firm's shares on more than one exchange.

duration (9)   a measure of bond price volatility, which captures both price and reinvestment risks, and which is used to indicate how a bond will react to different interest rate environments.

earnings per share (EPS) (5)   the amount of annual earnings available to common stockholders, as stated on a per share basis.

economic analysis (6)   a study of general economic conditions that is used in the valuation of common stock.

efficient frontier (16)   the leftmost boundary of the feasible (attainable) set of portfolios that includes all efficient portfolios—those providing the best attainable tradeoff between risk (measured by the standard deviation) and return.

efficient market (7)   a market in which securities reflect all possible information quickly and accurately.

efficient markets hypothesis (EMH) (7) basic theory of the behavior of efficient markets, in which there are a large number of knowledgeable investors, information is widely available to all investors, and they react quickly to new information, causing securities prices to adjust quickly and accurately.

efficient portfolio (16) a portfolio that provides the highest return for a given level of risk or that has the lowest risk for a given level of return.

environment (12) in real estate, the natural as well as aesthetic, socioeconomic, legal, and fiscal surroundings of a property.

equipment trust certificates (8) senior bonds secured by specific pieces of equipment; popular with transportation companies such as airlines.

equity (1) an ongoing ownership interest in a specific business or property.

equity capital (5) evidence of ownership position in a firm, in the form of shares of common stock.

equity kicker (10) another name for the conversion feature, giving the holder of a convertible security a deferred claim on the issuer's common stock.

equity-income fund (11) a mutual fund that emphasizes current income and capital preservation and invests primarily in high-yielding common stocks.

ethics (2) standards of conduct or moral judgment.

Eurodollar bonds (8) foreign bonds denominated in dollars but not registered with the SEC, thus restricting sales of new issues.

European option (14) an option that can be exercised only on the date of expiration.

event risk (4) risk that comes from a largely (or totally) unexpected event that has a significant and usually immediate effect on the underlying value of an investment.

ex-dividend date (5) the date three business days before the date of record; determines whether one is an official shareholder of a firm and thus eligible to receive a declared dividend.

excess margin (2) more equity than is required in a margin account.

exemption (13) a deduction from adjusted gross income for each qualifying dependent of a federal taxpayer.

exercise (subscription) price (14) with rights, the price at which a new share of common stock can be bought.

expectations hypothesis (9) theory that the shape of the yield curve reflects investor expectations of future interest rates.

expected inflation premium (4) the average rate of inflation expected in the future.

expected return (4, 9) the return an investor thinks an investment will earn in the future; the rate of return an investor can expect to earn by holding a bond over a period of time that's less than the life of the issue.

expiration date (14) the date at which an option expires.

financial futures (15) a type of futures contract in which the underlying "commodity" is a financial asset, such as debt securities, foreign currencies, or market baskets of common stocks.

financial institutions (1) organizations that channel the savings of governments, businesses, and individuals into loans or investments.

financial leverage (2)   the use of debt financing to magnify investment returns.

financial markets (1)   forums in which suppliers and demanders of funds are brought together to make financial transactions.

financial risk (4)   the degree of uncertainty associated with the mix of debt and equity used to finance a firm or property; the larger the proportion of debt financing, the greater this risk.

first and refunding bonds (8)   bonds secured in part with both first and second mortgages.

fixed annuity (13)   an annuity contract that pays an unchanging amount of monthly income during the distribution period.

fixed charge coverage (10)   a measure of how well a firm is able to cover its preferred stock dividends.

fixed-commission schedules (2)   fixed brokerage commissions that typically apply to small transactions.

fixed-income securities (1)   investment vehicles that offer a fixed periodic return.

fixed-weightings approach (16)   asset allocation plan in which a fixed percentage of the portfolio is allocated to each asset category.

flexible weightings approach (16)   asset allocation plan in which weights for each asset category are adjusted periodically based on market or technical analysis.

forced conversion (10)   the calling in of convertible bonds by the issuing firm.

foreign exchange rate (2)   the relationship between two currencies at a specific date.

foreign exchange risk (2)   the risk caused by varying exchange rates between the currencies of two countries.

foreign investments (1)   direct and indirect purchase of debt, equity, and derivative securities and property of foreign-based companies.

Form 10-K (3)   a statement that must be filed with the SEC by all firms having securities listed on an organized exchange or traded in the national OTC market.

formula plans (17)   mechanical methods of portfolio management that try to take advantage of price changes in securities that result from cyclical price movements.

forward contract (15)   agreement whereby a seller agrees to deliver a specific commodity or product to a buyer sometime in the future, at a price specified in the contract itself.

fourth market (2)   transactions made directly between large institutional buyers and sellers.

fully compounded rate of return (4)   the rate of return that includes interest earned on interest.

fund families (11)   different kinds of mutual funds offered by a single investment management company.

fundamental analysis (6)   the in-depth study of the financial condition and operating results of a firm.

future value (4) the amount to which a current deposit will grow over a period of time when it is placed in an account paying compound interest.

futures (1) legally binding obligations that the sellers of such contracts will make delivery and the buyers of the contracts will take delivery of a specified commodity or financial instrument at some specific date in the future at a price agreed upon at the time the contract is sold.

futures contract (15) a commitment to deliver a certain amount of some specified item at some specified date in the future.

futures market (15) the organized market for the trading of futures contracts.

futures options (15) options that give the holders the right to buy or sell a single standardized futures contract for a specified period of time at a specified striking price.

gemstones (12) diamonds and colored precious stones (rubies, sapphires, and emeralds).

general obligation bonds (8) municipal bonds backed by the full faith, credit, and taxing power of the issuer.

general partner (13) the managing partner who accepts unlimited liability and uses his expertise to manage the partnership.

general partnership (13) a joint venture in which all partners have management rights and all assume unlimited liability for any debts or obligations the partnership incurs.

government securities money funds (3) money market mutual funds that confine their investments to Treasury bills and other short-term securities of the U.S. government and its agencies.

gross income (13) all includable income for federal income tax purposes.

growth cycle (6) a reflection of the amount of business vitality that occurs within an industry (or company) over time.

growth fund (11) a mutual fund whose primary goals are capital gains and long-term growth.

growth-and-income fund (11) a mutual fund that seeks both long-term growth and current income, with primary emphasis on capital gains.

growth-oriented portfolio (16) a portfolio whose primary objective is long-term price appreciation.

guaranteed investment contracts (GICs) (13) portfolios of fixed-income securities with guaranteed competitive rates of return that are backed and sold by an insurance company.

hedge (14) a combination of two or more securities into a single investment position for the purpose of reducing or eliminating risk.

hedgers (15) producers and processors who use futures contracts to protect their interest in an underlying commodity or financial instrument.

holding period (4) the period of time over which one wishes to measure the return on an investment vehicle.

holding period return (HPR) (4) the total return earned from holding an investment for a specified holding period (usually one year or less).

immediate annuity (13)   an annuity contract under which payments to the annuitant begin as soon as it is purchased.

improvements (12)   in real estate, the additions to a site, such as buildings, sidewalks, and various on-site amenities.

in arrears (10)   having outstanding unfulfilled preferred dividend obligations.

in-the-money (14)   a call option with a strike price less than the market price of the underlying security; a put option whose strike price is greater than the market price of the underlying security.

income approach (12)   a real estate valuation approach that calculates a property's value as the present value of all its future income.

income bonds (8)   unsecured bonds requiring that interest be paid only after a specified amount of income is earned.

income property (12)   leased-out residential or commercial real estate that is expected to provide returns primarily from periodic rental income.

income statement (6)   a financial summary of the operating results of a firm covering a specified period of time, usually one year.

income-oriented portfolio (16)   a portfolio that stresses current dividend and interest returns.

index fund (11)   a mutual fund that buys and holds a portfolio of stocks (or bonds) equivalent to those in a specific market index.

index price (15)   technique used to price T-bill and other short-term securities futures contracts, by subtracting current yield from an index of 100.

indexes (3)   numbers used to measure the general behavior of stock prices by measuring the current price behavior of a representative group of stocks in relation to a base value set at an earlier point in time.

indirect investment (1)   investment made in a portfolio or group of securities or properties.

individual investors (1)   investors who manage their own funds.

individual retirement arrangements (IRAs) (13)   self-directed, tax-deferred retirement programs available to any gainfully employed individual, who can make up to a specified maximum annual contribution.

industry analysis (6)   study of industry groupings that looks at the competitive position of a particular industry in relation to others and identifies companies holding particular promise within an industry.

inflation (4)   a period of generally rising prices.

initial deposit (15)   the amount of investor capital that must be deposited with a broker at the time of a commodity transaction.

initial margin (2)   the minimum amount of equity that must be provided by a margin investor *at the time of purchase*.

initial public offering (IPO) (2, 5)   the public sale of common stock by a privately owned company; stock issued by (relatively) new firms going public for the first time.

insider trading (2)   the illegal use of material nonpublic information about a company to make profitable securities transactions.

installment annuity (13)   an annuity contract acquired by making payments over time; at a specified future date, the installment payments, plus interest earned on them, are used to purchase an annuity contract.

institutional investors (1)   investment professionals paid to manage other people's money.

insurance policy (3)   a contract between the insured and the insurer that requires the insured to make periodic premium payments in exchange for the insurer's promise to pay for losses according to specified terms.

interest (4)   the "rent" paid by a borrower to a lender for use of the lender's money.

interest rate futures (15)   futures contracts on debt securities.

interest rate options (14)   put and call options written on fixed-income (debt) securities.

interest rate risk (4)   the chance that changes in interest rates will adversely affect a security's value.

international fund (11)   a mutual fund that does all or most of its investing in foreign securities.

intrinsic value (6)   the underlying or inherent value of a stock, as determined through fundamental analysis.

investing (1)   the process of placing funds in selected investment vehicles with the expectation of generating positive income and/or preserving and increasing their value.

investment (1)   any vehicle into which funds can be placed with the expectation of receiving positive income and/or preserving or increasing its value.

investment advisers (3)   individuals or firms that provide investment advice, typically for a fee.

investment analysis (12)   approach to real estate valuation that not only considers what similar properties have sold for but also looks at the underlying determinants of value.

investment banker (2)   financial intermediary that purchases new securities from the issuing firm at an agreed-upon price and resells them to the public.

investment club (3)   a legal partnership through which a group of investors are bound to an organizational structure, operating procedures, and purpose, which is typically to earn favorable long-term returns from moderate-risk investments.

investment goals (1, 3)   statements of the timing, magnitude, form, and risk associated with a desired return; the financial objectives that one wishes to achieve by investing in any of a wide range of potential investment vehicles.

investment letters (3)   provide, on a subscription basis, the analyses, conclusions, and recommendations of experts in securities investment.

investment plan (3)   a written document describing how funds will be invested, the target date for achievement of each investment goal, and the associated amount of tolerable risk.

investment value (5, 10) the amount that investors believe a security should be trading for, or what they think it's worth; the price at which a convertible would trade if it were nonconvertible and priced at or near the prevailing market yields of comparable nonconvertible issues.

itemized deductions (13) personal living and family expenses that can be deducted from adjusted gross income.

Jensen's measure (Jensen's alpha) (17) a measure of portfolio performance that uses the portfolio's beta and CAPM to calculate its excess return, which may be positive, zero, or negative.

junior bonds (8) debt obligations backed only by the promise of the issuer to pay interest and principal on a timely basis.

junk bonds (8) high-risk securities that have low ratings but produce high yields.

Keogh plans (13) programs that allow self-employed individuals to establish self-directed, tax-deferred retirement plans for themselves and their employees.

LEAPS (14) long-term options.

leverage (12, 14) in real estate, the use of debt financing to purchase a piece of property and thereby affect its risk-return parameters; the ability to obtain a given investment position at a reduced capital investment, thereby magnifying returns.

leverage measures (6) financial ratios that measure the amount of debt being used to support operations and the ability of the firm to service its debt.

life insurance (3) a contract that provides financial protection for a family if the primary breadwinner or any other family member dies prematurely.

limit order (2) an order to buy at or below a specified price or to sell at or above a specified price.

limited partners (13) the passive investors in a partnership, who supply most of the capital and have liability limited to the amount of their investment.

limited partnership (LP) (13) vehicle in which the investor can passively invest with limited liability, receive the benefit of active professional management, and apply the resulting profit or loss (subject to limits) to his or her tax liability.

liquidity (1, 3) the ability to convert an investment into cash quickly and with little or no loss in value.

liquidity measures (6) financial ratios concerned with a firm's ability to meet its day-to-day operating expenses and satisfy its short-term obligations as they come due.

liquidity preference theory (9) theory that investors tend to prefer the greater liquidity of short-term securities and therefore require a premium to invest in long-term securities.

liquidity risk (4) the risk of not being able to liquidate an investment conveniently and at a reasonable price.

listed options (14) put and call options listed and traded on organized securities exchanges, such as the CBOE.

load fund (11) a mutual fund that charges a commission when shares are bought; also known as *front-end load fund*.

long purchase (2) a transaction in which investors buy securities in the hope that they will increase in value and can be sold at a later date for profit.

long-term investments (1) investments with maturities of longer than a year or with no maturity at all.

low-load fund (11) a mutual fund that charges a small commission (2 to 3 percent) when shares are bought.

maintenance deposit (15) the minimum amount of margin that must be kept in a margin account at all times.

maintenance margin (2) the minimum amount of margin (equity) that an investor must maintain in the margin account at all times.

management fee (11) a fee levied annually for professional mutual fund services provided; paid regardless of the performance of the portfolio.

margin account (2) a brokerage account in which the customer has been extended borrowing privileges by the brokerage firm; i.e., it is authorized for margin trading.

margin call (2) notification of the need to bring the equity of an account whose margin is below the maintenance level up to the initial margin level or have margined holdings sold to reach this point.

margin deposit (15) amount deposited with a broker to cover any loss in the market value of a futures contract that may result from adverse price movements.

margin loan (2) vehicle through which borrowed funds are made available, at a stated interest rate, in a margin transaction.

margin requirement (2) the minimum amount of equity (stated as a percentage) that must be a margin investor's own funds; set by the Federal Reserve Board.

margin trading (2) the use of borrowed funds to purchase securities; magnifies returns by reducing the amount of capital that must be put up by the investor.

marginal tax rate (13) the tax rate on additional income.

mark-to-the-market (15) a daily check of an investor's margin position, determined at the end of each session, at which time the broker debits or credits the account as needed.

market capitalization rate (12) the rate used to convert an income stream to a present value; used to estimate the value of real estate under the *income approach*.

market order (2) an order to buy or sell stock at the best price available when the order is placed.

market return (4) the average return on all (or a large sample of) stocks, such as those in Standard & Poor's 500 stock composite index.

market risk (4) risk of decline in investment returns due to market factors independent of the given security or property investment.

market segmentation theory (9) theory that the market for debt is segmented based on maturity, that supply and demand within each segment determines the prevailing interest rate, and that the slope of the yield curve depends on the relationship between the prevailing rates in each segment.

market value (5, 12) the prevailing market price of a security; in real estate, the actual worth of a property; indicates the price at which it would sell under current market conditions.

master limited partnerships (MLPs) (12) limited partnerships that are publicly traded on major stock exchanges.

maturity date (8) the date on which a bond matures and the principal must be repaid.

maximum daily price range (15) the amount a commodity price can change during a day; usually equal to twice the daily price limit.

minimum guaranteed interest rate (13) for a deferred annuity purchase contract, the minimum interest rate on contributions that the insurance company will guarantee over the full accumulation period.

mixed stream (4) a stream of returns that, unlike an annuity, exhibits no special pattern.

modern portfolio theory (MPT) (16) an approach to portfolio management that uses statistical measures to develop a portfolio plan.

money market (2) market in which short-term securities are bought and sold.

money market deposit accounts (MMDAs) (3) a bank deposit account with limited check-writing privileges; has no legal minimum balance, but many banks impose their own.

money market mutual fund (MMMF or money fund) (1, 3, 11) a mutual fund that pools the capital of a large number of investors and uses it to invest exclusively in high-yielding, short-term securities.

Moody's Investor Services (3) publisher of a variety of financial reference manuals, including *Moody's Manuals*.

mortgage bonds (8) senior bonds secured by real estate.

mortgage-backed bond (8) a debt issue secured by a pool of home mortgages; issued primarily by federal agencies.

multiple earnings approach (3) technique for estimating life insurance needs by applying a specified multiple to current gross annual earnings.

municipal bond guarantees (8) guarantees from a party other than the issuer that principal and interest payments will be made in a prompt and timely manner.

municipal bonds (8) debt securities issued by states, counties, cities, and other political subdivisions; most of these bonds are tax-exempt (free of federal income tax on interest income).

mutual fund (1, 11) a company that raises money from sale of its shares and invests in and professionally manages a diversified portfolio of securities.

naked options (14) options written on securities not owned by the writer.

Nasdaq (National Association of Securities Dealers Automated Quotation) system (2) an automated system that provides up-to-date bid and ask prices on certain selected, highly active OTC securities.

Nasdaq indexes (3) measures of current price behavior of securities sold OTC.

Nasdaq/National Market System (Nasdaq/NMS) (2) a list of Nasdaq stocks meeting certain qualification standards relative to financial size, performance, and trading activity.

needs approach (3) technique for estimating life insurance needs by considering a person's financial obligations and the financial resources currently available for meeting them.

negative leverage (12) a position in which, if a property's return is below its debt cost, the investor's return will be less than from an all-cash deal.

negatively correlated (16) describes two series that move in opposite directions.

negotiated commissions (2, 5) commissions on the sale and purchase of securities that are negotiated between brokers and institutional investors or individuals with large accounts.

net asset value (NAV) (11) the underlying value of a share of stock in a particular mutual fund.

net losses (3) the amount by which capital losses exceed capital gains; up to $3,000 of net losses can be applied against ordinary income in any year.

net operating income (NOI) (12) the amount left after subtracting vacancy and collection losses and property operating expenses from an income property's *gross potential* rental income.

net present value (NPV) (12) the difference between the present value of the cash flows and the amount of equity required to make an investment.

no-load fund (11) a mutual fund that does not charge a commission when shares are bought.

noncumulative provision (10) a provision found on some preferred stocks excusing the issuing firm from having to make up any passed dividends.

nondiversifiable (systematic) risk (4) the inescapable portion of an investment's risk attributable to forces that affect all investments and therefore are not unique to any given vehicle; also called *systematic risk*.

note (8) a debt security originally issued with a maturity of from 2 to 10 years.

NOW (negotiated order of withdrawal) account (3) a bank checking account that pays interest; has no legal minimum balance, but many banks impose their own.

NYSE composite index (3) measure of the current price behavior of the stocks listed on the NYSE.

odd lot (2) less than 100 shares of stock.

open interest (15) the number of contracts currently outstanding on a commodity or financial future.

open outcry auction (15)   in futures trading, an auction in which trading is done through a series of shouts, body motions, and hand signals.

open-end investment company (11)   a type of investment company in which investors buy shares from and sell them back to the mutual fund itself, with no limit on the number of shares the fund can issue.

option (14)   a security that gives the holder the right to buy or sell a certain amount of an underlying financial asset at a specified price for a specified period of time.

option maker (writer) (14)   the individual or institution that writes/creates put and call options.

option premium (14)   the quoted price the investor pays to buy a listed put or call option.

option spreading (14)   combining two or more options with different strike prices and/or expiration dates into a single transaction.

option straddle (14)   the simultaneous purchase (or sale) of a put and a call on the same underlying common stock (or financial asset).

options (1)   securities that provide the investor with an opportunity to sell or buy another security or property at a specified price over a given period of time.

ordinary annuity (4)   an annuity for which the cash flows occur at the *end* of each period.

organized securities exchanges (2)   centralized institutions in which transactions are made in already outstanding securities.

out-of-the-money (14)   a call option with no real value because the strike price exceeds the market price of the stock; a put option whose market price exceeds the strike price.

over-the-counter (OTC) market (2)   widely scattered telecommunications network through which sellers and buyers of certain securities can be brought together.

paper return (4)   a return that has been achieved but not yet realized by an investor during a given period.

par value (5)   the stated, or face, value of a stock.

passbook savings account (3)   a savings account, offered by banks, that generally pays a low rate of interest and has no minimum balance.

passive activity (13)   an investment in which the investor does not "materially participate" in its management or activity.

payback period (10)   the length of time it takes for the buyer of a convertible to recover the conversion premium from the extra current income earned on the convertible.

payout (13)   the investment return provided by an annuity contract; it is realized when the distribution period begins.

PERCs (10)   preferred equity redemption cumulative stock; preferred securities that carry conversion privileges and offer attractive dividend returns.

perfectly negatively correlated (16)   describes two negatively correlated series that have a correlation coefficient of -1.

perfectly positively correlated (16)   describes two positively correlated series that have a correlation coefficient of $+1$.

PIK-bond (8)   a payment-in-kind junk bond, which makes annual interest payments in new bonds rather than in cash.

point-and-figure charts (7)   charts used to keep track of emerging price patterns by plotting significant price changes with Xs and Os but with no time dimension used.

pooled diversification (11)   a process whereby investors buy into a diversified portfolio of securities for the collective benefit of the individual investors.

portfolio beta, b_p (16)   the beta of a portfolio; calculated as the weighted average of the betas of the individual assets the portfolio includes.

portfolio revision (17)   the process of selling certain issues in a portfolio and of purchasing new ones.

positive leverage (12)   a position in which, if a property's return is in excess of its debt cost, the investor's return will be increased to a level well above what could have been earned from an all-cash deal.

positively correlated (16)   describes two series that move in the same direction.

precious metals (12)   tangibles—like gold, silver, and platinum—that concentrate a great deal of value in a small amount of weight and volume.

preemptive right (14)   the right of existing stockholders to maintain their proportionate share of ownership in a firm.

preference (prior preferred) stock (10)   a type of preferred stock that has seniority over other preferred stock in its right to receive dividends and in its claim on assets.

preferred stock (1, 10)   ownership interest in a corporation; has a stated dividend rate, payment of which is given preference over common stock dividends of the same firm; the stock has a prior claim (ahead of common) on the income and assets of the issuing firm.

premium bond (8)   a bond with a market value in excess of par; occurs when interest rates drop below the coupon rate.

present value (4)   the value today of a sum to be received at some future date; the inverse of future value.

price/earnings (P/E) approach (7)   stock valuation approach that tries to find the P/E ratio that's most appropriate for the stock, which along with estimated EPS, is used to determine a reasonable stock price.

primary market (2)   market in which new issues of securities are sold to the public.

prime rate (2)   the lowest interest rate charged the best business borrowers.

principal (8)   on a bond, the amount of capital that must be paid at maturity.

principle of substitution (12)   the principle that people do not really buy or rent real estate per se but, instead, judge properties as different sets of benefits and costs.

private partnership (13)   a limited partnership that has a limited number of investors and is not registered with a public agency.

private placement (2)　the sale of new securities directly to selected groups of investors, without SEC registration.

profitability measures (6)　financial ratios that measure returns by relating the relative success of a firm through comparison of profits to sales, assets, or equity.

promised yield (9)　same as yield-to-maturity.

property (1)　investments in real property or in tangible personal property.

property management (12)　in real estate, finding the optimal level of benefits for a property and providing them at the lowest costs.

property transfer process (12)　the process of promotion and negotiation of real estate, which can significantly influence the cash flows a property will earn.

prospectus (2)　a portion of a security registration statement that details the key aspects of the issue, the issuer, and its management and financial position.

psychographics (12)　characteristics that describe people's mental dispositions, such as personality, lifestyle, and self-concept.

public offering (2, 5)　the sale of a firm's securities to the general public; an offer to sell to the investing public a set number of shares of a firm's stock at a specified price.

public partnership (13)　a limited partnership that is registered with state and/or federal regulators and usually has 35 or more investors.

publicly traded issues (5)　shares of stock readily available to the general public and bought and sold in the open market.

purchasing power risk (4)　the chance that changing price levels in the economy (inflation or deflation) will adversely affect the returns on a given investment.

put (13, 14)　an *option* that enables its holder to sell the underlying security at a specified price over a set period of time.

put hedge (13)　the purchase of a put option on shares currently owned, to lock in a profit and defer taxes on the profit to the next taxable year.

pyramiding (2)　the technique of using paper profits in margin accounts to partly or fully finance the acquisition of additional securities.

quotations (3)　ut various types of securities, including current price data and statistics on recent price behavior.

random walk hypothesis (7)　the theory that stock price movements are unpredictable and there's thus little way of knowing where future prices are headed.

rate of growth (4)　the compounded annual rate of change in the value of a stream of income.

ratio analysis (6)　the study of the relationships among and between various financial statement accounts.

real estate (1, 12)　entities such as residential homes, raw land, and income property.

real estate investment trust (REIT) (12)　a type of closed-end investment company that sells shares to investors and invests the proceeds in various types of real estate and real estate mortgages.

real estate limited partnership (RELP) (12) a professionally managed real estate syndicate that invests in various types of real estate; the managers take the role of general partner, with unlimited liability, and other investors are limited partners, with liability limited to the amount of their investment.

real rate of return (4) the rate of return that could be earned in a perfect world where all outcomes are known and certain.

realized return (4) current income actually received by an investor during a given period.

realized yield (9) same as expected return.

red herring (2) a preliminary prospectus made available to prospective investors after a registration statement's filing but before its approval.

refunding provisions (8) provisions that prohibit the premature retirement of an issue from the proceeds of a lower-coupon refunding bond.

reinvestment rate (4) the rate of return earned on interest or other income received from an investment over its investment horizon.

relative P/E multiple (7) the measure of how a stock's P/E behaves relative to the average market multiple.

relevant risk (16) risk that is nondiversifiable.

required rate of return (7) the return necessary to compensate an investor for the risk involved in an investment.

required return (4) the rate of return an investor must earn on an investment to be fully compensated for its risk.

residual owners (5) owners/stockholders of a firm, who are entitled to dividend income and a prorated share of the firm's earnings only after all the firm's other obligations have been met.

restricted account (2) a margin account whose equity is less than the initial margin requirement; the investor may not make further margin purchases and must bring the margin back to the initial level when securities are sold, as long as the account is restricted.

return (4) the level of profit from an investment, i.e., the reward for investing.

return on invested capital (15) return to investors based on the amount of money actually invested in a security, rather than the value of the contract itself.

revenue bonds (8) municipal bonds that require payment of principal and interest only if sufficient revenue is generated by the issuer.

reversion (17) the after-tax net proceeds received upon disposition of real property.

right (14) an option to buy shares of a new issue of common stock at a specified price, over a specified, fairly short period of time.

rights offering (2, 5) an offer of shares of stock to existing stockholders who may purchase new shares in proportion to their current ownership position.

rights-off (ex-rights) (14) a condition when a firm's common stock and its rights are trading in separate markets, separate from each other.

rights-on (14) a condition when a firm's common stock is trading with a stock right attached to it.

risk (1, 4) the chance that an investment's actual value or return will be less than its expected value or return.

risk premium (4) a return premium that reflects the issue and issuer characteristics associated with a given investment vehicle.

risk-averse (4) describes an investor who requires greater return in exchange for greater risk.

risk-free rate, R_F (4, 16) the return an investor can earn on a risk-free investment such as a U.S. Treasury bill or an insured money market account.

risk-indifferent (4) describes an investor who does not require a change in return as compensation for greater risk.

risk-return tradeoff (4, 16) the positive relationship between the risk associated with a given investment and its expected return; investments with more risk should provide higher returns, and vice versa.

risk-seeking (4) describes an investor who will accept a lower return in exchange for greater risk.

round lot (2) 100 share units of stock or multiples thereof.

round-trip commissions (15) the commission costs on both ends (buying and selling) of a securities transaction.

satisfactory investment (4) an investment whose present value of benefits (discounted at the appropriate rate) equals or exceeds the present value of its costs.

secondary distributions (2) the public sales of large blocks of previously issued securities held by large investors.

secondary market (2) the market in which securities are traded after they have been issued.

sector fund (11) a mutual fund that restricts its investments to a particular segment of the market.

Securities and Exchange Commission (SEC) (2) federal agency that regulates securities offerings and markets.

Securities Investor Protection Corporation (SIPC) (2) a nonprofit membership corporation, authorized by the federal government, that insures each brokerage customer's account for up to $500,000, with claims for cash limited to $100,000.

securities (1) investments that represent evidence of debt or ownership or the legal right to acquire or sell an ownership interest.

securities markets (2) a mechanism that allows suppliers and demanders of funds to make transactions; include both the *money market* and the *capital market*.

securitization (8) the process of transforming bank lending vehicles such as mortgages into marketable securities.

security analysis (6) the process of gathering and organizing information and then using it to determine the value of a share of common stock.

security market line (SML) (4) the graphic depiction of the capital asset pricing model; reflects the investor's required return for each level of nondiversifiable risk, measured by beta.

selling group (2) a large number of brokerage firms that join and accept responsibility for selling a certain portion of a new security issue.

semi-strong form (EMH) (7) form of the EMH holding that abnormally large profits cannot be consistently earned using publicly available information.

senior bonds (8) secured debt obligations, backed by a legal claim on specific property of the issuer.

serial bond (8) a bond that has a series of different maturity dates.

Series EE savings bonds (3) savings bonds issued by the U.S. Treasury and sold at banks and through payroll deduction plans, in varying denominations, at 50% of face value; pay a variable rate of interest tied to U.S. Treasury securities and calculated every six months in May and November.

settle price (15) the closing price (last price of the day) for commodities and financial futures.

Sharpe's measure (17) a measure of portfolio performance that measures the risk premium of a portfolio per unit of total risk, which is measured by the portfolio's standard deviation of return.

short interest (7) the number of stocks sold short in the market at any given time; a technical indicator believed to indicate future market demand.

short selling (2) the sale of borrowed securities, their eventual repurchase by the short seller, and their return to the lender.

short-term investments (1) investments that typically mature within one year.

short-term vehicles (1) savings instruments that usually have lives of one year or less.

shorting-against-the-box (2, 13) a conservative hedging technique used to protect existing security profits by following a profitable long purchase with a short sale of an equivalent number of the same shares; frequently used to lock in a security profit and defer the taxes on it to the following tax year by short selling a number of shares equal to those already owned.

simple interest (4) interest paid only on the initial deposit for the amount of time it is held.

single property syndicate (12) a type of RELP established to raise money to purchase a specific property (or properties).

single-premium annuity (13) an annuity contract purchased with a single lump-sum payment.

single-premium life insurance (SPLI) policy (13) an investment vehicle for which the policyholder purchases a whole life insurance policy that provides a stated death benefit and earns interest on the cash value buildup, which occurs over time on a tax-free basis.

sinking fund (8) a provision that stipulates the amount of principal that will be retired annually over the life of a bond.

Small Investor Index (3)   an index that measures gains and losses of the average investor relative to a base of 100; based on a portfolio that includes five types of investments held in proportions consistent with what the average small investor owns.

socially responsible fund (11)   a mutual fund that actively and directly incorporates ethics and morality into the investment decision.

specialist (2)   stock exchange member who specializes in making transactions in one or more stocks.

speculation (1)   the purchase of investment vehicles in which the levels of expected earnings and future value are highly uncertain.

speculative property (12)   raw land and real estate investment properties that are expected to provide returns primarily from appreciation in value.

split ratings (8)   different ratings given to a bond issue by the two major rating agencies.

Standard & Poor's Corporation (S&P) (3)   publisher of a variety of financial reports and services, including *Corporation Records* and *Stock Reports*.

Standard & Poor's indexes (3)   true indexes that measure the current price of a group of stocks relative to a base having an index value of 10.

standard deduction (13)   an amount, indexed to the cost of living, that taxpayers can elect to deduct from adjusted gross income without itemizing.

standard deviation, *s* (4)   a statistic used to measure the dispersion (variation) of returns around an asset's average or expected return, and the most common single indicator of an asset's risk.

stock dividend (5)   payment of a dividend in the form of additional shares of stock.

stock split (5)   a maneuver in which a company increases the number of shares outstanding by exchanging a specified number of new shares of stock for each outstanding share.

stock valuation (7)   the process by which the underlying value of a stock is established, as based on future risk and return performance of the security.

stock-index futures (15)   futures contracts written on broad based measures of stock market performance (e.g., the S&P 500 Stock Index), allowing investors to participate in the general movements of the stock market.

stock-index option (14)   a put or call option written on a specific stock market index, such as the S&P 500.

stockbrokers (2)   individuals licensed by stock exchanges to facilitate transactions between buyers and sellers of securities; also called *account executives*, *investment executives*, or *financial consultants*.

stockholders' (annual) report (3)   a report published yearly by a publicly held firm; contains a wide range of information, including financial statements for the most recent fiscal year.

stop-loss (stop) order (2)   an order to sell a stock when its market price reaches or drops below a specified level; can also be used to buy stock when its market price reaches or rises above a specified level.

straight annuity (13)   an annuity contract that provides for a series of payments for the rest of the annuitant's life.

street name (2)   stock certificates issued in the brokerage house's name but held in trust for its client, who actually owns them.

strike price (14)   the price contract between the buyer of an option and the writer; the stated price at which you can buy a security with a call or sell a security with a put.

strong form (EMH) (7)   form of the EMH that holds that there is no information, public or private, that allows investors to consistently earn abnormal profits.

subordinated debentures (8)   unsecured bonds whose claim is secondary to other debentures.

suitability rule (13)   a rule excluding investors who cannot bear a high amount of risk from buying limited partnership interests.

supply (12)   in real estate, the potential competitors available in the market.

syndicate (13)   a joint venture–general partnership, corporation, or limited partnership–in which investors pool their resources.

systematic withdrawal plan (11)   a mutual fund service that enables shareholders to automatically receive a predetermined amount of money every month or quarter.

tactical asset allocation (16)   asset allocation plan that uses stock-index futures and bond futures to change a portfolio's asset allocation.

tangibles (1, 12)   investment assets, other than real estate, which can be seen or touched.

tax avoidance (13)   reducing or eliminating taxes in legal ways.

tax credits (13)   tax reductions allowed by the IRS on a dollar-for-dollar basis under certain specified conditions.

tax deferral (13)   the strategy of delaying taxes by shifting income subject to tax into a later period.

tax evasion (13)   illegal activities designed to avoid paying taxes by omitting income or overstating deductions.

tax planning (3, 13)   the formulation of strategies that will exclude, defer, or reduce the taxes to be paid.

tax risk (4)   the chance that Congress will make unfavorable changes in the tax laws that drive down the after-tax returns and market values of certain investments.

tax shelter (13)   an investment vehicle that takes advantage of existing tax laws and offers potential reductions of taxable income.

tax swap (9, 13)   selling one security that has a capital loss and replacing it with another, similar security to offset, partially or fully, a capital gain that has been realized in another part of the investor's portfolio.

tax-advantaged investments (1, 13)   various vehicles and associated strategies for legally reducing one's tax liability.

tax-exempt money fund (3)   a money market mutual fund that limits its investments to tax-exempt municipal securities with very short (30 to 90 days) maturities.

tax-favored income (13)   an investment return that is not taxable, is taxed at a rate less than that on other similar investments, defers the payment of tax to a later period, or trades current income for capital gains.

tax-sheltered annuity (13)   an annuity contract that allows employees of certain institutions to make a *tax-free contribution* from current income to purchase a deferred annuity.

taxable equivalent yield (8)   the return a fully taxable bond would have to provide to match the after-tax return of a lower-yielding, tax-free municipal bond.

taxable income (13)   the income to which tax rates are applied; equals adjusted gross income minus itemized deductions and exemptions.

technical analysis (7)   the study of the various forces at work in the marketplace and their effect on stock prices.

term bond (8)   a bond that has a single, fairly lengthy maturity date.

term life insurance (3)   a policy in which the insurer is obligated to pay a specified amount if the insured dies within the policy period; does not contain a savings feature.

term structure of interest rates (9)   the relationship between the interest rate or rate of return (yield) on a bond and its time to maturity.

theory of contrary opinion (7)   a technical indicator that uses the amount and type of odd-lot trading as an indicator of the current state of the market and pending changes.

third market (2)   over-the-counter transactions made in securities listed on the NYSE, AMEX, or other organized exchanges.

time premium (14)   the amount by which the option price exceeds the option's fundamental value.

time value of money (4)   the fact that as long as an opportunity exists to earn interest, the value of money is affected by the point in time when the money is expected to be received.

total return (4)   the sum of the current income and the capital gain (or loss) earned on an investment over a specified period of time.

total risk (4)   the sum of an investment's nondiversifiable risk and diversifiable risk.

traditional portfolio management (16)   an approach to portfolio management that emphasizes "balancing" the portfolio with a variety of stocks and/or bonds of companies from a broad cross-section of industries.

Treasury bonds (8)   U.S. Treasury debt securities that are issued with maturities of more than 10 years—usually 20 years or more.

Treasury notes (8)   U.S. Treasury debt securities that are issued by the U.S. Treasury with maturities of 10 years or less.

Treasury Strips (Strip-Ts) (8)   zero-coupon bonds sold by the U.S. Treasury.

treasury stock (5) shares of stock that have been sold and subsequently repurchased (and held) by the issuing firm.

Treynor's measure (17) a measure of portfolio performance that measures the risk premium of a portfolio per unit of *nondiversifiable* risk, which is measured by the portfolio's beta.

U.S. Treasury bills (T-bills) (3) obligations of the U.S. Treasury, sold on a discount basis, and having varying short-term maturities; regarded as the safest of all investments.

uncorrelated (16) describes two series that lack any relationship or interaction and therefore have a correlation coefficient close to zero.

underwriting (2) the role of the investment banker in bearing the risk of reselling at a profit the securities purchased from an issuing corporation at an agreed-upon price.

underwriting syndicate (2) a group formed by an investment banker to spread the financial risk associated with the selling of new securities.

unit investment trust (11) a type of investment vehicle whereby the trust sponsors put together a fixed/unmanaged portfolio of securities and then sell ownership units in the portfolio to individual investors.

universal life insurance (3) a policy that combines term insurance with a tax-sheltered savings/investment account that pays interest at competitive rates.

unrealized capital gains (paper profits) (11) a capital gain made only "on paper," that is, not realized until the fund's holdings are sold.

valuation (1, 7) procedure for estimating the perceived worth of an investment vehicle, using measures of return and risk.

Value Line composite index (3) a stock index, published by Value Line, that reflects the percentage changes in share price of about 1,700 stocks traded on the NYSE, AMEX, and OTC market relative to a base of 100.

Value Line Investment Survey **(3)** one of the most popular subscription services used by individual investors; subscribers receive three basic reports.

variable annuity (13) an annuity contract that adjusts the monthly income it pays during the distribution period according to the investment experience (and sometimes the mortality experience) of the insurer.

variable life insurance (3) a policy that combines insurance coverage with a savings account that allows the insured to decide how it is invested; the amount of insurance coverage varies with the profit generated in the investment (savings) account.

variable-ratio plan (17) a formula plan for timing investment transactions, in which the ratio of the speculative portion to the total portfolio varies depending upon the movement in value of the speculative securities; when the ratio rises or falls by a predetermined amount, the amount committed to the speculative portion of the portfolio is reduced or increased, respectively.

Wall Street Journal **(3)** a daily business newspaper, published regionally; the most popular source of financial news.

warrant (14) a long-lived option that gives the holder the right to buy stock in a company at a price specified in the warrant itself.

warrant premium (14)   the difference between the true value of a warrant and its market price.

wash sale (13)   the procedure of selling securities on which capital losses can be realized and then immediately buying them back; disallowed under the tax law.

weak form (EMH) (7)   form of the EMH holding that past data on stock prices are of no use in predicting future prices.

whipsawing (17)   the situation where a stock temporarily drops in price and then bounces back upward.

whole life insurance (3)   a policy that provides coverage over the entire life of the insured; offers a savings benefit.

Wilshire 5000 Index (3)   measure of the total dollar value of 5,000 actively traded stocks, including all those on the NYSE and the AMEX in addition to active OTC stocks.

wrap account (2)   a brokerage account in which customers with large portfolios pay a flat annual fee that covers the cost of a money manager's services and the commissions on *all* trades.

Yankee bonds (2, 8)   dollar-denominated debt securities (bonds) issued by foreign governments or corporations and registered with the SEC and traded in U.S. securities markets.

yield (internal rate of return) (4)   the compounded annual rate of return earned by a long-term investment; the discount rate that produces a present value of the investment's benefits that just equals its cost.

yield curve (9)   a graph that represents the relationship between a bond's term to maturity and its yield at a given point in time.

yield pickup swap (9)   replacement of a low-coupon bond for a comparable higher-coupon bond in order to realize an increase in current yield and yield-to-maturity.

yield spreads (9)   differences in interest rates that exist in various sectors of the market.

yield-to-maturity (YTM) (9)   the fully compounded rate of return earned by an investor over the life of a bond, including interest income and price appreciation.

zero-coupon bonds (8)   bonds with no coupons that are sold at a deep discount from par value.

CREDITS

Text

Page 11, InvestorFacts: From FORTUNE, December 26, 1994, p. 60. Reprinted by permission. Page 14, InvestorFacts: From MONEY, June 1994, p. 76. Reprinted by permission. Page 33, InvestorFacts: Reprinted by permission of THE WALL STREET JOURNAL. Copyright © 1995 Dow Jones & Company Inc. All Rights Reserved Worldwide. Page 39, InvestorFacts: Reprinted by permission of THE WALL STREET JOURNAL. Copyright © 1995 Dow Jones & Company Inc. All Rights Reserved Worldwide. Page 79, InvestorFacts: From WORTH, June 1994, pp. 61, 64. Printed with permission from WORTH magazine. Page 101, InvestorFacts: Reprinted by permission of THE WALL STREET JOURNAL, Copyright © 1994 Dow Jones & Company, Inc. All Rights Reserved Worldwide. Page 103, Figure 3.4: Reprinted by permission of THE WALL STREET JOURNAL, Copyright © 1994 Dow Jones & Company, Inc. All Rights Reserved Worldwide. Page 104, Figure 3.5: Reprinted by permission of THE WALL STREET JOURNAL, Copyright © 1994 Dow Jones & Company, Inc. All Rights Reserved Worldwide. Page 118, Figure 3.7: Reprinted by permission of THE WALL STREET JOURNAL, Copyright © 1994 Dow Jones & Company, Inc. All Rights Reserved Worldwide. Page 133, InvestorFacts: Reprinted from FINANCIAL WORLD, 1328 Broadway, New York, NY 10001 © copyrighted 1995 by Financial World Partners. All rights reserved. Page 164, chart: Copyright 1995 by Value Line Publishing, Inc. Reprinted by Permission; All Rights Reserved. Page 168, InvestorFacts: Reprinted by permission of THE WALL STREET JOURNAL, Copyright © 1994 Dow Jones & Company, Inc. All Rights Reserved Worldwide. Page 189, Figure 5.1: Reprinted by permission of THE WALL STREET JOURNAL, Copyright © 1995 Dow Jones & Company, Inc. All Rights Reserved Worldwide. Page 191, InvestorFacts; From BOTTOM LINE PERSONAL, December 1, 1994, p. 9. Reprinted with permission of Bottom Line/Personal, 55 Railroad Avenue, Greenwich, CT 06830. Page 197, Figure 5.4: Reprinted by permission of THE WALL STREET JOURNAL, Copyright © 1994 Dow Jones & Company, Inc. All Rights Reserved Worldwide. Page 199, Investor Insights: From "Penny Stock Swindles Die Hard," WORTH Online, downloaded from America Online, transmitted January 2, 1993. Printed with permission of WORTH magazine. Page 206, Figure 5.6: Reprinted by permission of THE WALL STREET JOURNAL, All Rights Reserved Worldwide. Page 240: From "How to Play the Recovery," WORTH, August/September 1992, p. 32. Printed with permission of WORTH magazine. Page 246, Figure 6.1: From 1994 ANALYST'S HANDBOOK. Reprinted by permission of Standard & Poor's, a division of The McGraw-Hill Companies. Page 248, Figure 6.2: From STANDARD & POOR'S INDUSTRY SURVEYS. Reprinted by permission of Standard & Poor's, a division of The McGraw-Hill Companies. Page 263, Figure 6.3: From STANDARD & POOR'S NYSE REPORTS, August 23, 1994. Reprinted by permission of Standard & Poor's, a division of The McGraw-Hill Companies. Page 278, InvestorFacts: From SMART MONEY, March, 1994. Page 301, Figure 7.1: Reprinted by permission of THE WALL STREET JOURNAL, Copyright © 1994 Dow Jones & Company, Inc. All Rights Reserved Worldwide. Page 303, Figure 7.2: Reprinted by permission of THE WALL STREET JOURNAL, Copyright © 1994 Dow Jones & Company, Inc. All Rights Reserved Worldwide. Page 305, Figure 7.3: Graph reprinted with permission from Daliy Graphics, Inc., 12655 Beatrice Street, Los Angeles, CA 90066, 800-472-7479 310-448-6843. Page 340, Figure 8.4: Reprinted by permission of THE WALL STREET JOURNAL, Copyright © 1991 Dow Jones & Company, Inc.. All Rights Reserved Worldwide. Page 356, Figure 8.5: Reprinted by permission of THE WALL STREET JOURNAL, Copyright © 1994 Dow Jones & Company, Inc. All Rights Reserved Worldwide. Page 357: Investor Insights: Reprinted by permission of BARRON'S , Copyright © 1989 Dow Jones & Company, Inc. All Rights Reserved Worldwide. Page 370, Figure 9.1: Reprinted by permission of THE WALL STREET JOURNAL, Copyright © 1992 Dow Jones & Company, Inc. All Rights Reserved Worldwide. Page 382, Investor Insights: Reprinted by permission of THE WALL STREET JOURNAL, Copyright © 1992 Dow Jones & Company, Inc. All Rights Reserved Worldwide. Page 407, Figure 10.1: From "Average High-Grade Preferred Stock Yield Versus Average Market Yields on AA-Rated Corporate Bonds," STANDARD & POOR'S TRADE AND SECURITIES STATISTICS, 1991. Reprinted by permission of Standard & Poor's, a division of The McGraw-Hill Companies. Page 410, Figure 10.2: Reprinted by permission of THE WALL STREET JOURNAL, Copyright © 1994 Dow Jones & Company, Inc. All Rights Reserved Worldwide. Page 425, Figure 10.6: Reprinted by permission of THE WALL STREET JOURNAL, Copyright © 1994 Dow Jones & Company, Inc. All Rights Reserved Worldwide. Page 447, Investor Insights: From Russ Wiles, "Could Your Mutual Funds Go Under?" PERSONAL INVESTOR, September 1991. Reprinted by permission of Russ Wiles. Page 449, Figure 11.3: Reprinted by permission of THE WALL STREET JOURNAL, Copyright © 1994 Dow Jones & Company, Inc. All Rights Reserved Worldwide. Page 451, Table 11.1: Reprinted by permission of THE WALL STREET JOURNAL, Copyright © 1994 Dow Jones & Company, Inc. All Rights Reserved Worldwide. Page 453, Figure 11.4: Reprinted by permission of THE WALL STREET JOURNAL, Copyright © 1995 Dow Jones & Company, Inc. All Rights Reserved Worldwide. Page 454, InvestorFacts: Source 1994 Mutual Fund Fact Book, pp. 33, 86, and 87. Investment Company Institute, Washington, DC. Reprinted by permission. Page 464, InvestorFacts: Source 1994

THE INVESTMENT MANAGEMENT
DISK (IMD)

SYSTEM REQUIREMENTS

- Any IBM or IBM-compatible PC
- DOS version 3.3 or higher
- 640 KB of memory (500 KB free)
- Any of the following disk drive(s):
    1 1.2 MB 5.25" floppy disk drive
    1 1.44 MB 3.5" floppy disk drive
    1 fixed disk and any floppy disk drive
- Printer recommended but not required

USER INSTRUCTIONS

You may run the Investment Management Disk from a fixed disk or from a floppy disk that is large enough to hold the entire system. It is most satisfactory when run from a fixed disk.

From either a 5.25" or a 3.5" floppy disk system:

1. Insert your DOS diskette into drive A: (generally the one on the left or top of a dual disk drive.) Always insert disks with the label-side up.
2. Turn on the computer and respond to any date and time requests.
3. The computer will display the A: prompt.
4. Remove the DOS diskette and replace it with the IMD Program diskette if you have a single-drive system or will be using the A: drive to run the IMD. If you have a dual-drive system, you may place the IMD in the B: drive and change to the B: drive by typing B: followed by <Enter>.
5. With the computer at the A: or B: prompt, type START and press the <Enter> key.

To load the IMD to a fixed disk system:

1. Create a subdirectory called IMD on your fixed disk and copy all of the files from the IMD diskette to that subdirectory. For example, if you are at the C: prompt:
    C:\>**MD IMD**
    C:\>**CD IMD**
    C:\IMD>**COPY A:*.***
2. Rename the START.HD file to START.BAT. (Make this change only if you are running from a fixed disk, not a floppy disk system.)
    C:\IMD>**COPY START.HD START.BAT**
3. From the IMD subdirectory, you may then execute the IMD program by typing START and pressing the <Enter> key.
    C:\IMD>**START**

The IMD will load and the introductory screen will appear. Follow the instructions from the program. The IMD is menu-driven. Select the chapter and problems you wish to execute by highlighting the menu item and pressing <Enter> or by simply typing the letter of the menu item. Most of the routines in the IMD are keyed to equation numbers in the book for reference. You may choose to enable the printer with the <F9> key to print the results of the calculations.

SEE APPENDIX C FOR COMPLETE LIST OF
KEY EQUATIONS AND DISK ROUTINES.